Isobel Neill
H MOC Dept.

Management

Student:

To help you make the most of your study time and improve your grades, we have developed the following supplement designed to accompany Baird/Post/Mahon: *Management: Functions and Responsibilities:*

•Management Student's Handbook, by the text authors 0-06-0404470-7

You can order a copy at your local bookstore or call HarperCollins directly at 1-800-638-3030.

Management

Functions and Responsibilities

Lloyd S. Baird
Boston University

James E. Post
Boston University

John F. Mahon
Boston University

HarperCollins*Publishers*

TO COLEEN, JEANNETTE, AND JULIE

Editor-in-Chief	Judith L. Rothman
Sponsoring Editor	Debra Riegert
Development Editor	Robert Ginsberg
Project Editor	Paula Cousin
Art Direction	Teresa Delgado
Cover Design	Delgado Design, Inc.
Cover Photo	Copyright 1989, Comstock
Photo Research	Lynn Goldberg Biderman, Ilene Cherna Bellovin
Production Manager	Jeanie Berke
Production Assistant	Paula Roppolo

About the Cover

The cover photograph shows the inner workings of a solid gold Swiss watch. For centuries the Swiss watch has been an international symbol of effective design and performance.

Managers strive for effectiveness, too. They combine people, technology, and other resources to produce products and services and to meet financial goals. This text is crafted with these standards in mind.

MANAGEMENT: FUNCTIONS AND RESPONSIBILITIES

Copyright © 1990 by HarperCollins Publishers Inc.

Library of Congress Cataloging-in-Publication Data
Baird, Lloyd S.
   Management : functions and responsibilities / Lloyd S. Baird,
James E. Post, John F. Mahon.
     p.   cm.
   ISBN 0-06-040438-8
   1. Management. I. Post, James E. II. Mahon, John F.
(John Francis), 1948–   III. Title.
HD31.B324 1989
658.4—dc20

89-19986
CIP

92 9 8 7 6 5 4 3

Brief Contents

Detailed Contents   vii
Preface   xvii
About the Authors   xxvi

PART ONE ▮
MANAGEMENT
1

Chapter 1   Management: A Framework   3
Chapter 2   The Evolution of Modern Management   29
Chapter 3   Managerial Decision Making and Problem Solving   57
Comprehensive Case One Whatever Became of the Ringling Brothers' Moral, Elevating, Instructive, and Fascinating Concert and Variety Performance?   89

PART TWO ▮
PLANNING   94

Chapter 4   Organizational Planning   97
Chapter 5   Strategic Planning   124
Chapter 6   Strategic Management in Changing Environments   151
Comprehensive Case Two The Big Store   181

PART THREE ▮
ORGANIZING
188

Chapter 7   The Structure of Organizations   191
Chapter 8   Organizational Design and Culture   221
Chapter 9   Organizational Change, Conflict, and Development   249
Comprehensive Case Three Long-Term Survival: Lessons from a 750-Year-Old Organization   279

PART FOUR ▮
DIRECTING
284

Chapter 10   Leading and Directing   287
Chapter 11   Staffing and Human Resource Management   317
Chapter 12   Communicating   348
Chapter 13   Motivating for Productivity   380
Chapter 14   Managing Group Processes   413
Comprehensive Case Four Showtime at Motown Productions   443

PART FIVE ▮
CONTROL
448

Chapter 15   Controlling Performance   451
Chapter 16   Production and Operations Management   480
Chapter 17   MIS and Technology Management   511
Comprehensive Case Five Close Your Eyes for Two Seconds and You Lose   541

PART SIX ▮
MANAGEMENT
IN THE
EXTERNAL
ENVIRON-
MENT   548

Chapter 18   Ethics and Social Responsibility   551
Chapter 19   Managing in the Political and Legal Environment   581
Chapter 20   Managing in the International Environment   608
Chapter 21   Managing in the Future   635
Comprehensive Case Six The Smell of Huge Profits over Cocktails and Sushi   667

Appendix: Quantitative Management Tools   673

Notes   685
Glossary   697
Company Index   707
Name Index   710
Subject Index   715

Detailed Contents

Preface   xvii

About the Authors   xxvi

PART ONE ■ MANAGEMENT   1

Chapter 1   Management: A Framework   3

Focus Case: The Greatest Job on Earth   4
The Importance of Management   5
Management Defined   6
Decision Making and Management Functions   7
   Management Decision Making   8 ▪ The Basic Functions of
   Management   8 ▪ Planning   8 ▪ Organizing   10 ▪ Directing   12 ▪
   Controlling   13
Management Responsibilities   15
   Types of Responsibilities   16 ▪ The Levels of Management   17
Sources of Knowledge About Management   20
   Intuition   21 ▪ Experience   22 ▪ Research   22 ▪ Using All Three
   Sources   23

The Conference Table: Discussion Case 1.1   Jim Cavanaugh,
                                      Manager   24
The Conference Table: Discussion Case 1.2   Phillips   27

**Chapter 2   The Evolution of Modern
            Management   29**

Focus Case: The Mystery of the Buddhist Temple   30
Major Themes in Management History   31
Technical Issues   34
   Scientific Management   35 ▪ Other Contributions   38 ▪ Obstacles to
   Scientific Management   38 ▪ Automation and Operations Research   41
Administrative Issues   43
   Classical Organization Theory   44 ▪ Research in Human
   Behavior   46 ▪ The Human Relations Movement   47 ▪ World War II: A
   Turning Point   48
Institutional Issues   49
   Systems Concepts   49 ▪ Strategic Management and Contingency
   Theory   51 ▪ Social Responsibility   52

The Conference Table: Discussion Case 2.1   Pullman Standard
                                      Corporation   54

Chapter 3   Managerial Decision Making and Problem Solving   57

Focus Case: Coke Are It   58
What Is a Decision?   60
   Decision Making Defined   60 ▪ Choice Making, Decision Making, and Problem Solving   60 ▪ Relatedness of Decisions   61 ▪ Personal Versus Managerial Decision Making   62 ▪ Programmed Versus Nonprogrammed Decisions   62
Context of Decision Making   64
   Conditions of Certainty   65 ▪ Conditions of Risk   65 ▪ Conditions of Uncertainty   66 ▪ Optimal Versus Satisficing Decisions   69
The Decision-Making/Problem-Solving Process   70
   Define the Problem or Issue   71 ▪ Analyze the Issue and Generate Alternatives   71 ▪ Evaluate the Alternatives and Select the Best One   74 ▪ Implement the Decision   75 ▪ Monitor the Results and Evaluate the Impact   76
Improving Decision Making   78
   Quantitative and Qualitative Methods   78 ▪ Group and Committee Involvement   79

The Conference Table: Discussion Case 3.1   Bay Manufacturing   85
The Conference Table: Discussion Case 3.2   The Swine Flu Epidemic   86

Comprehensive Case One   Whatever Became of the Ringling Brothers' Moral, Elevating, Instructive, and Fascinating Concert and Variety Performance?   89

PART TWO ▪ PLANNING   94

Chapter 4   Organizational Planning   97

Focus Case: Olympic Gold   98
What Is Planning?   100
   Importance of Planning   100
Steps in the Planning Process   101
   Analyze Current Status and Forecast the Future Environment   102 ▪ Establish Goals and Objectives   104 ▪ Identify Alternatives   105 ▪ Select the Best Alternative   106 ▪ Implement the Plan   106 ▪ Criteria for a Good Plan   107
Types of Planning   109
   Scope of Activities Covered   109 ▪ Standing Plans and Single-Use Plans   112
Management by Objectives   115
   Goals and Objectives   115 ▪ The MBO Process   117 ▪ MBO Appraised   118

The Conference Table: Discussion Case 4.1   Ben and Jerry's   119
The Conference Table: Discussion Case 4.2   Osborne Computer   122

Chapter 5   Strategic Planning   124

Focus Case: USA Today . . . And Tomorrow   125
What Is Strategy?   127

Strategic Thinking 127 ▪ Modes of Strategy Making 128 ▪ Importance of Strategic Planning 128 ▪ Costs of Strategic Planning 130

Strategic Planning and Strategic Management   130

Analyze the Current Status and Forecast the Future Environment 133 ▪ Establish Mission and Goals 135 ▪ Develop Strategic Options 137 ▪ Choose the Best Option 137 ▪ Implement and Monitor the Strategic Plan 138

Strategic Planning in Organizations   141

Approaches to Strategic Planning 141 ▪ Levels of Strategic Planning 143 ▪ Contingency Planning 145

The Conference Table: Discussion Case 5.1   Tops in Toys   147
The Conference Table: Discussion Case 5.2   The Wonderful World of Money   149

Chapter 6 **Strategic Management in Changing Environments 151**

Focus Case: Shrimp Farming: Bountiful Harvest or Bust   152

Strategic Management in the Environment   154

Operating and General Environments 155 ▪ Degree of Complexity and Rate of Change 156 ▪ Economic, Technological, and Competitive Factors in the Operating Environment 157

Economic Factors   160

The GNP and the Federal Government's Role 161 ▪ Strategic Responses to Economic Fluctuations 162

Technological Factors   163

What Is Technology? 163 ▪ Effects on Organizational Strategy 165 ▪ Strategic Responses to Technological Changes 167

Competitive Factors   167

Strategic Responses to Competitive Forces 168 ▪ Basic Market Strategies 169 ▪ Portfolio Management 170 ▪ Choosing a Strategy 173

The Conference Table: Discussion Case 6.1   Timex Timing   176
The Conference Table: Discussion Case 6.2   Hitch Your Wagon to a Supercomputer   178

Comprehensive Case Two   The Big Store   181

PART THREE ▪ **ORGANIZING 188**

Chapter 7 **The Structure of Organizations 191**

Focus Case: From Strategy to Structure: Moments of Truth   192

Organizing for Goal Accomplishment   194

Structure and the Formal Organization 194 ▪ The Informal Organization 196

Division of Labor and Specialization   196

Line and Staff Work 199 ▪ Departmentalization 200 ▪ Departmentalization by Two Dimensions Simultaneously: The Matrix Concept 203 ▪ Overcoming Problems in Division of Labor and Specialization 205

Coordinating Work   208
Individual Coordinating Mechanisms 208 ▪ Structural Coordinating
Mechanisms 209 ▪ Issues in Coordination 213 ▪ Alternative
Organization Structures 214

The Conference Table: Discussion Case 7.1   Transnational Mergers   217
The Conference Table: Discussion Case 7.2   Hands Across America   218

Chapter 8   Organizational Design and Culture   221

Focus Case: Give Us a Ring   222
Organization Structure, Culture, and Strategy Relationships   224
Designing the Structure   225
Proponents of Bureaucracy 225 ▪ Critics of
Bureaucracy 226 ▪ Beyond Bureaucracy: The Contingency
Approach 227
Fitting the External Environment   227
The Degree of Complexity and the Rate of Change 228
Fitting the Internal Environment   230
Size of the Organization 230 ▪ Technology of
Production 231 ▪ Diversity of Products and Services 234
Designing the Individual Units Within the Organization   234
Organizational Culture and Strategy Relationships   236
Understanding Organizational Culture 237 ▪ Managing Organizational
Culture 240

The Conference Table: Discussion Case 8.1   No Desks, No Drawers   245
The Conference Table: Discussion Case 8.2   Roger Penske, Inc.   247

Chapter 9   Organizational Change, Conflict, and Development   249

Focus Case: Marketing Rainbows   250
Change: Catalyst for Development or Crisis   252
Force Field Analysis 254
The Nature of Conflict   256
Conflict Caused by Differences 256 ▪ Conflict Caused by Competition
for Limited Resources 258
Managing Conflict   258
Lose-Lose Resolutions 259 ▪ Win-Lose Resolutions 259 ▪ Win-Win
Resolutions 259
Managing Planned Change   261
Unfreezing, Change, Refreezing 261 ▪ A Six-Step Change
Process 263 ▪ Structural, Technological, Human, and Task
Approaches 265
Managing Organization Development   267
The Organization Development Process 267 ▪ Fostering a Creative
Climate 270 ▪ Fostering Innovation 270 ▪ Developing an Atmosphere
of Entrepreneurship 270

The Conference Table: Discussion Case 9.1   The Generic
(Un)revolution   275

The Conference Table: Discussion Case 9.2   McDentists   277

Comprehensive Case Three   Long-Term Survival: Lessons from a 750-Year-Old
                            Organization   279

PART FOUR ■ DIRECTING   284

Chapter 10   Leading and Directing   287

Focus Case: No, This *Is How You Run a Cookie Business   288*
Managing, Directing, and Leading   290
Leading and Influencing   290
   Authority   291 ▪ Power   292 ▪ Delegation   294 ▪ Responsibility and
   Accountability   295 ▪ Maintaining the Balance   296
Leadership Traits   297
Leadership Behaviors   299
   The University of Michigan Studies   300 ▪ The Ohio State
   Studies   300 ▪ The Implications of Behavioral Research   301
Situational Approaches to Leadership   302
   Fiedler's Contingency Model   304 ▪ Path-Goal Model   307 ▪ Life Cycle
   Model   308
Continuing Research   310
   Attribution Theory   310 ▪ Leadership Substitutes   311

The Conference Table: Discussion Case 10.1   Tips from the Top   314
The Conference Table: Discussion Case 10.2   Conflicts Between a
                                              Younger Leader and an
                                              Older Employee   315

Chapter 11   Staffing and Human Resource
                Management   317

Focus Case: Challenging the Theory of Potential Limit   318
The Human Resource System   320
   Elements of the Human Resource System   320 ▪ External
   Constraints   321 ▪ Internal Guidelines   324
Human Resource Planning   324
   Assessment of Needs   326 ▪ Evaluation of Current Human
   Resources   328 ▪ Analysis of Future Availability   328 ▪ Preparation of
   Recruitment and Development Plans   329
Recruitment and Selection   331
   Internal Recruiting   331 ▪ External Recruiting   331 ▪ Selection   332
Orientation, Training, and Development   334
   Orientation   334 ▪ Training and Development   335 ▪ Management
   Development Programs   335
Performance Appraisal   336
Rewarding   339
   Compensation   339 ▪ Promotions and Transfers   341 ▪ Demotions,
   Terminations, and Retirement: Leading to Replacement   341
Current Issues: Testing the Work Force   342

The Conference Table: Discussion Case 11.1   SafePlace   344
The Conference Table: Discussion Case 11.2   The British Nanny Carries
                                              On   346

Chapter 12   Communicating   348

Focus Case: A Script for Power 349
Communication and the Directing Function   351
The Communication Process   351
    Encoding the Meaning 354 ▪ Transmitting 355 ▪ Decoding and
    Interpreting 356
Problems and Barriers to Communication   357
    Noise 358 ▪ Differences in Perceptions 358 ▪
    Language 361 ▪ Status 363
One-Way Versus Two-Way Communication   364
Managing Interpersonal Communication   366
    Face-to-Face Communication 367 ▪ Listening 368
Organizational Communication   369
    Formal Channels 370 ▪ Informal Channels 372
Managing Organizational Communication   373

The Conference Table: Discussion Case 12.1   VNET or Gripenet?   376
The Conference Table: Discussion Case 12.2   Communication—
*   Sometimes the Difference*
*   Between Life and*
*   Death 378*

Chapter 13   Motivating for Productivity   380

Focus Case: Why Do You Work? 381
Understanding Motivation   382
What Do People Want?   383
    Maslow's Hierarchy of Needs Theory 384 ▪ Alderfer's ERG
    Theory 385 ▪ Acquired Needs Theory 387 ▪ Herzberg's Two-Factor
    Theory 390 ▪ Need Theories at Work 391
What Do People Expect?   391
    Expectancy Theory 391 ▪ Expectancy Theory at Work 393 ▪ Equity
    Theory 395 ▪ Equity Theory at Work 396
How Do People React to What They Get?   396
    Operant Conditioning 398 ▪ Organizational Behavior
    Modification 398 ▪ Operant Conditioning at Work 399
Which Theory to Use?   402
Participative Management   402
    Theory X 403 ▪ Theory Y 403 ▪ Quality of Work Life
    Projects 404 ▪ Quality Circles 405

The Conference Table: Discussion Case 13.1   Long Hours + Bad Pay =
*   Great Ads   408*
The Conference Table: Discussion Case 13.2   Adversity as a
*   Motivator 410*

Chapter 14   Managing Group Processes   413

Focus Case: USA for Africa 414
What Is a Group?   415
    Group Characteristics 416 ▪ Formal Groups 416 ▪ Informal
    Groups 418

Working with Groups in the Organization   420
   Advantages 420 ▪ Disadvantages 421
The Formation and Development of Groups   421
   Forming 421 ▪ Storming 423 ▪ Norming 423 ▪ Performing 424
Group Dynamics   424
   Required and Emergent Behaviors 425 ▪ Activities, Interactions,
   Sentiments 426 ▪ Managing Group Dynamics 426 ▪ Group
   Norms 427 ▪ Group Roles 428 ▪ Task and Maintenance Roles 431
Resolving Problems with Groups   431
   Ineffectiveness 432 ▪ Groupthink 433 ▪ Intergroup Conflict 435

The Conference Table: Discussion Case 14.1   High-Powered Inertia   439
The Conference Table: Discussion Case 14.2   The Visitor Who
                                          Stayed   441

Comprehensive Case Four   Showtime at Motown Productions   443

PART FIVE ▪ CONTROL 448

Chapter 15   Controlling Performance 451

Focus Case: The DIVAD, Out of Control   452
What Is Control?   454
   Control in Organizations 454 ▪ Levels of Control 455
Elements of the Control Process   457
   Setting Performance Objectives and Standards 458 ▪ Measuring and
   Evaluating Performance 460 ▪ Taking Corrective Action 462
Methods of Control   464
   Internal and External Control Methods 465 ▪ Formal and Informal
   Control Methods 465 ▪ Systematic and Ad Hoc Controls 466
Quality Control   466
   Total Quality Control 467
Financial Controls   468
   Budgets 468 ▪ The Balance Sheet, Income Statement, and Ratio
   Analysis 468 ▪ Cash Flow Analysis 470 ▪ Responsibility Centers 470
Control Through Performance Management   472
Effective Degrees of Control   474

The Conference Table: Discussion Case 15.1   Mills Brothers   476
The Conference Table: Discussion Case 15.2   They Called Us the Green
                                          Machine   478

Chapter 16   Production and Operations Management 480

Focus Case: The How-Not-To Book   481
Production/Operations Management   483
   The Operating System 483
Planning the Production/Operations Processes   486
   Unique Product and Batch Processing 486 ▪ Rigid Mass
   Production 487 ▪ Flexible Mass Production 487 ▪ Process or Flow
   Production 489

Designing the Production System   491
What to Produce: The Product Choice   491 ▪ How to Produce: The
Process Choice   492 ▪ How Many to Produce: Capacity
Planning   492 ▪ Who Will Produce: Facilities Location and Layout
Planning   494
Operating the System: Scheduling   495
Gantt Charts   496 ▪ Critical Path Method (CPM)   498 ▪ Program
Evaluation and Review Technique (PERT)   500
Operating the System: Controlling the Inventory   500
Ordering Quantities and Timing   502 ▪ Just-in-Time Delivery   504
Controlling the Production Process   505
Process Analysis   505 ▪ Trade-off Analysis   506

The Conference Table: Discussion Case 16.1   *TRW and*
Productivity   *507*
The Conference Table: Discussion Case 16.2   *Shaping Up Your*
Suppliers   *509*

Chapter 17   MIS and Technology
Management   511

Focus Case: The Hand-Held Solution   *512*
Management Information Systems (MIS)   514
Evolution of MIS   516 ▪ Basic Components of MIS   517
Balancing the Value and Cost of Information   518
Managerial Uses of Information   518 ▪ The Value of
Information   519 ▪ MIS—A Management Tool   520
Establishing an MIS   521
MIS Planning   521 ▪ MIS Design   522 ▪ MIS Implementation   524 ▪ MIS
Monitoring and Improvement   527
Decision Support Systems, Expert Systems, and Artificial Intelligence   528
Decision Support Systems   528 ▪ Expert Systems   530 ▪ Artificial
Intelligence   531
The Impact of Information Technology   531
Information Technology in the Manufacturing Sector   532 ▪ Information
Technology in the Service Sector   532

The Conference Table: Discussion Case 17.1   *Pharmacy Information*
Systems   *536*
The Conference Table: Discussion Case 17.2   *The Paperless Expense*
Account   *538*

Comprehensive Case Five   Close Your Eyes for Two Seconds and You
Lose   541

PART SIX ▪ **MANAGEMENT IN THE EXTERNAL
ENVIRONMENT   548**

Chapter 18   Ethics and Social Responsibility   551

Focus Case: The Outfit Responsible Goes out of Business   *552*
Foundations of Business Ethics and Social Responsibility   554

An Interactive Model of Business and Society 559
The Stakeholder Concept 559 ▪ An Ethical Decision-Making
Framework 562
Responsibility, Responsiveness, and Rectitude 564
Corporate Social Responsibility 564 ▪ Corporate Social
Responsiveness 566 ▪ Corporate Social Rectitude 566
Individual Ethics 568
Exit, Voice, or Loyalty 569 ▪ Making Difficult Decisions 571
Institutionalizing Ethical and Socially Responsible Behavior 573
Ethics Codes 574 ▪ Ethics Committees 575 ▪ Ethics Training
Programs 575 ▪ Ethics Audits 575

The Conference Table: Discussion Case 18.1 Out of South Africa 576
*The Conference Table: Discussion Case 18.2 Bhopal: A Question of
Response 579*

**Chapter 19 Managing in the Political and Legal
Environment 581**

Focus Case: The Great American Smokeout 582
Interplay Between Social, Political, and Legal Environments 584
Differing Priorities for Society, Business, and Government 584
The Political Environment 586
Public Issues 586 ▪ Mechanisms of Influence 588 ▪ Business
Issues 589 ▪ Public Policy and the Public-Policy Process 592
The Legal Environment 596
Sources of Law 597 ▪ The Impact of Law on Managers 597 ▪ Legal
Responsibilities of Organizations 600 ▪ Legal Responsibilities of
Managers 602

The Conference Table: Discussion Case 19.1 Acid Rain 604
*The Conference Table: Discussion Case 19.2 Drug Testing as Public
Policy 606*

**Chapter 20 Managing in the International
Environment 608**

Focus Case: Ford Comes Full Circle 609
What Is International Business? 611
Import-Export Trade 611 ▪ Portfolio Investment 613 ▪ Licensing and
Management Agreements 613 ▪ Direct Investment 614
Multinational Corporations 616
Development of Multinationals 618 ▪ Multinationals Today 620
Managing in the International Environment 621
Economic Factors 621 ▪ Political and Legal Factors 622 ▪ Cultural
Factors 624
Opportunities and Risks 627
Opportunities 627 ▪ Risks 628

*The Conference Table: Discussion Case 20.1 Dresser Industries and
Pipeline Politics 631*
*The Conference Table: Discussion Case 20.2 Apple Computer Goes
Mexican 633*

Chapter 21   Managing in the Future   635

Focus Case: Nor Rain Nor Sleet Nor Snow Nor Heated Competition   636
The Future: Scenarios   639
Trends   639
   Globalization 640 ▪ Demographic Changes 642 ▪ Resource
   Availability 642 ▪ Growth in the Service Economy 646 ▪ Revolutions
   in Information Technology 649
Organization Responses   650
   Any Time 650 ▪ Any Place 651 ▪ No-Matter 653 ▪ Mass
   Customizing 654
Technical, Administrative, and Institutional Issues in the Future   655
Management in the Future   657
   Decision Making 657 ▪ Planning 658 ▪ Organizing 658 ▪ Directing
   659 ▪ Controlling 660

*The Conference Table: Discussion Case 21.1   New Waves at
                                               NUMMI 661*
*The Conference Table: Discussion Case 21.2   Back to the Future in
                                               Health Care 664*

Comprehensive Case Six   The Smell of Huge Profits over Cocktails and
                          Sushi 667

Appendix: Quantitative Management Tools   673

Notes   685
Glossary   697
Company Index   707
Name Index   710
Subject Index   715

Preface

GUIDING PRINCIPLES

Management education is transforming itself. New ideas are challenging old doctrines. New examples of innovation and change occur daily. New instructional technologies, including computers, videocassettes, and global communication systems, make it possible to bring this excitement to any classroom anywhere in the world. Leading international businesses are already doing this in their training programs. University-based education is learning to do the same.

Our experience with many companies showed us the possibilities. Our roles as faculty members showed us the need. Thus, when we set out to do this project, we started with a commitment to develop more than a textbook. It was a commitment to create an integrated instructional system that would use the best current ideas, examples from real organizations, and available instructional technologies to bring management to life. To achieve this goal we have followed three guiding principles.

First: The material must retain the readers' interest. Each of us has been a manager and a consultant to managers in various organizations, and we have taught students at every level—community college, undergraduate, master, doctoral, and executive programs. Along the way, we have discovered that if we make the concepts of management useful and involve the student, the classroom is fun for both us and our students.

To capture student attention in the classroom, we would often enliven theory by telling stories about the companies we visited or consulted for. We found students to be very interested in our experiences with Travellers, Pillsbury, ITT, Union Carbide, General Motors, and many more. Thus, we have enlivened every part of this book and its supplements with cases and examples based on our experience and research.

We also believe that students learn more when they become active learners. To involve our students, we encourage them to think about, discuss, and apply their own intuitive judgment to real management decisions. We believe the cases, examples, and exercises throughout our text encourage this type of learning.

Our second principle was to produce a tightly integrated teaching/learning package that encompassed all the latest technologies. To achieve this, each and every supplement was developed simultaneously with the text, to ensure that these companion materials supported the goals and objectives of the text. To further ensure quality and consistency, the instructor's handbook, student handbook, and test bank have been extensively reviewed by a dedicated group of faculty around the country.

Our third guiding principle was that all materials be of the highest quality possible. We have been clear from the beginning about the need to stay in tune with our customers for the book. We invested a great deal of time, effort, and money in market research. We have constantly involved a team of students and other professors in criticizing and evaluating the presentation as well as the content of the book. These reviews helped us develop useful stylistic features, and avoid "cute" but useless devices.

As we considered publishers, we wanted a company that would commit to a very high standard of quality. We also wanted production, design, and marketing involved from the very beginning. As in all things, this has meant more time and energy, but we think our close work with the people at Harper & Row has been worth it. The production and design of the book and its package are of the highest quality.

SPECIAL CONTENT FEATURES

In consulting for organizations, we have found that much has changed in the last ten years that has dramatic implications for the future of management education. Many organizations have reorganized, retooled, and transformed themselves into vigorous competitors in global markets. We felt it was important to bring students close to the reality in which they would manage. The following features highlight these key themes.

Decision Making
We believe that management knowledge comes from a combination of theory, the experience of others, and, to some extent, one's own intuition. Together, these three sources affect a person's ability to make effective decisions. The test of learning, then, is not whether a person can memorize and recite information, but whether his or her application of knowledge is sharpened and more accurate. For this reason, we have chosen to present decision-making early, in Chapter 3, because it seems absolutely central to what all managers do. The decisions of managers vary greatly as to content, but the *process* of making decisions is one that can be understood early in a course, communicated in an interesting way, and used as a building block for all other areas of management activity in the text. Faculty members who have reviewed and commented on the placement and content of this chapter have found it to be a superior presentation. We hope that all of the readers of this book will come to agree with that assessment.

The Globalization of Management
Now more than ever students need to understand the intensity of foreign competition and the globalization of management ideas. We have addressed this issue in several ways. First, we have introduced relevant international ideas into each chapter. In addition, many of the examples and cases throughout the text deal with American companies as they operate overseas or, in other instances, with foreign organizations themselves.

Finally, we devote an entire chapter to the international environment. Here we discuss the challenges presented by the globalization of business, including the pitfalls of doing business in foreign cultures and the implications of foreign ownership of U.S. based businesses.

Environmental Influences
Today's managers find themselves charged with increasing responsibility for the social and ethical behavior of their organizations. Even introductory students must begin to be aware of this dimension of their future responsibility, and for this reason we have devoted separate chapters to ethics and social responsibility and to the political and legal environment. These chapters explain the ways society sets standards and formalizes ethi-

cal expectations in law and regulation. In designing these chapters, we have sought to find new and effective ways to assist faculty members who are trying to address the accreditation standards of the AACSB in the law and environment area.

Strategic Planning in Competitive Environments As competition has intensified in today's businesses, special attention has been given to charting strategic plans for success in competitive markets. Chapters 5 and 6 help readers better understand the importance and practice of strategic planning for the competitive environment of the 1990s.

Innovation and Entrepreneurship These two aspects of the modern business environment are highlighted throughout the book. The pressure to change the way things are done, to innovate, and to create new businesses is basic to understanding what drives managers and entrepreneurs. Case examples illustrate these influences in each chapter. Students will find additional examples in the *Management Student's Handbook*. Faculty will note that additional materials are contained in the *Management Instructor's Handbook*.

PEDAGOGY

Our goal has been to craft a text that presented material in ways that would interest, excite, and guide readers to new levels of understanding. The following features will help students get deeply involved in the learning process.

Focus Case Each chapter begins with a Focus Case that takes a real organization and describes a problem or situation that it faced. In the course of relating the story, the core concepts of the chapter are introduced. The case is then woven into the chapter to guide the student through the topics. This case provides a consistent reference for examining the concepts, and gives students great insight into the principles by seeing how they apply to a real organization. It is also a reference for comparison to other examples used in the chapter.

The Inside View To provide additional insights about the concepts as they exist in actual management situations, each chapter includes brief accounts of organizations, situations, or facets of the topics under discussion.

The Conference Table: Discussion Cases Management is learned by practicing. Discussion cases give the student an opportunity to practice the application of concepts covered in the chapter. Each case ends with a set of questions to stimulate thought and to lead to lively classroom exchanges.

Comprehensive Case An extended case is included at the end of each part. These cases provide the student with a chance to integrate concepts from all the chapters in the part. Each Comprehensive Case is based on the experience of a real organization.

Key Questions and Key Points We have also included learning aids for the student. Each chapter begins with a list of Key Questions. These identify the main concepts to be learned in the text and help the student put the material in the context of management issues and problems they will face. Each chapter then ends with Key Points. These function as the chapter summary and show how the answers to the Key Questions are drawn from the text.

Review Questions Each chapter ends with review questions and discussion topics. Some have been written to test students' ability to use the chapter's terminology to describe situations. Others are written to test their ability to analyze situations and assess what is happening and why. Still others present new problems for the student to solve.

Key Terms, Definitions, and Glossary To help the student learn the vocabulary of management we have highlighted the key terms and provided short definitions in the margins of the text. Key terms are then summarized at the end of each chapter, and a full glossary of terms is included at the end of the text.

ORGANIZATION OF THE BOOK

The chapters in *Management* are organized around the various functions that must be performed in all organizations and the responsibilities that all managers face in their work. The managerial functions include planning organizational activity, organizing work and designing appropriate structures to accomplish objectives, leading and guiding people, evaluating and measuring results with proper guidance-control systems, and shaping the organization's relations with the external world. These functions are related to many different types of technical, administrative, and institutional responsibilities that are shared by people in organizations.

Part One introduces the world of modern management, including the nature of managerial work, historical contributions to current practice, and the manager's responsibility as a decision maker. With a foundation of key ideas about management functions and responsibilities, sources of knowledge, and the decision-making process firmly in hand, the reader is well equipped to move into the study of major areas of managerial action.

Part Two focuses on the manager as a planner. Three chapters are devoted to the language and concepts of planning, different types of operational and strategic planning, and the role of strategic management in complex competitive environments.

Part Three is devoted to building effective organizations through the design of work activities and organization structures. These three chapters show how organization design and culture are used to build work units, adapt the organization to fit internal and external environmental factors, and create a framework in which people can be productive and innovative, and can work with minimal conflict.

Part Four deals with managing people. The importance and complexity of this area has led us to devote five chapters to such topics as motivating, directing, and leading people; developing human resource strategies within organizations; the critical role of communications; and the coordination of group activities in organizations.

Part Five focuses on the evaluation, measurement, and control of organizational performance. An introductory chapter reviews basic principles of evaluation and control. The crucial role of quality control and evaluation is extended in a separate chapter on operations and product management. Readers will also find a special new chapter on the role and uses of information systems and technology in enhancing organizational performance.

Part Six addresses the current and future impact of environmental influences on management. The responsibility of management to society and social expectations that organizations will behave in ethically appropriate ways are discussed in a separate chapter. The legal and political requirements facing organizations are also treated in a separate chapter, reflecting their special importance in the modern management environment and the need of faculty to find new and effective ways to respond to accreditation requirements in these areas. The unique requirements of operating in an international environment are addressed in a special chapter on international management. Finally, the full range of emerging technical, administrative, and institutional issues of the 1990s is drawn together in a concluding chapter.

For students who want or need a more extensive grounding in quantitative methods, we have included an appendix that reviews quantitative techniques commonly used by managers.

SUPPLEMENTS

An extensive set of supplements has been created by the authors to assist students and instructors. We have brought the same level of commitment to craftsmanship to all of these supplements.

Management Instructor's Handbook A good textbook is always enhanced by an instructor who is well prepared to guide student thinking about the usefulness of management education. To assist instructors, we have collaborated with Sandra A. Waddock of Boston College to develop an extensive handbook of resource materials. The handbook includes both material to help the instructor organize the classroom experience and enrichment material. It is organized so all materials necessary for each class are together. The instructor will not need to search through many sources to organize chapter materials. According to reviewers, the handbook sets a new standard for useful instructional support.

Each chapter of the text has a companion chapter in the *Management Instructor's Handbook* organized in the following manner.

Part I: Overview Chapter Overview; Learning Objectives; Focus Case Summary; Chapter Outline; Discussion and Review Questions; Discussion Cases; Teaching Notes.

Part II: Teaching Plan Key Concepts; Teaching Strategies; Class Plan/Teaching Tips.

Part III: Additional Resource Materials Lecture Supplements; More of "The Inside View"; Writing/Thinking Skills; Experiential Exercises; Suggested Assignments and Homework Questions; Suggested Films and Videos; Related Readings; Transparency Masters.

Management Student's Handbook   Management is a subject that is learned by practice. Concepts must be applied before they have meaning. To help students apply management concepts, we have developed cases for the student to analyze—integrative cases and comprehensive cases. The integrative cases take the student step-by-step through management situations. At critical points in the action the student is asked to analyze what is happening in the organization. Based on the analysis, the student presents recommendations for actions. These exercises sharpen a student's diagnostic abilities.

Each chapter also provides the student with a comprehensive case. This case presents a full management situation that the student must describe and analyze and for which he or she must present recommendations. The cases are developed to fit uniquely the concepts presented in the chapters. Questions help the student apply to real situations the concepts they have read in the text. The answer key contains guidance in how to analyze the situation.

In the handbook, we have also included special sections on how to study a text and analyze a case. Of added value to the students are six brief sections on how to manage their careers. The handbook also includes self-study true/false, multiple-choice, fill-in-the-blank, and essay questions.

Management Competencies Video   Watching others in management situations and analyzing their performance is an excellent way to learn how to apply management concepts. In the past, the closest students could come to management situations was through cases. In collaboration with Organizational Dynamics, Inc., a leading producer of executive educational materials, we have produced a video series that makes it possible for students to watch managers in action.

Unlike other management videos, this video focuses on the skills and competencies of management. Each situation focuses on the key skills or competencies an effective manager must have. Each situation is five to ten minutes long and each comes complete with a set of analytical assignments.

Management Competencies Video Handbook   We have written an instructor's handbook to provide guidance on how to lead discussions based on the video presentation. The handbook also includes the possible assignments for each of the video segments.

Additional Videos   Additional videos are available to supplement our text. Adopters may select from a number of videos including "The Winning Formula," "The New Entrepreneurs," "Industrial Design," and "Can America Compete?" Ideas for using the videos in the classroom are found in the *Management Competencies Video Handbook*.

Test Bank   Written by Ben Wieder (Queensborough Community College) with the text authors, it contains over 3500 extensively reviewed multiple-choice, true/false, completion, essay, and application questions. Each question is referenced by text page, cognitive type, and level of difficulty.

Harper Test The test bank is available on this highly acclaimed computerized test-generation system with full word-processing capabilities. Harper Test produces customized tests and allows instructors to scramble questions and/or add new ones. It is available for use on the Macintosh, IBM, and some compatibles.

Grades Harper & Row offers to adopters this grade-keeping and class-management package for the IBM-PC that maintains data for up to 200 students.

Transparencies A set of 100 full-color acetates of important figures and graphs from the text is available free to adopters.

Take Charge: A Management Simulation A computer simulation based on the integrative case in the study guide is available free to adopters.

ACKNOWLEDGMENTS

An enormous number of people have made important contributions to the development of this book and supplementary materials. A separate book could be written detailing all of their heroic efforts. Michelle Poirier deserves far more than a single sentence for her energy, enthusiasm, and dedication to all aspects of this project. Janet Murphy, Del Richmond, Bill Bird, Courtney Holt, Ray Moriarity, Tanya Phillips, Gina Pedley, Kay Beck, Julita Pomorska, Lani Mah, Lisa Horlick, and Bret Baird each provided valued editorial assistance at different stages of the project. Diane Lowry, Vince Mahler, Victoria Selden, and Mary Jane Curtenaz carefully edited and word processed every portion of the manuscript. Sandra A. Waddock has led the development of the *Management Instructor's Handbook,* with Mary Ellen Boyle providing valuable assistance. Mary Young has assisted in the development of the *Management Student's Handbook.* George Labovitz and Victor Rozansky of ODI, Inc., have been good friends and invaluable contributors to the development of the video materials that accompany this book.

Throughout the development, we have benefited greatly from a group of professionals whose reviews of the content and style have shaped every part of this book.

Peter Arlow, Youngstown State University
Debra A. Arvanites, Villanova University
Charna B. Blumberg, University of Texas at Arlington
Joseph E. Cantrell, De Anza College
Richard L. Clarke, Clemson University
Sharon Clinebell, University of Northern Colorado
Raymond L. Cook, University of Texas at Austin
John A. Drexler, Jr., Oregon State University
Jack R. Dustman, Northern Arizona University
James E. Estes, University of South Carolina
William Galle, University of New Orleans
Carol Harvey, Quinsigamond Community College
Phyllis G. Holland, Georgia State University

N. Larue Hubbard, Glendale Community College
Dewey E. Johnson, California State University at Fresno
Calvin Kellogg, University of Mississippi
Pamela S. Lewis, University of Central Florida
Edward Lyell, Metropolitan State College
Timothy A. Matherly, Florida State University
Donald R. McCarthy, Keene State College
James C. McElroy, Iowa State University
Robert P. McGowan, University of Denver
James Meszaros, County College of Morris
Elizabeth Peterson, University of Northern Iowa
Daniel Sauers, Louisiana Tech University
Joan Sepic-Mizis, St. Louis Community College
Eugene Schneider, Austin Community College
Mary S. Thibodeaux, University of Northern Texas
Keith F. Ward, Baylor University

We are also grateful to the following instructors for participating in two focus groups when we were in the early stages of writing. Although their names were not revealed to us at the time, their comments on the needs of those who teach the introductory management course played a major role in the shaping of this text.

Stephen C. Bushardt, University of Southern Mississippi
John A. Drexler, Jr., Oregon State University
William Galle, University of New Orleans
Douglas Grider, Louisiana Tech University
Carol Harvey, Quinsigamond Community College
Dewey E. Johnson, California State University, Fresno
James C. McElroy, Iowa State University
Robert P. McGowan, University of Denver
Daniel Sauers, Lousiana Tech University
Charles Schrader, Iowa State University
Pamela Van Epps, University of New Orleans

Each of us has made many friends in the publishing industry over the years, many of whom have influenced the look and feel of this book. Barbara Piercecchi was persuasive in convincing us that such a project could be done. Sue Gleason had an early, formative hand in making sure that it was done properly. Judy Rothman and Jayne Maerker of Harper & Row proved a dynamic duo in sponsoring the signing and development of the book. Robert Ginsberg set a superior standard of editorial craftsmanship. Paula Cousin and Joanne Goldfarb sweated over every word, line, and paragraph of this book. Debra Riegert has been tireless in bringing together all facets of this project; we award her a special "good manager" medal of author appreciation. Suzy Spivey has implemented a professional marketing plan of the highest caliber. Steve Eisen and Teresa Delgado have also provided assistance with supplements and design respectively. Harper & Row has provided us with an outstanding team of publishing professionals whose dedication to the production of highest quality books has been, and continues to be, a standard of industry excellence. We are grateful to each and every one of these people. They have earned a rest.

Families—personal and professional—pay a heavy price whenever books are written. There are activities foregone, moments lost never to be recovered. Our professional colleagues at Boston University have given freely of their knowledge, insight, and wisdom throughout the half-dozen years that this book has been in development. Our students and the managers in the many organizations we have visited, researched, and worked with as consultants have all shared far more with us through their interest and excitement than they could possibly know.

Finally, there are those spouses and children who have been so supportive for such a long time. To them, and to all who have shared in this work, we express our sincere thanks.

Lloyd S. Baird
James E. Post
John F. Mahon

About the Authors

The authors are well-known teachers, researchers, and consultants in management. This combination of academic and professional experience has influenced every facet of this book and accompanying supplementary materials.

 **LLOYD BAIRD** has taught at Boston University for 15 years. He is an expert in the study of organizational effectiveness, performance management, and human resources management. He has published widely in academic and applied journals and is the author of several books, including *Performance Management,* and editor of the popular *Sourcebook* series. Professor Baird has been a consultant and participant in executive education programs at such leading companies as the General Motors Corporation, ITT, Control Data, Digital Equipment Corporation, Union Carbide, John Hancock, and Honeywell. He has been professionally active in the Academy of Management, Human Resources Planning Society, and the American Society for Training and Development. He holds a Ph.D. from Michigan State University in Organizational Behavior and Human Resources.

JAMES E. POST is Professor of Management and Public Policy and chairman of the Management Policy Department of Boston University. He is internationally known for his research on business, government, and society relations. Professor Post has been a consultant to companies in the food, pharmaceutical, and insurance industries, an advisor to the World Health Organization and National Wildlife Federation and an expert witness before various committees of the U.S. Senate and House of Representatives. He has been chairperson of the Social Issues in Management division of the Academy of Management and a member of the editorial board of the *Academy of Management Review*. His numerous publications include five books and more than 50 papers and articles. He is the series editor of *Research in Corporate Social Performance and Policy*, an international research annual. Dr. Post holds a Ph.D. in Management and Public Policy from the State University of New York at Buffalo and a J.D. from Villanova University.

JOHN MAHON received his doctoral degree from Boston University where he is now Associate Professor of Management Policy. Professor Mahon has won numerous awards for teaching excellence and has served as a consultant and executive educator for Bell Communications Research, Bell South, Boston City Hospital, GTE, Georgia Pacific, Honeywell, NYNEX, Pillsbury, and many other private and public organizations. He is an active researcher in the areas of strategic management, regulatory effects on business, crisis management, and implementation of organization policy. His papers have appeared in the *Academy of Management Review*, *Business in the Contemporary World*, and *Strategic Management Journal*. He is a past winner of the A.T. Kearney Award for Outstanding Research in General Management, and has been recently selected as a Beta Gamma Sigma National Scholar.

PART ONE

Management

The basic principles of management had their beginnings in the birth of civilization, when people first began to live in groups and first sought to improve their lot in life. Over 2500 years ago, King Nebuchadnezzar of Babylon decided to turn his desert kingdom into an oasis to please his wife, Amytis. In the sixth century B.C., Nebuchadnezzar dug into the kingdom's treasury, hired laborers and technicians to construct a palace from the limited materials available, and had an elaborate system of aqueducts built to transport water from the local river to the palace. Construction completed, he planted beautiful and exotic trees and flowering shrubs on the terraces, and the Hanging Gardens of Babylon transformed the city.

Nebuchadnezzar set a goal: He would transform a desert metropolis into a garden oasis. He used and coordinated human, technical, and financial resources to accomplish this goal. He secured financing from the royal coffers, hired laborers and technicians, and acquired building materials from the surrounding areas. And he accomplished the goal in the context of his environment, which offered primitive plumbing and construction technology and limited means of acquiring materials from great distances. In the end, the efforts of everyone working on the project produced one of the Seven Wonders of the World.

Thus, even 2500 years ago people who wanted to accomplish large tasks used a process of management similar to the basic process used today. Management is the process of setting and accomplishing an organization's goals through the use and coordination of human, technical, and financial resources within the context of the environment. Managers undertake this process by breaking it down into its individual functions: planning, organizing, directing, and controlling.

The purpose of this book is to help you understand the management process and how it can be applied in the many different situations you will face. The principles of management you will study are tenets, rules, or codes of conduct that guide managers. They will provide a framework for action. To effectively use them, one must develop and use skills in decision making. Rational decision making is a process of identifying a problem or opportunity, developing alternative ways to address it, and selecting the best alternative. Managers must make decisions to carry out each of the functions of management and to determine which principles to apply to each situation. Thus, decision making is the most important managerial activity.

In Chapters 1 and 2, we will describe in more detail the management process and discuss the historical development of some basic principles of management. In Chapter 3 we will illustrate the process of decision making and describe tools and techniques managers can use to help them make effective decisions. In the remainder of the book we will cover in depth each of the four functions of management and the broader environment in which every organization must operate.

1 | Management: A Framework

FOCUS CASE / The Greatest Job on Earth

THE IMPORTANCE OF MANAGEMENT

MANAGEMENT DEFINED

DECISION MAKING AND MANAGEMENT FUNCTIONS
Management Decision Making
The Basic Functions of Management
Planning
Organizing
Directing
Controlling

MANAGEMENT RESPONSIBILITIES
Types of Responsibilities
The Levels of Management

SOURCES OF KNOWLEDGE ABOUT MANAGEMENT
Intuition
Experience
Research
Using All Three Sources

M anagement is the process of setting and accomplishing goals through the use of human, technical, and financial resources within the context of the environment. This process involves several core functions including planning, organizing, directing, and controlling. All managers engage in each of these functions, to a greater or lesser degree, based on the specific responsibilities they bear. This chapter explains these core functions and the way in which they are divided among managers with varying responsibilities.

KEY QUESTIONS

As you study this chapter, try to answer the following key questions:

1 Why is management important?
2 What is management?
3 Why is decision making important to management?
4 What are the four key functions that all managers perform?
5 What is the difference between efficiency and effectiveness, and why are they both important to management?
6 What are the three types of responsibilities that managers have in organizations?
7 What are the basic levels of management in an organization, and how does the mix of managerial responsibilities differ according to level?
8 What are the sources of our knowledge about management?

Focus Case

The Greatest Job on Earth

Kenneth Feld, president of Ringling Bros. and Barnum & Bailey Circus, has what he describes as "the greatest job on earth." Just like any other manager, he must plan, organize, direct, and control in order for the show to go on.

Kenneth Feld has what he calls "the greatest job on earth." He works long days and nights, often 18–20 hours at a stretch, and usually seven days a week. His job requires extensive travel throughout the United States and often to other nations. There are many headaches, usually brought on by people complaining about one thing or another. But through it all, Feld maintains that his is the greatest job on earth because he is the president of the "Greatest Show on Earth," Ringling Bros. and Barnum & Bailey Circus.

As smooth as a circus performance appears to the audience, many issues and problems confront a circus every day. Ringling Bros. is not only in the entertainment business, but also the transportation business, the restaurant business, the printing business, and the zoological business. Coordinating these businesses and keeping them running smoothly is Kenneth Feld's basic responsibility. He is a manager.

Feld's job is certainly not the typical management job. But his tasks and the skills and abilities he needs to meet those tasks are like those of any other manager. Like any manager, Feld must plan, organize, direct, and control. And like any manager, to undertake these functions he must make decisions.

Consider some of Feld's daily activities. Since Ringling Bros. and Barnum & Bailey Circus has two traveling shows, Feld has to plan which circus will travel to which cities. For example, if one circus works the western part of the United States and the other works the eastern half, which circus should visit Chicago? Dallas? St. Louis? The planning Ken Feld does has to be thorough so the overall circus operation meets its goal of being a profitable entertainment business.

The public sees only the staged performance of the circus. With split-second precision, performers cascade into the arena, undertake feats of skill and daring in rapid succession, bow, and flow back into the shadows. But the performance doesn't just happen. Extensive organizing enables the circus to be up and running within six hours of arrival in a new city and makes it possible for the acts to fit together and follow each other smoothly. Every person in the traveling show understands his or her responsibilities without having to worry about what anyone else is doing. Each person's actions fit together with the work of others because Feld has coordinated them well.

Ken Feld also directs the circus. He leads and coordinates the activities of hundreds of diverse employees—not only lion tamers, clowns, and other skilled entertainers, but also drivers, popcorn vendors, and hundreds of other employees. He sees that they are paid, transported, housed, and cared for.

Source: This case was prepared by the authors especially for this book. It is based on published information and interviews with Kenneth Feld.

Hiring, placing, motivating, and leading a staff of office workers is much different from staffing and directing a circus, but it is still a basic management function.

Directing a circus presents some unique challenges. "How do you negotiate salaries with performers who are risking their lives every day in different ways to please the audience?" asks Feld. And, he continues, "how do you supervise the world's tallest or shortest man?" Staffing the circus with special people is part of the job, but working with them is a challenge. As Feld says, "A lot of my job involves dealing with my employees, from salary negotiations, to listening to their complaints, to providing an ear as they talk through a problem."

Unexpected events also force good managers to adjust their plans, sometimes very quickly. Someone needs to control the money, operation, and people so that problems can be identified and solved to keep the circus on track. Ken Feld tells the story of receiving a telephone call from one of the traveling circus managers who informed him that the train carrying all the circus equipment, animals, and staff broke down about 50 miles from their destination. They were scheduled to perform in less than 12 hours, and there was no chance the train would arrive on time. Feld and his managers had to scramble to hire every available truck and van in the area; but the equipment, performers, and animals did get to the city on time, and the show did go on. ■

THE IMPORTANCE OF MANAGEMENT

All people, no matter what they do in life, must manage in order to accomplish almost any activity or task. Almost every person faces certain obligations each day: We must eat and sleep, go to school or work, care for our possessions. Each morning, we must determine what needs to be done, when to do it, and how to do it with limited time and money. Taking the car to the shop may mean taking a morning off from work or school and may mean forgoing a weekend vacation. In a simple sense, that is management: determining what to accomplish and allocating and coordinating resources to accomplish it in a given context.

The importance of management goes well beyond meeting personal needs, however. Modern society is characterized by people working together to accomplish tasks. One person can cut a lawn or make a dress. But most people do not build their own lawnmowers or make clothes for their entire family. We are not self-sufficient; we depend on other people and organizations to manufacture lawnmowers, clothing, and thousands of other products and to provide medical, financial, educational, and entertainment services. This interdependence, and the prominent role of organizations in our lives, highlights the importance of management.

Organizations bring together people and other resources for a common purpose, whether that purpose is to build computers, learn about human psychology, or ship food to starving people in Africa. Organizations are the means through which people coordinate their work in modern society. Just as we must manage ourselves to accomplish our objectives, managers must manage organizations to accomplish their objectives.

MANAGEMENT DEFINED

Management The process of setting and accomplishing goals through the use and coordination of human, technical, and financial resources within the context of the environment.

The term **management** has two important meanings. One dictionary defines management as "the act, art or manner of handling, controlling, or directing" and "the group of those who manage or direct an enterprise."[1] This definition suggests that management involves action directed toward some purpose and that managers are the people involved in this process. Managerial activities cannot be discussed without reference to the human beings performing them, and the position of managers within an organization is ultimately defined not by titles, but by the activities the managers perform.[2] We define management as (1) a process of setting and accomplishing goals (2) through the use and coordination of human, technical, and financial resources (3) within the context of the environment.

1. *Management Is a Process of Setting and Accomplishing Goals* Every organization is created and operated to accomplish *something*—usually many things—such as developing a state-of-the-art product or servicing a group of customers. The possibilities are endless. To achieve each goal, managers must break it down into objectives the organization can achieve. The broad goal of Ringling Bros. and Barnum & Bailey Circus, for example, is to entertain the public. To accomplish that broad purpose, Ken Feld may decide that the circus will perform in the 20 largest cities in the United States during the next 12 months. This objective is consistent with the broad goal, but it is more precise and enables other people in the circus to focus their activities so the desired results are produced. The person in charge of public relations can contact the media in each town, for example, and the people in charge of setting up or laying out the circus arena can study the facilities in each city. The activities of all the managers and employees of the circus, taken together, result in the accomplishment of the overall goal.

2. *Management Uses and Coordinates Human, Technological, and Financial Resources* To accomplish goals, managers bring together people, materials, money, and technology. This task involves determining what quantity of resources is necessary to accomplish a goal, finding these resources, and managing them so the task is accomplished in the best way possible. As you will see throughout this book, costs can often be reduced and benefits expanded through better use and coordination of resources. For example, reorganizing the way food is served in a dormitory dining hall can often reduce the length of time students must spend waiting. Reorganizing the way cars are produced on an assembly line has resulted in significant cost and time savings in the past decade alone. In short, management involves the creative use and coordination of resources to achieve the organization's goals.

3. *Management Operates Within the Context of the Environment* Management exists in an environment that includes competition, the demands of customers, the restrictions imposed by governments, the state of the economy, and even the actions of foreign governments in some cases. A general model of the organization and its environment is presented in Exhibit 1.1. We will discuss it further in Chapter 6.

Each factor in the environment may help, hinder, or otherwise influence the organization. For example, customer demand for a product might allow the organization to produce and sell large quantities of this product and make a sizable profit, while government restrictions such as mandatory safety attachments might make the product too expensive to be profitable.

EXHIBIT / 1.1
The Organization and Its Environment

International factors

Competition

Social factors

Organization

Political factors

Technological factors

Economical factors

Legal factors

Management would be a far less challenging task if not for the changes, threats, and opportunities the environment thrusts upon the organization. If the world around managers and their organizations was stable, they could quite easily determine a plan, set up the organization to achieve it, direct the organization's employees, and control the operation without incident. But there is no such thing as a stable environment. Learning how to manage in a changing environment is a manager's most difficult—and most exciting—challenge. We will discuss this further in several sections of the book, particularly Chapter 6, and also in Part Six, which covers the social, legal, political, and international components of the environment.

To summarize our definition of management, consider Ken Feld and the Ringling Bros. and Barnum & Bailey Circus. He and his managers continuously set goals and objectives for the circus and its component parts. To accomplish their objectives, they coordinate these parts with sufficient financing and technology (sound, special effects, lighting). Finally, they make management decisions in the context of a larger environment (e.g., population density, regulation of transportation, city ordinances for waste disposal).

DECISION MAKING AND MANAGEMENT FUNCTIONS

Although organizations vary greatly in terms of size, activities, and number of employees, every manager performs a critical role: decision making. To plan, organize, direct, and control, managers must make decisions: What will our course of action be? How will we structure ourselves to accomplish it? Who will we recruit to help us achieve our goals, and how will we direct them? What will we do if our plans fail or our goals are not met? Some decisions are very important and have broad consequences (We will close our Cleveland store); others are of more modest importance and consequence (We will use liquid soap in the lavatories). Whatever the specific job of the manager, all of his or her functions and activities involve decision making.

Management Decision Making

Management decision making Identifying a problem or opportunity, developing alternatives, and selecting the best.

Management decision making is a process of identifying a problem or opportunity, developing alternative ways to address it, and selecting the best alternative. Two characteristics distinguish management decisions from everyday, individual decisions: First, management decisions are made in the context of the organization. They affect various groups of people (employees, customers, suppliers), the plans or objectives of the organization or its subunits, or the methods of accomplishing those plans and objectives. Even minor decisions have organizational implication (e.g., powdered soap would more effectively remove greasy dirt than liquid soap, a relevant consideration in a machine shop). Second, many important managerial decisions involve large amounts of data, such as sales figures, production levels, or financing restrictions. Managers often must analyze and synthesize data from multiple sources to make decisions.

The basic skills for management decision making are discussed in Chapter 3, and the entire book deals with the various types of decisions that managers make as they carry out the other functions of management.

The Basic Functions of Management

Managers use decision-making skills and tools to perform the four basic functions of management: planning, organizing, directing, and controlling.[3] However, not all managers perform all the functions all of the time, for example, not every manager makes plans every day. Nor do managers necessarily perform the functions in sequence. But within any organization, all four functions must be performed by the managers together if the organization is to be successful over time. As an integrated team, the managers must plan, organize, direct, and control.

Assume a student organization decides to hold a fall festival weekend, including a concert by a popular musical group. The committee must first decide what group to hire and where to locate the festival, obtain approvals, and handle other specifics of production. These activities involve some planning, some organizing, and some controlling. The activities of the festival itself must then be determined and scheduled, funds collected, and tickets sold. Again, this involves several functions simultaneously. Finally, the committee must direct the operation and control the activities to meet its goals within the budget. If the planning, organizing, directing, and controlling are coordinated and handled effectively, the fall festival weekend can be a financial and social success; if they are not, the weekend will fall short of its objectives. The same is true for all organizations.

Planning

Planning The process of analyzing the environment, setting objectives, and designing courses of action to achieve them.

Managers must think ahead. Managers are responsible for accomplishing some objective and must be able to anticipate problems. **Planning** is a process by which managers analyze the organization and its environment, set objectives, and design courses of action to achieve them.

The planning function serves several purposes. First, planning identifies priorities and guides managers in acquiring and committing resources (people, money, etc.). Second, planning provides clear directions to organizational members, showing how their activities relate to overall organizational goals. Third, planning is a blueprint for action and a reference point for monitoring activities and measuring whether goals are being accomplished. Plans are also used to determine new courses of action, as illustrated in The Inside View 1.1.

Dayton Hudson's Creative Planning

Future-oriented companies do not want to fall into repetitious routines. Even a monthly planning meeting can take on a new color if it is held in an unusual and stimulating environment.

Planning for the future sometimes involves planning to stop doing what you've always been doing and do something else, as the executives of Dayton Hudson Corporation are well aware. Not only have their plans been departures from the mean, but their planning methods are somewhat eccentric as well. One monthly planning session was held in a historical mansion, another at a golf course, others in still stranger places—anywhere but the office, if possible. Says Chairman Kenneth A. Macke, "It seems ridiculous to hold meetings, where you talk about change, in the same place all the time."[1]

It should come as no surprise, therefore, that Dayton Hudson, a prominent department store chain for decades, should plan to move into a variety of nondepartment store enterprises and out of department stores. Dayton Hudson's five-year expansion plan calls for no department store openings at all but does call for the opening of 13 discount electronics and small appliance stores in New England. In addition, 90 percent of the $4 billion allotted to this expansion is expected to go to Target and Mervyn's stores, solidifying Dayton Hudson's position in the discount clothing market, which has been stealing business from other department store chains for years. If you can't beat'em, join'em.

This is not to say that Dayton Hudson has been ahead of, or on top of, every trend to come down

the pike. For example, the number of B. Dalton Bookseller stores (a subsidiary of Dayton Hudson), located primarily in shopping malls, expanded rapidly during the 1970s. In recent years, however, the number of openings dropped off, not because Dayton Hudson planned to cut back on the expansion, but because the number of mall openings decreased and because they failed to pick up on the extent to which discount bookselling had been drawing from the retail market. Dayton Hudson also abandoned plans to move into discount designer fashions after realizing that the market was too small. It sold off all four Plum's stores to another retailer.

But these shelved plans are the exception. Since George Draper Dayton founded the first store in Minneapolis in 1902, his five grandsons opened a string of shopping malls after World War II, and the company merged with J. L. Hudson Company in 1969, Dayton Hudson has continuously and ambitiously repositioned itself into fast-growing retail segments and out of stagnating ones. With creative, anticipative, and responsive planning and replanning, Dayton Hudson can expect continued success and growing profits. ∎

NOTE

1. Pitzer, Mary J., "Dayton Hudson Steals a Page from the Opposition's Playbook," *Business Week,* November 18, 1985, p. 70.

Managers throughout an organization must plan. For example, the supervisor of a local Burger King restaurant plans daily inventory levels, food and supply orders, and employee staffing. Because Burger King is a franchise operation, with thousands of branches throughout the United States, a central management staff manages overall Burger King operations. These managers plan such things as national marketing campaigns and the introduction of new foods and product lines (e.g., the fast-food salad bar). The president of overall Burger King operations plans for the continued growth of the restaurant chain. He considers such variables as restaurant location and sales volume per restaurant in developing this plan. The president and the local and regional Burger King restaurant managers all consider the same things when planning—goals, objectives, targets, adjustment to change—but each has a different focus.

We can extend this example further. Burger King is a division of the Pillsbury Co., which was once primarily in the grain-milling and bakery products business. Years ago, Pillsbury's top management, seeing the need to diversify in order to stabilize earnings and profits, created a plan: The company would acquire businesses with patterns of earnings that were immune to the volatile gluts and shortages that characterize the grain and flour business. Their search led them to Burger King, which needed money for continued expansion. Today, Burger King is a contributor to Pillsbury's annual sales and earnings, while Pillsbury facilitates Burger King's continued growth. More recently, Pillsbury was acquired by Grand Metropolitan, a British company. Now Pillsbury's sales and revenues are a part of Grand Metropolitan's income.

As the example illustrates, the planning that is done by different managers—at the local restaurant, the regional center, the national headquarters of Burger King, and Pillsbury—differs in scope and specifics but accomplishes similar purposes for each of the managers. The same is true in any organization. Planning is the tool that helps the manager connect present activities to future objectives. We will review the basic principles of planning in Chapters 4 through 6, but they are also relevant to functions discussed in the remainder of the book.

Organizing

Organizing Identifying the work to be done, dividing it into units, and coordinating efforts to accomplish the goals.

The **organizing** function requires identifying the work to be undertaken to accomplish objectives, dividing it into parts or units, assigning these parts to specific departments, and then coordinating the individual efforts with the available technical and financial resources. Organizing has two aspects—the organization of work (the responsibilities included in each job) and the structure of the organization itself (integration of the jobs and the organization's resources). The Inside View 1.2 illustrates what one company did to organize human and nonhuman resources to streamline its operations.

Certain characteristics of the organization and its environment will influence the way work is organized and job responsibilities are determined. For example, human skills and the availability and complexity of technology greatly affect the organization of work. Modern offices provide a good illustration of this point. Secretaries once had to answer telephones, take dictation, type letters and reports, and file materials. The introduction of word-processing equipment, however, greatly altered the nature and content of the secretary's job. Some secretaries will require special training in the use of word-processing equipment, and others may be eliminated entirely due to the speed of the equipment. Thus, the office of the future may have no secretaries as we know them today. Rather, there

Organizing Men and Machines at Knife River Coal Co.

Doug Kane, vice president of operations for Knife River Coal Co., has a problem common to many business executives: how to bring a long-established company into the computer age without alienating a dedicated staff, many of whom have been with the company for decades.

Knife River Coal, a wholly owned subsidiary of Montana Dakota Utilities with headquarters in Bismarck, North Dakota, mines coal in the lignite coal country of western North Dakota. With an equipment fleet worth nearly $100 million, the company works three surface mines 24 hours a day, seven days a week, feeding coal to the huge Coyote power plant at Beulah, North Dakota, and to the Bigstone power plant in South Dakota, as well as to other smaller plants.

To reach the coal, workers remove earth and rock to depths of 40 to 100 feet, a process that creates long, open pits and requires some of the largest earth-moving equipment made. Knife River has draglines with booms 310 feet long and 70-cubic-yard buckets, as well as a sizable fleet of large scrapers and dozers. During the company's busiest season, January and February, this equipment often works in sub-zero temperatures. Until now, the equipment has been managed and maintained by the supervisors.

"It's getting to be too much to keep track of," says Kane. "We've got more than $3 million worth of parts alone. We are getting so much equipment for the number of people we have that we have to computerize."

Computerizing meant adding information and computer specialists as well as experts who could develop and implement sophisticated maintenance and inventory systems. A big problem was how to organize these specialists.

Management decided to keep the number of experts to a minimum and have them work directly with the supervisors. As a consultant from Caterpillar said, "If we can show the supervisor in the field that it's going to benefit him by saving two hours a week doing reports or five hours a

Even coal mining is being affected by computerization. As new information technology is added, new types of organizations must be created.

month filling out paperwork, then the guy will see there's something in it for him."

Before installing the system, Kane and other company executives talked extensively with operations people at the Knife River mines, particularly the employees who would have the most exposure to hands-on computer work. As Kane said, "Based on our finding, we decided to push the installation of a maintenance and inventory system, even though it requires a lot of front-end money."

In introducing computers to the Knife River mines, the strategy has been to make each user a part of the system with a personal stake in making the system succeed. Management did not want a big centralized computer department responsible for the system. Satisfied that he and the other company executives have met these ends, Kane says Knife River will enter the computer age with a $300,000 expenditure in a maintenance and inventory system. By the end of the year all basic functions at Knife River will be computerized. ∎

Source: Adapted from Moghmer, P., "Mining Company Matches Computer System with People," *Construction Equipment,* February 15, 1985, p. 37.

will be word-processing operators, communication specialists, and office administrators. The content of each job will be different from what it is today. Managers must configure the jobs in the best way possible to accomplish organizational objectives.

The second aspect of organizing involves the structure of the entire organization. Once goals have been determined, plans have been made, and objectives specified, appropriate organizational structures must be developed to carry out these programs. The structure of a service organization, such as a college, will be quite different from that of a production organization, such as an air conditioner manufacturer. This is not a trivial issue since excellent plans and goals can be derailed by poor structure. The structure must fit both the internal characteristics of the organization and the characteristics of the organization's operating environment and must be able to change as these sets of characteristics change.

Decisions about the organizational structure and the jobs people do are highly interrelated, as Ken Feld is well aware. Because it is expensive to transport and feed people and animals, he must carefully determine the types of performers needed and the number of tasks each person must perform for the circus. The number and type of responsibilities included in each job will determine how the jobs can be coordinated to form the organizational structure of the circus. People must understand how their individual jobs relate to what others do for the circus to be a success.

Historically, the military and the Roman Catholic Church, with their emphasis on formal hierarchical structures and authority, served as models of how to structure organizations. Today, we are in the midst of a revolution in organizational structure and design. Formal, hierarchical structures are not as effective for organizations operating in a rapidly changing environment, and managers have learned to adapt and experiment with new, more flexible designs. "Tall" organizational structures, characterized by numerous levels of management and centralized control, are increasingly being replaced by "flat" organization structures, characterized by fewer management levels and greater independence of organizational units. High-technology companies such as Hewlett Packard and Apple Computer have succeeded, in part, because their organizational departments are highly autonomous and their employees work as equals.

There are many differing ideas about how best to organize work activities and build effective organizational structures and systems.[4] Many organizations have adopted principles from the Japanese, whose more flexible, less hierarchical organizations have proven more successful than the traditional rigid structure of American corporations.[5] Organizing, an area in which the principles of management have changed greatly during the past 100 years, is discussed in Part Three.

Directing

Directing Focusing people's skills, time, and energy on the goals to be accomplished.

Directing requires focusing people's skills, time, and energy on organizational goals. This function involves staffing, communicating, motivating, and coordinating groups.

Directing is the core of what is typically called human resource management, one of the primary responsibilities of all managers. Individual managers must motivate and direct their employees, must communicate goals and strategy, and must make sure their employees are working together effectively. In addition, they must keep the department fully staffed, make promotional recommendations, and manage many other human resource considerations. In most organizations a separate department, usually called the personnel department, helps the manager with hiring, training, compensating, and promoting activities and generally keeps track of all the organization's employees.

The directing function is challenging specifically because it involves people, the organization's most valuable and complex resource. Effective management of this function is crucial to an organization's success.

Controlling

Controlling Setting performance standards, comparing actual performance to these standards, and taking appropriate corrective action.

Controlling is the management function in which performance standards are set based on objectives and overall goals, actual performance is compared to the standards, and appropriate action is taken if performance does not meet these standards. If managers design creative, realistic plans, organize effectively to accomplish them, staff the organization with the most qualified people and direct them well, then lean back and relax, all their efforts may be wasted. Managers must constantly monitor progress; they must know whether the organization is, in fact, moving toward the accomplishment of its goals. Evaluation and control are the means of doing this. Assume, for example, that the standard level for the production of pens in a manufacturing operation is 60 pens per minute. If actual production is 40 pens per minute, managers know a goal is not being met. The standard is something against which the manager can compare actual performance. If performance doesn't meet the established standard, management must adjust by correcting performance or by altering the standard to reflect the changed circumstances.

Because controlling involves the setting of standards and the measurement of performance against them, managers often rely on quantitative standards and measurement devices. Suppose that Ken Feld sets a goal of increasing circus attendance and implements plans to promote ticket sales through advertising. His standard of comparison will be last year's ticket sales. If the number of tickets sold in Phoenix is greater than last year, but the number in Los Angeles is fewer, Feld will have to try to determine why the promotional campaign worked in Phoenix but not in L.A. These figures prompt questions, so managers look for explanations. This research points to problems and helps managers determine what to do next. Quantitative measures don't explain why something happened, but they illustrate discrepancies between actual performance and desired or anticipated performance.

Of course, controlling is much more complex than simply meeting numerical standards. It requires keeping the organization on track and responsive to its environment. In other words, managers must have some autonomy to allow them to be responsive but must also be restricted so that overall organizational performance can be controlled. As The Inside View 1.3 illustrates, it is not always easy to determine just how much control to exercise, how much freedom to allow, and how to correct an imbalance between these two.

Control can be a problematic function; it is difficult to measure performance and to balance control with freedom. To guide themselves, therefore, managers can ask two basic questions: Are we doing things right? (efficiency); and, Are we doing the right things? (effectiveness).[6] Control systems should be set up to help ensure both.

THE INSIDE VIEW / 1.3

A Fine Balance of Control

Thomas D. Sege, Chairman of Varian Associates, faces the challenge of providing freedom to workers and at the same time maintaining control.

Even the most experienced and knowledgeable managers can have difficulty achieving a balance between a desire to control and a need to delegate responsibility to others. Consider the case of Thomas D. Sege, chairman of Varian Associates, Inc., a high-tech electronic gear manufacturer in Palo Alto, California. After 16 years as an electrical engineer at Varian, Sege took the helm in 1981, as the company was experiencing its first loss in ten years. Immediately, he launched a three-year turnaround program that involved, among other extreme measures, selling off a dozen businesses. As hoped, in 1984 Varian achieved record earnings of $60 million.

Turnaround achieved, Sege decided to shift his responsibilities to strategy formulation and hired former Honeywell executive Jerome J. Meyer to be president. Having delegated day-to-day operational concerns to someone else, Sege was going to relax and enjoy the ride for a while, leaving day-to-day control to Meyer. The ride turned out to be short. In 1985, profits fell to $26 million, and Varian lost roughly $10 million in the fiscal year ending September 30. Meyer resigned and returned to Honeywell the following June, citing "different management styles." Sege reshuffled management duties, imposed layoffs, and cut executive salaries by 10 percent. It was expected that these measures would again turn the company around, but talk of takeover attempts had already hit the rumor mill.

What went wrong? Sege is self-admittedly a zealous manager who switches in and out of the tough-guy mode as the situation dictates. But many of his employees and associates have implied or stated outright that he "overmanages." Some former executives accused him of always staring over their shoulders. One manager said, "Jerry [Meyer] was never given the authority to do the things he would have done" to keep the company up and running profitably. Perhaps because Sege was so good at taking the helm, he was reluctant to turn it over to his new president. Apparently admitting that possibility, Sege recently installed new management in the major groups and product lines and promised to delegate more responsibility. "I'll stimulate and contribute," he said, "not take over." ■

Source: Wilson, John W., "Can a Tough Guy Approach Work Again at Varian?" *Business Week,* October 5, 1987, p. 103.

Efficiency The best possible use of time, money, and resources.

Efficiency is the best use of time, money, and resources. Nearly all resources are scarce, so it is important to gain the greatest output or value for whatever resources are utilized. This relationship of inputs (resources used) to outputs is essentially the level of productivity of a firm or operation. Consider an illustration: Assume there are two organizations, ABC Corp. and XYZ Corp. Each has 500 employees, a \$50 million annual budget, and a plant with an assembly line used to produce manual typewriters for office use. ABC Corp. has a steady output of 500 typewriters per month. At XYZ Corp., however, typewriter production vacillates between 100 and 350 per month. ABC Corp., by definition, is more efficient. **Effectiveness,** on the other hand, refers to the accomplishment of proper goals.[7] Managers must ask whether they are doing the right thing. Though ABC may be more efficient than XYZ in producing typewriters, both may be ineffective if more and more businesses are switching to electric typewriters and word-processing computers. Thus, it is possible to be efficient yet ineffective at the same time. Many organizations in fact are just that, at least temporarily, in times of rapid change. If new and improved products or services are introduced suddenly by an innovative firm, many of its competitors may continue to produce "outdated" ones efficiently for some time, until they can afford to develop and produce something for which the market demonstrates a greater demand.

Effectiveness The accomplishment of proper goals.

It is also possible to be effective and inefficient simultaneously. XYZ Corp. may decide that, because of changes in customer demand, they will switch to the manufacture of office computers for word processing. Because they have no experience, they may be very inefficient. Production levels may be low, quality uneven, inventory unpredictable, or resources misappropriated. But the company is still being effective, by definition, because customers want and buy word processors. No matter how efficiently ABC produces manual typewriters, it will never be effective as long as the customer wants word processors.

In practice, managers must balance the need for efficiency with the need for effectiveness. In Exhibit 1.2, we have suggested that the management process should ideally result in both effectiveness and efficiency.

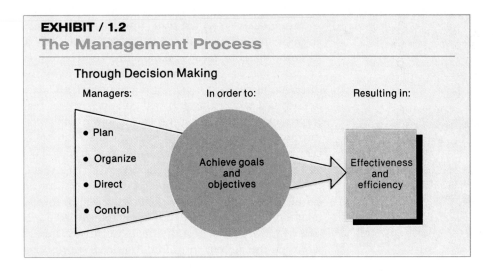

EXHIBIT / 1.2
The Management Process

Through Decision Making

Managers: In order to: Resulting in:

- Plan
- Organize   Achieve goals   Effectiveness
- Direct   and objectives   and
- Control   efficiency

MANAGEMENT RESPONSIBILITIES

All managers perform the functions of management. They plan, organize, direct, and control so that objectives are accomplished. However, the nature and focus of these functions vary according to the manager's responsibilities.[8] Some managers deal primarily with equipment and technology and are directly responsible for producing goods and services; they have technical responsibilities. Others deal primarily with people and are responsible for coordinating and directing work; they have administrative responsibilities. Still others are responsible for setting direction for the organization and managing its relationship with the environment; they have institutional responsibilities.[9] See Exhibit 1.3.

EXHIBIT / 1.3
Three Types of Management Responsibilities

Technical responsibility	Responsibility for the technical activity that produces the goods or services the organization provides
Administrative responsibility	Responsibility for guiding and coordinating the work of many people so that together they accomplish organizational objectives
Institutional responsibility	Responsibility for directing and guiding the organization and representing it to the public

---

Types of Responsibilities

The differences between technical, administrative, and institutional responsibilities of management are clear in many situations. Consider the responsibilities involved, for example, in sailing a three-masted ship. Someone must raise the sails, climb the rigging, and secure the ropes that hold the sails in place. These are technical responsibilities. In addition, since a large ship has many sails and sailors, someone, such as the first mate, must coordinate and direct the sailors so that the appropriate sails are unfurled at the right time and secured with the proper lines. In short, someone must assume administrative responsibility. Finally, even if sailors raise and lower sails properly and they work together as a team under the direction of the first mate, the whole effort will be useless unless someone has determined where the ship will go and for what reason. Someone must assume responsibility for guiding the entire ship on its journey to a destination. That is institutional responsibility. Let us discuss each of the responsibilities briefly as they apply to typical business situations.

Technical responsibility
Direct responsibility for producing goods and services.

Technical responsibility involves the work that directly produces goods and services. For example, a hospital provides medical assistance to sick and injured people, and banks provide financial services. Providing medical service is the function of the hospital that differentiates it from a bank. Managers and supervisors who work directly with the physicians and nurses, such as the nursing supervisor and the director of patient services, are responsible for the technical work of the hospital. Managers and supervisors who work directly with the accountants, tellers, and clerical personnel are responsible for the technical work of the bank.

Administrative responsibility Responsibility for directing and coordinating the work of other people.

Administrative responsibility involves coordinating the work of others. In the hospital, for instance, the head nurse coordinates the schedules of the nursing supervisors, who in turn coordinate the nurses throughout the hospital. The nursing activities also must be coordinated with patient record keeping, pharmacy inventory, and facilities maintenance. Support services are needed to transfer patients into and out of the intensive care unit. All these activities must be coordinated to provide patient care. The administrative responsibilities of management, with their heavy emphasis on coordination, communication, and interpersonal relations, require special skills in understanding and managing people.[10]

Institutional responsibility is quite different from technical and administrative responsibilities. Institutional responsibility involves guiding and directing the organization. To continue with the example of the hospital, it is important for a hospital to have a clear purpose, understand its customers and competitors, and operate within governmental guidelines and license requirements. Those with institutional responsibilities represent the hospital to the public and work to make sure the hospital serves the needs of its patients.

Institutional responsibility Responsibility for setting overall direction for the organization and managing relationships with the environment.

The Levels of Management

Although every management job involves some mixture of technical, administrative, and institutional responsibilities, different levels of management tend to emphasize one or another of the responsibilities. It is useful to think of a pyramid to represent levels of management as shown in Exhibit 1.4. We have emphasized that rigid hierarchies are increasingly being replaced with flatter, more flexible structures. However, the basic principle still holds that direction is to be set by a top management group, which is accountable for organizational success, and that managers and employees with various responsibilities will carry out these plans. Top managers oversee the entire organization. Reporting to top managers are the middle managers, who manage the individual units of the organization. Reporting to middle managers are first-line managers, or supervisors, who are directly involved in the technical work of the organization. The mix of responsibilities at each of these levels is different.

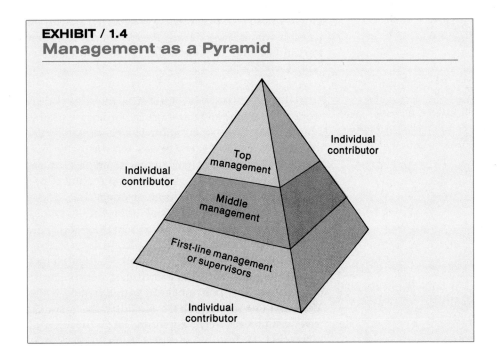

EXHIBIT / 1.4
Management as a Pyramid

Individual contributor

Top management

Individual contributor

Middle management

First-line management or supervisors

Individual contributor

Individual contributor

EXHIBIT / 1.5
Mix of Management Responsibilities

	First-Line Managers	Individual Contributors	Middle Managers	Top Managers
Dominant responsibilities	Mostly technical	Mostly technical	Mostly administrative	Mostly institutional
Examples				
Hospital	Shift supervisor; head nurse	Physician	Chief of surgery; director of nursing	Chief of staff; hospital director
High-technology company	Production supervisor	Software designer	Plant manager	Director of planning
Pharmaceutical company	Local sales manager	Research and development scientist Patent lawyer	Manager of East Coast marketing	Vice president of pharmaceutical operations
Real estate developer	Construction foreman	Architect	Project manager	Chief executive officer
Ringling Bros. and Barnum & Bailey Circus	Foreman of setup crew	Lion tamer	Ringmaster	Kenneth Feld, Chief Executive

Many organizations have a fourth type of manager—the individual contributor—whose role of providing specialized skills is becoming increasingly important but who doesn't fit into the traditional management hierarchy. Examples of top, middle, and first-line managers and individual contributors are listed in Exhibit 1.5.

First-line managers
Those who directly supervise the technical work force.

First-line Managers **First-line managers** directly supervise the technical work force of the organization. Subordinates of first-line managers perform the actual work of the organization. In an automobile plant, for example, the first-line managers supervise the workers who actually assemble automobiles, operate machines, order and deliver supplies, and perform repairs. First-line managers are responsible for spotting and resolving technical problems quickly with a minimum amount of work stoppage or down time. Today, supervisory work increasingly involves developing cooperation among employees. Thus, first-line managers are increasingly required to have good communication and interpersonal skills.

The jobs of first-line managers are dominated by technical responsibilities. In most organizations first-line managers coordinate their activities with those of other supervisory personnel and with the middle managers to whom they report. Thus, first-line managers have administrative responsibility as well. They may also have institutional responsibilities, as in the case of a nursing supervisor who represents the hospital at a professional conference.

Middle managers Those who direct and coordinate the efforts of supervisors and are the link between the operating level and top management.

Middle Managers **Middle managers** are those who direct and coordinate the efforts of the supervisors and are the link between top management and the operating level of the organization. Middle managers may actually run a subunit or part of the organization (the Baltimore plant, the software division) or be part of the chain of responsibility that oversees and evaluates the running of the organization's parts. Depending on the size of the organization, there may be one or many layers of middle management. The vast diversity of middle-manager positions makes it difficult to generalize about their responsibilities. However, middle managers are responsible for interpreting top management's broad plans and strategies and translating them into operational concepts and plans.

The middle manager's time is dominated by administrative responsibilities. Middle managers spend much time discussing ideas with managers above and below them in the organization. They spend some time directly supervising the work of managers who report to them and often must prepare and present information to those to whom they report. Coordination is the heart of a middle manager's administrative responsibility, although another responsibility is to troubleshoot, either as an expert on technical problems or as an implementor of new actions that top management has ordered. These responsibilities require that the middle manager possess technical as well as administrative skills.

In summary, middle management tends to be dominated by administrative responsibilities but involves substantial technical responsibilities as well. Middle managers have fewer institutional responsibilities than top management but do represent the organization to civic groups and professional organizations and also may be involved in helping to set the organization's direction.

Top managers Those responsible for the total organization.

Top Managers **Top managers** and senior executives are responsible for the total organization or unit. They make decisions about the long-term direction of the organization, its goals and objectives, and the basic plans for achieving those objectives. This group of managers also represents the organization to the outside world, often giving speeches to public groups, appearing before government agencies, and providing statements to the press. Today, much attention is given to the quality of life inside organizations and the culture of the organization, and much recent research has emphasized the important role that top managers play in creating and shaping the basic values of the organization. Top management, through its ability to set goals and objectives, reward others, and determine how resources will be invested, influences and shapes the organization's culture.

Most of top management's activities are related to the institutional responsibilities, but top management also has administrative responsibilities. The vice president of finance for a department store chain, for example, will outline broad priorities through budget allocations on the institutional level and will also spend considerable time coordinating the manner in which various stores deposit funds with banks and suppliers. In addition, a top manager, such as the vice president of finance, has some technical responsibilities, such as preparing and reviewing reports about the company's finances.

Individual contributors Unsupervised technical specialists who make independent or autonomous contributions.

Individual Contributor Modern organizations also have managers at all levels who have almost entirely technical responsibilities. These managers are known as **individual contributors.** These unsupervised technical specialists make independent or autonomous contributions to the organization and are responsible for accomplishing their own work and coordinating their work with that of others. In many organizations, for example, there are scientists, engineers, lawyers, and physicians whose work can only be managed by the professionals themselves. Physicians in hospitals are not employees in the same way that hospital nurses are. They are the center of the work activity, and they make decisions that determine how the work will progress.

Individual contributors typically do not fit neatly into the standard organizational structure. There are no first-line supervisors for physicians in an operating room. To the extent that there is supervision, it is done through a process known as peer review in which other physicians evaluate a doctor whose actions have been questioned. Similar forms of nonhierarchical reviews occur in other organizations where professionals are important contributors. More importantly, management of professionals is moving in the direction of equals managing equals rather than bosses managing workers. Some of the most successful companies in the computer industry, such as Hewlett Packard and Apple Computer, IBM, and Digital Equipment, encourage self-direction and self-supervision and have created innovative systems through which employees monitor and direct their own performance.

Individual contributors have a high degree of technical responsibility. The lion tamer at the Ringling Bros. and Barnum & Bailey Circus, for example, is an individual contributor. The lion tamer is responsible for putting on a good show each time and also for making certain that the lions are cared for, healthy, and trained. To arrange for all of these needs to be filled, the lion tamer must assume some administrative responsibilities. Because the lions and the lion tamer also represent the circus at media events and public appearances, this individual contributor also assumes some institutional responsibility. In short, the individual contributor's job is dominated by technical responsibility but also includes some administrative and institutional responsibilities.

Thus far, we have described the four basic functions of management and the types of responsibilities managers at the three basic levels of an organization have. Management scholar Henry Mintzberg offers another framework that is useful in understanding what managers do. He argues that managers at every level of an organization perform three basic sets of roles—behaviors and activities that are part of their jobs or that come with their positions.[11] These managerial activities are the interpersonal, informational, and decisional roles of managers and are illustrated in Exhibit 1.6.

SOURCES OF KNOWLEDGE ABOUT MANAGEMENT

At this point, you should have two basic understandings about management. First, to set and accomplish goals through the use of various resources in the context of the environment, management must plan, organize, direct, and control. Second, to ensure organizational success, management must meet its technical, administrative, and institutional responsibilities. Though this may sound simple, the development of these two principles took centuries. All the principles that will be discussed in this book were derived over time from various sources. Some principles are based on personal hunches and intuition, whereas others reflect the experience of successful entrepreneurs, celebrated tycoons, or innovative workers in organizations. Until the 1900s, experience and intuition were the primary sources of management know-how. With the development of the concept of functions of management, however, research has also become an important source of management principles.

EXHIBIT / 1.6
Mintzberg's Summary of Ten Roles of Managers

Role	Description
Interpersonal	
Figurehead	Symbolic head; obliged to perform routine duties of a legal or social nature
Leader	Responsible for the motivation and activation of subordinates; responsible for staffing, training, and associated duties
Liaison	Maintains self-developed network of outside contacts and informers who provide favors and information
Informational	
Monitor	Seeks and receives wide variety of special information (much of it current) to develop thorough understanding of organization and environment; emerges as nerve center of internal and external information of the organization
Disseminator	Transmits information received from outsiders or from other subordinates to members of the organization; some information factual, some involving interpretation and integration of diverse value positions of organizational influences
Spokesperson	Transmits information to outsiders on organization's plans, policies, actions, results, etc.; serves as expert on organization's industry
Decisional	
Entrepreneur	Searches organization and its environment for opportunities and initiates "improvement projects" to bring about change; supervises design of certain projects as well
Disturbance handler	Responsible for corrective action when organization faces important, unexpected disturbances
Resource allocator	Responsible for the allocation of organizational resources of all kinds—in effect the making or approval of all significant organizational decisions
Negotiator	Responsible for representing the organization at major negotiations

Source: Mintzberg, Henry, excerpt from *The Nature of Managerial Work,* copyright © 1977 by Henry Mintzberg. Reprinted by permission of Harper & Row, Publishers, Inc.

Intuition

Instinct and intuition were once the basis for business management. For example, if a customer ordered an unusually large wagon for hauling extremely heavy loads, a master cart maker might send one apprentice to find sturdier wood and another to fashion stronger pins and bolts, and might make a few sketches of stronger axle fittings or wagon beds. Through experience and intuition, he would construct a stronger wagon.

Entrepreneurs—people who start up new businesses—often manage on the basis of their instinct and intuition. In the computer industry during the 1970s and 1980s, hundreds of hardware and software companies were formed by entrepreneurs who knew a great deal about technology and much less about management. Some survived; many others did not.[12] A great number of these companies started off well because of the founder's technical instincts but then needed a professional manager to help overcome the problems of growth and size. In short, management by instinct and intuition alone is rarely successful today. There is simply too much to know about management for someone's instinct always to be correct. In an increasingly competitive world, even one small mistake can sometimes cause great damage.

Experience

Experience is a major source of management principles. Like the artisan who trained the apprentice, experienced managers train new managers. This is especially true in well-established companies, where rules and policies have been developed over many years. The experience of the railroads in overcoming the communications problems among operations that were spread over thousands of miles became the basis for other companies' approaches to the problem of geographic distance. The success of McDonald's inexpensive hamburgers of consistent quality provided an example to the many companies that followed it into the fast-food field. Sometimes the experience is directly applicable (How did we solve that problem in our plant in Peoria?), and sometimes it is indirect (A similar problem happened in the aerospace industry a few years ago.). As we shall see, good management often relies on the creative application of lessons learned through the experiences of others.

Research

The third way of developing good management practices is through systematic research and the refinement of knowledge. Although it has been going on for a much shorter period of time, research in management is similar in many ways to research in biology, chemistry, or psychology. As in clinical psychology, for example, some research in management is done by having experts study and analyze actual situations. The experts then suggest ways in which the situation can be improved. Hundreds of companies engaged in such consulting research provide advice to organizations and managers throughout the world. The roots of this consulting approach to management knowledge can be traced to Frederick Taylor, who, in the early 1900s, provided such advice to many companies in the steel industry based on his studies in plants across the United States and Europe (see Chapter 2).

Experimental research has also contributed to the development of management principles. An experiment is a controlled situation in which the researcher attempts to keep everything stable except the one or two variables being studied. Although experiments are somewhat difficult to organize in management research, there have been some notable and successful attempts to use them. Perhaps the best known were the Hawthorne studies conducted in a Western Electric plant in Chicago during the 1920s and 1930s. These experiments, which were intended to examine how people would react when certain conditions such as light, heat, and sound were altered, produced both expected and unexpected results. These results and their importance to management thinking are discussed in more detail in Chapter 2. Today researchers in such fields as social psychology, sociology, and psychology are engaged in experiments that may one day contribute new knowledge to management. In addition, through the use of computer simulations, even management practitioners can create hypothetical situations (management games) to see how a particular decision or action would affect the outcome.

A third type of research that has contributed to management thinking is theoretical research. Fields such as economics, psychology, and history have generated theories about what contributes to the successful management of organizations. Many of the older ideas about management were based on theories from fields such as economics, which has contributed to our understanding of costs, revenues, and human motivation. Today, management researchers use information from many different fields and integrate theories of their own to provide a more coherent understanding of how and why organizations behave as they do. In 1978, Herbert A. Simon won the Nobel Prize in Economic Science for his theoretical work in developing an understanding of decision-making processes in economic organizations. The nature of Simon's research makes it much less a theory of economics than a theory of human behavior in organizations—that is, much closer to management science than to conventional economic science.[13]

Using All Three Sources

The management principles that guide the actions of modern managers are derived from all three sources. Most are based on the accumulated wisdom and experience of past practice, coupled with the refinement and analysis that research in management and other fields has contributed. There is still room for intuition and instinctive action, however, and in many new and smaller companies, intuition is still the primary basis for decision making. Ideally, a manager should have a mixture of knowledge and skill based on research and formal learning, practical experience in organizations, and good hunches. The most important thing in managing is to use all of the available tools. An experienced manager is foolish to ignore either intuition or the information provided by new research; the newly graduated researcher should ignore neither personal hunches nor the advice of experienced managers; and the intuitive entrepreneur is wise to listen to both experienced managers and people who have studied management. Most managers benefit from using a mix of these sources of knowledge. As we discuss the principles of management, we will refer to all three sources of knowledge. Each provides valuable insights, and together they create an understanding of the richness and excitement of the practice of management.

▧ KEY POINTS

1 People depend on organizations to provide them with many of the goods and services they need in their daily lives. Organizations must be managed effectively and efficiently to provide these goods and services; thus management is extremely important.

2 Management is a process of setting and accomplishing organizational goals through the use of human, technical, and financial resources within the context of the environment.

3 In undertaking all management functions—planning, organizing, directing, and controlling—managers must make decisions. Thus, decision making is crucial to management.

4 The four basic functions of management are planning, organizing, directing, and controlling. Through these functions, managers set goals and objectives, determine how to carry them out, manage people so that the goals can be achieved, and monitor progress so that the organization achieves what it intends.

5 Efficiency is the best possible use of time, money, and resources. Effectiveness is the accomplishment of the proper goals. Because an organization's success depends on accomplishing the right objectives without wasting time, money, or resources, managers must be concerned with both efficiency and effectiveness.

6 Managers have three types of responsibilities. Technical responsibilities involve accomplishing the technical work of the organization. Administrative responsibilities involve coordinating operational activities and managing people. Institutional responsibilities involve setting the direction for the organization, guiding it, and representing it to the outside world.

7 The basic levels of management in an organization are top, middle, and first line. Though managers at each level all have some technical, administrative, and insti-

tutional responsibilities, the amount or degree of each differs based on the manager's level in the organization. Top managers have mostly institutional responsibilities; middle managers have mostly administrative responsibilities; first-line managers have mostly technical responsibilities; and another type of manager, the individual contributors, have mostly technical responsibilities.

8 Management knowledge and skill have been and still are acquired through the intuition of individual managers, the experience of managers and organizations, and research about the factors that improve managerial and organizational performance. Our knowledge of management principles has improved because experience and research are recorded and continually reapplied, tested, and improved.

▨ FOR DISCUSSION AND REVIEW

1. What are the management functions and responsibilities of Kenneth Feld at Ringling Bros. and Barnum & Bailey Circus? How are they different from the responsibilities of the person in charge of all concession stands at the circus?

2. Why is management considered vital to progress? Do governments and churches need management too? Explain.

3. What are the four functions that an organization's management must perform? What skills do managers need to perform these functions well?

4. Explain how organizations in the same business can be successful with different sets of goals and objectives. Consider, for example, Sears versus

Neiman-Marcus in retailing, or the University of Colorado versus the Air Force Academy in education.

5. How do the responsibilities of top managers differ from those of middle managers?

6. What types of responsibilities do the first-line, middle, and top managers of a software firm have? In a supermarket? A publishing house? A petroleum refinery? A charity? A cosmetics company? A physics lab?

7. What kind of organization are you a part of now? Can you identify who has technical, administrative, and institutional responsibilities in this organization?

▨ KEY TERMS

Administrative responsibility	Efficiency	Management decision making	Planning
Controlling	First-line managers	Middle managers	Technical responsibility
Directing	Individual contributors	Organizing	Top managers
Effectiveness	Institutional responsibility		
	Management		

THE CONFERENCE TABLE: DISCUSSION CASE / 1.1

Jim Cavanaugh, Manager

Jim Cavanaugh was the night shift manager for a Burger Chef restaurant directly across the street from a major university campus. The restaurant was growing and enjoying a profitable business, especially during the evenings. Other fast-food

In a busy fast-food restaurant, the manager must assign shift responsibilities and be ready to reassign workers in response to shifting customer demand. The young woman scooping ice cream may next have to help out at the steam table.

restaurants were at least three blocks from campus, and after the school's cafeteria closed for the night, Jim's business generally was brisk. His customers regularly engaged in plenty of fun-loving, creative hijinks, making Jim feel at times more like a circus manager than a food service manager.

As the night manager, Jim was directly responsible for handling the cash, maintaining the inventory, and scheduling and positioning his crew members. In order to organize his work, he came in half an hour before his shift each evening. This extra time allowed him to prioritize the shift's work and to make a general plan for the coming weeks. He had to take particular note of those evenings when the campus hosted large entertainment events to order extra supplies and schedule workers to serve a large crowd.

This particular Burger Chef had eight work stations:

Broiler	Dining room
Steamer	Counter
Specialty board	Drink stations
French fryer	Salad bar

During busy hours, each station needed at least one employee. It was Jim's job to monitor each employee's abilities and to schedule him or her at stations, allowing for the most efficient and effective operation. Jim had used "crosstraining" to teach new employees how to work at each of the eight stations. This gave him flexibility in assigning shift responsibilities and, during slower times, in having an employee cover more than one station. If a big crowd of students came in after the Friday night basketball game, Jim had to be prepared to rearrange workers or pitch in himself to handle the rush. He maintained close contact with the employees to make sure that each station was operating smoothly.

Jim was on his feet a lot but did delegate many of the jobs for which he was responsible. There were a few tasks, such as inventory and cleaning, that he could delegate entirely to employees. He also had help from Susan Swifton, a production leader, in coordinating and delegating work. Production leaders were able to perform many of a Burger Chef manager's duties, except for handling cash or disciplining, hiring, and firing staff. Susan had been very good at making sure that the work flowed smoothly. Customers received their food within a few minutes of placing an order. Burgers were cooked to order with only a few kept in stock. Susan made sure that a burger was never served if it was more than ten minutes old.

Friday night, Jim met with the managers of the daytime and morning shifts, Tom Miller and Linda Jenkins. He made notes on the following points:

1. *District Manager Inspection*   Tom reported that the district manager's most recent restaurant visitation report had been their best ever. The Burger Chef operations standards were being met, and the restaurant rating was improving gradually. However, there was one employee on Jim's shift, Charlie Pines, whom the district manager specifically mentioned to Jim during his inspection. Charlie usually worked in one of the operations in the rear of the kitchen area. He tended to neglect his work to socialize, and he slowed down and distracted the other employees. Jim had given him a first warning.

2. *Sales Promotions*   Jim noted an interesting phenomenon when looking over the quarterly figures. On the nights when the university had a sports event, the restaurant had more customers but lower dollar sales than on the nights when there were concerts. People coming in after concerts were apparently spending more per person than those coming from games. Jim suggested a promotional campaign in sports programs to help boost the sales after games. Tom and Linda agreed to the idea, and they decided to offer discount coupons on the higher-priced sandwiches. Jim made a note to check with the university about placing advertisements in the sports programs.

3. *Inventory*   When the last bill for bread products came in, Tom noted a drastic price increase from the prior month. Jim agreed to talk to other distributors in the area to find better prices.

4. *Litter*   Linda had recently read that a new Burger King restaurant was scheduled to open soon in an affluent college town in New Jersey. The mayor of the town, opposed to the fast-food franchise, had met with the franchise owner to discuss her misgivings. They had agreed that "burger patrols" would police the street a half mile in each direction, three times a day, picking up any litter bearing the Burger King logo. Because of the local town council's dislike for fast-food restaurants, Linda suggested Burger Chef ought to do something comparable. ■

DISCUSSION QUESTIONS

1. How does the definition of management offered in this chapter apply to Jim and his job at Burger Chef?

2. In what ways does Jim have to plan, organize, direct, and control? What decisions will he have to make in executing each of these functions?

3. Define Jim's technical responsibilities. What are his administrative and institu-

tional responsibilities? Compare Jim's list of responsibilities with those of Susan Swifton. Are there differences?

4. Where do you think Jim has gotten most of this managerial knowledge? Do you think he handles different situations based on different sources of knowledge?

THE CONFERENCE TABLE: DISCUSSION CASE / 1.2

Phillips

NV Phillips Gloeilampenfabrieken was established in 1891 as a small Dutch company that created some of the world's first incandescent light bulbs. Since then, Phillips has grown into one of the largest multinational companies, manufacturing everything from vacuum cleaners and color televisions to telephone transmission systems.

Even though the organization is constantly changing, some things remain the same. Phillips has stayed in tune with its customers by delegating marketing and manufacturing to national companies while retaining central direction of research, development, and strategy. It has also been able to recognize and capitalize on changes and developments in the technological environment.

Over the years, Phillips has had its ups and downs. Despite the oil crisis of the 1970s and increasing competition from Japan throughout the 1980s, however,

Phillips has grown into a multinational company by developing sophisticated electronics products like the compact disc.

the firm remains one of the most influential and powerful companies in the European Community. Phillips was largely responsible for the compact disc (CD) format for prerecorded music. Even so, it faces increasing challenges from the Japanese, who have recently introduced a recording process referred to as digital audio tape (DAT), which threatens to cut into the CD market. Phillips has kept DATs out of the public's hands for over a year using copyright laws and has even introduced a chip that prevents DATs from copying CDs. But these barriers are falling as the Japanese continue to develop new technology.

In order to better coordinate technological developments, Phillips has consolidated its audio and video divisions and has merged data systems with telecommunications. Medical systems, lighting, and defense remain self-contained. "We do not want to transform Phillips into a rigid, centrally controlled company," said one board member. "Not only would that be contradictory to the company culture, but it is the wrong prescription for the flexibility necessary to compete in today's environment."

In order to maintain its atmosphere of flexibility and responsiveness, Phillips has altered its management training and development approach. Before, it was believed that technical managers could run every factory and commercial managers could sell anything. Now those desiring general management positions must spend time learning technical, financial, and staff functions. Even aspiring engineers and scientists are now required to spend at least three months of their first year at Phillips working in manufacturing, development, and sometimes sales.

In an attempt to promote closeness within the huge organization, Phillips brings veteran middle managers together from different divisions and departments to discuss and investigate specific problems that cause the managers trouble. The managers are then given the opportunity to travel anywhere to interview other managers and specialists, inside and outside the company. The company asks the managers to spend at least two days a week on this for six months. Though it is a costly process, Phillips feels it is very useful in the solution of major problems. Kees Krombeen, a 24-year veteran managing director states, "the ultimate aim of management is to have 3000 potential candidates waiting in the wings for the 1000 top positions worldwide."

Phillips is a company bent on challenging the flourishing Japanese technological market face to face, and although they have lost a few battles, their war may just be beginning. ■

DISCUSSION QUESTIONS

1. In what ways does Phillips management reflect the ideas of planning, organizing, directing, and controlling?
2. Is the company putting too much emphasis on creating a strong, effective management staff? Do you feel it will give Phillips the edge it desires in the world market?
3. What are the costs and benefits of having engineers and scientists spend three months in manufacturing, development, or sales?

Sources: Hill, Roy, *International Management,* "Phillips Over the Years: A Model of the Maturing Multinational," (August 1986): 28–32; Borrus, Amy, *International Management,* "The Next High-Tech Gem from Japan," (May 1988): 48–50.

2 The Evolution of Modern Management

FOCUS CASE / The Mystery of the Buddhist Temple

MAJOR THEMES IN MANAGEMENT HISTORY

TECHNICAL ISSUES
Scientific Management
Other Contributions
Obstacles to Scientific Management
Automation and Operations Research

ADMINISTRATIVE ISSUES
Classical Organization Theory
Research in Human Behavior
The Human Relations Movement
World War II: A Turning Point

INSTITUTIONAL ISSUES
Systems Concepts
Strategic Management and Contingency Theory
Social Responsibility

Throughout history, people have faced great challenges and have set themselves far-reaching goals. And throughout history, people have combined intuition, experience, and trial-and-error methods to meet these challenges and accomplish these goals. The experience and ideas of yesterday's managers form the foundation for today's principles of management. By understanding the challenges they faced and the ideas they used to meet them, we may be better able to meet present challenges. The learning process is continuous. As the philosopher Sören Kierkegaard wrote, "Life can only be understood backwards, but it must be lived forwards."[1]

▧ KEY QUESTIONS

As you study this chapter, try to answer the following key questions:

1 Historically, what were the three themes that characterized the evolution of management theory?
2 What was the significance of the Industrial Revolution on management practices and principles?
3 How did people such as Frederick Taylor, Henry Ford, and Frank and Lillian Gilbreth contribute to the study of technical issues in management? What are some more recent developments in the area of technical management?
4 What were the problems and shortcomings of scientific management?
5 What did Henri Fayol contribute to principles of administrative management? What contributions came from the human relations movement?
6 How was World War II a turning point in the development of management principles?
7 What is the focus of research in institutional issues, and what are the primary theories related to managing the overall organization as an internally interdependent and dynamic system?
8 Why must organizations be concerned about issues of social responsibility?

Focus Case

The Mystery of the Buddhist Temple

Chandi Borobudur, which means "Temple on the Hill," was constructed 1000 years ago and stands today as a symbol of what people can do when they coordinate their efforts.

Deep in the jungles of central Java, the principal island of Indonesia, sits a spectacular Buddhist monument that was built more than 1000 years ago. Chandi Borobudur, which means "temple on the hill," was constructed as a stepped pyramid of unmortared volcanic rock standing 403 feet square and 105 feet high. The five ascending tiers of the temple, connected by narrow, steep stairways, are lined with thousands of carved stone panels that illustrate the various levels of life described in Buddhist teachings, ranging from the lower (World of Desire, World of Form) to the higher (World of Formlessness). To all who see it, Borobudur seems as great a human achievement as the cathedrals of Europe or the skyscrapers of New York.

Though no written documents about the construction of the monument exist, it is estimated that as many as 25,000 workers were involved. Since the construction is dated at 800 A.D., the machinery and tools available would have been, by our standards, extremely primitive. Thousands of sculptors must have carved the one million stone panels. Thousands of workers must have labored to transport the volcanic rock, build the foundation, and move the carved panels from the base of the monument to the various levels. Millions of worker-hours would have been needed to create the giant temple.

Unlike such "modern" architectural wonders as the Gothic cathedral of Notre Dame in Paris, which took several hundred years to complete, Borobudur is reputed to have been completely built within 80 years. Most engineers who have studied Borobudur consider the fact that it was finished in such a short period of time a great accomplishment, and also a great mystery.

Though the building of such a temple in the absence of advanced tools and machinery is universally applauded, certain oversights on the part of its designers contributed to its eventual decay. It was built, for example, around and over the top of a hill rather than on level ground. Evidence strongly suggests that the workers packed the loose earth and rubble before them, constructing the foundation and levels on landfill. Even during construction, this unstable fill caused parts of the temple to slide; thus, a retaining wall was added by the builders around the temple's base.

The more serious problem, however, was that Borobudur was built near an earthquake fault. In 1006, roughly 200 years after it was completed, the temple was severely damaged by an earthquake and the eruption of the nearby vol-

Source: This case was prepared by James E. Post and M. R. Poirier, based on notes from Professor Post's own visit to Indonesia and the following sources: Morton, W. Brown, III, "Indonesia Rescues Ancient Boropudur," *National Geographic* (January 1983): 126–142. Soekmono, R., "Boropudur, Indonesia's Buddhist Sanctuary—A Sermon in Stone," *UNESCO Courier* (February 1983): 8–15. Soekmono, R., and Voute, Ceasar, "How Boropudur Was Saved," *UNESCO Courier* (February 1983): 16–23.

cano, Merapi. The population fled, and the temple was lost in the jungle for 800 years.

Borobudur was rediscovered in 1814. Over the next 20 years, the jungle, earth, and rubble were peeled away, and the temple was completely uncovered by 1835. Some restoration was done between 1907 and 1911. Then, in the 1960s, the government of Indonesia began to call for assistance from the United Nations agency UNESCO and from all the nations of the world. In 1975, after funds had been collected and a consultative committee had determined the best course of action, reconstruction began.

Preliminary research synthesized information from many diverse disciplines: aerial photo analysis, archaeology, architecture, chemistry, conservation techniques, engineering seismology, foundation engineering, landscape planning, meteorology, microbiology, petrography, physics, soil mechanics, surveying, and terrestrial photogrammetry. Because the deterioration was so extensive, the temple had to be completely disassembled and reconstructed stone by stone. Through careful and innovative construction techniques, the monument was made more stable but still flexible enough to allow for the frequent tremors natural to the area.

Seven years and $20 million after reconstruction began, Borobudur was returned to its original splendor, and then some. Though 80 years of construction time seems painstakingly long in comparison to 7, the fact that the original builders built the temple at all without the knowledge and equipment available to the restoration team is still amazing.

The people who lived in that era cannot tell us what they knew about construction and engineering. From more recent, well-documented examples of great accomplishments, we can ascertain the principles, practices, and ideas that form the roots of modern management thought. The great temple itself, however, is proof that its builders knew much about how to plan, organize, direct, and control—they knew how to manage for goal accomplishment. Borobudur is a monument not only to spiritual growth, but to human potential and ability. ◼

MAJOR THEMES IN MANAGEMENT HISTORY

As Kierkegaard's statement at the beginning of this chapter suggests, the knowledge that we apply to current problems is derived from solutions to yesterday's problems and challenges. The reconstruction of Borobudur, the building of the Panama Canal, the mass production of automobiles, and hundreds of other projects taught our parents and grandparents important lessons that we can apply today.

Consider a familiar example. Most of us don't give much thought to the process by which fast food is produced. But turning out billions of hamburgers of uniform size and consistent quality at very high speed is actually a revolution in the delivery of food. Mass production of hamburgers is in fact an application to the restaurant business of assembly line techniques developed for the mass production of automobiles and appliances.[2] By applying these established management and production principles with imagination and creativity to a new set of problems, Ray Kroc created the McDonald's restaurant chain, made a fortune for himself, and created a new way of life for American families. Mass production was developed to allow a goal (high output) to be achieved using less time, money, and labor. It was an innovation that has been applied by countless managers and organizations since then. By understanding how managers have solved problems and accomplished major feats throughout history, we can better apply developments in the practice of management to problems and challenges today.

Throughout history, people who have managed organizations have been concerned with increasing productivity, improving performance, and learning new and better ways to accomplish objectives. Management practice and research have been aimed at improving managers' ability to perform better in all three areas of responsibility: technical, administrative, and institutional. See Exhibit 2.1.

Historically, the first set of issues dealt with by practitioners and management writers was productivity: how to accomplish tasks or work more rapidly and efficiently. Much of the effort focused on helping managers perform their technical responsibilities. The construction supervisor at Borobudur who was responsible for seeing that stones were carved and moved into position had to determine the best way to accomplish these tasks using the wooden poles and crude axes available. Though modern managers have much more sophisticated tools for production, they all still share the same concern: How can work be done most efficiently?

The second set of issues focused on how the whole organization, rather than each individual, could become more productive. There are two parallel developments here. Some researchers focused on improving an organization's performance by finding more effective ways to divide work among people and units and better ways to coordinate these efforts. That is, they focused on the way the organization itself was structured. Other researchers felt an organization's performance could be improved if its employees were more motivated to do their work. The new techniques employed to make workers more efficient in many cases demotivated them, as we will discuss later. Thus, researchers tried to determine how feelings and attitudes affected the performance of the work force. Researchers and writers began to study organizational structure and behavioral issues, which were and are particularly important to managers with administrative responsibilities.

The construction supervisor at Borobudur would also have been concerned with these issues. Of course, we know from history books that slaves, who may have comprised much of Borobudur's construction team, were "motivated" through force. But there is evidence to suggest that the artists who carved the stones were offered financial incentives and rewards similar to those offered to workers today. And even where people-oriented techniques of improving work performance were different from the techniques used today, the construction manager at Borobudur still faced an administrative challenge many managers face today: coordinating the efforts of the thousands of workers doing very different kinds of work, all directed at the achievement of one ultimate goal.

The third set of issues is broader and concerns guiding and directing the whole organization and managing it as a system that is influenced by its environment. These are institutional issues. The designers of the temple at Borobudur apparently were most successful in this respect: The precarious position and condition of the structure indicates some shortcomings on the technical and perhaps even administrative levels. But the temple was very effectively designed to guide its

EXHIBIT / 2.1
The Development of Management Theory

	Technical Issues	Administrative Issues	Institutional Issues
1900	Frederick Taylor, scientific management		
1910	The Gilbreths, time and motion studies, 1909–1911 Henry Ford, assembly lines, 1913	Henri Fayol, principles of administration and functions of management, 1917	
1920		Max Weber, bureaucratic management Hawthorne studies, 1924–1933	Ludwig von Bertalanffy, systems theory, 1920s
1930		Chester Barnard, the informal organization, 1938	Mary Parker Follett, the law of the situation
1940	Mass production of war equipment and supplies	Abraham Maslow, hierarchy of needs, 1943	
1950	Norbert Weiner, cybernetics, 1950s		Talcott Parsons, the social system
1960	Beginning of computer age Operations research	Douglas McGregor, theory X, theory Y, 1960	Open systems
1970			Strategy management and contingency theory
1980	Beginning of age of information technology Computer-aided design and manufacturing	William Ouchi, theory Z, 1981	Social responsibility
1990	Totally automated factories		

visitors along a course that illustrates the progress of spiritual development; visitors must "read" the panels in succession, not reaching the point of "ultimate enlightenment" until the end. In other words, this religious building, like many others, was probably designed to instill a universal belief system in the society and centralize power (in the form of spiritual knowledge) in the hands of the society's political and religious leaders. The temple's designers no doubt very carefully thought out the purpose of the building and determined how it would be used by both the public and political and religious leaders. Modern managers must give equal thought to the purpose of the organization and its relationship to society.

TECHNICAL ISSUES

In Chapter 1 we noted that technical activities actually accomplish the basic work of the organization. In building the Buddhist temple, technical activities included the carving and laying of the stones. In a manufacturing company, production processes make up the technical activities; in a university, the technical activity is the teaching of students and conducting of research. In short, technical issues involve the production methods and operations the organization uses to produce its products or services.

Technical issues involving production systems and the problem of how to increase efficiency came to the forefront during the Industrial Revolution.[3] Production "systems," per se, were almost nonexistent until the mid-1700s. In the early 1700s, for example, a barrel maker, or cooper, would assemble one barrel at a time. An especially good cooper whose barrels were in demand might have to hire an assistant or two. These assistants, or apprentices, would learn to construct barrels to the master cooper's specifications; then all three (or more) people would go about individually producing exceptional barrels, one by one.

By the late 1700s, with the invention of interchangeable parts and mass production techniques, the craft systems began to break down and hand tools gave way to machines and large-scale industrial production methods. Now barrels were made in large batches, instead of one by one. Work became specialized. Each person would do a small portion of the job and pass it on. A worker could become efficient at doing one piece of the job; costs would go down and productivity up. Because so many more people were now doing one limited section of a job, supervisors were needed to oversee and coordinate the laborers' work. The master and apprentice system was soon replaced with the supervisor and labor system.

This new method of production brought many changes, both to workers and to the way work was done. The factory system that emerged was built on the concept that specialization produced many social benefits.[4] The efficiency of the production system reduced the cost per unit of products such as shoes, cotton goods, and machinery. These items became more affordable, and at the same time, more jobs were created in the factories. However, during this early period, the factory system had negative effects as well. Workers began to lose their individuality and were transformed, essentially, into parts of an assembly process. Child labor in the factories, poor housing for the employees, dreadful safety problems from the machinery, and a lack of sanitary conditions also resulted.

These negative aspects led early researchers and managers to experiment with the idea of improving housing, working conditions, and the work environment. One such businessman was Robert Owen, who, at the age of 19, was general manager of an English cotton mill. Owen's greatest attempts at improving housing, working conditions, and educational opportunities for workers and their children were made in New Lanark, England, and New Harmony, Indiana. New Harmony, founded in 1825, was one of the most famous utopian experiments to be tried in America. During its early years, it sponsored the first kindergarten, the first trade school, the first free library, and the first community-sponsored public school in the United States. All were created to combat the problems created by early factories.

Scientific Management

Scientific management
A systematic method of determining the best way to do a job and specifying the skills needed to perform it.

By the late 1800s, business managers in many industries were concerned with efficiency. Several factors had created this concern, among them the rise of huge companies in industries such as oil (the Standard Oil Trust) and steel (United States Steel, the first $1 billion company in the world). Medium and small companies in these industries could survive against the giants only by achieving lower costs per unit of production. This led various engineers and experienced managers to experiment systematically with ideas to further improve productivity and efficiency.

Their systematic attempts to determine the best way to do a job and specify the skills needed to perform it were characteristic of the way scientists in chemistry, physics, and other fields developed and tested theories. Hence, it was not long before the work of these managers and researchers was called **scientific management,** a term coined by Frederick Winslow Taylor.[5]

Frederick Winslow Taylor (1856–1915) Frederick Winslow Taylor is generally known as the father of scientific management. He was, however, only one of a large number of people—mostly engineers—who worked in the late 1800s and early 1900s to improve efficiency in the production of industrial and consumer goods.

Taylor was born near Philadelphia in 1856, attended school and traveled in Europe, and, returning to the United States, became an apprentice machinist and pattern maker for a small hydraulic pump manufacturing company owned by family friends. After completing his apprenticeship in 1878, Taylor became a clerk at Midvale Steel Company, a manufacturer of locomotive wheels and axles. His talent for organizing and increasing efficiency was evident, and in eight years, at the age of 28, he was named chief engineer.

Having been a laborer himself, Taylor was convinced that the output at Midvale was significantly lower than it should have been. As he soon discovered, the laborers were deliberately working slowly, for fear that they would be laid off if they finished a job too quickly. This practice had gone undetected because no one had ever determined how long it should take to complete any of the laborers' work. Thus, Taylor proposed the basis of scientific management: Analyze the job to find out how long it should take and how best to do it, then train the employees to do the job, and pay them according to what they accomplish. Taylor anticipated that workers would be reluctant to work faster if their pay would be lowered when tasks were completed ahead of schedule. Therefore, he urged employers to pay workers on a differential rate system, wherein workers who met high standards ("first class men") would be rewarded with higher wages than those who fell below the standard (see The Inside View 2.1).

Taylor saw many advantages in the system he described, advantages that companies in many industries could achieve using similar systems. Among the best outcomes of the differential piece rate system, according to Taylor, was that it promoted "a most friendly feeling between the men and their employers" because it served both their best interests. Indeed, Taylor said that "no system or

Frederick Winslow Taylor (1856–1915)

THE INSIDE VIEW / 2.1

Frederick Taylor's "Piece-Rate System"

According to Frederick Taylor's piece-rate system, "Each man's wages, as far as possible, are fixed according to the skill and energy with which he performs his work and not according to the position which he fills."

Taylor wrote about the Midvale system in the following terms:

The ordinary piecework system involves a permanent antagonism between employers and men, and a certainty of punishment for each workman who reaches a high rate of efficiency. The demoralizing effect of this system is most serious. Under it, even the best workmen are forced continually to act the part of hypocrites to hold their own in the struggle against the encroachments of their employers.

The system introduced by the writer, however, is directly the opposite, both in theory and in its results. It makes each workman's interests the same as that of his employer, pays a premium for high efficiency, and soon convinces each man that it is for his permanent advantage to turn out each day the best quality and maximum quantity of work.

The differential rate system of piecework consists briefly in offering two different rates for the same job: a high price per piece, in case the work is finished in the shortest possible time and in perfect condition, and a low price if it takes a longer time to do the job or if there are any imperfections in the work. (The high rate should be such that the workman can earn more per day than is usually paid in smaller establishments.) This is directly the opposite of the ordinary plan of piecework, in which the wages of the workmen are reduced when they increase their productivity.

The system by which the writer proposes managing the men who are on daywork consists of paying *men* and not *positions*. Each man's wages, as far as possible, are fixed according to the skill and energy with which he performs his work and not according to the position which he fills.[1] ■

NOTE

1. Taylor, Frederick W, "A Piece-Rate System," *Transactions of American Society of Mechanical Engineers* (1895): 856–903.

scheme of management should be considered which does not in the long run give satisfaction to both employer and employee, which does not make it apparent that their best interests are mutual, and which does not bring about such thorough and hearty cooperation that they can pull together instead of apart."[6] Midvale suffered no strikes or labor disruptions during the ten years Taylor's system operated there, even though the steel industry as a whole was suffering numerous strikes and labor problems at that time. However, this system did cause conflicts elsewhere.

Taylor's consulting experience at the Bethlehem Steel Company in 1898 was an example of how he applied the principles of scientific management. One of his assignments was to increase the amount of raw materials—sand, iron ore, coal, limestone, coke—shoveled into the company's blast and open-hearth furnaces each day. To do this, Taylor selected one "first class man" and had him shovel various amounts of different materials each day. Through careful study, Taylor determined that a $21\frac{1}{2}$-pound load was the optimum weight, then designed new shovels so that for each substance being hauled, a full shovel would weigh $21\frac{1}{2}$ pounds. When the system was implemented, the average amount shoveled, per worker per day, increased from 16 to 59 long tons. Workers' wages increased from \$1.15 to \$1.88 per day, and the company saved 4¢ in labor costs per long ton shoveled. However, the number of shovelers needed was reduced from a high of 600 to 140. It was largely this result, which occurred in numerous organizations that adopted Taylor's systems, that provoked later opposition to scientific management.

Time and motion studies Studies that attempt to make operations more efficient by finding the best way to do them.

Frank Gilbreth and Lillian Gilbreth

Frank Gilbreth (1868–1924) and Lillian Gilbreth (1878–1972) Frank and Lillian Gilbreth, inspired by Taylor's early work, conducted a series of **time and motion studies.** In the early 1900s, researchers were attempting to make operations more efficient by altering the number of steps in a task and the way work was undertaken. Using a stopwatch to measure the length of time it took to perform an action, and motion analysis to subdivide a task (e.g., assembly of an item) into component actions (e.g., lift right arm 12 inches, twist right hand to screw cover onto jar), researchers were able to explore new combinations of actions to perform tasks in less time. Among the most celebrated of these efforts were the studies of Frank and Lillian Gilbreth, aimed at determining the "one best way" to accomplish work.[7] Frank Gilbreth was a contracting engineer and Lillian Moller a psychologist and teacher when they married in 1904. They collaborated on applying the social sciences to industrial management, emphasizing the worker rather than technological factors. His first important book was *Motion Study,* published in 1911; Lillian's book, *The Psychology of Management,* published in 1916, highlighted the importance of human factors in organizations.

In 1909, the Gilbreths studied the task of bricklaying and concluded that much motion was wasted by the workers, who had to bend down to pick up each brick, lay it in place, smooth the mortar, and then begin again. The Gilbreths designed an adjustable scaffold that eliminated stooping, thereby improving average work performance from 120 to 350 bricks per hour. Studies such as those done by the Gilbreths led hundreds of companies to use time and motion studies to improve productivity during the 1920s.

In time, Frank Gilbreth became the first researcher to use motion pictures to study work activities (in this instance, surgical operations). He also devised a method for classifying and studying hand motions, which he called *therbligs* (*Gilbreth* spelled backwards). After Frank's death in 1924, Lillian Gilbreth continued the consulting and teaching practices they had begun together. The Gilbreths' devotion to the study of efficiency extended to their life at home with 12 children. Two of the children published humorous remembrances in a book entitled *Cheaper by the Dozen* (1949), which was made into a movie in 1950.

Assembly line A production method whereby components to be worked on are cycled past a stationary worker.

Henry Ford (1893–1947)

Henry Ford (1896–1947) Two years after Taylor left the Bethlehem Steel Company in 1901, and less than a decade before the Gilbreths published their most important works, another management innovator was starting a revolution of a different sort in production methods. Trained as a mechanic's apprentice in Detroit, Henry Ford spent several years building racing cars, and then, in 1903, founded the Ford Motor Company. Ford wanted to build a car the average worker could afford. Mass production techniques and the **assembly line** were his solution because they allowed him to decrease the unit cost and increase the volume of sales.[8]

Henry Ford's assembly line began operation in 1913. Under the old system for making the chassis, parts were carried to a stationary assembly point; it took $12\frac{1}{2}$ hours to assemble each chassis. By using a rope to pull the chassis past workers and stockpiles of components, Ford cut the labor time to six hours. With further improvements, assembly time was reduced to 93 minutes by April 1914. Each reduction in time meant dollar savings for Ford. The company was able to reduce the price of its automobiles, making them affordable to more American families.

Assembly line techniques developed by Ford soon spread. For example, in meat-packing plants in Chicago and Cincinnati, overhead trolleys were used to move the carcasses of the slaughtered animals from worker to worker, each of whom had a specialized butchering job. When the trolleys were connected with chains and motorized, the carcasses would be moved at a steady rate. This was a true assembly line, with the machine dictating the pace of the work. Unnecessary movements were eliminated, specialization was increased, and productivity was improved dramatically.

Other Contributions

Henry Towne (1844–1924)

Many others contributed in the early years to the evolution of management thought.[9] Henry Towne (founder of Yale and Towne Lock Company), for example, was a professional manager who cared about the development and dissemination of better management techniques. As President of the American Society of Mechanical Engineers, he created the professional journal *Transactions,* which printed much of the writing of Taylor and others.

Another writer, Harrington Emerson, wrote and published *The Twelve Principles of Efficiency in 1912.* Those principles, like Taylor's principles of scientific management, still have followers today. Among the more practical and lasting technical developments in the management field was a scheduling system created by Henry L. Gantt, a student of Frederick Taylor. The Gantt chart proved an invaluable tool for helping managers oversee efficient production operations and still finds use today. Gantt charts and other tools for improving production operations are discussed in Chapter 16. Not all early developments were in research. Emily Roebling, who managed construction of the Brooklyn Bridge in the late 1800s, demonstrated much skill and creativity in overcoming production and management obstacles. See The Inside View 2.2.

Obstacles to Scientific Management

Two obstacles slowed the adoption of scientific management principles by the business community. First, scientific management posed a major threat to the powerful foremen and union chiefs who exercised ultimate control over job assignments and methods of operation in a plant. Using scientific management

Emily Roebling: Management Pioneer

The Brooklyn Bridge stands as a memorial to modern management techniques.

Much of the history of modern management is a story of how imaginative people used difficult problems to produce new ideas. The Brooklyn Bridge project is a fine example of this, with much of the credit for management expertise going to Emily Roebling.

The East River in New York separates Manhattan from Brooklyn. In 1857, John Roebling, a German-born engineer, proposed the building of "a wire suspension bridge crossing the East River by one single span at such an elevation as will not impede the navigation." It took five years for Roebling to convince investors, government officials, and others that his plan was feasible.

During this time, responsibility for the project eventually transferred from an aging John Roebling to his son, Washington, and from an ailing Washington—then chief engineer—to his wife, Emily. Construction finally began in 1869, and it took 14 years to complete the bridge. Many problems arose, including some that had never before been successfully managed. The East River has fierce currents, for example, and the size of the two towers from which the suspension cables were to be hung required especially sturdy support beneath the riverbed. To anchor these tow-

ers, huge airtight caissons (each more than half a city block long) had to be constructed, lowered into the riverbed, and filled with concrete. To do the excavation, workers had to descend through airlocks into small chambers where they dug away at the riverbed. There were dangers from flooding and from caisson disease (the bends). At one point, the workers went on strike, returning only when their pay was increased from $2.25 to $2.75 per day to compensate for the extra risk.

Initially, the bedridden Washington instructed Emily on how to handle these various problems. But ultimately, it was Emily Roebling who successfully oversaw the bridge construction project.

Emily did not "secretly take over as engineer of the bridge," said one author on the subject. However, he reported:

Since every piece of written communication from [Washington's] house on Columbia Heights to the bridge offices was in her hand, there was, understandably, a strong suspicion that she was doing more than merely taking down what her husband dictated. By and by, it was common gossip that hers was the real mind behind the great work and that this the most monumental engineering triumph of the age was actually the doing of a *woman*, which as a general proposition was taken

Emily Roebling, known as the "lady boss," was the driving force behind the construction of the Brooklyn Bridge.

in some quarters to be both preposterous and ca-lamitous.

[But] when bridge officials or representatives for various contractors were told it would be ac-ceptable for them to call at the Roebling house in Brooklyn, it was seldom if ever the Chief Engineer who received them. [Emily] would carry on the interview in his behalf, asking questions and an-swering theirs with perfect confidence and com-mand of the facts . . . so impressed were some that they went out the door convinced that they had met with the Chief Engineer after all and their future correspondence would be addressed di-rectly to her.

At one point in 1879, a controversy developed over the honesty of an important contractor, the Edge Moor Iron company. Ugly insinuations were traded back and forth in the papers, and it began to look as though there might be still another drawn out investigation. To assure the engineer-ing department of their honesty and good inten-tions, the firm addressed a formal written state-ment to the effect, not to the Chief Engineer, but to Mrs. Washington A. Roebling.[1]

On May 24, 1883, a huge celebration marked the dedication of the Brooklyn Bridge. Today, more than 100 years later, the Brooklyn Bridge is still a beautiful symbol of ingenuity and talent. The efforts of talented men and women to solve prob-lems led to the creation of new knowledge. The lessons the Roeblings had learned about construc-tion, design, and management would be available to all future bridge builders. ■

NOTE

1. McCullough, David, *The Great Bridge* (New York: Simon & Schuster, 1972), pp. 462–463.

principles, researchers determined how work was to be done, and people were assigned to jobs based on their test results and competencies. In companies such as Bethlehem Steel, there was a virtual battle for the factory floor between the researchers and the foremen, skilled workers, and union chiefs.

The second obstacle came from the workers themselves. Taylor and his disci-ples believed that employees wanted to work in the most efficient manner, to perform their work with a minimum of effort, and to be better paid for the increased productivity. They also assumed, quite incorrectly, that workers would submit to having their physical movements and thinking about the job standard-ized. Resentment and employee dissatisfaction grew when employers attempted to set higher norms for production and sped up the assembly line without im-proving wages. In the worst cases, management used increased productivity as a reason for laying people off. Though Bethlehem Steel saved on labor costs by using Taylor's system, 450 workers lost their jobs because of it. Abuses of the techniques led to strikes and work stoppages.

America's economic mobilization during the First World War, and the intro-duction of new worker-oriented management techniques (discussed in the fol-lowing section), eventually allowed the proliferation of scientific management techniques. America needed goods, and scientific management provided the most efficient ways of producing them. "The crush of industrial novelty—new military products, skills, tasks, and procedures—had disrupted traditional patterns in American manufacturing, and the patriotic clamor for speed and efficiency had dramatically accelerated the movement toward scientific management."[10] The efficiency of scientific approaches to production was too valuable to forgo. To overcome any resistance, managers continually revise and modify the techniques so that efficiency gains do not come at the expense of employee safety or satisfaction.

Automation and Operations Research

The headlong plunge into a scientific management revolution was slowed by the Great Depression of the 1930s. Little money was available for major investments in plants and equipment. Hence, it was not until World War II, which brought again both the need for more goods and the resources to produce them, that companies and managers returned their focus to innovating production methods. Two especially significant developments emerged that are still in use: automation and operations research.

Automation The automatic handling of parts in mass production processes.

Cybernetics A term used in the 1950s to describe the emerging computer field.

Automation   The term **automation** was coined in the 1940s to describe the automatic handling of parts in metalworking processes such as auto assembly. Automation and the development of computers went hand in hand. The field of computers was then called **cybernetics.** These new machines, which could make electronic calculations more rapidly and accurately than the human brain, were the solution to automation's major difficulty: coordination of the work of many different machines. But though they solved at least that problem, many feared they would cause other problems. In the 1950s, mathematician Norbert Wiener predicted that these computers would be widely used and would produce massive unemployment.[11] By the 1960s, this view became popular and caused great alarm as bookkeepers and file clerks were replaced by new technology. The issue was so politically potent that the federal government undertook a major job-retraining program to upgrade the skills of people who lost their jobs to automation and computerization.

The computer technology that Wiener and others foresaw in the workplace has now taken root. Computerized manufacturing equipment has helped transform workers from machine operators to machine supervisors, who coordinate and integrate rather than actually operate the equipment. Among the most important consequences of automation is the ability to guarantee uniform production and quality standards. Control systems have been designed around computer-directed machinery to reduce the risk of error in meeting product specifications. One example of current automation techniques is illustrated in The Inside View 2.3.

Operations research A management approach that uses mathematical models to analyze and compare situations and alternatives.

Operations Research   **Operations research** is a specialized field based on mathematical modeling of complex processes. Using computers to analyze the millions of possible ways to produce and assemble an airplane, for example, operations research specialists can find new ways of streamlining the production process. Such tools have now been applied to countless problems, including inventory scheduling, personnel planning, and financial and accounting control—all concerns of modern managers. Many writers refer to this phenomenon as the birth of management science.

The Factory that Made a Great Leap Forward

Gigantic gears and huge metal plates lie scattered on the floor. Welders and other workers tug them together to build massive gearboxes and other heavy-duty machinery. It could be a scene straight from the 1940s. But on the second floor of the new building next door, there is no doubt that this is the eighties: The glow of computer screens punctuates the bleak concrete walls.

This study in contrasts is China's prototype for future automated factories. Shanghai Metallurgical & Mining Machinery Mfg., better known as S4M, has installed a computer-aided design (CAD) system from Gerber Systems Technology Inc., of South Windsor, Connecticut, and a factory-control system from Hewlett-Packard Co. (HP). S4M's mission is to blaze a trail into the twenty-first century for China's 400,000 state-run factories. So far, only six have imported computers to help manage production, and only for selected functions. The vast majority still rely on manual controls.

But now that Beijing has given priority to renovating old factories, many Chinese managers are eagerly reviewing the latest in computer-aided manufacturing, mostly from U.S. suppliers. Beijing chose S4M as a pilot site because its managers are young, aggressive, and eager to computerize. So they got $750,000 in hard currency for the equipment. After studying several candidates, the factory's engineers negotiated extensively with Computervision Corp. and International Business Machines Corp. before settling on the HP and Gerber systems in 1985.

After the U.S. government cleared the sale, and the hardware was delivered last year, a team of S4M engineers spent a month in California learning the HP software inside-out so they could customize it and translate it into Chinese. So impressed was HP that it awarded S4M the rights to sell its materials-management software to other factories in China. Says John Sorensen, HP's market development manager for manufacturing systems in Asia: "In the way they are focused on what they

Automation has had dramatic effects on many organizations. This factory of Shanghai Metallurgical & Mining Machinery Mfg. in China is a good example.

want to get done, these guys could outdo anybody in the U.S."

Many of S4M's lower-level managers, used to the old ways, resisted the newfangled techniques and argued with the bespectacled computer whizzes. But after seeing the detailed monthly reports of work hours, units completed, and output value, one middle-aged warehouse manager grudgingly concedes: "The new system does have some merits."

S4M's top managers never had any doubts. They claim that within two years they will get a complete return on their investment. They expect not only to improve efficiency but also to shave 18 percent off their raw materials bill through better design and management. That is now crucial because Beijing, as part of its economic reforms, no longer provides S4M the materials it needs at low, state-fixed prices.

The first payoff came in July. The factory landed an $890,000 order from an Italian utility for an electrostatic precipitator to control air pollution at a power plant. What clinched the sale, says S4M, was the CAD system's ability to modify the precipitator's design within hours. With the proceeds of

that and other sales, S4M had repaid 90 percent of the loan used to buy its computers.

More than 1000 Chinese factory managers have flocked to S4M. But before many of them will be able to buy computers, Beijing will have to loosen its tight grip on foreign exchange. That could happen soon. And with China's current stress on renovating factories to increase exports, sellers of manufacturing-oriented systems may benefit most. ■

Source: Yang, Dori Jones, "The Factory that Made a Great Leap Forward," *Business Week,* November 2, 1987, p. 79.

The value of this approach in helping to solve complicated problems cannot be overstated. With modern computers, the manager can tackle problems that would have been insurmountable in earlier times. We could never have successfully launched a spacecraft or placed a man on the moon without such equipment. They are used in every field, from aerospace to medicine to politics. In fact, a team of archaeologists using a powerful IBM computer still took years to catalog and cross-reference the one million stones found at the Borobudur temple site. Only in this way could they have determined how to reconstruct the temple. In short, some of the greatest challenges today can be met only because we have these new tools of management.

Automation has improved efficiency and increased production in modern times just as the assembly lines and time and motion studies did in the early 1900s. Today technical innovation can be used to reduce drudgery and unpleasant work and provide people with opportunities for more meaningful work. In a world that faces so many genuine needs for improved products, services, and the efficient use of resources, the need to improve technical processes and systems will continue into the future. Current developments in information technology such as computer-aided design and manufacturing (which will be discussed in Part Five) are leading to totally automated factories in which robots replace all humans. Meanwhile, managers continue to refine the "fit" between people and machines in thousands of small ways to improve the way work is to be done and to eliminate unpleasant and unsafe jobs. The need to manage and improve the technical components of work continues.

ADMINISTRATIVE ISSUES

To enhance productivity beyond the levels achievable through technological innovation, managers and researchers designed methods to manage people, coordinate their work, and enhance their productivity. These methods were developed in two distinct but highly interdependent fields: organization theory and behavioral study.

Classical Organization Theory

Henri Fayol (1841–1925)

While Taylor, the Gilbreths, and Ford were focusing their attention on the technical activities of organizations, Henri Fayol (1841–1925), living in France and only partially aware of these developments, was devoting his life to understanding and improving managerial work.[12] Hired as an engineer by a French mining company, he worked his way up the ranks to manager, general manager, then member of the board of directors.

Fayol focused on the administrative level of organizations. From his extensive experience, he concluded that a company's success was due to managerial as well as engineering skill. Fayol determined that six basic activities were essential to the operation of any organization: technical, commercial, financial, security, accounting, and managerial. Of the six, managerial activity was the only one not yet clearly defined.

Fayol became a pioneer in the field of management thought, first for distinguishing managerial activity from all other activities in organizations, and second, for defining managerial activity in terms of its core functions. He described them as follows: planning—devising a course of action; organizing—mobilizing material and human resources; commanding—providing direction to employees; coordinating—making sure activities and resources are working well together toward the common goal; and controlling—monitoring progress to ensure that plans are being carried out properly. These functions of management were to be carried out in all aspects of the organization: technical production, marketing, finance, and accounting security.

Fayol was also the first to offer a list of principles of management to guide managers. Each of his principles, listed in Exhibit 2.2, is a general statement usually involving a single basic idea that can be applied in different kinds of organizations and in different ways. Though 14 are presented, Fayol stressed the fact that many others could be identified and that managers would have to apply them with discretion in each new set of circumstances.

Fayol's original work, *Administration Industrielle et Générale,* was published in French in 1917. It was not until the book was translated into English in 1930, several years after his death, that British and American managers began to take advantage of his contributions to the study of organizations.

Mary Parker Follett (1868–1933) was another scholar who contributed much to the study of administrative issues.[13] Like Fayol, she argued that principles and management techniques must be applied differently in each situation in accordance with its unique requirements—referring to this as *the law of the situation.* She also argued that managers could use superordinate goals—goals workers in all areas of an organization could hold in common—to reduce conflict and increase coordination between units. Follett's contributions were valuable, and still hold true today, but were given little credit by scholars in her time.

While Fayol focused on making management more effective, Max Weber (1864–1920) focused on structuring the organization.[14] His major contribution was an outline of what he called the characteristics of bureaucratic management. The characteristics he claimed were necessary for an organization to run smoothly are:

1. Division of labor: People should specialize and thus be able to learn how to do one set of activities well.

Mary Parker Follett (1868–1933)

Max Weber (1864–1920)

2. Authority hierarchy: A clear chain of command should be installed so workers clearly understand to whom they are responsible.
3. Formal selection: Employees should be hired and promoted based on merit and expertise.
4. Career orientation: Managers should be professionals devoted to the career of management.
5. Formal rules and controls: Formal rules and controls should be developed and used to guide and monitor employee behavior.
6. Impersonality: Rules should be impersonally and uniformly applied limiting the possibility that personalities and personal preferences affect management decision making and actions.

In these writings, Weber did not intend to create the atmosphere of red tape and slow response associated with the word *bureaucracy* today. He was concerned with creating a well-run organization where decisions were made based on facts and people were rewarded and punished according to their expertise and performance. These ideals still hold some validity in organizations and are discussed further in Chapter 8.

EXHIBIT / 2.2
Fayol's 14 Principles of Administration

Henri Fayol noted that administration was concerned with the human part of an undertaking. The following principles were to be applied in a flexible manner by administrators (managers) who could adapt them to the specific circumstance.

1. *Division of Labor*   Through specialization of labor, maximum efficiency can be achieved.
2. *Authority and Responsibility*   Authority is the right to command and the power to make oneself obeyed. Responsibility is the reward or penalty accompanying the use of power.
3. *Discipline*   The essence of discipline is "obedience, diligence, energy, correct attitude, and outward marks of respect, within the limits fixed by a concern (organization) and its employees."
4. *Unity of Command*   Everyone should have one, and only one, boss.
5. *Unity of Direction*   There should be only one manager and one plan for all operations of the same type. This assures consistency and responsibility.
6. *Subordination of Individual Interest to the Common Good*   The goals of the organization take precedence over the goal of the individual.
7. *Remuneration*   Employees should be paid fairly for their work, and the payment should be an incentive to perform well but not lead to unreasonable rewards.

8. *Centralization*   Authority and responsibility should not be too centralized in one manager. There should be enough delegation to others that subordinates are encouraged to work well, yet enough centralization to ensure accountability within the organization.
9. *Hierarchy*   The line of authority in an organization (scalar chain) runs from top to bottom in a straight line. Communications should normally follow this path, although administrators should be able to communicate across the organization to their peers at the same level of authority.
10. *Order*   To run well, an organization should have a place for everything and everything should be in its place.
11. *Equity*   The organization runs best when there is friendliness among employees and managers and when managers act fairly toward others.
12. *Stability of Staff*   Employee turnover is unhealthy for organizations. Good administration encourages commitment and long-term associations from employees.
13. *Initiative*   Subordinates should be given the opportunity and freedom to conceive and execute a plan, even if it sometimes fails.
14. *Esprit de Corps*   The morale of an organization's people is an asset and should be cultivated and encouraged by administrators whenever possible.

Source: Adapted from Fayol, Henri, *Industrial and General Administration*, trans. J. A. Courbrough (Geneva, Switzerland: International Management Institute, 1929).

Research in Human Behavior

To trace the development of managers' concern about human behavior, we must again turn back in time. Ideas about human behavior and motivation have existed since the beginning of recorded history. Some of the evidence found at Borobudur, for example, indicates that the artisans who carved the figures on each of the one million stones were "supervised" in a manner different from that used to direct the hundreds of workers who carried the stones to the temple for assembly. The transporters were virtual slaves, and physical punishment was used to "motivate" them. Physical punishments, however, were apparently unthinkable as a means of motivating stone carvers. These artisans responded better to incentives—rewards of food, for example—than threats.

In more modern times, the need for a better understanding of human behavior grew out of the inadequacies of scientific management as a comprehensive model for improving management effectiveness. The quest for efficient production methods, better technology, and more closely controlled work procedures often encountered resistance from workers. Though they were often justifiably rebelling against an increased work pace or low pay, their resistance led some supervisors to believe that workers were basically lazy and did not want to work more efficiently.

Some researchers and business managers saw the problem in different terms. Consultants found that motivation seemed related to the individual values and attitudes of workers themselves. For that reason, researchers concentrated on identifying the human factors that would stimulate people to be more productive. One important finding was that a sense of belonging or being part of a group was often vital to a person's job satisfaction.

Hawthorne studies
Studies conducted by Elton Mayo and his associates in the 1920s and 1930s which attempted to measure the effects of changes in physical environment on productivity.

The Hawthorne Studies   The best-known studies done during this era were the **Hawthorne studies,** begun in 1924 by Elton Mayo and his colleagues from Harvard University at a Western Electric plant in Hawthorne, near Chicago.[15] Following the traditions of scientific management, Mayo had previously studied the problems of physical fatigue among workers in a textile plant in Philadelphia. At the Hawthorne plant, the challenge was to study the effect that changes in illumination had on productivity. If the optimum level of illumination could be identified, all lights could be adjusted to that level and productivity could be increased. Mayo varied the lighting in several departments, in one case even decreasing it. All other working conditions were left as they were. To the researchers' surprise, the productivity of all groups increased. Even when the researchers told the women in one group that the light was going to be changed, and then did not change it, the women said that they liked the increased illumination. Productivity continued to rise. The first experiment indicated to Mayo that illumination was not the only variable affecting productivity and that no simple cause-and-effect relationship could be determined between lighting levels and productivity.

A second series of experiments was begun in 1927, partly to resolve the puzzle presented by the first set. These experiments were conducted over a five-year period and involved the assembly of telephone relays. A carefully selected test group was subjected to changes in wages, rest periods, duration of workweek, temperature, humidity, and other factors. The results again were puzzling. No matter what the change, productivity increased. Even when conditions were returned to their original state, productivity remained about 25 percent above its original level. Mayo concluded that the explanation must lie in the attitudes of the workers toward their jobs and toward the company. In changing workplace conditions experimentally, Mayo had unwittingly changed the relationship between management and the team of workers being studied. The test subjects were under less strict supervision than the other employees, became a cohesive group, and experienced a significant increase in morale. Their performance improved because these employees believed they were part of an important group whose help and advice were being sought by the company. They believed management was concerned about their welfare. In later years, the name *Hawthorne effect* was given to this phenomenon.

Recognizing that human relations, rather than physical workplace conditions, was the key variable in productivity levels, the Hawthorne researchers conducted a third experiment beginning in 1931. This experiment involved no changes in workroom conditions. This time, Mayo and his associates merely observed the behavior and interactions of a selected group of bank wiring technicians and conducted interviews. Through this experiment, Mayo identified the powerful and complex effect of group norms on productivity. Workers who produced above or below the norm set by the group met with some form of disapproval from the other members of the group. The group had developed informal mechanisms for enforcing its norms. Thus, again, human factors were found to have a significant impact on productivity.

By demonstrating that the human element was at least as important as physical conditions in influencing productivity, Mayo and his associates added a new dimension to the study of management.

The Human Relations Movement

Human relations A management approach that emphasizes people and their feelings and attitudes.

During the 1930s and 1940s, the work of Elton Mayo and others studying the psychology of workers became widely known. It became evident that workers often belonged to informal groups that greatly influenced whether a job would get done on time, whether a new employee would be accepted into the organization, or whether a managerial directive would be followed. Managers and researchers began to realize that people's needs and attitudes sometimes had as much or more influence on worker performance and productivity as the production system.

As researchers became more aware of the importance of people to the success of organizations, efforts were made to communicate these ideas to practicing managers. The term **human relations** was used to describe an entire approach toward management that emphasized people rather than machines, and this approach was quite different from the scientific management approach of Taylor and others. Many business executives supported the human relations approach to management, often because of personal experiences that confirmed or reinforced what researchers were saying.

One such executive was Chester I. Barnard, president of the New Jersey Bell Telephone Company in the late 1920s and the 1930s. Barnard, like Fayol, had learned much about successful management during his years as an executive. Among Barnard's most valuable contributions was the concept of the informal

Elton Mayo (1880–1949)

organization. He recognized that an organization's structure did not illustrate the informal groupings and networks of people that often had a powerful influence on whether the organization would run effectively. Taking it further, he also argued that employees had the free will not to follow orders from authority figures—and that they might not if they did not feel it was in their interest in some way. In his book *The Functions of the Executive* (1938), Barnard argued that successful managers learned how to work with people to harmonize labor and management objectives.[16] Implicitly, Barnard was suggesting that such an approach could minimize the need for labor unions, which were becoming increasingly powerful in many industries.

World War II: A Turning Point

The need to understand why people worked and what motivated them had special significance during World War II. With millions of young men in the armed forces, and with the war effort requiring huge amounts of equipment, munitions, and other goods, managers faced a difficult human resources problem. Older workers, including many who had previously retired, were called back to work. Women, who had not been widely employed in factories during the Depression of the 1930s, entered the work force in huge numbers. In fact, one of the most popular songs of the era was dedicated to and titled "Rosie the Riveter." Managers were faced with the necessity of meeting staggering production requirements with a work force made up of very different people from those whom they had been accustomed to directing.

Managers called on researchers for assistance in obtaining maximum effort from the work force. They needed help finding the right people, assigning them jobs they could best do, training them, and motivating them. Abraham Maslow, a psychologist from Brandeis University, was the first to articulate a new approach to management that focused on worker needs. He argued that people did not work primarily, or only, for money. Rather, they had a series of needs, including basic needs such as food and shelter and "higher needs for self-esteem and personal fulfillment," all of which could potentially be satisfied through work. In time, this became known as *Maslow's hierarchy of human needs* and inspired new ideas about how to motivate workers by filling their needs.[17] Motivational issues are discussed further in Chapter 11.

During the 1950s, a researcher named Douglas McGregor began to contrast the old assumptions about workers and their attitudes toward work with the new assumptions made by Mayo, Maslow, and other researchers of human behavior. In his 1960 book *The Human Side of Enterprise,* McGregor argued that the old assumptions about workers should be abandoned in favor of a humanistic approach.[18] Among the old assumptions, which McGregor called theory X, were the ideas that people didn't really want to work, that they needed to be closely supervised, and that they took little pride in their work. McGregor's counterpoints, which he called theory Y, were that people did want to work, that they could supervise themselves, and that they did take pride in their work. McGregor argued that if managers treated employees as responsible, intelligent, and productive, they would become just that.

Abraham Maslow (1908–1970)

**Douglas McGregor
(1906–1964)**

The book proved immensely popular and sparked a whole new discussion of how to manage work in large organizations by building positive, cooperative relationships among workers. The concepts of theory X and theory Y are an important part of our current understanding of how to manage people. In fact, in the 1980s, when Japanese management practices became a popular subject of discussion because of Japan's great commercial success, Professor William Ouchi of UCLA published a book titled *Theory Z* to illustrate how Japanese management practices differed from both theory X and theory Y practices found in the United States and Europe.[19] With the surge of interest in quality control, participative management, innovation, and decentralization, managers now more than ever are interested in the behavioral aspects of management.

It is clear that in contemporary Western societies, people in the work force expect to be treated as individuals with their own rights and interests. People are a valuable organizational resource. They must be managed carefully. Managers must recognize each individual's qualities to release the potential of their work force.

INSTITUTIONAL ISSUES

As research on technical and administrative issues was developing, a third approach to the study of management was introduced. This approach focused on the combined technical and human aspects of work and how they, as a system, fit into the environment. Writers in this area argued that the parts of the organization could not be perfected without understanding the whole and that the whole would not be successful without conforming to or suiting its environment. The organization was viewed as a total system. The focus of this branch of research was on integrating the parts of an organization and guiding the whole to respond to the environment.

Systems Concepts

The original ideas of systems were developed by Ludwig von Bertalanffy, a biologist who came to be known as the father of systems theory. Von Bertalanffy's work in the 1920s helped explain how living organisms functioned as systems. In simple terms, a system is an organized arrangement of interrelated parts. The human body is a system of organs, bones, muscles, and other parts. Flowers, trees, and other living organisms are also systems consisting of interrelated parts. Eventually, von Bertalanffy extended his thinking about systems to other types of "organisms," including organizations.[20]

Thinking about the whole as a system of interrelated parts led sociologists such as Talcott Parsons to question whether society could be understood in terms of social systems composed of structures, relationships, and interconnections that keep the society functioning.[21] This idea naturally led to the concept of organizations as social systems and scholars began to think about the interrelationships among parts of the organizational system. This was the beginning of **systems theory** applied to organizations. Although it was difficult at first for practicing managers to comprehend, it has since come to dominate many areas of management knowledge. Words such as *feedback, input, output,* and *subsystem,* familiar to most managers today, are derived directly from systems theory.

Systems theory A management theory that views the organization as a whole constructed of interrelated parts.

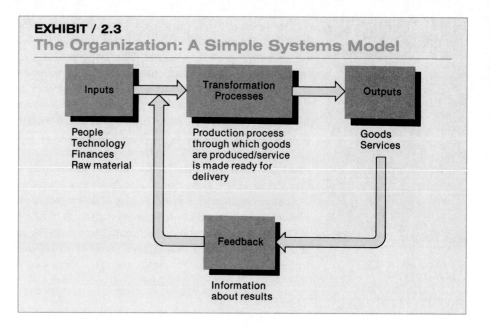

EXHIBIT / 2.3
The Organization: A Simple Systems Model

Inputs

People
Technology
Finances
Raw material

Transformation
Processes

Production process
through which goods
are produced/service
is made ready for
delivery

Outputs

Goods
Services

Feedback

Information
about results

A very simple illustration of the flow from inputs to outputs and back in an organizational system is shown in Exhibit 2.3. This picture illustrates the inputs—the human and nonhuman resources that are combined to create goods and services. These inputs are transformed in some way to produce outputs, which the organization sells as a service or a product. Feedback about what is accomplished then serves as the basis for deciding what inputs to use the next time. Thus, the organization consists of three essential elements: inputs, transformation processes, and outputs.

The value of the systems concept for managers is that it applies to all types of organizations. Automobile manufacturing can be thought of as a system of inputs, transformation, and outputs. The United States Postal Service can be understood in the same terms, as can a hospital, a canning plant, an insurance company, or a university. The quantitative techniques developed from systems theory can help managers gather valuable information by developing mathematical models that can compare the costs and benefits of various ways to use and coordinate resources.

Some of the most important innovations in productivity have occurred simply because it was possible for managers to reconceptualize their organization's activities. Advertising, sales, and distribution were once understood as very separate and distinct activities. By understanding them as related activities whose purpose is to distribute the organization's output, managers have redefined these activities as a single subsystem of marketing: Advertising lures new customers, sales efforts increase client contact while also producing orders for goods or services, and distribution systems bring the product or service to the customer. If any one of the components fails, the whole marketing system fails.

Another issue discussed in systems theory is adaptation. Researchers such as von Bertalanffy concentrated their efforts on understanding how organic systems survived under changing conditions, such as light and temperature variations. They learned that some systems are open to outside influences while others are closed and are relatively immune to such influences. For managers, the idea of an open system is a key concept in understanding how organizations behave in a changing environment.[22] Just as organic systems can be affected by variations in temperature and light, an organization can be affected by changing social values, economic trends, and political issues. Managers must guide the organization so that it adapts and responds to events and changes going on in its environment.

The story of Henry Ford's refusal to change the color of his automobiles illustrates the point. Ford believed that black was the perfect color for an automobile. During the 1920s, when other manufacturers began to produce cars in red, green, and blue, Ford is said to have told his managers that the "customer can have any color he wants as long as it's black!" Not surprisingly, customers who wanted cars of different colors bought them from other manufacturers. The Ford Motor Company slipped from being the largest in the industry, and it would have gone out of business had it not eventually adapted to consumer tastes. The lesson Ford learned was not the importance of offering automobiles in several choices of colors. It was that all organizations must adapt and respond to a changing environment.

Strategic Management and Contingency Theory

Systems theory, because it addressed issues of adaptiveness and responsiveness, ultimately fostered the development of another branch of study, one that asked the question, What can be done to anticipate changes and thereby increase responsiveness? This led to the development of the notion of strategic management. Strategy, as originally proposed, was an overall plan that served as a guide or reference point for accomplishing a future objective; by consulting it, managers could ensure that the organization's parts were integrated and that all energies and resources were directed toward the accomplishment of the overall mission. With a strategy, managers could think about where they wanted the organization to be in the future (e.g., the largest or most profitable in the industry) and organize resources in ways that would make the objective achievable. The idea of strategic management therefore came to refer to a process that guides the whole organization—operations, people, and resources—to move in a direction that will produce successful long-term as well as short-term results.[23] Chapter 5 explains these concepts in detail.

With the idea of strategy came a recognition that different organizations, even those in the same industry, could not be managed in the same way. There were different factors influencing each organization, and no one managerial tool could possibly work equally well in all circumstances. Instead, effective managers would carefully analyze all the factors that might influence a given situation, then determine an approach that would fit the situation. As you recall, Mary Parker Follett had referred to this in the 1920s as the law of the situation. In time, this general concept came to be known as the **contingency theory** of management.[24] For example, though the largest firm in an industry might be able to alter or cut its pricing to an extent that smaller firms could not, smaller firms might be able to be more flexible in arranging delivery schedules. Thus, to achieve "success," the larger firm should focus on competitive pricing while the smaller company's strategy should emphasize convenient delivery schedules.

Contingency theory A management philosophy that focuses on analyzing the situation and then fitting the management approach to the situation.

The importance of strategic management has grown over the past two decades. Today, virtually all large and medium-sized organizations, including hospitals, universities, and even government agencies, have some type of strategic plan. As organizations become more complex, more attention must be paid to coordinating the diverse units, defining opportunities to pursue, and handling increased competition.

Social Responsibility

Social responsibility
The idea that managers must meet the product and service needs of society while continuing to protect and enhance the resource base, the individuals, and the society itself.

Because strategic management involves fitting an organization to its environment, it also involves concepts of **social responsibility.** Organizations are becoming increasingly large and powerful; therefore, the public has begun to feel that managers and organizations should act in ethical, or socially responsible, ways. For the most part, this means meeting the product and service needs of society while protecting the environment, the people affected by the operation, and society itself. But since public opinions change, managers are required to pay constant attention to the ethical standards that prevail in society. Society's demands for protection of the air and water, equal employment opportunities for women and members of minority groups, and the protection of consumers against the risks of unsafe products have all contributed to the business sector's increased awareness of its responsibility to conduct its actions ethically. Because society relies on institutions to accomplish most large tasks, it maintains high expectations about the manner in which those activities will be conducted. This means that managers must be concerned about to whom and for what the organization is responsible.[25]

Many times the government provides answers to these questions. Government agencies are the means through which law and public policy are implemented in society, and they have a great influence on companies. In the automobile industry, for example, designs were once based on an engineer's ideas about what customers wanted in the area of performance and style. In the past 20 years, automobile designs have been dramatically affected by government specifications regarding safety standards, pollution control, and gasoline mileage requirements. Automobile design is no longer solely the job of the automobile companies but the joint responsibility of the companies and the government.

In addition to dealing with government regulation, managers have a responsibility to behave in accordance with socially accepted norms of "goodness." As companies become more international in their operations, managers must face the dilemmas of operating in other societies with different cultural and social standards. It is illegal for a foreign company to pay a local government official to speed up the issuance of a license or permit in the United States. And it is illegal for a U.S.-owned company to do the same in another country. But in some other countries, these are normal practices. How should the manager of a U.S. company operating in a foreign company behave when bribery is the normally accepted (and sometimes only) way to obtain large contracts?

Ideas and theories about management have been developing for centuries. Improvements and developments have been made in the principles and techniques used to manage on the technical, administrative, and institutional levels. Still, the basic process remains the same: Management is a process of setting and accomplishing goals through the use and coordination of human, technical, and financial resources, in the context of the environment.

■ KEY POINTS

1 Three broad themes characterize the evolution of management theory. The first emphasizes production efficiency, or methods of accomplishing tasks more rapidly and efficiently, and helping managers meet their technical responsibilities. The second emphasizes human behavior and principles of administration, especially the direction and coordination of people in organizations. The third addresses principles for managing the whole organization as a system. This has included strategic management and a concern for an institution's social responsibilities.

2 The Industrial Revolution, by changing the nature of work from an individual task to a group effort based on mass production, created many problems as the negative aspects of factories and production plants counteracted the productivity gains of mass production techniques. Many of the managerial principles we study and use today were initially developed to address these problems.

3 The early study of technical issues in management was led by Frederick Taylor, the father of scientific management, who developed the system of analyzing a job, determining how long it should take and how best to do it, then training workers to do it this way and paying them according to output. Henry Ford's assembly line and the time and motion studies of Frank and Lillian Gilbreth were also important technical-level developments. These experts were united in a desire to find more efficient ways to integrate humans and machines. In more recent times, automation, computerization, and the application of quantitative analysis have assisted managers in challenging technical barriers to improved efficiency. Some refer to this application of quantitative analysis to organizational problems as management science.

4 Though scientific management produced significant increases in production efficiency and speed, it was based partially on the notion that human beings are interchangeable parts of a machine. Through such research as the Hawthorne studies, an understanding of human behavior was introduced so techniques of scientific management could be applied more effectively.

5 Henri Fayol is credited with being the first to define management in terms of its core functions: planning, organizing, directing, and controlling. Thus, he offered the foundations of administrative management, the guiding and coordinating of the work force. The human relations movement, sparked by the Hawthorne studies in the 1920s, highlighted the significance of employee feelings, attitudes, and sense of belonging or importance to productivity and motivation.

6 During World War II managers were faced with a unique and difficult predicament: They had to meet staggering production requirements with a work force composed of women and older people, neither of whom the managers were accustomed to working with in large numbers. Thus, new methods of both production and human resource management were required, and researchers such as Abraham Maslow and Douglas McGregor made valuable contributions.

7 The primary focus of research in institutional issues is on integrating the parts of an organization and guiding the whole to respond to the environment. The main theories that relate to managing the overall organization as a system include systems theory, which views organizations as wholes constructed of interrelated parts; operations research, which provides mathematical models that can compare the costs and benefits of various ways to use and coordinate resources; strategic management, a process that guides a whole organization to move in a direction that produces long-term as well as short-term results; and contingency theory, the recognition that different organizations cannot be managed the same way and that no one managerial tool could possibly work equally well in all circumstances.

8 Because strategic management involves fitting an organization to its environment, it involves concepts of social responsibility. Organizations must meet the product and service needs of society while protecting the environment, the people affected by the operation, and society itself.

■ FOR DISCUSSION AND REVIEW

1. How does the building of the temple at Borobudar demonstrate knowledge of the four functions of management?
2. How did artisans get their work done before the Industrial Revolution, and what did the Industrial Revolution introduce to the old craft trades?
3. Name the three areas in which management principles have evolved.
4. Explain how engineering ideas, as seen in the work of Henry Ford, F. W. Taylor, and the Gilbreths, contributed to the development of scientific management.

5. What effects did the assembly line and scientific management have on production workers? What were the good and bad effects?
6. Discuss which of Henri Fayol's 14 principles of administrative management are still relevant to managers today. Do any of these principles seem outdated to you? If so, which ones? Why?
7. What were the designers of the Hawthorne studies trying to accomplish with their research, and what is the Hawthorne effect?
8. Explain what is meant by the claim that an organization is a *system* of interrelated parts and dependencies. Think of your own school—discuss how it is a system.

9. It is commonly said that today's organizations and managers have to think about where they want to be in the future as well as where they are today. Explain how the idea of *strategy* is used by managers to relate today's activities to tomorrow's goals.
10. Explain what is meant by the *contingency approach* to management. Does the contingency approach undermine the idea of principles of management?
11. Why must the modern manager be concerned with people and factors outside the organization as well as people and factors inside?

▪ KEY TERMS

Assembly line	Cybernetics	Operations research	Systems theory
Automation	Hawthorne studies	Scientific management	Time and motion
Contingency theory	Human relations	Social responsibility	studies

THE CONFERENCE TABLE: DISCUSSION CASE / 2.1

Pullman Standard Corporation

In the history of the American railroad industry, few names are better known than that of Pullman. George Pullman was the founder of a company whose name became synonomous with railroading, especially the design and production of railroad cars. For more than 100 years, the company led the industry in the production of railroad cars and benefited greatly when social or political events created a demand for them.

In 1972, for example, President Richard M. Nixon negotiated a wheat deal with the Soviet Union whereby U.S. grain was to be sold to the Soviets to help alleviate shortages there. The deal was a bonanza for U.S. farmers and American railroads. Much of the grain was shipped by rail to Gulf ports where it was loaded onto ships for transport to Russia. The ports were overloaded, however, and railroad cars were backed up for miles awaiting unloading. This backup created a shortage of hopper cars that were used to haul grain.

Sources: "What's Going on at Pullman?" *Forbes,* July 7, 1980, pp. 36–37; "A Bumper Crop—Without a Shortage of Boxcars," *Business Week,* August 9, 1982, p. 22; "Bye-bye, Boxcars," *Forbes,* June 7, 1982, pp. 135–138; "Pullman's Not a Sleeper Anymore," *Business Week,* July 22, 1985, pp. 86–87.

When the demand for railroad cars plummeted, Pullman's sales and production dropped drastically.

As the largest manufacturer in the industry, Pullman was ready to meet the demand. It expanded operations and hired more workers. Profits soared. By 1980, Pullman had reached a production capacity of 25,000 cars annually at its two plants in Butler, Pennsylvania, and Bessemer, Alabama. The pressure to produce more cars led the company to agree to some questionable labor contract terms. Pullman had a contract with the United Steel workers and paid steel industry wages. The Butler plant contract created direct labor costs of $11 per hour plus $7 per hour fringe benefits. An incentive plan paid workers 130 percent of an eight-hour wage for every 6½ hours of work. Half the work force was allowed 13 weeks' paid vacation every five years. Inefficiencies were introduced through an extensive job classification system; the Butler plant had 160 separate classes of jobs.

In 1980, the outlook for the railroad industry began to cloud. First, the Russians invaded Afghanistan and President Jimmy Carter imposed an embargo on the sale of wheat to the Soviet Union. The demand for railroad cars plummeted. Second, the U.S. Congress passed legislation that reduced the Interstate Commerce Commission's regulation of the railroads. Among the many changes that resulted was a severe pressure on the railroads to be cost competitive and efficient. Pullman's high costs of production made its cars less attractive than the lower-cost cars of its competitors. Third, the economy entered a recessionary phase, and the demand for railroad shipping declined during 1980 and 1982. Boxcars were idle in railway yards throughout the country. By one estimate, more than 25 percent of boxcars had been abandoned. In 1982, freight traffic on U.S. railroads was 12.3 percent below that of the previous year. New cars placed in service in 1982 totaled 18,000, the lowest number since 1938.

In 1982, all of Pullman's production facilities were closed. Over 5000 employees were discharged. Total sales and production were zero, and the company was on the verge of bankruptcy. The company's stock, which had sold for more than $43 per share only a few years before, sold at less than $2 per share. ■

1. What internal factors accounted for Pullman's disastrous performance? What external factors contributed to Pullman's problems?
2. Can you draw a diagram of the "system" at Pullman, including the internal and external relationships?
3. In 1980, when signs of trouble began to arise, what would those focusing on the technical issues of management suggest Pullman do? What would those focusing on administrative issues suggest? What would those focusing on institutional issues suggest?

3 Managerial Decision Making and Problem Solving

FOCUS CASE / Coke Are It

WHAT IS A DECISION?
Decision Making Defined
Choice Making, Decision Making, and Problem Solving
Relatedness of Decisions
Personal Versus Managerial Decision Making
Programmed Versus Nonprogrammed Decisions

CONTEXT OF DECISION MAKING
Conditions of Certainty
Conditions of Risk
Conditions of Uncertainty
Optimal Versus Satisficing Decisions

THE DECISION-MAKING/ PROBLEM-SOLVING PROCESS
Define the Problem or Issue
Analyze the Issue and Generate Alternatives
Evaluate the Alternatives and Select the Best One
Implement the Decision
Monitor Results and Evaluate the Impact

IMPROVING DECISION MAKING
Quantitative and Qualitative Methods
Group and Committee Involvement

very profession requires certain fundamental skills. In management, the fundamental skill is the ability to make decisions. Decision making is the basis of all the functions of management: planning, organizing, directing, and controlling. Peter Drucker, one of the foremost management scholars of modern times, has written:

> Whatever a manager does, he does through making decisions. These decisions may be made as a matter of routine. Indeed, he may not even realize that he is making them. Or they may affect the future existence of the enterprise and require years of systematic analysis. But management is always a decision-making process.[1]

This chapter presents an introduction to the context in which decisions are made, the process used to make them, and some tools to improve their accuracy and effectiveness.

KEY QUESTIONS

As you study this chapter, try to answer the following key questions:

1 In what broad sense can problem solving be defined, and in what way are decision making and choice making connected to this process?
2 What effect do past decisions have on current decisions, and what effect do current decisions have on the future?
3 Why should managerial decisions differ from personal ones?
4 What are the differences between programmed and nonprogrammed decisions?
5 What are conditions of certainty, risk, and uncertainty, and what must managers do to make effective decisions under each of these conditions?
6 How do optimal decisions differ from satisficing ones?
7 What are the intended and unintended effects of decision making? What are the primary and secondary impacts?
8 What is the difference between qualitative and quantitative methods of improving decision making, and what types of situations do they address?
9 What are the advantages and disadvantages of using groups in the decision-making process?

Focus Case

"Coke Are It"

Many consumers rebelled against New Coke. Some banded together to form "Old Cola Drinkers of America" to make their protest even more visible.

In 1886, Atlanta pharmacist John Styth Pemberton concocted a mixture in a 30-gallon brass kettle in his backyard. The formula for the soft drink he created lasted, virtually unaltered, for 99 years, and when it finally was changed, consumers mounted such a strong protest that the global company that grew from the sale of the soft drink was forced to do an about-face and reintroduce the original formula.

A copy of 7X, the original formula for Coca-Cola in Pemberton's handwriting, still lies in a company vault. For the first 95 years, this formula went unchallenged. Then a series of rapid changes took place. In 1982 Robert C. Goizueta, appointed Coca Cola Company's president in May 1980 and named chairman in March 1981, convinced corporate managers to introduce Diet Coke at great cost; it was a huge success. After having thus broken tradition, the company introduced caffeine-free Coke and Cherry Coke. In 1984, *Financial World* awarded Goizueta one of its 10 silver medals for CEO performance and "decisive ability."[2]

During this time, testing began for a new formula for Coke itself. A representative of Dean Witter Reynolds had asserted in 1980 that "Coke is no longer a steady growth company—it is a cyclical growth company."[3] Though still the market leader in 1984, Coke's market share was dropping while rival Pepsi's share was rising, and both companies were struggling with new competition from fruit juices, bottled water, and other "light" beverages. It seemed to be time for drastic action.

"In the course of developing Diet Coke," said Goizueta, "our expert taste testers came upon a taste better than the old Coca-Cola. We had two options: we could do nothing, put it on the shelf and forget we ever developed it. Or we could change the taste and give the world a new Coca-Cola."[4] Goizueta decided to do the latter. Taste tests performed over the course of four years, at a cost of $4 million, indicated that people would prefer the new Coke over both Pepsi and the original Coke. (The taste testers were not told that the original formula would be discontinued.) Goizueta was convinced. In 1981 he said, "There are no sacred cows in the way we manage our business, including the formulation of any or all of our products."[5] New Coke was introduced on April 23, 1985, and Goizueta said of the decision, "This is our surest move ever. The consumer made it."[6]

Source: This case was written by M. R. Poirier, based on the following sources: Greenwald, John, "Fiddling with the Real Thing," *Time,* May 6, 1985, pp. 54–56; "Will Things Still Go Better with Coke?" *U.S. News & World Report,* May 6, 1985, p. 14; Scredon, Scott, "Is Coke Fixing a Cola that Isn't Broken?" *Business Week,* May 6, 1985, p. 47; Fisher, Anne B., "Coke's Brand Loyalty Lesson," *Fortune,* August 5, 1985, pp. 44–45; Gelman, Eric, et al., "Hey America, Coke Are It!" *Newsweek,* July 22, 1985, p. 40.

Initial reactions were favorable. According to the *Wall Street Journal,* during May, shipments of new Coke to bottlers "rose by the highest percentage in five years. New Coke was tried by a record number of people for any product, and more than three-quarters of those who tried it indicated they would eagerly buy it again."[7] On the other hand, indications of trouble also showed almost immediately. Pepsi officials called the decision an admission by Coke that Pepsi tastes better and gave Pepsi employees the day off in celebration. And though Coke's stock climbed $1\frac{5}{8}$ points in anticipation of the announcement, it fell $2\frac{3}{4}$ points within two days of the introduction. Before May 30, more than half the people surveyed had said they liked new Coke. By the end of June, less than one-third liked it. One letter received by the company read: "Dear Chief Dodo: What ignoramus decided to change the formula of Coke?"[8] Bottlers at a convention in Dallas on June 18 circulated a petition demanding the return of the old formula. Meanwhile, in Seattle, Old Coca-Cola Drinkers of America was formed and decided to file a class action suit to get old Coke returned.

On July 3, corporate executives met with the five largest bottlers. On the fourth, the decision was made to reintroduce the original formula. On the fifth, orders had already gone out to the various departments to prepare for a relaunch. This abrupt decision surprised industry analysts as well as Coke's competitors, according to the *Wall Street Journal:* "Unlike its elaborate preparations for the introduction of reformulated Coke, the company didn't include outside consultants or ad agencies in its decision making until the last minute. As a result, when the company filmed the ads, it asked McCann Erickson [an advertising agency] to send a video crew to Atlanta without explaining why."[9]

In the week that Coke Classic was reintroduced, Coke's stock price jumped $5.50. In parts of the United States and most of Canada, new Coke was still outselling Coke Classic three months later, but in other areas Coke Classic was outselling new Coke, in some cases by a margin of nine to one. Despite the embarrassment involved with undoing over four years of elaborate planning, Coke may have solved its immediate problem of losing market share to Pepsi. "They stumbled into a way to beat Pepsi," an advertising executive stated. "They got every single American to think about Coca-Cola." Adding to this point, a *Newsweek* reporter stated that, "Coke has given its customers the rare satisfaction of forcing a giant corporation to do an about face."[10]

The irony of the situation is that "improved" taste was never the issue. As one restaurant owner put it, the extra bite that made the original Coke hard to guzzle was one of the things that distinguished Coke from Pepsi. "If everyone is going to be smooth and sweet, who's going to be Coke? Maybe Pepsi ought to come out with Coke's original formula; that would fill a void Coke is creating."[11] And Gay Mullins, the founder of Old Coca-Cola Drinkers of America, repeatedly failed to identify or prefer old Coke in taste tests. ■

WHAT IS A DECISION?

Every person makes many decisions every day. Most are small or inconsequential, and people rarely think about the act of making them. However, when people are faced with major decisions, such as buying a house, or a new car, they begin to think hard about the decision itself.

In the organizational context, where decisions are required for planning, organizing, directing, and controlling, effective decision-making skills are crucial. This chapter will introduce you to three important concepts: the context in which decisions are made, the steps in making them, and some methods useful for improving their accuracy and effectiveness. First, however, we will provide a broad definition of decision making.

Decision Making Defined

There are many ways to define the word *decision*. A decision can be thought of as the act of making up one's mind about something. It can be thought of as the ability to arrange facts and events into patterns, interpret them, and draw implications from them. Or it can be thought to involve a judgment that settles a matter in favor of one side or the other. In this book, we discuss decision making in terms of the differences and connections between choice making, decision making, and problem solving.

Choice Making, Decision Making, and Problem Solving

Problem solving
Making decisions, implementing the chosen solution, monitoring its impact, and making adjustments as necessary.

The simplest way to understand decision making is to realize that it is a part of a larger process of problem solving. As illustrated in Exhibit 3.1, **problem solving** can be described in terms of five types of activities. Identifying the problem or

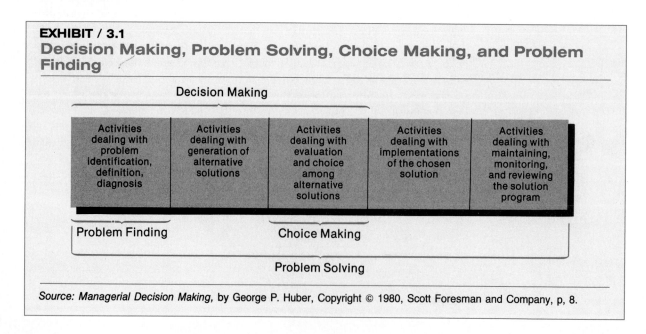

EXHIBIT / 3.1
Decision Making, Problem Solving, Choice Making, and Problem Finding

Decision Making

| Activities dealing with problem identification, definition, diagnosis | Activities dealing with generation of alternative solutions | Activities dealing with evaluation and choice among alternative solutions | Activities dealing with implementations of the chosen solution | Activities dealing with maintaining, monitoring, and reviewing the solution program |

Problem Finding   Choice Making

Problem Solving

Source: Managerial Decision Making, by George P. Huber, Copyright © 1980, Scott Foresman and Company, p, 8.

issue is the first step.[12] If no problem seems to exist, no efforts will be directed at solving it. Once the problem has been identified, the relevant issues can be explored and alternative solutions can be developed. When enough information exists about each alternative, they can be evaluated and the best one selected. The selected alternative must then be implemented; following this, it must be monitored for progress and effectiveness. If the problem still exists or a new one has developed, the problem solver(s) must return to the first step.

The first three steps in the problem-solving process—identifying the problem, developing alternatives, and selecting a solution—are the three basic components of **decision making.** The specific selection of one alternative is **choice making.** The last two steps, implementation and progress monitoring, are part of the broader process of problem solving. The overall process is cyclical, the last step always leading back into the first.[13]

The Coke case is a good illustration of the differences between problem solving, decision making, and choice making. The flattening soft-drink market, Coke's slipping market share, and Pepsi's growing market share were indications of a problem. Through the decision-making process, the problem was identified, information was gathered, alternatives were generated, and the "best" option—changing the formula—was selected. Choosing to change the formula, specifically, was choice making. The results of the implemented decision were unsatisfactory, so the monitoring and reviewing phases of the problem-solving process were used. Coke's actions during each of these steps will be discussed in more depth later in the chapter. First, however, we will cover several basic points to keep in mind about decisions and decision making.

Decision making
Identifying a problem, developing alternatives, and selecting a solution.

Choice making
Evaluating alternatives and selecting one that meets established criteria.

Relatedness of Decisions

No decision is completely independent of other decisions. Each decision is based on the outcome of previous decisions and in turn affects the context for future decisions. A decision to study at 9:00 P.M. on Tuesday, for example, may follow from a decision to play racquetball from 7:00 to 8:00. That decision, in turn, may have resulted from a decision not to schedule Tuesday night courses.

Similarly, decisions affect those that come after them. Take, for example, the decision to study or not to study. Deciding to study will presumably lead to an increased understanding of the material in your courses, which should allow you to do well on tests and papers and pass all your classes. This will leave you the option of deciding on a fresh set of classes for the next semester. If, on the other hand, you decide not to study but to play racquetball instead, you might have a very weak understanding of the material in your classes, fail your courses, and be forced to take them again in order to graduate. You will have eliminated the possibility of making a decision about new classes for the next semester.

Robert Goizueta's many decisions concerning Coca-Cola products were also closely related to each other. The early decision to introduce Diet Coke broke tradition, paving the way for later decisions to add other products and ultimately to change the original formula. The decision to change the formula was followed by decisions regarding methods of research and new lines of advertising. When the decision to change the formula was actually implemented, it produced a negative reaction and required the making of several more decisions rapidly to remedy the situation.

Personal Versus Managerial Decision Making

Managerial decision making Making judg-ments or decisions related to organization's goals.

It is useful to distinguish between personal and managerial decision making. Though no manager can make a decision that is completely unaffected by his or her personal experience, characteristics, and viewpoint, a manager has specific responsibilities for being rational and for safeguarding the organization's re-sources. Such responsibilities are not required in the personal domain. **Manage-rial decision making** is a process of making judgments or decisions related to the setting and accomplishment of an organization's goals,[14] involving the use of human, financial, and technological resources in the context of the environment. As an illustration, consider Rita Sanchez, a manager faced with two decisions. She is about to buy herself a new car because she just received a raise and a promo-tion. She also must purchase, as one of her new responsibilities, a fleet of cars for her service division. For herself, she might buy a red convertible sports coupe that is expensive to maintain and gets very low gas mileage because she person-ally likes fast, flashy cars. She can spend her own money without concern for efficiency or economy. For the division's fleet, however, which must be reliable and inexpensive to maintain, and which would not benefit from a flashy image, she would have to consider such factors as economy pricing, low maintenance costs, good gas mileage, and conservative styling when making her decision. She must allocate the organization's financial resources efficiently and economically.

The Inside View 3.1 provides a good example of the difference between per-sonal and managerial decisions. In one of the most publicized rounds of the "cola wars," managers at Pepsi-Cola decided to employ rock star Madonna in their advertisements. The managers involved may indeed like Madonna and purchase her records—those are personal decisions—but when they devote the organiza-tion's resources and pay for Madonna to be part of their advertising campaign, they are making managerial decisions. As can be seen in The Inside View 3.1, managerial decisions have very real consequences for the organization.

Programmed Versus Nonprogrammed Decisions

Programmed or routine decisions Decisions where the option to be chosen is identified by the circumstances of the situa-tion.

Nonprogrammed or nonroutine decisions Decisions for which no specific policy exists by which to choose a course of action.

Not every situation requires that a decision be made. A decision is not necessary when only one possible course of action is available, and no decision need be made when a set of mandated actions always applies in a given situation. In organizations, there are two broad, sometimes overlapping categories of deci-sions: those for which a set of mandated actions has been determined and those that require the discretion and judgment of the decision maker. These are re-ferred to as programmed and nonprogrammed decisions, respectively.[15]

For **programmed or routine decisions,** the option to be chosen is identified by the circumstances of the situation. All the decision maker need do is correctly assess the situation. Programmed decisions are essentially procedures or rules. For example, most department stores have set procedures for the return of mer-chandise. The clerks in the stores do not decide, each time a customer tries to return something, how to go about it. The decision is programmed: A standard policy, procedure, or rule exists, and the clerks need only refer to it.

For **nonprogrammed or nonroutine decisions,** no specific policy exists by which to choose a course of action. Nonprogrammed decisions are made in unique situations and require the judgment and discretion of the decision maker. In the example of the department store, a nonprogrammed decision would be the selection of new items for the floor. Buyers have to rely on their experience and skills at predicting fashion trends to select new lines of clothing. They cannot refer to a standard policy to determine what items to select.

The number of programmed and nonprogrammed decisions a manager makes varies according to his or her level in the organization (see Exhibit 3.2). Higher-

THE INSIDE VIEW / 3.1

Like a Prayer

A major Christian organization said it is prepared to boycott Pepsi-Cola Co. unless the company cancels its multimillion-dollar advertising contract with rock singer Madonna.

American Family Association, which publishes a monthly Christian magazine claiming a circulation of 380,000, cited a rock video starring Madonna that is running on MTV, the cable music station. The video, called "Like a Prayer," shows Madonna wearing a sexy black slip in a church in one scene, and dancing around flaming crosses in another.

"It is very offensive to Christians," said Donald Wildmon, executive director of the association, based in Tupelo, Miss.

Madonna sings her new song "Like a Prayer" in both the video and the Pepsi ad, but the story lines are completely different and Pepsi had nothing to do with the video. Still, said Mr. Wildmon, a Protestant minister, "They're putting money into this woman to make her a role model to sell soft drinks."

Responds a Madonna publicist: "I don't think it is an anti-Catholic or anti-religious video."

Mr. Wildmon said he contacted Pepsi to ask the soft-drink giant to drop Madonna, but Pepsi officials didn't return his phone calls. If Pepsi doesn't cancel its contract, valued at between $2 million and $5 million by industry sources, Mr. Wildmon's group would "encourage millions of Christians to quit drinking Pepsi and switch to Coca-Cola, 7 Up and Dr Pepper," the minister said.

Pepsi said it's keeping Madonna. "I'm not sure what the connection is between a video, which Pepsi had nothing to do with, and our ad," said a spokesman for the PepsiCo Inc. unit. ■

Pepsi managers found out not everyone likes Madonna's songs, and the negative attitude reflected badly on Pepsi. Using her as a spokesperson for their products did not turn out to be a good decision.

Source: McCarthy, Michael, *Wall Street Journal,* March 9, 1989, p. B7.

Author's Note: After running the ad only twice, the Pepsi-Cola Company decided to cancel any further use of the Madonna ad in the United States. The company cited confusion between its ad and Madonna's video, which was drawing negative reaction from religious groups, as the reason.

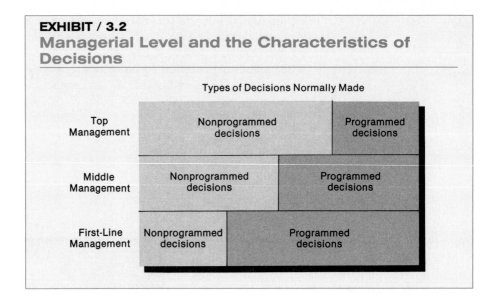

EXHIBIT / 3.2
Managerial Level and the Characteristics of Decisions

Types of Decisions Normally Made

Top Management	Nonprogrammed decisions	Programmed decisions
Middle Management	Nonprogrammed decisions	Programmed decisions
First-Line Management	Nonprogrammed decisions	Programmed decisions

level managers tend to make more nonprogrammed decisions, while lower-level managers usually make more programmed decisions. Regardless of managerial level, however, programmed and nonprogrammed decisions overlap. Most decisions can be resolved partially by referring to programs and partially by using discretion and experience. Buyers, for example, will have space constraints, quotas, or style restrictions as a framework for all their discretionary decisions. The clerks, though they have several procedures to follow in handling returned merchandise, may occasionally have to refer a customer to the floor manager to make a nonprogrammed decision. In some cases, the situation may not exactly fit the rules, or the customer may be particularly irate.

Both the decision to change Coke's original formula and the decision to reintroduce it were nonprogrammed decisions. The first decision broke 99 years of tradition, the second was made on extremely short notice, and it undid over four years of research. In both cases, the judgment and discretion of top management were called upon: No rule or procedure for changing the formula was written into the company's policy manual.

Since no decision-making skills are needed to implement a course of action that is already mandated, the remainder of this chapter will discuss nonprogrammed decision making only.

CONTEXT OF DECISION MAKING

Every problem exists, and every decision is made, within a specific context that gives the decision maker information for predicting decision outcomes. The less information available, the less accurate will be the prediction. Because all decisions have future consequences, decision makers need to anticipate these consequences to the greatest possible degree. The accuracy of their predictions will depend partially on the degree of certainty, risk, or uncertainty surrounding the decision.[16]

Conditions of Certainty

Conditions of certainty
A situation in which the decision maker knows precisely what consequences will follow from each alternative course of action.

Conditions of certainty exist when decision makers know precisely what consequences will follow from each course of action that can be selected. The manager need only compare the known outcome for each alternative against the given criteria for success (increased profits, number of jobs created, number of items sold) to make an effective decision. For example, assume you are responsible for a $5000 recreation fund for your organization. You want to achieve the highest possible return on an investment of the money before it is needed for next year's softball season. You have three investment alternatives: a checking account that will earn 5 percent interest and allows the depositer to write checks for a 10¢ service charge; a savings account that pays 6 percent interest and requires 30 days' notice before withdrawals; and a certificate of deposit that pays 10 percent interest and requires a $5000 minimum balance for a six-month period of deposit. The outcome of each of these alternatives is certain. Therefore, because you don't need any of the money for at least six months, the decision is quite easy to make. You should invest in the certificate of deposit (see Exhibit 3.3).

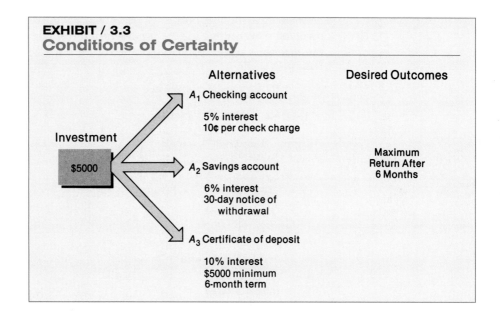

EXHIBIT / 3.3
Conditions of Certainty

Conditions of Risk

Conditions of risk
Circumstances in which a manager can identify several possible outcomes of decision alternatives but can only estimate the probability that each will occur.

Conditions of certainty rarely exist in the real world. Much more common are **conditions of risk,** in which a manager is able to identify several possible outcomes of various decision alternatives but can only estimate the probability that each will occur. There is some risk that the possible outcomes will not occur or will occur to a different degree than expected. A manager who has to allocate resources to three different product departments based on expected sales cannot be sure exactly how much each will sell and therefore how large an investment should be made in each department.

Risks can be minimized by gathering more information. If the information is accurate, it can help a manager assess the realistic probabilities that each specified outcome will occur. Suppose, for example, that Alpha Computer Company is considering borrowing $5 million at 10 percent interest to build a plant in Canada to produce component parts for personal computers. The Canadian government has been eager to develop the computer-manufacturing industry and is considering a program to provide low-cost loans at 5 percent interest to companies that invest in new manufacturing facilities. However, the law has not yet passed. Alpha's customers will need the component parts within 12 months, and it will take 6 months to set up the facility in Canada. What should Alpha's management do?

The decision must be made under conditions of risk. If Alpha's management borrows and invests the $5 million now, they are certain to be able to build the plant in time to deliver the parts to their customers. However, they will be paying 10 percent interest on the loan when they might have had to pay only 5 percent. On the other hand, if they wait to see if the law passes and it does not, they will still have to pay 10 percent (or more) on their loan and may not be able to build the facility in time. Because the decision makers at Alpha have no risk-free alternative, their best course of action is to gather as much information as possible within a reasonable time frame. If their lobbyists to the Canadian government discover that there is only a 20 percent chance that the bill will pass, the risks involved with waiting for the 5 percent interest rate increase greatly. Therefore, the managers would probably be better off borrowing at 10 percent now (see Exhibit 3.4).

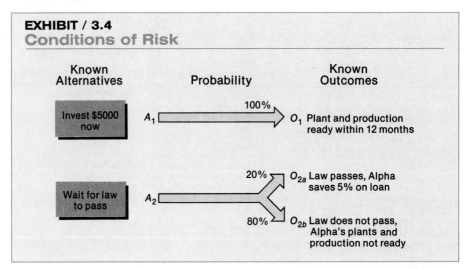

EXHIBIT / 3.4
Conditions of Risk

Known Alternatives	Probability	Known Outcomes

Invest $5000 now — A_1 — 100% → O_1 Plant and production ready within 12 months

Wait for law to pass — A_2 — 20% → O_{2a} Law passes, Alpha saves 5% on loan
80% → O_{2b} Law does not pass, Alpha's plants and production not ready

Conditions of Uncertainty

Conditions of uncertainty Situations in which neither the probabilities of certain outcomes nor even all possible outcomes can be identified.

Conditions of uncertainty exist when neither the probability of a certain outcome nor even all possible outcomes can be accurately identified (see Exhibit 3.5). Managers must gather more information about the known possible outcomes to clarify the probabilities of each occurring and also must gather more information about the entire issue to identify other possible outcomes. The decision to invest in a plant in a foreign country is frequently made under conditions of uncertainty. For example, as The Inside View 3.2 explains, the coming shifts in market conditions caused by the European agreement to move to a totally integrated market by 1992 will create great uncertainties for organizations doing business in Europe. Even if it were possible to make these forecasts with 99

A Unified European Market

Recently we visited Dr. Pierre Huemann, the financial/economic columnist for the *Die Weltwoche*, a prestigious Swiss weekly magazine. He claimed that he practices international trade on a weekly basis. Wondering why a reporter has to actually practice what he writes, we joined him for his weekly grocery shopping.

The excursion started in his hometown, Allschwil, a suburb of Basel. Driving northeast for 15 minutes, we crossed the Swiss border into Germany and found ourselves paying a butcher in deutsche marks. Dr. Huemann explained: "The meat in Germany is 30 to 50 percent cheaper than in Switzerland." Then, we headed west for another 20 minutes, crossing the border to France. Now Dr. Huemann used his French francs to buy wines, cheese, and vegetables. On the way back to Switzerland Dr. Huemann summarized his shopping strategy: "Different countries in Europe have different taxation and subsidization policies. You have to be foolish not to take advantage of the situation."

Easier said than done. Unlike Dr. Huemann, most Europeans don't live on the border. Furthermore, once one tries to transfer a large quantity of goods across Europe's borders, one starts hitting economic "walls." Eliminating these "walls" is the European Community's (EC) top priority.

Currently, protectionism in Europe means additional costs for both the producer and the consumer. The French pay 43 percent more for telephone equipment than necessary, according to an analysis conducted by the European Commission. Germans pay an extra 39 percent. Common switching systems could result in 60 percent lower telephone call charges in Belgium and as much as 70 percent lower in some other EC countries. In addition, both France and Germany have extremely stringent laws regulating the technical standards of building materials. Foreign producers must wait as long as five years to be certified to sell into these countries. Similarly, in most EC countries ludicrous health standards are applied to foreign but not to domestic food products.

Flags and symbols of the European Economic Community. Managers will have to learn to cope with the diversity of the expanded EC in order to successfully compete in Europe after 1992.

The Single European Act, which came into force on July 1, 1987, called for the completion of the integration process by 1992. If implemented, it will mean a free flow of goods, free capital movements, free trade in services, as well as the freedom of employees to look for jobs throughout the EC. Undoubtedly businesses will have to adapt quickly to these changes if they expect to compete successfully in Europe beyond 1992 ■

Source: Adapted from Michel, Allen and Shaked, Israel, "A Unified European Market: A Wonderful Dream or an Achievable Reality? *Bostonia Magazine*, summer, 1989.

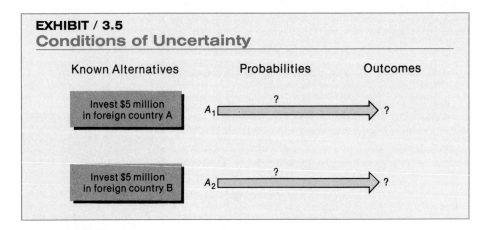

EXHIBIT / 3.5
Conditions of Uncertainty

Known Alternatives	Probabilities	Outcomes

percent accuracy, there might be other situations, such as sudden social upheaval, which had not even been considered as possibilities.

Under conditions of uncertainty, the chosen course of action will depend partly on the manager's values and the organization's priorities. If the organization has a very clear statement of priorities, managers can refer to it when making decisions in conditions of uncertainty. Consider the contrast between two mythical managers called Mini and Maxi. Mini believes that good managers strive to avoid the worst possible results of action. Given three possible alternatives in making a decision to invest in a new piece of machinery, Mini will select the alternative that will be the least damaging or costly if a "worst possible" scenario occurs. Mini is a conservative pessimist and believes that it is always best to minimize the maximum possible cost or loss to the organization. In technical terms, this is known as a **minimax**—minimize the maximum cost—decision.

In comparison, Maxi believes that it is always best to select the alternative with the biggest potential payoff, even if that alternative could result in a greater loss if something went wrong than other alternatives. Maxi is a risk-taking optimist. Thus, in deciding which machine to purchase, Maxi is likely to select the machine that promises the largest future payoff. In technical terms, this is known as a **maximax**—maximize the maximum payoff—decision.

In practice, managers are rarely so extreme in their views. A responsible manager will consider the degree of risk involved, gather as much additional information as time allows, then make the decision balancing the remaining risk with the organization's goals, resources, and values.

In reality, it is difficult to distinguish whether a decision is being made in conditions of risk or uncertainty, as the Coke case well illustrates. Goizueta's decision to change the formula was made in what Coke's managers would have considered conditions of risk. The formula they wished to change had 99 years of experience, and a $300 million company had been built on it. The only reason they considered changing the formula was because Coke appeared to be losing its hold on the number one position in a leveling soft-drink market. Therefore, the managers decided to conduct extensive research to reduce their risks to a reasonable level, and after four years, they were convinced the new formula they developed would be a hit.

Unfortunately, they didn't take into consideration certain factors that several market researchers were quick to point out, albeit after the fact. First, many

Minimax A decision that minimizes the maximum costs.

Maximax A decision that maximizes the maximum payoff.

researchers claimed that "in taste tests, the sweeter product almost invariably wins—but only once. Over the long haul, people may tire of it."[17] Second, even if taste tests are accurate predictions of long-term favor, they "don't take into account the emotional tie-in with the old brand, which is all wrapped up in people's childhoods."[18] In the case of Coke, taste seemed to be secondary to brand loyalty or familiarity.

In making the first decision, then, Coke's managers assumed they were operating in conditions of reduced risk: They had made a decision based on what they considered thorough research and analysis. However, not only had they failed to analyze the probability of the result that occurred, they had never even considered emotional reaction as a possible outcome. In deciding to reintroduce the original formula, Coke's managers were operating in conditions of uncertainty: There was no precedent for the situation and no way to determine what might happen next. Nevertheless, the company's executives consulted almost no one and spent only a few days in preparation, before announcing their decision. While this may seem ironic, the results are actually not surprising. The new formula was not selling, and the old formula always had. The only difficulty was the embarrassment of changing such a widely publicized decision. Profits obviously spoke louder than pride.

Optimal Versus Satisficing Decisions

Optimal decision A decision for which the decision maker has full knowledge of all alternatives and chooses the alternative producing the best possible outcomes.

Bounded rationality The natural limit on our ability to handle increased information.

Satisficing decision A decision that is satisfactory or acceptable given the limits on time and available information.

Thus far we have assumed that managers base decisions on unemotional reasoning and logic, a process called rational decision making. The rational decision maker attempts to identify all alternatives and gather all information related to a particular decision situation. In this manner, he or she can reach an **optimal decision,** one for which the decision maker had full knowledge of all information and alternatives and chose the alternative that would produce the best possible outcome. Unfortunately, optimal decision making almost never occurs in an organization because of the uncertainty in almost any situation and the tremendous resources required to achieve an optimal solution.

Organizations (and people) try to reduce the expense and complexity of making decisions primarily by using the concept of **bounded rationality,** the natural limit on our ability to handle increased amounts of information and complexity in a decision situation. We make problems more understandable and manageable by limiting the amount of information we consider and the alternatives we investigate. This process, called satisficing, is a consciously selective approach to decision making.[19] A **satisficing decision** is a decision that is satisfactory or acceptable given the narrow range of information or alternatives and the limits on time and available information. Satisficing decisions are often driven by the values of the decision maker.

The Coke case provides an interesting illustration of these concepts. By spending four years and $4 million on taste tests, and by thoroughly analyzing the results, Goizueta believed he had made an optimal decision and that the new formula would be a hit. However, in assuming that taste was the only issue, when in fact several other factors were involved, Goizueta failed to explore all possible alternatives. Thus the decision was, by definition, not optimal. It also did not meet the definition of satisficing, because Goizueta unconsciously, as opposed to consciously, overlooked certain important factors.

THE DECISION-MAKING/PROBLEM-SOLVING PROCESS

As we have stated, the decision-making process is complex.[20] All decisions are related to other decisions, and the contexts in which decisions must be made are usually far from ideal. Because managers at all levels must make many decisions pertaining to planning, organizing, directing, and controlling on a daily basis, and because the success of the organization depends on the effectiveness of these decisions, efforts have been made to systematize and improve the decision-making/problem-solving process. Five basic decision-making/problem-solving steps have been developed, but simply following the steps to the letter will not guarantee perfect decisions.[21] Managers are responsible for effectively applying their intuition, experience, and common sense to the following process (see Exhibit 3.6).

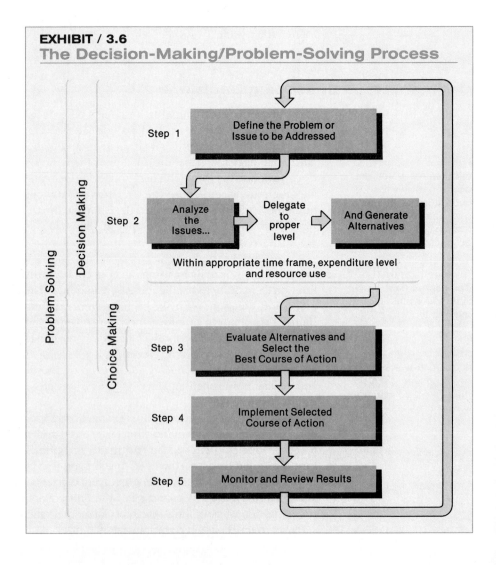

EXHIBIT / 3.6
The Decision-Making/Problem-Solving Process

Step 1 Define the Problem or Issue to be Addressed

Step 2 Analyze the Issues... → Delegate to proper level → And Generate Alternatives

Within appropriate time frame, expenditure level and resource use

Step 3 Evaluate Alternatives and Select the Best Course of Action

Step 4 Implement Selected Course of Action

Step 5 Monitor and Review Results

Problem Solving

Decision Making

Choice Making

1. *Define* the problem or issue to be addressed.
2. *Analyze* the issue and begin to generate alternative courses of action.
3. *Evaluate* the alternatives and select the one that meets the criteria previously established by the manager and/or organization.
4. *Implement* the decision or selected alternative.
5. *Monitor* its results and evaluate the impact, taking corrective action as necessary.

Define the Problem or Issue

In making good decisions, a manager must first properly define the problem or issue, that is, define its content. During this step, it is important to keep two points in mind: First, the existence of a problem indicates that there is a gap between what the organization intended and what actually occurred; second, the symptoms of the problem must be distinguished from the problem itself. Unfortunately, it is usually the symptoms that become evident first, after the problem has been developing for some time.

Suppose, for example, that the head of personnel, reviewing expenditure reports, finds that a disproportionately high share of the budget has gone to recruiting and training costs for the production department. During the past few quarters, production has overrun its portion and dipped slightly into the funds reserved for other departments. In other words, there is a gap between what was intended and what has occurred. A problem exists that will require a decision and corrective action.

The symptoms of this problem are evident: There are cost overruns and a considerably higher turnover rate in production than was anticipated. Defining the problem, however, is more difficult than identifying the symptoms. Some employees in production might complain of a lack of opportunities for advancement. Others might say that the supervisor is impossible to work with. The supervisor might claim that there is no problem at all, that due to the nature of the work people have always worked in the department for short periods of time. The personnel manager might even discover from an outside colleague that a local competitor has been hiring experienced production employees at a higher wage, saving itself the cost of a training program. The manager responsible for defining the problem may have to sift through conflicting reports and biased information before getting to the heart of the matter.

In the Coke case, the decision makers defined the problem as being the taste of their product. Though their taste-testing research seemed to support that conclusion, they found out that was not the problem. As the case demonstrates, incorrectly defining the problem or issue can adversely affect the organization's decision and course of action. As The Inside View 3.3 illustrates, it is important to be open-minded as you define the issue with which you are dealing.

Analyze the Issue and Generate Alternatives

Once the problem has been defined, relevant information must be gathered and analyzed. The speed and effectiveness of the analysis will depend on many things, such as the manager's skill and experience, the availability of information, and the complexity of the problem. The analysis phase contains three main components:

THE INSIDE VIEW / 3.3

Creative Problem Identification and Solution

Assume you are a golfer. You tee off on the fourth hole and hit a beautiful 140-yard drive up the center of the fairway. When you get to the ball, you find to your dismay that it has rolled into a spectator's empty paper lunch bag. You are in a close match and cannot delay play long without incurring a penalty. Additionally, if you move the ball you will receive at least a one-stroke penalty. How would you define this problem?

Most people immediately define the problem as getting the ball out of or away from the bag. This definition is often made subconsciously but causes the search for solutions to deal with the removal of the ball, a process that defies solution unless you are willing to incur a penalty.

A more creative definition of the problem is getting the bag away from the ball. This is more than just a semantic difference. The first definition tends to focus us on the ball; the second definition focuses on the bag. The solution is straightforward: Take a match and burn the bag. The wind will blow the ashes away, and you will have a clear shot without penalties. ■

a preliminary analysis to determine which level of the organization can best handle the issue; a more comprehensive analysis conducted at that level, during which alternatives are developed; and a control or review process to ensure that time and resources spent on analysis are appropriate for the situation.

A preliminary analysis must be completed so that the issue can be delegated to the appropriate organizational level. Simple or relatively insignificant problems can be handled effectively on a local level. Situations that are more involved and complicated require middle- or upper-management attention. If the personnel manager of our example discovers that the rapid turnover is being caused by poor supervisor-employee relations, the matter can probably be handled within the production department with the help of an on-site counselor or consultant. If the turnover is caused by lack of advancement opportunities, middle management from several departments or divisions might have to determine new avenues for employee development. If the turnover is caused specifically by the hiring practices of another organization, top management might have to consider redesigning its own policies or devising a way to combat the competition.

Once the issue or problem has been delegated to the appropriate level, the decision maker or decision-making group must propose and analyze alternatives. Analysis is needed to determine the strengths and weaknesses, costs and benefits, feasibility, and potential problems of each alternative. Creativity is crucial to this phase; after all, the outcome of the decision can only be as effective as the alternatives generated. It is important to generate several alternatives and withhold evaluation until all have been developed.

Often, managers will favor one option more than others if they have analyzed or lived with a problem for a long time. Unless they are forced to think out some alternatives, they will lean toward the decision that they instinctively "feel" is correct. This phenomenon is described by Peter Drucker in a story about Alfred P. Sloan, Jr., president of General Motors for more than 20 years. Sloan transformed GM into America's largest automobile manufacturer during the 1920s and 1930s:

> Alfred P. Sloan, Jr., is reported to have said at a meeting of one of the GM top committees, "Gentlemen, I take it we are all in complete agreement on the decision here." Everyone around the table nodded assent. "Then," continued Mr. Sloan, "I propose we postpone further discussion of this matter until our next meeting to give ourselves time to develop disagreement and perhaps gain some understanding of what the decision is all about." [22]

Sloan recognized that disagreement helps promote healthy discussion and analysis of an issue. Without alternatives, each with unique advantages and disadvantages, it is unlikely that all the important aspects of the decision will be understood and considered.

If the cause of the turnover in the production department has been identified as lack of advancement opportunities, the personnel manager should collect several alternative suggestions from different departments since lateral transfers may be necessary. The production manager and the sales manager might come up with an interesting idea over lunch, but if the personnel manager adopts it instantly, he or she will eliminate other ideas that might be more creative or effective or might address the needs of several departments.

Robert Goizueta is quoted in the opening case as seeing only two alternatives: either shelving the new formula or introducing it in place of the existing product. It is more than likely that several other alternatives existed. Just as Cherry Coke had been added to the line, the new formula could have been incorporated into some other flavor. However, because it was assumed from the beginning that the taste of the flagship product (Coke Classic, as it is now called) was at the root of the problem, options other than changing it were apparently not considered.

Finally, decision makers must closely monitor the analysis to ensure that the time and money spent are appropriate for the situation. Information gathering and analysis can be very costly. In order for the analysis to be effective, however, it must cost less than the problem itself costs and must be completed in time to be helpful. The personnel manager who analyzes the problem that is creating the high turnover might want to survey every department in the organization extensively, or might try to find out where every single former employee is currently working and for what salary. An analysis this thorough might take months or years and cost more than the production department's budget overruns. Most managerial decisions must be made with less than perfect information simply because of time and cost considerations. [23]

The analysis of future-oriented problems requires a different approach that often incorporates more risk than the analysis of current-time-frame problems. For example, auto manufacturers retool (change the production line to make a new type of car) every three years or so. Retooling is extremely expensive and time consuming. It is based on an assessment of the combination of car style and features that will sell in the future. If this prediction has been grossly inaccurate, the organization will suffer great financial losses.

Timeliness becomes problematic here. The only way to know with absolute certainty whether the analysis of some future condition has been accurate is to wait until this future condition becomes the present condition. If every manager waited to guarantee the accuracy of future predictions before putting anything into production, nothing would get produced. Consequently, managers must rely on a combination of experience, intuition, and knowledge in their analysis of future-oriented decisions.

Coca Cola was facing both an immediate and a long-term problem: It was losing market share in a flattening market. Time and money spent on analysis were certainly appropriate. The decision to change 99 years of tradition was delegated to the correct level of the organization: Such a major step was certainly in top management's realm of responsibility. But although it spent $4 million on taste tests, the company failed to use several more sophisticated methods of market research that were available at the time. *Newsweek*, for example, claimed that by using what is called psychographics, Coke would have discovered that its "largest and most loyal block of customers, mostly middle-class Americans, are disturbed by changes."[24] The decision makers also failed to take advantage of other programs that can "dramatically reduce the failure rate for new products (currently 60%), in some cases by as much as 30–50%."[25]

Evaluate the Alternatives and Select the Best One

In theory, selecting the best alternative should be a relatively easy task if the problem has been properly identified and analyzed and if a range of feasible alternatives has been proposed. The decision-making process is designed to encourage the manager to carefully consider all the factors that are important to the organization and relevant to the decision. The alternative that is both realistic in terms of goals and resources and that will actually achieve the desired results is the most rational choice. If an optimal decision is possible, of course it should be

"It's high time you became involved in the decision-making process. Take a straw!"

made. More often, however, the alternative that satisfies the most (and most important) criteria possible will become apparent as the less promising possibilities are eliminated.

Projected implementation costs can also influence the choice of an alternative. If two options will satisfy an equal number of important criteria, the less costly one will usually be chosen. For example, one of the options for improving advancement opportunities for the production staff might be an elaborate system to train and rotate experienced employees in production. This option might be so effective that it will completely eliminate the turnover, but if it is too costly to implement, a different alternative will have to be selected. Implementation costs should be considered during the generation of alternatives.

Implement the Decision

Once the most promising alternative has been selected, it must be implemented. Although it is crucial to the success of any decision, implementation rarely receives the level of attention and thoroughness that the decision itself receives. In the previous section, we pointed out that implementation costs must be taken into account during the alternative generation and selection phases. In addition, after making a decision, managers must consider who will implement the decision, how it should be implemented, and what should be done if problems occur during implementation.

Scope The degree of impact of a decision.

Managers need to assign specific responsibility for implementation, and this means determining on which organizational level—top, middle, or first-line management—this responsibility should lie. In general, the broader the **scope,** or degree of impact, of the decision, the higher the level of management in the organization that should handle it. Referring to our example, a decision to implement a training and rotation system would have a considerably broader scope than a decision to replace one supervisor with whom it is simply impossible to work.

Implementation involves not only the consideration of timelines (for example, deadlines for certain accomplishments) but raises the question of what role other parts of the organization will have. Will task forces be used? What proportion or amount of resources will be allocated? As the actual implementation proceeds, adjustments to the implementation process, to the decision itself, and to parts of the organization may be required.

Finally, potential implementation problems must be assessed before implementation for two important reasons. First, the organization or manager must be able to smooth out potential difficulties or at least anticipate trouble spots before they occur. Second, careful consideration of implementation problems may lead to revisions of decision alternatives as they are being generated. Although an alternative may appear to be the best choice, predicted problems with implementation may, in fact, make that particular choice impossible.

The process of decision making does not end with the decision choice itself. As we assess the success or failure of a particular decision, we must also assess its implementation. It is entirely possible that a "good" decision fails because of poor implementation and that a "poor" decision succeeds because of excellent implementation. Managers trying to position organizations for the future have to understand why a decision fails or succeeds.

Monitor Results and Evaluate the Impact

Much feedback and follow-up work will be necessary to ensure that the decisions produce the expected results. Often, as The Inside View 3.4 demonstrates, even though it looks like decisions are working out well, something might happen to throw them off course. Managers in the Apple Corporation, the computer firm, thought they had an ironclad deal with Apple Corps Limited, the music firm. The judge's decision could change the situation very quickly. Decisions can also have unintended effects. Consider our earlier example concerning the turnover problem in production. The training and rotation system would be expected to reduce turnover; a reduction in turnover would then be an intended effect. The unintended effects of a decision are the unexpected results it produces. Suppose, for

---

THE INSIDE VIEW / 3.4

Why Don't We Do It in the Courts?

George Harrison wrote a song about it: the "Sue Me, Sue You Blues." The "quiet one" was poking fun at the nasty legal battles the Beatles fought with one another after they split up in the early '70s. Now the Fab Four's old company, Apple Corps Limited, is back in court again. This time it's going after the other Apple—the Cupertino, Calif.–based computer maker—for playing its tune.

Four years after the American firm started up in 1977, the Beatles' company gave it a ticket to ride: the right to use the Apple name and a logo similar to its own. The only hitch: that the upstart stick to making computers, and not sell what the agreement calls machines "intended for synthesizing music." Now Apples, like many other computers, are used to compose and even play music, thanks to sound-processing microchips and connections that link computers with electronic instruments. Apple Corps claims this move into music violates the 1981 contract and has cried Help! to a British magistrate.

What does Apple 1 want Apple 2 to call its musical computers? "Banana is good," says Wayne Cooper, Apple Corps's San Francisco counsel. "We don't care what they use as long as it isn't Apple. Let them call it Cadillac." The British Apple is pushing for what one of its U.S. attorneys, Paul LiCalsi, calls "a substantial and large licensing fee." An Apple Computer spokesperson called the suit "without merit" and promised a formal rebuttal in

The Apple logo used by Apple computers. The use of Apple computers to program music has raised new questions and uncertainties. Managers at Apple computers thought they had an ironclad arrangement with Apple Corps Ltd to use the Apple name and logo concept, but the judge may decide differently.

30 days. With talks at an impasse, it may be a long and winding road before the two Apples come together. ∎

Source: "Why Don't We Do It in the Courts?" *Newsweek,* March 6, 1989, p. 44.

example, the training and rotation system was designed specifically for production employees. Their moving into higher-level slots in other departments might limit the advancement possibilities of employees in those departments. The unintended result, therefore, might be to increase turnover in some other departments.

Decisions should also be analyzed in terms of primary and secondary impacts. The primary impact of a decision should essentially be its intended effect. The first thing the implementation of an effective decision should achieve is the desired result; whatever the alternative chosen by the head of personnel, the primary impact should be a reduction in turnover in the production department. The primary impact can be something unintended, however. Secondary impacts, also known as the *ripple effect,* are the results of the primary impact. A reduction in turnover, the primary impact, will probably cause increased productivity and lower recruitment costs, and might produce tangible results such as increased morale in the production department (see Exhibit 3.7).

Managers usually consider the intended effects and primary impacts of alternatives during the analysis and selection phases of decision making. However, just as implementation costs should be analyzed prior to final selection, so should unintended effects and secondary impacts. Although the prediction of outcomes incorporates risk and uncertainty, a responsible manager will try to anticipate the future consequences of decisions, thereby reducing the dangers of unforeseen results.

In the Coke case, the primary impact was different from the intended effects (namely, to regain market share and increase sales), and the unintended effects and secondary impacts were so many and so unfavorable that they caused a second decision to be made immediately to correct the results of the first. Though at first record numbers of people tried the new formula and Coke shipments increased, the unintended primary effects included decreased sales, complaints from bottlers, unfavorable letters from customers, and celebrations at rival PepsiCo. The secondary impacts included the development of Coke boycotts, several spontaneous meetings among top executives, and demands for the return of the original product. Fortunately, the monitoring and reviewing phases of the problem-solving process were in full swing, and the original formula was reintroduced as a result.

EXHIBIT / 3.7
The Impact of Managerial Decisions

	Primary Impacts	Secondary Impacts
Intended/ Anticipated Effects	Desired outcome	Positive outcome caused directly by primary impact
Unintended/ Unanticipated Effects	Positive or negative first result or outcome	Positive or negative result caused directly by either intended or unintended primary impact

IMPROVING DECISION MAKING

The broader the scope of a decision and the less certain the context in which it is made, the more chances there will be for damaging unintended effects and secondary impacts. In addition to the five-step process just discussed, other tools have been developed that can reduce the risks in making decisions and help increase the effectiveness of those decisions.

Quantitative and Qualitative Methods

Several techniques that can measure the success of a given decision have been developed. Tools used to measure such numerical results as profits, costs, and levels of output are referred to as quantitative methods or techniques. Such techniques include probability theory, which was mentioned earlier with regard to certainty, uncertainty, and risk conditions; linear programming, which is a mathematical technique for allocation of resources to achieve either minimum (least cost) or maximum (greatest profits) results; and decision trees (see Exhibits 3.8 and 3.9), which show how a sequence of decisions leads to various outcomes. Decision trees can help the decision maker identify the estimated costs and probabilities of various outcomes.[26] Many of these techniques are used in production management for control of output. These and other quantitative techniques are described more fully in the Quantitative Appendix.

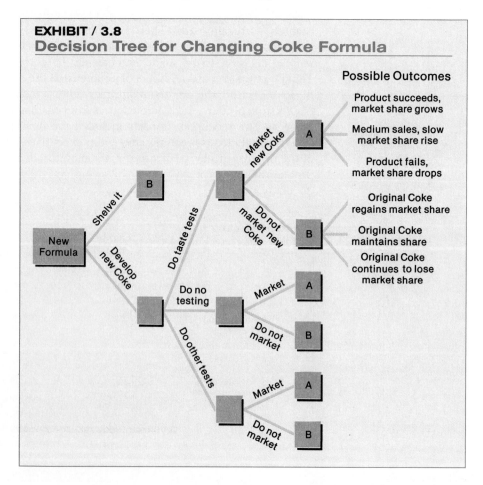

EXHIBIT / 3.8
Decision Tree for Changing Coke Formula

Possible Outcomes

Product succeeds, market share grows

Medium sales, slow market share rise

Product fails, market share drops

Original Coke regains market share

Original Coke maintains share

Original Coke continues to lose market share

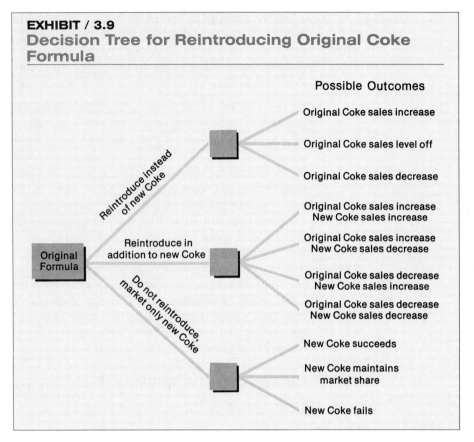

EXHIBIT / 3.9
Decision Tree for Reintroducing Original Coke Formula

Possible Outcomes

Original Formula

Reintroduce instead of new Coke
- Original Coke sales increase
- Original Coke sales level off
- Original Coke sales decrease

Reintroduce in addition to new Coke
- Original Coke sales increase / New Coke sales increase
- Original Coke sales increase / New Coke sales decrease
- Original Coke sales decrease / New Coke sales increase
- Original Coke sales decrease / New Coke sales decrease

Do not reintroduce, market only new Coke
- New Coke succeeds
- New Coke maintains market share
- New Coke fails

Not all information is quantifiable, and if managers focus only on the numbers, they may overlook other relevant considerations. The decision of whether to continue a training program, for example, cannot be made by simply counting how many hours people have spent in class. People's skills, motivation, and attitudes have to be assessed with the use of qualitative information involving feelings, attitudes, and ideas.

Most methods used to collect qualitative information use groups. The Delphi technique is one such method. Using this technique, a group goes through a process of reaching consensus on a view of the future (e.g., Will demand for this product increase next year?). Individuals are asked a set of questions, and after they have replied, all members are given the responses of the other group members. These steps are repeated until a consensus is reached. Other qualitative techniques include computer simulation, scenario building, and assumption testing. But even with the help of effective tools and techniques, decision makers still must use their experience, intuition, and judgment to make effective decisions.

Group and Committee Involvement

An individual manager regularly faces problems that he or she cannot deal with adequately for lack of time or information. Drawing other people into the decision-making process can allow a manager to handle complicated issues more effectively.[27] Top management frequently encourages managers to work in groups in order to produce decisions that achieve favorable outcomes with few unanticipated problems.

Before deciding to use group decision making, the manager must answer two questions. First, under what circumstances does it make sense to use a group rather than an individual manager to make the decision? Second, what degree of involvement should the group have in decision making? Each of these issues is discussed below.

Choosing to Involve a Group   In deciding whether to use a group in a problem situation, the manager should consider the advantages and disadvantages of group decision making.[28] The major advantage is that groups bring a broader perspective to the problem. They can improve the definition of an issue, expand the range of alternatives considered, and help identify potential problems with implementation. Second, a group allows for more information to be collected, analyzed, and synthesized. There are simply more hands to work on the task. Third, participants in the decision-making process are more likely to support the decision than those who have not participated, which usually makes implementation smoother. Fourth, there is a better chance of accurate communication throughout the organization about the decision. These advantages create a powerful incentive to involve groups in the decision-making process.

There are, however, several disadvantages to using groups. First, groups typically take longer to formulate and reach decisions than individuals. Second, groups sometimes produce decisions that appease various members but are not optimal for solving the problem. Third, if the group members disagree, the result may be no decision at all. Fourth, groups are sometimes subject to domination by strong personalities or members with special authority. People tend to defer to those with the highest rank, and members usually follow their boss's lead in developing a decision.[29]

Degree of Involvement   Group involvement in the decision-making process means that the manager gives up some authority and the subordinates or other group members have some influence on the decision. At one extreme, the manager merely announces a decision and the subordinates are expected to accept it. At the other extreme, the manager notes that a problem exists (but doesn't specify it) and provides limits on subordinates' action: "You can't spend more than $10,000," or "This has to be solved in 60 days." The manager then accepts the group's decision. Between these extremes lie varying levels of freedom of action for subordinates. Selection of the most effective level of group involvement depends on the individual manager and the given situation. The characteristics of the decision and the organizational situation are the keys to selecting an appropriate balance between individual and group decision making.

The Vroom-Yetton Model   One of the most systematic studies of managerial decision making was prepared by Victor Vroom and Philip Yetton in 1973.[30] It resulted in a method for choosing an appropriate decision-making style in either individual or group problem situations. An individual problem situation is one in which only the manager or leader and one employee are involved or will be affected by the decision. When several people are involved or will be affected, it is a group problem situation.

The Vroom-Yetton model is a decision tree in which managers answer a series of seven questions regarding their current situation (see Exhibit 3.10). The answers to the questions guide the decision maker from left to right along a decision tree to the appropriate method or style for handling the decision. In the model illustrated in Exhibit 3.11, if the answer to question A is no, you move upward

EXHIBIT / 3.10
Questions for Deciding How to Involve the Group

A. *Is there a quality requirement such that one solution is likely to be more rational than another?* If it matters what alternative is selected there is a quality requirement and the manager should be actively involved.

B. *Do I have sufficient information to make a high-quality decision?* If the manager does not have sufficient information to make the decision he or she should involve subordinates who do have the relevant information.

C. *Is the problem structured?* If the problem is ambiguous, the manager should work with subordinates to help clarify the problem and possible solutions.

D. *Is acceptance of decision by subordinates critical to implementation?* If implementation requires subordinates to understand and accept the decision, they should probably be involved in the decision process.

E. *If you were to make the decision by yourself, is it reasonably certain that it would be accepted by your subordinates?* If subordinates usually go along with what the manager decides, there is less need to have them involved in the decision process.

F. *Do subordinates share the organizational goals to be obtained in solving the problem?* If subordinates do not share the overall goals of the organization, they will likely make decisions contrary to what should be done. In this case, the manager should stay actively involved in the decision process.

G. *Is conflict among subordinates likely in the preferred solution?* If disagreements among subordinates are likely, the manager should stay actively involved to help resolve the conflicts.

along the path to the next question (D). If the answer is yes, you move downward along the alternative path (to question B). Once you have reached the far right side of the tree, there can be one or more "decision" styles, as described in Exhibit 3.12, indicated as appropriate for the situation; these can apply only to individual problems, only to group problems, or to both.

Use the Vroom-Yetton decision tree to analyze the following situation. Suppose you are the manager of a word-processing service, and you must decide whether your staff will be required to do transcribing work. Transcription requires typing from tape recordings, turning spoken words into written copy. It can be extremely lucrative work but is very time consuming and tedious. Tapes are often from meetings in which many people may talk at once, making it confusing to differentiate among speakers and hear what each one is saying. Most of the employees won't want to do transcription work in addition to the typing they already do, particularly because of the difficulty and the likelihood of error. Your problem is that, to provide full services and earn extra profits, you want to make it mandatory for employees to do all transcription work assigned them. Several options are available to you: You could simply assign the work randomly, as it comes in; you could offer it at an increased rate to employees who volunteer; or you could hire additional staff specifically for transcription work.

Using the decision tree, you would answer the following questions to determine how to address the issue:

A. *Does the decision possess a quality requirement?* Since it makes no difference to you which alternative is chosen, as long as it works, the answer is no. Move upward along the path to D.

D. *Is acceptance of the decision by subordinates important for effective implementation?* Yes; move downward to E.

E. *If you were to make the decision by yourself, is it reasonably certain that it would be accepted by your subordinates?* Not necessarily. The chosen decision style is therefore GII (see Exhibit 3.12): Share the problem with subordinates as a group, generate and evaluate alternatives together, and implement the solution upon which consensus has been reached.

EXHIBIT / 3.11
Decision Process Flowchart

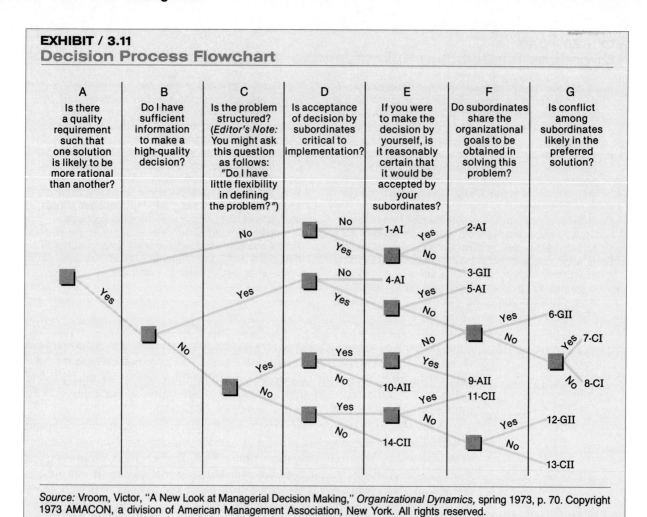

A	B	C	D	E	F	G
Is there a quality requirement such that one solution is likely to be more rational than another?	Do I have sufficient information to make a high-quality decision?	Is the problem structured? (*Editor's Note:* You might ask this question as follows: "Do I have little flexibility in defining the problem?")	Is acceptance of decision by subordinates critical to implementation?	If you were to make the decision by yourself, is it reasonably certain that it would be accepted by your subordinates?	Do subordinates share the organizational goals to be obtained in solving this problem?	Is conflict among subordinates likely in the preferred solution?

Several research studies have been done in an attempt to verify the Vroom-Yetton decision-making model, and the results have been supportive. In one study, a sample of decisions was analyzed. It was found that a large percentage (68 percent) of those made as illustrated in the model were successful, while a small percentage (22 percent) of those not made in accordance with the model were successful.[31] Though the model is somewhat complex and probably no practicing managers use it daily for every decision they make, it can be a very useful tool. It offers a method for understanding the specifics of one's circumstances and identifying one or more options that can be successful given these circumstances.

The Vroom-Yetton model is just one tool managers can use in making effective decisions. In a real-life situation, a manager may wish to choose other tools or follow a decision-making process similar to the one outlined in this chapter. Through the intelligent and skillful use of such tools and methods, managers can successfully make decisions regarding all levels of planning, organizing, directing, and controlling.

EXHIBIT / 3.12
Decision Styles for Leadership; Individuals and Groups

INDIVIDUAL

AI. You solve the problem or make the decision yourself, using information available to you at that time.

AII. You obtain necessary information from the subordinate, then decide on the solution to the problem yourself. You may or may not tell the subordinate what the problem is. The role played by your subordinate in making the decision is clearly one of providing specific information that you request rather than generating or evaluating alternative solutions.

CI. You share the problem with the relevant subordinates, getting ideas and suggestions. Then you make the decision, which may or may not reflect your subordinates' influence.

GI. You share the problem with one of your subordinates and together you analyze the problem and arrive at a mutually satisfactory solution in an atmosphere of free and open exchange of information and ideas. You both contribute to the resolution of the problem with the relative contribution of each being dependent on knowledge rather than formal authority.

DI. You delegate the problem to one of your subordinates providing him or her with any relevant information that you possess, but giving him or her responsibility for solving the problem alone. You will support any solution that the person reaches.

GROUP LEVEL

AI. You solve the problem or make the decision yourself, using information available to you at that time.

AII. You obtain necessary information from subordinates, then decide on the solution to the problem yourself. You may or may not tell the subordinates what the problem is. The role played by your subordinates in making the decision is clearly one of providing specific information that you request rather than generating or evaluating solutions.

CI. You share the problem with the relevant subordinates individually, getting their ideas and suggestions without bringing them together as a group. Then you make the decision, which may or may not reflect your subordinates' influence.

CII. You share the problem with your subordinates in a group meeting at which you obtain their ideas and suggestions. Then you make the decision, which may or may not reflect your subordinates' influence.

GII. You share the problem with your subordinates as a group. Together, you generate and evaluate alternatives and attempt to reach agreement (consensus) on a solution. You coordinate the discussion, keeping it focused on the problem and making sure that the critical issues are discussed. You do not try to influence the group to adopt "your" solution, and you are willing to accept and implement any solution that has the support of the entire group.

Source: Vroom, Victor, and Yetton, Philip, *Leadership and Decision Making* (Pittsburgh: University of Pittsburgh Press, 1973), p. 13.

■ KEY POINTS

1 Problem solving involves five basic activities: identifying a problem, analyzing it and generating alternative courses of action, evaluating them and selecting the best one, implementing the selected option, and monitoring the results. Decision making involves specifically the first three activities, and choice making involves specifically the third activity.

2 Past decisions affect current decisions by structuring opportunities and constraints, and current decisions similarly affect the opportunities and constraints that will exist in the future. Every decision is made within the context resulting from previous decisions and will in turn create (at least in part) the context for future decisions.

3 Because managers are responsible for efficiently and effectively allocating organizational resources, managerial decisions must be made on the basis of organizational goals and standards. Personal decisions can be made on the basis of whim or personal taste.

4 A programmed decision requires little analysis and is a straightforward implementation of decisions that have already been made. Nonprogrammed decisions are made in unique, one-time situations that require judgment or discretion. There is usually some overlap between programmed and nonprogrammed decisions.

5 In conditions of certainty, all possible outcomes of a decision and the probabilities of their occurring are known. In conditions of risk, all possible outcomes are known, but the probabilities of their occurring can only be estimated. In conditions of uncertainty, neither all possible outcomes nor the probabilities of their occurring are known. In the latter two conditions, information must be gathered to reduce risks. In conditions of uncertainty, a manager might choose to minimize the maximum cost of the decision, that is, make a minimax decision. At the opposite extreme, he or she might choose to maximize the maximum payoff of the decision, that is, make a maximax decision.

6 Optimal decisions can be reached when all relevant information about all possible alternatives has been analyzed fully and rationally. However, bounded rationality, a natural limit on an individual's ability to handle extensive complexity, makes satisficing decisions necessary in most circumstances. Satisficing decisions are reached when a sufficient amount of information has been analyzed—given time, money, and resource constraints—and enough important organizational criteria have been met.

7 Intended effects of a decision are the results that the decision maker expects it to produce; unintended effects are results that were not anticipated. The primary impact of a decision is its first result, while secondary impacts are those caused by the primary impact. Ideally, the primary impact will be the intended effect, though this is not always the case.

8 Quantitative methods of improving decision making involve measurements and usually focus on such factors as costs, outputs, and profits. Qualitative methods focus on feelings, attitudes, and ideas.

9 The main advantage to using groups in decision making is the variety of perspectives brought to the problem-solving process. Disadvantages include the length of time spent and difficulties evolving in intragroup relations. Advantages and disadvantages should be weighed when deciding whether to use a group or an individual in the decision-making or problem-solving process.

FOR DISCUSSION AND REVIEW

1. What decisions did Goizueta have to make before and after the introduction of new Coke? Name some factors that would have influenced each decision.

2. What are some major decisions being made in the automobile industry that are based on previous industry decisions?

3. If a company is introducing a new product (dissimilar to any already in the market), and extensive market research has been done, is the decision to produce being made under certainty, risk, or uncertainty, and why?

4. A secretary has programmed and nonprogrammed decisions to make each day. List examples of each type, and indicate what factors should influence the decisions.

5. In what types of industries or situations would minimax types of decisions be best suited? Maximax?

6. Will decisions made under risk conditions have greater scope than decisions made where uncertainty exists? Why or why not?

7. Was your decision to enter college made under uncertainty, risk, or certainty conditions? Why?

8. A robot is the perfect example of an optimal decision maker. Present an argument either for or against the use of machines in managerial decision making for producing optimal results.

9. What types of industries should focus more heavily on quantitative methods for decision making? Qualitative?

10. What are the advantages and disadvantages in utilizing groups to make decisions? Design a group that Coca Cola could have used effectively in their problem-solving process. Address the issues of advantages versus disadvantages and the appropriate degree of the group's involvement.

11. What is your opinion of the Vroom-Yetton decision-making model? In what situations should it be used? Should it be modified? Using the model, analyze either the first or second decision made by Coca Cola Co.

KEY TERMS

Bounded rationality
Choice making
Conditions of certainty
Conditions of risk
Conditions of uncertainty
Decision making
Managerial decision making
Maximax decision
Minimax decision
Nonprogrammed or nonroutine decisions
Optimal decision
Problem solving
Programmed or routine decisions
Satisficing decision
Scope

Bay Manufacturing

Sandra Johnson is the personnel manager for Bay Manufacturing, a small company in Seattle, Washington. She has seven people working directly for her and is responsible for all personnel matters involving the 600 managers and employees of Bay Manufacturing. At the management meeting this morning, the president of the firm revealed that the firm has landed a long-term contract with the Glencoe Corporation. The terms of the contract require that Bay provide on-site supervisors and technicians for product manufacturing in Tucson, Arizona. The president of Bay explained that placements would be handled by the personnel department. On Sandra's desk are the personnel files of 8 supervisors and 28 technicians who are fully qualified to perform the job. Two supervisors and 12 technicians are required to move to Tucson within one year.

Sandra knows that the quality of life and attractions of the Seattle area are quite different from those in Tucson. Additionally, the president assured her that success on this project would be very beneficial to the firm and to the individuals assigned. ■

The essence of management is decision making. Every manager must constantly make decisions which determine how people work and what they accomplish.

DISCUSSION QUESTIONS

1. What is the problem that Sandra faces? What decisions will have to be made? What choices?
2. How will the various decisions to be made by Sandra and those recruited be related? Which are personal, and which managerial? Which, if any, are programmed, and which nonprogrammed?
3. Is Sandra operating in conditions of certainty, risk, or uncertainty? On what conditions will the recruited personnel be operating? Can each make an optimal or a satisficing decision?
4. How should Sandra make her decisions and solve her problem? What steps should she go through? How could she improve the decision-making process?

THE CONFERENCE TABLE: DISCUSSION CASE / 3.2

The Swine Flu Epidemic

Army recruit David Lewis collapsed and died within hours of contracting a respiratory illness in February 1976 at Fort Dix, New Jersey. When blood samples from Lewis and several other recruits with a similar illness were analyzed at the federal Center for Disease Control (CDC) in Atlanta, Georgia, the CDC identified the disease as swine flu.

No cases of swine flu had been identified in humans in the previous 40 years, but some scientists believed that a swine virus had caused the terrible influenza epidemic that struck worldwide in 1918 and 1919, infecting more than 500,000 people in the United States. Over 20 million around the world died in that outbreak, and it killed more people in less time than any other natural disaster in history. Officials at the CDC believed that the swine flu virus that killed David Lewis might be related to the disease that caused the 1918 disaster, but they could not determine whether it would be as deadly as the 1918 flu.

Public health officials were worried for several reasons. Not only was there the possibility that swine flu was related to the virus that caused the 1918 pandemic, but recent research showed that influenza epidemics occurred in 10- to 12-year cycles. Since serious epidemics had occurred in 1957 and 1968, some scientists believed that 1976–1977 might be the next round in the cycle. In a normal year, flu causes 10,000 to 17,000 deaths in the United States. During an epidemic season, that figure doubles.

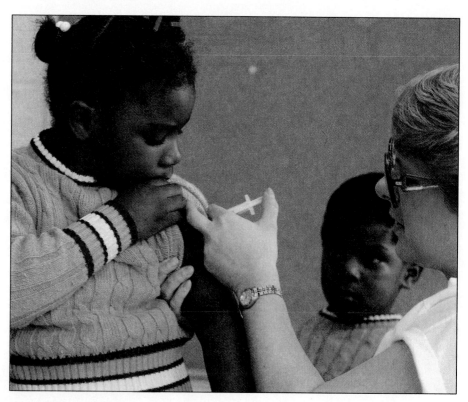

Public health officials feared that an epidemic of swine flu might claim hundreds of thousands of lives, so they recommended a mass-immunization program to forestall the outbreak.

TAKING ACTION

After a series of meetings in February and March, CDC officials reached a consensus that a swine flu epidemic was a possibility, that no assurances could be given as to its mildness, and that almost everyone under 50 years of age would be susceptible. Several participants thought that the early detection of an epidemic would provide a critical opportunity to demonstrate the virtues of preventive medicine through a mass immunization program. As one official stated, "for the first time, there was both the knowledge and the time to provide for vast immunization."[1]

Dr. David Sencer, head of the CDC, directed and coordinated the early government reaction to the swine flu problem. He saw his task as one of persuading his bosses at the Department of Health, Education, and Welfare (HEW) of the wisdom of a preventative program in this case. Under his direction, an action memorandum was prepared outlining what the government should do to prevent a national epidemic. Sencer believed there was a strong possibility that the United States would experience widespread influenza in 1976–1977 and recommended the following course of action:

1. The federal government would undertake a massive immunization of the public against the feared outbreak of flu.
2. The government would request drug manufacturers to produce 200 million doses of the vaccine and would purchase the entire lot.
3. The vaccine would be given free of charge to the public, with the actual vaccination programs administered through private physicians and state health services.
4. The CDC would monitor the administration and implementation of the entire program. The cost to the federal government would be $134 million.

Finally, Sencer concluded that the decision had to be made immediately. Sencer argued that because drug companies would need considerable lead time to produce the vaccine, a decision had to be made by the end of March, barely two weeks away.

MR. FORD'S DECISION

Incredibly enough, the wheels of government moved quickly. The secretary of HEW reviewed Sencer's plan and agreed with the need for the immunization and the efficiency of the proposed steps to implement it. On March 24, President Gerald Ford convened a blue-ribbon panel of experts from outside the government to discuss the recommendations. This group, including Dr. Jonas Salk and Dr. Albert Savin, creators of the polio vaccines (and bitter professional rivals), reviewed the plan and agreed with it.

President Ford faced a simple choice between accepting or rejecting the Sencer recommendation. Alternative courses of action had been raised during lower-level discussions at CDC and HEW, but these were not raised at the presidential level. Though not an expert in medical matters, Mr. Ford had to make a policy decision. There seemed to be four questions:

1. What were the odds that a swine flu epidemic would occur during 1976–1977?

2. What would be the likely consequences of such an epidemic if it did occur?
3. What was the likelihood that the immunization program would succeed in preventing the epidemic?
4. Would the costs of such a program be acceptable?   ■

DISCUSSION QUESTIONS

1. Define the problem President Ford faced.
2. HEW provided one recommendation to the president. Should he have asked for more options? Why or why not?
3. What was the purpose of the blue-ribbon panel? What did it accomplish?
4. Using a simple decision tree diagram, outline the risks, probabilities, and uncertainties that faced President Ford in making a go/no-go decision.

NOTE

1. Quoted in Neustadt, Richard E., and Fineberg, Harvey V., M.D., *The Swine Flu Affair* (Washington, D.C.: U.S. Department of Health, Education, and Welfare, 1978), pp. 11–12, 14.

Whatever Became of the Ringling Brothers' Moral, Elevating, Instructive, and Fascinating Concert and Variety Performance?

The Ringling Brothers' Circus had its beginning when five brothers pooled their talents to form a traveling troupe. Today it brings fun and laughter to millions of people.

In the winter of 1882, five brothers from Baraboo, Wisconsin, counted out $5 between them and planned their first performance as a traveling circus troupe. They designed an advertising poster and had it printed for $3.70 at a local print shop. It read: "Ringling Brothers' Moral, Elevating, Instructive, and Fascinating Concert and Variety Performance, One Night Only." Then the youngest brother headed out to post bills in a nearby town, and his four brothers followed the next morning. They rehearsed at 11:00 A.M. and delivered a single performance that afternoon. Al juggled plates and rolled bowling balls up and down the length of his arm and around his neck. Charlie played the trombone and violin, Alf T. played the cornet and organ, Otto acted out a comedy, and John did a dance in wooden shoes. By nightfall, they had more than doubled their money, leaving town with $13. Sensing great profits were theirs to be had, these five sons of German immigrant harness maker August Reungling set out in earnest to develop the greatest circus the world had ever seen.[1]

Within a decade the Ringling Brothers' Circus consisted of 18 railroad cars filled with animals, equipment, and performers. They performed from Connecticut to Texas and had become such a serious threat to their number one competitor, P. T. Barnum, that the two giants signed a pact dividing their territories. By 1929, the Ringlings had acquired virtually all of their competition, including the Barnum and

Source: This case was prepared by M. R. Poirier from published sources. See notes.

Bailey show, and still dominate the circus industry today.

The circus basically hasn't changed much in the past century. There are still high-wire acts, trapeze acts, acrobats and clowns, and exotic animals, and the music is still played by a live band. The basic jobs of the circus managers haven't changed much either. They still must provide entertainment by gathering together the most amazing acts, purchasing and utilizing vast amounts of equipment, and transporting the performance from city to city.

This is no small task. "Greater wonder by far than all the curiosities and the performance of the circus," wrote one author at the turn of the century, "is the really marvelous system which governs every element of its organization and makes possible its smooth and certain operation upon such a stupendous scale."[2] Said another a quarter century later, "The real marvel of the great American circus is . . . the fact that it is there today and gone tomorrow. A million-dollar manufactory is set up, operated, torn down, and moved scores of miles, in each twenty-four hours."[3] And, said a circus performer a decade later in 1936, "Whatever practice you find on the circus lot is being conducted in exactly the same way today as it always has been, even if its origins go back to the old circuses of Rome."[4]

But in the history of one circus, we can find evidence of vast changes, not in its basics, but in the opportunities available to it, the constraints placed upon it, and the methods and techniques its managers have developed over time to improve on the glittering, age-old tradition. The animal acts, for example, can now be more exotic than ever due to advances in climate control and veterinary care. The Ringling Brothers tried three times in the first quarter of this century to exhibit a gorilla. Each time, the beast died within a short period of time, being unable to adjust to a new diet and climate. In 1919, an observer wrote: "This [last] attempt to exhibit this rare beast in America proved a costly venture, and it was the only effort made in the last fifteen years. There will be no other. Animal men are now satisfied that it cannot be done, for this circus had three men caring for the gorilla, one of them an authority on the care of sick animals."[5] But in 1938, Ringling Brothers requisitioned a special air-conditioned cage not previously available and brought a 700-pound gorilla over from Africa. Gargantua was a main attraction for many years after.

THE CIRCUS CHANGES

On the other hand, some attractions that are a part of circus history are no longer found in circuses today. Death-defying thrillers were largely taken out of program by the 1920s. As John Ringling put it in 1919, there was a time when "the nearer a man or woman came to breaking his or her neck, the higher the salary. Now . . . the dangerous and seemingly dangerous acts have been cut out. This is because we discovered that at the climax of such acts, four out of five of the women and children turned away their faces and refused to look."[6] The performers also were opposed to acts that were nothing more than terrifying "because [their] appeal was wholly in [their] danger, and the question of skill did not enter at all."[7]

The freak show, or side show, is also a thing of the past. Early in the century, circuses had earned huge profits on the premise that people were more interested in seeing strange and exotic humans than strange and exotic animals. In 1910, it was reported that Millie Christine, the "two-headed nightingale," was being paid $1000 for appearing in a circus side show. Other popular attractions included the "Wild Man of Borneo" and midgets, dwarfs, and giants.[8] With shifts in the moral and ethical climate of society, however, these circus features are no longer accepted. Civil and human rights groups would bring the full weight of the law down on any show that exhibited human beings as freaks.

The basic operating routine of the circus has not changed much in the last hundred years. Until the 1870s, all circuses in the United States were wagon shows. Each would move all of its performers and equipment in wagons and carts drawn by horses and elephants from one town to the next every day for the six warm months of a year. The wagon train would usually arrive in a town at dawn; the tents and equipment would be removed from the wagons and set up, and the performers would prepare for the parade. At 9:00 A.M. or so, the parade would wind through town, piquing the local interest and drawing a crowd back to the grounds. The workers would sleep during the afternoon performance, then begin tearing down all unnecessary portions of the camp when the evening performance was under way. After the last bow, the performers would head back to their wagons to sleep, the workers would load all the gear, and the wagon train would be off to the next town.

Starting in the 1880s, when the Ringling brothers began their operation, most circuses took to the ever-expanding rail lines to move from town to town. This reduced the burden on the circus animals and shortened the traveling times but involved the extra work of moving the equipment between the rail station and the fairgrounds in each town. It also added to the manager's work, because he now had to familiarize himself with the fees of hundreds of short-hop rail lines, the construction and size of the rail cars used, and the location of each railyard in relation to the local fairgrounds.

FROM TRAINS TO TRUCKS

With the outbreak of the First World War, the circuses were forced off the rail lines, needed for military purposes, and found themselves back on the roads again. At the same time, however, automobiles were rapidly taking the place of horse-drawn transportation, and the circus was being moved via huge, custom-made trucks. There were arguments, initially, that the circus would never be "motorized." The tractors and trucks were slower and less reliable than wagons on the rough roads between small towns, and as one observer put it, "What would the [circus] parade be without its six, eight and twelve horse teams of dapple-greys, bays, blacks and whites? It wouldn't be the circus, would it?"[9]

The circus has not only motorized, but taken to the air as well. With improvements in both automotive technology and road surfaces, huge trucks now haul thousands of tons of equipment quite easily. These improvements have also made it possible for people to travel greater distances to see the circus; thus the shows needn't make 20-mile hops as they used to. The biggest shows now visit only major metropolitan centers. The Ringling Bros. and Barnum & Bailey Circus, now split into two regional circuses, plays only major cities across the United States and foreign countries. But technological developments aside, it is still necessary for the whole organization to move into a town, set up, deliver a show, then pack up and leave for the next engagement—if not within 24 hours, within a number of days.

The basic goals of the circus have always been to thrill and entertain, the basic resources used have always been exotic animals and skilled performers. The basic functions of the circus managers also have remained similar, but the environment in which they are undertaken has changed.

PLANNING

Planning has always been crucial to the success of the circus. The circus director would identify the constraints and opportunities and plan around them. When the Ringling brothers were just starting out, weather, road conditions, seasonal changes, and distances between towns were the most significant constraints on a traveling circus. The circus played only between April and November; for the remaining months, the performers and animals would live in winter quarters in Sarasota, Florida. During performance season, the planning of the route could make or break the circus.

Originally, a circus would determine which territory it would travel in—east, west, north, or south—then book the show straight through for the season based on the distance between towns. Often, the circus would make it halfway through the summer, then come across communities in financial hardship, weather problems, or ruthless competition from another circus and would go bankrupt. Later, circuses began to book only a few weeks in advance, leaving just enough time to send a crew ahead to post advertising bills, obtain licenses, and repair or adjust the roads, bridges, or fairground sites. That way, they could route themselves into only the communities that could afford them, and around those that could not.

Today, circuses are again booked far in advance. The Ringling Bros. and Barnum & Bailey Circus plays only indoor arenas in the major cities; transportation is much more reliable; farm cycles (it was said in 1910: "The circus that doesn't have regard for the farmer's busy season is courting disaster")[10] are no longer of significant impact on the general or even local economies. Therefore, Ringling Bros. can schedule performances for each of its performing groups in all the major cities in the country a year in advance. Indeed, such advance billing is necessary to book space in the arenas that host the circus. To plan a route today, Kenneth Feld, the current president of Ringling Bros. and Barnum & Bailey Circus, must decide which cities each circus will perform in, when, for how long, and in what order. Then the advertising, licensing, transportation, and setup details can be undertaken with the overall plan as a guide.

ORGANIZING

Organizing too has long been a crucial function for circus managers. The Ringling brothers knew this at the outset and organized their circus to give the best possible performance even when they were the only ones working for it. As John Ringling said in 1919, "Team work and strict attention to every detail of the circus business has been the key to the success of the Ringling Brothers."[11] In the earliest days, four of them would play instruments while the fifth performed stunts. Later, as they added equipment and hired performers, they divided management responsibilities among themselves according to their talents.

John's skills seemed to be in routing. It was a joke among them, he said, that "I can put my hand out of a car window at night, feel the air, and say 'six and a half miles from Abilene,' while Al frequently was known to inquire what city we were in after the tents were up."[12] Al, for his part, was "the greatest producing showman the world has ever known. He knew instinctively what the public would like or dislike, and his big success was in his ability to choose good features."[13] Otto, a financial and business wizard, was in charge of managing the troupe's cash. Alfred T. was in charge of publicity and knew "practically every newspaper man in the United States."[14] And Charles was in charge of billboard advertising and handling the "opposition." (Around the turn of the century, circuses often engaged in ruthless competitive practices, ranging from stealing promotional notices to kidnapping a competitor's top-billed performer to poisoning its featured animals.)

After the last of the original five brothers died in 1936, the management of the circus changed hands and duties were shifted and balanced between family members and hired managers. In 1937, John's nephew, John Ringling North, gained control, and the circus management was divided among three members of the Ringling clan. Unfortunately, the heirs of the original Ringlings did not have their predecessors' team spirit and unity of purpose. As a result, the circus during the late 1930s and into the 1950s was "managed by whichever two of the factions [were] able to agree long enough to gang up on the third."[15] The third, not content to remain powerless, "employ[ed] most of the weapons of psychological and of open warfare. The spreading of rumors and the spraying of subversive propaganda [were] commonplace."[16]

This constant shifting in organizational structure and division of responsibility eventually brought the circus to the verge of bankruptcy, and in 1955, Irvin and Israel Feld and an associate bought 95 percent of the stock in Ringling Bros.—Barnum & Bailey Combined Shows. The Feld brothers completely reorganized the circus, cutting its employee roster to one-tenth its size, greatly reducing its menagerie, and billing it only in arenas and auditoriums to save the expense of maintaining, transporting, and operating the big top. Today, Irvin Feld's son Kenneth has reorganized and streamlined the circus yet again. In doing so, he has doubled its profits from those earned under his father.

DIRECTING

Directing has also long been a part of the circus manager's job. Staffing, motivating, directing, facilitating communication, and leading have all been functions of a circus manager's job since the first troupe hired its first employee. But of course, as with the other functions, the specifics of directing a circus have changed over the years in response to changes in the environment.

Changes in staffing, for example, encompass the whole system of recruiting, compensating, and taking care of the employees as well as employees' skill bases. Clowns are no longer the most skilled riders and acrobats in the show; they are the sideline entertainment between acts. Performers no longer pay for their own medical services (salaries previously having been based on the hazards of the act); rather the circus covers these expenses for them. And the acts themselves are no longer recruited from a pool of home-grown talent; there are schools for clowns, for instance, and most of the Ringling Bros. star attractions are highly trained performers recruited from circuses around the world.

These performers and the workers supporting the show are not motivated in the same ways as in the past. Financial incentives used to be the predominant form of motivation for workers and performers alike. Performers' salaries increased with the degree of risk they assumed, and side show attractions' salaries increased with the degree of strangeness or deformity. Workers' salaries were constant, but the crew members were often fined if they slowed down the finely tuned moving, setting-up, operating, tearing down process. "The performance moves with a machine-like regularity," it was written in 1902, "which is obtained only by rigidly enforced discipline with a certain punishment by fines or dismissal following an infraction of rules that cover every phase of action and demeanor."[17] Today, motivation comes more from instilling the goals and purpose of the circus in each employee than from compensating the performers for taking risks or penalizing workers for violating schedules or rules.

From the time when the five brothers comprised the whole show, team efforts have been the foundation of the circus. An author writing in 1947 said: "The most impressive thing about any part of the circus teardown is the imparted sense of urgent necessity for speed, and the sight of many men simultaneously doing many things without many orders."[18] As the last performance of the day began under the big top, a group would disassemble and load the ticket booths. As the floats pulled out of the main tent after the final act, each would be pounced on by a small crew that covered and secured it and sent it on its way to the train. Even before the last spectator left the big top, "a swarm of men" began working from one end to the other, removing stakes and pulling out the seating.[19] To see the Ringling Bros. circus today, though it is held indoors, you might think the very same teams were moving the rigging, setting up and tearing down the apparatus for each performance, and keeping the whole show moving with split-second timing.

The success of any circus's operations depends largely on how effectively its goals are communicated to its employees and how effectively the employees are led and directed to work together. Each employee must know exactly what he or she must do, exactly when and where, and exactly what the accomplishment of this task means for the circus as a whole. Thus, directing is still one of the most crucial functions the circus manager must undertake.

CONTROLLING

The notion of control, the fourth basic function of management, is somewhat new to the circus. It wasn't until the Feld brothers took over in 1955 that rigorous business sense was brought to the management of the Ringling Bros. circus. The circus was a financial disaster at that time, but the Feld brothers cut expenses so significantly that the circus's profits have been virtually guaranteed ever since.

But as many have said, the more things change, the more they stay the same. Despite everything, current manager Ken Feld still describes his job in almost the same terms others have used over the decades and centuries: "We blow into town, set up a logistical nightmare, put on a spectacle for a few days and move on. We're the only living dinosaur."[20] ■

QUESTIONS

1. How specifically have the managers of the Ringling Bros. and Barnum & Bailey Circus planned, organized, directed, and controlled the circus during the past century?
2. What have been the various goals of the circus, and how have its managers achieved them?
3. What important decisions have the managers of the circus made over the years, and what effects have they had on the circus?
4. What institutional, administrative, and technical responsibilities do the managers of the Ringling Bros. and Barnum & Bailey Circus have?

NOTES

1. There is some discrepancy between published reports of the Ringling brothers' first show. The description in this paragraph was compiled from the following sources: Crooker, Orin, "'Al' Ringling," *The American Magazine* (February 1914): 64, 65; Ringling, John, "We Divided the Job—But Stuck Together," *The American Magazine* (September 1919): 56–58; "How Ringling Made the Greatest Show Greater," *Literary Digest*, October 5, 1929, pp. 36–40.
2. Allen, Whiting, "The Organization of a Modern Circus," *Cosmopolitan* (August 1902): 374.
3. May, Earl Chapin, "The Tougher the Job the Tighter They Stick," *The American Magazine* (August 1925): 46.
4. Miller, H. E., "The Sanitation of a Large Circus," *American Journal of Public Health* (November 1936): 1106.
5. Braden, Frank, "The Science of Running a Menagerie," *Illustrated World* (October 1919): 213.
6. Ringling, op. cit., p. 182.
7. Davis, Hartley, "The Business Side of the Circus," *Everybody's Magazine* (July 1910): 121.
8. Marcosson, Isaac F., "Sawdust and Gold Dust," *Bookman* (June 1910): 407.
9. Braden, Frank, "Why the Circus Will Never Be Motorized," *Illustrated World* (April 1920): 251.
10. Davis, op. cit., p. 126.
11. Ringling, op. cit., p. 56.
12. Ringling, op. cit., p. 57.
13. Ibid.
14. Ringling, op. cit., p. 57.
15. "Ringling Wrangling," *Fortune* (July 1947): 114.
16. Ibid.
17. Allen, op. cit., p. 380.
18. "Circus: Tearing Down, Moving, and Resettling the Ringling Circus," *Fortune* (July 1947): 108.
19. Ibid.
20. Recio, Maria E., "Ladies and Gentlemen, Presenting—Kenneth Feld," *Business Week*, June 8, 1987, p. 78.

Planning is the first function of management. Before managers can organize, direct, or control, they must set a course of action for the organization. Planning is a complex process, although the steps involved seem simple. The basic planning process consists of assessing the environment and predicting the future, setting goals, developing alternative courses of action, selecting the best one, implementing it, and monitoring progress. You frequently go through a process like this yourself, informally, and think nothing of it.

In applying to college, you went through a planning process. You assessed your academic standing and your strengths and weaknesses and predicted which of the schools that interested you the most would accept you. You also may have identified a number of majors that would make it easier for you to find a good job when you graduated. Then you set your goals: to go to the best school that offered the programs of greatest interest. Your alternatives were the list of schools you applied to. Assuming you were accepted by more than one, you selected the one that met the most criteria of importance to you—for example, the one that had the best management program, was located in your favorite region, or had the best athletic opportunities—and you enrolled. Now that you are a student at this university, you must assess the progress of your plan. Are you doing well here? Is your program of study as you expected? If not, should you transfer to another school? If so, which one?

You are the planner of your life. But planning in an organizational setting is more complex. As with decision making, management planning must be done in consideration of the resources and values of the organization. Planning in the organizational context takes on added dimension.

In Part Two, we will discuss organizational planning, strategic planning, and strategic management in changing environments. We will outline the basics of planning in Chapter 4, describing the steps in the planning process and showing how managers with different responsibilities (technical, administrative, and institutional) all plan in different ways. In Chapter 5, we will discuss strategic planning, describing its longer-term focus, outlining the steps in the strategic planning process, and discussing various approaches to strategic planning. In Chapter 6 we will describe how changes in an organization's operating environment—that is, technological developments, competitive shifts, and changes in the economy—make it necessary for managers to continually adapt and revise the strategic plans of the organization.

PART TWO

Planning

4 | Organizational Planning

FOCUS CASE / Olympic Gold

WHAT IS PLANNING?
Importance of Planning

STEPS IN THE PLANNING PROCESS
Analyze Current Status and Forecast the Future Environment
Establish Goals and Objectives
Identify Alternatives
Select the Best Alternative
Implement the Plan
Criteria for a Good Plan

TYPES OF PLANNING
Scope of Activities Covered
Standing Plans and Single-Use Plans

MANAGEMENT BY OBJECTIVES
Goals and Objectives
The MBO Process
MBO Appraised

M anagement requires planning, the process through which managers determine goals and devise ways of accomplishing them. Through planning, managers transform their ideas into actions and, ultimately, into results. On all levels—technical, administrative, and institutional—effective planning is crucial to organizational success.

▪ KEY QUESTIONS

As you study this chapter, try to answer the following key questions:

1 What is planning?
2 Why is planning important?
3 What are the basic steps in the planning process?
4 What elements do all good plans have in common?
5 What different types of plans do organizations use?
6 Explain management by objectives as it relates to planning. What are its advantages and disadvantages?

Focus Case

Olympic Gold

On cue, 92,000 members of the audience transformed the 1984 Olympic Stadium into a multicolored patchwork of the flags of the 140 participating nations. The plan worked to perfection.

At 4:00 P.M. on July 27, 1984, church bells all over Los Angeles, California, began chiming in unison. Then a voice booming over the loudspeaker at the Los Angeles Coliseum announced the start of the games of the twenty-third olympiad. Skywriting airplanes wrote the word *welcome* across the southern California skies, as a man wearing a jetpack swooped into the coliseum and flew around its circumference several times before landing. Then a 1200-member drill team performed, followed by an 800-member marching band, and then 92,000 members of the audience, on cue, transformed the stadium into a multicolored patchwork of the flags of the 140 nations participating in the games by raising colored plastic cards located at each seat. Finally, 84 pianists seated at 84 white baby grand pianos rolled into the coliseum playing George Gershwin's "Rhapsody in Blue," and thousands of Olympic athletes paraded into the arena. At this point, Lord Killanin, honorary life president of the International Olympic Committee—a man who had seen every Olympics since 1948—turned to Peter Ueberroth and said: "This is simply the best I have ever seen."

Not only did the opening ceremonies of the 1984 Olympic Games go off virtually without a hitch, the games themselves were a record-breaking success. Despite a boycott by 14 nations including the Soviet Union, 140 nations participated, 18 more than the previous attendance record set in 1972. And although the games had no funding from the federal or local government, the games ended with a surplus of $215 million, which was distributed to youth and sports interests in the United States. The success of the 1984 Olympic Games was no accident. It was due to the effective planning and leadership of Los Angeles Olympic Organizing Committee (LAOOC) president Peter Ueberroth who, with the help of 72,000 staff members and volunteers, "channeled the strength of private enterprise to . . . organize the Olympic Games . . . as it had never been done before."

Because Ueberroth had started an international business from scratch—First Travel Corporation, the second largest travel enterprise in North America in 1978—he seemed a good choice for president of the LAOOC. He accepted the position in March 1979 on a handshake with organizing committee member Paul Ziffren; Ueberroth would run the games with full authority for all personnel and expenditures as chief executive officer, and Ziffren, as chairman

Sources: This case prepared by M. R. Poirier and James E. Post, based on the following sources: Ueberroth, Peter, *Made in America* (New York: Fawcett Crest, 1985); "Critics Are Carping at Commercialization of Summer Olympics," *Wall Street Journal,* April 17, 1984, pp. 1, 20; "Success of Games in Los Angeles Likely to Change Future Olympics," *New York Times,* August 12, 1984, pp. 1, 10.

of the board, would serve as a buffer between political and special-interest groups and Ueberroth's day-to-day operations.

The first day on the job was a hint of things to come. Standing in the hallway outside of his new office, Ueberroth went over a checklist of operational details with an associate. The phones, desks, and chairs had arrived, the lease was signed, and the necessary files were en route. But the key wouldn't open the door. Negative sentiment toward the games (Montreal taxpayers were still paying for their games of 1976, and the murders of 11 Israeli athletes in Munich, Germany, in 1972 were still fresh in people's minds) had provoked the building owner to cancel the lease; the LAOOC had to find new office space as its first order of duty.

But Ueberroth had a list of goals clearly outlined in this mind, and for every setback—of which there were hundreds over the five-year period—he or one of his associates came up with a way to work around it. To obtain the nearly $400 million needed to stage the games, Ueberroth would rely entirely on the sale of television rights, tickets, and commercial sponsorships. Ueberroth's financial plan stated clearly that the games would operate at a surplus—a *real* surplus. He announced in May 1979 that the committee would spend about $350 million and net $20 million. Ueberroth had a detailed contingency plan that covered every possible problem and cost. That plan was more than simply achieved.

As money from sponsors began to roll in, Ueberroth faced the challenge of transforming an area 200 miles long by 50 miles wide into a giant Olympic playground. The task required the committee to manage 27 stadiums and facilities in 3 states, 9 counties, and 29 cities and would be "tougher than staging ten Super Bowls a day for sixteen straight days." To locate and secure sites for all events, Ueberroth and his associates, in fact, had to search the entire southern California area. Though they had identified ideal sites for each event, community resistance made it necessary for them to try three, four, or five successive avenues before finding—or constructing from scratch—the site ultimately used for each event.

When all sites had been settled upon, security became and remained Ueberroth's greatest concern. He assured a visiting White House representative in early 1983 that security was the LAOOC's "largest budget item. We'll do whatever it takes, regardless of cost." It turned out to be one of his biggest headaches. Facilities across hundreds of square miles were subject to bomb threats (an average of two per day, though no bombs were ever found), and Ueberroth and his family also were threatened and his two pet dogs were poisoned.

Ueberroth had to know which problems needed to be solved early in the five-year process and which could be postponed. Key decisions, such as how to raise money, had to be identified and made effectively before other decisions could follow. But even with the most effective planning, events occurred that required immediate, last-minute shuffling. Less than three months before the games were to begin, the Soviet Union announced that they would boycott the Olympic Games because of "security problems." Thirteen other Soviet-bloc nations also withdrew. But Ueberroth mobilized a task force responsible for getting attendance commitments from at least 123 nations, one more than the previous record; 140 ultimately participated. Ueberroth faced each crisis, met the challenge, and kept the overall plan for the games on course. ■

WHAT IS PLANNING?

Plan An agreed-upon set of means to achieve a goal within a specified time frame.

Planning The process through which managers determine goals and devise means to accomplish them.

A **plan** is an agreed-upon set of means for utilizing resources to achieve a goal within a specified time frame. **Planning** is the process through which managers determine goals and devise the means for utilizing resources to accomplish them. In the planning process, managers analyze the current status of the organization, predict the future environment, establish goals, and design and implement a course of action to achieve the goals within a specified time frame. In other words, planning involves identifying the organization's strengths and weaknesses and the opportunities and constraints in the environment, then deciding what to do and where, when, and how to do it.

Importance of Planning

Planning is a crucial function and precedes all the other management functions. Through planning, managers can anticipate how best to utilize the organization's resources. Successful organizations of all kinds, including businesses, churches, universities, sports teams, and government agencies, use plans.

For example, many in the LAOOC thought a coast-to-coast torch relay would be a "security nightmare," but Peter Ueberroth "believed [that] with good planning, we could eliminate the negatives and create a relay Americans would remember for the rest of their lives."[1] His original plan was to have runners start in New York in early May, travel 12,000 miles, and pass through all 50 states before arriving in Los Angeles at the end of July. But he later admitted that he'd "put the cart before the horse by announcing the torch relay before figuring out how to do it."[2] After consulting experts, he revised the plan. The relay ultimately traveled only 9000 miles and went through 30 states and the District of Columbia, but it was a major success. It reversed much of the negative sentiment directed at the games up to that point, and because each runner was required to be backed by a $3000 contribution to youth sports, the relay raised over $10 million.

Planning is not a perfect science, and there are probably no managers or organizations whose plans do not occasionally miss the mark. But the planning process is valuable to managers and organizations for many reasons.

Provide Direction The establishment of a plan can invigorate an organization and its employees by encouraging people to focus their activities on helping the organization achieve its goals. By setting a clear direction and continually emphasizing the importance of the event, Peter Ueberroth mobilized the efforts of thousands of volunteers and even gained the support of the Los Angeles community for the 1984 summer Olympics.

Make Difficult Decisions Managerial decision making can sometimes be difficult. When Lee Iacocca took over as chief executive of Chrysler Corporation in September 1979, Chrysler was on the brink of bankruptcy. Iacocca would have been unwise to make rapid, erratic decisions about who to save and who to fire, which cars to produce and which to cancel, and which production methods to keep and which to change. Therefore, he assessed the situation, set priorities, and developed a "survival plan"—a coherent idea of what problems needed to be attacked in what order—aimed largely at cutting costs drastically.[3] To reduce labor costs, for instance, Iacocca negotiated with the auto workers' union for wage concessions, which the workers fought vigorously. Ultimately, however,

Chrysler's survival plan took precedence over the difficulty of the decisions, and management and the labor unions reached an agreement.[4]

Stay on Track As organizations grow in size and complexity, they tend naturally to have difficulty meeting goals and staying on track. Planning helps managers follow developments and detect trouble spots. By identifying problem areas early, managers can quickly find the causes and either remedy the problem or adjust the plan to get the organization back on track.[5] To make the Los Angeles Olympics a success, Peter Ueberroth had to continually adjust his plans to compensate for problems in one area or take advantage of opportunities in another.

Avoid Surprises Planning enables managers and organizations to protect themselves against surprises caused by changes in the economic, technological, and political environment. For example, ever since the murder of athletes at the 1972 Olympics in Munich, Olympic officials have had to recognize that political instability is a potential threat to any international event. Not only was security the LAOOC's largest budget item, but Peter Ueberroth had a more difficult political problem with which to contend: the Soviet boycott of the games. Conflicts between the U.S. and Soviet governments prevented hundreds of athletes from participating in both Moscow's 1980 games and Los Angeles's 1984 games.

STEPS IN THE PLANNING PROCESS

Managers who plan usually go through a rational thought process involving careful research, analysis, and determination of a course of action. The basic steps managers follow in developing a plan are as follows (see Exhibit 4.1):

1. Analyze current status and forecast the future environment. What are the organization's strengths and weaknesses? What opportunities and threats will be present in the environment?
2. Establish goals and objectives. Given the predicted future, what do we want to do?
3. Identify alternative ways of achieving objectives in light of problems and opportunities likely to be encountered in the future.
4. Select the best alternative for achieving the objectives.
5. Implement the plan.

These basic steps can be applied to all planning activities. The planning process helps managers clarify where they are in relation to their long-term goals and helps them chart a course by which to achieve the organization's goals. After

EXHIBIT / 4.1
The Planning Process

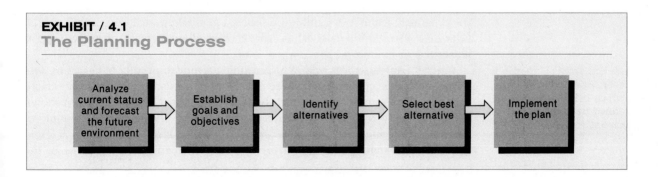

Analyze current status and forecast the future environment → Establish goals and objectives → Identify alternatives → Select best alternative → Implement the plan

plans are implemented, activities and results must be monitored and adjustments made. Monitoring and adjusting are aspects of the control function, which we will discuss in Chapter 15.

Analyze Current Status and Forecast the Future Environment

The first steps in the planning process are to analyze the organization's current status and forecast the future environment.[6] Analyzing current status requires determining the organization's strengths and weaknesses. For example, a broad-based cost-efficient distribution network or a powerful marketing operation would be strengths the organization could incorporate into a plan. On the other hand, an outdated production system or a shortage of skilled employees would be weaknesses the organization would have to remedy or work around in developing and carrying out a plan.

Forecasting   Predicting future circumstances.

Once the managers have determined the organization's current status, they must attempt to forecast the future environment. **Forecasting** is the act of predicting future organizational and environmental circumstances that will influence the effectiveness of plans and decisions. Three common types of forecasts are sales forecasts (predictions of the company's sales in a future time frame such as a month or a quarter), technological forecasts (predictions of advances in technology that will affect the company's operations), and human resource forecasts (estimates of the organization's labor needs in a future time frame such as one year or five years). Through forecasting, managers identify opportunities and threats that may affect plans in the future. Forecasting is crucial to planning but can be difficult and often involves guesswork. Researchers have therefore designed several sophisticated methods for reducing the uncertainty in decision-making and increasing the accuracy of forecasts and predictions. These methods are of two principal types: quantitative and qualitative.

Quantitative forecasting methods   Forecasting methods based on historic data used to project a trend or specify relationships among key variables.

Quantitative Methods   **Quantitative forecasting methods** are based on historic data and are used to project a trend or specify relationships among key variables, such as sales levels and inflation rates. Advances in computer technology have increased the accuracy and decreased the costs of these types of forecasts, even those incorporating many variables. There are several commonly used quantitative forecasting methods.

Time series analysis   A quantitative forecasting technique in which historical trends are used to project future events.

In **time series analysis,** one of the most popular forecasting methods, historical trends are used to project future events. Sales histories and inventory levels, for example, can be used to forecast future production requirements, especially for seasonal products (e.g., Christmas decorations). When data follow a general, steady pattern of movement up or down over time, they are said to exhibit a trend pattern. Panel A in Exhibit 4.2 shows a general upward sales trend pattern. Data may also exhibit cyclical, seasonal, or random patterns of movement, as illustrated in Exhibit 4.2.

Causal analysis methods   Forecasting techniques in which behavior is predicted by analyzing its causes.

Causal analysis methods of forecasting attempt to predict behavior by analyzing its causes and are used where excellent data exist for a number of related variables. For example, assume that the level of personal income has been shown to be positively related to the purchase of jewelry. The higher the income of persons in a community, the more jewelry they buy. If this relationship is found to exist consistently, it is logical for a jewelry firm to use the income of the

EXHIBIT / 4.2
Time Series Forecasting Patterns

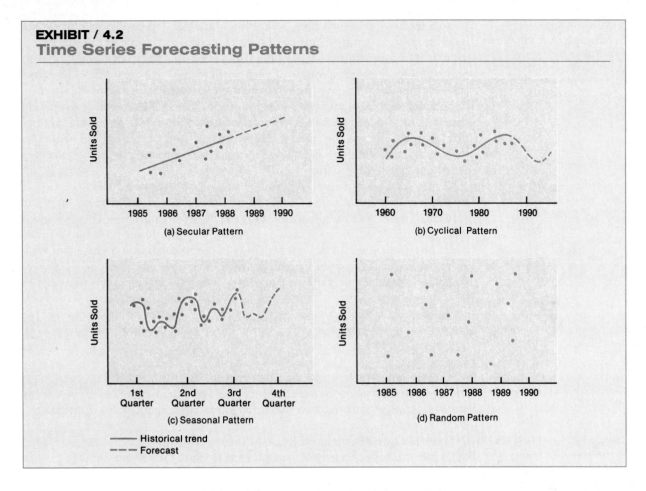

(a) Secular Pattern

(b) Cyclical Pattern

(c) Seasonal Pattern

(d) Random Pattern

——— Historical trend
- - - Forecast

community to predict sales. When income goes up, the firm should produce more jewelry; when it goes down, the firm should produce less.

Program Evaluation and Review Technique (PERT) is a quantitative method of planning, scheduling, and controlling with which the LAOOC experimented. PERT was created to track planning for the navy's Polaris submarine and is now often used to help managers identify and schedule the many interrelated activities of complex projects. For the LAOOC, PERT identified over 10,000 tasks and specified when each would be completed for the games to take place. Said Peter Ueberroth, "We continued experimenting with it for a year and a half before our planners became convinced its design was not compatible to solving illogical problems such as planning for an Olympic Games. According to PERT, we'd complete the tasks and be ready for the Games by 1988."[7] Ueberroth did, however, take advantage of the valuable data the tool provided—especially data concerning overlaps between security tasks and sports management and between the personnel function and individual departments. PERT is discussed further in Chapter 16.

Qualitative Methods **Qualitative forecasting methods** are based on the opinions and judgments of experts. They are particularly useful when precise data are scarce or difficult to use. There are several popular qualitative methods.

Qualitative forecasting methods Forecasting methods based on the opinions and judgments of experts.

Executive opinion jury
A forecasting technique in which a prediction is made from a composite of the opinions of a small group of executives.

An **executive opinion jury** is a small group of top executives who offer their opinions about what the future will hold in a given area, such as sales or rate of growth. The forecast the opinion jury produces tends to be an average or composite of the differing opinions of each participating manager. Sales force forecasts are composites or averages derived from the sales force's responses to questions concerning upcoming consumer buying patterns. The sales force usually has expert or intuitive information about fluctuations in trends or buying patterns that historical data will not reflect. Therefore, sales force forecasts can be used to determine marketing or sales budgets, inventory requirements, and production schedules and requirements.

Delphi technique   A forecasting technique in which a panel of experts develops a composite prediction.

The **Delphi technique** is probably the most sophisticated qualitative method for making forecasts. A panel of experts on a particular problem or business area is selected, usually from both inside and outside the organization. They are asked, in confidence, to make a forecast or answer a questionnaire about a future event or set of events. (The confidentiality prevents them from being influenced, intimidated, or confronted by one another.) For example, they may be asked when they think people will land on Mars or when video telephones will be common household items. The answers are then compiled and the composite results are sent back to each person. Further estimates of the future are requested using the composite view of the group as a starting point. This process is repeated until the members' estimates converge to produce an acceptable forecast.

Brainstorming   A group technique used to identify alternatives.

Another group technique is **brainstorming.** Groups focus on a given problem and generate as many solution alternatives as they can. Judgments of the relative merits or flaws of the proposed alternatives are withheld until a list of alternatives is developed.

Scenario building   A qualitative forecasting technique in which managers hypothesize future conditions.

Scenario building is a technique through which managers hypothesize about the future. To build scenarios, managers ask if/then types of questions (e.g., If oil prices double, then . . . ?). Each scenario is a description of a new environment. Scenario building helps managers consider possible future conditions and organizational responses to them. The probability of each scenario can be evaluated, and the most feasible-sounding scenario may be used as the forecast.

All qualitative methods suffer from the problems of limited input and a reliance on the opinions, judgments, and informed ideas of a small group of people. The forecasts produced through these methods may not be reliable, and it is often wise to supplement them with quantitative forecasts.

Establish Goals and Objectives

After the organization's strengths and weaknesses have been determined and upcoming threats and opportunities predicted, managers can establish goals and objectives. These two steps in the planning process—analysis and goal establishment—actually occur more simultaneously than in succession. That is, managers have some idea of what they would like to accomplish before they conduct an analysis. After conducting the analysis, they can more clearly outline goals and ensure that the goals and objectives are realistic given internal and external circumstances.

Goals   An organization's primary intended accomplishments.

Management literature draws a distinction between *goals* and *objectives,* two terms often used interchangeably. Throughout this chapter, **goals** will refer to the organization's primary intended accomplishments. Examples of goals are increasing profitability, sales, and assets or becoming an industry leader. Organizations often have multiple goals, some internally oriented (increasing profits per unit sold), others externally oriented (attracting more high-income people to purchase a product). Organizations also have both economic goals (increasing market share) and social goals (being a good citizen of the community).

Objectives The specific aims that managers accomplish to achieve organizational goals.

Objectives are the more precise aims of the organization; they are the specific aims that managers accomplish so that overall organizational goals are ultimately achieved.[8] A company might have a goal of growth in sales, for example, that could be translated into specific sales objectives for all the sales units.

Through advertisements, many of us are familiar with the goals of various organizations. One may want to be the market leader in quality (recall Ford's advertising that "Quality is Job 1"); another may want to carve out a niche for itself (like Yugo in the small-car segment of the automobile market). In achieving these goals, the managers of these companies will focus on accomplishing specific objectives: Ford's production department would have to meet increased quality standards, and Yugo's marketing department would have to design a campaign highlighting the small car's unique advantages for a sector of the market.

Goals and objectives, therefore, are highly interrelated. The broad purposes set by management must be translated into specific targets if employees are to know the precise results expected of them. Although Peter Ueberroth established goals throughout his term with the LAOOC—obtain $400 million in funding, guarantee the safety of all athletes and visitors, finish with a surplus instead of a deficit— a visit to the Moscow Olympics of 1980 clarified his overall goal and enabled him to establish more precise objectives. "Visiting Moscow . . . opened my eyes to the enormity and complexity of staging an Olympic Games," he said in 1985.

> What previously had been a kaleidoscope of images . . . crystallized into a reality from which we were able to set objectives and priorities. . . . [It] made me realize how vastly we had underestimated our staffing needs. . . . [We would have to] locate and lease suitable facilities and arrange for all necessary construction to be completed at least a year before the start of the Games. We needed solutions to traffic congestion. We had to find housing for the Olympic family and journalists. . . . Most important, to secure the Games we would need the cooperation and goodwill of the city, county, and state governments, and a federal overlay of 30 different agencies.[9]

Translation of goals into objectives was a complex and demanding task for the LAOOC.

In addition to being realistic in terms of environmental conditions, goals and objectives must be prioritized if the organization is to allocate its resources effectively. For example, a sales department's plan to boost sales may increase advertising and travel costs, while the organization's plan to raise profits may require decreases in these costs. To avoid conflicts and waste, the plans of various departments and levels must be made compatible. Assuming that increased overall profits will take precedence over increased sales, the sales department may have to revise its plan.

Identify Alternatives

Having selected goals and objectives based on a thorough analysis of the organization and the future environment, managers can develop alternative plans or courses of action. The identification of alternatives should be just that—

identification, not evaluation. For every situation, a number of options should be offered.

For example, General Motors (GM) had a goal in the early 1980s of meeting the small-car challenge from foreign producers. The alternative methods of achieving this goal ranged from signing joint agreements with Japanese or Korean firms and having them produce small cars to be sold under a GM name to retooling GM production plants in the United States to produce the cars. Each alternative would involve different costs and require different methods of allocating resources. Though either plan could achieve the overall goal, each would be very different in terms of its specifics.

Select the Best Alternative

The planning process is not complete until managers select an alternative. Normally, managers will select the alternative that, in their judgment, will best enable the organization to accomplish its goals. In choosing to implement one plan instead of another, the manager is engaging in choice making, as outlined in Chapter 3. Selecting the best plan, like selecting the best decision possibility, should be a relatively easy task if the situation has been thoroughly analyzed, the goals have been clearly defined, and feasible alternatives have been fully developed. The plan that promises to achieve the goals most effectively and at the least cost is, of course, the most rational choice. If more than one plan meets these criteria, the manager will have to weigh other relevant factors, such as long-term market position versus short-term profit considerations.

To continue our previous example, GM decided, after much debate, to enter the small-car market aggressively. The market was to be pursued on technological and production grounds, and the plan called for complete redesign of the production system. The project was code-named Saturn. (More details are provided in the opening case for Chapter 8.) The idea was to dramatically decrease the number of parts and the amount of labor needed to build a car and to gain a competitive edge by using robots. This alternative requires tremendous engineering and managerial talent; other options, such as retooling an existing production line to make smaller cars, would have been less costly to implement. With success, however, GM could become one of the lowest-cost auto producers in the world and force the competition to upgrade their production facilities at huge costs.[10]

Implement the Plan

Implementation The process of transforming plans into actions.

Once a plan has been chosen, it must be turned into reality. The process of transforming an idea or plan into actions that will achieve it is called **implementation.** This process requires managerial coordination and teamwork, and all participants must understand what goals are being sought and what specific objectives, if undertaken, will accomplish those goals. In practice, managers often have to "sell" the plan to the people who will personally be responsible for turning it into reality.

The LAOOC's security plans were among the most difficult to implement, and their complete success was crucial. As Ueberroth put it, "Law enforcement needed to be pulled together. There was a lack of unity that had begun to sow seeds of fear within the community and raise questions from overseas about our ability to stage and protect the games."[11] Therefore, he "sold" the Federal Bureau of Investigation (FBI) and the Los Angeles Police Department (LAPD) on the importance of their efforts by explaining that the LAOOC and its security forces were "undertaking the most visible law enforcement effort in peacetime in our country's history. We will only achieve success in this endeavor if we are able to coordinate our planning, communicate continuously, and, most important, put jurisdictional differences aside."[12]

Ueberroth placed Ed Best, the FBI's special agent in charge of Los Angeles, in charge of security. Referring to information on the security arrangements of other international sporting events, Best divided the Los Angeles area into three sectors and placed a top-level enforcement officer in charge of each. Then he devised a comprehensive system to guarantee the safe lodging and transportation of all athletes and officials during the games. This system included searching all transport vehicles before and after they delivered anyone anywhere. Best coordinated all security activities of each department and made special arrangements with the Israeli and Turkish guards who were brought along as extra protection for their own athletes.

Effective implementation of a plan is a continuing process that requires managers to keep a careful eye on progress and results. This is where the planning and control functions are most closely linked in an organization. Control involves constant monitoring of plans as they unfold so that adjustments and corrections can be made in a timely and relevant manner.

Criteria for a Good Plan

A plan should reflect certain characteristics that have been identified with successful plans. The plan should be relevant to the organization's needs and to environmental conditions. It should be realistic and achievable given the organization's financial, technical, marketing, managerial, and human resources.

In addition, a good plan should clearly identify expected results. To determine whether these results are in fact being achieved, the components or phases of the plan must produce results that are measurable, in either quantitative or qualitative terms, or both. The plan should have a clear time framework for completion, and managers should know exactly when each component of a plan should be completed. It is also important that an individual manager or group of managers be accountable and responsible for results.

All successful managers learn to adapt to new circumstances, so, finally, a good plan should be flexible. The plan should include some contingency actions in the event the environment changes significantly. One can determine when to switch to a contingency plan by monitoring the implementation of the original plan to see if it is working as expected. If not, new circumstances can be spotted quickly and appropriate corrective action can be taken.

When the planning process is effective, when "good" plans have been designed and implemented, the control function of management is facilitated. If a plan addresses organizational needs and is realistic given organizational resources, it is more likely to achieve desired and expected results. If the plan produces measurable results, managers can readily determine whether it is achieving the desired ends. And if the responsibility for the plan has been clearly defined, managers know whom to hold accountable for results that are not as intended. Finally, if

Calcium-Rich, Sodium-Free, Cherry-Flavored

All organizations must respond to changes in their environment. When Tums came out with a new commercial featuring the benefits of calcium in their antacid tablets, Rolaids' counterattack was several months in the planning. The effort paid off when the focus on their cherry flavor began to pay off.

The antacid story documents what it takes to survive in an innovate-or-perish world. Until about 1985, Rolaids, a Warner-Lambert product, had always shared two-thirds of the $300-million antacid tablet market with its only major competitor, Tums. Then Tums came out with a new commercial featuring a hitherto unexploited benefit, calcium, the standard neutralizer in antacid tablets. The timing was perfect. Physicians and the recently established National Osteoporosis Foundation had begun suggesting calcium supplements to meet the recommended amount in the daily diet. Tums' sales jumped more than 40 percent, challenging Warner-Lambert's decades-old position as number one.

Rolaids' counterattack was several months in the planning. It called for close collaboration between Warner-Lambert, focusing on why people buy antacids, and Young and Rubicam (Y&R), their advertising agency, focusing on what antacid buyers are like as people. First came the search for an unexploited exploitable. What about packing more pleasure into the tablet? Tums had already moved a step beyond the standard mint choices, offering fruit flavors as well.

In February, a preliminary survey conducted on more than 400 interviewees, male and female, in cities across the United States, revealed that Rolaids users had a very positive reaction to a cherry-flavored product. In April, a second, similar survey comparing Tums and Rolaids for cherry flavor gave clear-cut results. For all users, Rolaids' cherry flavor had "a dramatically stronger overall appeal" than Tums' cherry flavor.

Yet another survey suggested a good target group would be what might be called middle-American females who move in limited social circles, are home- and family-oriented, and watch a lot of television. Confirmation came from one-hour depth interviews with a dozen antacid-using women 35 and over (the age group especially concerned with indigestion and osteoporosis), observed through one-way mirrors and videotaped—a focus-group session.

The final push, turning strategy into message, involved Y&R's creative team. Think of what had to be jam-packed into one fleeting commercial: antacid, calcium-rich, sodium-free, cherry-flavored, good-tasting. It took some doing to translate each of these points, with emphasis, into attention-grabbing words and images—and all within that murderous time constraint.

It took 30 hours of brainstorming and 50 hours of revisions, both within the agency and by the client, to arrive at the final product. The agency came up with a half-dozen storyboards—scripts with rough sketches indicating action. Warner-Lambert selected two: "Face," which ended with a munched maraschino, and "Stack," which ended with the placing of a cherry on top of a stack of tablets. Before production started, there had to be one more survey to make sure the storyboards communicated what Warner-Lambert had set out to do. The two storyboards were shown to 20 women ages 45 to 54, all moderate to heavy antacid users. Both made the grade.

If the commercials work, all the research is justified. Jobs and lives are not on the line, but failures are much better remembered than successes. While it is too early to assess the full impact of

"Face" and "Stack," the cherry-flavored strategy seems to be paying off. But Rolaids and Tums both have top-secret plans ready to unfold at a moment's notice, and no one can predict tomorrow's market scores. ∎

Source: Adapted from Pfeiffer, John, "Six Months and Half a Million Dollars, All for 15 Seconds," *Smithsonian* 9(7) (October 1987): 134–145.

unexpected results do occur, a plan that is flexible can most easily be adjusted so that success becomes achievable. The Inside View 4.1 provides a good example how one organization uses the planning process to respond to sudden changes in the environment.

TYPES OF PLANNING

In modern organizations, planning creates a framework, or context, within which most managerial decisions take place. By preparing a plan, managers know where the organization is headed and basically how it is going to get there. All individual managerial decisions and actions can be related to one or more aspects of the basic plan. Plans for a department, for example, should be coordinated and integrated with the organization's overall business plan. This section introduces some of the key types of planning found in organizations, discussing them on the basis of the scope of activities covered and the uses to which the plan is placed.

Scope of Activities Covered

Some plans guide the entire organization, others only a small part of it. A means-ends chain is one way to illustrate the links between the various plans in an organization. Goals established by top management become the ends toward which the objectives of middle managers are directed. The objectives of the middle and first-line manager, achieved in concert, become the means of accomplishing the goals of the top managers (see Exhibit 4.3).

Plans vary in their focus as well: They may have a strategic, tactical, or operational emphasis.

Strategic planning The determination of the organization's basic mission and the means for achieving this mission.

Strategic Planning **Strategic planning** is the process through which managers determine the organization's basic mission and the set of means for achieving this mission. Strategic planning is normally done by top-level managers. The president, chief executive officer, or other senior executives are responsible for charting the organization's future course, so the task of answering the two key questions—what to do and how to do it—is theirs.[13] Peter Ueberroth determined a three-pronged strategy for the 1984 Olympics: to host 123 nations (140 participated) in events across the Los Angeles area; to realize a surplus of $20 million ($215 million resulted); and to benefit local, national, and international sporting interests.

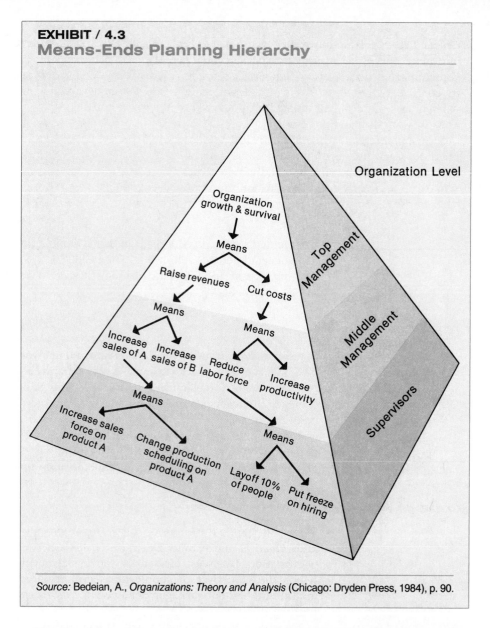

EXHIBIT / 4.3
Means-Ends Planning Hierarchy

Organization Level

Organization growth & survival

Means

Raise revenues   Cut costs

Means

Means

Increase sales of A   Increase sales of B   Reduce labor force   Increase productivity

Means

Increase sales force on product A   Change production scheduling on product A   Means

Layoff 10% of people   Put freeze on hiring

Top Management

Middle Management

Supervisors

Source: Bedeian, A., *Organizations: Theory and Analysis* (Chicago: Dryden Press, 1984), p. 90.

The time horizon for strategic plans tends to be long term, often three to five years. Thus strategic planning, by its very nature, requires managers to think about where they want the organization to be at some point in the future. The strategic plan of an organization is the basic context in which all other plans, at all other levels of the organization, must be designed and implemented. To carry off his strategy for the Olympic Games, Ueberroth and the managers working for him had to coordinate all tactical and operational plans under the general strategy.

Because strategic planning is so fundamental to the long-term success and direction of an organization, top management may create a specialized staff to assist with the various planning steps. The planning staff's role is advisory; only rarely will such staffs have the power to implement directly any of the recommendations of the plan itself.

Tactical planning The process through which managers design coherent groups of activities to accomplish a strategy.

Tactical Planning **Tactical planning,** a term derived from the military, is the process through which managers design coherent groups of activities to accomplish a strategy. The time frame for tactical planning tends to be shorter than that of strategic planning—usually no more than two years. Tactical planning is done by middle managers whose responsibilities include the direction of a department, division, or other subunits of the organization.

The 1984 Olympics provide a good example of how tactical planning fits with a larger strategic plan. One component of the strategy, for example, was to hold sporting events at various sites around the city since no single site was large enough to accommodate all the events. The strategic plan determined which sporting events would be held at which sites. With this strategic plan as a framework, tactical plans were developed outlining how and when athletes, officials, and fans could be moved and gathered so that all events would take place on schedule, even though some athletes had to compete in different events held at different sites in rapid succession. Individual managers or teams took responsibility for one area and spent their time assessing the problems, setting objectives, and developing alternative ways of meeting those objectives. In other words, they conducted the planning function discussed earlier in this chapter but with a special emphasis on one particular objective, not the entire strategic plan.

Operational planning The process through which managers design specific activities and steps to accomplish objectives.

Operational Planning **Operational planning** is the process through which managers design specific activities and steps to accomplish objectives. Whereas strategic and tactical planning have time horizons of a number of years, operational planning has a very short time frame, usually a few months.

Though operational planning is done by managers throughout the organization, it is most often done by managers who have a very limited responsibility for accomplishing a limited objective. For example, a manager responsible for testing toys for safety may have the objective of reducing the amount of time necessary to test the toys effectively. This manager therefore must develop an operational plan to help speed up delivery of finished toys to retail stores, yet still maintain proper quality standards.

Similarly, at the 1984 Olympics, individual managers were required to formulate operational plans to meet their objectives. One manager, for example, was responsible for maintaining crowd control at the Los Angeles Coliseum; another oversaw the swimming facilities at the University of Southern California. Each manager was responsible for developing operational plans to manage his or her area of responsibility. If all the managers met their objectives, they would contribute in turn to the overall goal of a well-run, successful Olympics. Each manager is a planner on his or her level in an organization. (See Exhibit 4.4.)

Interaction of Strategic, Tactical, and Operational Plans Strategic plans cannot be accomplished without the implementation of tactical and operational plans. Tactical and operational plans, on the other hand, do not make much sense if they are not coordinated through a broader strategic plan. Organizations use all three types of plans, and managers have to ensure that there is a smooth interaction among them.

In 1982, for example, IBM developed a strategic plan to enter the personal computer market. Until then, it focused on large computers for professional computer scientists and engineers. The shift to a computer that could be used by the average person required new products and services. Tactical plans were developed to produce, market, sell, and service the new personal computers, followed

EXHIBIT / 4.4
All Managers Are Planners

Management Level	Role	Type of Planning
Top management	Institutional: direction of the whole organization	Strategic: intermediate- to long-term focus
Middle management	Administrative: coordination within and among units of the organization	Tactical: short- to intermediate-term focus
Supervisory/first-line	Technical: directly supervise work	Operational: short-term focus

by operational plans specifying the design of the machine, including its "chiclet" keyboard. The chiclet keyboard was smaller than the normal typewriter keyboard and positioned some keys differently. When the first IBM PC was offered, however, severe marketing problems occurred because the chiclet keyboard was widely disliked by customers. It was clear that IBM's tactical plans for sales were being jeopardized by an operational decision, so the company replaced the chiclet keyboard with a more conventional keyboard. Had IBM's managers not recognized the significance of the customer objections, they might have persisted in trying to sell PCs with chiclet keyboards and made it impossible to achieve the company's strategic objectives.

Such examples illustrate the need for managers at all levels to remain flexible and respond to new information, to understand and recognize the importance of various types of plans that occur on other levels. Fortunately, not all plans have to be continually changed, updated, or adjusted. Good planning helps managers avoid problems, and a good plan may need only occasional modifications.

Standing Plans and Single-Use Plans

Standing plans Predetermined courses of action undertaken under specified circumstances.

Single-use plans Plans prepared for unique, one-of-a-kind situations.

Management by exception The principle that managers should concentrate on unusual events that require their skill, expertise, or managerial experience.

Different situations require the use of different types of plans. Some deal with routine matters, others with unique situations. (See Exhibits 4.5 and 4.6.) Repetitive or routine situations allow managers to develop **standing plans,** predetermined courses of action similar to programmed decisions in that they are undertaken when specified circumstances exist or arise.

Single-use plans are prepared for unique, one-of-a-kind situations. The steps in the planning process, however, remain the same for both types: assess the organization and its environment, set goals and objectives, and design alternatives before selecting and implementing the plan.

Standing Plans Standing plans provide clear guidelines for action under specific, identifiable circumstances. A standing plan eliminates the need for a new discussion and decision each time a situation recurs. Standing plans provide the basis for **management by exception,** the principle that managers should focus not on usual or recurring events, but on unusual events that require their skill, expertise, or managerial experience. Organizations use three types of standing plans: (1) policies, (2) procedures, and (3) rules. Policies, procedures, and rules

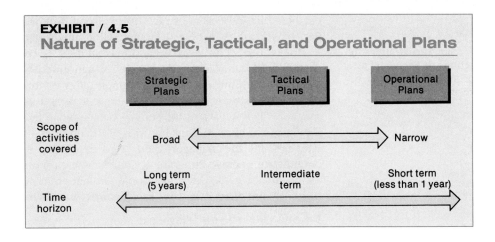

EXHIBIT / 4.5
Nature of Strategic, Tactical, and Operational Plans

Strategic Plans   Tactical Plans   Operational Plans

Scope of activities covered   Broad ⟵⟶ Narrow

Time horizon   Long term (5 years)   Intermediate term   Short term (less than 1 year)

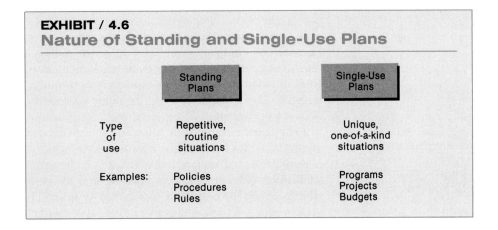

EXHIBIT / 4.6
Nature of Standing and Single-Use Plans

Standing Plans   Single-Use Plans

Type of use   Repetitive, routine situations   Unique, one-of-a-kind situations

Examples: Policies Procedures Rules   Programs Projects Budgets

should "handle" situations that are commonplace or routine and thereby limit the number of problems pushed upwards. Thus managers at higher levels are free to deal with the decisions affecting organizational health and direction.

Policies General guidelines for managers to follow in making decisions.

    Policies are general guidelines for managers to follow in making decisions. They set limitations on a manager's choice of alternatives and actions.

    Policies could be statements such as: "We will attempt to fill all vacancies by promotion from within the firm"; or "To be considered for a merit pay increase, employees must be with the firm for at least two years." A manager must work within the boundaries of the organization's policies to achieve the organization's goals. In securing funding for the 1984 Olympics, for example, Peter Ueberroth established a policy of limiting sponsors to 30—one in each category—to increase the value of the sponsorship and enable the LAOOC to charge more for each.

Procedures Step-by-step guides to action.

    Procedures are step-by-step guides to action. Procedures eliminate uncertainty in dealing with a recurring situation and ensure conformity and consistency in job performance. A predetermined procedure can eliminate excess work, reduce task completion time, and improve the overall level of performance. For example, the inspection of parts on an aircraft follows a standard procedure; each part or section is inspected in succession according to a detailed checklist.

Rules Specifications for actions that must be taken, or must not be taken, in particular circumstances.

Rules are specifications for actions that must be taken, or must not be taken, in particular circumstances. If a specific situation exists, then the rule must be followed. To continue the LAOOC example, after establishing a policy to limit sponsors to 30, Ueberroth established a rule setting a $4 million minimum for any sponsor. "This separates the serious businessman from the phonies," he said. "It also forces bidders to think in terms of the number you want to deal with."[14] The only task for the manager, then, is to determine whether or not the defined circumstances exist. Rules are designed to be clear and unambiguous. They allow for no flexibility or deviation. Some familiar rules seen in organizations are *No smoking* and *Hard hats and badges must be worn at all times.*

Single-Use Plans Single-use plans are for nonroutine situations and actions. Once accomplished, a single-use plan has no continuing value. For example, when Union Carbide Corporation's top management decided to relocate company headquarters, a specialized, one-time plan was designed to move the company's operations, employees, files, and equipment from midtown Manhattan to rural Connecticut. Union Carbide's relocation plan is not likely to be useful again because the company is unlikely to move its headquarters in the foreseeable future, and certainly not from midtown Manhattan to Danbury, Connecticut. If it were to move again, another single-use plan would have to be developed for that purpose. There are three types of single-use plans normally found in organizations: (1) programs, (2) projects, and (3) budgets.

Programs Plans that outline a variety of interdependent activities that must be coordinated to achieve a goal.

Programs are large-scale, single-use plans that outline a variety of interdepartmental activities that must be coordinated to achieve a goal. Programs detail who is responsible for each activity, when specific actions are to be accomplished, what milestones or deadlines must be met for completion of activities, and to whom reports of completed activity are to be sent. Programs can address a wide variety of issues such as university fund-raising and church membership development.

Projects Plans that are either smaller in scale than programs or part of a program.

Projects are single-use plans that are either smaller in scale than a program or part of a program. Aircraft construction, for example, is most often done by project teams. Each project team deals with a particular aspect of airplane design and construction. One team may deal with cockpit design and assembly, another with the wings, still another with the tail assembly. A product development program may be broken into many projects, each focused on a specific technology. Project plans reduce a very large, complex activity into a smaller, more manageable set of activities. One advantage of project teams is the pride and sense of accomplishment that project team members develop.

Budgets Financial plans for allocating resources to a program or project.

Budgets are single-use plans that detail the resources—usually financial—that will be required to complete a program, project, or other organizational activity. In one sense, a budget is a financial plan prepared by a manager to support a request for money, people, or other scarce resources. In the city of Philadelphia, for example, an urban redevelopment program of the city's center was begun in the 1960s. An early phase of that work centered around the reconstruction of an area known as Society Hill. Specific projects were designed, concentrating on the rebuilding of historically significant buildings. Each building project was given a budget detailing the amount of money, personnel, and other resources needed to restore the site.

Once budgets are approved, the manager responsible for the project or activity knows the financial and human limits within which the job must be completed. This helps other managers determine whether the project manager is on or off track. Thus, budgets help managers both plan and control to achieve organizational objectives. As The Inside View 4.2 illustrates, however, it becomes increasingly challenging to accomplish objectives when budgets are restricted.

MANAGEMENT BY OBJECTIVES

There was a time when it was believed that only top management needed to understand the organization's basic plan for the future and the planning process that was used to achieve it. That view receives little support today. Good organizational planning now commonly involves managers from the top of the organization to the bottom (though not necessarily in that order) and provides opportunities for everyone to make a contribution. In many organizations, this is done through a system of setting objectives known as management by objectives (MBO).

Management by objectives is generally understood to be the idea of management scholar Peter Drucker. In his book *The Practice of Management*,[15] Drucker suggested that a system of managing by objectives was a practical tool for motivating employees and providing direction to managers and employees at all levels. The heart of the MBO approach is the recognition that every person and every job in an organization exists for a reason. That reason can be expressed as an objective for the person and the job. By having all employees discuss their job and its objectives with those to whom they report, it is possible to increase a *common* understanding of personal and job expectations and responsibilities. A commonly accepted definition of **management by objectives** is as follows:

> A process whereby the superior and subordinate managers of an enterprise (organization) jointly identify its common goals, define each individual's major areas of responsibility in terms of the results expected of him, and use these measures as guides for operating the unit and assessing the contributions of each of its members.[16]

Management by objectives The mutual determination of objectives and goals by employees and their supervisors.

The key aspect of MBO in practice is the mutual determination of objectives and goals by both employee and supervisor. The two agree on what is expected of the employee and what performance criteria will be used in a specified time period. For example, a sales representative and sales manager agree that the representative will increase the number of potential clients visited in the next month from 40 to 48. The two have created a reference point against which the representative's actual performance can be judged. Of course, it is also important that the reward be tied to how well or poorly the salesperson performs in meeting the objective. A performance that reaches or exceeds the target should earn praise and reward; failure should earn neither.

Goals and Objectives

The integration of general goals and specific objectives works very well in an MBO system. Each person in the organization helps set objectives for himself or herself and his or her particular job. These targets are precise and can be mea-

Salvation Army's Job Is Growing Tougher

The Salvation Army was hurt by the 1987 stock market crash, not because the crash created so many more of the destitute people the organization helps, but because the Army, like most charities, depends heavily on year-end generosity. The October 19 crash lowered the generosity level considerably.

During October and November 1986, for example, contributors gave the Army's New York division about $200,000 in securities. The 1987 figure for the same two months *and* December was about $7000. But the division—which covers New York City, Long Island, and seven counties north of the city—marches on. It has a job on its hands, and the job is getting bigger.

The Salvation Army's resources are limited. Government contracts defray some of the costs. The city pays the organization to run city shelters, and the state provides money for the Salvation Army's work with parolees. But only one-fifth of the New York division's $39 million operating budget is covered by such funds; nearly half the budget depends on public contributions of one kind or another. The rest is covered by fees charged by such Salvation Army facilities as Booth Memorial Medical Center and residences for single women and the elderly.

The organization is frugal. An impressive 86 cents of every dollar goes into program, rather than administrative, expenses. The 163 commissioned officers, as Salvation Army ministers are called, work for allowances ranging from $107 to $122 a week, plus housing. Nevertheless, on September 30, the division ended the 1987 fiscal year $1 million in the red.

Nearly half of the $6 million that individuals contributed to the New York division in that fiscal year came in during the weeks between Thanksgiving and Christmas. Army officials launched the 1987–1988 year's holiday season campaign with a

The Salvation Army found raising money extremely difficult after the 1987 stock market crash.

mailing of about 250,000 fund-raising letters. A few days later, on the Friday after Thanksgiving, they stationed 170 of the familiar red kettles in front of department stores, tourist attractions, and other busy thoroughfares around the city.

But early returns were discouraging. More coins and bills were being tossed into the kettles, but the checks and gifts of securities that historically account for over 60 percent of the division's holiday donations were down. The response to the mail appeal was, in fact, dismal, and officials said the appeal would probably bring in $250,000 less than the previous year. The stock market crash was undoubtedly a factor. ■

Source: Simpson, Janice C., "Friend of the Poor, Salvation Army's Job Is Growing Tougher as the Cries for Help Rise," *Wall Street Journal,* December 21, 1987, p. 1.

sured. Since each person also confers with his or her supervisor, who communicates information about the organization's broad plans and goals, each individual can understand how his or her plan fits into the overall picture. Ideally, this arrangement enables every employee to participate in a commitment to the same broad goals. The steps in the MBO process and some examples of MBO objectives are illustrated in Exhibits 4.7 and 4.8.

EXHIBIT / 4.7
Steps in an MBO Program

1. Each person develops a description of his or her job, then discusses it with his or her superior.
2. The subordinate and the superior discuss and establish several short-term performance objectives.
3. During the time period of the MBO program, the subordinate meets regularly with the superior to discuss progress toward the objectives.

4. Checkpoints are established to measure progress toward the objectives.
5. At the end of the period of the entire MBO program, the subordinate and superior meet to review and evaluate the results of the efforts. If it is a continuing program, they set new objectives for the next time period.

EXHIBIT / 4.8
Examples of Objectives for an MBO Program

Position	Objective
Collections manager	To reduce the number of outstanding past due accounts by 10 percent in six months.
Marketing manager	To introduce an updated version of a product in the $75–$100 price range by November 1 and to reach 4000 units annual sales volume by July 1.
Production manager	To reduce product rejects from 8 percent to 5 percent by December 1.
Sales manager	To reduce salespersons' costs by 5 percent by consolidating sales districts (and thereby reducing travel expenses) by April 1.
Personnel manager	To update and computerize all personnel files by January 1.

The MBO Process

Although every MBO program is unique, each nonetheless is designed and implemented following a common process. The characteristics of this process are:

1. Top management is committed to the program and its success. This commitment requires action as well as verbal support.
2. All levels of management participate in order to link objectives and goals and reinforce overall organizational goals.
3. Communications between and among managers and subordinates are clear and frequent. Performance review, evaluation, and mutual adjustment of objectives are ongoing processes.
4. Great latitude is given in the methods used to achieve results.

MBO Appraised

MBO is definitely an asset to planning, but while it has compelling advantages, it also suffers from several shortcomings. The first problem sometimes encountered in implementing an MBO program is employee skepticism and suspicion. Why does the organization want my input now? How is it to be used? These questions are representative of real concerns shared by employees in MBO programs.

Even after the program is implemented, several problems can arise. The system can easily become an inflexible paperwork mill, in which case the goal of better planning and communications is lost. Additionally, unless carefully monitored, the objectives of each manager can become trivialized. That is, the objectives are set so low that those responsible for achieving them can easily do so and earn a reward. In some cases the feedback process grows so long that managers do not get timely evaluations, so they have no opportunity to adjust their goals as changing situations require.

Finally, there can sometimes be an overemphasis on evaluating and grading each other's performance, rather than on helping each other do a better job. This is a potential problem in any evaluation system, and managers should try to be genuinely helpful and still achieve the stated goals.

In many organizations, the problems are greatly outweighed by the benefits of an MBO approach. The MBO process focuses managerial attention and facilitates coordinated efforts to achieve individual, departmental, and organizational goals. Such direction can help reduce costs, increase profits and productivity, and foster innovation and creativity. The system also helps the organization allocate rewards, identify promising people for further advancement, and identify the needs of individual managers. Finally, the MBO process helps to instill flexibility and planning skills in all management levels.

Management by objectives is not the solution to all managerial problems. It does, if properly handled, provide a clear direction for the organization, improve planning skills, and produce clear, measurable results. Many organizations use some form of MBO, and recognition of its strengths and limitations are leading to more refined developments and use in the planning process. The important point to remember is that all organizational planning is for the purpose of goal accomplishment; therefore, managers should take advantage of planning tools and techniques that can help them in this process.

KEY POINTS

1 Planning involves deciding what to do and where, when, and how to do it. A plan outlines the agreed-upon set of means for using resources to achieve a goal or objective within a specified time frame.

2 Planning is important because it enables managers to anticipate how best to utilize the energies and resources of people in the organization, invigorates employees and the organization by providing direction, helps managers make difficult decisions, helps organizations stay on track, and protects them against unforeseen occurrences.

3 The planning process generally involves five steps: analysis of the organization and prediction of the future environment, establishment of goals and objectives,

identification of alternative courses of action, selection of the best alternative, and implementation of the plan.

4 Successful plans tend to have the following characteristics: They are relevant to the organization's needs and environmental conditions; they are realistic and achievable; they identify expected results; they incorporate methods or phases that are measurable; they specify a clear time framework; they specify accountability and responsibility for results; and they are flexible, incorporating ideas for contingency actions.

5 Organizations use various types of plans. Strategic, tactical, and operational plans differ in terms of the scope of activities they cover—strategic plans having the broadest focus and operational plans the narrow-

est. Standing plans, such as policies, procedures, and rules, are predetermined courses of action useful for routine situations. Single-use plans, such as programs, projects, and budgets, are unique plans used in one-of-a-kind situations.

6 Management by objectives is a process by which superiors and subordinates jointly determine goals, objectives, and expected results and measure and reward performance based on these results. The MBO process requires top management commitment, participation on all levels, effective communication between levels, and flexibility of methods used to achieve results. The disadvantages of the MBO system are that it can create excess paperwork; objectives can become trivialized; and evaluation of performance sometimes supersedes cooperative efforts. MBO systems must therefore be carefully designed and implemented.

▤ FOR DISCUSSION AND REVIEW

1. What objectives did Peter Ueberroth set for himself and for the Olympics? Did they meet the criteria for objectives discussed in the chapter?
2. Define MBO in your own terms. Does it make sense as an effective management tool?
3. Where are the major decision points in the planning process?
4. Explain how and why the objectives of a small manufacturer of pet food and other supplies might differ from those of Ralston Purina.
5. What constitutes the planning process? Does mechanical adherence to this process always produce good plans?
6. Describe the meaning of the term *scope.* How does scope affect the planning process?
7. What plans have you made recently and how well do the plans you made fit into the planning-process model?

▤ KEY TERMS

Brainstorming	Management by exception	Procedures	Rules
Budgets	Management by objectives	Programs	Scenario building
Causal analysis methods	Objectives	Projects	Single-use plans
Delphi technique	Operational planning	Qualitative forecasting	Standing plans
Executive opinion jury	Plan	methods	Strategic planning
Forecasting	Planning	Quantitative forecasting	Tactical planning
Goals	Policies	methods	Time series analysis
Implementation			

THE CONFERENCE TABLE: DISCUSSION CASE / 4.1

Ben and Jerry's

"We didn't have any intention of becoming businessmen. Neither of us was really into that image," remarked Ben Cohen in reference to the work he and his partner Jerry Greenfield did in turning a small Vermont ice cream parlor into a gold mine. To even consider Cohen and Greenfield as businessmen would be inappropriate; in college the two studied pottery, jewelry making, and even carnival techniques. They learned how to make ice cream through a five-dollar correspondence course, and they never thought or expected it to turn into a multimillion-dollar enterprise.

Ben and Jerry did not plan on creating a large organization, but now they are learning to deal with the problems of growth and success.

In 1987 Ben and Jerry's ice cream became the third largest selling premium ice cream in America, with $30 million in sales. This is quite an accomplishment considering that the company began on a mere $12,000 in 1978 as an experiment; a socially conscious "business" was founded on principles that have been forgotten in the corporate world.

When the two opened their original ice cream parlor in a renovated gas station, they questioned and feared the prospect of growth. They had planned to sell the business once it got going and move on to other projects. However, they were forced to expand the company to keep up with their cost. Ben and Jerry's was becoming more and more a business. They even found themselves hiring a businessman, Fred Lager, universally known as "Chico," as chief executive officer of the company. Chico's changes brought the company real money by slashing costs and boosting production.

All of this business nonsense became too much for Jerry. Becoming a successful businessman went against his beliefs, so he retired from the company in late 1982 and moved to Arizona with no intention of returning to the company (he came back in 1985). Though Ben stuck with the company, he felt no better about his position: "I was just a mindless cog in the overall economy, taking in money with one hand and paying it out with the other, adding nothing."

In order to justify the company's growth and ease his own conscience, Ben decided to turn the company into a force for social change and give something back to the community. The more it grew, the more good work it could achieve. This was best demonstrated when the company first sold stock in 1984; rather than deal with Wall Street, they offered the stock solely to Vermont residents, hoping to redistribute some of the wealth. Even though the stock has gone na-

Source: This case was written by C. William Jed Holt, based on the following sources: Larson, Erick, "Forever Young," *Inc.* (July 1988): 50–62; Adolph, Jonathan, and Graves, Florence, "Ben and Jerry Interview," *New Age* (March/April 1988): 33–72.

tional, more than half the shares still belong to people in Vermont. In 1985, Ben and Jerry's Foundation Inc. was created. It receives 7.5 percent of the company's pretax income and spends it on a wide variety of causes.

As the company grew, it began to face more and more competition from other companies like Steve's Homemade Ice Cream, which marketed their product on a national scale. Ben had originally planned to enter only one market per year, but in order to compete he found himself bringing Ben and Jerry's into eight new markets over a nine-month period—quite a change from a man who had questioned growth just a few years before.

Next, the company began to focus attention on its employees. A five-to-one salary ratio was established to keep the top managers from making more than five times that of any other worker in the company. This was quite a departure from the normal corporate ratio of about 100 to 1. For monthly staff meetings, the entire company shuts down to allow all employees to attend.

Though it appears that Ben and Jerry's growth was a simple fluke, many problems arose. The closeness among the employees at the beginning fell apart. Communication channels broke down all over the organization and departments began duplicating work. "Everybody was trying to do the right thing," recalls Ben, "everybody was putting out an incredible amount of effort." However, everything became complicated. Most of the blame for the company's problems was attributed to their lack of a standard operating system.

One major crisis arose in 1987 when Ben and Jerry's attempted to become the first ice cream manufacturer to produce a tamper-proof container for their product. The machinery was very high-tech and was designed to do tasks previously done by hand. The machines came late and proved very difficult to operate; and as demand went up, they found it harder and harder to keep up. The company eventually abandoned the whole project, resulting in a large loss.

Still, through all the problems, Ben and Jerry's manages to survive. "Some people feel the company's first goal is to make as much money as possible, and then spend it in a socially responsible way," states Ben. "I see those values as influencing the way the company does business in all facets, and influencing how it makes all its decisions."

Jerry says, "When Ben and I say that the purpose of our business is to spread joy and not to make money, I think that comes from a feeling or an understanding that throughout your life you're faced with a bunch of opportunities or situations and a lot of it is just challenges. I mean you're stuck here on earth and things come at you, and you're supposed to do things and learn from it. It's all a big experiment, and you never know how it's going to turn out. That's also what business is like. You start out knowing what's going to happen and it's not really a matter of winning or losing, it's how you face everything that comes up." ■

DISCUSSION QUESTIONS

1. Have Ben and Jerry been able to stick to the principles with which they began, or did they, in fact, sell out and become "corporate"?

2. Keeping in mind that Ben and Jerry's original plan for their business was not to become the third largest specialty ice cream company in America, is it possible for a business to succeed by planning around the type of values Ben and Jerry have? (Or simply, is it possible to plan a business based on social values rather than on typical business values?)

3. In what ways did Ben and Jerry's follow the planning process outlined in this chapter? In which ways didn't they? To what can we attribute their success?

THE CONFERENCE TABLE: DISCUSSION CASE / 4.2

Osborne Computer

Adam Osborne was one of the first to recognize the potential in a growing portable computer market.

Founded in 1980, the Osborne company sold 8000 of its units in 1981 and then skyrocketed to 110,000 units of sales in 1982. It looked as if nothing could stop this outstanding growth. However, in less than three years, Osborne Computer was forced to file for protection under Chapter 11 of the Bankruptcy Law on September 14, 1983. What went wrong?

Founded by Adam Osborne, Osborne Computer was the first major innovator in the personal computer field. Incorporating the latest technological advances, the first Osborne Computer was a runaway winner. In a single 24-pound plastic case, a user would find the computer, two disk drives for memory storage, and a keyboard for data entry. The computer could handle an array of popular programs (financial management and word processing, for example) and had an easy-to-grasp handle for carrying the machine around. In addition, the machine was attractively priced at $1795. This technological and price innovation gave Osborne a lead on its competitors in both distribution and name recognition. Orders came pouring in to corporate headquarters in Hayward, California, and they were filled as fast as possible.

Source: This case was written by Janet Murphy, based on the following sources: "Osborne Closes Plant," *New York Times,* August 3, 1983, p. D16; "Shaken Osborne Computer Seeking Suitor in the Face of Possible Failure," *Wall Street Journal,* September 12, 1983, p. 35; "Pacesetting Computer Maker Files for Bankruptcy," *New York Times,* September 15, 1983, pp. A1, D4; "The Osborne Collapse," *Boston Globe,* September 26, 1983, p. 45; and "Trouble in Computer Land," *Newsweek,* September 26, 1983, pp. 72–74.

The personal computer industry (over $1000 per unit) market had $3.8 billion in sales in 1982 and was expected to reach $6 billion on sales of 10.5 million units in 1983. With a 50 percent growth rate projected through 1985, the scramble among eager entrants for a sustainable market position in the early years was fierce. Industry analysts predicted that only 10 to 15 manufacturers would survive the competitive battle. Adam Osborne, founder of Osborne Computers, confidently predicted that 80 percent of all personal computers sold in 1985 would be portable models.

Osborne seemed to be an excellent soothsayer as sales of Osborne computers skyrocketed from nothing to over $100 million within 15 months. However, as competition heated up, the largest computer maker in the world, International Business Machines (IBM), decided to enter the market. Osborne, sensing an IBM onslaught, called industry and business reporters in to announce plans to build and market a new computer that would compete with the IBM model. The new computer, called the Executive II, would have a bigger screen than the first model and be able to operate with more programs. Osborne asked the participants not to publish word of this machine yet and forced them to sign agreements to that effect.

Despite these precautions, word of the new model leaked out; dealers and customers stopped buying the original Osborne, instead waiting for the newer model. An industry observer noted: "There were whole months when Osborne had virtually no cash flow. Sales of the Osborne I died." Contributing to the growing problem were delays in making the model available to distributors in a timely fashion. Osborne was forced to close two plants and lay off a third of his employees. When the new model finally made it to the market, it had to compete with IBM's personal computer, and the Osborne machine was not compatible with the IBM model or its computer systems. IBM quickly dominated the field with its personal computer and set the industry standard. By 1983, IBM held over 25 percent of the market. Although Osborne had an IBM-compatible model on the drawing boards, its development was undertaken too late.

The depth of Osborne's financial ills came as a surprise even to the executives of the firm. Trying to grow fast in order to keep up with the market, the firm spent freely and tolerated internal information systems that were insufficient to keep pace with order entry, inventory changes, expenditures, debt, and income. Expecting to see a profit on the bottom line for the 1983 fiscal year, Osborne managers were shocked to discover that they had a loss of $8 million instead. They quickly scrapped plans to make a public stock offering, cut back severely on expenses, and began to look for a merger partner or further private investment to salvage the firm.

Unfortunately, they had done too little too late. With $45 million owed to 600 creditors and only $40 million in assets, the firm filed for bankruptcy. The firm that was first to enter the industry was also the first to fail. ■

DISCUSSION QUESTIONS

1. Why was Osborne so successful in the beginning?
2. What were Osborne's key mistakes? Could they have been foreseen?
3. Would planning have helped in this situation? How?
4. Given the Osborne situation and experience, what advice would you give to an entrepreneur (someone starting his or her own business)? What are the key lessons here?

5 | Strategic Planning

FOCUS CASE / *USA Today*
. . . And Tomorrow

WHAT IS STRATEGY?
Strategic Thinking
Modes of Strategy Making
Importance of Strategic Planning
Costs of Strategic Planning

STRATEGIC PLANNING AND STRATEGIC MANAGEMENT
Analyze the Current Status and Forecast the Future Environment
Establish Mission and Goals
Develop Strategic Options
Choose the Best Option
Implement and Monitor the Strategic Plan

STRATEGIC PLANNING IN ORGANIZATIONS
Approaches to Strategic Planning
Levels of Strategic Planning
Contingency Planning

Chapter 4 outlined the basic planning process through which goals and objectives are translated into steps for action directed at achieving them. Strategic planning follows this same basic sequence to set the overall goals of the organization or unit. A strategic plan provides the framework that guides all other plans and actions. The strategic planning process is the process through which managers guide broad actions and through which strategy is continually adapted to changing conditions.

■ KEY QUESTIONS

As you study this chapter, try to answer the following key questions:

1 What is the basic definition of strategy?
2 What is strategic thinking, and how is it related to strategy?
3 Why is strategic planning important?
4 What are the costs of strategic planning?
5 What are the steps in the strategic planning process?
6 What two types of analysis are important to begin the strategic planning process?
7 In implementing a strategic plan, operating decisions must be made in consideration of what aspects of the organization?
8 Why is monitoring an important aspect of strategic planning?
9 What are several different approaches to strategic planning?
10 How does the strategic planning process vary between levels of an organization?
11 What is the basic purpose of contingency plans?

Focus Case

USA Today . . . And Tomorrow

Part of Allen H. Neuharth's marketing strategy for *USA Today* was to cover the street corners in every city and town in the country with it's blue and white vending boxes.

In 1981, 45 daily newspapers disappeared. During the decade prior to that, 165 papers either folded or merged. Meanwhile, shifting demographics, reports of declining literacy, and a nationwide dependence on quick, flashy, easily accessible television news coverage all indicated more trouble ahead for the newspaper industry. As if oblivious to all of this, Allen H. Neuharth, chairman of Gannett Co., introduced *USA Today* in September 1982. The nation's first national newspaper was born.

Most people in the industry said it couldn't be done, but from Neuharth's point of view, it was a logical move. Gannett is the largest newspaper chain in the country. It owns over 132 newspapers (93 of them dailies), 8 television stations, 18 radio stations, 40,300 billboards, and the Lou Harris poll. The year before *USA Today*'s introduction, Gannett had "reported record profits—despite strikes, paper shortfalls, recession, and whatever other pestilence has raged—since it went public 57 quarters ago."

Neuharth's strategy for creating *USA Today* was comprehensive. It involved channeling resources from Gannett papers around the country into the new one, picking a target audience, designing the paper to appeal to this audience, and marketing it in a fashion that would win readers over.

Neuharth kept start-up costs (roughly $50 million) down by recruiting roughly 75 percent of the new paper's staff from existing Gannett papers while keeping these people on their original payrolls. He also made extensive use of existing Gannett resources. As one reporter put it, "Physically, [Gannett] is a skeleton of a national newspaper ready to be fleshed out. Distribution routes and plants with available press time and labor are scattered across the country. The Gannett News Service is already in place, turning out features and local angles on major news stories for the chain."

Neuharth next worked on designing *USA Today* for a targeted audience and marketing it successfully. He aimed the paper at young, mobile readers who move frequently and want information about their hometowns. He realized that some would want a quick summary of the national news. All were weaned on television and would be attracted to the color pictures, the upbeat tone, and the impressive graphics on which he decided.

Sources: This case was written by M. R. Poirier, based on the following sources: Alter, Jonathan, et al., "Black and White and All Green," *Newsweek,* February 11, 1985, p. 54; Magnet, Myron, "Can Cathie Black Pull USA Today out of the Red?" *Fortune,* September 3, 1984, pp. 98–101; "Does America Want a National Daily?" *New York,* March 1, 1982, pp. 20, 23; Lewis, Mike, "Extra! Extra! Read About It All Over," *Nation's Business* (December 1984): 30R, 31R; Vaiser, Charles, with Stadtman, Nancy, "Gannett's National Gamble," *Newsweek,* September 20, 1982, pp. 101–102; DeParle, Jason, "Hi-Tech Trend-Speak," *The New Republic,* October 25, 1982, pp. 12–14; Vanner, Bernice, "Questions About 'USA Today,'" *New York,* March 5, 1984, pp. 20, 22, 24; Easterbrook, Gregg, "St. Louis Diarist: Take My Story, Please," *The New Republic,* August 8, 1983, p. 42.

The paper itself attempts to cover almost everything in almost no depth; most items are no more than six paragraphs long. The exceptions seem to be sports and weather: Sports is usually covered in 12 pages and the full-color "Accu-weather" map takes up one whole page. The paper has a flair for listing statistics, analyzing trends, and spotting fads, and it remains relentlessly optimistic about everything, including the economy.

USA Today's style and format have drawn criticism from many in the industry. From the outset, it was criticized for running lead stories on trivial subjects and was dubbed "McPaper," the too-short stories being called "McNuggets." After the slaughter of hundreds of Palestinians in Beirut's refugee camps, for example, *USA Today*'s lead story was "40 Million Take Time For Sports." Jokes were circulating that categories should be added to the Pulitzers for "investigative weather" and "best paragraph." But as one editor for the paper said, "We aren't going to ponder the world's imponderables on a daily basis."

Beyond these criticisms, *USA Today* also had great difficulties attracting advertisers. One problem was the ambiguity of *USA Today*'s market niche. For the first two years, only 30 percent of circulation was attributable to subscriptions. Most newspapers derive 75 percent of circulation from subscriptions. Subscriptions provide a stable, predictable advertising target, and by looking at the zip codes, advertisers can quite accurately identify the income levels of subscribers. The absence of one specific local focus also prevented *USA Today* from luring advertisers, since most papers make their profits from local advertisers.

The paper was under pressure from both external and internal sources. As part of the marketing strategy, Neuharth literally covered the street corners in every city and town in the country with the blue and white vending boxes—almost overnight. Community leaders then accused Gannett of corporate arrogance in disregarding civic protests against this proliferation of vending boxes and took the company to court. Gannett won. Meanwhile, Neuharth was constantly handling complaints from local Gannett papers regarding the borrowed staff. Local papers were forced to give up their "best" reporters while continuing to pay their high salaries, and therefore they couldn't afford to replace them. This issue remains unresolved.

Through 1986, the paper continued to lose money. Though the paper had the fastest circulation rise in newspaper history (to 1.3 million in 16 months), Neuharth admitted it was still behind in meeting its advertising revenue targets. After two years, pretax losses approached $250 million, and the paper lost another $100 million in 1984. However, losses decreased steadily throughout 1985 and 1986, with the exception of 1985's fourth quarter. Circulation reached just under 1.5 million in 1986 and continued to climb through the rest of the 1980s.

Given the paper's leadership, Neuharth's optimism is not unrealistic. As if to confirm his commitment to the paper, Neuharth moved Gannett's headquarters from Rochester, New York, to *USA Today*'s headquarters in Rosslyn, Virginia, just outside of Washington D.C. and Cathie Black, the paper's publisher since June 1984, said "I like dicey situations. . . . I like start-ups and new things and turnarounds." For Gannett and *USA Today*, that is fortunate, because *USA Today* is still here, today. ■

WHAT IS STRATEGY?

Strategy The overall mission of the organization and the set of means for utilizing resources to accomplish the mission.

Strategy is an abstract concept. In the most basic sense, **strategy** is the overall mission of the organization and the set of means for utilizing resources to accomplish the mission. H. Igor Ansoff, a leading expert, elaborates on the concept of strategy to suggest, "Basically, strategy is a set of decision-making rules for guidance of organizational behavior."[1] In this sense, strategy is a framework that guides managers in setting priorities and taking action to achieve goals. The term *strategy,* as commonly used, refers to both the ends—the overall goal or mission—and the means by which the ends will be achieved. In other words, the strategic plan is the system through which resources are organized and directed to achieve the strategic mission.[2]

Consider the example of Sara McIntosh, a marathon runner. Sara's resources include shoes and clothing, water and food, and strength and endurance. Assume her mission is to beat her own best time. She knows she will have to expend her resources carefully, so she must develop a strategy for accomplishing her overall objective. Her shoes and clothing will easily hold up, but she must design an eating and drinking schedule that will give her maximum energy and hydration without slowing her down or causing cramps. To set her pace, Sara will have to consider her strengths and weaknesses and the nature of the race course. If she can keep pace on inclines, a hilly course will not slow her down. If, however, her best time was made on a course with no hills and the current course has many, she might find it more difficult to beat her previous time.

If Sara changes her goal from beating her own best time to winning the race, she will have to change her strategy to consider several factors in addition to her own strengths and weaknesses. She will have to be somewhat familiar with the strengths and weaknesses of the other runners in the field and be able to make comparisons between these runners and herself in terms of endurance, overall speed, and success or failure rates on the type of course to be run. Based on these comparisons, Sara can design various strategies: for example, she could start out slow and save strength, take an early lead in hopes of holding it, or run with the leaders and try to break out ahead in the last few miles.

Regardless of the goals she chooses, Sara will have to adapt to unpredicted environmental changes. A sudden change in temperature or rain shower will affect all runners, either positively or negatively. Sara's strategy must leave room to make adjustments when unforeseen events cause problems or present opportunities.

The basic principles of strategic planning illustrated in the context of this race are the same as those that apply in organizational settings. An organization can have a variety of possible overall goals: to become the market leader in its field (to win the race), to improve over past performance (to beat its own time, so to speak), or simply to maintain its position (to run all 26 miles). Depending on the strategy chosen, resources will be allocated differently. If some aspect of the environment suddenly shifts, a contingency plan will have to be put into operation.

Strategic Thinking

Strategic thinking The thought process that actively creates a strategic plan and adapts it to changing circumstances.

Strategic thinking is closely related to strategy.[3] While a strategy is a plan or system, **strategic thinking** is the thought process that creates this plan and adapts it to changing circumstances. Strategic thinking requires an ability to relate action in present circumstances to future conditions and an overall mission.

The major similarity between strategic thinking in organizations and in marathon running is that the strategic planner and the marathon runner must each operate effectively on two levels at once. Each must understand the present conditions, taking advantage of all opportunities and working around all problems. At the same time, each must anticipate future conditions or events and design ways to take advantage of coming opportunities and avoid coming roadblocks.[4]

Allen Neuharth faced such a situation at Gannett: He had to consider the operating realities of both the Gannett chain and *USA Today* while taking action to achieve desired objectives. He could allocate only a limited amount of human and nonhuman resources from Gannett's local papers to *USA Today*. If he took too much, the locals would not be able to function effectively in their local markets. Many local papers did, in fact, complain that Neuharth had gone too far in taking their best reporters and editors while forcing them to continue paying their salaries. Eventually, a staff rotation plan was designed, allowing the expertise to be shared without being a drain on any one unit.

Neuharth also had to consider *USA Today*'s current needs for investment against the lower-than-expected increases in advertising revenue. At one point, for example, each new subscriber of *USA Today* was costing the company money because the subscription price was below the paper's cost. Neuharth knew that circulation would eventually attract advertising but that circulation increases in the short term actually increased the paper's losses. This was a clear example of the strategic thinker weighing current losses against a predicted future payoff.

Modes of Strategy Making

Organizations create strategy in many different ways. Sometimes the process may be very formal and other times very informal. Henry Mintzberg describes three general modes of strategic planning in organizations.[5]

Entrepreneurial: a mode in which the leader (often the founder) makes risk-taking decisions based on intuition, using very little of the formal process.

Adaptive (often called the science of "muddling through"): a reactive approach to change that focuses on the last steps of the strategic planning process (monitoring and reacting to change).

Planning: a mode that assumes that there is a systematic, formal approach to making risk-taking decisions and that goes through all the steps. (See Exhibit 5.1.)

Today, especially in large, complex organizations, the planning mode is increasingly used. Managers at all levels engage in some aspect of the strategic planning process.

Importance of Strategic Planning

Strategic planning The process through which managers determine the organization's mission and the set of means for utilizing resources to achieve it.

Strategic planning, the process through which managers determine the organization's mission and the set of means for utilizing resources to achieve it, has become an increasingly prominent organizational activity during the past two decades. Three factors have made effective strategic planning essential for modern organizations.

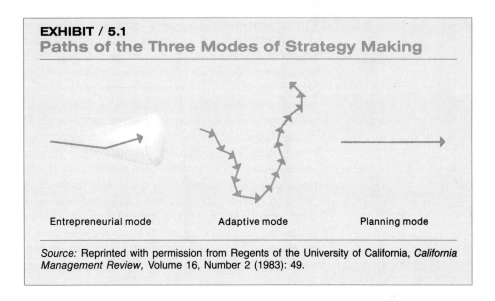

EXHIBIT / 5.1
Paths of the Three Modes of Strategy Making

Entrepreneurial mode   Adaptive mode   Planning mode

Source: Reprinted with permission from Regents of the University of California, *California Management Review,* Volume 16, Number 2 (1983): 49.

Organizational Growth   The increasing size of organizations has made strategic planning more important for two main reasons. First, as organizations grow, management is often increasingly reluctant to rethink the activities and direction of the organization. Sometimes, a management team will use a great amount of time, money, and human resources developing a seemingly flawless plan only to have it ruined by unpredicted events. Going through the steps of strategic planning provides a way for managers to constantly check their company's direction and adapt to new circumstances.

For example, during the 1970s it became fashionable for American businesses to expand away from their original products and acquire companies that provided a diverse product line. Unfortunately, many companies acquired new units that did not fit well into the organizations they joined. The net effect was unsatisfactory, if not disastrous. Although it would have been prudent to sell off the poorly fitting businesses, many organizations were unwilling to do so because of a strong belief—some would say a rigid belief—in the diversification approach. Avon Products, for example, became committed to diversification in the 1970s and was finally forced to sell off the Mallinkrodt Chemical Company in 1984 after continued efforts to incorporate it into the cosmetic business failed. By the mid-1980s, a number of corporate takeovers were launched because the conglomerates had failed to sell off poorly performing parts at an opportune time. Similarly, if after better-than-expected performance, *USA Today*'s losses should increase again, and Neuharth still remains committed to the paper, Gannett will also suffer financial losses. As in many areas of human endeavor, too great a faith in "one best way" is dangerous.

The second reason organizational size makes strategic planning important is that larger organizations require more effective monitoring and coordinating mechanisms. With multiple divisions scattered in various locations, it is easy for one or more of them to stray from the overall organizational plan. Strategic planning helps focus managerial attention on the question of whether the organization's objectives are the "right" ones and whether or not they are actually being accomplished effectively.

Organizational Diversity Strategic planning allows managers to set priorities among products or services, allocating human and nonhuman resources where they will be most effective and provide the greatest return. All organizations have a limited set of resources and must utilize them effectively on a limited set of projects or investments. This can mean that certain promising possibilities will go unexploited; few organizations can pursue all of the opportunities for growth and development available to them. Allen Neuharth, for example, chose to start an entirely new paper rather than purchase any other existing media enterprises. (Five years later, Gannett began purchasing other local newspapers as well.) Even if every investment made by the organization at least pays for itself, there may have been others that might have earned more. Effective strategic planning cannot guarantee that some excellent opportunities will not be left for others to pursue, but it can help managers pick those opportunities that have a promising future. As organizations become increasingly diverse, therefore, strategic planning becomes increasingly vital by providing the coherence necessary for success and survival.

Environmental Change The third reason for the increased importance of strategic planning is the pace of environmental change. As the context in which organizations operate changes more and more rapidly, organizations must be able to anticipate and respond to changes more and more effectively. If the outside world were more static, organizations could focus solely on making their operations efficient. Since this is not the case, they must also continually ask if they are headed in the right direction. They must be able to forecast and estimate changes in capital costs, government regulation, demand, and other variables. Strategic planning helps managers assess the organization's preparedness for an uncertain future. The Inside View 5.1 illustrates the hazards of not adhering to a strategic planning approach and failing to constantly reassess an organization's position.

Costs of Strategic Planning

Although strategic planning makes a valuable contribution to organizational success and survival, it is not problem-free. Strategic planning can be a very expensive activity. First, because it can involve a great amount of top management time and effort, strategic planning can reduce managers' productivity. Second, strategic plans often require current investments with potential future payoffs. Such investments can be risky because they might not provide as great a return as predicted or might even result in a loss. Third, organizations reviewing their strategic direction or considering major new activities will often call in outside experts for consultation. While consultants can be quite valuable to an organization, their fees are often high. Managers must carefully control costs in all strategic planning activities.

STRATEGIC PLANNING AND STRATEGIC MANAGEMENT

Managers use the strategic planning process to determine and reach an overall goal or mission. Strategic planning follows the planning process outlined in Chapter 4 but is conducted on a broader scale, with a longer time frame, and with greater consideration for present and future environmental conditions.

Pell-Mell Growth

People Express is an example of how hard it is to develop and make a strategic plan work.

People Express President Donald C. Burr announced on September 15, 1986, that the airline would be purchased for $125 million. This announcement came after nearly a year of multimillion-dollar losses and the bankruptcy of People's one-year-old acquisition, Frontier Airlines.

The news came as a blow not only to the airline's investors and employees but also to a growing portion of the business and academic world that viewed Donald Burr as the forerunner of a new breed of business manager.

The airline's difficulties were due not so much to Burr's unorthodox views on management and discounting as to a pell-mell rush toward expansion. Indeed, over the year and a half prior to the sale of the company, Mr. Burr and his fellow executives had been almost totally caught up in rapid expansion. A new city was added to the airline's routes about every 20 days. In the midst of such growth, People Express took on a major acquisition—the purchase of Frontier Airlines for $300 million. Two other large commuter airlines, Britt and Provincetown-Boston, were added later.

The preoccupation with growth led to major problems, tactical mistakes, and huge expansion costs. One of the mistakes was the elimination of free drinks, food, and baggage check-in for coach travelers on Frontier Airlines. "It was a mess; it was a disaster," Burr said in an interview in mid-summer 1986. Business travelers who had been loyal to Frontier did not want to reach into their pockets for 50 cents for a cup of coffee. Many turned to United and Continental.

People had pilots who also tended ticket counters, financial officers who also worked as flight attendants, and flight attendants who also tracked lost baggage. But as employee numbers increased rapidly, it was harder to find and train people to do two or three different jobs, and to keep everyone working productively. "Sometimes you get three pilots sitting in a room staring at a phone and wondering what to do next," said a former People Express pilot.

People's competition didn't sit still. Other carriers learned how to counter its low fares. American invented the Ultra Supersaver in 1986 which, with restrictions, matched or undercut People's fares. Other carriers followed, and People, lacking the sophisticated computers needed to handle restricted fares, was "in a bind," Burr said. The big carriers began taking passengers from People.

The combination of overcapacity, loss of customers, and high start-up costs on new routes brought the airline in September 1986 to the verge of bankruptcy. Texas Air, the company Don Burr left only five years earlier to found "a better airline," bought People Express, merged it with Continental Airlines, and signed on Burr as an executive vice president of Texas Air Corporation in February 1987. Burr stressed that he would attempt to transfer "the best of Peoples to the Continental system." ■

Sources: Salpukas, Agis, "The Woes of People Express," *New York Times,* June 25, 1986, pp. D1, D5; Carley, William, "People Express Is a Victim of Its Fast Growth," *Wall Street Journal,* June 25, 1986, p. 31; "People Express Head to Shift," *New York Times,* January 22, 1987, p. D5; Salpukas, Agis, "Texas Air Buying People Express for $125 Million," *New York Times,* September 16, 1986, pp. 1, D4.

As with the planning process, managers must monitor and adjust strategic plans in order to achieve success. By adding these aspects of the control function (which we will discuss in Chapter 15) to the strategic planning process, managers can keep the organization on track and up to date. This is **strategic management:** monitoring and adjusting the strategic plans so that they remain current and the organization remains responsive to its environment. The steps in the strategic management process are as follows:

1. Analyze the current status and forecast the future environment.
2. Establish the mission and goals of the organization.
3. Develop strategic options.
4. Choose the best option.
5. Implement and monitor the strategic plan.

As illustrated in Exhibit 5.2, the strategic management process is cyclical; assessment of the environment leads to the development of an overall purpose.

Strategic management Monitoring and adjusting strategic plans so that they remain current and the organization remains responsive to its environment.

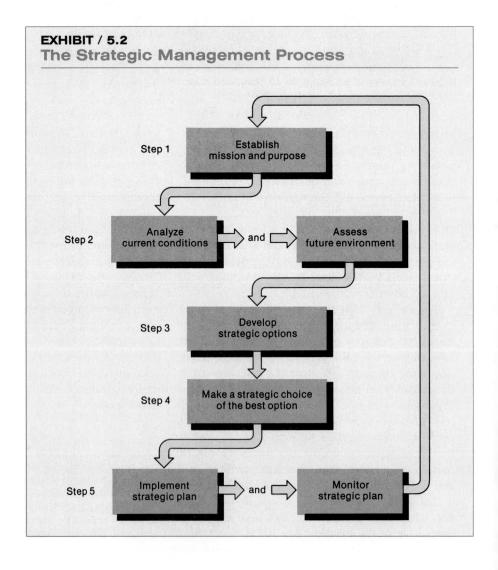

EXHIBIT / 5.2
The Strategic Management Process

Step 1 — Establish mission and purpose

Step 2 — Analyze current conditions and Assess future environment

Step 3 — Develop strategic options

Step 4 — Make a strategic choice of the best option

Step 5 — Implement strategic plan and Monitor strategic plan

Given a purpose, alternative strategies for achieving it can be designed. The selected option, once implemented, must be monitored. If the purpose is not being achieved, or if environmental conditions change such that the strategy is no longer appropriate, the plan must be reassessed, a new mission may be established, or a different strategy to achieve the same purpose may be designed.

Analyze the Current Status and Forecast the Future Environment

Strategic planning always requires the analysis of the current status and the prediction of future conditions to determine what threats and opportunities are likely to present themselves. In addition to utilizing forecasting techniques such as those discussed in Chapter 4, managers should conduct an organizational analysis and engage continuously in environmental scanning.

Organizational analysis *An analysis that provides information about an organization's strengths and weaknesses.*

An **organizational analysis** provides information about an organization's strengths and weaknesses. It is an assessment of current status: What do we do well? What areas of operation need improvement? Some organizations might find that they can develop new products more effectively than they can market or sell them. Other organizations might have highly efficient manufacturing capabilities but inefficient data-processing capabilities that inhibit their ability to coordinate orders and shipments. An organization's strengths and weaknesses determine its ability to pursue various strategic paths; some options simply will not be possible if the organization does not have the necessary resources, skills, equipment, or funding. It is sometimes quite difficult to assess an organization's strengths and weaknesses accurately. Managers may use consultants to help conduct an objective and accurate analysis of the organization. Exhibit 5.3 provides a framework for conducting a strategic analysis.

EXHIBIT / 5.3
A Strategy Evaluation Framework

	Company Objectives	Your Stakeholders' Objectives	Company Resources	Industry	Competition	Environment	Stakeholders
Past							
Current							
Near-term future							
Long-term future							
Strengths							
Weaknesses							
Opportunities							
Threats							

Source: Adapted from Hatten, K., and Hatten, M. L., *Strategic Management: Analysis and Action* (Englewood Cliffs, N.J.: Prentice-Hall, 1987), p. 143.

Environmental scanning
The process by which managers comprehensively research and analyze the environment.

The world outside the organization should also be analyzed. **Environmental scanning** is the process by which managers comprehensively research and analyze the environment. An effective environmental scan will take into consideration such factors as the national and global economy, changes in technology that could affect production processes or products, legal decisions made by state and federal courts, governmental policies and regulations, national and international political trends, demographic shifts, and changes in social values. Environmental scanning should be done systematically and regularly. It should address all possible influences on the organization or any of its component parts. To be an effective strategic planner, one must be a very well informed citizen of the world.

Allen Neuharth's scan of the general environment seems to have been quite accurate. He identified a large sector of the public—that is, mobile, middle- to upper-income, television-bred newspaper readers—and designed a product specifically for them. Neuharth's mission, to design and market a national newspaper, was based on his analysis of the people in the environment. The high circulation figures indicate that these people have been attracted to *USA Today*. Yet, as this case illustrates, accurate environmental scanning by itself is not enough to create a successful strategic plan.

Analysis of competitive factors, such as the products and services offered by all existing and potential rivals within the organization's competitive field, is a crucial part of environmental scanning. It is important to understand the strengths and vulnerabilities of a company's own products compared to those of others. Are its product sales growing or declining? What products or services are in highest demand? What can the organization do to improve its position in the field—how can it become more competitive? By understanding the characteristics of the most competitive, successful firms and their products, managers are in the best position to improve their own organization. Competitive strategies are discussed in Chapter 6.

USA Today is in the unique position of having virtually no direct competition. Most other newspapers have a different market focus, as illustrated in Exhibit 5.4. If, however, *USA Today* really is the nation's number one newspaper (based on number of readers daily) as Gannett's annual report claims, others may attempt to introduce similar products. Currently, Neuharth must keep track of what is in demand in the newspaper industry and attempt to provide it in his national news-

---

EXHIBIT / 5.4
Major Daily Newspapers and Their Focuses

Newspaper	Primary Market Focus
Washington Post	Metropolitan Washington, D.C.; influential national leaders
New York Times	Metropolitan New York City; northeastern U.S., major national markets (e.g., Chicago, San Francisco, Los Angeles).
Wall Street Journal	Business and investment community in all U.S. cities; European and Asian business communities through special editions
Dallas Morning News	Metropolitan Dallas, Texas; political leaders

paper. Later, he may have to devote increasing attention to other competitors who try to copy the *USA Today* formula.

Establish Mission and Goals

Organizational mission
An organization's reason for existence and overall purpose.

Given a thorough assessment of current and future environmental conditions, managers can develop a statement of organizational mission. A statement of **organizational mission** broadly addresses the overall goals of the organization. It states why the organization exists and what it should become. It is a frame of reference for everything that occurs in the organization and changes only as the environment, or the organization's position in it, changes. Most organizations have an ongoing mission. For example, a business stays alive to continue earning profits for investors and to provide products or services to customers. A university continues to exist because its mission—education of students—is also an ongoing one.

An organization's specific goals reflect the unique aims of the organization, as defined by its management, in order to accomplish the broad purpose.[6] The goals are concrete definitions of the organization's mission. For example, within the mission of "providing banking and financial services to those who need and desire them," a bank may have overall goals of

- Establishing an integrated network of checking, savings, retirement, and insurance accounts available to customers
- Providing a customer service agent who handles all business for an individual client

Exhibit 5.5 shows the relationship among an organization's mission, goals, and objectives.

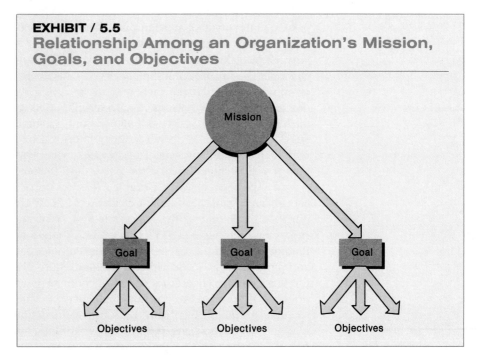

EXHIBIT / 5.5
Relationship Among an Organization's Mission, Goals, and Objectives

Four points should be kept in mind regarding an organization's mission. First, it should be broad enough to allow the organization to grow and to achieve the potential of its people and technology, given the constraints and opportunities identified in the environment. Second, managers must understand that mission statements are not cast in stone but must be adapted to changing conditions. The organization's mission and goals must be periodically reassessed: What business is the organization in, and should the firm continue to be in it? An old cliché states that "nothing breeds failure faster than success." The more successful an organization is in doing something, the less reason there tends to be for management to examine whether it is doing the proper thing. This problem is similar to the distinction drawn by Peter Drucker between efficiency—doing things right—and effectiveness—doing the right things. (See Chapter 1.) The organization can become so focused on doing things right (i.e., becoming efficient) that managers forget to step back and ask whether they are doing the proper things.

A third point to remember is that no strategy endures forever. Sometimes, managers are forced to reevaluate mission and purpose despite years of success. In 1982, for example, the Justice Department approved the breakup of the residential telephone company, AT&T. The breakup resulted in the creation of various local telephone companies (known as the operating companies) and a new company known as American Bell. Since American Bell was no longer to be in the residential telephone business, its management had to define its new mission— that is, what business it was going to be in. After months of management debate, American Bell announced that it would be in the telecommunications business, specializing in the development and manufacture of technologies on the frontier of information transfer. The management of American Bell had developed a mission for the company that was very different from that of the local telephone companies and very different from the mission of the previous AT&T.

Fourth, managers should use a common understanding of organizational purpose, or mission, as a starting point—not an endpoint—in the planning of the organization's future. Every manager must be able to translate the mission and purpose into the product or service, the technological strategy, and the type of customer the organization should serve. Managers in the American Red Cross, for example, must understand whether the purpose of the Red Cross is to provide only disaster relief or also general assistance. Will it provide short-term or long-term services? Will it serve populations only inside or also outside of the United States? The choice of overall strategy is critical because it has implications for what competition the organization faces, what regulations it must follow, and how it will be perceived by the public and various groups in society.

The experience of W. T. Grant is a good example of what happens when managers in an organization do not clearly understand the organization's mission and purpose. Once among the nation's largest retailers, W. T. Grant filed for bankruptcy on October 2, 1975.[7] Part of the problem was Grant's shift to high-cost durable goods in the 1970s. The strategic choice for Grant (in terms of mission and purpose) was to be either a discount store (like K-Mart at the time) or a full-service store (like Sears or J. C. Penney's). Grant, guided by its success up until the 1970s, tried to position itself "between the two and thus consequently stand for nothing." Eventually, both management and consumers became unsure of what the mission and purpose of W. T. Grant was, and the company's sales suffered to the point where it went bankrupt.

Develop Strategic Options

Given a thorough analysis of the environment and the determination of strategic mission, managers can develop options for achieving this mission. Top management is rarely satisfied when presented a single path to the future. Thus, planning staffs have become increasingly adept at developing multiple ways of increasing sales, market share, profitability, or other goals that top management may have established. Global expansion, regional growth, increasing product diversity, and retrenchment (making a current position more stable) are just a few of the options. With several alternatives before them, senior managers are able to select the approach, or strategy, that best fits their understanding of the organization's strengths, weaknesses, and future environment.

At Gannett, for example, Allen Neuharth probably had a number of alternative ways for developing a national newspaper. One might have been a national extension of the company's major city paper. (This is the type of strategy the *New York Times* has adopted as it expands its printing and delivery capabilities to an ever-increasing national market.) A second might have been the renaming of Gannett's existing newspapers around the country—abandoning old names for a new name such as "America Today." The development of a new newspaper, *USA Today*, may have been a third option.

Just as there are many ways to achieve success in the modern economy, there are usually several strategic paths an organization may pursue to fulfill its selected mission. The strategic planning process works well when several options are created, each with its strengths and weaknesses clearly understood.

Choose the Best Option

If several strategic options have been developed, it will be necessary for top management to choose which to follow. The final selection may depend on a variety of factors. If, for example, Allen Neuharth had the three previously mentioned options for developing a national newspaper, his staff would certainly have analyzed the strengths and weaknesses of each proposal. A selective national expansion strategy, similar to that implemented by the *New York Times* for example, may require selection of a "flagship" paper and a slow process of expansion. Thus, much time would be required. The renaming of local newspapers would be easier to do, but risky, since local communities are very loyal to traditional and long-established newspapers. Changing the name of such a paper might affect advertising revenues and circulation.

Beyond the obvious costs and benefits of various options, several intangible influences must also be considered when making a strategic choice. Management values or preferences, for example, can affect such decisions. If the idea of a new national newspaper strongly appealed to Neuharth and Gannett's managers, this may have affected the decision to pursue the *USA Today* option.

Neuharth obviously took many things into consideration when formualting his decision to introduce *USA Today*. He studied Gannett's structure, realizing that the abundance of printing facilities spread out across the country would be extremely helpful in putting out a national newspaper. Human resources could be drawn from Gannett's local papers. They would already have the editorial expertise, and the financial burden on *USA Today* could be minimized. In other words,

Neuharth studied the situation and found that the structure, human and non-human resources, expertise, production capacity, and financial strength of Gannett could, if effectively used, produce success for his new venture. This managerial vision is the heart of strategic choice making.

Implement and Monitor the Strategic Plan

In order to translate the chosen strategic option into a working system that achieves the desired outcomes, the organization must have a blueprint for action. The actual implementation of a strategic plan may be an even more difficult job than the creation of such a plan.[8] Implementation involves bringing the plan into reality. As such, it requires the full range of general management talents and skills for planning, organizing, directing, and controlling.

Implementation of strategy requires the structuring of activities within the organization and the design of the budgets, programs, and policies that enable each department to make some contribution to the overall purpose. The written plan produced by the strategic planning process should specify decisions that have been made with regard to the products, technologies, and expected benefits from the company's activities; targeted customers; the means of financing (debt, equity); channels of distribution; the targeted rate of return and level of risk; size and kind (structure) of organization; and the distinctive competencies to be developed.

The written plan is actually the beginning of the implementation process. It serves to get down on paper the consensus that has been reached on the direction and purpose of the organization. The written plan must also include operating decisions and action plans that enable the organization to reach the stated goals. For example, American Bell's strategic plan called for the production and development of high-technology communications equipment that would represent the state of the art in the field. Such a plan requires a large number of operational decisions before it can be successfully implemented. These decisions will be concerned with whether the organization is structured correctly, providing people with the correct skills, making sure people are rewarded properly, and establishing the proper production and finance systems.

Assume, for example, that an organization has had a human resources policy emphasizing development of managers from inside. Management believes that only by emphasizing internal development can they guarantee that they will have the managerial talent necessary to implement a strategy of technological superiority in the marketplace. Effective implementation of an internal management development policy requires numerous specific actions by managers at all levels.

First, a pool of talented managers must be trained and properly developed within the company. This, in turn, requires selection procedures to bring in promising management recruits and management training, consisting of in-house training and outside supplemental education. Capable managers may be rotated through a succession of executive responsibilities that exposes them to (and tests them in) various facets of the business. Financial incentives are needed that will induce successive generations of promising senior managers to stay with the organization until the current generation retires or leaves. If the budgets do not allow for selective recruitment and intensive training, the selection program will bring in managers who only stay in the organization a short time. Without opportunities for increased responsibilities, the training programs will develop skills managers cannot use within the organization. If the rotation program does not give managers the developmental experiences they need, the policy of promotion from within as a way of implementing strategy will fail.

For Allen Neuharth, implementing his plans for *USA Today* meant relocating personnel; electronically linking various printing plants and editorial offices via satellite; designing, manufacturing, and distributing hundreds of thousands of vending boxes in a very short period of time; and finally, putting out the paper. He kept his budgets trim by utilizing Gannett's human and nonhuman resources and then prioritized spending to focus on putting out a splashy, catchy package. Personnel programs included the regrouping of employees, retraining of some for new tasks, and assigning of others to specific sections of the paper. Editorial policies included focusing on the "up" side of the news and staying in the office until 2:00 or 3:00 A.M. to get the last bit of news ready for the next day's paper.

Monitoring progress and results includes an assessment of work done in previous steps in order to ensure that the strategic plan is being accomplished and that the strategy is still appropriate. The best formulated plan will be worthless if its implementation is not carefully monitored and adjustments made as necessary. Chapter 15 presents the techniques used for controlling organizational activity and performance so strategies are effectively implemented. Conflicts brought on by the borrowing of reporters for *USA Today*, for example, indicated that part of the strategy needed adjusting. Reporters now work on rotation. Monitoring makes adjustments possible. As the environment changes or events occur, the original strategic plans may not continue to be appropriate. Organizational performance may vary over time as the strategy is carried out, as illustrated in Exhibit 5.6. Managers need to know when strategic plans are not being accomplished and make changes as necessary.

When it becomes apparent that the desired results are not being achieved, action must be taken to adjust activities and programs. For an example, see The Inside View 5.2. Adjustment to change is an ongoing process. Monitoring, control, and adjustment are what make strategic planning a dynamic process.

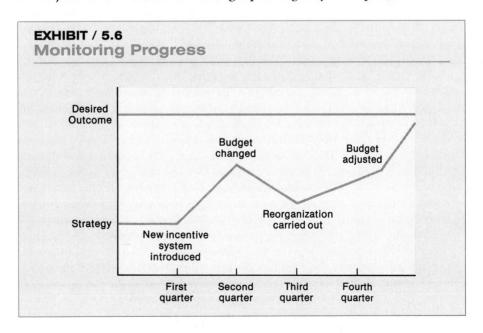

EXHIBIT / 5.6
Monitoring Progress

THE INSIDE VIEW / 5.2

Lighting a Fire Under 3M

Minnesota Mining & Manufacturing Co. (3M) has always been known as one of America's most advanced corporations. However, when Allen F. Jacobson took over as chairman in 1986, earnings for 3M had dropped off. His number one priority was restoring growth and earnings.

Minnesota Mining & Manufacturing Co. (3M) was in the top 50 of the *Fortune* 500 in 1987. It was listed second, after IBM, in *Fortune*'s 1986 list of America's most admired corporations. It had exhibited steady growth in all but one of the previous 10 years and had paid shareholders dividends every quarter since 1916. Nevertheless, this company, boasting 50,000 products ranging from Scotch tape to heart-lung machines, was known to be highly self-critical. Chairman Allen F. Jacobson, newly installed in March 1986, admitted he was worried; after virtually uninterrupted double-digit growth during the 1960s and 1970s, earnings had dropped off. Restoring growth thus became his number one priority, and he started revamping every sector of the business to achieve this goal.

Unlike the previous chairman, Lewis W. Lehr, who mapped broad directions for 3M, Jacobson planned to concentrate more on the nuts and bolts of implementing strategies and reaping the rewards of rising research and development spending. "Lehr got a lot of programs going," said Jacobson, who specialized in operations. "My feeling now is, 'Let's make them pay off.'"

Jacobson started revitalizing every aspect of the business from new product development, to marketing, to management accounting, to human resource management programs. New products were one area showing immediate payoffs. The company had long had a goal of achieving at least 25 percent of its annual sales from products less than five years old. The goal was not met in 1982 or 1983, but with the help of innovations such as a new way to make dental impressions, elastic waistbands for diapers, and a cardiovascular drug developed by a 3M medical research subsidiary, the 25 percent figure was met in the following two years.

In addition to boosting new product development, Jacobson focused on innovative marketing and business development techniques designed to boost sales of all products in all divisions. The Automotive Trades Division, for example, made no products of its own but served as a marketing arm to auto repair shops. To enhance performance in the office copier business, 3M entered into a joint venture with Harris Corporation and developed a program to substantially reduce manufacturing, labor, and quality control costs. And Jacobson authorized a major expenditure—40 percent of 3M's 1985 capital spending figure of $767 million—to rescue the company's sagging Electronics & Information Technologies sector.

To harness the potential of its highly entrepreneurial atmosphere, 3M developed an effective management accounting system. A network of good financial planning and tight cost controls extended from the upper levels of management to the center of every operating unit and was part of everyday decision making. In new product development, for example, a team of controllers spelled out the cost implications of bringing each proposed development to market, showed how it would affect the business segment, and indicated whether its financial targets were realistic. They worked together to prioritize product offerings.

3M was no longer content to fund a slew of small products. "We were the company that put a $2 bet on every horse," said Michael A. Tita, one of 3M's strategic planners. ■

Sources: Williams, Kathy, "How Jake Jacobson Is Lighting a Fire Under 3M," *Business Week,* July 21, 1986, pp. 106–107; "The Magic of 3M—Management Accounting Excellence," *Management Accounting* (February 1986): 20–21; Johnson, Cindy L., and Lewis, Artie S., "Program Replaces Flower for Office Support," *Management Solutions* (August 1986): 39–43.

STRATEGIC PLANNING IN ORGANIZATIONS

Approaches to Strategic Planning

Every organization has certain unique characteristics; therefore strategic planning activities will always vary, reflecting a variety of practical, situational considerations and management values. Exhibit 5.7 provides an illustration of the following approaches.

Inside/Outside Versus Outside/Inside

Inside/outside strategic planning An internal analysis of strengths that assumes that the organization will continue on its present course and seeks to identify the markets the organization should serve.

Strategic planning activities may have either an internal focus or an external focus. Using an **inside/outside strategic planning** approach, management begins with the assumption that the organization will probably continue on its present course into the future. This is an internal analysis that is then tested against outside realities. The organization begins by identifying its special strength (distinctive competence) and questioning which markets it can serve. This approach is common in companies that have highly specialized technical capabilities (e.g., chemical processing) or in industries where the companies have very large investments in capital equipment (e.g., steel, oil, utilities).

Outside/inside strategic planning An analysis of the external environment that seeks to identify opportunities the organization can take advantage of through internal adaptation.

The **outside/inside strategic planning** begins by looking at trends in the external environment. Companies such as General Electric have invested heavily in analyses of social trends and emerging issues. By examining economic, technological, political, and social trends, the companies' planning staffs are able to develop projections or scenarios of the future. The question is then posed, What opportunities will exist in this new environment? This approach assumes that there is little chance of influencing external trends but that internal adaptation is possible if management has enough forewarning. Users of this approach assume it is easier to sell off a business line that has a poor future than it is to change life-styles, cultural trends, or political pressures that have caused the business to become unprofitable. In short, the outside/inside approach assumes the world will keep changing and that the job of management is to fit the organization to the new realities.

Informal Versus Formal

Strategic planning activities may also vary according to degree of formality or structure. In many organizations strategic planning is done by senior managers in brainstorming sessions, whenever the chief executive feels the need. They do not necessarily go through all the steps of strategic plan-

EXHIBIT / 5.7
Approaches to Strategic Planning

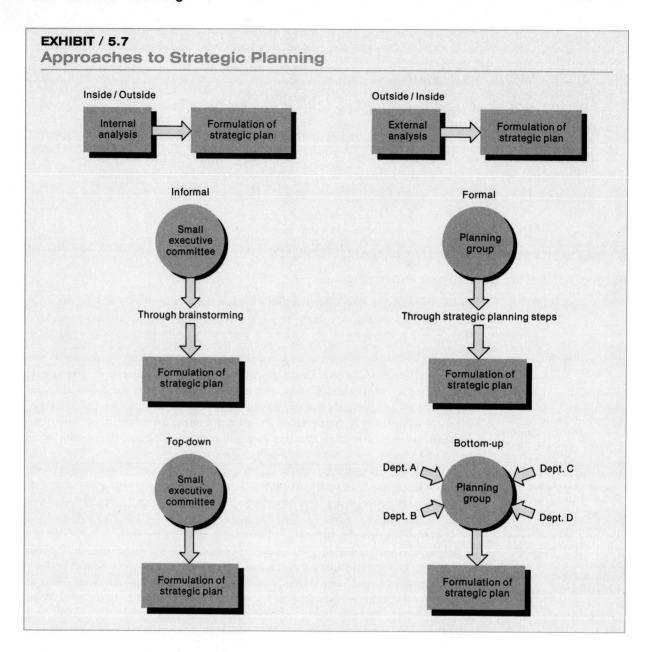

Informal strategic planning Planning conducted in brainstorming sessions without adherence to steps in the strategic planning sequence.

ning in sequence but discuss topics that seem important. This is **informal strategic planning.** Under the guidance of the chief executive, heads of various departments or subunits present their views about the next year's activities. Where there are problems and conflicts, discussion will follow until some resolution occurs. This informal approach to planning may require as much effort as a formal system, but it is done irregularly. An informal planning process will almost always be an inside/outside process, with the basic assumption being that the company will continue on its present course. There is little likelihood that an informal process will ever produce large shifts in the direction of the organization.

Formal strategic planning Planning that proceeds through a series of strategic planning steps.

The most important distinction between a formal and an informal process is that the **formal strategic planning** process systematically proceeds through the series of strategic planning steps previously discussed. When organizations formalize the planning process, they are committing themselves to repeated examination of the assumptions on which the business is built and the conditions that are affecting that business.

Top-Down Versus Bottom-Up Another way in which strategic planning differs from organization to organization is the extent to which it is done by a small group of senior-level managers or is a broad-based activity involving managers at all levels. There are advantages and disadvantages to either approach, and it appears that the selection of either a top-down or bottom-up process can be effective if it is consistent with the organizational situation.

Top-down strategic planning Planning conducted by a specialized planning staff and delivered to senior executives for analysis.

In **top-down strategic planning** systems, the organization usually has a small planning staff that functions as a consulting group to the senior managers. This planning staff conducts the environmental analysis and internal resource assessment and usually presents senior management with these findings in the form of a strategic assessment report. This may be followed by a discussion between the planning staff and the senior executives regarding the set of opportunities and threats and the possible courses of action that may be taken. Chief executives who enter a company that seems in need of strategic redirection often prefer this approach. A notable example of a top-down planning approach occurred at the Bendix Corporation in the late 1970s when, under the direction of chief executive William Agee, a small group of planners headed by Mary Cunningham planned a series of strategy changes that redirected the company. Bendix quickly changed from a stable manufacturing company to a rapidly changing, acquisition-oriented firm. It is unlikely that this shift could have been accomplished had the company engaged in a bottom-up planning process.

Bottom-up strategic planning Planning efforts involving managers from various levels in the development of organizational strategy.

Bottom-up strategic planning, in which managers from various levels are asked to contribute to the development of organizational strategy, has the advantage of drawing many managers into the process, giving them a sense that they are participating in the important activity of clarifying the organization's priorities and intentions. Management by objectives systems, discussed in Chapter 4, are one form of bottom-up planning. In large and complex organizations consisting of many different levels, bottom-up planning is an essential part to organizational strategy.

Levels of Strategic Planning

Managers at all levels of an organization, not just those at the top, are responsible for helping to develop and implement a viable strategy. All managers have some strategic planning responsibilities for both the overall organization and their specific units. While the chief executive and top management staff may be responsible for setting the direction for the entire organization, other managers will be responsible for setting the direction for their divisions and subdivisions. All managers may ask, "What business are we in, and how will we achieve our objectives?" As R. Edward Freeman points out, the "complicated nature of the modern corporation entails that we address these [strategic direction] questions at several levels."[9] Strategic planning needs answers to questions on at least four distinct levels in large, complex organizations.

Functional-Level Questions Functional-level questions normally focus on the maximization of resource productivity.[10] Planners are concerned with how much the organization is gaining from effective management of finance, marketing, and production operations. They are also concerned with identifying distinctive competence, that is, the particular arrangement of an organization's past and present resources and skill deployments that help it achieve goals and objectives. By using existing Gannett Co. printing presses and reporters for *USA Today*, Allen Neuharth was addressing these functional-level issues.

Business-Level Questions At the business level, strategic planning questions focus on how to compete in a particular industry or product/market segment. What are our competitive advantages? What product/market niches or segments should we pursue? How can we better integrate the functional areas to achieve advantage over our rivals? In designing *USA Today* to cater to a younger, transplanted, upwardly mobile, television-bred audience, Gannett's management was addressing these issues.

Corporate-Level Questions The dominant questions at the corporate level are: What business(es) should or will we be in? How shall we deploy our resources among our various businesses? How do our businesses relate to one another? What financial and managerial controls will we exercise? These are broad questions, usually focusing on the mission of the organization. In deploying resources from Gannett local papers to a new, national paper and in working to "create" a new market, Neuharth was addressing these issues.

Enterprise-Level Questions According to at least one author, there is a unique set of questions that is even broader than those posed at the corporate level. Because all organizations, and particularly large organizations, exist and operate in a world that is filled with values, social issues, and numerous groups with an interest in organization actions, it is legitimate and necessary for top management to think about the values that the entire enterprise represents. R. Edward Freeman views this as answering the question, For what do the corporation and its managers stand?[11] When blizzards rage in the upper Midwest, the blue and gold insignia of telephone company repair trucks is visible wherever service problems exist. The company "stands for" dedicated service. Peters and Waterman, in their book *In Search of Excellence,* describe the Frito-Lay Company's commitment to have their salespeople visit 95 percent of their customers daily, whether they are high-volume supermarkets in cities and towns or small-volume general stores in rural communities. Such actions reflect much more than administrative systems or even organizational policies: They are a tangible expression of what the former Bell Telephone and Frito-Lay stand for, the values of customer service that they believe in. They reflect the values the organization wants to represent to the world outside the organization.[12]

Enterprise-level questions are bound to be controversial. Critics have pointed out that *USA Today* stands for things that do not belong in the newspaper business, and further, if it succeeds, others will copy the format. "Gannett is known for expert marketing and mediocre journalism," said one critic.[13] And, as discussed in the opening case, many were critical of editorial decisions that put major stories on back pages. Finally, some are worried that in competing with television to produce easily consumable news, papers are sacrificing accurate, thorough coverage for simple, titillating, amusing packages. *USA Today*, they claim, is leading this trend. "For the moment, the marketing talents of Gannett have given us the brightest, slickest, fastest product on the streets, a paper of hi-tech and trend-speak," said one critic. "But apart from 'Buy Me,' does it have anything to say?"[14] In an era when "corporate cultures" are increasingly important to employees and customers, these value decisions may be some of the most important made by an organization's managers.

Contingency Planning

Contingency plans
Plans that identify alternative courses of action to be taken if events disrupt the completion or accomplishment of a plan.

While all organizations must have strategic plans, they cannot rely on them indefinitely without making adjustments as the environment changes. One way of preparing for unforeseen circumstances is to develop contingency plans.[15] **Contingency plans** identify alternative courses of action to be taken if events disrupt the completion or accomplishment of a plan. For example, as *USA Today* began circulation, it was important to make the public aware of the newspaper. To accomplish this, the Gannett Company provided millions of free copies to hotels and airlines, which in turn gave these complimentary copies to their clients. Hotel guests and airline passengers are traveling and are likely to be interested in more national news than the local papers provide. They are potential future customers of *USA Today;* an important part of implementing Gannett's strategy was getting the paper into their hands. Airlines and hotels across the nation cooperated, perhaps because the copies were free, maybe because this was a good way to provide a service for their clients. What if hotels had refused, or the *Wall Street Journal* or the *New York Times* had responded with more attractive offers for the hotels? Gannett would have needed a contingency plan, an alternative course of action for getting the paper into the hands of potential future subscribers.

In a much broader sense, Gannett needed a contingency plan in the event that *USA Today* failed. The staff on *USA Today* would have to be reassigned to their original papers or otherwise relocated; the resources would have to be channeled into areas where Gannett would need them the most; any new technologies developed would have to be put to use in other ways so as not to waste them. Neuharth was apparently aware of the need for a strong contingency plan; reorganizing resources in the manner he did allowed for relatively quick readjustments as conditions changed.

Contingency plans must be developed not only for problem areas but also for opportunities. What if a new market opened up for national news through telephone lines, satellites, and computers? What if people in Europe suddenly became very interested in a paper like *USA Today* in their own languages? What if local papers suddenly decided that the cost of production was so great they were going to cease operations, leaving big markets for *USA Today?* Management needs to be prepared to seize these opportunities as they arise. The strategic plans cannot be so rigid nor the steps for developing the strategic plans so carefully followed that opportunities are lost. Successful managers know how to adjust and modify their actions and plans to quickly correct arising problems and rapidly take advantage of new opportunities.

▧ KEY POINTS

1 Strategy is the overall mission of the organization and the set of means for utilizing resources to accomplish the mission.

2 Strategic thinking is a thought process that actively creates a strategic plan and adapts it to changing circumstances. The strategic thinker must be able to relate action in the present to future conditions and an overall mission.

3 Organizational growth and diversity and the constant environmental changes faced by a firm have forced organizations to reemphasize strategic planning to remain competitive.

4 Although strategic planning may prove very beneficial, it may involve costs such as decreased productivity of managers while they are engaged in the process, risks involved in making investments for future pay-offs, and the costs of outside consultants if they are used.

5 The basic steps in the strategic management process include analyzing current conditions and predicting the future environment, formulating mission and goals, developing strategic options for achieving the goals, choosing the best option, then implementing and monitoring the strategic plan.

6 It is important to begin the strategic planning process with two types of analysis: organizational analysis of the firm's strengths and weaknesses and environmental scanning that covers economic, technological, legal, political, and competitive factors.

7 The operating decisions that must be made in implementing a strategic plan concern organizational structure, human resources, expertise, production capacity, reward systems, financing, and acquisition of resources.

8 Monitoring strategic plans allows management to see whether the mission and goals are being achieved and serves as a guide for making adjustments if it is not.

9 Common approaches to strategic planning include inside/outside or outside/inside, informal or formal, and top-down or bottom-up. Often a combination will be used.

10 At the functional level of the organization, strategic planning activities focus on maximizing productivity. At the business level, they focus on maintaining or increasing market share. At the corporate level, they focus on organizational mission and purpose. At the enterprise level, they are concerned with determining the organization's position in the social or ethical environment.

11 Contingency plans identify an alternative course of action to be taken if events disrupt the completion or accomplishment of a plan. They help managers solve problems and take advantage of opportunities.

▧ FOR DISCUSSION AND REVIEW

1. What was Gannett's initial strategy for *USA Today*? How was strategic thinking involved in the decision to start publishing?

2. What is the strategic objective of a surgeon before performing a major operation? What must he or she incorporate in the strategic thinking process?

3. What is competitive analysis and why is it important?

4. How would the definition of strategy differ within organizations such as universities as opposed to organizations that produce durable manufactured goods? To such large companies as General Motors and AT&T and to smaller companies such as the local grocery store?

5. What major firms have been able to survive in the United States for the past 50 years? Why are these firms so successful? What role has strategic planning played in their success?

6. In the *USA Today* case, was the strategic planning top-down or bottom-up planning?

7. Think of a marketable product (completely new or an adaptation of a former product) and *briefly* present a written plan regarding the strategic planning process.

8. What types of industries would prefer formal planning? What types of approaches do you think are currently being used in the automobile industry? The home entertainment industry? The computer industry?

9. What business failure you are aware of can be attributed to poor analysis of current conditions? Which aspects of poor analysis were most crucial to this failure?

■ KEY TERMS

Bottom-up strategic
    planning
Contingency plans
Environmental scanning
Formal strategic
    planning

Informal strategic
    planning
Inside/outside strategic
    planning
Organizational analysis

Organizational mission
Outside/inside strategic
    planning
Strategic management
Strategic planning

Strategic thinking
Strategy
Top-down strategic
    planning

THE CONFERENCE TABLE: DISCUSSION CASE / 5.1

Tops in Toys

To implement the Toys 'R' Us strategy of selling large quantities of toys year round, the company created a supermarket atmosphere that provides a large selection of items for children of all ages and with diverse interests.

"Convenience. Large selection. Good Prices," said the mother of a one-year-old boy. That's why she and millions of other parents shop almost exclusively at Toys 'R' Us stores to buy everything from games and toys to baby furniture, clothing, diapers, and even baby food. "The Toys 'R' Us strategy," said one reporter, to "move mass quantities of toys year round at low prices—has destroyed the old-fashioned department store philosophy on how to sell toys: expand the toy section as Christmas approaches, set prices high, and shrink them again in January." And this strategy has been responsible for increasing the Toys 'R' Us market share from 5 to 20 percent between 1978 and 1988, making Toys 'R' Us the largest U.S. toy retailer: $20 out of every $100 spent in the United States on toys winds up in a cash register in one of the company's 313 stores across the country. The second-place toy retailer, Child World, commands only 6 percent of the market.

Sources: This case was written by M. R. Poirier, based on the following sources: Yip, Pamela, and Cauchon, Dennis, "Toy Chain Is Toughest Kid on the Block," *USA Today,* December 16, 1987, pp. 1B, 2B; Kerr, Peter, "The New Game at Toys 'R' Us," *New York Times,* September 4, 1983, p. F7; Ricci, Claudia, "Children's Wear Retailers Brace for Competition from Toys 'R' Us," *Wall Street Journal,* August 25, 1983, p. 21.

Toys 'R' Us founder Charles Lazarus seems to have had the same concept for his company since he opened the first store in his father's Washington, D.C., bicycle shop in 1948. In a 1987 interview he referred to the chain as a "supermarket for toys. Toys 'R' Us being out of Monopoly would be like Safeway being out of milk," he said; part of his strategy is to err on the side of too much inventory, rather than too little. The only reason he changed the original name for the store—the Baby Furniture & Toy Supermarket—was because the 27-letter name required small letters to fit on a sign. *Toys 'R' Us* could be written in much larger letters, easily readable from a distance. He had reversed the *r*'s in the original title to appeal to children, and he carried this over to the new store name.

In 1966, Lazarus sold his company, then consisting of only four stores, to Interstate Stores, Inc. for $7.5 million. He stayed on as manager, but other problems forced the owners into bankruptcy in roughly a decade. In 1978, Lazarus led the company out of bankruptcy and, in the next 10 years, expanded its network of stores and warehouses across the country and even entered foreign markets. He expanded his line of toys to include sophisticated electronic toys and video games to appeal to an older market and added designer clothing outlets for children. His goals for 1995 include increasing market share from 20 to 40 percent, increasing the number of toy stores in the United States from 313 to 700, increasing the number of foreign stores from 37 to 200, and increasing the number of Kids 'R' Us clothing stores from 74 to 350.

In taking the leading sales position, Toys 'R' Us has also become the toy manufacturers' number one customer, to the point where many manufacturers package their toys to meet Toys 'R' Us floor-to-ceiling stacking specifications. Toys 'R' Us also requests that packages be printed with a full description of the toy and its uses on all sides of the package, to reduce the burden on store employees to answer customer questions.

And Lazarus is so committed to his policy of keeping well stocked that he installed a $35 million computer tracking system that can display, even on his home computer, the rate of sales for any item, the current level in inventory of the item, and the name and phone number of the item's buyer. Lazarus feels customer satisfaction is worth the costs of overstocking inventory. Only that way can he ensure that customers get everything on their shopping lists in one trip to the store. ■

DISCUSSION QUESTIONS

1. Assume you are Charles Lazarus in 1978, and you went through the basic strategic planning process outlined in this chapter after pulling the company from bankruptcy. Describe each step (what were your goals, what did you perceive in the environment, what options did you have, etc.).

2. Assume you are the manager of a department store that has relied heavily on Christmas sales of toys to round out your sales figures for the year. In the past few years, more and more of your customers have been going to Toys 'R' Us for the wider selection and lower prices on toys. What strategy would you design to recoup your losses?

3. What "really crazy" things could Toys 'R' Us do to lose their leading position in the market? (Answer in terms of strategy—do not discuss tactics such as burning down all the stores or yelling at the customers to shop elsewhere).

4. What might one competitor or several competitors do to capture some of Toys 'R' Us market share?

The Wonderful World of Money

Under the leadership of Michael Eisner, the Walt Disney Company has dealt with major strategic issues very successfully.

In 1955 Walt Disney celebrated the opening of Disneyland in Anaheim, California. The next year, it generated revenues of $10 million, or about 30 percent of the total company revenues. It was a good start for the theme park, which would become the major source of revenues and profits for the company.

In addition to theme parks, Disney became famous for the characters developed by its animation studios and for the movies created by its live-action studios. All of the Disney elements together created what seemed like an absolutely unbeatable combination in the many years that Walt stood as the autocratic head of the company. But in 1966, he died, leaving the company locked in the path on which it had been going. There were a few memorable movies in the time after Walt died and before the mid-1980s, but for the most part, while the rest of the industry was making *Star Wars* and other exciting new movies, Disney was left muddling along with the same old formula that had been successful many years before. The problem was a management team that had no business plan, loyally following the direction Walt Disney had been going in when he died.

There were major events, such as the openings of the Magic Kingdom (Florida) in 1971, Epcot Center in 1982, and Tokyo Disneyland, and a few successful films. But when each of these projects had been completed, the company was left

Sources: This case was written by William Bird, based on the following sources: Taylor, John, *Storming the Magic Kingdom* (New York: Knopf, 1987); Koepp, Stephen, "Do You Believe in Magic?" *Time,* April 25, 1988, p. 68.

with staffs that had nothing to do. The company was always looking at the tails of the big studios. The environment had changed but Disney had not. The results were declining revenues, a depressed stock price, low profits and net income, and generally the signs of a sick company.

But when you are worth billions of dollars and your market price is less, it makes no difference to Wall Street if your name is Mickey Mouse or Big Blue. Anyone will buy a box with $100 in it for $89.99, and for brokers with the task of making money with money, Disney was a plum ripe for the picking.

So in 1984, Saul Steinberg, armed with Wall Street savvy, hungry investors to back him up, and years of experience at the game, went after Disney—and he won. After a long battle and several defensive moves, the Disney management ended up paying him greenmail (buying stocks back from hostile owners for a premium) and he left. Disney's problems were far from over after paying Steinberg off. It still had the basic problem that had caused the raid. Management was in poor shape, and toward the end of 1984 Disney reorganized under new leaders, Michael Eisner and Frank Wells.

Eisner set about refocusing Disney. He raised prices and profits at the two theme parks (Walt Disney Company owns only a small share of the revenues of Tokyo Disneyland) which had been held low to increase admissions. He pushed better development and marketing of the Disney characters on everything from high fashion to baby clothes. But one of the biggest changes Eisner introduced was the increased production of mainstream movies under the new label Touchstone Pictures. Having a second label allowed Disney to produce and market the hotter-selling "R" and "PG-13" movies without tainting the Disney name. This, plus increased budgets and benefits for stars (such as the chance to produce or direct), gave Disney a new look.

The company increased its net income from a fairly stable $98 million to $135 million between 1978 and 1984, to an all-time high of $445 million in 1987 and still growing. There are plans going for a EuroDisneyland, home videos sales revenues grew from $55 million in 1983 to $175 million in 1987, and the Disney channel has been the fastest-growing video channel, with over 4 million viewers in 1987.

The trick of the whole revitalization was identifying hidden wealth at Disney. The company needed to see opportunities still in television. The vaults of films, the many characters, and the ability to produce contemporary movies to attract adult crowds were strengths that lay latent but were still there. The vision to see that hidden treasure chest and new paths for a dynamic company were the strengths Eisner brought. Moreover, Eisner brought a team that could deal with Wall Street and the creative side of the business. It could appreciate the new stockholders and could meet the new environment rather than be surprised by it. ■

DISCUSSION QUESTIONS

1. At the beginning of 1984, before Disney was thrown into confusion, what were some of its main strategic problems?
2. Were Disney's actions adaptive or entrepreneurial?
3. Identify the major parts of Disney's business and spell out some of the new avenues for development facing them in the 1990s.
4. Can you see some coming problems either in the industry or in changing trends of consumers that might have an unexpected effect on Disney's business?

6 | Strategic Management in Changing Environments

FOCUS CASE / Shrimp Farming: Bountiful Harvest or Bust

STRATEGIC MANAGEMENT IN THE ENVIRONMENT
Operating and General Environments
Degree of Complexity and Rate of Change
Economic, Technological, and Competitive Factors in the Operating Environment

ECONOMIC FACTORS
The GNP and the Federal Government's Role
Strategic Responses to Economic Fluctuations

TECHNOLOGICAL FACTORS
What Is Technology?
Effects on Organizational Strategy
Strategic Responses to Technological Changes

COMPETITIVE FACTORS
Strategic Responses to Competitive Forces
Basic Market Strategies
Portfolio Management
Choosing a Strategy

The objectives, policies, and plans that express an organization's strategy cannot remain unchanged. The economy fluctuates, new technology renders the old obsolete continuously, and organizations continually respond to other organizations' actions. Thus, managers are always confronting the dilemma of strategic management in an increasingly complicated, ever-changing environment. This chapter focuses on some of the basic strategies businesses pursue and ways in which managers adjust those strategies to new realities in the environment.

▥ KEY QUESTIONS

As you study this chapter, try to answer the following key questions:

1 How does the context of the environment add depth and meaning to the five steps in the strategic planning process covered in Chapter 5?
2 What is the difference between the organization's operating environment and the general environment?
3 What is the relationship between the degree of complexity and the rate of change in an organization's operating environment?
4 How do changing economic factors influence organizational operations and strategy? What can the organization's managers do to respond to these influences?
5 What is technology, and what effects do technological developments have on organizational strategy? In what ways is technological change a source of opportunities, and in what ways is it a source of threats?
6 How can organizations best respond to or take control of technological change?
7 What are the basic competitive forces?
8 Describe the four basic market strategies.
9 What is a portfolio, and what is it designed to do?
10 What competitive forces must a strategist understand to position the organization in its industry so that it can best defend itself against competitive forces or can influence them in its favor?

Focus Case

Shrimp Farming: Bountiful Harvest or Bust

As the demand for shrimp increases, shrimp farming becomes profitable.

The ramshackle barn and sheds of a former tomato farm in South Carolina do not look like the headquarters of a pioneering, high-technology venture. But they are the home of Plantation Sea Farms, one of about 20 ventures across the United States in shrimp aquaculture: farming shrimp in ponds.

"It's an industry whose time is here," said Joe Alexander, president of the 115-acre farm 25 miles south of Charleston. "We're using an underutilized resource (the coastal waters); we are nonpolluting and creating new jobs."

They are also hoping for big profits. A shrimp crop had a value of $2000 to $4000 per acre in 1985, compared to $200 to $300 for an acre of grain sorghum or $400 to $500 for cotton. What makes shrimp so valuable? One reason is that shrimp are an efficient protein source: They convert two pounds of feed into a pound of protein; the ratio for pigs is 4 to 1, and for cattle it is 10 to 1. In addition, "We seem to have an insatiable demand for shrimp," said Bille Hougart, aquaculture coordinator for the U.S. Department of Agriculture. Americans consumed a record 591 million pounds of shrimp in 1986. Demand for seafood in general has also increased; in the 1970s, Americans consumed an average of 9 pounds per year. In 1987 that figure increased to over 15 pounds and was expected to reach 30 pounds by 1990.

Our appetite for shrimp has virtually outstripped the oceans' supply. "If we want more shrimp and shellfish, we are going to have to raise it on farms," Hougart said. Currently, this appetite is being satisfied by imports—71 percent of shrimp consumed in the United States comes from foreign fleets or farmers.

The only successful commercial shrimp farms are in Central and South America and Asia, where labor is cheaper, environmental rules are fewer, and the climate allows the harvesting of crops year-round. Several American companies, including Ralston Purina Co. and Baltek Corp., have invested overseas. Ecuador is the largest producer in this hemisphere, mostly by farming. This is due in large part to the abundance of salt flats and brackish marshes surrounded by mangrove trees, which are important to the survival of young shrimp. Ecuador exports 99 percent of its crop to the United States.

Plentiful imports have cut the wholesale price of medium-sized shrimp to $1.57 per pound from the 1982 price of $5.03. U.S. shrimp farmers say they can still get premium prices. Their crop is more uniform in flavor and texture and fresher than the ocean catches or imports. But no U.S. farm has returned a profit. The major drawback is production costs, which need to be cut by a

Sources: This case was written by M. R. Poirier, based on the following sources: Mariani, John F., "It's No Fish Story: We Love Seafood," *USA Today,* pp. 1D, 2D; Barnes, Jill, "Big on Shrimp Farming," *Nation's Business* (July 1986): 62; Blair, Jess F., "Interest in Fish Farming Increases Rapidly in Southwest," *Feedstuffs,* March 30, 1987, p. 11; Guy, Pat, "Our Appetite for Shrimp Swims Deep," *USA Today,* October 18, 1985, p. 1B.

third for domestic shrimp farms to be viable. "Until we have five companies out there (making money) . . . it's not commercial," said Addison Lawrence, project leader of the Shrimp Mariculture Program at Texas A&M University.

Aquaculture, or fish farming, has been around for centuries and accounts for about 11 percent of total U.S. fish production, 40 percent of the oysters and most of the catfish, crawfish, and rainbow trout. Only in the last decade have shrimp successfully been bred on farms. Hatcheries now produce larvae for "grow out" ponds, which are harvested 120 days later. Most shrimp farms circulate brackish (i.e., salty) water from the ocean in their ponds, but other methods are being tested.

Shrimp farming is a very costly, complicated business, which explains why it is not yet "commercial." The water in the ponds must be kept between three and four feet deep, at a constant temperature between 60 and 80 degrees, and at a constant salinity of roughly 8000 parts per million (ppm). Because the ponds are open to the elements, an extreme temperature change could cause the water temperature to soar above or drop below acceptable levels. Similarly, excessive evaporation, drainage, or rainfall could cause salinity levels to rise above or fall below the stated limits. One producer lost a crop of shrimp to a fungus disease after rainfalls dropped the salt content to 6000 ppm in his open pond.

One of the largest and best financed ventures is Marin Culture Enterprises in Kahuku, Hawaii, a partnership of W. R. Grace & Company and F. H. Prince & Company, Inc. The firm was mum in 1987 on details of its system of raceways under a plastic inflated cover. Ten years of research and about $25 million had been invested at that point. *Aquaculture Digest* editor and publisher Bob Rosenberry describes it as "one of the most exciting" ventures because it promises yields 80 times normal.

Texas United Fisheries invested $10 million at Port Mansfield, Texas, and has more than 100 acres of ponds. It expects its method to produce up to 10,000 pounds per acre. Sean McGowan, a marine biologist and vice president of Texas United, estimated production costs at $2 a pound for premium shrimp that could sell for up to $5. "I want to turn a profit in the next year," he said. "It certainly seems possible, at least on paper." The biggest obstacle for McGowan was to get three federal and state permits. It took nine months and a small fortune in consultant fees for clearances from 18 agencies. That kind of red tape drove Joe Ikeguchi out of business. His Marifarms, Inc., of Panama City, Florida, was one of the first shrimp farms in 1968. Almost $15 million later, Ikeguchi and his partners, "ran out of gas in 1981." When Marifarms wanted to expand in the marshlands, the Environmental Protection Agency "wouldn't budge," Ikeguchi said. "They said it destroyed the natural habitat."

Shrimp farming is a risky business with almost equal potential for large profits or losses. "You have to be crazy," said Jack Parker, general partner of Laguna Madre Shrimp Farms Ltd. of Harlingen, Texas. Parker developed the shrimp research program at Texas A&M from 1968 until 1980 when he joined eight partners in the venture. The farm—500 acres of ponds, a hatchery, and facilities to make dry-pellet shrimp food—produces more than 300,000 pounds. Its highest yield was 2500 pounds per acre. "We hope to be profitable this year," said Parker in 1985. "To a great extent we probably are writing the book, or at least the first chapter. That is exciting and fun to do, but it's painful." ■

As the preceding case illustrates, the future of companies such as Plantation Sea Farms and Laguna Madre Shrimp Farms Ltd., and the entire shrimp farming industry, depends on the effects of a complicated network of environmental factors such as the market demand for shrimp and the number and strengths of competitors. If demand is low, domestic producers stand little chance of breaking into a market already cornered by foreign producers. Similarly, if technology is not readily available, domestic producers again will have trouble turning a profit within a reasonable period of time, if ever. But if, for example, Marin Culture Enterprises can inexpensively and quickly develop and implement a production system that is 80 times more productive than most other systems, they stand to make a fortune.

These forces do not operate independently of each other. A "sure thing" is a situation where competition is low, demand for the product or service is high, and the resources and technology needed to produce it are inexpensive and readily available. But sure things, by nature, have a very short life span. If demand for something is high and production costs low, opportunity seekers will move in quickly. Then competition soars, resources are eaten up, technological development drains funds from other areas, and supply may even begin to outstrip demand, as profit-hungry producers saturate the market.

In reality, there are always trade-offs. The shrimp farmers are now in a situation where demand is high and natural resources are accessible, but efficient, productive technology is expensive and in the developmental stages, and competition from established producers is high. Thus, shrimp farmers will need effective and responsive strategies that consider these factors.

STRATEGIC MANAGEMENT IN THE ENVIRONMENT

Chapter 5 outlined strategic management in five steps: analyze current conditions and forecast the future environment; establish the purpose, mission, and goals; develop strategic options; choose the best one; and implement and monitor the strategic plan. Each step must be conducted within the environment in which the organization operates. Each step, viewed in the context of the environment, takes on new depth and meaning.

In analyzing current conditions and forecasting possible futures, managers must realize that, first, current conditions are not static—a host of environmental changes constantly influences any organization; and, second, because of this constant flux, many forecasts will be accurate for only a limited time. When establishing a purpose, within the context of the environment, the manager must ask not only, Why does this organization exist? but, Given an ever-changing environment, does the reason for this organization's existence remain valid?

When developing and selecting strategic options, managers must consider not only each situational factor but also the interplay and trade-offs among them and how they will change in the future. Which environmental forces are strongest; which are weakest? Which have positive and which have negative effects? Which strategic options are therefore the most feasible given the sum of pluses and minuses?

Implementation and monitoring are also more complex in a changing environment. Organizational resources, production capacity, and financial status—all aspects relevant to implementation of any strategy—will fluctuate in response to environmental conditions. Thus, implementation procedures must be designed or adapted to fit a changing framework. In monitoring the plan, once it is implemented managers must appreciate those uncontrollable external forces, as well as controllable internal activities, that will affect the outcome of the strategy.

Because the environment is so critical, it needs to be well understood. An in-depth analysis will provide the basis for developing successful organization plans.

Operating and General Environments

Environment The factors, forces, and influences outside the organization.

Operating environment The factors, forces, or influences in the environment that directly and immediately affect the organization—primarily economic, technological, and competitive forces.

The external **environment** consists of all those factors, forces, and influences outside the organization that define the reality within which the organization exists. It can be divided into two parts: the operating and the general environment. The **operating environment** is made up of the factors, forces, or influences in the environment that most directly and immediately affect the organization. The operating environment consists primarily of economic, technological, and competitive forces or influences. A hospital's operating environment includes the economic and competitive forces in the geographic area from which its patients, nurses, physicians, and other health workers come as well as the technology available nationwide. Because the hospital also has to recruit interns and residents from medical schools, some of which may be outside its geographic area, the nation's medical schools are part of its operating environment, too. In other words, all of the factors, forces, and influences that affect, in a reasonably direct way, the ability of the organization to exist, to pursue its mission, and to survive, are part of the operating environment.

General environment The factors, forces, or influences in the environment that indirectly affect the organization—primarily social, legal, ethical, and political influences.

The **general environment** consists of those factors, forces, and influences in the environment that indirectly affect the organization. These include social, legal, ethical, and political influences. Assume, for example, that a hospital runs an ambulance service to pick up and transfer patients within the city. If a military conflict in the Persian Gulf occurs, it has no direct impact on the hospital. But if the military conflict halts the shipment of oil, which causes international shortages of gasoline and thereby drives the price of gasoline up, the hospital's cost of running the ambulance service will rise. In this indirect manner, changes in the general environment can have an important impact on an organization. The impact of an oil shortage brought on by military conflict would be even more significant to a taxicab company or a trucking company. In these cases, the company's very ability to exist might be at risk.

Many scholars differentiate between operating and general environments, although they may refer to them by different terms such as "task" and "societal" environments, respectively. In addition, not all scholars include the same components in each environment; that is, some include political and legal factors in the "inner" circle, and technological factors in the "outer" circle. These distinctions, including our own, are somewhat arbitrary. That is to say, political factors may directly affect some organizations and/or industries more than others. One framework cannot accurately distinguish between the more and less influential factors for the entire spectrum of business. Therefore, in Exhibit 6.1, we have illustrated influential factors as part of each environment.

EXHIBIT / 6.1
Operating, General, and International Environments

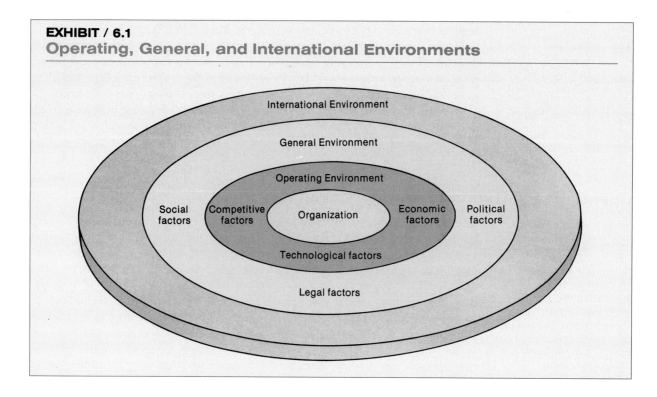

Degree of Complexity and Rate of Change

Degree of complexity
The number of forces or influences in the environment.

Rate of change   The speed or frequency with which environmental forces change in character.

One feature of the environment that managers particularly need to keep in mind is the relationship between the degree of complexity and the rate of change. These have distinct influences on an organization and do not necessarily operate in unison. **Degree of complexity** refers to the number of forces or influences in the environment that affect or are affected by an organization—forces the organization must keep track of or address. **Rate of change** refers to the speed or frequency with which these forces—whether there are very few or very many—change in character. Thus, an organization may operate in an environment that is both highly complex and changes very slowly, although this is highly unlikely, or an environment that is not highly complex but changes very rapidly. Shrimp farmers face the latter environment. There are relatively few producers and the economics of the industry are relatively stable, but each producer is developing technology that could revolutionize the industry overnight.

Typically, however, highly complex environments tend to change rapidly. Complexity alone is a surmountable problem for managers. But complexity combined with a rapid rate of change creates instability and uncertainty for managers. As Exhibit 6.2 illustrates, the most difficult environment to manage in is one in which there is high complexity and a high rate of change. A company that is operating in 140 nations, some of which are in the Persian Gulf, and operating petrochemical plants in nations requiring an uninterrupted flow of oil has both a very complex and a rapidly changing environment to deal with. This will make carrying out a strategy very challenging.

EXHIBIT / 6.2

Relationship Between Degree of Complexity and Rate of Change in the Environment

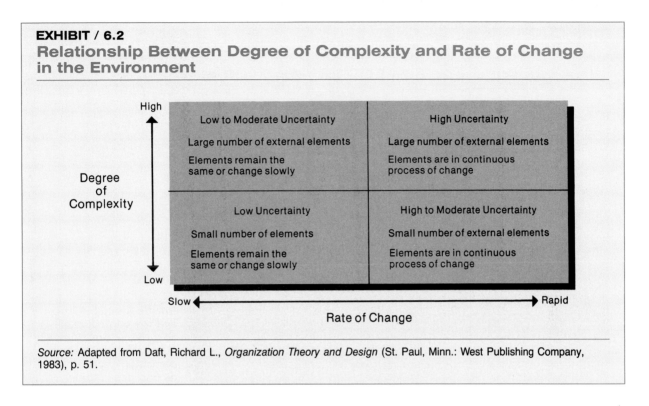

Source: Adapted from Daft, Richard L., *Organization Theory and Design* (St. Paul, Minn.: West Publishing Company, 1983), p. 51.

In this chapter we will discuss the operating environment because it has the most immediate affect on strategic management. In later chapters we will consider the general environment and the international environment.

Economic, Technological, and Competitive Factors in the Operating Environment

Because the operating environment has the most direct and immediate effect on the organization, factors and forces in it are critical to consider when formulating business strategies. In developing and implementing effective business strategies, management's objectives are:

1. To identify products or services that customers want and are willing to pay for. No matter how good the company's products or services are, if the customer does not want them the strategy has failed.
2. To acquire or develop the resources and technology necessary to produce these products/services. A strategy that cannot be implemented because resources are lacking is obviously a failure.
3. To gain a profit by ensuring that the market price is high enough to cover production costs but low enough to lure a sufficient number of buyers. Management's responsibility is deciding what profits and losses are acceptable and then establishing a strategy which will accomplish them.

Strategic Planning in the Oil and Gas Industry

Drastic swings in price and the unpredictable cost of exploration have made strategic planning particularly hard in the oil and gas industry.

Drastic price swings in the oil and gas industry over the past two decades have caused many in the industry to question whether entering other lines of business might not be wise, or at the very least, more relaxing. The experience of one Canadian oil and gas company is somewhat typical: In 1980, it was "riding the exploration wave" and was considered by many in the industry to be a "winner." In 1983, it was on the verge of bankruptcy. It recovered during 1984 and 1985, only to be in financial trouble again in 1986. Though the Canadian government's energy programs have been credited with some of the company's early problems, many of them can be attributed to strategic planning errors. A leading management consultant identified the following factors the firm should have considered.

ECONOMIC MARKETS

The supply and demand for petroleum is affected by the economic activity of industrial nations and the level of world oil and gas reserves. This supply/demand balance is particularly subject to the forces of the Organization of Petroleum Exporting

Countries (OPEC), which is able to influence the price and security of world oil supplies through its control of massive low-cost oil reserves (crude oil can be produced in quantity and profitably by OPEC countries at prices ranging down to $2 per barrel). When OPEC prices are high, companies are prompted to explore for reserves in what were previously considered uneconomic locations. They abandon such exploration initiatives when prices are low. Similarly, the development of nonindustrial nations has opened new markets for petroleum products and prompted the governments of these nations to offer attractive incentives for the development of domestic reserves where such reserves exist. Financial markets respond to change in the supply/demand balance by equating the cost of funds for exploration and development with the risks inherent in the particular strategy.

TECHNOLOGICAL FORCES

Strategic initiatives impose technological demands on oil and gas companies. These demands are in turn translated into financial and human resource capability requirements. For example, offshore and arctic exploration require different technologies than do conventional oil and gas exploration. Technology has made possible the development of alternative fuels and sources of supply impacting the economic potential of petroleum, both as a local and world commodity. Hence, the appropriateness of any organization's exploration strategy and research and development initiatives may be influenced by the technologies it employs and the geographic locations in which it operates.

COMPETITIVE FORCES

Oil and gas are commodities, and natural resource markets are entirely dependent upon supply and demand. Hence, the product of one company is comparable with, if not identical to, that of another. This same comparison does not hold, however, when we examine corporate strategies. An analysis of competitive forces should focus on an examination and comparison of the company's strategy in the context of the strategies followed by comparable oil and gas companies that are successful. For example, some oil and gas companies have pursued strategies of geographic diversification to exploit governmental incentives to minimize political risk. Other companies have attempted to mitigate the impact of cyclical fluctuations in the price of oil and gas by securing long-term contracts by innovative financing approaches such as interest rate or foreign currency swaps. However, no matter what strategy an oil firm adopts, it must consider what its competitors are doing. ■

Source: Howard, Thomas P., "Strategic Planning in the Oil and Gas Industry at $15 Per Barrel," *Business Quarterly* (November 1986): 56–61.

Economic factors
Factors that determine the cost of production and the prices for goods.

Technological factors
Factors that determine how and what products will be produced.

Competitive factors
Factors that determine what products at what prices will be successful.

Thus, **economic factors** (factors that determine the cost of production and the prices for goods), **technological factors** (factors that determine which products will be made and how they will be produced), and **competitive factors** (factors that determine what products at what prices will be successful) are all crucial in designing an effective strategy. The Inside View 6.1 illustrates how economic, technological, and competitive factors affect strategic planning in the oil industry. These factors affect each other and must be balanced.[1] Some shrimp-farming companies, for example, have been able to raise shrimp in an artificial environment but not at a cost-effective price; if they charge enough to cover costs, sales will be too low to break even or make a profit. If they lower prices, sales will go up, but profits still might be too low.

These concepts apply equally to service industries. For example, if the management of a health clinic recognizes that its clientele consists of people who come to the center for inexpensive, regular checkups and preventive medical care, then the type of technology available (X ray, CAT scan) is secondary to the quality of medical advice provided on a continuing basis. Buying expensive equipment will drive up costs unnecessarily, making the clinic inaccessible to the majority of its clientele. On the other hand, if the health center is a critical- or specialized-care facility, serving mostly patients with insurance or receiving government subsidies for providing critical care, it is clear that investments in technology such as X rays are really vital to providing a product (emergency care) demanded by the market.

Managers must design and adjust strategies so that the organization can respond to changes in all three areas of the operating environment. There is always a risk that some mismatch will develop among them, perhaps in the form of technological change, economic fluctuations that change demand for the product, or competitive pressure. To prevent mismatches, managers need to monitor those areas in which important, or potentially important, changes are occurring and be prepared to adapt to new circumstances. Because the economic environment is the broadest, encompassing all industries and not being subject to overriding influence by any one industry in particular, we will discuss it first.

ECONOMIC FACTORS

Economic factors have an impact on all organizations. For example, mortgage rates, unemployment levels, and the health of the economy form a very influential context for the entire housing market. Important economic issues include the national level of unemployment, productivity, savings, investment, inflation, and the supply and value of a nation's currency. These factors are important to managers because they form the context in which the individual decisions of consumers, producers, and distributors occur. During a recession, for example, the overall level of consumer demand is reduced, unemployment insurance costs increase, and interest rates for business loans rise. All of these conditions affect the company's profit, the tax revenue the government receives, and the products that will sell.

Long-term patterns of economic activity are difficult to predict but are very important for most industries. Changes in overall levels of economic activity—production, employment, investment—are called business cycles. Swings in the economy, such as the ups and downs of a typical business cycle, provide threats and opportunities to organizations and thus strongly affect the performance of existing strategic plans and options for new ones. A business cycle has four basic phases: trough, expansion, peak, and contraction.[2] A typical business cycle is illustrated in Exhibit 6.3.

An understanding of the business cycle is fundamental to any effective managerial planning activity. Such industries as housing, automobiles, and steel are especially sensitive to changes in the business cycle (they are sometimes referred to as cyclical industries). In hard times, people buy fewer cars and build fewer houses. The success of the firms in these industries very much depends on accurate forecasts of changing demand. Many new opportunities and threats accompany a shift in the cycle.

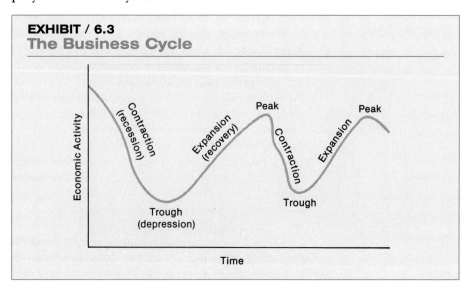

EXHIBIT / 6.3
The Business Cycle

The GNP and the Federal Government's Role

The federal government is the primary "manager" of the nation's economy. Through a set of policy tools—the interest rate, availability of money, tax policy, spending patterns—the federal government influences the growth rate of the gross national product (GNP), that is, the sum of the sale of all goods and services over a one-year period (these policy tools are more fully discussed in Chapter 19). The GNP is a measure of economic activity, a sort of barometer of the health and competitiveness of the U.S. economy.

The GNP is expected to grow from year to year (see Exhibit 6.4). There are three major forces at work. First, the number of working-age people tends to increase every year, meaning that more and more people are available to contribute to and consume national production. Second, business firms and governments tend to expand the capacity of their facilities to meet the demands of an increasingly large population. Finally, advances in technology and management tend to increase both the availability of goods and services and the efficiency with which they are produced so that more products become accessible to more buyers.[3]

Changes in GNP do show an upward trend, but they are far from steady. Economists and managers are concerned with both short-term and long-term fluctuations in economic activity. Seasonal changes in supply and demand can generally be predicted with some confidence; they depend on such annual cycles or events as crop harvests, holiday and vacation spending, and budgetary schedules. Different organizations have to deal with different seasonal patterns of supply and demand in their purchasing and sales plans. Consider, for example, the seasonal variations in the following industries: Christmas tree farming, rental of recreational vehicles, teaching, travel, and agriculture.

Until the Great Depression of the 1930s, the federal government's role was limited. The Depression, followed quickly by World War II, made government intervention in the economy a virtual necessity. Following World War II, the U.S.

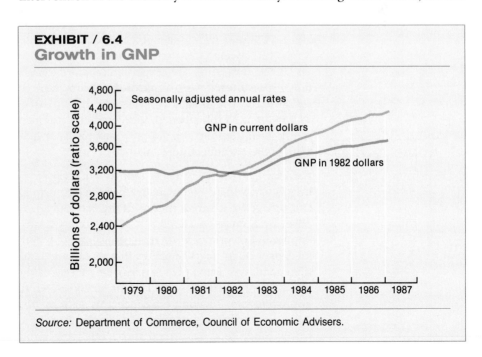

EXHIBIT / 6.4
Growth in GNP

Source: Department of Commerce, Council of Economic Advisers.

Congress cemented the federal government's responsibility for economic policy by passing the Employment Act of 1946. This piece of legislation gave Congress and the federal government the responsibility for maintaining full employment, stable price levels, and economic growth. Today, over 40 years later, those three goals—full employment, stable prices, and economic growth—remain the cornerstone of national economic policy.

Strategic Responses to Economic Fluctuations

The government's role as an economic stabilizer protects most organizations from failure due to violent economic fluctuations. For example, while thousands of businesses failed immediately after the stock market crash of 1929, very few suffered significantly immediately after the crash of 1987, largely as a result of stabilizing factors built into the economy following the first crash. However, economic forces still greatly influence what costs of production and what prices for goods will allow an organization to succeed and grow; therefore, managers must develop strategic responses that enable the organization to cope with negative economic developments and take advantage of positive ones.

Anticipation of Change   To remain aware of what is happening in the economy, many large organizations have research departments staffed with economists who interpret both national and international economic data and provide analyses to top management. While individual managers can increase their understanding through a careful reading of newspapers and business and economic magazines, many organizations also subscribe to economic research services.

By anticipating change, managers can prepare the organization to cope with its impact. If economic forecasters predict a downturn in the economy during the next year, decisions can be made to cut back new investments in buildings and machinery. If an upturn is predicted, long term investments can be increased with less risk.

Consider Marin Culture Enterprises, for example. If managers from W. R. Grace and F. H. Prince had anticipated a downturn or recession, they might have postponed or canceled plans to enter into the Marin partnership to produce shrimp. Or, if the downturn was experienced after the partnership was formed, they might have altered their plans for the shrimp farm so that development time was significantly shorter than 10 years and the investment was significantly less than $25 million. As it happened, they predicted the economy would remain consistently strong enough to support and justify a full-fledged effort to develop a state-of-the-art aquaculture facility.

Product Diversification   One way of preparing for future downturns in business is to diversify.[4] A company diversifies by developing and/or selling products and services in different sectors of the economy. Downturns in one sector can be offset by upturns in another. Assume, for example, that a company sells home improvement products to retail consumers. A careful study of this company's sales over many years indicates that its sales are directly affected by the state of the economy—when personal income increases, more home improvements are undertaken; when personal income declines, so, too, does spending on home improvements. To counterbalance this pattern of "boom-and-bust" sales revenues, the company's management might acquire a chain of supermarket food stores. Since food sales tend to be relatively stable regardless of the business cycle, the company's overall revenues would be more stable. Portfolio approaches, discussed later in this chapter, have the same balancing effect.

Shrimp farmers, too, could diversify to cushion the impact of economic fluctuations. Because shrimp are expensive, farmers could allocate smaller or larger sections of their "farms" to different types of fish. When the economy is strongest, they could produce only shrimp, which brings one of the highest prices in cultivated seafood. During downturns, they could produce redfish or catfish. Redfish is cheaper than shrimp and could be in higher demand during an economic slump. Catfish is presently in high demand only in the South, but because of its lower price, demand in those areas would go up in economic downturns. Because all three require similar water depth, changeovers would not be difficult. Of course, a shrimp farmer could produce shrimp and also diversify into unrelated businesses such as paper products, restaurants, or drive-in theaters.

TECHNOLOGICAL FACTORS

A strategy that makes sense in economic terms must also be technologically feasible. If it is not, it will be quickly outdated and the organization endangered.[5] Consider one of our shrimp farmers. In 1982, the going rate for shrimp was $5.03 per pound. Any farmer who had the technology to produce and distribute the shrimp for less than $5.03 per pound could have made a profit. However, because of plentiful, low-cost imports, the wholesale price per pound dropped to $1.57 by 1985. If the shrimp farmer has not developed or purchased technology since 1982 that will reduce costs to less than $1.57, what was once a technologically and economically sound strategy becomes a danger to organizational survival. Similarly, if Marin Culture enterprises can indeed develop the technology to increase yields 80 times above normal levels, but in so doing raises production costs too high to make a profit, the strategy does not make economic sense.

What Is Technology?

Technology   The science and study of the practical and industrial arts.

Technology is derived from the Greek words *techne,* meaning "art," and *logos,* meaning "word" or "discourse"; the Greek *technologia* translates to "systematic treatment." From these roots, our modern understanding of **technology** is the science and study of the practical and industrial arts.

Technologies can be thought of as the tools people and organizations apply to operations to get things done more quickly, more easily, or more efficiently. Jacques Ellul, in his book *The Technological Society,* describes the creation of bodies of knowledge that enable people to accomplish certain objectives, whether they apply to solving a manufacturing problem, writing a book, electing a political candidate, or marketing sugar-coated cereals on television.[6] The fact that these knowledge tools exist and can be used repeatedly to accomplish objectives means that they can be applied to the accomplishment of an organization's strategy. As The Inside View 6.2 illustrates, however, developing and implementing the new technology will take a conscious effort.

For decades, managers have believed that a successful business could only survive by building a "better mousetrap." That is, success could be guaranteed by continuing to offer buyers a product that did more, did it better, was more reliable, and cost less than any similar product on the market. From the late 1940s to the 1970s, the United States was in an era of "technological optimism" when

Finding the Right Fit for New Technologies

Frederick D. Buggie, president of Strategic Innovations International (SII) says he often gets calls from companies that have become uncompetitive because of old and outdated technologies. Typically, a company's research unit, attempting to correct the situation, will develop a new product that has nothing to do with the company's main business. According to Buggie, company scientists are likely to stand back and proudly say, "Hmmmm, that is an interesting product; something like that must be good for 100 applications." However, the product may be different from anything the company has dealt with, and finding applications may be difficult. That is when Buggie is called in.

First, Buggie meets with a team of high-level corporate managers, including representatives from research and development, marketing, and general management. That group reviews internal suggestions about what to do with the product and formulates criteria about attributes the company would like to see in a new business—financial goals, spending limits, manufacturing capabilities, even cultural preferences for commodities rather than specialties.

Then, Buggie gathers together a group of six to eight outside experts, chosen because of their perspective on the problem at hand, to provide input. Without revealing the corporate client or the exact nature of the prospective new product, Buggie gives panel members information to consider in advance of a meeting. At the meeting, they discuss the matter and are encouraged to come up with suggestions.

Ideas from that session, usually 60 to 80, are brought back to the client company's management group, which meets with Buggie to discuss the project and tries to assess the range of suggestions. The aim is to see how well those suggestions mesh with the original criteria.

Now, with a narrowed set of five to ten ideas, Buggie rounds up a new group of outside specialists and goes through another evaluation and review process. By this time, the ideas are more specific and the possibilities more sharply focused.

After that session with outside specialists, Buggie's firm takes the remaining ideas out to the field and conducts marketing research to obtain data that may help to show whether any of those ideas is realistic for the corporate client.

The final group of suggestions and Buggie's market research are submitted to the company's management, which then decides whether to go ahead with any of the suggestions or to drop the project. Even if the decision is no go, says Buggie, "the company has been saved from spending real money to develop a turkey." ■

Source: "Finding the Right Fit for New Technologies," *Chemical Week,* May 7, 1986, p. 76.

people generally believed that technology could solve virtually any problem.[7] After all, the United States had successfully placed a man on the moon. If that could be accomplished, what couldn't? As former Secretary of the Interior Stewart Udall said, "There were no problems, only solutions."[8]

Today we have a sharpened understanding of the limits of technology and realize that some current problems are beyond the scope of technology, even the technology in the imaginations of the brightest scientists. Nevertheless, technology remains one of the single most powerful forces of change in society. Knowing where technology is headed and the rate of technological change offers strategic opportunities for organizations of all types.

Effects on Organizational Strategy

Technological change affects managers and their organizations in two ways. One is the impact of technology on the products created by industry. A high rate of technological change means products are changing rapidly. Competition from organizations that produce state-of-the-art products often forces other firms out of the market. Changing technologies also affect the processes used to manufacture and create the products offered by the industry. Because technology is the core of the process that transforms inputs (resources) into outputs (goods and services), changes in production processes and activities (e.g., robotics) can have a dramatic effect on production efficiency and thus on the ability of an organization to meet the needs of its current and potential customers.

Technology as a Source of Opportunities Technological development offers organizations opportunities to grow, increase profits, and gain a larger share of a market. Some shrimp farmers, for example, claim they can provide a "new and improved" shrimp, fresher and more uniform in flavor than the currently marketed shrimp. Many are also trying new methods of production. Solar Aquafarms uses a filtered, recycled water system. Marin uses raceways under inflated plastic covers. Meanwhile, various aquaculture research facilities are continually developing new technologies and methods. The opportunities are there for all, not for just one organization. Thus, many organizations find themselves in a continuous war to be state of the art. "The competition" will always be developing something "new and improved," be it a product or a process.

However, organizations winning the technology battle may actually be creating problems for themselves. Biotechnological and nuclear energy developments, for example, have been met with heavy opposition from environmental protection and public interest groups. Questions of morals and ethics in the case of biotechnology, and questions of environmental hazards stemming from wastes and from potential accidents in both biotechnology and nuclear energy, have held up countless projects in both fields. Though firms in these industries may be able to work with government and society to resolve these issues and pave the way for profitable developments, the front-runners may go bankrupt in the process, leaving the profits to later entrants. Many firms have, in fact, taken advantage of following front-runners into a field or market, as illustrated in The Inside View 6.3.

Technology as a Source of Threats While technology is seen as an opportunity to some organizations, those who do not have the research and development capabilities to develop innovative technologies on their own, who do not have the financial resources to implement new technologies developed elsewhere, or who are reluctant to undertake the cost and effort of changing consider technology a source of threats. The American steel industry is one example. Following World War II, when European and Japanese steel industries were being reconstructed with highly modern production facilities, U.S. manufacturers continued to use blast furnaces dating back to the early 1900s. During the 1950s and 1960s, competition increased but did not become a critical threat to U.S. producers because the global demand for steel exceeded global production. Finally, during the 1970s, worldwide steel-making capacity surpassed the demand for steel. The price of the most efficient manufacturers dropped and began to

The Advantages of Coming in Second

The proliferation of fast-food businesses shows that the number 2s and number 3s in a market can do quite well if they can identify a niche that the number 1 company has not filled.

Being second into a market can be both advantageous and profitable, according to Peter J. Flatow, president of Brain Reserve, New York. He said that since many companies cannot always be first, they have to develop appropriate strategies for being a strong second- or third-place contender. Speaking in 1986, Flatow said that following a pioneer into the marketplace demands innovation—a key component for winning at the bank.

"There are discontinuities between the market as it could be and as it is created by No. 1," Flatow said. "The second entry has to locate these opportunity gaps—a task which requires considerable ingenuity.

"First, a new market has been identified which we can more fully exploit. Second, we can identify the chinks in No. 1's armor and exploit them. Third, the No. 1 entrant has deployed its funds to educate the consumer about a new idea, allowing us to deploy our funds to build consumer identification around our specific brand."

While No. 1 is off establishing the category or segment, it is forced almost by definition to be everything to everybody, Flatow said. Because the waters have already been charted, second entrants have the opportunity to modify the idea, give it better definition, effectively develop a more profitable business, take greater risks, and be more innovative.

He said the pioneer plays the critical role in identifying or creating the market, but that all too often, later entrants are designated as "me toos," while only the pioneer is thought of as the innovator. Using fast-food "burger wars" as an example, Flatow pointed out that although McDonald's developed the fast hamburger, Burger King fulfilled a specific consumer need with the "Have It Your Way" campaign, and by flame broiling instead of frying.

"This is a case of No. 2 saying, 'Okay, big guy, thanks for the great idea, but you missed the point,'" he said. "People don't just want fast food; they want real food, fast. The product created by the lead company cannot be equated with the real market opportunities. It is only a signpost." ■

Source: "No. 2 Can Be More Innovative than the Forerunner," *Marketing News,* November 21, 1986, p. 17.

draw sales away from the least efficient producers. Japanese and European manufacturers reaped the benefit of modern, low-cost steel manufacturing facilities, whereas American companies paid the price of antiquated plants. The technological advantages of the foreign steel manufacturers translated into serious cost and profit problems for U.S. manufacturers.

Polaroid is another example. For many years, the Polaroid Corporation was known only for its instant photography, holding exclusive patents on the technology. Despite the growth of the photography market during the 1970s and the increasing demand for 35-millimeter cameras, Polaroid failed to develop other photographic products. The company continued to offer new and advanced forms of instant photography while many amateur photographers remained convinced that instant photography was not "serious" photography. Eastman Kodak responded to market demands for more sophisticated, automated 35-millimeter photography equipment. For Polaroid, the popular identification with a single technology, instant photography, proved to be a strategic weakness. When Polaroid's exclusive rights to instant photography technology expired, they had neither a unique product others could not produce nor a variety of products with which to compete against others.

Strategic Responses to Technological Changes

The general manager responsible for shaping an organization's strategy must certainly be aware of the nature and types of technological change—in terms of both products and processes—that could affect the company's business.[9] One way of keeping track of such changes is to remain informed about investments in research and development related to the industry. In general, there are three main sources of research and development investment capable of generating technological change. First, there is commercial research and development, much of which is reported by companies in financial documents required by the government and available to the public. Second, there is government-sponsored research, especially basic research capable of producing revolutionary changes, that is reported in scientific and industry journals. Third, there is university research, such as the shrimp mariculture program being conducted at Texas A&M University, some of which is either industry- or government-financed. Each of these sources of technical research is likely to spark technological development and change. Thus, it remains an important job of the general manager to track such changes and assess their effects on the organization.

COMPETITIVE FACTORS

The third factor strategic planners must consider, in addition to technology and economic factors, is competitive forces. The most basic competitive forces are the going price of a good or service and the demand for it. What is the organization charging? Are customers willing to pay that amount? Can they get the same product or service from someone else cheaper? Overall, the relationship between price and demand is inverse; that is, as the price for an item increases, fewer people will be willing or able to buy it. Consider the fresh-shrimp market described in the preview case. Shrimp is a desirable product but not at all prices. When the price of shrimp is $5 per pound, for example, fewer people will purchase it than if the price is $4 per pound. At $2 per pound, even more people will be able to buy it. The implication is clear: If an organization wants to increase sales of a given product, it can do so by lowering the price. This principle applies to virtually all products, ranging from shrimp to candy bars, mortgages to automobiles, and shampoo to college textbooks.[10]

Of course if businesses were interested only in the quantity of units sold, we could expect to see rock-bottom prices for all things at all times. Obviously, that is not the case. The willingness of producers and sellers to deliver a good or service is dependent on their ability to make money. Shrimp farming is a relatively new industry: the number of "players" willing to join the "game" will depend on how much money they expect to make. That is, if the difference between what it costs to produce the good and what it sells for is large enough, many players will be lured to the market. Assume, for example, that the selling price of shrimp is $2 per pound. Few organizations will be willing to supply shrimp because they cannot produce it for less than $2. Only the most efficient companies using the most efficient techniques will produce shrimp. If the price of shrimp is $50 a pound, many organizations, even the most inefficient, will be willing to supply shrimp because they can profit from doing so. Likewise, those already producing shrimp will be willing to invest in even more facilities and technology to increase production.

By looking at both the demand and the supply for a product simultaneously, managers can predict how many pounds of shrimp can actually be sold at particular prices. Managers will be willing to sell at a price that allows the company to make a profit. The lower they make the price, the more consumers are willing to buy, but the smaller the profit per item sold.

Notice that the manager has three very distinct tasks in designing a strategy for selling shrimp. First, there is the task of analyzing internal costs of production to determine how much it will cost to produce various quantities of shrimp. Second, the manager must anticipate consumer demand and the willingness of buyers to purchase at various prices. Third, the manager must anticipate and take into account what other sellers will do; they may be able and willing to offer the product at a lower price.

Strategic Responses to Competitive Forces

A *market* consists of a group of buyers and sellers who interact with one another in order to exchange goods or services at a price each believes is acceptable. Understanding other buyers and sellers and the market they create is critical to a successful strategy. Sellers must know their customers, present and potential, and must know how to keep them and win them. Similarly, smart buyers must analyze the market to know who is selling the product, at what price, and on what terms. The number and type of buyers and sellers in a market determine the nature of competition.[11]

In the petroleum industry, for example, there are relatively few producers but many buyers for a limited quantity of oil. The major oil producers, therefore, are more powerful than their customers, and they are able to set prices, delivery schedules, and rates of production as they choose. Therefore, the oil producers must be more concerned with what their few competitors are doing than with what their many customers are doing. Farmers, on the other hand, are relatively numerous and control relatively small quantities of produce. Their customers (food processors) have much greater market power because they buy in large quantities and can fix the prices, delivery, and production schedules more effectively than the farmers. Farmers, therefore, need not be significantly concerned with how much grain a neighboring farmer is producing but must keep very close track of how much grain is being produced nationwide and what prices the large food processors are paying for the crops.

Basic Market Strategies

With an understanding of the market, managers can adapt their basic strategies to the competitive context of the environment. Any strategy must take into account what other firms in similar and related industries are doing. An organization may have an outstanding product, but if it is developed after similar products of competitors are already available, the organization may not be able to attract buyers away from the other products. The market may be too crowded. Exhibit 6.5 shows how the basic generic strategies of a business can be reformulated to consider the competition.

To achieve success against competitors, firms typically adopt one of four approaches: market penetration, market development, product development, and diversification.

Market Penetration   Market penetration refers to a business's commitment to expand sales or revenues from its current customer base, utilizing the same product. Managers can increase sales, as discussed above, by changing prices, offering special promotions (e.g., coupons), and increasing product advertising. Each of these actions is designed to help the company further penetrate the market it currently sells in, that is, get a larger share of the existing market for the particular product.

EXHIBIT / 6.5
Four Basic Market Strategies

	Products	
	Current	**New**
Customers Current	Market penetration	Product development
Customers New	Market development	Diversification

Market penetration:	Achieving more sales per capita; accomplished through changed prices, more advertising, aggressive promotion
Market development:	Finding and researching new customers for the same product; geographic expansion into new regions, territories, or countries; international sales
Product development:	Bringing new products to the attention of current customers; offering "new and improved" products
Diversification:	Using current knowledge to develop new products suitable for sale to new kinds of customers

Market Development   Market development is a strategy whereby the company continues to sell the same product but tries to find new customers for that product. For example, a local company operating in the upper Midwest may produce a meat sausage that is well known in that region. Market development would call for the company to expand sales activities to new geographic areas—for instance, the southeastern United States—until it reached a national or even international market. The essence of the market development strategy is the aggressive search for new customers who would be attracted to, and benefit from, the purchase of the company's present products.

Product Development   Even organizations with a well-developed base of customers find these customers may be induced to try new brands. In such instances, management may seek to preserve the current customer base by bringing out an improved version of the company's product. Thus, in the soap business, it is not surprising to see advertising claiming that Soap X is now "new and improved." Some years ago, Colgate toothpaste was changed into a "winterfresh gel" form, and many customers switched from the old toothpaste to the new gel. Of course, many users of other toothpastes were also induced to try the new gel formula and become Colgate customers.

In general, product development strategies assume that the company can reach its current base of customers and induce them to buy the new products it has developed. Product development is, in fact, one of the most reliable ways of preserving and expanding a company's market share in an industry.

Diversification   Diversification is based on the assumption that the company can develop and sell new products to new customers. This strategy does not require abandoning the company's original business. A company may believe that it knows how to reach a particular customer audience but will need a new product to do so. In the early 1970s, for example, the Gerber Products Company, makers of the well-known Gerber baby foods, saw that the birth rate was relatively flat and that baby food sales would be leveling off. By recognizing that they could easily reach the parents of young children, however, Gerber management knew it could sell new products to the parents of the children who ate baby food. The company diversified its sales by acquiring a manufacturer of vaporizers, an insurance company that sold life insurance on children to their parents, and a manufacturer of rubber pants that babies wear over diapers. The strategy of selling diversified products to the parents of children worked very well for Gerber.

You recall that we discussed diversification also as a strategic response to economic fluctuations. In that context, to diversify as a business referred to operating several different businesses that reacted differently to fluctuations in the economy. The ideal result is that one or some units of the organization will always be performing well, though others may be suffering the effects of an economic shift. This is diversification as an economic strategy. Diversification as a competitive strategy, on the other hand, refers to the production of a variety of products or services that can be sold to customers the organization already has.

Portfolio Management

An important concern of management in changing environments is stabilizing revenues and profits in ways that minimize the year-to-year variations while at the same time increasing earnings through innovation and exploitation of new mar-

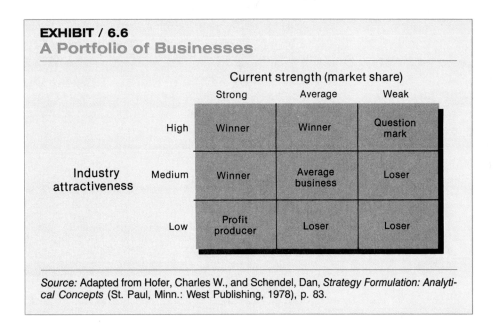

EXHIBIT / 6.6
A Portfolio of Businesses

Current strength (market share)

		Strong	Average	Weak
	High	Winner	Winner	Question mark
Industry attractiveness	Medium	Winner	Average business	Loser
	Low	Profit producer	Loser	Loser

Source: Adapted from Hofer, Charles W., and Schendel, Dan, *Strategy Formulation: Analytical Concepts* (St. Paul, Minn.: West Publishing, 1978), p. 83.

Portfolio A group of products, businesses, or companies assembled to achieve stability and growth.

kets. One way to obtain stability is to have many products and services that serve different markets and are at different stages of development. When one product is selling well, the money it makes can be taken to develop new products. When products and services sold in one market are not selling well, emphasis can be shifted to products in other markets. This is a portfolio approach, similar to a diversification strategy that could be used to protect an organization against fluctuations in the economy. Simply stated, a **portfolio** is a group of products, businesses, or even companies that is assembled for the purpose of achieving the twin goals of stability and growth.

Exhibit 6.6 provides a popular illustration of a portfolio. The horizontal axis represents the company's current market share (current strength); the vertical axis represents the outlook for the business in terms of overall industry growth (industry attractiveness). The various products can be analyzed in the matrix to assess them individually and show how they relate to each other. The best position for a company, of course, is to have products with a strong market share in an industry that is highly attractive. But even a small market share in a rapidly growing (attractive) industry may be acceptable if a strategy can be designed to help the organization expand its share as the industry grows. A company may take the cash generated by a profitable product and invest it in products that are struggling. The references to "winners" and "losers" should be clear. Obviously, a company would like to have all winners and no losers, but that is rarely the situation. Managers have to make careful decisions about how to balance all of the considerations relevant to a portfolio decision.

Business consultants have adopted colorful names to refer to the various positions: cash cows, dogs, question marks, and stars. (See Exhibit 6.7.)

Cash Cows Products and services that generate large amounts of cash. Typically, they are more mature products that the organization can produce very efficiently and that have a large share of a fairly stable market. They provide a predictable flow of cash to invest in other areas of the organization.

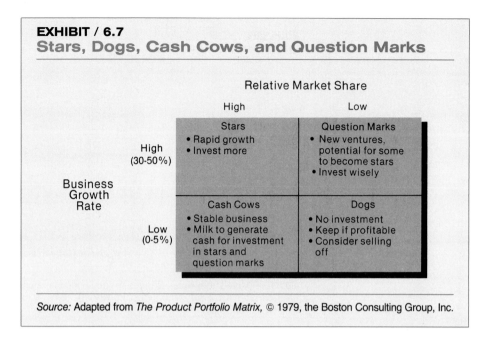

EXHIBIT / 6.7
Stars, Dogs, Cash Cows, and Question Marks

Relative Market Share

	High	Low
Business Growth Rate — High (30-50%)	**Stars** • Rapid growth • Invest more	**Question Marks** • New ventures, potential for some to become stars • Invest wisely
Business Growth Rate — Low (0-5%)	**Cash Cows** • Stable business • Milk to generate cash for investment in stars and question marks	**Dogs** • No investment • Keep if profitable • Consider selling off

Source: Adapted from *The Product Portfolio Matrix,* © 1979, the Boston Consulting Group, Inc.

Dogs   Products and services that have a low share of a stable or slowly growing market. They do not generate much cash nor do organizations typically spend money advertising and pushing them.

Question Marks   Products or services with a low share of a growing market. Because the market is growing and competition is usually heavy, large amounts of money must be spent attempting to gain market share. Their low market share usually means low profits and little excess cash being generated.

Stars   Products that have a high share of a fast-growing market. Because the market is expanding, investments must be made to increase production capability, make the organization efficient, and maintain and expand market share.

Once the positions of the various products have been identified, how they support and relate to each other can be analyzed. Cash generated by the cash cow can be used to develop new products or increase the market share of current products. Dogs can be discontinued and replaced with higher-potential products.

It is also possible, using the matrix, to anticipate and identify what should be done to maintain a healthy portfolio in the future. For example, if the market will be growing in the future, something must be done to maintain market share and prevent, for example, a cash cow from turning into a question mark. Money can be invested in question marks to increase their market share and move them to a star position. If competition is increasing, something must be done to protect market share so that cash cows do not become dogs and stars do not become question marks.

Portfolio analysis generally implies that money should be invested in areas where there are large potential payoffs. Many managers tend to overinvest in stable, productive areas—in products or services that are already doing as well as they should, or products and services that have already reached their peaks in terms of demand and sales. On the other hand, some managers tend to continue investing in failing products due to emotional attachments or a sunk-cost rationale. Rather than cut losses and get on to something new, an attachment or unfailing belief in the product (especially if it is a product the manager developed) causes the manager to believe that with just a little more cash, the product can be saved.

Choosing a Strategy

As outlined above, an organization can choose from several basic strategies or design a combination of competitive strategies to accomplish its goals and objectives. Each has merits and will be more or less effective for different organizations in different competitive situations. Michael E. Porter, a leading theorist in competitive strategy, argues that the state of competition in an industry depends on five basic forces: the ease or difficulty with which outsiders can enter the competitive field, the bargaining power of suppliers, the bargaining power of buyers, the availability and quality of substitute products or services, and the intensity of the rivalry among industry competitors.[12] (See Exhibit 6.8.) If a manager can understand all of these forces and the direction in or degree to which they are changing, he or she can position the organization most effectively within the competitive environment. "The strategist's goal," Porter argues, "is to find a position in the industry where his or her company can best defend itself against these forces or can influence them in its favor."[13]

The Threat of Entry   One aspect of the competitive environment a strategist must understand in order to select the appropriate competitive strategy is the number and strength of barriers to entry into the field. Companies seeking to

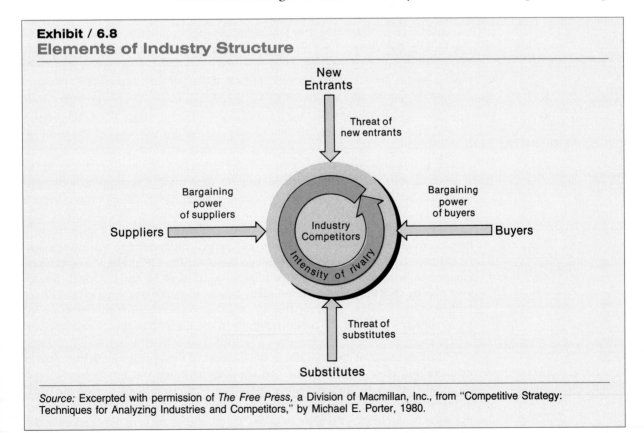

Exhibit / 6.8
Elements of Industry Structure

New Entrants

Threat of new entrants

Bargaining power of suppliers

Suppliers

Industry Competitors

Intensity of rivalry

Bargaining power of buyers

Buyers

Threat of substitutes

Substitutes

Source: Excerpted with permission of *The Free Press,* a Division of Macmillan, Inc., from "Competitive Strategy: Techniques for Analyzing Industries and Competitors," by Michael E. Porter, 1980.

enter a market or industry may be prevented from doing so for a number of reasons: Established firms may have significant advantages over new entrants in terms of research, marketing, service, and production capabilities; they may enjoy brand loyalty; they may have entered the industry at its inception, before costs and scale of operation were prohibitive (such as capital requirements for entering the automobile industry); they may have temporary but exclusive rights to internally developed technologies or exclusive relationships with one or more of a limited number of suppliers or buyers; or the government policy may restrict entry to an industry with licensing requirements and prohibitive regulations. Limited or weak barriers to entry make it possible for new entrants to enter easily. This is a threat to existing competitors but an opportunity to new entrants.

Powerful Suppliers and Buyers   Strategists must also consider the power of suppliers and buyers in an industry. By raising prices, a powerful supplier group (a group dominated by a few firms that offer unique products) can reduce the profit margins of the producers who depend on their products. A powerful buyer group (a group that purchases standard, widely available products in large volume and is not dependent on one supplier), by refusing to pay high prices or by demanding quality, can play competitors against each other and thereby lower profits in its industry. A strategist must understand the power of buyers and suppliers in a competitive market relative to each other and must know where his or her own company fits.

Substitute Products   The availability of substitute products or services limits the ability of members of a competitive group to raise prices. Above a certain price level, customers will turn to the substitute. The more attractive or adequate the substitute products are, the less members of a competitive field are able to manipulate the market. For example, though demand for insulation materials soared in the mid-1970s, makers of fiberglass insulation were prohibited from raising prices substantially because numerous substitute insulators (cellulose, rock wool, Styrofoam) were available.

Jockeying for Position   Finally, strategists must understand how heated the competition is within a given field in order to determine the best market strategy. When there are numerous competitors in a slowly growing industry of undifferentiated products or services, competition is likely to be the most heated. In these situations, strategists might be wise to determine a strategy that circumvents the battle so that resources are not wasted primarily on fighting competitors.

Once strategic planners have assessed the relative strengths of each force— barriers to entry, suppliers' power, buyers' power, availability of substitutes, and intensity of rivalry—and have determined the company's position, they can more effectively determine a successful competitive strategy for the company. Strategists may be able to position the company against the strongest competitive force, influence the balance of forces through strategic moves and therefore improve the company's position, or anticipate shifts in the balance of forces and respond to them.

Ultimately, to plan strategically in the context of the operating environment, a manager will have to understand and allow for competitive, technological, and economic factors. By understanding the influence these factors have on the organization, and by understanding in what ways and how quickly the factors change, the effective strategic planner can position the organization to succeed over the long term.

KEY POINTS

1 Each phase in the strategic planning process must be conducted with a consideration of environmental factors. The mission depends on environmental possibilities; analysis must be continuous due to an ever-changing environment; development and selection of options depends not on single factors but on the interplay between them as they all change; and implementation and monitoring are not only ongoing but subject to constant revision as environmental factors change and affect the performance of the strategy.

2 An organization's operating environment consists of economic, technological, and competitive forces that immediately and directly affect the organization. The general environment consists of social, legal, ethical, and political forces that indirectly affect the organization.

3 The degree of complexity in an organization's operating environment refers to the number of forces or influences an organization must attend. The rate of change refers to the speed or frequency with which these forces change. These influences do not necessarily act in unison. An organization may operate in a highly complex, slowly changing environment—though this is rare—or a rapidly changing environment that is not highly complex.

4 Swings in the economy, such as the ups and downs of a typical business cycle, provide threats and opportunities to organizations and thus strongly affect the performance of existing strategic plans and options for new ones. To respond to these influences, managers can anticipate change, can help the organization cope, and can diversify into different sectors of the economy to be protected from the poor performance of one sector.

5 Technologies are the tools organizations apply to operations to get things done more quickly, more easily, or more efficiently. Technology can be a great source of opportunity to grow, increase profits, or gain a larger share of a market. To those who do not or cannot purchase or develop new technologies, technology is seen as a source of threats and can cause both cost-ineffectiveness and product obsolescence.

6 Because technological developments can provide both opportunities and threats, managers should continuously survey the environment to remain aware of technological developments in three areas: commercial, government-sponsored, and university research.

7 The most basic competitive forces are the price and demand for goods and services. Overall, the relationship between price and demand is inverse; that is, as the price for an item increases, fewer people will be willing or able to buy it.

8 Four basic market strategies are market penetration, market development, product development, and diversification. Market penetration is an expansion of sales from a current customer base. Market development is a strategy of finding new customers in different areas to buy the same product. Product development refers to improving a product or service to preserve or expand an existing customer base. Diversification is a strategy of designing new but related products to sell to customers already buying the company's other products regularly.

9 A portfolio is a group of products, businesses, or even companies that is assembled for the purpose of achieving the twin goals of stability and growth.

10 A strategist must understand five basic competitive forces to position the organization to defend itself against them or influence them in its favor: the ease or difficulty with which outsiders can enter the competitive field, the bargaining power of suppliers, the bargaining power of buyers, the availability and quality of substitute products and services, and the intensity of the rivalry among industry competitors.

FOR DISCUSSION AND REVIEW

1. Look in the latest business periodicals and search for references concerning the shrimp farms in the opening case. Have any gone bankrupt or made a significant profit? What caused the results?

2. Your paper company in Pennsylvania has one-third of the market in the western half of the state. You want to diversify or expand into other geographical areas. What environmental factors might affect your success with either strategy, and what would you do about them?

3. Think of a company whose overall strategy or specific objective in one area has failed or is not succeeding. Of the environmental factors, which contributed most to its decline?

4. *Fortune* regularly makes economic predictions. What are some changes in store for the immediate and long-term future? Write recommendations for an organization in one of the soon-to-be-affected industries to combat or respond to these changes.

5. For each of the three sets of factors in the operating environment, give an industry-related example and tell why it is important.

6. Basic market and competitive forces are closely related to supply and demand. But supply and demand differ greatly for different items. In terms of profits to be made in the short or long run, how do competitive forces affect the production and sales of (a) pet rocks, (b) toilet paper, (c) shrimp?

7. Give an example of a cash cow, dog, wildcat, and star, according to the explanation in the text.
8. If you were choosing a house and a place to live right now, what factors would influence your pur-

chase? What role would the following factors play: (a) competition, (b) supply, (c) development of local area, (d) nearby towns and cities, (e) supply and quality of services?

KEY TERMS

Competitive factors	Environment	Portfolio	Technological factors
Degree of complexity	General environment	Rate of change	Technology
Economic factors	Operating environment		

THE CONFERENCE TABLE: DISCUSSION CASE / 6.1

Timex Timing

The watch continues to be a fashion item as well as a timepiece. Nicholas Hayek, chairman of Swatch, displays the range of watches which is making Swatch a formidable competitor to Timex.

In 1942, in the midst of World War II, Norwegian immigrant Joakim Lehmkuhl came up with an idea to turn a bankrupt company into a profitable enterprise by altering its capabilities to meet a market need. Seeing the need for bomb fuse timers, he and a group of businessmen acquired a majority interest in Connecticut's Waterbury Clock Company and converted it to fuse production. With Lehmkuhl as its president, the company quickly became the nation's largest producer of fuses.

But then the war ended. In 1945, sales dropped from $70 million to $300,000, easily one of the largest drops in the history of organized production. Lehmkuhl's only option was to convert the company back to watchmaking, but inflated costs made it economically unfeasible to manufacture the $1 Ingersoll watch that the company had produced before the war. Meanwhile, the Swiss were flooding the market with relatively inexpensive imports. Lehmkuhl's solution was to combine the precision tooling techniques designed to make fuse timers with a high degree of mechanization and to mass-produce high-quality watches.

Sources: This case was written by M. R. Poirier, based on the following sources: Tully, Shawn, "The Swiss Put Glitz in Cheap Quartz Watches," *Fortune,* August 20, 1984, p. 102; "Swatch's Bold Look Expands," *New York Times,* July 12, 1986, pp. 33, 44; "Sweet Success," *The Economist,* January 19, 1985, p. 71; Annual reports, Timex Corporation; Knickerbocker, F. T., "Timex Corporation" (#373-080), Harvard Business School Publishing, 1972; "A Time Bomb for Watchmakers," *Business Week,* November 16, 1963.

By 1949, Waterbury's engineers had succeeded in designing a simple watch mechanism, substituting a new alloy developed during the war (Armalloy) for jewels in the movement. This made the watch, according to the company, equal to jeweled-lever models and superior to the pin-lever models available at that time. Meanwhile, Lehmkuhl changed the name of the company to United States Time, changed the name of the watch from Ingersoll to Timex, and prepared to introduce his new product on the market.

The first Timexes out, in 1950, were men's watches designed to retail for between $7 and $8. Simple, tasteful, and modernistic, they represented an innovation in the low-priced watch market. Throughout the 1950s, new lines and variations were added: First came sweeping second hands, then shockproof, waterproof, and antimagnetic watches. In 1954, calendar and self-winding watches were added, and in 1958, a whole line of women's watches was developed. The company sold them with the pitch that a woman should have a wardrobe of watches, one for every occasion—dress, sports, general use—with the whole set for less than $50. By 1960, the company claimed it had attained more than 36 percent of the under-$50 women's watch market.

Timex had rebounded from virtual financial disaster in the mid-1940s with a very simple strategy: Make watches an everyday item, not just a seasonal-gift item, and make one for every personality, purpose, and purse. Having designed the product, they then set about reaching the market. In doing so, they violated almost all of the conservative practices in the watch business at the time.

Jewelers, not surprisingly, were not interested in distributing the low-cost watches. They could only expect a 30 percent margin on Timexes and easily made a 50 percent margin on their regular, higher-priced stock. So Timex took its wares to the highest-traffic outlets they could find: drugstores, hardware stores, and tobacco stores. At its high point, Timex was sold through 250,000 retail accounts. Early on, 80 percent of sales came from drugstores. To convince retailers to sell their lines, Timex salespersons relied almost completely on dramatic presentation, also unheard of in the watch business. They slammed watches against walls and dropped them into buckets of water and generally abused them until the owner agreed to sell them in his store.

In one decade, between 1950 and 1960, Timex sales went from zero to seven million annually. In 1962, it was estimated that one out of every three watches sold in the country was a Timex. Timex had captured the low-cost market, wrists down. The competition was essentially forced to stick to expensive, gift season watches, watches in the $30–$300 ranges. Those who tried to break into Timex's domain failed through lack of effective mass production and distribution systems. Without those, competitive (and very expensive) advertising campaigns made no sense. Although Timex had reshaped the watch industry and reaped most of the benefits of doing so, by the mid 1980s several players were now poised to grab a piece of the action.

Swatch watches, $30 plastic fashion accessories that happen to tell time, represented the most significant, if ironic, challenge. Having lost 21 percent of their 30 percent market share between 1974 and 1984, due mostly to Japan's dominance in the quartz watch market, the Swiss were looking for a way to get back into the market. So, just as Timex nosed out the Swiss by cleverly focusing on a market niche, the Swiss came full circle in 1983 with the Swatch watch, a more sporty, more fashionable time piece. Currently, there are over 140 models, in every imaginable color and pattern. Where Timex attempted to sell each person a watch for each activity, Swatch wants to sell each person a watch for every outfit.

The average buyer owns three, and probably wears them all at once.

Meanwhile, Swatch has developed a revolutionary manufacturing process. While most Japanese producers need three operations to manufacture watches (to Timex's original six), Swatches roll off a single assembly line. Robots insert all the parts into the plastic cases, and lasers seal the crystals. Swatches have only 51 parts (to Timex's original 98), far fewer than any current quartz watch. Manufacturing costs are "spectacularly low," says *Fortune* magazine, "labor minimal. Understandably, the technology is a closely guarded secret."

In the late-1980s, while Timex still sold more watches in the $10 to $50 market than all other brands combined, threats were appearing on the horizon. Swatch, for one, introduced a line of junior apparel to go with its watches. Other low-cost, high-fashion watches can be expected to come out of the woodwork to take advantage of yet another watch market: timepieces as fashion accessories. ■

DISCUSSION QUESTIONS

1. Describe Timex's operating environment in the 1950s and in the 1980s. How were economic, technological, and competitive factors interacting in each decade?
2. What threats and opportunities have existed over the course of the past three decades? Who has taken advantage of the opportunities, and who has lost to the threats?
3. Faced with the latest competitive pressures, what would you recommend Timex do? What should the makers of Swatches do? If both companies follow your advice, what will the outcome be?

THE CONFERENCE TABLE: DISCUSSION CASE / 6.2

Hitch Your Wagon to a Supercomputer

Seymour Cray had one goal in life: to design and build the world's fastest and most powerful computer. He frequently took time off from his job as a computer designer for Control Data Corporation (CDC) in Minneapolis and locked himself in his lakeside cabin in Wisconsin to scribble, dabble, and dream. It was at CDC, in the 1960s, that Cray developed the first practical supercomputer. It was a slow evolution: First germanium transmitters replaced vacuum tubes to increase speed, then Cray replaced the germanium transmitters themselves with silicon transistors, then further developments were added. CDC's 7600 model supercomputer was the result. Introduced in 1969, it pushed CDC into first position in its field.

In the early 1970s, however, a merger brought on changes in CDC's strategy and future plans, most notably its refusal to fund Cray's research to develop a computer more powerful than the 7600. This prompted Cray to move on. With $500,000 of his own money, $500,000 from CDC's merger partner, and $1.5

Sources: This case was written by M. R. Poirier, based on the following sources: Goldstein, Mark L., "Piloting Cray Without Cray," *Industry Week,* January 20, 1986, pp. 55, 56; Goldstein, Mark L., "The Quest for the Next Super Computer," *Industry Week,* May 12, 1986, pp. 41–43; Gibson, Richard, "Control Data Posts First-Period Profit; Cray Net Rose 86%," *Wall Street Journal,* April 24, 1987, p. 7; Houston, Patrick, et al., "Where Three Sales a Year Make You a Superstar," *Business Week,* February 17, 1986, pp. 76, 77; Knowles, Anne, "A New Computer Breed Tackles a Super Gap," *Electronic Business,* November 1, 1985, pp. 46–58; Aquillar, F. S., "Cray Research, Inc." (#385-011), Harvard Business School Publishing, 1984.

Cray Computer has always had one goal in mind: to build the world's fastest and biggest computer.

million from 14 other investors, he founded Cray Research, Inc., in 1972. It was his company, and he would run it his way: One computer at a time would be produced, each one would be a supercomputer, and each would be priced to allow a margin for future research. Cray himself would be left entirely free to develop his next supercomputer.

Research and development activities were carried out at breakneck speed, and although an additional $6.1 million in private financing was raised in the next three years, all the seed money ran out by the time the Cray-1 was ready to be introduced in 1976. John Rollwagon, a financial officer who had only been with Cray since 1975, was put in charge of fund-raising. He arranged a stock offering in March 1976. Despite the fact that the company had no sales, no earnings, a worldwide projected market of 80 customers, and a $2.4 million deficit that would be growing in the near future, Wall Street bought in. The offering raised $10 million. The first Cray-1, five times more powerful than CDC's 7600, was installed one month later on a trial basis at a government research lab in the Southwest.

Cray's first real sale, one and a half years later, was for over $8.8 million, and it finally pulled the company out of the red. The following three years were a boom: Cray sold five supercomputers in 1978, five in 1979, and nine in 1980. By 1981, 35 Cray systems ranging in price between $4 million and $17 million had been installed, revenues had topped $100 million, and Cray had resigned and contracted himself out to his own company to devote himself fully to research. The Cray-2 was on the drawing table. It would perform 500 million to 1 billion calculations per second, would be six to ten times more powerful than the Cray-1, and would be one-third the size. In 1983, the X-MP was introduced. Developed by one of Cray's researchers, it utilized technology even more advanced than miniaturization, and it was three to five times as powerful as the existing Cray models. By this time, Cray was solidly in the number one position in the very narrow supercomputer market, having knocked out CDC with the Cray-1 in the mid-1970s.

But growth brought with it problems. Public ownership, which had been necessary to keep the fledgling enterprise afloat, brought pressure for growth in earnings. This could only be achieved by serving a broader market than 80 or so high-powered scientific laboratories. Cray had to branch out into the industrial market, but this required shifts in research and production focus. While laboratories were more interested in hardware and raw power, which Cray was uniquely equipped to provide, industrial clients were more interested in software, service, and price.

Meanwhile, competition in the supercomputer field was beginning to perk up. Though 100 of the 150 supercomputers installed worldwide in the spring of 1986 were Cray's, the company's position was being threatened. In 1982, CDC Chairman William Norris founded the Microelectronic and Computer Technology Corporation, a nonprofit research and development organization based in Austin, Texas. Any company that wished to join would have to donate research talent for four years and fund the research. In return, the member companies would have the right to use the results. The corporation started with a roster of 11 companies and a budget of $75 million in 1983. By 1984 in Japan, $100 million was being invested in a supercomputer development project and $500 million in an artificial-intelligence project. The Pentagon requested $1 billion that same year to counter the Japanese on both fronts.

Meanwhile, corporations were scurrying to grab a piece of the high-dollar contracts market. ETA Systems sold three supercomputers by 1987 that were six times faster than the existing Cray models but no more expensive. IBM, Alliant Computer Systems Corp., Convex Computers, Inc., and a number of other manufacturers are also offering so-called Baby-Crays or Crayettes, minisupercomputers that are less powerful but more affordable and that are designed for a much larger market. These smaller firms have been able to increase demand without engaging in tough market share battles. Yet it seems that these "Baby-Crays" have only whetted the appetites of computer users for bigger, more powerful machines. New uses have been found for supercomputers by businesses such as banks, pharmaceutical companies, and large insurance brokers. Where there once was a market of 80 potential users, now there are over 1000.

But with the increased demand has come increased competition. For example, in December 1988, one of its former star designers formed a company to cooperate with IBM to design new supercomputers. Competition was coming from both American and Japanese companies. One Japanese company, Fujitsu, announced a new supercomputer, the UP-2000, at the end of 1988, which it claimed would be faster than any other supercomputer available. Meanwhile, Cray Research released its fastest computer ever, the Cray III, in 1989. ■

1. What factors in Cray's operating, general, and international environments have affected the company, and in what way?
2. What opportunities and threats does technological development, inside and outside Cray Research, offer the company? What is your advice to Rollwagon? To Cray?
3. What competitive forces are now acting in the supercomputer industry? How has the competitive situation changed since Cray introduced the first supercomputer in 1969?

Comprehensive Case Two

The Big Store

Although Sears started out as a mail-order company, by the 1930s it had become primarily a company of retail outlets which carried brand-name products as well as its own house brands.

Most successful business enterprises identify a need in the market and find a way to satisfy it. For 23-year-old Richard Warren Sears, the need in rural Minnesota in 1886 was watches. People in those parts had been using the sun to tell time. Dick Sears sold them on the idea of gold-filled pocket watches, available at low cost through the mail. By the time he moved his budding business to Chicago and teamed up with watchmaker Alvah Curtis Roebuck, he was recognized as a retailing genius. By being able to get suspicious farmers to buy things they'd never heard of from a man they'd never even seen, he became a legend.

THE CATALOG EMPIRE

"Within a decade of the company's founding," as Donald R. Katz put it, "Sears's inflammatory prose had spawned a breadth of popular desire that could only be served by a carefully organized and disciplined enterprise." Sears's first partner, Alvah Roebuck, sold out for $25,000 in 1895. His second partner, Julius Rosenwald, felt that the company couldn't survive forever solely on the momentum created by Sears's literary talents, though the Sears catalog was said to be one of the only two books the rural midwesterners read. First he forced Sears to edit some of the more questionable items from his catalog (such as the electrified waist belt that promised to cure "impotency, emissions, losses, and drains," but instead cauterized many a farmer). Second he cut back expenditures as an economic slump set in in 1907. Rosenwald's lack of soapbox retailing finesse and his reliance on systems led Sears to believe that his own company had passed him by. He resigned in 1908, sold all his stock in 1913, and died the following year.

Rosenwald, leaning on the strength of the Sears name, implemented his own vision for the company. He considered the company so central to so many people's daily lives that he called it "the buyer for the American farmer." Indeed, under Rosenwald's guidance, Sears, Roebuck became a catalog empire. He developed a network of suppliers and storage and distribution facilities so large that the company became "an economy unto itself." Some claimed that Sears encompassed more of the basic functions of a capitalist economy than any company in the history of American business.

But Sears, Roebuck's success under Rosenwald was based on the fact that over half the nation's population at that time lived in rural areas, where catalog sales were always the strongest; by the 1920s, the shift to urban living was already in full swing. During this decade, Rosenwald turned over leadership of the company to yet another visionary. General Robert E.

Source: This case was written by M. R. Poirier, based on the following source: Katz, Donald R., *The Big Store* (New York: Viking Press, 1987).

Wood took over in 1922 just as the so-called golden age of the American catalog was coming to a close.

Wood took advantage of Rosenwald's legacy of trust and reliability and sought to turn the company into "the purchasing agent for the American people." Having studied population and economic trends, he saw the country's urban-oriented future in the declining agrarian economy and the increasing prominence of automobile transportation. Wood's plan for transforming the company to fit its new environment involved converting the regional mail-order plants established under Rosenwald into retail outlets. These would serve people in the growing urban and suburban areas by being readily accessible and well-stocked. By 1928, he had established 27 stores. In one more year, he had established 324. Retail sales surpassed catalog sales, for good, in 1932.

Under "the General," Sears became "one of the most powerful economic organizations of all time" by virtue of the business system he built into it. Though he retired as president in 1937, he stayed on as chairman formally until 1954 (he wandered the halls at the Chicago headquarters until his death in 1969); with his shift in title, the real executive power in the company transferred from the presidency to the chairmanship.

Wood's legacy transcended the economic growth and strength of the company. He established a revolutionary "democratic" system of management under which people could "speak their minds and still roam free." The loyalty the company commanded from its employees because of this system was the envy of corporations across industries. In addition, Wood considered centralized authority a disadvantage in the business. Therefore, he divided the company into five regional territories, headquartered in Los Angeles, Dallas, Atlanta, Chicago, and Philadelphia. By the mid-1950s, Sears Roebuck was considered a model for organizational management. "There is no better illustration of what a business is and what managing it means," wrote Peter Drucker of the company in *The Practice of Management* in 1954.

NUMBER ONE RETAILER IN THE UNITED STATES

Those were the days when managing a regional territory for Sears had all the allure of a swashbuckling adventure. Regional managers were all-powerful. Vice presidents developed their own administrative procedures, could structure their staffs any way they chose, could borrow money and design and build stores at will, and had complete discretion over the selection and pricing of goods. The home office in Chicago was nothing more than a figurehead or anchor; "corporate directives from Chicago were rewritten when they weren't thrown away."

In the early 1970s, construction was completed on the tallest building in the world: the Sears Tower in Chicago. The irony of this did not make itself plain immediately, but the company was soon feeling the effects of having reached its pinnacle. "Sears, Roebuck was singular in the history of enterprise in that in less than a century it had been founded and refounded by three charismatic business geniuses, any one of whom could have created a significant corporate empire." But in the time it took to build the Tower, the world the company had banked on for decades, literally and figuratively, had begun to pull away from it.

The term *market saturation*, until that time, was not in the vocabulary of anyone at Sears. But the fact was, Sears had done such an effective job of reaching the whole of the population that by the early 1970s, there just were not many people left who had not already acquired their first refrigerator, color television, or wall-to-wall carpeting from the company. And *competition*, another term no one had bandied about in prior decades, was also beginning to creep in. Sears was being challenged on two fronts. On one side, the shops in the malls that had grown up as virtual appendages to a Sears store now offered variety and prestige that lured customers away. On the other side, discount retailers such as K Mart began to offer standard goods at lower prices than Sears was then offering.

END OF THE GROWTH AND SUCCESS ERA

The year 1974 marked the end of the growth, growth, and more growth strategy that had characterized Sears's first nine decades. New stores were still opened at the rate of almost one per week into the 1960s, but returns from these stores began to slack off. Retail sales fell across the nation in early 1973, just before oil prices quadrupled and the country sank into a recession. In 1974, profits at Sears dropped by $170 million; sales that were projected to increase by 15 percent increased by less than 7 percent. Layoffs across regional territories ran anywhere from 1 to 10 percent. Arthur Wood (a personal favorite of General Wood, though no relation) replaced Gordon Metcalf as chairman in late 1972. As Wood looked at Sears, Roebuck in 1975, "he perceived the makings of a humiliating business failure and possibly a civil war that could destroy the company."

A NEW CONCEPT: PLANNING

In 1978, the company underwent yet another change in leadership; Ed Telling took over as chairman from Arthur Wood who reached mandatory retirement age. Telling's first two major moves in the fight to save the company were instituting a planning staff in the executive office and hiring one of McKinsey's best officers, Phil Purcell, to head it.

Planning was, until then, almost a foreign concept. "Most insiders believed profits came to Sears by virtue of the confluent skills of talented individuals. Planning was a practice of the faceless organizations to which Sears served as a monument in counterpoint. The deal was between an individual and history, and how a fellow got the profit out was his personal and private business." Thus, Phil Purcell's planning group, called 702-P to designate its place at the top of the executive tower, was installed. Telling's orders to personnel were to get Purcell the "brightest, farthest-thinking people we've got. I want him to have people who aren't afraid to think about things."

The new era of planning to be ushered in by Telling tripped as it left the starting block. Telling's plan was to turn the great buying power of Sears loose. Buyers were told to find the products America wanted and make the best deals they could with suppliers. Stores were told to slash prices and sell as much as possible. Initially, sales increases of 20 percent between the Septembers of 1986 and 1987 resulted. But as Christmas approached, buyers and sellers alike took the strategy to heart, the former buying everything in sight and the latter marking items down like never before in the history of the company. Sales of some items increased by 200 and 300 percent, and the number of markdown items on the floor increased by 75 percent. By the time the holiday rush was over, however, the lack of control over the plan proved highly damaging. In the space of a few months, Sears sold a year's worth of merchandise at less than the company had paid for it. Financial losses were staggering.

But Ed Telling saw beyond the losses to the significance of the process involved:

For the first time, Sears executives in an office in Chicago had done something that translated into specific, simultaneous action everywhere in the far-flung kingdoms and baronies. Millions of private decisions between factories, buyers, truckers, bankers, warehousers, salesmen, and a significant portion of all the active consumers in America had harmonized in response to a system.

Planning efforts from that time on were given the benefit of a doubt, though many failed to achieve their purposes initially. McKinsey & Company, for example, drew up a decision tree matrix, in attempt to identify the source and path of decisions, and a planning matrix, in attempt to have buyers identify which goods should be promoted and which discontinued. Employees, however, found it quite impossible to map the path of decisions in an organization that had never had a practicing, formal chain of authority. And the planning matrix was a complete failure. Only one buyer in the whole organization identified a product he had chosen for purchase that he thought should be discontinued.

IMPLEMENTING THE STRATEGY

Joe Moran, an experienced insider hired as head of merchandising, had another approach. He cut 50 planned product promotions, put a mandatory limit on the number of days an item could be on sale, and restricted markdowns to 20 percent off the regular price. These measures put substantial limits on many stores. They often sold goods at 20 percent off the regular price on a daily basis, and this would eliminate markdown discretion entirely for them. Moreover, across-the-board standards had never been implemented at Sears since "Richard Sears stopped buying all the goods himself. The freedom to buy, promote, and to cut prices to the stores at will was an inalienable prerogative of a Sears buyer, akin to his right to establish personal relationships and cut his own deals with the factories."

Though the plan did cut losses and increase profits per item sold, Sears's overall sales did not grow. During September of that year, while other retailers were reaping soaring sales increases, Sears was selling 32 percent fewer goods. But Moran had called his mandate the "Final Solution for 1978" and he did not "expect or require . . . any further changes except in the event of fire, brimstone, catastrophe, or acts of a less than benevolent God."

As the plan struggled forward, Moran clarified his ideas for the company and set them down in the "Headquarters Merchandising Plan" for the executive office. The truth was, despite all recent efforts to increase profits and market share, Sears had not increased its share of the general merchandising market since 1965 and "had instead whittled down profit margins and besmirched its venerable reputation as a place where the great silent majority got good value for their money." Of Sears, Moran said, "We reflect the world of Middle America . . . and we must all look on what we are and pronounce it good! And seek to extend it. And not be swayed from it by the attraction of other markets, no matter how enticing they might be."

Sears quite probably would have saved itself significant trouble if a broad mission statement had been clarified earlier. However, by the time Moran had put his down on paper, the lack of an overriding purpose had already taken its toll across the company, from finance to human resource management to sales.

The lack of any but purely financial control and monitoring mechanisms was at the heart of the problem. Traditionally, the only way Sears measured progress was by looking at sales, incomes, and profit figures. If they were up, things were good. If they were down, things were bad. The accountants in the Sears network, under this arrangement, had become the only check-and-balance mechanism against the otherwise autonomous regional managers. They were all-powerful, and the degree of animosity between them and the sales branches was significant.

By the time Sears ushered in a new president, Edward Brennan, in 1980, the crisis at Sears was at its peak. Sales at the end of 1979 were even lower than those of 1978, despite soaring inflation that would have boosted even nominal increases. Brennan's impression was that the restrictions instituted in 1978 were an overreaction that had "crippled the delicate mechanism by which goods are bought with inspiration, quickly distributed, priced with a slender margin of error, powerfully advertised, and gracefully purveyed." The previous process had been "held together by thread, trust, hair triggers, and countless egos," but the across-the-board restrictions that had succeeded in reining in the autonomous regional managers had also caused the company to lose "its spirit and its will."

Massive layoffs seemed imminent, suggestions that the company's credit card system (which cost $20

Sears Tower. On June 26, 1989, Edward Brennan told a press conference that after 102 years, Sears would be leaving Chicago for a site 35 miles northwest of the city. The landmark Sears Tower will no longer be the company's headquarters; Sears intends to sell the building.

million a week in debt service) be discontinued were made by a number of executives, and there was a consensus among the upper echelons that an investment in advertising would be the company's only hope. But Brennan felt that layoffs would only destroy what little was left of the company's energy, that terminating the credit card system would do more harm than good, and that an advertising binge, no matter how large, would not bring about a sales increase significant enough to turn the company around. Thus, he devised a compromise. Extensive layoffs were ruled out, the credit card system was ruled in, and a highly focused and moderately expensive advertising and promotion campaign was implemented through which buyers selected a small number of bargain items that could be shipped to the stores and sold immediately; inventory was to be kept at 10 percent.

Beyond these measures, however, Brennan knew that broad changes in the entire operating system and philosophy would be needed to guarantee the company's long-term survival. The planning system had to be made to work. The best remedial measures he could design would still leave the company as "so much less than the sum of its parts that it would fail." Brennan saw that "the path into the future was going to require brand new tracks."

These brand new tracks were laid over the course of the following decade, slowly and painfully. Shifts in thinking about the company—its structure, products, image, competition, customers, and operating environment—were required of everyone from one end of the organization to the other. Brennan knew, by 1980, that "the dream of imposing his planning system upon the entire society of merchants would require the most titanic selling job of his career."

COMPETING IN THE NEW ENVIRONMENT

The first step was the sales pitch: 1981 would be The Challenge Year. Items hand-picked by buyers to move quickly and increase profit-per-sale ratios would be called Challenge Items. The convention, at which the pitch would be made and the items introduced in August 1980 at the Chicago headquarters, would be called The Challenge Meeting. This call to arms, if Brennan pulled it off, would remind everyone that the lifeblood of Sears flowed from baby cribs, bench power tools, bathrobes, hacksaws, and pantyhose and would reunite the whole company behind a common purpose.

At the convention, Brennan explained how the competition and customers had changed. Malls and discount and specialty stores had taken firm and permanent hold of sections of the market that used to belong to Sears. The competition would never go away and would get worse. Sears, which had formerly thought it was hundreds of individual kingdoms, was really just "one big store" and would have to realize it immediately. Nobody could sit around waiting for "them" to solve the problems; "them" was everyone, and the problems were everyone's equal responsibility to solve. And beyond reassessing its vision of itself, Brennan reminded the assembled throng of hundreds of managers that the company "has many purposes. Some are social, some are economic, all are directed at serving the many publics that are dependent on us . . . almost one out of 10 Americans depends on us in whole or in part for their economic well-being."

The next step was to trim the ranks. As opposed as the Sears culture had been to centralized planning or directives from Chicago, it was even more opposed to layoffs. But the company would have to be run with significantly fewer people if it was to compete in this new environment. Thus, Brennan designed the company's first retirement incentive plan to reduce operating costs. The "Early Retirement Incentive Plan" had several purposes: It sought to reduce the overall number of employees while increasing advancement opportunities for younger people, allowing Sears to demonstrate its commitment to affirmative action, and minimizing the necessity for mandatory layoffs. Almost 1500 executives took advantage of the offer by the end of 1980, at a cost of $77 million to the company.

By the end of 1983, the company had 100,000 fewer employees than it had when Brennan took over. The five territories were reduced to four, the number of distribution warehouses was cut to almost half the 1980 level of 110, and the number of freight carriers hauling Sears merchandise was reduced from over 4000 in 1980 to 210. The costs of running Sears, with cuts and consolidations, were about one-third the level predicted in 1980. "But the best thing about slimming down the Merchant," Brennan said of his company, "was that it was bringing the organization into contact with the state of the real working economy for the first time in years."

Meanwhile, various plans for reorganizing the company were under way. On the first day of 1981, after 1500 senior executives left the company, it was reorganized into three groups: the Seraco Real Estate Group, the Allstate Insurance Group, and the Sears Merchandise Group. By the mid-1970s, internal statistics indicated that the company's domination of American merchandising had peaked in 1969 and that there were simply too many new stores to allow Sears to grow. By the end of the 1970s, 75 percent of Sears's profits came from services (installation, credit extension, insurance), while in prior decades 80 to 90 percent of the profits had come from the sale of goods.

Brennan wanted Sears to diversify even further. He suggested that Sears become "The Great American Company" by acquiring another business; suggestions to acquire everything from fast-food chains to brokerage houses to movie studios were given serious consideration. Many of the suggestions, however, were doomed from the start: Telling's mandate that "We're just not gonna have anything to do with food or manure" ruled out acquiring the Wendy's fast-food chain and various other enterprises. John Deere, the farm machinery manufacturer, appeared ready to fight any acquisition attempt to the death. ABC and other movie studios were too tied to Hollywood and would pollute Sears's clean-cut, all-American image.

DIVERSIFYING INTO FINANCIAL SERVICES

But financial services was a field Sears was almost built for. Just after Sears's 1980 shareholders' meeting, a national polling organization released a report that placed Sears atop the list of most trusted American corporations. The planning staff was reaching a powerful consensus that "there could be no area of the economy in which the 'trust quotient' was more eminently exploitable . . . than in the organized act of storing and caring for people's money." Richard Sears himself had laid the groundwork for this strategy in 1899, when he offered his customers checking and savings services. Mail-order customers, when they were not inclined to buy, could receive 5 percent interest on their money; this was so Sears could still earn money and keep people involved with the store until they felt like buying again. But the final arguments for diversifying into financial services came from the economy: The savings industry was predicted in 1980 to grow by 15 percent per annum, while consumer spending was not expected to grow by more than 9 percent.

Ed Telling told the board of directors in May 1981 that he wanted to move Sears into financial services through acquisitions. By December, after a long weeding-out process, Sears had acquired Dean Witter Reynolds and Coldwell Banker. In this move, Brennan's dream that Sears could somehow become greater than the sum of its parts was realized. Sears could now "spin a grand, gilded net for the people that included housing, mortgages, all manner of insurance, variations on banking sources, investment services, and, of course, consumer goods." A person could purchase a house from Sears, finance the purchase through the company's mortgage services, furnish and fill the house through its merchandising services, and insure the lot of it, plus the car in the garage and the very life and health of the family, through the company's insurance services. Sears, Roebuck was on the way to becoming "the chassis for the whole of a citizen's material life."

And finally, merchandising, the traditional core of the company's existence, would get a long-awaited face-lift. The American marketplace had undergone significant changes over the preceding decades, and the Sears merchandising function had not changed with it. The middle class Sears had defined initially, and served uniquely thereafter, was dropping as a percentage of the population. Increasing competition from specialty and discount stores, and Sears's own haphazard merchandising strategy, only made the situation worse. The autonomy of the buying organization, which allowed the manager of stationery to sell cameras, phones, and clocks, and the manager of sporting goods to sell video games, tempted the already shrinking customer base to look elsewhere for their goods.

Thus, Brennan began a top-to-bottom analysis of the goods Sears had bought and sold. Motorcycles, uniforms, silos, surgical instruments, and live animals had long since been dropped from the listings; Brennan wanted to make sure everything left fit the image he was trying to create—or re-create—for Sears. Up to that point, there had been no clear philosophy of what things Sears should and shouldn't sell. "We have to mean something again," he told his planning committee in 1982 and the analysis was undertaken. "We have to stand for something in every line we carry. Where we can't purvey an image of 'dominance,' then let's get out of that business."

Statistics indicated that Sears was dominant in the bench power tool market (75 percent) and made a strong showing in automobile batteries (40 percent), laundry machines (37 percent), and lawnmowers (25 percent). But many other goods meant nothing to the public or Sears's customer base. To determine which goods should be chosen to fill the stores, Brennan and Moran asked buyers from every department to list which items fit the Sears image and which were expendable. Then they systematically eliminated the ones that did not fit. In the end, Brennan said, "These have been the most exciting days of my career, because now we can do anything we want."

Sears did an about-face in half a decade. Net income for the first three quarters of 1980 was $50 million, down from $236.3 million the year before. The firm needed $70 million to pay for the Early Retirement Incentive Program at the end of the year, and it came from Allstate's $450 million "contribution" to the bottom line. By 1983, however, the combination of increased sales and profits and decreased costs, according to Brennan, would have paid for the acquisition of Dean Witter.

On January 1, 1986, Ed Telling retired as chairman and CEO and was replaced by Ed Brennan. On June 30, the four remaining territorial headquarters were closed; merchandising is now administered from the Chicago headquarters. Meanwhile, the stores were renovated, layouts were made consistent, and the organization of goods was made more effective.

IDEAS FOR THE FUTURE

With the company firmly back in shape, Brennan had no lack of ideas for the future. One was a computerized, state-of-the-art information system through which all of Sears's already comprehensive services to the American public could be coordinated. A family's fluid capital could be stored in the system and moved laterally to make payments to the mortgage service on the home purchased from Caldwell Banker, to purchase goods to fill the home at a Sears store, to purchase insurance, and even to purchase Sears medical services. As automatic deductions are being made, the system could also automatically invest the balance or offer financial advice to the customer.

By the end of the 1980s, Sears was back in the mood for change once again. In 1989, the company announced three moves, each of which was historic in Sears' evolution as a company. In March, the company which pioneered the sales promotional event announced it would end that practice and offer discount prices on an everyday basis. This change was intended as a response to the advances made by retailers, such as Walmart and K-Mart, which discounted all merchandise all the time. Sears' management hoped that the adjustment would help the company retain its status as America's No. 1 retailer.

By mid year, the company was announcing more historic changes. The flagship of the giant enterprise has been the Sears Tower in Chicago. The announcement that the tower was being put up for sale sent shock waves through many quarters, but the expected sales price of more than $1 billion was expected to help the company improve its flagging earnings. Finally, the company announced that its 6,000 employee merchandising group would be relocating to the Chicago suburbs and away from the downtown location it had inhabited for 102 years. Once again, convention was being shattered in the name of new realities and new corporate needs.

Sears, an institution that became a leader in its industry on sheer selling ability and an aversion to almost all formal techniques of decision making and planning, has, with the help of all these techniques, pushed itself into the top of a whole new industry. And with a continual supply of the visionaries Sears has been blessed with from inception, there is no doubt it will be blazing new trails in the future. ■

QUESTIONS

1. Differentiate between the strategic plans of Richard Sears, Julius Rosenwald, General Wood, Arthur Wood, Ed Telling, and Edward Brennan. What environmental and organizational circumstances made it necessary for each to have a different strategy?
2. Outline several plans described in the case. On what level did (or do) they operate? Were they successful or did they fail, and in either case, why?
3. How does this case point up the importance of monitoring as the final phase of either the planning or strategic management process?
4. What different approaches to planning did the various CEOs in charge of Sears utilize? Which approaches were more successful and which were less successful? Was the approach the factor responsible for success, or were other factors involved?
5. What economic, technological, and competitive forces affected the strategies of Sears executives? Did they present constraints or opportunities? What might you have done differently in response to each situation?

PART ▲ THREE

Organizing

Planning and strategic planning, discussed in Part Two, are the tools managers use to guide the organization so that it can achieve its goals in a changing environment. But the setting of goals and objectives and the determination of plans by which to achieve them are only the first step in the overall process of management. To carry out any plan, a manager must organize people and resources. Thus, organizing logically follows planning as the second function of management.

Organizing is the process of dividing an overall task into parts that individuals, groups, or units can perform, then coordinating their efforts with each other and with financial and technical resources so that the overall goals are ultimately achieved. This is not to imply that organizing is a simple task or that there is one way to do it that suits every situation. Just the opposite is the case. Organizing, like strategic planning, must be undertaken in the context of the environment. Because the environment affects what is possible and what will be successful or unsuccessful, managers must always take it into consideration when determining how best to organize their people and resources for goal accomplishment.

In Chapter 7, The Structure of Organizations, we will discuss the basics of organizing: the various ways in which large tasks may be broken up into smaller ones that individuals and units can perform and the various ways in which these divided efforts can be coordinated. This will give you a general understanding of what is meant by the term *organizing* and what basic methods managers use to undertake the organizing function.

In Chapter 8, Organizational Design and Culture, we will expand on the basic principles of organizing. Once you have an understanding of the general methods of dividing and coordinating work, we will illustrate how certain methods are better suited to one type of environment or another. Factors in the organization's operating environment as well as characteristics of the organization itself influence the determination of the most appropriate methods of dividing and coordinating work. Just as it was important for strategic planning efforts to be responsive to the environment, so it is important for organizing efforts to be responsive to the environment.

In Chapter 9, Organizational Change, Conflict, and Development, we will take this issue of organizational responsiveness a step further. Managers cannot simply look at the organization and its environment, determine the best way to organize for goal accomplishment, then sit back and watch the organization perform. The relationship between the organization and its environment is dynamic. Thus, managers must continually monitor the condition of the organization and the risks and opportunities presented by its environment, and they must continually reshape and reorganize the organization to keep it responsive to these environmental fluctuations. Also in Chapter 9, we will discuss ways in which managers can continually guide the growth and development of their organizations in rapidly changing environments.

7 | The Structure of Organizations

FOCUS CASE / From Strategy to Structure: Moments of Truth

ORGANIZING FOR GOAL ACCOMPLISHMENT
Structure and the Formal Organization
The Informal Organization

DIVISION OF LABOR AND SPECIALIZATION
Line and Staff Work
Departmentalization
Departmentalization by Two Dimensions Simultaneously: The Matrix Concept
Overcoming Problems in Division of Labor and Specialization

COORDINATING WORK
Individual Coordinating Mechanisms
Structural Coordinating Mechanisms
Issues in Coordination
Alternative Organization Structures

An organization has many of the characteristics of music. Music is not constituted of the individual notes but the relationship among them. Just as each note would be meaningless if played by itself so would each task in an organization be ineffective if not coordinated with the others. The conductor's function is, in a figurative sense, similar to that of an organizer. Given a piece of music (a plan, of sorts), the conductor must select the musicians to play each instrument, determine the tempo, cue the musicians to enter at the right time, and ensure that everyone works together to complete the performance. Similarly, given a plan with specified objectives, the organizer must assign people to accomplish each objective and must coordinate their efforts so that each objective is accomplished and the goal is attained. If the conductor's efforts are successful, the results will be music, not noise. If the organizer's efforts are successful, the results will be accomplishment of the overall goals, not chaos.[1]

KEY QUESTIONS

As you study this chapter, try to answer the following key questions:

1 What are the three basic things managers must do to organize people and resources for goal accomplishment?
2 What are the differences and relationships between the formal and the informal organization?
3 What is the relationship between division of labor and specialization? What effect do they have on productivity?
4 What are the differences between line and staff work? To what conflicts are line and staff employees sometimes subjected?
5 What are three ways of departmentalizing, and what are their advantages and disadvantages?
6 What are some problems caused by division of labor and specialization? What are some methods that have been used to remedy these problems?
7 What are some individual mechanisms of coordination?
8 What are some structural mechanisms of coordination?
9 What is meant by centralization and decentralization?

Focus Case

From Strategy to Structure: Moments of Truth

The president of SAS believes that customer satisfaction determines whether the airline will succeed or fail to such a degree that he made his belief the basis of a major restructuring of the company.

In 1986, each of 10 million travelers came in contact with approximately five different employees of Scandinavian Airline System (SAS), a Swedish airline headquartered in Copenhagen. Each interaction lasted an average of 15 seconds. Thus, as SAS president Jan Carlzon put it, the image of SAS was " 'created' in the minds of our customers 50 million times a year, 15 seconds at a time. These 50 million 'moments of truth' are the moments that ultimately determine whether SAS will succeed or fail as a company. They are the moments when we must prove to our customers that SAS is their best alternative."

The importance of these moments of truth—of customer satisfaction—was the basis for Carlzon's restructuring of SAS when he became its president in 1981. From 1975 to 1985, competition became increasingly fierce and customers increasingly demanding. Between 1975 and 1980, SAS had lost 20 percent of its global market share. The company Carlzon joined at the turn of the decade was overstaffed, undermotivated, and suffering from productivity and punctuality problems.

Given the increased competitiveness of the industry and the emphasis on service, Carlzon recognized that the first step in formulating a strategy would be determining exactly in what business the company was. Thus he questioned himself, "Is SAS in the airline business? Or is it really in the business of transporting people from one place to another in the safest and most efficient way possible?"

Based on an analysis of the business environment and his customers' needs, Carlzon determined that the airline should be customer driven rather than product driven. In other words, money should be spent on customer service rather than new planes, and the convenience of the passengers should take precedence over the convenience of the airlines' employees. "We cannot rely on rule books and instructions from distant corporate offices (to service customers)," Carlzon argued. "We have to place responsibility for ideas, decisions, and actions with the people who *are* SAS during those 15 seconds: ticket agents, flight attendants, baggage handlers, and all the other frontline employees. If they have to go up the organizational chain of command for a decision on an individual problem, then those 15 golden seconds will elapse without a response, and we will have lost an opportunity to earn a loyal customer."

Thus, with customer service defined as the number one strategic priority, the top executives at SAS began putting in place a new organization. The

Sources: This case was written by M. R. Poirier, based on the following sources: Hill, Roy, "Personal Touch Pulls SAS out of Its Stall," *International Management* (December 1982): 19–22; Carlzon, Jan, *Moments of Truth* (Cambridge, Mass.: Ballinger, 1987).

guiding principle was to flatten the structure of the organization—to push responsibility and decision-making power to the front lines. Werner Tarnowski, manager of the SAS branch in Stuttgart, provides an excellent example of how this principle was implemented.

Before his arrival, the Stuttgart branch operated out of two locations: a downtown ticket sales office and the airport, where flight-related personnel worked. Since the only significant responsibility of the downtown office was ticket sales, they did not have the information necessary to answer questions about lost baggage, arrival times, or how to ship freight. Meanwhile, the airport personnel had highly uneven work loads. There was only one daily round-trip passenger connection, and that plane was only in the airport in the morning and evening. The company's only cargo plane also had only one regular daily stop, leaving most of the airport personnel unoccupied for long stretches each day.

Tarnowski closed the downtown office and moved all its personnel to the airport. He then trained everyone in all of the jobs necessary to serve each customer so that in any "golden moment" somebody would be available to handle the situation. Ticket agents learned how to ship freight, load baggage, and arrange special meals for passengers. Airport personnel learned how to write tickets for passengers, read fare charts, and handle money. Before the reorganization, if a passenger buying a ticket had questions about freight or needed special assistance boarding, the ticketing agent referred the passenger to someone else. Most often, the second person would simply refer the passenger to a third person. After the reorganization, everyone in the unit was made responsible for handling all passenger requests. Now the first person the passenger requested assistance from provided it.

This reciprocal training arrangement also broadened the employees' knowledge of the whole operation and made their jobs more challenging and interesting. As a result of Tarnowski's reorganization, the Stuttgart branch cost SAS less because fewer employees were needed, the employees wasted less time, and they needed less supervision. In addition, employee motivation was up, and customers were better served.

The whole SAS organization has undergone a similar "flattening" since Carlzon took over. At a meeting with 20 of his top managers in 1982, Carlzon drew a management pyramid to indicate the traditional structure of the organization. Then he rubbed it out and replaced it with a wheel, adding the operating departments around its hub. "I am the manager in the middle," he said. "I give a vision of the future of the company and formulate business strategy. But I delegate responsibility. I give everyone full authority to use his own initiative when dealing with passengers." As he put it in 1987, "Any business organization seeking to establish a customer orientation and create a good impression during its 'moments of truth' must flatten the pyramid—that is, eliminate the hierarchical tiers of responsibility in order to respond directly and quickly to customers' needs."

Employee initiative became the order of the day after the changes were implemented. Where previously customer requests for anything were shuffled from one person to another, now complete customer service was everybody's responsibility—even if that meant circumventing the management hierarchy.

Carlzon continually stressed the fact that serving the customer was now the front line's responsibility, and helping them do so is the responsibility of the middle managers.

The success of Carlzon's methods was evident almost immediately after he implemented them. The airline he took over in 1981 had racked up losses of $30 million in 1979 and 1980. SAS returned to profitability by 1982, a year in which the rest of the international airlines amassed a record $2 billion collective loss. It was rated the most punctual in the industry in 1983 and was voted *Air Transport World's* Airline of the Year in 1984. In early 1988, SAS ranked eighth in the newly deregulated European airline industry, and Carlzon's goal is to guarantee that it be one of the five major carriers expected to dominate that industry in the 1990s. ■

ORGANIZING FOR GOAL ACCOMPLISHMENT

Organizing The process of identifying what work needs to be done, dividing the work, and coordinating efforts to accomplish goals.

Organizing is the process through which managers identify what work needs to be done to accomplish the goals laid out in the planning process, divide work among units and individuals, and then coordinate the divided efforts so the goals can be accomplished.[2] At SAS, for example, Carlzon's major goal was to make the organization more responsive to customers. He chose to pursue that goal by pushing authority and responsibility into the hands of the people who had direct customer contact. To accomplish this goal through this method he had to change the way the airline's work was divided.

In the Stuttgart branch, for example, the employees in the downtown office handled ticket reservations, and the personnel at the airport handled everything else. The airport personnel all had distinct jobs and did not do each other's work. With the work divided this way, passengers had to go to different locations and different employees to obtain all the services they needed. The way the work was divided among the employees prevented the organization from achieving its new goal of being responsive to customers.

With all the work moved to the airport location and assigned not to distinct groups but to all employees, SAS employees could handle all customer requests right away. Carlzon organized work so that SAS could accomplish its goal.

An organization's goals and strategy should serve as the guide by which managers organize activities, resources, and technology.[3] In other words, goals and strategy should help managers determine how to structure the work of the organization. In this chapter, we will discuss the basics of organization structure, that is, some of the ways work can be divided and coordinated among people and groups.

Structure and the Formal Organization

Organization structure The defined set of relationships among divisions, departments, and managers in the organization, including the responsibilities of each unit.

Organization structure is the defined set of relationships among divisions, departments, and managers in the organization, including the responsibilities of each unit. According to John Child in his book *Organization,* there are four major components to the definition of structure:[4]

1. It describes the assignment of tasks and responsibilities to individuals and departments in the organization.
2. It designates formal reporting relationships, including the number of levels in the management hierarchy and the span of control of each.

3. It identifies the grouping of individuals into departments and departments into the organization.
4. It incorporates the design of systems to ensure effective communication, coordination, and integration of efforts among departments and across levels of the organization.

Essentially, structure is the way work is divided and coordinated among units of the organization. The organization structure put in place by management is the **formal organization.** The formal organization structure is easy to visualize using an organization chart.[5] Exhibit 7.1 illustrates the organization chart for SAS as of 1984.

The **organization chart** identifies many characteristics of the formal organization:

1. *Division of Labor*   How the total work of the organization is divided among its members or groups of members.
2. *Reporting Relationships*   The network linking all participants in the task of goal achievement; it indicates the path along which directives flow from the

Formal organization
The organization structure put in place by management.

Organization chart   A chart that identifies the division of labor, the reporting relationships, and the levels of management in the formal organization.

EXHIBIT / 7.1
Organization Chart for SAS as of 1984

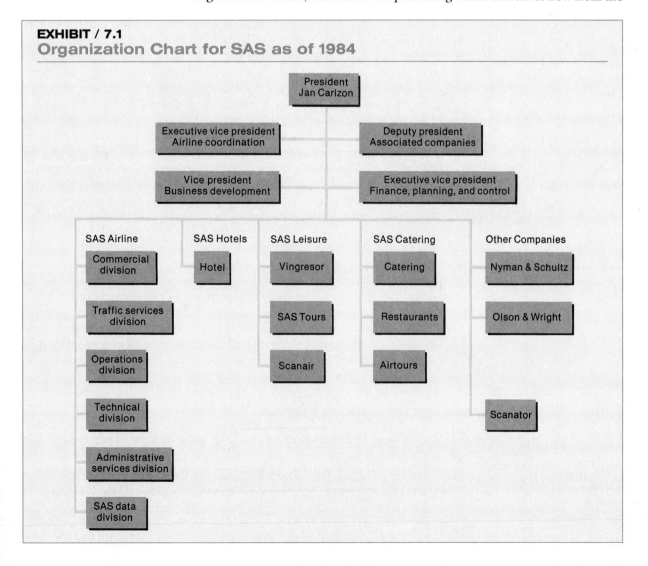

source to the parties responsible for carrying them out and the path along which information concerning results is fed back to the source.

3. ***Levels of Management***   Successive layers of reporting relationships.

In summary, the organization chart identifies the various components of the organization and the formal relationships among them. It identifies the formal structure of the organization.

The Informal Organization

Informal organization
The informal network of relationships in an organization.

Within every formal organization, there exists an **informal organization**—an informal network of reporting relationships, levels of management, and division of labor. Formal organizations are designed by management to establish reporting relationships, define responsibilities, and coordinate work. However, it would be unreasonable to assume that any group of five or ten top executives could define specific responsibilities and design a network of reporting relationships for hundreds or thousands of individuals that would function flawlessly, exactly as defined. In some cases, in fact, formally defined relationships do not actually facilitate the accomplishment of work.

For example, an SAS purser, given a new mandate to give customers top-priority treatment, decided independently to offer free coffee and biscuits to the passengers on a delayed flight. Knowing she would need about 40 extra servings since they would be free, she requested them from the SAS catering supervisor. She was turned down because it was against regulations to order more food than that allotted for any flight. Thinking of another way to compensate the passengers, she noticed a Finnair plane at a nearby gate. Because Finnair was an outside customer of SAS catering and therefore not subject to SAS regulations, the purser asked her counterpart on the Finnair plane to order the extra servings. She then bought them from Finnair with SAS petty cash and served them to her own passengers while they waited for takeoff. In this case, to accomplish a goal of customer service, the SAS employee circumvented the formal SAS organization.

In the course of their daily work, employees come up with methods of accomplishing things outside of the formal procedures, and they establish relationships with people outside of the formal divisions of work or lines of authority. The informal organization has a life of its own, which has the potential to be both constructive and destructive. If procedures, divisions of labor, or lines of authority that are effective are circumvented, the effects of the informal organization may be destructive; on the other hand, if formal structures and relationships are less effective than the ones created informally, the informal organization is constructive as in the example described above. Because of its power and its potential to do both harm and good, managers must monitor the informal organization closely and strive to guide it to constructive ends.[6]

DIVISION OF LABOR AND SPECIALIZATION

Division of labor and specialization, which go hand in hand, represent the first half of the organizing function. Once plans have specified what work must be accomplished, the work must be divided into segments individuals or units can actually accomplish. The people doing each task then tend to become experts, or specialists, at doing it.

The term *division of labor* was used by the economist and philosopher Adam Smith in the late 1700s. In his book *An Inquiry into the Nature and Causes of the*

Wealth of Nations,[7] Smith described the methods used in a pin-making factory in Great Britain. Each worker was responsible for only one aspect of the pin-making process: One would draw the steel, another would cut it to the proper length, another would sharpen the point, another attach the head, and still another would package the finished pins. By dividing the pin-making tasks among several individuals, instead of having each person create each pin from start to finish, the factory was able to greatly increase its output from an average of 200 pins per day to 48,000 pins per day. The productivity gains in the mid to late 1800s, and the Industrial Revolution itself, would never have been possible without the division of labor.

Division of labor The process of breaking a large task into components one person or group can accomplish.

We refer to **division of labor** as the process of breaking a large task into components an individual or group can accomplish and designing them specifically so they can be coordinated and the organization's goals can be achieved. Restaurants provide a simple illustration of how organizations must vary their division of labor according to their goals. Each restaurant has a number of tasks that must be performed: greeting patrons, taking drink and food orders, transferring food orders to the cooks, delivering food and drinks to patrons, cleaning the tables, calculating a bill, delivering a bill, collecting money, and preparing the table for the next patron. How these tasks are grouped, how employees are assigned to them, and how their work is coordinated is determined by the type of service that the restaurant wants to provide. Exhibit 7.2 illustrates the three organization structures described below.

Super service: At a deluxe restaurant, such as the Pillar House in Boston, for example, highly thorough and personal service is the business objective. The manager of this restaurant wants to provide every convenience and luxury for its patrons. For this reason, the waiters' work is divided into tasks focusing on individual service. Each table has one waiter or waitress who tends it almost exclusively, rather than waiting on a large number of tables. He or she takes the orders, serves the meals, responds to any requests, and collects payment for the meal. The same person also coordinates the work of bus persons and wine stewards so that the patron is well served. A head chef coordinates the sauce makers, salad preparers, dessert chefs, and assistant chefs so that the meals are prepared to the specifications of individual customers.

Standard service: Managers at the International House of Pancakes want to serve a large number of people a full meal in a reasonably short time. The work has therefore been divided into tasks focusing on efficiency without eliminating personal service. Waiters and waitresses are assigned sections of the dining area and wait on several tables simultaneously. One person fills water glasses for everyone in the restaurant, and another prepares and collects the bills at the cash register for each customer. The cash register attendant usually answers the phone and greets and seats the customers. In the kitchen, much of the food may be prepared in advance, and cooks often follow simple standard instructions for preparing each meal. One cook might work the grill, another the oven, and another the range. The work is organized for speed and efficiency. Instead of work being organized around the needs of each individual customer, as at the Pillar House, work is organized around each task. When integrated, these tasks provide the complete service.

Limited service: At McDonald's fast-food restaurants, where the main objective is high-volume sales of fast food, the work has been divided so that cooking, billing, and collecting can be done rapidly, and "service" is essentially left up to the customers. They order at the counter, pick up their own eating utensils, and

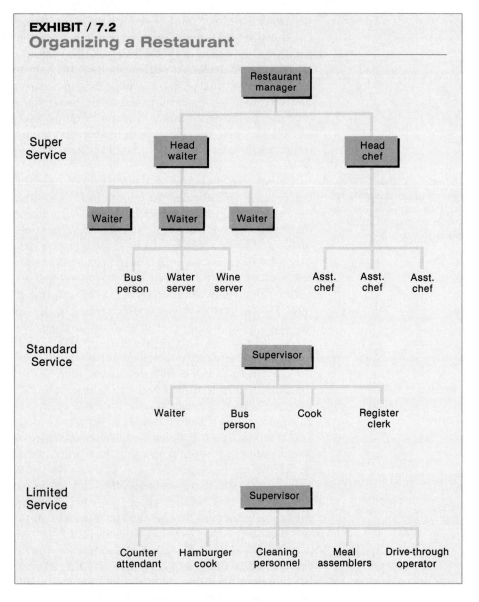

EXHIBIT / 7.2
Organizing a Restaurant

set their own tables, and it is expected that they will clear their tables when finished. The menu is very limited, and the food is prepared in assembly line fashion. The counter attendants serve drinks, take orders, and collect payment. There are fewer tasks to do than in either of the other restaurants, and they are grouped for optimum speed and economy rather than around individual or bulk service.

Each of the restaurants divides labor, but in different ways. Today, there are very few businesses that operate without dividing labor and work. Though some craftspeople still produce handmade wooden toys or handwoven hats and clothing individually, these enterprises tend to operate on a very small scale. Any company producing the types of toys or clothing more commonly seen advertised in the media, and attempting to reap large profits from doing so, is dependent on the productivity gains derived from the division of labor.

Specialization The designing of work so that each individual undertakes a limited set of activities.

Specialization refers to the designing of work so that each individual undertakes a limited set of activities. As labor is divided, people can focus on their particular jobs—they can specialize. There is evidence that the first known civilizations used the principle of specialization. When people began to live in tribal communities, work was divided among them. Over time, some people became better hunters, some became better builders, and some became better caretakers for the children. As young tribal members showed proficiency for certain tasks, or were born into a family known for its skills in a certain area, they were assigned work in that area. Work was assigned on the basis of specialized expertise.

Similarly, as the work necessary for producing one whole pin in the factory was broken down into smaller tasks, the people doing each of these tasks became specialized. The person drawing the steel, for example, became very experienced and proficient at drawing steel. If any individuals were suddenly assigned to other tasks in the pin-making process, they might be clumsy at first and would have to learn how it was done.

Specialization has taken on a different character today than it had in the last century. Specialization today refers to the design of the individual components of an organization's overall work. Modern factories do not employ workers to do such tasks as drawing steel and sharpening the heads of pins; these tasks can easily be done by machines. Specialized work today consists of more complicated tasks, such as balancing a budget, testing the properties of a biological compound, or building integrated circuit boards. Thus, workers today tend to be specialized before they take a job; many have been trained in universities or vocational schools to be proficient in one area or task, such as finance, biological research, or electrical engineering.

Line and Staff Work

Line employees Workers who are directly responsible for producing the organization's goods or services.

Division of labor and specialization can also be discussed in terms of line and staff work (see Exhibit 7.3). **Line employees** are those who are directly responsible

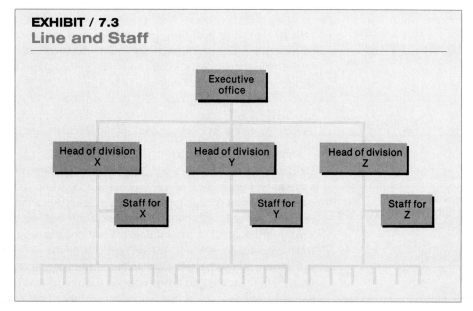

EXHIBIT / 7.3
Line and Staff

Staff employees
Workers in advisory positions who use specialized expertise to support the production efforts of line employees.

for producing the organization's goods or services. A plant manager, head waiter, executive in charge of the total organization, or machine shop supervisor are all line employees. The term was first used to describe employees working on an assembly line and has evolved to mean anyone with direct responsibility for producing goods or services. **Staff employees** are those in advisory positions who use specialized expertise to support the production efforts of line employees. The staff's role in production efforts is thus indirect. Examples of staff employees are lawyers who give legal counsel to managers, accountants who give financial advice, and personnel officers who advise the manager on how to work with employees. They provide advice to the line manager or supervisor. At the Stuttgart branch of SAS, Werner Tarnowski is the line manager in charge of the branch; he is responsible for making sure the customers are served. The accountant at the branch is a staff member responsible for handling financial transactions and making sure the financial accounting systems work. If, for example, the accounting system allows too many errors, the finance accountant can make recommendations to Tarnowski, who will decide what should be done.

Both line and staff employees do specialized work. Line employees usually have hands-on experience in whatever it is they do, and staff employees usually have training or some type of expertise in the area in which they provide advice. On paper, line and staff positions are designed to complement each other—line employees are strong in experience and practical knowledge, and staff employees are strong in theoretical knowledge and innovative techniques in their area of expertise. However, conflicts frequently arise when staff employees consider their training and education superior to the experiential knowledge of line employees, or when line employees feel that their experience is more useful than the intellectual or untested theories that staff often use as the basis of their recommendations.[8]

Departmentalization

Departmentalization
The grouping of activities and responsibilities by subunits of the organization.

Whereas division of labor between line and staff is on the individual level, departmentalization is division of labor on the unit or organizational level. **Departmentalization** is the grouping of activities and responsibilities by subunits of the organization. These subunits are called departments. Departments, in turn, further divide the work to be done and assign it to people. There are several ways to departmentalize work. People may be assigned to one department either because they all do the same type of work or because they are jointly responsible for some product, client, or market. These methods of departmentalization are referred to as departmentalization by function and departmentalization by purpose, respectively.

Departmentalization by function The grouping together of people who perform similar or closely related tasks.

Departmentalization by Function **Departmentalization by function** is a method of organizing work by grouping together people who perform similar or closely related tasks. For example, people in the accounting department all keep financial records and balance the books. People in the purchasing department acquire the products and equipment the organization needs. Before Werner Tarnowski reorganized SAS's Stuttgart branch, all the people who sold tickets were in one office, all the people who serviced the passengers were in the airline terminals, and all the people who serviced the planes were in the hangars. The entire SAS organization, in fact, was departmentalized by function before Jan Carlzon took over. (See Exhibit 7.4.) Consider another example, a manufacturer of printed T-shirts. People in one department would design and print the shirts, those in another department would be responsible for packaging them, another group would take orders and ship them, and still another would keep track of expenses and income.

One of the main advantages of departmentalizing by function is the development of localized expertise, or unit specialization. Each person within a functional unit gains knowledge and experience from working on one task for a long period of time. Working together, the people in the units become highly proficient in the tasks they are doing. Statistical experts (actuaries), for example, who mathematically estimate the risk of loss for many types of insurance protection, tend to develop a feel for trends in their area of analysis. Over time, many become skilled at producing highly accurate loss ratios and can therefore determine premium rate schedules that will ensure healthy profits for the insurance company. Their expertise is a valuable resource for the organization.

On the other hand, specialized expertise may cause the unit to develop a narrow view of problems and opportunities. Being so proficient in their work and limited in focus, the members of the units might be unable to best serve the organization's overall goals. In the case of the actuaries, for example, there is a risk that they will urge the insurance company not to enter into any field of activity where risks and probabilities cannot be statistically estimated with a high confidence of accuracy. While that position is understandable given their professional orientation, it is a narrow viewpoint and might prevent the company from adapting rapidly to changing environments.

In the case of SAS, being departmentalized by function prevented the organization from achieving its goal of improved customer service. In the Stuttgart branch, it slowed customer service. At the airport in Copenhagen, where SAS plane service crews were grouped according to the size of the planes they serviced, it caused flight delays and inconvenienced the passengers. Carlzon himself experienced problems with this arrangement. Upon arriving in Copenhagen from New York en route to Stockholm, he was informed that his connecting flight would leave from a gate in another concourse of the airport—half a mile away. After asking why passengers had to make such a trek, he was told that all wide-

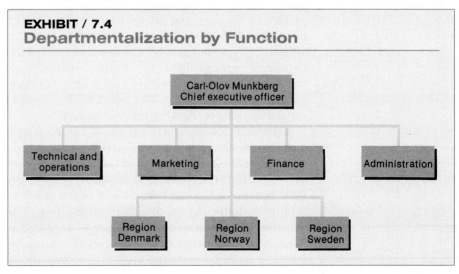

EXHIBIT / 7.4
Departmentalization by Function

Carl-Olov Munkberg
Chief executive officer

Technical and operations · Marketing · Finance · Administration

Region Denmark · Region Norway · Region Sweden

body planes, such as the one he had just arrived on, were always parked together near the hangar where they were serviced. All smaller planes and domestic flights used the gates on another concourse. In other words, the convenience of the ground personnel took precedence over the convenience of the passengers. After that experience, Carlzon restructured the servicing function so that it would be less dependent on the size of the planes. Planes were then towed from concourse to concourse, minimizing the distance passengers would have to walk between connections. Not only did that increase customer satisfaction, it minimized delays caused when planes were held for passengers running from one concourse to another.

Departmentalization by purpose The grouping together of people who are responsible for achieving a single purpose.

Departmentalization by Purpose **Departmentalization by purpose** is a method of organizing work by grouping together people who are responsible for achieving a single purpose. The employees in a given department are not necessarily doing the same tasks, but all of their work focuses on a common objective. Such departments are usually set up (1) to cater to a particular geographic region; (2) to produce, market, and sell one particular product from a broader family of products; or (3) to serve one particular client or group of clients.

Consider again the example of the T-shirt manufacturer. If this was a large operation, it might be departmentalized by purpose rather than by function. The entertainment department would be entirely responsible for designing, producing, marketing, selling, and shipping all T-shirts with rock stars or celebrities printed on them. Another department might be completely responsible for putting out institutional T-shirts, such as those worn by a corporate softball team. Each department would employ people doing very different tasks, all focused on a common result or outcome. Exhibit 7.5 presents examples of different ways of departmentalizing by purpose. The method chosen will depend on the managers' focus. If they want to focus on particular clients, for example, they will organize by client.

Units organized according to purpose can benefit from the variety of perspectives readily available; this can be useful for problem solving. For example, if the product of one of the product departments in Exhibit 7.5(a) is becoming unprofitable, the product manager can quickly bring together the marketing manager, purchasing manager, and personnel manager to determine whether sales, costs of raw materials, or labor costs are responsible. Most likely, it will be a combination of all three. In a functionally organized company, it might take months to identify the source of the problem. In purpose-oriented departments, all costs, revenues, and outputs are located within one group; therefore, responsibility for success and failure is easy to place. This responsibility for one client, one product, or one geographic area tends to motivate department members to work as a team.

A disadvantage of departmentalization by purpose is that because each department is somewhat self-contained, staff is often duplicated. This is an added cost. In addition, because the members of the unit do different types of work, there tends to be a lack of the specialized expertise that develops within functional units. When problems emerge that no one in the group has the skill, knowledge, or experience to handle, the organization may have to call in additional experts. For example, an insurance company organized by purpose (e.g., around one product) might have only one actuary assigned to the automobile insurance product group. If several statistical problems arose simultaneously, that actuary might need professional support. This is an area in which the line and staff relationship mentioned above can become particularly important. If there is an actuarial staff, then the actuary in the auto insurance department can get help from this staff and still meet the actuarial responsibilities in the auto insurance department.

Departmentalization by Two Dimensions Simultaneously: The Matrix Concept

Matrix organization
Departmentalization by two dimensions, such as function and purpose, simultaneously.

Departmentalization by any one dimension has both advantages and disadvantages. Therefore, managers have continued to experiment with approaches that organize by two dimensions simultaneously. The overall approach is referred to as **matrix organization.**

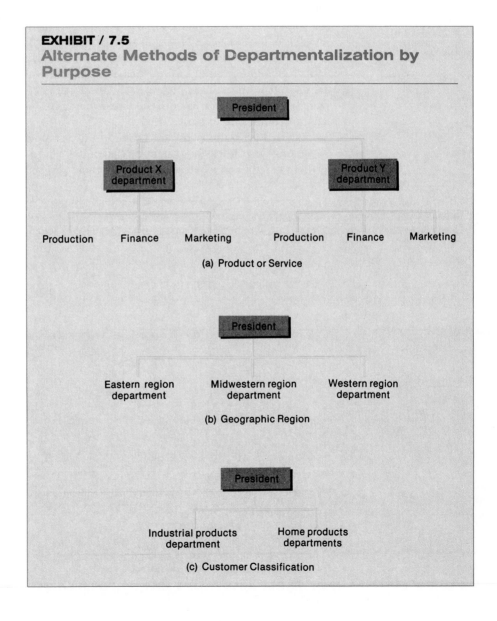

EXHIBIT / 7.5
Alternate Methods of Departmentalization by Purpose

The most common type of matrix organization departmentalizes by both function and purpose simultaneously. In a matrix organization, managers of individual units report to two different matrix bosses, one responsible for the functional aspects of the unit and one responsible for the objective or purpose of the unit. The matrix bosses, in turn, report to a chief executive, who is responsible for coordinating the efforts and activities of both the functional and objective-oriented sides of the organization. The actuarial manager in the insurance company, for example, might report to both the manager of the automobile insurance department and to the head of the actuarial department. The latter reflects a functional design, the former a purpose-oriented design. Together, they form a matrix.

Matrix organizations are found in all types of settings. Originally developed in aerospace companies, where project teams were frequently assembled to build different types of aircraft, the idea of the matrix spread rapidly to such diverse companies as General Electric, Dow Chemical, Citibank, and Shell Oil and is used in government agencies as well. One of its most prevalent uses has been in universities, where academic departments such as accounting, marketing, and finance (functional units) often form a "matrix" with undergraduate, master's, doctoral, or executive programs (purpose-oriented units). Faculty members in such a university are responsible to both the department chair and the program director or administrator (see Exhibit 7.6).

Matrix organizations are not limited to the combination of function and purpose. Any two dimensions could be combined. For example, a multinational corporation might choose to organize by product and geography. According to Stan-

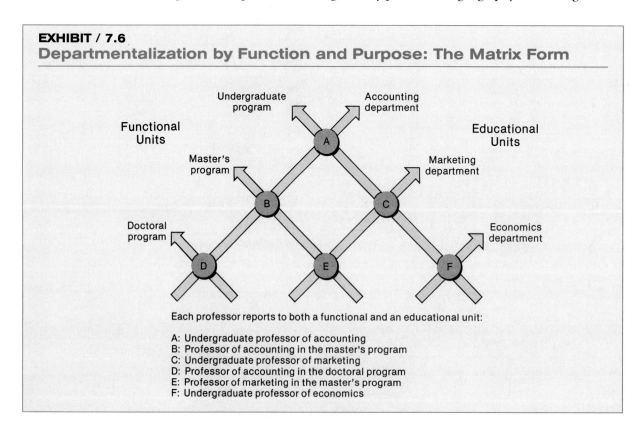

EXHIBIT / 7.6
Departmentalization by Function and Purpose: The Matrix Form

Functional Units

Educational Units

Undergraduate program

Accounting department

Master's program

Marketing department

Doctoral program

Economics department

A
B
C
D
E
F

Each professor reports to both a functional and an educational unit:

A: Undergraduate professor of accounting
B: Professor of accounting in the master's program
C: Undergraduate professor of marketing
D: Professor of accounting in the doctoral program
E: Professor of marketing in the master's program
F: Undergraduate professor of economics

ley M. Davis and Paul R. Lawrence, two of the leading experts on matrix design, organizations tend to use matrix forms in the following instances:[9]

- When it is essential that they be highly responsive to two sectors simultaneously, such as markets and technologies
- When they face uncertainty and have to be able to adjust and change quickly
- When they have to be able to share limited expertise across multiple products or projects

The primary advantage of the matrix organization is that it takes advantage of the best aspects of the other methods of departmentalization. Units and the people in them can still become efficiently specialized, as they do in functional departments, without losing contact with the broader goals and direction of the organization. And coherent teams of diverse specialists can still be formed as they are in objective-oriented departments, without sacrificing the efficiency of groups of specialists.

The matrix organization, however, is not without its problems.[10] Because each employee reports to two supervisors, he or she may receive conflicting directives. Conflict among those responsible for either dimension of the matrix also may be high, especially if team members are assembled from very diverse parts of the organization and have not developed the informal relationships that can help smooth normal conflicts. Because of these problems, many managers prefer the one-boss reporting relationships in simpler organization structures.

Overcoming Problems in Division of Labor and Specialization

The productivity gains from dividing and specializing labor have been enormous. Hundreds of consultants and researchers since the time of Frederick Taylor and the Gilbreths, with their time and motion studies, have attempted to improve the way work is conducted and organized. Today, the efficiency of such operations as automobile assembly lines and food-processing plants illustrates the success of the advances made. However, gains in productivity and efficiency have not come without problems and drawbacks.

Researchers have found that, when carried to extremes, the specialization of work left employees with jobs so repetitive and meaningless that the employees became bored, dissatisfied, and unproductive.[11] The initial gains in efficiency and productivity from specialization were offset by the slowdowns due to employee dissatisfaction. In some cases, overspecialization has resulted in excessive absenteeism, careless performance, and even sabotage. By 1960, several management scholars had suggested that work should be structured in ways that would give each employee a greater variety of tasks, more challenge, or more autonomy.[12] Three of the most commonly used techniques are job enlargement, job rotation, and job enrichment. Exhibit 7.7 illustrates productivity trade-offs associated with specialization and the various mechanisms of increasing the variety, challenge, and autonomy on a job.

Job enlargement A technique used to increase the number of tasks in a job.

Job scope The number of tasks in a job.

Job Enlargement **Job enlargement** is a technique used to increase the number of tasks in a job; that is, it increases **job scope.** Employees usually experience a greater job satisfaction when task variety increases. The employees at SAS, for example, benefitted significantly from being regrouped in client-oriented units and learning each other's jobs. "For many employees," said Carlzon, "work has become more fun and challenging."[13] Job enlargement is said to be a horizon-

---

EXHIBIT / 7.7
Positive and Negative Effects of Specialization and Job Enrichment

---

Specialization of Work

Positive Effects	Negative Effects
• Efficiency	• Boring jobs
• Increased output	• Worker unhappiness

Job Enlargement, Rotation, and Enrichment

Positive Effects	Negative Effects
• More interesting work activity	• Possible decrease in output per hour of work
• More worker involvement	• Greater cost and expense

---

tal expansion, because tasks of comparable nature are being combined. For example, on an automobile assembly line, four people might be responsible for attaching the wheels, the doors, and the bumpers. In a specialized system, each would attach only one item per car. Using job enlargement, the four people could be spread out over four cars, each attaching all three items on the car.

Job rotation The moving of employees between different jobs.

Job Rotation   **Job rotation** is another technique used to expand the variety of tasks. The movement of employees between very different jobs on an hourly, daily, or weekly basis allows the workers to learn and develop new skills. Work therefore becomes less monotonous and more challenging. This is also a horizontal expansion; employees rotate among comparable jobs on the same level. In a computer components plant, for example, an employee might spend mornings assembling circuit boards and afternoons wiring mainframes.

Job enrichment A technique that expands the number and variety of tasks in a job and expands worker responsibility.

Job depth The degree of control or autonomy an individual has over his or her own work.

Job Enrichment   **Job enrichment** is a technique in which employees are given autonomy to set their own work pace, design their own work methods, participate in making decisions affecting their work units, and evaluate their accomplishments. The major differences between the previous two techniques and job enrichment are that (1) job enlargement and job rotation are horizontal expansions while job enrichment is a vertical expansion; and (2) enlargement and rotation increase job scope while enrichment increases job depth. **Job depth** is the degree of control or autonomy an individual has over his or her own work. Frederick Herzberg recommends job enrichment over job enlargement and job rotation because he considers it a more meaningful improvement. Workers do not become more motivated when one or more meaningless tasks are added to tasks that are already meaningless.[14] Many scholars and practitioners currently consider job enrichment more effective than either job enlargement or job rotation. The Inside View 7.1 gives an example of how these concepts have been applied in one organization.

Job Characteristics   J. Richard Hackman and Greg R. Oldham developed the job diagnostic survey as a tool to help enrich jobs.[15] They identified five core dimensions that determine how enriched a job is. Exhibit 7.8 describes and gives examples of each of these dimensions. Hackman and Oldham argue that if jobs have skill variety, task identity, and task significance, people doing them are more likely to see their work as meaningful. If jobs give people the autonomy to make

Digital Tries a Bossless System

Working in teams is a way to increase each employee's sense of responsibility and involvement.

The inside of the Digital Equipment Corp. plant at Enfield looks less like a factory than a warehouse full of machines and office desks deposited haphazardly. The plant's 180 employees produce printed circuit board modules for computer storage systems. At other Digital plants, similar modules are made in assembly lines, where one person does the same job, or operates the same machine, all day. At Enfield, by contrast, each board is put together from start to finish by one of several teams. The 18 people on each team divide the work among themselves and assemble the modules from the moment the raw materials are delivered to the plant to the time the finished product is shipped out the door. Each person is expected to be able to do all the roughly 20 jobs involved in making a module.

Workers set their own hours, plan their own schedules, check their own work, and take team responsibility for each board. There are no time clocks, security guards, or quality control officers, and every employee has a key to the building.

Enfield plant manager Bruce Dillingham says the new system has decreased by 40 percent the time needed to produce one printed circuit board, reduced by half the amount of scrap that is common in the industry, and produced twice as many perfectly working modules as other production systems.

Team members interview and train new workers and give each other certification tests as they learn new parts of the manufacturing process. Pay increases are based on improved levels of skills, as opposed to seniority or authority. There are only three managers in addition to Dillingham. "Everybody is a teacher here, and everybody is a learner," Dillingham says.

Greg Plakias, Digital's group manufacturing manager of storage systems, says Digital wants to produce at the Enfield plant in one day what is produced at other plants in ten. But the real goal, he says, is to emphasize each worker's achievement and involvement. "Productivity is good, but it comes in many ways," he says. "Primarily, this is an investment in our most valued asset, and that's people. The concept we have designed here is one of very few layers of supervision and management. . . . We have an environment here that has no functional structure. It's a team concept."

Many workers do not want to work in a place where all workers are equal in terms of authority and there is no opportunity to become a supervisor. Plakias counters by saying, "Instead of getting better at what you're good at, you get better by adding to what you have. As you gain more knowledge about how to build a product and manage the administrative aspects of the product, you become more valuable." ■

Source: Fox, Wendy, "Digital Trying the Bossless System," *Boston Globe,* October 14, 1984, pp. A82, A89.

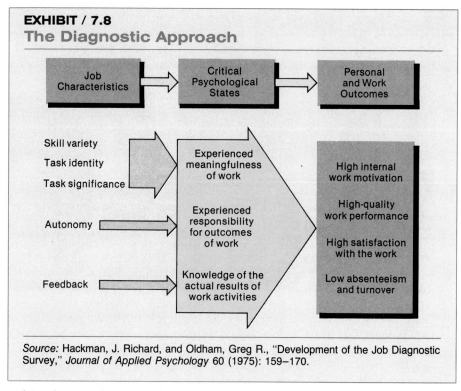

EXHIBIT / 7.8
The Diagnostic Approach

Job Characteristics → Critical Psychological States → Personal and Work Outcomes

Skill variety
Task identity
Task significance
→ Experienced meaningfulness of work

Autonomy → Experienced responsibility for outcomes of work

Feedback → Knowledge of the actual results of work activities

High internal work motivation

High-quality work performance

High satisfaction with the work

Low absenteeism and turnover

Source: Hackman, J. Richard, and Oldham, Greg R., "Development of the Job Diagnostic Survey," Journal of Applied Psychology 60 (1975): 159–170.

and implement decisions, they will feel more responsible for the outcomes. If people receive feedback concerning how well they are performing in their jobs, they will know more about what they are accomplishing and will have a clearer understanding of their responsibilities.

Hackman and Oldham suggest that workers who hold jobs they perceive as meaningful, workers who feel responsible for their work, and workers who know that they are accomplishing important tasks will be motivated, productive, and satisfied. Current research supports their contentions.[16]

COORDINATING WORK

After work is specialized and departmentalized, the activities and outcomes of each of the units and individuals must be coordinated. Organizations are systems; the parts are interdependent. A production department, for example, cannot operate if it has no raw materials and workers. Without connections to the purchasing and personnel departments, it cannot function. The successful organization must be organized into parts (departments) that allow it to do its work efficiently; yet those departments must be linked or coordinated with other units to accomplish the organization's overall purpose. There are two basic types of coordinating mechanisms: individual and structural.

Individual Coordinating Mechanisms

Liaison An individual who serves as the contact between his or her unit and another unit.

Several individual or human-oriented mechanisms are available for coordinating the work of units or departments. A **liaison** serves as the contact or communication channel between his or her own unit and another unit. A liaison is essentially an information conduit. For example, a member of the production department might be responsible for contacting the manager of the sales department on a regular basis so that both departments can be aware of how many items are being made and how many sold. The same information would be available in quarterly reports, of course, but a liaison could consistently keep sales and production figures balanced on a daily or weekly basis.[17]

Task force A temporary group assigned one problem or issue.

A **task force** is a coordination mechanism that temporarily unites people from several departments specifically for the purpose of solving a particular problem or addressing one issue. After they have achieved their objective, they are disbanded and the members return to their original departments. For example, a task force created by a city government for the purpose of developing plans for a new subway would probably include people drawn from the engineering, highway, waste management, and legal departments. These individuals might spend part of their time in their own departments and part with the task force. When the plans for the subway were completed, they would resume full-time work in their home units.

Committee A group assigned specific responsibilities on an ongoing basis.

Committees are similar to task forces, except that they are more permanent and formal. A **committee** unites people from inside and outside the organization to address certain issues on an ongoing basis. If a committee were formed to address public transportation issues on a regular basis, it might include some of the city government officials listed above and also community representatives. Committee members, like liaisons, task force members, and matrix organization managers, have dual reporting responsibilities. They have one duty to their own department and another to the committee. Exhibit 7.9 illustrates these methods of coordination.

Structural Coordinating Mechanisms

Structural coordinating mechanisms are connections between individuals and units that are built into the formal organizational hierarchy. Formal, established relationships between levels and units of the organization are structural coordinating mechanisms. The efforts of all people at all levels are integrated by using some variation of the chain of command, scalar process, and span of management.[18]

Chain of command The hierarchical reporting relationships that connect all units and levels of the organization.

Chain of Command   The **chain of command** is the hierarchical web of authority and reporting routes that connects all units and levels of the organization. Each person in one unit reports to a supervisor. This supervisor reports to his or her manager, who in turn reports to another, and so on up to the president and the chairman of the board. The army is an organization with a very clear chain of command: Privates report to corporals, corporals report to sergeants, sergeants report to lieutenants, lieutenants report to captains, captains report to majors, majors report to colonels, colonels report to generals. In an organization like the army, every person has one boss. A situation in which everyone reports to and receives instructions from one boss is said to possess **unity of command.** In such a system no person is without direct guidance, and the distinct connections between and among the bosses link the entire organization together. Together, the chain of command and unity of command provide clear directions and instructions for everyone in the organization and coordinate the efforts of people doing very diverse activities.

Unity of command A reporting relationship in which everyone reports to and receives instructions from one boss.

Scalar process The levels of authority and responsibility in an organization.

Scalar Process   The **scalar process** refers to levels of authority and responsibility in an organization, each of which is responsible for coordinating the work of the levels below. Top executives are responsible for coordinating the work of

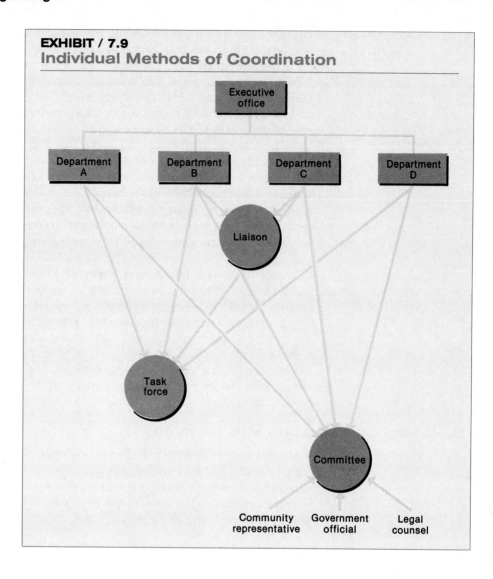

EXHIBIT / 7.9
Individual Methods of Coordination

middle-level managers, who in turn oversee supervisors, who then supervise technicians. These levels help workers understand to whom they can delegate and who can delegate to them. This establishment of a hierarchy of authority creates levels in the organization. The more supervisory levels that exist, the more difficult it will be to communicate clearly the intent and direction of the organization from the top to the bottom, and the less flexible an organization is likely to be.

Span of control The number of subordinates who report to a given manager.

Span of Management Span of management, originally called **span of control,** is simply the number of subordinates who report directly to a given manager.[19] Managers and scholars tend to favor the term *span of management* because they object to the connotations of manipulation in the word *control.* Depending on various factors, the span of management may be quite small (2, 3, or 4 employees) or quite large (10, 15, or 20 employees). According to several management historians, Napoleon was reported to have said that "no man can command more than five distinct bodies in the same theater of war."[20]

In the early 1900s, most organizations had "tall" organization structures such as that illustrated in Exhibit 7.10(a). These organizations had narrow spans of management with each manager closely supervising the work of subordinates. Sears, Roebuck revolutionized this tradition at that time by devising a "flat" organization structure such as that illustrated in Exhibit 7.10(b), in which managers had a broad span of management. The flat structure greatly affected how managers and workers behaved.[21] Managers had to delegate more work because they had more workers reporting to them. They simply could not be as attentive to the details of each employee's activity as they had been when the span of control was smaller. In addition, subordinates throughout the organization had more discretion and latitude in their work activity and had to spend more time managing themselves. Today, many of the techniques for involving people in the work process are modern versions of this earlier break from the tradition of the narrow span of management.

In the modern organization, managers recognize that the proper span of management depends on the following factors:

1. Competence of the workers and their supervisors: The more competent people are in an organization, the wider the span of management can be.
2. Coordination needs: Some types of work simply require more oversight, coordination, and direction than others.
3. Similarity of jobs performed: If everyone is doing the same type of work, it is easier for one supervisor to oversee their efforts. If, however, several types of work are being done, the span of management has to be narrower.
4. Location of work activity: When workers are geographically close to each other, the span of management can be quite wide. As the distance between workers increases, coordination becomes more difficult and the span must decrease.
5. Quality of work: When work is routine and predictable, the manager's task is to train employees and monitor performance. When the work is complex, the manager may also have to answer questions, help design solutions to new problems, and deal with nonroutine matters. This reduces the span.

EXHIBIT / 7.10
Structural Methods of Coordination

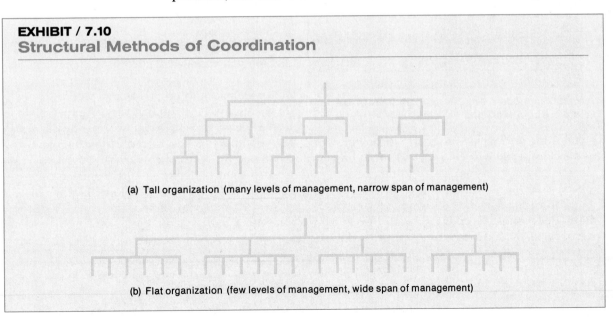

(a) Tall organization (many levels of management, narrow span of management)

(b) Flat organization (few levels of management, wide span of management)

These three principles—unity of command, scalar process, and span of management—are related, and together they determine the shape of the organization. However, as we discussed in Chapter 1, rigid hierarchical systems such as that used by the military are generally ineffective for organizations operating in rapidly changing environments. Thus, organizations often break away from the chain-of-command/unity-of-command approach. As illustrated in The Inside View 7.2, there has been a movement for quite some time to reduce the number of middle-level managers in organizations. Employees lower in the organizational hierarchy

THE INSIDE VIEW / 7.2

Management Layoffs Won't Quit

Middle managers are the main victims of corporate restructuring and "downsizing."

Following are exerpts from an article from *Fortune* magazine written in 1985. The pressure many organizations feel today to reduce staff existed even then.

These should be the best of times for managers. The U.S. economy is entering its fourth year of recovery; unemployment is near a five-year low; interest rates have dropped; inflation has been around 4 percent for more than three years. In such conditions, industry could be expected to add staff to accommodate rising demand. The last thing white-collar workers should have to worry about is job security. Yet they have rarely felt more vulnerable. Company after company is "downsizing," sometimes right up to the executive suite, as though the recession were still with us. As corporate bureaucracies shrink, middle managers are the main victims.

The phenomenon is not simply a case of trouble at the smokestack, of vanishing oil refineries, steel mills, or shoe factories. It cuts across industry lines. Over the past five years, U.S. companies have shed almost half a million managers—and the shedding continues. "We're reconstructing much of the U.S. economic system," says Eugene E. Jennings, a management professor at Michigan State University. "Eighty-nine of our 100 largest corporations—perhaps more—have gone to total corporate realignments." AT&T's Information Systems division will eliminate 24,000 jobs, 30 percent of them in management, by early next year. Ford Motor Co. plans to cut its salaried work force by 20 percent by 1990. Union Carbide Corp. will unload 4,000 white-collar employees during the next few months. CBS has offered early retirement to 2,000 people. Motorola has cut 7,500 employees from its semiconductor groups and is looking for 1,700 more. At Du Pont, 11,200 took early retirement, and the company wants to get a few thousand more out the door. ∎

Source: Nielsen, John, "Management Layoffs Won't Quit," *Fortune,* October 28, 1985, p. 46.

are gaining skills, and technology is making it possible for them to do much of the work middle-level managers used to do. Therefore, when cutbacks come or when organizations are trying to improve their efficiency, it is logical to remove middle layers in the organization. As this is done, however, spans of management are likely to be increased, and the organization will become much flatter. Management practices and procedures must be adapted to this new organization structure.

Issues in Coordination

Technology, competitive pressures, and constant fluctuations in the economy make the environment that organizations face very complex. Managers have adopted many ways of coping with this complexity. One common way to deal with it is to simultaneously use multiple coordinating mechanisms; another is to decentralize decision making so that those closest to existing problems and potential opportunities make the decisions.

Centralization Versus Decentralization   As organizations grow, coordination becomes increasingly difficult. Larger organizations tend to have more units and to undertake more numerous and diverse activities. It is difficult in large organizations to keep track of everything that is going on and to coordinate all of these efforts.

In these cases, some managers will want strict control over decision-making authority. That is, they may wish to ensure that all decisions that will significantly affect the organization are made either in the top executive office or with the direct authorization of that office. This is referred to as **centralization**—the degree to which decision making is concentrated at a single point (such as the executive office) in the organization.

Centralization The degree to which decision making is concentrated at a single point in the organization.

Centralization gives top managers control over most decisions, leaving to lower levels only the authority necessary to implement the decisions already made. In the centralized organization, top management tends to specify what lower levels are to do and how it is to be done. The rationale for centralizing decision making is to provide a central focus for direction and control.

However, though centralization eases the task of coordination in some ways and may give top executives the feeling that they are in complete control of the organization, it is not always effective strategically. In some circumstances, centralized authority and decision making make organizations too rigid and inflexible to respond to rapidly changing environments. It was a strategic necessity for SAS employees with direct customer contact to have the authority to make decisions about customer service. In the SAS organization, decision making and authority were decentralized, that is, dispersed among members of the organization with direct responsibility for customer service.

Decentralization The degree to which authority and responsibility are pushed down to the lowest level in the organization.

Decentralization tends to push authority and responsibility down to the lowest levels in the organization. Top management encourages lower-level managers to assume as much responsibility as possible. Decentralization encourages innovation and experimentation among units of the organization. Many writers have argued that organizations of the future will be much more decentralized than they are today.[22] The experts who know how to do the work will be at the bottom of the organization, and new information systems will provide them with the information they need to make decisions.

Though decentralization would seem to be in opposition to coordination efforts, this is not the case. If top managers have clearly expressed the overall goals of the organization, managers in the lower or outer areas of responsibility should be able to carry out their portions of this goal independently. Through reporting relationships, top managers can still coordinate and monitor all the organization's activities.

Alternative Organization Structures

Currently there is a trend toward simultaneous centralization and decentralization. Advances in information technology and theories of organization design are going hand in hand. More effective computerized communication systems allow a sort of centralized control over what appear to be decentralized systems. We will discuss communication systems and information technology in later chapters. Here we will introduce three forms of organization structure that combine principles of both centralization and decentralization.

Network structure A decentralized structure in which power is distributed among interdependent members.

A **network structure** is a decentralized structure in which power is distributed among interdependent members of a system.[23] Control over resources and decisions regarding their allocation is distributed radially (from the roots) among outer members of the organization. At their discretion, the members may delegate authority to coordinate their activities to a central body of representatives. Thus, a network organization differs from a hierarchy in that the "higher" levels are dependent on the "lower" levels, rather than vice versa. In hierarchies, decentralization occurs at the discretion of upper management. In network organizations, centralization occurs at the discretion of the "lower-level" managers. A network organization can be drawn in concentric circles (see Exhibit 7.11).

Collegial (collective) structure A structure created to allow individuals to assist each other.

A **collegial** or **collective structure** is a structure in which members who cannot achieve their individual goals without the assistance of others determine a means through which they can cooperate.[24] Beyond the goal of preserving the system, the members do not share common goals. The members share space, time, and energy, but not necessarily visions, aspirations, or intentions. Collegial structures depend on mutual interdependence. That is, the members must need each other's skills or contributions to accomplish their own ends and must be able to count on the reliable participation of the other members.

Loosely coupled structure A structure in which two systems are weakly related.

Loosely coupled organizations are similar to collegial systems. Two systems that are joined by few common variables or weak common variables are said to have a **loosely coupled structure**.[25] Each system has its own purposes and is influenced by independent factors, but the two are joined because the allegiance benefits both. Practically speaking, when one of the systems is disturbed, the effects will not greatly or immediately affect the functioning of the other.

The above methods of organizing are significant departures from traditional organization theory as we have outlined it in the chapter. They are still in the experimental stages today and not in wide usage. And though they appear to violate our basic premise—that organizing is done for the purpose of goal accomplishment—this is not really the case. Each system allows individual members or "outer" members to achieve their goals through the organization. The major difference is where in the structure the goals are determined. Though these alternative structures are characterized by power and authority being held by outer members, their reasons and purposes for organizing remain the same: to accomplish goals.

EXHIBIT / 7.11
Network Structure Versus Hierarchical Structure

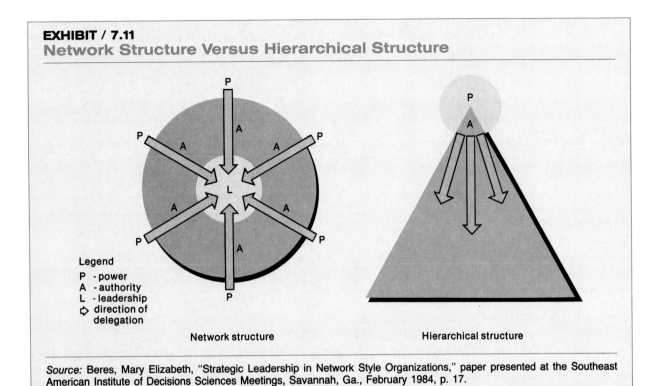

Legend
P - power
A - authority
L - leadership
▷ direction of delegation

Network structure   Hierarchical structure

Source: Beres, Mary Elizabeth, "Strategic Leadership in Network Style Organizations," paper presented at the Southeast American Institute of Decisions Sciences Meetings, Savannah, Ga., February 1984, p. 17.

◼ KEY POINTS

1 To organize people and resources for goal accomplishment, managers must clearly define goals, divide the overall goals into smaller tasks that one individual or unit can handle, and coordinate these divided efforts so that the goals are, in fact, accomplished.

2 The formal organization is put in place specifically by the managers of the organization and refers to the relationships among divisions, departments, and managers; it specifies division of labor, reporting relationships, and levels of management. The informal organization is the informal network of reporting relationships, division of labor, and levels of management organization lines. Activities in the informal organization that circumvent formal structures and relationships may or may not facilitate accomplishment of the organization's goals. Therefore, the informal organization should be carefully managed.

3 Division of labor is the breaking up of large tasks into small parts that one person or group can handle. Specialization, though originally referring to the specialized expertise that developed as a natural by-product of this process, today refers to designing components of an overall task in the process of division of labor. In the last century, division of labor and specialization were responsible for large gains in productivity.

4 Line employees are those who are responsible for producing the organization's goods or services. Staff employees are those with specialized training or expertise who are responsible for giving advice to line employees. Occasionally, the relationship between line and staff employees is tense because line employees feel they have experience and responsibility that staff does not, and staff employees resent line employees when the line will not accept their advice.

5 Departmentalization by function is the grouping together of people who perform a similar or closely related task. This method allows each unit to develop a high level of expertise in one area, but it sometimes narrows the unit's focus or viewpoint on problems or opportunities. Departmentalization by purpose groups people based on the product, the geographical area, or the client they are responsible for serving. This method allows an effective blending of various talents but sometimes results in a lack of necessary, specialized expertise in the unit. The matrix organization, in which department or unit supervisors report to both a functional manager and an objective-oriented manager, attempts to utilize both approaches to gain the advantages and minimize the disadvantages of each.

6 Excessive division of labor and specialization often result in boring, meaningless work and a corresponding drop in worker motivation and productivity, which may offset efficiency gains. Job enlargement and job rotation programs attempt to decrease boredom by increasing the number of similar tasks incorporated into the job. Job enrichment attempts to increase the meaningfulness of work by increasing autonomy, responsibility, and depth of the job.

7 Individual mechanisms of coordination include liaisons, who serve as information conduits between two units and report to both; task forces, temporary work groups formed with individuals from several units; and committees, more permanent work groups formed with individuals from several units and sometimes from the community or government.

8 Structural mechanisms of coordination are connections between individuals and units that are built into the formal organization hierarchy. These include the chain of command, a web of authority that illustrates which individuals report to which manager; the scalar process, which illustrates the levels of authority within which the chain of command operates; and the span of control, which illustrates how many people report to each manager.

9 In a centralized system, authority and decision making are concentrated at the top of the organization. In a decentralized system, authority and decision making are pushed to lower levels, allowing departments to function more independently, autonomously, and innovatively.

▥ FOR DISCUSSION AND REVIEW

1. How did the management of SAS organize for goal accomplishment? What was the situation, and how did they divide and coordinate the work?

2. Why is organizing an important process? Give an example where being disorganized caused severe performance problems.

3. Assume that you manage a department in which a line employee responsible for producing television sets refuses to take advice from a staff employee. How would you approach the problem and resolve the conflict?

4. Assume that you are responsible for producing a series of five floats for a parade, all with a related theme. How might you departmentalize your employees by function? By purpose? Using the matrix concept?

5. How could excessive specialization result in decreased worker motivation and productivity? Give an example. Why did this happen and what would you have done about it?

6. In what situations would job enlargement, job rotation, and job enrichment be least effective? Why?

7. In what situations would highly formalized, structural methods of coordination be most effective? Least effective? How would you adapt them to be more effective?

8. As the manager in charge of producing five floats for a parade, would you centralize or decentralize your operation? Explain why.

▥ KEY TERMS

Centralization	Departmentalization by purpose	Job rotation	Organization structure
Chain of command		Job scope	Organizing
Collegial (collective) structure	Division of labor	Liaison	Scalar process
	Formal organization	Line employees	Span of control
Committee	Informal organization	Loosely coupled structure	Specialization
Decentralization	Job depth	Matrix organization	Staff employees
Departmentalization	Job enlargement	Network structure	Task force
Departmentalization by function	Job enrichment	Organization chart	Unity of command

THE CONFERENCE TABLE: DISCUSSION CASE / 7.1

Transnational Mergers

The Celilo Converter Station in Dalles, Oregon, built by Asea Brown Boveri. Although the bulk of ABB's business is in Europe, they are getting a foothold in the United States as well.

Transnational mergers have a low success rate, but recently a man has decided to challenge the odds. The man, Percy Barnevik, is the head of a new European energy powerhouse called ABB. Barnevik presents the company with worldwide sales of $18 billion as a model for future transnational mergers that many people believe will be necessary for survival when trade barriers begin forming around Europe. "I'm anxious to set an example. ABB will be a success story."

ABB, headquartered in Switzerland, is the combination of Switzerland's Brown Boveri Company and Sweden's Asea. The company has 180,000 employees in 140 countries worldwide. Though the company is headquartered in Switzerland, which is not a member of the European Economic Community, it is trying to build its market within it. Over 70 percent of the company's employees are in Europe, and its largest single manufacturing operation is in Germany. But ABB has set its sights beyond Europe by forming two joint ventures with Westinghouse, giving them some power in the U.S. market as well. Barnevik is setting out to prove all the critics and analysts wrong.

ABB plans to build on the strength of Asea in applications-oriented research and BBC in basic research. They have already transferred several researchers from research and development facilities, which are located at corporate headquarters, to specific business units throughout Europe with the hope of bringing R&D closer together with the marketing function. "The (long-term) objective is to push down responsibility, authority, and accountability."

Barnevik's approach to restructuring is unique in a number of ways. First, he stressed the importance of quickness in implementing the changes. "It's better to move swiftly and correct an error here and there afterwards rather than leave people hanging in the air, uncertain about their future." Second, he dismissed the idea of bringing in outside consultants; instead he created an internal task force of five top managers from each of the former companies.

Source: Arbose, Jules, "ABB: The New Energy Powerhouse," *International Management* (June 1988): 24–30.

Whatever structure is finally chosen for ABB, there will undoubtedly be many managerial positions to be filled. To avoid any evidence of favoritism, Barnevik, ABB deputy chief officer Thomas Gasser, and the personnel directors of Asea and BBC cross-interviewed hundreds of applicants. The team was looking for individuals who showed flexibility and the desire to work in a multicultural environment along with a knack for innovation, risk taking, and the ability to motivate others. "We sought people capable of becoming superstars," said Barnevik. "For the merger to work, it is essential that we have managers who are open and generous and capable of thinking in group terms."

Barnevik's vision seems to be becoming a reality and if it doesn't work out, it can't be for lack of effort. ABB, with its ambition, technology, expertise, and determination may just be the company of the future. ■

DISCUSSION QUESTIONS

1. Assume that you have just been appointed to the internal task force responsible for making recommendations on organization structure. How should the new merged companies be organized? Why?
2. How would you recommend coordinating the work of the research and development facilities with the business units to which they are assigned?
3. What unique problems in organizing will ABB face because it is a multinational company with employees in 140 countries?

THE CONFERENCE TABLE: DISCUSSION CASE / 7.2

Hands Across America: Organizing a Mega-event

On October 22, 1985, Ken Kragen, Hollywood agent and creative genius behind USA for Africa's successful drive to raise funds for the starving people in Africa, held a press conference at the Essex House in New York. Kragen announced that in less than seven months millions of people would join "Hands Across America" to fight hunger and homelessness in America. Backing up this effort was USA for Africa, the parent organization, headed by executive director Marty Rogol. In addition to Kragen and USA for Africa, there existed an embryonic Hands organization of two employees and a promise of a sponsorship by the Coca-Cola Company.

Never before had six million people united to do *anything* at the same time in so many locations. The prospect boggled the minds of many who could just begin to conceive of the myriad details associated with getting permits, mapping out routes, informing and organizing participants, collecting donations, garnering media attention, working with celebrities, and drawing in corporate partners.

Yet, on May 25, 1986, five-and-a-half million people *did* join hands, sang "We Are the World," "America the Beautiful," and "Hands Across America," had a good time, and went home believing an important step had been taken toward solving hunger and homelessness in America. Another one million are estimated to have participated in related activities. Many people made donations, and some donated the $10 requested of them to join the line. Having grown from essentially nothing, the organization brought together more than six million people and raised more than $30 million in seven months.

Hands was to be a big event—a mega-event. It required organizing and informing millions of people about how they could donate, where the line would be,

Making "Hands Across America" happen required a vast and complex organization to coordinate promotion, marketing, celebrity relations, field activities, corporate support, and financial resources.

where they were needed, and what they were to do. A major organization framework would be needed. In addition, a substantial financial commitment was necessary to make it happen. Making Hands happen would require extensive staff and line support for promotion, marketing, celebrity relations, field activities in states along the line, corporate support, and financial resources to pay for all of this. The enormity of the undertaking was daunting to everyone except Kragen, who first contacted AT&T. While AT&T was interested, the timing was wrong. On Kragen's next try, he connected with the Coca-Cola Corporation. Coca-Cola was approaching its 100th anniversary and looking for projects that would bond Coke to America and demonstrate that the company cared about the country. It was only three minutes into Kragen's presentation before Sergio Zeman, vice president of marketing, exclaimed that Coke was "in." Following the formal agreement, Kragen was able to announce the May 25 event.

The interdependence of Hands with its corporate sponsors, and particularly with Coca-Cola, is highlighted by the admission of Hands' staff that "We couldn't have done it without Coke." Similarly, Coke needed the nonprofit, social cause-related organization that Hands provided. The benefits were mutual. Hands received direct financial support that allowed the elaborate state and national operation to be organized and enjoyed the power of Coke's mass marketing expertise, the access to 84 percent of the consumer market, and local partnerships through the Coca-Cola bottler network. Coke, in return, benefited from the idea, the media attention (1.2 billion impressions), the goodwill, and the use of the Hands

Source: Based on interviews conducted by James Post.

logo. Coke hired a full-time staff of nine to work on the project.

Going from virtually no employees in October, the Hands organization grew to 350 employees, located at the headquarters in Los Angeles and at field offices in the 16 states and the District of Columbia through which the line would pass. These employees organized more than six million people to participate, which required meeting three major organizational challenges. At the institutional level, Hands had to develop a centralized staff to support Kragen as he traveled around the country. It also had to build staff in such areas as corporate, celebrity, and media relations, and administration.

The technical task of filling the line was left to a growing field operation, which was adding dozens of people weekly, many with political campaign experience. Affectionately known as "political nomads," these people were experienced in short-term, highly visible "event management," using their expertise in organizing grass roots support. Fortunately for Hands, there were few major campaigns underway at the time and a number of experienced organizers were available. Considering the temporary nature of the jobs and the intensity of the work involved in developing state and local operations, it is remarkable that so many highly talented people signed on. In part, the explanation lies in the widely shared view that the issues of hunger and homelessness were important, that the timing was right, and that the concept of holding hands across the country was bold, "if a bit crazy." ■

DISCUSSION QUESTIONS

1. Given the goal of holding the "mega-event," what organization structure would you recommend to Ken Kragen? Draw an organization chart of the structure.

2. How would you coordinate the activities of the "Hands Across America" staff and the corporate sponsors?

3. How is the organization structure of a temporary organization such as "Hands Across America" different from a permanent organization? How is it similar?

8 | Organizational Design and Culture

FOCUS CASE / Give Us a Ring

**ORGANIZATION STRUC-
TURE, CULTURE, AND
STRATEGY RELATION-
SHIPS**

**DESIGNING THE STRUC-
TURE**
Proponents of Bureaucracy
Critics of Bureaucracy
Beyond Bureaucracy: The
Contingency Approach

**FITTING THE EXTERNAL
ENVIRONMENT**
The Degree of Complexity and
the Rate of Change

**FITTING THE INTERNAL
ENVIRONMENT**
Size of the Organization
Technology of Production
Diversity of Products and Ser-
vices

**DESIGNING THE INDIVID-
UAL UNITS WITHIN THE
ORGANIZATION**

**ORGANIZATIONAL CUL-
TURE AND STRATEGY
RELATIONSHIPS**
Understanding Organizational
Culture
Managing Organizational Cul-
ture

Chapter 7 defined the basics of the organizing function and illustrated several different ways to divide and coordinate work. But the choice of how best to divide and coordinate work is highly dependent on both the characteristics of the organization's operating environment and the characteristics of the organization itself, including its culture. This chapter analyzes how organizational structure can be designed and adjusted to help the organization accomplish its goals and objectives, and how an organization's culture can influence this process.

KEY QUESTIONS

As you study this chapter, try to answer the following key questions:

1 What are organizational structure and culture, and what influence and significance do they have on strategy?
2 What are the arguments for and against bureaucracy?
3 How does the contingency approach go beyond the argument of whether bureaucracy is good or bad?
4 In what ways do the degree of complexity and the rate of change in the external environment affect the determination of appropriate organization structure?
5 What internal characteristics influence the determination of appropriate organization structure?
6 What do the terms differentiation and integration refer to, and what influence does the environment have on them?
7 What is the relationship between culture and strategy, and how can culture be managed or guided so that it supports strategy?

Focus Case

Give Us a Ring

Roger B. Smith's plan to restructure General Motors to better cope with the changing environment was aimed at making the company more market responsive.

Over the past decade, General Motors Corporation (GM) has undergone sweeping changes in organization structure. The structure put in place by Alfred P. Sloan during the 1920s, considered revolutionary at the time, held its ground at least 50 years. His strategy was to maximize financial return and simultaneously decentralize operational decisions so that General Motors could more quickly respond to competitive pressures. Accordingly, he decentralized operations into the now famous divisions of Oldsmobile, Chevrolet, Pontiac, Buick, and Cadillac and centralized planning and financial controls.

Over the years, competition intensified, technology became a driving force for change in the industry, and the economy fluctuated drastically. GM's corporate structure and culture had to change in response. As the company added more and more lines of cars, the five different engineering and manufacturing departments became inefficient and expensive. They were duplicating each other's efforts. To increase efficiency, manufacturing was centralized during the 1960s in the General Motors Assembly Division. Engineering was specialized. Where previously "everyone was doing everything," now engineering units in each of the car groups were assigned specialized tasks. Buick, for example, might have specialized in brakes, Pontiac in rear suspensions, and other divisions in other areas, and each benefitted from the other's developments.

As the organization was becoming accustomed to these changes, the oil embargo of 1973 made necessary more drastic measures still. To develop and manufacture smaller cars, project centers were formed. Each one was responsible for developing all components of a new model and could produce innovative, highly marketable designs more quickly than if product development remained scattered throughout the organization. These small groups had more of a team culture than the larger, formal General Motors culture.

By 1980, GM faced even more pressure: New legislation regarding safety, pollution control, and fuel economy, coupled with increased competition from Japan and a general shift in market tastes, made it necessary for all auto

Sources: This case was written by M. R. Poirier, based on the following sources: "Can GM Solve Its Identity Crisis?" *Business Week,* January 23, 1984, pp. 32, 33; "GM Moves into a New Era," *Business Week,* July 16, 1984, pp. 48–54; Whiteside, David, et al., "How GM's Saturn Could Run Rings Around Old-Style Car Makers," *Business Week,* January 28, 1985, pp. 126, 128; Winter, Drew, and Lowell, Jon, "How Power Will Be Balanced on Saturn's Shop Floor," *WARD's Auto World* (March 1985): 55–60, 90–91; Reich, Cary, "The Innovator," *New York Times Magazine,* April 21, 1985, p. 29; Guiles, Melinda Grenier, "Hazardous Road: GM's Smith Presses for Sweeping Changes but Questions Arise," *Wall Street Journal,* March 14, 1985, p. 27; Richard Resciano's interview with Roger Smith, "What's Ahead for GM," *Barron's,* March 12, 1984, pp. 11, 28, 30, 32, 34; O'Reilly, Brian, "Is Perot Good for General Motors?" *Fortune,* August 6, 1984, p. 125.

makers to reengineer their cars top to bottom, very quickly. Faced with these pressures, along with increased domestic competition, technological changes, and growth, GM was in a far different environment than when Sloan put the car divisions in place. When Roger B. Smith became chief executive officer in 1981, it was apparent to him that major changes in structure were needed to cope with the changing environment GM faced. His aim was to make General Motors more market responsive.

The new structure Smith implemented in 1984 combined Buick, Oldsmobile, and Cadillac into one car group (BOC) and Chevrolet, Pontiac, and GM of Canada into another car group (CPC). The BOC group is responsible for producing big cars and for defending GM's dominant position in the upper size and price range. It is organized around product lines and has units responsible for making and selling each of the three nameplates. The CPC group is responsible for producing compact or small cars and for bolstering GM's share of the small-car, lower-priced market segment. It is organized around functional areas such as finance and operations rather than around any individual car line.

In addition, in 1984 GM acquired Electronic Data Services (EDS) for $2.5 billion to facilitate the streamlining of the company. The Dallas-based company specialized in overhauling chaotic computer systems, and GM's acquisition of it could revolutionize how big corporations structure themselves. "Companies once forced to decentralize because they lacked the means to manage a far-flung empire may gain the tools to respond quickly to changing market conditions."

Smith is aware of the problems that come with change. "It's coming slow," he said. "The easy thing is moving the boxes around on the organization chart. The hard part is changing the system." Many inside and outside the organization have recognized a significant change in corporate culture, an emphasis on innovation and risk taking, on searching for new developments. Some indicate that all the changes have made some people feel more insecure than creative. "So many people are being transferred that just finding a phone number can be a challenge." Or, as one executive put it, "The problem is there's no anchor anymore. There's no place to take your security blanket and go suck your thumb." Said Smith, "There are a lot of people here who are still clinging to that old faithful rock."

Smith had already introduced one plan to develop an entrepreneurial and innovative climate within GM in 1982: the Saturn project. As originally conceived, Saturn was to be an independent corporation utilizing revolutionary organizing and production systems to design and manufacture cars. It was to be a corporate laboratory of sorts. The latest systems and ideas in everything from technology to supplier relations to distribution of labor would all be tested there. Saturn was created as a new corporation from a blank slate, said Smith, because, "If we just threw Saturn in with what we had already, I thought it would just get swallowed up."

The idea of a totally new automobile corporation built from the ground up caught the imagination of many state governors. Here was a chance to have a major corporation appear in the state overnight, bringing with it jobs and economic benefits. Competition for being selected as the site was so keen the Economic Development Office of Missouri purchased billboard space all over

Detroit. Featured on the billboards was a picture of the planet Saturn and the words "Give us a ring."

However, by 1989 some said the project, which has yet to produce its first automobile, was already outdated. Low-priced models from Yugoslavia and Korea beat Saturn's comparable offering to the market, and GM was forced to reassess Saturn's goals and structure. While original plans called for a $5 billion investment to put out 400,000 low-price cars annually, the revised strategy is to spend $1.7 billion for a "first phase" plant that will produce 250,000 cars targeted for the middle of the import pack. And GM may yet again change the strategy for Saturn in response to further changes in the environment. ∎

ORGANIZATION STRUCTURE, CULTURE, AND STRATEGY RELATIONSHIPS

Organization design
The process of determining and implementing an appropriate organization structure.

Culture The values and beliefs that organization members hold in common as they relate to each other and do their jobs.

Both General Motors and the autonomous Saturn Corporation face tremendous opportunities and risks. To be successful, the top managers of each organization will have to manage both the structure and culture of the organizations carefully. Organization structure, as you recall from Chapter 7, is the defined set of relationships between divisions, departments, and managers in the organization. It is the formal organization. **Organization design** is the process of determining and implementing an appropriate organization structure. In a sense, it is managing the structure: continually reassessing the effectiveness of the structure as the environment changes and altering the structure to remain responsive.

Culture refers to the beliefs, behavioral patterns, ceremonies, and rituals that members of the organization hold in common as they relate to each other and do their jobs. Culture also shifts over time, though not necessarily in response to an external environment or managerial action. Culture often has a life of its own. Both structure and culture have a tremendous effect on whether organizational strategy is realized.[1]

As the opening case illustrated, General Motors is attempting to shift both its structure and culture in order to increase its ability to compete with the Japanese and to position itself in the forefront of the American automotive industry. It instituted a massive reorganization for greater efficiency, shrinking six divisions into two. And the acquisition of EDS may allow GM to develop a hybrid structure: If Roger Smith's changes have their intended effect, "GM will present an imposing combination—a powerful giant with the nimble reflexes of a small, entrepreneurial company."[2] If other automakers follow his lead, Smith feels, "Detroit may have a brand new look by the year 2000. . . . Ford, Chrysler Corporation, and American Motors cannot survive until the end of the century in their present form."[3]

Finally, as he initiated broad changes in the organization's structure, Smith is also working to bring about shifts in GM's traditional, slow-to-change culture. Though this might seem simpler than a top-to-bottom reorganization of an elephantine corporation, Smith explained that changing the culture is much more difficult than rearranging the boxes on the organization chart. How hard it is to successfully manage structure and culture is demonstrated by the fact that currently Ford appears to be more successful than General Motors.

Structure and culture are crucial to goal accomplishment in a changing environment. To achieve a goal, managers can change the structure of the organization, try to shift its culture or attempt to influence shifts in the environment to the company's advantage. As the opening case illustrated, Roger Smith is attempting to do all three. His success will be determined in large part by the marketplace.

There is no one best way to organize. The way large tasks are divided and work efforts are coordinated for goal accomplishment will depend on the organization's character, operating environment, and culture.

In the following sections, we will discuss the origins of theories arguing that organization structure should be designed with environmental conditions and organizational characteristics in mind. We will then discuss which types of structures are appropriate in different situations, how organization culture affects the implementation of structural and strategic changes, and how it can be guided to support these changes and facilitate the achievement of the organization's goals.

DESIGNING THE STRUCTURE

The German sociologist Max Weber was one of the first to offer the view that the efficiency of an organization could be improved by systematically designing its structure. He argued that structure could influence (positively or negatively) the organization's efforts to accomplish its strategy. His view was that organizations should be clearly structured so that employees know exactly what their job responsibilities are and to whom they report so that their efforts would be best harnessed in pursuit of the organization's goals. He referred to a rational, clearly defined organization as a bureaucracy.[4]

Proponents of Bureaucracy

Far from being the inflexible, burdensome organizations associated with the name today, bureaucracies were designed to offer the most efficient way to get work done. Each employee could precisely define his or her job and how it related to other jobs. The worker was protected from biased and arbitrary management by rules and regulations. Bureaucrats were the skilled managers that made the organization work. A **bureaucracy,** as originally conceived, has the following characteristics:

Bureaucracy An organization structure with a clear division of labor in which positions are arranged in a hierarchy of authority and filled based on technical competence.

1. Clear division of labor—each position is well defined, with responsibilities clearly specified and the appropriate authority delegated.
2. Positions arranged in a hierarchy of authority—each employee reports to a supervisor, and supervisors report to managers, thus forming the hierarchy along which the organization is structured.
3. Positions filled based on technical competence—because each job is clearly defined, the competence needed to do the job can be clearly identified. People are to be selected for jobs and promoted based on experience, knowledge, technical expertise, and competence.
4. A system of impersonal rules and standards to guide managerial decisions—uniformity and consistency in treatment of employees is ensured by the consistent and impartial application of rules and standards. Thus, no favoritism is shown.

5. Career appointment based on professionalism—professional managers are trained and placed in managerial jobs. They are paid a fixed salary to do their jobs.[5]

Proponents of bureaucracy argue that people need to clearly understand their jobs and know the standards against which they are being evaluated. Only then can they know whether they are completing their portions of the overall tasks and whether they are being evaluated fairly. Many organizations today could benefit from implementing some of the basic principles of a bureaucracy.

Critics of Bureaucracy

Those who challenge these principles argue that bureaucracy is a good idea gone bad. Clear job responsibilities, standard rules, and selection and promotion according to competence are fair, efficient, and rational but are difficult to put into practice and are not well suited to rapidly changing and uncertain environments. By clearly specifying all of the employees' responsibilities and structuring all actions and decisions, managers in effect take away employee initiative and limit organizational flexibility and responsiveness.

In 1966 one of the most outspoken critics of bureaucracy, Warren Bennis, wrote an article entitled "The Coming Death of Bureaucracy," in which he presented the following reasons for the decline of bureaucracy:[6]

> The bureaucratic "machine model" was developed as a reaction against the personal subjugation, nepotism, cruelty, and capricious and subjective judgments that passed for managerial practices during the early days of the industrial revolution. Bureaucracy emerged out of the organization's need for order and precision and the workers' demands for impartial treatment. It was an organization ideally suited to the values and demands of the Victorian era. And just as bureaucracy emerged as a creative response to a radically new age, so today new organizational shapes are surfacing before our eyes.
>
> I shall try to show why the conditions of our modern industrialized world will bring about the death of bureaucracy. There are at least four relevant threats to bureaucracy.
>
> 1. *Rapid and Unexpected Change* Bureaucracy's strength is its capacity to efficiently manage the routine and predictable in human affairs. Its nicely defined chain of command, its rules, and its rigidities are ill-adapted to the rapid change the environment now demands.
> 2. *Growth in Size* While, in theory, there may be no natural limit to the height of a bureaucratic pyramid, in practice the element of complexity is almost invariably introduced with great size.
> 3. *Complexity of Modern Technology* Today's activities require persons of very diverse, highly specialized competence. These changes break down the old, industrial trend toward more and more people doing either simple or undifferentiated chores. Hurried growth, rapid change, and increase in specialization pit these three factors against the pyramid structure. We should expect the pyramid of bureaucracy to begin crumbling.
> 4. *A Basically Psychological Threat Springing from a Change in Managerial Behavior* There is, I believe, a subtle but perceptible change in the philosophy underlying management behavior; a new concept of the human being, based on increased knowledge of complex and shifting needs; a new concept of power, based on collaboration and reason; and a new concept of organizational values, based on humanistic-democratic ideals.

Beyond Bureaucracy: The Contingency Approach

Contingency theory of organization The idea that the most effective structure for an organization depends on the characteristics of both the organization and its environment.

Neither Weber nor Bennis is totally right or wrong. By suggesting that structure is a tool used to implement strategy, we have gone beyond the argument of whether bureaucracy is good or bad. In some situations, a rigid structure is best; in others, a flexible, changeable structure is best. The most appropriate structure for an organization will depend on the characteristics of both the organization and its environment. This idea is referred to as the **contingency theory of organization.**[7] We will discuss contingency theory in terms of the external environment in the following section. Organizational characteristics—the internal environment—will be covered in a later section.

FITTING THE EXTERNAL ENVIRONMENT

Mechanistic organization An organization structure characterized by rules, procedures, a clear hierarchy of authority, and centralized decision making.

Organic organization An organization structure characterized by flexibility, decentralized decision making, and the absence of rules and procedures.

Tom Burns and George Stalker were two of the first researchers to investigate the concept that organizations interact with the environment and are more successful when their structure is compatible with it.[8] Based on their investigation of 20 manufacturing firms in England and Scotland, Burns and Stalker concluded that two very different forms of organizing—mechanistic and organic—could be successful, depending on the nature of the organization's environment. The **mechanistic organization,** characterized by rules, procedures, a clear hierarchy of authority, and centralized decision making (most decisions made by the top management group) was more successful when the environment was predictable and stable, and less successful as the environment became unpredictable. The **organic organization,** characterized by flexibility, decentralized decision making, and the absence of rules and procedures, was more successful in rapidly changing environments. Exhibit 8.1 describes more fully these organizational design alternatives.

Even at the outset, Alfred Sloan, the president and later chief operating officer of General Motors, had a great understanding of these issues. In his memoirs, he wrote, "any rigidity by an automobile manufacturer, no matter how large or well established, is severely penalized in the market."[9] From his time on, General Motors has tried to respond to environmental pressures by becoming more organic, sometimes successfully, sometimes unsuccessfully. In the 1970s, the company established project centers to speed up response times and increase innovativeness. These were loosely structured, autonomous units with the responsibility for designing new cars. In 1984 the organization was consolidated from six divisions into two, each responsible for catering to one of two basic market segments: luxury cars and economy cars. The Saturn Corporation, currently under development, is an experiment in designing a more organic corporation to fit the future's unpredictable environment. In order to keep pace with its dynamic, rapidly changing environment, GM "has undergone sweeping changes aimed at turning it into a quicker-acting, less bureaucracy-ridden and more entrepreneurial entity."[10]

The organization's operating environment, as we defined it in Chapter 6, includes primarily economic, technological, and competitive factors. Each of these forces changes at a different pace and in a different way from one industry to another. Managers of organizations in any industry must remain aware of how these forces are changing in order to determine what structure will be the most

EXHIBIT / 8.1
Characteristics of Mechanistic and Organic Systems

Stable Technologies and Markets, Mechanistic Systems Characterized by:	Rapidly Changing Technologies and Markets, Organic Systems Characterized by:
1. Highly specialized and separate jobs.	Individuals contribute as appropriate to overall goals.
2. Jobs pursued as distinct from company as a whole.	Jobs relate directly to company's current situation.
3. Coordination by hierarchic supervisory authority.	Coordination by mutual adjustment.
4. Precise definitions of rights and responsibilities.	Wide sharing of responsibility for outcomes.
5. Responsibility and commitment attached only to a single job.	Responsibility and commitment to company as a whole.
6. Hierarchic control, authority, and communication.	Network structure with pressure to serve the common interest.
7. Knowledge focused at top of hierarchy.	Knowledge located anywhere creates its own center of authority.
8. Primarily vertical interaction.	Lateral communication flow resembling consultation.
9. Work behavior governed by superiors' communications.	Communications are in the form of information and advice.
10. Insistence on loyalty and obedience.	Commitment to company goals valued over loyalty and obedience.
11. Local company knowledge and experience most important.	Knowledge and experience from wider professional and industry arena most important.

Source: Adapted from Burns, Tom, and Stalker, G. M., *The Management of Innovation* (London: Tavistock, 1961), pp. 120–122.

effective for the organization. Just as an understanding of these forces was crucial to designing an effective strategy, it is crucial to determining the structure most suited to carrying out that strategy.

The Degree of Complexity and the Rate of Change

To the extent that the economy, technological developments, and competition are stable and predictable, the organization can utilize a stable and predictable structure—a mechanistic structure. However, to the extent that factors in the environment change rapidly and unpredictably, the organization must be flexible and able to adapt; that is, the organization must be organic. Exhibit 8.2 is an extension of Exhibit 6.2, which illustrated the relationship between the degree of complexity and the rate of change in the environment. Exhibit 8.2 illustrates what types of structures are most effective in each of the four basic environmental conditions: low uncertainty, low moderate uncertainty, high moderate uncertainty, and high uncertainty.

Though the combination of the rate of change and the degree of complexity in all aspects of the operating environment are the criteria managers must be most concerned with in designing the structure of the organization, a change or condition in any individual area, such as the economic environment or the general environment, can also affect organization design decisions and efforts.

For example, in our discussion of economic forces in Chapter 6 we described the effects of fluctuations in the business cycle on organizations. One way organizations shield themselves from these fluctuations is by diversifying. That is, to

EXHIBIT / 8.2
Contingency Framework for Degree of Complexity and Rate of Change

	Slow ←→ Rapid
High	

Low Moderate Uncertainty	**High Uncertainty**
Mechanistic structure formal, centralized	Organic structure informal, decentralized
Many departments, buffers	Many departments, differentiated
Few integrating roles	Many integrating roles
Some planning	Extensive planning, forecasting
Low Uncertainty	**High Moderate Uncertainty**
Mechanistic structure formal, centralized	Organic structure informal, decentralized
Few departments	Few departments
No integrating roles	Few integrating roles
Operational orientation	Planning orientation

Degree of Complexity (vertical axis: High / Low)

Rate of Change (horizontal axis: Slow / Rapid)

Source: Adapted from Daft, Richard L., *Organization Theory and Design* (St. Paul, Minn.: West Publishing, 1983), p. 64.

accomplish a goal of growth or economic security, an organization can acquire different types of businesses, some of which do well while others do poorly in certain economic conditions. In doing so, the organization often alters its structure. Another way to respond to business fluctuations is to establish new units within the organization. The new units must be coordinated to the existing structure in some way. For example, one major economic condition affecting General Motors was the oil embargo in 1973. As prices for fuel escalated, demand for smaller, more fuel-efficient cars increased. To respond to these demands quickly, GM changed its structure, creating individual units—project centers—and gave them the responsibility of producing innovative designs quickly and efficiently.

As we discussed in Chapter 6, components of the general environment, namely social, legal, ethical, and political forces, also have an impact on an organization. Changes in the general environment in 1984, for example, affected General Motors's ability to implement a new structure. Said Smith in July of that year: "The ultimate goal [was] a broader, more flexible company that can react to the market faster."[11] However, GM could not move as fast as Smith wanted. Since 1970, GM has been forced to continually react to enormous pressure from the environment.

New pollution-control and fuel-economy laws forced a top-to-bottom reengineering of all its cars. Radical shifts in market tastes pushed the company to rethink sales techniques and marketing assumptions. The onset of intense Japanese competition compelled it to begin revamping its manufacturing and management methods for greater efficiency.[12]

Thus, forces in the general environment had great bearing not only on GM's ability to implement a new structure but also influenced the choice of structural design, Saturn Corporation being designed as a highly flexible and autonomous unit ideally capable of beating Japanese competition.

The organization must respond simultaneously to all environmental factors: competition, economic conditions, technology, and changes in the general environment. As these changing factors put pressure on the organization, it must adapt to them and develop. The more rapid or unpredictable the change in the environment, the more flexible the organization's structure will have to become. The organization must fit the external environment to survive.

FITTING THE INTERNAL ENVIRONMENT

Burns and Stalker's recommendations were the beginning of the contingency approach to organizational design. Other researchers have extended the contingency approach to show that internal characteristics, in addition to external characteristics, must be taken into consideration.[13] The organization structure must fit internal characteristics such as size, technology of production, and the diversity of the products and services. The nature of the relationship between structure and these internal and external characteristics is always changing.

Size of the Organization

Size is an obvious factor affecting organization design. As organizations grow, they can assume any one of many varying structures. Obviously, General Motors Corporation with 750,000 employees will be organized differently from Volvo in Sweden, which also makes cars but has only 25,000 employees. In general, as size increases, organizations become more formal and complex, have more levels in the hierarchy, have more different units and departments, and require more managers and administrative coordination mechanisms.

Size usually affects structure in three ways:

1. As organizations grow, they usually become increasingly departmentalized. More levels in the hierarchy and more administrative and management personnel are added to control the organization.
2. As the number of employees increases, coordinating through informal relationships becomes more difficult. Formal coordinating mechanisms, meetings, and reporting relationships must be established.
3. As size increases, the percentage of employees in advisory staff positions decreases in such areas as personnel, legal, and communications. A firm of 1,000 people may have 30 people in staff positions (3 percent). As it grows to 10,000 employees, it is likely only to have 100 in advisory staff positions (1 percent). This affects not only the internal structure of the department but also its relationship with other departments.

It is clear that as organizations grow they have a tendency to become more mechanistic. Some organizations control this tendency by forming more autonomous units within the organization. International Business Machines (IBM), for example, recognized that the development of a personal computer from scratch could best be accomplished within the flexibility and autonomy of a small group. IBM therefore established a personal computer development group in Boca Raton, Florida, and gave the staff the flexibility and autonomy they needed to develop the personal computer.

Technology of Production

Technology of production The tools, mechanical equipment, knowledge, and materials used to produce a good or service.

Technology of production refers to the tools, mechanical equipment, knowledge, and materials used to produce a good or service. All firms use technology of some sort.[14] For example, publishers have word processors, printing presses, and layout equipment; contractors have soil-testing equipment, bulldozers, cranes, drills, and hammers; telecommunications companies have complex information technology, computers, and switching equipment. To a great extent, the nature of technology affects how the organization should be structured.[15]

Joan Woodward was one of the first researchers to rigorously analyze the relationship between the nature of technology and organizational structure.[16] She studied the organizational structure and operating procedures of 100 British manufacturing firms and classified them into three types of technologies: In **unit production,** one person works on one product from beginning to end, as in the manufacture of custom clothing, furniture, or other specialized products; in **mass production,** each worker works on one portion of a product so that large numbers of this product can be produced rapidly, as in industrial-equipment manufacturing, large bakeries, or the automobile industry; and in **process production,** several workers monitor machinery and automated production processes, as with oil refineries or chemical plants. She also sorted them into three groups according to their success: average, above average, and below average.

Unit production A production process in which one person works on one product from beginning to end.

Mass production A production process in which each worker works on one portion of a product.

Process production A production process in which several workers monitor machinery and automated or continuous production processes.

Woodward found the following results:

1. The number of management levels tended to increase as technology moved from unit to mass to process production (see Exhibit 8.3). Unit production

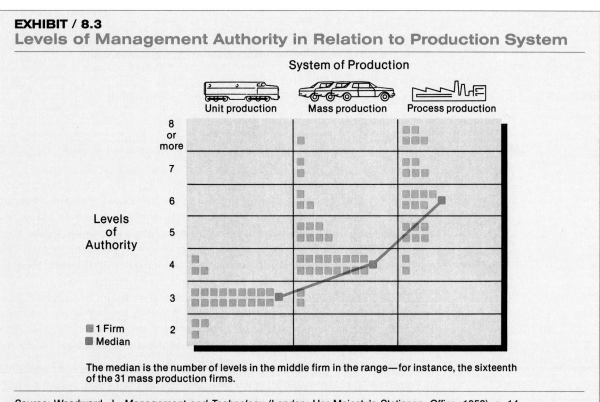

EXHIBIT / 8.3
Levels of Management Authority in Relation to Production System

The median is the number of levels in the middle firm in the range—for instance, the sixteenth of the 31 mass production firms.

Source: Woodward, J., *Management and Technology* (London: Her Majesty's Stationery Office, 1958), p. 14.

EXHIBIT / 8.4
Span of Control of First-Line Supervision in Relation to Production System

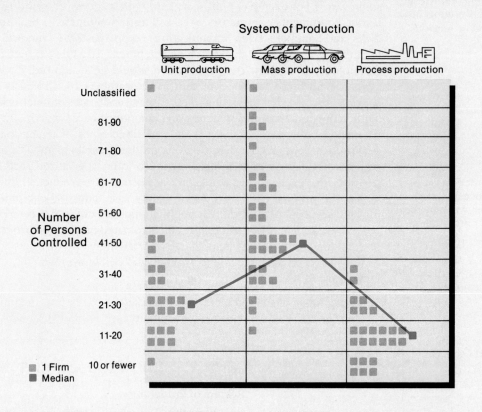

Source: Woodward, J., *Management and Technology* (London: Her Majesty's Stationery Office, 1958), p. 15.

firms average three levels of management; mass production four levels; and process production six levels. The most successful firms in each category of technology group were the ones that conformed to these averages.

2. The span of control of first-line supervisors varied in relation to the technology (see Exhibit 8.4). Span of control in mass production was the greatest because the machinery and the production process did most of the coordination and because the employees were all basically doing the same thing. In the other two technologies, more management supervision was needed because the work was not coordinated as much by the production process. Again, the most successful firms were the ones that followed these general trends.

3. Most firms had many different types of technology. In effective organizations, each subunit and level was organized to match the technology of its unit rather than conforming to one common organizational structure. Management was responsible for coordinating the activities of diversely structured units that existed simultaneously in the organization.

Woodward found that having the right combination of flexibility and technology was critical. Successful small-batch and continuous-process organizations had flexible structures while their less successful counterparts were more rigid. Successful mass production operations, on the other hand, were rigidly structured. Mass production operations with more flexible structures were less successful.

Based on these results, others have suggested that the more unpredictable and varied the technology, such as in unit and process production, the more flexibility and decentralization of the decision making are needed. Thus, the organization should be more organic. In contrast, the simpler, more predictable, and less varied the technology, as in mass production, the more centralized the decision-making process should be. That is, the structure should be more mechanistic.

Charles Perrow developed one of the most comprehensive frameworks for understanding the relationship between technology and structure.[17] Perrow specified two dimensions relevant to organizational structure and technology: task variety, the frequency with which unexpected events occur in the transformation (inputs to outputs) process; and analyzability, the degree to which unexpected problems can be easily solved by following an objective, step-by-step procedure. When individuals encounter a large number of unexpected problems, variety is high; when they must rely on experience, judgment, intuition, and trouble-shooting techniques to solve these problems, analyzability is low. In other words, the situation is not easily analyzed. Based on a matrix of these two dimensions, Perrow identified four types of technology: routine, craft, engineering, and nonroutine. Perrow's technology framework is illustrated in Exhibit 8.5.

In the most basic sense, mechanistic structures fit routine technologies, and organic structures fit nonroutine technologies. This is similar to the results Woodward found, but Perrow's framework applies to nonmanufacturing as well as manufacturing organizations.

EXHIBIT / 8.5
Perrow's Technology Framework

	Variety Low		Variety High
Analyzability Low	**Craft** Performing artists Manufacturers of fine glassware Tradespeople Personnel workers	University teachers General management	**Nonroutine** Strategic planners Social science researchers Applied researchers
Analyzability High	**Routine** Salespersons Bank tellers Clerks Machine shop workers	Drafters Auditors	**Engineering** Lawyers Engineers Tax accountants Accounting partners

Source: Adapted with permission from Daft, Richard, and McIntosh, Norman, "A New Approach to Design and Use of Management Information," *California Management Review* 21 (1978): 82–92. Copyright © 1978 by the Regents of the University of California. Reprinted by permission of the Regents.

Diversity of Products and Services

Another internal characteristic that influences structure is the diversity of products and services offered. The more products or services a firm offers, the more large and complex the organization will tend to be. For example, consider a hockey equipment store that employs ten people. The managers advertise on one radio station and in the local newspaper. The salespeople are all ex-hockey players extremely familiar with the sport. If the hockey store diversifies and becomes a sports equipment store, the managers will have to add employees who know about tennis, golf, and other sports. They may have to expand advertising and deal with new suppliers. If they decide to become a leisure time store and add camping equipment, motorcycles, jet skis, and dune buggies, the staff and structure will have to undergo another transformation. This time, the increase of suppliers and the increase in the number and variety of customers may be so great that they will have to add a purchasing department to handle the accounts, an advertising department to coordinate advertising across a broad spectrum of media, and a customer relations department to handle customer service effectively. The organization's structure must incorporate new departments and be changed to coordinate these new units with the others.

DESIGNING THE INDIVIDUAL UNITS WITHIN THE ORGANIZATION

Management theory recognizes that not only should organizations be structurally different, but units within organizations should and do vary. They are of different sizes, use different technologies, produce different products, perform different functions, and face different environments. Thus, they should be structured differently. General Motors provides an illustration of the utilization of different design structures for units with different purposes and technologies. In a design unit at the technology center in Warren, Michigan, where new car styles are developed, the technology is what Woodward termed small batch: Prototypes of new car models are designed in clay, then remolded and reshaped until the "right" design has been achieved. New information regarding competitors' designs or new materials may come in at any time, and the design staff may remold the prototype over and over again before settling on a final result. The unit is small, produces only one product, and requires very little management coordination. The structure of this unit is therefore highly flexible and decentralized.

A production plant, such as the one of Lansing, Michigan, requires a different structure. The unit is large, produces a wide variety of products, requires many levels of management, interacts minimally directly with the external environment, and employs mass production technology. The structure of this unit will therefore tend to be more mechanistic and the decision-making process more centralized.

One of the major studies analyzing differences among organizational units within the same firm was done by Paul Lawrence and Jay Lorsch in 1967.[18] They studied a variety of firms that faced different levels of environmental uncertainty. Plastics firms faced very uncertain, unpredictable, and ever-changing environments. Packaging firms faced very certain, slowly changing environments. Between these two extremes, consumer goods firms faced moderate uncertainty and change. Lawrence and Lorsch studied three firms in each of the industries, looking specifically at the relationships among the sales and marketing, production, and research and development units. They found the following results in their study:

1. The overall structure of successful organizations better matched their environment than unsuccessful organizations. For example, successful plastics firms in uncertain environments were more organic than unsuccessful plastic firms. Successful packaging firms in a stable, predictable environment were more mechanistic than unsuccessful ones.
2. Different units in the organization faced different degrees of uncertainty in their environment. For example, research and development units in all firms often faced far more uncertain environments than the marketing and production units.
3. Successful firms varied the structure of units to match the uncertainty that the units faced. Thus, because the marketing, production, and research and development units within an organization faced different environments, their structures were different. Production units that faced stable environments had a more fixed and stable structure. Research and development units that faced ever-changing and dynamic environments had a more flexible structure.
4. Even though the units within the organization had different structures to match their respective environments, they were well coordinated in the more successful firms.

Differentiation The differences in structure and orientation that exist among units within an organization.

Integration The degree to which separate organizational units are coordinated.

Lawrence and Lorsch refer to the findings in points 3 and 4 as differentiation and integration. **Differentiation** refers to the differences in structure and orientation that exist among units within an organization. If these differences are great, the units are said to be highly differentiated. If the units are similar, differentiation is low. **Integration** is the degree to which the separate units are coordinated.

Lawrence and Lorsch identified four dimensions along which units could be different: time orientation, goal orientation, interpersonal orientation, and structure.

1. *Time Orientation* The planning and action orientation of managers varies from short to long. For example, those in manufacturing often have a short time orientation concerned with meeting production deadlines and maintaining efficiency. Those in research and development typically have a longer time orientation. Their concerns are developing new products and markets.
2. *Goal Orientation* Perhaps because of their different responsibilities, employees in different units have difficult objectives. For example, production managers tend to be cost conscious, marketing managers style and product conscious, and research and development managers quality conscious.
3. *Interpersonal Orientation* Patterns of communication, decision-making style, leadership style, and type of interaction vary from unit to unit. For example, accounting personnel tend to feel more comfortable in structured environments than do research and development personnel.
4. *Structure* A mechanistic unit will have strict, regimented procedures to follow, whereas an organic unit will allow the manager more discretion. For example, the procedures or routines used by the unit producing a bar of soap are much more formalized than the procedures used by the marketing department for creatively developing a new ad campaign to sell it.

Lawrence and Lorsch suggest that in uncertain or unstable environments, these differences among the units will be the greatest. The research and development departments in the successful plastics firm had a long time orientation, a loose structure, and a flexible style of communications, whereas the production department in the plastics firm had a short time orientation, a formal structure, and a formal style of communication. The environment was so uncertain that the research and development department had to be highly flexible to be able to take advantage of new opportunities and respond to new markets. At the same time, the production department still needed to be fixed and predictable enough to get the right quantity of the product out on schedule. In the plastics firm, it is appropriate for these two departments to be highly differentiated. In the packaging firm, the research and development unit faced a predictable, stable environment similar to the one the production unit faced. It is therefore appropriate that these two units were not highly differentiated. In situations of increasing differentiation, the challenge for the firm is to improve integration and coordination systems.

For example, the General Motors plant in Pontiac, Michigan, manufactures cars. All of the units on the production floor focus on producing cars. There is little differentiation among the paint shop, the assembly line, and the parts department. The workers have similar work experiences and fairly common backgrounds, and they find it relatively easy to communicate with each other.

By contrast, at the same site are the headquarters offices for the Pontiac Motor Car Division of General Motors. Market analysts, controllers, accountants, sales managers, engineers, and a wide variety of other specialized personnel all work in the headquarters building. The marketing, accounting, and engineering departments in which they work are much more differentiated than the departments on the production floor. Consequently, they need to spend more time and effort coordinating their activities.

Jay Galbraith identifies several methods for accomplishing this coordination, each of which is useful in different types of situations (see Exhibit 8.6).[19] These methods are arranged in a hierarchy running from those that are most useful in a mechanistic organization to those most useful in an organic organization. In a mechanistic organization, rules and procedures provide the guidance necessary to coordinate the stable units. In an organic organization, more time and effort are required to coordinate the diverse, ever-changing units than can be provided by rules and regulations; task forces and interunit teams are needed.

Taken together, the above theories of organizational design suggest that structure is a very important organization component managers can control to implement strategy. If the structure is effective, it will be easier for employees to direct their time and energy in the right direction. If the structure is inappropriate, either employees will be focusing their efforts in the wrong direction, or they will have to develop informal ways of getting their work done, ignoring the structure that is in place.

ORGANIZATIONAL CULTURE AND STRATEGY RELATIONSHIPS

Along with organizational structure, culture is a critical component that must be managed if strategy is to be successfully implemented.[20] Culture, as we defined it earlier in the chapter, refers to the shared values and beliefs that members of an organization have about the way they should act, relate to each other, and do their jobs. These values become the basis of action. If the culture does not support the strategy, changes in structure designed to implement the strategy are not

---

EXHIBIT / 8.6
Types of Coordination Mechanisms

Useful in Mechanistic Structures ↑	**Rules and procedures:** Rules and procedures identify what actions are appropriate in various situations. They are standards to guide managers and employees.
	Hierarchical referral: When rules and procedures are inadequate to coordinate actions of separate units, coordination problems are referred upward to the common supervisor. The hierarchy acts as the integrator.
	Planning: Objectives are set to guide people's actions. How units within the organization relate to each other is determined by what needs to be accomplished. Plans define each unit's responsibilities and identify their relationships.
	Direct contact among managers: Managers from separate units work together to coordinate the work of their units.
	Liaisons: Specific people can be made responsible for providing communication and coordination among units.
	Task forces: Members of the separate units are combined in a task force to work together for a particular task or period of time.
	Teams: Teams are permanent task forces responsible for coordinating the work of separate units over a long time period and numerous projects.
↓ Useful in Organic Structures	**Matrix organization:** Matrix organizations give employees status in two or more groups simultaneously; coordination is done through the formal matrix organization.

---

likely to have the desired effect. General Motors's strategy, for example, is to respond quickly to market and competitive pressures and to redesign their cars more rapidly. To do this, they have reorganized and decentralized their structure to push decisions down in the organization so they can be made more quickly. However, if they are not successful in guiding their culture to become more risk taking, more innovative, and more forward and outward looking, the restructuring will have little impact. When the strategy changes, the culture must be guided to support it. Consider American Telephone and Telegraph's recent shift in strategy as discussed in The Inside View 8.1.

Understanding Organizational Culture

To manage culture, managers must first understand it and then determine how it can support their organization's strategy. Analyzing the organization's symbols, rituals, and ideologies is one way of understanding culture.[21]

Symbols The names, logos, and physical characteristics used to convey an organization's image.

Symbols **Symbols** of organizational culture include the name and logo that convey the organization's image, the office arrangements, the physical environment within which the work is conducted, and the use of job titles. When Trans World Airlines changed its name to Trans World Corporation, the company executives were indicating their diversification into businesses other than aviation. The people in the organization could no longer think of themselves only as airline employees but had to recognize that they were now employees dedicated to the

THE INSIDE VIEW / 8.1

American Telephone and Telegraph

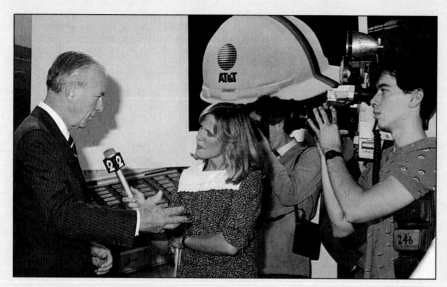

An AT&T executive discussing the breakup of the company with reporters after the announcement. The restructuring ordered by the court had vast repercussions throughout the country and within the company.

In August 1980, the justice department decreed that American Telephone and Telegraph (AT&T), which held a monopoly on telephone services across the United States, be split up into seven different companies and two centralized national and international divisions.

Before the split, AT&T had been like a miniature nation with a century of history, culture, government, and clarity of purpose. The company believed strongly in the precepts set down by two historic Bell System leaders. Theodore Vail provided the mission statement that guided the company for more than 70 years: One system, one policy, universal service. Vail's mission was supported by Walter Gifford's value system. Gifford's philosophy was to "furnish the lowest possible cost, consistent with fair treatment of employees and shareholders."

The culture shock generated by divestiture was difficult to exaggerate. "My initial reaction," said one company president, "was that my best horse had just been shot out from under me." Brooke Tunstall, writing for the *Sloan Management Review* in 1983, said, "every one of [AT&T's] million employees knew that the company would be

changed forever, that the post-divested entities would constitute a new ball game, and that they would be working for new companies requiring new skills and new ways of doing things." When the divestiture was announced in January 1982, the employees "spoke in metaphors of personal grief, almost as if they had been deserted or there had been a death in the family."

Said Tunstall, "With divestiture, AT&T will experience a metamorphosis that would challenge the most boastful caterpillar." Even the experts agree that managing culture change is difficult at best. As Allan Kennedy and Terrence Deal wrote, "Let's be candid about this. We do not know this area any better than anyone else. Cultural change is still a black art as far as we're concerned." Yet as of the fall of 1983, no manager, task force, or committee had been assigned to study and handle the task. In fact, the status control center for the staggering job of disaggregating the Bell System was located in one remote 20-by-32-foot room at AT&T Operational Headquarters in Basking Ridge, New Jersey.

"The culture must be reshaped, adapted, and reoriented to bring the value systems and expectations of AT&T people into congruence with the corporation's new mission and to prepare them for the competitive telecommunications battles looming ahead," said Tunstall. AT&T must change management's day-to-day focus from regulatory and legal matters to ways to gain market share. It must change the old method of basing prices on what most people can afford. This strategy priced some products below cost to sell at a loss and others well above cost to help balance the losses. The new strategy must be to price individual products based upon costs with a reasonable profit added. In the past, managers were chosen solely from the operating line division because they had firsthand experience providing customer service, the basis of all company profits. With reorganization, competitive strategies will provide the company's profits; therefore, managers from other divisions such as production, engineering, marketing, sales, and finance will have to provide leadership for the future. ∎

Sources: Tunstall, W. Brooke, "Cultural Transition at AT&T," *Sloan Management Review* (Fall 1983): 17, 18, 25; Langley, Monica, "AT&T Has Call for a New Corporate Culture," *Wall Street Journal,* February 28, 1984, p. 32; O'Reilly, Brian, "AT&T: What Was It We Were Trying to Fix?" *Fortune,* June 11, 1984, pp. 30–34.

service of broader objectives. As illustrated in The Inside View 8.2, changing a name or logo can be a costly undertaking.

Physical surroundings are another symbol of culture. The spartan decor, cement floors, and metal furniture of offices at Lincoln Electric in Cleveland, Ohio, indicate a serious, nuts-and-bolts orientation to business, while the thick carpets, tiled washrooms, and mahogany furniture of a Wall Street investment firm indicated an orientation to prestige. An office laid out with the desk in the middle, creating a physical barrier between the manager and the employee, denotes a culture that emphasizes authority, while an office with the desk pushed against the wall so there are no barriers denotes a culture that emphasizes teamwork and equality. The title of vice president implies more prestige and responsibility than that of supervisor. Many organizations now refer to line employees as problem-solving managers, to symbolize the importance the organization attributes to their jobs. Exhibit 8.7 illustrates the proposed new use of titles in the Saturn Corporation. In the old style plants, GM has six levels of management: plant manager, production manager, general superintendent, production superintendent, general supervisor, and foreman. As can be seen, the new levels and titles are quite different.

Rituals Customary and repeated actions within an organization.

Rituals **Rituals** are customary and repeated actions within an organization.[22] Law and consulting firms are often noted for the unwritten ritual of working on Saturday morning. Even if there is nothing to do, people show up at the office, unwilling to risk not being seen working. Three-martini lunches, evaluation and reward procedures, the nature and use of staff meetings, welcoming ceremonies, and farewell parties are all rituals that set the tone for the organization.

Ideologies The beliefs, moral principles, and values that provide a basis for organizational decision making.

Ideologies **Ideologies** are the beliefs, moral principles, and values that provide a basis for organizational decision making. Phillips and Kennedy found that companies with strong, clear expressions of corporate values tend to be more successful than those not having such clearly shared beliefs and values.[23] These values and beliefs serve to guide decision making in the organization.

Hewlett Packard, a maker of high-technology electronic equipment, has an ideology that focuses on involving employees in all aspects of the business and enhancing their commitment to the firm and its goals. For example, their corporate objectives related to people are "to help HP people share in the company's success, which they make possible; to provide job security based on their perfor-

THE INSIDE VIEW / 8.2

Logo Logistics

AT&T's experience shows that the financial implications of changing a company logo can be enormous.

In September 1983, the *Wall Street Journal* printed a brief article illustrating the financial drawbacks of changing a company logo. It read as follows:

AT&T says it's spending about $1 million to "de-identify" about 9,500 buildings—that is, to remove all traces of the Bell symbol that's being dropped (except by the seven companies that AT&T will spin off). Erecting the first wave of signs with the new globe symbol will cost about $9 million; a further $10 million or more will be spent eventually on signs. Then there's about $1,250,000 to be spent for symbols and stripes on 30,000 sedans, wagons, and vans.

The company's current ad campaign to introduce the globe symbol is costing about $10 million. Still other costs—for replacing stationery, business cards, and so on—are yet to be estimated. The company will even scrap 50,000 hard hats. "It's easier to replace them than to repaint them," an official says. Purging the Bell symbol "will take a long time," he adds. "It's something like getting Burma Shave signs down." ∎

Source: "Logo Logistics," *Wall Street Journal,* September 29, 1983, p. 1.

---

mance; to recognize their individual achievements; and to help them gain a sense of satisfaction and accomplishment from their work."[24]

Relationships within the company depend upon a spirit of cooperation among individuals and groups and an attitude of trust and understanding on the part of managers toward their employees. These relationships will be good only if employees have faith in the motives and integrity of their peers, supervisors, and the company itself.

Managing Organizational Culture

Symbols, rituals, and ideologies indicate what the organizational culture is; the strategy indicates what the culture should be. Management's challenge is to manage the fit between culture and strategy so that the organization's goals can be achieved.[25] As The Inside View 8.3 illustrates, however, this is a difficult, complicated task.

Because of the complexity of this task, many researchers have attempted to develop recommendations for managing the fit between culture and strategy. Howard Schwartz and Stanley M. Davis, for example, present the following hypothetical picture of the culture of a money center bank, which they developed from characteristics common across many banks.[26]

[The] summary of the international banking division culture characterized individual area managers as feudal barons. Each had been in place from five to seven years. As long as their profit contribution goals were met, they operated with almost complete autonomy. To preserve that autonomy, their concern for short-term performance was paramount. Planning and decision making were undisciplined, excessively personalized, and focused on each individual deal. Subordinates were highly averse to taking risks. So many people were involved in signing off on a loan decision that it was difficult to hold anyone truly accountable for results.

There was, furthermore, a veneer of mannerliness and colleagueship that inhibited frank and honest confrontations to resolve conflicts in the bank's best interest. Information, jealously guarded, was used to manipulate and control adversaries. Political intrigues abounded, with advancement often going to people most loyal to immediate supervisors. As a result of these culture aspects of our composite division, innovation was risky and received little support. Anything the area manager decided to address was quickly picked up by subordinates. Opportunism was more important than strategy.

The international division of this hypothetical bank adopted a strategy to expand its foreign banking operation that demanded several major changes: a shift in focus from geographic area to service to each foreign bank; a shift in structure

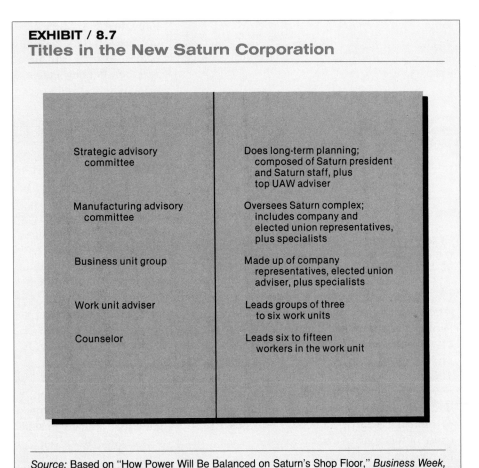

EXHIBIT / 8.7
Titles in the New Saturn Corporation

Strategic advisory committee	Does long-term planning; composed of Saturn president and Saturn staff, plus top UAW adviser
Manufacturing advisory committee	Oversees Saturn complex; includes company and elected union representatives, plus specialists
Business unit group	Made up of company representatives, elected union adviser, plus specialists
Work unit adviser	Leads groups of three to six work units
Counselor	Leads six to fifteen workers in the work unit

Source: Based on "How Power Will Be Balanced on Saturn's Shop Floor," *Business Week,* August 5, 1985, pp. 65–66.

Culture and Strategy: Portraits of J. C. Penney and Twentieth Century-Fox

"The Penney Idea" provides a guide for management decisions and helps establish the culture at J.C. Penney.

J. C. Penney and Twentieth Century-Fox have very different strategies and very different cultures. J. C. Penney has always had a paternalistic attitude and a well-entrenched culture aimed straight at the middle class. Employees are part of the family. This paternalism has meant that rather than fire marginally competent employees Penney tries to find new jobs for them. Stephen Temlock, manager of human resource strategy, concedes that because of this approach some workers "expect us to be papa and mama, and are not movitated enough to help themselves." He also admits that some-

times this means that the company also fails to reward outstanding performers. Consequently Penney is not known for its hard-charging, aggressive employees. Change comes slowly, and as new competitors come on the scene, Penney runs the risk of losing market share.

Penney's commitment to employees does, however, have payoffs. Penney employees consider the company their second home. Loyalty is high and people like to work for Penney. Penney is rightfully proud of being consistently named as one of the best places in the nation to work. As one former executive notes, "Everyone is treated as an individual." Another notes that Penney has "an openness in the organization that many large companies do not seem to achieve." The question is whether Penney can maintain these humanistic principles and keep pace with changing customer preferences.

While J. C. Penney's strategy is constrained by its culture, Twentieth Century-Fox's culture is constrained by its strategy. Dennis C. Stanfill took over as chief executive in 1971 and immediately ran into problems. He began acquiring other leisure-time businesses to balance the risk in the motion picture business. But he chose to keep tight control of the purse strings and run Twentieth Century-Fox like a "business."

What Stanfill overlooked was that creative people in the film business are different from other business employees. Creative people are self-motivated rather than motivated by the typical carrot-and-stick approach he was using to control them. What they want is support and freedom to produce their art.

Stanfill soon clashed with Alan Ladd, Jr., president of the film group, when he refused to give Ladd control over bonuses for his staff. Ladd argued that certainly a staff that had produced such hits as *Star Wars* ought to be rewarded. Stanfill argued that the traditional extravagances of the film company could not be afforded. Giving Ladd bonus money and the right to hand it out would simply put the company back on a shaky foundation. He wanted to maintain the balance between the art of film making and the bottom line of business.

Ladd's response was predictable: He quit, taking several key people with him. He complained that Stanfill did not understand what motivates creative people. They need the recognition and the freedom to perform. "You do not run a film business like a brokerage house." ■

Source: "Corporate Culture," *Business Week,* October 27, 1980, pp. 148–158.

from geographic breakdown to a matrix between geographic areas and individual banks; a decentralization of decision making, taking it out of the hands of the regional manager and placing it in the hands of those in charge of relations with the foreign banks; an increase in the quality and continuity of client relationships; and a decrease in response times to customers. The employees dealing with the customers needed to be well aware of the bank's strategy and to have the power to initiate deals and make decisions to implement those strategies. Obviously, the current culture was not at all consistent with the strategy. If the bank CEO in the example disregards the culture in place, the strategy will not be implemented effectively. The CEO has three basic options.

Option 1: Change the Culture to Fit the Strategy   Culture is perhaps the hardest component of an organization to change and will only change if top management sets the example, educates all employees regarding new desired ways of operating, and reinforces the desired norms and behaviors through compensation, rewards, or recognition. Culture will change over time as new procedures and practices are adopted. The new behavior, values, and expectations will be adopted as managers focus on and support the new practices and procedures. In the case of our hypothetical bank, the top managers would have to emphasize teamwork over autonomy, emphasize and reward accountability for loan decisions, and emphasize and reward innovation and dedication to customer service. Only then could the culture shift to support the new strategy.

Roger Smith recognized the need to change the culture at General Motors to fit the new strategy and decentralized structure. This change is, however, taking place gradually. Though most employees recognize the shift to a more entrepreneurial, innovative, and risk-taking culture, many are uncomfortable with it. They feel as if their stability and security have been taken away. Smith will have to manage this cultural change very carefully to ensure that the result is an entrepreneurial atmosphere and increased innovation rather than paralysis.[27]

Option 2: Change the Strategy to Fit the Culture   Changing the organization's strategy means deciding to pursue a different course. The major drawback of this approach is that strategies are normally designed with environmental demands in mind. Thus, changing the strategy for the sake of a stubborn culture tends to be counterproductive. Schwartz and Davis's hypothetical bank, for example, could have abandoned its strategy of expanding foreign banking operations because it required too great a shift in culture. However, this would not have helped the bank grow or increase its profits. It simply would put it back where it started, minus whatever investments were made in attempting to implement the strategic and cultural shifts. At GM, resistance to the new entrepreneurial, innovative climate could also lead management to revert back to the previous strategy, remaining more centralized and structured. However, changing the strategy so that it fit the old culture would only mean failure. The strategy of innovation and decentralization was adopted because it fit the competitive environment.

Option 3: Manage Around the Culture   Schwartz and Davis suggest that, in certain circumstances, culture should be "managed around." When it is not reasonable to change either the culture or the strategy, managing around the culture is the only option left. Consider, for example, a chemical firm interested in entering the field of ceramics. Ceramics have unlimited potential; prepared properly, they are stronger than iron or steel and wear longer than other substances. Some Japanese and American firms are making great strides in developing products such as automobile engines, machine parts, and computers with ceramic components.

The logical strategy for the chemical firm entering the ceramics business would be to combine a research-oriented unit and a production unit responsible for ceramics into one division. This would allow the firm to coordinate and quickly move their new products into production more easily. Unfortunately, the cultures of units from both areas probably would not be compatible. Research units tend to focus on technology and to have innovative, risk-oriented cultures with long-term focuses, while production units tend to have structured cultures with a focus on short-term returns.

As an alternative, the organization can manage around the cultures of the two units. In this case, the approach would not be to create a third unit to develop the ceramics business but to design ways of coordinating the work of the research and consumer products groups. Task forces and reporting structures could be established that would allow the units to remain separate but to draw upon each other's expertise in working toward their common objective: establishing a ceramics business.

Both structure and culture are critical components in implementing strategy, although the influence of culture has only recently been addressed. There is a dynamic relationship between all three: Changes in strategy often demand corresponding changes in structure and culture to support them. Similarly, aspects of culture and structure should be considered in the design of strategy due to their crucial role in helping to carry strategy out. In changing environments, managers must understand and guide culture, structure, and strategy together.

■ KEY POINTS

1 Organization structure is the defined set of relationships between divisions, departments, and managers in the organization. Culture is the beliefs, behavior patterns, ceremonies, and rituals that members of the organization hold in common as they relate to each other and do their jobs. Both structure and culture must be compatible with strategy, or its implementation will be ineffective.

2 Proponents of bureaucracy argue that only a rational, clearly defined organization allows people to understand their jobs and the standards against which they are being evaluated; thus, it allows them to determine whether they are completing their portions of the overall tasks and know whether they are being evaluated fairly. Critics of bureaucracy argue that clear job responsibilities and standard rules are difficult to put into practice and are not well suited to rapidly changing and uncertain environments.

3 By suggesting that structure is a tool used to implement strategy, the contingency approach goes beyond the argument of whether bureaucracy is good or bad. In some situations, a rigid, bureaucratic or mechanistic structure is best; in others, a flexible, changeable, organic structure is best.

4 The degree of complexity and the rate of change in an organization's external environment affect the determination of an appropriate structure. To the extent that factors in the operating environment are stable and predictable, the organization can utilize a stable structure, such as a bureaucracy or a mechanistic structure.

To the extent that factors in this environment change rapidly and unpredictably, the organization must utilize a flexible, organic structure.

5 The size of the organization, its technology of production, and the diversity of its products and services influence the determination of appropriate organization structure.

6 Differentiation refers to the differences in structure and orientation that exist among units within an organization; integration is the degree to which the separate units are coordinated. In more uncertain environments,

differentiation among units and the need for integration will be great. In more stable environments, differentiation and the need for integration will not be as great.

7 Symbols, rituals, and ideologies indicate what the organizational culture is; the strategy indicates what it should be. Managers have three basic options for managing the fit between culture and strategy so that the organization's goals can be achieved: They can change the culture to fit the strategy, change the strategy to fit the culture, or manage around the culture.

FOR DISCUSSION AND REVIEW

1. How has the structure of General Motors changed over the years? Evaluate the pros and cons of each structure the firm has had.

2. What are the relationships between organizational design and culture?

3. What aspects of the internal and external environment must an effective design take into consideration? How can this be done effectively?

4. What are the relationships between the Woodward and the Lawrence and Lorsch studies?

5. Carefully analyze the culture of a university, college, or high school with which you are familiar. How should its culture be changed to enhance its ability to accomplish its mission?

6. Describe the symbols, rituals, and ideologies of a company you know. How do they affect the performance of the organization?

KEY TERMS

Bureaucracy
Contingency theory of
   organization
Culture
Differentiation

Ideologies
Integration
Mass production
Mechanistic organization

Organic organization
Organization design
Process production
Rituals

Symbols
Technology of
   production
Unit production

THE CONFERENCE TABLE: DISCUSSION CASE / 8.1

No Desks, No Drawers

At the age of 81, Amador Aguiar, founder of the Banco Brasileiro de Descontos S.A. (Bradesco), was still putting in long hours at the Brazilian bank. Founded in 1943, Bradesco has over $8 billion in assets, operates 1650 branches nationwide, controls 15 percent of Brazil's retail market, and is the country's largest private retail bank. However, the structure and culture at Bradesco are far from the conservative atmosphere one would expect. According to director Dorival Bianchi, "We're more than a bank. We're a religion."

Source: Schuster, Lynda, "At a Bank in Brazil, Stress on Teamwork Pays Big Dividends," *Wall Street Journal,* August 22, 1985, pp. 1, 16.

Banco Brasileiro's headquarters in a suburb of Sao Paulo constitute a town within a town, reflecting the all-encompassing philosophy of its founder.

Executives not only are not allowed drawers in their desks ("Drawers are just a place to leave work for the next day," according to Aguiar), they do not even have their own desks. Nor offices, nor secretaries. They work together from 7 A.M. to 7 P.M., sitting around two large tables in one room. They share phones, listen to one another's business, and eat together in the dining room. It was all part of Aguiar's teamwork philosophy; he could be seen daily wandering the premises to enforce this precept, dressed in a suit, tie, and no socks.

When he founded the bank, Aguiar's strategy was simple: to provide loans to small coffee growers and ranchers. This group frequently had trouble funding their operations because most banks only lend to the old, landed families. In keeping with his strategy, he extended the bank's hours so the farmers could stop in on the way to or from the fields. He also required the branch managers to sit at open desks at the front of the bank so clients could easily approach them.

Statements of Aguiar's ideology can be found everywhere: "Only work can produce wealth" is emblazoned over a doorway at the bank's headquarters; "We trust in God" is printed on the stationery; a "thought on smiles" section is printed in the company's message and prayer books; and all workers are required to sign a declaration vowing to put the bank's interest above personal interests and to "love Brazil and work hard for the country." Employee promotions are based on how well one assimilates these principles; therefore almost no one is brought in from other banks.

Every employee starts out as an office boy and must work 15 years before even being considered for top managerial positions. Togetherness and teamwork training begin immediately. For example, the credit department is a football-field-sized room filled with tables where three or four sit together. They work on forms and "chatter away as though in a high school cafeteria." The bank dominates much of its employees' lives, running a hospital, a supermarket, a clinic, and almost 30 primary and elementary schools, which introduce the students to Bradesco's principles. Bradesco has an almost cultlike following among its 137,000 employees, all of whom are familiar with Aguiar's humble beginnings as a typesetter.

However, with the bank's success and unique operating methods have come certain sacrifices. Turnover among the lower levels is high; pay there is low even by Brazilian banking standards, and many are not willing to wait 15 years for meaningful promotions. One employee who finally resigned from the international division found Bradesco "ponderous and inflexible" and was soon earning twice his former Bradesco salary in his new job for an American bank. Not every employee feels this way, of course. The executive vice president for international business (as of 1987) started at 15 as a clerk. After 31 years, he says, "The bank has given me everything I ever dreamed of, a chance to learn, to work, to grow. . . . It let me realize myself in a way I never thought possible. All this, and without a high school education." ■

DISCUSSION QUESTIONS

1. In what way did Aguiar take Bradesco far beyond bureaucracy? How successfully or unsuccessfully has he utilized the contingency approach?
2. Does he match strategy to external or to internal conditions more effectively? What might you change for the better, if anything?
3. How effectively does the structure of individual units match the bank's strategy? How differentiated are they, and how well or poorly integrated?
4. How compatible is the culture with the structure and strategy of the bank? How is this managed, and how effectively or successfully?

THE CONFERENCE TABLE: DISCUSSION CASE / 8.2

Roger Penske, Inc.

Roger Penske, former race-car driver, still keeps his foot firmly on the accelerator. The only difference is that now he is a president and CEO of the thriving transportation leasing concern, Penske Corporation, as well as the head of the Penske Racing Team.

Hertz-Penske, the nation's second largest truck leasing and rental company, with a fleet of nearly 42,000 vehicles and 267 service facilities, was formed as a joint venture with Hertz in 1982. In 1981, a year before Penske became involved, Hertz's division registered a $40 million pretax loss. Under the aggressive management style of the new president, the division reached $575 million in sales with an estimated $31 million of pretax earnings in 1987. In 1988, the Penske Corporation acquired Detroit Diesel Corporation, the maker of diesel engines, and total revenues are expected to exceed $2.3 billion.

Some industry analysts think that the company is growing too fast and is taking on too much debt. But it is not in Penske's nature to coast. "We plan to keep on growing through acquisition. We are always looking at other companies." If you take a close look at Hertz-Penske, you will find a smoothly run organization that

Sources: "Roger Penske: Running on 16 Cylinders," *Business Week,* June 1, 1987, p. 71 and "Penske to End Hertz Venture, Start a GE One," *Wall Street Journal,* June 7, 1988, p. 24. Doron P. Levin, "Penske Wins Big at Detroit Diesel," *The New York Times,* May 29, 1989, p. 1.

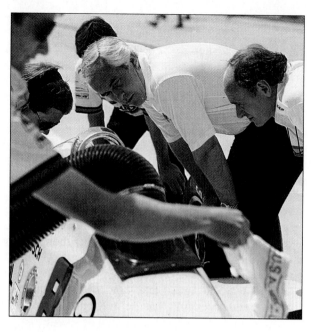

Roger Penske had a "brief but flashy" stint in racing before he became the head of a conglomerate worth $470 million.

functions as efficiently as a racing team. Penske demands attention to detail, as well as total cleanliness in all the facilities, from the boardroom to the body shop. At a recent meeting with his bankers, he showcased the company headquarters by serving lunch in the spotless garage.

Roger Penske is described as a hard-driving but fair man. He expects high performance from his cars and his employees. Hourly workers and union officials are described as giving Mr. Penske slack " . . . because they have been infused with a sense of involvement they never had before." Penske has dispensed with the chair of command and deals directly with the workers. For example, Jim Morrow, plant manager at Detroit Diesel, says he is no longer surprised when his memos to top managers and Penske are passed among hourly workers with Penske's notation, "Is this OK with you?"

These days Penske is focusing attention on his truck leasing business. His goal is to unseat a four-times larger Ryder System, Inc. as the industry leader. As unrealistic as it may sound, his associates warn not to take him too lightly. "He will run you off the road," says one of his friends. "He'll try to beat you any way he can."

In order to increase the profit margins to between seven and eight percent, in 1988 Roger Penske decided to sever his joint truck leasing venture with Hertz Corporation to form one with General Electric Company. Although his spokesman states that the move was caused by Ford's acquisition of ownership stake in Hertz and Penske's unwillingness to be associated with any other car manufacturer but GM, many analysts speculate that the real reason was to improve the competitive position against Ryder and increase annual revenues to $750 million. ■

DISCUSSION QUESTIONS

1. Considering some of the diverse units in which Roger Penske is involved—car rentals, racing, and truck leasing—how many organization structure(s) would you suggest? How should he coordinate his many activities?

2. How would you describe the culture at Hertz-Penske? How does it help the organization accomplish its strategy?

9 | Organizational Change, Conflict, and Development

FOCUS CASE / Marketing Rainbows

CHANGE: CATALYST FOR DEVELOPMENT OR CRISIS
Force Field Analysis

THE NATURE OF CONFLICT
Conflict Caused by Differences
Conflict Caused by Competition for Limited Resources

MANAGING CONFLICT
Lose-Lose Resolutions
Win-Lose Resolutions
Win-Win Resolutions

MANAGING PLANNED CHANGE
Unfreezing, Change, Refreezing
A Six-Step Change Process
Structural, Technological, Human, and Task Approaches

MANAGING ORGANIZATION DEVELOPMENT
The Organization Development Process
Fostering a Creative Climate
Fostering Innovation
Developing an Atmosphere of Entrepreneurship

An organization's structure must be compatible with the environment, as we illustrated in Chapter 8. But both the internal and external environments of an organization are dynamic. Forces from inside and outside the organization continually push and pull it in opposite directions. Change and conflict continually occur and must be managed if the organization is to operate effectively in the short term and grow and develop in the long term. Organizations must continually manage the fit between their structures, their cultures, and their environment. In this chapter, we will discuss change and its effects on organizations, and various methods for managing change and guiding organization development.

▓ KEY QUESTIONS

As you study this chapter, try to answer the following key questions:

1 What effect does environmental change have on organizations, and how should management cope with the effect?
2 How can force field analysis be used to diagnose and plan for change?
3 What are the major sources of conflict, and on what levels can organizational conflict exist?
4 What are three basic ways managers resolve conflicts, and which is the most successful in the long run?
5 Describe the change process in two ways, illustrating each phase.
6 What are four approaches to planned change?
7 What is organization development (OD), and what does the OD process involve?
8 What are three ways managers can enhance or facilitate the organization development process?

Focus Case

Marketing Rainbows

Giuliana Benneton. Her ability to design sweaters has been a major factor in the international success of the Benneton corporation.

As one reporter said of conditions in Italy during the 1970s, "There is a very thin line between chaos and vitality." Labor unrest in that country had been steadily increasing, and strikes were common. The government had set in motion a system of wage indexing to keep wages ahead of inflation, but this only steadily decreased the value of the Italian lira. Few businesses were willing or able to expand. The problems seemed to reach a crescendo in the fall of 1978, and the entire country was in a state of chaos. But "the crisis became a moment of profound change, not breakdown," said the reporter.

> There was a dramatic change in the attitudes of workers and managers. Old businesses were revitalized and new businesses created. Employment increased, inflation fell . . . but, as when a magician pulls a rabbit out of a hat, the rabbit has to be there in the first place; the potential for change was already there.

But economic upheaval was not the only factor affecting businesses. Relaxed restrictions brought with them a surge in business activity, and competition in many industries was heating up rapidly. This is the environment clothing manufacturer Benetton was facing in its first decade of operation. As a fashion-oriented company in a highly competitive environment, Benetton had to learn how to respond to labor unrest and chaotic economic conditions as well as competitors' advances and swings in customer preferences.

Sister and brother Giuliana and Luciano Benetton founded the company in 1965 in a villa north of Venice, combining her sweater-designing skills and his wholesaling connections. They started by distributing homemade sweaters to retail outlets. Their two brothers joined the partnership later: Gilberto in charge of administration and Carlo in charge of production. They opened their first store in 1968, and by 1978 they had 1000 stores worldwide and annual sales of $78 million.

After 1978, Benetton took advantage of the government's relaxed labor agreements and began to farm out more and more of its manufacturing to contractors. Local independent producers, employing about 10,000 people, became responsible for much of the knitting, assembly, and finishing operations. Benetton became increasingly decentralized. The company launched a major export program to the rest of Europe (previously 98 percent of their

Sources: This case was written by M. R. Poirier, based on the following sources: Sasseen, J., "A Nation of Workshops," *Forbes,* April 30, 1984, p. 80; "Benetton," Harvard Business School Case (#9-685-014), rev. September 1985; "Benetton: Bringing European Chic to Middle America," *Business Week,* June 11, 1984, pp. 109–110; Belkin, Lisa, "Benetton's Cluster Strategy," *New York Times,* January 16, 1986, pp. D1, D5; Resener, Madlyn, "Europe's Invasion," *Newsweek,* August 12, 1985, p. 55; Szanto, "Anarchy that Works," *Whole Earth Review* (May 1985): 36.

sales had been in Italy). Production processes were modernized, much of the factory was automated, and as Luciano Benetton summed it up, "We have kept the same strategy all along: to put fashion on an industrial level. Most of the rest of Italian fashion is still on an artisan level."

Today, Benetton has sales of almost $1 billion, has 5000 franchise shops that sell its wares exclusively, and has branched out into shirts, jeans, gloves, shoes, perfume, and even financial services. Expansion did not come easily, however. It required countless innovations, departures from the norm, and variations on accepted methods. Early developments were in the area of clothing production. Newly manufactured woolen clothing, for example, must be softened. Ten years before the development of machines to do this, Luciano Benetton devised a makeshift method, based upon one he had seen in Scotland, to soften clothing by beating it in water. The crude machine with wooden arms that he assembled was ungainly, but it did the job. To dry the wet garments without shrinking them, another unusual method was developed: They were placed in bags on sticks and rotated vertically in the air.

And the management at Benetton did not have a monopoly on creative ideas. In its early years, one of Benetton's employees recommended buying hosiery-knitting machines that had become obsolete when seamed stockings fell out of fashion. They could be bought very cheaply and needed relatively minor alterations to be converted to suit Benetton's purposes. Before being replaced by modern, computerized knitting machines, the converted ones provided about 90 percent of Benetton's knitting capacity.

Perhaps the most significant development in Benetton's operations—and one of its most unique features—occurred in 1972 when the company began dyeing assembled garments rather than yarn. Though the cost of dyeing assembled garments was about 10 percent higher in terms of labor and production overhead, it allowed Benetton a level of responsiveness to the market that is virtually unparalleled in any other manufacturer its size. Through an intricate communications network and computer system, Benetton can receive and deliver orders for garments of specific colors far faster than its competitors. Though the winter and summer lines are designed at least a year in advance, much of the stock is left undyed. That way, early orders can be altered, last-minute orders can be met easily, and "hot" items can be restocked throughout the season as soon as the information system (through sales data) identifies them. In addition to the regular seasonal lines, therefore, the "flash collection" of about 50 items of any color can be added in response to early customer requests for out-of-stock colors, and a "reassortment" collection can cover end-of-season requests.

To the individual consumer, Benetton may appear a small and simple operation. This is certainly not the case. Since it supplies clothing under several different "line" names, many people do not realize how extensive the operation is. Each line is sold in small shops with decor well suited to the consumers to whom it caters. The 012 Benetton shops, which supply children's wear, are decorated with stuffed animals. Young teens can shop in Tomato stores featuring rock music and flashing lights, and men and women looking for more sophisticated fashions can find what they are looking for in the more sedate, refined environments of the Sisley and Mercerie shops.

Benetton's success did not come easily, and it is not small. Internal innovations and creativity have transformed the small family business into the wildly successful multinational corporation it is today. As one reporter put it, the Benettons and many other Italian entrepreneurs may be abundantly possessed of what Italians call *fantasia,* something along the lines of creative imagination. "They see possibilities, they can imagine the new." Through their innovative efforts, the Benettons have come through a period of rapid change and conflict, creating not only their own rainbow but also the pot of gold at the end of it. ■

Like Benetton, all organizations exist within a changing environment that offers both threats and opportunities. In 1978, Benetton's challenge was to guide the organization through a chaotic environment characterized not only by political upheaval and labor unrest but also by increasing competition in the fashion and clothing industries. Today, businesses face increased challenges from an ever more complex and rapidly changing environment. In 1982, Thomas Peters and Robert Waterman, Jr., in their book *In Search of Excellence,* developed a list of traits they said characterized "excellent" firms. The list included such factors as "(being) close to the customer" and "productivity through people." In a 1987 interview, after he published his third book, *Thriving on Chaos,*[1] Peters explained that, "excellence at least as we talked about it in the first book," was no longer enough. The first book "talked about IBM and Procter & Gamble and institutions that had done incredibly well for a darn long time, but in an environment that was a lot more placid than it is today,"[2] said Peters. Peters's thoughts on chaos, change, and organizational development are quoted in The Inside View 9.1.

Change is a source of both threats and opportunities. It can be sudden or unpredictable, but, if the organization is carefully guided through it, it can have very positive, productive outcomes. The challenge is to manage the organization so that it is not damaged by the threats and so that it can take advantage of the opportunities.

CHANGE: CATALYST FOR DEVELOPMENT OR CRISIS

Change pervades modern society and is happening at an ever-increasing rate. More technological advancement and cultural change have happened in the past 200 years than in the previous 2000. To survive and develop, organizations must adapt to threatening changes and respond to opportunities for growth.[3] Shifts in any sector of an organization's operating environment (changes in the economy, developments in technology, or fluctuations in competition) as well as changes in the organization's general environment (changes in social, ethical, legal, and political forces) and shifts in the international environments combine to create a complex environment of dynamic and fast-moving change. An organization's management must understand and manage change if the organization is to thrive and grow.

The Benettons and their organization, for example, had to respond to many of these changes, particularly changes in the competitive environment. Starting in the 1960s, competitive strength was measured by the number and variety of

THE INSIDE VIEW / 9.1

Excellence Is No Longer Enough

According to Tom Peters, we are coming out of a predictable environment into a world where great flexibility is necessary in order to react to constant change.

I do not think [chaos is] around the corner. It's here. The question is: Will companies learn to deal with it? Now, when I say chaos, I do not mean the technical definition of "total disarray, randomness" and so on. What I mean is that back in the olden days—like five years ago—you had a reasonably good idea, whether you were a banker or even the head of a semiconductor company, who you might be competing against next week.

Today, literally, you have no idea who your competitors will be next week, whether the yen-dollar relationship is going to be at 80 or 300, what the price of money is going to be, what inflation is going to be. We are coming out of an environment that was reasonably predictable . . . cyclical, sure, your automatic once-every-eight-years recession . . . but the fundamentals tended to be somewhat the same. Now that's out the window. Now all bets are off. But I still believe there is

substantial control over one's own destiny. In fact, what I'm trying to say is that the world has changed, that the cycles have gotten shorter and incredible flexibility is required relative to the task, and that you've got to learn a totally new set of tricks.

But on net, my major concern over the last couple of years has been the slowness of big corporations to react to change, and I will be the unyielding fan of anybody who will scare the hell out of the chieftains of the Fortune 500.

Certainly I do not think the average raider—Boone Pickens or Carl Icahn or so on—is an altruist. They are greedy capitalists in the best sense of the word, but I think they are the rare institutions with the ability to scare the big guys into doing what they ought to do.

The average business school takes people that are technically trained in science or engineering and teaches them business as an abstraction. But business is not an abstraction. A relationship with an employee or customer or supplier is not an abstraction. It is blood and guts and human beings trying to figure out what makes somebody happy. We do not teach the value of that in our business schools.

But the one beautiful glowing light coming out of this country right now is the volatility of all of our marketplaces—from health care to financial services to the world of semiconductors and computers. Where there's chaos there's also opportunity. ■

Source: Interview by Michael S. Malone with Tom Peters, "Excellence Is No Longer Enough," *Boston Globe,* December 14, 1987, p. 18, 20.

goods a retailer could offer: the greater the number and variety, the greater the competitive advantage. But increased number and variety were costly. Therefore, to compete in the 1970s, many stores began specializing, offering fewer items at lower cost. Competitive advantages then came from the offering of unique, specialized items unavailable or unaffordable at department stores. During the 1980s, competitive advantage came from the mastering of both previous tactics: being able to produce a wide variety of specialized items without raising costs (or prices). The Japanese system of automobile production, which we will discuss in Chapter 16, utilized this strategy with such success that American manufacturers were forced to rethink their entire method of operation. In simplest terms, Japanese auto producers manufacture, exactly, only what is needed and only as it is needed. This eliminates inventory, decreases labor costs, and increases flexibility.

Benetton has been using a similar system since 1978: By manufacturing only the number of items that has already been ordered and by leaving finished garments undyed until requests for specific colors come in, Benetton can produce exactly what will sell, exactly when needed, and meet an extremely wide variety of customer needs. The savings in inventory largely make up for the 10 percent increase in the cost of dyeing whole garments. Thus, by anticipating a trend in the competitive environment, Benetton has placed itself in the forefront of the fashion-retailing industry.

Force Field Analysis

The Benetton case illustrates how one company reacted to pressure in the external environment. Management was quick to respond to events innovatively and creatively, taking advantage of opportunities and working around constraints as they arose. The company, partially because it was small and grew up in a highly dynamic atmosphere, was dynamic itself and eager to grow, change, and develop.

But many companies are not as open to change. Pressures from any source exerted on more rigid companies may result in crisis rather than adaptation and development. Often this happens because organizations remain static; that is, though outside pressures may demand change, equally strong pressures from within the organization resist changes. Thus, the organization remains as is when, to survive or remain competitive, it must change.

Force field analysis A tool used to diagnose and plan for change.

This phenomenon can be illustrated through the use of force field analysis.[4] **Force field analysis** is a tool used to diagnose and plan for change. By lining up forces that drive change and forces that resist it on opposite sides of a line denoting present circumstances, managers can determine how likely a system or organization is to change and what will cause it.

Consider the example of Benetton and a hypothetical competitor, Trendy Clothing Store. Let us assume both are using standard production techniques and both are subject to the same forces discussed above that are increasing the need for change. These forces are listed in the left-hand column of Exhibit 9.1. The center column describes standard industry practice: making garments from dyed yarn, producing in bulk and maintaining inventories, and shipping on demand.

In the right-hand column are listed factors that cause the organization to resist making the changes that the driving forces are demanding—in this case, changing the system so that product variety can be increased while costs decrease. For Trendy, there are several resistance forces. One is the cost of new technology; they would have to purchase equipment to dye the whole garments if they wanted to produce colors on demand, and they would need a new computer system to coordinate sales data with production. In addition, both the workers and the plant managers have always produced goods from dyed yarn and expect to meet a daily production run that does not vary. To make the changes, they would have to forgo their old habits and learn entirely new skills and production methods. The cost of technology and the resistance to learning new methods are

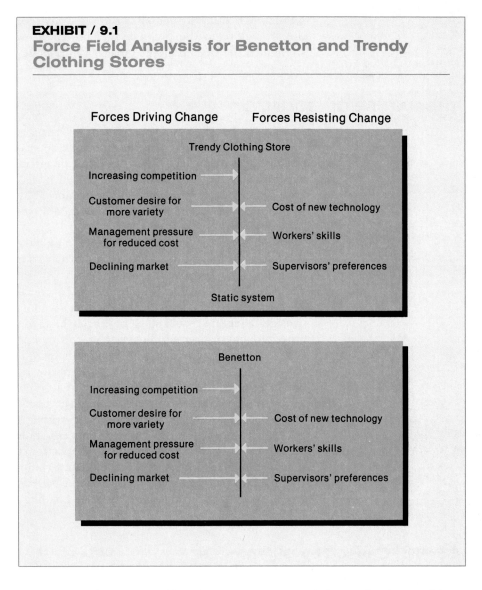

EXHIBIT / 9.1
Force Field Analysis for Benetton and Trendy Clothing Stores

strong enough forces in Trendy's case to counterbalance the forces driving change. Thus, Trendy will not change; the current system will remain.

Benetton, however, had ways of overcoming the barriers and reducing the resistance to change. Where new technology was needed, it was either developed from scratch (as with the softening and drying equipment) or a decision was made to invest in it and train the personnel in its use (as with the computer information system linking the stores to the production center). The company was innovative and flexible by nature. The forces driving change were strong, while the forces resisting it could be reduced. Thus, Benetton adopted a new system and gained a significant competitive advantage. Benetton was able to manage its own change and development.

In this chapter, we will discuss change, planned change, and organization development, beginning with a discussion of conflict and conflict resolution. The force field example above described opposing forces inside and outside the organization. If managers can understand the many sources of these opposing forces, they can develop the preliminary skills for managing conflict, and they will strengthen the organization so that it can operate more effectively.

THE NATURE OF CONFLICT

Conflict has been a prominent element in organizations for a long time, but only recently have scholars studied how it might be managed. Abraham Maslow credited this delay to society's fear of conflict, disagreement, and hostility. Traditionally, managers felt that conflict was caused by troublemakers or by failures of leadership. In other words, it was not the norm but the exception; it was avoidable. In situations where it did occur, it could be resolved by separating the warring factions as much as possible.

A more realistic view sees conflict as not only inevitable but potentially useful if managed correctly.[5] Since the 1970s, managers have recognized that absolute harmony within groups and organizations is impossible. In addition, lack of conflict is not always healthy, stimulating, or beneficial. When too little conflict exists, people are not confronting each other's assumptions and helping each other consider alternatives and solve problems. In such situations, conflict should be provoked and managed to help people and groups be more productive.[6]

This does not mean that more conflict is always better. When tensions are so high that people do not cooperate and are not productive, conflict should be reduced so that they can work together to accomplish their objectives. Modern managers do not necessarily try to eliminate conflict; rather, they manage it so that it contributes to the individuals' and organization's productivity.[7]

Conflict in organizations can exist between individuals, groups, units, departments, or organizational levels. It often results from two basic sources: differences (between people, groups, or situations) and competition for limited resources. There is nothing inherently wrong with differences or competition. Management's challenge is to find ways to make conflict productive.[8]

Conflict Caused by Differences

Differences that cause conflict can be inherent in the individual or group, such as differences in experience or characteristics; or they can be inherent to the situation, such as differences between levels or units in an organization's structure.

Differences in experience can enhance the organization's ability to solve complex problems because people with varied backgrounds can combine their experience and knowledge. These differences between people are natural in organizations. People who have spent many years in one department may resent newcomers who have no experience but are placed at a high level because they have college degrees. Both kinds of employees have valuable skills to offer, but they may be at odds with each other.

Line-staff conflicts can also be caused by differences in experience. As discussed in Chapter 7, line personnel often feel that because staff personnel are cut off from day-to-day operations they do not understand the operation well enough to make useful recommendations. Staff, on the other hand, feel the line does not have the expertise to make many of the decisions they are making and resent it when the line does not follow their recommendations.

Conflicts between groups or units may occur when two groups who must work together have developed incompatible methods of operation. A production department, for example, may have found that producing 500-unit lots of each product is most efficient or easy, while the packaging department may have developed a system in which 300-unit lots are handled most efficiently. Though both systems are internally efficient, the two groups will not work well together. After one round, there will be a 200-unit surplus in packaging; after the next round, there will be a 100-unit surplus. Not until the third round will production and packaging be on even terms again.

Differences in characteristics can also exist on several levels. Both individuals and groups may have different personalities, perspectives, or norms or different patterns of behavior.[9] One person may value teamwork and cooperation while another may consider individuality and personal success more important. Given the assignment to work together developing a new product, these two people may approach the task very differently. One person will want to work closely with the other, share ideas and resources, and cooperate to develop the new product. The other may want to work separately and in competition with the first. It is not likely that these two people will work together successfully for any length of time. Whole groups can also have these same characteristics, each group developing a style that makes it hard to work with other groups.

Differences inherent in organizational structure are another source of conflicts.[10] When separate production and marketing departments are created, as in a functionally departmentalized organization, differences in perspectives will emerge. The production department is responsible for producing certain quantities and types of products at the lowest price possible. They want standard products that can be produced efficiently. They will resist changes in the production system because changes take time and money—changes inhibit cost-efficient production. The marketing department, on the other hand, works directly with the customers. They want flexibility in the production system and large inventories of products in all shapes and sizes so that they can best respond to customer demands. The structure of the organization creates these differences in focus that can lead, in turn, to conflict.

Hierarchical conflict
Conflict caused by differences in the nature of managers' responsibilities and frames of reference across levels in the organization.

Differences in the nature of managers' responsibilities and frames of reference across levels in the organization create another source of conflict referred to as **hierarchical conflict.** Because people on different levels have different responsibilities, they may think and act differently. Those in top managerial positions may not understand the day-to-day operating realities of the first-line employees. These employees, in turn, may not fully understand the pressures and responsibilities of top management.

Benetton provides an illustration of how conflicts between units can be prevented through effective organizing. Giuliana's design unit, for example, wanted extensive variety in response to customers' needs. Carlo's production unit wanted predictable production schedules. What might have been a debilitating conflict was actually the source of one of Benetton's greatest innovations: dyeing the whole garment rather than the yarn. This innovation allowed production to make the garments on a continuous, fairly predictable schedule rather than requiring change every time a new color was needed. At the same time, Benetton could more quickly respond to customer demand because it did not have to wait for a full production run to be completed in order to obtain garments in the color and quantity it needed. Thus, Benetton has a tremendous competitive advantage over others who still manufacture bulk inventories of garments from dyed yarn.

Conflict Caused by Competition for Limited Resources

Competition exists whenever there are limited resources. The concept of zero-sum, which derives from military theory, describes these situations. A zero-sum situation exists when one individual, group, or organization (or country) wins at the expense of another. For instance, if there is only enough money in the budget for one project to be developed, then one person's or one unit's project will be selected, and the projects of the others will be passed over. Students experience a zero-sum situation whenever professors grade on a forced distribution. Only so many students can receive A grades. If 10 out of 70 students get the A's, the other 60 students cannot.

Being in a zero-sum situation causes individuals or groups to see others as the opposition, or enemy. Winning or losing aggravates this divisiveness. Winners feel confident and become more cohesive and supportive of each other. Losers are frustrated and angry. They may single out someone in the group or something to blame for their failure. Members of the losing group may become less tolerant of each other and less willing to work together in the future.

MANAGING CONFLICT

The challenge for managers is not to eliminate conflict but to manage it to contribute to the accomplishment of organizational objectives. As we have demonstrated in previous chapters, problems and challenges in organizations are often best addressed through a rational process. Conflict resolution can be managed through the five-step process described in Exhibit 9.2. Using this process, managers can usually reach successful, effective resolutions to conflict. However, if these solutions are to be lasting, the manager must ensure that both (or all) parties are truly satisfied by the resulting agreement. This is not always the case. Conflicts may be resolved in one of three basic ways: lose-lose, win-lose, and win-win.

EXHIBIT / 9.2
A Process for Conflict Resolution

1. *Identify the problem* to determine the basic reasons it exists. When conflict exists managers should identify the perceptions, assumptions, expected results, needs of individuals and proposed solutions.
2. *Approach the problem as an obstacle to be overcome or a goal to be accomplished.* Do not immediately jump to conclusions. First make sure you have carefully analyzed the problem and have a clear understanding of why it exists. Make sure everyone involved understands the obstacles preventing you from resolving the problem and what must be accomplished in order for these obstacles to be overcome.
3. *Depersonalize the problem.* Do not focus on the individuals or groups involved. Shift attention to differences that exist because of the nature of the situation or the organization.

4. *Achieve a common understanding.* Make sure everyone shares a common understanding of why the conflict exists. If people do not share a common definition of the problem it will be impossible for them to work together to solve it.
5. *Identify action steps.* Having spent the time to analyze the problem and identify solutions, people will want to see action taken and results produced. Identify those steps and get them involved in implementing the correct solutions.

Lose-Lose Resolutions

Lose-lose conflict resolution A resolution that does not completely satisfy the needs or criteria of either party.

Lose-lose conflict resolution occurs when compromises are reached that do not completely satisfy the needs or criteria of either party or when both parties have to sacrifice important objectives to reach a settlement. While sometimes there are no other alternatives, this type of resolution leaves people dissatisfied and searching for ways to increase equity. For example, some strikes end in both parties losing. The union is on strike so long that its membership becomes discouraged and loses commitment. The workers realize that they can never win back all that they have lost in wages and benefits, but to save face they hold a hard line. The company becomes so firm in its position during the length of the strike that it will not back off. The final agreement will probably be unsatisfactory to both sides, even if one side "loses" decisively. In these cases, any contract agreed to will probably not hold for the long term. The mutual lack of satisfaction will eventually provoke another conflict or strike.

Win-Lose Resolutions

Win-lose conflict resolution A resolution in which one party wins and one loses.

In a **win-lose conflict resolution,** one party wins and one loses. Most American sporting events are based on this concept. Only one team can win or take first place, at the expense of the others. Sometimes the teams tie, but often, if a tie exists, the teams are forced to keep playing until one team defeats the other.

Win-lose resolutions cause unique conditions in a group at work. For example, a supervisor may use the power of his or her position to force a subordinate's compliance. Thus, the supervisor "wins" and the employee "loses." A line manager may refuse to adopt the suggestions of a staff specialist. A group may vote on an issue and force the minority to accept its decisions. A clear us-versus-them distinction between the parties emerges, rather than a we-versus-the-problem orientation. The objective, in this case, becomes to beat the other party rather than to solve the particular problem or reach an overriding objective. Because the focus is on beating someone else, the conflict becomes inappropriately personalized. This decreases the possibility that the parties will be willing to work together in the future.

In addition, win-lose resolutions may inhibit the future performance of either group. The losing group may lose cohesiveness as members blame each other for the group's failure. Members of the winning group, on the other hand, may become complacent. They will assume their approach was right because they won. Rather than trying to understand the other side's approach or analyzing their own performance to see why it succeeded, they will continue to do what they have done in the past, thereby stifling their own potential.

Win-Win Resolutions

Win-win conflict resolution A situation in which both parties gain from the resolution.
Superordinate goal An overall goal that units working together can accomplish.

Win-win conflict resolution results when both parties gain from the resolution by developing solutions that meet both of their objectives. One way this can be done is by using a **superordinate goal,** a goal that is more important than the individual goals of separate units that are contributing to its achievement—a goal toward which both parties can work. The Inside View 9.2 illustrates that some psychologists consider win-win game techniques more constructive than the traditional win-lose formats.

THE INSIDE VIEW / 9.2

Group Winning

Some psychologists believe that excessive competitiveness is counterproductive and damaging because it teaches questionable values and takes the fun out of sports and games.

Some psychological game theorists feel that competitive natures are drilled into Americans from a very early age and that these characteristics are very damaging. Psychologist Terry Orlick thinks the notion that "winning is not everything, it is the only thing" permeates all sectors and levels of our society and that it is damaging and counterproductive because "it teaches children questionable values and takes the fun out of sports and games in the process." Society could benefit more, he feels, from espousing the Chinese concept that "winning or losing is only temporary, friendship is everlasting."

In his studies of the sports industry, he finds that competitive games serve only to breed suspicion and to provoke players into acting solely in their own interest.

> Self-acceptance, trust, self-confidence and personal identity are not fostered. Instead, sports are becoming "failure factories" that produce rejection, degradation, and fear . . . players are taught to care only about winning, and are not free to take chances, improvise, and be creative.

One of the major problems is that children who learn these habits are unable to shake them off later in life, even when cooperation is in their own best interest. "Confident, cooperative, joyous children, who will carry these qualities into adulthood, are becoming an endangered species."

As a remedy, Orlick suggests replacing competitive strategy with cooperative strategy in traditional games. In musical chairs, for example, a chair can still be taken away after each stop in the music, but all players can remain in the game until the end, having as their goal holding onto each other to fit everyone in the last chair. In volleyball, the objective for both sides could simply be to keep the ball aloft as long as possible. Or all the players could be on one side of the net and run under it as the ball is passed to the other side.

Studies have indicated a ready acceptance of these concepts if introduced early enough. After one such game, both teams ran off the field together, yelling "We won! We won!" In another group, after a 10-week exposure to the "new games," two-thirds of the boys and all of the girls said they preferred games in which neither side lost. ■

Source: "How We Lose by Winning," *The Futurist* (December 1979): 424.

The same principle applies in the business world. Take the example of salespeople who were selling inventory control systems for a computer software firm. Customers, including automobile, appliance, and furniture stores, were most commonly organizations whose products were of high value and who needed to keep exact count of what they had in stock. Five salespeople from the firm handled all new and ongoing customer sales accounts and received incentive payments according to their sales each month.

The salespeople were competing with each other for customers. Each had an expense budget, and each was going after the most lucrative accounts. Rather than referring a promising lead to a colleague, for example, one salesperson would drive hours to call on a large appliance dealer who was located very close to another salesperson. Because the incentive system put them in competition for the large accounts, the salespeople were wasting time and money and cutting into the organization's profits.

The firm decided to change the incentive system to cut down expenses and give their sales force an incentive to cooperate. Under the new system, salespeople received bonuses based on the total sales of the territory, and everyone received the same allowance out of which to pay their own expenses. Now the sales force had reason to cooperate. Rather than drive across town to make a sales call, they would refer customers to the closest salesperson. With the time they saved they also were able to call on the medium and small organizations they had previously overlooked. They found a vast new market for their computerized inventory systems in smaller hardware, music, and sports equipment stores. No longer in a win-lose situation, they found that the more they cooperated and helped each other, the more successful they became.

MANAGING PLANNED CHANGE

The previous example illustrates how a company can change its systems or organization to become more efficient or successful. As the world changes at an ever-increasing pace, this becomes ever more necessary. To survive and grow, organizations must change with the environment. They are much more likely to change in the proper direction if the process of change is skillfully managed.

Several models have been developed to help managers understand and manage the process of change.[11] Managers can adapt reactively, or they can anticipate, plan, and manage changes. Kurt Lewin and Larry Greiner both provide valuable models for understanding how to manage change.

Unfreezing, Change, Refreezing

Lewin suggests a three-step process for managing change: unfreezing, change, and refreezing.[12] (See Exhibit 9.3.) Often, managers assume that people blindly resist all changes: If the vacation schedules are adjusted, everyone might be dissatisfied; if the work schedule is changed, the union might threaten to strike; if a new plant is built, the employees might resist relocating; if new technology is introduced, employees might leave the organization rather than develop the new skills to use it. However, people do not resist all change, only change they do not understand or that they see as psychologically or economically threatening. Obviously, they do not resist increases in salary, upward job grade changes, or new conveniences that make their jobs easier.

Because people respond to change based on how they perceive the change will affect them, Kurt Lewin suggests that the first step in introducing change is **unfreezing:** reducing resistance to change by helping people understand the need for it and the benefits to be gained from it. Resistance is typically caused by people fearing the unknown, being economically or psychologically threatened

Unfreezing Reducing resistance to change by helping people understand the need for it.

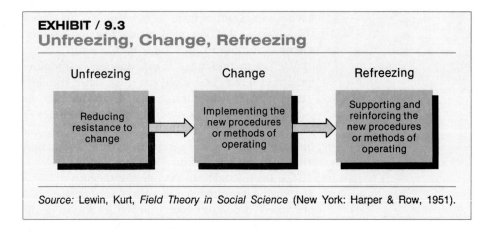

EXHIBIT / 9.3
Unfreezing, Change, Refreezing

Unfreezing → Change → Refreezing

Reducing resistance to change → Implementing the new procedures or methods of operating → Supporting and reinforcing the new procedures or methods of operating

Source: Lewin, Kurt, *Field Theory in Social Science* (New York: Harper & Row, 1951).

by new situations, or fearing the loss of things they value. In such cases, managers might assume that the resistance will go away and that the change will be made if pressure for the change is increased. But when people resist change, they are defending something they have. If a change is forced, it will remain in place only as long as pressure is applied. As we discussed in the presentation of force field analysis, the alternative is to reduce resistance to change first by reducing the fear or decreasing the threats involved, then introducing the change slowly and reinforcing it gradually.

Consider, for example, a college that introduced a new computer requirement into the junior year of the undergraduate curriculum. Initially, students took the class but could not see any application for the material presented. They disliked the new requirement and did not take it seriously. When the time came to apply the computer knowledge in their senior year, they could not remember anything they had been taught because they did not understand why the course was introduced or how the new material was to be used, and they had learned it only because of the pressure applied. As soon as they completed the class, and the pressure was gone, they forgot the material.

If the object is to get students to accept a new class and learn computer skills, the first step, according to Lewin's model, would be to reduce their resistance by helping them understand the need for the class. Professors should show them how the material will be used in later classes and in their professions. Students will learn and retain new material when they see a reason for it, when they understand that the material will help them in their future studies and in their careers. People will readily accept changes that improve their chances of success.

The second step in Lewin's model is the change itself. Once people realize that old values, attitudes, and behavior are no longer effective, they will be open to new ways. The change, whether it is a new procedure, a new technology, or a skill to be learned, can then be implemented. This calls for rearranging schedules, conducting training sessions, restructuring communications or transportation channels, or installing new equipment. In our example, once students have understood the need for the new computer skills and are ready to learn them, they will accept the new course and learn quickly.

Researchers John Kotter and Leonard Schlesinger determined that there are several ways to reduce resistance to change, each appropriate in different circumstances.[13] These are listed in Exhibit 9.4.

EXHIBIT / 9.4
Methods of Reducing Resistance to Change

1. Education and communication—effective in situations where participants lack information or the information available is inaccurate.
2. Participation and involvement—effective in situations where participants have information relevant for the change and have strong power to resist any imposed solutions.
3. Facilitation and support—effective in situations where participants are resisting change because of adjustment problems.

4. Negotiation and agreement—effective in situations where participants will clearly lose out in a change, and they have considerable power to resist.
5. Manipulation and co-optation—effective in situations where other tactics will not work or are too expensive.
6. Explicit and implicit coercion—effective in situations where speed is essential and participants have considerable power.

Source: Kotter, J. P., and Schlesinger, L. A., "Choosing Strategies for Change," *Harvard Business Review* (March–April 1979): 109–112.

Refreezing The process of supporting an implemented change.

The third step is refreezing the change. **Refreezing** is the process of supporting an implemented change through reinforcement and continued application. New skills will be retained only if they are used. New attitudes will remain only if they are supported. New procedures will be used continually only if they are productive. In other words, change must be stabilized and supported by continuing positive experience. In the university example, students must use their computer skills if they are to retain them. Students must be required to repeat the application of new skills immediately and frequently in order to become proficient. The class needs to be followed immediately by other classes in which the new computer skills are applied to practical problems.

In the above case, the administrators eventually redesigned the curriculum. Rather than offering a theoretical class with few applied examples, the school offered an applied class. Theory and applications were interwoven so that students learned the new skills by using them to solve specific organizational problems. Guest speakers demonstrated how the skills were used in the professions that students would be entering. The university also implemented follow-up classes. They were redesigned to integrate the use of the computer skills. Because the students immediately applied what they had learned, the learning experience was much more lasting and effective. In short, the students' resistance to the change had been reduced because they understood the purpose for the change. The change was then introduced, and finally the new skills and attitudes were refrozen and supported by continued positive experiences.

A Six-Step Change Process

Another approach to understanding and managing the process of change has been proposed by Larry Greiner.[14] After reviewing projects in many organizations, Greiner identified six steps in the change process. Consider the change in the computer requirement as an illustration of the steps.

1. *Pressure and Arousal*   The change process starts by a buildup in pressure to change a procedure that is ineffective or related to low performance. This pressure may come from inside or outside the organization and leads to arousal to take action. In the example we just discussed, there were really two

sources of pressure: one from inside and one from outside the university. Organizations were starting to look for computer literacy in the people they hired. They wanted graduates who could use the computer to solve real organizational problems; therefore, they created pressure for the university to add a computer course. Once the course was added, internal pressure for change arose. Professors were frustrated because students showed no interest, and students were frustrated because they did not understand why they were expected to take the classes.

2. ***Intervention and reorientation***   A change agent becomes active and focuses on the problem. The change agent may be a manager in the organization, a staff specialist in organizational development, or someone from outside the organization. After the course had been introduced and proved unsuccessful, the dean of the school in our example stepped in and requested a review of the curriculum to investigate the positioning of the course and to determine what changes should be made.

3. ***Diagnosis and Recognition***   Management and the change agent then involve those who are immediately affected by the change for fact-finding and problem solving. In Lewin's terms, unfreezing takes place. Employees learn the reasons for change and take part in its creation and design. At the university, a task force composed of professors and students was established to analyze the problems with the new computer requirements.

4. ***Invention and Commitment***   Solutions that have the support of management and employees are identified. Much of the commitment to making the change work comes from the fact that employees have helped create or invent the solution. Both professors and students at the university took part in redesigning the curriculum.

5. ***Experimentation and Search***   Experimentation and search are the first steps in implementing solutions to problems. Solutions are tested on a small scale prior to being adopted company-wide. What works can be adopted by the rest of the organization; what does not can be modified and changed so that it does work. For example, the dean could have recommended that a trial version of the new class be offered during the summer. Both students and faculty could have taken part in evaluating the class.

6. ***Reinforcement and Acceptance***   Changes that promise to be successful are introduced on a large scale and are eventually absorbed throughout the organization. This phase is characterized by management acceptance of employee participation in the change process. At the university, after initial problems with the new course were analyzed and understood, the curriculum was redesigned. The course was structured to combine theory and practice, and it was followed immediately by related courses. Students accepted the new course because they understood its practical applications.

Both the Lewin and Greiner models of organizational change are useful tools for understanding and managing the change process. Both suggest that managers must recognize that the impetus for productive change can come from anywhere in the organization, the lower levels as well as the top. Both encourage participation in the change process by those who will be affected. Their participation usually improves the likelihood that the change will be understood and implemented. Finally, both suggest that change is best managed by reducing resistance to it, not by increasing pressure for it. When managers and employees understand the need for change and see how it will improve their ability to perform in the organization, their resistance to change will diminish.

Structural, Technological, Human, and Task Approaches

Harold J. Leavitt suggests that organizations should be considered as interacting, interdependent systems of structure, technology, humans, and tasks.[15] By his definition, structure refers to how the work is divided among jobs and how the work of the many jobs is coordinated to accomplish the tasks. Technology refers to the technical tools and procedures the organization uses to accomplish its tasks. The human element is the people working within an organization. Tasks refer to the jobs and methods the organization uses in the production of goods and services. A change in any one of these will cause changes in the others. Effective, planned change may focus on one of these components, but it also recognizes and prepares for changes in the others (see Exhibit 9.5).

Structural approaches to change
Approaches that focus on modifying reporting relationships in a firm.

Structural approaches to change focus on modifying reporting relationships and on the way work is divided and organized within a firm. Benetton's decentralization of the knitting and dyeing processes are good examples of structural change. Leavitt divides structural change efforts into three categories:

1. *Classical design changes* address such factors as departmentalization, span of management, organizational hierarchy, and relationships among units within the organization.
2. *Decentralization efforts* focus on creating small, self-contained units within the organization to increase employee involvement, motivation, and productivity. Decentralization gives each unit the authority to adapt its own structure to change, to decide how work is divided and coordinated, and to decide how to ensure a compatible fit between tasks and people on the job. It gives a group of employees one whole job to do and allows them to determine how to do it.
3. *Work flow modifications* deal with how work passes from one individual and group to another. Individuals and groups should be arranged so that materials can be moved through production as efficiently as possible.

Technological approaches to change
Approaches that focus on modifying equipment and production methods.

Technological approaches to change focus on the modification of equipment and production methods. The introduction of the automated knitting machines at Benetton is an example of a technological change. Fredrick Taylor's "scientific management" was the first systematic application of the technological

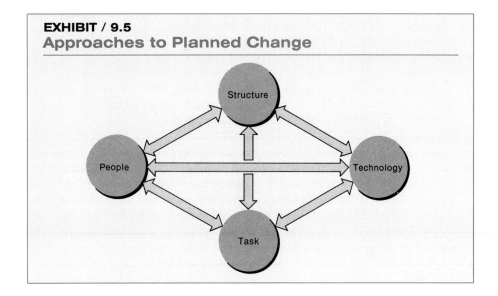

EXHIBIT / 9.5
Approaches to Planned Change

Structure

People

Technology

Task

THE INSIDE VIEW / 9.3

Ergonomics

A properly designed work station can contribute to an employee's comfort, job satisfaction, motivation, and sense of well-being and accomplishment.

The following guidelines on ergonomic systems are taken from the IBM *Ergonomics Handbook.*

WHY ERGONOMICS?

Ergonomics, the European word synonymous with human factors, was invented in the early 1950s by a group of scientists and engineers interested in the relationship between people and machines. The word is derived from the Greek *ergon,* "work," and *nomos,* "natural laws of." A properly designed work station can contribute to an employee's comfort, job satisfaction, motivation, and sense of well-being and accomplishment.

JOB DESIGN AND THE BACK

The best way to reduce back injuries is to design out the lifting tasks. This statement should be taken seriously and IBM Corporation strives to limit the weight of components in both manufacturing and service. Intelligent job design will reduce problems. For example, when you bend over and twist, the load is much heavier than when you simply bend over forward. (In the United States, the action of bending and twisting is the most common cause of back injuries.) Changing the layout of common lifting tasks, for example, moving boxes from the end of a roller conveyor onto a pallet, eliminates twisting actions at no cost.

THE HAND: TECHNIQUES FOR REDUCING REPETITIVE-TASK INJURIES

The basic technique for reducing hand and wrist injuries is to reduce the exposure of the hand to repetitive motion. This can be accomplished through good work practices, training procedures, and hand tool design.

NOISE

Noise can be very distracting and prevent concentrated mental work. In extreme cases, it can also result in physical disorders. Direct noise should be suppressed by placing covers over impact printers or by isolating sources of noise from the rest of the work area. Reflected noise can be reduced by introducing sound-absorbing materials into the environment.

LIGHTING

Different tasks require different lighting levels. Intricate assembly tasks require more lights than warehouse areas. Putting light where it is needed on the working plane and reducing general light levels can often improve lighting significantly.

Care should be taken to avoid glare. Dials, instruments panels, and visual display terminals (VDTs) should be very carefully positioned in relation to light sources so that the latter cannot produce glare from reflection in the glass fronts of the equipment, which makes them difficult to read. ■

Source: Adapted from *Ergonomics Handbook*, IBM Corporation.

Ergonomics The study of how best to design equipment to fit a worker's physical characteristics.

approach to organizational change. Taylor analyzed interactions between workers and machines. Based on this analysis (described more fully in Chapter 2), he established more efficient ways for workers to use machines. **Ergonomics,** the most recent approach to technological change, is the study of how best to design equipment to fit the worker's physical characteristics (see The Inside View 9.3).

Human approaches to change Approaches that attempt to improve productivity by changing employees' behavior, attitudes, skills, perceptions, and expectations.

Human approaches to change attempt to improve productivity by changing employees' behavior, attitudes, skills, perceptions, and expectations. Such changes may focus on individuals, groups, units, or the entire organization. In individual change, training and development efforts are designed to improve managers' or employees' performance by upgrading their interpersonal, leadership, or job skills. In group change, group training and development programs, often called team building, are designed to help small groups become more effective work units by improving group decision-making skills, interpersonal relations, and communication. At the level of the entire organization the programs focus on improving the effectiveness of the whole organization, improving relationships between units and improving the organization's ability to adjust and adapt to its environment.

Task approaches to change Approaches that focus on designing jobs to be as productive as possible.

Task approaches to change focus on designing jobs to be as productive as possible. Job enrichment, discussed in Chapter 7, is a current example of a task approach. Job enrichment is a method of organizing jobs so that they include a variety of activities, are challenging to the employee, include information about results, and give the employee the autonomy and responsibility to do the job.

MANAGING ORGANIZATION DEVELOPMENT

Organization development An approach to planned change that applies knowledge in a continuing effort to improve the organization.

Organization development, in a sense, is continuous change management. **Organization development** (OD) is an approach to planned change that applies knowledge in a continuing effort to improve the organization's ability to cope with change in its external environment and increase its internal problem-solving capabilities.[16]

The Organization Development Process

The organization development process involves diagnosis of a situation, intervention through specific activities to change the situation, and reinforcement of the new ways of operating. Thus, as illustrated in Exhibit 9.6, organization develop-

EXHIBIT / 9.6
The Organization Development Process

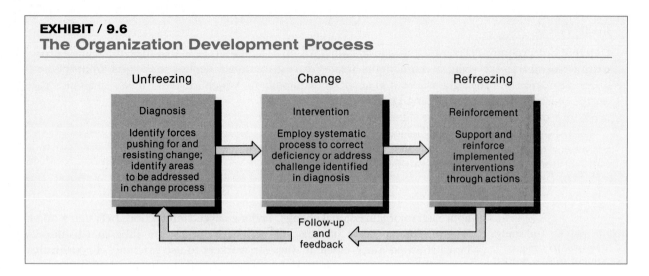

ment is similar to Lewin's unfreezing, change, and refreezing process of planned change, but it is continuous.

Diagnosis   Diagnosis is the first phase of the OD process. In this phase, managers may review corporate records, conduct interviews, administer questionnaires to selected groups or to the whole organization, and gather information through direct observation. This way, they can identify the forces pushing for change, the forces resisting change, and the specific areas that therefore must be addressed. In Benetton's case, for example, increased competition in the fashion and clothing industries was pushing for innovative mechanisms to produce high variety at low cost. The force restraining Benetton's ability to innovate was the problem of creating a system that could increase variety without increasing costs. Thus, diagnosis would reveal that the specific areas in need of change interventions would be production and distribution.

Intervention   An intervention is a systematic attempt to correct an organizational deficiency or address an environmental challenge indicated in the diagnosis phase. Traditionally, OD interventions were designed primarily to improve working relationships between people and groups in the organization. OD theory, in fact, was developed in response to the restrictive and authoritarian conditions in earlier bureaucracies, primarily in manufacturing industries. It was originally designed to enhance communication and involvement within rigorously structured well-ordered but restrictive systems. Thus, the OD interventions typically used, such as those we have listed in Exhibit 9.7, were human- and relationship-oriented tactics aimed at the individual, group, and organizational level.

Today, in some organizations, communication, involvement, and working relationships between people and groups are already very effective. In these cases, organization development can focus on helping the total organization renew its sense of direction and purpose and maintain or increase its competitive strength. Organization development can help the organization remain innovative and responsive to its environment.[17]

Consider again the example of Benetton: The Benetton organization is highly innovative, and its people are geared to participation, involvement, and change.

EXHIBIT / 9.7
Traditional OD Interventions

OD Interventions Designed to Increase Effectiveness on:

THE INDIVIDUAL LEVEL

Life and Career Planning   An analysis of personal strengths and weaknesses helps employees understand what they can do to take advantage of their strengths and limit their weaknesses.

Skill Development   Both managers and technicians can improve their abilities and skills; while managers can receive training in such areas as delegation, communication, and interpersonal relations, technicians can be trained in advanced techniques in their fields.

THE GROUP LEVEL

Role Analysis   Ideally, all organization members should understand exactly what role they play in the accomplishment of the organization's goals, and all the roles should be meshed so that goals can be achieved cooperatively.

Team Building   Enhancing the performance and developing the effectiveness of groups is one of the most popular OD interventions. Effective groups must be able to set goals and priorities, allocate work among themselves, and understand how group members relate to each other.

THE ORGANIZATIONAL LEVEL

Survey Feedback   To give everyone in the organization an understanding of its current status and an opportunity to participate in improving this status, some organizations use surveys and questionnaires. The information gathered is analyzed and fed back to those who supplied it in a format they can use for problem solving.

Grid® OD   Grid® OD was developed in the 1960s, based on Blake and Mouton's Managerial Grid®. It is a comprehensive, long-range training program that may unfold over four or more years. Participants work in teams to identify mission-oriented objectives, implement them, and simultaneously develop their problem-solving and conflict resolution skills.

Source: Adapted from information on Grid® OD, based on Blake, Robert R., and Mouton, Jane Srygley, *The New Managerial Grid* (Houston: Gulf Publishing, 1978).

To improve its ability to cope with change and increase its internal problem-solving capabilities, Benetton employed many interventions. The last-minute dyeing system and the computerized order and distribution systems were systematic interventions focused on production and distribution as warranted by the diagnosis. Essentially structural and technological design changes, they were designed to allow the company to respond rapidly to changes in the environment. And the Benettons' support of an innovative atmosphere enhances the company's internal problem-solving capabilities.

Reinforcement   Similar to the refreezing phase of the planned-change process, reinforcement is a process of supporting through action the changes or interventions implemented. Many believe reinforcement is a preferable term to refreezing because OD is a cyclical process; new changes will always be made, and nothing should be "frozen" permanently in place. Changes or interventions that increase the organization's ability to respond to change and that increase its internal ability to solve problems should be reinforced; programs, systems, or interventions that impede either of these abilities should be changed.

Fostering a Creative Climate

Today one of the main purposes of organization development is to foster a creative and innovative climate. Managers can support creativity by welcoming suggestions and ideas from employees, regardless of how far-fetched the ideas may seem. The recommendation by one of Benetton's employees to buy and convert machinery that had been used to knit seamed stockings saved the company millions of dollars. Benetton benefitted enormously from its openness to its employee's creative suggestion.

The overall attitude and climate of the organization must be tolerant of change, novelty, and even failure. Employees will hesitate to suggest changes if they fear they will lose their jobs or be punished in some way. For this reason, creative behavior should be stimulated in regular, day-to-day operations. Luciano Benetton, for example, set the receptive tone of his organization by himself introducing a variation of the Scottish wool-softening machine. Regardless of how unsophisticated or eccentric it seemed, it effectively accomplished its purpose. Management thereby demonstrated its priorities: Practicality and effectiveness were more important than appearances and following norms. The Inside View 9.4 illustrates a problem session in which a group was given a clear objective and the creative freedom to attain it.

Fostering Innovation

Another challenge of organization development is to foster innovation. As Robert A. Burgelman and Leonard R. Sayles argue in their book *Inside Corporate Innovation,* "The challenge for established firms . . . is not either to be well organized and act in unison or to be creative and entrepreneurial. The real challenge . . . is to be able to live with the tensions generated by both modes of action."[18] To accomplish this, they argue, management must exploit existing opportunities to the fullest (because only relatively few will be available), must generate entirely new opportunities (because today's success is not guarantee for tomorrow), and must balance this exploitation and generation over time (because resources are limited). "Strategic management approaches," they conclude, "will have to accomplish all three concerns simultaneously and virtually continually."[19]

Many companies have enjoyed significant success from promoting innovation. A 1984 study by *Fortune* magazine, for example, identified eight "masters of innovation" that held leading positions in their industries largely because of their ability to sustain inventiveness.[20] Results of the study are given in The Inside View 9.5.

Developing an Atmosphere of Entrepreneurship

Entrepreneur A person who undertakes a venture, organizes it, raises capital to finance it, and assumes most or all of the risk for it.

Finally, promoting entrepreneurship can facilitate organization development. Entrepreneurship is the act of being an **entrepreneur,** that is, a person who undertakes a venture, organizes it, raises capital to finance it, and assumes most or all of the risk for the project. Entrepreneurship usually refers to the independent start-up of a business venture, but many organizations find that there are significant

Panty Hose for the Guy Next Door

Panty hose manufacturers discovered a new flourishing underground market: men.

We talked about panty hose twice during the week. The first time, Stan played the role of a panty hose manufacturer who had discovered a flourishing new underground market: men. It seems that construction workers, football players, motorcyclists, policemen, and firemen are secretly wearing them for warmth because they are lighter and provide more support than long underwear.

While pleased with the new market, the manufacturer was troubled by the fact that none of the men dared buy the panty hose themselves; they either sent their wives or girlfriends or did without.

Our problem: how to market panty hose directly and openly to men in a way that avoids their embarrassment.

Two days later, we tackled a problem presented by No Nonsense Fashions, a mass marketer of panty hose. They currently sell the product from racks in supermarkets, drugstores, and other outlets. But the addition of new styles, colors and features through the years has turned the rack into a nightmare for buyers. The product now comes in two leg types (support and nonsupport), two panty types (with and without built-in underpants), two toe types (sheer and reinforced), three sizes, and six colors, more than 100 choices in all.

Our problem: how to simplify the display and selection process.

There are no "correct" solutions to these marketing problems, just potentially useful ideas. Compare your solutions with ours.

MOLLIFYING MALES

The first thing we concentrated on was finding a new name that would make panty hose more appealing to men. We came up with "Jox Sox," "Hot Sox," "Power Hose," and "Machose." Then we attacked the marketing problem: offer them in macho colors like forest green or fireman's red; add a Velcro fly; put odor-absorbent pads in the feet; package them in six-packs; sell them by "male order" or through the L.L. Bean catalogue; get famous athletes to wear and endorse them on television.

SIMPLIFYING SELECTION

Among the ideas we came up with for the display rack were: reduce the number of options, dropping those with lower sales; create a uniform system of color-coding to guide selection; separate the rack into smaller component racks according to category; put the packs on a rotating wheel, like a Rolodex.

Since the woman from No Nonsense told us that multiple options were one of the product's major marketing advantages, we finally settled on the idea of replacing the rack with a mechanical or even computerized vending machine; the consumer would make each choice by pressing a series of buttons (size, style, color, etc.), and a dispenser would produce the correct pair of panty hose. ■

Source: Rice, Berkeley, "Imagination to Go," *Psychology Today* (May 1984): 48–56.

THE INSIDE VIEW / 9.5

Eight Big Masters of Innovation

Intel is one of the U.S. industrial giants which sees the need to innovate and adopt new ideas as the essence of long-term survival.

The world has fallen in love with innovation. Ask a technocrat in Paris or a middle manager in Dayton who the heroes of contemporary capitalism are. You will hear excited tales about Silicon Valley, but few words about those heads of giant corporations who used to be known as the captains of industry.

But does big business have to be slow and stodgy? How does the management of a corporate colossus keep new ideas coming and nurture them into new ways of making money? Given the tendency of the innovation cult to consign most of the Fortune 1,000 to the dustbin of history, these seemed questions well worth asking.

Using *Fortune's* lists of the 500 largest industrial and service companies as a base, [researchers] asked business school professors, management consultants, and security analysts for nominations.

Each nominee was measured against peers in the same industry according to such objective criteria as research spending and the number of new product introductions. The final cut was necessarily subjective, particularly on the question of what constitutes a true innovation. Does Honey Nut Cheerios, a so-called brand-line extension of the original cereal, represent as much of an advance as a new micro-processor? We do not think so. We then interviewed managers at the companies on our list of finalists, in part to confirm our choices, in part to find out how they achieved and sustained such inventiveness.

Judged by these methods, eight of the most innovative giants of U.S. industry are American Airlines, Apple Computer, Campbell Soup, General Electric, Intel, Merck, Minnesota Mining & Manufacturing, and Philip Morris. They are nimble enough to put smaller companies to shame. While the eight differ in many ways, the techniques they use to foster innovation are sufficiently similar to provide clear-cut lessons. These techniques combine a let-a-thousand-flowers-bloom zest for new ideas with a rigid, almost martial discipline bred, finally, of fear.

The management of each of the eight is convinced of the *need* to innovate, regarding new ideas as the essence of long-term survival. No matter how dependent the companies are on purely technological advances, they are uniformly devoted to marketing. Their people believe that markets can speak, and routinely treat bureaucratic considerations—who works for what division—as entirely subservient to the goal of listening carefully to their customers. All the companies have clearly defined corporate cultures through which their strategic aims are widely, and convincingly, promulgated.

Not satisfied simply to indoctrinate employees in such mom-and-flag values as product quality, market leadership, and the necessity of invention—although they loudly preach these values—the eight companies also ruthlessly limit the search for new ideas to areas they are competent to exploit. Not one of these corporations is a gambler: financially disciplined sometimes to the point of parsimony, their top executives are convinced that the risk of experimentation can be carefully controlled.

The eight innovators are uniformly profitable and most are fast-growing compared with their competitors—even though their average age is a hoary 102 years. All are large enough to have tested the proposition that size necessitates idea-stifling bureaucracy: their 1983 sales range from Apple's $983 million to GE's $27 billion. ■

Source: Sherman, Stratford P., "Eight Big Masters of Innovation," *Fortune,* October 15, 1984, p. 66.

Intrapreneurship The act of fostering entrepreneurial spirit within an established organization.

benefits to be gained from fostering the same type of spirit within the company. This is usually referred to as **intrapreneurship.**

John G. Burch, in his book *Entrepreneurship,* provides a good description of the relationship between entrepreneurship and management in organizations:[21]

> Some may think that entrepreneurship is simply a form of management when, in fact, the essence of entrepreneurship is the initiation of change as opposed to management, which involves controlling and planning within a given structure. For example, when someone develops a new product, such as a human-intelligent computer, this constitutes an innovative change and hence involves entrepreneurship. But once the production of this new computer begins, then management takes over and coordinates and organizes for the continuing production of it in a well-defined structure. Entrepreneurship reappears, usually from outside the present structure (many large companies have, however, established venture or entrepreneurship departments), to initiate change in the computer or in the way it is produced. Once that change is initiated, management again takes charge of the production and distribution process.

The fact that innovation and entrepreneurship are considered hot topics does not mean that they are fads of temporary value. Rapidly changing environments demand new ideas, quick responses, and adaptability. New methods of organization development are being introduced constantly in response to new environmental demands or organization conditions. The important point for managers to keep in mind is that each successful move ahead should be considered not an achievement upon which to rest, but a starting point upon which to build yet again.

■ KEY POINTS

1 All organizations exist within a changing environment that offers both threats and opportunities. Management's challenge is to manage the organization so that it is not damaged by the threats and so that it can take advantage of the opportunities.

2 Force field analysis is a tool used to diagnose and plan for change. By lining up forces that provoke change and forces that resist it, managers can determine how likely an organization is to change and what will cause the change.

3 Conflict can be caused by differences (between people, groups, or situations) and by competition for limited resources. These conflicts can exist between individuals, groups, units, departments, or levels in the organization.

4 Lose-lose, win-lose, and win-win resolutions are the three basic ways in which conflict can be resolved, but managers should always strive to achieve win-win resolutions because the other two resolutions always leave at least one party unsatisfied and therefore tend to provoke further conflicts.

5 The change process can be understood as a process of unfreezing patterns of behavior, implementing change, and refreezing or reinforcing the new patterns of behavior. It can be thought of as a process of applying pressure and arousing interest in a change, followed in turn by intervention by a change agent, diagnosis of the situation, involvement and commitment by affected people, experimental implementation of change, and reinforcement of the change.

6 Approaches to planned change can focus on structure, technology, humans, or tasks. A change implemented in any one of these areas may make necessary corresponding changes in the others.

7 Organization development (OD) is an approach to planned change that applies knowledge in a continuing effort to improve the organization's ability to cope with change in its external environment and increase its internal problem-solving capabilities. The OD process involves diagnosis of a situation, intervention through specific activities to change the situation, and reinforcement of the new ways of operating.

8 Managers can enhance the organization development process by fostering a creative climate, fostering innovation, and developing an atmosphere of entrepreneurship.

FOR DISCUSSION AND REVIEW

1. What major economic, technological, competitive, or other changes do you see going on today, and how might they affect businesses in general? What effect do these pressures or opportunities have on Benetton?

2. Describe how two leading theories on the change process might apply to an organization you know. In what ways do these approaches illustrate the process differently?

3. What are the four basic approaches to managing the change process? On which aspect(s) of the organization does each focus? How do they interrelate?

4. Current periodicals are full of examples where two organizations, or an organization and some other group such as a town or public interest group, are involved in a conflict. Discuss and describe a situation in which both parties lost (lose-lose), both parties won (win-win), or one lost and the other won (win-lose).

5. Think of a time when you had a difficult problem to solve, whether it was a puzzle, a game, or a personal problem, task, or challenge. Did you go through some or all of the steps in the creative process to reach your solution? Did you solve the problem some other way? How?

6. How can a manager effectively manage the creative climate of his or her organization? Have you ever been in a work or classroom situation in which such a climate was effectively or ineffectively maintained? Why was, or was not, the "manager" of the situation successful in this regard?

7. Describe an incident from your own working or personal life where conflict arose based on differences as discussed in the text. Think of another situation where conflict arose based on competition for some limited resource. How was each situation resolved or not resolved? In retrospect, would you have done anything different?

8. What are three basic methods for managing organization development? How do they differ, and how might they all be used in one organization successfully?

KEY TERMS

Entrepreneur
Ergonomics
Force field analysis
Hierarchical conflict
Human approach to change

Intrapreneurship
Lose-lose conflict resolution
Organization development
Refreezing

Structural approach to change
Superordinate goal
Task approach to change
Technological approach to change

Unfreezing
Win-lose conflict resolution
Win-win conflict resolution

THE CONFERENCE TABLE: DISCUSSION CASE / 9.1

The Generic (Un)revolution

Generic food chains eliminate bagging, item pricing, check-cashing, and even the meat and produce sections, all in exchange for prices 20 percent below the market average.

A phenomenon that began in 1977 has demonstrated, painfully to some and profitably to others, that internal change and responsiveness to environmental changes are issues with which to be reckoned. This phenomenon was a trend toward, and then away from, generic merchandise. Germany's Albrecht Group opened its first Aldi store in the Midwest, offering one brand and one size of each product in 500 categories. It eliminated bagging, item pricing, check-cashing, and even the meat and produce sections, all in exchange for prices 20 percent below the market average. Though the customer had to give up the 12,000-category variety, the bakeries, delicatessens, and other services that standard stores provided, they still came, lured by low prices.

Aldi's success attracted other players, and coupled with a weak economy and a demographic trend away from the female grocery-store-brand expert, the generic food industry took off. Starting from nearly zero in 1977, no-frills operators selling generics or cut-price foods grabbed 5 percent of the grocery market in less than five years, at a time when the grocery market's real annual growth rate had sunk to 0.3 percent. Merchants who began offering generics claimed the generics quickly accounted for 15 percent of their sales and expected this figure to grow. Some experts went so far as to say that one-quarter of all national brands would be eliminated from supermarkets, and that no-frills retailing would capture 25 percent of the market during the 1980s.

Sources: This case was written by M. R. Poirier, based on the following sources: "No-Frills Food, New Power for the Supermarkets," *Business Week,* March 23, 1981, p. 76; Dunkin, Amy, "No-Frills Products: 'An Idea Whose Time Has Gone,'" *Business Week,* June 17, 1985, p. 65.

In response, several chains implemented changes in their operations. As broadscale policies, many national brand suppliers, such as Borden and Union Carbide, began producing and supplying generic goods to use up extra production capacity as demand for their name brands dropped. Borden's executive vice president, admitting that the policy involved competing against oneself, said, "Making a private label is a cancer. The better you do it, the worse things get, because you erode your own brand's share."

The chains then implemented changes on many levels. On the technological level, two contradictory changes were occurring simultaneously. In warehouse stores, since goods were literally left in their boxes and set out that way, there was no longer any need for price markers or display apparatus. In stores with no meat or bakery departments, there was no longer any need for meat slicers, fancy scales, or on-site baking and decorating equipment. On the other hand, automatic scanning systems were becoming popular, making it necessary not only for clerks to learn the new system but for computer programmers to design systems that keep track of inventory and isolate profitable from nonprofitable items.

On the task level, jobs had to be restructured in no-frills stores from very specialized and service oriented to simpler and more functionally oriented, toward moving merchandise only. In the case of standard stores adding generic merchandise to their regular stock, management had to decide on percentages of shelf space and methods of handling: Would the items be priced individually? Left in boxes? Put on shelves? These questions would affect the stock people's jobs.

Human-oriented changes would also have to correspond to the overall strategy. Some workers would have to alter their viewpoints or motivations. Some would have to learn new skills. Some might have to begin working regularly with new associates or cease working with familiar associates.

These changes, however, may be short-lived. Generics recorded their highest U.S. sale in 1982, during a period of high inflation and low purchasing power. Ever since then, sales of generics, the number of stores carrying them, and the amount of shelf space allotted to them have all been decreasing. According to one survey, less than 1 percent of the consumers were disturbed by this reverse trend. With the inflation rate back down, consumers became more interested in quality than low prices, and they became dissatisfied with generics. Paper goods, cigarettes, and FDA-approved generic drugs have held up, but as one supermarket chain chairman said, "People are very cautious when it comes to products they ingest." As for the producers of brand name items, they could not be happier. The popularity of generics had drawn them into a self-defeating cycle of trying to retain high standards while reducing prices and offering coupons on name items, and simultaneously offering generics to use up production capacity. "With the way everyone is dealing right now," said a Del Monte vice president at the time, "we all must be kamikaze pilots." ■

DISCUSSION QUESTIONS

1. Explain the technology, task, and human change necessary to successfully introduce generic brands into a local supermarket.
2. What conflicts will the introduction of generic brands cause in the supermarket, and how should they be managed?
3. What creative ways can you suggest for introducing and managing the generic foods portion of the supermarket so that it will be successful.

THE CONFERENCE TABLE: DISCUSSION CASE / 9.2

McDentists

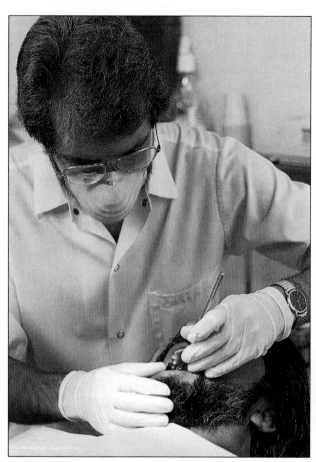

Retail franchise dentistry appeals to patients because it offers convenience and lower costs. It appeals to dentists because it offers visibility, low overhead, and a steady clientele.

"The trouble with that expansionist strategy is that it can blow up in your face," said a business reporter, referring to the rapid rise and fall of DentCare Systems. Retail franchise dentistry was just beginning to gain popularity in response to consumer demands for convenience, low costs, and visibility. The potential benefits to the franchisers, the franchisees, and the patients were inviting, but the DentCare "explosion" illustrated the importance of careful, systematic management of changes, conflicts, and development.

Started by lawyer Ronald F. Saverin and dentist Myles Sokolof in 1977, the venture showed some early success. Because they had no money, they decided to franchise and opened eight dental centers in Montgomery Ward stores east of the Rockies. They barely posted a small profit in 1980 when problems began. Many of them were caused by the newness of the whole situation. Franchise managers had to be licensed dentists by law but did very little dentistry, acting mostly as admin-

Source: Magnet, Myron, "Here Come McDentists," *Fortune,* February 21, 1983, pp. 135–138.

istrators. Dentists who practiced in the office had to adapt to whole new operating systems. No longer were they in charge of all facets of the business and involved with customers they had known for years. Now they were "hired hands," in a sense, doing nothing but the dentistry work alone and often for new patients all the time. The office personnel also had different task functions than those in traditional, family dentist offices and had to work with groups such as regional marketing and promotion staffs, with which they were unfamiliar.

Conflicts arose immediately. One franchisee alleged that the advertising was too expensive and basically inept. Others complained that equipment they requested arrived late; still others claimed that not only was it late, in some cases the franchisers never even ordered it. Meanwhile, DentCare went public through a New York brokerage in 1981, expanded to the point where "leases with no franchisee anywhere in sight proliferated," and then were left fundless when the broker went bankrupt.

As a result, franchises who never received promised equipment and services stopped paying royalties, and eventually Saverin and Sokolof "walked away from the enterprise, leaving . . . major creditors . . . to sue the empty corporate shell for hundreds of thousands of dollars."

Meanwhile, at least eight other franchise dentistry operations have joined the field. The advantages are there: Though the operators are only turning profits after two or three years, the stockholders are making small profits; newly graduated dentists are saved the trouble of building up a clientele and raising the $100,000 necessary to open their own offices; dentists with mature or lagging practices can augment their incomes with afternoons in the mall; and patients can take advantage of more convenient hours and locations, the acceptance of credit cards, and in some cases, the use of beepers that call them back from shopping when their children are done in the office. ■

DISCUSSION QUESTIONS

1. What types of changes will have to be managed for this new method of dentistry to succeed, and how can the changes be implemented successfully?
2. On what levels do conflicts exist, and what causes them?
3. What innovative or creative methods would you suggest for development of a franchise operation, taking into consideration the needs of the patients, the hired dentists, the franchisees, and the franchisers?

Comprehensive Case Three

Long-Term Survival: Lessons from a 750-Year-Old Organization

The Vatican, Rome. Even though the congregation of nuns of the Dominican order operates in the Midwest, it must still fit within the structure of the world-wide Catholic Church.

Scholars, researchers, and industry observers are all quick to point out modern success stories: the companies that made the grade or led the way in organization effectiveness through an ability to adapt and remain flexible in a changing environment. Most of these organizations are relatively new and were formed long after or at the tail end of the Industrial Revolution. The service organization described in this case, however, has survived for hundreds of years. Over its 750-year history it has expanded its operations from a small Bavarian town in Europe to cover the globe. It has changed from a rigid, bureaucratic hierarchy to a flexible, organic structure. The organization has demonstrated the flexibility and adaptability that organizations in many industries seek today.

The organization in question is a congregation of nuns of the Dominican order that operates within the framework of the Roman Catholic church. The relationship between the congregation and the church is similar to that between a corporation and a state: As the activities and policies of a corporation must conform to the laws and regulations of the state, so must the activities and policies of the congregation conform to the laws and dictates of the church.

Though the congregation remained cloistered in Bavaria for roughly 600 years, it branched out in the early 1800s and opened a school. Fifty years later, the congregation began sending its members to other countries to teach and serve "clients." The midwestern congregation that is the focus of this case was one of the first groups to set up operations away from the home congregation.

MOVING TO THE MIDWEST

The first group of four Dominican nuns from this congregation arrived in the United States in 1853. Missionary work was a radical change for these women, who had lived most of their adult lives in only one location and had virtually no contact with the outside environment. The four nuns expanded the congregation on the east coast, and in 1884, a group split off and moved into the midwestern territory to staff a hospital. This group became a province (a branch office, of sorts) in 1892 and was established as an independent congregation in 1923.

During its time as a province, the congregation formally shifted from a semicloistered group to an active outreach group. Between 1923 and 1960, the congregation was organized as a strict hierarchy,

Sources: This case was written by M. R. Poirier, based on the following sources: Beres, Mary Elizabeth, and Musser, Steven, "Avenues and Impediments to Transformation: Lessons from a Case of Bottom-up Change," in Ralph M. Kilman, Theresa Joyce Covin, and Associates, *Corporate Transformation: Revitalizing Organizations for a Competitive World* (San Francisco: Jossey-Bass, 1988), pp. 152–182; Beres, Mary Elizabeth, "Change in a Women's Religious Organization: The Impact of Individual Differences, Power, and the Environment," Ann Arbor, Mich.: VMI Dissertation Information Service, 1976; Musser, Steven, "The Momentum of the Power Redistribution Idea Among Lower Participants in an Organization," Ann Arbor, Mich.: UMI Dissertation Information Service, 1984; Beres, Mary Elizabeth, "Strategic Leadership in Network Style Organizations," paper presented at the Southeast American Institute of Decision Sciences meetings, Savannah, Ga., February 1984.

with the prioress general (essentially, the CEO) having direct and complete authority over all 2500 members. Until 1960, the prioress general appointed all local superiors and oversaw the regulation of all converts. Most of the congregation's members became professionals in education, health care, social services, or church ministry, and by 1960, all of them had earned a scholastic or professional degree.

THE NEW MANAGERIAL HIERARCHY

In 1960, the unity of command of the prioress general was abolished and the congregation was divided into five regional provinces. The new "managerial" hierarchy was still highly centralized and had three levels, as illustrated in the chart below. The prioress general and her councillors (the CEO and her executive staff) were at the top. The prioress general was ultimately responsible for seeing that the members of the congregation were properly trained and accredited as teachers and nurses, and that the congregation's missions were properly staffed and executed.

The provincials (division heads) and their staffs ran each of the five regional branches. They represented the second level of management—the middle manager. Their function was to help the prioress general in the administration of the provinces. The third level of management, the local superioresses (first-line managers), were directly responsible for the members-at-large, serving as house managers for the members who lived in groups of up to one hundred.

In 1962, the woman who had been prioress general of the midwestern congregation since 1934 died. The governing body met to reach major policy decisions and elect the top officials of the congregation. A new prioress general was elected and the congrega-

tion began to undergo its most significant transformation since its inception.

The main impetus for change was that the 1962 meeting coincided with the Second Vatican Council, which was convened by Pope John XXIII and ran from 1962 to 1965. In 1965, the pope issued his "Decree on the Appropriate Renewal of Religious Life," which directed all religious congregations of the faith to undertake intensive self-examination. He asked the congregations not simply to change in response to a changing environment, but to determine how the doctrines and precepts of the church might be made more pertinent to the issues of modern society.

Accordingly, between 1962 and 1968, the new prioress general introduced several changes into the congregation. In 1965, members were invited, for the first time, to recommend sisters for the position of local superioress. In 1967, workshops were instituted to prepare sisters for the duties of superioress. In 1965, after the Vatican decree was distributed, the prioress general directed all members to nominate and elect members to regional renewal committees. Each committee was to suggest constitutional changes and develop plans for consideration by a corporate assembly. As the committee began to gather opinions and suggestions for renewal, it became clear that a significant portion of the congregation's membership felt that the authority within the organization was too centralized. The midwestern congregation had operated hierarchically before the issuance of the decree. Though this organization frustrated many of the members, they simply assumed it was unchangeable. However, when the committees began to discuss the notion of a collegial organization, the membership began to question the existing structure and to express strong support for collegiality.

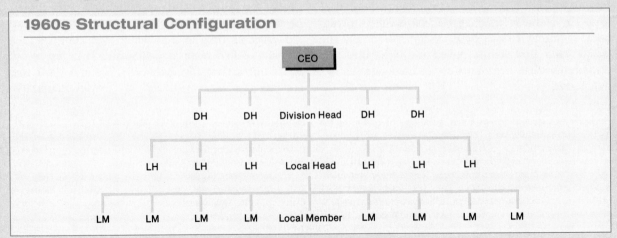

1960s Structural Configuration

Although the Dominican order has experienced changes in organizational structure and philosophy, the nuns and sisters have remained committed to education and to the care of those in need.

During the summer of 1967, the chairpersons of each committee met to discuss the results of their research. This central committee was to translate all the collected ideas and suggestions into specific proposals. Those proposals, approved by the corporate assembly in 1968, would in turn be sent to the Vatican for approval, after which they would become part of the organization's constitution.

But the committee also took action not requested by the prioress general. First, the members established a committee to represent the concerns and interests of the congregation until the corporate assembly met. The central committee also developed a proposal for a decentralized structure of government, which the prioress general rejected; a communications plan to allow open dialogue among congregation members at all levels; and proposals for member participation in the corporate assembly.

QUESTIONS ABOUT STRUCTURE

At this point, a rift developed between the top management of the organization and its membership. The prioress general had followed the Vatican directive in good faith but felt that the membership was misinterpreting the meaning of *self-reflection* and *spiritual renewal* by questioning the authority structure of the organization. The congregation, on the other hand, felt that questioning the governance structure and

proposing increased participation in decision making were precisely in the spirit of renewal.

The conflict between management and membership came to a head when the committee representing members' concerns (the prechapter commission) requested control over the agenda of the upcoming corporate assembly meeting. Of course, they wanted the assembly to address governmental structure as the priority concern. The prioress general rejected the idea and called in a church lawyer to convince the committee that the Vatican would never approve such changes in management structure and authority. Undaunted, the committee sent out a representative in early 1968 to share ideas with and garner support from the entire membership. The prioress general reacted to this by cutting off the committee's funding; the committee responded in turn by soliciting contributions from the membership, and it continued on its educational mission.

IMPLEMENTING DECENTRALIZATION

The prechapter commission won the right to control the corporate assembly's agenda—even if informally. When the commission members submitted the list of renewed proposals originally requested of them (1060 proposals, 69 of which suggested wide-ranging changes in governance structure), they also submitted the results of a general vote that indicated how the organization's membership felt about the proposals.

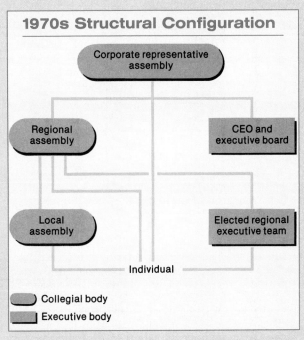

1970s Structural Configuration

- Corporate representative assembly
- Regional assembly
- CEO and executive board
- Local assembly
- Elected regional executive team
- Individual

◯ Collegial body
▮ Executive body

Sixty-one percent favored decentralized government, 24 percent opposed it, and 15 percent were undecided. Faced with this information, the assembly members had no choice but to address the question of decentralization. During the next two years, a conflict-charged debate continued over what the new structure should be. But the membership's desire for increased participation was answered. Three members of the prechapter commission were elected to the congregation's executive board during the 1968 meeting, and by 1970, the outlines of the new organization structure were finalized as illustrated in the chart on page 281.

As the new structure was put in place, so too were new policies stressing the rights of individuals to express themselves freely and to participate in decisions concerning congregational and work affairs. A summary of the differences in various organizational procedures and characteristics between 1962 and 1972 is presented in the table below.

The organization is now undergoing further changes. In the 1960s, executive positions dominated the structure, communication flowed through highly restricted channels, and deliberations in corporate-level assemblies were secret. By the 1970s,

Prechange and Postchange Characteristics

Characteristic	1962	1972
General mission	Praise of God and self-transformation	Share Christian love with each other and all people
Specific mission	Christian education, health care, and social service	Communication of the gospel individually and corporately
Corporate strategy	Focus on education; growth primarily through acquisition, some growth through internal development	Diversification based on social needs and members' abilities/interests Divestiture of institutional ownership
Structure	Centralized hierarchy; major decisions made by executive officers	Decentralized network; major decisions made in collegial assemblies
Functional Strategies		
Operations	Centrally formalized processes administered by local authority	Dependent on local initiative
Staffing	Assignment by regional unit head	Individual search in consultation with regional unit head
Marketing	CEO interacted with bishops and pastors to obtain schools to staff	Research on opportunities, information distributed to members
Finance	Compensation for members' services primary source of income	Compensation for members' services primary source of income, some investment income
	Finances managed centrally except for ordinary local expenses; all current income used for current operations	Finances managed centrally except for ordinary local expenses; income used for current operations and invested for future operations

Source: Beres, Mary Elizabeth, and Musser, Steven, "Avenues and Impediments to Transformation: Lessons from a Case of Bottom-up Change." Kilman, Ralph H., and Covin, Teresa Joyce, and Associates (eds.), *Corporate Transformation* (San Francisco: Jossey-Bass, 1988), p. 157.

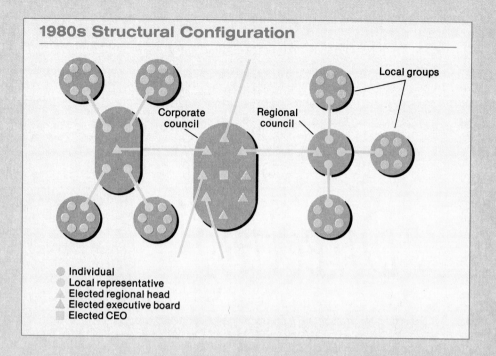

1980s Structural Configuration

- ● Individual
- ● Local representative
- ▲ Elected regional head
- ▲ Elected executive board
- ■ Elected CEO

Corporate council

Regional council

Local groups

collegial assemblies dominated the structure at the corporate, regional, and local levels, and these assemblies had broad authority over the organization's affairs.

By 1980, the relative authority of the prioress general and the corporate council at the center of the organization network has become ambiguous. The corporate assembly has been eliminated entirely from the organization chart, as illustrated in the chart above. Executive hierarchies have been replaced with a corporate network of linked groups. Individual members choose a local group through which they will be linked into the organization, and each local group elects a member to represent them at a regional council.

CHANGING STRATEGY AND STRUCTURE

In the course of the organization's transformation, it has undergone changes in mission, priorities, strategies, and structure. The organization's general mission became one of outward service rather than inward development. Its specific mission broadened from particular areas of service to a general philosophy of service. Priorities were shifted from an emphasis on the works of the congregation to an emphasis

on members as the primary vehicle for fulfilling the organization's mission. In business terminology, the organization has shifted from a product to a market orientation, using members' abilities to identify the markets that the organization is best equipped to serve. ■

QUESTIONS

1. At each stage in the transformation of the organization's structure (1960s, 1970s, 1980s), in what way was work divided or departmentalized, and what coordinating mechanisms were used to synthesize the efforts and guide the organization?
2. How did the organization change to fit its environment? What internal characteristics and external conditions had to be taken into consideration in this effort, and how did they ultimately determine the structure of the organization?
3. What were the sources of conflict during the organizational transformation during the 1960s and 1970s? How were the conflicts resolved, and how did the organization begin to manage planned change thereafter? How did the organization's culture change during this process?
4. What would you recommend the organization do to foster its own development in the future?

If organizations were entirely composed of machines that functioned precisely as required and with complete predictability, the planning and organizing functions might suffice on their own for organizations to accomplish goals. But organizations are composed of people as well as machines. People are an organization's most valuable resource.

This, many managers will tell you, is a mixed blessing, because people are also the most unpredictable and unstable resource. Each person working for an organization has different skills, interests, goals, motivations, and work habits, as well as a personal agenda that may not be compatible with the interests of the organization. Therefore, managers cannot simply set a course for the organization, outline objectives and goals, then organize the work and hope for the best. Rather, managers must continually work with people, the resource that in the end will determine whether the organization is a success or failure.

Directing

Through directing, managers harness the efforts of an organization's human resources. In Chapter 10, we will introduce directing and discuss leadership in particular as it relates to this function. Leadership is an ability, not an activity, and it is crucial to managing and directing and to all the activities necessary to be effective in both.

Organizations need people with skills, talents, and experience, who must be hired, trained, rewarded, and developed so that they can achieve the organization's goals as well as their own. In Chapter 11, we will discuss staffing, the combination of activities that brings people into the organization and helps to keep them performing effectively.

In Chapter 12, we will discuss communication, a primary activity for managers. Once the right people have been brought together to work on the organization's goals and objectives, managers must inform them of the company's strategies and their specific roles in attaining them. Managers must also ensure that information can flow freely through the organization so that the efforts of all of these people can be coordinated. Communication channels and activities are in a sense the glue that holds the organization together.

Chapter 13 discusses motivation, or how managers maintain high performance and satisfaction among their employees. This is a complex task because people are so different. Effective communication may produce informed employees but not necessarily enthusiastic ones. Work performance and organizational growth and development depend in large part on managers' abilities to release the potential of their work force through motivational strategies.

Because groups, such as departments, task forces, and committees, are the building blocks of organizations, a manager's skill in improving group effectiveness is crucial to organizational performance. In Chapter 14 we will discuss groups and the methods by which managers can improve group performance and enhance employees' abilities to work in teams.

10 Leading and Directing

FOCUS CASE / No, *This* Is How You Run a Cookie Business

MANAGING, DIRECTING, AND LEADING

LEADING AND INFLUENCING
Authority
Power
Delegation
Responsibility and Accountability
Maintaining the Balance

LEADERSHIP TRAITS

LEADERSHIP BEHAVIORS
The University of Michigan Studies
The Ohio State Studies
The Implications of Behavioral Research

SITUATIONAL APPROACHES TO LEADERSHIP
Fiedler's Contingency Model
Path-Goal Model
Life Cycle Model

CONTINUING RESEARCH
Attribution Theory
Leadership Substitutes

People ultimately determine the success or failure of any organization. Without the harnessed efforts of the organization's human resources, its plans will not be realized and the organization will not succeed. Directing the organization—harnessing the efforts of its human resources—is therefore the crucial third function of management. In this chapter, we will introduce the components of the directing function and discuss leadership as it relates to this function.

KEY QUESTIONS

As you study this chapter, try to answer the following key questions:

1 What is the relationship between leading and directing?
2 What are the five basic aspects of influence and leadership?
3 What is the difference between formal and informal authority?
4 What are five sources of power according to French and Raven?
5 What is delegation, and how should it be carried out? What are its advantages and disadvantages?
6 What are responsibility and accountability, and how are they best managed? What is the relationship between these two and delegation?
7 Describe the early research focusing on leadership traits. What useful information or concepts did it provide, and what were its shortcomings?
8 Describe the research focusing on leadership behaviors. What did it add to previous studies, and what did it fail to take into consideration?
9 What are the three major situational or contingency approaches to the study of leadership?
10 What three basic steps to fitting leadership style to the situation are incorporated in Fiedler's model?
11 What is the basis for House's path-goal model of leadership? What four basic leadership orientations does he describe, and in what situations would each be most effective?
12 Describe Hersey and Blanchard's life cycle theory. What are its implications for managers?

Focus Case

No, *This* Is How You Run a Cookie Business

Debbi Fields leads a "people company" in which she wants the employees to feel good about their work.

Quality is the top priority for both Debbi Fields and David Leiderman. Both use only fresh ingredients and nothing artificial. They refuse to sell cookies that are "old": David "will never knowingly sell a day-old cookie," and Debbi donates most cookies that have not been sold in two hours to the Red Cross "for blood-donor pick-me-ups." They are competing for the lion's share of the gourmet cookie market, even down to the nuts. David "would gladly show you the whole macadamia nuts he uses and compare them to the little pieces in a Mrs. Fields cookie." Debbi Fields, on the other hand, would be quick to respond that she uses 10 percent of the world's macadamia nut crop.

This mania for high-quality cookies is one of the few similarities David Leiderman, founder and chief executive officer (CEO) of David's Cookies, and Debbi Fields, founder and CEO of Mrs. Fields Cookies, have in common. Leiderman is essentially a businessman's businessman, always looking at the bottom line. Fields is much more concerned with improving and perfecting her products and developing her staff.

In 1977, Debbi Fields borrowed $50,000 from her husband to open a store in Palo Alto, California, to sell freshly baked cookies. With the opening of her second store, in San Francisco, she opted against the franchise system because she felt she would not be able to ensure her cookies' quality. From then on, the company grew in leaps and bounds. It had pretax profits of $17 million in 1986, up 154 percent from 1985, and in 1988 Mrs. Fields Cookies operated over 500 company-owned stores in 37 states and 5 other countries.

Debbi Fields believes that people want to get involved, accept responsibility, and "feel good" about their work. She has very definite ideas about what motivates her employees: "People come to work because they need to be productive. They need to feel successful in whatever they do. . . . Money is not the issue. . . . You know, everybody likes to be made to feel special and important. They like to be acknowledged. That's my real role, to make people feel important and to create an opportunity for them."

Though between Mrs. Fields and each store manager there are several traditional layers of hierarchy—an area sales manager, a district sales manager, a regional director of operations, and a vice president of operations—the degree and frequency of personal contact between them makes each store manager feel directly involved with the organization's success and with the upper management circle.

Sources: This case was written by M. R. Poirier, based on the following sources: Fabricant, Florence, "Cashing in His Chips," *Cuisine* (November 1984): 15, 17, 24; Furst, Alan, "The Golden Age of Goo," *Esquire* (December 1984): 324–330; Richman, Tom, "A Tale of Two Companies," *Inc.* (July 1984): 38–43; Richman, Tom, "Mrs. Fields' Secret Ingredient," *Inc.* (October 1987): 65–72; Fields, Debbie, and Furst, Alan, *One Smart Cookie* (New York: Simon & Schuster, 1987); Frydman, Ken, "David Leiderman: Cookie Goliath Sees No Bounds," *Restaurant News,* August 5, 1985, p. F 12; Burros, Marian, "Cookie Wars: David vs. Goliath," *New York Times,* January 17, 1987, p. 52.

Through computer hookups, the Park City, Utah, headquarters learns what every store is doing on a daily basis and feeds the information back to the managers immediately in terms of sale projections and customer counts. Each manager calls Park City several times a week and often receives a taped message from Debbi Fields herself. Ultimately, each manager runs his or her store essentially the same way Debbi ran her first one in 1977. The company's communications technology has "leveraged" Mrs. Fields's ability to influence operations in each of her 500 stores.

The company motto is, "Good Enough Never Is," and employees are encouraged to suggest ways to improve the business. Participation is encouraged: Workers take part in management activities, and managers stay in contact with customers by spending time behind the counter and making cookies. Debbi Fields travels constantly in order to visit every company store personally, and she holds regular "pep rallies" and training programs to encourage and sustain the cheerful enthusiasm employees are expected to maintain on the job. Quick to admit her own experience in underbaking and overbaking cookies, Fields considers herself a qualified instructor. "I've been there," she says. "I understand these things. And therefore I'm there to teach [the employees]. I'm their support system. We do it together, and we start feeling good about what we're doing. It's a people company. That's what it's all about," says Debbi.

While Mrs. Fields Cookies began on the West Coast, David's Cookies began operating in Manhattan in 1979. For founder David Leiderman, the business has two parts: making cookies and selling cookies. He strives to maintain close control over both tasks. Minimizing the probability of error, according to Leiderman, "means either minimizing the number of people involved or, when that is not practical, supervising them as closely as possible." From a Long Island plant, David's Cookies manufactures and ships cookie dough to over 180 franchised stores where employees place the dough on a baking sheet in an automatic oven of his own design, which bakes the cookies for exactly $7\frac{1}{2}$ minutes. In order to minimize problems at the franchise stores, everything is controlled by standard rules and regulations.

David Leiderman focuses on the task, on standardizing procedures, and on establishing guidelines.

David leaves the interpersonal problems and people management issues to the individual franchise owners. "The realities of the retail business in any typical urban environment," says David, "are not wonderful: the external robberies, the internal robberies, the motivation. You're dealing with kids who really are just passing through. . . . We have pretty good kids, but still we get these calls from Mrs. X who says so-and-so was rude. The kids are the Achilles' heel of retailing."

Leiderman encourages store owners to develop innovative menus and offer whatever products might sell. Some stores sell ice cream, soft drinks and milk, or even sandwiches, in addition to cookies. But David strictly regulates the franchises in regard to how the cookies are baked and sold. David Leiderman says he is "terrified of sending anything out there where an employee has to do anything to the food. You have to think in the lowest common denominator. One of the reasons we do so well in the cookie business is that a chimpanzee could take cookies out of that bag, and more often than not put them on the tray properly." David's cookies had sales of $60 million in fiscal 1985, and Leiderman has expanded his business by opening kiosks in malls across the country and by selling tubes of prepared cookie dough in grocery stores. ∎

Neither David Leiderman nor Debbi Fields has *the* one right method of directing a business. Both built multimillion-dollar enterprises in less than a decade. Both companies are opening new stores and branching out internationally. Both companies consistently provide an excellent product, but their founders have radically different notions of how to run their businesses. Debbi Fields directs her enterprise by focusing on managing people, making them feel important, maintaining close contact with them, creating opportunities for them, and managing the way they work together. David Leiderman directs his enterprise by focusing on the task, standardizing procedures, and establishing guidelines for all activities.

MANAGING, DIRECTING, AND LEADING

Directing The process of guiding organization members in their activities toward goal accomplishment.

It is important to differentiate between managing, directing, and leading. Managing, as defined in Part One, is a process of setting and accomplishing goals through the use of human, technical, and financial resources within the context of the environment. Managing requires the undertaking of four basic functions: planning, organizing, directing, and controlling. **Directing** is a general term that refers to guiding the activities of organization members toward the accomplishment of some goal or goals. The director of a play, for example, assigns people to roles, explains what he or she expects of them, and then guides or leads them so that the play is performed—the goal is achieved. Through directing, managers harness the efforts of the organization's human resources. And just as management involved four functions, directing involves four basic activities: staffing, communicating, motivating, and developing group performance.

Through staffing, managers locate, hire, train, and reward employees for accomplishing the tasks needed for overall goal accomplishment. Through communicating, they keep employees informed of organization strategy and progress toward organizational goals. Using motivational techniques, managers keep the employees energized in their work and involved in the organization's progress. And by enhancing the performance of groups and facilitating the ability of people to work with each other, managers improve the organization's ability to accomplish large tasks.

All of these directing activities, if undertaken effectively, enhance each other: effective compensation, reward systems, and regular communication about strategy and progress tend to increase motivation. Improved group dynamics tend to improve communication and motivation.

Beyond the undertaking of these basic activities, however, directing requires specific abilities. Just as decision-making skills and abilities are the most crucial to management in general, leadership skills and abilities are the most crucial to directing. To direct a play, the director must not only understand the overall play and each part, but also be able to get people to perform. Likewise, a manager must not only understand the organization's goals and each job, but also be able to get people to perform. He or she must be able to influence them in their activities.[1]

Leadership The ability to influence people toward goal achievement.

Leadership, defined as the ability to influence people toward goal achievement, is one of the most important skills. In the remainder of this chapter, we will discuss influence, leadership, and various methods of identifying and developing leadership skills and abilities.

LEADING AND INFLUENCING

Influence The capacity or power to affect others' actions.

Influence is the capacity or power to affect others by intangible or indirect means.[2] Thus, it is a key aspect of leadership. There are, however, many intangible and indirect ways to affect others or influence their activities. A person's actions may be influenced actively by orders from a superior or passively by his or her own sense of responsibility and accountability. In either case, the person will *act* to achieve something. Authority, power, responsibility, accountability, and delegation are all interrelated aspects of influence and leadership. If balanced effectively, they can help managers influence workers to do the jobs created by organizations.

Authority

Authority The right to influence others to act.

Authority, simply put, is the right to influence others and request action.[3] For a manager, authority is the right to require subordinates to do the jobs they are assigned. A theater manager has the right to ask assistants to sell tickets and clean the theater. A teacher has the right to ask students to prepare an assignment. Each of these people has the authority to make these requests because the organization has given it to him or her. It is an integral part of the job.

Authority can also be considered the right to act. Managers give subordinates some authority to accomplish their jobs. Certain bank employees have the right to enter the safe. Certain insurance company employees have the right to sign policies as representatives of the company. The organization gives each of these people the authority to undertake certain actions.

Formal authority The right to influence others given a person because of the job he or she holds.

The positions employees hold determine their formal authority. **Formal authority** is the right, inherent in one's position, to influence others and request action. Debbi Fields and David Leiderman have formal authority; they have the right to request action of others because of the positions they hold. The clearest examples of formal authority can be found in the military, where authority is visibly specified by the insignia worn. First lieutenants, identified with silver bars, have authority over second lieutenants, identified with gold bars. Members of other organizations do not often wear insignia to indicate their authority, but formal authority has the same characteristics: It goes with position and rank in an organization.

Disagreements sometimes arise concerning what a person with formal authority has the right to request. Two people might read the same description of a person's job and have different perceptions of the authority designated with it. Two store clerks might have completely different understandings of what the store manager has the authority to ask them to do. One employee may accept the manager's right to request overtime or to request personal errands, the other may not. In recent years, one of the most common disagreements concerning the limits of authority was over a manager's right to request that a secretary make coffee in the office. In most organizations today, this task is often informally delegated to whomever arrives first and wants a cup. Because descriptions of authority can be vague or subjective, it is important for managers and those over whom they have authority to discuss openly and agree on the boundaries of the manager's authority.

Informal authority The ability to influence others without having formal authority.

The right to influence others or request action does not only come from formal position, however. A person can be given this right, informally, by members of a group because the members feel he or she is capable of leading them. In this case, the person has **informal authority**, the ability to influence others without having the formal authority of a position or title in the organization. A person with informal authority can spontaneously take charge and direct the activities of members of a group or unit.

Power

Power The ability to influence others to act.

While authority is the formal or informal right to influence others, **power** is the ability to influence others to act. That is, while formal authority may give one person the right to request that another clean the washroom, and informal authority may give one person the right to tell another the best way to accomplish a task, neither type of authority gives a person the ability to make the other comply. The only guarantee that requests will be acted upon is through power—the ability to get others to act on one's requests, demands, or directives.

It is important not to think of power as an inherent quality in a leader; it is an attribute one possesses in relation to others. Power in relationships comes from several sources. John R. P. French, Jr., and Bertram Raven refer to the power that comes from one's formal position in authority over others as legitimate power, but they propose that power can come from five different sources:[4]

Legitimate power The authority to influence others because of the position held.

1. **Legitimate power:** The authority to influence others because of the position one holds. Subordinates will follow a manager's orders because the organization defines him or her as the boss.

Reward power The ability to influence others by giving or withholding rewards.

2. **Reward power:** The ability to influence others by giving or withholding rewards. Rewards that the manager controls include salary increases, bonuses, promotion recommendations, praise, recognition, and interesting job assignments.[5]

Coercive power The ability to influence others by punishment.

3. **Coercive power:** The ability to influence others by punishment or threats of punishment. Coercion can take many forms. Any form of psychological, emotional, or physical threat can be a basis for coercive power. In extreme cases, one might even use verbal abuse, humiliation, and physical deprivation. As The Inside View 10.1 illustrates, coercive power, though not the most morally admirable method of influencing behavior, may be the most common in American society.

Expert power The ability to influence others because of specialized skills or knowledge.

4. **Expert power:** The ability to influence others because of specialized skills or knowledge. People will follow the lead of one who possesses important information and valuable skills. The more important the information, the more power accompanies it.

Referent power The ability to influence others based on personal magnetism and charisma.

5. **Referent power:** The ability to influence others is based on personal magnetism and charisma. Charisma is a personal quality that inspires popular allegiance. Lee Iaccoca is one leader whose charismatic style helped him rescue his company (Chrysler Corp.) from bankruptcy. Both Debbi Fields and David Leiderman have been described as charismatic, but they still have very different leadership styles. Exhibit 10.1 presents a list of attributes that distinguishes charismatic from noncharismatic leaders.

As can be seen from French and Raven's list of sources of power, the "boss" (the person to whom the organization assigns authority) may not always be the leader (the person who influences what others do). Even if the designated boss has legitimate power, reward power, or coercive power, informal leaders may still have more influence over their groups. The expert with necessary skills or the individual with referent power, perhaps a subordinate, will be the one with actual influence. It is crucial for a manager to identify the leaders and work with them in motivating the work force to achieve organizational objectives.

THE INSIDE VIEW / 10.1

The Power of Fear and Greed

Fear is a motivator in even the most benign relationships, such as that of doctor and patient.

Instilling fear and appealing to greed are the two most commonly used motivators in a business organization, or, for that matter, in any other kind of human organization. They help to hold society together.

To pretend it is not so is to bury your head in the sand.

We think of fear and greed as being negative forces—not nice things like praise, challenge, reward, service, duty, competitive spirit. Yet the fact cannot be denied that consciously or subconsciously, directly or subtly, fear and greed are used in every organization to apply control and purpose.

Just a couple of humble examples. Why do employees go through the hassle of getting to work on time? Because they are afraid of the consequences of not doing so ("You don't come to work, you get fired"). Why do financial incentives work best when they are designed to reward individual performance? Because we are all motivated primarily by personal self-interest ("More earnings up 10 percent and we'll pay you a big bonus").

Take lawyers. I'm sure there is no special course in law school to teach attorneys how to instill fear in their clients. Nevertheless, they get the message. Instilling fear becomes implicit in just about everything a lawyer does. I defy you to talk to a lawyer about anything without him or her pointing out the possible dire consequences of what you propose to do. You buy a house, and the attorney says, "Maybe the title will stand up and maybe it won't." In essence what he or she is telling you is "You really need me, mister."

It's not just attorneys who use fear to get what they want from us. Physicians use it: "Take these pills, or you may not be long for this world." The police use it: "Let me see your license and registration." Religions use it: "Believe what we tell you, or you'll go to hell."

In fact, we all use it. If I'm selling umbrellas on a street corner, I'm not going to smile and tell you it's going to be a bright and sunny day.

If you are a boss, it is important to recognize that you are using fear as a technique of motivation. You may be using it unconsciously or subliminally, but why not recognize it for what it is? ■

Source: Mahoney, David, *Confessions of a Street Smart Manager* (New York: Simon & Schuster, 1988), pp. 80, 81.

EXHIBIT / 10.1
Distinguishing Attributes of Charismatic and Noncharismatic Leaders

Attribute	Noncharismatic Leader	Charismatic Leader
Relation to status quo	Essentially agrees with status quo and strives to maintain it	Essentially opposed to status quo and strives to change it
Future goal	Goal not too discrepant from status quo	Idealized vision that is highly discrepant from status quo
Expertise	Expert in using available means to achieve goals within the framework of the existing order	Expert in using unconventional means to transcend the existing order
Behavior	Conventional, conforming to existing norms	Unconventional, countercultural, or counternormative
Environmental sensitivity	Low need for environmental sensitivity to maintain status quo	High need for environmental sensitivity for changing the status quo
Articulation	Weak articulation of goals and motivation to lead	Strong articulation of future vision and motivation to lead
Leader-follower relationship	Egalitarian, consensus seeking, or directive. Nudges or orders people to share his or her views	Elitist, entrepreneurial, and exemplary. Transforms people to share the radical changes advocated

Source: Conger, Jay A., and Kanungo, Rabindra N., "Developing a Questionnaire Measure of Charismatic Leadership," paper submitted to the Organizational Behavior Division of the 1988 Academy of Management Annual Meeting.

Delegation

Delegation The process by which a supervisor gives a subordinate the authority to act.

Managers sometimes give a subordinate the authority to act,[6] a process called **delegation.**[7] Delegation allows supervisors to break up and distribute parts of their work to subordinates. A manager assigns duties to subordinates, gives them authority to carry out those duties and establishes a system for evaluating each person's execution of the duties.

The connection between delegation and organization is clear. Organizing requires breaking up parts of an overall task and delegating them to others. Through this delegation, managers decentralize the responsibility for completing the work—they assign it to different people or units.

Obviously, when managers delegate, they accept some risks. They expand their own ability to get the job done by having others help, but at the same time they increase the chances that the work will be done differently or even incorrectly. Further, by delegating some tasks, they in fact create another organizational task for themselves: the task of coordinating work.[8] As soon as Debbi Fields and David Leiderman opened new stores after their first successful efforts, they had to delegate work and authority and coordinate overall performance. Each approached this task in a different manner.

Fields and Leiderman both delegate to expand their ability to produce while maintaining control over quality, but they delegate different types of work and different amounts of authority. Debbi Fields appears to have delegated almost the whole management and cookie-making process to her store managers since there is only one headquarters staffer to every five store managers. Store managers and employees mix their own dough, time their own baking, and come up with their own promotion schemes. But at her Park City headquarters, Fields receives daily and weekly reports and guides the store managers in setting hourly selling goals and increasing customer counts. In addition, Debbi Fields set up a "cookie school" at the company headquarters in Utah, where regional and district managers are trained. To ensure the quality of her product, she had the personnel department develop and distribute a detailed manual of operating procedures. Though the store managers have few supervisors and thus broad responsibility for achieving results, the specifics of their jobs are closely monitored and guided from headquarters. But Debbi Fields does not see herself as a tight-fisted administrator. "I see myself as a team player," she says. "I owe my success to the family of superstars that make up our company."[9]

David Leiderman, on the other hand, delegates almost the entire management process to his franchisees but tightly controls the cookie-making process. His franchisees hire and schedule employees at their own discretion, have no set measures for increasing sales, and are responsible for inventory and maintenance on their own. Leiderman monitors only the actual food-making process, though he does allow franchisees to develop and sell food items other than his cookies. For example, one new product, David's Brownies, was put "on hold because the formula for them requires store employees to add an egg, a culinary tour de force the boss fears may be beyond some of them."[10]

Responsibility and Accountability

Responsibility The obligation to perform a task, function, or assignment.

Accountability The obligation to report back the results of the responsibilities undertaken.

Responsibility is the obligation to perform a task, function, or assignment. **Accountability** is the obligation to report back the results of the responsibilities undertaken. Responsibility cannot be reduced by delegating assignments to others. Delegating does not decrease a person's responsibility for the job but merely involves someone else in helping to accomplish it. A teacher may temporarily turn the classroom over to a guest speaker. But by delegating the authority to

teach the class, the teacher does not reduce his or her own responsibility. If the class degenerates into violent arguments and a physical fight, the school will hold the teacher, not the guest lecturer, responsible.

Though ultimate responsibility always rests with the top delegator, responsibility for a task is accepted with the acceptance of that task. The sales clerk accepts the responsibility of serving the customer, the engineer accepts the responsibility of completing a design project, and the teacher accepts the responsibility of teaching and guiding the students. Each person assigned to accomplishing a task is responsible for accomplishing it, but overall responsibility for accomplishing all tasks rests with the head of the organization.

Like responsibility, accountability is not diminished by delegating job assignments to others. Supervisors who assign jobs to their subordinates are still accountable to their managers and must still collect information from the subordinates. These reports might be evaluations, feedback, production statistics, or sales figures. Whatever the format, the individual responsible for the work is also held accountable for reporting the results. Ultimately, the head of an organization is both responsible and accountable for every job and action undertaken, from major business plans to daily accounting jobs to emptying the trash.

Again, David Leiderman and Debbi Fields do not assign responsibility and accountability the same way. By franchising, David Leiderman remains more an entrepreneur than a leader; he has brought "responsibility and accountability down to the store level in a far-flung, multi-store organization. For this, [he] trades off revenues and profits that would otherwise be his and a large measure of flexibility."[11] In other words, by decreasing his own responsibility for in-store management through franchising, he also sacrifices profits and limits his ability to control what all his stores do.

Debbi Fields, on the other hand, retains complete responsibility and accountability for all 500 stores. Her company's extensive communications system "gives top management a dimension of personal control over dispersed operations that small companies otherwise find impossible to achieve."[12] Though she is not physically present in each store baking the cookies, she is ultimately responsible for the cookies' quality. Fields continues to make unannounced visits to her stores and "thinks nothing of throwing $500 worth of cookies into the garbage if they aren't up to her standards."[13] She therefore retains responsibility over all day-to-day operations and retains the profits Leiderman turns over to franchisees.

Maintaining the Balance

To be effective, an organization must maintain a balanced array of authority, power, delegation, responsibility, and accountability among its employees. Whenever these five components are out of balance, people will not be able to do their jobs effectively. For example, if one clerk in a Mrs. Fields cookie store is responsible for keeping an area of the store clean but has no authority to ask that other assistants clean up their messes, to order needed cleaning supplies, or to request help when the crowd gets too large, he or she will not be able to keep the store clean. Authority must support and be equal to responsibility.

An imbalance between authority and accountability is another common and frustrating occurrence in organizations. A person may be given authority to accomplish one task but is held accountable for another. A teacher is responsible for educating the students but is sometimes held accountable for students' behavior outside the classroom. An engineer may be responsible for completing a particular project but is sometimes held accountable for project costs controlled by others.

Understanding these concepts and the interplay between them is essential to understanding the influence process and, thus, leadership in general. For decades people have wondered about influence and leadership. The Inside View 10.2 provides several leaders' ideas about leadership. The research analyzing influence and leadership has focused on three different aspects: leadership traits, leadership behaviors, and the nature of leader-follower situations.

LEADERSHIP TRAITS

In the early 1900s, researchers studied leadership as a collection of personal traits and characteristics. They tried to identify a set of intellectual, emotional, and even physical traits that were generally characteristic of people who successfully influenced others. The rationale was that if they could identify these traits they could then select those who possessed them and be almost guaranteed effective leaders. The underlying argument of the trait research was that leadership ability is a function of personality attributes. By implication, organizations could improve their overall performance and success if they selected people with the appropriate traits to be managers or leaders.

Research focusing on the development of a list of leadership traits was most intense during World War II, but it continues even today. Edwin Ghiselli's research in the 1960s and 1970s produced one of the most comprehensive lists. Ghiselli examined 13 personality and motivational traits to determine how these traits related to managerial success.[14] Not surprisingly, the most significant trait of managerial success he identified was supervisory ability—the ability to direct the work of others and to organize them so that they can work together to accomplish common objectives.

Many studies of the traits of leaders have been conducted in the past several decades. For example, in 1980 Harry Levinson offered a list of 20 dimensions of personality that he recommended be used as a basis for selecting chief executives.[15] The list, however, was prefaced with a caution: "No one person has all qualities of an ideal leader. No one is at one time far-seeing, sensitive, analytical, energetic, well-spoken, active, wise, and involved. Real people are more like diamonds . . . with facets of personality, and flaws . . . some . . . more important than others depending on the company and its environment."[16]

Other studies have focused on specific traits, such as intelligence. A report released in 1984, for example, indicated that high IQ test scores did not necessarily correspond to leadership or executive success. This finding led researchers to begin searching for what they called a measure of practical intelligence, or a highly complex style of thinking. "The hallmarks of cognitive complexity," according to Dr. Siegfried Streutfort of Pennsylvania State University, "include the ability to plan strategically without being rigidly locked into one course of events; the capacity to acquire ample information for decision-making without being overwhelmed and being able to group relationships between rapidly changing events."[17] A recent summary of the most researched leadership traits is listed in Exhibit 10.2.

Leaders Talk About Leadership

James Baker, now secretary of state and one-time White House chief of staff, says that the White House chief of staff must make quick decisions and know how to say no in an agreeable manner.

In May 1985, *U.S. News and World Report* interviewed several political leaders and asked them what the challenges were for a chief decision maker. Did they have any special techniques for wielding power effectively? How burdensome are the responsibilities of leadership? Here is what they said:

You Have to Roll with the Punches—*James Baker, ex-secretary of the treasury*

An effective White House chief of staff must have some management experience and be a people person. You have so many things coming at you that are divisive, that involve disputes. You have to be able to hear people out and to roll with the punches. Ninety percent of the job involves saying no. And you must be able to do so agreeably.

What surprised me most about the exercise of power in the White House was the speed with which issues moved and required resolution.

You're hitting everything right at the very top. You really don't have a chance to get into things in the depth I was used to in the private sector. You've got to be able to make decisions.

Needed: Strong Nerves, Thick Skin—*Zbigniew Brzezinski, former national security advisor.*

You are also continuously under pressure. If you are at the very top in the White House, you are working 14 to 16 hours a day in 5-to-7 minute fragments, occasionally interspersed with sessions of up to an hour that shift from topic to topic, from event to event. That imposes enormous strains.

When the pressure is high, it's essential to be very low-key and to cool everybody's moods rather than contribute to a heightened sense of anxiety and tension. One should never scream or stomp—and I never did.

It's important not only to have control over your emotions but also over your schedule and work habits. That means discriminating about what you want to do and, once you have made that decision, acting expeditiously.

You're on Stage Every Waking Moment—*Edward Koch, mayor, New York City.*

In running a major city, it is important to exercise leadership. That means if you think what you're doing is right, do it. If you make a mistake and it becomes evident to you that you have, correct it.

[It is] important to never let department heads take the flak while I only accept applause. I stand with them when they're under attack, whether unfairly or when they've made an error. You get loyalty that way, and if your administration is first rate, as I hope mine is, the applause for them and me far outweighs the flak.

Yet what has surprised me is that things I thought would be done immediately upon my having requested them take much longer. There is a resistance on the part of the government officials . . . while they want to carry out what you want [they] will nevertheless second guess you. ■

Source: "Price of Power: What It's Like on the Inside," *U.S. News & World Report,* May 20, 1985, pp. 65–68

EXHIBIT / 10.2
The Most Researched Leadership Traits

Intelligence

Judgment
Decisiveness
Knowledge
Fluency of speech

Personality

Adaptability
Alertness
Creativity
Personal integrity
Self-confidence
Emotional balance and control
Independence

Abilities

Ability to enlist cooperation
Cooperativeness
Popularity and prestige
Sociability
Social participation
Tact, diplomacy

Source: Adapted from Bernard M. Bass, *Stodgill's Handbook of Leadership* (New York: Free Press, 1981), pp. 75–76.

Researchers have been unable to isolate a definitive list of leadership traits. Ralph Stodgill, a famous leadership researcher, provided a logical explanation for this in 1948, before much of the ensuing research had even been undertaken:[18]

> It is primarily by virtue of participating in group activities and demonstrating the capacity for expediting the work of the group that a person becomes endowed with leadership status. . . . A person does not become a leader by virtue of the possession of some combination of traits, but the pattern of personal characteristics, activities and goals of the followers.

Stodgill added, however, that to assume that leadership could be analyzed entirely from the situational perspective would be to underestimate the personal nature of leadership.

That one set of leadership traits cannot identify all effective leaders is illustrated well by the fact that David Leiderman and Debbi Fields—both successful leaders of their businesses—have extremely different leadership or personality traits. Leiderman "is a crammer," said one reporter. "He talks loud, fast, and constantly, and works the same way."[19] Said another, "Leiderman pursues his enterprise with all the hustle of a small business owner still struggling to make ends meet."[20] On the other hand, Fields was described as a manager who treats her employees "with great tenderness and respect,"[21] a vibrant and energetic, yet patient and maternal type. One reporter, after getting altitude sickness while interviewing Fields at a mountaintop restaurant and being sent home to rest, said of Fields: "She's a lady who would, if she could, tiptoe into the world's room at night and throw a giant blanket over it."[22]

LEADERSHIP BEHAVIORS

Partly in response to the inconclusive results of the research of traits, researchers in the late 1940s began to focus their studies on what leaders did rather than on who they were. These behavioral theories of leadership focused on the relationship between leaders' behavior and subordinates' performance and satisfaction.

Behavioral researchers were trying to identify specific leadership behaviors common to the best leaders.

Two research groups are noted for their work on leadership behavior, one at the University of Michigan and one at Ohio State University. Both groups were seeking to determine which leadership style was most effective. They came to similar conclusions even though their approaches were different.[23]

The University of Michigan Studies

The University of Michigan (UM) studies initiated in 1947 by Rensis Likert and his associates compared how group effectiveness varied depending on the leader's behavior. Their goal was to determine the basic principles and methods of effective leadership necessary to achieve desired performance and satisfaction levels.[24] From the information they gathered, the researchers identified two types of leadership behavior.

Job-centered behavior Leadership behavior characterized by a concern for job performance.

Job-centered behavior: Leadership behavior that focused on the job was characterized by close supervision, pressure for better performance, a concern for meeting deadlines, and a close evaluation of output. Supervisors whose behavior was job-centered were detached from those they supervised and considered their main objective just getting the work done. To them, subordinates were instruments for goal attainment or task performance rather than people with needs and emotions similar to their own. David Leiderman is an example of a job-centered leader.

Employee-centered behavior Leadership behavior characterized by an orientation toward human aspects of work and problems.

Employee-centered behavior: Leadership behavior that focused on the employee was characterized by an orientation toward human aspects of work and toward developing effective work groups with high performance goals. Employee-centered leaders focused their behavior on supervision of people rather than on expediting production. They were concerned with employee needs, advancement, and personal and professional growth. Debbi Fields is a good example of an employee-centered leader.

The UM researchers found that production (as measured by number of claims processed in an insurance company, for example) was higher in the employee-centered units than in the job-centered units. They also found that the attitudes and behaviors in the two groups were very different. In the units having leaders with employee-centered styles, satisfaction was high and turnover and absenteeism were low. In the units with leaders who were job-centered, production was not much lower, but satisfaction among the workers was low and turnover and absenteeism were high. Their initial conclusion was that successful leaders had supportive, human-relations-oriented, employee-centered behavior patterns.

The Ohio State Studies

During the same time frame as the UM studies, E. A. Fleishman and his associates at Ohio State University (OSU) were conducting comparable studies.[25] The OSU studies originally identified ten categories in which leadership behavior could differ. Eventually, two leadership dimensions, referred to as consideration and initiation of structure, were isolated. *Consideration* referred to a manager's concern for people, relationships among people on the job and between leaders and followers, mutual trust, respect, and friendship (in other words, the extent to which the leader showed consideration for the followers). *Initiating structure* referred to the manager's tendency to structure the task, to clearly define relationships among the group, and to define channels of communication (in other words, the extent to which the leader initiated or created the structure of the followers' work). The studies indicated that a leader's behavior could vary along each of these dimensions, and a leader's position within each dimension could be measured with one of two questionnaires (one for each dimension).

The OSU researchers found that foremen working in production jobs who were rated high on proficiency were evaluated by their subordinates as having high initiating structure ratings and low consideration ratings. In office settings they found the reverse. Supervisors with high proficiency ratings were rated high on consideration and low on initiating structure. In their many additional studies, the OSU researchers found in general that high initiating structure and low consideration measures were related to more absenteeism, accidents, grievances, and turnover.

The two dimensions can be combined as shown in the matrix in Exhibit 10.3. A person's leadership style can be described as varying along both dimensions. Exhibit 10.3 shows where three managers fall into the matrix. Manager A demonstrates a strong tendency to structure work to get the job done but also spends time and energy managing interpersonal relationships. Manager B is very concerned about the relationships of people in the group he supervises and very interested in maintaining good relations between the group and himself. However, he shows little concern for structuring communications or job assignments. Manager C does not spend more time managing either the task or the employees process. She balances her time between managing relationships and managing work flows and communications channels. Notice that the matrix does not show whether manager A, B, or C is more or less effective as a leader. As later research discovered, each may be effective depending on the nature of the situation.

The Implications of Behavioral Research

Behavioral research, like trait theories, has not provided universally applicable guidelines for identifying leaders; the OSU studies in particular have been criticized for being too simple, for being inapplicable to a broader range of situations,

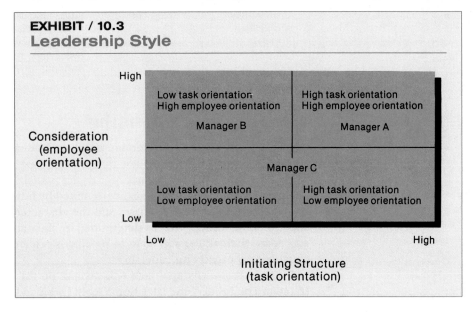

EXHIBIT / 10.3
Leadership Style

and for relying on questionnaires to measure leadership effectiveness. However, many important implications can be drawn from the behavioral studies:

1. Leadership is multidimensional. The dimensions of concern for people and concern for task have both been identified as important components of leadership.
2. Effective leadership behavior varies according to the situation. Contrary to initial beliefs, no one best style consistently corresponds with high levels of performance. There is no one best way to lead others.
3. Leadership skills can be taught. Once it has been demonstrated that the abilities to manage the task and the people are both important, these skills can be taught to those wanting to improve their leadership.

A summary of the two behavioral studies discussed is presented in Exhibit 10.4. Research to investigate the relationship between a high focus on each of these dimensions and effective leadership performance has found no absolute relationship. Effectiveness of leaders was found to be determined by the compatibility of the leaders' behavior with the needs of the subordinates and the characteristics of the situation. These conclusions led to the next phase of leadership research: situational approaches.

EXHIBIT / 10.4
Behavioral Studies of Leadership

Origin of Study	Leadership Dimensions Identified	Conclusions
University of Michigan (Likert)	Employee-centered Job-centered	Though both employee-centered and job-centered styles can increase production, over the longer term, job-centered styles tended to decrease employee satisfaction and increase turnover and absenteeism.
Ohio State University (Fleishman)	Initiating structure Consideration	In general, high initiating structure measures and low consideration measures were associated with increases in absenteeism, grievances, and turnover; however, the most effective combination depends on the nature of the situation.

SITUATIONAL APPROACHES TO LEADERSHIP

The results of trait and behavioral research on leadership increasingly led managers and researchers to conclude that no one best approach to understanding leadership exists. A leader's success may be partially due to certain traits or behaviors of the leader, but it is also determined by how well the traits or behaviors suit the needs of the subordinates and the characteristics of the situation.[26] The success of the leaders is often determined by their ability to analyze the situation and adapt their leadership style to it. This is referred to as the contingency or situational approach to leadership.

The success of any approach will depend on the particular situation, as illustrated in The Inside View 10.3. Both Debbi Fields and David Leiderman, who have

The Need for Benevolent Tyrants

Stephen Wozniak, Steven Jobs, and John Sculley. Wozniak and Jobs founded Apple Computer and ran it in a loose and personal way. When Apple grew into a giant corporation, Sculley was brought in and Jobs was forced to leave.

Plato was perceptive enough to see that leading must sometimes be a solo act, that leaders must be more concerned with the good of the enterprise than with pleasing the multitude. On those frequent occasions when the two are compatible, an easygoing, democratic, management-by-consensus style works and works well. But Plato knew that when the going gets tough, it might be time for a benevolent tyrant to take the helm.

A tough-minded leader might have saved Studebaker, the now-defunct automobile company. Studebaker's demise was caused by its interest in furthering industrial democracy rather than in meeting the developing threat from General Motors. Managing by committee and making excessive concessions to its unions, Studebaker lost sight of its economic objectives. Meanwhile, GM focused with Spartan tenacity on the business of survival. Its authoritarianism worked. Today, GM is the largest automaker in the world. Studebaker went out of business in 1964.

Consider a more recent example. Apple Computer practiced radical democratic and egalitarian management under Steven Jobs's leadership during Silicon Valley's heyday. But when IBM launched its personal computer, the "good ol' days" were gone forever. Jobs wisely brought in John Sculley, from Eastern-establishment PepsiCo, who immediately put an end to laissez-faire management at Apple.

At a meeting of financial analysts just before Jobs departed, Sculley threw down the gauntlet. "There is," he said, "no role for Steven Jobs in the operations of Apple now or in the future." He did not ask for a show of hands. Described as a manager who can be tough, even ruthless, Sculley is clearly in charge at Apple. A recent statement that he made says it all: "I am alone at the top now."

As Plato suggested, democratic management is not a cure-all. It is not the only type of management that works. Often there is not time for a vote. Even if there is, employees may not know enough about what it is they are voting on to make the wisest choice. Good management is sometimes a solo act, relying less on democratic consensus than on individual judgment. ■

Source: Clemens, John, and Mayer, Douglas, *The Classic Touch* (Homewood, Ill.: Dow Jones–Irwin, 1987), pp. 42, 43.

very different styles, are successful. Instead of searching for the one best leadership style, managers should learn to understand the fit between themselves, the situation, and the nature of their subordinates.

Three leadership theories that focus on attaining compatibility between the leadership style and the management situation are Fiedler's contingency model, House's path-goal model, and Hersey and Blanchard's life cycle model.

Fiedler's Contingency Model

Fred E. Fiedler's model is based on the notion that successful leadership depends on a match between the leader, the situation, and the subordinate.[27] He suggests that there is no one best style. The effectiveness of a leader is determined by how well his or her style fits the situation. To sum up Fiedler's theory, a manager can maintain this fit by:

1. Understanding his or her own leadership style.
2. Analyzing the situation.
3. Matching the style to the situation either by placing himself or herself in situations to which the style is suited or by altering a given situation so that it is compatible with the style.

Step 1: Understand Your Own Leadership Style   Leadership style is most often described in terms of the extent to which the manager focuses on the task or the people involved. Exhibit 10.5 presents the least preferred co-worker scale (LPC) Fiedler developed to help managers determine on which aspect they tend to focus. His underlying assumption was that by discovering what a manager felt about the person he or she had the most difficulty with, he would discover whether the manager tended to focus more on task or on people. By marking one number on the scale in each line in Exhibit 10.5, then totaling all the numbers from top to bottom, the manager would obtain a numerical score. A score of 64 or higher would indicate that the manager viewed his or her least preferred co-worker in a positive light. Fiedler defines such a person as a people- or relationship-oriented leader.

A score of 57 or lower would indicate that a manager viewed his or her least preferred co-worker in unfavorable terms. Fiedler defines such people as task-oriented leaders. Scores falling between 57 and 64 indicate a manager who vacillates between styles.

Step 2: Analyze the Situation   The next step is to analyze the situation in order to understand whether the manager's style will be effective. Fiedler suggests three variables that are essential to understanding a situation:

1. Leader-member relations—the degree to which the group accepts and supports the leader.
2. Task structure—the degree to which the task, its goals, and the procedures and practices it requires are clearly specified.
3. Position power—the degree to which the position gives the leader power to reward and punish subordinates.

According to Fiedler, each characteristic can vary: leader-member relations can be good or poor; task structure can be high or low; and leader position power can be strong or weak. Combining each possible combination of these variances produces eight different leadership situations or conditions, as illustrated in

EXHIBIT / 10.5
Fiedler's Least Preferred Co-worker Scale

Think of the person with whom you work least well. He or she may be someone you work with now or someone you knew in the past. This person does not have to be someone you like least, but should be the person with whom you have had the most difficulty in getting a job done. Describe this person.

	8	7	6	5	4	3	2	1	
Pleasant	: ___ : ___ : ___ : ___ : ___ : ___ : ___ : ___ :								Unpleasant
Friendly	: ___ : ___ : ___ : ___ : ___ : ___ : ___ : ___ :								Unfriendly

	8	7	6	5	4	3	2	1

Pleasant : ___ : ___ : ___ : ___ : ___ : ___ : ___ : ___ : Unpleasant
        8   7   6   5   4   3   2   1

Friendly : ___ : ___ : ___ : ___ : ___ : ___ : ___ : ___ : Unfriendly
        8   7   6   5   4   3   2   1

Rejecting : ___ : ___ : ___ : ___ : ___ : ___ : ___ : ___ : Accepting
        1   2   3   4   5   6   7   8

Helpful : ___ : ___ : ___ : ___ : ___ : ___ : ___ : ___ : Frustrating
        8   7   6   5   4   3   2   1

Unenthusiastic : ___ : ___ : ___ : ___ : ___ : ___ : ___ : ___ : Enthusiastic
        1   2   3   4   5   6   7   8

Tense : ___ : ___ : ___ : ___ : ___ : ___ : ___ : ___ : Relaxed
        1   2   3   4   5   6   7   8

Distant : ___ : ___ : ___ : ___ : ___ : ___ : ___ : ___ : Close
        1   2   3   4   5   6   7   8

Cold : ___ : ___ : ___ : ___ : ___ : ___ : ___ : ___ : Warm
        1   2   3   4   5   6   7   8

Cooperative : ___ : ___ : ___ : ___ : ___ : ___ : ___ : ___ : Uncooperative
        8   7   6   5   4   3   2   1

Supportive : ___ : ___ : ___ : ___ : ___ : ___ : ___ : ___ : Hostile
        8   7   6   5   4   3   2   1

Boring : ___ : ___ : ___ : ___ : ___ : ___ : ___ : ___ : Interesting
        1   2   3   4   5   6   7   8

Quarrelsome : ___ : ___ : ___ : ___ : ___ : ___ : ___ : ___ : Harmonious
        1   2   3   4   5   6   7   8

Self-assured : ___ : ___ : ___ : ___ : ___ : ___ : ___ : ___ : Hesitant
        8   7   6   5   4   3   2   1

Efficient : ___ : ___ : ___ : ___ : ___ : ___ : ___ : ___ : Inefficient
        8   7   6   5   4   3   2   1

Gloomy : ___ : ___ : ___ : ___ : ___ : ___ : ___ : ___ : Cheerful
        1   2   3   4   5   6   7   8

Open : ___ : ___ : ___ : ___ : ___ : ___ : ___ : ___ : Guarded
        8   7   6   5   4   3   2   1

Source: Adapted from Fiedler, Fred E., *Theory of Leadership Effectiveness* (New York: McGraw-Hill, 1967), pp. 2, 41.

Exhibit 10.6. These eight conditions range, from left to right on the figure, from favorable to unfavorable. Conditions are favorable when the leader can exert influence over the group, for example, when leader-member relations are good, task structure is high, and leader position power is high (situation I). Conditions are unfavorable when the leader cannot exert influence over the group, for example, when leader-member relations are poor, task structure is low, and leader position power is weak (situation VIII).

Step 3: Match the Situation to Your Style Finally, Fiedler suggests that leaders are most effective when their style matches the situation. Given eight possible situations ranging from favorable to moderate to unfavorable:

1. Task-oriented leaders will be most successful in either very favorable or very unfavorable situations, that is, situations in which the leader is either very able or very unable to influence the group.

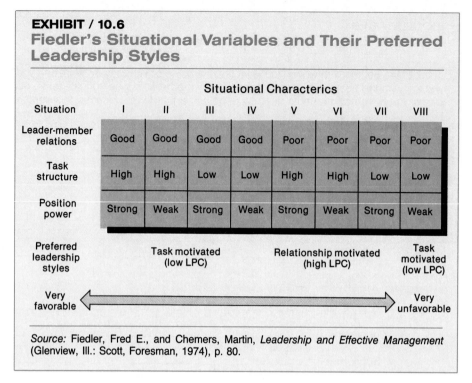

EXHIBIT / 10.6
Fiedler's Situational Variables and Their Preferred Leadership Styles

Situational Characterics

Situation	I	II	III	IV	V	VI	VII	VIII
Leader-member relations	Good	Good	Good	Good	Poor	Poor	Poor	Poor
Task structure	High	High	Low	Low	High	High	Low	Low
Position power	Strong	Weak	Strong	Weak	Strong	Weak	Strong	Weak
Preferred leadership styles	Task motivated (low LPC)				Relationship motivated (high LPC)			Task motivated (low LPC)

Very favorable ⟵⟶ Very unfavorable

Source: Fiedler, Fred E., and Chemers, Martin, *Leadership and Effective Management* (Glenview, Ill.: Scott, Foresman, 1974), p. 80.

2. Relationship-oriented leaders will be most successful in moderately favorable situations, that is, situations in which the leader is moderately able to influence the group.

Consider the following examples. Assume you are the manager of a neighborhood 7-11 store. Your assistants are supportive and want to see the store succeed. Because the store is a franchise of a larger national chain, your job is well defined. You have a schedule of what needs to be done and when. You are responsible for evaluating the performance of your assistants and making pay and promotion recommendations. This type of situation is characterized by good leader-member relations, high task structure, and strong position power. A task-oriented leader is the most effective.

Assume, in another example, that you are the head of the investment unit of the Continental Bank of Illinois. Those you supervise are investment bankers and are used to working independently. They resent your being appointed boss. They question your knowledge of the investment market and see no need for supervision. Policies and procedures greatly structure the job because the buying and selling of stocks and bonds is highly technical and must be done according to applicable laws and restrictions. You have little power over the investment counselors because their salary and promotions are determined by their sales, not by your evaluations. This is a situation that Fiedler would rate as poor on leader-member relations, high on task structure, and weak on position power. A relationship-oriented leader will be most effective. The situational variables of Fiedler's theory, and their corresponding "preferred" leadership style, are illustrated in Exhibit 10.6.

As can be seen from these situations, Fiedler's recommendation is that effective leadership results from matching the leader's style to the situation. Fiedler believes that leadership style is a fairly fixed human characteristic and therefore recommends either changing the situation so that it matches the leader's style or selecting situations that already match the leader's style. He believes that trying to change one's style will not be successful.

Fiedler's model has met with criticism, largely because of its complexity. Several researchers have questioned the validity of the model and of the LPC questionnaire specifically.[28] In addition, some consider the definitions of the variables in the model vague and unclear. Yet, it clarifies some elements of the leadership process.

Path-Goal Model

Another contingency theory of leadership draws heavily on the expectancy theory of motivation, which will be discussed in Chapter 13. Expectancy theory holds that people will do what they expect to result in rewards they want. This is the basis for the path-goal model of leadership. Developed by Robert J. House, it proposes that leaders influence subordinates by clarifying what must be done (the path) to obtain rewards they want (the goal).[29] House suggests that the rewards leaders offer vary according to their leadership style.

For example, an employee-centered leader such as Debbi Fields offers a wide range of not only tangible rewards such as pay and promotions but also intangible rewards such as support, recognition, and praise. A task-oriented leader such as David Leiderman is more likely to focus on fewer and more tangible rewards, such as money and promotions.

House also suggests that leaders can best help subordinates clarify what they should do (the path) to get the rewards they want by adopting different leadership styles—directive, supportive, participative, and achievement-oriented—in different situations. These leadership styles are defined as follows:

1. Directive behavior: leadership activities focused on scheduling work, establishing performance standards, and clarifying expectations regarding employee performance. (This is very similar to job-centered behavior and initiating structure.)
2. Supportive behavior: leadership behaviors focused on improving interpersonal relationships and being generally supportive, accessible, and friendly. (This is very similar to employee-centered behavior and consideration.)
3. Participative behavior: leadership behavior focused on including and involving employees in work-related decisions and generally soliciting their opinions.
4. Achievement-oriented behavior: leadership behavior focused on building employee confidence, encouraging high performance, and energizing employees so that they will strive to achieve challenging goals.

According to House's model, each of these types of behavior is effective in different situations. For example:

Situation A   Sue wants to do well on the job. She would enjoy doing well on the job, but she does not believe she has the ability to perform. Consequently, she is not trying.

Leader Behavior A   The leader can assist Sue by using *directive* leadership: making sure she understands the job and establishing a plan Sue can follow to do well on the job. He or she can also show Sue how her skills fit the job and how to use them.

Situation B   Bob enjoys being around and working with other people. He has been on his job for several years and has not had many opportunities to develop lasting associations with a work group. He works by himself and does not see how doing well on the job will give him any more contact with others.

Leader Behavior B   To assist Bob, the leader in this case should be *supportive* and provide social rewards. He or she should display concern for Bob's well-being and give Bob more of a chance to work with others. The leader should make sure Bob receives praise and recognition when he peforms well.

Situation C   Maria is a very capable person with many years of experience who feels frustrated because her ideas and inputs do not seem to be utilized or taken seriously by management. She likes to be involved and see her ideas used.

Leader Behavior C   The leader in this situation should be *participative,* consulting with Maria, seeking her suggestions, and helping her understand how her skills are used to help solve organizational problems.

Situation D   Herman believes he has the skill to perform well on his job, but he does not perceive that his performance will provide great personal satisfaction. He feels his work is too easy, his best skills and abilities being wasted.

Leader Behavior D   In this case, the leader should be *achievement-oriented.* He or she can help Herman by setting challenging goals, expecting good performance, and continually clarifying for him the rewards available for good performance. When Herman performs well, the leader should make sure he receives the rewards he values, such as challenge and responsibility.

The path-goal model suggests that leaders should select the leadership style that best fits the characteristics of the situation, the subordinates, and the demands of their jobs. In general, leaders should choose styles that improve employees' perceptions of their own abilities to perform and thereby to earn rewards they value.

One of the main strengths of the path-goal model is that it considers both behavioral and situational factors in its analysis of appropriate leadership style, and it attempts to illustrate why one approach works better or worse in motivating performance in each circumstance. However, as with the other models, this one is not without its critics. Some question the validity of House's basic hypotheses,[30] and one researcher argues that it may be changes in employee ability and performance that cause changes in leadership behavior, rather than the other way around.[31]

Life Cycle Model

Another contingency theory is the life cycle model of leadership developed by Paul Hersey and Kenneth Blanchard.[32] It proposes that the leadership style that will be most effective is determined by the maturity of the subordinates. Maturity is defined as the subordinates' desire for achievement, willingness to accept responsibility, and task-related ability and experience.

Hersey and Blanchard use as their basic model the four quadrants (see Exhibit 10.7) developed by combining task and employee orientation, as we did in Exhibit 10.3.[33] When subordinates are not mature and must learn their jobs, the leader should be operating in quadrant I. In this quadrant leaders adopt a highly directive task-oriented style, helping the subordinates learn the basic procedures and telling them how to do their jobs. As subordinates begin to accept responsibility, the leader's orientation moves into quadrant II, managing both task and relationships. In this phase leaders should focus on coaching and teaching subordinates, helping them clarify how they could perform. As subordinates become

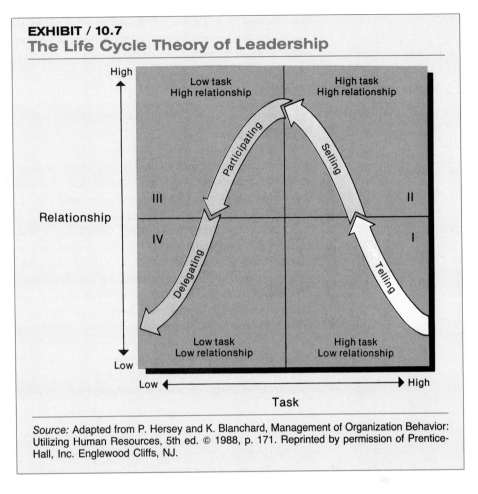

EXHIBIT / 10.7
The Life Cycle Theory of Leadership

Source: Adapted from P. Hersey and K. Blanchard, Management of Organization Behavior: Utilizing Human Resources, 5th ed. © 1988, p. 171. Reprinted by permission of Prentice-Hall, Inc. Englewood Cliffs, NJ.

increasingly proficient at the task and learn to work with others in their unit, moving into quadrant III, they need less direct task help from the supervisor. Now they need support. Supervisors can then move into quadrant III and spend their time sharing ideas and facilitating the problem-solving process. As subordinates gain even more experience, they gradually learn how to manage themselves. They resolve their own conflicts, manage their own professional growth, and develop the ability to work effectively within a group. At this stage (quadrant IV) supervisors can delegate responsibility for decisions and their implementation to the group. They can then spend their time representing the group to the rest of the organization.

In the life cycle model, leadership style should change as the group develops and matures. To be successful, leaders must be able to assess the situation, determine what types of support or guidance are necessary, and then adapt their own style as the situation changes.

The advantage of the life cycle model is that it encourages leaders to work with subordinates, developing their abilities to manage themselves and the process. The difficulty in implementing the life cycle model is that people move through the cycle at different rates. Managers will have to consider each employee individually as well as guiding them all together as a group. Additionally, once subordinates have developed to the level of quadrant IV, they tend to be ripe for promotions or transfers. If the organization wants to move them into other positions, the manager who worked with them from the beginning must start all over with new employees.

CONTINUING RESEARCH

The trait, behavioral, and situational approaches to the study of leadership have greatly expanded researchers' and practitioners' understandings of leadership and influence in organizations. However, each has shortcomings. No one group of traits is characteristic of all leaders, no one type of behavior works in all situations with all people, and situational approaches have tended to assume that the impetus for behavior changes is always one-directional, always flowing from the top down.

Current research tries to study leadership as a dynamic interaction between leaders and followers. James McGregor Burns, for example, defines transformational leadership as the ability of a leader to cause followers to operate on a higher value plane, such as making decisions for the good of society.[34] Two theories are of particular interest. Attribution theory suggests that leaders search for clues or reasons why followers behave one way or another, and then adjust their own behavior to guide the followers. A second branch of research has identified several environmental, individual, and task-related factors that will influence employee satisfaction and performance outside of leadership behavior. They act, in a sense, as substitutes for leadership in influencing employee behavior. These two areas of research will be discussed briefly below.

Attribution Theory

Attribution theory assumes a leader is essentially an information processor.[35] Unlike theories suggesting that subordinates' behaviors directly determine appropriate leader behavior, attribution theory adds a conceptual middle step. It assumes a leader will take time to understand what specifically is causing a follower's behavior, such as low performance, rather than arbitrarily selecting a leadership style in response to the behavior.

The leader's responsibility, according to this theory, is to determine whether the employee's behavior was caused by the employee, by the nature of the task, or by the circumstances or context of the situation. In other words, the leader can categorize the employee's behavior into one of three dimensions: person, entity (task), and context.

To determine an appropriate course of action, the leader must then seek to identify three types of information. First, the leader must determine the *consistency* of the employee's performance; has it been poor over a long period of time or only recently? Second, the leader must determine whether the behavior is *distinctive* to the task, that is, whether the employee performs poorly on that task alone or on others as well. Finally, the leader must determine the extent to which the employee's co-workers react or behave similarly with respect to the same task; that is, whether there is a high or low *consensus* of behavior among all the employees relative to the task.

Once the source or cause of the undesirable follower behavior has been identified, whether it be internal (resting with the employee) or external (inherent in

EXHIBIT / 10.8
Attribution Theory

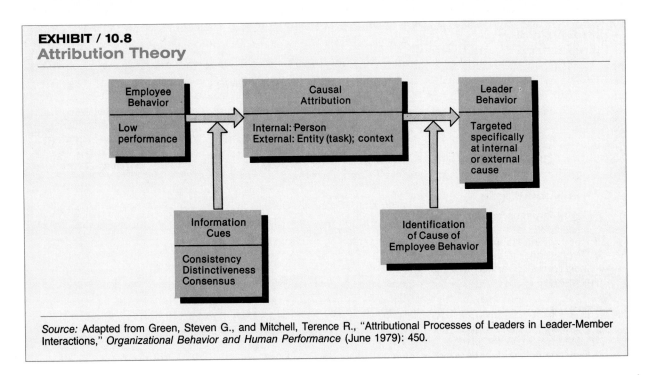

Source: Adapted from Green, Steven G., and Mitchell, Terence R., "Attributional Processes of Leaders in Leader-Member Interactions," *Organizational Behavior and Human Performance* (June 1979): 450.

the task or context), the leader can then determine an effective leadership response. A model of this flow from analysis to response is presented in Exhibit 10.8. Attribution theory is a valuable contribution to the study of leadership in that it addresses effective leaders carefully to assess the causes of follower behavior before determining appropriate leadership behavior.

Leadership Substitutes

The theories discussed above generally assume that follower behavior, satisfaction, and performance are formally and/or directly tied to the behavior of leaders. They assume that employees' performance depends almost entirely on motivation, support, and rewards from leaders. However, recent research has identified several factors internal and external to the employee that affect both satisfaction and performance and that do not emanate from leaders.[36] The characteristics of the employee, of the tasks, and of the organization listed in Exhibit 10.9 all can either serve as a substitute for what would be an appropriate leadership style in a given situation or neutralize the effects of a leadership behavior—appropriate or inappropriate—used in a given situation.

Research into the behavior of leaders and followers, and into the leader-follower relationship, continues today. Organizations such as the Center for Creative Leadership in Greensboro, North Carolina, continually develop and test new theories. Although no single, best theory will ever exist, each one offers new insights into how managers can influence their employees and gain their enthusiastic cooperation in the progress toward goal achievement.

EXHIBIT / 10.9
Leadership Substitutes

Characteristics	Will Tend to Neutralize	
	Relationship-oriented, Supportive, People-centered Leadership: Consideration, Support	Task-oriented, Instrumental, Job-centered Leadership: Initiating, Structure
Of the Subordinate		
1. Ability, experience, training, knowledge		X
2. Need for independence	X	X
3. "Professional" orientation	X	X
4. Indifference toward orgainzational rewards	X	X
Of the Task		
5. Unambiguous and routine		X
6. Methodologically routine		X
7. Provides its own feedback concerning accomplishment		X
8. Intrinsically satisfying	X	
Of the Organization		
9. Formalization (explicit plans, goals, and areas of responsibility)		X
10. Inflexibility (rigid, unbending rules and procedures)		X
11. Highly specified and active advisory and staff functions		X
12. Closely knit; cohesive work groups	X	X
13. Organizational rewards not within the leader's control	X	X
14. Spatial distance between superior and subordinates	X	X

Source: Adapted from Kerr, Steven, and Jermier, John M., "Substitutes for Leadership: Their Meaning and Measurement," *Organizational Behavior and Human Performance* (December 1978): 376–405.

▓ KEY POINTS

1 Directing, the process of guiding the activities of a group of people toward goal accomplishment, involves staffing, communicating, motivating, and working with groups. Directing is highly dependent on leadership abilities. Leadership, a concept of narrower scope than directing, is the active process of influencing others in their activities toward goal accomplishment.

2 Authority, power, delegation, responsibility, and ac-

countability are the five basic aspects of influence and leadership. All must be in balance if an organization is to function effectively.

3 Formal authority is the right to request action that is assigned by an organization to a person and/or position. Informal authority is the ability to influence others and can come from several sources (such as expertise and charisma), but it is not designated by the organization. Managers in an organization are wise to identify informal leaders and gain their support so that, together, they can influence and motivate the workforce.

4 According to French and Raven, power can come from five sources: Legitimate power is formally assigned and specifically attributable to a title or position; reward power is the ability to influence others by giving or withholding rewards; coercive power derives from the ability to mete out punishment or simply from the delivery of threats; expert power derives from the possession of specialized skills or knowledge; referent power derives from the possession of charismatic or attractive characteristics.

5 Delegation is the process by which a supervisor gives a subordinate the authority to act. It allows managers to split up their own jobs, expanding their abilities to complete these jobs. However, by delegating, managers accept the risk that the jobs will be done differently or incorrectly, and they add to their own job the task of coordinating the subdivided work.

6 Responsibility is the obligation to perform a task; accountability is the obligation to report the results or accomplishment of the undertaken responsibilities. Ideally, the person responsible for completing the task should also be held accountable for it. Ultimate responsibility and accountability always rest with the head of an organization. Delegating a job and the responsibility to do it does not decrease the delegator's responsibility, nor can accountability be delegated.

7 In the early 1900s, researchers tried to identify a set of individual traits that were generally characteristic of effective leaders. Although the resulting list of personality and motivational traits was useful, not one list best described characteristics common to all effective leaders.

8 Starting in the late 1940s, the focus of leadership studies shifted from trait identification to behavioral analysis. Behavioral studies attempted to identify what effective leaders did rather than who they were. These studies indicated that leadership is multidimensional, that leadership style is flexible, and that leadership skills can be learned. However, no one set of behaviors was found universally effective; effective leadership behavior was determined to be largely contingent on the needs of followers and on situational factors.

9 The three major situational approaches to the study of leadership are Fiedler's contingency model, focusing on the fit between leadership style and the characteristics of the situation; House's path-goal model of leadership, based on the expectancy theory of motivation; and Hersey and Blanchards' life cycle model, focusing on employee development and maturity.

10 According to Fiedler's model, essentially, leaders should first gain an understanding of their own leadership style, then analyze the situation in terms of leader-member relations, task structure, and position power, and finally adapt the situation to fit their style.

11 House bases his path-goal theory of leadership on the expectancy theory of motivation. He states that leaders should be directive in situations where employees do not believe they have the ability to perform, supportive in situations where employees need to improve their interpersonal relations, participative when employees need to feel involved and useful, and achievement-oriented where employees need motivation to perform at their highest level.

12 Hersey and Blanchard state that the most effective leadership style will depend on the maturity and development of the subordinates. New employees will need leaders who are task-oriented, developing employees will need leaders who are less task-oriented and more process-oriented, and highly developed or mature employees will need managers who give them much freedom and autonomy.

FOR DISCUSSION AND REVIEW

1. Is David or Debbi a better leader? Which one of their leadership styles would fit a company in Japan? Germany? France? China?

2. Give an example of a situation you are familiar with where a person's responsibility was less than his or her authority. What problems did it create?

3. Describe French and Raven's five sources of power. What type of power does a police officer have? A politician? Your teacher?

4. Contrast the University of Michigan studies with the Ohio State studies. What did each discover? After reading results of the studies, how would you characterize an effective group leader?

5. Contingency theory states that a leader's style should fit the situation. Give an example where a leader who had been doing well moved to a new situation and did poorly.

6. Why is the life cycle model different from Fiedler's and House's work? Think of a situation for each and describe it.

7. Think of a leader whom you have known and admired. Describe the aspects of that person's leadership that you have noticed or admired.

▦ KEY TERMS

Accountability	Employee-centered	Informal authority	Power
Authority	behavior	Job-centered behavior	Referent power
Coercive power	Expert power	Leadership	Responsibility
Delegation	Formal authority	Legitimate power	Reward power
Directing	Influence		

THE CONFERENCE TABLE: DISCUSSION CASE / 10.1

Tips from the Top

If you could give one best piece of advice to managers today, what would that be? *Industry Week* asked leading CEOs and other corporate chiefs just that question. Here are some of their responses.

"Communicate"
Jerry Benefield
President/CEO
Nissan Motor Manufac-turing Corporation, USA

Communicate, communicate, communicate. Open communication up, down, and across the organization is the most important ingredient for success, particularly in these days of participative management, employee involvement, and productivity and quality improvements. And when I say communication, I don't mean just talking, I also mean listening.

"Persistence"
Ellen Gordon
President/COO
Tootsie Roll Industries, Inc.

Persistence. We have a saying here: Don't be stopped by the first blade of grass. If there's something you want and you know it's right, keep going after it. The other advice is: Work hard. There's no substitute for really hard work—and persistence.

"Know your customer"
Daniel Krumm
Chairman/CEO
Maytag Corporation

Keep your eye on your ultimate customer. Constantly determine and be confident that you know what that customer really wants and needs. It's so easy to get so involved in filling all the responsibilities of a manager that you forget that sometimes. The [domestic] auto industry kind of lost track of what the consumer really wanted and that's when the Japanese really got a toehold in this country. That could happen very easily to us in appliances.

Source: Brahm, James, "Tips from the Top." Reprinted with permission from *Industry Week,* July 4, 1988, © Penton Publishing Inc., Cleveland, OH.

"Tell it like it is"
Vaughn Beals, Jr.
Chairman/CEO Harley-
Davidson, Inc.

Tell it like it is. That's a two-way street. Senior management's got to set the environment [to] eliminate fear, so that people are comfortable [telling you]. But middle managers have to give you all the facts, as they understand them. That's not always been the case in my experience. You can get in an awful lot of trouble by not getting well-informed by the guys down the line. Give your full professional opinion as to what the problem is, what the solution might be, and don't pull your punches. Sometimes people don't like to be bearers of bad tidings.

"Keep employees
happy"
Joseph "Rod" Canion
President/CEO
Compaq Computer Cor-
poration

If you had to put your finger on the most important thing that will ensure success, I think it would have to be how you deal with your people. You have to, first, be fortunate enough to attract the right people for the job. Then you need to create an environment where they can accomplish things and take personal satisfaction. This results in happier employees. The result is the most powerful retention mechanism you can have. That stability from continuity pays all kinds of benefits. ■

DISCUSSION
QUESTIONS

1. Which of these CEOs are examples of a leadership style that emphasizes employee-centered behaviors? Job-centered?
2. Which CEOs would you like to work for? Why?
3. If their corporations suddenly were in real trouble, sales down, morale low, and products and services poor, how do you think each of the CEOs would respond?

THE CONFERENCE TABLE: DISCUSSION CASE / 10.2

Conflicts Between a Younger Leader and an Older Employee

When older employees work for young bosses, conflicts that upset the corporate balance often result.

After 20 years of cooking, cleaning, and kids, a middle-aged woman gets a job and finds herself working for a woman 10 or more years her junior. How does she feel?

"It's a double whammy," says 45-year-old Joanna Henderson, who helped organize a seminar at Boston's Simmons College on the subject after she was hired by a younger woman. "The stigma is more intense if your boss is both younger and a woman."

The phenomenon of older women working for younger women is the latest of a series of social upheavals unsettling corporate psyches. While older women long have accepted the inevitability of working for younger men in a largely male domain, and even older men know that aggressive younger men may surpass them, other pairings meet greater resistance. Many white workers still resent taking orders from blacks, and many men chafe at working for women.

The older woman generally has entered the work force late after raising a family or has been stuck for years in a dead-end, traditionally female job—secretary, nurse, or teacher. So she often resents younger managers, who have advantages she generally was denied—a business-school education, specialized training, and fewer barriers to the corporate fast track.

Meanwhile, the younger women managers harbor their own resentments toward their older colleagues. And because this situation was once so rare, younger women managers have few role models who have handled such conflicts.

Today more than 1.3 million women under age 35 hold managerial or administrative posts, up from only 322,000 a dozen years ago. Meanwhile, more than half the women over age 45 also work. "Your first reaction" to having a younger woman boss, says Eileen Bergquist, a 39-year-old Wheaton College career counselor, "is 'what the heck does this kid know?'"

Older women workers admit that they are sometimes deferential with colleagues and maternal with superiors. "I freaked out when I started working for younger people," says a 46-year-old software specialist at Data General Corp. "You sort of want to pick up after them and wipe their noses."

But such an attitude infuriates younger women managers, raised on the feminism of the 1970s. "I don't respond to a mother, because I've got one and that was plenty," says Lori King, a Boston University career counselor, who supervises women 10 and 20 years older.

And those older women have not been easy to manage, she concedes. She claims they resist her directives and become dismayed when she treats them as employees instead of sisters. "They say, 'I expected something different from a woman,'" she says, and accuse her of being "pro-male" in making assignments and doling out criticism.

Younger women managers also run into conflicts with long-time women employees who may feel they know better how things should be done. Bosses grow annoyed when their older secretaries "come in and tell you perhaps your letter needs to be revised or they don't like the word you used," says Jayne Hurley Morgan, a 30-year-old Air Force contracting officer. ■

DISCUSSION QUESTIONS

1. In circumstances like those described above, what forces are operating to upset the balance between authority, power, responsibility, accountability, and delegation? How could these problems be remedied and balance restored?
2. How would leadership trait researchers describe this situation? How would behavioral researchers describe it?
3. Based on the leadership theories discussed in the chapter, what recommendations would you have for a younger, female leader or manager, in order for her to be effective and successful when managing older women and men?

Source: Glickman, Amy, "Women Clash: Older Worker vs. Young Boss," *Wall Street Journal,* February 19, 1985, p. 37.

11 Staffing and Human Resource Management

To direct, a manager or leader must harness the efforts of the organization's human resources. People are an essential ingredient of every organization's success. They are one of the most valuable resources used by organizations to produce goods and services. One of management's greatest challenges is finding good people, integrating their efforts into the organization's activities, and guiding them so that they contribute to the accomplishment of the organization's goals. Staffing and the effective management of human resources are critical to organizational success.

KEY QUESTIONS

As you study this chapter, try to answer the following key questions:

1 What are the basic elements of the human resource system?
2 What external constraints and internal guidelines typically affect the way in which an organization can undertake its human resource management activities?
3 What is human resource planning?
4 What are the advantages and disadvantages of recruiting internally and externally to fill jobs?
5 What is selection? Of those prospective employees found through recruiting, which ones should be offered the jobs?
6 What is the purpose of orientation and training in organizations?
7 What are the purposes and uses of performance appraisals in organizations?
8 What purpose does compensation play in the organization?
9 What purpose does replacement play in the human resource system?

FOCUS CASE / Challenging the Theory of Potential Limit

THE HUMAN RESOURCE SYSTEM
Elements of the Human Resource System
External Constraints
Internal Guidelines

HUMAN RESOURCE PLANNING
Assessment of Needs
Evaluation of Current Human Resources
Analysis of Future Availability
Preparation of Recruitment and Development Plans

RECRUITMENT AND SELECTION
Internal Recruiting
External Recruiting
Selection

ORIENTATION, TRAINING, AND DEVELOPMENT
Orientation
Training and Development
Management Development Programs

PERFORMANCE APPRAISAL

REWARDING
Compensation
Promotions and Transfers
Demotions, Terminations, and Retirement: Leading to Replacement

CURRENT ISSUES: TESTING THE WORK FORCE

Focus Case

Challenging the Theory of Potential Limit

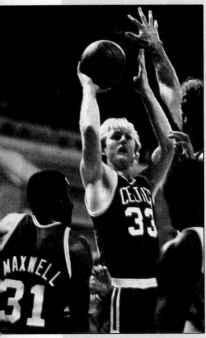

The great Celtics' coach and general manager "Red" Auerbach picked Larry Bird for the team because of his shooting ability, and he immediately became a star. But Bird still considers himself just part of the team.

Before he became coach of the Boston Celtics in 1950, before he rose to general manager, and before he became president of the Celtics organization, Arnold "Red" Auerbach had developed what he called his potential limit theory to keep his high school students on their toes. As he saw it, everyone is born with a certain potential. How close people come to achieving their full potential depends on how much effort they put into what they are doing, how willing they are to pay the price, and how well their efforts are directed by those in a position to teach or guide them.

Based on this theory, Auerbach saw his role in the Celtics organization very clearly: He would find the basketball players who were born with the highest potential, motivate them so that they would be willing and eager to give their best effort to the team, and train them so that their unique talents would be developed to the fullest. If he could succeed in these things, he would have the winningest team in basketball history. After 36 years with the Celtics, most people—except Auerbach himself—would say he challenged his own theory of potential limit. "Auerbach's brand of manipulation has garnered the 16 World Champion banners that hang from the rafters of the Boston Garden, a record no other sports franchise in *any* venue comes close to rivaling," said one reporter. "Not only does Auerbach know how to extract the most from his present players, but he is equally astute when it's necessary to choose new members to fit within the prevailing framework of his team." But, says Auerbach, he only led the team to 16 championships in 36 seasons—and that is far short of the Celtics' potential.

According to Auerbach, managing the Celtics is similar to managing any competitive, fast-paced business. And his human resource strategy—the key to the organization's success—is also similar. In his early days with the team, one of its former owners made a player trade that ended up costing the team millions and "ruining" its performance ability. Said Auerbach, "I had to start from scratch" after that. "I picked out the best team in the league and said, 'We've got to put a team together that's competitive with that team.'" Auerbach's human resource strategy was simple: He identified the needs of the team and the organization, identified the availability of the necessary talent in both college teams and other pro clubs, and made whatever arrangements needed to put together the most competitive team.

Sources: This case was written by M. R. Poirier, based on the following sources: Auerbach, Red, with Joe Fitzgerald, *On and Off the Court* (New York: Bantam Books, 1986); Jones, K. C., with Jack Warner, *Rebound* (Boston: Quinlan Press, 1986); "Red Auerbach on Management," interview with Alan M. Webber, *Harvard Business Review* (March–April 1987): 84–91; "Arnold 'Red' Auerbach," *Pan Am Airlines Magazine* (February 1988).

In 1956, for example, a player who could block shots, catch rebounds, and keep the ball in the Celtics' possession was "the one missing element that could make us a great, great team." On a tip from his old college coach, Auerbach decided to draft Bill Russell, a student at San Francisco. He worked out a deal with St. Louis, giving that team the Celtics all-star center and a forward in return for their first pick in the draft that same year. Russell joined the Celtics in December 1956.

Russell was not much of a scorer, but he never got fooled the same way twice, and "he turned shot-blocking into an art." Said Auerbach, "Russell took that one great skill and revolutionized the game by terrorizing the league." And Auerbach never tried to teach Russell to shoot. During his tenure with the Celtics, he sought to develop highly talented specialists and meld them into a tight-knit team in which everybody, scoring statistics aside, was a crucial player.

The Celtics were the first organization to popularize the use of "role player" positions. Auerbach was always able to convince a player to take on the "thankless job that has to be done in order to make the whole package fly," such as spending the whole game guarding the toughest member of the other team. The Celtics also invented the "sixth man" concept, the strategy by which the coach does not send out the best or strongest five players at the opening of the game. Auerbach sent out four of his best; then, when both teams began to wear out, he would send out the sixth man, increasing the Celtics' effectiveness while the other team was losing stamina.

Always, Auerbach strove to find the best, develop their unique strengths, and place them in positions that would help the team win. Statistics were never considered first, only performance, drive, and contribution to the overall effectiveness of the team. As the players learn what their positions are and what contributions they, uniquely, can make, individual stardom becomes less important.

This is true even today, despite the obvious popularity of one of the team's players. In 1977, the Celtics needed a great shooter. Just as Auerbach had singled out Russell 20 years earlier and paid the price, he hedged his bets on a kid from Indiana State who was passed over by the first five picks because he would still be in school for a year before he could play. Larry Bird joined the team in the fall of 1979, and there has not been an empty seat in the Boston Garden during a home game since. Though he has sold more tickets as an individual attraction than any other player before him, and though he has developed not only his ability to shoot, but to pass, rebound, block, and even motivate the other players, he still considers himself just part of the team. He gets as big a thrill out of making the connecting pass as making the actual shot, and before the big game, says Auerbach, Bird will say, "'We're going to win this thing.' Not I'm going to win it . . . 'We're going to win it.'" ■

It is important for all managers to understand what types of people their organizations need, where to find them, and how to harness their best efforts after they are employed. The need to locate, hire, train, and develop employees exists in every organization, whether it is the Red Cross, a high-technology manufacturer, a bank, or a sports franchise.

The ability to manage other people effectively is one of the most important talents an executive or administrator can possess. Of all the resources that need to be gathered and managed in the modern organization, none is as potentially productive as the human resource.[1] Money, machinery, and standard capital investments, while they are much more stable and predictable, do not have the imagination, intelligence, or capacity for learning that human beings possess.

Red Auerbach was just one manager who was pleasantly surprised by the potential of many of his recruits. Of Russell, he said he did not really know what he was getting, beyond a great rebounder. "I knew nothing about his character, his smarts, his heart [and I] certainly didn't know what was about to happen: 11 Boston championships in the next 13 years."[2] And though he knew Larry Bird was a great shooter and had the potential to make a "major impact" on the team, he said:[3]

> I didn't even dream of the surprises which were to come. I didn't realize how quick he was. I had no knowledge of his rebounding abilities. . . . I had no sense of his leadership qualities, or his ability to motivate other people as well as motivating himself. . . . He keeps coming up with the damnedest plays I've ever seen.

No two people will think or act in precisely the same way; they will always vary in intelligence, enthusiasm, mechanical skill, and personality. For an organization to really tap the potential of its human resources, then, it has to invest in learning about them and in finding ways to get the most from them. In its very simplest form, that is what human resources management is: staffing the organization with people and managing those people so they perform. In this chapter, we discuss some of the basic principles of human resource management.

THE HUMAN RESOURCE SYSTEM

Staffing The continuous process of identifying the types of jobs that need to be done, filling these positions with appropriate people, and managing their performance.

The human resource system of an organization consists of all those activities necessary to ensure that the proper mix of people is attracted to the organization, trained to accomplish tasks that contribute to the achievement of objectives, and developed to achieve their potential within the organization.[4] **Staffing** is the process of continuously identifying the types of jobs that need to be done, filling these positions with appropriate people, and managing their performance so they operate at peak effectiveness.

Elements of the Human Resource System

In most organizations, there are always jobs to be filled, employees to be evaluated, training to be completed, and new skills to be learned. There are seven key elements to the human resource system: human resource planning, recruitment, selection, orientation, training and development, performance appraisal, and rewarding.

These elements, shown in Exhibit 11.1, describe the activities management must undertake if the organization is to be successful in attracting, keeping, and developing its people. However, managers do not have complete discretion over how they will undertake these activities. A number of internal and external restrictions and constraints limit a manager's ability to hire, fire, promote, or compensate any employee in any way the managers choose.

EXHIBIT / 11.1
The Human Resource System

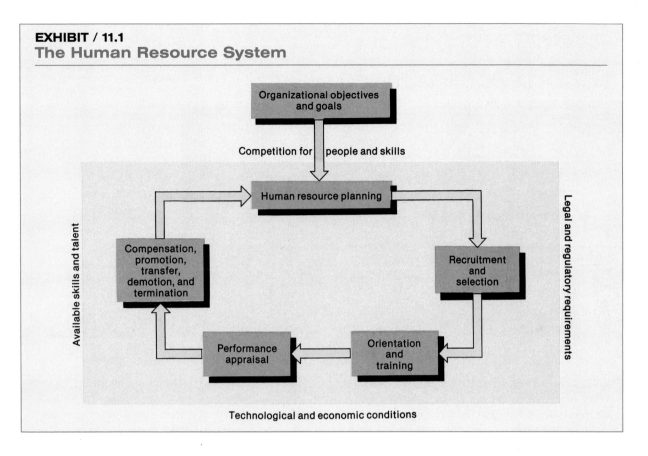

External Constraints

The entire human resources system exists within a set of constraints external to the organization. One of these is the availability of skilled or trained potential recruits. For the Celtics, there are a limited number of players, college or pro, who will meet the team's needs. Similarly, if a company wishes to hire ten electrical engineers and there is a shortage of electrical engineers in the country or even the region, those skills may not be readily available. In addition, the company may be competing against other firms for electrical engineers, in which case salaries, benefits, and other factors may determine which firms get the new engineers. Technological demands, such as computer-programming skills, and economic conditions in the nation or region may also affect a company's success or failure in managing the human resource system. All of these factors limit or constrain an organization's ability to find, recruit, and keep the people who will help it achieve organizational goals and objectives. Moreover, as The Inside View 11.1 shows, women coming to work are greatly changing the nature of the labor force.

Perhaps the most important external constraint is the law. In Chapters 1 and 2, we described some human resource management policies and procedures that would obviously be illegal today. Corporations cannot hire young children, force employees to work long hours, or, in general, hire and fire employees at will or without cause. We take these standards for granted, but they were a long time in coming and only came into being after much pressure was exerted on government.

THE INSIDE VIEW / 11.1

Women at Work in the United States

The number of women in the labor force has been steadily increasing since 1947. Over 38.8 percent of all managerial, executive, and administrative workers now are women.

Following are some statistics about women in the work force, and although statistics alone mean little, these do show us some very important trends.

Over half of all women (56.0 percent) were in the labor force in 1987, employed or looking for work.

The number of women in the labor force increased by 173 percent (from 16.7 million to 45.6 million) between 1947 and 1980. Since then, it has grown even more, to 53.9 million in 1987. About 50.6 million women were employed and 3.3 million were unemployed and looking for work in 1987.

Today, women make up 44.3 percent of the labor force. By the start of the twenty-first century they will make up nearly half (47.3 percent).

As women have moved into the labor force they've decided to have fewer children; the fertility rate for American women is now 1.8, compared to 3.7 in the late 1950s at the height of the baby boom.

About half of all women (49 percent) with children under the age of 1 are working.

Even though more women are working, more women are living in poverty. About 25 million mothers and their children now live in poverty.

Women earned only 69.2 cents for every dollar men made in 1986, indicating that the wage gap between men and women has improved somewhat since 1955, when women made 65 cents for every dollar men did.

Only 11 percent of all women fit the stereotype of a housewife—a married woman, not in the labor force, with children at home.

Over 38.8 percent of all managerial, executive, and administrative workers were women in 1986. There are about 3.8 million women managers, executives, and administrators, up from 2.2 million in 1972, when women were 27.5 percent of the total.

Yet the single most common occupation for women is still secretary. ■

Source: Rukeyser, Louis, *Business Almanac* (New York: Simon & Schuster, 1988), pp. 39–40.

Equal employment opportunity and affirmative action are two of the most significant legal mandates affecting employers today. During the 1960s, civil and women's rights groups began to raise their voices against discriminatory human resource practices. The results of these pressures were several pieces of legislation that guarantee the rights of women and minorities in the workplace.

The Civil Rights Act of 1964 (amended in 1972) and the 1978 Uniform Guidelines on Employee Selection procedures prohibit discrimination on the basis of race, sex, religion, color, or national origin in employment decisions such as "promotions, demotions, retention, and transfer . . . and other decisions [that] lead to any decision listed above."[5] These protections are referred to as *equal employment opportunity* (EEO) requirements. All public and private organizations employing 15 or more people must conform to them or face possible legal action. The Equal Pay Act of 1963 prohibits discrimination in pay for substantially equal work on the basis of sex. Exhibit 11.2 illustrates the changes in the employ-

EXHIBIT / 11.2
Employment and Earnings Patterns of Women

Median Annual Earnings for Full-Time Workers

1960	Women $3,293
	Men $5,417
1970	Women $5,323
	Men $8,966
1980	Women $11,197
	Men $18,612
1983	Women $13,915
	Men $21,881

Number of Women in Selected Positions

Job Category	1972 (nos. in thousands)	1984 (nos. in thousands)	Percent change
Professional, technical, and managerial	6,054	11,856	+95.8
Executive, administrative, and managerial	1,433	3,889	+171.4
Professional specialty	3,881	6,440	+65.9
Technician and related support	740	1,527	+106.4
Sales occupations	3,473	6,032	+73.7
Administrative support, including clerical	9,845	13,361	+35.7
Service occupations	6,614	8,607	+30.1
Precision production, craft, and repair	493	1,112	+125.6
Operators, fabricators, and laborers	4,183	4,385	+4.8
Farming, forestry, and fishing	593	562	-5.2
Total	31,257	45,916	+46.9%

Sources: Serrin, William, "Experts Say Job Bias Against Women Persists," *New York Times,* November 25, 1984, pp. A1, A32; U.S. Bureau of Labor Statistics, *Employment and Earnings* 32(1) (January 1985): 174.

ment and earnings patterns of women since the EEO requirements and the Equal Pay Act of 1963 were enacted. The results are mixed: Though women's earnings have increased significantly, they are still 30 to 40 percent lower than men's. And though the number of women in higher-paying, higher-status positions has also increased, the proportion of women to men in these positions is still low.

Affirmative action (AA) requirements, based on executive orders issued by President Lyndon Johnson in 1965 and 1968 (and amended in 1977), were also enacted to prevent discrimination in human resource practices. *Affirmative action programs* ensure that firms doing business with the federal government make special efforts to hire and promote women, veterans, the handicapped, the aged, and members of minority groups. Many states have similar laws. Although recent Supreme Court decisions have lessened the requirements, many organizations continue to believe affirmative action is good human resource management.

In addition to AA, EEO, and the Equal Pay Act, several other pieces of legislation have been enacted in the past three decades to protect the rights of various members of society. These are listed in Exhibit 11.3. Each act or law places certain requirements or restrictions on human resource practices, preventing managers from exercising ultimate discretion in all of the human resource activities we will discuss in the remainder of this chapter.

Internal Guidelines

Organizations often have well-established and long-standing guidelines and policies for dealing with their people. Japanese companies, for example, traditionally hire selectively, train, and then provide lifetime employment for their workers. Being hired by a company such as Sony, therefore, will assure a young Japanese worker of future employment for as long as the company continues in operation. Such a policy also means that companies emphasize training, developing, and promoting people from within the organization and almost never hire from outside to fill middle- or top-management positions.

American management traditions are quite different. Most companies provide neither lifetime employment nor guarantees that new job opportunities will be filled by current employees rather than outsiders. Obviously, these internal policies have a dramatic effect on how managers work with people. Both external constraints and internal policies shape the way the human resources system of the organization is managed. Legislation determines which pool of applicants the organization may choose from in hiring and also provides a framework for how employees may be treated. Internal guidelines also affect the options available to managers as they make staffing decisions. In the following sections, we will discuss the specific components of the human resource management process.

HUMAN RESOURCE PLANNING

Human resource planning The process of deciding the type and number of employees that the organization will need.

The first step in human resource management is determining who is needed and will be needed to accomplish organizational objectives. The organization's objectives determine the number and type of employees needed. Because organizations tend to be future-oriented in their goals and objectives, managers must pay attention to future as well as current personnel needs. This is the heart of **human resource planning**—the process of deciding what types of employees and how many will be needed for the organization to accomplish its objectives now and in the future.[6]

EXHIBIT / 11.3
Legal Requirements Pertaining to Human Resource Practices

Year	Legislation	Impact
1963	Equal Pay Act	Requires equal pay for equal work regardless of sex
1964	Title VII of the Civil Rights Act; amended as Equal Opportunity Employment Act, 1972	Prohibits employment discrimination on the basis of race, sex, age, religion, color, or national origin
1965	Executive orders for affirmative action	Requires firms doing business with the federal government to make special efforts to hire and promote women and members of minorities proportionate to their representation in the work force
1967	Age Discrimination in Employment Act; amended in 1978	Prohibits employment discrimination on the basis of age; specifically protects people in the 40- to 70-year-old age group
1973	Vocational Rehabilitation Act; amended in 1974	Requires affirmative action programs for the physically and mentally handicapped, provided they are qualified to perform job tasks with reasonable accommodation by the employer
1974	Mandatory Retirement Act	Prohibits mandatory retirement before age 70
1974	Employee Retirement Income Security Act	Guarantees certain pension vesting rights for employees
1974	Vietnam-era Veteran's Readjustment Act	Requires organizations doing business with the federal government to extend affirmative action programs to Vietnam veterans and disabled veterans in general
1978	Pregnancy Discrimination Act	Prohibits the dismissal of women due to pregnancy and protects their job security during maternity leave

For example, many public school systems in the United States face the problem of human resources planning in the 1980s and 1990s. For years, school populations declined as the 1960s "baby boom" passed through the educational system. The need for teachers declined as classes decreased in size. However, in the 1990s, it is likely that the children of parents born in the fifties and sixties will begin their passage through the educational system, creating another "boom" and a need for more teachers. The dilemma facing some school administrators is whether to lay off good teachers today because classes are smaller, knowing that in several years it will be hard to find well-qualified teachers. Compounding this problem is the fact that, on the average, current teachers are getting older and will be retiring. In school districts where budgets are very tight, managers may be forced to let some teachers go, even though it will be more expensive to find qualified replacements in the future. Such dilemmas emphasize the reasons human resource planning is such an important part of managing an organization.[7]

Human resource planning is done through a series of four steps: assessment of needs, evaluation of current human resources, analysis of future availability, and preparation of recruitment and development plans.[8]

Assessment of Needs

What are the predicted future employment needs of the organization? How many and what type of employees will the organization require in the future? Answers to these questions will be determined by forecasts of the organization's future size, products and services, and technological demands. Some organizations are growing rapidly and changing their products and services drastically.

Job analysis is the method used to clearly define staffing needs. It includes analysis of:

Job analysis The method used to clearly define staffing needs.

- Work activities—what needs to be done
- Work tools and technology—what machines, tools, and technology people will use
- Knowledge required—what people must know to perform the job
- Personal requirements—what skills and experience people must possess to perform well
- Job context—the work schedules, physical conditions, and social environment of the job
- Performance standards—expected results

Job description An outline of the specific responsibilities and duties of a job.

Job specification An outline of the education, experience, and skills necessary to perform well on the job.

The two most important components of the job analysis are the descriptions of what is to be done on the job and what skills a person will need to do it. These two components are often individually addressed in a **job description,** which outlines the specific duties and responsibilities of the job, and a **job specification,** which outlines the education, experience, and skills necessary to perform well on the job. Exhibit 11.4 presents, as an example, the job description and specification for the position of corporate loan officer of a bank.

The job descriptions and specifications are the basis of staffing. With a good job description and specification in hand, the manager is prepared to search for people who can do the job. Though Red Auerbach did not develop formal job descriptions and specifications for each position on the team, he had a very clear picture of the specific skills needed to round out the team during each draft. Bill Russell was picked because the team needed a rebounder. Larry Bird was picked because the team needed a great shooter and a forward who could handle the ball well. Auerbach even picked players rejected by other teams because he knew he could fit them into "the Celtics' scheme of things." After the Los Angeles Lakers dropped Don Nelson in 1965, and no other team picked him up, the Celtics took him and kept him for 11 seasons. They helped him focus on his ability to shoot after faking out the other team and his knack for boxing the opposition out of shooting range. "If we had just turned him loose and allowed him to float in the general swing of things—hey that's why L.A. let him go! He wasn't productive that way."[9] When Auerbach saw a hole in his team, he went looking for the skill that could fill it, even if it meant looking in less than obvious places.

EXHIBIT / 11.4
A Job Description for a Corporate Loan Assistant

JOB DESCRIPTION
Exempt

Functional Title: Corporate Loan Assistant   Department: Corporate Banking
Function Code: Division:
Incumbent: Location: Head Office
                                                  Date: June 19—

Note: Statements included in this description are intended to reflect in general the duties and responsibilities of this classification and are not to be interpreted as being all-inclusive.

Relationships:

Reports to: Corporate account officer A or AA; or senior corporate account officer B or BB
Subordinate staff: None
Other internal contacts: Various levels of management within the corporate banking department
Extenal contacts: Major bank customers

SUMMARY STATEMENT

Assist in the administration of commercial accounts, to ensure maintenance of profitable bank relationships.

Under the direction of a supervising loan officer: Analyze a customer company's history, industry position, present condition, accounting procedures, and debt requirements. Review credit reports, summarizing analysis and recommending course of action for potential borrowers; review and summarize performance of existing borrowers. Prepare and follow up on credit communications and reports and Loan Agreement Compliance sheets. Help customers with banking problems and needs. Give out customer credit information to valid inquirers. Analyze profitability and compliance with balance arrangements; distribute to customer. Direct the Corporate Loan Note Department in receiving and disbursing funds and in booking loans.

Correct internal errors.

Prepare credit reports, describing and analyzing customer relationship and loan commitments; prepare for input into information system. Monitor credit reports for accuracy.

JOB SPECIFICATIONS

Knowledge, Skills, and Abilities

Oral communication skills, including listening and questioning. Intermediate accounting skills. Writing skills. Researching/reading skills to understand legal financial documents. Organizational/analytical skills. Social skills to represent the bank and strengthen its image. Sales skills. Knowledge of bank credit policy and services. Skill to use bank computer terminal. Knowledge of bank-related legal terminology. Independent work skills. Work efficiently under pressure. Courtesy and tactfulness. Interfacing skills. Knowledge of basic business (corporate) finance. Skill to interpret economic/political events.

Physical Requirements

See to read fine print and numbers. Hear speaker 20 feet away. Speak to address a group of five. Mobility to tour customer facilities (may include climbing stairs). Use of hands and fingers to write, operate a calculator.

Other Requirements

Driver's license. Willing to: work overtime and weekends occasionally; travel out of state every three months/locally weekly; attend activities after work hours; wear clear, neat businesslike attire.

Typical Line of Promotion:

    From:
    To: Corporate Account Officer

Analyst	Incumbent	Date
	Superior	Date

Source: Adapted from Biddle & Associates, Inc., Sacramento, Calif. Reproduced with permission.

Evaluation of Current Human Resources

The second step is to evaluate the status of current human resources. What skills, interests, and experiences do current employees have? What jobs are being done? How many employees are doing particular jobs? Current employees are the most likely candidates to meet future needs and should be the first ones considered for new positions. When Auerbach retired as coach in 1966, for example, Bill Russell replaced him in that role. Team players with on-the-court experience often become effective coaches when they retire from playing.

Information about employees in business organizations is contained in a human resource information system. Exhibit 11.5 shows a sample of the information kept on each employee at one organization. Using this type of information, managers maintain and update profiles of each employee in order to assess the available skills, interests, and experiences and to identify departments with surplus or insufficient skills or employees.

Analysis of Future Availability

The next step is to determine the jobs that employees are likely to hold in the future. The positions employees will hold in the future will be affected by promotions, transfers, and terminations. Some moves are easier to predict than others. Consider the firm in Exhibit 11.6. The chart shows the employees' positions in the organization, performance ratings, and promotability. It also lists the two employees most qualified and likely to fill the job if the person holding it were to move.

EXHIBIT / 11.5
Sample Human Resource Information

Name of Employee	Depart- ment (1)	Current Perform- ance Level (1–5: 5 is highest) (2)	Age (3)	Present Manage- ment Level in Hierarchy (1–7: 1 is highest) (4)	Current Mana- gerial Skill Level (6–30: 30 is highest) (5)	Education (highest degree) (6)	Potential Level Rating (1–10: 10 is highest) (8)	Current salary ($/yr.) (9)	Time in Present Job (mos.) (10)	Minority Status (minority = 1) (11)	Sex (M/F) (12)
Frank R. Shanks	ACC	5	43	2	028	BA	10	54700.	61	0	M
Jeffrey Neal Marks	ACC	1	52	3	009	MBA/CPA	4	44800.	92	0	M
Stanley F. Allen	ACC	2	38	4	010	BS	2	37700.	43	0	M
Michael Kennelly	ACC	5	36	4	028	MBA	9	39400.	83	0	M
Lance W. Weintraub	ACC	4	52	5	024	MBA	4	32700.	46	0	M
Sean Jones	ACC	4	54	3	027	MBA	9	31250.	26	0	M
Robert N. Nilsen	ACC	4	61	5	026	HS	5	35700.	81	0	M

Source: Beatty, R. W., and Schneier, C. E., *Personnel Administration: An Experiential/Skill-Building Approach,* 2nd ed. (Reading, Mass.: Addison-Wesley, 1981), p. 56.

Certain changes, such as retirements and some terminations, are easily predictable. For example, Miguel is due to retire next year, which will leave a vacant position. Shaw's performance is so poor, his skills and potential so low, that he will probably be removed, leaving another vacant slot. Managers can also predict promotions and transfers. Miguel's and Shaw's positions will need to be filled. Elsie is a likely candidate for Miguel's job because her performance and potential are both high. Peter is a likely candidate for Shaw's position for the same reason.

Predicting who will be promoted, transferred, or fired allows managers to predict what jobs will be vacant. These vacancies are the basis for the organization's recruiting and training plans. On a basketball or other sports team, players rarely move from one position to another in a hierarchical fashion, except in cases where a player moves into a managerial position. Nevertheless, the person in charge of staffing the team must remain aware of when each player will retire so he or she can plan to have this player replaced.

For the Celtics, this planning process became particularly crucial in 1988 and 1989. Both years, the Celtics lost to the Detroit Pistons, failing to make it into the finals for the National Basketball Association's championship for the first time since 1983. Many people began to say that the Celtics were getting old. "The fact is, it will be a constantly deteriorating team," predicted one sports reporter.[10] Only one of the team's five superstar starters was under 30, and the team was slated for the twenty-fourth pick (out of 25 teams) for the midsummer college draft. It will take some fancy footwork and a lot of back-court shuffling for the Celtics' management to rebuild a championship team when its starting lineup retires.

Preparation of Recruitment and Development Plans

Vacant jobs can be filled from sources outside or inside the organization; usually recruits come from both. Training and development programs can be developed to prepare those already in the organization for the jobs available in the future. Recruiting programs can be mounted to find new employees to fill slots that will be vacant after internal moves have been made.

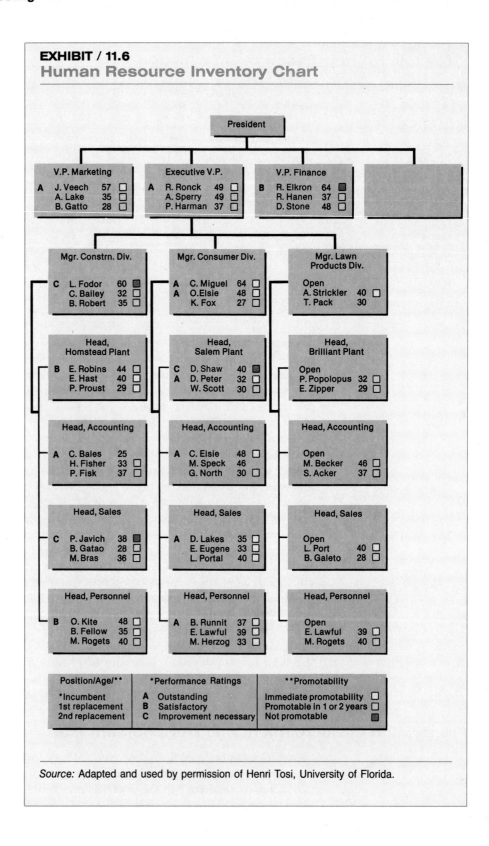

EXHIBIT / 11.6
Human Resource Inventory Chart

President

V.P. Marketing		
A	J. Veech	57 ☐
	A. Lake	35 ☐
	B. Gatto	28 ☐

Executive V.P.		
A	R. Ronck	49 ☐
	A. Sperry	49 ☐
	P. Harman	37 ☐

V.P. Finance		
B	R. Elkron	64 ■
	R. Hanen	37 ☐
	D. Stone	48 ☐

Mgr. Constrn. Div.		
C	L. Fodor	60 ■
	C. Bailey	32 ☐
	B. Robert	35 ☐

Mgr. Consumer Div.		
A	C. Miguel	64 ☐
A	O. Elsie	48 ☐
	K. Fox	27 ☐

Mgr. Lawn Products Div.		
	Open	
	A. Strickler	40 ☐
	T. Pack	30

Head, Homstead Plant		
B	E. Robins	44 ☐
	E. Hast	40 ☐
	P. Proust	29 ☐

Head, Salem Plant		
C	D. Shaw	40 ■
A	D. Peter	32 ☐
	W. Scott	30 ☐

Head, Brilliant Plant		
	Open	
	P. Popolopus	32 ☐
	E. Zipper	29 ☐

Head, Accounting		
A	C. Bales	25
	H. Fisher	33 ☐
	P. Fisk	37 ☐

Head, Accounting		
A	C. Elsie	48 ☐
	M. Speck	46
	G. North	30

Head, Accounting		
	Open	
	M. Becker	46 ☐
	S. Acker	37 ☐

Head, Sales		
C	P. Javich	38 ■
	B. Gatao	28 ☐
	M. Bras	36 ☐

Head, Sales		
A	D. Lakes	35 ☐
	E. Eugene	33 ☐
	L. Portal	40 ☐

Head, Sales		
	Open	
	L. Port	40 ☐
	B. Galeto	28 ☐

Head, Personnel		
B	O. Kite	48 ☐
	B. Fellow	35 ☐
	M. Rogets	40 ☐

Head, Personnel		
A	B. Runnit	37 ☐
	E. Lawful	39 ☐
	M. Herzog	33 ☐

Head, Personnel		
	Open	
	E. Lawful	39 ☐
	M. Rogets	40 ☐

Position/Age/**	*Performance Ratings		**Promotability	
*Incumbent	**A**	Outstanding	Immediate promotability	☐
1st replacement	**B**	Satisfactory	Promotable in 1 or 2 years	☐
2nd replacement	**C**	Improvement necessary	Not promotable	■

Source: Adapted and used by permission of Henri Tosi, University of Florida.

Invasion of the Body Snatchers

Money is not always the sole factor in executive recruitment. When Lester Korn recruited Peter Ueberroth to become head of the Los Angeles Olympics, the lure was the challenge inherent in the job.

Bruce Dahltorp, a 46-year-old financial consultant, was relaxing in his Geneva, Illinois home one Friday evening when the executive recruiter phoned. Would Dahltorp consider a job as president of a Midwestern bank, the caller wanted to know. That unexpected opportunity was too good to refuse.

Hiring companies pay headhunters up to one-third of an executive's salary, and so profits for recruiters are also high. Search firms earned some $1.2 billion in fees in 1983, or about 20 percent more than in 1982. Their total earnings could climb to $1.5 billion in 1984.

Companies making consumer products from computers to packaged foods are the most active in the talent hunt. The buoyant spending tide lifted consumer firms' demand for executives by 33 percent (in 1983). The financial services field, meanwhile, recorded a 23 percent gain. Commercial bankers have been in especially short supply.

As the competition grows, companies are finding that they must offer increasingly tempting bait to lure top personnel. Executive pay packages climbed some 7 percent in 1983, well ahead of the 3.8 percent inflation rate, and as much as 10 percent in 1984. Companies in growing industries frequently must offer up to 50 percent more than an executive's current pay in order to win him. Like star athletes, some job hoppers are receiving one time bonuses to sign with new companies. These often range from $25,000 to $100,000.

Wage considerations alone, however, may not be enough. Says Norman Keider, managing director of the Chicago office of Arthur Young & Company's recruitment service, "For an executive with a job already paying $100,000 and above, salary can be fifth, sixth, or even seventh on the priority list. To recruit these executives you have got to show them a job with challenge." Korn/Ferry did just that when it approached Peter Ueberroth, who had been running his own travel agency chain, about becoming president of the Los Angeles Olympic Organizing Committee for this year's Summer Games. Ueberroth, who went on to become commissioner of baseball in October 1984, took a salary cut to accept the $115,000-a-year Olympics job. Says Korn/Ferry President Richard Ferry, "The challenge of putting on a private Olympics for the first time was the selling tool."

A ticklish difficulty for search firms is families in which both the husband and the wife have careers. "This can be a substantial problem for some employers," says John Sibbald, who runs his own firm in Chicago. "Some clients go out of their way to identify opportunities for the recruit's spouse."

Despite the salary increases or challenges, many people when first approached by a headhunter turn down the proposal. Says Richard Ferry, "Often the reaction is, 'Why should I look at it? I've got everything going for me now. Why should I change direction?'" Recruiters reply that managers should at least listen. They can always say no, and in any case, an unexpected job offer is flattering to an executive ego. ■

Source: "Invasion of the Body Snatchers," *Time* (April 1984): 69.

given a preview, they know what to expect. The system also helps the company cut down on training costs, which can be quite high. By giving job applicants an opportunity to get some first-hand experience before hiring them and giving managers an opportunity to see how well these applicants perform, the process gives a better match between the company and prospective employees. This type of selection process is effective for locating people who will perform on the job, but it is very costly. Special machinery, supervision, counseling, and so forth, are required.

In recruiting for professional sports teams, scouts have other ways to assess the abilities of prospective players. Potential recruits are either college ballplayers or members of other professional teams. Scouts have numerous opportunities to see them perform in a variety of situations before making a selection decision. However, there is still room for uncertainty. After the Celtics made the deal to sign Bill Russell, Auerbach and then-owner Walter Brown went to see him play in an exhibition game at the University of Maryland. Said Auerbach, "He was terrible. Just awful! Walter and I sat there looking at each other all night. What in the world had we done?"[15] Fortunately, they kept him.

ORIENTATION, TRAINING, AND DEVELOPMENT

Once applicants have been selected for new jobs, they must be helped to adjust to their new job and surroundings. Not only will the new recruits need to be introduced to their environment, they will need to be trained in the jobs they will be performing. Ultimately, they will also need help turning these new jobs into satisfying careers. The activities managers undertake to assist employees in these ways are orientation, training, and development.

Orientation

Orientation The process of introducing new employees to the organization, their jobs, and their co-workers.

The principal purpose of orientation programs is to socialize new employees into the organization.[16] **Orientation** is the process of introducing new employees to the jobs they will be doing, the people with whom they will be working, and the ways in which the organization operates. An orientation may involve as little as a quick tour of the job area, pointing out the work area, the cafeteria, and the bathroom. Such an introduction is not likely to make the new employee feel particularly welcome, but it may serve to meet the basic requirements of orientation. Most organizations try to do more than provide a quick tour by introducing new employees to their co-workers and the new environment.[17]

Helping the players understand how they fit into the team has always been one of the main goals of the Celtics' coaching staff. Retired player Satch Sanders did not become oriented to this philosophy early, but he never forgot it after he did. During his third or fourth year with the team, he decided he would rather score points than play defense so he started taking more shots as the opportunities arose. Once he scored 15 points, then 18. Then one night he scored 20 points, and the team lost. "It bothered him all the way home,"[18] said Auerbach. Sanders's conclusion the next day was, "All it takes to upset the balance of this beautiful machine of ours is one man crossing over into another man's specialty. So I decided [last] night that it was a much bigger claim to say that I was a member of the world champions than it was to say I averaged 35 points a game."[19]

In business organizations, there are usually more formal methods of orientation. In production facilities, for example, it is common for a supervisor to show new workers the machinery they will be using and to make sure they understand how to operate the equipment. If there are safety rules in the facility, new employees may be given a special safety briefing. In an office or clerical setting, where coordination with other office employees is especially important, the new employee may be introduced to all the other people working in the facility. Orientation procedures must always be adapted to the specific setting, but the purpose remains similar in any workplace: making the new employees feel comfortable enough to begin to do their jobs.

Training and Development

Training and development Joint activities to teach people the skills, activities, and behavior necessary to perform their jobs well.

Among the millions of people who start new jobs each year, there are relatively few—perhaps less than 10 percent by one estimate—who are fully qualified for their new position. This means that the vast majority of people starting new jobs need some additional training for their position. **Training and development** are joint activities used to teach people the various skills, activities, and behaviors necessary to perform their jobs well and to help them advance in their chosen career paths.

Training can take a wide variety of forms. In some instances, one hour of a supervisor's time may be sufficient to familiarize the new employee with the equipment, operating procedures, and requirements of the organization. In others, new employees may need several days, or perhaps weeks, of specialized job training.

In modern organizations, it is not just new employees who need training. Because the environment changes rapidly, even veteran employees may be working under new circumstances. Consider a department store clerk who has handled cash and credit sales for ten years. If the store implements a complex computerized credit authorization and sales information system, the clerk will become increasingly ineffective unless he or she learns to handle transactions with the new computerized terminal. In this case, management would provide a brief computer training program for its staff.

As soon as an organization has more than just a few employees, managers must begin to think systematically about training and development needs.[20] There are many different types of training and development programs, ranging from apprenticeship arrangements (an inexperienced employee works closely with a very experienced employee), to on-the-job programs, to formal classroom teaching programs. The computer is providing even more options. The choice of program should be determined by the needs of participants.

Management Development Programs

The specialized training of managers is a modern phenomenon. One of the earliest management training programs was developed in 1901 by James Cash Penney, founder of the J. C. Penney department store chain. Penney developed a system whereby the manager-partner of each dry-goods store in the chain selected and trained one prospective manager, who would then be sent to another community to start a new store.

Modern organizations face increasing needs for well-trained and capable managers. In the private sector, where growth is an important goal of businesses, there is a need for managers who are able to move from technical to administrative types of work, where management of other people is important, and from administrative to institutional management, which requires the skills to manage entire units of the organization.

Even people at the very top of the organization—chief executives, members of the board of directors, and trustees—need additional training and the opportunity to grow in their management thinking. At the Aspen Institute in the United States and the Niagara Institute in Canada, for example, senior managers of companies and nonprofit organizations spend weeks discussing values and their influence on society in general. This experience enhances their understanding of the basic responsibilities of all organizations to the societies in which they exist. Does it make them better managers? Participants believe that it does, if only by sharpening their understanding of the forces of social change that ultimately affect organizations and their members. Learning is a lifelong responsibility and challenge. Management development programs will continue to grow in number and variety as long as there are new types and levels of knowledge to be used in the effective management of organizations.[21]

PERFORMANCE APPRAISAL

Performance appraisal
The assessment of employee performance and potential.

The contribution of each employee to the accomplishment of the organization's objectives is evaluated through performance appraisal.[22] The **performance appraisal** is the process through which managers assess employees' present performance and potential for future development. Appraisals form the basis for rewards, the identification of skills on which the employee needs training, or even reprimands. All of us receive some form of rewards for our work and some amount of feedback about our performance. Feedback is the foundation upon which learning and job improvement are based in an organization.[23] However, in the absence of a carefully planned method of assessing performance, feedback and rewards may be inconsistent.

For example, consider the job performance of two employees, Smith and Jones, who have identical job responsibilities. The supervisor is impressed with Smith, who often stays late to complete assigned tasks. Jones, who never stays late because of family responsibilities, almost always completes assigned work during regular hours and, when necessary, arrives early. Since the supervisor never shows up early, but does stay late, Smith appears "more dedicated" than Jones. If Smith receives a raise and/or promotion and Jones does not, the latter could rightly complain of inconsistency in the performance appraisal system. Such inconsistencies are an inherent hazard of an unplanned or ad hoc system; there are no checks and balances to guarantee that people are being evaluated on a consistent basis.

To avoid inconsistencies, many organizations carefully plan performance appraisal systems. Although organizations modify formal systems to meet their specific circumstances, formal appraisal systems have three critical components, as illustrated in Exhibit 11.7. First, performance standards are established based on the job description and the organization's objectives. The specifics of the job description and the organizational objectives form the broad criteria against which individual performance is measured. Second, the formal appraisal is con-

EXHIBIT / 11.7
The Appraisal System

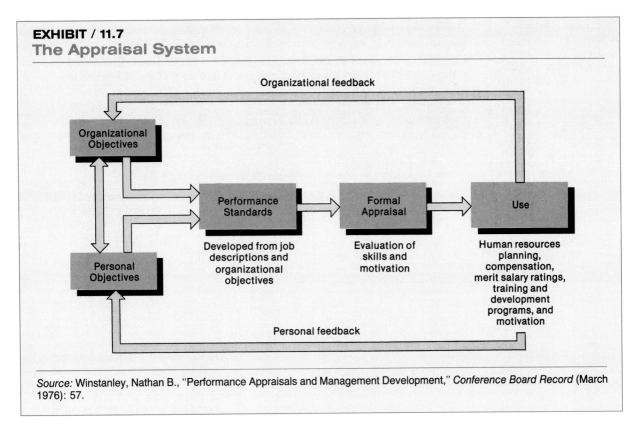

Organizational feedback

Organizational Objectives

Performance Standards

Developed from job descriptions and organizational objectives

Formal Appraisal

Evaluation of skills and motivation

Use

Human resources planning, compensation, merit salary ratings, training and development programs, and motivation

Personal Objectives

Personal feedback

Source: Winstanley, Nathan B., "Performance Appraisals and Management Development," *Conference Board Record* (March 1976): 57.

ducted by evaluating the actual performance of the employee. Third, the information from the appraisal review is used to provide feedback to the employee. In the case of Jones and Smith, the existence of performance standards ("complete all work during regular hours") would show that both people have to use extra hours to complete their work.

The formal appraisal would not indicate that Smith's staying late was superior to Jones's coming in early, only that both were unable to complete their work during regular hours and that both were dedicated, hard-working employees. The supervisor might then recommend that organizational objectives be revised to either lessen the work load or allow for extra hours (e. g., overtime) and also reward Smith and Jones for their performance. This system can enable the supervisor to discover important information about the effectiveness of the organization's policy as well as disclose any real differences between Smith's and Jones's performances.

Performance evaluations must accurately measure what the employee has accomplished on the job. In most organizations, however, that is not a mechanical process because good performance reflects an employee's attitudes, output, and interaction with others. To deal with this, managers often attempt to isolate three distinct factors for measurement:[24] (1) trait measures, (2) process measures, and (3) output measures.

Trait measures
Indications of the characteristics a person brings to the job.

Trait measures reflect the characteristics that a person brings to the job. Common trait measures are skill, dependability, enthusiasm, initiative, and job knowledge. These measures are among the most important to the management and coaching staff of the Celtics and other sports teams.

Process measures
Indications of the way
people go about their
work and interact with
others on the job.

Process measures focus on the way people go about their work and interact with one another. Process measures focus on behaviors.[25] Exhibit 11.8 illustrates a process scale used to evaluate a manager on his or her organization of work activities. Notice how many of the items relate to quality of interaction.

EXHIBIT / 11.8
Sample Managerial Process Scale

Position _____ Manager _____

Job Dimension _____ Scale for Organization of Work Activities _____

Plans work and organizes time carefully so as to maximize resources and meet commitments.	9	Even though this associate has a report due on another project, he or she would be well prepared for the assigned discussion on your project.
	8	
	7	This associate would keep a calendar or schedule on which deadlines and activities are carefully noted, and which would be consulted before making new commitments.
	6	As program chief, this associate would manage arrangements for enlisting resources for a special project reasonably well, but would probably omit one or two details that would have to be handled by improvisation.
Plans and organizes time and effort primarily for large segments of a task. Usually meets commitments, but may overlook what are considered secondary details.	5	This associate would meet a deadline in handling in a report, but the report might be below usual standard if other deadlines occur on the same date the report is due.
	4	This associate's evaluations are likely not to reflect abilities because of overcommitments in other activities.
	3	This associate would plan more by enthusiasm than by timetable and frequently have to work late the night before an assignment is due, although it would be completed on time.
Appears to do little planning. May perform effectively despite what seems to be a disorganized approach by concerted effort, although deadlines may be missed.	2	This associate would often be late for meetings, although others in similar circumstances do not seem to find it difficult to be on time.
	1	This associate never makes a deadline, even with sufficient notice.

Source: Beatty, R. W., and Schneier, C. E., *Personnel Administration: An Experiential/Skill-Building Approach,* 2nd ed. (Reading, Mass.: Addison-Wesley, 1981), p. 135.

Output measures
Indications of the results actually accomplished by the employee on the job.

Output measures focus on the results actually achieved by the employee on the job. For example, a consumer products company may have an 800 telephone number for customers to use for making complaints. A customer representative answering the calls could be assessed on the basis of the number of calls handled. Thus, a representative who dealt with 400 calls in one week (80 per day, 10 calls per hour), would have a higher output than one who handled 300 calls in one week (60 per day, 7.5 per hour). This does not mean, however, that the first representative is really doing a better job. The person who handled 100 fewer calls may have been more helpful or more thorough.

Though many sports franchises focus on scoring and other statistics as the output measures by which they evaluate a player's performance, Red Auerbach continually stresses the value of contribution to a win or to the team effort over such statistics. In fact, he takes pride in the fact that the Celtics have never had the league's top scorer. "Individual honors are nice," he said, "but no Celtic has ever gone out of his way to achieve them. In fact, we've won seven championships without placing even one Celtic among the league's Top 10."[26]

REWARDING

People expect to be rewarded for jobs well done, and managers spend a great deal of time trying to match the available rewards to the needs and expectations of employees.[27] Obviously, money, in the form of wage and salary increases, is one of the most common rewards.[28] But there are nonmonetary rewards as well, such as promotions or jobs with increasing amounts of responsibility and authority. Many organizations use devices such as "Employee of the Month" designations to highlight the special efforts of productive persons. The rewards available in an organization are an important means for encouraging the accomplishment of its goals and objectives. Thus, managers need to understand the organization's reward system and find ways to use it creatively to encourage others to improve their job performance.

Compensation

Compensation The financial payment package an organization provides to its employees in exchange for their work.

Compensation is the term most commonly used for the financial payment package an organization provides its employees in exchange for their work and performance on the job.[29] Some portions of a compensation system are standardized for all employees, some are standardized for particular groups of employees (e.g., union members), and some are individualized to reward the unique performance accomplishments of particular employees.

An organization's compensation package is affected by several internal and external factors.[30] For example, a company in an industry such as steel that has been suffering through an economic recession will surely be less generous in its compensation package than a company that is enjoying boom times, such as the computer industry. An organization's compensation structure is also affected by the national economic and political environment and by unionization. A company considering building a plant in either the United States or South Korea during this time would quickly recognize that the average hourly wages of South Korean manufacturing employees were only one-tenth of those paid to unionized U.S. manufacturing workers. All other things being equal, the labor costs for hourly employees in the United States would be ten times greater than those in South Korea. Such total compensation calculations strongly influence managerial decisions about where to locate new plants and whether to transfer operations from one location to another.

Red Auerbach has a very simple notion of compensation: "A player's salary is determined by what the coaches see and what I see. What determines a player's salary is his contribution to winning—not his statistical accomplishments."[31]

Compensation consists of wages and salaries, benefits, bonuses, incentives, stock options, profit sharing, and perquisites (perks).[32] **Wages** are payments based on the number of units (hours, days) that a person works for the organization or the number of units produced (piece rate system). **Salary** is the annual amount paid to an employee irrespective of the number of units of time spent on the job or the units produced. Most managerial jobs are salaried, with no extra compensation paid by the organization for extra hours spent on the job.

Benefits are noncash compensation an employee receives. Currently, they account for 37 percent of a company's total employment costs on average. Typically, benefits consist of life insurance, paid vacation time, pensions, medical insurance, and accident insurance. Many corporations are adding legal counseling, day care services, dental insurance, and personal counseling benefits to their standard benefits packages. Of course these additional benefits help recruiters lure talented employees, but each is an added expense.

One way organizations have been able to increase the number of benefits available to employees without suffering excessive cost increases is to provide flexible benefits packages, also referred to as cafeteria benefit plans because employees can pick and choose among coverage items. Under a flexible benefits program, each employee can choose the specific benefits most valuable to him or her. These packages are a particular boon to dual-career families. For example, when one working person's medical insurance covers all family members, it does not make sense for that person's working spouse also to have family medical coverage as a benefit. The spouse could choose access to legal aid, dental insurance, or added vacation time. If both people work for companies (or the same company) that offer flexible benefits, they can structure a package providing them a wide variety of benefits and coverage.

Bonuses are single, lump-sum payments that are given in recognition of employees' (managerial or nonmanagerial) performance. **Incentives** are financial payments offered for the accomplishment of specified objectives, for example, $1000 for each 1000 units sold. **Stock options** are rights to purchase company stock at a reduced price. The option can be exercised at some time in the future when, it is hoped, the company's stock price will have risen. **Profit sharing** is a distribution of a portion of business profits to a pool of employees (managers or all employees) in recognition of their contribution to the success of the organization during the preceding year. **Perquisites (perks)** are noncash additions to salary including automobiles (company cars), reserved parking spaces, low-cost loans, memberships in clubs, medical examinations, health club facilities, and expense accounts.

The needs of the organization and the employee determine which combination of these is offered in a financial package. Ultimately, management has to decide what is best. Auerbach, for example, feels perks are just confusing and shift the focus from basketball. "How much does it cost for you to play basketball?" he'll ask. "Let's set a figure and do that. You want a car, buy a car."[33]

Wages Payments based on the number of time units a person works or on the number of units produced.

Salary The annual amount paid to an employee irrespective of the number of time units spent on the job.

Benefits Noncash compensation.

Bonuses Single, lump-sum payments.

Incentives Financial payments offered for the accomplishment of specified objectives.

Stock options Rights to purchase company stock at a reduced price.

Profit sharing The distribution of a portion of business profits to a pool of employees.

Perquisites (perks) Noncash additions to salary such as cars, expense accounts, and club memberships.

Promotions and Transfers

Promotion A movement to a position of higher responsibility.

People rarely enter an organization at one job level and stay in the same position for many years. The normal course is for individuals to move from one position to another through a process of promotions and transfers. A **promotion** is a movement to a position of higher responsibility, often with higher pay and almost always with increased authority and status. People are promoted for several basic reasons. They may have demonstrated outstanding performance (merit) or capability for the new position; they may have seniority rights based on length of service; or they may have a unique ability that is required in the new position.

Transfer A lateral move into a position at the same or a comparable level of responsibility.

A **transfer** is a lateral move into a position at the same or a comparable level of responsibility in the organization. Normally, such job moves do not include higher pay or increased responsibility. Employees may be transferred, either temporarily or permanently, to broaden their skills so that they will be qualified to assume higher positions in the future or to meet an organizational need. Young managers, in particular, are often willing—even eager—to take transfers in order to broaden their exposure to different parts of an organization and expand their skills.

Demotions, Terminations, and Retirement: Leading to Replacement

Demotion A movement to a position of lesser responsibility and status.

Inevitably, there are times when employees do not perform satisfactorily, and efforts to improve their performance through training, development, or other means fail. Managers faced with such a situation cannot ignore poor performance and must take action. **Demotion** is a movement to a position of lesser responsibility and status. Often, the employee will resist such action, particularly if it involves a pay reduction.

Termination The final separation of an employee from the organization.

A **termination** is the final separation of an employee from the organization. There are many reasons for terminations, some related to employees' performance and some to factors beyond their control, such as economic recessions or a change in the organization's direction. During the 1980s, Monsanto, the large U.S. chemical company, shifted its business focus from chemical manufacturing to biogenetic products. This shift eliminated the jobs of hundreds of chemical engineers, technicians, and others. The company began a program to retrain chemical engineers with skills that would enable them to move into other areas of the company's operations. Those who could not transfer were given a severance, or separation, package of benefits to ease the difficulty of the termination. Monsanto, like many other companies, also established a very aggressive outplacement program. Stated simply, **outplacement programs** are designed to help terminated or laid-off employees find employment in other organizations.

Outplacement programs Programs designed to help terminated or laid-off employees find employment in other organizations.

Retirement When an employee stops working in an organization and shifts to nonwork activities or a different career.

Retirement occurs when an employee stops working in an organization and shifts to nonwork activities or a different career. For the Celtic basketball players, retirement usually happens in their mid-30s. For most of us, it will happen some time after age 65.

The most difficult termination for both employer and employee is the involuntary dismissal for nonperformance. Firing an employee is one of a manager's most unpleasant responsibilities. By its nature it is painful for the employee who is being terminated and often produces outright hostility and anger. In companies with very expensive equipment or highly sensitive, top-secret data, it is normal practice for a fired employee to be immediately escorted from the plant by a security guard to prevent the possibility of damage or sabotage.

DUFFY®   by **Bruce Hammond**

Terminations of any kind may lead to a reassessment of staffing needs. Thus, the human resources system is cyclical in nature: Replacement, the final phase, leads back into human resource planning, the first phase. This cycle provides an ongoing challenge for managers who must keep the organization staffed with a skilled, high-performance work force.

CURRENT ISSUES: TESTING THE WORK FORCE

Many human resource researchers and practitioners think the challenges of finding and managing human resources are increasing. As the costs of making wrong decisions about people increase, managers will spend more time and money getting as much information about an employee as possible. One way of getting information is by screening and testing employees for characteristics, habits, or tendencies that would impair their performance. Currently, there is much debate about whether testing for acquired immune deficiency syndrome (AIDS) or drug use helps managers make better decisions and whether it is legal to do so. Many argue it violates an employee's constitutional right to privacy. Testing of employees and job applicants is the issue of greatest concern to employers, employees, and legislative bodies alike; by one account, this "will prove one of the most difficult and explosive workplace issues over the next ten years."[34]

Testing for HIV (the virus that causes AIDS) is at the center of heated debates. Millions of workers may be carrying the virus or come down with the fatal disease, and the implications of this are severe. According to a random survey of 2000 people across the United States, more than 60 percent expressed concern over sharing bathroom facilities with an infected individual, and roughly 40 percent expressed concern about sharing a cafeteria and sharing work equipment.[35] Said David M. Herold, who conducted the survey, "If people are catatonic because they have a co-worker with AIDS, the impact on productivity and efficiency is going to be great."[36]

Under these circumstances, many employers have a great interest in knowing whether current or potential employees carry the virus. They do not want to undermine the productivity of 50 percent of their work force, nor do they want to be responsible for the medical benefits of the potentially large number of employees who might come down with the disease. However, civil rights groups and legal activists argue that mandatory AIDs testing of both employees and job applicants is a violation of an individual's right to privacy afforded by the Constitution and a violation of equal protection guaranteed to all citizens. In numerous cases already, employers have been ordered to reinstate employees fired for having the virus, and schools have been ordered to allow infected students to attend classes. This issue may remain unresolved for quite some time.

Another complex and heated testing issue concerns drug use among employees and job applicants. The employer's interest in this issue, again, is sound. Not only can drug use decrease employee performance, it can also increase the risk of injury on the job to the drug user and his or her co-workers. The importance of maintaining a drug-free work force is especially significant in the airline and public transportation industries but is also important on the shop floor, on the construction site, and in any situation where employees' fast reflexes and alertness are critically important.

Many companies in all industries have tested employees for drug use. In 1986, about 25 percent of the Fortune 500 companies conducted tests in one form or another, up from 5 percent in 1982.[37] Reportedly, IBM, Exxon, DuPont, Lockheed, Federal Express, Shearson Lehman, the New York Times, United Airlines, and Trans World Airlines (TWA) use urinalysis to screen all job applicants for drug use, and many private and public organizations utilize the same technique on existing employees.

Again, the legal implications of the issue are not clear-cut. Many argue that people responsible for the health and safety of others should be required to undergo drug testing. Others argue that all employees have their right to privacy and that drug testing is a violation of that right. In the coming decade, testing issues are likely to come to the legislative battleground, and their resolution will add to the legal framework within which every organization's human resources system must operate.

■ KEY POINTS

1 The basic elements of the human resource system include human resource planning, recruitment and selection, orientation, training and development, performance appraisal, compensation, promotion, and replacement (transfer, demotion, and termination).

2 Human resource management activities must be conducted within certain external constraints and internal guidelines. External constraints include the availability of skilled resources, competition for employees, technological demands, economic conditions, and most importantly, legal requirements. Most organizations also have internal guidelines that dictate how people are to be managed.

3 Human resource planning is the process of deciding how many and what types of people are needed to perform the work of the organization. There are four steps to human resource planning: assessing the needs of the organization, evaluating the current human resources, analyzing the future availability, and preparing recruitment and development plans.

4 Recruiting is the process through which managers attempt to locate and secure people to fill the organization's available jobs. Those recruited internally through job posting, the human resource information systems, or a referral system are already familiar with the organization. The main problem of recruiting internally is that it creates a domino effect. If a new position is filled by

an internal candidate, another vacancy is created. Recruiting externally through college recruiting, employment agencies, professional organizations, or unions is usually more expensive than recruiting internally, but it provides a much broader range of people.

5 Selection is the process of determining which people in the pool that has been found through recruiting will be best able to perform the available jobs. The decision to whom to offer the job is based on predictors of performance. Tests, interviews, and reviews of background and experience are all used to predict how well a person will be able to do the job.

6 Orientation is the process of introducing new employees to the jobs they will be doing, the people with whom they will be working, and the ways in which the organization operates. Training and development are joint activities used to build skills that employees need, now or in the future, in order to improve their performance.

7 Performance appraisal is the process through which managers assess employees' present performance and potential for future development. It is done to evaluate the contribution of each employee to the accomplishment of the organization's objectives. These evaluations serve as the basis of rewards, determine what skills the employee needs to improve, and provide feedback to the employee on how he or she is doing.

8 Compensation, including wages, salaries, and benefits,

is the payment package employers pay to employees for performance of the job. Promotions and transfers are used, respectively, to reward employees by giving increased salaries, position, and/or responsibility or to give them opportunity to broaden their skill and experience bases.

9 Replacement, the process of filling a position vacated by a demotion, termination, transfer, promotion, or retirement, is the "final phase" of the human resource system that leads back to the first.

FOR DISCUSSION AND REVIEW

1. Explain how Red Auerbach's potential limit theory would apply in other types of businesses.

2. When recruiting to fill positions, why does a manager assess the skills, interests, and experiences of employees who are already working in the organization?

3. How can organizations locate potential employees?

4. Of those potential employees found through the recruiting effort, to which ones should the organization offer jobs?

5. Through what selection process is a potential employee likely to go?

6. What are the advantages and disadvantages of concentrating more efforts on developing present employees rather than recruiting new employees with the required skills?

7. How can the organization determine what training programs are needed?

8. Why should the reward system be consistent with the objectives of the organizations? What might be a good indication, in general terms, of whether or not a reward system is consistent?

KEY TERMS

Benefits	Job analysis	Perquisites (perks)	Staffing
Bonuses	Job description	Process measures	Stock options
Compensation	Job posting	Profit sharing	Termination
Demotion	Job specification	Promotion	Training and development
Human resource planning	Orientation	Recruitment	Trait measures
Human resources information system	Outplacement programs	Retirement	Transfer
	Output measures	Salary	Wages
Incentives	Performance appraisal	Selection	

THE CONFERENCE TABLE: DISCUSSION CASE / 11.1

SafePlace

SafePlace, a short-term children's shelter in a major metropolitan area, is a small human services agency. Its mission is to provide a temporary and safe haven for abused, neglected, and runaway children 8 to 15 years old. With a professional staff of nine supplemented by volunteers and interns, SafePlace provides emergency shelter 24 hours a day, 365 days a year, primarily to children from the local area.

The agency is supported by the State Department of Social Services, which through its massive bureaucracy provides funding on a day-to-day basis for each child taken in. But while the agency depends on the state for funding support, it

Source: Prepared by Sandra Waddock and used with permission.

Children's shelters provide a temporary haven for abused, neglected, and runaway children.

is an "open" shelter, meaning that anyone can refer a child for short-term shelter and the state will pay the costs. A youngster can walk in off the street in the middle of the night seeking a place to stay or can be referred by the police, a parent, a teacher, or a social worker.

However, with only eight beds available, and with one of those kept as an emergency bed specifically for local children, the agency is faced with far more demand for its services than it can possibly supply. In the last year alone, more than 1200 youngsters were referred to it, but it could serve only 150. Obviously, the staff requires considerable skill in dealing with the referring agency or individual, especially when the child is to be turned away, as well as in handling children with problems.

In addition to maintaining its relationships with the state and the community, the management staff must be able to deal effectively with the occasional crisis— the suicidal or violent child, the psychotic, or the delinquent. Although all the children are carefully screened to assure that they are not dangerous to themselves or others, mistakes are sometimes made. All staff must be capable of dealing with these crises.

SafePlace has had a high employee turnover in recent months, which has caused some internal turmoil. Six months ago, the board of directors recruited Allen Richardson to the position of executive director after the previous executive director had proved incompetent. Richardson took charge quickly, establishing numerous new systems and structures, rebuilding a badly deteriorated relationship with the state, and ensuring that the agency was on solid financial ground. He is energetically pursuing new initiatives that will expand SafePlace's visibility and contact with the community in the future.

Now Richardson is faced with a new set of staffing issues, particularly with hiring a new clinical coordinator. The clinical coordinator is in charge of all the clinical and treatment aspects of the program, including assessing the suitability of youngsters for acceptance in the program, working with the state on a permanent solution to the shelter's problems, and supervising the staff that provides individual counseling. Bill Chaffe, a senior counselor at the agency, is interested in the position but has had only three years of full-time experience, all at the agency. Richardson and the board, who will actually choose the new clinical coordinator, are reluctant to hire from within since the last clinical coordinator had been promoted from within and had understood few of her managerial or administrative duties. While Chaffe has the technical qualifications for the job, Richardson is worried that he lacks the experience, especially with regard to working with the state systems and the community, that are needed for effectiveness in the job. ■

DISCUSSION QUESTIONS

1. What particular skills and abilities does SafePlace need in a clinical coordinator? What kind of educational and work background should the person have?
2. What would a job description for the position of clinical coordinator entail?
3. What kind of recruitment plan should Richardson develop to find the new clinical coordinator? Should he look internally or externally or both? What are the possible sources of qualified individuals?

THE CONFERENCE TABLE: DISCUSSION CASE / 11.2

The British Nanny Carries On

A nanny will devote her entire attention to a child, live with the child's family for many years, and earn a good salary. Selecting the proper nanny is a critical decision for a family.

If you lived in London and needed someone to perform live-in child care for your precocious five-year-old, would you recruit for a mother's helper or a nanny?

If you sought a mother's helper, you would probably advertise in the countryside among teenage girls who probably had no formal training and were from large working-class families where they gained practical experiences in child care by looking after younger siblings. They would be fairly adaptable and flexible in helping out around the house and would perform chores and run errands as well as take care of your child. You might expect them to move on to a different job, perhaps in a shop or office, after a few months or a year or two, and because of their lack of experience or training, their ability to meet your standards of child care might be erratic. Nonetheless, other than providing room and board, you would not be expected to pay more than $50 a week in wages.

If you sought a nanny, however, you would recruit in a far different way. You would probably seek older applicants, who might ask what other domestic staff you have working for you since they will not do any household chores at all, but will devote their entire attention to the child and expect to live with your family for many years, perhaps until your child is grown. You would expect a nanny to know as much about child rearing as you, the parent. Prim and proper English nannies are a breed apart. Being a nanny is as much a profession as being a teacher. Nannies today are expected to have completed a two-year course in child care and have received the National Nursery Examination Board certificate. With several years' experience, a nanny would expect a fairly high salary as well as room and board.

One place you would probably look is the Norland Nursery Training College in Berkshire, established in 1892. Norland nannies are easy to identify. They wear uniforms, crisp brown dresses with stiff collars and cuffs, sensible shoes, and good brown coats. Because of their extensive training, they are in great demand and can expect to have their pick of well-paying jobs. A Norland nanny can expect up to $220 per week salary with a few years' experience, in addition to receiving room and board, and often such perks as her own apartment, the use of a car, and family holidays abroad with the children. ■

DISCUSSION QUESTIONS

1. What type of orientation and training program would you design for future nannies?
2. Assume you needed a nanny. How would you select from those available?
3. Design a compensation program that would include wages plus incentives for nannies. What would be the advantages and disadvantages of such a system?

Source: Adapted from Arnold, S., "The British Nanny Carries on, Though She's Being Updated," *Smithsonian* 14 (January 1984): 96–105.

12 | Communicating

FOCUS CASE / A Script for Power

COMMUNICATION AND THE DIRECTING FUNCTION

THE COMMUNICATION PROCESS
Encoding the Meaning
Transmitting
Decoding and Interpreting

PROBLEMS AND BARRIERS TO COMMUNICATION
Noise
Differences in Perceptions
Language
Status

ONE-WAY VERSUS TWO-WAY COMMUNICATION

MANAGING INTERPERSONAL COMMUNICATION
Face-to-Face Communication
Listening

ORGANIZATIONAL COMMUNICATION
Formal Channels
Informal Channels

MANAGING ORGANIZATIONAL COMMUNICATION

Organization is based on coordination and cooperation, both of which are impossible without communication. Therefore, communication is not only a crucial aspect of the directing function but also crucial to the effectiveness and success of the management process. Through communication, managers keep all organization members aware of the organization's strategy and its progress toward achieving its goals. Through communication, all members of the organization work out new and better ways of achieving results and accomplishing the organization's goals. In this chapter, we will review the basics of communication and illustrate how information flows in an organization and how individuals and groups communicate with each other.

KEY QUESTIONS

As you study this chapter, try to answer the following key questions:

1 What does the communication process consist of?
2 What barriers and problems can disrupt accurate communication?
3 What are the differences between one-way and two-way communication?
4 What are the advantages and disadvantages of two-way communication?
5 Why is face-to-face communication important?
6 Why is the ability to listen so essential for effective communication? How can one improve listening abilities?
7 Through what formal and informal channels does organizational communication flow?

Focus Case

A Script for Power

As the Writer's Guild of America (WGA) discovered, the ability to manage a strike successfully depends on the ability to communicate.

On April 10, 1981, the 8300 members of the Writers Guild of America (WGA) went on strike after rejecting wage packages offered by television producers at ABC, NBC, and CBS. The writers had demanded a 100 percent increase in minimum pay for prime-time one-hour television and movie scripts (at that time, $9,434 and $26,326, respectively) while the producers only offered a 5 percent-per-year increase for television scripts and 7 percent for movies in a four-year package.

The main point of contention was pay-TV royalties: Producers had offered writers 1.5 percent of the distributor's gross revenue from made-for-pay-TV shows, after a show had played for ten days or after the first year, whichever came first. In other words, said one writer, "we'll get 1.5 percent of nothing." Writers demanded 6 percent of the gross revenues from the first playing and 8 percent of the revenues from the first sales of videocassettes and videodiscs.

The strike dragged on for 13 weeks, production for the fall 1981 television season was delayed, and half of the 30,000 members of the behind-the-scenes unions were laid off before the WGA accepted a 2 percent share of pay-TV revenues and a 65 percent pay increase over four years. However, the 1981 strike marked the beginning of factionalization in the union and thus the beginning of the end of effective internal communications in the WGA.

This internal dissent would sabotage the union's strength in later years. In 1983, the WGA's administrator of royalty payments discovered that the screenwriter for a 1981 movie was being grossly underpaid on videocassette sales by the film's producers. According to her reading of the contract language, the writer should have been paid a royalty based on 100 percent of the wholesale price of a cassette, or roughly one dollar per cassette, but he was only receiving about 20 cents per cassette. After an in-depth review of residual payments, the union concluded that all its writers had been shortchanged up to $800 million since 1973. The producers, on the other hand, argued that the contract language specified that writers were to be paid a royalty based on 20 percent of a cassette's wholesale price, not 100 percent. They asserted that all writers had been compensated fairly.

Sources: This case was written by M. R. Poirier, based on the following sources: "The Writers' Strike Fires up the Script," *Business Week,* April 27, 1981, pp. 44, 48; "A Real-Life Cliff-hanger," *Newsweek,* June 1, 1981, p. 80; "Pact Ratified, Writers Return," *New York Times,* July 16, 1981, II, p. 20; Horn, John, "Gunfight at the Writers Guild Corral," *Los Angeles Times,* Calendar section, September 1, 1985, pp. 14–20; Horn, John, "Writers Guild Runoff Set," *Los Angeles Times,* September 26, 1985, pp. 1, 2; Billingsley, Lloyd, "Writers Guild in Need of Revision," *Wall Street Journal,* January 12, 1987, p. 24(E); Boyer, Peter G., "Writers Guild Strikes ABC and CBS Newsrooms," *New York Times,* March 3, 1987, III, p. 16; Belkin, Lisa, "Unit at Writers Guild Endorses CBS Contract Proposal," *New York Times,* April 15, 1987, p. C24; "Writers Guild Supports Proposed ABC Contract," *Wall Street Journal,* April 24, 1987, p. 7.

In April 1984, the WGA initiated 51 labor arbitrations against the 17 largest film companies in an effort to recoup the alleged underpayments. The producing companies stalled for over a year, so the arbitrations came to be heard just as the WGA's contract was due to expire in mid-1985. Thinking it could use the arbitrations as leverage in new contract negotiations, the WGA went out on strike.

The WGA's position was strong this time. The union could have offered to drop the arbitrations in exchange for possessive credits for writers. In other words, writers would gain name recognition (and thus personal advertising) by having the films attributed to them instead of to a producer or director. The union could also have used the $800 million bargaining chip to increase writers' creative control over their work or to raise minimum salaries again. "For the first time," said a union board member, "the guild sat in the catbird seat with a weapon that scared the *hell* out of management."

However, even as the strike began to cripple television production, the WGA dropped the arbitrations and accepted a contract that, according to one union member, was "little more than a joke." This was largely because the union's membership was divided over its priorities. Only 60 percent had voted to strike, a percentage that seemed to slip as the strike wore on. One large faction, calling itself the Union Blues, was pressing heavily to drop the strike regardless of terms, and some members of the faction threatened to go back to work during the strike.

The major cause of the lack of cohesion among WGA members was the shortage of work. While membership had increased ten times since 1958, the number of writing jobs had remained almost static. Since the union could not create or guarantee work, its members were not supportive of it. Though the WGA had an advantage over producers, it had lost control of its own membership. "Guild leaders—who make their livings communicating to millions of moviegoers and TV watchers—seemed unable to convince their increasingly fractious members that the videocassette issue was crucial to their future. . . . [And] because they were unable to adequately communicate, the rank and file began to side with the Union Blues, which, at least, was speaking with a clear voice."

In short, the strike and the arbitrations were dropped to unify the guild. But because the settlement fell so far short of its potential, the membership remained divided, and in fact, the union's executive director was fired by a vote of 10 to 9 only a few weeks later.

The guild's internal strike continued into 1987 and 1988. Though the WGA won newswriters' strikes over job security against CBS and ABC in spring 1987, internal divisiveness makes it difficult for the union's leadership to communicate a strategy and gain the whole membership's commitment. Said one member running for union office in 1987, "We furnish product. We're an indispensable monopoly." Said another, "When we stop, everything stops. That's power, my friends." But internal struggles between staff writers and freelancers, and struggles between union members and nonunion writers, are a continual drain on union power. "The WGA has won important battles in the past," said one screenwriter. But its inability to communicate internally and reach a consensus "could wind up destroying the Guild itself," he said. ■

COMMUNICATION AND THE DIRECTING FUNCTION

Communication is one of the most crucial aspects of the directing function. To direct, one must be able to influence the behavior of others, and to do so, one must be able to communicate. A leader or director must be able to communicate goals to followers and spell out clearly how those followers are to be involved in the achievement of those goals. In addition, people at all organizational levels must be able to reach understandings with each other so that the interdependent units can function effectively as a system. As the focus case illustrated, the different factions in the WGA—the Union Blues and the WGA's leadership—could not reach a consensus that allowed them to establish a strong position in 1985. In addition, the board simply could not effectively communicate its negotiating strategy to the rank and file, and the union may have lost hundreds of millions of dollars in back pay because of it.

Thus, communication is crucial to organizational success and is a primary component of every manager's job. Managers must ensure that the flow of information between people and units in the organization is both timely and appropriate. All needed information must reach the right people at the right time. Communication is especially necessary for problem solving. As progress toward goal accomplishment is made, organization members must be able to address snags, impediments, and unforeseen circumstances. They must be able to reach understandings about the causes of and solutions to problems.

Managers do not spend most of their time sitting at their desks planning and thinking.[1] They spend it talking with supervisors, peers, or subordinates, writing memos and notes, evaluating data, and preparing and giving presentations. They conduct group meetings, give speeches, and communicate decisions that are relevant to some or all members of the organization. A major part of every manager's job is transmitting and receiving information, as indicated in Exhibit 12.1.

Communication The exchange of ideas, opinions, and information through written or spoken words, symbols, or actions.

Communication is the exchange of ideas, opinions, and information through written or spoken words, symbols, or actions.[2] It is the method by which we coordinate our activities with the activities of others. The Inside View 12.1 hypothesizes on the historical development of communication efforts. Speaking and writing are in themselves relatively easy, but achieving an understanding is a challenge. Each of us has a different background, different experiences, and different personal needs, which affect personal understanding.[3] A word or a facial expression can have different meanings for different people depending on their perceptions, background, and experiences. One of a manager's major challenges is to ensure that his or her statements are conveyed clearly and accurately so that employees can work together effectively.

This chapter explains the communication process people use to influence each other, transfer information, and solve problems. It then identifies some factors that can disrupt communication and considers the importance of such aspects of communication as body language and listening.

THE COMMUNICATION PROCESS

We all communicate every day, although almost no one thinks of it as a process involving formal steps. When you engage in a conversation with someone, you listen to what he or she says. From words and gestures, you infer the other person's meaning, and then you respond. Your conversational partner then inter-

EXHIBIT / 12.1
Communication as a Percentage* of a Manager's Work

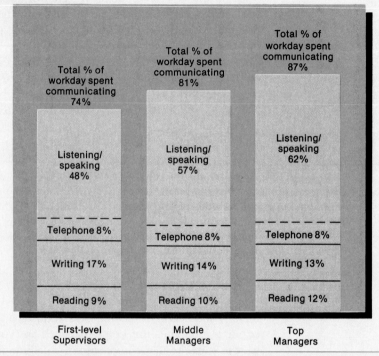

	First-level Supervisors	Middle Managers	Top Managers
Total % of workday spent communicating	74%	81%	87%
Listening/speaking	48%	57%	62%
Telephone	8%	8%	8%
Writing	17%	14%	13%
Reading	9%	10%	12%

Source: Adapted from Hinrichs, John R., "Communications Activity of Industrial Research Personnel," *Personnel Psychology* 17 (Summer 1964): 199.

*Percentage of 8-hour workday.

prets your message and responds in turn. A manager and an employee, or any two employees, may have a conversation about some aspect of work. Each listens to the other's words, looks at the gestures, reads the relevant documents, or looks over the equipment to understand what the other means. When the two achieve a mutual understanding about what is to be done in the work situation, they have communicated effectively.

As indicated in the WGA case, however, misunderstandings often occur, even when people share the same information. The producers and the WGA, for example, both read the same contract but understood it to say something different regarding payment to writers on videocassette sales. To see how misunderstandings occur in the communication process, it is helpful to look at the distinct steps and components of the process.

The communication process requires at least two people, a sender and a receiver. The sender initiates the communication. To transfer information, such as ideas, facts, feelings, or opinions, the sender creates a message using symbols, such as words, actions, or expressions. These symbols are then transmitted to the receiver visually, verbally, or by some other channel. From this transmitted message, the receiver attempts to reconstruct the sender's original thought. When the receiver responds, giving feedback to the sender, the roles are reversed: Now the receiver is the sender and vice versa.[4]

THE INSIDE VIEW / 12.1

Symbols of Mankind

The Pioneer spacecraft carries on board a line drawing of two humans and the solar system depicting where the spacecraft came from. Pictures are more effective than words at communicating ideas when the communicators have no language in common.

The first written messages were simply pictures relating to familiar objects in some meaningful way—pictographs. Yet there were no images for much that was important in human life. What, for instance, was the image for sorrow or bravery? So from pictographs humans developed ideograms to represent more abstract ideas. An eye flowing with tears could represent sorrow, and a man with the head of a lion might be bravery.

The next leap occurred when the figures became independent of things or ideas and came to stand for spoken sounds. Written figures were free to lose all resemblance to actual objects.

At first, ideas flowed only slightly faster when written than they had through speech. But as technologies evolved, humans embodied their thoughts in new ways through the printing press, in Morse code, in electromagnetic waves bouncing through the atmosphere, and in the binary language of computers.

Today, when the Earth is covered with a swarming interchange of ideas, we are even trying to send our thoughts beyond our planet to other minds in the universe. Our first efforts at sending our thoughts beyond Earth have taken a very an-

cient form: pictographs. The first message on plaques aboard Pioneer spacecraft launched in 1972 and 1973 featured a simple line drawing of two humans, one male and one female, the male holding up his hand in greeting. Behind them was an outline of the Pioneer spacecraft, from which the size of the humans could be judged. The plaque also included the "address" of the two human figures: a picture of the solar system, with a spacecraft emerging from the third planet. Most scientists believe that when other civilizations attempt to communicate with us they, too, will use pictures.

All the accomplishments since humans first scribbled in the sand have led us back to where we began. Written language only works when two individuals know what the symbols mean. We can only return to the simplest form of symbol available and work from there. In interstellar communication, we are at the same stage our ancestors were when they used sticks to trace a few simple images in the sand. ■

Source: Lago, Don, "Symbols of Mankind," *Science Digest* (March 1981): 16.

To understand the mechanics of this process, it is useful to refer to the sequence developed by communications researchers.[5] Though many models of the communication process have been developed, the general consensus is that it consists of encoding a meaning, transmitting a message, and decoding and interpretating. Usually, the flow of information between parties is continuous and reciprocal; that is, it involves feedback (see Exhibit 12.2). This model uses only two people, mainly for illustrative purposes. Often several people are involved. In some cases, such as television broadcasts, millions of people may receive a message. Of course in this case, communication is not reciprocal—a million viewers will not feed back a response.

Encoding the Meaning

Encoding Selecting symbols to convey the meaning of a message.

The first step in communicating is encoding. A sender who has a message to convey must begin by **encoding** it by selecting symbols to relay the meaning of this message. Symbols can be words, pictures, facial expressions, signals, or actions. The word *cat* is a symbol in English for the feline animal. Similarly, a frown is a symbol for the feeling of displeasure; a clenched fist raised to the sky might be a symbol for anger, victory, or jubilation; and a red light in a traffic signal is a symbol for the word *stop*.

But all these symbols are ambiguous; that is, they may be interpreted differently by some people, especially those not familiar with American culture or the English language. Often an action or gesture meant to convey one meaning is misunderstood by the receiver and, in fact, conveys a different meaning. This is particularly true between people from different cultures. In the United States, for example, the gesture of slitting one's throat with a finger implies "I've had it," or "you're a dead man." Yet this gesture conveys quite a different message in Swaziland; there it means "I love you!"

Americans make no distinction between gesturing for silence to an adult or to a child. An American puts one finger to the lips for both, while an Ethiopian will use only one finger to a child and four fingers for an adult. In Ethiopia, to use only one finger for an adult is disrespectful. On the other hand, Ethiopians make no distinction in gesturing to indicate emphatic negation. They shake their index fingers from side to side to an adult as well as to a child. In the United States, on

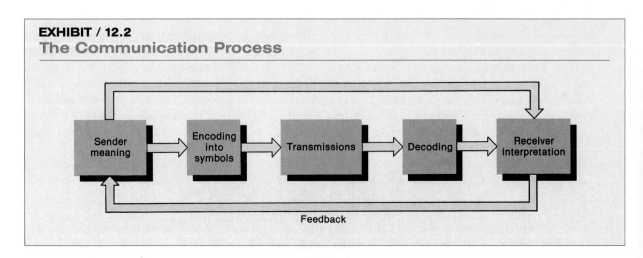

EXHIBIT / 12.2
The Communication Process

Sender meaning → Encoding into symbols → Transmissions → Decoding → Receiver interpretation

Feedback

the other hand, this gesture is used only for children and would be considered an insult by an adult. Even colors connote different meanings in different countries. For example, when President Nixon visited China in the 1970s, his wife wore a red coat. She would not have done so had she known that in China, only prostitutes wore red.

Words can be as easily misunderstood as physical symbols, even within one culture. Meanings are not inherent in words. Some of these differences exist because of varying definitions of words. Consider, for example, some of the meanings of the word *run*: Babe Ruth scored a *run*. I have a *run* in my stocking. Did he *run* the ship aground? I have to *run* downtown. You have the *run* of the place. Also, recall the conflicting interpretation of the wording in the WGA contract discussed earlier. The main point is clear: The sender should encode the message in words or actions that will have the same meaning, or the intended meaning, to the receiver.[6]

In some cases, it is necessary to go even beyond ensuring that a receiver has the same understanding of the words or symbols the sender has chosen. For example, encoding a message by using direct, accurate words may allow the receiver to understand it, but the directness of the message may cause a conflict that will hamper understanding between the sender and receiver. If a student, for example, tells his or her parents: "I flunked two courses in school," the parents may become enraged or upset, thus preventing continued conversation. But one student devised a way to cushion the message so that an understanding was achieved: "Dear Mom and Dad," she wrote,

> I'm sorry I haven't written in a long time, but since our dormitory was burned down during the student demonstration, I haven't been able to see very well. But don't worry. The doctor says there is a good chance I'll get my sight back. While in the hospital I met a wonderful man who works as an orderly there. He is an atheist and has convinced me to renounce Christianity. You'll soon have your wish of becoming grandparents. We are moving to New Zealand and expect to be married. Love, Mary.
>
> P.S. There was no demonstration or fire. I wasn't in the hospital. I'm not pregnant. I don't even have a boyfriend. But I did flunk chemistry and economics and I wanted you to view these problems in proper perspective.[7]

Transmitting

Transmitting Passing a message from sender to receiver.

Transmitting the message means passing the encoded message from the sender to the receiver over auditory, visual, tactical, electronic, or other communication channels. Many people mistake the sending of a message for transmission, but no transmission has occurred unless the intended person has received it. Typical examples of transmission include passing a typed letter to a receiver, speaking words so the intended receiver can hear them, or enacting a gesture so a person can see it.

Transmission occurred on many levels in the WGA case: In each strike, union members and producers exchanged lists of demands, either orally or in writing. Meanwhile, news of the strike was printed in newspapers read by the public, and broadcasts of the strike were transmitted over radios and television sets. Messages were transmitted on paper, electronically, verbally, and visually among thousands of writers, negotiators, and producers, and also to millions of "receivers" in the general population.

The sender of a message must ensure it is transmitted along appropriate lines. The best mode of transmission is determined by the message to be sent because the mode of transmission becomes part of the message. As Marshall McLuhan said in his book *Understanding Media,* "The medium is the message."[8] Even if the selected words—the symbols—are the same, a formal telegram conveys a greater sense of urgency than a first-class letter.

Decoding and Interpreting

Decoding The process of assigning meaning to transmitted symbols.

Interpretation The process of assigning meaning to a message.

Once the message is received, the receiver must translate the transmitted symbols into feelings, impressions, or thoughts that have meaning to him or her, in an attempt to reconstruct the original idea of the sender. **Decoding** is the process of assigning meaning to each symbol; **interpretation** is the process of assigning meaning to the entire message. These two processes are influenced by the receiver's past experience, particularly with the sender of the message, and the receiver's expectations of what the message is supposed to mean and skills in decoding and interpretation. These last steps clarify whether communication has occurred. They determine whether the sender and receiver understand the message the same way. The meaning of the symbolized feelings and thoughts as decoded by the receiver may be totally different from that intended by the sender. That is why the sender must pick symbols known to have the desired meaning for the receiver. The greater the difference between sender's intent and receiver's interpretation, the greater the distortion of the message.

Filter A limit on a person's capacity to sense or perceive stimuli.

Message distortion is often attributed to filtering. A **filter** is a limit on a person's capacity to sense or perceive stimuli.[9] This limit may be physiological or psychological. All human beings have natural, biological (physiological) limits on their ability to perceive stimuli or messages in the environment. We cannot see infrared or ultraviolet light with the naked eye, and we cannot hear tones as high-pitched as a dog whistle. Some people, such as those who are blind or deaf, also have additional physiological limits. Physiological filters, depending on their nature and extent, can limit a person's ability to perceive and therefore to understand or interpret a message.

Psychological filters, sometimes referred to as mind-sets, are expectancies or predispositions that affect what is perceived and how it is interpreted. Two people may view the same segment of a film or hear the same portion of a speech and still interpret the messages contained differently. One person may read subtle facial expressions differently or react differently to the use of certain words, phrases, or tones of voice. We will talk more about perceptual differences in the following section.

Communication is never as simple as the step-by-step process just described. More than one medium can be used to transmit messages. For example, while you talk with someone, your face and hands may be delivering supporting or contradictory messages. A manager's words may indicate that an employee is doing well on the job, while his or her facial expression may indicate that the employee is failing. Meanwhile, a written performance appraisal may indicate that the employee is average. In addition, similar messages coming from more than one sender can conceal very different meanings. One supervisor might ask the employee to stay late and finish a report, indicating by tone of voice that serious consequences may result if it is not done. Another supervisor saying the same thing may indicate through gestures or tone of voice that the report is not crucial.

To illustrate the complexities of the communication process and show how breakdowns can occur in the various phases, consider the example of Dick Olen, president of Thornton Associates. Olen wanted to share with the employees his excitement about the corporation's potential growth in the future, so he decided to tell them about the search for new and larger facilities. He called a staff meeting for all 50 employees to announce the search and describe the possible relocation sites.

However, the employees interpreted the announcement in different ways, depending on their perspectives. The head of production saw the move as a threat to his job. He believed that new facilities would bring in new, unfamiliar technology that he did not know how to use. Several production line employees interpreted the move as an opportunity for advancement. Growth would mean new supervisor slots for them. Other employees did not believe that the company would move. They saw the announcement as a managerial ploy to make the workers believe that the corporation was doing well when in fact it was failing and they were soon to be laid off. Many engineers, on hearing the announcement, decided to start looking for new jobs. Their specialized skills were in high demand in many organizations, and they did not welcome the idea of increased commuting time.

Obviously, Olen's announcement did not universally convey the point he was trying to make. Breakdowns occurred in various phases of the communication process. Several employees, based on their differing predispositions, interpreted Olen's message differently. Some had a history of losing jobs when their company moved, and some had a history of winning promotions in the same circumstances. Some were suspicious, some afraid, and some enthusiastic. If he had been aware of each employee's mind-set, Olen might have been able to encode and transmit the message differently so that all would react enthusiastically.

Even though communications can become complicated, the basic process remains the same: encoding the meaning, transmitting the message, and decoding and interpreting the meaning. If information is not being understood similarly by all involved parties, one should refer to this simple three-step model to find the source of the problems. Has the sender clarified and defined the message? Has the most effective mode of transmission been chosen? What are the perceptions of the receivers? Has the message been correctly interpreted?

PROBLEMS AND BARRIERS TO COMMUNICATION

If communication was perfect, the receiver would always understand the message in the same way the sender meant it. Communication, of course, is never perfect. People interpret information from their own perspectives, words are often ineffective for communicating feelings or attitudes, and social and organizational positions affect how people send and receive information. These problems highlight how important it is for both the sender and receiver to clarify communication.

One cannot assume that the message sent is the message received, because breakdowns and barriers can exist at any phase in the communication process. The nature and sources of the problems must be clearly understood. Four major problems that prevent accurate communication are noise, differences in perception, language usage, and status differences.

Noise

Noise Anything that physically interferes with or distorts the transmission process.

Noise is anything that interferes with or distorts the transmission process. The sender may use so many words that the message gets lost in the transmission. The Inside View 12.2 gives an example of how memos should be written. The words used may be accurate, but there are so many and they may be so complex that the message is lost. Noise may also be competing messages. One person may receive several different or conflicting orders from people who have equal authority or influence over him or her. Noise may be the actual clanging and banging of machinery or static on a telephone line that makes transmission of the message impossible.

In one of the worst cases, noise may be verbal—too many people talking at once or trying to be heard over each other. This was often the case in the board meetings at the WGA during the 1985 strike. According to one board member, the meetings were characterized by "screaming and name-calling," and a general summary of opinions described the WGA board room as "a snake pit of personal attacks and innuendo, self-aggrandizing politicking and demagoguery. Even the most trivial of agenda items . . . bog down in . . . quarrels."[10]

Whenever noise interferes with communication, the receiver must piece together information and guess at the meaning of the message. Consider, for example, trying to hear someone speaking at a construction site. The noise of the jackhammers may drown out the words so the receiver will be forced to piece together the message by reading lips or watching gestures.

Differences in Perceptions

Differences in needs and experiences cause people to see the world differently. Certainly the WGA members saw things differently than the producers, and even the Union Blues, the WGA subgroup, had different perceptions of what was important than the rest of the union.

Interpretations are often based on what one expects to see rather than what actually exists, and information that does not correspond with one's expectations is often received slowly. As an example, consider Exhibit 12.3. Count the number of times the letter *F* appears in the statement. People usually find three. Now read the statement backwards and count the *F*'s. You will probably find more because now you are not reading words that cause you to expect *F* only in certain places. Read backwards, the sentence makes no sense anyway, so there are no expectations of where the *F*'s should be. Having fewer preconceived notions, you should obtain more accurate results.

EXHIBIT / 12.3
Count The Number of F's

FINISHED FILES ARE THE RE-
SULT OF YEARS OF SCIENTIFIC
STUDY COMBINED WITH THE EX-
PERIENCE OF MANY YEARS.

Source: Kossen, S. *The Human Side of Organizations,* 2nd Edition, (San Francisco, CA: Canfield Press, 1978), p. 27.

THE INSIDE VIEW / 12.2

Brevity Is All: How to Write a Memo

THE WRONG WAY

MEMO TO: All Departments
FROM: D. Frizee, Vice President, Training
RE: Memos

It has come to the attention of this department that the general run of company memos are neither impactful nor effective, with sentences that run on too long, an excess of verbiage, and a failure to come to the point briefly and expeditiously, a matter that has been noted by many, but most recently by Chairman Curtis, who has elected my department to bring our standards up to snuff.

Chairman Curtis feels that, above all else, memos should be terse, not given to long exposition on the subject but simply laying out what needs to be said without redundancy; that is, saying what needs to be said correctly the first time, not the second or third. In short, brevity is all.

THE RIGHT WAY

MEMO TO: Everyone
FROM: Doug Frizee
RE: Bad memos

As we all know, the memo situation is terrible:
• There are too many of them.
• Most are boring and hard to read.
• Mr. Curtis feels they should be more concise. Therefore:
• Any memo over one page should be cut to one page.
• Don't write a memo if a phone call will do. ■

Source: Bing, Stanley, "Take a Memo . . . Please," *Esquire* (May 1985): 66.

DUFFY®   by **BRUCE HAMMOND**

Perceptions also vary according to the objectivity of the information. For example, physical objects such as a desk or a car are familiar to most people. The transfer of meaning about them is particularly clear if both persons have actually seen and felt the object: a desk both have used or a car in which both have ridden. Whether or not information is communicated depends on how accurate the description is. If I am trying to explain to you what elevator to take or when the project is due, I can easily tell whether I have communicated to you accurately. You either get on the elevator I described or you do not; you hand in the project on the designated day or you do not. Exhibit 12.4 presents examples of this type of problem. A perceptual distortion exists, but there are correct responses against

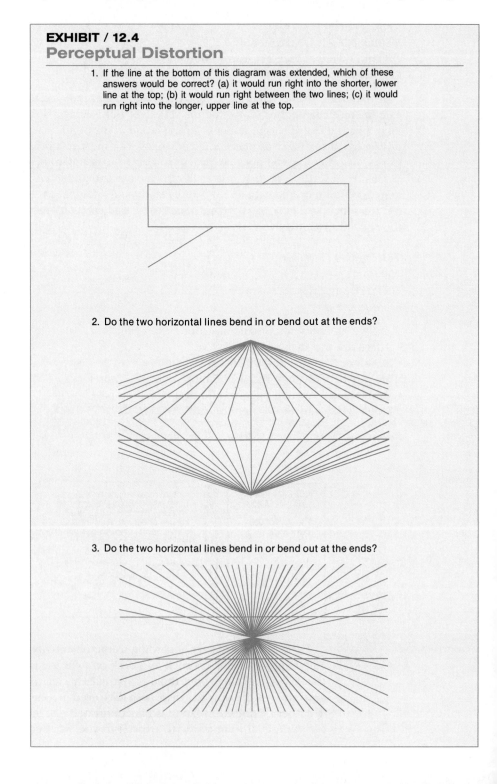

EXHIBIT / 12.4
Perceptual Distortion

1. If the line at the bottom of this diagram was extended, which of these answers would be correct? (a) it would run right into the shorter, lower line at the top; (b) it would run right between the two lines; (c) it would run right into the longer, upper line at the top.

2. Do the two horizontal lines bend in or bend out at the ends?

3. Do the two horizontal lines bend in or bend out at the ends?

which appropriate responses can be tested. In the case of disagreement, the length or straightness of the lines can be measured.

As the object of the communication becomes subjective, the transfer of meaning from one person to another becomes harder. There are no correct answers when people are asked to interpret subjective feelings, attitudes, and impressions. The criteria against which to check interpretations or to determine whether a person has understood correctly are much more vague in these cases. Exhibit 12.5 shows a drawing that is an example of this type of problem. People will interpret the drawing differently, but there is no one correct interpretation. A number of feasible, "accurate" interpretations exist: When people look at the drawing, 55 percent see a duck, 25 percent see an island, and 20 percent see a rabbit. None of these is right or wrong; they are all different interpretations of the same picture. In situations in which no objective reality exists against which to compare interpretations, people must be sure that they understand how others perceive the situation. It is unwise to proceed assuming that others see things the same way we do.

An organization's culture is particularly subjective. A hundred different people could offer a hundred descriptions of one company's culture, and they all could be "right." Consequently, communications regarding cultural characteristics such as supportiveness of supervisors, conformity to rules, and even openness of communication are often problematic. Both sender and receiver have to make a concerted effort to understand each other.

Language

The variety of meanings that many words have is a prime cause of confusion and misunderstanding during communication. When these words are part of a message without accompanying words to explain them, the message is often distorted. For example, directing a subordinate to "handle some calls" may result in a pile of messages on the manager's desk. The manager may have wanted the subordinate to answer all the questions and respond to all the requests, while the subordinate thought the manager wanted messages taken. The misunderstanding occurred over the meaning of the word *handle*.

Occasionally, however, confusing and incomprehensible language is used deliberately by people who stand to gain from confusing their audience. Advertisers are especially guilty of this, as explained in The Inside View 12.3.

EXHIBIT / 12.5
What Do You See?

But Does Anybody Understand It?

The 1988 Honda Prelude SI. Most cars will get you where you want to go, but the advertising emphasizes a technology that most consumers don't understand.

More and more high-tech lingo is appearing in car commercials nowadays, even though anybody hardly understands it and the advertising rarely explains what the whiz-bang features do. Consider these examples:

General Motors's Oldsmobile division touts the "16-valve, dual-overhead-cam Quad 4 engine and power-assisted rack-and-pinion steering" on its LeBaron coupe. American Honda Motor Co. boasts that all its 1988 models have "double-wishbone suspension."

Those who create such ads insist there is method to their madness. By making the explanation of four-wheel steering "purposefully confusing," Honda hopes to "pique people's curiosity and get them into the showroom to ask about it," says Kevin McKeon, the copywriter at Korey, Kay & Partners in New York who wrote Honda's Prelude ad.

That is one theory. A nearly opposite explanation is that any high-tech term "sounds impressive, and a lot of consumers are afraid to ask what it is because they don't want to sound dumb," says advertiser Roy Grace, who tried to avoid technical talk in the Volkswagen ads he created for 20 years.

"To be honest," said Honda salesman David M. Walls, "it would be easier for me to give you a brochure than to try to explain it." For what it is worth, the term "wishbone" refers to U-shaped

control arms that connect a car's suspension apparatus to its body. Honda says they provide more stability and a smoother ride than conventional, A-shaped control arms. (That is what you thought, right?)

Then there is Quad 4, a term that graces many GM ads. "Isn't that four-wheel steering?" asks Judy Hegarty as she enters a suburban Detroit Chrysler-Plymouth showroom. "Could that be four-wheel drive?" asks Max Schwandt, who was shopping for a minivan. Well, no. It refers to an engine with four valves instead of two on each of four cylinders. The extra valves are supposed to mix air with the fuel in the combustion chamber more efficiently, boosting power without sacrificing gas mileage.

Some auto makers say they hope that touting technology will set their models apart. Only 20 percent of consumers understand car technology, estimates Ford Motor Co. executive Thomas J. Wagner, but the company emphasizes it anyway in the advertising for the new Lincoln Continental.

Mr. Wagner explains: "If we tell them about our dual-damping, electronically controlled air suspension, and they go over to Cadillac and say, 'Where's yours?' and Cadillac says, 'We don't have it,' then buyers have to believe we're better."

Other auto executives, though, offer a different philosophy. "Our advertising is common sense, logical, and simple," says Thomas Mignanelli, head of Nissan Motor Co.'s U.S. sales operations.

Still, Nissan's magazine ads talk about the "DOHC 16-valve fuel-injected engine" on one model, and the "normally aspirated" engine on another. Translation: The former has dual overhead camshafts, and they operate the 16 intake and exhaust valves, from above the cylinders, more efficiently than a single camshaft would. The latter lacks a supercharger or tubocharger to force air into the engine and so is said to breathe on its own.

Or, in other words, you put the car in drive and it goes. ◼

Source: Witcher, Gregory, "Car Ads Turn to High-Tech Talk—But Does Anybody Understand It?" *Wall Street Journal,* March 7, 1988, p. 19, sec. 2.

Status

Status, or the relative position of the sender and the receiver, often affects communication. A receiver who sees the sender as having low status in the organization might discount messages from him or her, even if the sender is actually well informed. Conversely, a sender regarded as possessing high status may be considered correct and well informed regardless of the facts. His or her messages may be interpreted as accurate even if they are not. In this sense, status differences can affect the communication between managers and employees. Managers, perceived to have the higher-status position, are sometimes assumed to be more knowledgeable and to have more power to implement action. Their opinions and recommendations may be accepted more than those of an employee who is seen to have a lower-status position.

In other cases, status simply affects the perception some employees have of others. Subordinates may be suspicious of a supervisor's actions simply because the person is a supervisor and not because there is anything suspicious about the actions. For example, a floor manager for Sears walked through the department she supervised six times a day, asking subordinates individually about any problems they had. She perceived herself as showing sincere interest in each person. The workers, however, saw her as the boss and interpreted her many trips as a sign that she did not trust them. They resented her always checking on them. The manager thought she was being helpful, but the employees perceived her, because of her position, as being overbearing and untrusting.

Status can also affect communication between two competing departments. For example, a chemical firm had two product units, one focusing on consumer products and the other on military products. Each considered itself the primary contributor to the organization's profits and considered the other unit a sideline that only marginally contributed to profits. Over the years, a natural conflict emerged between the two units because they competed for the same resources—people and money—from the organization. Each came to view the other as an enemy and of lower status. Communication between these units was extremely poor since messages from either unit were always perceived as having ulterior meanings by the receiving unit.

The consumer products department then discovered that new federal legislation was being considered that would greatly and adversely affect both departments. Knowing it would be wise for both departments to forget their differences for a while and focus on the "common enemy" (Washington), it sent the military unit information about the new legislation. The military department, because of the previous antagonistic relationship, assumed this was a ploy to throw them off the track and refused to believe the information, much to their detriment.

ONE-WAY VERSUS TWO-WAY COMMUNICATION

One-way communication Communication efforts in which a message is passed from sender to receiver without feedback from the receiver.

Two-way communication Communication efforts in which sender and receiver exchange feedback messages.

Because so many possible barriers to effective communication exist, communicators must make special efforts to ensure that their intended messages are conveyed. It is rarely effective for one person simply to speak and assume that the listener has understood. This is **one-way communication,** communication efforts in which a message travels from sender to receiver without feedback from the receiver. In such cases, it is impossible to check whether the meaning received matches what the sender intended. To verify that the meanings are the same, sender and receiver must be able to exchange messages in turn. This is called feedback, and it is characteristic of **two-way communication.** Feedback is essential for successful communication, and it can often be immediate, as in face-to-face conversation. Feedback can come in many forms: verbal reactions, facial expressions, follow-up actions, return signals, letters, and memos.[11]

Harold Leavitt, a professor of management at Stanford University, developed an exercise that demonstrates the difference between one-way and two-way communication.[12] Using the diagrams in Exhibit 12.6, the sender verbally explains the diagram on the left while facing away from the audience, which cannot see the diagram. During the explanation the receivers cannot ask questions, make noises, or in any way provide feedback. The communication usually appears orderly, the person with the diagram appears to be in control, and both the sender and the receivers seem to feel that there is a mutual understanding. However, very few of the receivers ever draw the diagram the way the sender sees it—the way it actually exists.

The second time, the sender faces the receiver(s) and explains the diagram on the right. The sender is still limited only to verbal communication, but this time the receivers can also speak. They can ask the sender questions and make sugges-

EXHIBIT / 12.6
One-Way Versus Two-Way Communication Experiment

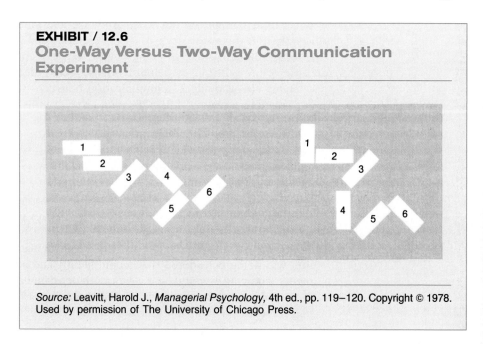

Source: Leavitt, Harold J., *Managerial Psychology,* 4th ed., pp. 119–120. Copyright © 1978. Used by permission of The University of Chicago Press.

tions and comments. Communication becomes a two-way process. During this second try, the communication usually appears disorganized. If a group is involved, many people usually talk at the same time. The sender may come under attack if the receivers think he or she is not communicating accurately. Group members often start helping each other verbally; they often converse more among themselves than with the person who sees the diagram. At this point, the receivers seem to be more in control than the sender. In addition, neither the sender nor all of the receivers feel sure that they understand each other, specifically because questions have arisen. Despite the apparent confusion and disorder, however, most of the receivers are able to draw the diagram so that it matches what the sender is describing.

Despite the appearance of confusion in the process, two-way communication illustrates the importance of feedback. People need to be able to say "I do not understand" or "Let me tell you what I heard you say and see if that is correct." Though the one-way process in the first attempt appears more orderly, the two-way process in the second attempt tends to be more effective.

Including feedback in the communication process turns one-way into two-way communication. Two-way communication is more accurate because the original message can be clarified and redefined. Consider, for example, a discussion that took place between Eric Lundquist, president of a manufacturing firm, and June Inaki, a financial analyst on the staff.

Eric: June, the figures for March are not good. Go back and do a more thorough analysis of the sales figures for our overseas operations.

June assumed that Eric was concerned that her work, and particularly the numbers for the overseas operations, be accurate. After thoroughly checking her report for accuracy, she reported to Eric that everything was OK. Eric's response indicated a misunderstanding:

Eric: What do you mean they are OK? They are not OK at all. Sales are down by 30 percent and we are losing business like crazy to the Japanese. I guess I am going to have to get someone else to find out what is happening.

June: I didn't know you wanted me to do an analysis. I thought you were questioning whether the numbers were accurate.

Eric: No, no. We have a competent staff. I assume the figures are accurate. What I want to know is, why are we losing sales? Do an analysis to find out where we are losing money overseas and why. Look at inventory, operations, and transportation costs. Look at sales figures by region. Consider our price relative to the competition. Do an analysis of our product and competitive position. I need you to tell me why we are losing money, not whether the numbers are accurate.

If two-way communication had been used initially, Eric and June could have saved a lot of time and frustration. June could have asked what Eric meant by *analysis* or suggested what areas should be looked at to make sure she understood what Eric wanted. She may even have been able to explain the problem to Eric immediately, or at least give him her impressions of what was happening.

Two-way communication also has some disadvantages. It takes much more time. Communication becomes a discussion. In some cases, one-way communication is more effective. In an operating room, for example, many patients might die if the chief surgeon allowed the nurses and assistants to question directives or discuss the procedures at length.

In addition to being faster than two-way communication, one-way communication occasionally is more effective. For example, recently it became necessary for a large industrial manufacturer that was committed to continuous employment for its workers to close one of its plants. The company was prepared to help employees find alternative employment either within the company or at other companies and also intended to arrange for early retirement to help those who were close to it. However, management concluded that employees would be upset and concerned when informed of the decision to close the plant. If the news was announced at a meeting, employees would probably not listen carefully to the company's pleas and would focus more on their worries and objections than on how to handle the situation.

To combat this, management decided to send a detailed letter to the employees explaining why the plant was being closed and describing the relocation, job search, and early retirement efforts of the organization. The letter was then followed up with question-and-answer sessions with management. The employees had time to assimilate the relevant information in the letter and to develop specific, pertinent questions about the options open to them. At the question-and-answer sessions held three days later, they were agitated, but they were able to discuss the problems and situation with management in a constructive manner. By combining one- and two-way communication with effective timing, management was able to provide employees with information, answer questions, and begin to solve the problems.

MANAGING INTERPERSONAL COMMUNICATION

Management of the communication process is complex and requires a manager's constant attention. Breakdowns in communication must be located and repaired. When information is not transmitted properly, the communication channels must be improved. When misunderstandings and disagreements exist because of lack of information or differences in perceptions, interpersonal communication must be improved. Exhibit 12.7 provides a list of "ten commandments of good communication" that the American Management Association suggested 35 years ago for improving communication. In addition to these classic rules, the use of face-to-face communication and effective listening are the main tools to help managers solve communication problems.

EXHIBIT / 12.7
Ten Commandments of Good Communication

1. *Seek to Clarify Your Ideas Before Communicating* The more systematically the problem or idea to be communicated is analyzed, the clearer it becomes. Many communications fail because of inadequate planning. One should consider the goals and attitudes of those who will receive the communication and those who will be affected by it.

2. *Examine the True Purpose of Each Communication* Before communicating, define specifically what the message is supposed to accomplish. Is it to obtain information, initiate action, change another person's attitude? Identify the most impor-

tant goal and then adapt the language, tone, and overall approach to serve that specific objective. Do not try to accomplish too much with each communication. The sharper the focus of the message, the greater its chances of being successfully communicated.

3. *Consider the Total Physical and Human Setting Whenever Communicating* Meaning and intent are conveyed by more than words alone. Many other factors influence the overall impact of a communication, and managers must be sensitive to the context in which they communicate. Consider

timing, that is, the circumstances under which an announcement is made or a decision rendered; the social climate, the work relationships within the company or a department, the tone of its communications; custom and practice—the degree to which communication conforms to, or departs from, the expectations of the audience. The physical setting: Is it private? Is there much interference? Be constantly aware of the total setting in which communication is taking place.

4. *Consult with Others, When Appropriate, in Planning Communications* Frequently, it is desirable or necessary to seek the participation of others in planning to communicate or developing the facts on which to base the communication. Such consultation often lends additional insight and objectivity to your message. Moreover, those who have helped plan the communication will probably give it their active support.

5. *Be Mindful, While Communicating, of the Overtones as Well as the Basic Content of the Message* Tone of voice, expression, apparent receptiveness to the responses of others—all have tremendous impact on the audience. Frequently overlooked, these subtleties of communication often affect a listener's reaction to a message even more than its basic content. Similarly, choice of language, particularly an awareness of the fine shades of meaning and emotion in the words used, predetermine in large part the reactions of the listeners.

6. *Take the Opportunity, When It Arises, to Convey Something of Help or Value to the Receiver* Consideration of the other person's interests and needs—trying to look at things from the other person's point of view—frequently provides opportunities to convey something of immediate benefit or long-range value to that person. Subordinates are most responsive to managers whose messages take the subordinates' interests into account.

7. *Follow up on Communications* The best efforts at communication may be wasted if they are not followed up. One may never know whether he or she has succeeded in expressing the true meaning and intent of the message if it is just delivered once and forgotten. By asking questions, by encouraging the receiver to express his or her reactions, by follow-up contacts, and by subsequent review of performance, one can determine whether the message was accurately received. Make certain that every important communication receives feedback so that complete understanding and appropriate action result.

8. *Communicate for Tomorrow as Well as Today* While communications may be aimed primarily at meeting the demands of an immediate situation, they must be planned with the past in mind if they are to maintain consistency in the receiver's view. More importantly, however, communications must be consistent with long-range interests and goals. For example, it is not easy to communicate frankly on such matters as poor performance or the shortcomings of a loyal subordinate, but postponing disagreeable communications makes these matters more difficult in the long run and is actually unfair to subordinates and the company.

9. *Be Sure Actions Support Communications* In the final analysis, the most persuasive kind of communication is not what is said, but what is done. When actions or attitudes contradict words, others tend to discount what is said. For every manager, this means that good supervisory practices—such as clear assignment of responsibility and authority, fair rewards for effort, and sound policy enforcement—serve to communicate more than all the gifts of oratory.

10. *Seek Not Only to Be Understood but to Understand—Be a Good Listener* When people start talking, they often stop listening. They become less attuned to the other person's unspoken reactions and attitudes. Listening is one of the most important, most difficult, and most neglected skills in communication. It demands concentration on the explicit meanings, unspoken words, and undertones that may be far more significant than the basic message.

Source: Adapted by permission of the publisher from "Ten Commandments of Good Communication," *Management Review*, Vol. 44 (October 1955): 704–705. Copyright 1955 by AMACOM, a division of American Management Associations. All rights reserved.

Face-to-Face Communication

Face-to-face communication is often more accurate than other forms of communication because gestures and actions can supplement words and provide immediate feedback. Nonverbal communication, or body language, is an important part of face-to-face communication. It includes posture, facial expressions, body movement, eye contact, and physical contact. Although nonverbal communication is often combined with verbal, it can also be very effective by itself.[13]

When one person approaches another to speak, the second person immediately takes mental note of the speaker's mannerisms: hand waving, head nodding, and other physical expressions. Often the receiver will be able to estimate the nature of the communication before the sender speaks a word. In this way, communication begins immediately and is supplemented by several types of messages. Feedback is also immediate.[14]

People react to face-to-face messages, revealing whether they agree or disagree with the statements or how they feel in general. By reading each other's expressions and gestures, people can determine right away whether they are being understood and can clarify their points as necessary. Exhibit 12.8 gives some examples of how body language communicates.

The power of nonverbal communication is demonstrated when the verbal and the nonverbal do not agree. People are much more likely to believe nonverbal than verbal communication. Managers, therefore, must carefully control facial expressions and other nonverbal methods of communicating so that they are compatible with the words they use. When the two are incompatible, employees may perceive the wrong messages, because they watch the manager and may believe what they see rather than what they hear.[15]

Listening

To be effective communicators, people must be skilled at both sides of the communication process: sending and receiving, or listening.[16] Many managers spend half their workday listening to subordinates, other managers, superiors, or clients

---

EXHIBIT / 12.8
Body Language

Superiority

Fists reinforcing the defensive position

The girl is bored. The giveaway gestures are head in the palm of her hand and body pointing toward an exit.

Source: Neirenberg, G., and Caler, H., *How to Read a Person Like a Book* (New York: Pocket Books, 1973).

and customers. Listening carefully to these messages is as important to managerial success as sending good messages.[17] Some of the messages will contain new information useful in decision making, and some will contain feedback to messages previously sent. In either case, the information is important and the ability to listen is essential.

Every message carries with it the underlying feelings or emotions of the sender. Understanding both the words or actions sent and the feelings and emotions behind them is important for effective listening. For example, speakers who use overstatement, irony, sarcasm, or hyperbole in their messages are certainly trying to convey something other than what is actually stated. A perceptive listener will hear both the words and the emotions that underlie them, as illustrated in The Inside View 12.4.

Active listening
Attempting to read the message beyond the words spoken.

Several researchers have studied the listening process and tried to determine how people can listen more effectively. Carl Rogers popularized the term **active listening** from his work in this field.[18] This concept recognizes that talking is simply the action taken by the sender to communicate a message; the original meaning of the message may or may not come across through talking. Thus, people should be active listeners and attempt to read the message beyond the words spoken.

There are five basic guidelines to active listening:

1. Listen for message content—make an effort to hear exactly what is being said.
2. Listen for feelings—try to perceive the sender's feelings about the subject matter (as reflected in tone of voice, rate of speed of talking, facial expressions, and gestures, for example).
3. Respond to feelings—demonstrate to the sender that you recognize and understand his or her feelings.
4. Note all cues verbal and nonverbal—in being sensitive to nonverbal messages (as indicated above in point 2), attempt to identify mixed messages and contradicting messages.
5. Reflect back to the source what you think you are hearing—restate in your own words, after interpreting both verbal and nonverbal messages, what you think the sender meant. Allow the sender to respond, confirming or contradicting your assumptions or adding further information.

Active listening is one technique for improving communication, but it is only applicable in small-group situations that allow a two-way exchange of information. But other techniques facilitate an organization's ability to keep all its members informed of goals and progress, enhance the exchange of information between interdependent units, or facilitate members' abilities to solve problems. In directing, managers must ensure that communications on and between all levels in the organization are effective.

ORGANIZATIONAL COMMUNICATION

Organizational communication follows the process outlined earlier in the chapter and is subject to the same dysfunctions. But many of the communication efforts and activities undertaken in organizations are formalized or systematic. Managers plan and design communication mechanisms specifically to facilitate understanding and coordination among levels and departments in the organization.

THE INSIDE VIEW / 12.4

Words and Images

An entrepreneurial personality will express itself with characteristic verbal images and metaphors.

A senior vice president in a large New York bank is talking about the group he formerly worked with: "You hit the bird cage and everyone is on a new perch. People are always moving there. People move so fast, and they—whew! I got out of there before it all came down."

The imagery is very graphic and tells a lot about this man and the world in which he lives. If you could listen to him a little more, you would not be surprised to learn that he does not have a traditional banking background. He sees himself as an entrepreneur and feels that, while most of them are attractively dressed and schooled, the other executives in the bank do not have any fire in their guts. En masse (he does not see them as individuals) "they" are "birds," which suggests he thinks they are pretty, caged, and—quite likely—fragile. One can sense the relief this man felt when he moved to a part of the bank where he could be active, be himself, be entrepreneurial.

When you pay close attention to the words other people use, you notice that most people draw characteristic verbal pictures of themselves and the world around them. The imagery and metaphors that a person most frequently uses can be clues to understanding the world he or she inhabits. The imagery shows what's valued, what's feared, and what the speaker's behavioral rules are. ∎

Source: McCaskey, Michael B., "The Hidden Messages Managers Send," *Harvard Business Review* (November–December 1979): 136.

Formal Channels

Formal channels
Communication channels planned and established by the organization.

Downward communication Communication initiated from upper management.

Formal channels of communication are planned and established by the organization to carry information between units and levels. The formal lines of communication most often follow the reporting relationships in the organization and travel in three general directions: downward, upward, and laterally.

Downward communication is communication initiated from top management and directed at levels below. It may contain directives from managers to subordinates concerning work activities, explanations of strategy, or reports on progress toward goals. Downward communication messages may be broad statements on the objectives of a particular unit or job, or they may be specific directions for performing certain activities. The WGA used downward communication to try to convince its membership that the videocassette royalty arbitrations were crucial to the union's bargaining strength. The union's management, however, was unable to effectively communicate this strategy to the rank and file.

The main problem with downward communication is that the message is distorted as it is passed from one level to another.[19] Each level reinterprets the message based on its own perspective. By the time the message reaches the bottom of the organization, it may be nothing like what was intended. In highly autocratic organizations, downward communication may be the only channel through which information flows—communication may be essentially a one-way process—and the errors and distortions may never be corrected. Downward communication is most effective in conjunction with upward communication; with feedback and a continual exchange of information, errors and distortions can be corrected.

Upward communication

Information passed from subordinates to supervisors or upper levels of management.

Upward communication is information passed from subordinates to supervisors or upper levels of management. It is essential to the effective functioning of the organization.[20] Bruce Harriman, in his theory of ups and downs, provides a colorful description of the differences between upward and downward communication. His theory is that "communications in a hierarchical society or organization work according to the principle that governs gravity. Downward communications are usually better than anyone realizes and frequently more accurate than those at higher levels want them to be. Conversely, upward communications have to be pumped and piped, with a minimum of filters, in order to be effective."[21]

Upward communication can be threatening to supervisors. For example, if the information concerns recommendations about the job or procedures, supervisors may fear that it makes them look uninformed; it may make the subordinate look more competent. If the information is feedback, supervisors may feel the subordinate is trying to evaluate them. Complaints from customers, reports on problems by subordinates, and feedback on failures are all threatening upward communications because they all contain negative information. Even so, supervisors need subordinates' information to make corrections and do their job properly. If the information is discarded or ignored because it is a threat, the result may be decreased productivity, continued problems, or alienation of the employees. For a healthy organization to exist, managers must make special efforts to obtain and respond to subordinates' opinions and suggestions.

Some organizations use surveys and suggestion systems to improve upward communication. Surveys are questionnaires asking specific questions about problem areas, attitudes, and suggestions for improvement. Employees typically fill out the questionnaires anonymously. The results are tabulated, summarized, and used to identify and solve organizational problems. As you recall from Chapter 9, survey questionnaires are also used to facilitate organization development.

Suggestion systems work much the same way, but they are not structured questions. Employees are given the opportunity to identify specific problems and solutions. Some suggestion systems provide forms for employees to complete and send to management anonymously. Others provide boxes or drop-off points where employees leave suggestions. No matter how the information is collected, the purpose is the same: to give employees a mechanism for feeding upward information about the organization's performance and ways to improve it.

Lateral communication
Information passed between persons or units at the same level in the organization.

Lateral communication is information passed between persons or units at the same level in the organizational hierarchy. These messages usually help coordinate the activities of the various departments. Lateral communication is particularly important when units depend on each other to accomplish organizational objectives.[22] For example, for a hospital nursing staff to be effective, it must be able to communicate effectively with X-ray technicians and medical records personnel; for the X-ray and medical records departments to be successful, they must be able to communicate effectively with the nurses. Their ability to cooperate is determined by the effectiveness of lateral communication.

Informal Channels

The best communication network for an organization uses all three channels. Managers should initiate two-way communication, upward and downward, whenever possible.[23] They should also coordinate their activities with others in the organization through lateral communication.

Informal channels
Communication channels, such as the grapevine, that allow messages to travel outside of the formal communication structure.

But not all communication in an organization is transmitted through formal channels. **Informal channels** of communication are additional routes for communication that allow messages to travel outside of the formal communication structure (see Exhibit 12.9). Because informal communication often flows between friends and acquaintances, flow is determined haphazardly by informal contacts.

Informal communication transcends the barriers of status and hierarchy and can quickly transmit news. The informal network can communicate information; the formal network cannot. Consider the example of Thornton Associates moving to a new location. The president may hesitate to make a formal announcement or directly ask employees how they feel about the move because this might generate many anxieties, questions, and demands. He could, however, use the informal network to spread the word about the possibility of a move and see how people react. If confronted, he could say no such decision has been made. Though no formal communication channels have been used, the president still receives valuable information about how people might react to a decision to move.

Grapevine An informal, person-to-person communication network not officially sanctioned by the organization.

The most common and predominant informal channel of communication in an organization is the grapevine. The **grapevine** is an informal, person-to-person communication network not officially sanctioned by the organization.[24] Grapevines and rumor mills exist in every organization and can form links between any level or department from the president to the line employees. Primarily, the grapevine is used by employees to make sense of unclear or confusing management actions or to fill in information missing from formal communication channels. Thus, the grapevine is most active when the organization is undergoing change and/or is threatened by events in the environment.

Despite the lack of organizational sanction, grapevine communications tend to be both highly accurate and highly relevant to organizational activities. According to one study, about 80 percent of grapevine communications are business-related rather than personal. In addition, 70 to 90 percent of the facts and details transmitted through the grapevine were accurate.[25] This is partly because, typically, only a few people are actively involved in transmitting information, so distortions are less likely to occur. Several grapevine networks are illustrated in Exhibit 12.10.

EXHIBIT / 12.9
Formal and Informal Channels of Communication

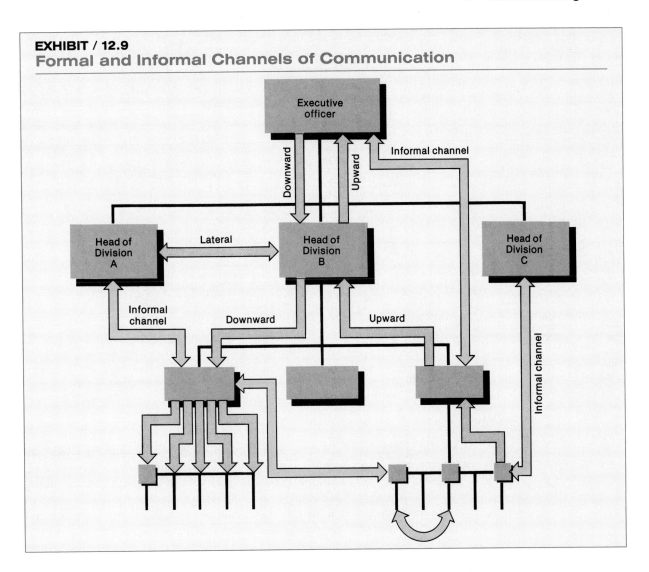

Grapevines are valuable communication networks in organizations because of their speed and informality, but they do have one potential drawback: They may run out of control. Rumors often begin from fears or suspicions of workers that some unwanted occurrence will happen in the organization. Managers must keep track of rumors, preventing the damaging ones from spreading out of control.

MANAGING ORGANIZATIONAL COMMUNICATION

The communication process in organizations is highly complex and quite difficult to define or identify specifically. That is, although formal communications, networks, and channels can be drawn on an organization chart, the ways that information flows or does not flow among people, units, and levels are virtually impossible to pin down. Informal communication channels have a life of their own; they grow and change as people come and go and as the organization grows or shifts in structure.

EXHIBIT / 12.10
Grapevine Networks

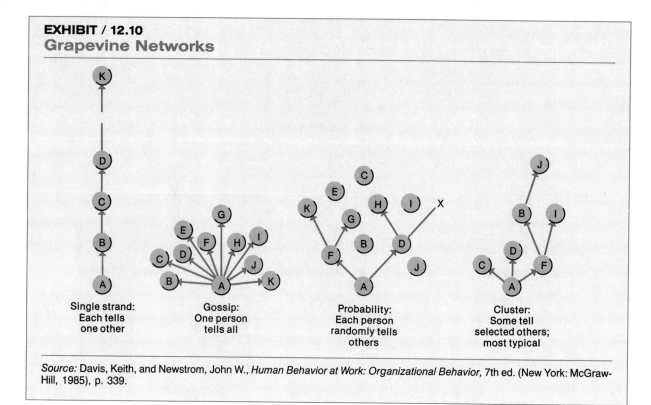

| Single strand: Each tells one other | Gossip: One person tells all | Probability: Each person randomly tells others | Cluster: Some tell selected others; most typical |

Source: Davis, Keith, and Newstrom, John W., *Human Behavior at Work: Organizational Behavior*, 7th ed. (New York: McGraw-Hill, 1985), p. 339.

Managing organizational communications is, therefore, an ongoing challenge. Managers must design upward, downward, and lateral networks that operate reciprocally (two-way communications) and that keep information flowing among people so that they can accomplish their objectives. Managers must also seek to harness informal channels to take advantage of their speed and accuracy and minimize the potential for damaging rumors.

The task of managing the communication process is, in a sense, becoming both more challenging and less challenging with developments in other aspects of business. Advances in organization structure, which we discussed in Chapter 7, are creating structures that would not benefit from the standard communication networks outlined here. For example, downward communication systems would not be used in a network organization. Most communication would be lateral, but even so, it would not flow laterally as it would in a more traditionally structured organization.

While it may seem as though managing communications in such "loose" organizations would be more challenging, developments in information technology (which we will cover in Chapter 17) are actually making it less so. Members of an organization spread around the world can now "talk" to each other any time, via computer, electronic mail, facsimile transmission, or just the telephone. Widely dispersed units engaged in various activities can integrate their efforts smoothly and simply through telecommunications and information technology. So while the challenge of managing communications may increase, new advances will make it more exciting and open up whole new opportunities.

KEY POINTS

1 The communication process consists of encoding, transmitting, decoding, and interpreting ideas, information, and messages. Each step must be carefully managed to ensure accurate communication and understanding.

2 Communication is never perfect—the message or idea sent will never exactly match the one received and interpreted. Several barriers to accurate communication are noise (distortions), differences in perceptions and experience, and differences in status and language.

3 One-way communication allows no exchange of information between sender and receiver; the sender transmits all of the messages, and the receiver interprets them without responding. Though it appears orderly and controlled, it is less accurate than two-way communication, which allows both parties to verify their interpretations through questions and feedback.

4 Two-way communication is essential to ensuring understanding. It provides feedback unavailable in one-way communication and thereby measures the accuracy of the communication process. However, it is time consuming and in some cases, especially emergencies, feedback may confuse the issues or delay response times.

5 Face-to-face communication is important, as it is often more accurate than other forms of communication; gestures and actions supplement words and provide immediate feedback.

6 The ability to listen is essential to communication because it ensures that important information is received and understood; communication is strengthened by asking important questions and paying attention to answers; by preventing expectations from altering perceptions; by being attentive, unprejudiced and responsive; and by keeping in mind the whole picture rather than focusing on one point. In order to improve listening skills, one must listen for message content and feelings behind it, note verbal and nonverbal cues, and provide feedback.

7 Organizational communication can flow in formal or informal channels: Formal channels can move downward, upward, or laterally; informal channels consist of grapevines and gossip. Effective communication requires a combination of the two. Managers have to take advantage of the strong points of each channel and minimize their damaging potentials.

FOR DISCUSSION AND REVIEW

1. What problems with the communication process developed in the Writers' Guild of America? How were they manifested?

2. In what ways is communication more than having a conversation or getting a letter? What else does it include?

3. Describe an everyday form of communication in terms of the communication process in the text.

4. How would communication differ in a small company like a local accounting firm as opposed to a large company like IBM or GM? What are some forms or channels that they might share?

5. Give an example of a situation where a psychological filter would affect communications. Tell how it would work.

6. Define perception and discuss how it affects communication. How does it affect feedback?

7. Discuss an experience in bad communication you have had. How would the situation have improved if the "ten commandments of good communication" had been followed?

KEY TERMS

Active listening
Communication
Decoding
Downward communication
Encoding
Filter
Formal channels
Informal channels
Interpretation
Lateral communication
Noise
One-way communication
Grapevine
Transmitting
Two-way communication
Upward communication

THE CONFERENCE TABLE: DISCUSSION CASE / 12.1

VNET or Gripenet?

A programmer at work in an IBM computer room. Ironically, as IBM found out, computers can be used for internal personal communications as well as for doing assigned work.

In October 1981, a group of IBM software developers sent a "catalogue of their grievances" to the company's top executives. This "plea for reform . . . was compiled from individual submissions sent over IBM's massive internal electronic mail network, VNET." What makes this situation so striking is that, first, the top management at IBM was not even aware of the VNET system until two years after it had been "born"; and second, this independently started and operated system "grew with little or no mandate, direction, or control by IBM management" to have 10,000 subscribers by 1978 and to cost IBM roughly $1 million annually in line costs alone.

It is ironic that such a vast communications system could operate for so long and so extensively without the knowledge of those who were funding it. The reasons for this, however, may lie in the purposes the system's developers had for it. The authors of the network, Edson Hendricks and T. C. Hartmann, claimed that "it has materialized quite spontaneously without any explicit mandate or governing organization." Starting in 1976, VNET grew into a system that facilitated the transference of job and data information at IBM research sites worldwide. "Subscribers" used it to send job resumes and, in some cases, to announce resignations. With time, one source said, "it has evolved into an enormous broadcast mechanism or mouthpiece for workers to let out steam and get out old hurts."

Most of these so-called old hurts arose from what some workers have called a "systematic de-skilling" in the data-processing department. In addition, employees of this section felt that they were stuck in a career that lacked upward mobility. They attributed much of this to being tied to the development of IBM's

Source: Emmet, Ralph, "VNET or Gripenet?" *Datamation* (November 1981): 48–58.

VM 370 (virtual machine computer mainframe) as opposed to IBM's operating system for large mainframes to the MVS (multiple virtual storage) system. IBM management policy seemed to favor the MVS and as a result wanted to push the VM 370 aside.

In 1976, "IBM decided to kill off its VM Product Development facility in Burlington, Massachusetts and move its people into the MVS fold at Poughkeepsie, New York. . . . Some of the current crop of VM dissidents . . . say that the Burlington incident was probably a calculated attempt by IBM to reduce VM support." Only one-third of the Burlington group actually moved to the Poughkeepsie branch. Another third moved to VM research jobs at local branches, and the other third left the company.

Most of those who left complained of a lack of autonomy, merit incentives, and career opportunities. One employee found he could only log onto the computer for half of each day, at most. "For somebody who wants to do something meaningful, that can be frustrating," he said. Another, who left and started his own company, said IBM did not support or reward "entrepreneurial-minded" employees. After being denied office time to work on a project, he developed it at home. When he brought in the finished product, which was developed at no cost to IBM and which pulled in $500,000 almost immediately, his commission was only $11,000. Said another ex-VM employee, "Today it doesn't really pay to be a professional and a conscientious programmer at IBM."

The VM rebellion found voice through the VNET system. IBM considered dismantling the system but soon found that too many vital research projects depended on it. As a result, IBM beefed up its fight against the rebellious employee users, and the working climate began to change. In secrecy, after hours, IBM began to audit the user files to find out which employees were misusing the system. Although an IBM spokesman said, "The whole exercise was conducted with the highest sensitivity to personal privacy," many employees disagreed. They began using the system to broadcast their concerns about the audit and to devise methods of confusing the auditors. The selective purging of various VNET user files merely added ammunition to this communication battle. The VNET became a medium where "electronic conversations turned into electronic complaints."

Finally, Lyn Wheeler, a "father figure" in the data-processing division, sent a collection of these angry memos to IBM's top management as a warning from an employee. An IBM spokesman said, "IBM management certainly considers all constructive and valid criticisms, no matter what the source may be."

Recently, IBM began to enhance some of its VM products, largely due to the demand for them in the marketplace. In the end, it may seem that a treaty of sorts has been negotiated and the revolution quelled, but at what price? The casualties were heavy as many key personnel defected, and morale was heavily damaged. Employees were not allowed to be heard, and IBM has paid the price. ■

DISCUSSION QUESTIONS

1. What do you think was the most significant barrier to the communication process at IBM as expressed in this case?
2. Do you think the situation that transpired is unique to IBM merely because of the technology involved?
3. What communication guidelines would you have recommended to top managers *and* to VM developers to have prevented the "rebellion"?

THE CONFERENCE TABLE: DISCUSSION CASE / 12.2

Communication—Sometimes the Difference Between Life and Death

Air Florida's Flight 90 after it crashed into the Potomac River. The cockpit of an airplane is one place where clear communication can be a matter of life and death.

The National Aeronautics and Space Administration (NASA) Aviation Safety Reporting System shows that 70 percent of all civil aviation incidents during a five-year period from the mid-1970s to the early 1980s were attributable to human error, mainly when information was improperly transferred from one crew member to another or was not transferred at all.

Several causes of poor communication and misunderstanding were cited. Close cooperation is difficult in large airlines where pilots and co-pilots bid for routes based on seniority and therefore often fly with colleagues they have never seen before. Another problem is that many pilots, 90 percent of whom have come from the military, tend to be domineering and assertive. They often interpret assistance by crew members as interference and inhibit participation. Captains may also be overly assertive as an acquired response to operating within very short decision times; they may feel that anything less than absolute firmness with co-pilots may allow for arguments in emergencies when time is desperately short.

The results of these on-board communication problems can be tragic. On January 13, 1982, Air Florida Flight 90's co-pilot Roger Pettit told pilot Larry Wheaton four times before takeoff from Washington National Airport that conditions were "not right" and that there were engine problems. Wheaton took off anyway, and only minutes later the plane crashed into the 4th Street bridge and then into the ice-covered Potomac River, killing 74 persons on board (including the pilot and co-pilot) and four motorists on the bridge.

Source: Burrows, William E., "Cockpit Encounters," *Psychology Today* (November 1982): 43–47.

On May 8, 1978, National Airlines Flight 193 turned into its final approach to Pensacola Regional Airport in Florida. Four miles from the runway, still over Escambria Bay, the Ground-Proximity Warning System (GPWS) went off with a loud whooping sound and a flashing red light on the instrument panel, warning that the plane was too close to the ground or water, or dropping altitude too quickly for where it was supposed to be. The on-board computer said "Pull up! Pull up!" in authoritative, urgent recorded English. The alarm was so loud that it made conversation difficult. The pilot, having forgotten his glasses, thought he was descending at a rate of 2000 feet per minute from 1500 feet, so he slowed the rate of descent slightly. The altimeter actually read 500 feet. The flight engineer, in all the confusion, turned off the GPWS, thinking the pilot had told him to. The pilot, noticing that the alarm had stopped, continued to descend without checking the altimeter, which by then read 50 feet. Seconds later, the plane hit the water—three miles short of the runway. Though the water was only 12 feet deep and the plane remained virtually intact, three people drowned before rescuers arrived.

To investigate the extent to which communications problems contribute to airplane accidents, the Aviation Reporting System conducted a survey of pilots with the following results: 35 percent felt crew coordination, poor understanding, and division of responsibilities were major problems; 16 percent said that extraneous conversation, which interfered with important cockpit conversation, reflected an overly relaxed atmosphere; 15 percent reported incidents where information was believed to have been transmitted by crew members when in fact it had not been; 12 percent cited total lack of communication, sometimes arising from personality conflicts; 10 percent cited deficient communications due to complacency (the assumption that everyone understood when they did not); and 5 percent reported that a lack of confidence in their subordinates prompted them to take on too many duties themselves.

The airline industry has found that technical malfunctions are easier to correct and prevent than human performance problems. Though it is evident that airlines need pilots who are both great leaders and great communicators, combining these qualities with cooperative crews is not easy. Producing an effective, efficient, tightly knit team for every flight will be a major undertaking, if it is ever achieved at all. ■

DISCUSSION QUESTIONS

1. What barriers to the communication process occurred in this case, and what phase or phases of the process (encoding, transmission, decoding) did they affect specifically?
2. How would two-way communication have helped in this situation, and why do you think it is not used extensively in cockpit environments?
3. Based on the results of the Aviation Reporting System survey, what recommendations would you make?

13 | Motivating for Productivity

FOCUS CASE / Why Do You Work?

UNDERSTANDING MOTIVATION

WHAT DO PEOPLE WANT?
Maslow's Hierarchy of Needs Theory
Alderfer's ERG Theory
Acquired Needs Theory
Herzberg's Two-Factor Theory
Need Theories at Work

WHAT DO PEOPLE EXPECT?
Expectancy Theory
Expectancy Theory at Work
Equity Theory
Equity Theory at Work

HOW DO PEOPLE REACT TO WHAT THEY GET?
Operant Conditioning
Organizational Behavior Modification
Operant Conditioning at Work

WHICH THEORY TO USE?

PARTICIPATIVE MANAGEMENT
Theory X
Theory Y
Quality of Work Life Projects
Quality Circles

Motivating the work force is one of the most crucial aspects of the directing function. Through staffing activities, managers fill the organization with competent employees, and through communication activities, they keep these employees informed and aware. But it is through motivational techniques, and a manager's ability to influence behavior, that the maximum efforts are obtained from these people. Only by understanding what people want from work, how they perceive their work situation, and how they respond to rewards will managers be able to harness the great potential of the organization's human resources.

KEY QUESTIONS

As you study this chapter, try to answer the following questions:

1 Why is understanding motivation important from a managerial perspective?
2 What are the three basic categories of motivational theory?
3 Describe Maslow's hierarchy of needs. What are its advantages and disadvantages?
4 What is Alderfer's ERG theory? What are its advantages and disadvantages?
5 How did Murray's acquired needs theory differ from later revisions by McClelland and Atkinson?
6 Describe Herzberg's two-factor theory. What are its advantages and disadvantages?
7 What are the managerial implications of need theories?
8 What is expectancy theory, and what are its managerial implications?
9 What is equity theory, and what are its managerial implications?
10 What are reinforcement theory and operant conditioning, and what are the managerial implications of these theories?
11 How is participative management a combination of the three categories of theories discussed in the chapter?
12 What are theory X and theory Y? What are their managerial implications?
13 What are quality-of-work life projects? How do they affect performance?

Focus Case

Why Do You Work?

People work for an infinite number of personal reasons. Managers must identify the principles that underlie individual choice and design jobs to accommodate individual motivations.

People have many reasons for working. Some may sound rational, other frivolous or misguided. In any case, managers must realize that the workers determine what motivates them. Managers must design the job, the work, and the rewards to fit the individual. The following quotes provide good examples of the broad spectrum of what motivates people at work.

> I own this cab. The medallion, which is the license to drive it, cost $21,000 when I bought it seven years ago. It is now worth $85,000. When I first got here from Russia, I worked for someone else. I lived in the cab. I mean really lived in it. I had no other home. I showered at the bus station, had all my clothes and shaving equipment in the trunk, and ate in the cab. I drove the cab 20 hours a day. After three years, I had enough money to buy my own cab and medallion. It is mine. Back in Russia my brother still owns nothing, and here I am a capitalist pig.
>
> Russian immigrant taxi driver,
> New York City

> Why do I work four days a week? Because I cannot make enough money to live by only working three days a week. It's the people here that make it bearable. My real love is painting, and I do not mean houses. I am a darn good artist and getting better slowly, but I do not have enough time to get really good. I had my first one-man show last week. Only problem is you cannot make enough money painting. So I put in my time and wait for the day when I can get out of here.
>
> Automobile assembly line worker

> I work here because this is a great job. The cars we make are the best in the world, and I am good at what I do. The pay is good, benefits excellent; I have seniority so I do not have to worry about being laid off. Sure the work is a little monotonous and dirty, but what job isn't? Here at least when you're done you can all get together and see what you have accomplished and be proud of it.
>
> Automobile assembly line worker

> Where else can you get paid for exercising? I run my route, always have. I finish about one o'clock and spend the rest of my time fixing up our house. We buy old houses, live in them a couple of years while we are fixing them, sell it and buy another old house. I really get a sense of achievement taking an old house and fixing it up. We have made enough money over the last 20 years that I don't need to work at the post office. I like the people on my route, I do it fast and get back to the house.
>
> Postman

> I wear fancy clothes, go to parties continually, eat exotic food, and generally am responsible for making sure everyone is having a good time. I get paid to party all of the time. I really enjoy the people. You could take all the clothes and food

Source: The quotations were taken from interviews conducted by the authors.

away, and I would still love this job, because of the people I get to work with. I would not change jobs for anything.

Professional events coordinator

I quit. No more responsibility, no more being in charge. Forget the suits, the tie, the constant pressure, the million dollars a year. Who needs it? The government just takes it all, anyway. Everyone here is money hungry. There has to be more to life than this. They throw any more money at me, and I will scream. I just bought a condominium in Colorado and plan to become a serious ski bum. Someone else can lead this crazy life. Split-second decisions, constant pressure, no control of your life, total subservience to the market.

Investment banker

Promotion? Why would I want a promotion and the money that goes with it? Increased headaches, increased responsibility, for what? I give them a good hard 40 hours a week, but when I am done, I forget about the job. Let management worry about it. This is the third time I have refused a promotion and if they ask again, there will be a fourth time. You'd think they would learn.

Wholesale grocery distributor, grocery store chain

Yeah, the work is OK, and the pay is OK. What I really enjoy is managing an auditing team. When I am in charge, we really fly.

Auditor, big eight accounting firm

Why study? I never have been able to do case analyses. I thought I had a shot at it at the beginning of the semester but no more. Besides, this teacher is crazy. I'm sure she grades by the weight method. You know, throw the papers down the stairs. The ones which go farthest are the heaviest so they get the best grades. ■

Student

People have different reasons for working and for performing well. Some people want money, some want recognition, and some just want to feel like part of a group. Consider the two automobile assembly line workers previously mentioned. The first views his job as a means of supporting himself until he can earn enough money with his painting. The second likes the pay and benefits and loves the cars.

Regardless of individuals' reasons for working, management must motivate each of them to perform. Understanding and influencing behavior are vital to successful management and organizational effectiveness. To motivate employees, a manager must, at various times, structure the work to satisfy employees' personal needs, identify those who are excited about doing the job and give them the opportunity to succeed, provide clear direction and even restrict what people can do, or give people the freedom to experiment.

UNDERSTANDING MOTIVATION

Most managers will agree that organizational objectives are best accomplished when workers with the proper skills apply their best efforts to the necessary tasks. But getting the employees to apply effort to organizational work often involves much more than hiring them, placing them in positions, and telling them their responsibilities. It hinges on managers' ability to motivate employees on the job.

There are many motivational theories, each based on different assumptions about human behavior. Some theorists argue that needs determine people's behavior; others argue that it is expectations or rewards. Combining all of these approaches can provide a simple yet comprehensive definition: **Motivation** is a desire and enthusiasm to act that results from processes internal (needs, expectations) and external (results, rewards) to an individual. For example, people may be enthusiastic to act because they are trying to satisfy an internal need, such as security or fulfillment, or because they expect their effort to lead to rewards they want. If the activity actually results in rewards, they will be satisfied and will be likely to engage in the same activity again.[1]

Motivation A desire and enthusiasm to act.

The Russian taxi driver needs food and shelter, and he expects that driving a taxi will provide him the money he needs to buy them. He has driven taxis so well and so long that he now owns his cab. His activities provided the rewards he sought. He will probably continue to drive a cab because it provides him with the rewards he wants.

Motivation theories focus on different aspects of this process:

1. *Need theories* argue that motivation derives from the efforts people exert to satisfy needs.
2. *Expectancy and equity theories* argue that motivation derives from what people expect to happen as a result of their actions and how fair they perceive these results to be.
3. *Reinforcement theories* hold that motivation and behavior derive from the consequences of action.

Before going into a detailed discussion of these three approaches, it is important to remember two things: First, performance depends not only on motivation but on ability. As we discussed in Chapter 11 on staffing, it is very important not only to place qualified people in appropriate positions but to train them to be competent at their work. Ability and motivation are both important in determining performance. Some even describe their relationship in an equation: performance = motivation $\times$ ability.

Second, motivation is an individual phenomenon. No two people are alike. As evidenced by the quotations at the beginning of the chapter people work for very different reasons, and they are motivated or unmotivated for very different reasons. Management's role is to create a work situation in which individuals with different needs, personalities, and expectations can remain motivated and satisfied while accomplishing the organization's objectives. Management's role is to create or increase motivation in their employees by integrating organizational and individual objectives.

WHAT DO PEOPLE WANT?

Need theories Theories that motivation derives from efforts people exert to satisfy needs.

One way to integrate organizational and individual objectives and to increase employee motivation is to try to understand people's needs and give them the opportunity to satisfy these needs through their work. **Need theories** assume motivation derives from efforts people exert to satisfy their needs. For example, the professional events coordinator wants to be with other people to satisfy a social need. The investment banker wants the slower pace of being a ski bum to satisfy a need for freedom. Each would respond differently to the same work situation. The first step, then, is understanding people's wants and needs. The most popular need theories assume that people have a variety of physiological or psychological needs and will be motivated to satisfy those that are the most important to them at a given time.

Maslow's Hierarchy of Needs Theory

The most widely known of the theories is Abraham Maslow's hierarchy of needs theory, which he developed in 1954.[2] It outlines five types of needs, arranged in a hierarchy. People are motivated to satisfy each need roughly in turn from the lowest to the highest. As each need is satisfied, it decreases in importance and the next highest need increases in importance. The process is continuous. Maslow's theory assumes that humans always want more, and what they want depends on what they already have. The five basic needs Maslow cites are:

1. *Physiological Needs*   These include needs for food, air, water, sex, rest, activity, and temperature regulation. From a managerial perspective, employees will want comfortable environments within which to work and enough money (income, wages) to support themselves and their families. If they do not find these in the job or workplace, they will not be motivated to work, but they will probably be motivated to find another workplace or to have the conditions changed.
2. *Safety Needs*   People also want security, stability, and freedom from fear or threat in their environment. At work, people feel the need for such things as steady employment, health insurance, and pensions. Given basic physical comforts, people will be motivated to seek security and stability.
3. *Social Needs*   Social needs include the need for friendship, love, affection, acceptance, and interpersonal interaction. Some employees have a strong need to be identified with or belong to a group or department. Given comfort and security, this will become the most important need to be satisfied.
4. *Esteem Needs*   Esteem needs include needs for achievement, recognition, self-esteem, and respect for oneself. These are needs for a favorable reputation and increased competence and knowledge. Some employees will strive to satisfy these needs through development of expertise on the job or through upward progress in a career, after more basic needs have been satisfied.
5. *Self-actualization Needs*   People have needs for self-fulfillment, for realization of their full potential, and for self-expression, accomplishment, and growth. Managers can allow some employees to satisfy these needs on the job by allowing them full responsibility and control over projects of great personal interest to them.

According to Maslow's theory, employees work to satisfy their most important needs. For example, Maslow would suggest that the first auto assembly line worker quoted is working in the car plant to satisfy his physiological and safety needs; that is, he works to earn income to support himself. He would like to paint, to satisfy an esteem or self-actualization need, but cannot because his basic need for financial security has not yet been satisfied and would, in fact, be jeopardized if he stopped working. According to Maslow's theory, he will work to satisfy his basic needs first and then move on to satisfying his social needs, his esteem needs, and eventually the self-actualization needs associated with his art work.

Managers can motivate employees by providing work-related opportunities for them to satisfy their needs. Exhibit 13.1 lists Maslow's categories of needs and

EXHIBIT / 13.1
Maslow's Needs Hierarchy

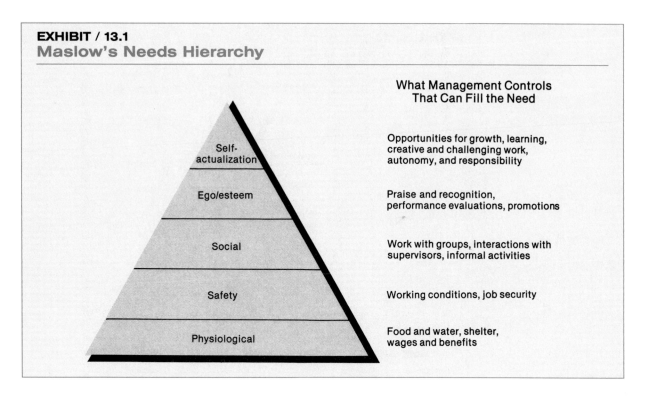

What Management Controls
That Can Fill the Need

Self-actualization — Opportunities for growth, learning, creative and challenging work, autonomy, and responsibility

Ego/esteem — Praise and recognition, performance evaluations, promotions

Social — Work with groups, interactions with supervisors, informal activities

Safety — Working conditions, job security

Physiological — Food and water, shelter, wages and benefits

identifies the variables managers can control to help employees satisfy them. According to this theory, if the manager can identify unsatisfied needs and provide an opportunity for individuals to satisfy them through their work, the employees' on-the-job performance will improve.

Although theorists and researchers tend to accept the ability of Maslow's theory to predict and explain human behavior in general terms, subsequent research in organizations has not supported the specifics of his theory.[3] Primarily, the concept of progression up a hierarchy has not been supported.[4] For example, there is no evidence that satisfying one need decreases its importance and leads to the increased importance of the next-higher-level need. It also does not appear to be true that a person deprived of two needs simultaneously will strive to satisfy the more basic of the two. Despite concerns about his methodology and the scope of application of his theory, however, scholars still generally consider Maslow's hierarchy of needs a valid conceptualization of human needs and behavior. The importance of Maslow's work is his identification of need categories to which managers can respond.

Alderfer's ERG Theory

Clayton P. Alderfer offers another motivational theory based on needs with his ERG theory (1972).[5] He simplifies Maslow's five needs into three: *existence, relatedness,* and *growth,* hence ERG theory (see Exhibit 13.2). His existence needs are analogous to Maslow's physiological and safety needs. Relatedness needs refer to social needs and some ego-esteem needs as Maslow defines them. Growth needs also refer to some ego-esteem needs, but correspond more directly with Maslow's self-actualization needs.

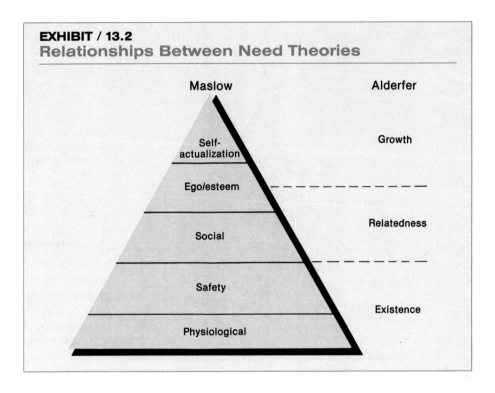

EXHIBIT / 13.2
Relationships Between Need Theories

Maslow

Alderfer

Growth

Self-actualization

Ego/esteem

Social

Relatedness

Safety

Existence

Physiological

The theory is quite similar to Maslow's, although it eliminates the hierarchy. Alderfer argues that two needs may be important simultaneously or that people move from one need to another when one is satisfied or because they are frustrated by attempting to satisfy one and have given up and moved on to another.[6] A person whose need for growth is frustrated, for example, may place increased importance on relatedness needs, at least for the time being. The auto assembly line worker interested in being an artist may focus more on social needs than he would if he were able to work full time developing his artistic talents. The professional events coordinator, on the other hand, works to satisfy two needs simultaneously: existence and relatedness. Moreover, if some physiological or safety need should suddenly be pressing, relatedness needs may be temporarily shelved until the more important need is satisfied. If the professional events coordinator suddenly found herself with no upcoming work, her main concern would probably not be enjoying herself at a party but rather just being hired for a party. ERG theory puts little emphasis on any succession up or down; rather it portrays need satisfaction on all levels as a more simultaneous process.

Maslow's hierarchy of needs and Alderfer's ERG theory share a common disadvantage. They are easy to explain but hard to use in the field to explain or influence behavior. In order to determine what will motivate an employee, a manager would have to assess each individual and isolate which of his or her needs was currently being satisfied or frustrated. It is doubtful that any manager could or would spend the time calculating all these factors for each employee in each situation. Maslow's hierarchy and Alderfer's ERG theory do, however, help managers understand and identify the many factors they can manage to meet their employees' needs.

Acquired Needs Theory

A third theory of motivation based on needs is Henry A. Murray's acquired needs theory, originally developed in 1938.[7] It has been refined and modified more recently by David C. McClelland and John W. Atkinson.[8] The theory holds that the will to perform, that is, the motivation to perform, is a function of the strengths of various *personality-need factors.* These factors may be active or inactive, and behavior is directed toward satisfying the more active ones. Because they are derived from experience, they are referred to as acquired needs. One of the strongest personality-need factors in the taxi driver is a need to achieve financial success and autonomy at work. He strives to achieve because it is the dominant part of his personality. The investment banker's dominant personality-need factor had at one time been the need to achieve position and wealth but is now the need for a slower pace and a simple life. These personality-need factors have apparently been dominant in the wholesale grocery distributor for some time, since he continually turns down promotions. The acquired needs theory operates on two premises: that people have a reservoir of potential energy and that basic, learned needs regulate and direct the flow of this energy.

Murray originally outlined over 20 different needs that, if activated or supported by environmental cues, influenced behavior. Unlike Maslow's, they are not hierarchical, but innate in each individual and are activated at random by an individual's interaction with the environment. Murray's original theory explained a wide range of behavior and specifically suggested why one action resulted as opposed to another. Such a large number of needs, however, made his theory too complex to use. One would have to measure the strength of over 20 needs to explain and predict what would motivate a person in a specific situation. For that reason, researchers McClelland and Atkinson later narrowed the field to three basic needs:

1. *Achievement*   People who place most importance on achievement set difficult goals for themselves, take moderate risks, look for feedback on their actions, and take responsibility for solving problems. A manager can motivate an achievement-oriented employee by linking pay to task because the reward is tangible, positive feedback on his or her performance.
2. *Affiliation*   People who consider affiliation and social contacts most important will seek personal reassurance from others, often conform to group norms, and show sincere interest in others. Where satisfaction of achievement needs leaves one with a feeling of accomplishment, satisfaction of affiliation needs leaves a feeling of warmth.
3. *Power*   Those who wish to have power will try to influence others in desired directions and to control not only the social but also the physical environment. Since they are motivated by being in positions of control or influence, managers may help them satisfy these needs by assigning them to positions that allow for a certain amount of autonomy.

McClelland claims that these three orientations are acquired over time through experience. Those who have been successful achievers will be oriented toward achievement and be motivated by achievement opportunities.[9] The postman is likely to continue buying and renovating houses, and the second automobile assembly line worker will probably continue to work hard making "the best

---

EXHIBIT / 13.3

Work Preferences of Persons High in Need for Achievement, Power, and Affiliation

Individual Need	Work Preferences	Example
High need for achievement	Individual responsibility; challenging but achievable goals; feedback on performance	Field salesperson with challenging quota and opportunity to earn individual bonus
High need for affiliation	Interpersonal relationships; opportunities to communicate	Customer service representative; member of work unit subject to group wage-bonus plan
High need for power	Control over other persons; attention; recognition	Formal position of supervisory responsibility; appointment as head of special task force or committee

Source: Schermerhorn, John R., Jr., Hunt, James G., and Osborn, Richard N., *Managing Organizational Behavior* (New York: Wiley, 1982), p. 113. Used by permission.

---

cars in the world." Those who have had good experiences working with others, such as the professional events coordinator, will be oriented toward affiliation and motivated by affiliation opportunities. Those who have had success at influencing others or in holding positions of leadership will be motivated by opportunities to have power or autonomy. The auditor will probably continue in management roles.

Understanding a person's acquired needs allows the manager to construct the most motivational work situation for that individual. Exhibit 13.3 gives examples of the work situations that persons oriented toward the three acquired needs will prefer and in which they will perform best.

Referring to these orientations as acquired needs has interesting implications: People can be taught to adopt the needs required to be successful in various types of jobs. To make a shift in the salience of a given personality-need factor, one starts by assessing his or her present acquired needs using a process referred to as imaging. Through imaging, a person is shown a picture and is asked to write a brief description of what is happening. Exhibit 13.4 shows a picture that is often used to measure acquired needs.

In one study, three managers each wrote a one-page story about the picture.[10] The first wrote about an engineer who was daydreaming about a family outing planned for the next day. He would be scored as low on need for achievement and high on need for affiliation. The second wrote about an engineer who picked up an idea for a new product from discussions with his family. He would be scored medium on both affiliation and achievement. The third discussed an engineer who was working on a bridge stress problem that he was sure he could solve. He would have scored low on affiliation needs and high on need for achievement. The achievement scores of each of the managers were:

Person daydreaming about family outing	Achievement = +1
Person thinking about new product	Achievement = +2
Person working on bridge stress problem	Achievement = +4

The procedures for scoring stories are formalized and well established. An extensive analysis of the personality implications of each story is given in *The Achieving Society* by David McClelland. You can write a story yourself about the picture to analyze the relative strengths of your personality need factors.

Keep in mind, however, that a high score on one dimension does not imply or mandate a low score on others. The three acquired needs combine in various levels to form a person's personality profile. Though most people tend to be strongly oriented toward only one of these needs categories, some may score high on all three. An individual's profile indicates the types of situations in which he or she will perform well and how he or she might respond to others. According to this theory, people will perform well in situations that allow them to satisfy their greatest personal needs.

McClelland further suggests that people who are not highly oriented to one of the needs, and thus perform poorly in a particular situation, can increase their acquired needs in that area through imaging. For instance, the first manager in our example, who scored low on need for achievement after writing the first story, could increase this need by deliberately writing stories that included specific goals, feedback, accomplishments, and responsibility. McClelland's argument is that the low need may derive from an inability to focus on or visualize goals and the path to achieving them. By writing about them, people can develop a need for achievement. With this developed need, the person should be able to perform better in achievement-oriented situations.

EXHIBIT / 13.4
Picture for Measuring Acquired Needs

Source: Reprinted with permission of the Tests and Scoring Division, McBer and Company, 137 Newbury Street, Boston, MA.

Herzberg's Two-Factor Theory

Another needs-oriented theory is Frederick Herzberg's two-factor, or motivation-hygiene, theory, developed in the late 1950s.[11] In essence, this theory takes all the various need types discussed by the others and divides them into two categories: motivation factors and hygiene factors.

Motivation factors
Factors that if present, produce satisfaction.

Hygiene factors Factors that, if present, prevent dissatisfaction but do not necessarily lead to satisfaction.

According to Herzberg, **motivation factors** are those factors that, if present, produce satisfaction. They include aspects of job content such as responsibility, achievement, advancement, increased competence, and recognition. Motivators correspond to Maslow's higher levels of need, namely esteem and self-actualization. **Hygiene factors,** when present, prevent dissatisfaction. They include aspects of job context or environment such as pay, policies, working conditions, job security, and relations with co-workers and supervisors. The presence of these does not lead to satisfaction; it just rules out dissatisfaction. Exhibit 13.5 compares Herzberg's hygiene and motivating factors to Maslow's and Alderfer's need lists.

As with all other theories, there are advantages and disadvantages to Herzberg's theory. One advantage is that it demonstrates that employees can be both satisfied and dissatisfied simultaneously. Second, it points out that traditional rewards, such as increased benefits and better working conditions, may not necessarily increase motivation. By Herzberg's definition, these may be hygiene factors, which simply prevent dissatisfaction. Finally, the theory indicates that hygiene and motivation factors must be incorporated into job design and built into the work situation.

There are also problems with the two-factor theory.[12] It is doubtful that the 200 accountants and engineers on whom Herzberg originally based his theory are representative of the national work force. Some question the validity of the re-

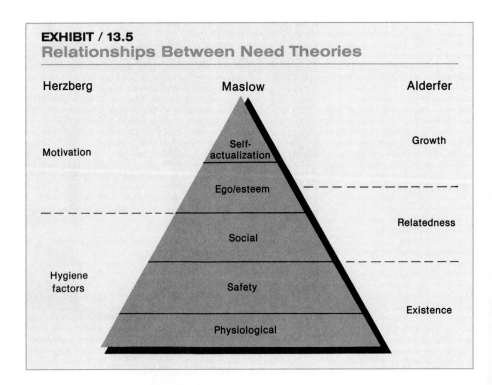

EXHIBIT / 13.5
Relationships Between Need Theories

Herzberg	Maslow	Alderfer
Motivation	Self-actualization	Growth
	Ego/esteem	
	Social	Relatedness
Hygiene factors	Safety	
	Physiological	Existence

sults and wonder how broadly they can be applied because of the small, specialized sample size. Second, research has not supported the assertion that hygiene factors can prevent dissatisfaction but cannot produce satisfaction. It has been demonstrated that supervision, achievement, and pay are directly associated with both satisfaction and dissatisfaction. Third, other theories have indicated that a lack of what Herzberg calls motivators, such as esteem, accomplishment, and achievement, can cause dissatisfaction. Finally, research has indicated that some people are not motivated to perform beyond a certain level; if their lower-level, physiological, or hygiene needs are adequately satisfied, they will not move on to higher needs, whether or not Herzberg's motivators are present.

Need Theories at Work

Need theories focus on individual differences in what people want and need from work. They argue that people will devote effort to satisfying unmet needs. Managers can motivate employees by giving them opportunities to meet their needs by performing on the job. When using need theories to motivate workers it is important to remember that:

1. *People have different wants and needs.* The auditor quoted at the beginning of the chapter wants power and control. The investment banker wants freedom and flexibility. The professional events coordinator wants to be with interesting people. A manager cannot treat them all the same. In fact, the responsibility that motivates the auditor drove the investment banker away. By understanding the individual wants and needs of employees, managers can more effectively give them opportunities to meet their needs.
2. *The worker, not the manager, decides what is satisfying.* The manager may be able to give or withhold rewards, but if the workers do not want them, the manager will have no influence over them. Managers can motivate workers by providing them with what they want, based on their performance.
3. *Employees' wants and needs change.* One need may be filled, or other needs may become more important. The wholesale grocer's children are young, but as they approach college age, his attitude toward a promotion, increased responsibility, and money may change. Managers must make an effort to be constantly in tune with the changing needs of their employees.

WHAT DO PEOPLE EXPECT?

Many theories of motivation focus on what people expect and perceive. **Expectancy theory** holds that motivation derives from what people expect to happen as a result of their efforts. **Equity theory** states that motivation derives from the equity people perceive to exist between their circumstances and comparable situations.

Expectancy Theory

Expectancy theory The theory that motivation derives from what people expect to happen as a result of their efforts.

Expectancy theory was originally formulated by Kurt Lewin but later refined and developed by Victor H. Vroom[13] and by Lyman W. Porter and Edward E. Lawler.[14] In its original form, the theory stated that motivation is equal to the product of *expectancy* and *valence.* That is,

$$M = E \times V$$

where

   M = motivation

   E = expectancy, perception, or prediction of the probability that a specific action will have a specific result

   V = the positive or negative value attached to the expected outcome

Because motivation is a product of expectancy and valence, if either is absent or zero, then motivation will also be absent. In the same sense, the higher the expectancy and/or valence, the higher the level of motivation.

Porter and Lawler developed the theory further to include the following points:

1. _There are two types of expectancy._ The first is concerned with whether effort put forth will result in some level of performance, or E → P expectancy. If a worker assumes that no amount of increased effort will be enough to complete a certain assigned task, then his motivation to begin working on it will be either very low or nonexistent. The second type of expectancy is concerned with whether the completed performance will result in a specific desired outcome, or P → O expectancy. If an employee is confident that the task is doable but feels she will not get credit or a reward for it, then her motivation to engage in it will again be very low.

For example, assume the student quoted at the beginning of the chapter is preparing for an exam early in the semester. The class is based on case analyses with which he has not had experience. He is, however, good at memorizing and understanding theories and assumes that this will enable him to perform well. He expects effort will lead to a high level of performance, that is, that he will be able to list and describe the theories accurately on the exam.

The student also expects his performance, the accurate lists and descriptions, to lead to a reward: an A on the exam. Because he expects to obtain a reward he values, he is motivated—he devotes considerable energy to studying and preparing for the exam. After the exam, he is confident he has done well. A week later when he gets the exam back he discovers that he has received a C+ grade. He reads over the exam carefully but cannot discover what he did wrong.

The student brings his exam to the professor to find out what he did wrong, and the following conversation takes place:

Student: I was wondering what I did wrong on my exam.
Teacher: Well, let's look at it. Interesting, but I wanted an analysis of the case, not a repetition of theories you had memorized.
Student: How did you grade the exams?
Teacher: Based on your ability to analyze cases.
Student: I thought you were going to grade the exams based on our understanding of the facts in the theories.
Teacher: No, you have to be able to use the theories to analyze the cases. That is a far different skill than the ability to memorize theories and explain them.
Student: What will the next exam be based on?
Teacher: The same. Your ability to analyze cases.
Student: I don't understand how you can grade cases. It seems awfully arbitrary.

The first time he prepared for the exam, he expected that his efforts would result in the desired grade. Now, however, he realizes that his ability to understand and remember theories is not what will be rewarded. Because he feels he does not have the ability to analyze cases—that is, he does not expect that efforts devoted to studying cases will enable him to analyze them—and because he thinks the teacher grades arbitrarily, he will be less motivated to exert effort in the future.

2.   *Rewards can be either intrinsic or extrinsic.* Intrinsic rewards are inherent in doing the work itself. They include the excitement that comes from doing the work, feelings of accomplishment and competence, and the satisfaction of growing and developing. Some students enjoy reading and writing for a class because they enjoy the material and the concepts they are learning. They are motivated because they find learning satisfying and rewarding in and of itself. Extrinsic rewards come from others and include such things as pay, promotions, and praise for performance. Students can receive both intrinsic and extrinsic rewards from their work. Grades are extrinsic rewards for academic performance. The feelings of advancing one's knowledge and accomplishing something academically are the intrinsic rewards controlled by the student.

3.   *Feelings of satisfaction or dissatisfaction depend on the value the individual attaches to the outcome received.*[15] For example, a student who attaches a negative value to a B grade will not be satisfied to receive one, even if the teacher or other students claim that a B is very good. Students who attach a very high value to a B grade will be excited and pleased to receive one. The Inside View 13.1 shows how some people motivate themselves by giving themselves rewards that they value.

4.   *Performance influences future behavior by altering the effort-to-performance and performance-to-outcome expectations.* After people try to accomplish a simple or difficult task and fail, their expectations that they will be able to accomplish a similar task on the second attempt may decrease. For example, the student thought that with enough effort he could perform well on the exam and would be rewarded for doing so. However, after exerting great effort he found that a different type of performance was expected in order to receive the highest grades. Next time, his expectation that effort (studying) will lead to the correct performance (case analysis), and that performance will be rewarded (with what he considers a good grade), will be lower.[16]

Another highly poignant example of this point was demonstrated by an American figure skater during the 1988 Winter Olympics. Before her final performance, which was to contain several difficult jumps, Debbie Thomas reportedly said, "If I can make the first one, I'll be okay." Unfortunately, she landed awkwardly on the first jump. This lowered her expectation that she could succeed on the rest of her jumps and give her best performance. She landed awkwardly on two more jumps and ultimately moved herself from first to third place in the competition.

Expectancy Theory at Work

Expectancy theory is a useful tool with implications for management practices. Its recommendations focus on creating realistic expectations. In organizations, training and modeling can be used to define what is meant by good performance and

THE INSIDE VIEW / 13.1

Carrots and Sticks

Film critic Roger Ebert believes that personal goals should be their own reward.

Freelance writer Jerry C. Hunter once wrote and asked some of America's most successful authors how they motivated themselves to write. Here are the replies:

> As a long-promised reward for finishing *Pilgrim at Tinker Creek,* I re-read *Moby Dick.* While I'm writing, I reward myself almost hourly by . . . *changing pens.* It is the smallest of pleasures. I'm sure it keeps advanced sensory deprivation at bay. After long days in which I have written much or well, I get into bed with a bowl of buttered popcorn and read French recipes. If other writers are half so tasteless, the arts shall indeed decline.
>
> Annie Dillard
> *Pilgrim at Tinker Creek*

Now, in my affluent dotage, I will sometimes reward a finished chapter or solved (seemingly) problem by an afternoon movie, replete with a Cadbury or Hershey very-much-overpriced chocolate bar. Aside from the prime condition of having earned the treat, the other conditions are: (1) that the movie be of the questionable kind my wife wouldn't have wanted to see anyway, and (2) that the candy be bought *in the movie.*

Seymour Epstein
Leah, Looking for Fred Schmidt

The only reward I look forward to is seeing the finished piece of writing in hand. And if I should find myself in a lazy spell, all I have to do to get active again is to remember how miserable life was for me when I was trying to get published.

Erskine Caldwell
Tobacco Road, God's Little Acre

My feeling is: if you need a reward to tempt yourself to reach a personal goal, the goal may not be worth reaching. A better approach is to set up your life so that personal goals are their own reward. If your life isn't organized that way, it might be well to reorganize it . . . with a higher caliber of goals. What you do instead of your real work is your real work.

Roger Ebert
film critic, *Chicago Sun Times*

It is not the thought of rewarding myself that drives me to write. As a matter of fact, when I finish a novel, I go into a shattering depression, an unbelievable funk, filled with panic and anxiety. The only way to beat the funk is to begin again. Whatever money or praise that comes from writing seems totally unreal to me. The money always seems like play money or found money, totally unrelated to the writing that brought it.

Harry Crews
The Gospel Singer, A Childhood

Whenever I have endured or accomplished some difficult task—such as watching television, going out socially, or sleeping—I always look forward to rewarding myself with the small pleasure of getting back to my typewriter and writing something. This enables me to store up enough strength to endure the next interruption. ■

Isaac Asimov
I Robot, Foundation

Source: Hunter, Jerry C., "Small Pleasures," *Writer's Digest* (June 1982): 30–32.

to show employees how good performance will be rewarded. Managers can motivate their employees by (1) convincing them that they have the ability to perform by structuring the job and providing training so they can perform well; (2) finding out what rewards workers value and convincing them that management does control these rewards; and (3) providing rewards based on performance.

Equity Theory

Equity theory The theory that motivation derives from the equity people perceive to exist between their circumstances and comparable situations.

A second theory dealing with expectations and perceptions is **equity theory,** developed by J. Stacy Adams.[17] This theory emphasizes that motivation levels are a function of perceived fairness and equity.[18] Adams holds that if people feel underrewarded or overrewarded for their work efforts, they will be dissatisfied and will be motivated to restore equity. Perceived inequity results when people feel that the rewards they receive for their efforts are unequal to the rewards other persons appear to have received for similar efforts. A comparison of inputs and outcomes may be made within one organization or between organizations. As Adams defines them, *inputs* include such things as intelligence, education, training, experience, effort, and seniority. *Outcomes* include pay, promotions, raises, praise, esteem of co-workers, and feelings of accomplishment. According to this theory, people who feel that their ratio of inputs to outcomes is less—or more—than that of others will be dissatisfied and will strive to restore equity (see Exhibit 13.6).

Adams's conclusions are based on extensive laboratory research. In one set of studies, an experimenter, posing as an employer, advertised for part-time interviewers for an attitude survey. The inequity was created by paying various subjects more or less than the publicized going rate and telling all subjects that their qualifications for the job were lower than others doing the same work.[19] In general, subjects who were overpaid increased their productivity as a way of bringing inputs and outcomes into balance and thus reducing their feelings of inequity. Those who were underpaid decreased their inputs; that is, they became less productive in order to achieve input-outcome balance.

Equity comparisons are especially likely to be made regarding money. Most people are concerned that they be paid fairly.[20] Interestingly, the definition of what is fair is determined by who makes the comparison. Most people will compare themselves first with others doing similar work within their organization and then with those doing similar work in other organizations. Consider the quotes in the beginning of the chapter. According to the theory, the postman's co-workers should not be concerned that he is very wealthy and receives far more money for fixing houses than they do for delivering mail. That is not a relevant comparison. They should only be concerned if his pay for delivering mail is not the same as their pay for delivering mail.

The less similar jobs are to each other, the less useful or meaningful an equity comparison between them will be. Sociology professors are usually not concerned that their salaries match those of engineering school professors, unless there are tremendous inequities. Because engineering professors are in demand, schools competing for them have to pay them an average of $5,000 to $10,000 a year more than they have to pay sociology professors. Sociology professors are first concerned that they be paid fairly in comparison to other sociology professors. They may be somewhat concerned that they be paid fairly in comparison with engineering school professors who are earning $10,000 more per year, and

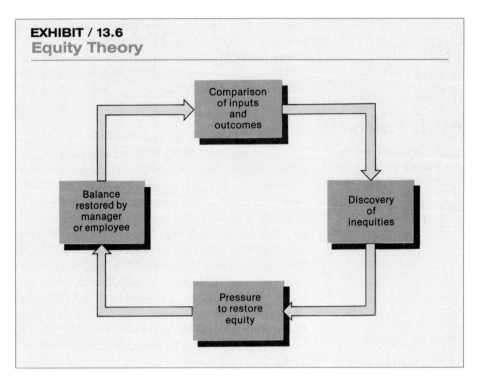

EXHIBIT / 13.6
Equity Theory

they should not be concerned about being paid less than professional basketball players. Professional athletes, however, are sometimes extremely concerned about pay equity. Consider the case of Eric Dickerson presented in The Inside View 13.2.

Equity Theory at Work

Equity theory points out the importance of the equitable distribution of rewards and compensation. People will make comparisons and be satisfied or dissatisfied based on how they feel they are being treated relative to others. Equity theory suggests that to motivate people managers should:

1. Recognize that employees will make comparisons. What each employee receives should be directly related to what he or she accomplishes. Managers should be able to explain or justify differences in rewards based on differences in accomplishments.
2. Always be aware of what others in the industry or field are receiving for work comparable to what their own employees are doing. General comparative salary statistics are published annually; therefore, managers can conduct salary surveys every year. A salary survey identifies the highest, lowest, and average salaries paid for various jobs in various industries. This provides managers useful information on which to base their salary decisions.

HOW DO PEOPLE REACT TO WHAT THEY GET?

The theories we have reviewed up to this point are cognitive theories; they focus on feelings, attitudes, perceptions, and expectations. Reinforcement theories are behavioral theories; they focus on actions, behavior, and tangible responses.

The Rams Got Me Cheap

Even though he was making over $500,000 a year, Eric Dickerson felt he was underpaid compared to what other football players in his class were making.

"I'd settle on a million [for each of his last two years]. I don't like saying this because I like it here, I'm treated right, and I love playing for [coach] John Robinson. But the Rams got me cheap, and everybody knows it."

In early July 1985, Eric Dickerson, the record-setting Los Angeles Rams running back, expressed discontent with his present four-year, $2.2 million contract. On July 29, 1985, the eve of the training camp for the 1985–1986 season, Dickerson announced that he would be a holdout. At a cost of $1000 per day, Dickerson sat at home in Sealy, Texas, while in Los Angeles, his agent, Jack Rodri, pleaded his case.

By the end of his first National Football League season, Eric Dickerson broke the rookie rushing record. In his second year, Dickerson broke O. J. Simpson's long-held single-season rushing record. For these reasons, Dickerson felt that he should receive at least as much as Marcus Allen, the former league rushing leader, received for his service with the Los Angeles Raiders. And until he did, Eric Dickerson was content to bide his time rather than play for only $350,000 per year (for 1985).

In addition, Dickerson was holding out for a contract guarantee that would insure him against career-ending injuries. Since other big-name players have them, he felt he deserved one also. In most cases, these policies provide an annuity that lasts until retirement.

Meanwhile, in Los Angeles, his Rams teammates were not taking the situation well. Left tackle Bill Bairn had this to say on the situation: "He should have done it differently. Everyone's upset at him, the way he listed his priorities." However, at Rams headquarters, hope remained high that a settlement could be reached as they worked to bridge the gap between Dickerson's notion of what he is now worth and what they can afford to pay him. ■

Sources: This article was written by F. Andrade, based on the following sources: "Is Dickerson the Best Ever?" *Sporting News,* November 26, 1984, p. 33; "Mr. Smooth Rushes into the Record Books," *Sports Illustrated,* September 4, 1985, pp. 150+; "Rams Boss Admits There's Little for Eric to Learn," *Jet,* October 7, 1985, p. 5; "Rams Dickerson Awards Team for Record Assists," *Jet,* April 29, 1985, p. 50; "Rams No. 29 Is Human Too," *Sporting News,* October 14, 1985, p. 38.

Reinforcement theory
The theory that motivation and behavior derive from the consequences of action.

Reinforcement theories hold that motivation and behavior derive from the consequences of action. For example, cognitive theorists studying an employee who is consistently late for work would look at the employee's attitude toward work, unmet needs, and satisfaction with the work in general. Behavioral theorists would focus on the rewards and punishments the employee receives by coming to work. Instead of assuming that a thought process determines behavior, reinforcement theorists assume that behavior is determined by the consequences— rewards or punishments—of previous actions. Psychologists refer to this as the law of effect. The **law of effect** states that behavior that results in pleasant outcomes is likely to be repeated; behavior that results in unpleasant outcomes is not likely to be repeated. The organizational implication of the law of effect is that managers can influence behavior by controlling rewards. Psychologist B. F. Skinner referred to this as operant conditioning.

Law of effect   The principle that behavior that results in pleasant outcomes is likely to be repeated.

Operant Conditioning

Operant conditioning
The process of controlling behavior by manipulating its consequences.

B. F. Skinner popularized the term **operant conditioning** to refer to the process of controlling behavior by manipulating its consequences.[21] As an example of operant conditioning, consider the employee who is asked to come in early to work on an important project. The employee will be motivated to come or not based on whether coming to work early in the past has been rewarding. If in the past he or she has accomplished the task successfully and received praise and a merit increase for coming in early, the employee will be highly motivated to come in early again. On the other hand, if in the past coming in early has meant having no supplies, being unable to reach people by phone, or getting little accomplished, the employee will not be motivated to come in early.

Organizational Behavior Modification

Organizational behavior modification is the application of operant conditioning to human behavior in work settings.[22] Managers can try to influence behavior by controlling rewards and punishments. Four basic behavior modification strategies have been proposed as means for influencing behavior: positive reinforcement, avoidance, punishment, and extinction (see Exhibit 13.7).

1.   *Positive reinforcement exists where a reward or consequence is given in return for some action desired by the manager.*   Positive reinforcement may take the form of bonuses for higher productivity, publicity for successful research, or a promotion for exceptional handling of a specific deal or project. A reward may be anything the employee values.

2.   *Avoidance or negative reinforcement occurs when one eliminates undesirable consequences when appropriate behavior is displayed.*   For example, if workers know that the supervisor reprimands and criticizes those who come in late, they are likely to avoid reprimands by showing up on time.

3.   *Punishment is the providing of a negative consequence in response to an undesirable behavior with the intent of stopping or decreasing that behavior.*   For example, a person may be demoted or lose privileges for stealing supplies. By providing consequences that are known to be

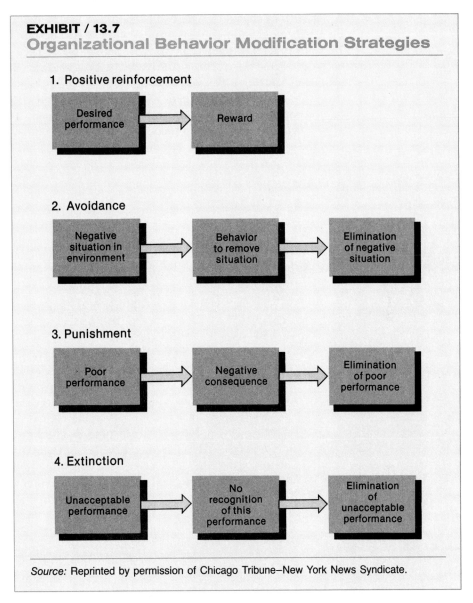

EXHIBIT / 13.7
Organizational Behavior Modification Strategies

1. Positive reinforcement

Desired performance → Reward

2. Avoidance

Negative situation in environment → Behavior to remove situation → Elimination of negative situation

3. Punishment

Poor performance → Negative consequence → Elimination of poor performance

4. Extinction

Unacceptable performance → No recognition of this performance → Elimination of unacceptable performance

Source: Reprinted by permission of Chicago Tribune–New York News Syndicate.

unpleasant to the employee, the manager hopes to prevent the employee from continuing to perform poorly. If the employee's performance improves, the punishment can be removed.

4. ***Extinction is the elimination of an undesirable behavior by a lack of response to it.*** A person might make outrageous comments or ridiculous recommendations in a group, looking for social approval. If the group does not respond either positively or negatively, the undesirable behavior, the comments, will eventually cease.

Operant Conditioning at Work

Operant conditioning is a controversial theory. Those in favor argue that management is responsible for affecting what employees do. Managers with this view think they should reward and punish based on results, and they will readily provide examples of where this approach has worked. Those opposed argue that operant conditioning is manipulation. They question the moral validity of manipulating employees to perform in certain ways. They cite Machiavelli's advice to the Prince (see The Inside View 13.3) as an example of the type of managerial behavior to which manipulation can lead.

Whether they agree or disagree with operant conditioning, managers are responsible for motivating employees to perform effectively. Managers must make sure rewards are given based on performance, not on factors unrelated to perfor-

THE INSIDE VIEW / 13.3

Advice to a Prince

Niccolo Machiavelli (1469–1527) lived in a period of severe political uncertainty, in which leaders ("princes") exercised immense personal power. His advice to them was to inspire fear rather than love in order to motivate people to be loyal.

Upon this a question arises: whether it be better to be loved than feared or feared than loved? It may be answered that one should wish to be both, but, because it is difficult to unite them in one person, it is much safer to be feared than loved, when, of the two, either must be dispensed. Because this is to be asserted in general of men, that they are ungrateful, fickle, false, cowardly, covetous, and as long as you succeed, they are yours entirely; they will offer you their blood, property, life, and children, as is said above, when the need is far distant; but when it approaches, they turn against you. And that prince who, relying entirely on their promises, has neglected other precautions, is ruined; because friendships that are obtained by payments, and not by greatness or nobility of mind, may indeed be earned, but they are not secured, and in time of need cannot be relied upon; and men have less scruple in offending one who is beloved than one who is feared, for love is preserved by the link of obligation which, owing to the baseness of men, is broken at every opportunity for their advantage; but fear preserves you by a dread of punishment which never fails.

Nevertheless, a prince ought to inspire fear in such a way that, if he does not win love, he avoids hatred; because he can endure very well being feared whilst he is not hated, which will always be as long as he abstains from the property of his citizens and subjects and from their women. But when it is necessary for him to proceed against the life of someone, he must do it on proper justification and for manifest cause, but above all things he must keep his hands off the property of others, because men more quickly forget the death of their father than the loss of their patrimony. ■

Source: Machiavelli, Niccolo, *The Prince,* trans. W. K. Marriot (London: D. M. Dent and Sons, 1958), 1974 ed., pp. 92–93.

mance. Exhibit 13.8 gives examples of how behavior modification programs have been used in organizations. Based on operant conditioning, we can suggest the following rules for management:[23]

> ***Rule 1***   Failure to respond has reinforcing consequences. Extinction, or lack of response, affects behavior by not reinforcing it. It can be very powerful, especially when combined with positive reinforcement. The behavior that is not

EXHIBIT / 13.8
Behavior Modification Programs

Organization	Participants	Program Goals	Reinforcers Use	Results
Michigan Bell Operator Services	2000 of 5500 employees at all levels in services	a. Decrease turnover and absenteeism b. Increase productivity c. Improve union-management relations	a. Praise and recognition b. Opportunity to see oneself become better	a. Attendance performance improved by 50% b. Productivity and efficiency has continued to be above standard
Michigan Bell Maintenance Services	220 of 5500	Improve: a. Productivity b. Quality c. Safety d. Customer-employee relations	a. Self-feedback b. Supervisory feedback	a. Cost efficiency increased b. Safety improved c. Service improved d. No change in absenteeism e. Satisfaction with superior and co-workers improved f. Satisfaction with pay increased
B. F. Goodrich Chemical Co.	100 of 420	a. Develop better meeting schedules b. Increase productivity	a. Praise and recognition b. Freedom to choose one's own activity	Production increased over 300%
General Electric	1000 employees at all levels	a. Meet EEO objectives b. Decrease absenteeism and turnover c. Improve training d. Increase productivity	Social reinforcers (praise, rewards, and constructive feedback)	a. Cost savings can be directly attributed to the program b. Productivity has increased c. Worked extremely well in training minorities and raising their self-esteem d. Direct labor cost decreased

Source: Reprinted by permission of the publisher from Hammer, W. C., and Hammer, E. R., "Behavior Modification on the Bottom Line," *Organizational Dynamics* 4 (Spring 1976): 12–14.

appropriate is ignored, so it decreases, while another desired behavior is positively reinforced. Managers must be careful to monitor the results of their inaction as well as their action.

Rule 2   Employees must understand what management will be reinforcing. Reinforcement theory assumes that people do what they are rewarded for doing. By specifying what will be rewarded, managers can increase the likelihood that employees will respond properly. Without this information, employees are forced to search for the contingency on their own; this often takes time and yields inaccurate conclusions.

Rule 3   Managers must tell the employees what they are doing wrong. When people fail, they want to understand why so that they can determine how to succeed next time.

Rule 4   Managers must not punish employees in front of others. Whenever rewards or punishment are given in front of others, the effect is doubled: The person is positively or negatively reinforced not only by the supervisor, but by the observers. An employee who is praised publicly may be much more positively motivated, but an employee who is punished publicly may be too upset to think about why his or her performance fell short. Public reprimands rarely yield constructive, positive, or instructional results.

WHICH THEORY TO USE?

Despite their various shortcomings, motivation theories can be useful to managers. While no theory is entirely applicable in every situation, an understanding of the mechanics of each, and of human behavior, will always be beneficial. A manager's method or strategy will vary depending on whether the problem seems to stem from individual needs, expectations, perceived inequities, rewards, or a combination of these factors.

In addition to considering the nature of the problem, managers must consider what they can actually control in order to determine which theory to use. Rewards may be at the heart of the problem, but many managers do not control rewards such as raises or promotions; in these cases, the managers will have to rely on other methods of motivating employees, such as offering more autonomy or more support, depending on the employee's needs.

In sum, then, managers should use the theory or combination of theories that best suits the situation and that focuses on the aspects of the situation that they can control.

PARTICIPATIVE MANAGEMENT

Participative management   The involvement of all organizational members in the management decision-making process.

An approach to management that combines need, expectancy, and reinforcement theories is **participative management**.[24] Participative management is the involvement of organizational members in the management decision-making process. It is built on the assumption that most people have a need to take part in decisions that affect them at work. By taking part and gaining an understanding of the situation, their perceptions and expectations will be more accurate. Ultimately, they will be more likely to receive rewards that they value.

The foundation of participative management was laid by Douglas McGregor.[25] He outlined two extreme positions on human nature that managers might take, and asserted that these attitudes direct management strategies and affect employee behavior in positive or negative directions.

Theory X

Theory X The assumption that people inherently dislike work and must be coerced and directed at work.

Theory X is the set of assumptions regarding human nature at the negative extreme. Managers espousing this set of assumptions feel that:

1. The average person has an inherent dislike of work and will avoid it if possible.
2. Because of this human characteristic, managers must coerce, control, direct, or threaten most people to get them to put forth adequate effort.
3. The average person prefers to be directed, wishes to avoid responsibility, has little ambition, and wants security above all.

As McGregor points out, these attitudes may have originated during and after the Industrial Revolution. The restrictive, demanding, depersonalized production systems often left workers feeling resentful and unmotivated. Management therefore assumed that, in general, workers were unmotivated, rebellious, and in need of tight controls. McGregor's warning is to "watch out for self-fulfilling prophecies": Management created the conditions that caused employees to fit theory X descriptions, and by assuming that employees were lazy, unmotivated, and in need of strict control, managers reinforced the conditions that made the employees that way in the first place. Even today, managers who think workers are lazy and irresponsible may lose or frustrate valuable employees.

Theory Y

Theory Y The assumption that people inherently like to work, like to accept responsibility, and are creative.

Theory Y represents the opposite extreme in terms of assumptions about human nature. A person who believes in the assumptions of theory Y feels that:

1. The average person does not inherently dislike work. The expenditure of physical and mental effort is as natural as play or rest. Depending on controllable conditions, work may be a source of satisfaction (and will be voluntarily performed) or a source of punishment (and will be avoided if possible).
2. External control and the threat of punishment are not the only means for bringing about effort toward organizational objectives. People will exercise self-direction and self-control in the service of objectives to which they are committed.
3. Commitment to objectives is a result of the rewards associated with their achievement. The most significant of such rewards—for example, the satisfaction of ego and self-actualization needs—can be the direct products of people's efforts.
4. The average person learns, under proper conditions, not only to accept but to seek responsibility. Avoidance of responsibility, lack of ambition, and emphasis on security are generally consequences of experience, not inherent human characteristics.
5. The capacity to exercise a relatively high degree of imagination, ingenuity, and creativity in the solution of organizational problems is widely, not narrowly, distributed in the population.

Based on this belief system, participative management can be practiced. McGregor feels that managers should strive to espouse theory Y beliefs for the same reason that they should not espouse theory X beliefs: If believing the assumptions of theory X leads to theory X behavior in employees, believing the assumptions of theory Y may lead to theory Y behavior in employees.

Research supports McGregor's findings, with some reservations and modifications. To an extent, and in varying situations, both theory X and theory Y have been found applicable and useful. Theory X seems most valid when applied to jobs where outputs are measured very objectively. Such jobs generally offer little intrinsic satisfaction and are held by people who tend to satisfy their higher-level needs off the job. The postman and the would-be painter, for example, satisfy their higher-level needs off the job rather than on it. The people on these jobs tend to need more direction, guidance, and predictability on the job than others.

Theory Y tends to be most successful when applied to situations where outputs are more difficult to measure and where jobs tend to offer much greater intrinsic rewards. The people holding these types of jobs try to satisfy some of their higher-level needs for growth and accomplishment while at work; therefore, theory Y assumptions are applicable to them. The auditor and the second assembly line worker try to satisfy their higher-level needs on the job. Theory X and theory Y may be successfully employed simultaneously in different departments within the same company.

The general assumptions of theory Y and participative management are that employees want to share in making decisions that affect them. They gain a clearer understanding of the situation, become more committed to successfully implementing the decisions that are made, and gain a feeling of satisfaction from being responsible for things going well.

Marshall Sashkin argues that participation in decision making fulfills three basic human work needs: the need for autonomy or control over one's behavior, the need for completion or achievement of a whole task, and the need for interpersonal contact.[26] Failure to fulfill these needs can have serious negative consequences. After reviewing much of the research, Edwin A. Locke comes to the conclusion that participation does not necessarily lead to higher performance but might have an impact on motivation through two mechanisms.[27] It can lead to the setting of higher goals and to greater acceptance and commitment to accomplishing the goal. Both are reasons many managers are enlisting employees in decision making. Many of the attempts to include workers are introduced into organizations under the name of quality of work life projects.

Quality of Work Life Projects

Quality of work life (QWL) project An approach to improving the motivation and productivity of workers.

Quality of work life (QWL) project is the general name given to many approaches to improving the motivation and productivity of workers.[28] Those who advocate such projects argue that when employees become more responsible for managing themselves and their jobs are expanded to include more responsibilities, they will be more motivated and productive. Exhibit 13.9 presents a list and brief description of eight quality of work life projects. The list illustrates the diversity of approaches used. Each was designed to meet the unique needs of a specific group of employees and the organizations in which they worked. No matter what approach was adopted:[29]

1. The current levels of productivity and the needs of employees were analyzed.

2. Employees helped identify productivity problems and design the programs to solve them.

3. It was determined what programs or combinations of programs would increase productivity by improving the quality of work life.

4. The programs were implemented with the aid of employees.

5. Results were evaluated and adjustments made.

Quality Circles

Quality circles Problem-solving groups in which workers and their supervisors meet to identify, analyze, and solve productivity problems.

One type of quality of work life program that deserves special mention because of its growing popularity is the quality circle. A **quality circle** is a problem-solving group in which workers and their supervisors meet to identify, analyze, and solve productivity problems. When they develop solutions, they become responsible for implementing them.[30] The Inside View 13.4 describes the quality circle process and some of the problems and payoffs of using this approach. The key factor is that work groups identify and solve problems in areas of their own responsibility. To do so, they usually learn some statistical and problem-solving techniques for tackling productivity problems.

EXHIBIT / 13.9
Productivity Effects of Quality of Work Life Projects

Type of Organization	Was Productivity Data Analyzed?	Some Productivity-related Changes Attempted in Project	Productivity Outcomes
1. Coal mine	Yes	Autonomous work groups job training; supervisor training; pay changes; intershift communication	Slight but statistically nonsignificant increase
2. Auto parts factory	Yes	Time-off bonus incentives; training; union-management cost reduction to retain business; safety program; plant newsletter	Significant positive increase
3. Wood products plants	No	Survey feedback and other communication activities	(No data available, but probably no change)
4. Bakery	Yes	Survey feedback; newsletter; new equipment; job training; interdepartmental coordination	No significant change
5. Federal utility company (engineering division)	No	Merit pay; performance appraisal; four-day workweek; survey feedback; other communication activities	?
6. Hospital	No	Survey feedback; staff meetings and training; management development; attempts to increase interdepartmental coordination	?
7. Municipal transit system	No	Survey feedback; management development; work team system; communication efforts	?
8. Municipal government	No	Better equipment; increased communication	?

Source: Lawler, Edward E., III, and Ledford, Gerald E., Jr., "Productivity and the Quality of Work Life," *National Productivity Review* (Winter 1981–1982): 34.

THE INSIDE VIEW / 13.4

Using Groups to Improve Quality

Quality circles allow workers to take part in identifying and solving problems, which often leads to better-quality products.

Quality circles are groups of workers who meet regularly to discuss work problems (particularly in product quality), to determine causes of those problems, to recommend solutions, and to take appropriate actions. Quality circles originated in the United States, but Japanese industry is largely responsible for their development and popularity.

American industry, impressed by the excellence of many Japanese products, has adopted the quality circle concept to improve worker commitment to quality and to take advantage of worker expertise in solving problems related to work. Recently, their use has expanded to service organizations, hospitals, accounting, engineering, and other nonindustrial firms in both this country and Japan.

Although the process varies from company to company, a typical quality circle is a voluntary group of people who work in the same work area or who do similar work. The size of groups may vary from 3 to 15 or more, but 7 or 8 is considered ideal for maintaining cohesiveness and enabling each member to contribute. A supervisor usually leads the group, which meets for an hour or so once a week to discuss problems. Problems may be identified by the group as a whole or by a single member, the supervisor, management, or staff personnel, such as quality control experts.

Groups usually decide which problems to work on and often call for outside assistance when problems exceed their expertise. If the solution is something they can implement themselves, they do so. If the solution requires resources or changes that must be approved by management, the group makes a formal presentation to solicit its approval and support.

Honeywell assigned the problem of reducing the cost of an electronics product in order to win a government contract that was being sought by several highly competitive firms. The quality circle suggested a way to automate a manufacturing process that improved costs by 20 percent and enabled Honeywell to win the contract. Lockheed credited nearly $3 million in savings to 15 circles in their first two years of operation. In one situation, a quality circle helped reduce rejects from 25 per thousand products to 6 per thousand. Other documented success stories include bank employees who cut the time in half for processing commercial customer's accounts and insurance company employees who cut absenteeism in half. ■

Source: Dewar, D. L., *The Quality Circle Guide to Participation Management* (Englewood Cliffs, N.J.: Prentice Hall, 1980); Yager, E. G., "The Quality Control Circle Explosion," *Training and Development Journal* 35(4) (April 1981): 98–105.

KEY POINTS

1 Understanding and influencing behavior are vital to successful management and organizational effectiveness. Only by understanding what people want from work, what they expect from it, and how they respond to its rewards or outcomes can managers harness their potential.

2 Three types of motivation theory focus on different causes of behavior: Need theories state that needs are motivators; expectancy and equity theories state that people will be motivated (or demotivated) by what they expect to result from their efforts, and how fair they perceive the rewards for their efforts to be, and reinforcement theories suggest that actual results of actions are motivators of behavior.

3 Maslow outlines five categories of needs that he claims people will be motivated to satisfy in hierarchical order from the lowest to the highest: physiological safety, social, esteem, and self-actualization needs. His theory is a valuable tool for understanding and studying motivation, though it is difficult to put into actual practice.

4 Alderfer simplified Maslow's five needs into three: existence, relatedness, and growth. He claims that the needs are not satisfied in hierarchical order. Though simpler and more flexible than Maslow's theory, ERG theory is also difficult to practice in the field.

5 Murray originally developed a list of over 20 personality-need factors that motivate an individual when activated or supported by environmental cues. McClelland and Atkinson simplified this list to three acquired needs: achievement, affiliation, and power, each of which motivates those who succeed in fulfilling it. They claimed these needs can be learned, developed, or strengthened.

6 Herzberg divided all the earlier types of needs into two categories: motivational factors, which, when present, produce satisfaction but do not dissatisfy when absent; and hygiene factors, which, when present, prevent dissatisfaction but do not satisfy. Though his theory recognizes that a person can simultaneously experience satisfaction and dissatisfaction, more recent research questions the validity and applicability of study.

7 In order for managers to motivate their employees based on need theories, they must keep in mind that (1) each employee is different and will have different needs; (2) the employees decide what is valuable to them; (3) needs change continually.

8 Expectancy theory states that people are motivated when they expect that their effort will result in correct performance and that their performance will be rewarded with something they value. To motivate based on this theory, managers should help employees understand their abilities, explain what is meant by correct performance, and provide rewards the employees value based on this performance.

9 Equity theory holds that people will be motivated to restore equity if they are either underrewarded or overrewarded. To motivate based on this theory, managers should recognize that employees will compare their inputs and outcomes to those of others and should reward fairly based on industry and company standards.

10 Reinforcement theory holds that behavior is influenced by its consequences, specifically that behavior resulting in pleasant outcomes will probably be repeated and behavior resulting in negative outcomes probably will not be repeated. Operant conditioning is the process of controlling behavior by manipulating its consequences. To motivate workers using reinforcement theory, managers should clearly define good performance, find rewards that the employee values, and reward the employee based on performance.

11 Participative management combines all of these approaches. It suggests that employees need to be involved in decisions regarding their work situations. This involvement gives employees more realistic expectations about correct performance and its rewards and therefore increases their chances of receiving rewards they value based on their performance.

12 McGregor's theory X and theory Y were the foundation of participative management theory. Theory X outlines a list of highly negative assumptions about human nature and employee work attitudes; theory Y outlines an extremely positive list. Since McGregor considers these assumptions, when held by managers, self-fulfilling, he recommends managers espouse theory Y. By doing so, they can make participative management effective.

13 Quality of work life projects and quality circles are participative management techniques designed to increase employee involvement, motivation, and productivity.

FOR DISCUSSION AND REVIEW

1. What motivates the various people quoted at the beginning of the chapter? How are they different? How are they similar?

2. According to Maslow's hierarchy, at what point is the investment banker? What needs has he satis-fied, and what needs is he trying to satisfy? What about the student?

3. Using Alderfer's categories of growth, relatedness, and existence, classify Maslow's five different categories of needs. Can you identify some needs that

are not specifically covered by these theories?

4. According to equity theory people will seek balance in a situation. Does this theory apply to the student quoted in the beginning? What would the student say if he were working in a shoe factory as a shoe assembler rather than being a student?

5. Reviewing the four theories of behavior modification, discuss a solution to the problem of a warehouse clerk who continually shows up late, and misses work. With which theory would you approach the problem? Why?

6. Many people criticize the study of motivation and behavior modification as being manipulation. In what kinds of cases might it be manipulation, and in what kinds of cases would it not be manipulation?

■ KEY TERMS

Equity theory

Expectancy theory

Hygiene factors

Law of effect

Motivation

Motivation factors

Need theories

Operant conditioning

Participative management

Quality circles

Quality of work life
  (QWL) project

Reinforcement theory

Theory X

Theory Y

THE CONFERENCE TABLE: DISCUSSION CASE / 13.1

Long Hours + Bad Pay = Great Ads

Jay Chiat of the Chiat/ Day advertising agency. Chiat's dedication to quality challenges his employees and motivates them to excel.

"If you don't come in Saturday, don't bother coming in Sunday," it is said at Chiat/Day. This highly successful bi-coastal (Los Angeles and New York) advertising agency is "an unabashed sweatshop" in which employees have been wearing "Chiat/Day & Night" T-shirts. And then there's the pay. Co-founder Jay Chiat does not hesitate to tell applicants that they could find better salaries elsewhere. In fact, if they went elsewhere they could also expect to have their own office, with a door, a secretary to answer their phone, and a nice view from a top floor in a fancy high-rise. None of these can be expected at Chiat/Day.

Source: "Long Hours + Bad Pay = Great Ads," *Fortune,* July 23, 1984, pp. 77–79.

Nevertheless, some people have gone to remarkable lengths to land jobs with the 17-year-old company. Creative director Lee Clow, who has been with Chiat/Day for almost 15 years, was perhaps the most determined job seeker the company has seen. Referring to his ill-behaved beard and hair, he waged an ad campaign to sell himself to them. His slogan was "Hire the Hairy"; he sent the agency executives posters, buttons, bumper stickers, and even a look-alike jack-in-the-box from which a hairy little figure popped. After nearly a year, he finally made them an offer they could not refuse: If they agreed to hire him for a year, he would work free for three months. If they hired him for a month, he would give them a free lighter. They hired him.

Though not all employees were quite that industrious or determined to work for the agency, those who do usually give it their all. People who last more than a few months tend to stay put for the long term. There is a great feeling of kinship among the employees resulting from their respect for Jay Chiat, their fervent reverence for their work, and the extensive amount of time they all spend in the office.

Much of his employees' motivation can be attributed directly to Chiat himself. An "uncommonly funny and intelligent man," he is respected by his staff for his toughness. Obsessed with the quality of the output, he says, "We're building an elitist organization. It has nothing to do with fairness, only with people culturally dedicated to doing the best work." To guarantee this level of quality, he covers all the bases. Each account is assigned a research and strategy specialist with direct responsibility for the advertising's effectiveness. Unlike the traditional staff-function research departments, this system isolates the source of failure or the source of success. The research specialist will fight to do his or her best "because if the ads don't work, [he's] in trouble."

Chiat also defends his choice of office locations. Neither the Los Angeles nor the New York office is located in the prime areas of town (Wilshire Boulevard and Madison Avenue, respectively). Chiat feels that spending more money on salaries than on rent produces better ads and also thinks the locations keeps his employees in touch with the real world. "It's hard to shop for a $200 pair of shoes on your lunch hour," he says (referring to the posh shopping available on Wilshire and Madison), "and then write good beer copy in the afternoon."

Whatever his strategies and whatever the source of his employees' motivation, it is all paying off. Though Chiat/Day is still a small agency, at ceremony after ceremony it picks up more awards and honors than agencies ten times its size. The agency's ads challenge convention, break rules, and most importantly, sell products. Perhaps its most celebrated ad was for Apple Computer's MacIntosh. The 60-second epic "1984" was aired only once on network television during the 1984 Super Bowl. The cost of the spot was $800,000, but the ad was responsible for millions of dollars in sales when the computer was released. Some praised it and some criticized it, but it provoked more discussion in advertising circles than any ad in years.

Having recently picked up such conservative clients as General Electric and the Wall Street securities firm of Drexel Burnham Lambert, and maintaining the accounts of Apple, Nike, and Yamaha, Chiat/Day's billings (essentially, sales of advertising) have risen an average of 50 percent a year since 1978. Aware that becoming successful and "comfortable" is sometimes hazardous to creativity, Chiat's management made itself a promise. "They insist that the moment the agency can't give its smallest client the same creative energy it gives its biggest, it will voluntarily cease to grow." ■

DISCUSSION
QUESTIONS
1. Does Jay Chiat use any of the concepts of need theory to motivate his employees? If so, which ones, and how effective is his utilization (or nonutilization) of them?
2. How does Chiat clarify or fail to clarify for his employees what they can expect? Does this seem to have a positive, negative, or neutral effect on his employees and/or the company's success?
3. What would Chiat have to say about operant conditioning? About theory X and theory Y? Participative management?

THE CONFERENCE TABLE: DISCUSSION CASE / 13.2

Luck and Hate as Motivators

John E. Murray's military career illustrates three major motivational incidents.

John E. Murray, vice president of the Association of American Railroads, gave a speech to the Command Junior Officer Council in Washington, D.C., in June 1982. Discussing his 20-year career in the army, he told how he was motivated

Source: Murray, John E., "Sweet Adversity: The U.S. Army, How It Motivates," *Vital Speeches of the Day* (July 1982): 650–653.

and eventually went from private to general. According to Murray:

> The main motivations in my military life were probably hate and accident. I was a great hater and exploiter of chance. . . . My first inspiration to rise above the ruck came from an illiterate regular Army sergeant of Battery F, 35th Field Artillery in 1941 at Camp Blanding, Florida. . . . Sergeant Clements was a connoisseur of latrines. He led me to one and made me clean it with a Q-tip. . . . I was nauseous. I retched. I sought the name of the deity, but not in prayer. I thought, "My God, if I can do this, I can do anything. . . . " That was the motivation from the dregs.

LUCK

> The next fillip [push] I received was the result of an accident. . . . One day my laundry was mixed up, and I received an almost Cloroxed-white set of fatigues. What's more, the blouse had two dark blue chevron outlines, where the original chevrons had been. The sign of a busted sergeant. . . . I soon found, as I wandered around the regiment sent by Sergeant Clements on what were called "craps" details, that the emblem of the busted sergeant was well recognized, and in those times of NCO shortages, I was pulled out of the work squads and platoons to take over the detail. . . . This was motivation from the sudden knowledge that rank indeed had its privileges.

HATE AGAIN

> My third inspiration did not come from mixed up laundry. It came from an officer who, in charity I readily acknowledge, must have had a lot of good left in him because none of it ever came out. . . . I was squatting in Camp Blanding sand with my precious shirt off, near the signal shack, splicing wire. To tell the truth, while I had pliers in my hand, I guess I could have been accused of basking in the Florida sun. A bass voice roared, "Get up." I looked up at a large red-faced captain who seemed entirely polished. Shoes, belt buckle, insignia, and face. He was a gleaming masterpiece of Shinola, Brasso, and sweat. . . . I came to attention and stood stiffly, as with a snapping swagger stick, Captain Oswald berated me, and treated me like scum. I've never gone along with officer fragging, but at the moment I must admit that I fantasized about the use of hand grenade suppositories. . . . As a result of the episode, I was hate-motivated again. I decided that if the Army could make the mistake of commissioning such an officer, it could no doubt make the mistake of commissioning me. . . . When the Battery Bulletin Board called for volunteers for the infantry, against all counsel I volunteered. And with the aid of prestige of my faded shirt, I was immediately promoted to corporal.
>
> If you think as you rise in rank you escape the wrath of your superiors, then think otherwise. Generals get chewed out too. . . . How does this relate to my near sacking as a general? Well here again, as with the early-day sergeant, I swear I was innocent. I was only trying to be artful. . . . Reviewing cablegrams from the Joint Chiefs of Staff, I saw an ambiguity in one of them (not unusual) that might lead to an interpretation in favor of more resources for the remnant organization that I was to head after MACV (Military Assistance Command Vietnam) dissolved. In a Top Secret message I asked "for guidance. . . . " The message went with a hundred others in the Commander's reading file. The next thing I knew I was literally on the carpet. You would have thought I'd been en flagrante, cutting up Old Glory's stars for rifle patches. . . . My message asking 'for guidance' was sternly ordered withdrawn. I was told in terms as shocking as an early reveille and with intonations of taps, that I was to follow the unassailable commandment of General Creighton Abrams, who had laid it down in terms I'll sanitize: "Never ask for guidance from Washington. If you do, they'll only screw it up worse than you can ever do in all your misbegotten life." ■

1. John Murray illustrates three major "motivational incidents" in his military career. In each situation, what was the basis for his motivation?

2. Assuming Murray's speech is accurate, summarize the concepts or theories that explain motivation in the military. How effective or ineffective would they be in an organization? Would they depend on the organization, the division within an organization, or some other relevant factors?

3. What might need theorists have to say about military motivation strategies and practices as explained by Murray? What would expectancy or equity theorists say? Behavioral (results-oriented) theorists?

14 Managing Group Processes

FOCUS CASE / USA for Africa: Please Check Your Egos at the Door

WHAT IS A GROUP?
Group Characteristics
Formal Groups
Informal Groups

WORKING WITH GROUPS IN THE ORGANIZATION
Advantages
Disadvantages

THE FORMATION AND DEVELOPMENT OF GROUPS
Forming
Storming
Norming
Performing

GROUP DYNAMICS
Required and Emergent Behaviors
Activities, Interactions, Sentiments
Managing Group Dynamics
Group Norms
Group Roles
Task and Maintenance Roles

RESOLVING PROBLEMS WITH GROUPS
Ineffectiveness
Groupthink
Intergroup Conflict

People are social animals. We spend much of our lives in groups, and we cannot achieve many of our goals without the cooperation and coordination of others. Individual motivation is important, but often what people do and accomplish is determined not only by their own motivation but also by how well they work with others. Directing, therefore, also involves structuring groups and improving group performance. As organizations are growing more complex and the environment more dynamic, groups are becoming increasingly important to goal accomplishment. In this chapter we will discuss what groups are, what different types of groups exist, and how they are formed. We will also describe how group-related issues can be managed so that both group members and the organization can accomplish their objectives.

▪ KEY QUESTIONS

As you study this chapter, try to answer the following key questions:

1 What are groups, and in what five basic ways can groups differ?
2 What are the differences between formal and informal groups?
3 What are the advantages and disadvantages of working with groups?
4 How do groups develop over time?
5 Based on the Homans model, how could managers best guide or control what is accomplished and the way people work together in the group?
6 How do roles and norms affect what individuals in a group do?
7 How is team building used as group "tune-up"?
8 What are the positive and negative results of groupthink, and how can the optimum balance between these be achieved?
9 What are the positive and negative results of intergroup conflict, and how can managers achieve the most effective balance between them?

Focus Case

USA for Africa: Please Check Your Egos at the Door

Stevie Wonder, Paul Simon, Kenny Rogers, Tina Turner, and Billy Joel at the "We Are the World" recording session. The organizers of the benefit had to meld 45 of the biggest, most independent musical talents into a single, cohesive group.

From the standpoint of group dynamics and group management, the USA (United Support of Artists) for Africa benefit recording session of the song "We Are the World" was a monumental accomplishment. It was a unique example of individuals working together in a group to accomplish a common purpose: to raise money to aid victims of famine in Ethiopia and other areas of Africa. The recording session was held January 28, 1985, and the single, released March 7, sold over 1 million copies in the first week, providing over $12.5 million in aid for famine relief.

Harry Belafonte initiated the USA for Africa project and had the support of several other influential people in the music and entertainment business. Manager Ken Kragen, producer Quincy Jones, and songwriters Michael Jackson and Lionel Richie had countless obstacles to overcome in making the dream a reality. How could 45 of America's biggest, most heavily booked musical stars be collected in the same place at the same time? How could the project initiators ensure that these highly independent, diversely talented, creative, and successful people would form a cohesive group? How could the group directors ensure that it would not be paralyzed by conflict?

The project's success was due partly to the skill of the group leaders, partly to the unity of purpose of the participants, and partly to luck.

The group members were chosen in a somewhat random "grass roots" fashion: Belafonte called Kragen, Kragen called Jones and Richie, Richie called Jackson, and Richie's wife ran into Stevie Wonder in a jewelry store. Kragen then started at the top of the pop music charts and kept calling. A group of 45 was collected—all of whom volunteered their time and effort. Another fifty were turned away.

Meanwhile, Richie and Jackson wrote the song, recorded it in Kenny Rogers's studio, and sent copies to all the selected singers. When they had familiarized themselves with it and were ready to record, one tough question remained: how to get all the artists together. Here luck helped out. Most of the stars would be attending the American Music Awards in Los Angeles on January 28, 1985. It was agreed that the session would take place immediately after the ceremony. Those not present in Los Angeles agreed to fly in between recording sessions, concert tour stops, and performance rehearsals, coming through all kinds of weather and from cities all over the United States and Europe.

Sources: This case was prepared by M. R. Poirier and F. Andrade, based on the following sources: "There Comes a Time When We Heed a Certain Call," *Life* (April 1985); Gold, Todd, "Rock's Finest Hour," *People*, July 29, 1985, p. 32; Loderand, Kurt, and Goldberg, Michael, "Inside the USA for Africa Session," *Rolling Stone,* March 28, 1985, p. 24.

Though the potential for personality conflict was high, the group formed a community spirit almost effortlessly. Everybody seemed to want to break the ice. A sign posted in the lobby read: "Please check your egos at the door." Ruth Pointer snapped pictures of Michael Jackson for her children. Diana Ross started passing around her sheet music for autographs, and everyone followed suit. A major argument about background vocal themes temporarily subdued everyone, but Stevie Wonder relieved the tension by breaking into a version of Belafonte's "Banana Boat Song" and everyone joined in.

The problem of vocal arranging was difficult in the presence of such vast and varied talent: Although the vocal arranger felt it was "like vocal arranging in a perfect world," the producer felt it was as challenging as "putting a watermelon into a Coke bottle." In the end, however, the chorus, the solos, and the brief duets were all arranged to everyone's satisfaction.

The success of USA for Africa had much to do with consensus—all involved believed in the importance of the project. Said Kenny Loggins at the recording session: "I've never before felt that strong a sense of community." Bette Midler added: "It was heartbreaking, just beautiful. There wasn't a dry eye in the house." "There was something in that room," said Al Jarreau, "We brought it . . . but we had a visitation, too."

Many left the recording session taking the spirit of the group's purpose—to band together to help others in need—with them. The morning after the recording session, Steve Perry ordered room service in his hotel, and as he took the silver cover off his food, he began to cry. And Harry Belafonte, making a stand against South Africa's system of apartheid (forced segregation) two days later was arrested in Washington, D.C., while picketing outside the South African embassy. ■

WHAT IS A GROUP?

Group Two or more persons working together to accomplish a common goal.

The people riding a subway or waiting in a checkout line are not a group; they are a collection of individuals, but all they have in common is the space in which they are standing. Groups have characteristics that go beyond just being in the same place at the same time. A **group** consists of two or more persons working together to accomplish a common goal.[1] Group members (1) depend on each other, (2) have a common purpose, (3) perceive themselves to be part of a group, and (4) assume different responsibilities.

The collection of artists at the American Music Awards may have talked with each other during the event and were all there for the same or similar reasons, but they were simply a collection of individuals attending an award ceremony. However, the ones who got together after the ceremony specifically to tape "We Are the World" became a group. They had a reason for interacting and working together, they depended on each other, and they perceived themselves as members of the group. As Kenny Loggins said, "I've never before felt that strong a sense of community." And each assumed different responsibilities: Michael Jackson and Lionel Richie wrote the song, Kenny Rogers provided the facilities, Quincy Jones produced the recording, and each artist sang a solo or sang in the chorus.

Group Characteristics

The nature of groups varies substantially. Some are very structured: Specific responsibilities are assigned to each member. Others are very flexible: Members have no specific responsibilities and go about accomplishing their task or objective in a random fashion. In some, all members are equally responsible for providing suggestions or direction. In other groups, one person dominates. Exhibit 14.1 presents some of the characteristics that must be managed if groups are to function successfully.

EXHIBIT / 14.1
Group Characteristics

Patterns of Participation   How active are people in the group? In some groups members participate freely and openly; in others, one person dominates.

Understanding   Do members understand and agree with the ideals, values, and objectives of the group?

Cohesion   How strong are the bonds and attractions of individuals in the group? Some groups are so cohesive that they are the main source of strength, values, and identity for the individuals in the group. Other groups exist very loosely because the members do not identify strongly with the group and do not seem very involved.

Atmosphere   What is the social climate of the group, the ambience, the feeling that a group carries with it? Some are freewheeling and spontaneous, allowing lengthy, heated discussions and the freedom to disagree and ask questions. Others are very structured and controlled.

Structure   What is the nature of the positions in the group and how do they relate to each other? Some groups are very structured: Relationships within the group are clearly defined, procedures for doing the work are clearly established, and goals are very specific. Others are flexible and adaptable: Relationships vary according to the situation, procedures for doing work are determined by each individual, and the goals of the group are established only in broad terms.

The characteristics in Exhibit 14.1 may create the impression that working with groups involves excessive time and energy. Managers must determine how to get the job done, what the group's structure will be, and how active each group member should be in the group. In addition, they must ensure that all members understand the group's objectives, that they remain cohesive, and that the group's atmosphere be conducive to its effective functioning. Each takes time and attention to manage, but if managers do not address these issues, the group may not be productive.[2] Although group management requires a great deal of effort, people working together in groups can often accomplish more than individuals working separately.

Groups may be formal or informal and may vary in structure. Our discussions of the formal and informal organization in Chapter 7 and formal and informal communications channels in Chapter 12 lend some insight to this discussion. Just as relationships develop informally across formal organizational lines, groups can also develop outside of formal organizational specifications for them.

Formal Groups

Formal groups   Groups created by someone with formal authority.

Formal groups exist because someone with formal authority has created them. Formal groups can be created by all levels of management and function at all levels of the organization. Executives create some groups to develop and implement organization strategy; middle managers create some groups to develop and manage operational procedures; and supervisors work with some groups to solve job performance problems.

Work group A group composed of a supervisor and those who report to him or her.

Linking pins Group members responsible for coordinating the work of their group with the work of other groups.

Permanent groups Groups that exist over time and whose structure remains constant.

Temporary groups Groups created for a specific purpose, that disband when the purpose is achieved.

The most common formal group in organizations is the **work group**, which is composed of the supervisor and those who report directly to him or her. In fact, Rensis Likert proposes that the organization can be viewed as nothing more than overlapping work groups coordinating their activities to accomplish an overall objective. Exhibit 14.2 presents a picture of an organization viewed as overlapping groups. Seen this way, managers become what Likert refers to as **linking pins**:[3] members of one group responsible for coordinating the work of that group with the work of other groups. They are managers or supervisors in one group and subordinates in the next higher level group. Based on this conception, the group is the basic building block of the organization.

Formal groups may also be either permanent or temporary. **Permanent groups** are the departments and divisions that make up the formal organization chart. They exist over time and their structure usually remains constant, even though the membership may change. **Temporary groups** are created for a specific purpose, and when the purpose is achieved—when the problem is solved or the analysis is completed—the group disbands and the members return to their original work groups.

The USA for Africa recording group was a temporary group put together to accomplish a specific purpose. It was structured, in the sense that responsibilities and roles were clearly specified. Quincy Jones directed, the chorus sang, and the soloists took turns recording their individual tracks. Yet it was temporary: After the song was recorded, the artists returned to their other projects and activities.

Task forces are the most common example of temporary groups in organizations, and they are becoming very important in planning, coordinating, and directing. They may be formed to develop plans or new products, monitor customer preferences, or analyze production problems. Committees, on the other hand, tend to have longer life spans than task forces. They may be either temporary or permanent; some are incorporated into an organization's formal structure.

EXHIBIT / 14.2
Groups as Organization Linking Pins

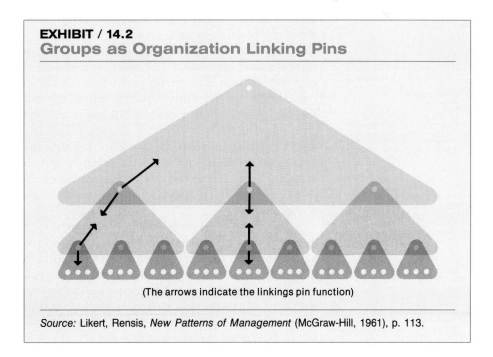

(The arrows indicate the linkings pin function)

Source: Likert, Rensis, *New Patterns of Management* (McGraw-Hill, 1961), p. 113.

EXHIBIT / 14.3
Procedures for Committee Management

The committee's goals should be clearly defined, preferably in writing. This will focus the committee's activities and reduce discussion of what the committee is supposed to do.

The committee's authority should be specified. Can the committee merely investigate, advise, and recommend, or is it authorized to implement decisions?

The optimum size of the committee should be determined. With fewer than five members, the advantages of group work may be diminished. Potential resources increase as group size increases. With more than 10 to 15, a committee may become unwieldy, and it may be difficult for each member to enter and influence the work.

A chairperson should be selected on the basis of his or her ability to run an efficient meeting—that is, the ability to encourage the participation of all committee members, to keep the committee meetings from getting bogged down in irrelevancies, and to see that the necessary paperwork gets done.

Appointing a permanent secretary to handle communications is often useful. The agenda and all supporting material for the meeting should be distributed before the meeting. When members can prepare in advance, they are more likely to stick to the point and to be ready with informed contributions. Meetings should start and end on time. The time when they will end should be announced at the outset.

Source: O'Donnel, C., "Ground Rules for Using Committees," *Management Review* 50(10) (October 1961): 63–67.

As organizations become more complex and the environment more dynamic, it is increasingly important that committees and task forces be managed effectively. Exhibit 14.3 presents some suggestions.

Informal Groups

Informal groups
Groups formed haphazardly, spontaneously, and naturally as people interact.

Unlike formal groups, which are formed and structured for a specific purpose, **informal groups** form haphazardly, spontaneously, and naturally as people interact. The activities of informal groups are not specified by management and may not be consistent with the organization's objectives. These groups may be based on common interests or personal relationships and may consist of people from different departments or the same department.

Informal groups can be very useful in organizations. They establish linkages across formal organization structures and communication channels. They provide peer support and allow employees to discuss and solve organization problems. For example, the inventory department of an electronics firm was responsible for sending kits (Styrofoam carriers holding all the parts necessary to assemble a given product) to the assembly department so that assembly could put them together. For many years, the assembly department had kept a separate cache of spare parts to use as substitutes for defective parts in the kits. When this system was terminated due to the cost of maintaining double inventories, assembly was simply advised to use up what they had and not order any spares. Inventory was not informed.

At the end of one month, inventory ran out of a part for the kits. The workers in inventory assumed that the assembly department had its own supply of spare parts and would request more when they ran out, and therefore inventory did not rush order the missing part. In fact, though, assembly did not have any of the needed spare parts and had been storing the kits on shelves in the basement to wait until the spare parts arrived. Having never heard from assembly, inventory assumed everything was going fine and therefore did not order the missing parts. In the meantime, nothing was being produced.

The problem remained undiscovered until an informal group who usually ate lunch together started discussing the issue. In the group were three people from assembly, one from inventory, a supervisor from quality control, and the bookkeeper for the purchasing department. As soon as they began talking, the inventory worker realized that his department had been incorrectly assuming that assembly had parts, and the assembly workers realized that inventory did not know what parts they needed. After that day, the two departments developed an ongoing feedback mechanism to remedy the problem.

Informal groups may also have negative effects. Employees may spend so much time with their informal group that they are unproductive on the job. They may learn things about other departments and units that anger or demoralize them. If these sentiments are strong enough, informal groups may deliberately restrict production.

Sociometry A process of identifying how group members interact.

One method of studying groups is **sociometry**, a process of identifying how members of a group interact. Through interviews or questionnaires, employees are asked with whom they spend their time or with whom they would like to spend their time. A diagram is then drawn illustrating the informal relationships among people. Those most often identified as the person with whom others spend most time are often the informal leaders. They are the people to whom employees turn for support and guidance. Exhibit 14.4 presents a diagram of two quality circle groups. In the first diagram, Juan is clearly the person to whom most people are drawn. In the second diagram, no one emerges as the dominant person; the interaction is evenly dispersed among the group.

Diagrams need not be formally drawn. Much can be understood about groups just by watching whom people talk with and when. By understanding the relationships among people, managers are better able to help the informal group focus its energy on accomplishing organization objectives.

It is inevitable that informal groups will form in organizations. Whether they help or hinder the organization often depends on the actions of the manager. If managers recognize the power of the informal group and identify the influential leaders, the group can be incorporated into the activities of the organization and

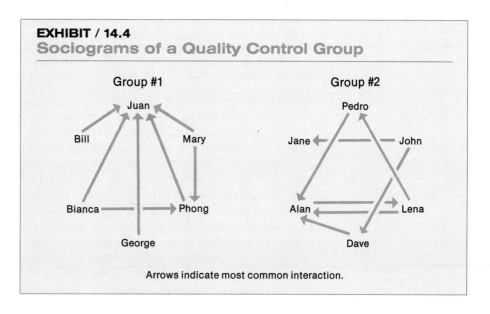

EXHIBIT / 14.4
Sociograms of a Quality Control Group

Group #1

Group #2

Arrows indicate most common interaction.

even accomplish things that the formally designated groups in the organization cannot.

WORKING WITH GROUPS IN THE ORGANIZATION

Though an organization can be considered a system of interlocking groups, not everything should always be done in groups. If managers never did anything without consulting a group, they would accomplish very little. Additionally, in a crisis there is rarely enough time to consult a group. However, when working with a group is appropriate, individuals and the organization as a whole can both benefit. Working with formal and informal groups in organizations has many advantages and disadvantages.

Advantages

As we discussed in Chapter 13, people have many needs that can be satisfied by working with others. Some of these are security needs, social and affiliation needs, and identity and esteem needs. Whether in formal or informal groups, people can satisfy these needs.

Security Needs   Most people like to have predictability and support in both their work and social environments. An employee who is having trouble completing a task or solving a problem at work likes to know that someone in the work group will offer assistance. The same is true for social situations. Groups can provide a sense of security and support.

Social and Affiliation Needs   Most people want to be liked by others and to feel as though they belong. Members of a task force or committee may share as strong an affiliation as a group of people who regularly meet during coffee breaks. Both work groups and social groups allow a feeling of belonging.

Identity and Esteem Needs   Groups provide a framework within which individuals define part of who they are and of how they fit. By sharing certain norms, members of the group may experience an increased sense of self worth and strength. Membership in both work and social groups provides a sense of safety in numbers, a sense of identity and esteem.

By having employees work in groups, organizations can also gain several benefits: socialization of new employees, task accomplishment, and problem solving.

Socialization of New Employees   Both work and social groups give employees an understanding of the beliefs, norms, and expectations of the organization. The experienced sales representative can train the new sales representative. Experienced managers can help new managers learn the ropes. College freshmen can find out from juniors and seniors what classes to take from which professors, how to use the library, and where the local hot spots are.

Task Accomplishment   The very essence of organizations is coordinating the work of many people for the accomplishment of overall objectives. Work groups provide a way to accomplish complex tasks beyond the capacity of any single individual. Ideally, each individual focuses on doing what he or she is most skilled and experienced at, and then the group coordinates the work.

Problem Solving and Decision Making   Groups are more effective than individuals at solving certain problems and making certain decisions.[4] For example, whenever the correct decision is not clear, when no individual has all the information to make a decision, or when the problem involves many people, groups tend to perform better than any individual alone.

Disadvantages

From an organizational standpoint, formal groups also have some disadvantages and are sometimes hard to run. The Inside View 14.1 provides one illustration. These disadvantages may also apply to informal groups, but in those cases, the impact might not affect organizational performance.

Group decisions take longer: Groups take longer to make decisions because the thoughts and ideas of many people have to be coordinated. Whenever people work together, their feelings, attitudes, and relationships must be sorted out and stabilized before objectives can be addressed. Coordinating individual talents to accomplish a common purpose takes time and energy, or as Quincy Jones, producer of "We Are the World," said, it may be "like putting a watermelon into a Coke bottle." Group members need time to reach an understanding, to come to agreement on the purpose and objectives of the group, and to manage the relationships among group members. Organizational performance may suffer when formal work groups are slow to act; informal relationships among members may help or impede the process further.

Groups force conformity: Most groups exert pressure for conformity,[5] but excessive pressure will suppress creativity and discourage risk taking. This works to the disadvantage of individuals, who feel forced to keep back some of their feelings and ideas, and to the organization, which may never hear about a creative, innovative solution to a problem.

Groups are susceptible to pressures of rank and status: Low-status group members may feel inhibited by those with higher status. Higher-status members may be able to influence the group not because their suggestions are better or more effective, but simply because they are generated by those with authority or power. The ideas of lower-status members are stifled and lost. From an individual standpoint, group members may feel unimportant; from an organizational standpoint, the best solutions may remain undiscovered if pressures of rank and status inhibit open group interaction.

THE FORMATION AND DEVELOPMENT OF GROUPS

Whether temporary like the USA for Africa group or permanent like an organization committee, groups usually go through a basic sequence of development: "forming, storming, norming, performing."[6] By recognizing this sequence and guiding groups through it, managers can improve group productivity.

Forming

Forming The first stage of group development, in which the basic ground rules and initial structure are established.

The first stage a group goes through is **forming.** Although the forming stage is somewhat different for formal and informal groups, and for temporary and permanent groups, basically it is the period in which the basic ground rules and an initial structure are established. During the forming stage, members of the group become acquainted with each other and begin to see how compatible they are and how they are going to relate to each other.[7] This stage is often characterized

Making Millions Was Easier

The skills needed to succeed as a commodities trader or investment banker do not necessarily translate into other fields.

Establishing teams for specific and often short-term purposes can be very useful and productive and can produce quality results not available through individual efforts. Think tanks are such an example—bringing experts together from various but related areas to develop strategies and solve problems. However, just because the results are desirable does not mean the process is simple or easy to pull off. Commodity trader Richard Dennis found out the hard way.

Having racked up trading profits of $40 million on the Chicago Board of Trade and other exchanges, he decided to put his "iconoclastic idealism" into practice in the realm of Washington policy-making. After studying the possibilities of buying out a local think tank, he eventually decided to set up his own. In 1982 he pledged $5 million to the setup and continuance of his brand new think tank: the Roosevelt Center for American Policy Studies. Senator Sam Nunn and former Deputy Secretary of Defense Frank Carlucci were taken on immediately and began "kicking around the big issues" as members of the center's study committees, and former Assistant Secretary of State (in the Carter administration) Douglas Bennett was hand-picked as president.

Despite his high-powered staff, it was a short-lived endeavor. "Bulls and bears in the soybean pit turned out to be easier to manage than a think tank," said *Fortune* magazine in August 1983. Ben-

nett and Dennis "could not be more different." Dennis himself said, "We could never be friends in the best of circumstances."

Harvard-educated Bennett, "with the looks of a well-tailored Secret Service agent," was considered a "classic insider": big names in the right place were all important in his eyes. "If you want an institution to be effective, you have to be credible and that means accepting the rules of the game," said Bennett. Dennis considered that a cop-out of sorts: a "bias toward the traditional way of doing things."

Beyond the basic personality conflict between founder and president, however, was a more serious problem: lack of direction. The think tank was launched with "some high sounding but vague ideas. It would be dedicated to activism but not advocacy . . . our heads would be in Washington but our hearts would be outside." According to *Fortune* reporters, "Dennis seems never to have got across what he wanted to do, and possibly wasn't sure himself."

It takes more than financial acumen to run a think tank—skills in one field do not always apply in others. Dennis found it easier to sit in his office making millions of dollars than to run a successful Washington think tank. ■

Source: "Making Millions Was Easier," *Fortune*, August 22, 1983, p. 89.

by good-natured bantering or ice-breaking, as when Ruth Pointer took pictures and Diana Ross collected autographs at the start of the USA for Africa recording session. These activities gave participants a way to get to know each other.

In the USA for Africa group, the forming state was rapid due to time constraints; the group's purpose had to be achieved in one night. In a formal organizational task force, time constraints also speed up the forming stage, but the formality of the setting usually prevents such ice-breaking antics as exhibited by the USA for Africa group. In the forming stage of the task force, a group leader or secretary may read a list of rules and objectives, and members may begin interacting by asking each other about their jobs, backgrounds, or interests.

Informal groups in organizations often have the slowest, least-heated forming stages largely because their members are not required to spend time or accomplish anything together. People often meet under casual circumstances, and an informal group may build slowly over time. The forming stage for an informal group could go on for months or a year, whereas formal work groups—especially temporary ones—must pass onto the next phases in much less time.

Storming

Storming The second stage of group development, in which members begin to sort out personal and operating relationships.

As people begin to feel familiar with the basic rules and objectives, and begin to know what to expect from each other, the group enters the storming stage. In the **storming** phase, members begin to sort out personal and operating relationships and make their own personal goals, needs, and expectations clear. Tensions are usually high, and periods of conflict may be frequent as the group members jockey for position. The USA for Africa group, for example, was unable to focus on its objectives during this phase, until one member intervened to reduce the tension. When the singers were arguing about the background vocal themes, Stevie Wonder started to sing Harry Belafonte's "Banana Boat Song." Everyone joined in, the tension evaporated, and the group members were in a better frame of mind to reach agreement on the vocal track.

Similary, in the case of a task force or committee, the lack of unity during the storming stage means that the objectives of the group are temporarily sidestepped. Time must be spent on coordinating interpersonal styles and individual needs and on clarifying personal objectives. It is also in the storming stage that each person's responsibilities and place in the group become more clearly defined.

Norming

Norming The third stage of group development, in which the collection of people starts to see itself as a group.

From the storming phase, a group consensus should emerge. Members should agree on the group's purpose or function, the responsibilities of each member, and the norms or rules of how they will work together.[8] This is called the **norming** stage, when the collection of people finally starts to see itself, and to be seen, as a group. Group members begin to develop a group identity; they can describe what it means to belong to the group and what the group does. In the case of a work group, the consensus makes it easier for members to focus on goals and objectives.

The norming stage is the starting point for action. At this stage, the group may be unstable, but its members have come to accept and understand their roles and will strive to maintain harmony and work toward objectives. At the USA for Africa recording session, the norming stage was reached when the chorus and duets had been agreed upon, the solos had been assigned, and the group was ready to begin recording.

Performing

Performing is the final stage of group development. It is the phase in which permanent formal groups (structural units) ideally remain, and the phase in which temporary formal groups (task forces, committees) achieve their objectives—the phase in which members know how to work together to accomplish the group's goals and objectives. Group structure, norms, and behaviors are no longer debated. The group is mature, organized, and effective. Members can handle disagreements and misunderstandings. Differences are dealt with unemotionally, before decisions are made. The group finally gets to complete the project, finish the analysis, or, as in our introductory case, record the song.

The performing stage is the phase in which group members can relate to each other constructively and can begin to satisfy individual needs. The members' relative positions in the group are established; for example, one person may be known as the sympathetic listener, another as the tension stabilizer. In the performing stage, members know who to turn to, for instance, for help with personal or technical problems.

Management must recognize that both formal and informal groups go through these developmental stages, that the development of both types of groups may influence the other, and that at each stage the groups need different types of support and guidance.[9] In the forming stage, work group members may need help in understanding what their mutual interests are and how they can work together. In the storming stage, the work group members may need help in understanding each other's goals, needs, and expectations and will need guidance in becoming more compatible. In the norming stage, managers should try to ensure that the organization's overall cultural norms are reflected in the norms and patterns adopted by the group, and that conflicts do not inhibit performance. In the performing stage, managers may have only to clarify the group's common objectives, provide all the resources and support necessary, and help the members address problems or constraints arising from outside the group.

Managers must also recognize that different types of groups go through the stages at different speeds. Informal groups tend to form more slowly because they have no predetermined objective. A consensus of what their purpose is needs time to emerge. Formal committees appointed to accomplish certain tasks already have a purpose. They can develop more quickly because at each stage the members have a common purpose around which to manage their relationships.

Exhibit 14.5 provides a checklist useful for identifying a group's developmental stage. After identifying this stage, managers can focus on helping the group progress to the next stage and eventually achieve effective performance. They can also guide informal groups to assist or enhance this process.

GROUP DYNAMICS

Group dynamics are the interaction patterns that evolve in groups. These patterns or forces influence how well the members can accomplish their common purpose and how satisfied and cohesive they are. Consider, for example, a task force in which a dominant personality has emerged. Other group members may

EXHIBIT / 14.5
Checklist for Identifying Group Stage of Development

FORMING

_____ Members of the group get acquainted with each other.

_____ Members have established initial ground rules and a tentative way of working with each other.

_____ Members of the group are testing each other to see how compatible they are.

STORMING

_____ Members are jockeying for position, trying to determine how they will work together.

_____ Conflict is frequent.

_____ Members are making their personal goals and needs clear.

_____ Members are becoming aware of their differences.

_____ There is a lack of unity.

NORMING

_____ The group has come to agreement on its purpose.

_____ Members are clear what their roles and responsibilities are and how they fit into the group.

_____ The group has a sense of identity.

_____ The group members strive to work together.

PERFORMING

_____ Group structure, norms, and behavior are understood and accepted.

_____ Members know how to work with each other.

_____ Members can effectively handle disagreements and misunderstandings.

_____ Differences have surfaced and members have dealt with them.

_____ The group is focused on accomplishing its purpose.

---

be reluctant to offer their genuine opinions or be vocal about different ideas. Additionally, although each member may contribute according to his or her expected role (one records the minutes, one collects data, one conducts interviews with outsiders), the group's functioning may be strongly influenced by the dominant personality. The data collector, for example, might disregard information he or she feels is important if he or she expects the dominant personality to reject it. The interaction pattern, or group dynamics, may therefore inhibit the task force in its efforts to accomplish its task and leave some members feeling unsatisfied.

George Homans provides a two-part model useful for analyzing the dynamics in a group.[10] It distinguishes between required and emergent behaviors and then discusses the activities, interactions, and sentiments characteristic of each. Combined, these concepts provide a useful model for analyzing and managing group dynamics.

Required and Emergent Behaviors

Required behaviors
Those actions a group expects from members as a condition or requirement of their membership.

Required behaviors are those actions a group expects from members as a condition or requirement of their membership. They include those actions that, at a minimum, must be performed for the group to accomplish its purpose. Each member of an assembly line team has specific duties to perform for a product to be assembled. Each member of a task force or committee is assigned a specific portion of that group's work and is also expected to attend regular meetings to report on progress. Each member of the USA for Africa recording group was required to perform part of the song, and specific individuals were required to write the song, direct it, and produce the recording. Members of informal groups are also typically "required" to meet at designated times, contact other members if schedules must be changed, or perform other basic social duties.

Emergent behaviors
Those actions group members do in addition to or in place of behaviors required by the organization.

Emergent behaviors are those actions members do in addition to or in place of behaviors required by the organization. For example, showing up from eight to five every weekday and taking only a half an hour for lunch may be required of members of the accounting department group, whereas coming in early, working through lunch, or taking over some work for a sick co-worker would be emergent behaviors. A task force member required to produce data may take extra time to put it into a more easily accessible format for the benefit of the other group members. And a member of a neighborhood social group who agrees to collect a neighbor's mail while the family is on vacation may also keep an eye on the house and water the garden.

Activities, Interactions, Sentiments

Activities, interactions, and sentiments, the second aspect of Homan's model, can be characteristic of both required and emergent behaviors.

Activities   Physical movements or verbal or nonverbal behaviors in which group members engage.

Activities are any physical movements or verbal or nonverbal behaviors in which group members engage. The required behaviors of an assembly line worker might be to show up from nine to five and do the work assigned. The required activities are the movements and actions—welding, bolting, lifting—necessary to complete the work. Emergent activities are actions members perform beyond those required, for example, polishing the chrome just attached, moving tools off the walkways, or cleaning the work area before lunch breaks.

Interactions   Two-way communications between group members.

Interactions are two-way communications between group members. Required interactions are the communications necessary for a group to accomplish its purpose. Members of a task force may be required to give each other certain reports or information. Emergent interactions are voluntary communications between members. A task force member may take extra time to explain a report to another member.

Sentiments   The feelings, attitudes, and beliefs held by group members.

Sentiments are the least tangible aspect of group dynamics. **Sentiments** are the feelings, attitudes, and beliefs held by group members. All members of a work or informal group generally believe they should be considerate and polite. But some may also be thoughtful, sensitive, or compassionate. Sentiments are much less controllable than activities or interactions and can have a powerful influence on the performance of a formal work group. Management can specify the activities and communications employees must engage in, but they cannot control the attitudes, feelings, and beliefs that people have on the job.

This is not to imply that one type of "sentiment" is better than another, or that the presence of many different types in one group is necessarily detrimental to group performance. Though the USA for Africa artists all had very different "sentiments" (Michael Jackson and Bob Dylan are described as shy and sometimes even withdrawn, Bruce Springsteen thinks it is important to remain simple and unglamorous, Cyndi Lauper is outgoing), all were comfortable with each other's differing attitudes, and the variety of the group members contributed to the great commercial success of the recording.

Managing Group Dynamics

Exhibit 14.6 illustrates Homan's model of group dynamics. Managers must perceive and understand not only what group members are expected to do and expect of each other in terms of activities, interactions, and sentiments, but also

EXHIBIT / 14.6
Homan's Model of Group Dynamics

	Activities	Interactions	Sentiments
Required Behaviors	Work 8-5 Park truck across street from mail box	Report problems to supervisor Accept mail from patrons	Maintain a positive attitude toward customers
Emergent Behaviors	Go wherever necessary to deliver mail Work late to deliver special services	Help patrons understand mail system Work closely with other postal workers to solve problems as they emerge	Help others solve personal problems Encourage others with enthusiasm Work effectively with the group

what spontaneously and informally occurs that may help or hinder the group. Addressing only required behaviors—for example, job descriptions, rules, and regulations—is not enough to get the job done. Managers must also remain aware of and guide emergent behaviors. Consider the following examples:[11]

> The U.S. postal system has many formal rules, policies, and activities that route-delivery workers are supposed to follow. However, none of these men and women can perform their work satisfactorily while following all of these rules rigorously. Complete conformity is so impractical that postal employees have chosen to follow rules perfectly only when they wish to "strike." In such cases the strike is called a "work-by-the-rules strike." The deliverers leave in the morning, park on the opposite side of the street from their postal box (a rule), unlock their trucks, get their bags out, lock the trucks (a rule), go across the street, come back, unlock the trucks, put the mail in, lock their trucks, etc. Thus, by following rules perfectly, the deliverers come in late from their daily activities with only half the mail delivered, and free from any possible prosecution.
>
> Similarly, when New York City police officers wish to register a grievance about pay and working conditions, they simply ticket every car in New York City that they see in violation of the law. The New York traffic department's activities come to a screeching halt. Again, it is made clear that observing required methods of working without balancing them with effective emergent behavior is not always satisfactory.

Group Norms

Group norms Proper or expected ways of acting in a group.

Norms can also be used to analyze group dynamics. **Group norms** are expected or proper ways of acting that have been determined appropriate by members of a group. Given a set of goals, norms define the kind of behavior believed necessary to accomplish the goals.[12] Norms become fully developed and reinforced among group members during the third phase of group development, norming.[13]

How strongly norms are enforced is determined by four conditions. First, norms are most likely to be enforced if they aid in group survival or provide benefits to group members. For example, employees at a pizza parlor might develop an unspoken rule regarding what to do with "mistakes": pizzas made not to customer specifications and, therefore, not servable or sellable. The norm might be to put these mistakes in a certain place and not mention them to the manager. Then the group members divide the goods at closing time. The norm is likely to be enforced because of the benefit provided: free pizza.

Second, norms will be enforced if they simplify or make predictable the behavior expected of group members. For example, a group of employees who regularly eat together may develop a norm of splitting the check evenly and covering the tip in rotation to save the time and effort of calculating exact costs per person. However, if benefits are not provided evenly this way, that is, if one person consistently orders the most expensive menu item or consistently undertips, the norm may not be enforced even if it does simplify things.

Third, norms are likely to be enforced if they help the group avoid embarrassing interpersonal problems. A discussion group, for example, might agree always to meet in a neutral location rather than in each other's homes. This way, information about each person's taste, income level, or family relations remains confidential.

Fourth, norms are likely to be enforced if they express the central values and identity of the group. Members of the executive staff of an insurance company may have an unspoken agreement to drive large luxury cars rather than small economy cars. They may wish to convey an image of wealth and conservatism. Similarly, the employees at a rock club or second-hand record store may all dress eccentricly to convey the image that they are "with it," or better yet, "ahead of it." These norms establish the basis of the culture of a group.

Once a group has developed a set of norms, new members are usually expected to conform to them. Sometimes new members easily conform because the norms are compatible with their habits, behavior, or values. Most young pizza parlor employees, for example, will accept the leftovers. Other times, members may feel they are being pressured to comply with norms to which they are opposed. A stickler for detail, for example, might not be comfortable splitting a check evenly when menu items differ in price.

From an organizational standpoint, compliance with norms among group members can be beneficial: Ideally, a group will develop such norms as *never produce anything that isn't your best effort* or *strive for perfection*. Unfortunately, norms may also be detrimental to group performance. For example, members of a production team may set an easy-to-meet production rate that is far lower than their capability and uneconomical for the department. Nevertheless, they can easily reach a consensus regarding the rate at which they wish to work collectively. The Inside View 14.2 provides one illustration of this point.

Norms held by a work group or by an informal group overlapping the work group may be beneficial or detrimental to the accomplishment of the group's objectives. Therefore, because managers are responsible for the productivity and effectiveness of any group of which they are in charge, they should always strive to support norms that are benefical to group performances and work to alter detrimental norms so that group effectiveness can increase.

Group Roles

Another way to study group dynamics is in terms of roles. The word *role* often connotes the idea of an actor in theatrical production. Roles in any work group

THE INSIDE VIEW / 14.2

Eighty Pieces Is Fair

For 18 years Ginny had been doing about the same thing: packing expandrium fittings for shipment. She was so well practiced that she could do the job perfectly without paying the slightest attention. This, of course, left her free to socialize and observe the life of the company around her. Today, Ginny was breaking in a new packer.

"No, not that way. Look, Jim, if you hold it that way, well, then you have to twist your arm when you pack this corner, see. This way it's easier."

"But that's the way Mr. Wolf [the methods engineer] said we had to do it."

"Sure he did, Jim. But he's never had to do it eight hours a day like me. You just pay attention to what I say."

"But what if he comes around and says I should pack the other way?"

"Oh, that's easy. When he's here you do it his way. Anyway, after a couple of weeks you won't see him again. Slow down. You'll wear yourself out. No one's going to expect you to do eighty pieces for a week anyway."

"But Mr. Wolf said ninety."

"Sure he did. Let him do it. Look, here's how to pace yourself. It's the way I was taught, and it works. You know the 'Battle Hymn of the Republic'?" Ginny hummed a few bars. "Well, you just work to that, hum it to yourself, use the way I showed you, and you'll be doing eighty next week."

"But what if they make me do ninety?"

"They can't. Y'know, you start making mistakes when you go that fast. No, eighty is right. I always say, a fair day's work for a fair day's pay." ■

Source: Ritti, R., and Funkhouser, G. R., *The Ropes to Skip and the Ropes to Know*, third edition, (New York: John Wiley and Sons, 1987), p. 71.

Role The set of activities a group member is expected to perform.

are quite similar: A **role** is the set of activities a group member is expected to perform in his or her position in the group. Formal and informal groups both have members who adopt different roles in the group. A formal committee may have a chairperson, a secretary, a treasurer, and a liaison responsible for working with other groups. An informal group may include someone who is the sympathetic listener, someone who tends to organize social events, and someone who is good at resolving group conflicts.

To understand how roles work in groups, it is useful to consider the role episode, which occurs in four steps:

1. *Expected Role* What other members of the group expect you to do. In a formal work group, members have assigned tasks and behaviors that are expected of them—their job roles. In an informal group, after group members have become acquainted, they begin to expect certain behaviors of each other.
2. *Sent Role* The information that group members transmit through messages and cues to communicate their expectations. A manager tells a group member what behavior is expected, or a social companion drops a hint that a behavior is expected.
3. *Perceived Role* What you perceive the sent role to mean. Your interpretation of what other group members expect you to do.
4. *Enacted Role* What you actually do in the role.

The process is cyclical. The enacted role has a direct effect on the expected role. What a group member does affects what others expect of him or her. This, in turn, affects what group members communicate to the member in terms of expectations, which again affects how the new information is perceived and what the member will do in response. And this leads us back to step 1. (See Exhibit 14.7.)

Consider the case of Ralph, who recently took a job at a Ralston Purina factory that produces dog food. At the factory, the production workers are organized in teams, each of which manages itself. They develop their own work plan and schedule. When there is a vacancy in the team, the members conduct interviews and hire the replacements themselves. The team has a supervisor for coordination purposes, but this person is considered just another member of the group with a different role to play and is not perceived as having a higher status.

Before beginning to recruit for a replacement, the group met and agreed on what type of person they wanted. Their main concerns were that the person be energetic and have the dexterity and skills necessary to do the assembly line work of the group. In addition, because the group was self-managed, the new member would need to have a good understanding of planning and work flow scheduling. They outlined the *expected role* of the person they would hire and described the requirements in a thorough job description. After reviewing the resumes of the ten people who applied for the job, they invited Ralph for an interview, during which they explained the job description to him. This was the *sent role.*

Ralph understood from the interview that he would be expected to do not only the type of assembly line work that he had done at his former job but also to take part in the management process of the work. This was the *perceived role.* It was different from the type of work he was used to, but he felt he was capable of it and thought he would enjoy the new responsibilities. The group also saw a good match and offered Ralph the job. He started work the next week and, using his previous experience, immediately offered the group some new ideas about how to plan their work. However, he was hesitant to assume managerial responsibilities, such as taking charge of the implementation of his ideas. This was the *enacted role.* After working with him for a while, the group's members explained that they really did want him to assume more management responsibilities. This was a *sent role,* a return to the first phase.

Obviously, each role is different, despite the fact that it belongs to one individual. This is partially due to the cyclical nature of the process, and partly because each step in the process is subject to distortions. The group members may choose the wrong messages or cues to send, they might not perceive the cues properly, or the individual may not have the ability to carry out the role. The results of these breakdowns are role ambiguity, role conflict, or role overload.

EXHIBIT / 14.7
Role Episode

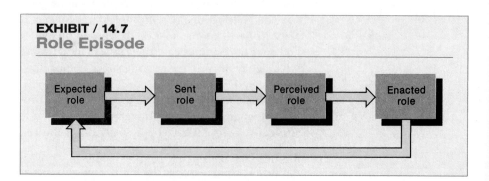

Role ambiguity A case where a person is unsure of what others expect of him or her.

Role ambiguity, the case where a person is unsure of what others expect of him or her, results from an unclear sent role, vague job descriptions, incomplete instructions from management, or confusing, unclear cues from co-workers. For example, if the job description that the group presented to Ralph did not clearly specify the management responsibilities of the job, he would not have known what was really expected of him or what to do. Role ambiguity is best managed by creating clear and reasonable expectations and communicating precisely what needs to be done. Clear job descriptions, precise goals, and specific feedback reduce and eliminate confusion and role ambiguity.

Role conflict A case where a person cannot simultaneously meet the expectations of two or more other group members.

Role conflict is the case where a person cannot simultaneously meet the expectations of two or more other group members. Messages sent by two people may be clear but either contradictory or impossible for one person to act on simultaneously. Role conflict can be reduced by coordinating the expectations of the many people who work with employees. Managers should understand the pressures that employees face from many sources in the organization. They should develop methods that keep them informed of what the employees are doing and schedule regular meetings with the employees to review the requests and assignments they are receiving from others.

Role overload The case where one person is expected to do more than he or she can possibly do.

Role overload exists when one person is expected to do more than he or she can possibly do in a given time frame. When an individual receives too many requests or does not have enough time or resources to meet the expectations of others, he or she is experiencing role overload. Role overload can be averted by helping employees be realistic about their skills and abilities and the amount of work they can accomplish. Both the manager and the employees should understand clearly what they can accomplish and how well or poorly the assignments they receive match their skills.

Task and Maintenance Roles

Two roles in groups deserve special mention because of their importance. The *task role* is the role necessary for the accomplishment of the group's purpose. Many people in a group have task roles. Some obtain resources and information, some evaluate progress, some serve as liaisons to outside groups, and together they focus on accomplishing the group purpose. *Maintenance roles* are necessary to maintain effective group functioning. A person with a maintenance role manages interpersonal relations, conflict resolution, member involvement, and personal and group development. Both roles are critical to group success. Tasks must be performed and relationships and conflict must be managed. Stevie Wonder took a turn at both roles during the USA for Africa recording session. He broke into song once to reduce tensions, then again later to contribute his solo—his task—to the group's performance.

Exhibit 14.8 provides a list of questions for evaluating how well members in a group are playing the task and maintenance roles.

RESOLVING PROBLEMS WITH GROUPS

Three important problems that may arise in the management of groups are ineffectiveness, groupthink, and intergroup conflict. Each can seriously affect the ability of the group to function and must be carefully managed.

EXHIBIT / 14.8
Task and Maintenance Roles

TASK ROLES

1. Was the group clear about their objective? Did they discuss it before making the decision?
2. Did the group clarify facts and assumptions before trying to make a decision?
3. Was the decision-making process appropriate (objectives, facts, assumptions, problem definition, alternatives, solution)? How could the group have improved?
4. Did the group stay on target? How did they get back on target when they started rambling?
5. Did the group evaluate its decision in light of their objectives? Did they talk about how they might improve?

MAINTENANCE ROLES

1. Was everyone appropriately involved in the discussion? How did the group get everyone involved?
2. Did the group assess the resources and skills everyone brought to the discussion? Did they use everyone effectively?
3. Did the group help everyone get their ideas across? Were some members preoccupied and not listening? Did some members attempt to help others clarify and express their ideas?
4. Did the group effectively manage their disagreements? Were conflicts brought to the surface and dealt with?
5. How did the group reject ideas? How did members react when their ideas were rejected? Was the climate supportive?

Ineffectiveness

Any group—a sports team, a rock band, a Senate subcommittee, or a management task force—will change, evolve, and suffer breakdowns in effectiveness.[14] Several factors can contribute to ineffectiveness: A change in membership may produce conflicts, a reduction of available resources may block a previously designed system of operations, an addition or innovation in technology may make new systems necessary, or increased competition may cause tensions. When pressures cause a breakdown in group effectiveness, team-building activities can be undertaken to restore it. Team building is, in essence, group tune-up. It is also an effective method of organization development discussed in Chapter 9.

Group members work together in team building (1) to identify a problem that exists or may develop, (2) to gather data and analyze the problem to specifically diagnose the situation, (3) to determine the root causes of the problem, and (4) to develop and implement a plan for corrective action. When enough time has passed for results to be obvious, the results can be evaluated and any new or remaining problems can be identified.

Team building should not be used as a last resort; it should be built into the group's general agenda. It also should be relatively unstructured; that is, members' individuality and creativity should not be stifled. This way a wide variety of data can be gathered and analyzed in many different ways, many different suggestions for action can be produced, and the overall results may be much more effective than if a structured list were followed.

The following method is often used as an introduction to team-building exercises. After preliminary remarks by the manager, group members can be asked: "In order for us to get a picture of how you see our group functioning, would each of you take a few minutes to describe our group as a kind of animal or combination of animals, a kind of machine, a kind of person, or whatever image comes to mind?" During one such session, the descriptions offered were:[15]

1. *A Hunting Dog—A Pointer*   We run around and locate problems, then stop and point and hope somebody else will take the action.

2. *A Cadillac with No Engine and Pedals*   We look good on the outside, but there is no real power to get us moving.
3. *A Rube Goldberg Device*   Everything looks crazy and you cannot imagine anything will ever happen, but in some way, for some reason, we do get results at the end.
4. *An Octopus*   Each tentacle is out grasping anything it can, unaware of what the other tentacles are doing.

As people share their images and explain what elicits the image, other questions should be asked: "What are the common elements in these images? Do we like these images of ourselves? What do we need to do to change our image?" The answers to these questions can become the major agenda items for subsequent group meetings, and they can help carry out the team-building process.

Whatever the methods employed, structured or loose, it is important that all members take part in discussing their views and feelings about the group. Task performance and member satisfaction should be carefully assessed. Each member should be aware of his or her contributions and those of the others, and the source of both successful and unsuccessful results should be identified.

Groupthink

Groupthink The tendency of group members to overemphasize the importance of agreement and thus lose their ability to evaluate and solve problems.

One responsibility of a group manager is to prevent or minimize the phenomenon of groupthink. **Groupthink** is the tendency of group members to overemphasize the importance of agreement and thus cause the group to lose its ability to evaluate and solve problems critically.[16] What makes groupthink most difficult to avoid and control is the fact that members tend to be unaware that it is occurring. The Inside View 14.3 provides one humorous illustration, and the following example gives an illustration in a business context.

The Ozyx Corporation is a relatively small industrial company.[17] The president of Ozyx has hired a consultant to help discover the reasons for the company's poor profits and specifically isolate the causes of the low morale and productivity in the research and development division. During the investigation, the consultant becomes aware of a research project in which the company has invested a sizable proportion of its R&D budget.

When asked about the project by the consultant in the privacy of their offices, the president, the vice president for research, and the research manager each describe it as an idea that looks great on paper but will ultimately fail because the technology required to make it work is unavailable. Each also acknowledges that continued support of the project will create cash flow problems that will jeopardize the very existence of the organization. Furthermore, each individual indicates that he or she has not told the others about his or her reactions. When asked why, the president says he cannot reveal his "true" feelings because abandoning the project, which has been widely publicized, would make the company look bad in the press. In addition, it would probably cause his vice president's ulcer to kick up or perhaps even cause her to quit, "Because she has staked her professional reputation on the project's success."

Similarly, the vice president for research says she cannot let the president or the research manager know her reservations because the president is so committed to it that "I would probably get fired for insubordination if I questioned the project." Finally, the research manager says he cannot let the president or vice president know of his doubts about the project because of their extreme commitment to the project's success.

The Trip to Abilene

Why would four reasonable adults take a 100-mile trip across the desert to eat unpalatable food at a bad restaurant in Abilene?

The July afternoon in Coleman, Texas (population 5,607) was particularly hot—104 degrees as measured by the Walgreen's Rexall Ex-Lax temperature gauge. In addition, the wind was blowing fine-grained West Texas topsoil through the house. But the afternoon was still tolerable—even potentially enjoyable. There was a fan going on the back porch; there was cold lemonade; and finally, there was entertainment. Dominoes. Perfect for the conditions. The game required little more physical exertion than an occasional mumbled comment, "Shuffle 'em," and an unhurried movement of the arm to place the spots in the appropriate perspective on the table. All in all, it had the makings of an agreeable Sunday afternoon in Coleman—that is, until my father-in-law suddenly said, "Let's get in

the car and go to Abilene and have dinner at the cafeteria."

I thought: "What, go to Abilene? Fifty-three miles? In this dust storm and heat? And in an unair-conditioned 1958 Buick?"

But my wife chimed in with, "Sounds like a great idea. I'd like to go. How about you, Jerry?" Since my own preferences were obviously out of step with the rest I replied, "Sounds good to me," and added, "I just hope your mother wants to go."

"Of course I want to go," said my mother-in-law. "I haven't been to Abilene in a long time."

So into the car and off to Abilene we went. My predictions were fulfilled. The heat was brutal. We were coated with a fine layer of dust that was cemented by the time we arrived. The food at the cafeteria provided first-rate testimonial for antacid commercials.

Some four hours and 106 miles later we returned to Coleman, hot and exhausted. We sat in front of the fan for a long time in silence. Then, both to be sociable and to break the silence, I said, "It was a great trip, wasn't it?"

No one spoke.

Finally my mother-in-law said, with some irritation, "Well, to tell the truth, I really didn't enjoy it much and would rather have stayed here. I just went along because the three of you were so enthusiastic about going. I wouldn't have gone if you all hadn't pressured me into it."

I could not believe it. "What do you mean 'you all'?" I said. "Don't put me in the 'you all' group. I was delighted to be doing what we were doing. I didn't want to go. I only went to satisfy the rest of you. You're the culprits."

My wife looked shocked. "Don't call me a culprit. You and Daddy and Mama were the ones who wanted to go. I just went along to be sociable and to keep you happy. I would have had to be crazy to want to go out in heat like that."

Her father entered the conversation abruptly. "Hell!" he said.

He proceeded to expand on what was already absolutely clear. "Listen, I never wanted to go to Abilene. I just thought you might be bored. You visit so seldom I wanted to be sure you enjoyed it. I would have preferred to play another game of dominoes and eat the leftovers in the icebox."

After the outburst of recrimination we all sat back in silence. Here we were, four reasonable sensible people who, of our own volition, had just taken a 106-mile trip across a Godforsaken desert in a furnace-like temperature through a cloud-like dust storm to eat unpalatable food at a hole-in-the-wall cafeteria in Abilene, when none of us had really wanted to go. In fact, to be more accurate, we'd done just the opposite of what we wanted to do. The whole situation simply did not make sense. ▪

Source: Harvey, Jerry B., "The Abilene Paradox: The Management of Agreement," *Organizational Dynamics* (Summer 1974): 63–80.

All indicate that they try to maintain an optimistic facade in meetings with one another, so that the others will not worry unduly about the project. The research director, in particular, admits to writing ambiguous progress reports so the president and vice president can "interpret them to suit themselves." He says he tends to slant them to the "positive" side, "given how committed the brass are." Left as it is, this situation can only lead to disaster.

Many studies have been done on the phenomenon of groupthink, but social psychologist Irving Janis provides some of the most useful insights into what its symptoms are and how to avoid its negative consequences (see Exhibit 14.9).

The potential advantages and disadvantages of groupthink depend on its degree and the situation. In one sense, groupthink can be more damaging than complete lack of consensus: When there is a consensus, however false or unsatisfactory, action will probably result, and it may have serious negative consequences. With lack of consensus, no action results and perhaps no damage is done.

Intergroup Conflict

Group effectiveness is not enough for organizational success. If each group achieves its own goals without coordination with the other groups, the organization will achieve little. Conflict in intergroup interactions can take many forms.[18] In a robot-manufacturing company, for example, research and development teams may be designing products that manufacturing does not have the machinery or expertise to build. They will blame each other when the new robots are not produced. Each group might do its job, but the overall objective will not be accomplished because their efforts have not been coordinated.

Marketing and manufacturing groups may disagree over the variety of the products offered. Marketing will want a wide variety of choices to offer customers, while manufacturing will object to the costs of constantly changing the production line. The goals of individual groups and departments in organizations are naturally in conflict, and their focuses are different. Research and development groups are future-oriented, marketing groups are oriented toward the customers, and production groups are concerned about producing the highest-quality prod-

EXHIBIT / 14.9
Symptoms and Cures of Groupthink

SYMPTOMS

Illusions of Group Invulnerability Members of the group feel that as a whole it is basically beyond criticism, attack, or failure.

Rationalizing Unpleasant and Disconfirming Data Refusal to accept contradictory data or consider alternatives thoroughly.

Belief in Inherent Group Morality Members of the group feel it is "right" and above any reproach by outsiders.

Stereotyping Competitors as Weak, Evil, and Stupid Refusal to look realistically at other groups.

Applying Direct Pressure to Deviants to Conform to Group Wishes Refusal to tolerate a member who suggests the group may be wrong.

Self-censorship by Members Refusal by members to communicate personal concerns to the group as a whole.

Illusions of Unanimity Accepting consensus prematurely, without testing its completeness.

Mind Guarding Members of the group protecting the group from hearing disturbing ideas or viewpoints from outsiders.

CURES

Provoke and encourage a sharing of all members' opinions by making each member play the role of critical evaluator.

As a manager or group leader, cover your own biases—never appear to favor or disfavor one particular course of action.

Divide the group up and have several subgroups discuss the same issue, then reconvene the larger group and discuss the alternatives.

Encourage group members to think about and discuss the problems outside of the group, then share their reactions and new information.

Invite observers and experts who are not in the group to sit in on sessions, to provide an objective viewpoint about group processes and decisions.

Create a rabble-rouser or devil's advocate—assign one member to deliberately counter consensus decisions with any different and valid point he or she can suggest.

Make the final session a "second-chance" meeting to allow members to contribute anything they may have previously left out and test the consensus one last time.

Source: Janis, Irving, *Victims of Groupthink* (Boston: Houghton Mifflin, 1972).

uct at the cheapest price. If they all focus solely on their own objectives, they will naturally conflict with each other.

Ideally, groups should cooperate with each other while accomplishing goals, but to some degree, competition between groups is good. It can potentially raise the productivity of all the groups. Managers must coordinate the efforts of various groups, balancing individual group identification with productive levels of intergroup competition.

It is important to recognize and control intergroup conflict early. When too much antagonism builds up, little gets accomplished. Some characteristics typically can be observed within groups in conflict:

1. There is a strong group cohesion and loyalty as members band together against their "common enemy."
2. Task orientation increases as goal accomplishment becomes more important.
3. Authority centralizes; group members look toward a single leader to focus their efforts.
4. Group activities become increasingly organized and efficient; structure becomes more mechanized.

In addition, certain characteristics are common between competing groups:

1. Each group considers the other an "enemy."

2. Group self-images become positively biased. Members overestimate their own strengths and other groups' weaknesses.
3. Communications decrease or break down entirely, and hostilities increase.
4. Groups tend to listen to each other through predisposition filters: They hear what they already believe and block out anything contradictory to that.

Managers can use several tactics to reduce damaging levels of intergroup conflict.[19] Groups will work with each other when cooperation is in their common interest. A manager, therefore, can emphasize a common enemy or common goal that the groups can only overcome or achieve, respectively, by working together. In a business organization, the common enemy is competition from other firms. Research and development, marketing, and production groups must work together if the organization is to prosper. Conflicts arising during the USA for Africa recording session could have been resolved easily by having the disagreeing parties focus on their goal: to generate funds for African famine relief.

One useful way of focusing groups on a common goal is to establish systems that reward the group based on their contributions to the accomplishment of the goal. In other words, rather than rewarding the production group for a high-quality product, reward them for a high-quality product that sells. Rather than rewarding the marketing groups for sales, reward them for profit. When groups are rewarded on the basis of their contributions to the whole, their orientation will be less self-focused and more cooperative. Whatever techniques are used, managers are responsible for maintaining and improving group effectiveness.

KEY POINTS

1 Groups consist of two or more people working to accomplish a common goal, and they can vary in terms of participation patterns, levels of understanding, cohesion, atmosphere, and structure.

2 Formal groups may be either temporary or permanent and are created by someone in authority to accomplish specific organizational objectives. Informal groups form spontaneously based on common interests or personal relationships. The activities and goals of the informal groups may or may not be related to organizational objectives.

3 Groups have many advantages: They fill people's social, security, and identity needs. They can be used to socialize new employees, accomplish tasks, and solve problems. Working with groups also has disadvantages: Group decisions take longer, and groups force conformity and are susceptible to pressures of rank and status.

4 Groups develop through a predictable sequence: forming, storming, norming, and performing. At each stage they need different types of support and guidance to be effective.

5 In the Homans model, required and emergent behaviors exist simultaneously in groups. Managers must guide and control both for groups to be effective.

6 Norms, the rules of behavior for group members, and roles, the set of expectations a person fills in a group, have a great effect on how people behave in a group.

7 Team building is a cyclical, continuing process in which groups identify and analyze breakdowns in their effectiveness, determine and implement solutions, and evaluate the results.

8 Groupthink is the phenomenon of overemphasizing the importance of consensus and conformity. Too much of it decreases a group's critical and evaluative abilities; too little of it may prevent the group from ever reaching a consensus or solution. Managers must encourage the sharing of opinions even though they may conflict, identify differences and talk about them, and critically analyze the group's problem-solving ability to keep it effective.

9 The differing characteristics and orientations of organizational departments, units, or levels naturally result in intergroup conflict. Too much of it inhibits or prevents overall organizational effectiveness, but too little may decrease innovation, production, or creativeness. By identifying or emphasizing a common enemy to competing groups, managers can achieve an effective level of competition or conflict.

FOR DISCUSSION AND REVIEW

1. Both individual motivation and group participation are necessary for the accomplishment of certain goals or objectives. When have you been in a situation where cooperation achieved a goal that individual action could not, or when group action slowed progress because individual action would have sufficed?

2. The text describes several characteristics of groups. Think of several groups you have seen or had contact with in various settings. What characteristics do they possess? How are they similar or different from each other?

3. Consider two organizations: one a small, owner-managed retail store in any town or city, the other an extensive chain operation with stores in many cities. In each situation, which tasks—such as inventory/buying decisions, marketing problems, layout/design issues, employee morale problems—would you recommend be handled by groups, and which by individuals?

4. The text lists several advantages and disadvantages, both on a personal level and an organizational level, to working in or with groups. Which of these have you experienced in a group situation?

5. Group development is defined, basically, as a four-step process. In what way do these four steps apply, or not apply, to the USA for Africa recording session?

6. We frequently read in the news of individuals who do something "above and beyond the call of duty" in an emergency situation, jeopardizing their own safety to rescue a person from a burning building or a frozen lake. Can you think of an example of a group exhibiting similar emergent behaviors?

7. Some tasks are best accomplished by specifying formal job descriptions and structures and others by managing and guiding informal relationships and group dynamics. Cite specific examples of such tasks.

8. What are the positive and negative effects on the organization of group norms and roles? Describe any that you have seen in action.

9. In some previous employment or academic situation, did you become aware that there was a discrepancy between an expected role, a sent role, a perceived role, and an enacted role? Did you experience this yourself or see it happen to someone else? What were the results?

10. What factors can cause a breakdown in the effectiveness of a functioning group? In what ways can this be beneficial? Harmful? How can effectiveness be restored?

11. What factors cause groupthink? When can groupthink be beneficial and when harmful? There have been many examples, quite a few in the military, of the harmful effects of groupthink. Why might the military be especially prone to this phenomenon, and how might you recommend this tendency be overcome?

12. A healthy balance of intergroup cooperation and conflict is beneficial to organizations. How can it be maintained, and what happens if the balance tips in either direction?

KEY TERMS

Activities	Group norms	Performing	Role overload
Emergent behaviors	Groupthink	Permanent groups	Sentiments
Formal groups	Informal groups	Required behaviors	Sociometry
Forming	Interactions	Role	Storming
Group	Linking pins	Role ambiguity	Temporary groups
Group dynamics	Norming	Role conflict	Work group

THE CONFERENCE TABLE: DISCUSSION CASE / 14.1

High-Powered Inertia

The Joint Chiefs of Staff. Although they are well-informed and powerful, the need to reach a consensus often waters down their advice.

What do you get when you combine the top military officers of the army, navy, marine corps, and air force with one chairman to coordinate them and 650 officers to support them in their strategy-making function? In the case of the U.S. Joint Chiefs of Staff (JCS), not particularly effective decision making. President Carter's secretary of defense, Harold Brown, went so far as to say that the recommendations he received during his four years in office had been "almost without exception either not very useful or the reverse of being helpful. That is, worse than nothing."

The five chiefs meet three afternoons a week in "the tank" in the Pentagon to thrash out differences among the services and determine long-term strategy. The Joint Staff, 650 officers drawn from the various services, supports the chiefs by providing accurate and impartial information upon which to base their decisions. Though the chiefs and the staff are all highly intelligent and experienced, the advice produced from the strategy sessions is often so useless and bland that Brown referred to it as "a bowl of oatmeal."

Several factors contribute to the impotency of the JCS. The "Byzantine bureaucracy" in which they operate has a tendency to stifle or water down any bold, creative approaches to the nation's defense that the JCS might devise. Each JCS

Sources: This case was written by M. R. Poirier, based on the following sources: "House Panel to Study Proposal to Revamp Joint Chiefs of Staff, *Wall Street Journal*, January 23, 1985, p. 12; Walloran, Richard, "Do Too Many Chiefs Spoil the Military?" *New York Times*, January 29, 1985, sec. 4, p. 22; Martin, David C., and Lerner, Michael A., "Why the General Can't Command," *Newsweek*, February 14, 1983, pp. 22–24.

recommendation must go through a series of drafts, called "flimsy," "buff," and "green," before being voted on and issued to the secretary of defense as "red stripe." At each step, any member of the JCS may "nonconcur" until the recommendation is amended and adapted and a consensus is reached. By this time, the red-stripe report may be too late or too thin to be of any use. William Brehm, who headed a 1982 study of the JCS, said that "the chiefs have written themselves out of the role [of military advisors to the secretary of defense] because they have these highly stylized procedures that drive content out. You get not the essence, but that portion of the military advice which is least contentious . . . They keep massaging it until the nonconcurrence disappears."

A second factor impeding the effectiveness of the JCS is that each member essentially wears two hats. Except for the chairman, each member serves both his individual service and the Joint Chiefs. A combination of pride in his service and fear of losing its loyalty provokes each chief to side with his own service on every issue. This problem also affects the Joint Staff. Each officer serves a tour with the JCS, afterwards returning to his or her own service. Since their service commanders maintain control over future promotions and assignments, the staffers feel they must constantly act on their service's behalf. Consequently, the information they provide is selective at best, and biased or inaccurate at worst. Though it would appear to be a prestigious assignment, serving on the Joint Staff, according to Brehm, is "perceived as a meaningless duty. The only thing it can do is hurt one's career."

Beyond being a waste in peacetime, an ineffective JCS is a disaster in war. Therefore, three years after Brehm's study, the issue was finally taken up by Congress. Several changes were proposed. The legislation proposed would provide the chairman of the JCS with more authority in planning and conducting military operations and in dividing funds among the services. This would prevent internal squabbling over funds and assignments. Local commanders would be given more authority to impose cooperation and cost controls among their services. The secretary of defense would have less power over day-to-day management of the military and more responsibility for broad defense strategy planning. The civilian department officials would take less part in planning and weapons procurement. Finally, multiyear budgeting has been proposed, which would call procurement specialists to plan further into the future and take advantage of lower unit costs of military equipment through economies of scale.

None of these measures will be passed without a fight because there are many who benefit from the current system. The new system would allow members of each service to have some control and influence over the operations of other services; obviously this ruffles some of the top brass. But no one claims the current system is adequate. "The disagreement is not between those who say the JCS works and those who say it doesn't," said one reporter. It is "between those who want it to work and those who don't." ■

DISCUSSION QUESTIONS

1. Using the concepts from the chapter, explain how you would manage the Joint Chiefs to improve their effectiveness.
2. How do groupthink and intergroup conflicts affect the Joint Chiefs, the Joint Staff, and the individual services?
3. How do you think the changes proposed by Congress will affect how the Joint Chiefs work together as a group?

THE CONFERENCE TABLE: DISCUSSION CASE / 14.2

The Visitor Who Stayed

In making a success of an inner-city farm, Gary Waldron found that groups can form even when the members have little in common, and that they can be effective even under adverse circumstances.

Many groups are formed to be temporary. They get together for a specific, predetermined amount of time, and when their task is finished, they disband. IBM Corporation has an executive loan program in which managers are sent for predetermined periods to work on community service projects. They continue to collect their salary, and at the end of the term, they return to their previous positions. Usually.

Gary Waldron was part of IBM's executive loan program in 1979. He went to the Bronx, in New York City, to help plan a group live-in experience (GLIE) farm. He was to be there for a year and then return to his position as a financial manager and controller. Instead, he stayed.

Waldron had worked most of his childhood summers on a farm in Pennsylvania, and he was raised and schooled a few blocks from the GLIE farm. From the beginning, it was his intention to make the GLIE more than just a token patch of green that would brown out when the grant money ran dry. Since his arrival, he has devoted his career to making the "temporary" project permanent and self-supporting, and he hopes to set up satellite farms in other parts of the city.

Based on what they were up against, this must be considered a fantastic example of group achievement. The first problem was the members themselves: one

Source: Gilbert, Susan, "Cities: A Real Farm Thrives Amidst the Rubble of a Blitzed South Bronx," *Audubon* (September 1983): 122–124.

executive from IBM, one office assistant, a horticulturist, a crew of runaway youths from the Bronx, a few children who for some reason could not live at home, and several adults who had been unemployed and on welfare for up to five years. Hardly a homogeneous bunch. The second problem was their resources: They were given a substantial grant and a vacant lot filled with "rusted box springs and car chassis, bricks, splintered doors, broken bottles, gashed tabletops, tires, and other city refuse," which was situated between three vacant tenements and the Cross Bronx Expressway.

Looking at their eventual accomplishments, it becomes obvious that the group was dedicated, determined, and united enough to overcome these obstacles. They cleared the lot and filled it with tons of fertile soil. They built a vast greenhouse on it from the pilings up, and planted, watered, tended, and nurtured the lot into a productive farm (recognized as such by the U.S. Census Bureau). Ironically, that same plot of land was a tomato farm a hundred years ago and is still zoned for farming.

After testing the feasibility and marketability of several crops, the farm decided to specialize in producing herbs: They are small enough to be cultivated in large quantities in greenhouses and small plots, and there is a large market for them in the city. Several of New York's finest restaurants, as well as hotels and restaurants in Boston, Connecticut, and cities as far away as Montreal, are among GLIE's customers. "Word has traveled from one chef to another that the farm in the South Bronx grows herbs that are difficult to find elsewhere . . . and that their quality is high."

The farm has had virtually no operating problems. The greenhouses around the corner—offshoots of the original—have no running water, so the crew runs hoses from the nearest fire hydrant to water the plants. And despite the farm's location and the fact that the greenhouse doors are unlocked and their only security is an ordinary chain-link fence, they have had only one run-in with vandals. In 1982, just before Mother's Day, some local kids climbed the fence and "went shopping" for flowers. "We weren't really angry," said Waldron, "because we felt the plants were being used in a productive way." Now that they specialize in herbs, Waldron expects no further incidents. "Some silly marigolds in bloom have street value, but what's a kid going to do with a pot of mint?"

The GLIE is a productive, self-supporting business now partially owned by its principal employees. Waldron has hopes for spinoffs of this group project, including a mushroom farm in an abandoned tenement. Experiments that they conducted convinced Waldron and his horticulturist that up to 2 million pounds of mushrooms could be raised each year in just one building. "This could alter the economics of the city," he said, "There's probably enough abandoned space to grow a hundred space-intensive crops. This could create tremendous local employment." What began for Waldron as a temporary group-leader assignment truly blossomed into much more. ■

DISCUSSION QUESTIONS

1. What characteristics did the GLIE group have that made it successful?
2. Considering the vast social and economic differences between the members, but also their desire to cooperate and make the project work, how would you say they progressed through the formation and development stages?
3. How might required and emergent behaviors, as well as activities, interactions and sentiments, come into play?

Comprehensive Case Four

Showtime at Motown Productions

Suzanne de Passe received her second Emmy award for producing the three-hour television concert *Motown Returns to the Apollo.* Her success in bringing off such complex projects depends on her ability to work with people, her skill as a television producer, and her ability to combine artists and concepts effectively.

From the moment of creative inspiration to the moment the last touches are put on the recording of the production, every new television or movie project is an ongoing administrative and logistical song and dance at Motown Productions. Every week, the executives and artists at the company meet to discuss each of up to 50 projects in some phase of development. First they talk about new inspirations and reach a consensus on which are "hot" enough to sell and which will never make it off the drawing board.

Then they discuss projects in development phases: Has the project manager for such-and-such production secured a contact with the necessary stars or producers? If not, will the project have any hopes of success, or could an alternative "name" be booked instead? How should the project manager proceed? Next on the agenda: An artist withdrew his tentative commitment to XYZ project after receiving a better offer from another studio for a different production. Should the project manager for the XYZ production offer the artist more money, or more creative control over the project? Or can the artist be replaced and the project proceed on schedule?

THE MANY ROLES OF SUZANNE DE PASSE

Suzanne de Passe, president of Motown Productions since 1980, presides over the staff meetings. She listens to the suggestions and opinions of all the artists and executives, always aware of the three strategic components of getting a production off the ground: (1) tying scripts or concepts together with

Sources: This case was written by M. R. Poirier, based on the following sources: Hopewell, Joan, "Motown's Other Mogul," *Channels* (September 1987): 38–39; Bray, Rosemary L., "Suzanne de Passe," *Ms.* (January 1986): 64–66. "Suzanne de Passe at Motown Productions," (#9-487-042, rev. 10/87), Harvard Business School Publishing, 1987; "Suzanne de Passe at Motown Productions," a Harvard Business School teaching note, 5-487-010.

artists and directors, (2) making packages attractive enough to secure financing from distributors, and (3) producing the project within budget and on schedule. Suzanne de Passe, as the driving force behind Motown Productions, makes sure her team knows where they stand on these strategic issues at every turn.

At the conclusion of each meeting, de Passe assigns each newly selected project to one of the executives for follow-up and developmental action, and delegates responsibility for each problem or issue concerning ongoing productions to whomever can handle it most effectively. Though the meetings are often heated and conflict-ridden from start to finish— largely because each person's pet projects are being openly criticized and analyzed—no staff members feel inhibited in voicing their honest opinions. All final decisions usually have the consensus support of the entire staff.

Finally, projects that have made it through all the development phases—from concept, to signing artists and talent, to designing a package to lure backers and distributors—can begin production. This is not the end of the road, it is just the beginning of yet another trying phase of project management. Not only must all expenses be considered carefully in regard to the allocated budget, but filming schedules must be balanced with two, often conflicting, constraints in mind: the availability of the artists involved, many of whom are working on more than one production simultaneously, and the deadlines set by the project's financial backers. For de Passe, this often requires a shift in roles from her job as president. While she assures the backers that everything is proceeding smoothly, she also goes out of her way to ensure the satisfaction of the contracted artists.

Meanwhile, de Passe, or the executive in charge of productions, must negotiate an endless number of unforeseen hurdles that arise during production. Each film or television special requires the contributions of hundreds of artists: technical crews; designers and makeup artists; script writers, musical composers, musicians, and performing artists. Each of these people has his or her own personal concept of the best way to do something: the most sensitive way to light a scene, the most upbeat musical score to support a scene, the most powerful way to portray the character's emotions at a given point. A line producer is generally charged with coordinating the work efforts and making sure that all the parts fit together. But the artists often come to de Passe to re-solve their conflicts; and her solution is always to call the parties in conflict to a meeting to resolve their differences among themselves.

MANAGEMENT STYLE AT MOTOWN

Her methods are not typical; heads of production companies are often characterized, based on many real-life examples, as tyrannical in their authority and determination to control all aspects of production. And her company is not run in a typical fashion. In most production companies, development and production functions are handled by separate divisions of the organization, while both are handled by one central group at Motown Productions. And in most other companies, one executive has complete control over each project, while at Motown, executives share responsibilities on projects as expertise suggests, and the creative development of each project is very much a group process.

But these eccentric methods have been quite successful for de Passe. Motown Productions started in the early 1970s as a movie production arm of Motown Records, a musical recording and distribution company founded in 1959 in Detroit by Berry Gordy. After two hits in 1972 and 1975—*Lady Sings the Blues* and *Mahogany*, respectively—the production arm put out a series of five failures. *The Wiz*, released in 1975, lost more than $20 million for its distributor, Universal Studios. Then, in 1981, Gordy spun Motown Productions off from the parent company, then renamed Motown Industries, as an independent subsidiary. Gordy offered Suzanne de Passe, who at age 34 was then his executive vice president, the presidency of the new company. By 1986, she had won Emmy awards for two of her productions (*Motown 25: Yesterday, Today and Forever*, and *Motown Returns to the Apollo*), had increased the company's revenues by more than five times, and was honored in 1986 as *Ms.* magazine's "Woman of the Year" for "leadership in combining art, business, and history."

Suzanne de Passe has been widely recognized not only for her leadership ability but for her ability to work with people, her skill and finesse in television production, her ability to pick and choose among concepts and artists and among combinations of them, and her success in reestablishing the reputation of Motown in the film industry. Now, in the late 1980s and 1990s, her skills and abilities will be put to the test. With new avenues opening up constantly, particularly in cable and video venues, de Passe is

Suzanne de Passe's management style emphasizes employee participation and hands-on involvement in all phases of development and production. It is her overall vision that enables her to shape the environment in which her staff works.

shifting the company's strategy from producing one project at a time (though many were always waiting in the wings) to producing several simultaneously. To accomplish this, she will draw largely on her experience in taking the floundering company from the brink of artistic and financial demise to its current position as a highly successful, innovative, independent production company.

BERRY GORDY'S TIMES

She did not have much to work with in 1980. On top of its recent string of production failures, the fledgling production company had a somewhat hostile relationship with the entertainment industry. Berry Gordy, as head of the company during its first decade, had alienated many artists and producers in the industry. Though his "unquestioned leadership, his emphasis on 'quality control,' and his ability to determine all facets of an artist's career combined to provide a balance between internal competition and cooperation" in both the recording and production arms of his company, these qualities also provoked many artists who gained fame under his tutelage to sign up with other companies later in order to gain greater financial rewards and more artistic freedom.

Meanwhile, Gordy developed a reputation for having poor relationships with directors and producers, often initiating heated battles for creative control over projects. After the failure of *The Wiz* in 1975, and Universal's substantial losses, Motown's reputation made it just about impossible to raise money for new projects. So, in 1980, Gordy handed de Passe a crippled company with a bad reputation, but also complete autonomy and a $10 million development budget. Fortunately, Gordy has a keen sense for leadership ability; de Passe was undaunted. She started from scratch and worked with what she had.

To staff the company, she turned to the people who had worked with her at Motown records. As a vice president, she brought in her creative assistant of 12 years, Suzanne Coston. Chris Clark, who worked on the screenplay for *Lady Sings the Blues*, was put in charge of internal development. Carol Caruso, who had been a production executive for Motown Production under Gordy, was hired as vice president for external development. In the spirit of the business, these four women who made up the core of the new company dubbed themselves the "Moettes."

Suzanne de Passe felt that the all-female executive staff worked to the company's advantage, though many in the field argued that they lacked experience and would never be able to pull projects off the ground in a male-dominated industry. But the group ignored the criticism. And de Passe argued that because the staff shared responsibilities on projects, filling in for each other at meetings and jointly reviewing progress and problems, they had an advantage over companies whose executives worked on projects individually.

THE EARLY PROJECTS

With this foundation, the group began to develop projects, though not surprisingly, the lack of support from the entertainment community hampered their initial efforts. Most of their early projects never got off the ground. But the staff was not easily worn down. As they stumbled, they learned, and they kept trying.

Meanwhile, de Passe honed her skills in deal making and negotiation, which were crucial to securing financial and artistic commitments, and her skills in planning, organizing, directing, and controlling, which were crucial to managing the production of projects once the commitments had been made. She emphasized employee participation and hands-on involvement in all phases of development and production, actively encouraging both artists and technicians to experiment and devise new concepts. She maintained control and influence over her staff not by instituting formal systems, but by providing an overall vision and developing a supportive culture within the organization. She remained the authority to which all of her co-workers turn, not because of her title as president, but because of her sheer volume of ideas, her personal magnetism, and her knowledge and reputation in the industry. From the beginning, she saw her job as primarily one of establishing an "esprit de corps" and making every employee in every position feel like they owned their projects and were crucially important to and responsible for results.

Her leadership style not only enables her to effectively manage an ever-changing roster of project teams and production efforts within the company, but it has helped her develop positive, productive relationships with the producers, artists, and financial backers in the industry upon whom the success of her projects depends. Thus, she has simultaneously reversed the financial and artistic slump of the company and has made its reputation in the industry do an about-face.

FIRST SUCCESSES AND FAILURES

In 1983, the new Motown Productions released its first production: *Motown 25: Yesterday, Today and Forever*. De Passe reunited the Jackson Five and the Supremes for the two-hour television special celebrating the twenty-fifth anniversary of the Motown label. The show was one of the highest-rated entertainment programs for the 1982–1983 television season, and de Passe won an Emmy for producing the best music/variety special of the year. This was the first significant boost to Motown Productions' credibility since de Passe took over.

In 1985, the second production was released: *Motown Returns to the Apollo*. The three-hour television concert production celebrated the reopening of New York's famed Apollo theater, and again, de Passe ensured the success of the project by securing the talent necessary to pull it off. After she gained Bill Cosby's commitment to host the program, the rest of the artists signed on in rapid succession. Ultimately, de Passe created a menu combining over 100 artists from various musical backgrounds and wove a production that thrilled the critics. For this production, she received a second Emmy for her role as executive producer.

Of course, not all of the productions released since de Passe took over were so highly successful. *Smokey Robinson and the Motown Revue*, for example, a variety series aired during the summer of 1985, was a critical failure. But while such a failure might have resulted in heated criticism and termination at another production company, the philosophy and culture at Motown Productions emphasizes the educational aspects of failure. De Passe took the blame for the production's shortcomings herself, then pointed out that the company had gained valuable experience in how and how not to put on a weekly variety show.

Following the success of the earlier ventures, de Passe determined that it was time to expand and that the company was ready to handle more than one production at a time. This strategic decision, however, would require several shifts in the established policies at Motown Productions. For example, though de Passe always made a point of hiring and promoting from within, she found that she would now have to search outside for the additional talent and expertise necessary to handle multiple projects and develop new markets.

This switch in policy caused some friction among the existing ranks. The new executives, for example, were paid higher salaries than those who had worked themselves up through the ranks. However, because the new executives had more industry experience and were being hired specifically for their specialized skills, their valuable connections, or their credibility in the various sectors of the market de Passe wished the company to enter, she had to "buy" these people from the market. As much as possible, she rewarded her other staff members with special projects, assignments, and creative freedoms. Beyond that, she relied on the strength of the long-term relationships she had built with them to keep them satisfied and motivated. The excitement her employees felt from working on innovative projects and the feeling of pride they gained from working for the company were both enormously helpful in her efforts.

As for the new recruits, de Passe faced the additional challenge of blending them into the existing culture. "I realized that it is vital when you bring someone in, you don't lose the group," she said.

OUTLOOK FOR THE FUTURE

In 1987, Motown Productions had 4 projects in production and 18 firmly in development. De Passe commanded a budget of over $70 million, up from $10 million in her first year there, and a staff of 23, up from the original four Moettes. The coming years will be trying for de Passe as she goes through the process of delegating control of Motown Productions' projects to outsiders, institutes some of the formal procedures and systems that will become necessary as the organization expands, delegates more operational responsibilities to Motown Productions staff members, and transfers the responsibility for maintaining crucial relationships with artists and financial backers to other executives. ■

QUESTIONS

1. Describe Suzanne de Passe as a manager, a director, and a leader. What type of leader is she, and would any of the researchers cited in Chapter 10 suggest she do anything to change? What would you suggest she change, if anything, to be an effective director, leader, or manager in the future?

2. How are staffing activities different for de Passe than for the manager of, for example, an insurance company or a more standard business? Are they more or less complex? How well do you think she has handled them, and what do you recommend she do in the future?

3. Consider one production, such as *Motown 25* or *Motown Returns to the Apollo*. How do you assume communication was involved from the initiation of the concept to the final production, based on the description of how a production unfolds offered at the beginning of the case? Where would breakdowns be likely to occur, what effects could they have on the project, and how would you guard against them or address them as they occurred?

4. How does de Passe motivate her staff? The artists she contracts? What factors can you see as likely to decrease or increase an employee's motivation in her company? Discuss her methods in terms of the three basic types of motivation theory discussed in Chapter 13.

5. Groups are obviously used extensively at Motown Productions. Describe the group dynamics of de Passe's weekly staff meetings. How effectively do you feel de Passe is at managing groups in her organization?

The final phase of the management process is controlling: monitoring and adjusting activities and resource utilization to accomplish organization goals. Without this phase, the process would be incomplete. Goals and plans would be established, but there would be no way to ensure that they would be realized. Managers could design the organization to achieve the plans and goals, but without monitoring and adjustment activities, there would be no way to ensure that organizational efforts actually achieved the goals. Managers could communicate strategy, motivate their work force, and strive to enhance its effectiveness through directing activities; but without monitoring and adjustment, no one at any level would be able to stay on track toward goal achievement.

Control is the function through which managers ensure that the goals they set are the goals that are achieved. It is the activity through which they adjust the performance and course of the organization continually so that it remains on track and effective.

In this part, we will discuss some of the tools managers can use to monitor, adjust, and control organizational performance. In Chapter 15, we will define control, outline the steps in the control process, describe several methods of control, and discuss some of the aspects of organizational performance on which managers tend to focus their control activities.

In Chapter 16, we will discuss production management as a subset of the control function. We will describe various operating systems and ways to choose the most effective one for a given situation, and we will discuss several specific tools managers use to control aspects of the production system.

The control of any organization depends significantly on information and the way it circulates throughout the organization. Therefore, in Chapter 17, we will discuss the purpose that information systems serve in organizations, the process through which managers establish information systems, several new developments in information technology, and the impacts these have on service and manufacturing industries.

PART ▲ FIVE

Control

15 Controlling Performance

Focus Case / The DIVAD, Out of Control

WHAT IS CONTROL?
Control in Organizations
Levels of Control

ELEMENTS OF THE CONTROL PROCESS
Setting Performance Objectives and Standards
Measuring and Evaluating Performance
Taking Corrective Action

METHODS OF CONTROL
Internal and External Control Methods
Formal and Informal Control Methods
Systematic and Ad Hoc Controls

QUALITY CONTROL
Total Quality Control

FINANCIAL CONTROLS
Budgets
The Balance Sheet, Income Statement, and Ratio Analysis
Cash Flow Analysis
Responsibility Centers

CONTROL THROUGH PERFORMANCE MANAGEMENT

EFFECTIVE DEGREES OF CONTROL

Managers make things happen, and good managers make sure that the right things happen in the right way and at the right time. Planning, organizing, and directing are therefore crucial managerial functions, but alone they are not enough. It is essential that managers also monitor organizational progress and operations to ensure that goals are actually being met, that resources are not being wasted, and that people are performing effectively. In this chapter, we will discuss how managers design systems of checks and balances and how they ensure that organizations perform as intended.

▪ KEY QUESTIONS

As you study this chapter, try to answer the following key questions:

1 What is control? What are its key steps or components?
2 What is the basic purpose of control in organizations?
3 What factors do control mechanisms on each level of an organization address?
4 What are two basic types of standards, and on what basis might they be determined?
5 In what different ways can controls be timed?
6 What are three methods of controls, and how do they differ?
7 What three areas of control are top priorities in organizations?
8 What degree of control is optimal?

Focus Case

The DIVAD, Out of Control

When managers lose control of a project, the result can be the expenditure of $1.8 billion for a technological marvel like the DIVAD—which cannot do any of the things it was intended to do.

In its conceptual stage during the 1970s, the Sergeant York gun was widely considered the solution to the army's ground defense problems. The army's only other antiaircraft weapons system, the Vulcan, carried missiles that were too large and elaborate to move around during combat and thus were only useful for protecting rear-area installations rather than tanks and troops in combat. The smaller missiles, called Stingers, were easy to carry but less effective in bringing down attacking aircraft. So no one disputed the army's need for a new antiaircraft weapons system.

In addition, no one disputed the army's insistence that it be a high-technology, "all singing, all dancing" ground defense system. During the mid-1970s, both enlistment and the quality of troops were down. Congress expected the army to operate with as few people as possible and to use weapons that required little skill to operate. "Putting the brains into the machine" became the slogan of the decade as Congress sought to promote wonder weapons that offered a hope of fewer deaths in the field.

But the effectiveness and value of the system never made it past the conceptual stage. The first problem was, in fact, the army's insistence that the weapon, also referred to as division air defense (DIVAD), be an ultra-technology system that could find targets with radar and aim itself using fully automated computer systems. It was designed to go wherever tanks could go and participate in ground fighting when not firing at the sky.

The army had tried to develop such weapons twice previously, with no success. During the 1960s, Army engineers testing an earlier such weapon produced a report (declassified in 1983) stating that radar-computer directed antiaircraft fire was a technological impossibility. While radar can tell with high precision where an airplane is, it cannot tell where the plane is going. The head of the DIVAD project, Lt. General James Maloney, admitted, "Of course DIVAD will miss if the target jerks [maneuvers]. No computer can handle a jerking target." In other words, there is no shame in failing to do that which cannot be done.

The army proceeded to look for a contractor to build the weapon. By 1980, two competing prototypes had been built, one by the Ford Aerospace division of Ford Motors and one by General Dynamics. Though neither did particularly well in tests, Ford's was less effective, recording only 9 hits to 19 for the General Dynamics contender. However, in 1981 Ford declared the largest

Sources: Easterbrook, Gregg, "Why DIVAD Wouldn't Die," *Washington Monthly* (November 1984): 10–22; Budiansky, Steven, "After DIVAD, an $11-Billion Plan," *Science Magazine,* April 10, 1987, pp. 137–140; Easterbrook, Gregg, "York, York, York," *The New Republic,* December 30, 1985, pp. 17–20.

corporate loss in U.S. history; in the White House, there was fear that Ford would declare bankruptcy or demand a Chrysler-style bailout. Government officials were inclined to throw Ford some business on the argument that production lines would be kept open. Ford won the contract in 1981.

At this point, army inspectors went over the prototype with a fine-toothed comb and found so many deficiencies that the production award was withheld for one year, subject to review in the spring of 1982. In September 1981, James Ambrose, vice president of Ford Aerospace in charge of the DIVAD project, was appointed undersecretary of the army. With Ambrose as the highest-ranking official present on the May 1982 review board, the board approved DIVAD production.

The first DIVADs came off the line six months late and in such shoddy condition that the army had to waive its contract requirement in order to accept them. During one test, a DIVAD locked onto a latrine fan. Of course, DIVAD's condition was not entirely Ford's fault, since the company was sent on a technological run-around. Nonetheless, in February 1984, the army formally notified Ford that its performance had been "totally unacceptable," and suspended DIVAD production.

After being challenged by Secretary of Defense Caspar Weinberger to show cause why the project should not be canceled completely, DIVAD's project managers staged a "realistic test" of the system in July 1984. During this test, the weapon was confined to shooting at a helicopter drone equipped with radar amplifiers. The amplifiers [Lunenberg lenses] refocus radar beams to make them easier for the sending unit to detect. At first the drone was fitted with only one Lunenberg lens, but that wasn't enough; DIVAD couldn't find it. With four amplifiers DIVAD finally scored a hit, and the tests were pronounced a success. In other words, this test was like testing a bloodhound's ability to track a human covered with beefsteaks standing alone and upright in the middle of a parking lot.

After this test demonstrated DIVAD's major flaws—its radar could track maneuvering planes but its computer could not aim at them, and its computer could handle hovering helicopters, but its radar could not track them—the project's proponents announced that the system's ineffectiveness could be cured by adding $1 billion worth of Stinger antiaircraft missiles to the gun. In other words, the antiaircraft weapon would carry an antiaircraft weapon to protect it from aircraft.

Despite all the evidence that the weapons system was ineffective, the army pleaded that stopping it at that point would mean that the $1.5 billion already spent would have been wasted.

In October 1984, Weinberger acted on pressure from Congress and suspended production for one year. In August 1985, the system was formally canceled after a final "realistic" but rigged test solidly demonstrated the system's inherent flaws. Total cost was $1.8 billion.

In retrospect, army officials have argued that DIVAD was the unfortunate victim of an "accelerated development" program. It was given only seven years from proposal to production, instead of "the normal 14." However, there are numerous examples of other systems that were more effective and less expensive, and that were designed and built in much less time. For example, the army's own internal weapons development unit, exempt from R&D regulations, took an automated antiaircraft weapon from inspiration to working prototype in eight months for less than $2.5 million. Mounted on an advanced jeep and operated by one person, it successfully hit a moving target on its first test while moving along at 20 miles per hour down a dirt road. ■

WHAT IS CONTROL?

Admittedly, the preceding example is extreme. However, it is a good illustration of the ways in which managers can lose control over a project or over progress toward objectives or goals. Numerous lapses in control are exhibited in the case: First, the less effective demonstration model was chosen to receive the manufacturing contract. Then, when the first prototypes were found defective, the buyer (the army) waived the quality specifications in the contract. Later, tests undertaken to prove the capabilities of the weapon system were rigged to produce positive, but inaccurate, results; people who knew that the technology did not work obscured this information from those in a position to cancel the project. Meanwhile, expenditures on the project increased almost unchecked, even as the system was found to be completely ineffective and cheaper alternatives to the system were discovered. In fact, the high expenditures themselves were to justify still more expenditures.

This case quite powerfully demonstrates the importance of control as a function of management. Every organization requires systems, procedures, and mechanisms to monitor what is going on in the organization, how this performance compares to goals and objectives, and what to do when discrepancies between goals and performance are revealed.

Control The process of monitoring performance and taking action to ensure intended or desired results.

Control is a process of monitoring performance and taking action to ensure intended or desired results. Controlling requires three basic steps or components: (1) setting performance standards and objectives, (2) analyzing how well activities and results compare against the standards, and (3) correcting performance that does not meet expectations, altering standards that are unsatisfactory, or acting to take advantage of opportunities that have been revealed.[1]

A managerial control system is similar to a household thermostat. The selected temperature is the performance objective, the standard against which the actual temperature of the room will be measured. The thermostat is the tool of control. It continually monitors the temperature of the room and sends information to the furnace when the temperature falls below or rises above the standard. The furnace—the performance corrector—acts on this information, emitting heat if the room is too cold or shutting itself off if the selected temperature has been reached. When new information is sent from the thermostat, the furnace will again make the necessary adjustments; the control process is an endless cycle.

Control in Organizations

Control mechanisms in organizations are of course much more complex than thermostats: All organizations have more than one objective, and all of these objectives are far more ambitious than the maintenance of a certain temperature. In a manufacturing organization, for example, managers will want to control the quality of the products produced; the costs of labor, resources, and energy; the time taken to produce and ship goods; and the cleanliness and safety of the work areas. In addition, they will want to monitor and control the performance, attendance, turnover, and satisfaction levels of all its employees as well as the progress of all units toward goals. In a service organization, managers will wish to monitor and control the same factors concerning their employees and organization goals but will also be concerned with the speed and quality of the service, the quality of relationships between employees and customers, and the costs of producing and delivering the service. In addition, all organizations are subject to certain legal requirements and limitations, and managers will have to control the activities of their firm or their employees to ensure compliance with these regulations.

Obviously, numerous control mechanisms of different types will be needed to address each of these issues. Some, such as measuring inventory, may be simple. Corrections in inventory are easy to make: If there are too few items, more can be ordered; if too many, orders can be withheld. Some things may be easy to measure but difficult to correct. For example, it is easy to count defective items or customer complaints, but it may be difficult to identify the cause of the defects or the reasons for the complaints. Without knowing either of these causes, managers will not be able to determine what corrective action is necessary. Finally, some things are both hard to measure and hard to correct: How can you really tell how satisfied your employees are? How do you measure the quality of relationships between employees and customers? Even if you could measure each of these things, what would you do to increase employee satisfaction or improve employee-customer relations?

In complex organizations, effective performance can be disrupted in hundreds of ways. Many of these will be difficult to measure, and many will affect other aspects of the operation. The basic purpose of control is to intercept these disturbances and to respond with appropriate action.[2] According to William Ross Ashby, a prominent early cyberneticist, a control system will be effective only if the number and variety of responses it is capable of exceeds the number and variety of disturbances the system it is controlling faces.[3] Because of the extent and complexity of the control function, many organizations have multilevel control systems to deal with the size, extent, and diversity of organizational activity.

Levels of Control

All organizations require three basic levels of management—technical, administrative, and institutional. Similarly, control systems should also be designed to operate on these three levels.[4] The activities undertaken at each level will differ, but if designed to work effectively as a system, together they will allow the organization to respond to a large number and variety of disturbances.

On the technical level, the most common type of controls are those similar to the thermostat. **Technical-level controls** monitor and provide feedback on operational performance and are aimed at standardizing performance to accomplish predetermined objectives. They clarify standards for correct or ideal performance and specify the corrective action to be taken when performance deviates from the standard. Monitoring that determines whether all size 8 dresses are exactly the same size, whether all fast-food hamburgers contain exactly four ounces of meat, or whether defect and complaint rates are up are technical-level controls. In the DIVAD case, reports concerning the number of targets accurately

Technical-level controls Controls that monitor and provide feedback on operational performance and that are aimed at standardizing performance.

hit or the number of tests taken before "acceptable" performance was reached were technical-level controls. Obviously, these controls were not useful because the reports were made from rigged tests.

Administrative-level controls Controls that regulate and monitor technical controls and ensure that appropriate technical controls are in place.

Administrative-level controls monitor performance of organization units, track how resources are being used, and make sure the objectives or standards on the technical level are correct. In addition, administrative-level controls address the question of whether the technical-level controls are appropriate. Referring to our thermostat example, an administrative control would question whether temperature is the only appropriate measure of comfort; perhaps humidity, light, and airflow should be included as comfort criteria. Using administrative controls, managers can coordinate work activities and resource allocations across units or adjust the controls on the technical level.

Budgets are one of the most common administrative-level control tools. In the DIVAD case, it was not determined until after the project was finally canceled in 1985 that the contractor had overbilled the army by $84 million. It was discovered that, in many cases, Ford Aerospace had given the army an estimated price for subcontracted components, then obtained the components for less, pocketing the difference. This was just one way cost overruns built up and reflected the weaknesses in the administrative control systems used.

Institutional-level controls Systems or frameworks that guide action and decision making affecting the total organization.

Institutional-level controls are "guidance systems," or mission and value frameworks that guide action and decision making affecting the total organization. At this level, the question becomes whether the right objective and strategy have been adopted. To continue the thermostat analogy, controls at the institutional level would help determine whether comfort was sufficiently important to be the objective. Perhaps the building is scheduled to be converted or sold and other objectives become more important.

Organizations are also controlled, by external forces. As we discussed in Chapter 6, every organization operates within a changing environment, and is affected by legal, competitive, and social forces. **Social control** of organizations is society's control over organizational action. Society expects clean, safe environments and pure, safe, reliable products and services. The government enforces these expectations through regulation and inspection. Regulatory agencies set standards for performance, and their inspectors regularly check to see that these standards are being met. If not, the organization in violation is expected to correct the deficiency and may also be fined or shut down temporarily. The Inside View 15.1 provides one illustration of social control.

Social control Society's control, especially through government regulation.

At each level—technical, administrative, and institutional—managers commonly use a technique referred to as management by exception. Acceptable limits are set, and as long as performance remains within these levels, no corrective action is taken.[5] Management only gives attention to exceptions. For example, at the institutional level, executives may outline acceptable levels of return on investment, market share, and product quality. As long as performance remains within acceptable levels, middle-level managers are given discretion to act. If performance is too low, top management will step in to correct the situation. At the technical level, management may define acceptable levels of quality. As long as production is within the acceptable levels, management lets the production line run; only when it deviates does management step in and implement changes.

In the remainder of this chapter, we will discuss the elements of the control process, various methods and types of control, and ways to determine the most effective degrees of control.

Bank of Boston

Sloppy financial controls cost Bank of Boston a $500,000 fine and a loss of investor and customer confidence.

bank employees and a sloppy control system. The bank, the largest in New England and the sixteenth largest bank in the country, paid a $500,000 fine after pleading guilty to a felony—handling millions of dollars of cash for a reputed organized-crime boss without alerting the government. Three congressional committees have investigated this laundering scheme and have put the bank in the spotlight. In addition the bank did not report shipments of U.S. currency to and from Swiss banks (in the amount of $1.22 billion) as required by law. Despite official letters and at least one telephone call with a senior Treasury official alerting the bank to the legal requirements, the practice continued.

The source of these problems has been blamed on poor judgment and a systems failure in the international funds transfer area. Whatever the cause, the problems demonstrate sloppy controls for a $22 billion bank and have created a public relations crisis that has been poorly handled. Since banks deal in confidence, errors and problems like this can shake investor and customer confidence alike. As yet, the final costs of this problem on the bank, its profitability, and its image are not yet in. ■

In early 1985, the staid and conservative Bank of Boston was rocked by a public scandal that was attributable to the mistake of some lower-level

Source: Wessel, D., and Davis, B., "Bank of Boston Faces Image Problem Likely to Linger for Years," *Wall Street Journal*, March 7, 1985, pp. 1, 29.

ELEMENTS OF THE CONTROL PROCESS

Every level of management has some responsibility for control, though the specifics of that responsibility will differ with the situation each manager faces. The manager designing a control system to guarantee product quality in a packaging operation has different responsibilities than the vice president of finance in charge of designing a financial control system, but both will utilize the same basic elements of the control process. The three steps in the design of a control system (see Exhibit 15.1) are:[6]

1. Set performance standards and objectives
2. Measure and evaluate performance against the standards
3. Take corrective action, adjust the standards, or act to take advantage of an opportunity revealed.

Setting Performance Objectives and Standards

Standard A specific criterion against which actual performance can be compared.

The first step in designing the control system is to specify the performance objectives and standards. A **standard** is a value or specific criterion against which actual performance can be compared. Whether the objective is the responsibility of a manager at the technical, administrative, or institutional level, the standards should be derived from the goals and objectives that have been set. At Zayre Department Stores, for example, top managers had a goal of improving customer satisfaction. After asking store managers to monitor customer satisfaction in the store, they found that their main service problem was that customers got angry when they had to wait in long checkout lines. Therefore, reducing waiting time (shortening the queue) became an objective. After additional monitoring, store personnel discovered that it was not the time spent waiting that seemed to bother people but the length of the line. Customers didn't seem to mind waiting when

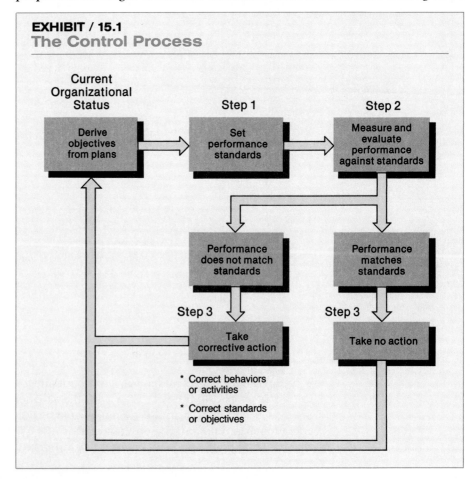

EXHIBIT / 15.1
The Control Process

the line was only two or three people long but became irate when it was five or more people in length.[7] Management set a performance standard: When more than three people were in a checkout line, a new checkout line would be opened. This standard clearly specified to checkout clerks when they were to open new lines rather than attend to other duties.

Types of Standards   Managers can set and use many types of standards. At Zayre, the length of the line was correlated with customer tolerance for waiting. In addition to time, standards are most often developed around quantity measures (units of output, turnover rates, days absent), quality measures (zero defects), or cost measures (dollar amounts or percentage of budget). In the DIVAD case, several standards were not met: The first units were six months late coming out of production. Each unit hit very few targets and, for the most part, only did so in rigged conditions that "bore no relationship whatsoever to any condition the DIVAD would encounter in wartime."[8] Finally, the army spent almost $2 billion, and did not wind up with a usable product. Each of these standards—time, quality, quantity, and cost—establishes a desired level of results and are referred to as **output standards.**

Output standards
Standards that establish a desired level of results, such as time, quality, quantity, or cost.

These output standards are the most common ones used by managers at all levels to measure performance inside the organization, but it is important also to set output of standards for the organization as a whole in consideration of the environment—the outside world.[9] Returns to shareholders and price-earnings ratios are two examples; they are easy to measure and compare against those of other organizations. However, corporate "good citizenship" is an output standard for the whole organization that is difficult to measure or compare. An organization may abide by laws, strive to maintain a clean environment, and support the local charities but this may not correspond to any particular corporate "citizenship" rating or ranking. And the issue becomes more complex when, for example, maintaining the environment is accomplished only by increasing internal costs or at the expense of the organization's profitability. In the DIVAD case, high costs were justified because it was believed they would result ultimately in more saved lives, which everyone would favor. However, this is only a valid justification if the high expenditures actually produce an effective product. For these reasons, it is most important that output standards at all levels of the organization be integrated and be designed with overall strategic priorities in mind.

Behavioral standards
Standards that address the way an activity is to be performed and the steps in its performance.

Behavioral standards address the way an activity is to be performed and the steps in its performance. They are generally used in situations where output standards are not applicable or are difficult to determine. For example, output standards would not apply in determining how well a service representative managed relationships with customers or how well an administrative manager developed subordinates for increased responsibility. In these situations, standards would have to focus on specific behaviors or activities. Does the service representative respond to inquiries quickly, circumvent conflict, and make the customer feel that the organization values his or her business? Does the administrative manager provide training, coaching, and opportunities for the subordinates to demonstrate their potential?

Historical standards
Standards based on individual or corporate experience.

Basis of Standard Setting   Determining standards for performance is a difficult task. One method of standard setting is to base the standard on individual or corporate experience. These standards are generally referred to as **historical standards.** Previous sales, profits, quality, and quantity levels can be evaluated to serve as a basis for future expectations. If in the past year the assembly line has maintained an output of 2000 units per day with an average of 20 defective units, the new standard may be to increase output to 2500 units and/or to decrease defects to 10 or zero. If historically the division managers of a large corporation have successfully developed and promoted 70 percent of their staff internally and lost 30 percent to turnover, a standard might be set to improve that ratio to 80 to 20 or 90 to 10. The army's Vulcan antiaircraft weapon had an effective range of one kilometer (it could effectively shoot down targets within a distance of one kilometer). The DIVAD had a planned range of four kilometers, and the weapon system currently being designed to replace DIVAD has a range between six and eight kilometers.

Comparative standards
Standards based on the experience of others.

Comparative standards, standards based on the experience of others, can also be used to manage organizations. On the institutional level, for example, the financial performance of one company is often compared against others in the same industry to measure both progress and success. One advantage of these standards over historical ones is that they are oriented toward the present and force the organization to keep pace with external conditions. One reason the DIVAD was deemed ineffective even when it did accurately hit targets was that it was designed to have a four-kilometer range, and immediately after it was produced, the Soviets produced an attack helicopter that could hover and attack effectively from six kilometers.

Measuring and Evaluating Performance

The second step in the control process is to measure and evaluate performance. Actual performance must be compared against desired performance as set by the standard. Measurement can be continuous, as with air quality in nuclear facilities, or infrequent, as with progress checkpoints on long-term research and development projects.

Timing of Control   There are three general time periods in which control mechanisms can be undertaken: (1) precontrols, (2) concurrent controls, and (3) postcontrols. See Exhibit 15.2.

Precontrols   Controls performed before work takes place; also referred to as feed forward controls.

Controls performed before work takes place are referred to as *feed forward* or **precontrols.**[10] The goal of precontrols is to eliminate activities and behavior that are foreseen to cause performance failures. Precontrols therefore serve a preventative maintenance function. Clear job descriptions, training programs, and effective communication of task requirements are examples of precontrols.

For example, the U.S. Navy uses an administrative-level control program called "preventive maintenance system" on all equipment and machinery. Before any check or test is undertaken, a project manager consults a preprinted card about the equipment. The card lists all the required materials, the skill level required to accomplish the task, the amount of time necessary to do the job, and a complete step-by-step set of instructions, including any special requirements or actions. The card also lists all the relevant reference manuals needed and the acceptable range of performance for the equipment. As a consequence, the manager knows before the task is begun what is needed, how long it should take, the steps necessary to do the task, and the standards of performance for the equipment once the task is accomplished. This system reduces the likelihood of failure or deviation from the standard.

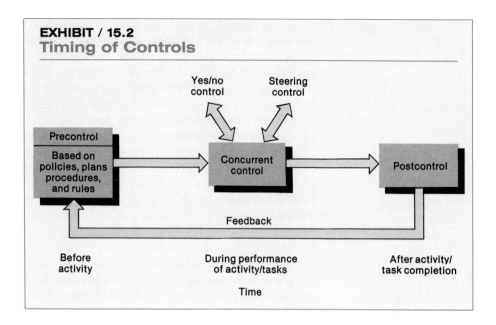

EXHIBIT / 15.2
Timing of Controls

Yes/no control — Steering control

Precontrol
Based on policies, plans procedures, and rules

Concurrent control

Postcontrol

Feedback

Before activity — During performance of activity/tasks — After activity/ task completion

Time

Concurrent controls
Control mechanisms used as work is being performed; also called steering controls.

Yes/no controls
Concurrent controls that act as checkpoints at transitional phases of an operation.

Postcontrols Controls undertaken when an activity or task has reached completion and is undergoing final inspection.

The control mechanisms used as work is being performed are called **concurrent controls** or *steering controls*. Inventory control is an example of concurrent control. Through analysis of past ordering practices and requirements, an organization knows when to reorder certain parts to keep inventory at acceptable levels. Reordering at this time ensures that enough parts will be on hand when needed and that the optimal ordering size is used for volume discounts and rapid delivery.

Yes/no controls are common concurrent controls that serve as checkpoints or screening points at transitional phases of an operation. When a product or service arrives at a designated critical phase, it must meet a specific standard or criterion before it moves on to the next phase. These controls can operate at many points in a process. On the technical level, component parts of a machine may be inspected before being sent to the production area; if they are found unsatisfactory, they will not be sent. The completed prototype of the DIVAD was checked in 1981; considering it unsatisfactory, the army withheld the fund award until a second check a year later. The prototype was approved the second time around. During phases of production, machines or products also may be tested to see that they meet specifications; if some do not, they can be taken from production and improvements can be made. Yes/no controls, when used effectively, can be both preventive and corrective in function.

Postcontrols are undertaken when the activity or task has reached completion and is undergoing final inspection. These controls tend to be corrective, and they have the built-in advantage of identifying who is responsible for success or failure. Strategy and customer responses are postcontrols at the institutional level. For example, Ford Motor Company's strategy in the early 1980s was "Quality Is Job 1." While the army was accepting DIVADs that did not work from the Aerospace Division, the automotive division was suspending production of its Tempo and Topaz models because of a manufacturing defect. Ford voluntarily halted production because the customers, American car buyers, would have reacted immediately and negatively if defective cars had been sold. But the DIVAD buyer, the army, not only did not complain, it covered up many of the product's major flaws. This put Ford Aerospace in a difficult position: They were already building the Sidewinder missiles, one of the most cost-effective weapons in the military arsenal at the time. If they withdrew from the DIVAD project, realizing it was a technological impossibility, they risked making the government look bad and thus risked losing much-needed defense contracts.

In performance evaluation it is important to keep in mind that priorities change when environmental conditions change. Assume, for example, that because of recent governmental budget cuts, the funds available to support some health programs in a certain large metropolitan hospital are reduced. Because of the budget cuts, some of the performances may fall below historical standards. Patient satisfaction with nursing service may decline because there are fewer nurses and support staff working in each patient area, but at the same time the hospital may actually be doing a more efficient job than in the past, getting better performance from the resources (people, money) it does have. The sacrifice of extra personnel for in-patient care may have been made in order to fund the continuation of a community health clinic run by the hospital. In this case, the overall delivery of service to the community may be greater despite a decrease in patient satisfaction. As The Inside View 15.2 illustrates, to gain an overall picture, it is important to measure performance across many activities even ones that are not so easily measured.

Understanding Deviations   As the hospital example indicates, when performance is evaluated it is not enough to know that deviations occurred. Managers also need to understand why the established standards were not met. Was a shortcoming in one area necessary for an improvement in another? Were the deviations the fault of the managers involved, or did conditions beyond the control of anyone in the organization affect performance?

There may be more complex reasons why an organization's actual performance does not meet the standards set by management. Exhibit 15.3 provides a list of common reasons for deviations from standards that has been drawn from a study of well-known accidents and problems in organizations.

Taking Corrective Action

Managers have several options after evaluating performance and identifying causes of deviation from standards: (1) do nothing, (2) correct the problem, (3) revise or alter the standard being used, or (4) take advantage of an opportunity revealed. Often, a control system will indicate to the manager that deviations are small or nonexistent, and the organization's performance is on track. If problems are not significant and remedying them is costly or time consuming, it is probably wise for the manager to do nothing.

Significant problems, however, require decisive managerial action. Identifying the reasons why standards were not met often helps managers determine what corrective action should be taken. For example, if a firm is experiencing a 50 percent employee turnover rate when the industry norm is 20 percent, there is a problem. The causes for turnover can range from poor pay to lack of advancement opportunities to uncomfortable or unsafe working conditions to poor supervision. If the cause is poor pay, corrective action will mean salary reviews. If the cause is unsafe working conditions, corrective action will mean plant or office remodeling.

THE INSIDE VIEW / 15.2

Quality Is Free

One sign of a decline in quality control is when customers start returning faulty goods.

The following is a description of a management monthly status review meeting, quoted by Philip B. Crosby in his book *Quality Is Free,* based on his experience at ITT:

"Inventory increased $270,358 this month for a total of $21,978,375.18. This is still $9981 below budget, but I think it requires a good look because the rate of increase is getting steeper."

"Good point," says the boss, who then directs purchasing to see if they are bringing material in quicker than needed and asks material control to give him a detailed report on in-process versus finished-goods inventory.

"Sales are directly on budget except for the hotel operation, where occupancy is falling off. During the week occupancy is running 98 percent, but this is dragged down by the weekend rate of 35 percent."

"Hmmm," says the boss. "Marketing better get hopping on putting together some weekend specials. 'Take the little lady away from it all' sort of thing. Give them a special rate and a bottle of bubbly. That should take care of it."

"Employee compensation is over budget. We've been paying too much overtime in the foundry and electronic test operations. This is caused by delinquent schedules in the assembly group. They got 2 days late last month and haven't been able to catch up." "Production," frowns the boss, "hasn't been paying enough attention to scheduling. I think it's all due to that new and expensive computer operation. Set up a task team to find out what's wrong and give me a daily report."

"Our quality is falling off—we've had several customer complaints."

"There's no excuse for low quality. The quality department has to get on the ball," growls the boss. "Maybe we need a new quality manager. I want high quality. Meeting adjourned."

At this point, Crosby points out that "everything in the above report is quite precise, even down to the last 18 cents of inventory." Quality, however, is merely described as "falling off." Why isn't that portion of the company not reported in numbers? Crosby asks.

Why is it left dangling in midair? Why is the quality manager suddenly considered inadequate when the other functional managers who have troubles are not? Why wasn't he there?

(*Continued on next page.*)

How come there wasn't a report on quality? Something like this:

"Our receiving inspection rejection rate has climbed from 2.5 to 4 percent in the last month. This is due to purchase orders on standard hardware not calling out the proper plating requirements. Printed circuit board rejections have risen from 4 to 6 percent due to untrained assemblers being placed on the line. Production has pulled them back for training. Customer returns have dropped from 3 to 1.2 percent, but this has cost us $35,491 in overtime due to the additional testing required. An engineering error was responsible for the defect. Changes have been issued and the problem will be corrected by the 18th of next month. The cost of quality is running at 6.1 percent of sale, and we plan to meet the year-end objective of 5.9 percent."

"Great," beams the boss. "As long as we can find these situations early and take action, we will be able to have confidence in our conformance. Quality is doing a fine job."

Quality is free, says Crosby, but no one is ever going to know it if there isn't some sort of agreed-on system of measurement. ∎

Source: Crosby, Philip B., *Quality Is Free* (New York: McGraw-Hill, 1979), pp. 101–102.

Sometimes the goals and standards will have to be revised. For example, assume that, after using the best forecasts available, an investment firm has set a goal of a 12 percent sales increase for next year. Managers will set up marketing, sales, and financial goals consistent with that increase in sales. The control system will be adjusted to measure performance (e.g., each broker must increase clientele by 2 percent and increase overall sales by 1 percent per month) against that organizational goal. If a recession occurs in the middle of the year, however, sales will be far below predicted levels and clientele may not increase at all. One reasonable course of action in this situation will be to modify the goals and standards downward to reflect the overall economic slowdown.

In the DIVAD case, this type of response was actually abused. When it was determined that the weapon could not hit a maneuvering target, and thus could not serve its purpose of protecting soldiers from attacking aircraft, the project manager simply said of course it could not, because no computer could. Army officials basically said that "DIVAD's inability to handle jerking targets is not an issue because everybody knows DIVAD can't handle jerking targets."[11]

In the opposite case, if an organization or project is exceeding the standards, they should be readjusted upward. Standards that are either too low or too high, too easy or too difficult to reach, are an organizational liability. They encourage employee distrust for, and contempt of, the entire control system and process. Any organization (or individual) that finds itself continually revising standards is exhibiting serious problems of incompatibility between its control system and its planning process.

Finally, measurement and monitoring activities may reveal an opportunity rather than a problem or deficiency. In the investment firm example, the recession resulting in lower overall sales may open up increased sales opportunities for certain types of investment products that thrive in recessions. The firm's management should then revise standards to increase the focus on sales of these items.

METHODS OF CONTROL

There are several different ways in which managers can undertake the control function. These methods can be internal or external, formal or informal, systematic or ad hoc. Most organizations use some combination of these methods.

Internal and External Control Methods

Internal control A control method in which an individual or group sets its own standards and monitors and corrects its own performance.

External control Control carried out through the organization's formal authority systems.

Internal control is essentially self-control or self-discipline. Internal control occurs when an individual or group determines how a specific objective is to be achieved, carries out the tasks to achieve it, monitors its own progress, and corrects itself as necessary during the process. **External control** includes rules, procedures, hierarchical reporting routes, and direct supervision imposed by others. External controls form a framework within which employees can exercise their own discretion.

Formal and Informal Control Methods

Formal controls Arrangements in which managers determine standards of performance, monitor performance and feedback, and take corrective action.

Informal controls Methods of standard setting, monitoring, and adjustment that do not conform to formal procedures.

Formal controls are arrangements in which managers determine standards of performance, monitor performance and feedback, and take corrective action. In other words, formal controls follow very specifically the three-step process discussed above. Most of the controls we have discussed so far are formal controls. **Informal controls** are methods of standard setting, monitoring, and adjustment that are done spontaneously in the normal course of work. Hewlett Packard, the California computer company, for example, emphasizes the importance of having managers "walk around" as a means of informal hands-on management control. According to Hewlett Packard research and development executive John Doyle:[12]

> Once a division or department has developed a plan of its own—a set of working objectives—it's important for managers and supervisors to keep it in operating con-

---

EXHIBIT / 15.3
Reasons for Deviations from Standards

1. *Faulty Planning* Were unreasonable assumptions made by management when they developed the plan and standards?
2. *Fuzzy Standards* Were the standards unclear, difficult to measure, or highly subjective? Did the standards make sense in light of the conditions that prevailed in the organization?
3. *Inappropriate Controls* Were the standards inappropriate to the performance that management was trying to oversee? If performance could fall into an acceptable range of values, were the boundaries accurate (just as ideal tire pressure is 32 pound per square inch and acceptable pressure is 28 to 36 pounds per square inch)?
4. *Failure to Identify Significant Deviations* The exception principle holds that managers should pay attention only to significant problems, leaving less significant problems for lower-level staff to solve. Sometimes, however, an employee may underestimate the importance or significance of a problem and fail to bring it to the attention of the appropriate manager. In the worst case, the manager may not recognize the problem's significance or may deliberately downplay its importance.
5. *Insufficient Frequency of Measurement* Because it is costly to evaluate performance, managers have to decide whether the benefit to be derived from the evaluation is equal to or greater than the cost. This may lead to relatively less frequent performance reviews, and hence more opportunity for deviations to creep into the system.
6. *Personnel-Related Causes* People are a highly variable resource, and even the best selection process will not perfectly prevent human error. Ineptitude, negligence, or lack of knowledge are but a few of the human factors that may contribute to deviations from standards of performance.
7. *External Forces* All organizations exist and operate in a changing external environment over which they have little or no control. These environmental forces can range from the weather (blizzards, sandstorms, and hurricanes), to the actions of competitors, to government decisions.

Source: Newman, W. H., *Constructive Control* (Englewood Cliffs, N.J.: Prentice-Hall, 1975).

dition. This is where observation, measurement, feedback, and guidance come in . . . management by wandering around is the business of staying in touch with the territory all the time. . . . By wandering around I literally mean moving around and talking to people. It's all done on a very informal and spontaneous basis, but it's important in the course of time to cover the whole territory. You start out by being accessible and approachable, but the main thing is to realize that you're there to listen. The second is that it is vital to keep people informed about what's going on in the company, especially those things that are important to them. The third reason for doing this is because it is just plain fun.

Management researchers have also discovered that organizational norms become informal controls. Norms are the unwritten rules of behavior for a group. As we discussed in Chapter 12, groups often develop norms about the pace of work, the quality of work, and acceptable "down time," or relaxing time. Such group norms can have either a positive or negative influence on organizational performance, and managers must creatively mesh these informal means with more formal systems.

Systematic and Ad Hoc Controls

Systematic controls Controls that produce information about activities on a routine or predictable basis.

Ad hoc controls Control activities undertaken apart from the routine reporting processes of the organization.

Many control systems, and certainly most formal control systems, are designed to produce information about a particular activity or set of activities on a routine and predictable basis. These are **systematic controls. Ad hoc controls** are undertaken apart from the routine reporting schedules of the organization. For example, if management becomes concerned about the accounting practices of a particular department, it may appoint an accounting firm to conduct a special audit of the unit's practices. Managers often engage in special studies of problems or activities in the organization.

Ad hoc control procedures may exist for a short time, or they may become part of the ongoing reporting system of an organization. In other words, the ad hoc controls may become systematic, formal controls. During the early 1970s, for example, oil prices escalated rapidly, sometimes doubling and tripling the cost of energy for residential and commercial users. Management task forces were formed in many organizations to monitor oil consumption and devise ways to conserve energy. In some organizations, special energy audit units were created to redesign energy usage. This activity proved so vital that the units were continued long after the crisis was over.[13]

You should by now have a thorough understanding of the methods of control, the general process of establishing control systems, and the need to integrate controls across organizational levels. We will now discuss three areas of control that are top priorities in organizations: quality control, financial control, and control of human resources performance.

QUALITY CONTROL

Quality control The process of maintaining and guaranteeing a given level of product or service quality.

Quality control is the process of maintaining and guaranteeing a given level of quality in the product or service delivered. It is extremely difficult to do, but nonetheless important. Manufacturing, by its nature, allows for large-scale product testing, quality checks, and the establishment of rigid acceptance standards to ensure quality in products before they are delivered. Guaranteeing quality of services is harder because they are consumed at the same time they are produced. No one would recommend that doctors make a few practice incisions to test their abilities before an operation. It is possible, however, to manage quality by evaluating incisions as they are made. The result with each patient becomes a quality check for succeeding patients.

Quality assurance An organized attempt to ensure quality before a product or service is marketed.

Quality assurance (QA) has a much broader focus than quality control. Quality assurance is concerned not just with the detection of problems but with the prevention of quality problems. It is an organized attempt to ensure quality before a product or service is marketed.

With every measure taken to increase quality, production costs can rise. A point will normally be reached at which the costs of further quality increases will outweigh their benefits. In other words, it might cost an organization hundreds of thousands of dollars to develop and implement a product improvement that does little or nothing to increase the sales value of the product and that is of virtually no significance to any consumer. In the worst case, the improvements, though impressive conceptually, will not be realizable, as happened in the DIVAD case. As one author put it: "Basing procurement decisions on what weapons do in theory is like my saying it will take me an hour to get from Washington to Philadelphia because my car has a top speed of 120 miles per hour. I could get into serious trouble if I confused what my car is capable of doing with how I use it under real-world conditions."[14]

Total Quality Control

Traditionally, quality control was the responsibility of a quality control department. Whatever level of defects the department set as acceptable was the level the production department would adhere to. Whichever defects the department caught would be corrected. But recently, organizations have been striving to achieve and maintain quality in a more comprehensive, integrated way.[15]

Today, many organizations have adopted a strategy of total quality control. The concept was originated in 1961 in the United States by A. V. Feigenbaum in his book *Total Quality Control,*[16] but it has taken more than 20 years to catch on. In fact, the successful use of such techniques by the Japanese and their growing competitive strength in the previous decades provided the primary impetus for American companies to adopt the techniques.

Total quality control A quality control process that assigns responsibility for quality to workers rather than managers.

Total quality control (TQC) is a quality control process that assigns responsibility for quality to every worker rather than a handful of managers. The process is an end in itself and stresses that all errors or defects be identified and resolved at their source. Krajewski and Ritzman offer the following example of TQC: "At Kawasaki's U.S. plant, lights of different colors strung along the assembly lines indicate the severity of the quality problem detected. Workers activate a yellow light to indicate that a problem has been detected and a red light when the problem is serious enough to stop the production line."[17]

The TQC process is a commitment to control. It emphasizes full participation of all employees; all workers are responsible for preventing and correcting defects. Considering the DIVAD case, had the army adopted a total quality control program, everyone from the technicians who tested the first prototypes to the project managers would have considered it their responsibility to stop the project or demand improvements from the contractor.

FINANCIAL CONTROLS

In addition to guaranteeing quality, organizations are always interested in controlling costs—for example, managing the trade-off between increases in quality and increases in costs. Financial controls are commonly used to monitor the sources and uses of cash during an operating period (generally a year in length). The DIVAD case, beyond highlighting the extensive failure of a control system, indicates the critical importance of financial control systems. The most common financial controls are budgets, ratio analysis of financial statements, and cash flow analysis.[18]

Budgets

Budgets Financial controls that present the projected and approved expenditures of an organization's financial resources.

The most common financial control technique is the budget. All firms have limited resources and must balance expenditures against income. **Budgets** present the projected and approved expenditures of an organization's financial resources—for the firm as a whole, for its individual units, and for any substantive project about to be undertaken. As such, budgets are a preventive and corrective tool. The approved expenditures and plans are preventive in nature, limiting a manager's authority to commit the firm's financial resources. The original budget allocation for DIVAD was $4.5 billion; $1.8 billion was spent before the project was canceled in 1985. Budgets are also corrective, because deviations from the approved expenditures are readily apparent to management. If expenditures exceed budgeted amounts, corrective action is required. The DIVAD units were supposed to cost between $7 million and $8 million each; by the time the program was canceled, 80 were purchased and $1.8 billion had been spent. That amounts to an average $22.5 million per unit. Obviously, production was not kept within budget.

Variable budgeting A budgeting process that recognizes that expenditures will change as the volume of sales and/or production is altered.

The two most common forms of budgeting are variable and zero-based. **Variable budgeting** is based on the recognition that expenditures will change as the volume of sales and/or production is altered. Variable budgets include fixed and variable costs. Fixed costs are constant regardless of volume. The cost of renting a building is an example of a fixed cost: It does not vary with the amount produced and sold. Variable costs change in relation to production or sales volume. Raw materials and salespersons' commissions are examples of variable costs. Good management control would closely monitor variable costs to ensure that they change appropriately in proportion to changes in sales and production.

Zero-based budgeting A budgeting process that requires managers to justify their entire budget and every portion of it for the year.

Zero-based budgeting (zbb) was begun by Texas Instruments in the 1970s. It requires managers to justify their entire budget, and each portion of that budget, every year. This justification effort is quite time consuming and generates numerous reports, but it does force a thorough evaluation of all expenditures.

The Balance Sheet, Income Statement, and Ratio Analysis

Balance sheet A report that illustrates the firm's financial position at a given point in time.

Organizational budgets are often derived from an overall assessment of what the organization's goals are, what it has to spend, and what it owes, all of which are reflected in the firm's balance sheet and income statement. The **balance sheet** shows the firm's financial position, that is, a comparison of how much it is worth and how much it owes, as of a given point in time. Exhibit 15.4 is a sample balance sheet. Assets are things of value owned by the firm and are generally

EXHIBIT / 15.4
Sample Balance Sheet

BPM Industries, Inc.
Balance Sheet as of December 31, 1990

Assets		Liabilities	
Current assets		Current liabilities	
Cash	$29,500	Accounts payable	$15,500
Inventory	21,000	Notes payable	75,000
Accounts receivable	12,000	Total current liabilities	90,500
Total current assets	62,500		
		Long-term liabilities	
Fixed assets		Bonds payable	72,000
Buildings	175,000	Mortgage payable	112,000
Less depreciation	35,000	Total long-term liabilities	184,000
	140,000		
		Owners' equity	
Equipment	80,000	Common stock, 10,000	
Less depreciation	18,000	shares	120,000
	62,000	Retained earnings	68,000
		Total owners' equity	188,000
Land	198,000		
Total fixed assets	400,000	Total liabilities and	
Total assets	462,500	equity	462,500

divided up into current and fixed assets. Current assets are those assets that are expected to be converted into cash, sold, or used up within one year. Examples of long-term fixed assets are land, buildings, and equipment.

Liabilities are the organization's debts. They reflect what the firm owes to others in both the long and short term. Current liabilities include payments that are due within one year, such as accounts payable, current taxes due, and short-term notes. Long-term liabilities are payments due in more than one year and include such items as bond or mortgage payables.

Owners' equity refers to the funds that owners have invested in the business plus any earnings retained by the organization. Equity is examined by banks and other financial institutions and markets when a firm wishes to borrow money or sell stock.

Income statement A report that illustrates the money an organization made or lost during a particular period.

The **income statement** reflects the money that the organization made or lost during a particular period (see Exhibit 15.5). It is also known as a profit and loss statement. While the balance sheet shows the financial position of a company at a given date, the income statement shows the record of the company's activities for an operating cycle, usually a year. It is made up of three parts and shows (1) the revenue taken in for the period shown and the associated cost of goods sold; (2) the firm's expenses during the same period; and (3) the net income or profit from operations. Although these statements must be prepared annually, many organizations prepare quarterly and even monthly statements.

Ratio analysis An assessment of a firm's performance and financial condition based on comparisons of balance sheets and income statements.

Ratio analysis uses the information contained in a balance sheet and an income statement to assess the firm's performance and financial condition. This assessment is made by comparing the firm's present performance against its past performance or against its industry competitors. Some representative ratios are

---

EXHIBIT / 15.5
Sample Income Statement

BPM Industries, Inc.
Income Statement for the Year Ending December 31, 1990

Revenue	$2,687,000	
Cost of goods sold	1,633,500	
Gross income (or gross profit)		$1,053,500
Less expenses:		
Depreciation	22,000	
Salaries	310,000	
Commissions	160,000	
Utilities	108,440	
Miscellaneous	12,630	613,070
Net profit before tax		440,430
Estimated income tax expense (48%)		211,406
Net income (net earnings)		229,024

---

shown in Exhibit 15.6. The use of ratio analysis can highlight a firm's successful and unsuccessful performance and suggest where corrective action is required. Ratio analysis is a type of historical standard. Ratios of an organization are compared against similar organizations and against the given organization's past performance. Ratio analysis and other financial analyses are used extensively by investors and lenders to assess the overall performance of the organization and the relative safety of investment in that organization.

Cash Flow Analysis

Cash flow analysis The assessment of the cash sources available to a firm, their uses, and their availability in time.

The control of the flow of cash into and out of an organization is an important issue. Although a firm may have great potential for earning profits, without cash it cannot operate very long. If a firm cannot meet its cash needs and required expenses, it is considered bankrupt. **Cash flow analysis** is an assessment of the cash sources available to a firm, their uses, and their timing. Cash management may require, for example, that the organization postpone expenses because cash is unavailable or that the organization attempt to collect payments owed to it ahead of schedule to make cash available for expenses.

Responsibility Centers

Responsibility center An organizational unit under the direction of a person who is responsible for its activity.

In order to determine and manage a budget, managers must know what each unit in the organization is responsible for. A **responsibility center** is an organizational unit under the direction of a person who is responsible for its activity. There are four basic types of responsibility centers: cost centers, revenue centers, profit centers, and investment centers. These responsibility centers enable an organization to exercise the proper amount of control at the appropriate level of activity.

EXHIBIT / 15.6
**Some Key Financial Ratios You Should Be Aware of
(and Capable of Using)**

1. Liquidity ratios: Measure the firm's ability to meet its maturing short-term debt.

$$\text{Current:} \quad \frac{\text{current assets}}{\text{current liabilities}}$$

$$\text{Quick (or acid):} \quad \frac{\text{current assets} - \text{inventory}}{\text{current liabilities}}$$

The quick (or acid test) shows the ability of the firm to pay off short-term debt without relying on the sale of inventories.

2. Leverage: Measures funds supplied by owners as compared to funds supplied by firm's creditors.

$$\text{Debt:} \quad \frac{\text{total debt}}{\text{total assets}}$$

Times interest earned:

$$\frac{\text{gross income}}{\text{interest charges}} =$$

$$\frac{\text{profit before taxes} + \text{interest charges}}{\text{interest charges}}$$

Fixed charge:

$$\frac{\text{profit before taxes} + \text{interest charges} + \text{lease obligations}}{\text{interest charges} + \text{lease obligations}}$$

3. Activity ratios: Measure how effectively the firm employs the resources at its command.

$$\text{Inventory turnover:} \quad \frac{\text{sales}}{\text{inventory}}$$

$$\text{Fixed asset turnover:} \quad \frac{\text{sales}}{\text{net fixed assets}}$$

$$\text{Total asset turnover:} \quad \frac{\text{sales}}{\text{total assets}}$$

4. Profitability ratios: Measure how effectively the firm is being managed.

$$\text{Profit margin on sales:} \quad \frac{\text{net profit after taxes}}{\text{sales}}$$

$$\text{Return on total assets:} \quad \frac{\text{net profit after taxes}}{\text{total assets}}$$

$$\text{Return on net worth:} \quad \frac{\text{net profit after taxes}}{\text{net worth}}$$

Please note that the use of these ratios without comparable data is a useless exercise. There are two broad ways that we compare data of this nature:

1. Against the performance of the rest of the industry.
2. Against the firm's own past performance: This serves as a yardstick of comparison in terms of how the firm has previously done.

A *cost center* is a responsibility center in which the manager is held responsible for controlling the costs of the unit's operations, such as salaries and supplies. Personnel, research and development, and accounting departments are usually cost centers. In each, the manager must keep operating costs with the budget.

A *revenue center* is a responsibility center in which the manager is held responsible for generating a certain level of income or revenue, for example, a sales or marketing department. In this case, budget allocations are based on the revenue goal; the number of salespersons hired and the amount they are paid will depend on what the sales goal is and how much each contributes to it.

In a *profit center,* the manager is responsible for maintaining a specified balance between costs and revenue, that is, a certain level of profit. Each unit is essentially autonomous and can make budget allocation decisions independently, provided the specified profit level is achieved. Unlike cost and revenue centers, which tend to be found in organizations that are departmentalized by function (refer to Chapter 7), profit centers tend to be found in organizations that are departmentalized by purpose.

An *investment center* is a responsibility center in which the manager is responsible for a specified return on the investment of the assets in the division. Subsidiaries are usually investment centers; if a company acquires a subsidiary for $10 million, it may require the manager of that subsidiary to produce a 10 percent return on that investment, regardless of how the manager allocates his or her budget.

Budgets and responsibility centers are tools for monitoring and controlling costs and balancing them against benefits and revenues received.

CONTROL THROUGH PERFORMANCE MANAGEMENT

Just as all organizations are concerned with producing goods and services of high quality, while controlling the costs of producing these goods and services, they are also concerned with managing the performance of their work force. In other words, organizations want to ensure that their employees are contributing to organizational goal accomplishment.

In Chapter 11, we discussed the role of performance appraisals, which evaluate the contribution of each employee to the accomplishment of the organization's objectives. Through performance evaluation, managers can identify what an employee is or is not accomplishing, what the cause of unsatisfactory performance may be, and what the best course of action is under the circumstances. One technique for performance management and evaluation is statistical process control.

Statistical process control The use of data and statistical information to evaluate the quality and productivity of employee performance.

Statistical process control (SPC) is the use of data and statistical information to evaluate employee performance in terms of quality and productivity. Due to its quantitative nature, it is used most often in manufacturing departments where employee activities are highly measurable. However, the technique can be used in any situation in which worker tasks can be defined in terms of individual, measurable elements. The process for carrying out statistical process control is simple: Managers define what high-quality output is, divide a worker's job into the tasks necessary to achieve this output, communicate the performance expectations clearly to the worker, collect performance data on checklists that correspond to the outlined tasks, and evaluate employee performance regularly based on the tabulated results. This process can greatly assist managers in monitoring and improving employee performance, but as The Inside View 15.3 points out, a balance should always be maintained between statistical and other methods of performance evaluation.

In Chapter 4, we also discussed management by objectives, a planning and motivation tool that spanned levels of the organization. MBO, as defined in that chapter, is a process in which managers and employees across levels jointly identify goals, define each person's responsibility for results with respect to these, and use the measures as guides for assessing the contribution of each person to the unit's performance. By referring to agreed-upon measures for performance or contribution, managers can monitor performance and take action when it is unsatisfactory.

At this point, some of the connections between the functions of management should be clear. Planning and control can be integrated through MBO systems. Organizing and control can be integrated through the establishment of financial responsibility centers. Directing and control can be integrated through performance management or appraisal systems.

The Data Doesn't Tell Me the Why

The overview system at Cedar Bluff was designed to help managers achieve better process control and to provide them with better information, but it also put them out of touch with their employees.

Cedar Bluff is one of the most automated pulp mills in the world. Its work force was newly recruited in the early 1980s and thus had no prior experience with other forms of pulping technology. Cedar Bluff's work system had been designed to achieve high levels of employee involvement and commitment; it emphasized worker teams and a pay-for-skills approach to compensation.

The managers at Cedar Bluff designed an overview system, referred to informally as a "snapshot" of what was happening at any given time or place in the organization; one glance at a summary screen and the operations of the entire plant were visible. The system was designed to help managers achieve better process control and higher levels of reliability and to provide better information for the purpose of performance improvement.

Some of the managers at Cedar Bluff discovered that the impartiality and detail of data from the overview system provided an ironclad basis for some difficult personnel decisions that in a conventional context would have taken months or years to execute. As the plant manager described it:

> We have disciplined and terminated people based on information from the Overview System. It pro-

vided information on incidents which showed that the individual was not performing to basic knowledge requirements. By recording what happens to all of the instrumentation in a given part of the process on a five-second basis, we can see exactly what was done, what should have been done, and what was not done. Since you know the people that were there, you know what they did or did not perform. This becomes independently verifiable because the system knows it.

You can take a piece of paper right out of the Overview System and put into someone's performance file, and this contributes to their promotion. It can be used for counseling, for guidance, for promotion, and for discipline. Without the information coming from the system, it would be difficult to have absolute proof of poor performance. If the poor performance had occurred on shift, maybe it would have been picked up. In general, it would have been deduced at some point through greater accumulation of incidents. Therefore, the termination might have occurred a year later because a case would have had to be built, and it would have cost the company a lot more.

Other managers saw a tendency for some to use the overview system as a substitute for personal supervision. They believed that it allowed managers to distance themselves from the kind of qualitative knowledge about one's subordinates that was so vital in maintaining good reciprocal relations. Said one:

> If I didn't have the Overview System, I would walk around and talk to people more. I would make more phone calls and digress, like asking someone about their family. I would be more interested in what people were thinking about and what

stresses they were under. When I managed in another plant without it, I had a better feeling of the human dynamics. Now we have all the data, but we don't know why. The system can't give you the heartbeat of the plant; it puts you out of touch. ■

Source: Zuboff, Shoshana, *In the Age of the Smart Machine* (New York: Basic Books, 1988), pp. 4, 15, 324, 326.

EFFECTIVE DEGREES OF CONTROL

Though we have illustrated the importance and uses of control mechanisms in organizations, some people still consider *control* a term with somewhat negative connotations. The idea seems to conflict with such valued concepts as personal freedom, creativity, and autonomy. Achieving an effective balance between them and control is often an ongoing challenge for managers.

Too much control can cause just as much damage as too little control. Too much control will, first of all, be very costly. Designing and implementing extensive control systems can be a great drain on human and nonhuman resources. Secondly, too much control will have serious negative effects on employee morale, motivation, and creativity. Limiting, restricting, or guiding employee behavior too extensively will only cause organizational performance to suffer. In learning how to drive, most new drivers "oversteer" and in effect overcontrol the car. The movements of the vehicle become exaggerated, and the driver can totally lose control of the car. The DIVAD case may have been merely a matter of overzealous control by the army and Ford to make a bad decision and product work no matter what the costs.

Too little control, on the other hand, will waste time and resources and will jeopardize organizational survival. With little direction and no monitoring systems, the organization will not be able to achieve its goals. Further, less control does not necessarily result in more autonomy. Freedom and autonomy are to some degree dependent on the predictability of events or of others' actions. Managers can be free to solve problems or design projects only if they can expect resources to be provided, funds to be available, the staff to be paid, and the working area to be maintained. Without control systems, none of this would necessarily take place. The anarchy resulting from complete lack of control would not increase freedom; it could, in fact, result in increased or oppressive personal supervision by managers over their employees.

There is no "correct" amount of control; appropriate levels are largely determined by the situation. Quality control systems in a hospital, for example, have to be much more rigorous than those at a clothing manufacturing plant. If the clothing dyes are not mixed quite right or if the sizes are slightly off, the merchandise will still be marketable. In a hospital, medicines must be measured and prescribed precisely, surgical procedures must be performed with meticulous care, and germfree environments must be maintained continuously.

Essentially, each organization and manager must maintain control systems that have a balance of "looseness" and "tightness" that is appropriate for the situation. Thomas Peters and Robert Waterman refer to this as "simultaneous loose-tight properties," one of the basic characteristics of excellent organizations. "It is in essence," they say,

> the co-existence of firm central direction and maximum individual autonomy—what we have called "having one's cake and eating it too." Organizations that live by the loose-tight principle are on the one hand rigidly controlled, yet at the same time allow (indeed, insist on) autonomy, entrepreneurship, and innovation from the rank and file. They do this literally through "faith"—through value systems which . . . most managers avoid like the plague. They do it also through painstaking attention to detail, to getting the "itty-bitty, teeny-tiny things" right.[19]

KEY POINTS

1 Control is a process of monitoring performance and taking action to ensure intended or desired results. It requires (1) setting performance standards and objectives, (2) analyzing how well activities and results compare against the standards, and (3) correcting performance, altering standards, or acting to take advantage of opportunities.

2 In complex organizations, performance can be disrupted in hundreds of ways, many of which will be difficult to measure, and all of which will affect other areas of the organization. The basic purpose of control is to intercept these disturbances and respond with appropriate action. A control system will be effective if the number and variety of responses it is capable of exceeds the number and variety of disturbances the system faces.

3 Technical-level controls monitor and provide feedback on operational performance and are aimed at standardizing performance. Administrative-level controls regulate and monitor technical controls and monitor and control performance of organization units. Institutional-level controls are systems or frameworks that guide action and decision making affecting the total organization. Society also controls organizations through regulation and social control.

4 Setting performance standards is the first step in the control process. Output standards, such as time, quality, quantity, or cost, establish a desired level of results. Behavioral standards address the way an activity is to be performed and the steps in its performance. These standards may be historical, based on the organization's previous performance, or comparative, based on the performance of other organizations.

5 Performance measurement, the second step in the control process, can take place in three general time periods. Precontrols are performed before work takes place; they are preventive in nature. Concurrent controls are used while work is being performed; they are both preventive and corrective. Postcontrols are undertaken when the activity or task is complete; they are primarily corrective in nature.

6 Control methods may be internal, that is, based on principles of self-control and autonomy, or external, that is, implemented through the normal authority framework of an organization. Controls may be formal, that is, standardized to follow a written process, or informal, such as random observation. Finally, controls may be systematic, that is, regularly scheduled, or ad hoc, that is, done sporadically to solve specific problems or address unique situations.

7 Quality control (the process used to maintain and guarantee a given level of product or service quality), financial control (utilized to monitor the sources and uses of cash during an operating period), and control through human resources performance management (used to ensure that employees are contributing to organizational goals) are top priorities in every organization.

8 Too much control can be just as damaging to an organization as too little control; each manager and organization must maintain control systems that have a balance of "looseness" and "tightness" that is appropriate for the situation.

FOR DISCUSSION AND REVIEW

1. Explain the relationship between planning and controlling.
2. Describe a control system and its key elements.
3. Develop a control system for an activity in which you are engaged. Share it with a peer and evaluate the control system.

4. What are *standards?* How are standards used in designing control systems and procedures?
5. Why do deviations from standards frequently occur?
6. Explain why control is needed, and identify the four major types of control. Give an example of each in an organization.
7. What are alternate methods of control for an example (for question 6)?
8. Describe the potential barriers to successful control.
9. What actions can managers take to ensure a successful control system?
10. What do you see as the control problem in the following examples?

a. In the 1970s H. J. Heinz, Inc. had a very strong management incentive program. Later the corporation added an ethical policy. Managers at the top levels of the organization "bent" the ethical rules in order to achieve stated financial goals and personal rewards.
b. In midsummer 1983, an Eastern Airlines plane cruising off the coast of Florida lost all engine power. The plane fell several thousand feet before the pilot was able to start one engine. It was later discovered that "O" rings, which provide a seal against the loss of engine oil, were not installed. Records showed that a maintenance person and supervisor had signed off on the installation of the "O" rings.

KEY TERMS

Ad hoc controls
Administrative-level controls
Balance sheet
Behavioral standards
Budgets
Cash flow analysis
Comparative standards
Concurrent controls
Control
External control
Formal controls
Historical standards
Income statement
Informal controls
Institutional-level controls
Internal control
Output standards
Postcontrols
Precontrols
Quality assurance
Quality control
Ratio analysis
Responsibility center
Social control
Standard
Statistical process control
Systematic controls
Technical-level controls
Total quality control
Variable budgeting
Yes/no controls
Zero-based budgeting

THE CONFERENCE TABLE: DISCUSSION CASE / 15.1

Mills Brothers

Mills Brothers was one of Chicago's most prestigious retail chains. During September 1973, Mills Brothers opened another in a growing chain of discount stores with the name of Violet. When the store opened, it appeared that it would be the pride of the Violet Division. The general operation of the store was the responsibility of the manager, assistant manager, and personnel director.

The manager, Rita Mellon was 30 years old and had been with Mills Brothers for six years. She worked herself up through the ranks from stock clerk to her present position. She had a Bachelor of Science degree in animal husbandry. The assistant store manager, Jake Freidman, was 26 years old. He had worked for Violet since his graduation from college, where he majored in history. He also started as a stock clerk. Ari Meyer, the personnel manager, was 28 years old and had worked in various capacities for Mills Brothers ranging from stock clerk to receiving manager. He had taken some college business courses and was currently enrolled in night school.

Source: Gatza, J., Milutinovich, J. S., and Boseman, F. G., *Decision Making in Administration: Text, Critical Incidents and Cases* (Philadelphia: Saunders, 1979), pp. 252–253.

A major cost for many stores is shoplifting or other unexplained shortages.

The profitability of the new store appeared to be growing steadily until January 1977, when the results from the year-end inventory were published. The sales volume was as expected. However, there was a steep decline in the net profits.

Inventory shortages in every department were found. They were far above all predictions and acceptable limits. Missing material in some departments accounted for over 15 percent of the cost of goods sold. Results from the physical inventory were easily matched with purchases and cash register receipts since all cash registers were part of the store's perpetual inventory system.

Upon disclosure of the year-end financial results, Rita called the security department. She asked members of the security staff if they knew why so much merchandise was missing. The response of the head of security was vague. In a nice way he told Rita to check the figures again. She did review the inventory and financial figures and then returned to the security department and demanded an explanation.

The head of security said that he had experienced a similar situation before but that "to steal that much merchandise, shoplifters would need trucks." Rita asked each department manager about the apparent inventory shortage. In every department the answer from the manager was essentially, "I don't know."

Mills Brothers executives demanded an explanation of the shortages. They also initiated an investigation into the high labor turnover in the store. It was found that there was general dissatisfaction among employees, who felt a growing dislike for the store managers. The major complaints by employees were low pay and harassment by the assistant manager. Jake had been promoted to his position with the recommendation of the store manager. Further investigation showed that Rita had attempted to intimidate the department managers by subtly threatening to discharge them if they did not work more than the required 40 hours. (Department managers did not use time cards.) ■

DISCUSSION QUESTIONS

1. What control problems exist in the case?
2. Who or what is to blame for them?
3. How would you gain control and prevent this situation from developing again?

THE CONFERENCE TABLE: DISCUSSION CASE / 15.2

They Called Us the Green Machine

At McDonald's "the procedures make the burgers."

When properly used, the techniques and functions of control make an organization more efficient, helping it survive in a competitive business environment. But control may also be taken too far, as Barbara Garson writes in her book, *The Electronic Sweatshop.* Following are some excerpts describing some real experiences at McDonald's.

> "They called us the Green Machine," says Jason Pratt, recently retired McDonald's griddleman, "'cause the crew had green uniforms then. And that's what it is, a machine. You don't have to know how to cook, you don't have to know how to think. There's a procedure for everything and you just follow the procedures."
>
> "Like?" I asked. I was interviewing Jason in the Pizza Hut across from his old McDonald's.
>
> "Like, uh," the wiry teenager searched for a word to describe the all-encompassing procedure. "O.K., we'll start you off on something simple. You're on the ten-in-one grill, ten patties in a pound. Your basic burger. The guy on the bin calls, 'Six hamburgers.' So you lay your six pieces of meat on the grill and set the timer." Before my eyes Jason conjures up the gleaming, mechanized McDonald's kitchen. "Beep-beep, beep-beep, beep-beep. That's the beeper to sear 'em. It goes off in twenty seconds. Sup, sup, sup, sup, sup, sup." He presses each of the six patties down on the sizzling grill with an imaginary silver disk. "Now you turn off the sear beeper, put the buns in the oven, set the oven timer, and then the next beeper is to turn the

Source: This case was prepared using excerpts from Garson, Barbara, *The Electronic Sweatshop* (New York: Simon & Schuster, 1988).

meat. This one goes beep-beep-beep, beep-beep-beep. So you turn your patties, and then you drop your re-cons on the meat, t-con, t-con, t-con." Here Jason takes two imaginary handfuls of reconstituted onions out of water and sets them out, two blops at a time, on top of the six patties he's arranged in two neat rows on our grill. "Now the bun oven buzzes" (there are over a half dozen different timers with distinct beeps and buzzes in a McDonald's kitchen). "This one turns itself off when you open the oven door so you just take out your crowns, line 'em up and give 'em each a squirt of mustard and a squirt of ketchup." With mustard in his right hand and ketchup in his left, Jason wields the dispensers like a pair of six-shooters up and down the lines of buns. Each dispenser has two triggers. One fires the premeasured squirt for ten-in-ones—the second is set for quarter-pounders.

"Now," says Jason, slowing down, "now you get to put on the pickles. Two if they're regular, three if they're small. That's the creative part. Then the lettuce, then you ask for a cheese count ('cheese on four please'). Finally the last beep goes off and you lay your burger on the crowns."

"On the crown of the buns?" I ask, unable to visualize. "On top?"

"Yeah, you dress 'em upside down. Put 'em in the box upside down too. They flip 'em over when they serve 'em."

"Oh, I think I see."

"Then scoop up the heels (the bun bottoms) which are on top of the bun warmer, take the heels with one hand and push the tray out from underneath and they land (plip) one on each burger, right on top of the re-cons, neat and perfect. [The official time allotted by Hamburger Central, the McDonald's headquarters in Oak Brook, Illinois, is ninety seconds to prepare and serve a burger.] It's like I told you. The procedures make the burgers. You don't have to know a thing." ■

DISCUSSION QUESTIONS

1. What are some of the mechanisms for control used at McDonald's?
2. In the example, from what level of management—technical, administrative, institutional—do you think the control is being imposed?
3. Do you see the effects of control at McDonald's as being positive or negative factors for the organizations?
4. Would you want to work there?

16 | Production and Operations Management

Focus Case / The How-Not-To Book

PRODUCTION/OPERATIONS MANAGEMENT
The Operating System

PLANNING THE PRODUCTION/OPERATIONS PROCESSES
Unique Product and Batch Processing
Rigid Mass Production
Flexible Mass Production
Process or Flow Production

DESIGNING THE PRODUCTION SYSTEM
What to Produce: The Product Choice
How to Produce: The Process Choice
How Many to Produce: Capacity Planning
Who Will Produce: Facilities Location and Layout Planning

OPERATING THE SYSTEM: SCHEDULING
Gantt Charts
Critical Path Method (CPM)
Program Evaluation and Review Technique (PERT)

OPERATING THE SYSTEM: CONTROLLING THE INVENTORY
Ordering Quantities and Timing
Just-in-Time Delivery

CONTROLLING THE PRODUCTION PROCESS
Process Analysis
Trade-off Analysis

M anagement attention has continually focused on finding ways to make an organization's production of goods and services as effective and efficient as possible.[1] As the world entered the industrial age with its increased demands for goods and services, managers needed to develop stronger skills to utilize people and machinery in the best possible combinations. From the days of Frederick Taylor to today, managers and researchers have developed new methods of producing goods and services and monitoring and controlling these processes.

▪ KEY QUESTIONS

As you study this chapter, try to answer the following key questions:

1 What is production/operations management?
2 What are the key elements of the operating system, and what five basic points should be kept in mind concerning it?
3 What are the required activities for production/operations management?
4 What are the four basic types of production processes?
5 What are the crucial decisions involved in production design?
6 What are two major aspects of operating a production system?
7 What are the more commonly used scheduling techniques, and in what situations are they applicable?
8 What are various methods for controlling inventory?
9 What are two tools that help managers control and update the production system?

Focus Case

The How-Not-To Book

The audience for cable television is large and growing quickly, but production problems turned *TV-Cable Week* into a financial debacle for Time Inc.

In 1981, Time Inc., one of the largest and most successful publishing firms in the world, began laying the groundwork for a new publication to be called *TV-Cable Week.* Backed by a $100 million investment, the weekly magazine was to be sold by subscription for 69 cents and was to provide comprehensive TV and cable listings tailored to individual cable systems and broadcast areas. After researching the feasibility of *TV-Cable Week,* the project's managing editor concluded that "people were fed up with snowshoeing through several different sources for programming. If they had one inclusive guide that showed them what was available, they would buy it."

In 1980, if a cable subscriber wanted to know what was on television that night, the easiest way to find out was to flip through the 47 channels that were available in many localities. This was not an efficient way to see what was on, but few local cable TV guides existed at the time. In this void, Time saw an opportunity to link its publishing strengths with its growing presence in the cable television business by publishing a comprehensive guide to the available services.

Time published *Life, Sports Illustrated, People,* and the flagship publication of the firm, *Time* magazine itself. Time bought Home Box Office in 1974, and in the ensuing 11 years, HBO's enormous growth pushed the value of its stock up to more than 14 times earnings—the highest annual multiple of price to earnings in a decade. HBO was so successful that it achieved a market penetration rate of more than 60 percent; in other words, 6 out of every 10 cable subscribers bought HBO.

However, there were over 4000 cable systems in the United States. Some had as few as 100 subscribers and some had over 100,000. The systems were scattered across several different time zones and offered different menus of programming. The actual channel on which an HBO or Cox program would appear, for example, differed widely from system to system. A Time task force spent 18 months analyzing market share data, the results of test marketing, pricing possibilities, and the comprehensive nature of the new magazine in detail. In order to compete successfully, particularly with *TV Guide,* the second largest money-maker among magazines after *Time,* the publication would have to be a weekly, would have to have feature stories, and would have to be specific to each cable system.

Sources: This case was written by John F. Mahon and M. R. Poirier, based on the following sources: Byron, C., *The Fanciest Dive* (New York: Norton, 1986); "Time Inc. Takes on *TV Guide,*" *Business Week,* April 18, 1983, p. 68; Byron, Christopher, in an address at Boston University, April 25, 1986; "Spreading the Word of *Cable Guide,*" *New York Times,* January 6, 1988, p. 19c.

The managers would have to resolve many production problems. First was the question of where the program listing information would come from. Determining that it would be unwise and unfeasible for Time Inc. to use its work force and computers to keep track of TV and cable listings for thousands of broadcast companies and cable TV systems, the managers decided to buy the listings from an outside source. However, after touring the premises of the most likely source the managing editor of the project became concerned. This source already supplied listings to nearly 2000 newspapers across the country, and the listings were apparently compiled by several dozen keyboard operators in a haphazard office located in a shopping mall. The editor feared not only that the listings would contain errors, but that *TV-Cable Week* subscribers would feel ripped off if they noticed the *same* errors in the magazine as in the newspaper. The best solution seemed to be to buy the listings and edit them carefully.

The second problem was coordination: Split-second timing and coordination would be required to produce the editions and get them to the right spot at the right time. The plain television listings bought from the outside source and the program lists obtained from the cable companies would be flown to New York on Wednesday night. The editors would carefully proofread, correct, and customize the list Thursday and Friday, add prewritten movie descriptions from an in-house data base, and then transmit each edition electronically to different parts of the country on Friday and Saturday night to be printed locally. Other plants would print the national stories that the magazine would carry in all editions, and trucking firms would transfer the national parts to binderies where the listings, stories, and system-specific material would be stapled together. The completed editions would be taken to postal mail drops by 6:00 A.M. Monday. If any deadlines were missed, even by an hour, the whole edition could be ruined.

The first edition of *TV-Cable Week* was mailed in the first week of April 1983, to 150,000 subscribers in five market areas. It was printed on heavy paper, had national articles and over 50,000 interrelated, cross-referenced listings. But the first may have been the best. Deadlines missed by editors soon raised havoc with printers. National stories did not fit with local formats. Completed editions missed postal deadlines for mailing. To top it all off, the expected number of customers never materialized. The major cable companies had no interest in turning over their mailing lists to Time (from which Time would secure subscribers), because Time could turn around and use these lists to promote HBO, a competitor, or any of its various magazines. And besides, these companies already provided their subscribers with program listings.

In addition, competitor *TV Guide* began to experiment with cable-specific listings, updated its program schedules and feature inclusions, and increased its budget for cable coverage by 25 percent. And *TV Guide* was not *TV-Cable Week*'s only competition. *On Cable* already had over a million readers when *TV-Cable Week* was introduced, and it was only one of over a dozen such publications.

Finally, costs began to run out of control as the project managers added staff and equipment in efforts to save the floundering weekly. On Friday, September 16, 1983, the twenty-fifth and last edition of *TV-Cable Week* was mailed off.

During the preceding three months the stock price of Time was on a roller coaster, as the failings of the new magazine became better known outside the firm. One member of the Time staff, when asked what was gained from their direct cash losses of over $47 million, and an indirect loss of $750 million in the value of Time's stock, replied: "A much improved *TV Guide*." And to TVSM, Inc., the publishers of *The Cable Guide,* one of the current leading comprehensive system-specific program guides, "*TV-Cable Week* is considered a how-not-to book." ■

PRODUCTION/OPERATIONS MANAGEMENT

Production/operations management The undertaking of activities that ensure that a product is manufactured or a service performed in manner that meets the needs of the customer and allows the organization to realize its overall objectives.

Production/operations management can be defined as the undertaking of activities that ensure a product is manufactured or a service performed in a manner both meeting the needs of the customer and allowing the organization to realize its overall goals. The required activities for production/operations management are selecting, designing, operating, updating, and controlling the production system,[2] each of which will be discussed in the following sections. First, however, we will discuss the basic operating system.

The Operating System

Operating system The activities and processes necessary to transform supplier inputs into goods and services, or outputs.

The core of production is the operating system. The **operating system** is comprised of the activities and processes necessary to transform supplier inputs into goods and services, or outputs. A common and widely accepted model for illustrating such a system is shown in Exhibit 16.1. The figure reflects the process

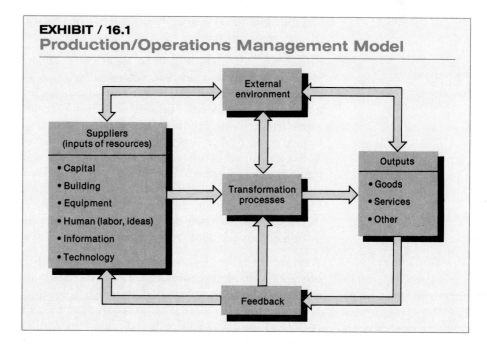

EXHIBIT / 16.1
Production/Operations Management Model

through which goods or services purchased from suppliers are transformed into outputs of value to the organization's customers. This input-transformation-output process, introduced in Chapter 2, has been the basis of production/operations management virtually since organizations have existed. Before we discuss it further, however, we will stress several important points concerning production processes.

Interdependence with the Environment The relationship between an organization's operating system and the environment is dynamic: The two influence each other. As an example, consider mass production techniques introduced in the early 1930s. Assembly line production techniques (the operating system) were used to meet increasing demands for products and services. Although assembly lines greatly improved output, many of these processes caused environmental damage and endangered the lives of both workers and the residents of towns hosting the plants. Initially, society (the environment) did not effectively challenge these practices. However, as the problems continued to build, government and society took action. Today, operating systems in organizations meet government-imposed safety and health standards that were unimagined 50 years ago.

As a different example, the production of *TV-Cable Week* provoked reactions in competitors that were in part responsible for the failure of the product. *TV Guide,* for example, improved its cable listings and updated its feature format. In addition, *Cable Guide* was designed to be profitable on advertising revenues, not subscriptions as a result of *TV-Cable Week*'s failure.

Interdependence with Other Organizations The operating systems of different organizations are interconnected. That is, outputs from one organization often serve as inputs for another. Consider the steel industry. Steel inputs include iron and coal, which are the outputs of the mining industry. The steel industry's finished steel is sold to the automotive and shipbuilding industries as one of their inputs. As another example, the output of the television program listing source was the input for *TV-Cable Week*'s program list, as well as for the program lists of thousands of newspapers.

Variation in Transformation Systems The heart of the operating system is the transformation process, where things "get done" in organizations. This process can take a variety of forms,[3] and it is here that the key to high productivity in organizations will (or will not) be found. It can be physical, as in the manufacture of any product. Automobiles, for example, are the output of transformed steel, rubber, glass, electronic, and plastic inputs. A weekly cable magazine is the output of information from compiled stories and program listings. The transformation process also applies to services, such as the delivery of flowers or telegrams. The transformation consists of taking the raw materials (flowers and messages), assembling them into useful packages (floral arrangements, typed messages), and then delivering them. Exhibit 16.2 presents sample input-transformation-output relationships for typical operating systems.

Transformation Process Is a Value-Adding Link The production/ operations function should be viewed as the link between suppliers of goods and services and the consumers of these outputs. A central assumption in this model is that the transformation process adds value to the inputs that the organization's customers want. If this were not true, the organization could cease to exist or the

EXHIBIT / 16.2
Sample Input-Transformational-Output Relationships

System	Inputs, Primary	Components	Transformation	Output, Desired
Hospital	Patients	MDs, nurses, medical supplies, equipment	Health care (physical)	Healthy individuals
Restaurant	Hungry customers	Food, chefs, waiters and waitresses, retail space	Well-prepared, well-served food; agreeable environment (physical and exchange)	Satisfied customers
Automobile factory	Raw materials	Tools, equipment, workers	Fabrication and assembly of cars (physical)	Complete automobiles
College or university	High school graduates	Teachers, books, classrooms	Imparting knowledge and skills (informational)	Educated individuals
Department store	Shoppers	Displays, stock of goods, sales clerks	Attract shoppers, promote products, fill orders (exchange)	Sales to satisfied customers

Source: Chase, R. B., and Aquilano, N. J., *Production and Operations Management* (Homewood, Ill.: Irwin, 1977), p. 12. Copyright © 1977 by Richard D. Irwin, Inc.; used by permission.

product in question could be discontinued. *TV-Cable Week,* for example, did not add sufficient value to program listings; they were readily available to viewers from other sources. Subscribers did not materialize in the numbers expected, and the publication was canceled.

The notion of value added, which has been developed by industrial economists, is a useful tool to analyze value creation in a business.[4] In its simplest form, a value-added chain shows the discrete activities in which a firm engages to produce and market products or services. Value-added components reflect either significant cost or value for a product or service. A sample value-added chain is shown in Exhibit 16.3.

EXHIBIT / 16.3
Typical Value-Added Chain

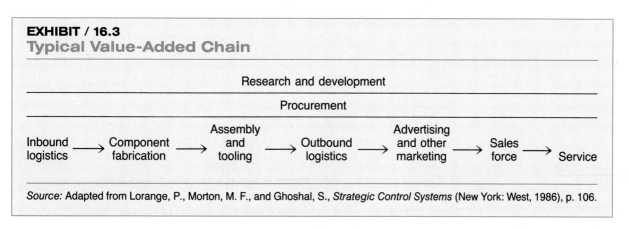

Source: Adapted from Lorange, P., Morton, M. F., and Ghoshal, S., *Strategic Control Systems* (New York: West, 1986), p. 106.

The Importance of the Feedback Loop   The feedback loop enables management to assess organization or production progress and to address issues of efficiency and effectiveness; that is, are we doing the right things, and are we doing things right?[5] The feedback loop caused the editors at Time, Inc. to cancel *TV-Cable Week* in a matter of months, although they initially did not project profits for the first three years.

PLANNING THE PRODUCTION/OPERATIONS PROCESSES

Several different kinds of production processes exist, ranging from assembly line techniques, such as those used to make cars, to craft techniques, such as those used to produce one unique item—a painting or statue, for example. The organization must select the optimal method for transforming inputs into desired outputs. Management theorist Peter Drucker cites four distinct production process choices: (1) unique-product production, (2) rigid mass production, (3) flexible mass production, and (4) process or "flow" production. Each of these choices makes its own demands on management and each has its own specifications.[6] In addition, the choice of production process greatly affects the way an organization is structured, the specific tasks that are to be performed, and the overall strategy utilized. These are discussed below.

Unique Product and Batch Processing

Unique-product production   A production process in which each product or service is one of a kind and is designed and produced or delivered to specifications.

In truly **unique-product production,** each product or service is one of a kind and it is designed and produced or delivered to specifications. Works of art, tailored clothing, and some custom-designed homes are examples of products produced this way. However, such specialized products are usually very expensive, and a producer can make only a limited number of them in a given time frame. Therefore, producers wishing to expand their output capabilities without sacrificing individualized customer service often apply this type of production to larger batches of products that are grouped together. Each batch with similar characteristics is operated on using similar techniques and tools.

Consider a repair facility for cars, for example. As the car enters the repair shop, an initial diagnosis is made: If engine work is needed it is sent to one area of the shop; if the exhaust system needs to be changed it is sent to another area; and if the body needs work, it is sent to a third. Each location has a set of tools and specialists to work on specific problems. Individual orders flow through the production facility in different patterns, starting and stopping at various points depending on what needs to be done. This procedure is referred to as *job shop* or **batch processing.** Characteristics of batch production processes include:[7]

Batch processing   A production process in which individual orders flow through the production facility in different patterns.

1. The potential for many different types of products.
2. A variable routing of jobs (that is, not all units of production will go through every operation).
3. Production for individual customers.
4. General-purpose facilities and equipment (that is, the operations of machines) that have high flexibility and are easily transformed to perform different tasks.

Unique-product production and batch processing focus both on the product and on customer satisfaction. Because everything must be customized, these types of systems are usually labor intensive and may require rigorous coordination and careful timing. The success of such systems depends almost entirely on the ability to obtain customer orders and fill them on schedule.

Rigid Mass Production

Rigid mass production A process characterized by the production of large quantities of the same product following the same series of operations.

Rigid mass production techniques are characterized by the production of large quantities of the same product following the same series of operations. Assembly line work is an excellent example of rigid mass production. Automobiles, appliances, and electronic components are produced by this type of process, as is most fast food. One of the earliest examples of rigid mass production is described in The Inside View 16.1.

In rigid mass production, standard and uniform products are assembled out of standard parts in fixed sequence. Unlike unique-product processes, this process is most efficient in dealing with high and continued volume. Production managers in charge of rigid mass production systems tend to avoid variations because they require halting the production process to change it. In illustration, Peter Drucker cites Henry Ford:[8]

> When Henry Ford said, "The customer can have a car in any color as long as it's black," he was not joking. He meant to express the essence of mass production as the manufacture of uniform products in large quantity. Of course, he knew it would be easy enough to give his customer a choice of color; all that was needed was to give the painter at the end of the assembly line three or four spray guns instead of one. But Ford also realized rightly that the uniformity of the product would soon be gone altogether once he made any concession to diversity. To him the uniformity of the product was the key to mass production.

Flexible Mass Production

Flexible mass production A process in which standardized processes and parts are used to make diverse products.

If Henry Ford had accepted more than one color for his cars, his production process would essentially have been transformed from rigid to flexible mass production. **Flexible mass production** is the use of standardized processes and parts to make diverse products. Early in the development of the automobile industry, General Motors became the pioneer of flexible mass production in automobiles. The autos that GM assembled used a great number of similar parts, but options at the end of the process, such as color, body styles, seat fabrics, and accessories, enabled them to manufacture a wide variety of products with broad customer appeal. General Motors' motto: "A car for every pocket and purse," indicated that they were trying to achieve diversity in output.

In some respects, flexible mass production can be thought of as the mass production of the unique, though it is not synonymous with batch processing. In batch processing, the producer never knows which route each product will take through the various different operating locations in the plant. Each car coming into the service shop is diagnosed, then routed through the system accordingly. In flexible mass production, all products travel through the same system at a constant or predictable rate, but each receives different components. Once the different components are identified, the process can be organized to make the maximum quantity of diverse products.

TV-Cable Week was produced by a system of flexible mass production. Each week, the capsule movie reviews were electronically drawn from the data base and integrated into customized program schedules for each edition. Then listings

The Arsenal of Venice

In the sixteenth century, Venice had the largest industrial plant in the world.

Production systems are considered an invention of modern civilization, but in the Middle Ages the Italian city-state of Venice, because of necessity, developed a production system for ships that was the envy of its neighbors and the comfort of its friends.

For Venice, trade was crucial to survival. As early as 1436, Venice operated its own shipyard for the protection of its citizens and its shipping. By the sixteenth century, the city was at its zenith as a maritime power, and its production facility became known as the Arsenal of Venice. It was, at the time, the largest industrial plant in the world. It covered over 60 acres of water and ground and employed from 1000 to 2000 people. The Arsenal not only built ships, but also stored equipment until it was needed, and assembled and refitted the ships kept in reserve.

The ships (called galleys) were rather small by today's standards. They were 106 feet long and about 15 to 22 feet wide at the beam. The method by which ships were outfitted with equipment, however, was quite extraordinary for its time. The canals of Venice were used much like an assembly line today. As each ship was towed past the warehouses, arms and equipment were passed out to it through windows. All parts and equipment were placed in the proper and required order. The Arsenal could outfit ships very quickly. When Henry III of France visited Venice in 1574, the workers assembled a galley and completely outfitted it for launch within one hour. More impressive was their response to a Turkish plan to attack Cyprus. In 1570, between January 28 and early April, the Arsenal put together an order of 100 ships. ■

Source: Lane, Frederic C., *Venetian Ships and Shipbuilders of the Renaissance* (Baltimore: Johns Hopkins Press, 1934).

and reviews were merged with the feature stories and all were transmitted to regional printing plants and finally mailed to subscribers. The ultimate goal was to produce a cable guide that was adapted to local or regional cable systems and that also had articles and features of national interest.

Until the last 20 or so years, flexible mass production was difficult to achieve because of inflexibility in the tools of production. Today the increased use of computers in manufacturing and design has greatly increased the flexibility of the production process itself. Flexible mass production, however, is more capital intensive than rigid mass production because tools and equipment must be provided for each variation. Ford only needed one spray gun and one color of paint. GM needed one spray gun for each different color. The heavy use of equipment and machinery is costly and requires excellent system design and maintenance skills.

In both of these mass production techniques, managers want to maximize output in the minimum amount of time, achieving a smooth work flow with minimum idle time in labor or equipment. As The Inside View 16.2 illustrates, this can be very challenging. Also in both cases, the customer must know about the quality and availability of the products. By definition, mass-produced items are not made to order. Therefore, producers must advertise, often heavily, to move massive amounts of product. *TV-Cable Week* was unable to do this. Customers were never sufficiently convinced of the value of the product to purchase it. In addition, the costs of production were never low enough to make the magazine profitable at the price for which it was selling.

Process or Flow Production

Flow production The continuous production of a product or service. Also called *process production.*

Process or **flow production** is the continuous production of a product or service. Examples are chemicals and beer production, and telephone and electrical service. Flow production is rigid; the process is standardized. The telephone lines and switching stations are in place; in the brewery, the distilling and fermenting equipment is stationary. There is also very little flexibility. The operations and machines have very special purposes and tasks and they cannot be easily interchanged or adapted to perform different tasks. Finally, process production is integrated; that is, the system provides for one continuous flow. A telephone caller's voice flows electronically through an integrated network of lines to the person receiving the call.

In process or flow production, it is essential to manage the smoothness of the product flow, because any break in the process shuts down the entire operation. One inoperative switching station makes it impossible to place a telephone call. Economies of scale are lost unless continuous, high-production volume is maintained. It is also crucial to design such systems for the long term, since they can produce only those products for which they have been designed, and since flow production requires tremendous costs and time. Because of the continuous flow, high-level skill is also required in their operation.

A major advantage of process production is that it has very large economies of scale and is tremendously productive. The principle underlying an economy of scale is that large plants with very high production volumes can produce goods at a lower cost per unit of output than small plants with low production volumes.

Managers must understand the characteristics, capabilities, limitations, and requirements of each type of production system so that they can choose systems

Getting 41427 out the Door

The production process has to be carefully controlled. Sudden changes or pressure to expedite a special order often will cause serious problems.

In his book, *The Goal,* Eli Goldratt offers the following description of a confrontation between Bill Peach, division vice president of UniCo, and plant manager Al Rogo concerning a delayed customer order. Peach had stormed into the plant first thing in the morning, after receiving a call the night before from one of UniCo's biggest customers asking why his order was seven weeks late. It was 7:30 A.M. and Rogo was heading from the parking lot to the plant.

I stop as four people come bursting out of a door on the side of the plant. I see Dempsey, the shift supervisor; Martinez, the union steward; some hourly guy; and a machining center foreman named Ray. And they're all talking at the same time. Dempsey is telling me we've got a problem. Martinez is shouting about how there is going to be a walkout. The hourly guy is saying something about harassment. Ray is yelling that we can't finish some damn thing because we don't have all the parts.

When I finally get everyone calmed down enough to ask what's going on, I learn that Mr. Peach arrived about an hour before me, walked into my plant, and demanded to be shown the status of Customer Order Number 41427.

Well, as fate would have it, nobody happened to know about Customer Order 41427. So Peach had everybody stepping and fetching to chase down the story on it. And it turns out to be a fairly big order. Also a late one. So what else is new? Everything in this plant is late. Based on observation, I'd say this plant has four ranks of priority for orders: Hot . . . Very Hot . . . Red Hot . . . and Do It NOW! We just can't keep ahead of anything.

As soon as he discovers 41427 is nowhere close to being shipped, Peach starts playing expeditor. He's storming around, yelling orders at Dempsey. Finally, it's determined almost all the parts needed are ready and waiting—stacks of them. But they can't be assembled. One part of some subassembly is missing; it still has to be run through some other operation yet. If the guys don't have the part, they can't assemble, and if they can't assemble, naturally, they can't ship.

They find out the pieces for the missing subassembly are sitting over by one of the n/c machines, where they're waiting their turn to be run. But when they go to that department, they find the machinists are not setting up to run the part in question, but instead some other do-it-now job which somebody imposed upon them for some other product.

Peach doesn't give a damn about the other do-it-now job. All he cares about is getting 41427 out the door. So he tells Dempsey to direct his foreman, Ray, to instruct his master machinist to forget about the other super-hot gizmo and get ready to run the missing part for 41427. Whereupon the master machinist looks from Ray to Dempsey to Peach, throws down his wrench, and tells them they're all crazy. It just took him and his helper an hour and a half to set up for the other part that everyone needed so desperately. Now they want to forget about it and set up for something else instead? The hell with it! So, Peach, always the diplomat, walks past my supervisor and my foreman, and tells the master machinist that if he doesn't do what he's told, he's fired. More words are exchanged. The machinist threatens to walk off the job. The union steward shows up. Everybody is greeting me bright and early in front of an idle plant.

"So where is Bill Peach now?" I ask.

"He's in your office," says Dempsey.

"Okay, would you tell him I'll be in to talk to him in a minute," I ask.

Dempsey gratefully hurries toward the office doors. I turn to Martinez and the hourly guy, who I discover is the machinist. I tell them that as far as I'm concerned there aren't going to be any firings or suspensions—that the whole thing is just a misunderstanding.

Realizing he can't do anything more before talking to the local president, Mike O'Donnell, anyway, Martinez finally accepts that, and he and the hourly guy start walking back to the plant.

"So let's get them back to work," I tell Ray.

"Sure, but uh, what should we be working on?" asks Ray. "The job we're set up to run or the one Peach wants?"

"Do the one Peach wants," I tell him.

"Okay, but we'll be wasting a set-up," says Ray.

"So we waste it!" I tell him, "Ray, I don't even know what the situation is. But for Bill to be there, there must be some kind of emergency. Doesn't that seem logical?"

"Yeah, sure," says Ray. "Hey, I just want to know what to do."

"Okay, I know you were just caught in the middle of all this," I say to try to make him feel better. "Let's just get that setup done as quick as we can and start running that part."

"Right," he says. ∎

Source: Goldratt, Eliyahu, and Cox, Jeff, *The Goal: A Process of Ongoing Improvement* (Croton-on-Hudson, N.Y.: North River Press, 1986), pp. 1–3.

intelligently. If a person or group of people have a highly specialized skill and believe they can profit from the production and sale of a few customized products or services, then unique or batch processing may be most appropriate. If an organization can produce and market large volumes of standardized products, mass production is the best choice.

DESIGNING THE PRODUCTION SYSTEM

The selection and design of a production system requires decisions about what to produce, how to produce it, how many to produce, and who will produce.

What to Produce: The Product Choice

The choice of product obviously influences the choice of production system. Determining which products to produce generally includes three basic steps:

1. A search for consumer needs: What do our customers want?
2. The comparison of products with organizational goals and objectives to see if they are compatible.
3. The development of specific product specifications. These specifications are important because they lay the basis for several other operational decisions (materials, process system layout, worker selection, and equipment).

For example, after 18 months of research, the managing editors at Time determined that consumers needed "one inclusive guide that showed them what was available." With Time's publishing strength and strong presence in the cable industry (through HBO), they determined that the product was compatible with the organization's goals. Finally, they determined just what each edition of the weekly would include. Given this understanding of the product, the editors could then begin to design a system to produce it. However, the three-step process described above is not always formally undertaken. Managers can determine product specifications in many ways, one of which is illustrated in The Inside View 16.3.

How to Produce: The Process Choice

Process choice addresses the specific issue of how the selected product or service will be produced. Managers making this decision must consider what currently exists at the facility: the specific equipment used (and its flexibility, reliability, and capacity), the feasibility of making the product, and the work flow. A potentially profitable product may, at this stage of analysis, be found to be impossible or too costly to produce. The editors at Time, for example, determined that setting up and monitoring their own program listings would not be feasible given their current work force and computer-processing capabilities. Instead of deciding not to produce it at all, they decided to purchase the lists from outside sources and use their flexible mass production system only to compile and ship "bottled" information.

How Many to Produce: Capacity Planning

Capacity planning An attempt to determine how much input will be converted into how many different products within a given time period.

After managers understand what the product must be like and how they will produce it, they must determine how much of it to produce. **Capacity planning** is a process through which managers attempt to determine how much input will be converted into how many different products within a given time period. It addresses the questions, How fast and how long can the people and the machines work, and how much product will the market absorb? Capacity planning is a complex process that involves six steps:[9]

1. The prediction of future demands, including competitive reaction. The editors at Time, determining that there was demand for a cable magazine, had to estimate how great that demand would be and how much of the market might be taken by existing or new cable magazines offered by competitors.
2. The shaping of these assessments into physical capacity requirements. Given the above estimates, the editors had to determine how many of each edition they could put out with the company's staff and computer equipment.
3. The development of alternate capacity plans. Understanding what the market could absorb and what the organization could produce, the editors could develop several options in terms of the number of different editions and the volume of each edition.
4. Analysis of the economic considerations of each alternative. The greater the number of editions and the greater the volume of each, the more costly the operation. Increased costs are only acceptable if they will result, in the long or short term, in increased payoffs.
5. The identification of risks and opportunities associated with each choice. Inundating the market might result in significant sales or it might just use up resources and result in no significant capture of market share.

THE INSIDE VIEW / 16.3

It May Hurt to Bend a Little

Designing dishwasher racks that pull out makes it possible to load and unload dishes without squatting or stooping.

In a conversation I once had in the mid-1950s with a friend who was a manager in a large company that manufactures major household appliances, I happened to say that in the long run consumers were seldom irrational—but I could not say the same for producers of consumer products. He challenged my statement and offered some counterexamples.

He claimed that since the electric refrigerator first had appeared on the market there had been a number of household appliance successes and failures that could not be explained by consumer rationality. Rather, he said, they demonstrated consumer irrationality. Then he cited examples of what he maintained were an irrational failure and an irrational success.

Market surveys, he said, indicated that housewives considered dishwashing to be the most unpleasant household task. Yet his company had only recently introduced an automatic dishwasher that had been poorly received by customers. On the other hand, he pointed out, the counter-top cooking range and built-in oven and broiler were very successful—even though they did nothing not done by the "old-fashioned" range and together were more expensive than the "old-fashioned" range. How, he asked, could I explain this on the basis of consumer rationality?

I replied that such answers were not easy to come by. They usually required extensive research. He was skeptical about the value of such an effort but indicated a willingness to take a "quick-and-dirty" look at the problem. As a first step, I asked him to gather all the appliances his company had produced in one showroom. I asked him further to put the successful appliances on one side of the room and the unsuccessful appliances on the other side. I also asked that he not enter the showroom until I was with him. He wanted to know why, but, frankly, I could not give him a good reason. I simply asked that he indulge my whim and he agreed.

A few days later he called me and said that the room was ready. We met and with mock ceremony entered the room. Neither of us said a word when we entered; we just looked. Within two minutes he admitted that my assertion about consumer rationality was correct.

All of the *successful* appliances had a common characteristic. They could be used without bending or climbing. In contrast, every one of the *unsuccessful* appliances required the discomfort of bending or squatting, climbing or stretching. For example, the unsuccessful dishwasher required that dishes be loaded from the front; the racks did not pull out. Therefore, it could not be loaded or unloaded without squatting. On the other hand, the successful built-in oven could be used while standing, whereas the oven in the traditional range still required bending.

Before we left, my friend initiated work on two ideas which occurred to him right in the showroom. First, that a dishwasher be designed with pull-out drawers so that they could be top-loaded, hence used without squatting. Second, that a cooking range be designed with the oven and broiler above the cooking unit, using the space below it for storage.

In time both of these modified appliances were introduced and met with success.

MORAL: Be sure that your behavior is not causing the problem before trying to change the apparently deficient behavior of others. ■

Source: Ackoff, Russell L., "Ackoff's Fables: It May Hurt to Bend a Little," *Wharton Magazine* 2(4) (Summer 1978): 66.

6. The choice and implementation of a given capacity plan. Ultimately, Time created five different editions for five market areas and sent a total of 150,000 issues. Had the weekly been a success, the number of editions and the volume of each—the production capacity—would have been increased over time.

Capacity planning is a reflection of the organization's long-range operations strategy. It helps managers determine how many and what type of buildings must be available, what technology will be needed, and how many people will be hired. Capacity planning is so closely related to facilities location that they are often considered and decided upon simultaneously.

Who Will Produce: Facilities Location and Layout Planning

The major objective of facilities location planning is to position the operating system to minimize production and distribution costs. The questions are, How large a facility should be built, and where should it be built?

The clearest trade-off in facilities location is whether to locate near the suppliers and supplies or to locate where the customers are. By locating near suppliers, organizations can reduce the costs of raw materials, their transportation, and the need for a large raw-materials inventory. However, the distribution costs associated with getting the product to the customer may more than offset any savings achieved by being close to the supplier. For example, the producers of *TV-Cable Week* decided to transfer electronically the listings and stories to printers located geographically near the customers in order to cut the transportation cost and time needed to get the magazine to the customer. For a service organization, the choice of location is heavily influenced by where customers are located.

Layout planning The determination of the actual placement of work stations, machinery, inventory areas, and departments within the production facility.

Layout planning is a process through which managers determine the actual placement of work stations, machinery, inventory areas, and departments within the production facility. As noted earlier, the overall goal here is to achieve the smoothest possible flow of operations given the organization's product-service mix. Some characteristics of good layouts are listed in Exhibit 16.4. Layout can be designed in terms of work flow or in terms of function.[10]

Work flow layouts Layouts designed to facilitate the flow of work.

Work flow layouts are designed to facilitate the flow of work. Three are commonly used. A product layout arranges the work according to the progressive steps in the making of a single product, as in automobile manufacturing or making

EXHIBIT / 16.4
Characteristics of a Good Plant Layout

1. Planned activity interrelationship
2. Planned material flow pattern
3. Straight-line flow
4. Minimum back-tracking
5. Auxiliary flow lines
6. Straight aisles
7. Minimum handling between operations
8. Planned material-handling methods
9. Minimum handling distances
10. Processes combined with material handling
11. Movement progresses from receiving toward shipping
12. First operations near shipping
13. Last operations near shipping
14. Point-of-use storage where appropriate
15. Layout adaptable to changing conditions
16. Planned for orderly expansion
17. Minimum goods in process
18. Minimum material in process
19. Maximum use of all plant levels
20. Adequate storage space
21. Adequate spacing between facilities
22. Building constructed around planned layout
23. Material delivered to employees and removed from work areas
24. Minimum walking by production operators
25. Proper location of production and employee service facilities
26. Mechanical handling installed where practicable
27. Adequate employee service functions
28. Planned control of noise, dirt, fumes, dust, humidity, etc.
29. Maximum processing time to overall production time
30. Minimum manual handling
31. Minimum rehandling
32. Partitions do not impede material flow
33. Minimum handling by direct labor
34. Planned scrap removal
35. Receiving and shipping in logical locations

Source: Apple, James M., *Plant Layout and Materials Handling,* 3rd ed., pp. 18–19. Copyright © 1977 by John Wiley & Sons, Inc. (Used by permission.)

a hamburger at a fast-food restaurant. Process layout calls for grouping the system components according to what is done in the process, as in hospitals and in college registration systems, with similar process operations in one place. Fixed-position layouts are generally used for heavy and bulky products that remain in one position or area while work is conducted around them, as in shipbuilding.

Function layouts
Layouts designed to facilitate the carrying out of a given function.

Function layouts are designed to facilitate the carrying out of a given function. Storage layout, for example, is a function layout based on the ideal location of parts or components in the storeroom and production area for ease of access and reduced inventory costs. Retail store displays on the other hand, are excellent examples of marketing layouts, in which work and merchandise are arranged to facilitate the sale of a product. Finally, project layout is designed and used for one-shot products, as in the building of a dam or nuclear-power facility. Although similar to fixed-position layouts, project layouts result in unique products, while fixed-position layouts can be used to provide many similar products.

OPERATING THE SYSTEM: SCHEDULING

During the design phase, managers establish product specifications, determine how to produce the products, determine capacity, and establish the layout of the operation. At this point, managers must determine how quickly or on what schedule the products should move through the production system. If too many move through too quickly, a backlog in production will develop. If too few move through too slowly, the system will be wasteful. Managers must therefore carefully determine how much capacity is available (what the machines and people are capable of producing in a given time frame, such as a day or week) and how many hours of capacity will be needed for each product. Two basic scheduling techniques that help managers control these operations are aggregate scheduling and master scheduling.

Aggregate scheduling is essentially an approximation of how much of each resource must be made available to satisfy output specifications (the amount of product to be produced to meet forecasted demand). This type of scheduling focuses on groups of products and services rather than on individual products. For example, some large manufacturing organizations may decide to produce goods in large quantities, shipping them from storage (e.g., toy manufacturers preparing for the Christmas season), while some smaller firms might produce goods on demand, shipping them as they are completed (e.g., unique products such as machine tools). Each organization will attempt to meet demands efficiently and at minimum cost. Aggregate scheduling allows managers to design the strategies for the utilization of resources that will be most effective for the organization over the long term.

Master scheduling is most often derived from aggregate scheduling; it provides details and specifics for each product for the short term. While aggregate schedules are concerned with groups of products or services over monthly or yearly time frames, master schedules are concerned with individual products over a daily or weekly time frame. Hospitals, in fact, will use master scheduling to assign rooms and equipment on an hourly basis. Master scheduling is based on demand forecasts and resource requirements.

Managers are often responsible for the planning, controlling, and scheduling of very large, complex projects. These may be one-time events (building a prototype of a new spacecraft), or very large, complicated, recurring projects (building multistory office buildings). Both often require unique production techniques, as defined earlier. Problems of coordination and control on projects like these often become critical issues, particularly since large dollar penalties and rewards are associated with untimely or timely completion dates. Some tools used in the production control process are Gantt charts, critical path methods, and performance evaluation and review techniques.[11]

Aggregate scheduling
An approximation of how much of each type of resource must be made available to satisfy forecasted demand.

Master scheduling
Scheduling that details the daily and weekly resource use and production specifics for each product or service.

Gantt Charts

Gantt chart A scheduling tool that (1) illustrates the work planned and the work accomplished in relation to each other and in relation to time and (2) identifies work delays.

One of the earliest scheduling techniques was developed by Henry L. Gantt in the early 1900s. Two distinguishing features of a **Gantt chart** are that (1) the work planned and the work accomplished are shown in relation to each other and in relation to time; and (2) the actual or potential work delays can easily be identified. Exhibit 16.5 is a typical Gantt chart. From the beginning, a criticism of Gantt charts has been the amount of time necessary to incorporate schedule changes and rush orders. The advent of the computer, however, has considerably reduced this task.

Gantt's approach helped to form the foundation for two similar control techniques developed in the late 1950s. These techniques are the critical path method (CPM) and program evaluation and review technique (PERT), both of

EXHIBIT / 16.5
Sample Gantt Chart

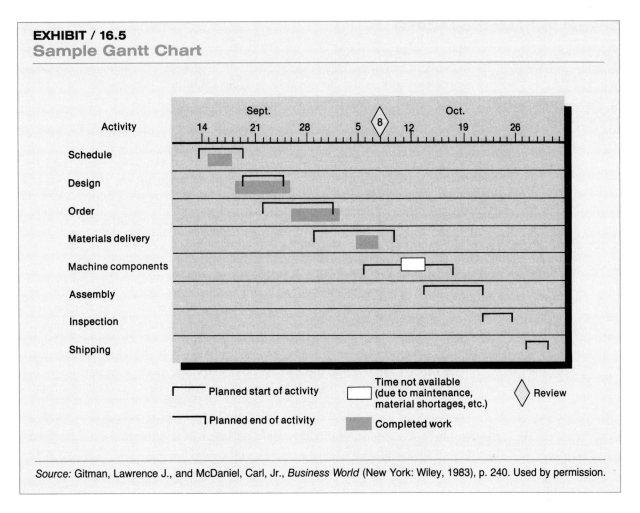

Source: Gitman, Lawrence J., and McDaniel, Carl, Jr., *Business World* (New York: Wiley, 1983), p. 240. Used by permission.

which track the progress of a project by monitoring the completion of its successive component activities.

Diverse kinds of projects lend themselves to analysis by either PERT or CPM. They include:

• Construction of highways and buildings
• Installation and debugging of a computer system
• Missile and satellite countdown procedures
• Major maintenance on installed operating systems
• Planning and launching of new products

Each of these projects has several characteristics that lend themselves to CPM/PERT analysis. First, the projects consist of a well-articulated and well-defined collection of jobs or activities which, upon completion, mark the end of the project. Second, all component jobs may be started and stopped independently of one another, within a given sequence. Finally, jobs may be prioritized or ordered. They must be performed in a given sequence. Continuous-processing jobs (oil refining) are therefore not subject to CPM/PERT because all jobs occur sequentially with little or no time separation.

Critical Path Method (CPM)

Critical path method (CPM) A scheduling tool that identifies the longest path in a network of activities, to determine a project's duration.

The **critical path method (CPM)** is used to determine the critical path in a given network of activities. This critical path is the longest path, or sequence of related activities, through the network. Its length determines the duration of a given project. The CPM is generally used for activities whose times are well known and well documented.

Suppose two salespersons for BPM Industries meet for dinner in Philadelphia. They discover that they are both going to New York City the next day and decide to continue their conversation at dinner in New York. Mrs. Aakers, the first salesperson, lives in Elizabeth, New Jersey, and plans to go through Elizabeth for a luncheon meeting with her husband, then travel to Stamford, Connecticut, for a business appointment, and then come back to New York. Ms. Strange, the other salesperson, has a lunch appointment in Washington, D.C., and then will head for New York. Both will spend about two hours at lunch. As both have a very busy day in New York, they want to meet for dinner as early as possible. They will both begin their journey at 9:30 A.M. the next morning.

The driving time from Philadelphia to Elizabeth is about two hours. The time and activities for all the legs of both women's trips are shown in Exhibit 16.6. Their travel to New York can be described as a project. The project's activities are given in Exhibit 16.6, with their immediate predecessors, travel routes and times are given in Exhibit 16.7, and the network diagram is shown in Exhibit 16.8.

In order to determine the earliest possible dinner time, we must determine who will take longer to reach New York. From Exhibit 16.8 it is clear that Aakers will take 10 hours (2 hours from Philadelphia to Elizabeth, 2 hours for lunch with her husband, 2.5 hours to Stamford from Elizabeth, 1.5 hours with her customer, and then 2 hours to New York), while Strange will require only 8 hours. Therefore, if they both leave Philadelphia at 9:30 A.M., the earliest dinner appointment possible is 7:30 P.M. (9:30 A.M. plus 10 hours).

The *critical path* is the longest path in a project's network. There are two paths in Exhibit 16.7, 1-2-3-4-5-8 and 1-6-7-8. Aakers's path is the critical path in traveling to Philadelphia. Activities or jobs on critical paths are referred to as critical jobs or critical activities. These jobs are crucial in determining the project's length; if a project is to be shortened, jobs or activities on the critical path must be reduced. In the above case, Aakers, not Strange, must reduce, for example, the time of her lunch in order for the dinner appointment to be held earlier.

EXHIBIT / 16.6
Projections of Traveling to New York

Job Name (node)	Activity	Activity Description	Immediate Predecessor	Time (hr)
a	(1–2)	Aakers drives to Elizabeth	—	2
b	(2–3)	Aakers lunches with husband	a	2
c	(3–4)	Aakers drives to Stamford	b	2.5
d	(4–5)	Aakers deals with customer	c	1.5
e	(5–8)	Aakers drives to New York	d	2.0
f	(1–6)	Strange drives to Washington, D.C.	—	2.0
g	(6–7)	Strange lunches with customer	f	2.0
h	(7–8)	Strange drives to New York	g	4.0

EXHIBIT / 16.7
Travel Routes and Times

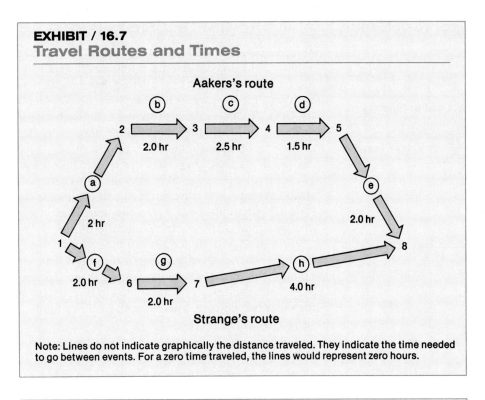

Note: Lines do not indicate graphically the distance traveled. They indicate the time needed to go between events. For a zero time traveled, the lines would represent zero hours.

EXHIBIT / 16.8
Sample Critical Path Chart

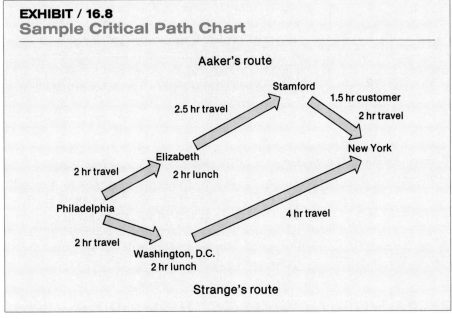

This is a very simplified example of CPM. Its utility lies in allowing managers to determine which path is critical for project duration and then to assess how that path can be shortened. There are, however, projects that may have multiple critical paths. The considerations are the same as noted above, but two or more paths would have to be reduced at the same time in order to produce a time savings for the entire project.

Program Evaluation and Review Technique (PERT)

Program evaluation and review technique (PERT) A scheduling tool that assumes well-defined relationships between activities, but variations in activity durations.

Another network model uses the notion of critical path but is most frequently applicable to nonstandard products and projects. **Program evaluation and review technique (PERT)** is a scheduling tool that assumes that the relationships between activities are well defined, but activity durations are subject to variability. In PERT, three estimates are made for each activity time. The first is the most probable (or likely) time to complete the activity. The second estimate is a pessimistic one: an educated guess as to how long the activity would take if bad luck and problems arose at every opportunity. This estimate does not include disasters or catastrophes (earthquakes, floods, bombs) but reflects inherent design or construction problems. The third is an optimistic estimate; that is, the minimum time for activity completion if everything goes perfectly well. The greater the uncertainties of the activities, the wider the estimates of completion time.

PERT deals with uncertainty in the estimates through the calculation of activity time as a weighted average of the three time estimates. PERT assumes that optimistic (T_o) and pessimistic activity times (T_p) are equally likely to occur. The most probable time (T_m) is assumed to be four times more likely to happen than the other two choices. Therefore, the formula for the average or expected time of an activity (T_e) is:

$$T_e = \frac{T_o + 4T_m + T_p}{6}$$

Expected time is what the activity's duration would probably be if the activity were repeated a large number of times. To make this clear, let us look at a simple example.

A small project is made up of seven activities whose time estimates are listed in Exhibit 16.9. Activities are listed at their beginning (b) and ending (e) node numbers, and T_e can be developed for each path. The expected times are then used, as in CPM, to determine the critical path. In this short example, the path lengths are as follows:

1-2-5-6 = 11

1-3-5-6 = 16

1-4-6 = 10

Therefore, the critical path for this example is 1-3-5-6 with an expected duration of 16 weeks. As in CPM, if the project is to be completed sooner, activities along that path will have to be reduced. Unlike CPM, PERT is useful in situations where the precise duration of activities is not known with certainty, but reliable estimates can be made.

OPERATING THE SYSTEM: CONTROLLING THE INVENTORY

Operating a production system requires controlling and managing the inventory of supplies that go into production—the inputs in the transformation process—and the inventory of finished goods. Because inventories are essentially inactive stored goods or parts, it is easy to consider them a "nonissue" in terms of management responsibility. One might think that just stacking things up and drawing from them as necessary would be the simplest of all management tasks. This,

EXHIBIT / 16.9
Expected Time of Activity

Activity		Estimated Duration (weeks)		
(begin)	(end)	Optimistic	Most Likely	Pessimistic
1	2	1	3	5
1	3	1	4	7
1	4	3	3	9
2	5	1	1	1
3	5	2	5	6
4	6	2	5	14
5	6	3	6	15

The network for this project is shown below. The ordering of times shown above the network paths is T_o, T_m, T_p, and in the figure below the path is the expected time for the activity, t_e, using the formula noted earlier.

For example, the expected time of activity 4 to 6 is:

$$\frac{2 + 4(5) + 14}{6} = \frac{2 + 20 + 14}{6} = \frac{36}{6} = 6$$

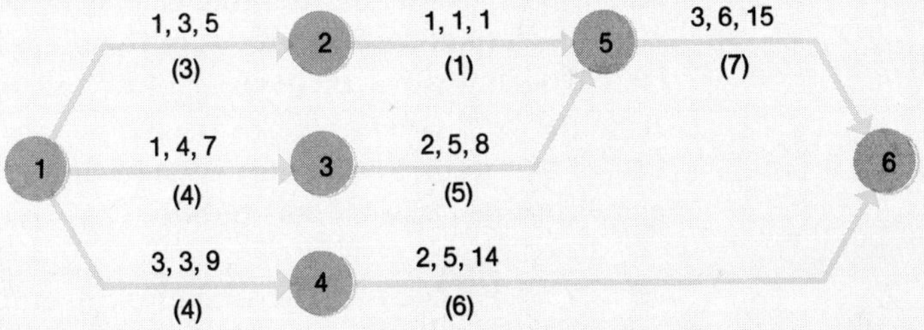

however, is not the case. There are several costs associated with maintaining inventories: storage space, personnel, equipment, capital costs of investment in inventory, and other carrying costs are just some of them. The organization can incur costs if either too much or not enough inventory is on hand. A shortage of parts could cause production delays, and insufficient finished stock could cause customers to go to other suppliers. On the other hand, a surplus of certain items, especially perishable goods, can be equally costly; anything that is not used up within a certain time will have to be thrown away.

There are three types of **inventory**: raw materials, work-in-process, and finished goods. The raw-materials inventory serves as a buffer between purchasing and production. The plain television listings were the raw material for *TV-Cable Week.* Parts are purchased in economical quantities, stored as efficiently as possible, and used up gradually by the production process. Work-in-process inventories are those goods that are partly finished or assembled. They allow for flexibility in the rates of flow through the production/operation processes. Finished-goods inventories—the accumulation of finished products—serve as a buffer between production and shipping. If a large order comes in before a production run of items is completed, finished goods can be drawn from inventory.

Inventory Stored goods including raw materials, work in process, or finished goods.

Inventories allow both flexibility and control. Through effective use of inventories, managers can:[12]

1. Purchase, produce, and ship goods in economic lot sizes rather than in small jobs.
2. Produce goods on a smooth, continuous basis even though the demand for the finished product or raw material may fluctuate.
3. Prevent major problems when forecasts of demand are in error or when there are unforeseen slowdowns or stoppages in supply or production.

Inventory control is done to maintain the most effective, efficient operations, and attention is often focused on when to order the needed parts and equipment.

Ordering Quantities and Timing

When controlling inventory, managers must decide when and how much to reorder. There are several mechanisms for helping managers make these decisions scientifically and therefore more accurately than through guesswork or intuition. One easy method is ABC analysis. A typical organization holds thousands of items in inventory, but only a few of them deserve management attention and tight control. ABC analysis is a management-by-exception principle (see Chapter 15) that divides inventory into three categories according to their use of dollars. Class A items account for 80 percent of the dollar usage and 20 percent of inventory; class B accounts for 15 percent of dollars and 30 percent of inventory; class C accounts for 5 percent of dollars and 50 percent of inventory. ABC analysis consists of two steps: (1) identify each inventory item by class and (2) have management control class A items tightly.[13]

When to Reorder   The timing of inventory levels and flows can be complicated. There must be enough goods on hand for production or shipping needs, but not so much that storage, spoilage, or obsolescence costs become too great. The reorder point for inventory can be determined by either the elapsed time period or the quantity on hand. These are referred to as the fixed order period and the fixed order quantity methods, respectively.

Fixed order period An inventory control technique in which inventory is ordered on a predetermined schedule.

Under the **fixed order period** method, inventory is reordered on a predetermined schedule, that is, after a specified number of weeks or months have elapsed. The size of the order will depend on the amount of inventory on hand when the order is placed. This system is convenient because managers need only measure present inventory levels. However, it cannot be used in all circumstances. It works well when demand for products is predictable. For example, the demand for milk and eggs is fairly predictable—they are perishable and must be restocked. The fixed order period method does not work well where demand is unpredictable. For example, the demand for fashion items, which follow fads, is so unpredictable that ordering supplies on a fixed schedule would be foolish.

Fixed order quantity An inventory control technique in which inventory is reordered whenever inventory levels reach a certain predetermined point.

Under the **fixed order quantity** method, parts or inventory items are reordered whenever levels reach a certain predetermined point. When there are only X number of item P left in stock, an order for a fixed amount of P will be placed. Timing of orders varies based on demand and depletion in inventory levels. This system should be used when inventory demand fluctuates. Using it when inventory falls at more predictable rates would be a waste of valuable managerial time.

These two methods can be very effective when used in the appropriate situations, but neither is flawless. For this reason, most organizations use what is called **safety stock:** extra inventory kept on hand in case of sudden, unpredicted changes in demand or late deliveries. The size of this safety stock can be determined by balancing the costs of carrying the extra items with the costs of running out of inventory.

Safety stock Extra inventory kept on hand in case of sudden, unpredicted changes in demand or late deliveries.

How Much to Reorder: Economic Order Quantity

Economic order quantity (EOQ) is the optimum order size, and it is a fixed order quantity method of inventory control. That is, when inventory drops to a certain level, the EOQ is determined and the order placed. To determine the optimum number of items to be ordered, the manager must consider certain costs. The costs of ordering include the costs of the labor, equipment, and material required to place and receive orders. Carrying costs include the costs of storing and insuring the inventory, as well as the opportunity cost of tying up funds in inventory rather than investing them elsewhere. Ordering and carrying costs have a natural tendency to balance each other out: If orders are made frequently, they also tend to be small. This means that ordering costs are high, but carrying costs are lower. On the other hand, if orders are made infrequently, they also tend to be large. In this case, ordering costs are lower but carrying costs are high. Basically, economic order quantity is the quantity at which ordering costs equal carrying costs, or the level at which the combination of these two is the lowest.

Economic order quantity The optimum order size, which balances ordering costs and carrying costs.

The mathematical formula for determining EOQ is as follows:

$$EOQ = \sqrt{\frac{2DO}{C}}$$

Where:
  D = actual annual demand for inventory use
  O = ordering cost of inventory
  C = carrying cost per unit of inventory

The accuracy of the EOQ figure depends on the accuracy of the predicted demand and ordering and carrying costs. The appropriate use of forecasting methods will help ensure the accuracy of the figures used in this model.

Material Requirements Planning

EOQ is most useful when inventory levels fall slowly and continuously and when demand is predictable. But when production is done by lots, and demand fluctuates, **material requirements planning** (MRP) is more effective. MRP, using the demand for the final product as a basis, generates a complete list of the parts and subassemblies required to produce the final product along with the required amounts and the correct timing to release the orders for these items. The Arsenal of Venice is an example of MRP in action because the Venetians had limited storage space. Their material had to be delivered when needed and not earlier. The MRP system is easily adaptable to computer programming and has been very effective in reducing costs, improving customer service times, and decreasing the costs of production.[14]

Material requirements planning An inventory planning technique that generates a list of the parts and subassemblies needed.

Just-in-Time Delivery

Just-in-time delivery
An inventory control
method that schedules
parts to arrive on the production line precisely
when they are needed.

A recent development in inventory and production control is **just-in-time** (JIT) **delivery** or the *kanban* system of component delivery. This system was developed by Toyota in Japan, and its name comes from the Japanese word for card, *kanban.* It works as follows: Each part or component necessary for the production of a certain item is assigned a card or pair of cards. An example is illustrated in Exhibit 16.10. One signifies the need for more of the part, the other signifies that a quantity of the part has been delivered. When a worker runs out of a particular item, he or she takes a card to the inventory or part production area, takes a container of the needed part, and leaves the identification card in a dispatch box. The card serves as a notice that more of the part must be ordered.

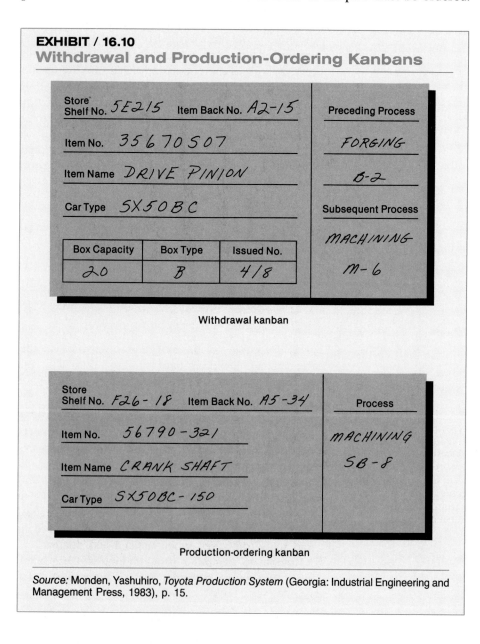

EXHIBIT / 16.10
Withdrawal and Production-Ordering Kanbans

Store Shelf No. *5E215*   Item Back No. *A2-15*

Item No. *35670S07*

Item Name *DRIVE PINION*

Car Type *SX50BC*

Box Capacity	Box Type	Issued No.
20	*B*	*4/8*

Preceding Process

FORGING

B-2

Subsequent Process

MACHINING

m-6

Withdrawal kanban

Store Shelf No. *F26-18*   Item Back No. *A5-34*

Item No. *56790-321*

Item Name *CRANK SHAFT*

Car Type *SX50BC-150*

Process

MACHINING

SB-8

Production-ordering kanban

Source: Monden, Yashuhiro, *Toyota Production System* (Georgia: Industrial Engineering and Management Press, 1983), p. 15.

Later applications of the system include just-in-time production, in which finished goods are produced just in time to meet orders or demand.

The major advantages of this system are its simplicity and the low carrying costs that result from having just enough inventory in stock. However, the savings in carrying costs are countered by increased ordering costs, and the system is not easy to implement in American companies without some major revisions and adjustments to management thinking and production operations. Several factors must be present if the JIT system is to be effective:[15]

1. Geographic concentration: Short distances between suppliers and consumers (production plants) are necessary for rapid delivery.
2. Dependable quality: Because there is no time to reorder, all parts received must be of good quality.
3. Manageable supplier network: The number of suppliers should be as small as possible, and they should be under long-term contracts so that relations are smooth and predictable.
4. Efficient transportation, reception and delivery of materials: Ordered parts must be received and delivered as close as possible to the point of use.
5. Strong management commitment: Managers must supply the necessary resources to make the system work, and they must be supportive during the transition from traditional methods to JIT methods.

CONTROLLING THE PRODUCTION PROCESS

The final activities in production/operations management are updating and controlling the system. Several key goals in the management of an operating system are maximizing profits, minimizing costs, increasing the level of quality in the products, and maintaining the optimal flow of goods and services through the system. Objectives and measurements like these are often in conflict, and to control and update the system, managers often must choose among them. Two tools that have proved helpful in making these decisions are process analysis and trade-off analysis.

Process Analysis

Process analysis A technique by which managers evaluate the efficiency of a process by determining whether it is level and balanced.

Process analysis is a technique by which managers evaluate the efficiency of a process by determining whether it is level and balanced. Process analysis utilizes the following steps:[16]

1. Make a list of all the steps in sequence from the beginning to the end of the process. Note steps such as movement, storage, inspection, and the specific tasks performed on the product.
2. Diagram the work flow of the product through the system.
3. For each specific operation, determine the capacity or rate of production using a common, appropriate unit of measurement.
4. Assess customer needs along with the potential demand for the product or service.
5. Analyze each step in the process and address bottlenecks.

A process analysis, for example, would have revealed what caused some of *TV-Cable Week*'s editors to miss printers' deadlines and what caused finished editions to miss postal deadlines. There were numerous bottlenecks and disruptions in the process used to produce the weekly magazine that could have been addressed through this technique.

Trade-off Analysis

Trade-off analysis   A logical method of choosing between courses of action.

Trade-off analysis is a logical method of choosing between alternative courses of action. It helps to answer the question, Is there a better way? Also, it helps to identify explicitly the criteria used in the decision choice. The generalized sequence of steps in trade-off analysis is:[17]

1. Continuously look for possible trade-off situations.
2. List available alternatives.
3. Specify costs, savings, advantages, and disadvantages for each alternative. List all quantitative and qualitative aspects of each alternative.
4. In step 3, use a common unit of measure—money is a frequent choice. This is not easy, as assigning monetary values to qualitative measures is difficult.
5. Select the course of action that results in the largest positive gain. It is at this step that there is no substitute for sound, experienced managerial judgment.

All organizations exist to produce goods and/or services. Thus, the production/operations system is essentially the core function of all organizations. Planning, organizing, and directing exist to provide support to the productive system. How well management integrates these functions in a rational, comprehensive manner will be a major determinant in the overall survival and success of the organization.

▪ KEY POINTS

1 Production/operations management is the undertaking of activities that ensure that a product is manufactured or a service performed in a manner that both meets the needs of the customer and allows the organization to realize its overall goals.

2 The required activities for production/operations management are selecting, designing, operating, updating, and controlling the production system.

3 The operating system is comprised of those activities and processes that are necessary to transform supplier inputs into goods and services, or outputs. Several important points about operating systems are (1) the relationship between an organization's operating system and the environment is dynamic; (2) the operating systems of different organizations are interconnected—outputs from one serve as inputs for another; (3) the transformation process can be physical or can be the delivery of a service; (4) the transformation process is a value-adding link between suppliers and consumers; and (5) the feedback loop in the operating system enables management to assess organization or production progress.

4 There are four major types of production process: unique product or batch processing, rigid mass production, flexible mass production, and process production.

5 The crucial decisions involved in production design include the product choice, the process choice, capacity planning, and facilities location and layout planning.

6 Two major aspects of operating a production system are scheduling and inventory control.

7 Projects can be scheduled using Gantt charts, CPM, and PERT. Gantt charts illustrate the relationship between finished work and work in progress. CPM and PERT were designed based on this early tool; both are used to illustrate the time frames between component activities of an overall task or project.

8 There are various methods of controlling inventory so that neither shortages nor surpluses cause undue expense. Goods can be reordered by the fixed order period or fixed order quantity method; amounts of goods to be ordered can be determined using the techniques of economic order quantity or material requirements planning. Just-in-time delivery, developed originally in Japan, is a newer technique for scheduling and controlling inventory. Each method has strengths and weaknesses and is well-suited to some situations more than others.

9 Process analysis is a tool used to determine the efficiency of a process by diagraming and analyzing all of its component parts. Trade-off analysis is a tool used to analyze various possible courses of action. It identifies the best option based on cost and benefit data. Both tools help managers control and update the production system.

FOR DISCUSSION AND REVIEW

1. In relation to production/operations, describe the operating system for *TV-Cable Week* noting interdependencies with other groups.
2. What is meant by production/operations management, and why is it a unique approach to the study of management?
3. Describe the five managerial activities in production/operations management.
4. What are the types of production processes? How do you differentiate between them? Give examples of each type.
5. What are the key aspects of production design, and what is meant by capacity planning?
6. Why do custom operations frequently tend to use process layouts? Give an example.
7. Choose an organization in which you are interested. Identify the production processes used, and describe how the system is designed. What are the inputs and outputs of this system? What transformations are performed? How would you measure output?
8. What kinds of inventories are there? Why are the distinctions important?
9. What decisions are involved in trade-off and process analysis?
10. What is quality control? Where is it appropriate?

KEY TERMS

Aggregate scheduling
Batch processing
Capacity planning
Critical path method (CPM)
Economic order quantity
Fixed order period
Fixed order quantity

Flexible mass production
Flow production
Function layouts
Gantt chart
Inventory
Just-in-time delivery
Layout planning
Master scheduling

Material requirements planning
Operating system
Process analysis
Production/operations management
Program evaluation and review technique (PERT)

Rigid mass production
Safety stock
Trade-off analysis
Unique-product production
Work flow layouts

THE CONFERENCE TABLE: DISCUSSION CASE / 16.1

TRW and Productivity

In 1981, blue-collar workers made up about 31 percent of the nation's nonfarm work force. By the year 2000, it is predicted, this figure will drop to about 23 percent. But at TRW, Inc., a widely diversified, Cleveland-based firm with 80,000 employees, the drop may be even sharper. Top management there estimates that their manufacturing work force could fall from 40 percent to 5 percent by the turn of the century.

Consequently, management faces the need to raise the productivity of white-collar office and managerial workers. Most advances in productivity measurement concentrated on manufacturing operations in the past and had little relevance to, or impact on, white-collar workers. Realizing that an upheaval in the nature of work within TRW was occurring, Ruben R. Mettler, TRW's chairman and chief executive officer, began an effort to increase white-collar productivity in 1980. The firm has since earned a reputation as an innovative leader in white-collar productivity.

Source: Brooks, G., "Faced with Changing Work Force, TRW Pushes to Raise White-Collar Productivity," *Wall Street Journal,* September 22, 1983, p. 33.

As the percentage of blue-collar workers in the work force steadily decreases, management faces the need to raise productivity of white-collar workers.

TRW's vice president for productivity first focused efforts on a group of 35 software writers in the Redondo Beach, California, facility. The choice came partly from necessity: "We wanted to participate in the growing market for software, but there is a shortage of qualified people to hire, so you have to get more from those you do have," according to the vice president. It was also an area that lent itself to a straightforward measurement system: the number of bug-free lines of computer code per hour worked.

Interviews with the software writers revealed major sources of production problems: distractions from office mates, meetings, phone calls, and the need to run new code to central processing for testing. At a cost of $10,000 per writer, TRW had private offices built, each with a well-designed chair, white board, work space, bookshelf, and computer terminal. The offices were small, soundproof, windowless, and painted beige. The programmers were able to communicate with each other through conference calls and electronic mail on their computer screens.

"The results were so good we were reluctant to believe them," said Robert Williams, vice president of Systems Information and Software Development. Productivity among the group shot up as much as 39 percent in the first year. Prior to these efforts, the division had posted a respectable 40 percent improvement during the decade of the 1970s. Estimated productivity growth for the 1980s was between 400 and 500 percent.

Industrial psychologists warn, however, that the effects of isolation on workers to improve their productivity is not yet completely understood. They caution that prolonged isolation may bring on dangerous psychological and physiological consequences and that worker productivity may suffer in the long term.

At least one participant in the original experiment was enthusiastic about it. While he initially missed feeling like part of a team, he came to appreciate his solitude. "I'd close the door and grind away at my work, and the next thing I knew I was hungry. I realized that it was 6 P.M. and I'd worked right through the day." When the project was completed, he returned to his old surroundings and reported feeling "an immediate decrease" in his productivity. Furthermore, he said that he learned to prefer a conference call on his computer screen to a casual chat in the corridor. ■

DISCUSSION QUESTIONS

1. How would you evaluate this experiment? Critically analyze the techniques and their results.
2. What types of business or production processes would lend themselves to isolation like this?
3. What kind of harm might result from the experiment?
4. What trade-offs do managers have to make between productivity and people? Where do you draw the line?
5. Would you want to work in a similar environment?

THE CONFERENCE TABLE: DISCUSSION CASE / 16.2

Shaping Up Your Suppliers

The managers of Cessna Aircraft in Wichita prefer to deal with suppliers in the local area.

Small manufacturing companies are in crisis. Their main customers, the big boys of U.S. industry, have been humbled by global competition and are seeking their salvation in higher standards of quality and productivity. The big companies can't find redemption alone. So, like passionate converts, they are spreading the gospel of efficiency to their suppliers. Suddenly, small companies whose greatest con-

Source: Dreyfuss, Joel, *Fortune,* April 10, 1989, p. 116.

cern was once to simply get the product out the door are under pressure to adopt the latest technologies, use quality control methods, *and* slash prices.

The suppliers often do not understand the new processes and management techniques their customers want them to embrace. Says L. Joseph Thompson, professor of manufacturing at Cornell's Johnson School of Management: "Small companies are less likely than large companies to have made improvements for productivity. They're concerned about meeting the payroll and not about the longer term." Besides, if the suppliers do manage to come up to their customers' idea of quality, they expect to be paid more, not less. They're not the world's best experts in management.

Suppliers had better learn fast. Most large U.S. manufacturers are reducing their number of vendors in order to control quality. Says Charles E. Lucier, a Booz Allen & Hamilton vice president: "Most want two or three suppliers instead of ten or 12." They will give preference to those close to home. Russell W. Meyer, the chairman of Cessna Aircraft, the small-plane manufacturer headquartered in Wichita, says: "We spend a lot of time with subcontractors. It's a lot easier to work with someone in Wichita than with someone in Los Angeles."

To make the cut, suppliers will have to go through a rigorous survival drill. Buyers routinely send inspection teams to rate a small company's plants. They want to see Japanese-style just-in-time manufacturing and delivery techniques, statistical process controls that identify causes of defects, and the ability to handle data electronically.

Some small companies resist, either from ignorance or from fear. Says Joseph A. Bockerstette, a manufacturing specialist at consultant Coopers & Lybrand: "Many suppliers feel just-in-time is a way for Fortune 500 companies to dump on them." When a large company begins asking for three deliveries a day, a small supplier may end up stockpiling the goods the customer wants. Craig Skevington, president of Factory Automation & Computer Technologies, a consulting firm near Albany, New York, that specializes in manufacturing, says, "Just-in-time becomes just-in-case."

The stringent requirements could bring a wave of restructuring among little manufacturers as wrenching as the one the large companies went through. Because the small fry are great sources of innovation and new jobs, Skevington and others worry that a weakened small manufacturing sector could chill entrepreneurship and hurt the ability of the U.S. to generate new products. ■

DISCUSSION QUESTIONS

1. What advantages does an organization gain by reducing the number of suppliers (vendors)?
2. Do you agree or disagree that just-in-time is a way for Fortune 500 companies to force smaller companies to carry their inventory?
3. How would you improve relationships with suppliers?

17 | MIS and Technology Management

An integral and crucial aspect of the control function is the use and management of information and technology. The survival of organizations in the 1990s and beyond will depend on their ability to collect, interpret, and effectively utilize information. This task will be both assisted and complicated by the rapid introduction of new technologies. In this chapter we will discuss the value and costs of information, methods for establishing information systems in an organization, and methods for managing technological advances.

FOCUS CASE / The Hand-Held Solution

MANAGEMENT INFORMATION SYSTEMS (MIS)
Evolution of MIS
Basic Components of MIS

BALANCING THE VALUE AND COST OF INFORMATION
Managerial Uses of Information
The Value of Information
MIS—A Management Tool

ESTABLISHING AN MIS
MIS Planning
MIS Design
MIS Implementation
MIS Monitoring and Improvement

DECISION SUPPORT SYSTEMS, EXPERT SYSTEMS, AND ARTIFICIAL INTELLIGENCE
Decision Support Systems
Expert Systems
Artificial Intelligence

THE IMPACT OF INFORMATION TECHNOLOGY
Information Technology in the Manufacturing Sector
Information Technology in the Service Sector

■ KEY QUESTIONS

As you study this chapter, try to answer the following key questions:

1 What is a management information system?
2 What are the basic components of an MIS?
3 What is the trade-off between the value and cost of information?
4 What types of information are needed by managers at different levels of the organization, and what factors determine the value of information?
5 What are the four steps in establishing an MIS?
6 What are the elements in a computer system?
7 What are some guidelines for effective design?
8 What are four methods of MIS implementation?
9 What are decision support systems, expert systems, and artificial intelligence?
10 Briefly summarize the impact information technology is having on the manufacturing and service sectors.

Focus Case

The Hand-Held Solution

A Frito-Lay salesperson entering an order into a hand-held computer. By automating its ordering system, Frito-Lay expects to reduce the time its salespeople spend on processing paperwork and to increase the productivity of its sales force.

Frito-Lay, Inc., the Texas-based giant snack food division of PepsiCo, had $2.6 billion in sales and $430 million in operating income in 1985. Despite its size, the $7 billion snack food industry experienced only a 5 percent growth rate that year, down from 11 percent in 1984 and its slowest since 1980.

Realizing that the chances for increasing sales were limited, Frito-Lay in 1984 decided to move to new technologies as a way of serving their customers better and hence stimulating market growth. The most significant management initiative was to distribute hand-held computers to 10,000 truck route sales representatives who deliver the products to 400,000 locations varying in size from huge metropolitan grocery store chains to rural general stores.

The company could now use the hand-held computers to better monitor the movement of its snack food products. The salesperson would enter all information about an order into the hand-held computer. The computer would automatically price and print the order and record the transactions for later use in the sales reporting. The hand-helds also could be used to make route drivers more productive and to automate the inventory and ordering process. Data captured by the devices would help Frito-Lay show retailers what products were moving and help justify its share of shelf space to grocers.

In 1987 the sales force started using the Fujitsu manufactured computers to track 100 branded products in 250 sizes. This new technology improved efficiency of operations so drastically that the company estimated the $45 million investment in hand-held computers (HHC) project and upgrading of the data center could be recovered within two years.

"We have made significant, concrete savings," says Charles S. Feld, vice president of management services, who, along with sales operations vice president Ronald A. Rittenmeyer, won the award for the HHC project from the Society for Information Management. "The ramifications have been in sales and stales. If we manufactured durables and we made a few extra, it wouldn't make any difference," explains Feld. "But the cost of stales is very high. We take them off the shelf because quality is the issue. We're not willing to lose any customers."

Because the hand-held computers reduce the amount of paperwork that needs to be done, sales reps can spend an average of three to five hours more a week to call on customers with new promotions and merchandising proposals. Managers have also benefited, as the up-to-date reports of activities on each route make them better equipped to monitor individual work-loads, trade off stops between sales reps, or consolidate routes.

Other strategic advantages gained from installing the system are the following:

Sources: Crutchfield, R. J., "Getting a leg up by using handhelds," *Datamation*, January 1, 1987, pp. 32–33; Winkler, C., "More sales, fewer 'stales'," *Computer Decisions*, November 1988, pp. 26–27. "Frito-Lay, Inc.: A Strategic Transition," (9-187-065), Harvard Business School Publishing, 1986.

- Better control of marketing programs. The effect of a new promotional campaign on sales can now be estimated and evaluated in two days. Before, Frito-Lay had to wait until a campaign had run its course to determine its success.
- Closer links between raw materials purchasing and manufacturing, distribution, and inventory systems. Such links are critical for a business in perishable products.
- More chances at future business opportunities, including links from the hand-held computers into a supermarket's computer system, an experiment that is underway in California.

Before the hand-held computers—the last of which were installed in June 1988—Frito-Lay's inventory and order process was done on paper. Sales reps filled out five-part forms, which were then scanned by optical character recognition systems manned by 150 technicians. The process was extremely time consuming and often did not allow the reps to spend sufficient amount of time on the promotions.

Fujitsu worked with Frito-Lay in defining and designing the system. The computers are sturdy, small and rubberized, and tolerate rugged conditions such as extreme temperatures inside the trucks. Feld's team had also invested a tremendous amount of time in the software development. Additional effort went into training the 10,000 route representatives. Both the sales and information systems departments dedicated employees to the design and implementation of the project.

On the job, the computers are used first to inventory the product left on the shelf: Information is entered into the computer in the same order that product appears on the shelves. Back in the truck, the computer is inserted into a cradle and attached to a printer which generates a list for restocking and the sales ticket which accounts for sales taxes, discounts and promotions. This sales invoice is given to the store personnel. At day's end, the rep returns the computer to one of Frito-Lay's 200 distribution centers, where overnight the data from the machine are downloaded into an IBM minicomputer and then transmitted to the IBM host computer. New pricing data and promotional information are uploaded for the following day. Within 24–36 hours, Frito-Lay aggregates and decodes the route information that was downloaded from the hand-held machines.

"For the first time," says Rittenmeyer, "we have a clear idea of what happened in the marketplace—what's selling, where, and through which channels. We always had all this information, but most of it was four weeks old by the time the invoices were processed."

With the new system, the marketing department can easily follow product trends and successes. The success of any given promotion can quickly be measured, and its life shortened or lengthened accordingly.

Frito-Lay also compares its internal market information against industry intelligence, most frequently gathered by supermarket checkout scanning systems, to screen its performance on various product categories. For Frito-Lay, it's critical that sales data are closely linked to the entire operation. "By tying into the whole manufacturing, purchasing, distribution and inventory complex," says Feld, "we're getting closer and closer to just-in-time production.

Right now, we're just about producing to order." Product is coming out of manufacturing in three days, another three days are needed for distribution, and sales reps have six days to get products on store shelves.

Frito-Lay is now prototyping a system that transfers billing information from the hand-held computers directly to a store's own computer system. "We are literally showing up at the back door and plugging our hand-helds into their units," says Rittenmeyer. He predicts this further extension of electronic data interchange between vendors and customers "will grow as fast as the industry will allow." ■

The preceding case is one illustration of the value of information systems. The hand-held computer project was an integral and crucial part of Frito-Lay's strategy for achieving its growth in sales and profits. Though the system cost the company $3 million more per year to run than the previous system, the strategic benefits it produced far outweighed its costs. First of all, the hand-held computers greatly simplified the route salesperson's job. In addition, the computers made it possible for Frito-Lay to begin accomplishing its goals: higher sales productivity in existing territories, increased ability to promote a wider variety of products, and increased ability to tailor marketing strategies to individual retailers, thus enabling the salespeople to justify more shelf space in each store.

All organizations benefit from effective management information systems. Managers must have constant access to information concerning the organization's operations: What progress is being made toward goals; how many people, with which skills, are making what contributions; how much money is being spent and with what results; how many resources are being consumed and with what results? In addition, they must have constant access to information concerning the organization's environment: Where does the organization stand in relation to its competition; what new trends and developments are unfolding that may affect the organization; what shifts in legal, social, or economic conditions may have an impact, and what will it be?

The purpose of a management information system (MIS) is to provide information selectively to people in the organization to help them do their jobs. If effective, the MIS can help the organization achieve a wide variety of objectives, such as increasing efficiency, lowering operating costs, improving customer service, and strengthening an organization's competitive position. Two examples are presented in The Inside View 17.1.

MANAGEMENT INFORMATION SYSTEMS (MIS)

Management information system (MIS) An organized method of providing past, present, and projected information relating to internal and external operations.

Although there is disagreement over the most "accurate" definition of an MIS,[1] J. M. Kenneran's definition, based on some of the earliest research in the MIS field, is comprehensive. A **management information system (MIS)**

> . . . is an organized method of providing past, present, and projected information relating to internal and external operations. An MIS supports the planning, control, and operational functions of an organization by furnishing uniform and useful information in the proper time frame to assist the decision-making process of the organization.[2]

Using Information Systems to Accomplish Strategy

American Airlines' on-line reservation system is utilized even by competing airlines to manage ticket sales and passenger check-ins.

The following are two examples of companies that have used information systems to achieve a variety of strategic benefits.

AMERICAN AIRLINES

In the 1960s American Airlines (AA) was one of two airlines—United was the other—to see the huge efficiency gains that an automated booking system could bring. If the travel agent body (the 27,000 entities that account for the bulk of all airline ticket sales) could get instant access to automatically updated flight and reservations information, this would save AA millions of dollars in clerical time and in overbooking and underbooking losses. Over time, however, many more benefits of Sabre, as its on-line reservations systems is called, became apparent.

- Having a distribution network reaching into the heart of its client body, the travel agents, made AA the logical system to use to book other airline tickets, make hotel and car rental reservations, and place such other orders as foreign currency requests.
- Enhanced offerings, such as travel agency management software, could be marketed through the same channel.
- The system became central to the accounting apparatus of the travel agents, giving AA a further leverage over its distribution network.
- AA could have its own flights show up first on the screen for any origin/destination pair being explored by the travel agent.
- Prices could be changed as frequently as was wished—daily if needed—by simply altering part of the central data base held in the Fort Worth mainframes.
- The system became a source of revenue in itself, with other airlines paying AA to be listed on it.
- By changing from "dumb" terminals to personal computers, AA could let important business accounts access Sabre directly. Easy-Sabre, introduced in 1986, allows large corporate customers to bypass their travel agent to some degree (although not to the extent of actually issuing tickets, since all ticket issuers have to be bonded).
- Over time, the system became a powerful barrier to entry to new competitors. Airlines without a good centralized reservations system, such as, People Express, suffered from chronic overbooking at the same time as excess capacity.

By 1986, AA's Sabre accounted for no less than 45 percent of the computerized air ticket sales made in the United States, with about 70 percent of all air tickets being issued by computerized systems. United Airline's Apollo system held the next highest market share, at 29 percent. Thus, its striving for efficiency in the 1960s led AA to a position where, in the 1980s, its technology offers it considerable effectiveness and strategy advantages.

AMERICAN HOSPITAL SUPPLY CORPORATION (AHSC)

The problem facing AHSC was to consolidate and build market share in its core business, supplying drugs and supplies to hospitals. Its innovative solution was to provide appropriate people in its client hospitals with terminals on which they could order directly from AHSC the items they needed. The advantages for the hospitals were so great that they naturally were drawn to AHSC for their supplies, since:

- Their own inventories could be reduced, since they had a direct and immediate way to replenish their stocks.
- The costs of ordering fell.
- The uncertain time lag involved in ordering was mitigated.

- Their bookkeeping was simplified, since paper-based accounting was replaced by an automated system.

For AHSC, on the other hand, the advantages were equally impressive. They included:

- Creating considerable exit barriers or problems in ending the relationship with AHSC.
- Creating a distribution network, down which new items, needed information, and sales material could be pushed.
- Creating the ability to integrate into hospitals' bookkeeping and record-keeping departments, thus further raising revenue per client.

In this case, AHSC has utilized a relatively unsophisticated level of technology but has used it with sufficient imagination to create a truly strategic redefinition of the business. ■

Source: Sinclair, Stuart W., "Information Technology and Strategy Revisited," *Multinational Business* (1986, no. 4): pp. 12, 13.

Consider Frito-Lay's hand-held computer project, one component of its information system. The system can provide information on past sales levels for various products, as well as daily sales counts, and can be used to predict future demand for products. With this information, marketing managers can plan what to promote, salespeople can plan what to carry, and the production staff can plan how much of each item to produce. The flow of goods to customers and the flow of revenues back to the company can be monitored and controlled. With detailed information on sales levels per item and per customer, salespeople, marketing managers, production managers, and the organization as a whole will be able to make decisions that will benefit the company strategically.

Frito-Lay was the first snack food vendor to utilize the hand-held computers, and that gave it a very significant competitive edge. An integrated system with such potential for customized ordering and billing was new. Most other snack food vendors still used more manual systems of ordering, selling, and billing, perhaps similar to Frito-Lay's previous system. But developments in computer technology, which we will now discuss, have made possible increased savings in time, effort, and money.

Evolution of MIS

Electronic data processing (EDP) The use of computers to process information.

The first applications of computers to information-processing tasks were quite simple. The use of computers to process information is commonly referred to as **electronic data processing** (EDP). MIS is much more complex than EDP and, in fact, uses EDP as a base or foundation. Initially, computers were used in organiza-

Transaction-processing systems EDP systems used by organizations to perform routine, recurring transactions, such as bill and invoice processing.

tions only for limited functions, such as inventory and billing. **Transaction-processing systems** (TPS) were one of the earliest applications of EDP; they were used by organizations to perform routine, recurring transactions, such as processing bills and invoices or recording payments and receipts. Because of their limited applications and because of the specialized skills needed to operate the earliest models, really powerful computers that could undertake more complicated functions were used only by computer scientists.

Computer-based information systems (CBIS) Information systems developed to coordinate the compilation of data and its dissemination to the appropriate individuals.

As computer applications in the organization expanded and more types of tasks were done using the EDP system, information systems were developed to coordinate the compilation of data and its dissemination to the appropriate individuals. These **computer-based information systems** (CBIS) were easier to use and more widely applicable. Computer-based management information systems gave way to MIS and continued to evolve. Further developments in MIS have resulted in decision support systems (DSS) and expert systems (ES), both of which will be discussed in more detail later in the chapter.

Basic Components of MIS

Inputs Data from internal and external sources.

Every MIS has four basic components: inputs, processing, outputs, and feedback. **Inputs** are data; the necessary data may already exist in the organization, or it may have to be gathered from external sources. Data in Frito-Lay's HHC system include volume and sales figures for various products and customers. Typically, the process of inputting the collected data is done by a computer operator. In this case, the HHCs unload the information into the central computer themselves, when plugged in by the operators. The input phase is ongoing; new data are continually added to the system as transactions are made.

Processing The phase during which the computer transforms, organizes, and stores the data collected during input.

During the **processing** phase, the computer transforms, organizes, and stores the data collected during input. Collected data are stored, analyzed, and manipulated by the computers; in-depth analysis of extensive numbers of facts, figures, and other data cannot be done quickly or effectively without them. It is during this phase that data become information. The central system at Frito-Lay manipulates data on sales rates for various products, the sales volume produced by various promotions, and even the differences in sales levels for various products between different stores.

Outputs Reports, printouts, charts, screen displays, or written summaries compiled and produced during the processing phase.

Outputs are the reports, printouts, charts, screen displays, or written summaries that are produced during the processing phase. Because they are used to make decisions, outputs should be produced in a format that is readily accessible to the end user: a 50-page printout of complex terms and data might tell a computer programmer what the facts are, but it will tell the general manager nothing. A graph with lines, curves, and numbers might indicate a trend or condition, but without the appropriate titles and keys for interpreting it, it will be useless. The output report given to each of Frito-Lay's 10,000 salespeople is customized to each person's route and may include information about hundreds of products. It allows the salespeople to customize product line, promotional strategy, and pricing arrangements to each retailer, whereas previously such information was produced in one national pattern, dictating layouts, promotions, and pricing strategies uniformly across the country.

Feedback Built-in check-and-balance mechanisms that help managers determine whether the information generated is accurate.

Feedback, the final component in an MIS, refers to the built-in check-and-balance mechanisms that help managers determine whether the information generated is accurate. Reports can be compared against predictions, standards, or other measuring sticks. Additionally, results and outputs are themselves feedback;

based on outputs, one can determine whether different types of information might be needed as inputs or whether different processing techniques might be more effective in analyzing and transforming the data. Through each report, a Frito-Lay salesperson can determine whether to cut back or increase the volume of each item. The better the salesperson is able to tailor orders to the demand of the retailer's customers, the more likely the retailer is to allocate more shelf space.

BALANCING THE VALUE AND COST OF INFORMATION

Data   Raw facts and figures concerning results, events, conditions, or trends.

Managers need information to make decisions and manage the organization, and obtaining it costs money. For this reason, there will always be a trade-off between the value and the cost of information.[3] Collecting **data,** which are raw facts and figures concerning results, events, conditions, or trends, costs the organization money, work force time, computer time, and filing space. The more data collected and entered, the greater the costs. Transforming these data into **information,** which is organized, analyzed, packaged data that contains meaning beyond the individual facts and which is useful to the manager in decision making, is also costly. Data can be transformed into information in many ways, and each additional type of analysis and degree of depth in the transformation is an added cost. According to the concept of bounded rationality, discussed in Chapter 3, there are natural limits to each person's ability to synthesize and use information. After a certain point, more data and more information are simply not useful, and generating more will therefore not be cost-efficient. An effective information system will collect the needed data, analyze and organize it into useful information, and disseminate it to the appropriate individuals in a timely and efficient manner.

Information   Organized, analyzed, packaged data that contains meaning beyond the individual facts and is used by managers in decision making.

Managerial Uses of Information

Obviously, all managers need information to do their jobs. Not all of them need all the information available, however. Managers in different departments or on different organizational levels need different types of information. Top-level managers need information to assist them in future-oriented strategic planning and control activities. They need external data on the actions of competitors and new legislation and internal data concerning the operational and financial performance of the firm. The top managers at Frito-Lay needed to know that the snack food industry's growth was only 5 percent in 1985, that the company's growth rate dropped from 11 percent in 1984 to 5 percent in 1985, and that the company's chances for increasing sales through geographic expansion were limited. Thus, increasing sales productivity in existing regions was one of the few ways the company could increase sales, and the HHC project was determined to be crucial to this effort. Top managers need a wide variety of information from diverse sources to help them in their role as the chief nonprogrammed decision makers of the firm.

Middle-level managers need information to help them manage their respective units, the output of the unit, its relationships with other units, and its financial performance. The data they receive from internal and external sources has to be transformed to help them in their role as coordinators of action and translators of strategic plans into operational results. Marketing managers at Frito-Lay need information on the products of competitors and on the effectiveness of various sales promotions. Production managers need information on quotas per product and on techniques for producing higher-quality products.

Supervisors need information about schedules, inventories, and activity plans for the group they supervise. Therefore, the data they collect primarily from internal sources often has a past-performance focus rather than a future-direction focus. Salespeople at Frito-Lay recorded their sales at the end of each day. Each level in an organization—top, middle, and supervisory—needs unique types of information from different sources, on different time schedules, to serve different purposes. See Exhibit 17.1.

The Value of Information

Just as information serves no purpose unless it is needed by the person receiving it to accomplish a purpose, it will be useless unless it meets several other criteria for value. Robert H. Gregory and Richard L. Van Horn have suggested that the value of information depends on four factors: its timeliness, quality, quantity, and relevance to management's ability to take action.[4]

Timeliness of Information The importance of timeliness of information should be obvious. Managers must know that products are defective before they are shipped; they must know that turnover is increasing in a given unit before that department is empty; they must know that organizational growth is being inhibited by the introduction of a competitor's product before the organization loses all of its market share to that competitor.

Quality of Information Information must not only be timely, it must be of high quality to be useful and valuable. The quality of information depends on its accuracy. In other words, the information must reflect reality. The cost of obtaining more accurate information increases as more accuracy is demanded, and the time required for increased accuracy also grows. Here the trade-off between cost and value of information becomes clear. If the information's quality does not increase or aid in the accuracy of the decision or in the success of its results, it is not worth the costs involved. For example, at small horse racing tracks scattered

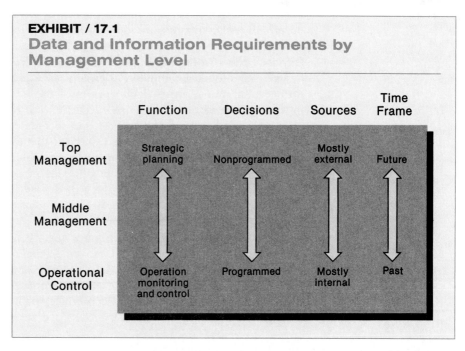

EXHIBIT / 17.1
Data and Information Requirements by Management Level

	Function	Decisions	Sources	Time Frame
Top Management	Strategic planning	Nonprogrammed	Mostly external	Future
Middle Management				
Operational Control	Operation monitoring and control	Programmed	Mostly internal	Past

through the West photographers are hired to take photo finishes of races. If there are disputes, the parties need only look at the photos. Photographers, however, sometimes make mistakes: The camera is not aimed right, the timing is off, the exposures can be incorrect. To help race course managers decide which photographer to hire, the American Quarterhorse Association publishes a list of certified photographers and their history of errors. The fewer the mistakes, the higher the billing rate. A photographer who has made no mistakes charges a premium rate; someone who constantly makes mistakes is cheap. The racing manager has to decide how much the increased accuracy is worth.

Quantity of Information   It is difficult for managers to make competent decisions without sufficient information. Recall from Chapter 3 our discussion of optimal decisions, in which managers know all outcomes of alternative courses of action, and satisficing decisions, in which managers make the best possible choice given the available but incomplete information. But again, *more* information is not always *better* information. An overabundance of information, known as data overload, can cause indecision and error, so managers must sift through a great deal of material to find what is relevant and important. If there is too much extraneous information, costs are increased, decision making is delayed, and errors can occur.

Relevance of Information   The information managers receive has to be relevant to the tasks or decisions at hand. The finance manager does not need detailed information on the personal career paths and employment histories of the staff, and the personnel manager does not need detailed information on the budgets for supplies for each department in the firm.

MIS—A Management Tool

Before we discuss the establishment and design of an MIS, a word of caution is in order. MIS and computers are *tools* managers use to accomplish objectives. Ray Mortiz, the vice president of service for Computervision, a high-tech firm that is recognized as a world leader in computer-aided design and manufacturing, says he would not touch a computer. After 20 years in the computer business, he has no need for one. Mortiz's employees must use computers to do analysis and make recommendations, but as an executive, Mortiz is responsible for the total operation and thus uses the analysis and recommendations others have done. His point is overstated, but he makes it clear that the value of the computer or the MIS is only in its utility for his purposes: If he can accomplish his objectives without spending time in front of a video display terminal, then he need not use one.

Another illustration should also make this point clear. Few of us are familiar with the mechanics of making long-distance telephone calls, but all of us, even children, know how to use the telephone. Mortiz is operating on the same principle: By his account, he does not need to understand anything about computers or how they work. He only needs employees who can give him timely, accurate, high-quality, relevant information useful to him in decision making. Even in this technological age, management skills produce results through other people, not through flashy displays of technology.[5]

ROTHCO

ESTABLISHING AN MIS

Given the need for so many different types of information by so many people in different areas of the organization, managers must make significant efforts to set up an effective MIS. To do so, they may follow four basic stages of design and implementation: (1) MIS planning, (2) MIS design, (3) implementation of MIS, and (4) monitoring and improvement of MIS.[6]

MIS Planning

Planning the process and design is absolutely essential if a successful MIS program is to be introduced and operated. The equipment needed for an MIS requires long ordering times and the establishment of an MIS calls for the commitment of large financial and managerial resources. The HHC project cost Frito-Lay not only $2100 for computers for each of 10,000 salespeople, but it also required $1.2 million for an upgrade of the company's data center to handle the volumes of information that would come pouring in. In addition, there were training costs, costs of miscellaneous supplies such as computer forms and batteries, and maintenance costs for the machines. The company also had to plan to establish a central support network to assist the salespeople right away if they had equipment trouble in the field. Total costs were projected to be $45 million.

Effective MIS planning begins with an assessment of organizational goals and objectives, as well as relevant environmental constraints and opportunities. After this initial analysis phase, the specific purpose the MIS will serve and the limits within which it must operate can be defined. The form taken by the resulting plans will vary greatly with the type of organization. As with any endeavor, the more thorough the planning stage, the greater the probability of success.

MIS Design

One major purpose of an MIS is to give managers information they will need to make decisions. The design of an MIS should begin with an analysis of the types of decisions that managers actually make on the job in a particular organization. Knowing what types of decisions are to be made and who is responsible for them allows management to specify what data is needed, how it should be gathered and organized, and what process will be used to ensure that the information gets to the right person. With this information the manager is ready to design the computer system.

Almost invariably, large organizations choose to computerize their information systems. Because so many transactions are repeated and so much data is used, it would be impossible for them to use noncomputerized information systems. There are three basic components in the design of the computer system: hardware, software, and structure.

Hardware is the physical equipment in the system, which consists of four primary elements. The **central processing unit (CPU)** is the core of the system, containing all the logic that guides processing functions. **Data storage devices** contain all the data that will be processed by the CPU. **Input/output devices,** such as the keyboard, display screen, and printer, are communication channels between the user and the computer. Finally, the **data channel** connects the input/output devices and the CPU.

Software comprises the programs and instructions that dictate how data will be manipulated or organized. Mathematical software contains instructions for various numerical calculations. Word-processing software contains instructions for moving, highlighting, deleting, adding, or spatially arranging written text. Electronic mail, spread sheets, and word processing are some of the commonly used software programs. Managers must select software that will manipulate the types of information they need into information or reports that will be useful to them.

System structure basically refers to the physical and spatial relationship between the hardware and the software. Many large computerized information systems today consist of some type of structural hierarchy between a mainframe and remote minicomputers or personal computers. A **mainframe** is a powerful computer that has extensive data-processing and storage capabilities; it can hold and process more data in more ways in a shorter time period than most or all smaller minicomputers. However, its capabilities are constrained by its cost and size; mainframes are too large and expensive for companies to place throughout their operations. Therefore, the mainframe and its input/output often are centralized in one location. In a **centralized processing system,** the hardware and the software are centralized in one location and are operated by a centralized group of computer specialists. The earliest organizational computer systems were all centralized. In modern applications of this approach, individual managers and users can gain access to the central mainframe by using remote terminals.

Hardware The physical equipment in a computer system.

Central processing unit (CPU) The core of the computer system containing the logic that guides processing functions.

Data storage devices Devices that contain all the data to be processed by the CPU.

Input/output devices Communication channels between the user and the computer.

Data channel The connector between the input/output devices and the CPU.

Software Programs and instructions that dictate how data will be manipulated and organized.

System structure The physical and spatial relationship between hardware and software.

Mainframe A powerful computer that has extensive data-processing and storage capabilities.

Centralized processing system A system in which hardware and software are centralized in one location.

Distributed processing system A system in which packages of hardware and software are spread throughout the organization.

Today, most organizations do not rely on mainframes or centralized processing systems for all their computer processing needs. They may use a mainframe to store and process large amounts of data on an ongoing basis, but they will rely on personal or minicomputers for day-to-day activities. In a **distributed processing system,** "packages" of hardware and software are spread out where needed throughout the organization. Organizations with personal computers in their various departments are using the distributed processing approach. While responsiveness to individual needs is very high, the degree of coordination between processing of all organizational information is much lower. Separate data bases are maintained and reports are generated at different locations. For example, the sales department might know how many of each item are sold in a month, the marketing department may know which types of products are or will be in highest demand in the coming month, and the production department will know how many of each item they can produce in that month with no changes in the production system. However, if the sales manager wants to revise sales goals based on demand, or if the production department wants to know how many of each product the sales force expects to sell, individual managers will have to coordinate that data between themselves; it is not stored, processed, or coordinated in a central location.

Local area networks Groups of computers that communicate with one another and share common resources such as data, hardware, and software.

One recent development attempts to minimize these problems: **Local area networks** are groups of computers that communicate with one another and share common resources such as data, hardware, and software. For example, a network may link an auto manufacturer, dealers, part suppliers, other suppliers, and the assembly line itself. When a customer orders a car with specific features, the dealer puts the order into a computer terminal; the network then orders parts, schedules shipment of the parts from suppliers to the factory, and orders the assembly line to start (or schedule) the production. This type of networking provides enormous cost and production benefits for the customer, dealer, supplier, and manufacturer.[7]

After managers have determined what types, combination, and structure of hardware and software will be used they can design the functions of the system. To help ensure effective design of an MIS, managers should keep in mind several guidelines.

1. *Include the end users in the design team.* Including end users will help ensure that the system meets the needs of the users. It can also help prevent the system from collecting and disseminating information that is useless, though perhaps impressive looking, to computer specialists. If the end users have defined their needs precisely, chances are that the system will process important and useful information rather than trivial, tangential, or unnecessary information. Close cooperation between systems designers, who have experience in implementation, and systems users, who know their own needs, will produce the best system.[8] Leo Kiely, senior vice president of sales and marketing for Frito-Lay, explained in 1986 how he would involve users in the system design: "We will put a couple of prime movers against the problem—full-time, director-level people. They'll ask themselves, 'If I were regional marketing manager in Boston, what would I do differently?' and 'If I were a district manager, how would I use the data?' Then they'll figure out the answers."[9]

2. *Balance the time and money costs with relevance of information.* Not every organization needs a mainframe to accomplish its goals, nor will every

organization truly benefit if every employee has a personal computer on his or her desk. In Frito-Lay's case, an expense of $2100 per salesperson for a hand-held computer—and an overall expense of $45 million—was justified because the strategic benefits were predicted to outweigh the costs. Even though actual operating costs would be $3 million higher annually, increased sales productivity and customer service were considered priority goals, worth the extra expense.

Information need only be gathered, processed, and disseminated to the appropriate individuals quickly enough to be useful in decision making and problem solving. If the cost of an information gathering and processing system exceeds its benefits, the system is not cost-effective.[10] An effective MIS will filter information so that users will receive information relevant to their work and condense it so that it is easy to use.[11]

3.   *Pretest the MIS prior to installation on the actual site.*   Pretesting serves a dual purpose. First, it allows faults or omissions in the planning phase to manifest themselves, and therefore be corrected before they cause problems in the organization. Second, the trial run can serve as a training ground for managers and operators of the system.

4.   *Provide training and written documentation to all users of the system.*   All those who received no instruction during the pretest will need adequate on-site training if the system is to work effectively. In addition, all users and operators should be given written documentation, such as instruction or operating manuals, to which they can refer to whenever they have problems with the system. At this point, an organization is ready to implement an MIS.

MIS Implementation

Effective planning and design are essential to successful implementation of an MIS, but several factors during the implementation phase must be taken into consideration as well. Various methods can be used to install the system, not all of which will be effective in a given situation.

Crash implementation
The installation of a newly designed system all at once, completely replacing the previous system.

Parallel implementation
Simultaneous operation of new and old systems to allow debugging of the new system and performance comparison between the two.

Modular implementation   Direct implementation of a new system by one organizational unit at a time. Also called pilot implementation.

Implementation Methods[12]   There are four basic methods of MIS implementation. In *direct* or **crash implementation,** the newly designed system is installed all at once, completely replacing the previous system. Extensive pretesting is required in this case, because the old system will not be available as a backup if the new system fails. In **parallel implementation,** the new and old systems are operated simultaneously for a period long enough to allow a debugging of the new system and a comparison of performance between the two. Pretest costs can be saved using this approach, but they are easily offset by the costs of operating two systems at once. In some cases, for example if a hospital is shifting from manual to computer filing of patient records, maintaining both old and new is absolutely essential until the new system is totally functioning. In these situations, backup systems are designed as part of the MIS. In such a system, backup records are maintained on the computer and updated weekly. If anything goes wrong in the computers, only one week's worth of information is lost. The old manual system may be discontinued when it is absolutely certain that both the primary and backup records in the computer system are accurate and not at risk of being erased, and that the new system is functioning effectively.

In **modular** or *pilot* **implementation,** individual units of the organization adopt the new system (through direct implementation) one at a time. This pro-

Phased implementation
Segment-by-segment installation of a system throughout the organization.

cess saves both pretest costs and the costs of operating two systems throughout the organization, but there may be problems in coordination between departments during the installation period. **Phased implementation** is a process of installing a system in pieces, or segment by segment, throughout the entire organization. As each component is adopted, part of the old system is dropped. While potentially economical, this method is difficult to design; at each stage, the new components must be able to work effectively with the old ones.

Each organization has different needs and situational factors that will make the use of one of these methods more effective than the others. Managers must analyze these factors and choose the most appropriate method.[13] Frito-Lay implemented its HHC project in several phases. Initially, 200 Fujitsu hand-held computers were tested in the Dallas and Minneapolis areas. By the end of 1987, half of the sales force was equipped with the units, and by 1988 the remaining sales reps received the computers. Thus the installation of the system, originally scheduled to be completed in 1989, was finalized far ahead of schedule. "Feld's organization works very hard to make the complexity totally transparent to the user, and at being a service organization that's sensitive to users' needs,"[14] Rittenmeyer said.

Implementation Problems   As discussed in Chapter 9, the implementation of any major change in an organization can be source of concern, confusion, and challenge for all employees. Technical problems in implementing an MIS must be handled by the managers in charge of the implementation, along with the end users and any specialists or suppliers involved in the project. But another, often more difficult problem is the potential negative human reaction to computers.

G. W. Dickson and J. K. Simmons have analyzed this human problem and identified several factors of MIS resistance.[15] The first is the effect of an MIS on the organization's structure. A new MIS often disrupts organizational units. Some departments, such as inventory and purchasing, may be merged; other departments may be completely abolished. Individuals may resent or resist the need to change work habits and/or to leave current colleagues.

Second, an MIS disrupts the informal organizational systems. Individuals may resist new formal channels of communication or prefer other channels. They may also feel threatened by having to provide new types of information or more detailed and revealing information about their activities or the performance of their department. Or, as The Inside View 17.2 illustrates, they may simply feel intimidated by having to rely on a system they do not fully understand.

Individual characteristics are the third major factor in MIS resistance. Different individuals need different types of information, as was illustrated in Exhibit 17.2. The new system may not meet their needs, or they may perceive that it will not. If it does not, they will not be motivated to spend the time and energy required to provide the data and reports necessary to make it work.

The fourth factor is organizational culture. People may resist the implementation of an MIS if it disrupts normal behavior or interaction patterns. In fact, resistance to change itself may be a strong component of the organization's culture, as we discussed in Chapters 8 and 9.

Finally, the manner in which the change is implemented affects the resistance level of employees. If it is autocratically imposed, people will resist. If the end users are included in the development of the MIS, it will be more likely to meet their needs, and they will be more likely to accept it.

THE INSIDE VIEW / 17.2

I'd Rather Have My Hand in the Pulp

Operators of fully automated control systems often find it difficult to translate information displayed on the terminal screen into what is actually happening in the plant.

Shoshana Zuboff studied several companies' information systems during the 1980s, including those at three wood pulp processing plants. She discovered that some operating personnel were uncomfortable with the new information systems. Operators seemed to have difficulty translating the data displayed on video display terminals to the reality of what was happening on the plant floor. Typically, when she asked an operator what the data on the screen meant, the operator would point to the screen and discuss the data in terms of its spatial relationship to other data on the screen rather than in terms of the information it was providing. The following is an example taken from her notes:

> Today I spent the afternoon in Piney Wood's bleach plant control room. Because it was Saturday, there were less people in the mill, and I had a great deal of time to speak with Gregory, who was in the control room most of the afternoon. . . . I asked Gregory, as I had asked so many operators, "How do you operate with the computer?" Each time he began to explain his answer, he used his index finger to point to different readings on the screen and trace a path from one reading to another. His utterances consisted exclusively of statements such as "When this (pointing to one reading) moves up here (pointing to a location on the screen), then this one (another reading indicated) will move down here (another location on the screen)." Each question I asked . . . elicited more of the same. Finally, after about one half hour, Gregory seemed agitated and frustrated. The agitation was not directed toward me, at least

I had no indication of that. Instead, he seemed frustrated by the limits of his ability to explain anything to me. He stood up abruptly and said, "Come on, I'll show you." With this, he guided me out into the bleach plant and gave me a tour of the equipment. He showed me the washers and the old instrument panels by the side of each washer that used to be the way variables such as viscosity levels were monitored. At each washer he stopped, stuck his hand into the vat, and brought out a fistful of wet pulp. Rolling it between his fingers, squeezing it, and sniffing it, he explained what stage each sample was in. After the tour, his tone was that of someone speaking in secrecy and confidence. "Using the computer might be easier if the screens were arranged like the physical things on the floor. I don't really work this computer stuff that well; I don't really understand it all that well."

Gregory was unable to bring the external world of the plant into the computer control room. His methods of explanation relied upon being able to touch and exhibit the real thing. The screen was an encapsulated, formal space unrelated to the plant beyond the control room door. He knew his way around the screen, not because he could give meaning to what he saw there, but because he had noticed through trial and error how data elements were arrayed in relation to one another. ■

Source: Zuboff, Shoshana, *In the Age of the Smart Machine* (New York: Basic Books, 1988), pp. 87, 88.

The Frito-Lay system was specifically designed with users in mind. And as one salesperson who was part of the pilot implementation group put it, the system definitely met their needs: "The sales calls go faster, the end of the day process is a snap, and my wife and I don't have to spend an hour every night going over the paperwork to make sure I did the multiplication right." In fact, he stated, "when we have problems with the hand-held computers, no one wants to tell headquarters for fear they might take them away from us!"[16]

MIS Monitoring and Improvement

To monitor MIS performance and use, a manager should be aware of the symptoms of an inadequate MIS. Bertram A. Colbert developed one list of such symptoms that is applicable to organizations today; examples of these, given in Exhibit 17.2 fall into the general categories of operational, psychological, and report

---

EXHIBIT / 17.2
Symptoms of an Inadequate MIS

Operational	Psychological	Report Content
Large physical inventory adjustments	Surprise at financial results	Excessive use of tabulations of figures
Capital expenditures overruns	Poor attitude of executives about usefulness of information	Multiple preparation and distribution of identical data
Inability of executives to explain changes from year to year in operating results	Lack of understanding of financial information on part of nonfinancial executives	Disagreeing information from different sources
Uncertain direction of company growth	Lack of concern for environmental changes	Lack of periodic comparative information and trends
Unexplainable cost variances	Executive homework reviewing reports considered excessive	Lateness of information
No order backlog awareness		Too little or excess detail
No internal discussion of reported data		Inaccurate information
Insufficient knowledge about competition		Lack of standards for comparison
Purchasing of parts from outside vendors despite internal capability to make them		Failure to identify variances by cause and responsibility
Record of some "sour" investment in facilities, or in programs such as R&D and advertising		Inadequate externally generated information

Source: Reprinted by permission of the Institute of Management Services from Colbert, Bertram A., "The Management Information System," *Management Services* 4(5) (September–October 1967): 15–24.

content symptoms. Operational inadequacies of an MIS include inventory imbalances, project failure, and an inability to use MIS outputs to explain any of these problems. Psychological inadequacies include resistance and system-defeating behavior on the part of managers. Report content inadequacies include overlapping or contradictory reports, overuse or underuse of detail, vagueness in outputs, and lateness of reports. In addition to addressing Colbert's list, managers can often pinpoint weaknesses by answering the following questions:

1. Where and how do managers get information?
2. Can managers make better use of their contacts to get information?
3. In what areas are managers' knowledge weakest, and how can they be given information to minimize these weaknesses?
4. Do managers tend to act before receiving information?
5. Do managers wait so long for information that opportunities pass them by and the organization gets tied up in bottlenecks?

The problems with MIS vary from situation to situation, depending on the organization, the individuals, and the specific features of the MIS. Therefore, it will be an ongoing challenge for managers to maintain and improve MIS performance in the organization. One of the most important things managers can do "is to constantly keep the goal of MIS clear: to provide decision-making information to managers."[17]

DECISION SUPPORT SYSTEMS, EXPERT SYSTEMS, AND ARTIFICIAL INTELLIGENCE

Decision support systems (DSS), expert systems (ES), and artificial intelligence (AI), are extended developments of MIS. They not only provide managers with effectively packaged information, which is the basic purpose of MIS, but assist in its analysis and in decision making. While supercomputers are still being developed to process more information more rapidly, so-called thinking computers are being developed to analyze information using humanlike reasoning. The two developments are independent, but as The Inside View 17.3 illustrates, they will eventually merge.

Decision Support Systems

Decision support system
An interactive computerized information system that assists the user in making decisions.

A **decision support system** is an interactive computerized information system that provides the user with an easily accessible question-and-answer framework for making decisions. Ideally, a DSS solicits input data from the user and then prompts him or her to consider all significant decision points.[18] The user can pose problems or hypothetical questions, allowing the computer to run through tests of alternative courses of action. Using the results, the decision maker has a better feel for what might happen if various decisions are made and so can lower their risks in decision making (as was discussed in Chapter 3). A DSS can help managers make nonprogrammed decisions in semistructured or uncertain conditions.

DSS essentially takes MIS a step further in terms of providing repackaged data as information. An MIS serves mainly to collect and disseminate information; it produces routine, standardized reports. DSS manipulates the data much more extensively and analytically. It can test solution options on any topic for which

THE INSIDE VIEW / 17.3

Fast and Smart

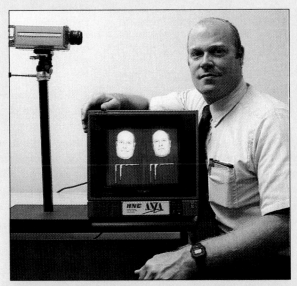

Traditional computers have trouble recognizing faces because they bog down in the details; people may smile one minute and frown the next. Newer computers are beginning to be able to discriminate.

The computer at the University of Illinois is simulating something that no one saw: the evolution of the universe in the aftermath of the Big Bang. Recreating conditions that may have prevailed billions of years ago, the computer reveals on a remote screen how massive clouds of subatomic particles, tugged by their own gravity, might have coalesced into filaments and flattened disks. The vivid reds, greens, and blues of the shapes are not merely decorative but represent the various densities of the first large structures as they emerged from primordial chaos in the near vacuum of space.

At the Massachusetts Institute of Technology, another computer is struggling to learn what any three-year-old already knows: the difference between a cup and a saucer. What the youngster sees at a glance, the computer must be taught, painstakingly, one step at a time. First it must comprehend the concept of an object, a physical thing distinguished from the space around it by edges and surfaces. Then it must grasp the essential attributes of cupness: the handle, the leakproof central cavity, the stable base. Finally, it must deal with the exceptions, like the foam-plastic cup whose heat-insulting properties are so good that it does not need a handle.

These experiments illustrate the paradox at the heart of today's computer science. The most powerful computing machines—giant number crunchers possessed of speed and storage capacities beyond human comprehension—are essentially dumb brutes with no more intellectual depth than a light bulb. At the other extreme are computers that have begun to exhibit the first glimmers of humanlike reasoning, but only within the confines of narrowly defined tasks.

For 40 years scientists have labored to make headway at these two frontiers of computer research. One group, working with the lightning-fast machines known as supercomputers, is always pushing for more raw power, more blazing speed. The other group, writing programs that show the rudiments of artificial intelligence, explores the mysteries of human thought. Each of these two grand scientific enterprises, backed by billions of research dollars and blessed with some of the century's best minds, has proceeded as if the other did not exist.

But there are signs that the two broad avenues of computer research may be starting to converge, that today's most advanced machines may someday evolve into electronic brains that are not just incredibly fast but smart as well. The quest has been taken up by almost every major nation. And no wonder: The potential rewards—in industrial productivity, scientific research, and national security—are staggering. Grown men glow with childlike excitement when they describe robots that will see their way around a factory, typewriters that will take dictation, defense systems that will make the world safe from nuclear arms.

The two fields of computer research are at different stages in their life cycles. Artificial intelligence is just getting started: The first commercial projects appeared less than five years ago, and are now finding widespread application. The supercomputer manufacturers, on the other hand, having supplied high-speed processors to government labs and intelligence agencies for a quarter-century, are now experiencing a growth so explosive that it has taken even the most optimistic in- dustry leaders by surprise. Sales of the machines, which cost $5 million to $25 million each, have increased 25 percent a year or more over the past decade, and in 1988 will pass the $1 billion-a-year mark for the first time. ■

Source: "Fast and Smart: Designers Race to Build the Supercomputers of the Future," *Time*, March 28, 1988, pp. 54, 55.

data exists. However, both MIS and DSSs are limited in that they incorporate no judgment. A manager reading a report from the MIS department about lower sales levels or increased service calls still has to assign meaning to the information and take action. A DSS programmed with various assumptions about the effects of an early retirement program can produce an "answer" for each set of assumptions (concerning program features and acceptance rates, for example); however, the *manager* must judge which assumptions are more accurate, which answer is the best, and what course of action to pursue.

Expert Systems

Expert systems
Knowledge-based computer systems that try to mimic human expertise and produce decisions requiring judgment.

Expert systems take DSS a step further by incorporating judgment. They are also called knowledge-based systems, because they include "intelligent response" capabilities. **Expert systems** are computer systems that try to mimic human expertise and produce decisions requiring judgment.[19] They can select the appropriate information to apply to a given situation and can update themselves based on experience and mistakes.

ESs, like DSSs, are interactive and can manipulate data, run tests, or create models. ES also diagnoses problems, recommends strategy or alternative courses of action, explains its rationale, and learns from its experience by "remembering" previous problem-solving exercises.[20] Additionally, users do not have to develop their own alternatives, as with a DSS, but only need to evaluate the alternatives and explanations provided by the ES. The ES can save time and be especially helpful in solving complex problems with many variables, but it should still be considered a managerial tool, not a managerial replacement.

Expert systems, because their effectiveness and scope are limited to the capabilities of the humans who program them, are inherently limited in making judgments. However, the *ideal* expert system "asks the 'right' questions, considers the 'right' factors, and delivers the 'right' decision, within a specialized field of knowledge. It 'guesses' when it has to, and when it is outside the range of its expertise, its proficiency degrades gradually and gracefully. When asked, it can explain precisely how it reached its conclusions."[21]

Expert systems are often used to duplicate or replace expertise needed by an organization. For example, if a manufacturing organization with several plants that conduct similar operations using similar equipment has only one highly effective troubleshooter, it might program this person's expertise into a system that could be accessed by the operations personnel in the other plants, to help them solve technical problems. The expertise of a number of technical specialists could in fact be incorporated into one system.[22]

Artificial Intelligence

Artificial intelligence
Information technology
that attempts to mimic
human thinking, seeing,
talking, and listening processes.

Expert systems are one branch of a broader field of computing called artificial intelligence (AI), which also incorporates such areas as robotics, natural language processing, speech recognition and synthesis, and vision. **Artificial intelligence** is information technology that attempts to mimic human activities requiring intelligence, such as thinking, seeing, talking, and listening.[23]

AI operates much like expert systems, but in "more human" ways. Facts, rules, and other input can enter the system through a voice receptor or some other sense receiver. The computer then takes the information, applies rules stored in its knowledge base, makes inferences, and produces a response—also perhaps in a "human" manner.

Consider the example of the Powercise machine, an exercise machine developed by LivingWell, Inc., a Houston-based health club chain. "Chester" is a chest press machine that, using artificial intelligence, holds personal workout records for club members and offers personalized workout regimes. Throughout the course of the workout, Chester will correct the club member's form, monitor the pace of the workout, and offer encouraging words like "You're halfway there!" and "Good job! Your dad would be proud."[24]

THE IMPACT OF INFORMATION TECHNOLOGY

Networks, expert systems, and artificial intelligences are just three technological developments that fall into the category of information technology. Telecommunications technology is another large branch of this field; using electronic mail, people within an organization or in different organizations around the world can send each other messages via computer faster and cheaper than by mail. Computer conferencing allows an ongoing exchange of information via computer hookup between several people simultaneously, and videoconferencing adds the benefit of a live television hookup so that conference members can see each other.

Automated offices combine several types of telecommunications and computerized information technology to help managers perform their duties. Each manager, for example, has a personal computer that not only holds all the types of information and software he or she needs but also may be hooked into decision support systems or central MIS files. The manager's office also has access to other offices within or outside of the organization via one or more of the telecommunications technologies discussed above.

The information technology options for organizations are virtually limitless. But the purpose and the value is the same in every case: Information technology is "technology that dramatically increases the ability to record, store, analyze, and transmit information in ways that permit flexibility, accuracy, immediacy, geographic independence, volume, and complexity."[25]

The speed and effectiveness of information and computer-based technologies has increased dramatically over the past five decades, while costs for capabilities have dropped just as precipitously. One study determined that the cost of computer power relative to the cost of information processing is at least 8000 times less now than it was 30 years ago. And between roughly 1960 and 1980, the amount of time needed by a computer to conduct one electronic operation fell by a factor of 80 million. As one author put it, "If the automotive industry had paralleled the advances that the computer industry has experienced in the last 25 years, a Rolls Royce would cost 50 cents and would deliver 15 million miles to the gallon."[26]

Information technology is affecting the work of people in virtually every job in organizations and is affecting the structure and strategy of virtually every organization. However, there are differences between the way it is affecting the manufacturing sector and the service sector.

Information Technology in the Manufacturing Sector

Information technology has affected both mass production and process production systems in manufacturing industries. In mass production systems, computer-aided design (CAD) allows drafting and engineering personnel to more easily and effectively develop new designs by simply altering, on the computer, existing designs. They can also generate hundreds of design variations with very little extra work, whereas previously it would have been too time consuming and costly to generate more than three or four prototypes.

On the production line, robots have taken over many of the routine, mechanical tasks formerly done by people, and computer-numerically-controlled machine tools have assumed the tasks of fashioning metal parts and components to desired dimensions and specifications. Flexible manufacturing systems (FMS) integrate all of these developments: Computer-controlled machining centers sculpt a variety of complex metal parts at high speed with great reliability; robots handle and move the parts and assemble them on the production line. All the phases of the process are linked by a central computer that guides production from design to output. Computer-integrated manufacturing (CIM) and FMS are often used interchangeably, but Krajewski and Ritzman argue that CIM is "an umbrella term that means a total integration of product design, engineering, process planning, and manufacturing through complex computer systems."[27]

One example of an FMS is Yamazaki Machinery Works Ltd. in Japan, which opened a machine tool factory that is essentially run by telephone from corporate headquarters. The plant has 65 computer-controlled machine tools and 34 robots, all linked via fiber-optic cables to corporate headquarters; 215 workers produce what formerly required 2000 employees. As demand fluctuates, the factory can reduce output from a maximum of $230 million worth of machine tools a year to $80 million worth a year without laying off one worker.

Continuous process production has also benefited from advances in information technology. Whereas previously computers simply alerted operating personnel to critical changes in processing conditions, they now can take their own readings, monitor conditions, perform computations, and adjust the system. However, with all this sophistication, there are still places where people perform best, as The Inside View 17.4 illustrates.

Information Technology in the Service Sector

Paperwork is fast becoming a thing of the past. In the service sector, information technology has primarily been used to speed up and simplify the work normally done by clerical personnel: the handling and processing of ever-increasing amounts of information. Today, word processors and personal computers allow

Where Robots Can't Yet Compete

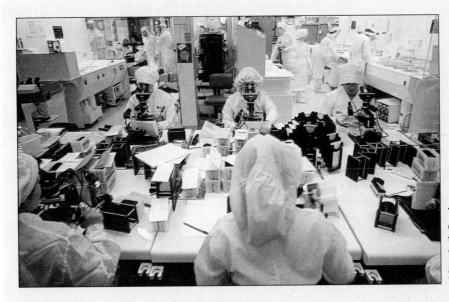

The manufacture of computer chips is one task that still requires the skill, dexterity, and judgment of a human worker.

The plant looks like the industrial exhibit at the Smithsonian Institution come to life, so old is much of its machinery. But in a world being engulfed by computerized automation, Briggs & Stratton Corp.'s maverick Wauwatosa, Wisconsin, factory towers as a stronghold of human skill, agility, and high productivity.

Briggs & Stratton is the world's leading and lowest-cost producer of small engines. The company has been consistently profitable; in its last fiscal year it toted up a net of $39.4 million on sales of $636 million. In the 1982 Fortune 500, it ranked 422nd in sales but 167th in total return to investors.

The company's secret technology is the most flexible of all manufacturing systems: the human being. "We find that people are best at doing the work that needs dexterity and a lot of repetition," says Laverne J. Socks, Briggs & Stratton's executive vice president for manufacturing. "We will consider automation wherever possible, practical, and economical. But if you are talking about one of those unmanned factories, you'll never see our operation all automated like that."

Part of the reason is that the firm's principal products, small air-cooled engines used mainly in lawn mowers and garden tractors, do not readily lend themselves to automation, at least not in assembly. While it is true that Fanuc Ltd. in Japan assembles electric motors with robots, internal combustion engines are more complicated. Even the small one- and two-cylinder Briggs & Stratton engines have as many as 500 parts.

But Briggs & Stratton has also achieved robot-like productivity by astute management of its factory. It minimizes the number of managers, and those managers, as Socks puts it, "communicate with the workers constantly, on the floor." Quality control is bolstered through employee participation. Housekeeping awards are issued to keep the plant clean.

The mainstay of this policy is a piecework incentive system, and visitors invariably marvel at the intensity of the work force. Workers don't linger over coffee breaks (there's only one a day, of six-minute duration). Says one impressed visitor, "They even run to and from the bathrooms." Sixty percent are on either group or incentive income pay; some workers earn as much as $30,000 a year. The union, local 232 of the Allied Industrial Workers, has no problem with piecework. "The people have a preference for the incentive plans," says a union official.

It remains to be seen, though, how long the people at Briggs & Stratton can hold out against the new machines. There's nothing in theory to stop others—the Japanese, for instance—from redesigning engines for easier automatic assembly. ■

Source: Bylinsky, G., "The Race to the Automatic Factory," *Fortune* 21 (February 1983): 52–64.

almost anyone in the organization to retrieve and manipulate data, generate reports and graphic displays, and communicate with each other across organizational and even national boundaries.

Though most service organizations still require large staffs of service personnel to input data and contact customers there is a trend toward eliminating these functions entirely. For example, most banks now provide their customers with access to their accounts through the use of 24-hour teller machines. Customers serve themselves and directly enter the data, which is automatically transmitted into the bank's central information system, bypassing what was previously a clerical function.

In the 1950s, when computers were first being introduced into the workplace, cyberneticist Norbert Wiener predicted that they would cause massive unemployment. Obviously, that has not transpired. Organizations today still use large clerical and production staffs, and these workers are much more effective utilizing the advanced technology that was rumored to make them obsolete. Although there is ongoing debate about the consequences of technological development on employment, it is likely that more people will be employed to do jobs related to the new technologies than will be unemployed completely because of the developments.

■ KEY POINTS

1 An MIS is an organized method of providing past, present, and projected information relating to internal and external operations. An MIS supports planning, control, and operational functions by furnishing uniform and useful information in the proper time frame to assist the decision-making process of the organization. Basically, the purpose of an MIS is to provide information selectively to people in the organization to help them do their jobs.

2 The basic components of an MIS are inputs (data), processing (computer transformation of the data), outputs and feedback.

3 Collecting data and transforming it into information are costly. Thus, both activities must be limited to useful levels. An effective MIS will collect only needed data, analyze and organize it into useful information, and disseminate it to the appropriate individuals in a timely and efficient manner.

4 Top-level managers need information to assist them in future-oriented strategic planning and control activities. Middle-level managers need information to help

them manage their units and coordinate them with others in the organization. Supervisors need information about schedules, inventories, and activity plans for the group they supervise. Information will be valuable to people if it helps them do their jobs and if it is timely, of good quality, of sufficient quantity, and relevant to the decisions and tasks at hand.

5 The four steps needed to establish an MIS are MIS planning, MIS design, MIS implementation, and MIS monitoring and improvement.

6 There are three basic elements of the computer system: hardware, which includes the central processing unit, data storage devices, input/output devices, and the data channel; software, which are the programs that manipulate and organize data; and structure, which is the physical and spatial relationship between the hardware and software.

7 In order to help ensure effective MIS design, a manager or designer should include end users in the design team, balance the time and money costs of the system, favor relevance and selectivity over quantity

of information, pretest the system prior to installation, and provide training and written documentation to all users of the system.

8 The four basic methods of MIS implementation are crash or direct implementation, in which the new system entirely and immediately replaces the old; parallel implementation, in which new and old operate simultaneously for a brief period; modular or pilot implementation, in which the new system is adopted by one organizational unit at a time; and phased implementation, in which segments of the new system gradually replace segments of the old one.

9 Decision support systems are interactive systems that provide users with question-and-answer frameworks useful in decision-making situations. DSSs allow users to test the merits of various courses of action. Expert systems are computer systems that try to mimic human expertise and produce decisions requiring judgment. They can select information that is applicable to a situation and can update their "reason-ing" capabilities based on experience. Expert systems are one branch of a broader field of computing called artificial intelligence. Artificial intelligence is information technology that attempts to mimic human activities that require intelligence, such as thinking, seeing, talking, and listening.

10 The information technology options for organizations are virtually limitless; information technology is affecting the work of people in virtually every job and is affecting the structure and strategy of virtually every organization. In the manufacturing sector, through computer-aided design, robotics, and flexible manufacturing systems, mass production processes can be run and controlled by computer. Continuous production processes can virtually monitor and control themselves. In the service sector paperwork is becoming a thing of the past, clerical work has been simplified or eliminated, and in many cases people can service themselves through computers.

FOR DISCUSSION AND REVIEW

1. Define an MIS in your own terms. What would characterize adequate information from such a system?
2. What is the difference between data and information? Give several examples from a job you have held recently.
3. Suppose that you were preparing to get married. What kinds of information would you need to make a good decision?
4. Define the major factors that influence the value of information.
5. Why would managers and employees resist an MIS? What would you do about this?
6. How would you define data overload? Is less information ever better than more?
7. Pick an organization with which you are familiar and explain how an MIS would work there. What would be its main components? What value could it provide to the firm you selected?
8. What is DSS, and how does it differ from MIS?
9. How can a DSS be used?
10. What is an expert system? How does it differ from an MIS and a DSS?
11. Explain how technology and an MIS interface. How do they affect one another?

KEY TERMS

Artificial intelligence
Central processing unit (CPU)
Centralized processing system
Computer-based information systems (CBIS)
Crash implementation
Data
Data channel
Data storage devices
Decision support system
Distributed processing system
Electronic data processing (EDP)
Expert systems
Feedback
Hardware
Information
Input/output devices
Inputs
Local area networks
Mainframe
Management information system (MIS)
Modular implementation
Outputs
Parallel implementation
Phased implementation
Processing
Software
System structure
Transaction-processing systems

THE CONFERENCE TABLE: DISCUSSION CASE / 17.1

Pharmacy Information Systems

Computers can now help pharmacists and patients by compiling information about individual drug reactions and giving an overall picture of all prescribed medications.

Inappropriately prescribed medications cost Americans over $4.5 billion in hospital expenses and billions of dollars more in physicians' bills, not to mention the fear and pain that can result from a bad drug reaction. Allergic reactions and harmful combinations of medications can kill. The problem is of great concern to patients, their families, physicians, and pharmacists.

Increasingly, pharmacies are taking steps to battle the problem. They are finding that affordable computers and software enable them to protect their custom-

Sources: Englemayer, P. A., "Safety Prompts Computer Use in Drugstore," *Wall Street Journal*, September 28, 1983, pp. 31, 51; and Ehrlich, P., "Court Sides with Computers in Medicine," *MIS Week*, January 27, 1982, p. 4.

ers' health, assist them in consultations with physicians, and provide them with a good competitive advantage. At first, as the price of computers fell, many pharmacies adapted computers for inventory and billing. Software that dealt specifically with drug interactions was developed much later, as a logical growth of the computer usage in this industry. About half of the nation's 25 largest drug chains are now adding drug interaction or customer information programs to their computer networks.

The new systems allow the pharmacist to check the compatibility of a drug with other medications the customer may be using, as well as with the customer's record of dietary restrictions and allergies, before a new prescription is filled. When problems turn up, the physician can be consulted. Pharmacists report that inappropriate combinations of prescriptions often result when patients consult different physicians. The information system is being developed so that eventually pharmacists can check not only their own records but those in the computers at other pharmacies across the state and maybe even across the nation.

Currently the information is transferred by the patient. For example, in Massachusetts, the Massachusetts Medical Society Auxiliary provides doctors with Medex cards that they give to patients. Each patient's card contains a list of prescriptions and any reactions the patient has had to them. The patient submits the card to the pharmacists with prescriptions. Computerizing the records at one drug store will greatly improve the ability of doctors and pharmacists to meet the needs of their patients.

Although the use of computers and software to prevent serious drug interactions in prescription users is attractive, the system is not without problems. Privacy of records is a major concern. Most pharmacies note that it is impossible to secure terminals and data from computer thieves. Legal liability is another problem. For example, if a person whose records are on the pharmacy's computer system takes a drug that causes a severe interaction, who is responsible?

Druggists using the new information systems report an increase in customer loyalty in filling their prescriptions. "It's a good selling point," says one. "It allows us to practice even more professionally than we did before. It's good for business. It's beyond me how anybody couldn't want it."

The concerns over the use of computers in medicine go well beyond the neighborhood pharmacy. Physicians and hospitals that have not bought or used computer-based technology in the diagnosis and treatment of patients may find themselves liable in a court of law. Several court decisions have gone against doctors whose failure to use the latest available technology resulted in serious injury to patients. ▪

DISCUSSION QUESTIONS

1. Have pharmacy information systems developed similarly to the evolution of MIS? What future developments in information technology would you expect to be applied in this field, and what purpose would they serve?

2. How does the value of information as discussed in the text apply in this case? How does the trade-off between the value and cost of information apply in this case?

3. Which method of MIS implementation would you recommend for a pharmacy information system, and why?

THE CONFERENCE TABLE: DISCUSSION CASE / 17.2

The Paperless Expense Account

Automation has made it much easier to record and analyze such accounting items as employee travel and expenses.

Adrienne Marchese is the travel manager at Barclays Bank in New York. Every day, she and her staff are bombarded with handwritten, miscoded expense reports stapled haphazardly together. They have to plow through hundreds of receipts, add and code travel and expense (T&E) report columns, and reconcile what was spent against what was drawn by the 1400 Barclays employees who will travel this year.

Trying to monitor and control how much money employees spend on T&E is painstaking but essential. For most companies T&E is the third-largest controllable expense, after salaries and data processing. In 1986, $85 billion was spent on T&E, and that figure will rise to $100 billion by 1990, American Express Co. predicted in a recent business-travel survey. To get a grip on the problem, 24 percent of all large companies now have travel managers, up from 7.5 percent in 1982.

Controlling T&E costs is so complex that only 35 percent of senior managements think their companies do it well, American Express reports. Now, though, a number of services are springing up to help. Airlines, travel agencies, and credit card companies are all building systems that track T&E information so that companies can better manage costs—before they go out of control.

In the latest development on August 31, 1987, American Airlines Inc. introduced Capture, a service that lets companies automate their T&E information, so that they can instantly see what is being booked. Capture automatically transmits booking information from American's Sabre reservation system—and eventually

Source: "Now, the 'Paperless' Expense Account," *Business Week*, September 7, 1987, p. 106.

from other systems—directly to corporate clients' headquarters. The idea is to create an electronic T&E report for each traveler, eliminating the need for a paper one.

When travelers return, they simply complete the report on-line, updating the company's travel data base. Programmed into Capture's software is the company's travel policy, with everything from preferred airlines to who can fly first-class, so the company can spot transgressions before money is spent.

With Capture, which costs companies $50,000 for a five-year lease, corporate travel and accounting departments can analyze T&E costs anytime. Eventually, Capture President Albert R. Ramacciotti hopes to negotiate deals to have hotel chains, rental car companies, and credit card issuers send data to Capture. With such participants on-line, Ramacciotti believes that customers will save as much as 20 percent on T&E.

Capture is likely to knock heads with a similar system introduced last November: the American Express Expense Management System. Aimed at customers of American Express's Corporate Card and Business Travel Service, EMS also allows companies to create electronic T&E forms. But American Express, which collects commissions on bookings and credit card use, will do all the processing for free.

Equipped with more reliable data from such services, companies will have a powerful tool to negotiate better deals with providers of services. "Airlines and hotels are going to suddenly wake up to the fact that customers are armed with data," says Peter M. Sontag, chairman of U.S. Travel Systems Inc. in Rockville, Maryland. For instance, companies splitting business between Marriott and Sheraton hotels might be able to wring greater rate concessions in exchange for the promise of more business. "For the first time," Sontag says, "travel agents and companies are going to be able to wheel and deal."

Automating T&E is not the only new trend in travel management. Several airlines, seeking to provide incentives to customers to start using or keep using their profitable reservation systems, are creating new software to help find the best fares. In June 1987, Texas Air Corp. purchased Airplan Systems Inc., a Chicago-based software developer. Now, corporate travel agents who use Texas Air's on-line reservation system, System One, can program their clients' travel policies into Airplan's software. The program breaks out only the flights that adhere to the policy. American's Sabre and United's Apollo system will offer similar software this fall.

Without such help, finding the right flight can be no small feat. As many as 300,000 air fare changes are made daily to the more than 32 million flights listed on American's Sabre, so travel agents often can't find the cheapest flights on their own. And with air travel accounting for 41 percent of all T&E costs, the extra expense can add up.

Travel agencies are designing "intelligent" reservation systems, too. Travelmation Corp., a Stamford (Connecticut) agency, has been marketing its Trip Planner program directly to corporate travel departments since January. This program works off the customer's personal computer. Travelers, or their travel managers, type where they want to go and when, then send the information to Travelmation by modem. Travelmation's software, customized to adhere to each company's travel policy, pulls out appropriate flights and sends the information back in seconds. The software also handles hotel reservations and car rentals. Louis Van Leeuwen, president of Travelmation, claims that Trip Planner may save companies up to 40 percent on air fares.

At first glance, the onslaught of corporate travel managers and sophisticated electronic systems would seem to threaten travel agents, who now book 80 percent of all business travel. But few observers think that will happen. "In the old days, the travel agent wrote the ticket and hustled it over to the company," says Vince Vitti, president of New York-based VTS Travel Enterprises, Inc. Now, he adds, armed with a lot more data, travel management firms will spend more time negotiating better for their clients. ■

DISCUSSION
QUESTIONS

1. Refer to our discussion of the uses and values of information; in this case, who now has access to what types of information, and in what ways is it valuable to them? Is Capture, for example, worth $50,000 over five years in your estimation?

2. What developments in artificial intelligence have or will affect this field, and how?

3. How does this change demonstrate the impact of information technology in the service sector?

Comprehensive Case Five

Close Your Eyes for Two Seconds and You Lose

The Xerox 914 copier was introduced in September 1959. It took 15 seconds to make one copy. In one fell swoop the machine created and cornered a market.

During the winter of 1959–1960, in an old building in Rochester, New York, a group of engineers worked around the clock seven days a week testing their new machines. To save money, Haloid Co. chose not to pay for heat after 5:00 P.M., so the landlord shut it off at the end of every workday. All night the engineers wore their hunting jackets and boots and bundled under tentlike canvases thrown over each machine to capture whatever heat the prototypes would throw off. By morning their feet were freezing, their hands were cold, and they were exhausted. But when the tests were finished, thousands of dollars later, a whole new industry was born.

Chester Carlson invented what he called electrophotography—later referred to as xerography (Greek for "dry writing") in 1937. Though he offered the technology to RCA, Remington Rand, General Electric, Kodak, and IBM, they all turned him down. The first models were excruciatingly slow, so no one

wanted to invest thousands of dollars in a machine that took twice as long to do what carbon paper did for pennies. Carlson finally entered into a development and production agreement with Haloid Co. in 1947, and though ten years had gone by since the technology had been invented, the first model still could only be operated by trained technicians and took two to three minutes to make one copy. Haloid's brochure for the machine, the Model A Xerox, was titled "Thirty-Nine Steps" (for making good copies).

Sources: This case was based on the following sources: Jacobson, Gary, and Hillkirk, John, *Xerox: American Samurai* (New York: Macmillan, 1986); Tannenbaum, Jeffrey A., "Xerox Unveils Line of Six New Copiers, Expects to Boost Its U.S. Market Share," *Wall Street Journal,* May 4, 1988, p. 8; Eichenwald, Kurt, "Copier Line Introduced by Xerox," *New York Times,* May 4, 1988, p. D4; Mitchell, R., "How Top Brass Is Taking to the Keyboard at Xerox," *Business Week,* June 27, 1988, p. 86; Xerox Corporation, Annual Reports, 1980–1988.

But with the new and faster model 914, Carlson's dream for instant, automatic copying became a reality. In the final stages of development, Haloid Co. changed its name to Xerox. Just prior to the introduction of the Xerox 914, Joe Wilson, president of Haloid and then of Xerox, made IBM another offer to buy the copying business. Xerox provided the consulting firm of Arthur D. Little a complete description of the technical aspects of the machine, but never provided a rundown of their pricing scheme: to lease the machines for $95 a month plus 4 cents for every copy over 2000. Using the incomplete information, the consultants informed IBM that the nationwide market for Xerox 914s would be no more than 5000. IBM turned down the offer again.

INITIAL SUCCESS

On September 16, 1959, the Xerox 914 copier was announced. It cost $2000 to produce and could make copies up to 9 to 14 inches in size (thus the name). It took about 15 seconds to produce the first copy and half that time for every copy thereafter made from the same original. It was over 3 feet tall, almost 4 feet long and wide, and weighed 648 pounds.

The production operation at that time was somewhat haphazard. The original plan was to produce 5 914s a day, 25 a week. But demand was so high that the output level was increased to 25 a day almost immediately, and eventually reached 90 a day. This surge in volume not only made it necessary to monitor production much more carefully, but made it crucial that parts from suppliers meet strict requirements. At one point, Horace Becker, once Xerox's head of manufacturing, visited the supplier of the fur brushes installed to clean the selenium drum after the image had been transferred to the paper. To be effective, the outer diameter of the fur layer could vary by no more than $\frac{1}{64}$ of an inch. The supplier was a furrier used to making women's fur coats in custom sizes, give or take half an inch. "What is a sixty-fourth?" he asked. Becker promptly provided him with sophisticated measuring equipment, and he was soon producing brushes "by the thousands" to specifications.

Due to the almost insatiable demand, the engineering on the early 914s was never completed. Said Becker: "After we shipped them, because we rented

them, we would keep improving them until they became dependable enough." Because Xerox had no competition, and because service cost the customers nothing, the customers allowed the intermittent improvements. "Today," said Becker, "the minute it goes out the door it's got to be there. We no longer have the luxury of being the only company in the marketplace with the technology."

Through a combination of technical superiority and marketing genius, the machine created and cornered a market in one fell swoop. In the 1950s, 20 million copies a day were made in the United States on such equipment as Diazo machines and the Kodak Verifax, both of which were messy, complicated, and time consuming. Five years after the 914 was introduced, offering push-button simplicity, America was making 9.5 billion copies per year. *Fortune* magazine later referred to the 914 as "the most successful product ever marketed in America." In 1959, Joe Wilson predicted that the 914 would double Haloid's sales volume to $60 million by 1965. Sales in 1965 were actually just short of $400 million. Xerox made it onto the bottom of the Fortune 500 two years after the 914 was introduced and racked up sales of $1 billion six years after that. Carlson made over $200 million on his invention, and Joe Wilson made over $100 million. One of the original 914s now rests in the Smithsonian Museum.

THE GOLDEN ERA ENDS

But it was a short, though ecstatic, decade for Xerox. In April 1970, IBM introduced its first office copying machine, the Copier I. Xerox purchased one and tested it for three months: It was unsophisticated, but it made ten copies per minute (cpm) and was reliable enough to make 50,000 copies a month. Xerox's success had baited the competition. The monopoly was over.

The 1970s were essentially a lost decade for Xerox, characterized by increased competition, stagnating product development, and constant litigation concerning patent infringements and antitrust violations. Xerox officials became afraid to move for fear of the legal ramifications; the formerly courageous company became overly conservative. Though hundreds of millions of dollars went into product development, only three products came out during that decade: the 7000, which could run 60 cpm but which was essentially only an update of an earlier machine; the 4000, which failed in the market; and the 8200, which could do 70 cpm but was not introduced until 1979. "We had nothing but refried beans in the marketplace," said Shelby Carter, head of the U.S. sales divisions from 1975 to 1981.

Meanwhile, other competitors began diving into the market. IBM followed its own Copier I with Copier II, which could make 25 cpm. By mid-decade, Kodak came out with a copier that could make 70 cpm and did everything Xerox was trying to do but better. As Kodak leapfrogged Xerox with reliability and technology, Xerox found it was no longer setting the tone for the industry, but rather playing defense and reacting to competition. By the end of the decade, several Japanese companies had introduced copiers that had higher cpm levels, were more reliable, and were selling for the same price that it cost Xerox to make theirs. Between 1971 and 1978, 77 different plain-paper copiers were introduced in the United States. From 1978 to 1980, another 77 were introduced. Between 1976 and 1982, Xerox lost half its market share, which dropped from 82 percent to 41 percent, primarily to the Japanese companies.

GRINDING TO A HALT

There were many reasons why Xerox ground to a halt during the 1970s. One was the stage of the market and Xerox's position in it. The market for copiers was mushrooming, and Xerox was accustomed to being able to sell any product at any price. Therefore, all product development efforts were aimed at producing the biggest, fastest, most sophisticated machines, despite the fact that competitors were coming out with cheaper, more reliable copiers. As one executive said, "We were looking for the champagne, candlelight, and nice steak dinner when what we really needed was hamburger. We needed a good, solid meat-and-potatoes product" in the market.

The product planners were changing their minds so fast the engineers could not keep up with them. Bob Gundlach, one of the company's most prolific inventors with more than 130 patents, said, "more than 50 percent of our product programs during that span were aborted before marketing." One project, code-named Moses, absorbed $90 million in development costs and the efforts of 1000 employees during the 1975 and 1976 before it was canceled due to overly complex, unworkable technology. "What we

missed in the seventies," said Gundlach, "was the opportunity to maintain unquestioned, unchallenged leadership in xerography. Why did Kodak first come out with a copier that everybody perceived as the most reliable machine in the marketplace? There's no question we could have done that if that had been set as a goal."

Second, the way the company was organized, the functions of product planning, engineering, and manufacturing did not come together below the level of the president's office at Stamford, Connecticut. The company's matrix management system ultimately made too many people responsible for project completion. No one was taking personal responsibility. Problems that should have been solved by planners and engineers at Rochester wound up being debated in executive-level meetings in Stamford. Compounding this problem was the fact that each branch of the company—the United States, Canada, Latin America, Europe—had its own product planners so that individual units could develop machines tailored to the needs of their local markets. The ideas and needs of all the customers were to be brought together in a strategy department in Rochester. The problem with that, according to Wayland Hicks, the head of Xerox copier development and production since 1983, was that no one in the department could agree on anything.

Finally, productivity suffered due to the rapid growth of the company. Throughout the 1960s and 1970s, the business was growing so fast that if someone needed someone, they hired the person. The sheer number of layers in the organization and its staged program management system slowed everything down. An engineer's design went from his or her desk to a drafter who drew it, to a detailer who finished it, to a service engineer who checked to see if it was practical for field maintenance, then to a manufacturing engineer who determined if it could be manufactured. At any point, it could be sent back to the engineer to be scrapped or reworked. Every phase of every project was reviewed endlessly. It could take months even for one component of one machine to make it from one desk to another before final approval, which also had to be circulated between managers in numerous departments. Each department was concerned only with its own functional responsibility. No overriding cost, product goal, or scheduling objectives kept product development efficient.

At the end of the decade, executives finally realized that the huge layers of bureaucracy would only slow the company down and make it less effective. They realized that throwing millions of dollars into research and development hoping to produce a few winners was only a waste of money. They realized that the "old American strategy of throwing people at problems, and raising prices as cost went up, just couldn't compete against the Japanese." And they finally realized that the Japanese, not Kodak and IBM, were their major threat.

THE NEW COMPETITIVE ENVIRONMENT

Xerox chairman and CEO (as of 1982) David Kearns wanted Xerox to be remembered as the first company to beat the Japanese at their own game by regaining its lost market share. However, the market had changed by the 1980s, and though still the leader in the high end (powerful, expensive copiers leased to high-volume users), Xerox would be coming in from behind in the middle-range and low end, or personal copier markets. And the company simply could not bank on its name: "There's no loyalty in the copier market today," said IBM executive Proctor Houston, summing up the environment of the 1980s. "A customer will sign a contract with IBM today. At the end of three years, if we don't continue to be the best-priced performer, we're going to be out. That's what happens. It's very tough, very demanding. Close your eyes for two seconds and you lose."

The challenge was particularly great for Xerox because it was the only full-line supplier, producing high-, mid-, and low-volume copiers, as well as paper and copier supplies, and having a full-service network. Although the company had an advantage in that many customers liked dealing with only one company for all their needs, it also had more flanks to protect than its competitors.

In 1980, three factors became clear to Xerox's executives. First, they realized the extent of the cost gap between Japanese producers and themselves. "Our costs were not only way out in left field," said Kearns, "they were not even in the ballpark." Second, there was a marked difference in the success of Fuji Xerox, a 50-50 joint venture between Rank Xerox of Europe and Fuji Film of Japan, started in the 1960s. Started as a marketing subsidiary to sell American-made equipment in Japan, it became an expert in design and manufacturing that turned around and began

In 1988 Xerox introduced the 50 series, its first major foray into the field of personal copiers.

selling Japanese equipment in the United States. Third, the consulting firm of McKinsey & Co. conducted a study of the organization that revealed, among other things, that those on the product development side believed that "you couldn't possibly design anything any good without 1000 people working on it," and that as late as 1975, most people in the company had never even heard of the term *market share*, had no market share information, and considered IBM their only significant competition.

In 1981, then-president Kearns called 24 of his top people from all branches of the company, including executives from Fuji Xerox, to Rochester, New York, for two weeks of intensive discussions. He told them that he wanted to know, no holds barred, what Xerox had to do to turn the company around. "He felt we were stagnant, that we took too long to do almost everything," said Wayland Hicks. "And he was determined that if we didn't change that, we would not survive."

TURNING THE COMPANY AROUND

Since those 1981 meetings, Xerox has done several major things and thousands of little things to streamline and improve the company and turn it around. Two major steps were to trim the work force and reorganize the business into more entrepreneurial units, each responsible for its own goal and accountable for costs and results. Employment at Xerox had swelled to 117,247 worldwide by 1980. By the end of 1981, voluntary and involuntary cuts trimmed the work force by 2000, including several hundred at the Stamford headquarters. Some departments had been cut in half, others eliminated entirely. In 1982 and 1983, almost 14,000 more employees were cut before Kearns announced that the layoffs were over. After the generous settlements, the company ultimately saved $600 million a year in salaries.

In a related development, the union began to see things from a more competitive perspective. Threatened with the layoff of 180 workers in a wire harness production unit, which executives argued was necessary to save $3.2 million in production costs, the union workers studied the problem and developed a way to produce the harnesses at a $3.7 million cost savings—without sacrificing the jobs.

The reorganization inside Xerox began in the early 1980s, just as it was completing work on its first major product offering for the decade: the Xerox 10 series. The series was introduced in September 1982 and offered highly competitive products in both the high-volume (the 1075) and mid-volume (1045) business segments, and almost instantly caused Xerox to begin regaining market share from the Japanese. In 1983, two Fuji models designed for the low-volume segment (the 1026 and the 1035) were also added to the 10 series. However, the 10 series on the domestic side had taken seven years and 1000 to 1500 people to develop. By Wayland Hicks's estimation, it should have been done in four years with 300 people.

Using the McKinsey study as a guide, Kearns divided the copier division into four strategic business units (SBUs)—low-volume, mid-volume, and high-volume copiers, and supplies—and put Hicks in charge of the mid-volume unit. Each unit has a centrally located product delivery team composed of multifunction engineers (rather than scattered specialists). The teams are as self-sufficient as possible and are directly responsible for developing the product and delivering it to market. If the chief engineer keeps the project within cost and time targets, there will be no reviews. This move eliminated the endless stream of go/no go reviews that slowed development and production, and the matrix that had service engineers checking design engineers and gave no one ultimate responsibility to get a product out.

Xerox also began analyzing both internal operations and the operations and products of competitors. In the latter task it had the significant advantage of Fuji Xerox, the company's "mole" in Japan. Not only could Fuji Xerox share its Japanese production techniques with European and American plants, it also had a much more developed competitive analysis function than its American counterpart. Tadashi Kobayashi became Fuji Xerox's manager for competitive analysis in 1976 and has since kept the executives at Stamford up to date on developments and strategies at the Japanese copier makers. He is an expert: "You give me a copy made from any one of the major Japanese machines and 80 percent of the time I can tell you which company it is," he says. Kobayashi draws his information from a variety of sources: publications, research studies, patent analyses, dealers (both Fuji's and the competitors'), vendors, salespersons, internal market research, trade shows, analysis of competitors' products, and the annual worldwide competitive conference held by Xerox Group.

IMPROVING EFFICIENCY

In 1984, Xerox sent Wayland Hicks on a tour of its plants in Europe to "wake Xerox people up" and "make them understand the competitive battle they're in." As head of copier development and production, he oversees engineering and copier plants in North America and Europe, decides what products will be manufactured, and sets sales targets and product prices. Over the course of four days, Hicks attacked whatever inefficient management or production practices he came across and reminded every employee he met that this was a new, more entrepreneurial Xerox—a Xerox in which they should not be afraid to try something new or to take risks in the name of competitive strength.

The first stop was an engineering center in Welwyn, England, just north of London. Here Hicks reviewed the 1048, a follow-up to the mid-volume 1045 introduced two years earlier. It had been on the market for six months, and the customer complaints were pouring in: It had noise and paper feeder problems, the two-sided copy function (its major distinguishing feature from the 1045) did not work well, it left too much background on copies, and the machines were just plain unreliable.

Several of the problems, it was discovered, were caused by faulty parts from vendors; in addition, the machine was promoted as a mid-volume copier, designed to make 12,500 copies a month. But customers were using it to make as many as 100,000, thus causing the machine to break down more frequently. One Welwyn employee suggested putting each machine through a 1000 copy burn-in (test run) at the end of the production line before shipping, but Hicks said "all burning them in at the end of the line will tell me is that I have a problem. I already know I have a problem." He also knew the Fuji Xerox did not use end-of-the-line burn-ins because they are "just an excuse for poor quality." The next time Welwyn launched a product, he said, "I want you to be crawling all over it from the start. If we have a problem, I want us to find it before it finds us."

Hicks's next step was a production plant in Lille, France, that made typewriters and sorters for the 1045 and 1048 copiers. The typewriter assembly line at Lille is controlled by a Digital Equipment Corporation computer. All the incoming parts and kits and outgoing machines are computer coded, and the monitoring computer alerts workers when inventory levels drop and the line must be resupplied with parts. All of Xerox's plants around the world have adopted similar control methods. However, the process is complicated at Lille by the fact that Lille makes six models of Memorywriter in 14 different languages; it is crucial that the right parts make it to the right spot at the right time. At the time of Hicks's visit, the plant was also gearing up to produce the high-volume 1075s, which had previously been produced in Venray, Holland.

The next day Hicks toured the Venray plant. Two projects were being developed there simultaneously, and both were in danger of falling behind schedule. The Somerset project had a launch date of April 1, 1985, and the Andes project a launch date of May 1.

Both had problems that still needed to be solved before production could begin. The plant was currently producing 1045s and 1048s that had the same quality problems as the 1048s in the Welwyn plant. To retool the plant completely so that the new machines would come out on schedule would require full manpower at an additional cost of $500,000, and initial output would be 25 machines per day while the workers learned how to build them. Output would ultimately be 140 machines per day. The plant had an obligation to supply new machines to the Xerox operating companies by the scheduled launch dates.

Hicks made several decisions, none of which completely pleased him. First, production of 1048s would be cut back from 180 a day to 90 until the quality problems were solved. Second, the Somerset project was to proceed on schedule, but extra parts for 3000 1045s were to be ordered as a backup so that the operating companies would receive machines even if the Somerset project did not meet its launch date. If Somerset met its launch date, the extra 1045 parts would be shipped to the plant in Mexico for use. And finally, the launch date for the Andes project was pushed back. "I'm certainly disappointed," said Hicks. "I don't want anyone to let up. The Japanese aren't."

The final stop on his tour was Coslada, Spain, where Xerox has a plant that makes toner and cleaning brushes like the ones made for the original 914. Coslada provided a powerful example of how exchange rates can affect an operation's performance. Since 1981, Coslada's output in pesetas (the Spanish currency) had grown more than 250 percent. Output in dollars, however, had actually shrunk. In 1981, there were 70 pesetas to a dollar. By the time of Hicks's visit, a dollar was worth 170 pesetas.

The trip to Coslada ended on a high note, however. While there, Hicks discovered that the plant had enough space for an additional toner processor. The Venray plant, he was told, had an extra toner processor with a capacity of 1.5 million kilos. If Venray's processor was transferred to Coslada, the plant could put out enough toner to sell it to Canon's European operations. "You see why I go on the tours," said Hicks. A new product and market had been discovered.

WINNING THE BATTLE

Since the turn of the decade, Xerox has done an about-face. With faster product development, automation, strict quality control, and technological advances, Xerox is rapidly wiping out Japan's cost advantage and regaining its lost market share. The Xerox 10 series introduced in 1983 is the most successful new copier line in history, accounting for 38 percent of the world's 2 million plus copiers in use. The 1075, in fact, was the first American-made product to win the Japanese Grand Prize for Good Design.

In May 1988, Xerox introduced another new line of copiers. The 50 series, named after the fiftieth anniversary of the invention of xerography, is Xerox's first major foray into the personal copier market. By overcoming the problem of competing with the Japanese in a market they created, Xerox expects the machines to be a major boon to the company. They are 20 to 30 percent less expensive to manufacture, yet they will sell for 5 to 10 percent more than earlier models. Thus, profit margins will be higher than on the older models.

In addition, an effort to computerize the corporate staff, begun in 1985, is beginning to pay off. Xerox employees have always been able to communicate with one another worldwide from some 15,000 work stations. Now the top executives are also hooked into the system and have custom software that helps them in every aspect of their jobs. With the ability to exchange information between each other more smoothly and rapidly, executives are more prepared for meetings, the meetings run more smoothly, and a great deal of time is saved in planning. Kearns and other top executives have also begun using the system to scan corporate data bases looking for trends.

All of these measures exemplify Xerox's renewed strategy: a commitment to quality. By the end of 1987, all 100,000 Xerox employees around the world had completed 48 hours of formal training in quality. Kearns is determined that as he leaves the company in the 1990s he will leave it as one of the premier copier companies in the world. ∎

QUESTIONS

1. In what ways have Xerox executives utilized the control process (or not) in this case? What methods of control were used? Which were not used but should have been? What factors did the company control well, and which did it not control well? What suggestions would you have made at any given point to have solved or prevented some of the problems the company encountered?

2. Can you describe an operating system in one of Xerox's plants? What production system is used? Given the situation at Lille, Venray, or Coslada, how would you design (or redesign) the production system? How would you schedule production and/or control inventory?

3. What types of information systems are in place at Xerox? Which would you have recommended in the 1970s, and what benefits would they have brought? How could Xerox utilize decision systems, expert systems, or artificial intelligence?

4. How does this case illustrate the connections between control, production management, and MIS and technology management?

The impact of the external environment on organizations and on the management process cannot be overstated. The effects of the environment and organizations on each other are numerous and complex. The number of factors involved and the number of ways in which they influence each other are limitless and constantly changing. We will discuss three environmental dimensions that have major significance: ethical and social issues, legal and political issues, and international issues.

In Chapter 18, we will discuss corporate ethics and social responsibility. We will describe the roots of these concepts and the ways in which organizations and managers can maintain ethical and socially responsible behavior.

In Chapter 19, we will define the legal and political environment and discuss the interrelationships among business, government, and society. Often, the moral and the ethical expectations society has with respect to the business sector become formalized in the legal framework of the nation. At the same time, the interests of business are also protected and furthered by the legal system. We will also discuss the sources of law and the legal responsibilities of managers and organizations.

In Chapter 20, we will discuss the international environment. Because many management issues and concerns apply across national boundaries, we will describe several ways in which organizations conduct international business. The impact of economic, political, legal, and cultural factors specifically on international operations is also discussed.

Chapter 21, the final chapter in the book, is at once both a summary and an introduction. In it, we will provide an encapsulated review of the major trends changing and shaping the business environment and the impact they will have on organizations. We will also describe several possible organizational responses to those changes and developments: methods and techniques managers can employ to keep their organizations current, flexible, and successful. Finally, we will review the basic functions and responsibilities of management, illustrating how they are likely to be carried on in the future.

PART ▲ SIX

Management in the External Environment

18 | Ethics and Social Responsibility

FOCUS CASE / The Outfit Responsible Goes out of Business

FOUNDATIONS OF BUSINESS ETHICS AND SOCIAL RESPONSIBILITY

AN INTERACTIVE MODEL OF BUSINESS AND SOCIETY
The Stakeholder Concept
An Ethical Decision-Making Framework

RESPONSIBILITY, RESPONSIVENESS, AND RECTITUDE
Corporate Social Responsibility
Corporate Social Responsiveness
Corporate Social Rectitude

INDIVIDUAL ETHICS
Exit, Voice, or Loyalty
Making Difficult Decisions

INSTITUTIONALIZING ETHICAL AND SOCIALLY RESPONSIBLE BEHAVIOR
Ethics Codes
Ethics Committees
Ethics Training Programs
Ethics Audits

S weeping changes in the relationship between organizations and society over the past three decades have dramatically altered the responsibilities of management. Society is no longer willing simply to accept the discretion of business leaders. People demand a voice in many aspects of organizational life: where plants are to be located, how they produce their products and services, what these products and services are, and what is done with the wastes of production. If a company's practices or outputs do not meet the expectations of the public or the government, the company will come under pressure to improve its performance.

▪ KEY QUESTIONS

As you study this chapter, try to answer the following key questions:

1 What are the foundations of modern concepts of corporate ethics and social responsibility?
2 Who or what are stakeholders?
3 Describe the difference between three general notions of the relationship between organizations and society: corporate social responsibility, corporate social responsiveness, and corporate social rectitude.
4 How can organizations institutionalize ethical and socially responsible behavior?

Focus Case

The Outfit Responsible Goes out of Business

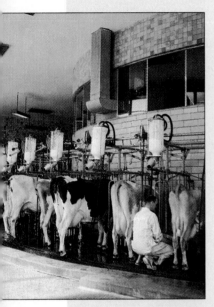

A modern dairy operation. Food producers have an ethical responsibility to insure the purity and healthfulness of their product.

In March and April 1985, the nation's most extensive outbreak of food poisoning struck the Chicago area. During roughly two weeks around Easter, an estimated 20,000 people came down with symptoms of salmonella poisoning. The dairy that produced the tainted milk believed to have caused the problem was eventually closed. Before the dust had settled, however, several people had died and the company that owned the dairy faced hundreds of individual and group lawsuits. The case provoked questions about managerial responsibility and about the appropriate and ethical response to such a crisis. It is tragic that lives were lost, but the outbreak and its results eventually provoked changes in the way poisoning outbreaks are handled by agencies and officials across the country.

The response of Jewel Companies Inc., the owner and operator of the dairy that produced the tainted milk, unfolded as follows. On Friday, March 29, 1985, the Lake County (Illinois) Health Department (LCHD) received reports of people suffering diarrhea and abdominal pain, symptoms of salmonella poisoning. Through preliminary interviews, it was determined that the product responsible was most likely Bluebrook 2% milk produced on March 20 by the Hillfarm Dairy. The LCHD contacted Jewel, informed management of the reports, and asked whether Jewel would voluntarily withdraw the milk from sale. Jewel's manager at Hillfarm Dairy said there was not enough information. Therefore, the milk would not be withdrawn, and the plant would remain open. Hillfarm Dairy's head of quality assurance threatened to sue the LCHD's executive director if he took "independent" action to close the dairy or warn Jewel customers.

The company and the government agencies began to act. Jewel officials began an internal study and hired a private testing lab to survey the plant and determine the cause and extent of possible contamination. The Center for Disease Control (CDC), a federal government agency based in Atlanta, was contacted and sent a special study team to Chicago to see if there was a significant statistical association between the Bluebrook 2% milk and the reported cases of salmonella poisoning. CDC officials stated that there was only a "one-in-a-million chance" that any other milk products were contaminated. The Hillfarm Dairy, acting on that information and believing the outbreak was limited to only the Bluebrook 2% milk produced on March 20, continued produc-

Sources: This case was based on the following sources: "Postponed Closing of Dairy Explained," *Chicago Tribune,* November 20, 1986, p. 5; "Jewel Wins 1st Verdict in Salmonella Suits," *Chicago Tribune,* January 23, 1987, pp. 1–2; "Jewel Dairy's Piping Violated Federal Code, Task Force Found," *Chicago Tribune,* January 15, 1987, p. 9; "Saying 'Never Again' to Salmonella Crisis," *Chicago Tribune,* March 23, 1986, pp. 1, 2.

tion of all milk products. The batch of milk presumed to be contaminated had a code date that expired on March 29, the same day the first salmonella reports were received. Therefore, it should no longer have been on store shelves. Local health departments, however, continued to receive reports of salmonella poisoning after that date as people used the milk they had purchased. Bluebrook 2% milk produced on March 20 was finally recalled by Jewel on Monday, April 1.

By Tuesday, April 2, the number of daily customer complaints continued and had risen to 360. Because the private testing lab had not completed its investigation, the federal Food and Drug Administration sent in an inspection team. Jewel's chief executive, James Hensen, continued to assert that it was not necessary to close the plant based on information provided to him by an Illinois Department of Health sanitarian who was at the dairy. No causal connection had been proved. The following day, the private lab released a "positive presumptive" finding: Evidence strongly indicated that the salmonella contamination originated in the Hillfarm Dairy. At a management meeting that day, opinions were divided as to whether the plant should be closed. One of Jewel's senior marketing managers thought it should be closed, but others disagreed. Hensen decided not to close the plant.

On Thursday, additional studies confirmed the link between the outbreak and the Hillfarm Bluebrook 2% milk. The number of reported salmonella poisoning cases now exceeded 1000. The dairy continued to produce and sell all products, relying on information that indicated that the Bluebrook 2% milk produced on March 20, and no longer on sale after March 29, was the only contaminated product. According to Hensen, "We were told [by government officials] that the outbreak would crest and then decline and that it would be just (the) one product produced on one day."

On Monday, April 8, the day after Easter, public health officials received a report of salmonella poisoning in another batch of Hillfarm milk not tied to the recalled Bluebrook 2% milk. James Hensen heard about it on his car radio en route to work. Upon arriving at his office, he ordered a recall of milk. Later in the morning, an official from the health department offered Jewel an ultimatum: The company could voluntarily close the Hillfarm Dairy or wait for the state director of public health to order it closed. At 1:30 P.M., 11 days after the first reported case of salmonella poisoning, and after thousands of people had been hospitalized or treated for the poisoning, Jewel announced that the dairy would be shut down that day.

Jewel's response to the salmonella poisoning outbreak was widely criticized. Months later, at a trial in Chicago, an attorney representing some 20,000 people in a class action lawsuit against the company asked Hensen: "What were you waiting for? Why didn't you halt milk production?" When Hensen responded that he was waiting for input from experts inside the plant, the attorney asked again: "Why did you need an expert? Didn't common sense tell you to do something?"

Hensen agreed that thousands of victims would not have contracted food poisoning had he recalled the milk and shut down the plant after the first report. He claimed that he was unaware that the dairy's head of quality assurance had threatened the health department officials and claimed that he would have "disciplined" the employee if he had known. He acknowledged that Easter was a time of high-volume sales for the dairy products business but adamantly denied that profit concerns were the reason he continued production and distribution. He asserted that Jewel's image and profits would suffer "substantially" if the company's products were found to be contaminated.

In the wake of the tragedy, many valuable lessons were learned by all who were or could have been involved. Said one attorney for the plaintiffs: "The notoriety and publicity sent a message . . . that purity of food is one of the principal qualities we desire for our citizens." Though the specific source of the contamination was never absolutely pinpointed, one lab worker said that it rarely is, and that "the only thing we can be certain about is that the outfit responsible goes out of business." State and national efforts to tighten the standards for milk and dairy product processing were initiated. Legislation was introduced in Illinois to curtail future outbreaks by allowing the department of health to shut down a food facility that is even suspected of producing contaminated products. "We have the legal authority to err on the side of public safety," said the new head of the health department. ■

FOUNDATIONS OF BUSINESS ETHICS AND SOCIAL RESPONSIBILITY

Charity principle
Wealthier members of society should provide assistance to the poorer members.

Stewardship principle
Those in positions of power and control should use their position for the good of society.

The idea that managers have a responsibility for the welfare of their customers and society in general is deeply ingrained in our society. Concepts of ethics and responsibility to others are not new. Charity, for example, is an ancient concept. During the Industrial Revolution, captains of industry made donations to community institutions such as churches and missions that ministered to the unemployed, the physically handicapped, the elderly, the sick, and the poor. The Community Chest movement of the 1920s was one the major manifestations of the **charity principle:** the notion that the wealthier members of society should provide assistance for the poorer members.

The **stewardship principle,** the notion that those in positions of power or control should use their positions for the good of society, is another key concept with historical roots. If organizations prudently and wisely used resources, their profits (and society's wealth) would increase. Thus, the organization would be acting as a responsible steward of society's resources. The foundations of our modern concepts of ethics and corporate social responsibility rest heavily on these two principles.[1]

Crises can be the catalyst for changes in the relationship between business and society,[2] as The Inside View 18.1 illustrates. In the early industrial era, many manufacturers legally engaged in practices that would bring jail sentences today. Young children were forced to work for 10 to 15 hours a day, food was often produced in extremely unsanitary conditions, and work spaces were littered with hazards and dangerous machinery. Eventually, the social harm and injury resulting from such practices led society to question business's right to increase profits at any cost. Public outrage became political pressure, and where organizations did not voluntarily consider the public welfare, the government eventually intervened. Over the course of the century, the result was a change in the relationship between business and society and their responsibilities to each other.

Three Crises of Corporate Responsibility

In the 1870s, farmers organized Granges to protect themselves against abuses by the growing industrial trusts.

According to Starhl Edmonds, historical crises have had a dramatic effect on the relationship between business and society. He points to three periods of crisis.

THE FIRST CRISIS—1870

The first corporations, born in the 1850s, were "trusts," which arose in response to pressures for Civil War mobilization, the drive to open up the American West, and general industrialization. These trusts had immense powers, and in many cases they abused them through such practices as kickbacks, discriminatory pricing, labor lockouts, and manipulation of commodity prices. In response to these abuses, groups of farmers organized the grange and populist movements, and groups of workers organized labor unions. Public pressure led legislators to force a higher level of social responsibility on big business, commensurate with their larger powers.

THE SECOND CRISIS—1930

Though the Sherman Anti-Trust Act (1890) greatly impeded monopolistic practices, it did not slow the trend toward larger and larger corporations. Mobilization for another war, this time World War I, was again the major impetus for this growth. However, just as the public came to feel comfortable with these large organizations, their trust in them was shattered by the stock market crash in 1929 and the Great Depression of the 1930s. A rash of social and labor legislation passed during this time interposed government as the manager of the nation's economy, the regulator of business, and the employer of last resort. The government had again forced business to accept a level of social responsibility commensurate with its increased power over the livelihood of individuals.

THE THIRD CRISIS—1970

World War II again renewed the population's faith in the ability of business to provide for society. After the war, corporations shifted swiftly to peacetime production, and the standard of living in the United States reached heights it had never before seen. The public expected much more of its business corporations in the postwar decades than it had in 1870, or in the 1920s and 1930s, but another shift in these expectations was on the horizon.

By 1960, a balance had been achieved between the public economy, controlled by the government, and the private economy, controlled by the free market.

By 1970, however, this relatively smooth balance was disrupted by a rise in antiestablishment sentiment, much of which was brought on by the Vietnam War and the Watergate debacle. Consum-

erism and environmentalism became leading causes, and public pressures for the third time forced government to impose new responsibilities on business commensurate with its power to affect society. ■

Source: Edmonds, Starhl W., "Unifying Concepts in Social Responsibility," *Academy of Management Review* (January 1977): 38–45.

There are many differing views of an organization's social responsibility. Some believe that a corporation's primary responsibility, perhaps its only responsibility, is to produce profits for its owners.[3] Others feel that the only responsibilities owed to employees, customers, and others in society are those obligations imposed by law. Still others believe companies must resolve social problems, and some say that business must anticipate social demands, not just react to them.

Social responsibility To whom and for what a modern organization is considered responsible.

Despite these differences, it is widely agreed that the practical definition of **social responsibility** for managers boils down to understanding what organizations must do to meet the legitimate expectations of the public. The critical questions are *to whom* and *for what* is the organization responsible. As The Inside View 18.2 illustrates, those questions must be answered in the context of specific events. Consider the cases of Johnson & Johnson and the Gerber baby food company. In the fall of 1982, seven people died after consuming Tylenol capsules tainted with cyanide. The manufacturer, Johnson & Johnson (J&J), immediately recalled all packages of the pain reliever, opened itself to the press, and put its chairman on the air in commercials designed to explain the situation and what was being done about it, so that the public's faith in the company would be restored. Roughly 6000 criminal leads were generated, but the killer who laced the capsules with poison was never identified. Families of the victims were compensated, J&J designed better, tamper-resistant packaging, and Tylenol capsules were again marketed.[4] When a second shipment was tainted with a different type of cyanide three years later and another person died, a similar pattern of response was followed, and J&J announced it would discontinue production of Tylenol in capsule form.

In response to a similar crisis, Gerber Products Co. reacted differently. In 1984, the company received reports that glass shards had been found in jars of its baby food and juice. It recalled the products and conducted extensive tests but found no glass. Gerber then put the products back on the market and tried to recoup the drop of sales brought on by the publicity. In early 1986, hundreds of reports came in that glass shards were again being found in jars of baby food. Food and Drug Administration officials toured manufacturing plants and tested 30,000 unopened jars of baby food. Five were found to contain bits of glass, all smaller than a pinhead. The FDA determined that this was consistent with state-of-the-art bottling techniques and did not order a recall.

The second time around, Gerber took the hard line. Said Gerber's chairman, "We have found no reason to suspect our product," and he stated that changing the company's packaging was not feasible. "When we tried to quiet the press with

Wreck of the Exxon Valdez

The Exxon Valdez oil tanker spilled 11 million gallons of oil into Prince William Sound in Alaska, creating an environmental disaster.

Business is a system that is subject to "normal accidents." As the wreck of the Exxon Valdez demonstrates, preparing for catastrophes is as much a management responsibility as is avoiding them.

The voyage of the Exxon Valdez started in a normal way. The huge oil supertanker was being loaded with Alaskan oil at the port of Valdez on March 23, 1989. About 9:00 P.M., the ship left port under the command of Captain Joseph Hazelwood, an experienced Exxon supertanker skipper. Maneuvering out of the harbor and into Port William Sound, Hazelwood turned over control of the ship to Third Mate Gregory Cousins at 11:50 P.M. with instructions to make a right turn at a navigational point three miles north of Bligh Reef. For unknown reasons, the turn was not started until seven minutes after the point had been passed, and the ship was unable to avoid hitting the rocky reef. Cousins called Hazelwood, who had gone to his cabin, and said, "We are in trouble!" The captain rushed to the bridge and worked to stabilize the ship on the reef to keep it from capsizing.

The collision had gashed the huge supertanker below the waterline, thereby allowing thousands of gallons of oil to gush into the water. The Coast Guard and Exxon officials began to respond to the Valdez's plight. Coast Guard officials boarded the ship and began an emergency response plan to contain the oil. As dawn broke on March 24, however, the magnitude of the spill became painfully evident. The oil slick was growing rapidly, and the estimated loss of oil began climbing from thousands to hundreds of thousands to millions of gallons. Months later, official reports would claim that more than 11 million gallons of oil had spilled into Prince William Sound.

In the days and weeks that followed, the Exxon Valdez would become synonymous with the nation's largest oil spill catastrophe. The beautiful Sound with its rocky shoreline, inlets, outcroppings, and islands became a disaster area. Fish, sea otters, and birds by the thousands perished in the aftermath of the oil spill. Environmentalists considered the spill to be one of the worst ever. Not only was the environmental damage severe, but Exxon's response was deemed woeful by many people. At one point, public anger with the company produced a one-day boycott of Exxon products and the threat of longer-term retaliation. Following a meeting with environmental leaders several weeks after the incident, Exxon's chief executive officer, Lawrence Rawl, announced that the company would take a number of actions, including the nomination of a qualified environmentalist to its board of directors.

Immediate press reports attributed the accident to Captain Hazelwood's alleged drinking both before the ship left Valdez and while he was in his cabin. In fact, Hazelwood, who left Alaska days after the crash, was arrested at his New York home, arraigned on criminal charges, and called by an assistant attorney general "the architect of an American tragedy." The judge claimed that the damage was comparable to the destruction of Hiroshima after the atomic bomb. Hazelwood's record of alcoholism was made public. Hazelwood was vilified, and his record of alcoholism quickly became the butt of vicious comedy. David Letterman, for example, gave as one of Hazelwood's "Top Ten Excuses" for the accident: "I was just trying to scrape some ice off the reef for my margarita."

The true causes were much more complicated and less colorful. Instead of a boozy sea captain, it appears that weak management systems within Exxon, the Coast Guard, and the oil industry contributed much more to the accident than Hazelwood's drinking. In July, 1989, Alaska released an official report of the accident that concluded that poor management by Exxon Shipping (the transportation subsidiary of Exxon Corporation) was at fault. "Exxon Shipping's failures and lapses in management were so numerous and pervasive that it is

a wonder the Exxon Valdez was the first tanker grounded," said the report.

Among the contributing management failures were the following:

- The decision to cut crew size, which probably contributed to fatigue among crew members of the ship.
- The decision to require the ship to leave the port on March 23 after a full day of loading, rather than waiting until daybreak on March 24.
- Altered federal regulations governing "pilotage endorsements" (i.e., qualifications) for piloting a ship at that point in Port William Sound. Both the industry and the Coast Guard held responsibility for changing standards and uncertainty in this area.
- Exxon's failure to monitor and oversee the rehabilitation of a sea captain who had undergone alcoholism treatment.
- Exxon's supplying of low-alcohol beer to tanker crewmen, despite the company's stated policy of banning drinking aboard its ships.

The tragedy in Prince William Sound will not end soon. But the shipping of Alaskan oil cannot stop. The world needs it, and with hundreds of oil tankers travelling all of the seas, it remains the responsibility of industry and government managers to protect against the next "normal accident." ∎

Sources: Behar, Richard, "Joe's Bad Trip," *Time* (July 24, 1989), pp. 42–47; "In Ten Years, You'll See Nothing," (An Interview with Lawrence Rawl), *Fortune* (May 8, 1989), pp. 50–54; "Lujan Criticizes Congress for Oil Plan," *New York Times* (July 19, 1989), p. A10; Nulty, Peter, "The Future of Big Oil," *Fortune* (May 8, 1989), pp. 46–49; "Alaska Blames Exxon for Oil Spill," *New York Times,* July 19, 1989, p. A10; Perrow, Charles, *Normal Accidents* (New York: Basic Books, 1984); Wald, Matthew, "Exxon Estimating $1.28 Billion Cost for Spill Clean-Up," *New York Times,* (July 25, 1989), p. A1.

an unjustified recall," he said, in reference to the 1984 scare, "it didn't work. So why should we do it again?"[5] The company even sued the state of Maryland for $150 million when the state ordered retailers to withdraw jars of baby food from the shelves. However, the chairman of another major food company thought Gerber should have been as responsive as J&J. "You must err on the side of going overboard to do what's right in view of the public."[6]

Though the situations are not identical, it is clear that the managers of Johnson & Johnson and Gerber have different ideas about **to whom** and **for what** they are responsible. Despite the costs, J&J changed both the packaging and the product to protect the public. Gerber, on the other hand, went only so far as to comply with the law, as confirmed by the FDA. Gerber decided not to change either its packaging or its production processes to further guarantee the safety of its products. And in the focus case, managers at Jewel Companies, acting on information from various government officials and health agencies, removed only one product from the market instead of closing the production facility entirely.

AN INTERACTIVE MODEL OF BUSINESS AND SOCIETY

To answer the questions of to whom and for what the organization is responsible, managers must be aware of all the people and groups on which the organization can or does have some impact.

The Stakeholder Concept

Stakeholders All groups that affect or are affected by an organization's actions or inaction.

As Exhibit 18.1 illustrates, organizations interact with many different groups in different environments. All groups that affect or are affected by an organization's actions are called **stakeholders;**[7] they have an interest—they hold a stake—in company operations. Different companies will have different stakeholders, but in general, interested parties include employees; owners and stockholders; suppliers; creditors; competitors; customers and clients (individuals or retailers and wholesalers); local communities and the general public; local, national, and foreign governments; and public-interest groups.

Employees By law, employers must meet certain minimum health and safety requirements for their employees. Workplaces must be hazard-free, and the general health and safety of employees must be protected. In production plants, areas must be clean and free of toxins and physical dangers; in offices, signs must be

EXHIBIT / 18.1
Stakeholders Are Part of the Organization's Environment

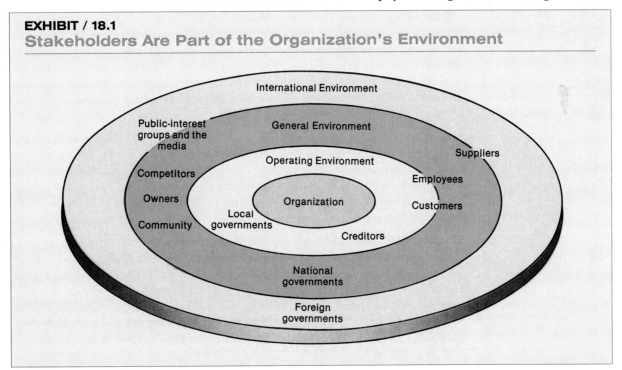

posted when floors are wet or when repairs are being made. Employers must also comply with hiring and firing regulations such as the Equal Employment Opportunity guidelines that protect the rights of minorities. Employees also have a stake in the general success of the organization; the employees at the Hillfarm Dairy, which was closed down, lost their jobs and income. Beyond legal responsibilities, however, many employers voluntarily provide counseling, special training opportunities, daycare centers, counseling and therapy for emotional or substance-abuse problems, and many other benefits that are not legally required.

Owners and Stockholders   Many firms are required by law to report to stockholders fully and accurately the financial status or condition of the organization. Stockholders have provided resources and are entitled to know how these resources are used. Traditionally, management's responsibility to provide stockholders a healthy return on investments has been considered its first priority. When managers trade on inside information that is unavailable to others, they undermine stockholders' interests. In the 1980s, many instances of insider trading were disclosed and legal action taken was against companies and investors. Many companies now pursue courses of action that appear to treat stockholders equally with other stakeholders. And some institutional investors, such as churches and universities, refuse to invest in companies that are not socially responsible and actually achieve higher long-term returns.[8] (See Exhibit 18.2.)

Suppliers   Suppliers depend for their survival on the organizations that use their materials. They have a stake in the regularity with which orders are placed, in the promptness with which they are paid, and in the stability and soundness of the organizations with which they deal. Organizations have a responsibility to consider bids fairly and to maintain stable, equitable relationships with suppliers. If they do not, they will jeopardize their reputation and credibility.

Creditors   Creditors, by having lent money to an organization, have a stake similar to that of stockholders and owners. They are mainly interested in the liquidity and financial health of the organization. For creditors to survive, loan payments must be regular and all debts must be repaid. Like owners and stockholders, creditors may be less interested in the organization's social responsibilities than in its profitability. But since many creditors are the pension funds of labor unions or other social institutions, they often have both financial and social interests in the organization.

Competitors   Competitors also have a stake in the performance of an organization. While all competing organizations have an interest in seeing the industry or market grow, each will contend for a larger portion of this market. One company's innovation may expand opportunities for all players, but will also probably strengthen its competitive position relative to them. Competitors may cooperate in responding to political or social issues.

Customers and Clients   Customers and clients, whether individuals or re-tailers/wholesalers, have a dual stake in the organization. Customers expect goods and services to be available at a fair price to meet their needs. In addition they demand products that are not hazardous or dangerous; that are reliable; durable, and of high quality; and that can be readily used. They also expect advertisements for these products to portray the products' features or capabilities accurately. The failure to meet these expectations can harm a company's reputation and ability to stay in business.

EXHIBIT / 18.2
Happy Returns for Do-Gooders

Some industry members estimate that assets managed according to ethical considerations—the most impassioned being the quest to eliminate apartheid in South Africa—have been growing rapidly for the past decade. The nine "ethical funds" surveyed by Lipper Analytical Securities Corp. produced an average yield of 25.24 percent, while the average mutual fund yielded 24.95 percent.

"CONSCIENCE-FOLLOWING" FUNDS

Instrument	Assets* ($ mil)	Minimum Invest.	Return (% 1985)	Return (% 10 yr)
Mutual Funds				
Calvert Social Inv.	$36.5	$1,000	26.97	N/A
Dreyfus Third Century	182.0	2,500	30.16	412.97
New Alternatives	0.8	2,650	24.96	N/A
Parmassus†	1.4	5,000	18.60	N/A
Pax World	33.5	250	25.89	257.73
Pioneer Bond Fund	22.1	1,000	20.06	N/A
Pioneer Fund	1,200.0	250	26.03	357.05
Pioneer II	2,200.0	250	31.41	756.33
Pioneer III	434.0	1,000	24.06	N/A
Money Market Funds				
Calvert Money Market	52.2	1,000	7.77	N/A
Working Assets	74.0	1,000	7.59	N/A
Asset Management				
U.S. Trust (Boston)	160.0	500,000	27.60	N/A
Franklin Mgmt.	65.0	250,000	24.94	N/A

*As of 1/31/86.
†Parmassus Fund began operations in early 1985 but did not become 50% invested until June. Source: Lipper Analytical Securities; JAM Research.
Source: Martin, Josh, "Happy Returns for Do-Gooders," Financial World, March 18, 1986, pp. 32–33.

Community   The community hosting an organization also has a dual stake in it. On the one hand, the community benefits from the jobs and local development the organization provides. New roads, parks, or even schools and hospitals may be built to induce an organization to locate in a particular area. On the other hand, producers can endanger their host communities by contaminating local water supplies with the wastes of production, or, as was the case in Bhopal, India, and Institute, West Virginia, by contaminating the environment in an industrial accident. The public concern over nuclear hazards illustrates the salience of these issues. The Seabrook nuclear power plant in New Hampshire may never become operational because of opposition from nearby communities; and citizens near plants in Savannah River, South Carolina, and Marion, Ohio, and Rocky Flats, Colorado, have discovered serious nuclear exposure hazards.

Local, National, and Foreign Governments   Governments on all levels are stakeholders in organizations for a variety of reasons. Local and federal governments depend on organizations for tax revenues and economic development.

Foreign governments sometimes depend on investments from outside organizations to develop their local economies, employ their citizens, and improve their undeveloped regions. Governments also have a responsibility to regulate the practices of these organizations. They must ensure that environments are not spoiled, that employees are protected, that public health and safety are safeguarded, and that competitive practices are lawful. For example, Illinois state legislators, after the salmonella outbreak in 1985, tightened requirements and safety standards in the dairy-processing industry.

Public-Interest Groups and the Media   Public-interest groups and the media are also, in a sense, stakeholders. Though members of these groups may not be directly affected by something the organization does, they represent the interests of other stakeholders, such as the general public or the work force. The media keep the public informed on issues relevant to its health, welfare, and safety. By reporting the outbreak of salmonella poisoning, Chicago-area media informed members of the community and undoubtedly prevented thousands of people from drinking tainted milk. Social activists monitor company actions and policies to ensure that they conform to legal and ethical standards and that they protect the public's safety and act responsibly. Because the media and certain public-interest groups can mobilize support in both government and society, they are a force to which managers respond in meeting social expectations.

Most organizations consider the needs and interests of a variety of stakeholders such as those described above. These are the groups to whom management believes some responsibility is owed. Exactly what to do, and how, requires additional thought.

An Ethical Decision-Making Framework

There is much debate over the question of what the organization is to do in regard to its stakeholders. To guide them, managers often refer to a framework for ethical decision making. Three approaches can be combined to provide such a framework: the utilitarian theory, the theory of rights, and the theory of justice.[9]

Utilitarian theory The goal of decisions is to do the most good for the greatest number of people.

Utilitarian Theory   Under the **utilitarian theory,** actions are judged based on their impact on the persons affected, and the goal is to serve the greatest good for the greatest number of people. In a decision situation, alternative actions and their consequences are weighed in terms of costs and benefits. It is assumed that each alternative will harm, inconvenience, or somehow deprive some number of people. However, as long as the alternative selected benefits the most people and harms the fewest, it will be considered the best, most ethical choice. Johnson & Johnson's initial decision to recall Tylenol capsules, and then to cease producing them entirely, was based on the premise that this action would benefit the most people; customers would be protected, and J&J's image would be improved in the long run, even if profits suffered in the short run. Jewel and Gerber, however, obviously weighed their options differently. Given information from government officials that allowed them legally to continue operations, they chose to continue selling their products.

America's capitalist economic tradition relies heavily on the utilitarian approach. Though the survival and success of some enterprises may cause the failure of others, free enterprise and the right of each organization to compete for market share are highly valued in this society. It is felt that the greatest good for the greatest number of people is served under a free-enterprise system because

Author's note: In 1989, Mobil announced it would stop doing business in South Africa. (See also the Discussion Case 18.1.)

competition keeps prices lower and quality higher than under other economic systems. Lost jobs and business failures, when kept to reasonably low levels, are considered inevitable, acceptable by-products of the system.

Utilitarian theory can help guide organizations. Under this approach, satisfying the stakeholders in an organization's operating environment is a priority. By satisfying customers, suppliers, creditors, and employees, the organization can be said to be serving the greatest good of the greatest number. Efficiency is also a paramount concern with this approach: The greatest good for the greatest number can be served if the organization uses only the resources it needs and minimizes production wastes.

Theory of rights   A decision-making approach that stresses minority rights or benefits.

Theory of Rights   The **theory of rights,** or moral-rights, approach stresses minority rather than majority rights or benefits. Decisions made based on the moral-rights approach emphasize the importance of protecting the fundamental liberties and privileges of all individuals and groups.

From this perspective, the greatest good for the greatest number is no longer an acceptable moral measuring stick on its own. If serving the interests of the majority infringes on the rights of even a small minority, the act or decision is not ethical under this definition. Corporate smoking policies are a modern example of this principle in action. Less than 20 years ago, a person could light up and smoke almost anywhere, anytime. After statistics on the dangers of passive smoke inhalation were released, smokers were denied the freedom to smoke anywhere they chose because it threatened the health and safety of nonsmokers. By instituting nonsmoking policies (even if more employees smoke than not), organizations demonstrate their belief that the freedom to smoke is secondary to the right to life and health.

Although much legislation has been enacted to enforce basic moral rights (the Occupational Health and Safety Act of 1970 safeguards a person's right to life and

Theory of justice A decision-making approach that stresses fairness, equity, and impartiality.

Liberty principle All people have the same rights.

Difference principle Disadvantaged people should be given proportionately more to balance out the social system.

health; The U.S. Privacy Act of 1974 safeguards a person's right to limit government access to personal information; Michigan's Whistle-blowers Protection Act of 1981 protects employees' rights to free speech without penalty, such as being fired for exposing controversial company practices), many organizations protect the moral rights of their various stakeholders out of more than legal obligation.

Theory of Justice   The **theory of justice** approach emphasizes the principles of fairness, equity, and impartiality. Measurement of fairness, equity, and impartiality are based on two principles under this approach: the liberty principle and the difference principle.[10] The **liberty principle** states that each person is entitled to liberties comparable to the liberties afforded all other people. The **difference principle** states that the most disadvantaged are the ones to whom the most benefits should be directed until social and economic balance, or equity, are achieved. Under affirmative action programs, for example, underrepresented groups are hired until balance is achieved. The hiring and promoting of minorities by quota has, however, led to charges of reverse discrimination in some cases.

Legislation based on the justice principle includes the 1964 Civil Rights Act and legislation guaranteeing similar wages for similar work, regardless of sex or other considerations not relevant to the ability to do a job. However, as with the other approaches, many organizations apply the justice approach above and beyond legislative requirements. Fair work assignments and rewards, equal wages and benefits, and impartial disciplinary action are all examples of the justice approach applied within organizations. External applications include hiring or helping the disadvantaged and helping to create access for the handicapped to public facilities.

Within the framework formed by the preceding theories, organizations should strive to serve the greatest good for the greatest number of people, to protect the rights of minorities, and to treat all their stakeholders fairly. Obviously, it is often impossible to do all this at once. Conflicts can occur, as when striving to serve the greatest good of the greatest number may mean failing to protect the rights of minorities or not treating all groups equally.

RESPONSIBILITY, RESPONSIVENESS, AND RECTITUDE

The modern view of business ethics and social responsibility evolved in three overlapping phases, beginning in the 1960s. In one sense, each phase posed a different question to managers and scholars of American business: What is the scope of responsibility? How can business more effectively respond to social demands? What ethical and moral values are at stake in each issue? The answers developed to each question created, in turn, the next logical question.

William Frederick has captured the flow of these ideas by terming them corporate social responsibility (CSR1), corporate social responsiveness (CSR2), and corporate social rectitude (CSR3).[11] These theories overlap and contribute to our understanding of corporate social responsibility. (See Exhibit 18.3.)

Corporate Social Responsibility

Corporate social responsibility The theory that business has responsibilities beyond the management of the organization itself.

Based primarily on the principles of charity and stewardship, the theory of **corporate social responsibility** argues that business has responsibilities and obligations beyond the management of the organization itself. As a fully developed point of view, CSR1 rests on six fundamental principles:[12]

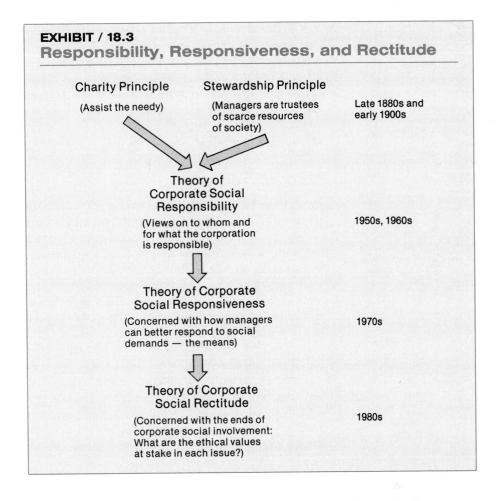

EXHIBIT / 18.3
Responsibility, Responsiveness, and Rectitude

Charity Principle
(Assist the needy)

Stewardship Principle
(Managers are trustees
of scarce resources
of society)

Late 1880s and
early 1900s

Theory of
Corporate Social
Responsibility
(Views on to whom and
for what the corporation
is responsible)

1950s, 1960s

Theory of Corporate
Social Responsiveness
(Concerned with how managers
can better respond to social
demands — the means)

1970s

Theory of Corporate
Social Rectitude
(Concerned with the ends of
corporate social involvement:
What are the ethical values
at stake in each issue?)

1980s

1. Power begets responsibility. Because business firms often control enormous wealth and resources and affect the livelihood of many people, they automatically incur a degree of responsibility that matches their power.

2. A voluntary assumption of responsibility is preferable to government intervention and regulation. The preservation of businesses' autonomy and power of decision is paramount, and voluntary social action is believed to forestall social criticism and government intervention.

3. Voluntary social responsibility requires business leaders to acknowledge and accept the legitimate claims, rights, and needs of other groups in society. Within an organization's economic means, it is obligated to address stakeholder interests.

4. Corporate social responsibility requires respect for law and for the rules that govern marketplace relations. Adherence to legal and market rules is essential for maintaining the stability that permits the pursuit of profits.

5. An attitude of enlightened self-interest leads socially responsible firms to take a long-run view of profits. Short-run costs, for example those incurred in product recall, are necessary for the sake of long-run profits resulting from an improved public image and confidence in the company.

6. Greater economic, social, and political stability, and therefore less social criticism, will result if all businesses adopt a socially responsible posture.

CSR1 offered an alternative to government intervention and social criticism that would curb businesses' autonomy. This theory, however, had several inherent problems. First, there was no clear definition of socially responsible behavior. Second was the problem of conflict between demands for socially responsible action and fiduciary responsibility: How much should an organization invest to serve a stakeholder interest at the expense of stockholders? Ultimately, the business community's efforts under CSR1 fell short of meeting its obligations to society, and some of these responsibilities were then legislated by the government.

Corporate Social Responsiveness

Corporate social responsiveness The theory that business should aggressively identify and manage social problems before they occur.

In the early 1970s, a shift in the notion of business-society relations began to take place. A new concept of **corporate social responsiveness** began to emerge which was more action- and result-oriented; corporations, responding to pressures in the social environment, began aggressively identifying and managing social problems before they occurred.

During the 1970s, managers started to deal with social-responsiveness problems as they did other business problems: goals were agreed on, priorities set, authority and responsibility for resolution of the problem assigned, budgets allocated, rewards for performance established, action and results monitored. For every problem, including issues of social action, a managerial solution could be found and implemented.

However, as with CSR1, definitions of responsible behavior were ambiguous, and concerns arose that while managers and corporations were becoming more skillful in using tools and techniques to manage issues, they were paying too little attention to the values that were at stake. The need to focus on the ends as well as the means of corporate responsiveness led to a new concern with ethical values.

Corporate Social Rectitude

Corporate social rectitude The theory that values and ethics are part of business decisions.

By the mid-1970s, the theory of **corporate social rectitude** was taking shape by incorporating two distinct but highly related components: a value component and an ethics component.

CSR3 took the theories of responsibility and responsiveness a step further by challenging the notion that business and social values are separate and distinct. CSR3 is based on the premise that no business decision is value-free and that business must make known the values upon which it bases its decisions and actions. In developing and publicizing a value orientation, business is given a guide for all of its actions, behaviors, and decisions, and society can determine which of business's values (if any) are inconsistent with its own. Under this framework, the traditional value system of business, based almost entirely on profits, growth, and technological efficiency, is called into question.

Equally important in judging the social performance of business is the ethical component. As CSR3 increased in prominence, the understanding and use of theories of ethics increased. Where organizations used to adopt one approach to ethical decision making—utilitarian, rights, or justice—more organizations began to incorporate all three. As William C. Frederick argued, "Making decisions from this broader ethical perspective would infuse a sense of moral goodness into corporate affairs that is often lacking or underemphasized."[13]

Business is increasingly expected to have a solid underlying moral and ethical framework upon which all of its decisions and actions are based. Some organizations also take the lead in serving society and protecting not only their own immediate stakeholders but also other groups and individuals in need. These are, in a sense, ethical innovators: organizations that take a proactive stance toward issues of ethics and social responsibility. They go well beyond their own economic and legally mandated responsibilities. They accept a full range of ethical responsibilities raised by their public value statements and even search out opportunities to have an affect on values and ethics (see Exhibit 18.4).

Sun Ship, Inc., is one such proactive company. Sun Ship operated a shipbuilding subsidiary for 64 years in Chester, Pennsylvania, an industrial city 15 miles south of Philadelphia. In January 1981, the company announced that it planned to get out of the shipbuilding business but that it would retain roughly 1100 of its 4200 employees for a modest ship repair and industrial metal fabricating business. Sun Ship sold its assets in early 1982 to the Pennsylvania Shipping Company, which agreed to retain an additional 1100 of Sun's employees.

However, Sun Ship went well beyond this to minimize the damage and impact of its business decision. Dismissed employees were offered generous early retirement and severance pay benefits, career counseling, and job placement assistance, including contacts with other employers in the area, educational assistance, and retraining programs. Sun Ship also agreed to make payments in lieu of taxes to the city of Chester and the adjacent Eddystone Township, in which part of the plant was located, to compensate the municipalities for loss of revenue for several years. The company also made substantial contributions to the Chamber of Commerce and the United Way and donated $360,000 to the Riverfront Development Corporation (RDC), a regional nonprofit organization established to find means of reviving the area's economy in the wake of numerous plant closings.

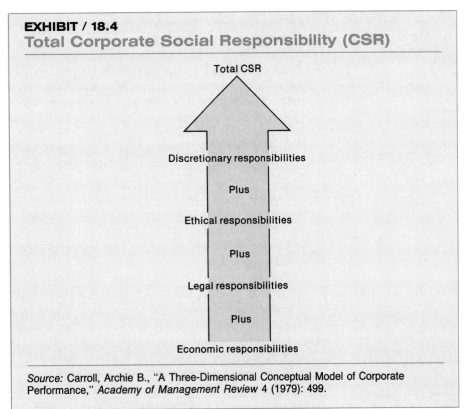

EXHIBIT / 18.4
Total Corporate Social Responsibility (CSR)

Total CSR

Discretionary responsibilities

Plus

Ethical responsibilities

Plus

Legal responsibilities

Plus

Economic responsibilities

Source: Carroll, Archie B., "A Three-Dimensional Conceptual Model of Corporate Performance," *Academy of Management Review* 4 (1979): 499.

Finally, Sun Ship offered a challenge grant of up to $1 million to match contributions from other industries and charitable foundations for the purpose of establishing a capital fund to stimulate development of new business. In all, the company spent or planned to spend tens of millions of dollars to repair the damage (real and potential) that the closing of its shipbuilding operation would have on the community.[14]

INDIVIDUAL ETHICS

People come to an organization with a set of personal values and moral standards, or ethics. In the selection process, prospective employees get an opportunity to see whether their values fit with the norms of the organization. As people work in an organization, this fit between the person and the organization becomes clearer. Individuals who are unhappy in an organization's climate or culture will probably want to leave. Organizations with very high turnover rates may find that their internal values and norms are a contributing factor.

Like organizations, individuals usually have numerous values or beliefs that are important to them. Occasionally, those beliefs conflict with the values and beliefs of the organization. For example, if a manager who believes that job promotions should always be based strictly on merit is asked by a superior to promote the boss's nephew, the manager will have to choose between the belief in merit as a basis for promotion and a belief that one should accommodate the wishes of a higher-level manager. Such common dilemmas force individual managers to clarify their own thinking about how to make a decision.

Individuals are the ones who must ultimately confront the moral and ethical dilemmas mentioned above. No one is exempt from these challenges, but managers face more of these situations and often face situations that affect many other people in the organization.[15]

The culture of an organization (see Chapter 8) reflects the values and beliefs that are important in that organization. In some companies, profitability is clearly the most important value; in many others, however, this value is tempered by the value placed on quality of work environment. Often people who have changed jobs note how different the culture or climate of the new organization differs from that of their previous employer.

The central role of culture has two implications. First, the behavior of people has to be understood in the organizational context. People respond to the cues that a system of values and beliefs provides. Second, managers must know what cues are being sent to people through the culture and be sure that people are not receiving signals to act irresponsibly. The company whose managers preach that the only thing that matters is sales will get a very different response from its employees than the company whose managers preach that their job is to give the customer good value.

Interviews conducted with managers in two different organizations, a high-technology manufacturer, and a large regional bank, disclosed that employees saw sharp differences in the importance of various values and in the number of high-score (or very important) values. This finding, illustrated in Exhibit 18.5, makes clear that not only were the ultimate values of the organizations (the ends) seen as different but also the instrumental values (the means) that managers believed they were to use in accomplishing those ends.

When these values conflict with an individual's personal values and beliefs, a dilemma is likely to result. How it is resolved will say much about the fit between

EXHIBIT / 18.5
A Comparison of Organizational Values

	High-Technology Company	Large Regional Bank
Industry leadership	6.4	5.6
Reputation of the firm	6.1	5.9
Employee welfare	5.0	3.0
Tolerance for diversity	5.0	3.0
Service to the general public	3.6	3.7
Organizational growth	5.2	4.9
Stability of the organization	5.3	3.3
Profit maximization	5.6	6.7
Innovation	5.7	4.0
Honesty	5.9	4.7
Integrity	6.0	4.4
Product quality	6.0	4.0
Customer service	5.0	4.0

Summary

End values	Customer service, quality, technological leadership, employee welfare	Maximize profits
Instrumental values	Openness, integrity, honesty	Follow orders

Note: Scores are based on a scale of 1 (least important) to 7 (most important) and are based on statistical analysis of employee perspectives of what is important in their organization.
Source: Liedtke, Jeanne, "Managerial Values and Corporate Decision Making: An Empirical Analysis of Value Congruence in Two Organizations," in J. Post, ed., *Research in Corporate Social Performance and Policy,* vol. II, Greenwich, CT: JAI Press, 1989, pp. 55–91.

the organization and its people and, in turn, about the effectiveness of the entire organization.

Exit, Voice, or Loyalty

People facing such dilemmas are likely to resort to one of three basic options for action.[16] The individual may subordinate his or her own beliefs and simply comply with the request of the superior. This option may be termed *loyalty* to the organizational principle of authority. The individual may object to the request and ask that his or her superior consider the merit of the various people involved. This response is called *voice* because the individual speaks out and describes his or her conflict with the requested action. If the individual is unable to either comply or resolve the issue by speaking out, the issue may be important enough to lead him or her to leave the organization, or *exit*. Naturally, there are personal stakes involved in either speaking out or exiting the organization (e.g., job security), but if the issue is sufficiently important, it may be the best course of action for the individual.

"Whistle-blowing" incidents, such as that described in The Inside View 18.3, illustrate the conflicts that can occur between individuals and their employers. Many employees have sacrificed their jobs rather than take part in a project or procedure that went against their own values. Ideally, people who are in strong

Do I Keep My Values or My Job?

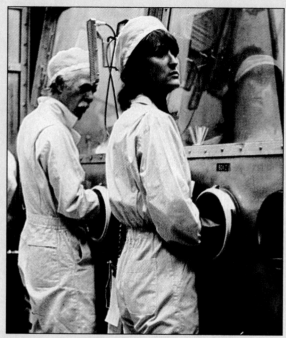

Although being a whistle-blower may mean losing a job, increasing numbers of employees, driven by conscience, are reporting illegal actions to government agencies. The movie *Silkwood*, starring Meryl Streep, is an account of what happened to one whistle-blower in the nuclear-power industry.

Individuals working for corporations have a number of responsibilities. They are responsible to the organization for doing what they are paid to do, and they are responsible for meeting their own needs and protecting their own values. If, in completing a job, the individual must violate a personal value, the responsibility to self and to the organization come in conflict.

One prime example is the case of Charles Atchison, at one time the quality control inspector for a construction company that builds nuclear power plants. When he worked on the site of the Comanche nuclear power plant for the Texas Utilities Electric Company, Atchison had a good salary, an expensive house, new cars, and most of the luxuries that he or his family wanted. He felt, then, that

he had met both his responsibility to do his job and his responsibility to provide for his security and protect his values.

When he became aware of numerous infractions of safety regulations at the site, he stood up before regulatory committees and exposed the problems. "It was sort of like I was barreling along, and I suddenly shifted into reverse," he said. He began to receive harassing telephone calls, was blacklisted by the nuclear power industry across the country, was refused jobs for being a "trouble-maker," and experienced many financial hardships caused by his subsequent litigation attempts. Now Atchison has another job, in an unrelated field, is six to eight months behind in the rent on the property his mobile home sits on, and says about his action, "I've got nothing to show . . . except the losses I've had. But I know I was on the cutting edge of the knife that prevented them from getting their license and sent them back to do repairs. I know I did right. And I know I'll always sleep right. I'll sleep just like a baby."

Other whistle-blowers can expect to pay similar high prices for their ethical behavior. According to Bertrand Berube, who counsels whistle-blowers and works closely with the nonprofit Government Accountability Project (GAP), which provides expense-only legal help for whistle-blowers, a whistle-blower can expect to pay anywhere from $20,000 to $700,000 and might spend six months to six years pursuing the case depending on whether the job was for a government agency or a private firm and whether he or she wants the job back.

But the fact is that more and more people, driven by conscience, are reporting illegal and unethical actions to the proper authorities regardless, or in spite of, the high price to themselves. Between 1978 and 1986, the GAP has represented more than 100 cases and has refused, due to lack of funds, just as many. Though this is not a recent problem, legislation has recently been proposed in favor of whistle-blowers. And an old law, signed in 1863 by Abraham Lincoln, known as the Civil

False Claims Act, has been targeted for major changes that would allow whistle-blowers to recoup as much as 30 percent of their legal costs. Thirty percent of $20,000 is little comfort, though, for a family in financial hardship, and it makes telling the truth very expensive. ■

Sources: Kleinfeld, N. R., "The Whistle Blowers' Morning After," *New York Times,* November 9, 1986, p. 1; Bradley, Barbara, "High Cost of Conscience," *Christian Science Monitor,* December 8, 1986, p. 24; Archer, Lawrence, "The Moral Minority," *Canadian Business* (January 1986): 56; Miller, William H., "Abe Lincoln Lives," *Industry Week,* August 28, 1986, p. 24.

moral or ethical opposition to a certain practice or operation should be allowed to discuss the reasons with management and work out a mutually satisfactory solution short of termination. The Inside View 18.4 illustrates ethical dilemmas many individuals face in organizations.

Making Difficult Decisions

Because managers will always face difficult decisions in their work, it is important they be clear about their own moral standards, values, and beliefs. Every difficult decision involves a subjective element in which the individual perceives the problem, assesses its importance, and decides whether there is a conflict. Beyond this subjective element, there is a need for individuals to use an ethical system of beliefs. These parallel the three approaches described earlier in this chapter. Some individuals take a utilitarian approach, weighing the respective costs and benefits of each course of action. The outcome with the most benefits and fewest costs is considered the best.

Other individuals take a moral rights approach. This view argues that the moral worth of a decision depends on the intentions of the actor, not only the outcome of the decision. No action can be worthy if it disregards the personal moral rights of others. Thus, individuals following this approach tend to favor two prescriptions: (1) act only as I would wish others to act, faced with the same set of circumstances; and (2) always treat people with dignity and respect. This view acknowledges that everyone has rights and implies that no one set of rights should be subordinated in favor of another set of rights.

Still other individuals prefer the justice approach. With this approach some rights can be subordinated to benefit the least advantaged. In this way, everyone benefits because the least advantaged are aided to become cooperative and contributing members of society.

Because none of these views is complete and perfect in itself, individual managers need to consider all in making difficult decisions. This can be done by asking some key questions:

• Is this a situation for which a preexisting law or precedent applies?
• What are the costs of acting this way? What are the benefits to the various stakeholders?
• Is there some net good that results? Would I want another person to act this way if I were a stakeholder? Does this decision give each person involved his or her rightful due?
• Does this decision help the most needy so that all stakeholders are left better off as a result?

The answers to these questions may not be easily reached, but they will give managers a clearer sense of the reasons for and consequences of their decisions.

The Decision to Launch the Shuttle *Challenger*

The explosion of the Challenger space shuttle resulted in the death of seven astronauts. The tragedy was caused by communication problems and by the conflicting priorities of NASA, Morton Thiokol, and Rockwell International.

The decision to launch the space shuttle *Challenger* in January 1986 is a powerful illustration of how ethical considerations affect individual managers and of how the choices of individuals have broad ethical implications.

On January 28, 1986, *Challenger* exploded one minute after takeoff from Kennedy Space Center in Florida. All seven crew members, including a civilian grade school teacher, were killed. In the aftermath, all scheduled shuttle flights were canceled until researchers could determine what went wrong and could guarantee that future missions would not meet the same fate.

In-depth analysis of debris collected from the ocean and records available from the National Aeronautics and Space Administration (NASA) and its hired contractors revealed some very unsettling information: The explosion was the result of a long string of related technical and managerial shortcomings that dated back to the first shuttle mission in 1981. From the time of the first test flight to virtually minutes prior to the January 28 flight, information was discovered and either hidden, disregarded, or blocked from reaching those who might have used it to stop the flight and prevent the tragedy.

For example, information available for several years indicated that low temperatures would increase the risks of O-ring failure. On the morning of the flight, the temperature was at least 15 degrees colder than it had been for any previous flight. The ice inspection team discovered heavy ice formations on several parts of the launch structure and, using infrared temperature sensors, found two extremely cold spots on the right rocket booster casing in the area of the seal that was later found to have failed. The head of the ice inspection team informed Kennedy Space Center's director of engineering that "the only choice you got today is not to go." The information did not reach those in a position to postpone the launch.

Officials from Rockwell International, which built the shuttle's orbiter, also advised Kennedy Space Center's launch team on the morning of the flight that the extremely cold temperatures on the pad posed too great a risk and that "it was not safe to fly." And two engineers from Morton Thiokol personally warned against the January 28 launch, fearing that the cold temperatures would cause a failure in the O-ring system they had helped design. (The engineers were demoted by Morton Thiokol after the accident but later reinstated to their original positions.) Ultimately, the temperature readings, like the data concerning the O-ring damage, were used to change the minimum criteria for launching. Tragically, the launch was approved.

Many have hypothesized about the reasons why so many serious problems could have been overlooked. A federal investigative committee found that shuttle workers were motivated to make unsound decisions such as those described above in large part because of pressure to achieve a planned flight rate of 24 missions per year. The committee's report specifically stated that "pressure on NASA to achieve flight rates was so pervasive that it undoubtedly adversely affected attitudes regarding safety. It has become clear that the shuttle launch system was not functioning well and was becoming increasingly unsafe as the flight rate was increased."

In this situation, individuals were faced with a number of decisions with ethical and social responsibility implications. In deciding to launch rather than postpone the mission, managers at NASA gave top priority to the flight schedule rather than to safety considerations. In not reporting information to senior launch committee officials, and in altering temperature criteria for launching, NASA technicians were also placing safety considerations second to schedule priorities. But by advising NASA not to launch, Rockwell International's managers demonstrated their concern about a disaster occurring. In deciding to warn NASA officials about the increased risks of the O-ring system in cold weather, the Morton Thiokol engineers gave top priority to the safety of the crew rather than to the reputation of their company or to their own job security. The organizations themselves—NASA, Morton Thiokol, and Rockwell International—did not make these decisions. Each decision was made by an individual or team of individuals, and each had ethical and social responsibility implications. ■

Sources: "Morton Thiokol Engineers Testify NASA Rejected Warnings on Launch," *Aviation Week & Space Technology,* March 3, 1986, pp. 18–20; "Faulty Joint Behind Space Shuttle Disaster," *Chemical and Engineering News,* June 23, 1986, pp. 9–15; "Rockwell Claims It Opposed Challenger Launch," *Aviation Week & Space Technology,* March 3, 1986, p. 14; "Transcript Reveals Launch Controllers Waived Challenger Temperature Warnings," *Aviation Week & Space Technology,* November 27, 1986, pp. 57–62; "Rogers Commission Charges NASA with Ineffective Safety Program," *Aviation Week & Space Technology,* June 16, 1986, pp. 18–22; "Missed Opportunities . . . ," *Aviation Week & Space Technology,* February 17, 1986, p. 13.

INSTITUTIONALIZING ETHICAL AND SOCIALLY RESPONSIBLE BEHAVIOR

As the preceding sections have illustrated, there is much ambiguity in corporate ethics and social responsibility. Definitions of terms are unclear, and even well-meant actions can have adverse, unexpected results. For these reasons, techniques have been developed to assist managers increase their awareness of social issues and their socially responsible behavior. As Theodore Purcell and James Weber argued in an important study, "Instituting ethics may sound ponderous, but its meaning is straightforward. It means getting ethics formally and explicitly into daily business life. It means getting ethics into company policy formation at the board and top management levels and, through a formal code, getting ethics into all daily decision-making and work practices down the line, at all levels of employment. It means grafting a new branch on the corporate decision tree—a branch that reads 'right/wrong.' "[17] Several methods of institutionalizing ethics include the establishment of formal codes of ethics, ethics committees, ethics training programs, and ethics audits.

Ethics Codes

An ethics code describes the general value system, ethical principles, or specific ethical rules that are supposed to guide employees in their everyday behavior. Codes vary considerably among companies, but Exhibit 18.6 shows some of the most commonly included provisions. According to a study conducted by the Ethics Resource Center, over 90 percent of large U.S. corporations had ethics codes in 1985.[18] IBM Corporation has had a code of conduct for many years. It begins with a letter from the chairman of the board.[19]

> If there is a single, overriding message in this book, it is that IBM expects every employee to act, in every instance, according to the highest standards of business conduct.

While some companies provide very detailed code statements, others offer more general statements of principles to guide employees' behavior. For example, the actions of Johnson & Johnson, in recalling Tylenol when it was related to the deaths of seven people, were guided by the company's "credo," which stated: "We believe our first responsibility is to the doctors, nurses and patients, to mothers and all others who use our products and services." Experts generally agree that the most effective codes are those drawn up with the cooperation and participation of employees and those having specific rewards and penalties that are spelled out and enforced. Surveys report that the majority of managers think

EXHIBIT / 18.6
Provisions of Ethics Codes

Policy Area	Percent of Codes Discussing It
Conduct on Behalf of the Firm	
Relations with U.S. governments	76.7
Relations with customers/suppliers	75.0
Employee relations*	52.6
Relations with competitors*	50.0
Relations with foreign governments	42.2
Relations with investing public*	41.4
Civic and community affairs	34.5
Transactions with agents, consultants, and distributors	26.7
Environmental affairs	19.8
Host-country commercial relations	12.1
Other	2.6
Conduct Against the Firm	
Conflict of interest*	69.0
Other white-collar crimes (e.g., embezzlement)	16.4
Personal character matters	9.6
Other	1.7

*Items receiving relatively greater emphasis by more detailed discussion.
Source: Cressey, Donald R., and Moore, Charles A., "Managerial Values and Corporate Codes of Ethics," California Management Review (Summer 1983): 56. Used with permission.

that a self-developed code will help improve ethical behavior in their industries.[20] Some companies have found it helpful to supplement codes with an employee advisory committee to provide confidential advice to personnel faced with an ethical dilemma.

Ethics Committees

Some corporations maintain a committee of the board of directors to consider the ethical dimensions of company policies and practices. These committees can make a difference in two ways: First, they can inject ethics into discussions at the highest levels of policy-making. Second, they symbolize to employees and external stakeholders the company's formal commitment to ethical behavior.[21]

Ethics Training Programs

In the 1980s, many companies started ethics training programs to raise employee awareness. Johnson & Johnson (J&J) is one of a number of companies that make an effort to include issues as part of its training programs for new employees.

At J&J, all new company managers are instructed in the firm's credo and have discussions with experienced executives about its usefulness and its application to real problems. Other companies include discussions of common types of ethical problems in their continuing education programs for managers. Defense contractors were forced to put such material in their programs after ethics scandals in the 1980s. Ethics training programs acquaint employees with official company policy on ethical issues and show how those policies can be translated into the specifics of everyday decision making. Simulated case studies, based on actual events in the company, are often used to illustrate how to apply ethical principles to on-the-job problems.[22]

Ethics Audits

Periodic ethics audits also tend to build an awareness of ethical issues into a company's regular routines. These audits attempt to uncover opportunities for unethical behavior that might exist or that have occurred in the company. Managers can then judge how actual practices vary from the company's code and can estimate the economic and public relations costs of correcting them and the costs of not correcting them. Action plans can then be designed to change the situation.

▨ KEY POINTS

1 Today's concepts of corporate ethics and social responsibility are derived from earlier principles of charity and stewardship. Three crises in the past century have increased public demand that corporations conduct business ethically and responsibly in order to be legitimate and credible in society's eyes.

2 Stakeholders are those groups or factions that have an interest in or are affected by an organization's operations. For the average organization, stakeholders include employees; owners and stockholders; suppliers; creditors; competitors; customers and clients; the community; local, national, and foreign governments; and public-interest groups and the media.

3 The theory of corporate social responsibility assumes that corporations have responsibilities and obligations beyond profitability. They have a responsibility to maintain and enhance society. An alternative view, social responsiveness, argues that corporations should not sit and wait for problems to occur but aggressively identify and manage them. Some who propose corporate social rectitude say that managers must also make known the value bases of their decisions. They should make

all decisions in light of their values and social impact.
4 An organization can institutionalize ethical and socially responsible behavior by establishing codes of ethics, setting up ethics committees or ethics training programs, or conducting ethics audits.

FOR DISCUSSION AND REVIEW

1. Did the people in control at Jewel use their power responsibly? What considerations did they balance during the crisis? Explain your answer.

2. Think of some ways the principles of stewardship and charity are manifested in today's business world. What are some of the social and economic benefits of charity and stewardship?

3. Who or what are the stakeholders in an urban hospital? In what large organizations are you a stakeholder?

4. Many groups affect the operating environment of a company and are affected by its actions and policies. How far does corporate social responsibility extend outside of a company?

5. In the chapter, three theories of ethical decision making were discussed. What guidelines for managers making decisions do these theories affect?

6. Using the theory of corporate social responsibility, what would you have done as the manager of Hillfarm Dairy? What about under the theory of corporate social responsiveness? Corporate social rectitude?

7. What role can or does a code of ethics play in a large organization? Try writing a code of ethics for a company. What values and principles should be stated?

KEY TERMS

Charity principle
Corporate social rectitude
Corporate social responsibility
Corporate social responsiveness
Difference principle
Liberty principle
Social responsibility
Stakeholders
Stewardship principle
Theory of justice
Theory of rights
Utilitarian theory

THE CONFERENCE TABLE: DISCUSSION CASE / 18.1

Out of South Africa

For General Electric (GE), pulling out of South Africa in 1986 was an especially painful period. GE had been doing business there since 1894. But most of the American businesses that had set up operations in South Africa were pulling out by the end of 1986. After a long and difficult struggle, they felt it was no longer feasible to operate there.

The South African government enforces a policy of apartheid, under which the black and white populations of the country are legally segregated. This policy was challenged for decades by the black people living in the country, but it did not

Sources: "Local Boycotts Power Pullouts by U.S. Business," *Washington Post,* November 17, 1986, p. A20; Tsifkoff, Michael, "Threat to Profits Spurs U.S. Exodus from South Africa," *Washington Post,* November 17, 1986, pp. A1, A20; Hammonds, Keith N., "Out of Africa?" *New York Times,* August 17, 1986, p. F4; Thurow, Roger, "South Africans Face Hard Time Living Without U.S. Companies," *Wall Street Journal,* October 24, 1986, p. 2; Thurow, Roger, "U.S. Exodus Touches Many South Africans," *Wall Street Journal,* November 6, 1986, p. 36; Davidson, Joe, "South Africa Blacks Believe Divestment Is Worth the Pain It Would Cause Them," *Wall Street Journal,* June 27, 1986, p. 30; Smith, Lee, "South Africa: Time to Stay—Or Go?" *Fortune,* August 4, 1986, pp. 46–48.

Public interest groups and students at numerous universities in the United States often hold demonstrations to demand that American corporations pull out of South Africa.

receive worldwide attention until white South African police officers armed with machine guns killed 69 peaceful black protesters in the township of Sharpeville in 1960. Since then, there have been calls from around the world for economic and other sanctions against South Africa, in hopes that they will pressure the government to abolish its racist policy.

These pressures did not severely affect the corporations operations in South Africa until the late 1970s and early 1980s. As violence escalated and more people died, public interest groups in the United States and elsewhere began to demand that the corporations pull out. Pullouts, it was felt, would jeopardize the South African economy, put pressure on its government, and prevent multinationals from profiting from the hardships of the black population.

As late as 1984, however, very few American multinationals seriously considered leaving. The general consensus among them was that they benefited the black population and would cause more harm than good by leaving. Multinationals had contributed 25 percent of the gross national product in 1984 and provided 84 percent of the social welfare funds not provided by the government. In addition, only a very small percentage of each company's local profits came from sales to government agencies, so the companies felt that they were neither supporting the system nor profiting from it. The majority of these companies had already signed the Sullivan principles, a list of recommendations laid down by the Reverend Leon Sullivan in 1980, and by doing so had pledged to maintain desegregated workplaces, pay equal wages and offer equal promotional opportunities to black and white workers, and contribute to social development by subsidizing schools, housing, and medical facilities. Most of the American companies operating in South Africa were model employers, offering equal rights and desegregated facilities even in violation of South African law.

Though black activists agreed that the companies were making valuable contributions, they felt this was only slowing down the change process. Violence in South Africa was increasing, and protests in the United States were stronger and more frequent. Sit-ins and shantytowns sprung up on college campuses all across the United States. Everywhere, groups that could influence investment boards were demanding that these boards divest all stock in companies doing business in or with South Africa. Finally, in the fall of 1986, California Governor George Deukmajian signed a sweeping divestment measure that mandated the sale of $9.5 billion worth of securities held by the state in companies doing business in South Africa. By the end of the year, 116 colleges and universities, 19 state governments, and 83 cities had passed similar measures.

One of the most effective measures, however, was the passage of so-called selective purchasing laws, under which public contracts cannot be awarded to companies with direct investments in South Africa. Thirty-one local governments and two states had enacted such laws by the end of 1986. The experience of Bell & Howell provides a good illustration of the dilemma in which most multinationals found themselves. Bell & Howell had been in South Africa for over ten years and had complied with the Sullivan principles, built a local hospital, and successfully trained and promoted black managers. But after years of thriving growth, it lost $500,000 for two years running in 1984 and 1985. Back home, dealers in the company's textbook division, which provided 50 percent of the company's revenue and depended almost entirely on public school systems, were about to come head to head with selective purchasing laws across the country. "We weren't going to endanger 11,000 jobs [in the United States] for the sake of 150 in South Africa," said a company representative. "We have a responsibility to our shareholders to make money." Bell & Howell sold its South African assets for one-fifth their estimated value and pulled out in April 1986.

Suddenly, multinationals found themselves fighting not only the South African government but their own governments if they stayed. As one reporter put it, "Perhaps no other market has ever required so much anguish for so little reward as South Africa." Corporations began leaving in droves. Of the 325 U.S. companies with factories or offices in South Africa in 1984, 85 had divested to some degree by the end of 1986 or had announced plans to do so. General Motors, Xerox, and many others, some with relationships dating back 60 or 70 years, all sold their facilities. Many, however, have retained licensing, distribution, or management agreements with the succeeding owners.

As the companies pull out, their early predictions are coming true. Those who have taken over their operations generally do not comply with the Sullivan principles and do not contribute to local social development. Many blacks have lost their jobs or had their wages cut as the new managers struggle to turn around the companies, which had been losing money for years before the American parents sold them. One former Ford employee put it graphically: "The poverty and suffering in Port Elizabeth brought on by Ford's departure is so pervasive that a blind man can feel it with a stick." Nonetheless, most companies finally realized South Africa was a no-win situation. These multinationals have pulled out with no intention of going back. ∎

DISCUSSION QUESTIONS

1. Was it more ethical for the U.S. companies to stay in South Africa or to leave? Can you argue both sides? How do the ethical theories apply?

2. Who are the stakeholders in this case, and what is the nature of their interest in multinationals' staying or leaving?

3. Where on the continuum of socially responsible behavior would you place Bell & Howell? Any of the other companies? Why?

THE CONFERENCE TABLE: DISCUSSION CASE / 18.2

Bhopal: A Question of Response

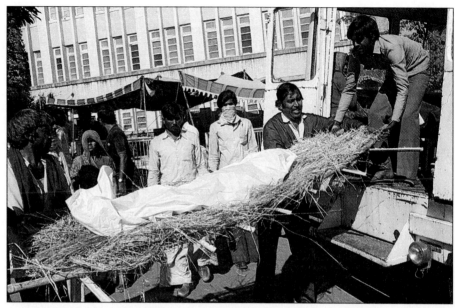

After the accident in Bhopal, India, in which toxic gases killed 2000 people, managers in the chemical industry, public officials, and the general public recognized the need for increased regulation and control.

On August 11, 1985, at Institute, West Virginia, a cloud of toxic chemical vapor was released into the air from a Union Carbide plant. The chemical cloud struck hundreds of people in its path. More than 130 were sent to hospitals for treatment. Subsequent investigations showed that the chemical leak was the result of equipment flaws and violations of operating and safety procedures at the plant by Union Carbide employees.

The Institute, West Virginia, chemical leak was an almost unthinkable and unbelievable event. Less than a year before, in December 1984, a chemical leak at a plant of a Union Carbide subsidiary in Bhopal, India, had created a killer cloud of toxic gases that killed more than 2000 people and injured tens of thousands more. The horror at Bhopal focused intense public attention on Union Carbide and the chemical industry. Union Carbide, headquartered in Danbury, Connecticut, pledged an intensive effort to find safer, more effective ways to make, distribute, and transport chemical products at its facilities around the world. The company's chairman and chief executive officer, Warren Anderson, repeatedly pledged that Carbide would lead the industry in finding improved means to protect workers and the public against toxic chemicals. In a statement before a congressional committee in March, 1985, Anderson said, "There will be intensi-

Sources: Shrivastava, Paul, *Bhopal: Anatomy of a Crisis* (Cambridge, Mass.: Ballinger, 1987); Mahon, John F., and Kelley, Patricia, "The Politics of Toxic Waste: Multinational Corporations as Facilitators of Transnational Public Policy," in Lee E. Preston, *Research in Corporate Social Performance and Policy,* vol. 10 (Greenwich, Conn.: JAI Press, 1988).

fied sampling procedures, training and retraining sessions, process reviews, and countless administrative and physical changes." Promises and public attention notwithstanding, the equipment and employee failures at the Institute facility created still another public and political crisis for Carbide.

The chemical leaks at Bhopal and Institute were crises for the chemical industry as well. Anyone who has driven near a chemical manufacturing facility knows that it is usually a smelly, unpleasant environment. Since the 1970s, however, the public has learned that chemical plants are much more than noxious neighbors: They are downright dangerous. Toxic fumes can kill anyone in their path. Chemicals that leak into the ground can enter groundwater supplies, and contaminate the drinking water for entire communities. Scientific research has produced increasingly convincing evidence of the link between chemicals and dozens of types of cancer in humans. In the 1960s, fears were raised about the "chemical feast" of dangerous chemicals in our food supplies and daily lives; by the 1970s, it was clear that society could not do without chemicals; in the 1980s, the general public saw the horrors of the "chemical beast" in the tragedies at Bhopal and Institute.

Public outrage and concern had a number of effects. People living in communities in which chemical plants were located put direct pressure on company managements and public officials to ensure a higher degree of safety. Public concern led state and federal officials to consider new laws to regulate chemical operations and safeguard employees and the general public. After the Bhopal and Institute crises, managers in the chemical industry, public officials, and the general public sensed that increased regulation and legal control was virtually inevitable. To many, there seemed no other way to ensure public safety. ■

DISCUSSION QUESTIONS

1. Where on the continuum of socially responsible behavior would you place Union Carbide in respect to the Bhopal, India, and Institute, West Virginia, incidents?
2. Did Union Carbide meet the needs of any of its stakeholders in either incident?
3. Which ethical principles did Union Carbide exhibit in each case?

19 | Managing in the Political and Legal Environment

FOCUS CASE / The Great American Smokeout

INTERPLAY BETWEEN SOCIAL, POLITICAL, AND LEGAL ENVIRONMENTS
Differing Priorities for Society, Business, and Government

THE POLITICAL ENVIRONMENT
Public Issues
Mechanisms of Influence
Business Issues
Public Policy and the Public-Policy Process

THE LEGAL ENVIRONMENT
Sources of Law
The Impact of Law on Managers
Legal Responsibilities of Organizations
Legal Responsibilities of Managers

Today, social expectations and requirements are often formalized in the political and legal standards of a nation. In the United States, no organization can operate without an eye toward federal, state, or local politics and laws. Through the political process, stakeholders influence the legal requirements that govern how organizations operate. Standards for dealing with employees, customers, competitors, local communities, and even foreign nations are specified through legislation and regulation. Government can also be a mighty ally for an industry or group of organizations. Politics and the law can influence and shape markets as well as determine what organizations can and cannot do. Dealing with legal and political environment is therefore as much a part of the manager's responsibility as dealing with owners, employees, and the customers.

KEY QUESTIONS

As you study this chapter, try to answer the following key questions:

1 What differences exist in the priorities of business, government, and society?
2 Through what mechanisms do society and business influence government to act on these interests?
3 What is the public-policy process, and how does it address the differing or compatible interests of various factions in society?
4 What is the difference between the political environment and the legal environment?
5 What is the legal basis for regulation in the United States?
6 What are the basic regulatory mechanisms in the American government system?
7 What are the basic types of regulations?
8 What types of civil-law and criminal-law responsibilities do managers face?

Focus Case

The Great American Smokeout

Up until the 1960s, cigarette smoking was a social norm. Today it is the subject of a bitter debate that affects individuals, businesses, and government.

Smoking at one time was a societal norm. As late as 1967, almost half the adult population of the United States smoked. Representatives from tobacco companies would swarm over college campuses, handing out free packages of cigarettes, usually filterless, and delivering elaborate sales pitches to convince young students to buy their brands. Smoking was a status symbol. The most beautiful and exciting movie stars smoked, and so did national heroes and society's movers and shakers.

Then, in 1964, Dr. Luther Terry published a book titled *Report of the Surgeon General's Advisory Committee on Smoking and Health,* which declared flatly that cigarette smoking caused lung cancer and increased the risk of heart disease. That 387-page report, and later studies confirming its findings, transformed smoking from a personal habit into a public issue.

Action followed quickly from that initial report. One year later, legislation was passed requiring cigarette companies to put labels warning of health dangers on all cigarette packages. In 1971, largely because the Federal Communications Commission's fairness doctrine allowed equal broadcast time for anti-smoking messages, cigarette manufacturers withdrew from television and radio advertising. In 1972, the surgeon general issued a report suggesting that secondhand smoke was a danger to nonsmokers. Minnesota passed the first state law in 1985 requiring businesses, restaurants, and other institutions to establish nonsmoking areas; San Francisco limited smoking in the workplace in 1983, and in 1986, Surgeon General C. Everett Koop and the National Research Council published a report linking secondhand smoke inhalation to lung cancer and respiratory disease in nonsmokers (i.e., passive smoking).

By 1987, 13 states and over 250 communities and municipalities enacted laws restricting smoking in the workplace, and 24 states had restricted smoking in public places. In 1980, fewer than 8 percent of U.S. companies provided nonsmoking areas; by 1987, 36 percent did. Some small firms have refused to hire smokers, and one major corporation, USG Corp. of Chicago, banned smoking both on and off the job for its 1300 plant workers. Because these workers handle mineral fibers that are a potential risk to respiratory health, the company is taking no chances that smoking-related diseases exacerbate the problem. Meanwhile, the Defense Department has imposed smoking restrictions in the military; Congress is considering substantial increases in the tax on ciga-

Sources: This case was written by M. R. Poirier, based on the following sources: Hamilton, Joan O'C., et al., "'No Smoking' Sweeps America," *Business Week,* July 27, 1987, pp. 40–46; Pertschuck, Michael, "Cigarette Ads and the Press," *The Nation,* March 7, 1987, pp. 283–399; Corelli, Rae, et al., "Crackdown on Smoking," *MacLeans,* June 22, 1987, pp. 24–27; Finch, Peter, "Crusader Who Helps Offices Go Smoke-Free," *Business Week,* March 23, 1987, p. 105; Moskal, Brian S., "Hup 2-3-4! No Smoking!" *Industry Week,* February 9, 1987, pp. 24–25; Voluck, Philip R., "Burning Legal Issues of Smoking in the Workplace," *Personnel Journal* (June 1987): 140–143; Gruson, Lindsey, "Employers Get Tough on Smoking at Work," *New York Times,* March 14, 1985, pp. B1, B8; "The FTC vs. R. J. Reynolds," *Newsweek,* June 30, 1986, p. 48; Wolf, Melvin L., "Advertising Pleads the First," *Commonweal,* February 13, 1987, pp. 75–79.

rettes; smoking on airline flights shorter than two hours has been banned; and legislation to restrict smoking in federal workplaces has been introduced in both the U.S. House of Representatives and the U.S. Senate.

This significant turnaround in events is the result of the balancing of pressures from many factions in society. Though antismoking sentiment had existed for some time (in 1604, for example, King James I called smoking "a custome loathsome to the eye, hateful to the nose, harmful to the brain, and dangerous to the lungs"), antismoking activists had no power, authority, or backing. However, with the 1964 and 1986 reports from the surgeon general's office to back them up, the nonsmoking public felt increasingly justified in challenging smokers.

As the nonsmoking public began to realize its size, it began to flex its muscle by forming antismoking groups and pushing nonsmokers' rights. One major group is the Group Against Smoking Pollution (GASP), which initially represented people complaining of illness caused by inhalation of secondhand smoke, and which later began helping corporations design and implement smoking policies. The actions of this and other groups have been greatly facilitated by the courts' position on the issue. EPA statistics have indicated that as many as 5000 people die each year from lung cancer and respiratory ailments caused by secondhand smoke; thus, in lawsuits since 1975 in which a nonsmoker has sued a corporation for failing to protect him or her from secondhand smoke, the courts have sided with the nonsmoker.

Most corporations are more than willing to restrict smoking in their facilities. Not only do they avoid lawsuits that could cost them millions of dollars, they save millions in many other ways. For example, an in-house survey conducted at Goodyear estimated that the almost 3000 employees at the company's Akron headquarters cost the company roughly $2 million annually in smoking-related problems. Smokers were out sick more often, and they took more time off from the job to smoke or even to buy cigarettes. Aside from these direct costs, an insurance company in Washington State even saved money on cleaning bills. The company's janitorial service gave it a $500 rebate after it imposed a smoking ban because the janitorial staff did not have to dump ashtrays, and the cleaning of desktops, upholstery, and windows was both easier and not needed as frequently.

Tobacco companies are, of course, reacting to these societal and governmental pressures. Though some are diversifying to make up for lost profits as cigarette sales decline, they are also devising new lines of attack, or defense, against the antismoking movement. R. J. Reynolds, for example, published an advertisement in 1985 that claimed that there was no proof that smoking increased health risks and that the "controversy over smoking and health remains an open one." Ironically, this ad jeopardized the tobacco industry's position. The Federal Trade Commission denounced the ad as misleading and inaccurate and challenged the right of tobacco producers to advertise at all. The tobacco producers claim that their right is protected by the First Amendment.

Cigarettes, only a few inches long, weighing a fraction of an ounce each, have gone from personal habit, to a public issue, to a subject of debate and contention at the highest levels of government. The debate over smokers' and nonsmokers' rights is a powerful illustration of the dynamics of the relationship between business, government, and society. ■

INTERPLAY BETWEEN SOCIAL, POLITICAL, AND LEGAL ENVIRONMENTS

All people in society have a voice. They are not only allowed but expected to make their interests known. Of course, as all these voices are raised, many highly differing opinions will be heard. Though there are thousands of formal voices (interest groups, ethnic groups, communities, business coalitions), a major division has traditionally existed between two of these: business and society, where business is the collection of organizations responsible for producing goods and services and society is the collection of individuals who consumes goods and services. In the United States, government action has often been undertaken to balance and adjust the interests and rights of each of these factions with respect to the other.

Differing Priorities for Society, Business, and Government

The interests of society and business are perhaps the most divergent in times of great institutional transformation. In the late 1800s, as the Industrial Revolution was nearing its peak, business was viewed as an opponent: Businesses exploited workers, maintained unsafe workplaces, manufactured shoddy and unsafe products, and generally did whatever they could to increase their own profits regardless of the effect it had on society. This behavior prompted the public to demand government action. Businesses often considered the public, including unions, as their opponents. Unions demanded more money for less work, and various "agitators" wanted production slowed for the sake of quality, worker safety, and what we now call environmental protection.

The relationship between business and society has shifted continually since then: It has been more harmonious during times of economic boom, such as during mobilization for both world wars, and less harmonious at other times, such as during the Great Depression and in the 1960s when antiestablishment sentiment ran high. For much of the 1980s, a so-called honeymoon existed between business and the American people. "Captains of Industry such as Chrysler's Lee A. Iaccoca, and successful entrepreneurs such as Apple Computer co-founder Steven P. Jobs, became national heroes."[1] But in the wake of insider trading scandals on Wall Street and other corporate excesses, a public skepticism of business grew. A late 1980s' Harris poll showed that 82 percent of Americans believed that businesses were predominantly motivated by greed.[2]

Business and society are interdependent. Society needs the jobs, products, and services business provides, and business needs the markets and skills society provides. However, the interests of the two still often differ. It is government's job to harmonize these interests and protect the rights and freedoms of all.

The Priorities of Society At different times in history, society has assigned greater or lesser priority to differing issues. Some of these had to do specifically with business, others with government's role in society. At the turn of the century, protection from the power and abuses of big business was one of society's most pressing causes. After 1929 and through most of the 1930s, unemployment levels and general public welfare became the top priorities. During the 1960s, with the country fully back on its economic feet, environmental and health issues moved into the top slot. Smoking, for example, became a public concern during that decade, after 1964 when the surgeon general released his report, and it has become an increasingly prominent issue since then. Today, a great variety of economic and social issues have come to the forefront of the public's conscience, encompassing many areas of society. Society's agenda is perhaps more complex than at any other time in history.

The demand for jobs, and government guarantees for those jobs, is now coupled with a demand for meaningful employment. While some employment guarantees can be legislated, meaningfulness cannot. Action here is required on the part of both business and government. The environment also remains a great concern, but it is not simply the actions of one company in one area that provoke interest and concern. Exposure to certain toxic and cancer-causing substances, such as asbestos, PCBs, and dioxin, is a national—and even international—danger that reflects the practices of thousands of companies over the past several decades. Acid rain and global warming are especially complex since pollutants from a wide variety of sources enter the atmosphere and contaminate environments irrespective of national boundaries.

The Priorities of Business Business also has an agenda: Business wants to protect its interests and further causes of its own. Deregulation, for example, was one of business's top priorities in the 1970s. Over the years, increasing regulations had imposed a variety of costs, in terms of both time and money, on organizations. Costs of compliance can be so high that they force smaller companies out of business. Deregulation of the airline, communications, and financial services industries during the late 1970s and 1980s came about largely in response to lobbying efforts on the part of business.

In the mid-1980s, the "new competitiveness" moved into the top position on business's agenda. The push for increased competitiveness was supported by all three factions. In 1987, Speaker of the U.S. House of Representatives Jim Wright predicted that the competitiveness craze might remain the dominant issue for the rest of the twentieth century.[3] The competitiveness issue is based on the notion that government must devise and implement a systematic policy to bolster U.S. industry's sagging ability to compete in world markets. Though Americans are skeptical of permanent government economic planning mechanisms (they are embraced only in times of national economic crisis), they appreciate the importance of regaining lost jobs and reestablishing America in the forefront of world trade. "People are losing jobs in every district," said a California congressional staffer. "It's not just the sunset, smokestack industries. It's the sunrise industries, too. Silicon Valley is getting hammered."[4]

Many of business's agenda items, such as efforts to limit the costs of environmental regulation, have been at cross-purposes to the goals of government and/or society. On the other hand, business efforts to establish and enforce smoking restrictions in the workplace have been welcomed by both. Because antismoking policies may prevent organizations from becoming entangled in secondhand smoke lawsuits, may reduce employee sick time, and may even save on cleaning bills, it is easy to understand how a consensus can be achieved. Even smokers tend to agree that the policies are beneficial to all, except in circumstances where their own jobs are placed on the line.

The Priorities of Government The U.S. government was designed specifically to protect each person's right to life, liberty, and the pursuit of happiness. As business and society position themselves around various issues, government must maintain harmony between them and guarantee that freedom remains balanced. As businesses pursue legitimate goals of profits and growth, society's right to life

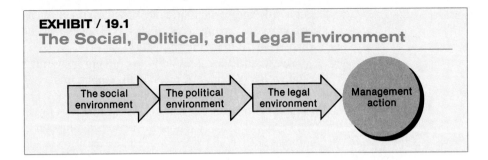

EXHIBIT / 19.1
The Social, Political, and Legal Environment

(or health and safety) must not be compromised. Similarly, society's efforts to control the actions of business must not unreasonably restrict business's liberty to pursue growth while still protecting people and the environment. In some cases, government must impose regulations or require businesses to meet their responsibilities to protect the health and welfare of society. The Inside View 19.1 illustrates how this issue has affected the Ford Motor Company, though the story is similar for many organizations across the country. In many cases, laws such as those restricting smoking or implementing policies, are intended to benefit both business and society.

This system is highly complex, and the momentum behind various issues and the powers of various coalitions shift continually. Because all factions have their own unique interests, and the right and ability to attempt to enforce them, conflict is inevitable. The political process and the laws that emerge are attempts by society to guide and control that conflict. To fully appreciate the laws within which they operate, managers need to understand the political environment within which laws are created. (See Exhibit 19.1.)

THE POLITICAL ENVIRONMENT

Public Issues

In a democratic society, business and individuals both have access to the political process that creates the law. What issues they promote and how they promote them is determined not only by their own interests and concerns but by the opportunities and crises they face.[5] An issue that is eventually brought forward and codified as a law usually goes through four stages of development. In stage 1, some segment of society begins to bring pressure for change because their expectations are not being met. For example, a group of residents in a neighborhood may object to the odor or smoke from a local manufacturer, or a group may protest the use of monkeys for scientific research at a local university. Or, as illustrated in the opening case, an employee may claim that he or she became ill after working in an area in which smoking was not restricted.[6] Once a gap develops between the expectations of an organization's performance and the actual performance, the seeds of a public issue have been sown.

At this point, an unhappy or concerned group may try to build a base of support by recruiting other citizens. They may form a group and print pamphlets, newsletters, or brochures or engage in other forms of communication. Ultimately, they are striving for visibility. The residents of a community may picket the plant that is spewing foul smoke into the air. Animal rights groups may contact their local representatives and demand that a university or commercial laboratory be

Changes at Ford Motor Company

As head of the Ford Motor Company, Henry Ford II faced more government oversights, labor relations laws, and consumer protection laws than his grandfather could ever have imagined.

When Henry Ford organized the Ford Motor Company in 1903, his relationships with government were relatively simple. There was only one important antitrust law on the books, and his business was too small to be bothered by it. The federal government did not tax the income of the company, its employees, or its capital gains. Although rival carmakers in this country were gearing up to compete with Ford, foreign competitors were no threat. No unions were permitted in the Ford plant, and government regulations concerning wages, hours, working conditions, and safety and health were unheard of. The government exacted

no payments from the company for employee retirement and pension plans for the simple reason that no such plans existed. Nor was the fledgling automaker plagued with problems of a polluted environment, an energy shortage, or consumer complaints about auto safety, all of which in later years would bring the wrath of the government down on the Ford company. Ford's main legal worry in those early years was a patent infringement suit brought against him by competitors, but he eventually won the suit in the courts.

By the late 1970s, Henry Ford II, the founder's grandson and the chief executive officer of the company, faced a different world. He could scarcely make a move without the government taking an active hand or peering over his shoulder. That single antitrust law known to his grandfather had grown into a tangle of antitrust law and court rulings regulating competition, pricing practices, mergers, and acquisitions. Labor laws legalized unions and controlled wages, hours, working conditions, safety and health, and employee discrimination. Federal, state, local, and foreign governments levied taxes on company income, its plants and equipment, capital gains, auto and truck sales, and salaries.

Decisions about the size and weight of cars, the types of engines, and gasoline consumption rates were shared with government regulators. Still another group of government officials were concerned with auto and plant emissions, effluent discharges, plant noise, and solid-waste disposal. Consumer protection laws dictated guidelines on matters ranging from safety belts to recalls for defective work to the terms of a loan to finance the auto's purchase.

Nor was this all. Henry Ford II—unlike the founder, who was a staunch believer in laissez faire—depended on the federal government to maintain general business prosperity, stabilize the dollar, and combat both inflation and recession. Such ideas were as wild and unlikely to the older

Ford as if someone had told him that his grandson would live to see astronauts walking on the moon!

The older and the younger Henry Fords have lived and managed their company in truly different worlds. What was insignificant to the one—government intervention—had become central to the other. ■

Source: Frederick, William, Davis, Keith, and Post, James, *Business and Society: Corporate Strategy, Public Policy, and Ethics,* 6th ed. (New York: McGraw-Hill, 1988), pp. 152–153.

prohibited from conducting painful experiments on animals. The groups opposing animal experiments have developed extensive public awareness campaigns: posters and stickers detailing the horrors of the experiments can be found on city streets and subway cars in many metropolitan areas.

GASP is one of the nonsmokers' main interest groups. It represents nonsmokers in claims against companies and helps organizations establish smoking policies. The growth in the antismoking movement, and in the support for GASP, has been profound. As one reporter put it, "For 25 years, anti-smokers fought the tobacco industry on a shoestring. But suddenly the movement looks like a juggernaut."[7] And Regina L. Carson, executive director of GASP, predicts that "in 20 years, we'll shake our heads and say: 'How could anyone ever have smoked?' "[8]

Americans for Nonsmokers Rights (ANR) is the nation's largest antismoking lobby. Formed in 1981, it now has 15,000 members and an annual budget of $300,000. Its hundreds of volunteers have helped push through most of the 250 local and state ordinances restricting smoking both in the workplace and in public facilities.

As public concern grows and pressure from groups mounts, political leaders begin to press the issue by introducing laws and regulation in various bodies of government (stage 2). If enough support is found, formal legislation is created (stage 3). At this stage, managers must comply with the law or face legal enforcement activities. Eventually organizations comply with the law (stage 4). (See Exhibit 19.2.)

Public issues do not always or exclusively focus on the performance of business corporations. Sometimes public pressure evolves in response to government actions or to a general situation in society. Protests against wars and military involvement, for example, have been prominent public issues in the past three decades, first in response to the United States' intervention in Vietnam in the 1960s, and in the 1980s to its intervention in Central America. Other current public issues concern the mass media campaigns to prevent drug abuse and to prevent people from driving under the influence of alcohol.

Mechanisms of Influence

The right to vote is the public's most fundamental mechanism for expressing its will and influencing what laws are eventually passed. On an individual level, however, the value of the vote as a tool of influence may seem more symbolic than real. The value of the vote as a tool of influence increases with the number of people voting for a given candidate or ballot item. Thus, people with an interest in seeing a specific law enacted may attempt to solicit votes from others who agree that the law would be valuable. **Canvassing** is the door-to-door solicitation of signatures on a petition, contributions to a cause, or pledges of support. It is the

Canvassing Door-to-door solicitation of signatures on a petition, contributions to a campaign, or pledges of support.

EXHIBIT / 19.2
How Public Issues Develop

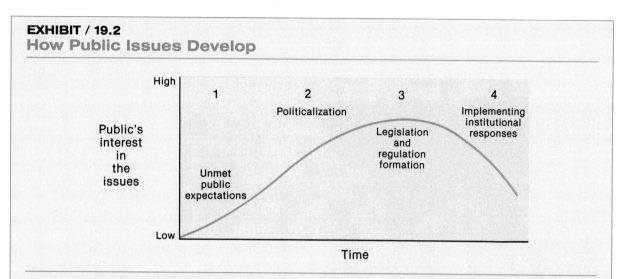

Source: Frederick, William F., Davis, Keith, and Post, James E., *Business and Society: Corporate Strategy, Public Policy, and Ethics,* 6th ed. (New York: McGraw-Hill, 1988). Originally presented in Post, James E., *Corporate Behavior and Social Change* (Reston, Va.: Reston Publishing, 1978).

concept of strength in numbers that makes interest groups one of society's most effective mechanisms of influence.

Special-interest groups in the United States are abundant and extremely diverse. Each interest group develops its own strategy for influencing other political actors. The success of its efforts depends on several factors: how well the group manages itself, the group's level of activity, its size (in terms of membership), its financial and other resources, the skill of its leadership, its social status, the presence or absence of competing organizations, and the attitudes of public officials.[9] For example, repeated attempts to pass the Equal Rights Amendment (ERA) on both the federal and state levels have failed. Despite the fact that the ERA's major supporters, such as the National Organization for Women (NOW), are well organized, well financed, and have an extensive membership, the ERA has not had the political support to be passed as a law. On the other hand, very small, underfinanced groups have sometimes been able to prevail on specific issues, as illustrated in The Inside View 19.2.

Business Issues

Businesses are also concerned about public issues such as environmental protection. Since environmentalists are extremely active and have been able to mobilize extensive support, almost no organization has been able to avoid responding to pressures from them. Thus, business is responding to public demands that operations be safe for both people and environments. If public pressure is leading to legislation or regulations, business will seek to influence the outcome or structure of the legislation. The establishment of corporate smoking policies, for example, has often been provoked by the threat of lawsuits brought on by nonsmokers; the record shows that the law is on the side of the nonsmokers.

In some cases, business will attempt to persuade lawmakers to structure legislation so it helps them produce products and services. Business's push for deregulation of various industries during the decade between 1975 and 1985 was one

You, Too, Can Be a Lawmaker

Although it is illegal to sell cigarettes to anyone under the age of 18, clearly children have easy access to cigarettes. Local anti-smoking campaigns are aimed at increasing the penalties for those who sell cigarettes to minors.

The job of making laws is not reserved just for elected officials. Draft laws are often prepared by advocacy groups as models for legislators to consider. Usually, the drafters of these models are experienced, politically-savvy professionals. Occasionally, they are regular Main-Street citizens. And once in a while, they may be kids like the seventh graders from a junior-senior high school in Sandwich, Massachusetts.

On October 4, 1985, thirty students from this Cape Cod community saw Gov. Michael Dukakis officially sign into law a piece of legislation of which they had been primary creators and sponsors. The story behind their effort is a reminder that the political process is both open to all citizens and responsive to the issues and concerns that people share.

These students had all been members of a health class taught by teacher Bill Sangster. During a lecture by Mr. Sangster on the hazards of smoking, students learned that there was a state law that prohibited the sale of cigarettes to anyone under the age of 18. The students were surprised because they knew that the law was not being enforced in their own community. The class decided to form an action group, Students Against Smoking (SAS), with the purpose of making their town a place that would be impossible for minors to buy cigarettes.

The students contacted a local elected official, Selectman Bruce Stanford, who suggested that the students draft a cigarette sales law for Sandwich and present it to the annual town meeting at which local laws are considered for adoption. From November through May, the students drummed up support for their proposal. TV interviews, newspaper coverage, and more than 1,000 signatures from local citizens lent support to the campaign. Although some teenage smokers and a few local merchants objected, the students presented their proposal at the town meeting and received both a standing ovation and adoption of the law.

Local success bred higher ambition, and SAS members set their sights on a state-wide sales ban on cigarette sales to minors. They persuaded a state senator and state representative to introduce a bill that was based on their original proposal. The students then set about lobbying for the legislation by contacting legislators and their home district constituents. The campaign had great success, and the Massachusetts legislature passed the bill and sent it to the governor for signature. As the students stood in the governor's office watching him sign the bill, they could not help but feel proud and excited at their success.

As the signing ceremony ended, reporters asked the students questions about their future. A few said they thought SAS should fight for a national law; a few said they were looking forward to summer vacation! Whatever the case, Mr. Sangster's class of 13- and 14-year-old students proved that committed people, whatever their age, can make a difference. ■

Source: "Law Makers—Not Law Breakers," *Good Housekeeping* (March 1987): 96.

such issue. The momentum for deregulation came largely from lobbying efforts by business leaders themselves in the mid-1970s. By 1980, it had become a rallying call of such political potency that Ronald Reagan used it as the core of his campaign platform. His success was attributable in part to his promise to "get government off the backs" of both business and the public.

The major ways business exerts influence are (1) through efforts to shape government policies, proposed legislation, and the actions of regulatory agencies, and (2) through efforts to influence the outcome of elections.

The most popular means of influencing government include lobbying, financial support through political action committee contributions, trade association representation, and correspondence. (See Exhibit 19.3.)

Lobbyists
Representatives hired to inform organizations of legislative developments and to influence legislation to protect the organizations' interests.

Hired representatives, or **lobbyists,** are used by large and small corporations alike to keep the companies abreast of legislative developments in local and national government and to voice the company's opinions in these arenas. On a broader scale, corporations may join **trade associations;** with the strength of greater numbers and the advantage of a centralized staff, these associations are significantly more effective than individual lobbyists in promoting the interests of an industry segment or group of organizations.

Trade associations
Groups formed by companies in the same industry to protect their interests and seek protection in numbers.

The Tobacco Institute is the trade association representing the interests of tobacco growers and cigarette manufacturers. It was formed in 1958 by several manufacturers and is now financed largely by R. J. Reynolds Tobacco Co., a subsidiary of RJR Nabisco, and Phillip Morris Co. Experts estimate that the association's annual budget exceeds $20 million.[10]

In addition, tobacco companies have contributed heavily to black and Latin political groups, such as the National Association for the Advancement of Colored People (NAACP) and the League of United Latin American Citizens. Because black and Latin minorities are the only segments of the population in which cigarette consumption is increasing, the tobacco companies argue that antismoking policies are discriminatory. Thus, tobacco interests urge groups like the NAACP to oppose the smoking restrictions.

EXHIBIT / 19.3
How Businesses Influence Government: Tools and Techniques of Political Action

Type of Activity	Percent of Companies Using this Technique	Effectiveness Rank (1 = highest)
Lobbying	78	1
Political action committees (campaign donations)	70	2
Correspondence (with elected officials)	89	3
Trade associations	70	N/A
Plant visits (for elective officials)	55	4
Visits to officials by top management	58	N/A

Source: Boston University Public Affairs Research Group, *Public Affairs Offices and Their Functions,* Boston University, 1981, 1987.

Political action committee (PAC) A group formed to solicit contributions and channel funds to political office seekers.

To influence the outcome of elections, businesses rely heavily on political action committees. A **political action committee (PAC)** is "an entity formed by a corporation, labor union, trade association, or membership organization, to accept voluntary contributions which are used on behalf of candidates for federal office, and for political committees."[11] Direct contributions by corporations to political candidates running for federal, and in some cases state, elections are prohibited by law. In the mid-1970s, however, an important court decision gave corporations the right to create and administer PACs to solicit contributions and channel the funds to those seeking political office.

The Federal Election Commission has established rules regarding the administration and functioning of these PACs. The Inside View 19.3 describes how PACs operate. The primary rule is that PACs are not allowed to give more than $5000 to any candidate in any election. However, the winner of the primary election may be given another $5000 for the general election. Of course, many loopholes exist. For example, as the rulings are worded, the spending limitations refer only to direct contributions. Therefore, during the elections of 1986 and 1988, PACs spent millions of dollars—indirectly—on television commercials, telephone banks, and mass mailings.

Business corporations are not the only organizations forming PACs. Though corporate PACs are the largest in number, they spend proportionately less than labor union and other types of PACs. For example, there are almost six times as many corporate PACs as labor PACs, but corporate PAC spending is only twice that of labor PACs. The sums of money contributed indicate that PACs are a significant tool of influence, although there is continuing debate on this point.[12] Some experts claim that PACs have now become tools of the representatives, rather than the other way around. "It used to be that PACs gave money in order to assure access. Now the candidates demand money as a price for access."[13] Clearly, each serves the purposes of the other.

Public Policy and the Public-Policy Process

Public policy A plan of action undertaken by government to achieve some broad purpose affecting a large segment of the citizenry.

Government, through the public-policy process, mediates the conflicts between business and society and enacts or implements policies to protect the rights and freedoms of each faction. Broadly defined, a **public policy** is a plan of action undertaken by government to achieve some broad purpose affecting a large segment of the citizenry.[14] In the form of a law, a rule or regulation, an executive order, or a judicial opinion and ruling, a public policy addresses and resolves the conflicting interests of all involved parties.

The public-policy process is a political process through which issues come to the attention of government, are argued for and against by various interested parties, are resolved one way or the other, and eventually are implemented as law or policy. The government's role is similar to that of corporations when they try to balance the interests of their stakeholders, except that the government's field of stakeholders is much larger and more complex. In addition, the government is subject to many more rules and restrictions in balancing these interests. The public-policy process is outlined in Exhibit 19.4.

Agenda Building   The public-policy agenda consists of the major issues or problems to which officials give serious attention and upon which they feel compelled to act.[15] Society will be more vocal about some issues than others: Issues of

How Political Action Committees Operate

Political Action Committees depend upon the ability to raise money. The Federal Election Commission Act (FECA) created detailed regulations for PACS to follow in their appeals for voluntary contributions.

UNIONS AND CORPORATIONS

For union and corporation employers soliciting from their employees, FECA requires that the employee be informed of the political purpose of the PAC and the right to refuse to contribute without any fear of reprisal. Corporations may solicit contributions only from administrative personnel, executive personnel, stockholders, and their families.

Unions are allowed to solicit contributions only from their members and their respective families. Both corporations and unions are allowed to solicit in writing or orally. No limitation has been placed on the number of solicitations that may be made each year. Corporation fund-raising methods must also be made available to labor unions. Corporations using payroll deductions, a check-off system, computer-addressed envelopes, or other use of corporate facilities for PAC fund-raising events must also make the same methods available to unions representing their employees.

TRADE ASSOCIATIONS

Trade associations must have prior approval from corporations to solicit administrative and executive personnel, families, and stockholders. Corporations may limit the number of solicitations that the trade association can make each year. Nonconnected PACs may solicit from anyone, at any time, through any vehicle.

PAC GROWTH

The FEC notes that the number of political action committees has increased. The following figures highlight PAC growth from the mid-1970s to the mid-1980s.

Type	1974	1986
Corporate	89	1,734
Labor	201	386
Trade/membership/health	318	707
Nonconnected	—	1,063
Cooperative	—	56
Corporation without stock	—	146
Total	608	4,092

Following are FEC figures for PAC contributions made January 1, 1985, through June 30, 1986, for the 1986 election.

Type	Senate	House
Corporate	$12,660,804	$17,447,197
Labor	4,291,542	12,107,593
Trade/membership/ health	6,001,945	13,621,265
Nonconnected	4,391,032	4,540,875
Cooperative	454,994	1,223,322
Corporation without stock	652,245	812,777
Total	$28,452,562	$49,753,029

Sources: "How PACs Operate," *Congressional Digest* (February 1987): 36–37. "Pac Scope," *Congressional Digest* (February 1987): 38.

environmental safety, product safety, equal rights for women and minorities, nuclear power and weapons reductions, and nonsmokers' rights have all been forced onto the government's agenda based on the extent of public pressure concerning them. Other issues have been raised and dismissed for lack of a broad consensus.

EXHIBIT / 19.4
The Public-Policy Process

Agenda building	An issue gets the attention of the government
↓	
Policy formulation	Individuals or groups take a position and fight for it
↓	
Policy decision	Government authorizes action
↓	
Policy implementation	Government enforces the policy
↓	
Policy evaluation	Judgments are made about the policy's effectiveness

Source: Frederick, William, Davis, Keith, and Post, James, *Business and Society: Corporate Strategy, Public Policy, and Ethics,* 6th ed. (New York: McGraw-Hill, 1988), p. 185.

Business also has pushed various issues onto the policy agenda through PACs and lobbies. Lobbying and pressure from the auto industry in the early 1980s resulted in tariffs and import fees to protect American producers from the influx of cheaper, high-quality Japanese and European imports. The steel industry was able to achieve the same result in the 1970s and renew it through the early 1990s. And again, not every interest group makes it to the political bargaining table.

Each year, factions from both business and society ask the government to respond to thousands of issues and problems; very few of these actually become topics of serious debate. Certain initiating factors must be present to push an item onto the agenda. These include:

1. A charismatic leader, as in the case of Ralph Nader's push for auto safety in the 1960s or Jesse Jackson's efforts to convince corporations to divest from South African operations in the 1980s.
2. A dramatic crisis, such as a toxic waste spill or oil spill such as the Exxon Valdez or a chemical leak such as that in Bhopal, India.
3. Interest group pressure on the part of society (e.g., for industrial safety) or business (e.g., for protection from foreign competition).
4. Media publicity; for example, when Vietnam veteran Brian Wilson, protesting munitions shipments to Central America, was struck by a naval train carrying weapons and lost his leg in September 1987, photos were on the front pages of newspapers across the country.
5. Political leadership, such as a high government official who personally pushes for a given policy. President Reagan, for example, long advocated deregulation and increased defense spending. President Bush declared he wanted to be known as the environmental president. He named William K. Reilly, a leading environmentalist, as head of the Environmental Protection Agency.

Policy Formulation   After an issue has received sufficient support and/or publicity and has been placed on the government's policy agenda, policy formulation begins. Interested groups take a position on a given issue and then try to persuade others to adopt their viewpoint in order to have the policy designed and implemented in their favor. If a consensus can easily be reached, the process is brief and policy can be constructed quickly, but if the various sides hold fast to their priorities, the debate may carry on for years.

Immigration reform was one such issue in the 1980s. Though there was a consensus that antiquated immigration laws needed to be overhauled, the issue was debated for over four years before a new policy was implemented. The major points of contention were the type and nature of penalties to be imposed on businesses that hired illegal aliens and whether to legalize the status of illegal aliens already in the country. The implications were far reaching in either case: Severe penalties would meet with resistance from the business community (especially in the Mexican border region); lax penalties would allow for the continued hiring and exploitation of aliens. If illegal aliens already living in the United States (for a given number of years) were made legal, millions of people would formally enter the work force. If not, millions of people would be deported or go into hiding.

Policy Decision At some point an appropriate government agency makes a policy decision authorizing, or failing to authorize, a course of action. At the end of each year, many bills "die" in Congress, while others are left to wait for future action. Policy decisions take the form of laws, executive orders, court rulings, or legislated regulations, but failure to act is also a policy decision because it results in an outcome that affects all the parties concerned. For example, the immigration bill finally signed in November 1986 contained an amnesty provision offering temporary residence status to some, but not all, of the 10 million illegal aliens living in the United States. Some could become citizens, but millions who arrived after that date could be forced to flee or go underground. However, if no bill had been passed, all of the aliens could have been forced to return to their homelands.

Interest groups are much less influential in this phase than prior to and after it. They can force an issue onto the agenda and argue the specifics of the policy, but they cannot determine whether, or when, the policy decision will be made. That decision is made by government leaders.

Policy Implementation Policies must be implemented to have a real effect; it is enforcement of the decision that brings results. However, there is always some ambiguity in the implementation process. For example, though a regulatory agency may be charged with inspecting plants, lab facilities, or mines, the agency itself, not the piece of legislation, may determine how many sites it visits and how frequently. The agency also may have broad discretionary power over thoroughness of inspections and severity of penalties.

Special-interest groups may influence the specifics of the outcome. In the case of environmental legislation, for example, a corporation may negotiate with a regulatory agency to gain extensions on the deadlines for compliance or the acceptable level or rate of the given standard. The Corporate Average Fuel Economy (CAFE) standards, enacted by Congress in 1975, provide one such example. After the oil crisis in 1973, the standards, which mandated increases in new-car miles-per-gallon (mpg) ratings, were implemented to promote energy conservation. Manufacturers were required to increase the ratings each year from 14 mpg, the average in 1978, to 27.5 mpg in 1985. As a result of this legislation, the mileage ratings for cars built in the United States almost doubled in less than a decade, and the owner of the average 1987 car paid roughly $500 less per year on fuel than the owner of the average 1975 car.[16]

However, not all automakers benefited from this regulation. In 1985 both General Motors and Ford missed the federally mandated mileage standard for the third straight year. Under the law they could have been fined $5 per car for each tenth of a mile by which they missed the CAFE standard, multiplied by the number of cars sold. These fines would cost Ford roughly $160 million and GM roughly $600 million. To escape the fines, they argued (through lobbyists) that shifts in consumer demand to larger, less fuel-efficient cars had made it impossible for the companies to survive if they complied with the standards. "We've designed smaller, more fuel-efficient cars," said GM's public affairs director, "but the public keeps buying big cars. The CAFE law has been superceded by the law of supply and demand."[17] Chrysler, on the other hand, lobbied for the enforcement of the original annual increases. As one Chrysler executive put it, the company changed almost its "entire product line in the midst of a recession at great expense and sacrifice" (roughly $4 billion), to produce a fleet that met the CAFE standards. If the standards were relaxed for Ford and GM, he said, the government "ironically penalizes those auto companies which have already paid the price."[18] Ford and GM successfully lobbied the Reagan administration, and the 1987 model standard was reduced to 26 mpg.

Policy Evaluation   Once a policy has been implemented, many people and groups assess its effects. As we saw in Chapter 3, a decision may have unintended as well as intended effects, and secondary as well as primary impacts. The same concept applies here; the public policy may achieve the results that were intended, but unintended and secondary effects may also result. For this reason, it is normal for those who have an interest in the outcome to review the results of the policy.

New results may rekindle the initial conflict or debate. If the policy has a disadvantageous side effect, those who argued against it in the beginning may come back to argue for its repeal or alteration. In this situation, those who initially fought for the policy may be tempted to minimize its shortcomings, or they may argue that it needs more time to achieve the intended results. Because they have put so much time, effort, and money into the cause, they may be unwilling to sacrifice it even to the most rational arguments of the opposition.

Even if major conflicts do not resurface, concerned people in and out of government will monitor the policy in terms of costs, benefits, and effectiveness. Cause-and-effect relationships of broad public policies, however, are difficult to determine. If a national antidrug campaign is waged for a year, and teenage drug use as well as drug-related crimes and deaths decline, a relationship between the cause of the policy and its effects can be assumed. But if the economy recovers from a recession after a tax cut is implemented by Congress, it is not so obvious whether the tax cut was responsible. Interpretations may differ and thereby stimulate another round of policy debate and action.

THE LEGAL ENVIRONMENT

The political process produces laws that guide and control managers' decisions. Political decisions are implemented through the legal process, or what has been called *the rule of law*. This phrase refers to the formal process of setting legal standards, communicating them to the public, and enforcing them through a process of judicial or court review. While there are some variations, there is a great similarity in the way governments formalize the rules and standards that govern the actions of business and other organizations. The legal environment, then, is this system of establishing and maintaining rule of law.

Sources of Law

Common law A body of customs and legal precedents built up over time.

The authority for government action in the United States comes from two basic sources: the common law and the Constitution. The common law predates American independence and the U.S. Constitution. Derived from English legal tradition, the **common law** is a body of customs and legal precedents built up over time through trial and error, experience, and court rulings. The common law gives judges and courts the authority to decide cases individually based on the principles built up over many years of earlier decisions. From the common law have come such principles as trial by jury, rights to and protection of property, and the enforcement of contracts. Laws forcing businesses to refrain from fraud and unscrupulous practices are a very old type of regulation supported by the common law.

The U.S. Constitution is the second source of law and the foundation of most modern legislation and lawmaking. Every law must pass the basic test: If it is not constitutional, it will not be upheld. Many older laws and regulations have in fact been overturned because it was successfully argued that they violated the principles of the Constitution.

The Constitution contains four important provisions that are the basis for laws controlling managers' actions: (1) the power to regulate interstate and foreign commerce, (2) the power to tax and spend, (3) the power to borrow, and (4) the power to promote the general welfare. The government is authorized to design and implement policy on virtually any issue involving business or the general welfare, and it is authorized to spend public or borrowed money in the process. The power of government to implement policies that are not connected to these basic provisions is limited. For example, the government may regulate the size and placement of exit doors in production plants, but not their color. The government can legislate levels of emissions or fuel economy standards for automobiles, but not the type of radio included or the pattern of the upholstery. Exit door and emission standards are related to the safety of workers and public health (general welfare), while door colors and upholstery patterns are not.

As shown in Exhibit 19.5, there are four specific instruments government uses to affect management's actions: statutes passed by a legislature, orders issued by executive officers or agencies, regulations issued by regulatory agencies of government, and decisions of courts and judicial bodies. In the United States, the fact that these instruments exist at both the federal and state levels make compliance by managers very complex. For example, a company such as McDonald's must deal with 51 different governments (federal and state), each with the power to issue statutes, executive orders, regulations, and court decisions. And, of course, this is not the full set of legal actors. Local communities also have the power to issue rules and legislation, as do foreign governments. Thus, a multinational company may have to deal with thousands of legal bodies.

The Impact of Law on Managers

The legal environment has two principal impacts on managers. First, the law empowers managers. Various kinds of laws, such as contract law, property law, and corporation law, create rights that are enforced by the courts. The ability to make contracts, own property, and exist as a corporation (which has unlimited life and can survive the death of its founders) are vital powers if organizations are to perform the function for which they were created.

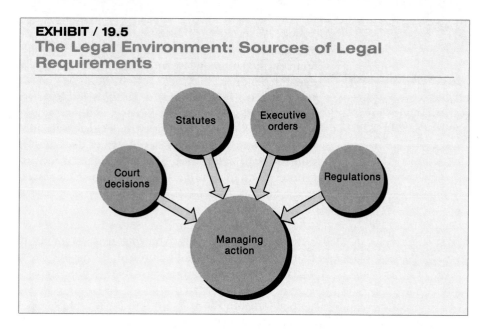

EXHIBIT / 19.5
The Legal Environment: Sources of Legal Requirements

The second impact of the law is in controlling managers. The social control of managers is exercised through legal requirements. The Inside View 19.4 provides examples of one area of control. Laws and regulations are the means societies use to define responsibilities and duties of people and organizations to one another. New laws and regulations are sometimes challenged by organizations. In such cases, courts determine their constitutionality.

Because society is affected in important ways by all aspects of organizational activity, activities are governed by laws or regulations. These can be divided into three categories: industry-specific, general social, and functional regulations.

Industry-Specific Regulations   Some of the earliest regulations, such as those drafted at the turn of the century to control the activities of the sugar, tobacco, and railroad industries, were industry-specific. Through combining into very large trusts, these economic giants abused their economic power. **Industry-specific regulations** were drafted to restrict price-setting, capital expansion, quality of services, customers served (or not served), and entry conditions for new competitors. Railroads, for example, were required to obtain permission from the Interstate Commerce Commission before raising shipping rates to customers.

Industry-specific regulations Laws passed to control the economic practices of certain industries.

Social Regulations   From time to time, the government has expanded its role to affect the social environment of all organizations. Four major areas are the target of most **social regulations:** pollution control, workplace health and safety, consumer protection, and equal employment opportunity. Almost any law addressing one of these issues applies to all industries. In every business in every industry, for example, job candidates cannot legally be denied equal employment opportunity because of race, religion, or sex, nor can employees be paid different salaries on the basis of race, religion, or sex.

Social regulations Laws passed to affect the social environment of most companies.

There has been much discussion about the costs of these regulations on industry. Enforcement agencies, such as the Environmental Protection Agency or the Occupational Safety and Health Administration, have not always considered the

Defense Contractor Fraud Exposed

Defense procurement funding by the Pentagon is so vast that it seems inevitable that some defense contractors will be tempted to commit bribery and other kinds of fraud.

In the late 1980s, numerous defense contractors were accused, tried, and convicted of schemes to defraud the U.S. government through overbilling for work performed, false billing for work not done, and direct and indirect bribery of former Defense Department officials. The pattern of fraud was so extensive in the defense industry that sweeping new rules were developed by the Defense Department and the Congress. One area of change involved the eligibility of companies to continue to do business with the federal government.

In October 1988, the Pentagon suspended the Sundstrand Corporation as a government contractor. The action followed the company's admission in court to procurement fraud. Sundstrand, which had 1987 revenues of $550 million, did more than 40 percent of its business with the U.S. government. A lengthy suspension could, therefore, have jeopardized well over $200 million of sales. The Pentagon indicated that the suspension would be "temporary" but that the precise duration would depend on the company's actions to ensure the integrity of its dealings with the government.

The court proceedings that led to Sundstrand's admission of guilt involved a criminal case in an Illinois federal court in which Sundstrand pleaded guilty to four criminal counts. The company agreed to pay more than $127 million in penalties as part of its punishment. At the time the penalties were handed down, the Sundstrand fraud case was "the largest military fraud in history."

According to the government auditor who led federal prosecutors to the case, the scheme was designed by upper- and middle-management Sundstrand executives. Because Sundstrand did so much defense business, its executives could successfully bid for competitive contracts by stating projected costs that were lower than they really expected. The added costs were then shifted to other contracts where the company either had no cost recovery cap or was operating on a cost-plus (i.e., incurred costs plus a percentage profit) basis. In such instances, the false billings were very difficult for auditors to trace. The company's guilty plea also included an admission that it had improperly billed the government for such personal expenses as baby-sitting costs, dog kennel fees, liquor, and country club memberships. Federal regulations do not allow taxpayer funds to be used for such purposes.

To restore itself as a government contractor, Sundstrand was forced not only to reimburse the government for the fraud but to fire or otherwise remove many of the managers who were involved in these schemes. Careers were damaged or destroyed, and several of the ringleaders actually faced criminal charges and possible jail sentences. In the end, not only the government and taxpayers lost. Honest employees at Sundstrand—of whom there were many thousands—were also damaged by the procurement fraud. Their jobs were put at risk, their personal reputations placed under a cloud, and their futures made uncertain. But lawyers who closely follow such corruption cases do not believe such tragic effects will stop procurement fraud. As long as the sums of money involved are so large, and the opportunities for fraud exist, many people will be tempted and a few will inevitably give in. No one has yet found a perfect way to manage that problem. ■

Sources: Cushman, John H., Jr., "Sundstrand Suspended by Pentagon," *New York Times,* October 20, 1988, p. D1; Glaberson, William, "Auditor Says Contractor Tried to Impede Search," *New York Times,* October 21, 1988, p. D4.

financial impact of their recommendations on the regulated firms or industries. Some organizations were unable to afford costly pollution control devices and were forced to either install them at the expense of overall profits, violate the law and risk severe penalties, or go out of business. Many governments now require that such costs be considered by the agency before issuing new regulations.

Functional regulations
Laws aimed at a specific area, such as minimum wage laws.

Functional Regulations **Functional regulations** are aimed at specific aspects or functions of business. Labor laws regulate employment practices for all types of businesses. Antitrust laws, which attempt to prevent monopolies, preserve competitive pricing, and protect consumers against unfair business practices, also apply to virtually all industries. Some functional regulations, such as those governing stock exchange and securities practices, focus on one industry (securities) but also affect all companies that wish to issue stocks or bonds to the public.

Legal Responsibilities of Organizations

While each organization will have a different mix of legal problems, several major areas of law concern nearly all organizations: product liability, antitrust law, employment and labor law, and securities law.

Product liability The responsibility a manufacturer has for the product it makes.

Product Liability An organization that sells products or services to customers must bear responsibility for their quality and performance: That is the concept of **product liability,** a principle of law that has been a part of the Anglo-American legal system for several hundred years. Today, the interests of customers are protected through laws, regulations (e.g., Consumer Product Safety Commission), and court decisions designed to place maximum responsibility on the producer, manufacturer, or seller of products. If a product or service is defective, the customer is normally entitled to recover damages to compensate for the injury. If the defect is especially serious, or the perpetrator seems particularly unscrupulous, the court may also award punitive damages.

Antitrust Law Antitrust law is designed to protect competitors against unreasonable behavior in the marketplace. The antitrust laws were first written in the late 1800s to attack the power of the oil, sugar, and tobacco trusts. The Sherman Act (1890) makes it illegal for an organization to be a monopoly or to engage in monopolization behavior toward others. Subsequent laws, such as the Clayton

Act (1914), Federal Trade Commission Act (1914), and Robinson Patman Act (1932), expanded the powers of the government and injured parties, primarily competitors, to fight anticompetitive behavior. One of the more noteworthy requirements is the right of an injured party who proves monopolization behavior occurred to receive damages three times greater than the actual damage done by the defendant. This treble-damages rule has led to some huge awards: In the late 1970s, for example, Berkey Photo sued Eastman Kodak, charging that Kodak had monopolized the amateur film and color paper markets. The jury found Kodak guilty and awarded Berkey $37.6 million for actual damages. This amount was then tripled to $112.8 million.[19] (Kodak later won an appeal in a higher court.)

Antitrust policy continues to evolve in the United States. The traditional concerns have been market structure (monopoly, oligopoly, competitive market) and market behavior (unfair, predatory, or other unreasonable conduct) that have injured competitors and the consumer interests that are served by competitive markets. More recently, antitrust experts have been concerned with the absolute size of the nation's largest corporations and the side effects of the wave of mergers, corporate takeovers, and leveraged buyouts (LBOs) that occurred in the past ten years.

Employment and Labor Law   The rights of employees have been a subject of legal definition and decision for 100 years. For the most part, labor laws have dealt with the rights of employees to form, join, and participate in labor unions. As in other areas of law, labor law has undergone several periods of great change. In the late 1800s, the first labor organizations were formed. In the 1930s, New Deal legislation gave unions new powers and required that employers bargain with unions that were duly elected to represent a company's employees. In the 1950s, the internal operations of unions were the subject of major reforms in the Taft-Hartley and, subsequently, the Landrum-Griffin acts.

More recently, the focus of labor and employment law has turned to such issues as equal employment opportunity for members of minority groups, women, the disabled, and other groups that have suffered from discrimination. During the 1970s, affirmative action programs were required by federal laws, and in some situations employment quotas were established. The 1980s saw a major reassessment of those affirmative action and quota laws by government agencies and the U.S. Supreme Court. The terms of these laws continue to reflect efforts to balance the interests of employers, current employees, and others who claim to have been disadvantaged by previous practices.

Securities Law   Following the collapse of financial markets during the Great Depression, the federal government moved to protect investors by creating a number of securities laws to set rules for the disclosure and reporting of financial information. Today, the Securities and Exchange Commission (SEC), together with the accounting profession, have established an elaborate network of rules and regulations covering the behavior of corporations and their managers. This system was reviewed extensively following the October 1987 stock market crash, but only minor adjustments were made. Unlike the crash of 1929, the crash of 1987 did not create a vast new set of laws.

False and misleading information is a particularly serious legal issue for organizations because it can lead investors to act in ways that might affect millions of dollars of a company's stock or bonds. It is especially important that managers take the highest degree of care not to erroneously report financial or other material information about the organization and not to use secret information through insider trading. In many companies, offices of investor relations have been designated as the only source through which financial information about the company is released. In some, only top management is allowed to make financial statements to the press or public.

Legal Responsibilities of Managers

Two broad categories of legal responsibilities affect managers as individuals. First, civil liabilities affect compliance with various statutes and regulations. The environmental protection field, for example, has laws that impose a fine on both the company and the manager in charge for illegal dumping of pollutants. Similar civil liabilities fall upon managers whose responsibility involves public health and safety. For example, a supermarket manager is responsible for the proper movement of dated inventory to prevent contaminated or dangerously old products from being consumed by the public.

Second, managers can be held criminally responsible for some actions. In most cases of corporate negligence, wrongdoing, or crime, the organization itself is charged and penalized. That was the case, for example, when E. F. Hutton & Co. pleaded guilty to 2000 counts in a check-kiting scheme and was fined $2 million. But when an employee collapsed and died on the job at Film Recovery Systems, Inc., near Chicago, the courts did not stop at slapping the company with a fine.

Film Recovery Systems (FRS) used a cyanide bath technique to extract silver from used X-ray and photographic film. The plant floor was filled with open vats of bubbling cyanide. Witnesses testified that on February 10, 1983, Polish immigrant Stefan Golab staggered from one of the tanks into the employee lunchroom, shaking violently and foaming from the mouth. He died shortly thereafter. An autopsy revealed that Golab had inhaled a lethal dose of cyanide. The defense attorneys claimed that Golab's death was a heart attack.

The judge rejected the heart attack defense and ruled that the executives had "knowingly created a strong probability of death"[20] and were thus guilty of murder. Golab spoke no English, and the only warning signs in the plant were in English and Spanish, so they were of no use to him. Witnesses testified that management had often seen workers get sick, was familiar with the symptoms and what caused them, and had in fact scraped the skull-and-crossbones insignia off several cyanide tanks.

Because the company was small, blame was easily traceable to the top management group. The president, plant manager, and a foreman were sentenced to 25 years in prison and fined $10,000 each. "This is not a case of taking a gun and shooting someone," said Judge Ronald J. P. Banks. "It is more like leaving a time bomb in an airport. The bomb kept ticking . . . until Stefan Golab died."[21]

Each of the legal areas mentioned in the preceding section has some potential personal responsibility for managers. Managers who have engaged in price fixing in violation of the antitrust laws, for example, have been fined and jailed. Others, like Ivan Boesky, who have violated securities laws by taking advantage of insider information about a company's plans have been forced to pay large penalties, give up their jobs, and face jail sentences.

Top management is responsible to the board of directors who, in turn, are elected by shareholders of a corporation. Occasionally, stockholders sue directors and top officers of the company for negligence. If the stockholders win, the directors and executives may be liable for many millions of dollars of damages to stockholders who lost money because the organization was improperly managed. There is every reason to believe that managers, like physicians, lawyers, and other professionals, will increasingly be held accountable for negligence in the way they practice their profession.

KEY POINTS

1 Throughout history, business and society have each had different priorities; business's primary interest has been to protect its right and ability to operate unrestricted in the free marketplace, while society's primary interests have been to protect jobs and the right to health, safety, and a clean environment. Government's role is to balance these interests and protect the rights and freedoms of all.

2 Society's main mechanisms for influencing government are through voting and interest group pressures. Business's primary mechanisms of influence include lobbyists and political action committees.

3 The interests of both business and society are addressed through the public-policy process. All important issues are placed on the public-policy agenda, where policy is formulated and argued for or against; a policy decision is made, the policy is implemented, and its effects are evaluated. Thus, the process may be cyclical.

4 The interests of all factions in a society are voiced in the political environment. Once a policy decision has been made, it is implemented in the legal environment through the executive, legislative, or judicial actions of the government.

5 The common law, which authorizes government inter-

vention in societal affairs for the purposes of fairness and justice, along with the United States Constitution, which is designed to protect the rights and freedoms of all people and factions in society, provide the legal basis for regulation.

6 The legislative branch of government, which includes the Congress, all state legislatures and city councils; the executive branch, including the president and Cabinet; and the judicial branch, including the Supreme Court and all other courts, are the three basic regulatory mechanisms in the American government system.

7 The three basic types of regulation are industry-specific regulations, which regulate the economic practices of specific industries; general social regulations, which regulate all business in terms of societal rights and protections; and functional regulations, which regulate specific aspects or functions of business and which may apply either within an industry or across many industries.

8 Managers have civil-law responsibilities to comply with regulations and laws to protect the health, safety, and welfare of stakeholders such as employees, customers, and the general public. Criminal liability for some actions is increasingly found in extreme cases of managerial neglect.

FOR DISCUSSION AND REVIEW

1. What factors have contributed to the success of interest groups in the Great American Smokeout?
2. Explain how the priorities of business might conflict with those of government, and give examples.
3. What channels do businesses have open to them to respond to public pressure and to help them represent themselves in government?
4. What sort of event or action might take an issue out of obscurity and push it into the public spotlight? Find a recent event and discuss its impact on business and society.

5. Since its introduction as a public issue in 1964, smoking has been evolving through the public-policy process. Where in the process is it at present? According to the process described in this chapter, what is the next step?
6. How do laws empower managers? How do laws control managers?
7. What are some of the major regulations and laws by which all managers must abide? Do you know of any recent examples where a manager has not complied with one of the laws?

KEY TERMS

Canvassing

Common law

Functional regulations

Industry-specific regulations

Lobbyists

Political action committee (PAC)

Product liability

Public policy

Social regulations

Trade associations

THE CONFERENCE TABLE: DISCUSSION CASE / 19.1

Acid Rain

Environmentalists and scientists argue that acid rain is produced by sulfur dioxide emitted from coal-burning plants and nitrogen oxide emitted from cars, while industrialists claim that the acidity levels in water and land are mainly influenced by natural processes.

Where acid rain comes from and how much damage it actually causes have been a topic of heated debate since at least 1980. Arguments on each side are equally feasible, and proponents of each are equally adamant. Environmentalists and scientists agree that acid rain is produced, at least to some degree, by sulfur dioxide emitted from coal-burning plants and by nitrogen oxide emitted from cars and trucks. Canadian officials argue that the United States, particularly the "rust belt" in the central northern states, produces most of these emissions, which are then carried hundreds of miles by the wind into Canadian territory, where they cause extensive environmental damage. According to Canadian government officials, acid rainfall generated largely in the United States has rendered some 14,000 lakes in eastern Canada and 13 salmon-bearing rivers in Nova Scotia "acid dead." One study also claimed that Canada's maple syrup industry was halved in some areas, due to the acid-rain-induced death or damage of maple trees.

Sources: "Industry Changes Acid-Rain Benefit Report Misleading," *Electrical World* (March 1987): 17; "Acid Rain: Bills Flood the New Congress," *Chemical and Engineering News,* January 26, 1987, p. 4; "Acid-Rain-Control Picture Exposes 'Ruinous' Costs," *Electrical World* (February 1987): 15; Shabecoff, Philip, "Byrd Opposes Legislation to Curb Pollution that Causes Acid Rain," *New York Times,* April 9, 1987, p. A22; Peterson, Cass R., "5 Lawmakers to Seek Action, not Research, on Acid Rain," *Washington Post,* April 4, 1987, p. A7; Wantuck, Mary-Margaret, "Little Is Plain About Acid Rain," *Nation's Business* (November 1984): 29–30; "Canada's Club," *Wall Street Journal,* April 3, 1987, p. 30; Brown, William M., "Mysteria About Acid Rain," *Fortune,* April 14, 1986, pp. 125–126; Ray, Mel, "Acid Rain and Public Health," *Electrical World* (March 1987): 8; "Sip, While the Sap Lasts," *Economist,* April 4, 1987, p. 63; Willey, Fay, et al., "Reagan and Mulroney: The Bloom Is off the Shamrock," *Newsweek,* April 6, 1987, pp. 34–35.

Some studies conducted in the United States have supported these claims. The National Research Council, for example, published a 500-page report in early 1986 that supported the claims that American power plants produce sulfurous emissions, that these are carried on the wind into Canada, and that they have contributed to the decay of hundreds of lakes on both sides of the U.S.-Canadian border. The Natural Resources Defense Council (NRDC) further argues that acid rain may hurt more than the natural environment. One NRDC official asserted that acid rain has accelerated the corrosion and wear of bridges, highways, buildings, and monuments; that it has substantially reduced visibility in the eastern United States; and that it has substantially elevated the levels of heavy metals in underground water sources. He also argued that acid rain might be tied to crop damage and premature death in humans. The president of the American Lung Association, in fact, declared that significant evidence exists to link acid rain to lung disease in both healthy and high-risk individuals.

There are equally strong arguments, however, claiming that land and water acidity levels are influenced more by nature than industry and that the relationship of industrial emissions either to acid rain or to environmental damage has not been solidly established. One expert argues that the acidity of a lake, for example, can vary with the time of day, the season, the amount of cloud cover, or the depth and distance from the shore at which the samples were taken. "As far as lakes are concerned," he argues, "the principal sources of damage are likely to be natural sources of acid." These might even include bird droppings. The 150 tons of droppings per year outweigh industrial sulfur dioxide emissions by roughly six to one. A scientific review panel commissioned by the Environmental Protection Agency reported that the Northeast was actually in a steady state. Of the few lakes in that region that showed a variation in acidity levels since 1930, the majority showed an increase in alkalinity, not acidity.

Policy on acid rain has struggled forward haltingly. Members of the House and Senate have begun taking positions on the issue, proposing various acid rain bills they hope to pass into law. One five-member team of senators and representatives announced in April 1987 that they would fight to defeat Reagan's $2.5 billion budget request, calling it a "bad environmental policy, bad budget policy, and bad foreign policy." Because it was earmarked for research rather than action, they considered it little more than "corporate welfare." They argued that technologies already existed that could, if forced into implementation, sufficiently combat the acid rain problem.

Meanwhile, many bills have been proposed by other members of Congress, and by the Bush administration. Some would mandate a decrease of 45 to 60 percent in sulfur dioxide emissions. One report indicated that under these proposals, utility rates in many major companies could increase from 20 to 50 percent. In West Virginia, for example, electricity rates would have to increase by 5 to 40 percent, depending on the proposal finally accepted. In addition, individual power companies would be affected differently. Monongahela Power Co. in West Virginia would face a 63 percent hike under one proposal, while Ohio Power (in the same state) would face a 40 percent increase. In either case, the six states of West Virginia, Ohio, Missouri, Indiana, Pennsylvania, and Illinois would be the most severely affected, having to meet between 55 and 60 percent (depending on the bill) of the national emissions reduction goals.

As new studies are released that argue that emissions are either more or less responsible for acid rain, that American emissions are either more or less responsible for acid rain in Canada, and that acid rain itself causes either more or less damage than previously argued, contenders line up on either side of the issue and ready themselves for battle. The highly influential Senate Democratic leader Robert C. Byrd, who represents West Virginia, argued strongly against strict proposals. Senator Stafford, who represents Vermont, a state that suffers from acid rain damage but whose power industry would be virtually unaffected by the enactment of tough new standards, argued strongly for passage of stricter measures. Byrd argued that jobs and community welfare are on the line while Stafford argued that human welfare and the environment are on the line. In the end, another form of generating electricity—namely, nuclear power—might appear more financially attractive. In this case, the debate would start over from the beginning. ■

DISCUSSION
QUESTIONS

1. What are society's interests in the acid rain issue? What are business's interests (keeping in mind that the power industry has a different interest than others)?
2. What type of regulation would either proposed bill be, and through what mechanism would it be enacted?
3. What will be the effects of the various proposed policies on constituents in both the business community and the larger society?

THE CONFERENCE TABLE: DISCUSSION CASE / 19.2

Drug Testing as Public Policy

More than one-quarter of the Fortune 500 companies test job applicants for drug use, and a few firms have begun testing their current employees. This crackdown has been foreseen for many years as the focus of the nationwide war on drug use has been slowly shifting from drug dealers to drug users. Studies indicate that almost one-fourth of the American population has tried marijuana, and 20 million people use it regularly. Between 5 million and 6 million people are regular cocaine users, and half a million are addicted to heroin.

Thus, authorities have decided that the problem can better be controlled by reducing demand than by attempting to control supply. The first and most logical or effective step, they have decided, is drug testing of workers.

Some of the arguments against drug testing center on employee rights versus employer rights. Those in favor of testing insist that the employer has the right to demand a drug-free work force because drug use reduces productivity and increases accidents and absenteeism. Opponents of testing, however, claim that is it both unconstitutional and inaccurate. Several studies have indicated that many legal and commonly used substances can produce positive results in drug testing. Among them are nasal sprays, poppy seeds, and the painkiller ibuprofen used in many over-the-counter aspirin substitutes. Some people even claim that the tests have a built-in racial bias due to the similarity between the chemical composition of the pigment melanin, found in high levels in blacks and Hispanics, and the active ingredient in marijuana. Finally, opponents claim that employers are not simply interested in performance but in enforcing their own brand of morality.

Source: Frederick, William, Davis, Keith, and Post, James, *Business and Society: Corporate Strategy, Public Policy, and Ethics,* 6th ed. (New York: McGraw-Hill, 1988), pp. 203–204.

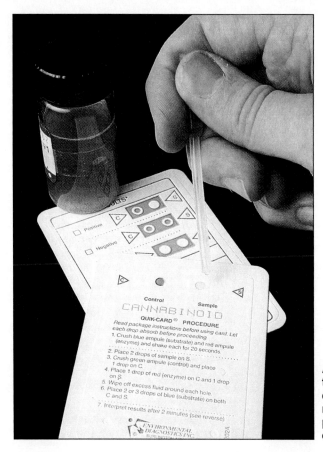

Arguments against drug testing focus on the conflict between the rights of individual employees and the rights of their employers.

These critics think that an employee should be able to smoke marijuana on a weekend, provided that he or she shows up and performs effectively on Monday morning.

More complex arguments are taking place on the national legislative level. Several issues are being debated, the most important being the gaps in coverage provided by the Fourth Amendment. The Bill of Rights restrains only the actions of government officials or those acting closely in concert with them. Thus, this amendment protects government employees from unreasonable searches and seizures but not private employees, because private employers have not been held subject to the strictures of the amendment. Another issue concerns the applicability of the term *administrative search* to drug testing. Administrative searches are those conducted regularly and indiscriminately for justifiable reasons, such as searches at airport departure gates. Some people claim that drug testing should not be included in this category because it is often conducted in the absence of valid suspicions and without overriding urgency (it certainly is not as urgent as preventing the presence of weapons or bombs on an airplane.) ■

DISCUSSION QUESTIONS

1. What is your personal position on drug testing as a public policy, and why?
2. What mechanisms of influence are available to the various parties interested in this issue, and which do you think are the most powerful?
3. What do you think the legal basis for such a policy would be, and which regulatory mechanism (or branch of government) do you think would be most likely to enact it?

20 Managing in the International Environment

FOCUS CASE / Ford Comes
Full Circle

**WHAT IS INTERNATIONAL
BUSINESS?**
Import-Export Trade
Portfolio Investment
Licensing and Management
Agreements
Direct Investment

**MULTINATIONAL CORPO-
RATIONS**
Development of Multination-
als
Multinationals Today

**MANAGING IN THE INTER-
NATIONAL ENVIRON-
MENT**
Economic Factors
Political and Legal Factors
Cultural Factors

**OPPORTUNITIES AND
RISKS**
Opportunities
Risks

The world has become a global community, and business is increasingly international. Very few large corporations operate in only one country today. Even small firms may get materials from foreign suppliers or have sales contracts with businesses in other countries. Since 1950, international trade and U.S. direct investment in foreign countries has increased dramatically. Today, many foreign businesses are investing directly in the United States. This explosion of activity between nations and peoples creates many new challenges, risks, and opportunities for managers.

▪ KEY QUESTIONS

As you study this chapter, try to answer the following key questions:

1 What is international business?
2 What are the different types of international business?
3 How did most modern multinational corporations get started and/or develop in the middle of this century?
4 What changes have recently occurred in the international environment to alter levels and patterns of international direct investment?
5 What opportunities cause many organizations to conduct business abroad?
6 What risks are involved in international business?
7 How can managers operate effectively in the international environment?

Focus Case

Ford Comes Full Circle

In an effort to tap world markets, Ford Motor Company joined forces with car producers in many countries to help them reach the American market.

On June 16, 1903, the Ford Motor Company was incorporated in Lansing, Michigan. In August, the sixth car Ford had ever built was shipped to a distributor in Canada. In September, Henry Ford placed one of his executives in charge of all marketing abroad and gave him 3000 catalogs "appropriate for introducing to the export trade in foreign countries the [Ford] business." And on October 15, 1903, Ford's stockholders urged the directors to "take the necessary steps to obtain foreign business." Thus, when the company was barely four months old, it had committed itself to selling its products around the world.

Ford was, however, a late arrival in both the international automobile market and the global business market. President Theodore Roosevelt had voiced the opinion of American business when he declared in April 1903, "as a nation, we stand in the very forefront in the giant international competition of the day." By 1900, 28 American-owned manufacturing plants were already located on the European continent, and one-third of American export trade was in manufactured goods (the rest was in agricultural and forest products). Automotive exports for the year ending June 1903, as reported by the magazine *Horseless Age,* were just over $1.2 million (roughly 1200 cars). R. E. Olds had sold the first American car abroad in 1893, and Cadillac, Pope, White, Waltham, and Locomobile had all beaten Ford to the starting gate.

However, Europeans were not particularly fond of American automobiles. Some with "narrow seats (and) hard springs . . . were simply torture machines." The 1902 Oldsmobile had a "coughing, spitting, one-cylinder engine that seemed to be suffering the final stages of shaking palsy." French cars, at that time, were in the highest demand by Europeans and wealthy vacationers from other continents. The only advantage that Ford had was advanced tooling and assembly line technology. Because the European firms produced each car individually and by hand, production levels were much lower and prices for both cars and replacement parts were, on the average, twice as high. Thus, the life of the American cars was longer and the upkeep cheaper.

With increases in quality, Ford's international sales increased, and in 1919, foreign and domestic sales topped one million, a level surpassing that of every other manufacturer. Ford came to virtually dominate the national *and* international markets for cars. Over the next 50 years, Ford opened operations in 45 countries on six continents. Typically, the company would branch into a new

Sources: This case was written by M. R. Poirier, based on the following sources: Wilkins, Mira, and Hill, Frank Ernest, *American Business Abroad: Ford on Six Continents* (Detroit: Wayne State University Press, 1964); Nevins, Allan, *Ford: The Times, the Man, the Company* (New York: Scribner, 1954); Emrich, Mary, "'Some Assembly—and Invention—Required' . . . ," *Manufacturing Systems* (March 1988): 26–29; "Ford-Mazda Car Is Shown," *New York Times,* February 11, 1988, p. D4.

country by exporting. If the market absorbed the cars, Ford would set up an assembly operation. Roughly one-quarter of the assembly operations were followed by manufacturing operations, though many of these have since been closed. During this time, Ford continued to upgrade its manufacturing processes, technology, product lines, even managerial talent. Plant location site decisions were made with much consideration for the benefits each might offer.

By the end of the 1950s, however, Ford and most other American automakers began to lose their dominant position in world markets. American automakers were essentially the victims of their own early advances. They had automated, at great cost, before their foreign competitors. They were hesitant to scrap these investments for the entirely new and more efficient processes introduced by the Europeans in the 1950s, processes that ironically were based on lessons learned directly from Henry Ford. By the late 1950s, production had become so expensive in the United States that models from Volkswagon, Renault, Fiat, and many other European automakers began to flood not only the American market but the world market. In 1957, for the first time since 1906, the value of automobile imports into the United States exceeded the value of exports.

The situation worsened in the 1960s and 1970s. The Japanese had developed production processes that were more efficient than those of either the Europeans or the Americans. Their low-cost production methods, higher quality, and better service records made it close to impossible for the Americans to compete in any but the high-price, luxury car market.

In the 1980s, the globalization of Ford came full circle. Ford reinstated quality as a top priority and reconsidered its strategies for tapping world markets. Instead of setting up plants in foreign countries merely to gain access to local markets, Ford and other American automakers were joining forces with producers in these countries to help them reach into the American market itself. Ford became a major importer of foreign-made cars and components, in addition to being an exporter of American cars. In 1988, Ford introduced a Japanese-American car called the Probe; its interior and exterior were designed by Ford, but the detailed engineering was done by Japan's Mazda Motor Corporation, which is 25 percent owned by Ford. The car was assembled in a plant Mazda built on the site of an old Ford factory in Flat Rock, Michigan.

In addition, Ford holds biannual technology exchange meetings during which representatives from each plant around the world share information on flexible manufacturing systems, body assembly, and even developments in durable paint. "If Europe comes up with a better way of doing something, it can be implemented into North America and Australia," says Morgan Whitney, director of the engineering and manufacturing staff at Ford's Robotics and Applications Consulting Center in Dearborn, Michigan. "The left hand knows what the right hand is doing." Ford's ultimate aim is to engineer a car or truck entirely in one place. Eighty to 90 percent of the car would be the same in all manufacturing locations around the world, with a small margin left over to handle differences required in each local market. With this achieved, Ford will go beyond being a multinational company; it will be a global manufacturer. ■

WHAT IS INTERNATIONAL BUSINESS?

International business
Financial and commercial
linkages between the peoples, businesses, and governments of two or more
countries.

A wealth of statistics have been published to illustrate how organizations are becoming involved in **international business,** trade and commercial transactions across national, geographic, or political boundaries. International trade has undergone explosive growth since the end of World War II, and nations have expanded trade to a point where we are truly becoming one closely integrated economy. American investment in other nations has increased steadily for over 40 years. Recently, foreign direct investment in the United States has increased rapidly as well. A broad range of financial and commercial linkages between the peoples, businesses, and governments of two or more countries has been established. Some common forms of international business today include import-export trade, portfolio investment, licensing and management agreements, direct investment, and multinational corporations. By understanding these linkages, we can better understand the challenges and opportunities managers face operating within the global community.

Import-Export Trade

Trade   The buying and
selling of goods, materials,
and services between
countries.

Imports   Goods, materials, and services a country
buys from other countries
and brings in.

Exports   Goods, materials, and services a country
makes or grows and sells
to other countries.

Trade is the buying and selling of goods, materials, and services between countries. **Imports** are goods, materials, or services one country buys from another country and brings in; **exports** are goods, materials, or services a country makes or grows and sells to another country. Ford's very first international business initiatives, for example, were in export trade, and each country Ford operated in after Canada was entered first through sales of automobiles. In the 1980s, however, Ford began to import not only parts for its automobiles, but whole cars from Japanese producers.

Managers' decisions about importing or exporting depend on many factors. The relative strengths of currencies have perhaps the broadest effect, making it more or less likely for all businesses in a country to import or export. For example, the weakening of the American dollar against foreign currencies—that is, the trend in which each unit of foreign currency was able to buy more and more American dollars—was credited with starting a surge of exports from the United States in the late 1980s. American goods simply became cheaper to foreign buyers. Since 1971, the United States has experienced a trade deficit (that is, it imported more than it exported) for every year but two. But the dollar dropped 50 percent in value between 1985 and 1988, and merchandise exports rose 19 percent throughout 1987 while imports increased 5 percent. Some economists predicted that the deficit would continue to decline and that there would be a surplus by 1991 or 1992. Countries whose currencies are essentially uncompetitive on the foreign exchange—mainly Third World countries—often engage in **countertrade,** which is the exchange of goods for goods rather than the purchase of goods for money.

Countertrade   The exchange of goods for goods
rather than the sale of
goods for currency.

Other factors also influence a manager's choice or ability to import or export. Managers in manufacturing companies usually import parts for their products if these parts are more cheaply obtained overseas. They may export their products if there is a large market for them in another country or if they bring a better price there. In some cases, managers may export a product that has been legislated out of the domestic market; that is, if domestic authorities determine that a product does not meet national health and safety standards, managers may export it to a country that has more relaxed standards. As we discussed in Chapter 18, however, this is not considered ethical business behavior.

Managers do not always have the option to import or export at will to realize economic advantages. To protect their national economies or various industries, governments may ban the import of goods or impose tariffs that make it uneconomical for an organization to sell its goods there. For example, South Korea maintained a ban on all car imports in the mid-1980s, making it impossible for Ford and other automakers to export cars to that country. When South Korea dropped the ban in 1988, Ford began to export Lincoln Continentals and Mercury Sables to that country. However, the tariffs, taxes, and fees Ford must pay to get the cars into the country force the prices of the cars up to $42,000 and $75,000, respectively, three times what they cost in the United States. These prices make it difficult for Ford to sell many of the cars in South Korea.

Relationships between governments have significant influence on what managers can trade with other countries. Consider trade relationships between the United States and two other countries: China and the Soviet Union. The United States traded with neither of these countries for decades in the middle of this century, because of their Communist socioeconomic systems. Then, in 1972, the Nixon-Brezhnev summit resulted in major grain and maritime trade agreements between the United States and the Soviet Union. In 1979, diplomatic relations were established in China. Since then, however, trade with China has continually increased, while trade with the Soviet Union peaked in 1976 and has dropped off through the 1980s.

This decline was mainly due to the strained relationship between the United States and the USSR. When the Soviets invaded Afghanistan, the United States responded with a grain embargo and boycotted the 1980 Moscow Olympic Games. The Soviets, in turn, boycotted the 1984 Olympic Games in Los Angeles. Exports of machinery and transportation equipment, goods considered particularly sensitive, were roughly one-sixth in 1984 what they were in 1976.[1] When the relationship between the USSR and the United States improved dramatically at the end of the Reagan administration, and the Soviets began their pullout of Afghanistan in 1988, President Reagan and Soviet General Secretary Gorbachev agreed to increase technological and commercial exchanges between the countries. This continued during the Bush administration.

Portfolio Investment

Portfolio investment
The purchase of stocks, bonds, or other securities in businesses in foreign countries in order to obtain interest, dividends, or capital gains.

Portfolio investment is a simple and limited form of international activity: It is the purchase of stocks, bonds, and other securities in businesses operating in and/or native to foreign countries for the purpose of obtaining interest, dividends, or capital gains. In other words, international portfolio investment amounts to managers from one organization buying an interest in an organization overseas and receiving a return on this investment. This activity helps protect against currency changes because assets are owned in a variety of nations. Such investments are often subject to extensive political and societal pressure, however. Organizations holding stock in businesses operating in countries that violate human rights have been under pressure to divest this stock since the late 1970s. Many argue that those holding the stock and receiving dividends were making money at the expense of other peoples' suffering. Student groups at several universities, for example, successfully convinced their boards of trustees to sell all stocks their universities held in businesses operating in South Africa, which maintains the segregationist policy of apartheid. As stockholders (such as universities) began to sell their stock in the organizations operating there, managers in these organizations were pressured to cease operating in South Africa. Many large corporations with huge holdings in South Africa eliminated or substantially reduced their direct investments there during the 1980s.

Licensing and Management Agreements

Licensing agreements
Agreements in which a licensor in one country contracts to provide technology, skills, or trademark rights to a licensee in another country so that the licensee can produce a product similar to that of the licensor.

Management agreements Agreements in which a licensor in one country agrees to provide management and direction for the licensee's enterprise in another country.

Licensing and management agreements are more participatory forms of involvement than portfolio investment. Under **licensing agreements,** managers in one company—the licensor—contract to provide technology, skills, and/or trademark rights to a company in another country—the licensee—so that the licensee can produce a product similar to that of the licensor. For example, Siltec Corporation of Menlo Park, California, licensed its silicon wafer technology to Lucky Advanced Materials, Inc., of Korea. Siltec received $4 million and royalty payments on future production.[2] Under **management agreements,** similarly, the licensor agrees to provide management and direction for the licensee's enterprise in another country. Licensing and management agreements came into great use in the 1970s. By 1977, in fact, the Commerce Department reported that the number of independent licenses exceeded that of fully or partly owned affiliates of U.S. companies.[3]

These arrangements became especially popular alternatives to direct investment in South Africa after public pressures demanded divestment. Corporations with plants or operations in South Africa in many cases sold them to the local managerial staff and/or set up agreements through which their products could still be produced or bought there. This satisfied the requirements of many managers of "socially responsible" portfolios.[4]

Direct Investment

Direct foreign investment Buying or owning of property or assets in another nation.

Turnkey projects Projects set up and managed by international enterprises, then turned over to local managers after completion.

Wholly owned subsidiaries Foreign operations in which multinationals hold 100 percent ownership.

Joint venture An agreement between two or more parties to share the costs and benefits of production.

Direct foreign investment involves buying or building a plant, factory, or resort in another nation. It is one of the most costly, resource-consuming types of international business. However, many managers consider the setting up and the risks of the undertaking worth the benefits—most importantly, cheaper labor and materials, even if the country is unstable. E. I. duPont de Nemours & Co., for example, had allocated between 16 and 17 percent of annual capital spending for overseas projects in the decade between 1975 and 1985. In 1986, it allocated 26 percent. "You get more bang for your bucks building overseas than in the U.S.," said Vice Chairman Richard E. Heckert. If a company can choose between building a plant in New Jersey and building one in Asia, "the plant will be built in Asia because the cost of capital is cheaper and so are materials."[5] The Inside View 20.1 illustrates some views of the location advantages of foreign sites.

There are several types of direct investment. **Turnkey projects** are set up and managed by international enterprises, then turned over to local managers after completion. The construction of dams, refineries, generators, or aqueducts are typical turnkey projects. **Wholly owned subsidiaries** are foreign operations in which multinationals hold 100 percent ownership. Such a subsidiary may or may not be in an industry related to that of the multinational. IBM, for example, owns 100 percent of roughly 100 subsidiaries in 40 countries, all of which are in the information systems and communications industries. Primerica (formerly American Can Company), on the other hand, originally engaged only in the manufacture of cans, now owns subsidiaries around the world in life insurance, mutual funds, mortgage banking, specialty retailing, and packaging.

Ford also has wholly owned auto production subsidiaries in several countries. Even Ford Motor Co. of Canada, Ltd. (91.8 percent owned by Ford Motor Co.) itself wholly owns subsidiaries in Australia and New Zealand. Some principal subsidiaries of Ford that are not auto production plants include Parker Chemical Co. in Japan; Ford Aerospace & Communications Corp. in Finland, Venezuela, and Australia; First Nationwide Financial Corp. & First Nationwide Savings in Mexico; Ford Motor Land Development Corp. in New Zealand; and Transcon Insurance Ltd., in Bermuda.

Some countries restrict the percentage of ownership by foreign firms. In such cases a popular alternative is the **joint venture,** in which two or more parties agree to share the costs and responsibilities of production. Joint ventures allow for the sharing of expertise and the realization of certain economies without demanding prohibitively heavy commitments or capital outlays from any of the participants. The auto industry especially favors this method of investment today.[6] The Inside View 20.2 gives examples of some options for dealing with these restrictions.

Highly industrialized countries are not the only ones engaged in joint ventures. Six members of the Union of Banana Exporting Countries in Latin America set up a venture called Comumbana in 1977 for the production, distribution, and international trade of bananas. In Africa, the countries of Ghana, Togo, and Benin set

Examples of Location Advantages for Foreign Business

Calgary in Alberta, Canada, with a long list of favorable characteristics, is one city that is very aggressively recruiting foreign businesses.

CALGARY, ALBERTA

Center of research and high-tech companies in western Canada; well-trained and educated work force; high quality of schooling; research facilities; available real estate for purchase or lease at competitive prices. Financial and tax inducements: lowest personal and corporate income taxes in Canada; no sales tax; favorable property taxes; research grants. Transportation: international airport; Canadian Pacific & Canadian National Railways; Trans-Canada & North/South highways. Attractions for employees: four-season activities including all amenities, recreational as well as cultural; professional sports; summer and winter recreational sports.

CHIHUAHUA, MEXICO

Facilities can be 100 percent owned by foreign companies; abundant, trainable labor; located 220 miles south of El Paso; offering shelter plan, regular in-bond industry-developed sites, world class industrial buildings for lease or purchase. Financial

and tax inducements: low Mexican minimum wage; no import taxes on equipment, raw materials brought into country under Maquiladora Program as long as they are eventually exported; U.S. duty paid only on value added to product in Mexico. Transportation: El Paso International Airport (220 miles); intercontinental highway network; national railroad system; two airlines in Chihuahua City. Attractions for employees: Sierra Madre Mountains, Mexico's Copper Canyon, Pacific coast beaches; all sports, ski resorts; three theaters, art center, museums, country club; national basketball team; amateur rodeos.

IRELAND

Availability of suitably skilled, educated work force; 30 percent plus return on electronics investments. Financial and tax inducements: 10 percent maximum corporate tax up to the year 2000; 45 percent maximum capital grants on buildings and equipment (60 percent maximum in underdeveloped areas); 100 percent training grants on approved programs; up to 50 percent support for approved R&D programs; low-cost financing schemes. Transportation: three international airports; regional airport network; excellent shipping facilities; comprehensive, efficient railroad; highway systems. Attractions for employees: moderate climate (low 35°F high 75°F); largest number of golf courses per capita in the world; many sports; broad range of cultural activities.

COLOMBO, SRI LANKA

Stable government; both major political parties favor foreign investment; low-cost, productive, educated labor; 85 percent literacy rate, modern infractructure; 100 percent foreign ownership; abundant training facilities; investments guaran-

teed by constitution and by U.S. Investment Protection Agreement. Financial and tax inducements: tax holiday up to 10 years, thereafter 2 to 5 percent tax on turnover for next 15 years; free repatriation of profits; no tax on remuneration of foreign personnel or on transfer of capital, proceeds of liquidation; duty-free imports, exports; unlimited equity holdings for foreign investors; free remittance of profits, dividends. Transportation: Colombo International Airport; free trade zone; port of Colombo; railroad, highway networks. Attractions for employees: tropical climate; modern, reasonably priced housing; free education from kindergarten through university; English widely spoken. ■

Source: "International Plant Sites," *Electronic Business,* May 15, 1985, pp. 131–162.

up a joint venture called Cimao for the exploitation of Togo's limestone deposits. In Asia, Indonesia, Malaysia, the Philippines, Thailand, and Singapore set up P.T. ASEAN Aceh Fertilizer in 1979 for the production and distribution of fertilizer and related chemicals.[7]

MULTINATIONAL CORPORATIONS

Multinational corporation A corporation engaged in several types of international business participation; each affiliate in each country is considered a separate enterprise whose purpose is to serve the local area.

Multinational corporations, or MNCs, usually incorporate all of the various types of international participation just discussed. A **multinational corporation** may invest in securities of foreign enterprises, import and export, set up licensing and management agreements for the production or sale of components or materials, and wholly or partly own plants or operations in foreign countries. When Ford first moved overseas, less than 30 American manufacturers had set up shop in Europe. This handful were the only multinationals world wide, and most of them were based in the United States and Europe. Today, the *Principal International Businesses Directory* lists 50,000 multinational companies in 133 countries.

Some writers differentiate between multinational corporations and global corporations. Multinational corporations consider each affiliate in each country a separate enterprise whose purpose is to serve the local area. Each subsidiary operates independently of the others, and they may be completely different enterprises.

Global corporation A corporation that engages almost exclusively in one type of business or produces one main product line but utilizes operations around the world to do so.

A **global corporation,** on the other hand, engages almost exclusively in one type of business, or produces one main product line, but utilizes operations around the world to do so. A global corporation might have component or unit production facilities in several different countries, as IBM and Ford do. The manufactured components are then shipped to assembly plants in other countries, and the assembled products might then be shipped to different market centers for finishing and distribution.

THE INSIDE VIEW / 20.2

Working Around India's Restrictions

A Colgate-Palmolive salesman in India. In order to continue producing and marketing toothpaste in India, Colgate agreed to sell a majority of shares in its Indian operation to local investors.

India's Foreign Exchange Regulation Act, or FERA, of 1983 restricts foreign equity participation in local operations to 40 percent. As in other countries, however, several exemptions can apply. If the company operates in high-priority industries that require "sophisticated technology," for example, or if it exports a "significant proportion" of output, officials may grant an exemption of up to 74 percent. And if the company exports its entire output, 100 percent foreign equity may be allowed. But intense negotiations between country managers and government regulators invariably precede extension of these exemptions.

India's rationale for regulating foreign investment this way is similar to that found elsewhere. The perceived economic benefits that flow from retaining more corporate earnings and the managerial control that presumably would follow a change in ownership are among the chief arguments for forced equity dilutions. In addition, such regulations respond to pressure from local competitors, who invoke nationalistic sentiment to support their claims on the government.

Managers compelled to reduce foreign equity holdings have at least four options: strict compliance, exit, negotiation, and preemptive action.

OPTION 1

Follow the letter of the law. Companies that sought to maintain existing operations typically sold a majority of their foreign shares to local investors and kept total equity constant. This strategy allowed Colgate-Palmolive (India) to continue producing and marketing a low-technology product line, toothpaste, for which local substitutes existed.

OPTION 2

Leave the country. As the widely publicized divestitures of IBM and Coca Cola illustrate, Indian local ownership requirements forced some companies to leave the country during the late 1970s. Still, exit was not the managers' first choice at any of these companies. Rather, the decision followed a long process of negotiation with government agencies.

OPTION 3

Negotiate under the law. For some multinationals, the equity dilution requirement became an opportunity to grow and diversify because their managers used it as a negotiating tool to raise funds, obtain government licenses, and win approval for new product lines.

Issuing fresh equity exclusively to local investors and leaving the absolute number of shares held by the parent constant was the most common dilution scheme. In this way, Purolator, Ciba-Geigy, and other multinationals used dilution to raise funds for expansion. Ciba-Geigy's dilution scheme, for example, increased the total equity

base of its subsidiary, Hindustan Ciba-Geigy, by 27 percent, to $17.7 million.

OPTION 4

Take preemptive action. Unlike the companies described so far, some multinationals initiated defensive strategies, such as preemptive diversification, phased "Indianization," and joint partnerships, well before FERA's final passage. Still others, like Cummins Engine, deflected political pressure by continuously updating their technology and bringing in valuable foreign exchange through exports. ■

Source: Encarnation, Dennis J., and Vachani, Sushil, "Foreign Ownership: When Hosts Change the Rules," *Harvard Business Review* (September–October 1985): 152–160.

Though there were relatively few multinational corporations even in the 1950s, multinational business has an ancient history. In 1100 B.C. the Phoenicians were trading with various Mediterranean countries. They exported cedar and pine from Lebanon, linen from territories north of Jerusalem, and metalwork, glass, wine, salt, and dried fish from other areas. In return for these goods, they received from African, Aegean, and western Mediterranean countries raw materials such as papyrus, ivory, silk, gold, silver, spices, horses, copper, iron, tin, and even ostrich eggs. They established a network of trading stations in this region, and even shared craft and manufacturing technologies. Over 2000 years later, Marco Polo was voyaging from that same area to the Far East in search of silks, spices, and other Oriental riches. In the fifteenth century, Christopher Columbus sailed in the opposite direction in search of the "West Indies," and brought with him cheap, manufactured merchandise "to relieve the aborigines of their gold."[8] Having landed in the New World quite by accident, early explorers established trading posts there, and these eventually grew into lively commercial centers.

Development of Multinationals

Early international business in the colonies consisted largely of trade rather than direct investments in foreign countries. America was still a colony itself, and manufacturing, which had been restricted under the British, spread rapidly after independence was won. Eli Whitney's manufacture of rifles with interchangeable parts started a revolution in American and world manufacturing in the early 1800s. By 1840, Colt revolvers were being sold in Europe. Yankee locks followed in a decade, and Waltham watches in 20 years more. Soon, American manufacturers began setting up shop abroad: Singer began producing sewing machines in Scotland in 1867, and Burroughs established a plant in England in 1896. Standard Oil, Eastman Kodak, American Radiator, National Cash Register, and Diamond Match all had operations in Europe before Ford was incorporated. In addition, more than 100 companies in Canada in 1900 were controlled by, or affiliated with, American firms. Diamond Match also held a controlling interest in a factory in Lima, Peru; Edison had a sales office in Buenos Aires; and Frazer & Company founded an importing office in Yokohama in 1867, through which the Edison electric system, the Baldwin locomotive, and many other American products were introduced to the Orient.

Many of today's multinationals arose from opportunities associated with the colonization of less developed countries (LDCs) before World War II.[9] Up to that time, these countries were characterized by farming populations that served the export and political interests of the colonial powers. As the LDCs achieved independence after the war, they tried to take over complete control of their resources, production facilities, and economy. Lack of experience and financing made this difficult or impossible in many cases, so multinationals would move in, stabilize and develop the area, and reap enormous profits from the inexpensive labor and materials.

Trade expanded rapidly after World War II. Many of the U.S. companies that had made direct manufacturing investments in the late 1800s expanded these into other developed nations. The greatest surge in the internationalization of American business came between the 1950s and the 1970s. Ford sales, for example, increased from $4.8 billion in the early 1950s to $8 billion in the early 1960s and to over $20 billion by 1970, primarily as a result of increases in international operations.

Direct investments in manufacturing were expanded first in Canada and Western Europe. Crude oil and petroleum operations were also undertaken in the Middle East and Africa, in such countries as Saudi Arabia, Iran, Kuwait, Libya, Nigeria, and Algeria. In addition, to protect themselves from trade barriers, American companies undertook manufacturing investments in Latin America and Asia. Initially, these manufacturing enterprises produced mostly standardized products, taking advantage of the large supply of low-cost, relatively unskilled labor. The complexity of these operations and the skills they required have been upgraded over time, as the multinationals have educated workers and built up local social infrastructures.

In the 1960s and 1970s, service industries began expanding overseas as well. Commercial banks, insurance companies, investment houses, accounting firms, advertising agencies, consulting firms, and market research firms began to set up offices in Western Europe, and they have since expanded to other continents. As service and manufacturing firms moved overseas, they brought with them valuable technology, management and business know-how, and training capabilities that have increased opportunities for both multinationals and host nations in many ways. In roughly three decades, U.S. multinationals became the third largest economy in the world, outranked only by the domestic economies of the United States and the Soviet Union. Exhibit 20.1 compares the income of several multinational firms to the gross national product of various countries.

U.S. firms were not the only ones making large investments in other countries. Western European firms, such as Unilever, Nestle, and Ciba-Geigy, had made significant manufacturing investments in other Western European nations since the late 1800s, and they expanded these before and after World War II. During the 1960s and 1970s, many of these multinationals began undertaking direct investments in the United States, particularly in chemical, pharmaceutical, and electrical equipment operations. Most of these investments followed a typical pattern:

EXHIBIT / 20.1

Comparison of Multinational's Sales to the GNPs of Various Countries

Company Sales 1987 (thousands)		Country Gross National Product 1987 (thousands)	
General Motors	$102,813,700	Thailand	$37,204,000
Exxon	69,888,000	Pakistan	35,831,000
Ford Motor	62,715,800	Sri Lanka	5,808,018
IBM	51,250,000	Paraguay	5,807,000
Mobil	44,866,000	Zimbabwe	5,791,814
General Electric	35,211,000	Honduras	3,359,500
AT&T	34,087,000	Nicaragua	4,479,402

Sources: "The Fortune 500 Largest U.S. Industrial Corporations," *Fortune,* April 27, 1987, pp. 364–365; *The European Yearbook (1987): A World Survey* (London: Europa Publications Limited, 1987).

---

distinctive innovation, followed by export, then by manufacturing and production in another country.[10] This pattern allowed European multinationals to circumvent actual or potential trade barriers.

Japanese firms also expanded overseas operations greatly after World War II, though expansion there started mainly with exports of textiles, consumer electronics, and automobiles. Trading firms initially set up branches in major metropolitan locations around the world, then Japanese industrials undertook direct investments in manufacturing in nearby Asian countries to protect their markets from trade restrictions. In the 1960s and 1970s, Japanese industrials such as Sony, Mitsubishi, and Honda began to set up plants in the United States in order to take advantage of the great demand for high-quality, differentiated products in the American market.

In recent years, Third World nations have been producing their own multinationals. These firms are typically much smaller than multinationals from developed countries, and they are designed to serve the smaller, local markets of the developing countries that host them. They generally use more labor-intensive manufacturing processes and have lower management and overhead costs. Based in such countries as Hong Kong, Brazil, Argentina, India, Korea, and Taiwan, these multinationals have been able to compete successfully with larger multinationals almost entirely on price.

Multinationals Today

The 1980s have seen the first turnaround in this explosion of foreign investment activity. While initially, many less developed countries felt that "a better life could be anticipated by emulating Western ways, which were largely introduced by multinationals,"[11] this sentiment was virtually reversed by the 1980s. Because LDC governments had been eager to attract multinationals in the 1950s and 1960s, they were extremely lenient in their regulations of these firms and they imposed almost no structural or behavioral restrictions. Thus, the multinationals were free to use (or abuse, as was often the case) local human and nonhuman resources and to show little regard for the local environment. Eventually, multinationals began to be viewed as threats to the economic and political independence of the host countries. In some cases, the LDCs rebelled, sometimes even nationalizing (taking over with or without compensation) the assets of the multinationals.

Increased restrictions by foreign governments, increased competition from Third World multinationals, and increased political and economic instability in the international environment have, together, greatly slowed the expansion in direct foreign investment worldwide. In addition, "when one realizes that [the multinationals'] environment-spanning boundary is so vast and complex that their management decisions must deal with an exhaustive number of strategic goals: maximization of profit, minimization of chances for losses and risk, thinking competitively, and devising alternatives and contingency plans to confront the changing market situation," the motivation to reinvest on national soil is understandable.[12] Exhibit 20.2 illustrates direct investment trends since the 1950s; the slowdown in U.S. direct investment abroad after 1980 is readily apparent, especially in comparison to foreign investment in the United States since then.

MANAGING IN THE INTERNATIONAL ENVIRONMENT

Because of the changing risks and opportunities of doing business abroad, managers must constantly be aware of the international environment. Multinationals must deal not only with a set of social, economic, legal, and political factors and stakeholders in the home nation, but with entirely different sets of these in each country of operation.

Economic Factors

There are vast economic imbalances in the world today. Economic growth rates differ widely from country to country; inflation is rampant in some areas, very low

---

EXHIBIT / 20.2

U.S.-Based Firms' Direct Investment in Foreign Countries and Foreign-Based Firms' Direct Investment in the United States

Based on Year-End Book Values in Billions of U.S. Dollars

	1950	1960	1970	1980	1985
U.S.-Based Firms in Foreign Countries					
Manufacturing	$ 3.8	$11.0	31.0	$89.0	$87.1
Petroleum	3.4	10.8	19.8	47.0	55.0
Other	4.6	10.0	24.7	77.5	109.6
Total	11.8	31.9	75.5	213.5	251.7
Foreign-Based Firms in the U.S.					
Manufacturing	N/A	2.6	6.1	24.1	60.8
Petroleum	N/A	1.2	3.0	12.3	28.1
Other	N/A	3.1	4.2	29.1	94.0
Total	N/A	6.1	13.3	65.5	183.0

*Note: N/A—not available.
Sources: Various issues of Survey of Current Business. See also Glickman, N.J. and Woodward, D.P., The New Competitors: How Foreign Investors Are Changing the U.S. Economy, New York: Basic Books, 1989.

in others. Some nations are considered highly developed, while others, including many LDCs, seem almost archaic by Western standards. People living a mile apart, separated only by a political border, sometimes live under completely different economic structures and may have widely different income levels and standards of living. This contrast is readily apparent in East and West Berlin, for example. In addition, the economic stability of various countries changes. An apparently stable economy might collapse very suddenly, or an unstable economy might be stabilized through a government policy or even a new government.

In very broad terms, there are two basic economic structures operating in the world today: free-market economies and centralized-planning economies. These correspond to the capitalist economies of America and most Western nations, and to the Communist systems of the Soviet Union and most Eastern Bloc countries, respectively. **Free-market economies** basically operate on principles of supply and demand, allowing business a great deal of autonomy. Government regulation does, however, temper this arrangement. In the 1930s, to help bring the United States out of the Great Depression, a great deal of social and economic legislation was passed which some argued bordered on socialism (a system falling between capitalism and communism in terms of government control of the economy).

Free-market economies Economies that operate on the principles of supply and demand.

Centralized-planning economies are planned and operated through a central governmental system. The government decides how much of what should be produced, where, made available to whom, and at what cost. In other words, the government makes virtually all the decisions that business makes in a free-market economy. Of course, just as most free-market economies are regulated and controlled to some extent for the benefit of society, many planned economies allow certain business freedoms, also for the benefit of society. Hungary, for example, is a Communist state in the Eastern Bloc that operates as a planned economy but allows citizens to engage in free enterprise after hours to supplement their own incomes and boost the economy.

Centralized-planning economies Economies planned and operated through a central governmental system.

International managers need skill in dealing with the variations in economic factors between nations. LDCs with weak economies may seek investors and offer strong incentives, but multinationals may be concerned about these nations' economic stability or support systems (utilities, transportation, and communications systems). A planned economy might contain a large market, but operating restrictions might be too severe to make an investment pay off. Managers have to consider a wide variety of factors in making every location, product, or market decision in the international environment.

Political and Legal Factors

Just as economic conditions vary greatly between countries, so too do political and legal conditions. Some governments are hostile toward foreign investors, some are eager to have them. Some governments are stable, some unstable. Some are highly efficient, others are overly bureaucratic and inefficient, or they may be newly installed and still in the process of implementing basic policies. Though one might break down world legal structures into two political extremes—totalitarian states, allowing no public input into decision making, and democratic states, theoretically ruled by the public—the variety of legal and political structures is far too vast to define here.

The complexity of the situation poses two major problems for multinationals: First, legal and political aspects of the environment are highly volatile, that is, they are always changing. Thus, strategic and long-range planning require contingency planning as well. Complete turnarounds in political structure are common enough and costly enough (e.g., China in 1989) to make managers think very carefully about where to locate their operations and how to limit the extent of their investment and risk. Second, because multinationals are expected to act within the laws of host countries, a multinational with branches or operations in many countries must juggle each operation so that it conforms to the host nation's laws while at the same time conforming to the home nation's laws.[13]

The Foreign Corrupt Practices Act   Several mechanisms have been developed as guidelines to help organizations conform to a number of potentially conflicting legal systems simultaneously. The *Foreign Corrupt Practices Act* for example, regulates payments made to foreign agents or officials. At one time, the bribery of government officials in foreign countries was a common practice to gain business favors or privileges. Though bribery is now illegal in the United States, in many other countries it is a normal part of business interaction. However, bribery sometimes gave certain firms an unfair competitive edge over others and was generally considered unethical. Thus, to protect the right of all firms to a fair market, and also to protect them from prosecution in the event of extortion or other forced illegal behavior, Congress passed the Foreign Corrupt Practices Act in 1977. It has the following provisions, which apply even if a payment is legal in the nation where it is made:

- It is a criminal offense for a firm to make payments to a foreign government official, political party, party official, or candidate for political office to secure or retain business in another nation.
- Sales commissions to independent agents are illegal if the business has knowledge that any part of the commission is being passed to foreign officials.
- Government employees "whose duties are essentially ministerial or clerical" are excluded, so expediting payments to persons such as customs agents and bureaucrats is permitted.

OECD Guidelines for Multinational Enterprises   The Foreign Corrupt Practices Act is America's major legislated action regarding the conduct of business in the international environment. However, other mechanisms have been developed by outside organizations for the same purposes. Though it was widely agreed that the expansion of multinational business in the 1950s and 1960s had brought many benefits to developing nations, many later became concerned about the power these multinationals had accrued. In the 1970s many countries began to fear that the explosion of multinational business might result in the loss of national control or could undermine established economic, political, and social values and structures.

In 1976, based on these concerns, the 24 member countries of the Organization for Economic Cooperation and Development (OECD) set forth a list of guidelines that could be followed voluntarily by the multinational enterprises operating within their boundaries. The general policies of the *OECD Guidelines for Multinational Enterprises* are listed in The Inside View 20.3, but the guidelines also address specific areas of business, including disclosure of information, competition, financing, taxation, employment, industrial relations, and science and technology. The United States supports the OECD guidelines.

General Policies of the OECD Guidelines

Enterprises should:

1. Take fully into account established general policy objectives of the member countries in which they operate.
2. In particular, give due consideration to those countries' aims and priorities with regard to economic and social progress, including industrial and regional development, the protection of the environment and consumer interest, the creation of employment opportunities, the promotion of innovation, and the transfer of technology.
3. While observing their legal obligations concerning information, supply their entities with supplementary information the latter may need in order to meet requests by the authorities of the countries in which those entities are located for information relevant to the activities of those entities, taking into account legitimate requirements of business confidentiality.
4. Favor close cooperation with the local community and business interest.

5. Allow their component entities freedom to develop their activities and to exploit their competitive advantage in domestic and foreign markets, consistent with the need for specialization and sound commercial practice.
6. When filling responsible posts in each country of operation, take due account of individual qualifications without discrimination as to nationality, subject to particular national requirements in this respect.
7. Not render—and they should not be solicited or expected to render—any bribe or other improper benefit, direct or indirect, to any public servant or holder of public office.
8. Unless legally permissible, not make contributions to candidates for public office or to political parties of other political organizations.
9. Abstain from any improper involvement in local political activities. ■

Source: "OECD Guidelines for Multinational Firms Remain Relevant After Ten Years," *Business America*, September 1, 1986, pp. 11–14.

Cultural Factors

Cultural factors are the most difficult to define, and their influence on managers in multinational organizations is equally difficult to pinpoint. Culture encompasses morals, ethics, beliefs, customs, values, arts, and even knowledge and history. Managers, in order to operate effectively in any country, must understand and respect the culture of the society. This can be especially challenging to managers charged with directing a staff of people who may look at the world in a completely different light. The same set of methods for motivating, rewarding, and managing people will not be effective in every country.

For most managers, the greatest challenge associated with international business activity is dealing with the cultural differences among nations and different parts of the world. Being a manager in Tokyo is very different from being a manager in Brussels. Language, history, ethics, values, beliefs, arts, and so forth, are very diverse. Managers and their families may find new surroundings to be quite interesting but also quite challenging. Little things such as customs and holidays are magnified by different types of food, educational systems, and cultural beliefs.

Geert Hofstede, of the Netherlands, has spent many years studying the cultural factors that define individual nations.[14] Dr. Hofstede has emphasized the importance of national values as a society's cultural preferences. There are four dimensions to these national values that distinguish one nation from all others:

1. *Power Distance*   "All societies are unequal, but some are more unequal than others," according to Hofstede. Power distance defines the extent to which the less powerful person in society accepts inequality in power and considers it normal.

2. *Individualism Versus Collectivism*   This refers to who bears primary responsibility for the welfare of the person: the individual or the entire community (collectively). In some nations, the degree of social integration is relatively low, emphasizing individual responsibility; in others, the integration is relatively high, emphasizing collective responsibility for others.

3. *Masculinity Versus Femininity*   Hofstede says that masculine cultures develop distinct social roles for men and women in which the latter tend to care for children, home, and spouse. In feminine cultures, social roles are relatively overlapping, and material success and assertiveness are not as dominant as in masculine cultures.

4. *Uncertainty Avoidance*   This factor refers to the tendency of national culture to try to avoid uncertainty and unpredictability through such devices as strict social and moral codes. Cultures with a weak uncertainty avoidance are relatively tolerant, accepting personal risk, and somewhat unemotional and aggressive.

Exhibit 20.3 illustrates how Hofstede clusters national cultures along some of these dimensions. National cultures were scored along the dimensions of power distance and individualism, then plotted on the graph. Not surprisingly, the United States is clustered with Canada, Great Britain, New Zealand, and the Netherlands, where there is a relatively small power distance and a high degree of individualism. In contrast, nations such as Guatemala, Panama, South Korea, and Taiwan are grouped in clusters where there is a relatively large power distance and a relatively low degree of individualism. It is not surprising, then, that families that are moved from the United States to another nation find it somewhat easier to adapt to cultural norms in Great Britain, Australia, or Canada than in Korea, Taiwan, or Panama. Companies that frequently move their managers from one nation to another must be very conscious of the need to accustom their managers to different cultural settings and also of the difficulty that can accompany those transfers and relocations.

In addition to differences in values, managers operating in the international environment have to face many other differences in culture; some of the most common are attitudes toward time, space, and language.

In the United States, time and space are highly valued resources. We use expressions such as "Time is of the essence" and rigorously schedule our days. In other countries, time is much less regimented, and daily activities are much more loosely scheduled. In some Eastern and South American cultures, for example, it is normal to show up for a meeting one or two hours after its scheduled time, whereas in others it is a great insult to be late for an appointment.

Space is also a carefully metered resource in the United States. Americans who have never met or who are engaged in formal relations typically do not stand or sit closer than two feet apart. An American's concept of personal space is, essentially, a circle two feet in diameter that surrounds him or her at all times, and into

Exhibit 20.3
Comparison of National Cultures

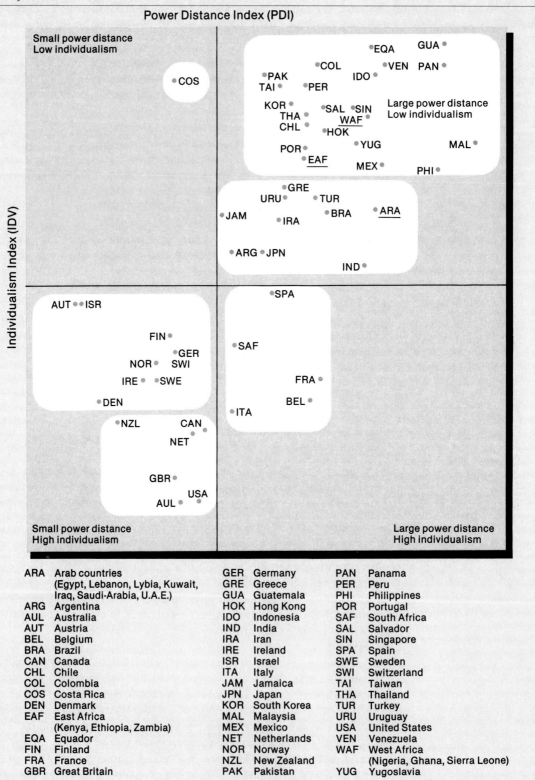

Power Distance Index (PDI)

Small power distance
Low individualism

COS

EQA GUA
COL VEN PAN
PAK IDO
TAI PER
KOR SAL SIN
THA WAF
CHL HOK
POR YUG MAL
EAF MEX PHI

Large power distance
Low individualism

GRE
URU TUR
JAM BRA ARA
IRA
ARG JPN
IND

Individualism Index (IDV)

AUT ISR
FIN
GER
NOR SWI
IRE SWE
DEN
NZL CAN
NET
GBR USA
AUL

SPA
SAF
FRA
BEL
ITA

Small power distance
High individualism

Large power distance
High individualism

ARA	Arab countries (Egypt, Lebanon, Lybia, Kuwait, Iraq, Saudi-Arabia, U.A.E.)	
ARG	Argentina	
AUL	Australia	
AUT	Austria	
BEL	Belgium	
BRA	Brazil	
CAN	Canada	
CHL	Chile	
COL	Colombia	
COS	Costa Rica	
DEN	Denmark	
EAF	East Africa (Kenya, Ethiopia, Zambia)	
EQA	Equador	
FIN	Finland	
FRA	France	
GBR	Great Britain	
GER	Germany	
GRE	Greece	
GUA	Guatemala	
HOK	Hong Kong	
IDO	Indonesia	
IND	India	
IRA	Iran	
IRE	Ireland	
ISR	Israel	
ITA	Italy	
JAM	Jamaica	
JPN	Japan	
KOR	South Korea	
MAL	Malaysia	
MEX	Mexico	
NET	Netherlands	
NOR	Norway	
NZL	New Zealand	
PAK	Pakistan	
PAN	Panama	
PER	Peru	
PHI	Philippines	
POR	Portugal	
SAF	South Africa	
SAL	Salvador	
SIN	Singapore	
SPA	Spain	
SWE	Sweden	
SWI	Switzerland	
TAI	Taiwan	
THA	Thailand	
TUR	Turkey	
URU	Uruguay	
USA	United States	
VEN	Venezuela	
WAF	West Africa (Nigeria, Ghana, Sierra Leone)	
YUG	Yugoslavia	

Source: G. Hofstede, "The Interaction Between National and Organizational Value Systems," *Journal of Management Studies* 22 (1985) pp. 347–357.

which only a chosen few may venture. In France and many European countries, however, "personal space" is a much smaller circle. Americans traveling in these areas have often been surprised to have people speak to them virtually inches from their noses.

Language barriers are an obvious problem. Even when expatriate managers have learned the language of the country to which they are assigned, nuances still exist that the foreigner may not understand. Nonverbal, or body, language also differs between cultures. As we illustrated in Chapter 12, managers must be very careful of the gestures they use to make a point. A thumbs up works very well in America, but it could cause an international incident if used in certain other countries.

These variations in culture provide constant challenges for managers, especially in the area of human resource management. To be effective, managers must keep abreast of changes in all aspects of the international environment: economic, political/legal, and cultural. Only by doing so can they minimize the risks and maximize the opportunities of conducting business beyond their own shores.

OPPORTUNITIES AND RISKS

The global community has an endless variety of factions, host nations, home nations, foreign and domestic competitors, international organizations, financial institutions, labor unions, consumers, environmentalists, and many others. Many benefits and opportunities exist, but there are also substantial risks. Some risks may be controlled or minimized, but others must be taken.

Opportunities

Operating domestically is relatively simple and uncomplicated in comparison to operating internationally. Risks are fewer, the environment is more stable, the culture and language are familiar, the currency is uniform, and the government is basically friendly, predictable, and subject to a certain amount of influence. Nonetheless, many managers undertake international operations for a variety of reasons.

Growth Certain domestic conditions may make it necessary for organizations to expand overseas to continue growing: Higher taxes, slower economic growth, burdensome legislation, and saturated markets are some examples. In other countries, managers might find more favorable tax structures, untapped markets, or fewer operating restrictions. When American business first began expanding overseas, environmental pressure was one of the main reasons: Less affluent countries often accepted operations or even products that affluent countries refused due to environmental or safety hazards. Ford and many other automakers benefited from the relaxed emissions standards in foreign countries after these were made stricter in the United States. In recent years, however LDCs have become much less lenient about these issues, especially in the wake of the Bhopal tragedy. Thus, if managers are looking to circumvent domestic regulations or operating restrictions, they must shop around considerably more than in the past.

Increased Economic Efficiency Desires for lower production costs and the benefits of vertical integration might also lead managers overseas. Most companies find it less expensive to produce anything, from watches to appliances to automobiles, abroad. Both labor and materials still tend to be cheaper in developing nations than elsewhere in the world. In addition, economic efficiency can sometimes be increased through international vertical integration. A company with oil-drilling operations in one country might set up refining and distribution operations in another country to get access to its market for refined products. A food processing operation might set up plants in countries around the world to save shipping and distribution costs. The costs of shipping canned or bottled Coca-Cola, for example, exceed the costs of production. Thus, Coca Cola Co. has syrup and/or concentrate manufacturing plants in 33 countries and offices or other operations in almost 150.

Competitive Pressures   As U.S. auto manufacturers painfully learned, many foreign producers, especially the Japanese, have been able to produce higher-quality cars at lower cost than Americans. To be competitive, U.S. manufacturers were essentially forced to go overseas with either independent direct investments or joint ventures. Some domestic manufacturers, not necessarily in the auto industry, even went so far as to purchase foreign firms to eliminate them as competitors.

Attain Larger Shares of Foreign Markets   Similarly, by locating in foreign countries, many managers are able to attain a market share much larger than would be available if they only traded with that country or if they only engaged in other limited forms of international investment. Moreover, by being the first to locate in a foreign country, a multinational might be able to prevent others from gaining a significant share of the local market. Some companies have actually been forced to shift from trade to manufacture in a country to avoid prohibitive tariffs and import quotas. It was for this reason that Japanese auto manufacturers first began locating in the United States: Import quotas imposed by the U.S. government in the early 1980s made it an economic and competitive necessity.

Incentives from Host Countries   Some countries eagerly recruit foreign organizations for the developmental benefits they can bring. These countries might offer tax breaks, low-cost loans for construction of plants, or even free use of land. In the 1950s and 1960s, incentives were often offered virtually without restriction. Currently, however, many countries temper their offerings with stipulations or conditions that will protect their environment or certain groups of local stakeholders. For example, a government might award licenses, permits, or privileges to only those companies that engage in behaviors considered desirable by the host nation.[15]

Ford's experience in the USSR in the early 1970s is an interesting example of the use of incentives by foreign nations. The Kama Motor Works was to use $600 million in U.S. equipment and multiply U.S. exports to the Soviet Union by nearly tenfold. Ford was offered a contract to produce 150,000 vehicles per year and was offered the opportunity to plan, supervise, and outfit the production plant. In addition, the Soviet Union would export finished trucks for sale abroad by Ford. However, due to political conflicts between the Soviets and U.S. governments, these incentives were never utilized.

Risks

If the opportunities illustrated above were all there was to international business, every manager would choose to locate on foreign soil. This is, of course, not the case. In addition to added complexity, there are a number of significant risks and problems that can accompany international operations.

Political Risk   Political risk encompasses a large number of potential hazards. Domestic instability, foreign conflict, and unstable political and economic climates are the major factors. **Political risk** is the probability that political events and actions, especially new government policies or the institution of an entirely new government, will endanger or negatively affect business investments in a given country.[16] These policies may include increased taxation as well as restrictions on imports and exports, on the hiring or employment of expatriate personnel, on repatriation of capital and earnings, and even on transfers of technology and information. In the most serious cases, organizations might find their assets entirely frozen or seized, virtually overnight, in the event of a violent change in government or laws.

American businesses have lost significant sums to nationalization in the past (e.g., $1.5 billion between 1959 and 1960 to Cuba alone[17]). Ford's Cuban credit company, known as Credesco, was nationalized by Fidel Castro in October 1960. Fortunately for Ford, the assets held in this subsidiary were minimal, and Ford's losses were not substantial. As the threat of nationalization continued into the 1980s, political-risk insurance became both very popular and very expensive. The dollar volume of this coverage, which reimburses companies for the value of assets lost in conflict or nationalization, grew 50 percent annually between 1980 and 1984, then leveled off. After Lloyds of London paid out $20 million in 1984 when Sudan failed to pay off a debt, insurance companies cut back on the amount of political-risk coverage they were willing to write by 30 to 40 percent.[18] Thus instability in the international environment, coupled with the difficulty of acquiring insurance coverage against it, are great concerns of multinational managers today.

Other Risks and Problems   Currently two other risks to international business have become prominent: terrorism and the trend toward foreign governments demanding percentages of ownership and/or control in "visiting" businesses. Terrorism has become a growing factor in location decisions of multinationals. Several areas of the world have already been rendered "off limits" since World War II, including most Eastern Bloc countries, Cuba, Libya, Iran, Nicaragua, and others. In addition, there are many other countries that "have such inept or corrupt governments that they cannot or will not preserve law and order."[19] Terrorism makes such countries far too risky to operate in. Of the 200 nations recognized by the United Nations, "fewer than 50 are currently secure and stable enough to receive serious and consistent consideration as investment locations by free-enterprise ventures."[20]

In those countries considered feasible for investments, there is another difficulty: More and more governments are demanding increasing percentages of control or ownership in multinationals. These demands will leave few multinationals unaffected. Whether the company under duress is Unilever in Canada or Coca Cola in India, the story remains the same. Governments of every political stripe are vying for greater domestic ownership of foreign operations within their borders.[21] India is perhaps at the top of the list in this respect.

Short of major upheavals or political turmoil, there are many other risks for multinational businesses. In some cases, host governments may favor local organi-

Political risk   The probability that political events and actions will endanger or negatively affect business investments in a given country.

zations over multinationals, allowing the former competitive or economic advantages. In addition, even in relatively stable economic environments, currency exchange rates may fluctuate, costing (or earning) multinationals millions of dollars. Other problems include low skill levels of employees in LDCs and activism by home country citizens opposed to a multinational's operations in a given country or situation.

KEY POINTS

1 International business is the financial and commercial linkage between the peoples, businesses, and governments of two or more countries.

2 International business can take the form of trade, portfolio investment, import-export trade, licensing and management agreements, direct investments, or multinational corporations.

3 The greatest surge in international direct investment on the part of multinational corporations was between 1950 and 1970, when new and established multinationals responded to opportunities in newly liberated developing countries.

4 Freedom allowed to multinationals by LDCs in the 1950s and 1960s was often abused; by the late 1970s, many LDC governments were imposing restrictions on foreign investments. Increased risks in the environment caused a downturn in direct international investment.

5 Opportunities for growth, increased economic efficiency, competitive advantage, access to foreign markets, and incentives from host countries have led many organizations to conduct business abroad.

6 Political risk, including domestic instability, foreign conflict, and unstable political and economic climate, is a major risk to international business. Other risks include terrorism, increasing trends toward host country control or ownership of local multinational operations, favoritism, and pressures from home country citizens or action groups.

7 To be effective in the international environment, managers must understand and keep aware of changes in economic, political, and cultural factors, the most influential aspects of the international business environment.

FOR DISCUSSION AND REVIEW

1. What are some of the factors that led to Ford's success in the international market?

2. How can foreign governments act to limit or prohibit trade in their countries? What factors can cause these actions?

3. What are some of the dangers associated with direct investment in foreign countries?

4. Of the many advantages discussed pertaining to overseas production possibilities, which might be most evident to a company investing in Japan from the United States? What about from Japan to the United States?

5. What risks would a company face as it prepared to invest in a less developed country like Peru? In Hungary?

6. What is covered under the Foreign Corrupt Practices Act, and how does it affect U.S. businesses operating abroad?

7. As a contractor contacting a prospective client in a country like the Philippines, what cultural differences would you expect to encounter? How would you handle them?

KEY TERMS

Centralized-planning economies	Free-market economies	Licensing agreements	Portfolio investment
Countertrade	Global corporation	Management agreements	Trade
Direct foreign investment	Imports	Multinational corporation	Turnkey projects
Exports	International business	Political risk	Wholly owned subsidiaries
	Joint venture		

THE CONFERENCE TABLE: DISCUSSION CASE / 20.1

Dresser Industries and Pipeline Politics

The construction of two Siberian gas pipelines meant an increase not only in energy supplies and in the number of jobs, but also in the hope of diplomatic cooperation between the USSR and Western European countries.

On August 3, 1982, Robert Tron of Dresser-France, a corporation owned by a multinational firm based in the United States, found himself in an unprecedented situation. As president of the French manufacturer, he had contracted with a Soviet trading agency and another French firm to deliver equipment to be used in the construction of a major Russian pipeline. Three of his mammoth natural gas compressors stood ready for shipment on a waiting Soviet freighter at Le Havre. Three documents in Tron's possession awaited reconciliation:

1. The contract with the Soviets, which specified meeting a delivery schedule or incurring a large penalty.
2. An order from the U.S. home office which forbade any work or shipments related to the Soviet contract, a matter of U.S. foreign policy.
3. A direct order from the French government to load the finished compressors and to continue work on the remainder of the contract.

Each government threatened severe punishment for noncompliance with its orders. Caught in the crossfire among three powerful countries, Tron saw that his options were fraught with dangers and potential disaster.

Since mid-1981, the Soviet Union and seven Western European countries had been negotiating the details of one of the biggest construction projects in history. Two pipelines were to be laid from western Siberia to Western Europe to carry natural gas. To the countries involved, the pipeline agreement meant not only energy supplies but also many new jobs and important diplomatic cooperation among historically antagonistic neighbors. European leaders looked forward to improved relations with the Communist leaders partly in deference to domestic political parties, but also because they desperately needed new export opportunities.

Source: Murphy, Janet, "Dresser Industries and Pipeline Politics," Boston University, Public Affairs Research Program, 1983. Reprinted in William Frederick, Keith Davis, and James Post, *Business and Society* (New York: McGraw-Hill, 1988), pp. 502–512.

The U.S. administration objected to the pipeline project for two reasons. First, it feared that its European allies could become dependent on Communist sources of energy, a development that might well compromise allied unity in trade and foreign affairs. Second, the uses to which the Soviets could put future natural gas revenues of between $7.5 billion and $12 billion a year caused conservative government officials to blanch. It was their opinion that the Russian economy was on the verge of collapse; the natural gas deal could help Russia to become strong once again.

President Ronald Reagan found a way to apply pressure to the pipeline plans. In December 1981, the government of Poland was placed under martial law, and many thousands of union leaders, popular activists, journalists, artists, and intellectuals were arrested and interned. Civil and union rights were suspended, strikes were broken, and the major Polish cities were occupied by military tanks and troops. While there was no direct military intervention by Soviet forces, Russian troops and equipment were present, and speculation ran strong that their influence was instrumental to the takeover.

Most Western leaders reacted cautiously to the Polish coup, but President Reagan reacted forcefully. In a series of speeches and presidential orders, he announced increasingly stringent measures against Polish and Soviet concerns. Expecting that certain well-placed economic and technological obstacles could pressure the Communists into easing the political situation in Poland, the president immediately imposed a trade embargo on certain high-technology goods and information. One of the direct effects of this order was to stop the release of all U.S. refining equipment and technology to the Soviet Union. U.S. firms complied with the president's directives. In June, the president further extended his embargo to include foreign subsidiaries of U.S. corporations. There was no known precedent in international law to give one world leader the right to apply political policies to foreign entities.

Dresser-France was only one of several firms that was affected seriously by the president's embargo policies, but it was the firm for which events came to a flashpoint first.

All of the blueprints and technical information that Tron required for his Soviet contract had been passed from Dresser's U.S. engineering group before the imposition of the embargo. After the first stage of the embargo, the home office was not permitted to engage in any further exchanges regarding the pipeline contract, but this posed no obstacle to the French unit, which continued to operate as before. When President Reagan extended the embargo to the foreign subsidiaries of U.S. firms, however, Tron received orders from Dresser headquarters to stop work on the Soviet pipeline products. Tron quickly complied, reassigning his personnel and canceling work orders.

The international situation grew increasingly dangerous after the president issued his extended embargo. The top leaders of the European countries protested that the U.S. order was a direct interference with their own sovereignty. U.S. officials warned foreign executives of U.S. subsidiaries that they would face criminal prosecution and fines if they were to violate the president's orders.

On August 10, Tron received a directive from the French minister for research and industry. The message stated that the French government desired that work resume immediately. Still under a stop order from the United States, Tron did not comply and sent his regrets to the French ministry. Nine days later, he received a telegram from the U.S. Department of Commerce, in which he was informed of the sanctions that the U.S. government claimed it could impose against his firm if the pipeline embargo were not respected.

Monday morning, August 23, Tron was summoned to the office of the French Ministry of Research and Industry. There, the minister served him with an order, legally binding and enforceable under French law, to manufacture and ship the goods required in his contract with the Soviet agency.

Edward R. Luter, Dresser Industries' vice president for finance, summed up the company's position:

> We're between a rock and a hard place. As an American company, we fully intend to obey the U.S. law. But it is our position that our French subsidiary is a French company that must obey the laws of that country. We dearly hope the matter can be resolved diplomatically between the two governments. I don't see any other way to get us off the hook. ■

DISCUSSION QUESTIONS

1. Could Dresser Industries have foreseen the problems that occurred? Discuss them in terms of the pressures brought on them from different governments.
2. How should managers at Dresser have responded to the pressures?
3. What responsibilities do managers operating overseas have to uphold foreign governments' policies?

THE CONFERENCE TABLE: DISCUSSION CASE / 20.2

Apple Computer Goes Mexican

Personal desktop computers were one of the hottest new products of the early 1980s. Manufacturers waged a fierce competition to establish a strong position, anticipating that IBM would soon introduce its first personal computer and begin to push the weaker competitors toward early graves. As part of its strategic thrust, Apple Computer decided to strengthen its international sales position.

Apple already had an impressive standing in its foreign markets. In 1983 the company could boast of a 70 percent share of the Latin American market and almost 20,000 personal computers working in Mexico alone. Industry watchers predicted a strong and growing market despite continuing difficulties in national economies. "In hard times, business will gladly buy a half-dozen Apple IIe's instead of a half-million dollar mainframe," explained the company's Latin American business manager.

Although the market demand looked rosy, Apple's ability to supply its products to its Latin American buyers was developing important problems. The Mexican government's import regulations restricted how many units could be shipped into the country and imposed a stiff tariff that more than tripled the computer's price. The company learned that about a third of the Apples in Mexico had entered the country illegally, circumventing the quota and tariff barriers. It became clear that the firm's international operations needed some changes in order to meet its customers' needs and stay in the good graces of the Mexican government.

Apple managers were required to negotiate business development plans with the Mexican government. The only acceptable way around the import limits, they

Sources: "Apple Stirs Up Mexican PC Market" *Electronics,* April 14, 1986, p. 18; Lineback, J. R., "Computer Makers Head South of the Border for New Markets," *Electronics,* July 8, 1985, pp. 28–29.

The only acceptable way for Apple to get around import limits placed on them by the Mexican government was to assemble the units inside the country. This fit the government's agenda because it helped to build the local Mexican economy.

agreed, was to assemble the units inside the country. But they disagreed on the best way to accomplish this. The government argued that Apple should show its commitment to the business by investing heavily in a factory and equipment and sharing ownership with a local partner. The firm's managers preferred to plan a licensing deal, where a local assembler would gain production rights, but Apple would not need to make a major investment or share ownership of assets. In addition, the parties would have to work out standards for export sales, local content, reinvestment, employment, unionization, and tax treatments.

The process and results of the government negotiations were important to Apple. Not only was it concerned with improving its position in Latin America, but it was also testing its ability to conduct a sensitive international discussion. The firm's managers hoped that the process and the agreement would be good enough to serve as models for further international expansions around the world.

The Apple deal was important to the government of Mexico, too. The country was feeling the effects of 70 percent inflation, a shrinking national output, and a large trade deficit in 1983. Its union leaders were demanding a 50 percent wage hike, and officials could not promise that social unrest due to economic hardship was not in the offing. New business that promised growth and exports was essential for economic recovery and social stability. ∎

DISCUSSION QUESTIONS

1. What options, in terms of the types of multinational business, are available to Apple?
2. What risks and opportunities exist for the company, especially with respect to the description of Chihuahua, Mexico, in The Inside View 20.1?
3. Which economic, political/legal, and cultural factors have come into play in this case?

21 | Managing in the Future

FOCUS CASE / Nor Rain Nor Sleet Nor Snow Nor Heated Competition

THE FUTURE: SCENARIOS

TRENDS
Globalization
Demographic Changes
Resource Availability
Growth in the Service Economy
Revolutions in Information Technology

ORGANIZATION RESPONSES
Any Time
Any Place
No-Matter
Mass Customizing

TECHNICAL, ADMINISTRATIVE, AND INSTITUTIONAL ISSUES IN THE FUTURE

MANAGEMENT IN THE FUTURE
Decision Making
Planning
Organizing
Directing
Controlling

Thus far, we have provided a comprehensive picture of management as it exists today. Years from now, things will be much different. The future will offer challenges and opportunities that we cannot even imagine today. Only looking back can we glean some amount of understanding; looking forward, it is all hypotheses. In this chapter, we will discuss some of the major trends in the national and international environments and their possible impact on the functions of management.

KEY QUESTIONS

As you study this chapter, try to answer the following key questions:

1 What are five major trends that will change the world environment in the coming decades?
2 What four conceptual shifts are occurring in the business environment?
3 What effect will these trends and shifts in conception have on technical, administrative, and institutional issues in the future?
4 Will the functions of management change in the future?

Focus Case

Nor Rain Nor Sleet Nor Snow Nor Heated Competition

Despite its extraordinary growth and admirable efficiency, Federal Express is now a company under siege as its operating conditions rapidly change.

While attending Yale University, Frederick W. Smith wrote a term paper describing a new air freight distribution system. He predicted a high demand for a rapid, efficient shipping service for urgently needed packages and documents. He got a C on the paper, but he decided to put the idea to the test nonetheless. In April 1973, in Memphis, Tennessee, he launched Federal Express Corporation. In its first month, the company transported only 20 packages—using 14 planes. Ten years and a billion dollars in sales later, it was a world-renowned business success. By 1990, sales exceeded $4 billion.

To accomplish his goal of next-day, door-to-door delivery of small packages and information throughout the United States and abroad, Smith needed a highly efficient moving and sorting network. Federal uses a simple but extremely efficient flow system. Packages enter the system through one of 9,000 drop boxes, 300 business centers, 400 walk-up counters, 700 transformed Fox Photo kiosks, 12,000 door-to-door van couriers, or 6,000 vanless couriers in large office buildings. Zip codes are entered into the central tracking network within two minutes of pickup. All the packages are then shipped to the Memphis distribution hub, arriving by 11:00 P.M. In the 17.3-acre hub complex, 3,000 employees along 65 miles of conveyor belts sort the 880,000 or so packages according to destination and then reload them onto the waiting jets, which leave by 2:45 A.M. The packages are picked up by couriers waiting at the destination airports, who hand deliver them by 10:30 A.M. Every delivery van and transition point is equipped with a bar code scanner and a computer, so every package can be traced from the beginning to the end of the journey.

Federal will transport any package weighing less than 150 pounds, from legal documents to flowers to fresh fruit to organs for transplant. Customer service is extensive. Operators give callers directions to the nearest drop-off location or schedule a pickup within an hour. Most packages can be tracked within 30 minutes, some while the customer is on the phone. Because client information is instantly retrievable by keying in the account number, the service representative can virtually greet the caller by name.

Sources: This case was written by M. R. Poirier, based on the following sources: "Europe in a Day—Or Less?" *Distribution* (January 1987): 36–42; Ott, James, "Federal Express Starts 24-Hr. Weather Forecasting System," *Aviation Week & Space Technology,* February 2, 1987, pp. 38–40; Ott, James, "Federal Express Plans New Hub, Buys McDonnell Douglas Freighters," *Aviation Week & Space Technology,* January 26, 1987, pp. 45–49; Gelfond, Susan M., "It's a Fax, Fax, Fax, Fax World," *Business Week,* March 21, 1988, p. 136; Reibstein, Larry, "Turbulence Ahead: Federal Express Faces Challenges to Its Grip on Overnight Delivery," *Wall Street Journal,* January 8, 1988, pp. 1, 10; Davis, Stanley M., *Future Perfect* (Reading, Mass.: Addison-Wesley, 1987).

In the future, executives hope to shorten pickup times from within one hour to within minutes of the call, and to shorten delivery times to either first thing in the morning or same-day-delivery. Through computer linkups, Federal hopes to enable each customer to track his or her own packages within minutes.

In addition, Federal has developed several new services. Federal Express Aviation Services, Inc. (FEASI), for example, provides aircraft marketing services to financial institutions and consults on aircraft modifications, purchases, leases, and sales. It has launched a worldwide transport fleet information service that provides detailed scheduling and maintenance information on more than 8100 aircraft. Federal Express also introduced a round-the-clock satellite-based meteorology service, currently used in a dozen locations, primarily by the government. The Man-Computer Integrative Data Access System (McIDAS) integrates weather information from many sources, permitting Federal to provide its fleet and its customers with "nowcasts," current weather forecasts for any point on the globe.

Of course, success like Federal's does not go unnoticed; by early 1988, the growth rate of Federal's overnight business was cut in half, to 25 percent, from its peak a year earlier, and the competition is heating up rapidly. Federal still took in over half of the $6 billion overnight package delivery market, but United Parcel Service (UPS) was fast on its heels, increasing its overnight business from zero to $1.3 billion in just five years. In addition, UPS spent millions to develop a central tracking and sorting system that allow it to offer service comparable to Federal Express at a price of $8.50 per package to Federal Express's $11.00. To compound the problem, as UPS attacked Federal's position in the saturated overnight letter market, Federal can expand only into large-package, or "back-door" delivery, in which UPS is the major contender. Federal's cleaner trucks and two-hour time advantage (UPS delivers by noon) may not be worth the money to "back-door" loading dock customers.

Meanwhile, as UPS is moving in on Federal's overnight express business, and Federal is trying to move into UPS's primary market with few advantages, the overnight letter business itself is under a major threat from the facsimile transmission business. Anticipating the threat, Federal developed Zap Mail service in 1984, a complex and sophisticated satellite-based network designed to transmit facsimiles of documents between Federal Express locations within minutes. However, the shuttle disaster in 1986 caused the price of satellites to soar, and the advances of such Japanese companies as Ricoh, Canon, and Sharp caused the prices of fax machines to plummet, allowing any business to buy one. Fax technology was becoming available and affordable by business. Costs of the project grew too high, demand for the service—because businesses had machines of their own—was too low, and after two years and $200 million, the service was canceled. Said company executives: "It was an idea ahead of its time."

However, where Federal Express failed, many others with less ambitious, and less risky, systems are beginning to succeed. FastFax, for example, is a service offered by Sir Speedy, an instant printing franchise with 800 locations nationwide. It offers fax services over the counter, via phone lines rather than satellites, to customers who do not have fax machines. U.S. Faxsys, on the other hand, offers service to businesses that do have fax machines. The sending machine can dial into a central network and transmit, via phone line, a facsimile to the receiving machine. Meanwhile, DHL International, one of Federal's major competitors in the overnight delivery business, has also developed a fax system that transmits documents via satellite across the United States and also between the United States, and Europe, Japan, Hong Kong, and Bahrain. It has the most rapid transmission speed (3 seconds per page to the average 20) and the highest-quality resolution (400 lines per inch to the standard 200).

Overnight Mail and Facsimile Market Statistics

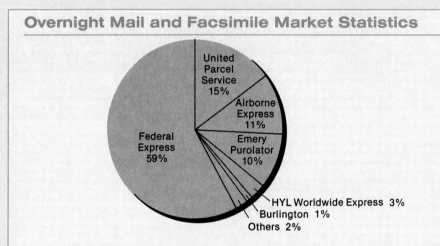

(a) 1986 Shares of the Overnight Air Express Package Delivery Market

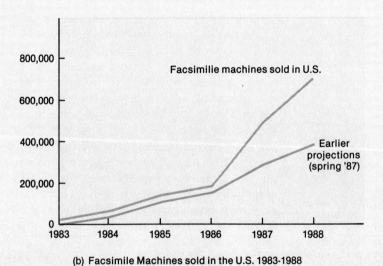

(b) Facsimile Machines sold in the U.S. 1983-1988

Sources: "Turbulence Ahead: Federal Express Faces Challenge to Its Dominance in Overnight Delivery from UPS," *Wall Street Journal,* January 8, 1988, p. 1. "It's a Fax, Fax, Fax, Fax World," *Business Week,* March 21, 1988, p. 136.

Federal Express has been a future-oriented innovator in two fields: overnight delivery and facsimile transmission. But it is now a company under siege on both fronts. The market share of the leading overnight carriers and the growth of sales of facsimile machines in the United States are shown in the charts on page 638. What the future holds for Federal Express is still very much in the air. ■

THE FUTURE: SCENARIOS

Most of us, as a high school English class requirement, read George Orwell's *1984,* Aldous Huxley's *Brave New World,* or Alvin Toffler's *Future Shock.* Orwell described a totalitarian state that vaporizes human beings, erases memory and history, and is always watched over by Big Brother. Huxley described a world of mass production of genetically predestined workers, all conditioned before their test-tube birth to love the work they are created to do. And Toffler illustrated a society beset with problems brought on by too much change in too short a period of time. All these authors offered scenarios, pictures of what life could be like in the future. Some were frightening, some were amazing, some were thrilling; all were very different from the present.

Researchers have also offered scenarios for the future. John Naisbitt, in his book *Megatrends,* described the trends that he predicted would dominate the conduct of business in the future.[1] These are listed in Exhibit 21.1. Between them all, futurists agree that major changes are on the immediate horizon.

TRENDS

The past 200 years have seen more growth and change in human civilization than the 3 or 4 million before them. From the dawn of humankind until 1787, when the first steam-powered boat was made operational, people traveled entirely under their own or nature's power. Journeys of 100 miles could take days. Voyages across the sea could take months, even years. But the invention of steam engines—virtually seconds ago in terms of human history—brought trains and steamships, which led to cars and planes, and now every corner of the globe is virtually a day away.

EXHIBIT / 21.1
Megatrends

1. From an industrial society to an information society
2. From forced technology to high tech/high touch
3. A change from a national economy to a world economy
4. Reorientation of management from the short term to the long term
5. From centralized to decentralized structures
6. From institutional help to self-help
7. From representative democracy to participatory democracy
8. From hierarchies to networking
9. Demographic shift from North to South
10. Either/or to multiple options

Source: Naisbitt, John, *Megatrends* (New York: Warner Books, 1984).

Before 1879, when Edison invented the light bulb, if you wanted to see in the dark, you had to use fire. Until 1844, when the Baltimore-to-Washington Morse telegraph was installed, and 1876, when telephones were introduced, messages could only be transmitted as fast as a person could get from one place to another on foot or on horseback. Printed news, outside of personal letters, was virtually unavailable before 1792 when the first daily paper was printed in London. Before 1798 and the invention of interchangeable parts and assembly line types of production, nearly everything was made individually, by hand, one at a time. If you owned a rifle, or any "small household appliance" of the time, and a piece of it broke, you would either scrap the whole item or have to pay to have another piece custom made.

Imagine trying to conduct even the most routine business operation under these conditions. So many of the tools and techniques we now use to manage were unavailable. Management has changed, organizations have changed, and they continue to change at an ever-increasing rate. We look back and are amazed at how simple and unsophisticated the world of management was. Managers in the future may also look back to today in wonder at the simplicity of the world, the lack of technological sophistication, and the inconveniences with which managers put up.

In general, there are five major trends that researchers and observers in almost any industry agree will create tremendous changes and new challenges with which future managers will have to deal. These trends include globalization, major shifts in population demographics, changes in resource availability, increasing growth of the service economy, and revolutions in information technology.

Globalization

The world is getting smaller every day. People can travel anywhere in the world within roughly 24 hours, and any daily paper will fill you in on events in China, Australia, Chile, or Antarctica. All over the world, people use or consume things that came from distant shores: Japanese sushi is available all over the West, Australian boomerangs are sold in California, South American wool ponchos can be found in the Orient.

Globalize To change operation and communication as the world gets "smaller."

Faced with these challenges, corporations must **globalize.** They can no longer consider one country to be their only, or even primary, place of business. The globe is their place of business, and global competition and markets are their concerns. Organizations set up factories, plants, and offices wherever it is most advantageous. Competition for goods, services, and ideas pays no respect to national borders or to the geopolitical divisions that supposedly separate north from south, east from west.[2] Build a better microchip in Omaha, Nebraska, and buyers will be there from Osaka, Japan, to Oslo, Norway. Fail to keep up with the latest technological developments in the industry, as USX (Steel) did, and you will find your survival threatened even by fledgling Third World producers. Workers in every country might be receiving paychecks from foreign owners; in the United States, almost half of the American chemical workers are employed by foreign owners. And since SONY bought CBS, Michael Jackson and Bruce Springsteen are working for the Japanese. But the increase in globalization brings not only challenges but opportunities. Companies in every industry have the chance to reap benefits by expanding overseas. Service industries in particular are expanding overseas, with Federal Express being just one example. The market for international overnight mail delivery is virtually untapped, and Federal and its competitors will be lining up to corner a piece of it.

Many governments are aiding this increase in globalization by offering foreign businesses incentives to operate within their shores and bring jobs with them. The Inside View 21.1 illustrates what several countries are doing to attract direct investors. And there are many other reasons for corporations to invest overseas: They can secure long-term sources of raw materials; establish or tap local markets; facilitate exports from the home country; avoid trade barriers in the host country; lower costs for materials, production, and transportation; and diversify internationally to stabilize the overall business portfolio.

THE INSIDE VIEW / 21.1

Luring Investors

Cyprus is not just a lovely place to visit; it offers investment incentives to foreign companies in order to draw in business to help fight unemployment.

Government involvement in business is a fact of life all over the world. It has become particularly apparent in the role that national, regional, and local governments are playing in an effort to attract new investment. Much of the investment that economic development agencies are vying for is foreign. For example:

- Cyprus is well known as a lovely place to visit. But several hundred foreign companies now do business in Cyprus, attracted partly by the country's investment incentives. Non-Cypriot corporations have their profits only lightly taxed. The national government is pleased just to have new jobs created for those who are unemployed. Never mind the loss of tax revenue.
- At the American Embassy's commercial library in Tokyo, there are "Invest in . . . " brochures from several of the states, all colorfully illustrated and written in Japanese. Each one tries to convince the Japanese reader that Alabama, or

wherever, is the right place to be. The pictures of the beaches, golf courses, and fishing spots are attractive, but the prose tells about tax exemptions for new investments, lowered real estate taxes, cash grants, and other financial attractions that affect profits on new ventures.
- Bulgaria loosened its tight control over local investment opportunities a few years ago when it said that it would allow Western capital to come in on a joint venture basis. Not many Western companies were very excited, so the Foreign Trade Ministry announced that it would loan money to its venture partners at rates lower than would be available from Western financial institutions. In short, the Bulgarians would subsidize their profit-seeking partners if the venture would suit the state's needs. ■

Source: Weigand, Robert E., "Searching for Investments—The Race is on, the Runner Should Be Wary," *Business Horizons* (March–April 1985): 46–52.

Demographic Changes

Demographics The way populations are distributed.

While people and organizations are spreading themselves among the various nations and turning the world into a global community, the distribution and size of the world's population, the **demographics,** continue to change.[3] The world's population expanded for millions of years before it reached 1 billion in 1830. It took only a century after that to hit 2 billion, and since then it has multiplied almost exponentially: It hit 3 billion in 1960, 4 billion in 1975, 5 billion in 1987, and it is projected to hit 6 billion before the year 2000. Some analysts predict it will hit 10 or 11 billion in the next 125 years before it stabilizes.

As The Inside View 21.2 illustrates, the growth in our overall numbers is more significant than the mere numerical increase; however, this increase is not the issue that concerns most observers. It is the geographical unevenness of this growth. In many Western nations, and especially in West Germany, Hungary, Sweden, Great Britain, and the United States, birth rates have fallen below the level necessary to replace population; in other words, the native population will actually decrease in these countries over the long term. Rates in the United States have been this low for more than a decade, meaning that, without immigration, population levels will begin falling by 2020. As Exhibit 21.2 illustrates, the U.S. population will have a much different character and composition in the next 50 years.

The opposite is true in the developing nations. The populations in Kenya and Syria are doubling every 20 years. Many African and Southeast Asian countries have birth rates significantly higher than those needed to replace population. And even if new population control measures in India and Nigeria are highly successful, by 2010 India will add to its population as many people as now live in China, and by 2035 Nigeria's population will exceed the current population of the entire continent of Africa. In 1940, 65 percent of the people on the earth lived in developing countries. In the early 1980s, the number was roughly 75 percent. By the year 2000, this percentage is predicted to rise to 78 percent, and in 2034 to 93 percent.

With such great divergence in growth rates between developed and developing nations, analysts predict two things: First, the rich countries will become richer while poor countries become poorer, not being able to support their own inhabitants. Second, because of this, mass migrations from these poorer, grossly overcrowded nations will flood the developed nations. The implications of these trends are certainly significant in a human sense, but also from a business perspective. First, organizations will, as never before, be considered responsible for contributing to the quality of life in every nation. Second, with such vast changes in the composition of the work force, organizations will find themselves drawing talent and labor from completely different sources than today. Therefore, demographic changes will force business to become more global in its sense of social responsibility and in its view of an international labor pool.

Resource Availability

Resource availability The ability of companies to get the raw materials they need to function.

As the numbers above indicate, increasing billions of people are drawing on the planet's resources. And because many essential resources exist in finite amounts and are not recyclable, specifically ores and fossil fuels, many observers predict **resource availability** will be an increasing problem for companies.

Problems Multiply Faster than People

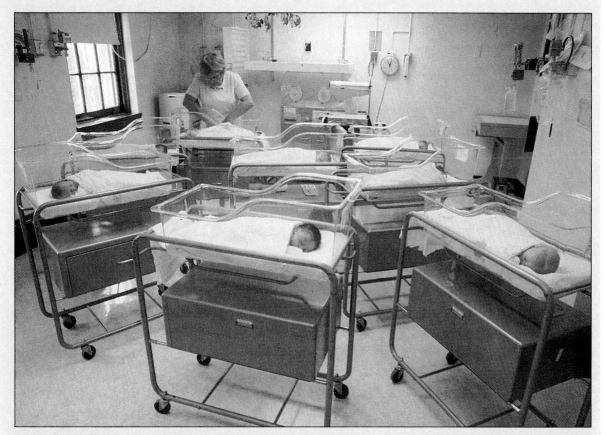

Those who believe that as a population grows the social problems increase recommend limiting population growth.

Economic and social systems respond to absolute numbers as well as to rates of growth. There is every reason to believe that most aspects of these systems have long since passed the point where economies of scale become diseconomies of scale. Twenty years ago, English writer C. P. Snow, commenting on the declining quality of English telephone services, generated what we might call Snow's law: "The difficulties of a service increase roughly by the square of the number of people using it."

Snow saw that when the number of people using a service grows, the number of service problems grows at an even faster rate, proportional to the number of possible connections between users. The diagram on page 644 illustrates this principle. For example, when the number of nodes doubles from four to eight, the number of connections between them more than quadruples. This law of connections helps explain many of the problems of an expanding, ever more complex, global society. From 1930 to 1976, the number of people on earth doubled from 2 billion to 4 billion, and the number of possible connections quadrupled. Based on current growth rates, the population could be expected to double again to 8

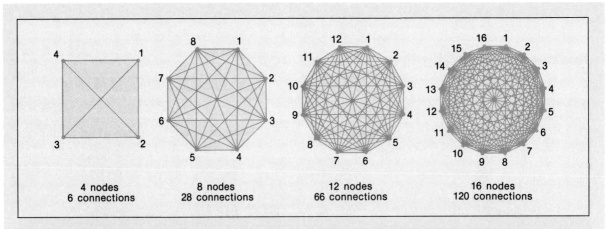

billion by 2020, bringing another quadrupling of possible connections and of Snow's "service difficulties."

That growing numbers of people are deleterious can be seen in the increased costs of supplying them with goods.

If today's population were of constant size, it still would have to run continually just to stay in place. Technology would have to be constantly improved to compensate for depleted supplies of fuels, declining quality of ores, and deterioration of soils, and to protect people from the environmental consequences of using both old and new technologies. But today's population is growing. Each additional person, on average, must be cared for by using lower-quality resources that must be transported further and by food grown on more marginal land. Supplying the additional energy needed for these tasks creates both economic and environmental problems.

Although population growth rates are highest in poor countries, overpopulation and continuing population growth in rich countries are the prime threat to global resources and environmental systems, simply because the average individual in rich nations has a large impact on resources and environment. One of the best available measures of that impact is a nation's per capita use of commercially produced energy. In the United States, the average person uses the commercial energy equivalent of about 10,000 kilograms of coal annually. In contrast, an average South American uses about 1,000 kilograms, an Asian about 600, and an African about 425. By this measure, the birth of an average baby in the United States will be about 200 times as disastrous for the world as the birth of an average Bangladeshi, who will consume the commercial equivalent of some 45 kilograms of coal annually. ■

Source: C. P. Snow quoted in Ehrlich, Paul R., and Ehrlich, Anne M., "World Population Crisis," *Bulletin of the Atomic Scientists* (April 1986): 13–18.

Resource depletion is a two-pronged problem. On the one hand, there are those resources that will be depleted: cheap oil in 100 years, coal in 300 to 500 years, various ores and chemicals sooner than that. Thus far, every prediction like this has been wrong, and with advances in technology, some of these resources could be made recyclable; others could be replaced by synthetic or other natural substances that possess the same necessary properties. On the other hand, there are those resources that are being depleted without being actually used. Emissions from automobile and airplane engines, and from factories and production methods, are affecting the earth's atmosphere so severely that within 100 to 200 years the climate on the planet may be completely different, perhaps not even livable without special protection. In June 1988, an international panel of scien-

EXHIBIT / 21.2
Americans in 2033

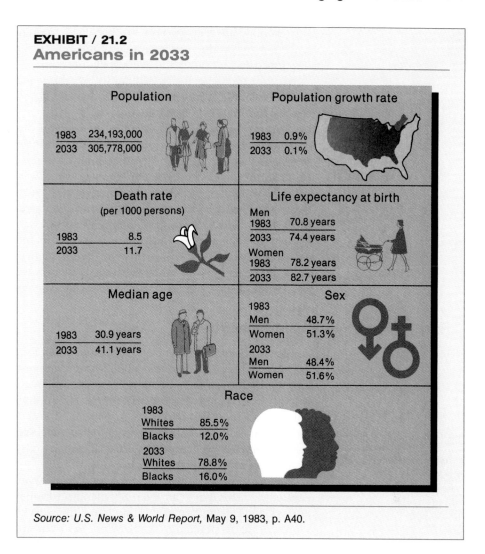

Population		Population growth rate	
1983	234,193,000	1983	0.9%
2033	305,778,000	2033	0.1%

Death rate
(per 1000 persons)

1983	8.5
2033	11.7

Life expectancy at birth

Men	
1983	70.8 years
2033	74.4 years
Women	
1983	78.2 years
2033	82.7 years

Median age

1983	30.9 years
2033	41.1 years

Sex

1983	
Men	48.7%
Women	51.3%
2033	
Men	48.4%
Women	51.6%

Race

1983	
Whites	85.5%
Blacks	12.0%
2033	
Whites	78.8%
Blacks	16.0%

Source: *U.S. News & World Report,* May 9, 1983, p. A40.

tists reported that a rapid rise in the earth's temperature was already under way and that if world and business leaders did not do something to reverse the trend, the global temperatures would rise much faster than human societies or ecosystems would be able to tolerate.

Water pollution is currently a major problem. Even today, many people in cities drink only bottled water imported from wells and springs. Chemical spills in the Rhine River in 1986 killed hundreds of thousands of fish and eels and forced many riverside inhabitants of West Germany, France, Luxembourg, the Netherlands, and Belgium to go elsewhere for drinking water. In Woburn, Massachusetts, in the 1970s and 1980s, 11 children died of leukemia brought on by drinking contaminated groundwater. And India's sacred Ganges River is a dumping ground for animal carcasses, partially cremated human remains, and tons of human and industrial wastes.[4]

The resource problem becomes more complex and severe when viewed in terms of uneven demographic bulges. For example, the United States, Europe, and the Soviet Union, three of the most highly developed areas with some of the slowest population growth rates, represent a combined total of 50 percent of the world's grain production. Africa and Latin America, containing some of the least developed and most quickly overpopulating countries, represent only 5 percent.[5]

Because more people are filling the world, demanding more goods and services, depleting more resources, and producing more wastes that contaminate the air and water, it is hardly surprising when researchers publish doomsday predictions. However, necessity has always bred invention and will continue to do so. The Inside View 21.3 describes the priorities for action outlined by an international panel of scientists to counteract the rise in the earth's temperature. In addition, to replace depleted resources, ocean waters will be desalinated to increase supplies of fresh water, minerals and ores will be mined from the sea floor—perhaps even the moon—and new food sources will be developed. In fact, in the early 1960s, a group of economists even devised a "minimum diet" and learned that one person could buy a balanced diet for what was then $79 per year and would today be $283 per year.[6] From an organizational perspective, the immense challenges posed by resource depletion will be turned into opportunities; organizations will be responsible for making what little there is go around.

Growth in the Service Economy

Service sector The portion of the economy that focuses on delivering a service.

For decades, organizations have been streamlining their operations in attempts to utilize all of their human and nonhuman resources more efficiently, though in most cases this has had more to do with the desire to increase profits and competitive position than with a concern for the environment. The emphasis on streamlining manufacturing operations is one of the factors responsible for the boom in the service industry. Assistance from the **service sector,** communications, banking, investments, and consulting have all been used by the manufacturing industry to increase efficiency and effectiveness.

America's manufacturing sector was at its peak in 1945, representing 35 percent of the GNP that year. By 1985, manufacturing represented only 28 percent of the GNP. During that same time frame, the service sector grew considerably, representing 56 percent of the GNP in 1945 and roughly 70 percent by 1985.[7] Shifts in employment and GNP percentages for the agricultural, industrial, and service sector in the past century are illustrated in Exhibit 21.3. Several manufacturing concerns have even shifted into the service economy. William S. Woodside, chief executive officer of American Can Co., described the shift in his company's position in 1987: "American Can is an extreme example. We had $4 billion worth of container and paper products manufacturing businesses six years ago; now we have no manufacturing but $4 billion worth of life insurance, mutual funds, and specialty retailing businesses."[8]

The differences between these two sectors in terms of profits and earnings are significant and do much to explain strategies like Woodside's. Though overall profits in the service sector were smaller than in manufacturing in 1983 ($46.5 billion and $68.8 billion, respectively), growth in service sector profits has far outstripped growth in manufacturing. In 1984, *Fortune* magazine studied six major service sector fields and found that each one came in far ahead of manufacturing's 77.8 percent rise in profits between 1973 and 1983: transportation companies' earnings rose 342.4 percent, retailers 243.6 percent, diversified financial companies 189.1 percent, commercial banks 174.4 percent, utilities 108.6 percent, and life insurance companies 101.7 percent.[9] As Woodside commented, "A

Counteracting the Greenhouse Effect

Many scientists believe that increasing pollution is creating a "greenhouse effect" that is causing atmospheric temperatures to rise. Such temperature increases could cause dramatic changes in climate and disrupt ecosystems and human societies.

In a report released in Washington, Toronto, Stockholm, and Geneva, an international panel of scientists convened by the World Meteorological Organization and the United Nations Environment Program concluded that the planet is warming much faster than human societies or ecosystems will be able to tolerate.

Given the present pollution trends, the panel says, global temperature will rise over the next century at a rate six times faster than what has been experienced in human history.

This warming is occurring because carbon dioxide and other insulating "greenhouse gases" released by human activity are building up in the earth's atmosphere and trapping heat from the sun that would otherwise escape back to space. Carbon dioxide, which is responsible for roughly half of the global warming, is released in the burning of fossil fuels such as coal and oil.

"The climate is going to warm faster than anything we're used to as a human race," said Michael Oppenheimer, an atmospheric scientist with the Environmental Defense Fund and a member of this panel, which reviewed the impact of the greenhouse effect and what can be done to address it.

By the end of the next century, Oppenheimer noted, the global average temperture could be nine degrees Fahrenheit warmer than it is now—equivalent to the warming that has occurred since the last ice age. While nine degrees may not sound like a lot, Oppenheimer said, it is the difference between the Boston of today and a Boston covered by an ice sheet.

As a first step, the panel recommended that world leaders try to slow the warming to roughly two degrees Fahrenheit over the next century, which historical experience indicates that natural ecosystems and societies can tolerate. To do this, Oppenheimer said, will require a 60 percent reduction in the current rate of carbon dioxide emissions, a halt to deforestation in the tropics and elsewhere, and at least a 50 percent cut in the release of other greenhouse gases such as methane and nitrous oxide.

"It's a tall order," he acknowledged, "but it's not impossible," noting that the United States can probably cut its carbon dioxide emissions in half by applying current technology aggressively to energy conservation.

He said slowing warming will give the world a couple of decades to speed the development on nonfossil technologies, such as solar, wind, and geothermal energy.

According to the panel, uncontrolled rising temperatures will cause dramatic climate changes across the face of the planet that will disrupt human societies and important ecosystems like forests and wetlands.

Coastal areas will be hard hit by rising sea levels that will accelerate erosion, devastate coastal wetlands that are vital to fisheries, damage port facilities, and increase the severity and frequency of flooding. In low-lying countries like Bangladesh, large areas of land may be lost to rising seas.

Semiarid tropical regions such as Africa, which are already plagued by recurring drought and famine, may be visited by even hotter temperatures and less rain. ■

Source: "Panel Calls for Action to Slow Rising Earth Temperature," *Boston Globe,* June 7, 1988, p. 10.

friend of mine used to tell me we were following a high risk strategy by going into financial services. I argued that the only higher risk strategy was staying where we were."[10]

Federal Express hopes to capitalize on this boom. As services expand both domestically and internationally, there will be more offices for Federal to service, in more places. Banking, insurances, investments, and many other service industries produce reams of legal documents that *must* make it from point A to point B overnight. Even competition from facsimile operations can not take the place of delivering an original, signed in ink, overnight.

The boom in the service economy, however, has many observers concerned. The low wage base of the nation may mean less private spending and an economic slump. And though profits have soared and service's percent of the GNP has increased, productivity has not grown, as indicated in Exhibit 21.4. Several experts have also claimed that a service economy simply cannot survive in the absence of a strong manufacturing base. Manufacturing and goods-producing in-

---

EXHIBIT / 21.3
U.S. Employment and GNP, by Selected Years, for Agricultural, Industrial, and Service Sectors

Year	Sector	Employment (%)	GNP (%)
1865	Agriculture	48	22
	Industry	14	22
	Service	38	56
1929	Agriculture	8	9
	Industry	37	28
	Service	55	63
1945	Agriculture	4	9
	Industry	39	35
	Service	57	56
1985	Agriculture	2	2
	Industry	21	28
	Service	77	70
2001	Agriculture	2	3
	Industry	5	24
	Service	93	73

Source: Davis, Stanley M., *Future Perfect* (Reading, Mass.: Addison-Wesley, 1987), p. 97.

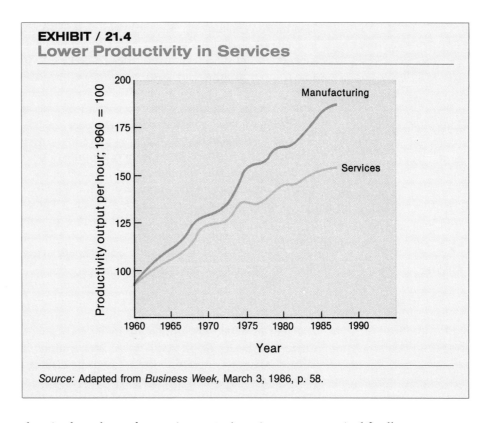

EXHIBIT / 21.4
Lower Productivity in Services

Source: Adapted from *Business Week,* March 3, 1986, p. 58.

dustries have been the service sector's major customers. And finally, many warn that, just as the manufacturing sector was vulnerable to international competition—and indeed lost prominence in many areas because of it—so too are services. There is evidence of this danger already: The U.S. share of global trade in such business services as engineering, consulting, and brokerage fell from 15 percent in 1973 to 8 percent in 1983.[11] As foreign countries imposed trade restrictions and other impediments, the nation's net positive trade balance continued to decline, falling from $41 billion in 1981 to $21.4 billion in 1985.[12]

Revolutions in Information Technology

Information technology
The use of computers to resolve communication needs.

Hand in hand with the growth in the service sector, **information technology**—the product of the convergence between the computer and communications industries—has boomed. Where computers used to be considered tools for the faster, more efficient handling of routine organizational tasks, they now are considered indispensable partners in activities as diverse as marketing, product development, customer service, human resource management, and strategic planning. Federal Express has already felt the pressure from computer linkup competition, which may ultimately force it to shift its focus from overnight mail delivery. Business is redesigning itself, incorporating entirely new approaches to existing markets and product lines; relationships and extensions of the business that never would have occurred previously are sprouting up in all industries.

For example, retailer J. C. Penney now processes credit card transactions for Shell Oil and Gulf Refining and Marketing in order to leverage its investment in information technology. American Hospital Supply Corporation achieved extensive market share gains in the 1970s when it set up a computer network between customers and suppliers. Inventories could be cut down, orders placed and filled much more rapidly, and customer service improved. As one Harvard business professor put it, "The diffusion of technology is changing the way we do business and the way companies relate to customers and suppliers. This is no longer a technological phenomenon but a social one."[13]

Artificial intelligence, or the knowledge-based system, is on the leading edge of advances in computer processing capabilities. Where the first computers were used simply to crunch numbers, artificial intelligence programs are designed, in essence, to transcend their own programming. These systems go many steps beyond rigid calculation and data processing. Though these developments will greatly increase the ability of managers and organizations to accomplish countless objectives, computers are still tools. The results obtained will be only as valuable as the uses to which they are put; powerful processing and infinite storage mean nothing without effective application.

Globalization, demographic shifts, availability of resources, service sector growth, and technological trends are all aspects of the changing environment. Together, these five overall trends provide a very general illustration of the environment in which we all may be living and in which all business will be conducted in 10, 20, or 50 years. Some corporations, anticipating the future, have already begun to respond to these trends by making changes in the products and services they produce, the way they produce them, the space in which they produce them, and the way they offer them to their markets.

ORGANIZATION RESPONSES

Stanley M. Davis, in his book *Future Perfect,* provides a picture of the changes some organizations have begun to make in order to cope with the complexity they will face in the future.[14] Davis argues that organizations will change their concepts of the time involved in production, the space utilized or required, the physical facilities and materials necessary, and what used to be the trade-off between economies of mass production and the market benefits of customization. Simply put, Davis explains that organizations will come to realize they can produce all goods and services in any time, any place, with any matter (including "no-matter"), and can mass-produce and customize simultaneously.

Any Time

People have lived and organizations have operated and produced things based on their concepts of time. At the turn of the century, halfway through the industrial era, Frederick Taylor invented the concept of time management. In the industrial model of time, each person had a place on the production line, performed the designated task over and over all day until closing, then started again the next day. Time was a cyclical, endless repetition of events.

Concepts of time in the business world are changing dramatically. Business managers do not look at things in 9-to-5 time, or one-week-turnaround time, or some other repeated constant block of time, but rather are striving for "zero-

Any time A concept of operation in which less time is needed for tasks, which in the future may require little enough time to be almost instantaneous.

based time" schedules, so that products and services are available at **any time.** Over the years, organizations have been manufacturing products and delivering services increasingly rapidly. In the past five years, Matsushita's refrigeration factory reduced its average manufacture time from 360 to less than 3 hours. And just as manufacturing itself is now faster, switching among the manufacture of various products in one production system is also faster. With the help of various new technologies, alterations in production runs now cause neither delays nor cost increases. For example, garment manufacturers now use computerized lasers rather than mechanized cutting blades to cut garments to different sizes. Dimensions can be changed instantly by computer with no machinery downtime.

Service delivery times have also been dramatically cut. Stratus Corporation can service its mainframes virtually before customers request it. When a part in the mainframe computer malfunctions, a backup part takes over and a signal is automatically sent to the Stratus factory requesting a backup part. The customer will not even know there is anything wrong until the replacement part arrives (via Federal Express) the next morning.

Hotels are another example. Currently they structure check-in and checkout times to allow several hours between patrons so that rooms can be cleaned. A traveler must be in no earlier than, say, 4:00 in the afternoon, and out by, usually, 12:00 noon. However, with a "real-time" (zero lag time) service network, rooms could be cleaned virtually within minutes between the departure and arrival of patrons. Imagine the competitive advantage a hotel might have if it could offer completely unstructured check-in and checkout times.

Federal Express has already made a fortune by shortening lag times in mail delivery: The firm delivered overnight when everyone else delivered in three days or more. Federal is making further strides by shortening the lag time between the last plane into the sorting facility and the first plane out. This will allow later mail pickups and earlier deliveries. Lag time in customer service at Federal Express is also being shortened. Packages can be traced almost immediately and customers are offered the option to hook their computer systems directly into Federal's tracking system so that they can service themselves without delay.

The trend in the future for all businesses is to achieve zero-based time lag in production and service. The point in time when a customer identifies a need is the point in time when it should be satisfied—not during working hours, not the next day, not when the next representative is free, but anytime, instantaneously. So far, business has been making marginal improvements (say 10 to 20 percent increased speed or efficiency) by charting the elapsed time for each step from conception (or request) to consumption (or delivery) and working to reduce it. But to reduce the elapsed time by multiples (50–100+ percent) will require a complete reconceptualization of the production, distribution, and/or delivery processes themselves.

Any Place

Business also will be changing its conception of place, or space. In early history, place requirements completely dominated survival. That is, humans hunted beasts to survive, and they were obliged to be in the place where the beasts were in order to catch them. The development of an agrarian economy relaxed those requirements: People could live in a number of places, provided the terrain supported crops. With industrialization, a living could be earned and food purchased almost anywhere. For purposes of basic survival, place no longer dominated human decision making, but for purposes of production, geographical and spatial considerations were still of major importance.

Any place A changing concept of space involving the elimination or reduction of space as a limit to human activities.

Any place concepts, where space and distance are constantly reduced, will revolutionize all aspects of business, from the locations in which it operates and the space its operations take up, to the size of its products, to the structure of its relationship to the marketplace. Products and services will virtually be available anywhere. One organization can produce products all over the world—not just different products in different factories, but one product through a linkage of factories anywhere on the globe, as Ford is currently doing. The transformation process we introduced in Chapter 2 and described further in Chapter 16 will look less like a structural block between supplier inputs and consumable outputs and more like an invisible link. (See Exhibit 21.5.) For example, the transformation process in overnight mail delivery is still the physical carrying of a package from one place to another. In facsimile transmission, it is the instant electronic transmission of an image from one place to another. If sent over phone lines, this is still a physical process. But if sent by satellite, it becomes even more intangible: an invisible, virtually instantaneous link.

The size and space of products will also change dramatically. Perhaps you recall seeing an early model of a personal calculator in the 1960s, a thing the size of a manual typewriter. Calculators are now the size of credit cards, and could easily be smaller except that the buttons have to be large enough for our fingers.

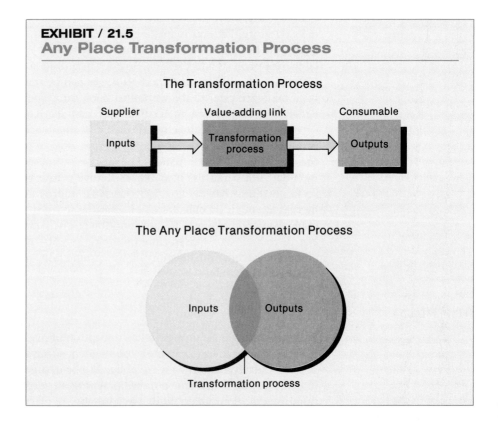

EXHIBIT / 21.5
Any Place Transformation Process

The Transformation Process

Supplier / Value-adding link / Consumable

Inputs → Transformation process → Outputs

The Any Place Transformation Process

Inputs / Outputs

Transformation process

Almost all electronic gadgets are getting smaller and less expensive in correspondence with developments in computer chips. Today, 2000 transistors could line up neatly on the head of a pin. And miniaturization is not the only spatial trend in products; organizations are also experimenting with three-dimensional television and video display screens.

The concept of space as it applies to an organization's relationship to markets is also changing. In early economies, the "market" was the central meeting place in town where goods were sold or exchanged. It was a very definable "place." The "place" of an organization's market will change dramatically in the future. Products and services virtually will not have to be taken from one place to another. Federal Express, for example, takes a letter from the doorstep of point A to the doorstep of point B. FastFax electronically transmits the letter from one of its offices to another, leaving the sender and receiver responsible for being in their respective offices. U.S. Faxsys electronically transmits the letter from the sender's desk to the receiver's. The delivery of service is handled in a different place and method in each case. Today, computers allow home banking, technology brings the phone into the car and plane, or wherever you are, and shopping can be done through the television set. A person could virtually live and work indefinitely at home and never want for anything, except perhaps a change of scenery.

No-Matter

No-matter Value that comes from intangibles.

According to the concept of **no-matter,** in future economic and business environments value will come from intangibles; that is, value will lie outside of tangible, material existence. This will be a difficult conceptual shift for many managers to make. They are used to allocating tangible resources (labor, capital, equipment) to create tangible products (food, cars, houses) and tangible services (restaurants, telephones, cleaners) for tangible market segments (middle-class male professionals, teenage suburban athletes). They are not accustomed to allocating intangible resources (mind, time, information) to create intangible products (software, advertisements, investments) and intangible services (health, education, personal shoppers) for intangible market segments (conservatives, compulsives, swingers).

The concept of no-matter will affect organizations in as many ways as the concepts of no time and no space. Not only are products themselves being developed that minimize their reliance of "matter" (for example, Fuji sells film in disposable cameras for $7 a roll, eliminating the need for an actual camera, and Canon is developing an electronic camera that produces images without film), but the difference between manufacturing (material) and service (nonmaterial) production is becoming moot. As illustrated in Exhibit 21.3, the U.S. Department of Commerce still classifies employment and GNP percentages into agriculture, industry, and service, yet a significant portion of manufacturing's percentage of the GNP is created in the service and administrative areas of these firms. For example, only 6 percent of IBM's employees worldwide are in industrial manufacturing; less than 20,000 out of 400,000 are production employees. Yet IBM is classified as part of the industrial sector. A third of the revenues at General Electric and half at Westinghouse come from services, and these too are considered industrial-sector firms.

The most important things for managers to realize are that employment in manufacturing is declining, service employment within manufacturing is increasing, and it is making less and less sense to differentiate between industrial and service companies. Service now plays a major role in every sector of the economy. In the future, intangibles themselves will be more valuable than tangibles, and they will also add value to tangibles.

Federal Express will find this trend a great challenge. If, for example, facsimile and electronic data transmission services are authorized to transmit legal documents in lieu of actual, signed originals, Federal will be forced to redevelop something along the lines of Zap Mail or concentrate entirely on package delivery. There will be no advantage to overnight or even same-day mail delivery; it will be valueless.

Mass Customizing

Mass customizing The mass production of customized products and services.

The fourth major development that will alter the shape of things to come is the trend toward **mass customizing,** or the mass production of customized products or services. Mass customization of products has already begun, to a greater or lesser extent, in several countries, with the United States not necessarily leading the way. Shoes and clothing are still sold in standard whole sizes, except in special-size stores. Audiovisual components are mass-produced but are modular; a customer can select a number of standard components and combine them to suit specific needs. For bigger, more complicated items, this is less the case. Houses are one example. In the United States, people who wish to buy new homes must either buy one of perhaps five models available in a real estate development, differentiated mostly by the number of bedrooms rather than the style or layout, or they must pay an architect to custom design an original home for them. In Japan, however, mass customization of homes is in full swing.

The real estate sales representative has access to a computer bank of 20,000 combinable parts, which the customers can put together in virtually any framework they desire. As the selections are made—living room on the east side, tea room off the kitchen, hallway wider—the pieces are put together on the screen. When the design is finished, the plans are sent electronically to the factory. The walls and roof are prefabricated and put up in one day by seven construction workers and one crane. Building and construction are completely finished within two months. Prefabricated home construction in the United States is considerably less advanced; the largest prefab manufacturer can produce about 2,000 units per year, while a major Japanese firm can produce 40,000.

Services are also being mass customized as a competitive strategy. Burger King, for example, has designed a strategy whereby a mass-produced product, the hamburger, is differentiated by customized service: Hold the pickles, hold the lettuce. Advertising too is on the verge of mass customizing; with pay-per-program technology, broadcasters are able to transmit different commercials to people in one area who are all watching the same program.

Markets, in addition to products and services, can also be mass customized. Formerly, producers had one of two basic choices: They could target the mass market (everyone) with a general campaign and product, or they could target a segment of the mass market—males or females, people in the Southwest, teens, white-collar workers—with a specific campaign or product. However, as market segments are increasingly divided into niches (young white-collar men, teenage girls in the Northeast), the mass market becomes an accumulation of ever-

EXHIBIT / 21.6
Market Development

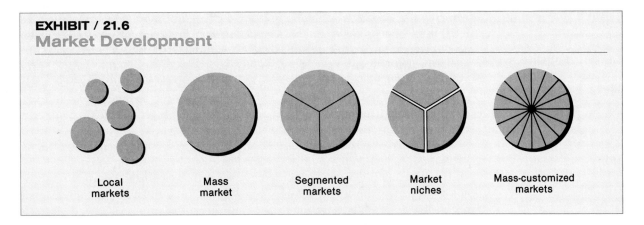

| Local markets | Mass market | Segmented markets | Market niches | Mass-customized markets |

narrower segments. (See Exhibit 21.6.) Ultimately, even finer differentiation will lead to the meeting of individual needs on a mass market basis.

Retailers are already experimenting with computerized techniques to yield these results. Some hardware stores, for example, have computerized color-swatching machines, which allow customers to choose the precise color of the commodity (paint) they are after. A light-sensitive reader can analyze the colors in a paint card or even a swatch of fabric that the customer brings in, compensate for the refraction of light off the solid object, and automatically mix the paint to match.

Federal Express, too, is experimenting in mass customization. It already allows customers to tailor shipping and billing systems to their own needs, providing greater customer-tailored service than any of its competitors. In addition, clients are able to hook directly into the Federal Express tracking network to locate their own packages at any time they wish, without relying on customer service representatives.

TECHNICAL, ADMINISTRATIVE, AND INSTITUTIONAL ISSUES IN THE FUTURE

It would be impossible to outline all the challenges, opportunities, and threats that increasingly rapid change will create. But the framework laid out in the opening chapters helps put it in context: in all three areas of management responsibilities—technical, administrative, and institutional—these trends will leave their mark.

In the technical area, increasing globalization and an expanding service base will have two effects simultaneously: Less complex manufacturing jobs will migrate overseas to developing nations, and technical jobs in the United States will be increasingly clerical and specialized. The revolution in information technology will make these clerical jobs increasingly computer-oriented. Thus, the average first-line manager with technical responsibilities is now beginning to manage a group of technical specialists who are running the machines that are performing the tasks the first-line personnel used to perform.

Meanwhile, diminishing lag times coupled with mass customization technologies in production will require changes in output standards. If lag times or downtimes are reduced to near zero, output standards will no longer be concerned with making incremental speed and efficiency improvements in the production of one product, but rather with how many different products can be produced from one production system or how quickly changes can be made to put out each different item. The trend toward "no-matter" production will present even greater challenges: The tangible resources of yesterday and today, such as labor, capital, and equipment, will be replaced by the intangible resources of tomorrow: mind, time, and information. Allocating the latter instead of the former will require entirely new skills and techniques.

Administrative responsibilities will also change in the future environment. As Exhibit 21.2 illustrated, America's work force will be changing in composition. And as the economy becomes increasingly service-oriented and information technologies change, the combination of a new work force and a new set of jobs will necessitate great shifts in the methods of human resource. In addition, administrative managers overseas will need different skills than those at home since the people employed and the work undertaken in various countries will be different.

The concepts of time, space, matter, and customization will also change administrative responsibilities. The no-lag-time customer service system in a hotel, for example, would require significantly more sophisticated personnel management techniques than the four- or five-hour lag time commonly allowed today. If customer service at Federal Express shifts completely into the hands of the customer, a whole department will be eliminated or take on a completely different function. "Any place" production, whereby parts of a whole could come from anywhere on the globe, would require more sophisticated coordination mechanisms than those currently used.

The conceptual shift in thinking for the institutional responsibilities, however, may be the most dramatic in the coming years. The how, what, where, when, and why of business will all change, subtly in some cases, drastically in others. The depletion of certain basic resources, such as fossil fuels, will necessitate entirely new ways of fueling or configuring production systems while technological developments will allow for the use of currently unheard of resources, expanding options on many levels. Population explosions in the developing nations, those nations that will probably host the bulk of the world's basic manufacturing capacity, will highlight new responsibilities for organizations to improve the quality of life in their operating environments. Increasing globalization, global competition, and the uneven imposition of trade restrictions will necessitate highly creative competitive strategies. And the growth in service industries and information technology will force many industries to rethink their main purpose, goal, and identity.

New methods, technologies, and opportunities will also allow or require shifts in strategic thinking and planning on the institutional level. How will you conduct strategic planning activities if lag times between idea and implementation approach virtual zero? Since information technologies increasingly allow "any place" production and operation, the possibilities are endless. If intangible goods, such as information, become the major products in the economy, how will you produce them? How will you use them to increase the productivity profits or efficiency of your organization?

This is not to say that, one day, ten years from now, you as a manager will wake up, go to work, find your office gone, your calendar replaced with a "relative time" monitor, your pens and note pads replaced with thought sensors, and everything you ever held as stable and solid, a memory. All the changes and developments we have discussed are only predictions and are still subject to what people, organizations, and nations do about or in response to them.

Though some of this may appear mind-boggling and intimidating, people living 200 years ago would have been boggled by the concepts of communications through copper or optical-fiber wires, moving pictures broadcast through the air and reproduced on little boxes in front of the living room sofa, and huge metal tubelike structures with wings flying through the air.

MANAGEMENT IN THE FUTURE

Though the environment will be vastly different in coming years, managers will still have to manage, still have to make decisions, and still engage in the same basic functions they do today: planning, organizing, directing, and controlling. The methods by which they undertake these activities, however, will be quite different.

Decision Making

Even major developments in artificial intelligence will not preempt human decision making. Computers with "reasoning" capabilities can still only "deduce" to the extent that they are programmed by humans. The inference bank is filled with inferences humans have made, and the conclusion-drawing mechanisms are limited to mechanisms people have written into the system. Though the artificially intelligent computer will be able to sort through possible solutions much more rapidly than a person or a team of experts, the outcome will always be subject to the discretion of the end user: the human being, or manager.

The decisions necessary and the way they are reached will change over time, though the basic principles discussed in Chapter 3 will not change. One decision will still be related to the next and to the previous one; all decisions will still affect future decision possibilities. If a company decides to set up mining operations on the moon, it may have to forgo the opportunity to mine on Mars. And although the moon may provide valuable ores or minerals, substances native to Mars may be in higher demand and bring a better price. There will still be programmed and nonprogrammed decisions; though many of today's nonprogrammed decisions may be programmed tomorrow, changing environments will always create new challenges requiring new decisions.

Similarly, the context of decision making will still include conditions of certainty, risk, and uncertainty. Information-processing capabilities will be increasing dramatically, but the world will always be full of unknowns. Consider extraterrestrial mining operations. On Earth, sensitive equipment and careful analysis can indicate where the richest stores of fuels, ores, and minerals lie under the soil or water. On other planets, similar techniques might give misleading results since the composition of these planets will be quite different from that of Earth. Even at home, conditions of risk and uncertainty will abound. A technological breakthrough in electronic data transmission, or even solid mass transmission, would render Federal Express's overnight mail service obsolete.

The basic steps in the decision-making process will also remain useful, despite extensive environmental changes. The issues will still need to be defined, relevant information analyzed, alternatives evaluated, options selected and implemented, results monitored, and corrections made. Though the time frame for many currently lengthy decisions will probably be shortened dramatically, new, more complicated issues will evolve that will take more time again to work through. And though new qualitative and quantitative methods to aid in decision making will be developed, new issues will put these methods to the test. Unless time does really become reversible in a practical sense, allowing us to evaluate the results of our decisions before we make them, decision making will continue to be one of the manager's most important and most challenging activities.

Planning

Planning, too, will continue to be an important managerial function. It will still be used to help the organization avoid unforeseen problems, to establish a clear purpose and direction, and to keep the organization on track, even if that track is completely different tomorrow than it is today. Where an organization might previously have planned to increase production of type X widgets, it might soon plan to increase the possible variety of widgets or might plan to go out of widget production entirely and go into consulting for widget production.

The steps in the planning process will also hold as they did with decision making. Goals will need to be established, future scenarios predicted, alternatives developed, and the plan selected, implemented, and monitored. Today, the prediction of future scenarios may be the most exciting or intimidating part of the process. With possibilities abounding, options for all organizations are increasing almost exponentially.

Planning will still be conducted on several levels: strategic, operational, and tactical, though not necessarily by different people. That is, although major directional courses and the specific methods for carrying them out will still need to be set, it is probable that the responsibility for these levels of planning will not be divided by hierarchy as much as it is today. Many individuals in the organization will participate in all aspects of a plan—for the overall strategy as well as for the technical details.

Not surprisingly, the barriers and obstacles to planning described in Chapter 4 will also exist, and in many cases may even become stronger. With environmental changes occurring ever more rapidly, and competitive development always on the immediate horizon, many managers might be tempted to just lock up a seemingly stable course of action and withdraw from the race. This, of course, will only mean complete or partial business failure at some point. While the rapid changes make planning more risky, they also make it more necessary and important.

Organizing

Organizational issues will undergo major revisions—they have already. When environmental change is slow, organizations can be stable and inflexible quite successfully. This is no longer the case. Every organization must incorporate some type or degree of flexibility to be able to respond to increasingly rapid developments. At any time, a competitor could come up with a new product or production method that places other companies at a great disadvantage. A certain resource could run low and become too expensive to use; another could be discovered that replaces something in common use and could allow great cost savings or result in completely new products.

Organization structure must still be utilized as a tool for goal accomplishment, and since the goals will change, the organizing methods and techniques must change in concert with them. All the ideas covered in Chapter 7, while they will hold in a general sense, may be applied very differently in the future. Division of labor may not refer to assembly line production in one plant but rather to component production spread out all over the world. It might also be used to refer to parallel processing by computers, through which separate units of a computer process parts of one whole transaction. Line and staff functions might not be divided between two groups of people in one organization. Since information will be a major product, "staff" may be composed entirely of external consultants.

When the place of operation of any one company is spread out around the globe, coordination of efforts is more complex and more crucial. The matrix organization, a balance of departmentalization by both function and purpose, may become the dominant organization structure. Creative systems allowing both tight centralization for efficiency and control, and far-flung decentralization for flexibility and market responsiveness, will become most prominent.

Directing

Robots, computers, and machines will not take over the world. And even if they took over the business sector, people would still be needed to program them, operate them, improve them, and nurse them back to health. Therefore it will always be necessary for managers to guide people in their work and to provide the appropriate environments for these people to work in effectively. Staffing, motivating, leading, working with groups, and communicating—all aspects of the directing function—will continue to be important.

In staffing, people will still be recruited from both inside and outside the organization; they will still need to be oriented and trained, compensated, promoted, or otherwise developed. But the specifics will change. The definitions of compensation and promotion, for example, can be expected to change significantly; employees may wish to be rewarded with something other than money or a step up the ladder. Project options, autonomy, creative work packages, or even royalty arrangements for new developments are already becoming more common compensation and motivation tools than incremental raises or promotions.

The ability of people to work in groups will become increasingly important. New production technology and work design will require even better techniques for creativity and problem solving. Leadership concepts are already shifting. Effective leadership requires the knowledge, experience, and skill needed to allow others to direct themselves independently, yet ensure that the overall goals are still achieved.

Communication, as we have seen already, will never be the same. The entire process of encoding, transmission, decoding, and interpretation, though still identifiable as a process, is undertaken in hundreds of new and different ways. Though communication problems still exist, and still can be broken down into the basic categories of noise, difference in perceptions, language, and status, the meaning of these terms is not the same. Noise on copper phone wires has been decreased through the use of fiber-optic cable, but noise in the sense of densely packed transmissions is a problem. Differences in perception, though they will always exist between people, also exist between computer programs, specifically those that do not "speak the same language."

Controlling

In an environment as unpredictable as the near future will be, control might seem close to impossible, although certainly it will be a necessity. How can a manager standardize performance and quality for the sake of efficiency and effectiveness without becoming too rigid to respond to the environment?

Mechanisms of control, just like mechanisms of organization, will simply be adjusted to reflect new realities. Performance standards will be set, performance will be measured against them, and corrective action will be taken; but the standards will tend to reflect variety, innovation, and intangible factors more than number, size, or other standard tangible factors. In many cases, informal, internal, and ad hoc methods of control will take precedence over formal, external, and systematic methods. As pointed out previously, in the increasingly service-oriented economy, controls must precede production, since production, delivery, and consumption are virtually simultaneous.

Management in the future will still be management. The challenges and opportunities will come in different shapes and sizes, but they will come, and the effective managers of tomorrow will be there to meet them head on.

▓ KEY POINTS

1 Five major trends that are changing the world environment are increasing globalization; shifts in the demographic characteristics of nations—some increasing their populations rapidly, others gradually leveling off; depletion or pollution of many of the resources organizations rely on today to produce their goods and services; continuing growth in the service economy; and continuing revolutions in information technology. These shifting trends will make it even more important for organizations to effectively manage themselves and to effectively manage their social responsibilities to the world.

2 Business is shifting its concepts of time (of production, distribution, and/or delivery processes), place (location of operatives, size of products, structure of market relationship), matter (as the economy shifts increasingly to services from manufacturing, value will be centered increasingly in intangibles over tangibles), and customization (ultimately, organizations will be able to mass produce a virtually unlimited number of "different" products).

3 On all three levels of organizational management—

technical, administrative, and institutional—environmental trends and conceptual shifts in the business environment will leave their mark. Technical managers will be managing machine specialists rather than laborers who work with their hands. Administrative managers will be faced with increased challenges of coordination as centralized/decentralized structures become the norm. And institutional managers will face the tremendous challenges of planning strategically in a world that can change drastically in very short time frames, while also having to assure the highest standards of socially responsible behavior in a world with many upcoming environmental and societal challenges.

4 The basic functions of management—planning, organizing, directing, and controlling—will remain necessities for organizational survival although the specifics of their application will change with the changes in the business and world environments. In addition, decision making will still be a manager's most crucial responsibility, and it will still have great bearing on the success and survival of the organization.

▓ FOR DISCUSSION AND REVIEW

1. Federal Express faces many challenges in the coming years as the environment in which it operates changes. Of the five trends discussed in the beginning of the chapter, which will cause the greatest change for Federal Express, and why?

2. Which of the five trends will cause the greatest

stress for a manager in the United States in the future? Which will cause the least? Why?

3. What are some examples of revolutions in information technology that you have recently heard about?

4. How will the concept of "any time" manufacturing affect industries such as the U.S. Postal Service which rely on time to add value to their services?

5. What evidence of the approach of "any place"

manufacturing can you see in today's business world, and how is it changing?

6. Of the five traditional management functions—decision making, planning, organizing, directing, and controlling—which do you think might be eliminated or become less important in the future?

7. Describe yourself in a future-oriented organization. How does the organization operate to help it deal with a changing environment?

KEY TERMS

Any place	Globalize	Mass customizing	Resource availability
Any time	Information technology	No-matter	Service sector
Demographics			

THE CONFERENCE TABLE: DISCUSSION CASE / 21.1

New Waves at NUMMI

In 1978, 7100 workers were employed in General Motors' Fremont, California, production plant. They worked under a 400-page union-management contract with 5000 labor agreements and 82 job descriptions. Labor-management relations were highly adversarial. During a normal workweek, the union steward would come in on Monday to collect a list of disciplinary actions the company had taken over the weekend. List in hand, the steward then wandered around the plant looking for company violations to the contract. At the next grievance meeting, the violations would be traded off for the disciplinary actions, and work would go on, antagonistically, as usual. Problems and slowdowns were rampant, the plant had one of the worst disciplinary records in the GM system, and absenteeism stood at about 20 percent at any given time.

Meanwhile, imports had gobbled up 20 percent of the market and had sent unemployment in the auto industry soaring. In Detroit, American autoworkers were venting their frustrations by destroying Japanese cars with sledgehammers and baseball bats.

In March 1982, the Fremont plant closed its doors. The remaining 5000 hourly workers were let go, and 800 grievances were left outstanding. General Motors was sitting on an aged, vacant, 200-acre plant complex in an ugly sprawl of factories, subdivisions, and shopping centers on the fringe of San Francisco Bay. The

Sources: Rehder, Robert R., and Smith, Marta Medaris, "Kaizen and the Art of Labor Relations," *Personnel Journal* (December 1986): 83–93; Schwartz, Jim, "Detroit's New Mentors in Managing Americans—The Japanese," *International Management* (September 1986): 81–83; Brody, Michael, "Toyota Meets U.S. Auto Workers," *Fortune,* July 9, 1984, pp. 54–64; Zonana, Victor F., "Auto Venture at Roadblock," *Los Angeles Times,* December 21, 1987, pp. 1, 8, pt. IV.

Through a joint venture agreement between General Motors and Toyota, the GM Fremont production plant was reorganized based upon Japanese management principles.

solution? Management got on the phone with Toyota, and an agreement was reached through which each party would sink $100 million into the plant and start the whole thing over from the ground up.

Not that this agreement was easy to reach. The United Auto Workers (UAW) had threatened to block the joint venture, called New United Motor Manufacturing, Inc. (NUMMI), if the bulk of Fremont's unionized employees were not rehired. But Toyota was not much interested in working with American unions, famous for rigid work rules that made Japanese production efficiency impossible. "Commies and drug addicts, gambling, fighting, refusing to work, that was Toyota's idea of a unionized American work force," said Toyota's senior advisor and labor relations consultant. For their part, the unions were not interested in working under Japanese management. They had no desire to use break time to discuss production problems and were not excited about the prospect of early-morning calisthenics to Japanese music.

But the deal went through, and by early 1984 the plant was being retooled for the new venture. Under the new management, the UAW retained bargaining power and the laid-off workers were considered the primary source for hiring. Many of the executive perks that the workers had resented, such as reserved parking spaces and a separate cafeteria, were eliminated. The union-management contract was now only 15 pages long (double-spaced) and incorporated only 20 labor agreements. Toyota agreed to provide the standard American wage and benefit package, though it cut costs by using more flexible health plans. In return, the UAW accepted the joint venture as a new company, not bound by the previous seniority rights, work rules, and job classifications of the GM contract. The union also agreed to work under the team-oriented, less hierarchical Japanese management system.

NUMMI's flat, democratic organization structure was built on teams from the bottom up. Originally, there were 2500 employees (in late 1987 the number fell to 1600, largely through attrition). The employees were all informally titled "problem-solving managers" and divided into 300 teams of five to eight; each team could decide how best to accomplish its own segment of the production work. Team members were trained to do each task in that segment so that they could rotate jobs. Job classifications have been narrowed down to four: three for skilled trades and one for production workers. Previously, hours could be lost for the sake of an unhooked wire simply because union restrictions prevented unauthorized workers from doing work outside their classifications. Now, no time is lost locating specialists; almost anybody in the vicinity can solve any problem.

In addition, establishment of harmony between humans and machines is a top priority. Though some state-of-the-art technology has been introduced, the Japanese managers do not consider increased automation the key to productivity. The combination of continuous collaborative problem solving, team control of the production systems, and a sociotechnical quality control system (problem-solving managers and machines, working together, identify and solve problems, continuously improving operations) is the synergistic key to increased success and productivity.

Production and cost efficiency have soared under the new management. Where a typical American manufacturing operation requires 27 worker-hours to assemble a subcompact car, the Japanese system requires only 15. And though the average Japanese product has a $1500 to $2500 estimated cost advantage, NUMMI is importing engines, transaxles, and other components—totaling more than 50 percent of costs—from Japan. Thus, NUMMI cars will be at a cost advantage over American-made vehicles.

The Fremont plant is transformed in all aspects. Grievances have hovered under 20, and absenteeism has dropped to less than 3 percent. Though none of the workers participate in the preshift calisthenics program, the belligerent, antagonistic atmosphere on the plant floor has been replaced with high-energy enthusiasm. Production began in 1985, and peak production of 20,000 models per month (Chevy Novas and Toyota Corollas) was reached in the spring of 1986. The Nova has fewer defects per vehicle than any other domestic car, and one market researcher called NUMMI "an unqualified success" in which both partners met their objectives: Toyota won valuable experience with an American work force and got around U.S. import quotas, while GM gained firsthand knowledge of Toyota's production system. ■

DISCUSSION
QUESTIONS

1. Which environmental trends contributed to the Fremont plant's original closing and NUMMI's subsequent opening?
2. How has NUMMI addressed such issues as time, place, matter, and customization in its operation?
3. How do operational, administrative, and strategic management differ in the NUMMI operation from the Fremont operation?

THE CONFERENCE TABLE: DISCUSSION CASE / 21.2

Back to the Future in Health Care

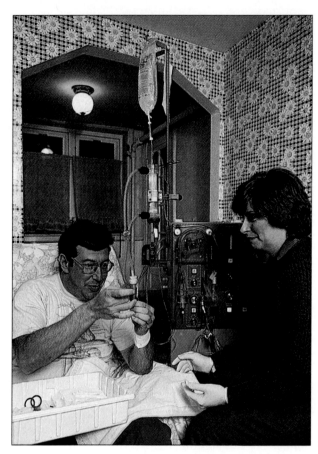

Lower costs and advanced technology are the main reasons for moving a patient from a hospital to home care.

Wherever one looks today, one sees trends that are changing the way we travel, work, communicate, and live. Producers are moving production facilities closer to the consumers for profit and service goals, and consumers are demanding increasingly better service and attention to their needs.

Nowhere is this more evident than in the field of health care. People, of course, would rather be healthy than sick, but if they must be sick, they would like to be as comfortable as possible. In a market driven by consumer tastes, one of the biggest barriers to comfort used to be expense. A stay in a hospital will cost hundreds of dollars or more a day, and insurance will not cover it all.

In the old days, health care was for the most part performed in the home. House calls were not an expensive option but rather a practical necessity. Only in the booming industrial era, as everything became more mass produced, did hospi-

Sources: Lutz, Sandy, "Home I.V. Therapy Companies Target Insurers, HMOs for Future Growth," *Modern Healthcare,* March 13, 1987, p. 96 (chart); Rublin, Lauren R., "Just What the Doctor Ordered," *Barron's,* December 1, 1986, p. 13.

tals come to dominate our way of treating the sick. In a hospital, a large number of sick people could be taken care of by a small number of trained professionals and support staff. By the twentieth century and the great world wars, hospitals became the only reasonable method of health care for seriously and chronically ill people. The cost of one $2 million heart machine could be shared among many different users and not borne by just one. As a benefit of the concentrated revenues, these same hospitals also frequently yielded the most exciting medical advances. Where there were many subjects to study, much was learned.

In recent years, however, health care costs have skyrocketed. The increase in the cost of hospital stays and the implementation of methods of cost control such as diagnostically related groups have produced more discomfort for patients both while they are sick and after they get the bill. In response to these problems of cost and comfort, increasing numbers of different methods of health care have arrived to meet our needs. One of the most exciting is home health care, and one of the most thriving companies in the business at present is Baxter Travenol Laboratories in Deerfield, Illinois. Moving the patient from the hospital to home saves hundreds of dollars a day and has inspired many of the newest technological innovations for health care such as the portable IV pump, the pacemaker, insulin pumps for diabetics, and fetal monitors for the home. These are the same reasons that the shift occurred in the first place: lower cost and advanced technology.

One area in which Baxter Travenol has been a leader for many years is the administration of home care kidney dialysis. One of the trends of the future is that producers and consumers will move closer to each other. Advances in technology and delivery services will allow many things to be made, or services performed, in the very lap of the customer. Travenol pioneered the delivery of kidney dialysis at home in the late 1960s. Kidney dialysis removes waste products from the blood of a patient, a job done by healthy kidneys, and then replaces the "clean" blood in the patient's body. Until home care kidney dialysis came around, patients with renal failure had to undergo dialysis at hospitals where the complex and expensive machinery was stored. Treatment required periodic, lengthy visits away from familiar surroundings, a problem which was solved by home care: moving the treatment to the patient rather than the patient to the treatment.

Two recent moves have thrust the former maker of intravenous solutions and blood preparations into the spotlight of home health care. One was the 1985 merger with the country's largest hospital supply chain, American Hospital Supply Corporation (AHSC), which very nearly tripled its size and doubled its revenues, and the 1987 acquisition of Caremark, a provider of specialized medical products to seriously ill patients in their homes. Before the merger with AHSC, Travenol was characterized as a producer of high-quality products. What Travenol got from the two other companies was an expanded range of products to serve new markets. AHSC supplied a market for its supplies, and Caremark will greatly expand its home care market. As was written recently about Travenol's expansions and improvements, "No doubt the company sensed at least the partial shape of things to come in establishing an early and significant presence in the alternate-site healthcare business."

Travenol also supplies services such as respiratory therapy, nutrition therapy, antibiotic therapy, and chemotherapy for patients in the home. In addition, the company services an estimated $10 billion a year alternate-site health care market that provides the company with $800 million in revenues a year. Technological breakthroughs, like the company's new patient-controlled analgesic device to administer pain-controlling intravenous drugs, which is the size of a wristwatch, have made the process of home care quicker, easier, and more comfortable, and it has cut the cost of treatment immensely for patients with these problems. The size of the home care market is predicted to more than triple from a total of $869 million in 1986 to an estimated $2.8 billion in 1990. In 1986, Caremark and Baxter Travenol were at the top of the list with combined revenues of $227 million. In 1990, revenues are projected to have grown to $585 million for nearly one-quarter of the market. And Travenol will be at the top. ■

DISCUSSION QUESTIONS

1. How has the health care industry been transformed over time in terms of the concept of space or place?
2. Which trends is Baxter Travenol taking into consideration in its operations, and how?
3. How has Baxter Travenol addressed the issues of time, space, and matter in its operating strategy?
4. With health care moving increasingly back into the home, how will the operational, administrative, and strategic responsibilities change for hospitals?

The Smell of Huge Profits over Cocktails and Sushi

On July 20, 1987, Japan's Toshiba Corporation ran a full-page advertisement in major metropolitan newspapers across the United States, which opened with the following:

Joichi Aoi, president and chief executive officer of Toshiba Corporation.

Toshiba Corporation Extends Its Deepest Regrets to the American People.

Toshiba Corporation shares the shock and anger of the American people, the Administration and Congress at the recent conduct of one of our 50 major subsidiaries, Toshiba Machine Company. We are equally concerned about the serious impact of TMC's diversion on the security of the United States, Japan, and other countries of the Free World.

Toshiba Corporation had no knowledge of this unauthorized action by TMC. And the United States and Japanese Governments have not claimed that Toshiba Corporation itself had any knowledge or involvement.

Nevertheless, Toshiba Corporation, as a majority shareholder of TMC, profoundly apologizes for these past actions by a subsidiary of Toshiba.

For the future, Toshiba Corporation takes full responsibility to ensure that never again will such activity take place within the Toshiba Group of companies.

- We are working with the Governments of the United States and Japan in this endeavor.

The relationship of Toshiba Corporation, its subsidiaries, and their American employees with the American people, one marked by mutual trust and cooperation, has developed over many years of doing business together. We pledge to do whatever it takes to repair, preserve, and enhance this relationship.

Toshiba Corporation already has begun to take corrective measures throughout its hundreds of subsidiaries and affilitate companies:

- We immediately directed all our companies to institute stringent measures guarding more securely against this kind of misconduct.

Sources: This case was written by M. R. Poirier, based on the following sources: "Toshiba Corporation Extends Its Deepest Regrets to the American People," *Boston Globe,* July 20, 1987, p. 7; Bennett, Ralph Kinney, "The Toshiba Scandal: Anatomy of a Betrayal," *Reader's Digest* (December 1987): 96; Rubinfien, Elisabeth, "Japan's Companies Wary of Joining Star Wars Research," *Wall Street Journal,* July 15, 1987, p. 24; Carrington, Tim, "Japan to Take Part in SDI; Toshiba Barred for a While," *Wall Street Journal,* July 22, 1987, p. 6; Farnsworth, Clyde H., "Senators Ease Trade Penalty Bill," *New York Times,* March 9, 1988, p. D1; Smart, Tim, and Webes, Joseph, "Why Congress Is Letting Toshiba off the Hook," *Business Week,* April 4, 1988, p. 39.

- We obtained the resignation of the President of TMC and the three other Board members who had corporate responsibility for the conduct of those TMC employees actually involved.

- We also obtained TMC's commitment to stop exports to the Soviet Bloc countries for an unlimited time.

- We have authorized an extensive investigation to find all the facts concerning TMC's actions and to design safeguards to prevent repetition of such conduct. This investigation is being directed by American counsel, assisted by a major independent accounting firm.

- We will discharge all officers and employees found to have knowingly participated in this wrongful export sale.

- We have appointed the former senior auditing official of Toshiba Corporation to TMC's Board with direct responsibility for Toshiba's policy of full observance of the law and of Japan's security arrangements with its allies.

- We are going to develop a rigid compliance program in cooperation with the Governments of Japan and the United States.

- We intend to estabish Toshiba's new compliance program as a model of future export controls throughout Japanese industry.

In its 22 years of doing business with the United States, Toshiba Corporation has been a leader in introducing American products to the Japanese market and also has significantly shifted the manufacture of Toshiba products to the United States. At a time when many of the U.S.-based corporations competing with Toshiba are moving production facilities and jobs abroad, Toshiba's American companies are steadily expanding the extent to which their products are manufactured in the United States. Today, Toshiba employs thousands of Americans in 21 states from New York to Texas to California. It is these Americans who have played a large and crucial part in earning Toshiba its reputation for producing top quality products, reliable service, and ongoing innovation that millions of American consumers and industrial customers know they can trust.

These bonds of cooperation are signs of our commitment to America. We earnestly wish to continue our efforts to develop our relationship with America.

We ask our American friends to work with us and help us to do so.

Joichi Aoi
President/CEO
Toshiba Corporation

THE PRESIDENT OF TOSHIBA APOLOGIZES

The advertisement was signed by Joichi Aoi, the president and chief executive officer of Toshiba Corporation. It was in response to revelations that its subsidiary, Toshiba Machine Company, had sold sensitive technology to the Soviet Union, violating NATO and other bans on the export of technology that could jeopardize Western military security. The advertisement also outlined what Toshiba Corporation was doing to repair the damage done by the unauthorized sale, including more closely monitoring its exports to the Soviet Union and firing and prosecuting those parties directly responsible for the violations. The chairman and the president of Toshiba Corporation both resigned, which, the letter explained, was "the highest form of apology" for the Japanese business world.

Ironically, the first episode in the story occurred in 1970 at the height of American-Soviet detente, a time when exchanges of technology and other types of information were being promoted by both governments. At a machine tool trade show in Chicago that year, a group of Soviets saw a milling machine that was used to manufacture ultraquiet U.S. submarine propellers. It was much more advanced than anything the Soviets themselves had and was largely responsible for the significant advantage the United States had always had over the Soviets in submarine-tracking maneuvers. The Soviets ordered six of the milling machines, but the U.S. Navy intervened and prevented the sale.

From that point on, the Soviets began undertaking more covert efforts to duplicate the technology. They acquired some less sophisticated machines from the Japanese and the French but made no significant advances for almost a decade. Then, in 1979, a meeting between Soviet trade officials and a Japanese trading company called Wako Koeki provided the Soviets their opportunity. Wako representatives were entertaining the Soviet trade officials over cocktails and sushi when Igor Aleksandrovich Osipov, vice president of Techmashimport, the Soviet agency that handles the purchase of foreign machinery, specifically requested a propeller-milling machine such as the one shown at the Chicago trade show nine years earlier. It seemed apparent to the Wako representatives that Osipov must be a KGB agent looking to acquire the machinery for military use; thus, the sale would be against Cocom (the Coordinating Committee on Multilateral Export Controls, based in Paris) restriction. Nonetheless, said one Wako official, the sale had "the smell of huge profits."

SELLING TO THE SOVIETS

A Wako representative took the request to Toshiba Machine Company (TMC), and in late 1980, a representative of TMC arrived in Moscow with a machine tool catalog. He met with Anatoly Troitsky, who was a representative of Techmashimport and also a KGB officer. Troitsky picked out what he wanted immediately: a nine-axis numerically controlled milling machine that could grind a ship propeller 30 feet in diameter and hold an almost infinite number of positions while its computerized "brain" directed the multiple cutting heads to carve and finish the blades to submillimeter tolerances. The machine, listed in Toshiba's catalog as an MBP-110, had such extensive capabilities that it was banned from export to the Soviet Union by the Western-based Cocom. Troitsky ordered it.

In working out the sales agreement, however, Troitsky specified that the machine tool be fitted not with Toshiba's computerized controllers, but with those of a company called Konsberg. Konsberg was owned by the Norwegian government, a NATO ally, and produced most of the computers used throughout the Soviet Union. The controllers the Soviet agent specified were not banned by Cocom because they were typically used to control the much simpler two-axis machines. However, with a minimum effort they could be converted to control nine-axis machines. Konsberg agreed, in a separate negotiation, to produce the two-axis controllers.

On April 24, 1981, TMC representatives signed a contract with Soviet trade officials in TMC's export office in Moscow. The 120-page contract specified that TMC would be delivering two-axis machine tools not banned by Cocom; in a "secret protocol," TMC and the Soviets, including Osipov and Troitsky, agreed that the machines would be upgraded to have nine axes.

One month later, the basic contract was submitted by TMC to Japan's Ministry of International Trade and Industry (MITI), a nonregulatory Japanese agency whose function is to nurture Japanese industry. As a noble gesture of sorts, it also strives to monitor export activities to ensure that they fall within international regulations (such as those outlined by Cocom). MITI officials quickly approved TMC's application to export the two-axis machine tools, one of 5000 applications it handled that year for goods going to Communist countries.

Over the course of the next two years, the two-axis machines were upgraded to nine-axis machines, the Konsberg two-axis controllers were shipped to TMC and upgraded to nine-axis controllers, and the controllers were mounted on the machine tools. In the spring of 1983, the finished machines were loaded onto the Soviet cargo ship *Starry Bolshevic* in Yokohama, Japan. Customs officials approved the paperwork, describing two-axis machine tools, without checking the contents of any of the crates. By August 1983, U.S. officials later estimated, all four nine-axis machines were in operation at the Baltic Shipyard in Leningrad. Over the course of the year, Konsberg and TMC technicians made regular trips to the shipyard to service and align the machines.

The Baltic Shipyards where reconnaissance photos showed restricted Western technology installed in Soviet facilities.

At this point, TMC and Konsberg had just about collected their money and walked away. However, in December 1985, a TMC employee involved in a dispute with his employer, and also uncomfortable with the arrangements that had been made with the Soviets, left his job and sent the story directly to the chairman of Cocom, Ranieri Tallarigo.

Tallarigo showed the TMC employee's letter to Cocom's Japanese delegate, who in turn reported the violation to MITI. MITI investigated the charge, TMC denied it, and the long chain of paperwork from TMC to Konsberg to the Japanese customs officials essentially backed up TMC's claims that they were guilty of no Cocom violations. MITI reported this back to the Japanese Cocom delegate, who in turn reported it to the Cocom chairman, who then declared the case closed.

THE UNITED STATES BECOMES CONCERNED

However, the United States Defense Technology Administration (DTSA) was not so easily convinced. For years, DTSA had been collecting bits and pieces of information that indicated that the Soviets had been on a worldwide hunt for submarine technology, that machinery was being secretly shipped through the Netherlands to the Soviet Union, and that the Soviets had very recently deployed submarines with propellers remarkably more quiet and sophisticated than they had ever had. Finally, reconnaisance photos

of the Baltic Shipyard were produced that very clearly showed Norwegian control devices mounted on two-story-high Japanese milling machines that were used to produce marine propellers.

The information was shuffled among MITI, Cocom, and Japanese government officials for several months. Then, in mid-April 1987, in preparation for his visit to the United States, Japanese Prime Minister Nakasone received a full briefing of the case. In his estimation, much had been covered up. On April 30, Japanese police arrived en masse at TMC's headquarters and seized virtually every file in the building. What followed was "an avalanche of confessions, resignations, explanations, and apologies."

But this was only the beginning. The repercussions of the events, all undertaken among a handful of individuals, reverberated across companies, industries, and countries around the world. Some events occurred immediately: Several top Toshiba Machine Co. and Toshiba Corporation executives resigned, and the main parties involved in the transgressions were fired and placed under investigation. The Norwegian government apologized for Konsberg's role in the scheme, halted all of Konsberg's ongoing deals with the Eastern Bloc, and closed its office in Moscow, but charged only one member of the company's sales department with various infractions. The employee is reportedly now working for a private Norwegian firm seeking to expand business with the Soviets.

THE UNITED STATES REACTS

Other impacts developed in the ensuing months. In the United States, the Reagan administration acted swiftly to punish the Japanese for Toshiba's violations of the Cocom export restriction. On June 30, the Senate approved a measure by a 95 to 2 vote to ban the sale in the United States of most Toshiba and Konsberg products for at least two years. Also at this time Japan and the United States had been on the verge of signing an agreement for the Japanese to join in the research of Reagan's strategic defense initiative (SDI) defense program. But government officials, as well as American executives in other participating corporations, began to consider Japanese companies a security risk. MITI, it appeared, was an ineffective monitoring agency incapable of ensuring that Western technology stayed in Western hands. In addition, if Japanese companies were offered participation in the project, the project might receive negative international attention and restrictions would be so tight that the costs of the project would skyrocket. Said one Japanese Foreign Ministry official, "The Toshiba case has taught companies that this time they had better stay out of any risky business that might put them on the front page of a newspaper."

Japan's minister of international trade, Hajime Tamura, arrived in the United States in mid-June to apologize for Toshiba's actions and appeal to Congress and the administration not to implement import bans of Japanese goods or prohibit Japanese companies from participating in such major lucrative projects as the SDI research. During meetings with U.S. officials, he assured them that Japan would strengthen its export-screening bureaucracy, expand its contribution of Cocom, and toughen its laws against diversions of militarily sensitive technologies to the Soviet Bloc.

On July 20, Toshiba Corporation published an apology in major newspapers across the United States. In addition to the opening remarks, quoted in the beginning of this case, Toshiba Corporation's president outlined an extensive list of actions the company was taking to ensure that such infractions would not be repeated, to emphasize the value it attributed to its relationship with the American people, and to express its sincere desire to continue developing that relationship.

Despite Tamura's visit and Toshiba's public apology, Toshiba Corporation was barred from obtaining SDI contracts, pending a Pentagon investigation into the diversion itself and the methods by which Japan would prevent another such incident. However, Defense Department officials considered Japan "a treasure trove of sophisticated technologies for the SDI project," specifying that Japan was expected to make significant contributions in the areas of "radar transmitters, semiconductors, superconductors, software systems, and optical systems." Thus, Japan's ban from participation was considered temporary.

One year after the story broke, pressure from many sources led Senate conferees to begin rethinking sections of the trade bill calling for sanctions against Toshiba and Konsberg. An amendment to the original bill called for the ban of all imports (except

F-16 fighter jets. American and Japanese interests are so intertwined that trade sanctions cannot realistically be imposed. Japan will help upgrade the F-16s.

products essential for American users) for two to five years from Konsberg and Toshiba as well as any companies found to have violated the Cocom restrictions since January 1, 1980. Investigations in early 1988 revealed that several Western allies, including companies within the 12-nation European Economic Community (EEC), were guilty of such violations. In March 1988, therefore, the Senate rewrote a portion of the bill so that it limited the sanctions to Toshiba and Konsberg and did not apply them retroactively to other companies whose export control violations resulted in "a substantial serious adverse impact on the strategic balance of forces." A House amendment also added that the president would have a list of sanctions from which to choose, such as import bans, bans from government contracts, or bans from American suppliers, and that he could apply these with discretion to the specific subsidiaries (such as Toshiba Machine) responsible for the violations. These would leave unaffected the parent's (Toshiba Corporation) sales of computers, chips, and other electronic equipment.

THE UNITED STATES BACKS OFF

Ultimately, it was argued, that amended trade bill one year later subjects Toshiba Corporation to "sanctions that, at worst, make only a slight dent in Toshiba's annual U.S. sales of $2.7 billion. The reasons: the U.S. has too much at stake in its political and economic relations with Japan to take drastic action." Japan had offered to pay one-half of the estimated $1 billion cost of civilian employees at U.S bases; it will increase its military spending by 5.2 percent in 1988; it will join General Dynamics Corporation in a $1.3 billion project to upgrade the F-16 fighter jet; and it will buy several state-of-the-art Aegis air defense systems at $500 million each to help fulfill its promise to monitor the sea lanes within 1000 miles of Japan.

According to some in the government, Toshiba should have been made an example. In March 1988, when a Tokyo court fined Toshiba Machine Co. $15,750 and gave two executives implicated in the scandal suspended sentences, Senator Jake Garn (R-Utah) called the verdict "nothing more than a slap on the wrist with a wet noodle." But other government officials and trade experts feel that Japan has in fact tightened up its export control mechanisms and heightened its concern for protecting sensitive technologies. Thus, some in Congress want the trade bill to let Toshiba off the hook while still allowing for sanctions against corporations that violate the export restrictions in the future. Therefore, "despite its initial anger," one reporter argued, "Congress appeared to accept the view that the cold realities of interdependence rule out tougher action." ∎

QUESTIONS

1. How many different instances of behavior can you identify in this case that are in some way unethical or not socially responsible? Based on the concepts in Chapter 18, why would you define them as such? Do you think Toshiba Corporation's proposed actions, outlined in Joichi Aoi's letter, will effectively correct these ethical shortcomings (at least those attributable to Toshiba employees)? Why or why not? What might you recommend in addition?

2. How does this case illustrate the interrelationship between society, business, and government? What effect do legal and political factors have on business in this case? As a top manager for an American company whose main supplier was Toshiba (at the time of the ban on imports of Toshiba products), what might you have been forced to do in this case?

3. What risks and opportunities of international business are illustrated in this case? What economic, legal, political, and cultural factors come into play? How do the political issues discussed in Chapter 18 and the legal and political issues discussed in Chapter 19 become more complicated when business is conducted across national borders?

Appendix: Quantitative Management Tools

We have noted that everyone makes decisions. How we make decisions can affect the survival and functioning of the organizations where we work and can influence our own quality of life. Typically we must make decisions with limited information and within numerous physical, financial, and societal constraints. Quantitative analysis can be helpful in two ways: First, it can help us analyze the particular situation; second, the formal procedures and rigorous analysis provide us with a way of thinking about the problem.

Most real-world decisions are subjective and require our intuitive judgment. The use of quantitative tools contributes to the refinement of our intuitive processes, making us more alert to the important factors and uncertainties we face and better able to deal with complex decisions.

In this appendix we will look at the development of management science and operations research and their contributions to management. We will also look at the two basic states of nature, certainty and risk/uncertainty, and see how they affect our decision making and our selection of quantitative techniques. The quantitative techniques chosen were selected because of their wide use in business and managerial decision making.

OPERATIONS RESEARCH AND MODEL BUILDING

Operations research is the application of the scientific method to problem solving; management science is the application of operations research to business and managerial decisions. The distinctions between these two disciplines are extremely fine, and in practice the two terms are used interchangeably.

History of Operations Research

Operations research has its roots in World War II, primarily in the solving of military problems. Morse and Kimball give the following example.[1]

During World War II, the Allies were greatly disturbed over the success of German U-boat attacks on Allied shipping. Operations research revealed two key facts: (1) The quantity of Allied ships lost per attack seemed to be independent (i.e., not related) of the convoy's size, and (2) the ratio of U-boats destroyed to Allied ships sunk appeared to be proportional to the square of the number of escort ships. In essence, as the number of escorts increased, this ratio changed (squared) due to an increase in the number of U-boats sunk and a decrease in the number of lost Allied ships. The recommendation from this analysis, which was followed, was to increase the average size of convoys and the average number of escorts. The benefits achieved were greater than expected: U-boat losses became so high and Allied losses so low that U-boats left the Atlantic for other battle areas.

Based on this and other successes, efforts were made to expand the use of operations research into business and industry. George Dantzig, Marshall Wood, and their associates made a major breakthrough in 1947. Their discovery was the development of the simplex algorithm, a computational technique for solving linear programming problems. Linear programming enables decision makers to explicitly state objectives in mathematically measurable terms. In addition, the method allows a decision maker simultaneously to maximize (profits, for example) and minimize (cost, for example) given combinations of resources and constraints. Over the past 35 years, linear programming has proven to be one of the most widely used quantitative techniques.

Rapid advances in queuing theory (the analysis of how long people or products have to wait before they are serviced), project scheduling techniques (e.g., PERT and CPM), and gaming theory (the analysis of a large number of different competitive situations where conflicts exist, and no single actor determines the outcome) soon followed, and operations research grew into a collection of techniques applicable to a wide variety of business problems. This expansion of operations research was made possible by equally rapid developments in computers. Since many of the quantitative procedures mentioned involved a large amount of computation, the advent of high-speed computers made these techniques widely available and greatly simplified their use by managers and decision makers.

According to Hiller and Lieberman[2] the contributions to management from operations research stem from:

1. Structuring real-life situations into a mathematical model and abstracting the essential elements so that a solution relevant to the decision makers's objective can be sought. This involves looking at the problem in the context of the entire system.
2. Exploring the structure of such solutions and developing systematic procedures for obtaining them.
3. Developing a solution including the mathematical theory, if necessary, that yields an optimal value of the system measure of desirability (or possibly comparing alternative courses of action by evaluating their measure of desirability).

Model Building and the Operations Research Process

The essential characteristic of operations research is its use of the scientific method of inquiry. The scientific method uses systematic and objective repetition of observation, measurement, and experimentation. It is similar to the rational problem-solving process discussed in Chapter 3. Differences between the two processes lie in the operations researcher's use of the scientific method to build mathematical models. Exhibit A.1 details the scientific method. The first of six

EXHIBIT / A.1
Scientific Method of Operations Research

Specific Activities and Decisions
I. Problem formulation
   A. Define objective of study
   B. Define measures of effectiveness and efficiency
   C. Define the relevant boundaries of the system
      1. Controllable variables
      2. Uncontrollable variables
II. Model construction
   A. Specify:
      1. Variables
      2. Parameters
      3. The relationship between variables and parameters
      4. Whether the relationship is deterministic or stochastic
III. Model validation
   A. Does the model fulfill the purpose for which it was intended?
   B. Does it predict the real-world behavior of the system?
   C. Are assumptions, variables, parameters, and relationships valid?
   D. Expert evaluation
IV. Derivation of solution
   A. Mathematical
   B. Iterative
   C. Simulation
   D. Experimental optimization
V. Evaluation of results
   A. Does the model provide valid information for decision making?
   B. Compare solutions with system behavior
VI. Implementing the model
VII. Update and revise the model

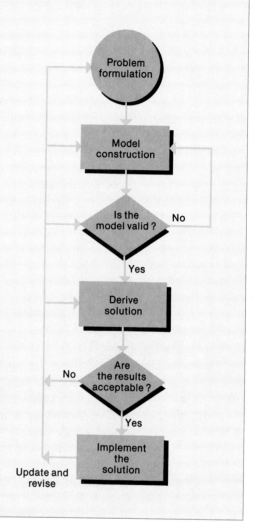

Source: Adapted From: Kwak, N., K., and DeLurgio, S. A., *Quantitative Models for Business Decisions* (North Scituate, Mass.: Duxbury Press, 1980), p. 3.

stages, problem formulation, involves defining and quantifying the objective, what we are trying to accomplish (increased profits, reduced cost, etc.). We then need to state measures of effectiveness (achievement of goals) and measures of efficiency (how much we produce with a given input) for what we are trying to accomplish.

In constructing the model, we must then specify quantities that vary (variables), quantities that are held constant (parameters), and the relationships between variables and parameters usually expressed in mathematical form (stage 2). Kwak and Delurgio offer the following example:[3]

$$P_{ii} = F(x_i d_i)$$

Where:

P_{ii} = profits (measure of performance or effectiveness)
$F(\ )$ = functional notation stating a relationship between P, x, and d
x_i = quantity demanded (uncontrollable variable)
d_i = quantity produced (controllable variable)

The uncontrollable variables (x_i) are often referred to as states of nature, whereas the controllable variables (d_i) are called decisions or actions. From this simple arrangement we can present the relationship in a tabular form called a payoff table or matrix. It reflects each combination of states of nature (x_i) and decisions (d_i) that result in different payoffs (P_{ii}). (See Exhibit A.2.)

EXHIBIT / A.2
General Payoff Table for $P_{ii} = F(x_i d_i)$

		Decisions d_i			
		d_i	d_2	...	d_n
States of nature	x_1	P_{11}	P_{12}		P_{1n}
	x_2	P_{21}	P_{22}		P_{2n}

This model incorporates the important elements of the decision situation and allows for testing of various combinations of the variable. The manager can then mathematically see how changing controllable variables affects the results.

Once constructed, the model has to be validated (stage 3). Essentially the key questions are, does the model fulfill the purpose for which it is intended, and does it provide accurate predictions?

The solution and results of a model (stage 4) are then evaluated (stage 5) to see if the model is useful and valid. If it is, the results are implemented (stage 6). If not, the managers involved must assess reasons why the model does not work. Based on experience, the model is then updated and revised.

STATES OF NATURE

Today's decisions affect tomorrow's personal and organizational performance. Since managers are attempting to make decisions about the future, they need to specify what they must know about the future to assess the impact and risk of their decisions. The first step in addressing the future is to recognize the existence of two basic states of nature: (1) conditions of certainty and (2) conditions of risk/uncertainty. Broadly speaking, states of nature refers to the set of possible random events that affect the outcomes of decisions. We review them here as background for the different types of decision-making tools. More complete explanations can be found in Chapter 3.

Conditions of Certainty

Conditions of certainty exist when a decision maker knows exactly what will happen in the future as a consequence of decisions made now. Each course of action (decision) is clearly identified with one and only one outcome (payoff). There is no randomness in the outcomes of decisions under certainty conditions. Models that operate under conditions of certainty are called deterministic models. In the real world, unfortunately, few important decisions are made under conditions of certainty.

Conditions of Risk/Uncertainty

Situations with known randomness, in the state of nature, are called conditions of risk. By known randomness we mean the ability to assign (to a decision) a number of possible outcomes and the probability that each outcome will happen. An example of this situation is the probability associated with the roll of one die. Each number (one through six) stands a 1 in 6 probability of coming up on a die roll. We know what might happen (outcomes) and the chance that they will happen (probabilities). Models under conditions of risk are called stochastic models.

One of the most difficult situations in which to make decisions is under conditions of uncertainty. In this state, we may be able to identify some or all of the outcomes associated with a decision but none of the probabilities of these outcomes. Quantitative aids to decision making are extremely helpful to managers in these situations because they help focus on key assumptions and provide some measure of risk.

DECISION MAKING UNDER CERTAINTY

There are several quantitative techniques available for decision makers operating under conditions of certainty. In this section we shall consider the following: inventory decision models, linear programming, and the critical path method (an example of network models).

Inventory Decision Models

Inventory models attempt to provide answers to two seemingly simple questions, How much inventory should we have, and when should we have it? If we define inventory creatively as idle resources, then we may think of resources as anything usable for obtaining something of value: people, money, equipment, and parts.

Business is concerned with making money and minimizing costs, objectives that are often in conflict. As managers we want to invest the minimum amount of money in inventories (idle resources) yet maintain maximum productivity. If inventory is too high, we lose the use of our money (it is tied up in inventory), increase our expenses (insurance and storage for inventory), and lose usable space for production. If inventory is too low, we lose sales because products are not available. We will have workers standing idly by waiting for parts and equipment. As a result, we would like to keep inventories high enough to make the products we can sell but not any higher.

One model developed to deal with this issue is called economic order quantity (EOQ). This model identifies how much and when inventory should be ordered. It is based on the following assumptions:

- Demand for the product is known, constant, and uniform.
- Lead time (from order to receipt) is constant.
- Price per unit of product is constant.
- Holding cost per unit per year is constant.
- Cost per order is constant.
- Setup costs are constant.
- No shortages or back orders are allowed.

This model helps us determine the specific point in time, T, at which an order will be placed and the size of that order, Q. The order point, T, will always be a specific number of actual units in inventory. An EOQ solution might be something like this: When the number of units in inventory drops to 50, place an order for 112 more units. Exhibit A.3 shows this in a graphic format.

Mathematically, the model is expressed as follows:

$$Q = \sqrt{\frac{2DO}{H}}$$

Where:

Q = economic order quantity (EOQ)
D = annual demand
O = cost of placing an order or making a setup
H = annual holding and storage cost per unit of average inventory

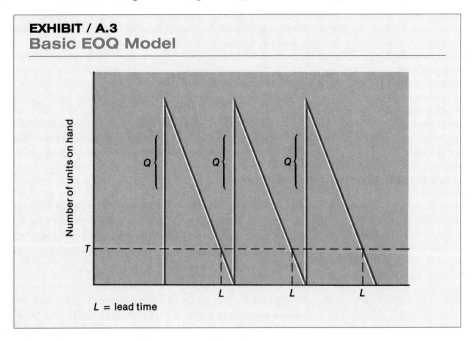

EXHIBIT / A.3
Basic EOQ Model

L = lead time

Linear Programming

Linear programming is a set of related mathematical techniques used to allocate limited resources among competing demands in an optimal way. The key assumption in linear programming is that relationships among variables are directly proportional (linear). This means that a change in variable X produces a consistent and constant change in variable Y. Graphically, the relationship would result in a

---

EXHIBIT / A.4
Data for Television Example

	Color Television	Black and White Television	Constraints
Profit	$40 (per unit)	$50 (per unit)	
Labor required	1 hour per unit	2 hours per unit	80 hours total available
Specialized color television expertise required	1 unit of capacity needed per color television	0 unit of capacity needed per black and white television	50 units total capacity available

---

straight line. Assume you work for a small manufacturer and you make televisions, one black and white model and one color. The key relationships are shown in Exhibit A.4.

In using this model, we need to state our objective in mathematical terms. This is called an objective function and either maximizes something or minimizes something. Since we are in business to make money, we would like to maximize our profit. We make $40 of profit on each color television and $50 on each black and white television we sell. Our total profit is equal to $40 X_1 + $50 X_2, where X_1 is the number of color televisions sold and X_2 is the number of black and white televisions sold. In producing these televisions we operate under two constraints. First, our capacity is limited by the number of technicians familiar with color television technology. We have only enough trained technicians to produce 50 color televisions. This can be expressed as $X_1 \le 50$. In a similar fashion, the number of hours available is constrained as follows: $1X_1 + 2X_2 \le 80$. That is, it takes one hour to make each color television and two hours to make each black and white television, and we have only 80 hours available in each production period. We can graph the objective function and constraints as shown in Exhibit A.5.

The feasible region is the graphic portrayal of the area where a solution to the problem will maximize the objective function and satisfy all the constraints. You might graph this chart on graph paper as an exercise. The optimal solution to the problem will occur within the feasible region. It is the production of 50 color and 15 black and white televisions. That will yield a profit of 50 × $40 = $2000 plus 15 × $50 = $750 for a total of $2750. This combination also satisfies the capacity and hour constraints. The capacity constraint is satisfied because we are producing only 50 color televisions. The formula for our hour constraint is $1X_1 + 2X_2 \le$ 80. Substituting in $X_1 = 50$, we find that we have 30 hours left to make black and white televisions, so we can make 15 of them.

$$1(50) + 2(X_2) = 80$$
$$2(X_2) = 80$$
$$X_2 = 15$$

This makes intuitive sense. We make a $10 higher profit on black and white televisions, but they take twice as many hours to make. So for the same amount of time it takes us to make one black and white television generating a $50 profit, we

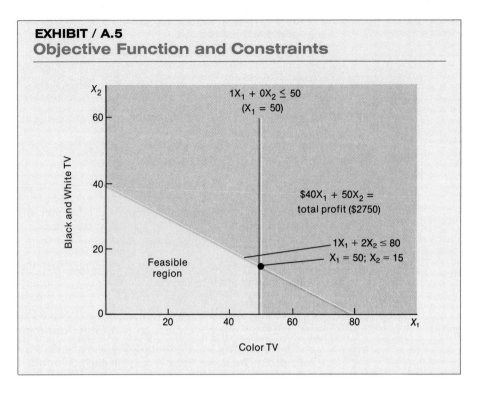

EXHIBIT / A.5
Objective Function and Constraints

could make two color televisions generating an $80 profit. It is logical to make as many color televisions as possible and then use whatever hours we have left to make black and white televisions.

Note that this is a simple problem with only two constraints. Problems with more than two constraints are best solved on a computer with the simplex algorithm. An algorithm is an interactive (repetitive) solution procedure. The computer will use the algorithm to run the linear programming until the best solution is achieved.

The key in using linear programming from a practical standpoint is not the solution of the problem on the computer. In fact, many college courses on linear programming do not address solutions. Instead, the focus is on the issue of problem formulation. The most successful users of linear programming spend most of their time defining the problem. Problem formulation skills are developed over time by experience with linear programming. They require the exercise of logical and vigorous managerial judgment.

Network Models

Managers are often responsible for the planning, controlling, and scheduling of very large, messy projects. These may be one-time events (e.g., building a new plant) or large recurring projects (e.g., managing the building of large orders of ships). Problems of coordination on such projects often become critical issues, particularly since dollar penalties and rewards are dependent on achieving contractual completion dates.

Two similar control techniques for these types of projects were developed in the late 1950s. The two techniques are the critical path method (CPM) and the program evaluation and review technique (PERT). Each method identifies a network of activities and events. Activities representing work in progress and events are performance milestones that represent either the start or finish of some activity. The major difference between PERT and CPM is on the estimate of activity time. CPM is used for activity times that are well known and documented. PERT uses estimates of activity time (optimistic, pessimistic, and most likely) in its construction. Both network methods provide a great deal of information about the relationships between activities. The overall objective of PERT and CPM is to improve the management of large projects.

Through any path there are one or more time routes having the longest sequence of activities. These paths are known as critical paths and deserve increased managerial attentions. Critical paths are defined specifically as the longest time path through a network of activities. Delays along these paths will lengthen the entire project. CPM is the obvious choice of network models under conditions of certainty. Under conditions of risk/uncertainty, PERT is the more appropriate and powerful tool. These techniques are reviewed more fully in Chapter 16.

DECISION MAKING UNDER RISK/UNCERTAINTY

Decisions made under risk and uncertainty are more representative of the problems that managers deal with in actual situations; the specific outcome of a decision is rarely known with certainty. Probability and expected-value tools have been developed to help managers make decisions in these situations.

Uncertainty/Risk

In conditions of uncertainty, we have no knowledge of the probability of a certain outcome occurring and no knowledge of all possible actions. For example, what problems are likely to be encountered in sending people to Mars? Can we identify all of the possible problems (outcomes) and the probability of their occurrence? This is highly unlikely and is illustrative of uncertain states of nature. One can easily conceive of many decision-making situations in which no prior experience or data is available. The manager planning a new research and development project would like to know the chances of success for the project but has no prior history from which to make a guess. Sports fans betting on the Super Bowl are frequently faced with a situation in which the two teams have never met in competition during the regular season, or possibly not at all. Nevertheless, in these and many other situations, probability assessments must be made, at least implicitly, in arriving at a decision on whether to embark on the R&D project or on which team to bet in the Super Bowl. The probability assessments made under these conditions are the individual's best guesses and are referred to as subjective (or personal) probabilities. The decision as to what the probability will be is a reflection of the individual's personal value, experience, and intuition.

In conditions of risk, we know all the possible outcomes and their associated probabilities. In flipping a coin, there is a 50/50 chance that it will come up either heads or tails. The probability is 50, and all outcomes are known.

Rules of Probability

Rules of probability help managers understand how to deal with risk. In attempting to describe and qualify uncertainty and risk, the manager must list the possible outcomes that will be considered in arriving at a decision. This comprehensive listing of all possible outcomes in an uncertain situation is defined as the sample space. A sample space is made up of a collection of elements each of which represents a single possible occurrence in the uncertain situation. It is assumed that the elements (outcomes) are such that one and only one of them will occur as a result of the decision. Think of one die. If you decide to toss it, then only one of the six elements (1, 2, 3, 4, 5, or 6) can occur.

Within this sample space, a manager might be concerned only with outcomes having a specific value or attribute and not all individual outcomes. An event is defined as a set or collection of outcomes within the sample space that possesses some specified property. In our die example, the player may only be concerned with outcomes represented by even numbers (2, 4, 6). The event "one even number is tossed" corresponds to the three elements, 2, 4, and 6, out of the total sample space of six elements. Simply put, an event represents a combination (or set) of elements that the decision maker has selected (based on his interest or other criteria) from the sample space for particular attention.

This background on sample space, elements, and events is necessary for an understanding of the fundamental laws of probability. The first law, or axiom, is that the probability of each event (X) in the sample space is nonnegative and less than or equal to 1. Numerically this is shown as $0 \leq P(X) \leq 1$. The second law of probability is that the sum of the probability of all events in the sample space is equal to 1; that is, $P(S) = 1$. The third axiom is that if X and Y are two events in S (the sample space) and are mutually exclusive, then the probability that at least one of these events occurs is: $P(X \text{ or } Y) = P(X) + P(Y)$. Exhibit A.6 portrays these rules for our one-die example.

EXHIBIT / A.6
Toss of One Die as a Sample Space

Probability	Element
1	1/6
2	1/6
3	1/6
4	1/6
5	1/6
6	1/6
	6/6 = 1

The probability of any element is 1/6, which is greater than 0 and less than 1. The probability of the event (all even numbers) is 3/6, which is also greater than 0 and less than 1. The sum of the probability of all elements in the sample space is equal to 1. The probability of rolling a 2 or a 5 (that is, that either a 2 or 5 will occur) is:

$$P(2 \text{ or } 5) = P(2) + P(5)$$
$$= 1/6 + 1/6$$
$$= 2/6$$
$$= 1/3$$

In conditions of uncertainty, decision makers use several criteria depending on organizational objectives and personal levels of risk. In Chapter 3, minimum and maximum criteria have already been discussed. A criterion that is often used to analyze long-run profit is expected value.

Expected value is the long-run average payoff of a random variable (or event). It is obtained by multiplying each value (or payoff) of the decision by the probability of its occurrence, and then summing the products of this process. For example, if a coin is flipped there is a 50 percent probability that it will come up heads or tails. Suppose that the payoffs are as follows: If the coin shows tails you pay (lose) $5.00, and if it shows heads you receive (win) $10.00. Would you play this game? If we use expected-value criteria, the long-run average payoff to you would be: 50% × $10.00 = +$5.00 minus 50% × $5.00 = $2.50, or a net gain to you in the long run (e.g., 100 flips of the coin) of $2.50 per flip. The expected value of this decision is $2.50.

Probability Distributions

Aiding in our quantification of problems are the concepts of discrete and continuous probability distributions. If any possible outcome of a decision can be represented by a discrete variable (e.g., 1, 2, 3, or 6), it is considered a discrete probability distribution. For example, a bike dealer placing an order for new ten-speed bikes prior to the start of the best selling season places such an order on some estimate of initial demand for these bikes. The demand for bikes can only assume a finite number of values (e.g., 1, 10, 50, etc.). This is an example of a problem that utilizes a discrete probability distribution.

There are times, however, when managers are faced with data that is not discrete, but continuous. The temperature at a certain location or monthly rainfall are two examples of such data. In these cases, it makes better sense to address the probability that the temperature or rainfall will fall within a given interval. This is where continuous probability distributions (e.g., uniform or normal distributions) are useful. The forecasting of electric power usage by utilities and the estimating of heating fuel demands in winter months are two examples of business applications of continuous probability functions.

Revisions of Probabilities

In assessing probabilities, managers often make estimates before any observations of the relevant events have been made. These are referred to as prior probabilities. The manager in this situation is making a decision about what he or she thinks the future state of nature will be.

When the probability of a given event is affected by the occurrence of another event, we call that probability conditional. That is, the probability of event A is conditional on the occurrence of event B. The construction of decision trees uses this notion of conditional probability and a theorem about these relationships called Bayes's theorem. Bayes's theorem specifically addresses the procedure for revising prior probabilities given the observation of the occurrence of particular events. As an example, suppose you arise this morning and the shade to your window is drawn. As you dress, you try to assess the probability of rain for that day and assume it is low, say 10 percent. You then go to the window with this prior probability estimate and draw the shade. You note that the sky is very dark and threatening and revise your probability of rain to a 50 percent chance. Your estimate of rain (50 percent) is conditioned by the event of cloudy, threatening skies. Simply put, conditional probabilities are our estimates of the states of nature, given a sample result or observation.

These estimates of probabilities are based in general on managers' prior experiences and judgments. The development of conditional probabilities is made possible by the use of sampling techniques and experiments. These methods are designed to improve the accuracy of probability estimates, and, as a consequence, they improve the quality of managerial decisions. The case that follows is offered to test your knowledge of risk and the applications of probability theory.

THE CONFERENCE TABLE: DISCUSSION CASE / A.1

Fish Forwarders

Fish Forwarders supplies fresh shrimp to a variety of customers in the New Orleans area. It places orders for cases of shrimp from fleet representatives at the beginning of each week to meet a demand from its customers at the middle of the week. The shrimp are subsequently delivered to Fish Forwarders and then, at the end of the week, to its customers.

Both the weekly supply of and demand for shrimp are uncertain. Supply may vary as much as plus or minus 10 percent from the amount ordered, and, by contract, Fish Forwarders must purchase this supply. Fish Forwarders has determined that the probability of this variation is as follows:

−10 percent from amount ordered: 30 percent of the time
  0 percent from amount ordered: 50 percent of the time
+10 percent from amount ordered: 20 percent of the time

Similarly, the demand for shrimp varies as follows:

600 cases: 5 percent of the time
700 cases: 15 percent of the time
800 cases: 60 percent of the time
900 cases: 15 percent of the time
1000 cases: 5 percent of the time

A case of shrimp costs Fish Forwarders $30 and sells for $50. Any shrimp not sold at the end of the week are sold to a cat food company at $4 per case. Fish Forwarders may, if it chooses, order the shrimp "flash-frozen" by the supplier at dockside, but this raises the cost of a case by $4, to $34 per case. Flash-freezing enables Fish Forwarders to maintain an inventory of shrimp, but it costs $2 per case per week to store the shrimp at a local icehouse. The customers are indifferent to whether they get regular or flash-frozen shrimp. Fish Forwarders figures that its shortage cost is equal to its markup; that is, each case demanded but not available costs the company $50 − $30, or $20. The order quantity for each may be in any amount. Assume that there is no opening inventory of flash-frozen shrimp. ∎

Source: Adapted, with permission from Chase, R. B., and Aquilano, N. J., *Production and Operations Management,* rev. ed. Homewood, IL: Richard D. Irwin Inc., 1977, pp. 295–296.

**DISCUSSION
QUESTIONS**

1. What decisions must the managers at Fish Forwarders make?
2. What amount of shrimp (fresh and/or flash-frozen) would you order for week 1? Week 2? Week 5?
3. How can Fish Forwarders improve its chances; that is, how can it minimize risk and optimize its profits?

NOTES

1. Morse, P. M., and Kimball, *Methods of Operations Research* (New York: Wiley, 1951).
2. Hillier, F. S., and Lieberman, G. J., *Operations Research,* 2nd ed. (San Francisco: Holden-Day, 1974), p. 4.
3. Kwak, N. K., and Delurgio, S. A., *Quantitative Models for Business Decisions* (North Scituate, Mass.: Duxbury Press, 1980), p. 1.

Notes

CHAPTER 1

1. *Webster's New Twentieth Century Dictionary of the English Language* (Unabridged) (Chicago: Consolidated Book Publishers, 1975), p. 1093.
2. Preston, Lee E., and Post, James E., *Private Management and Public Policy: The Principle of Public Responsibility* (Englewood Cliffs, N.J.: Prentice-Hall, 1975), ch. 1.
3. For a review of the usefulness of these functions as a way to describe managerial work, see Carroll, Stephen, and Gillen, Dennis J., "Are the Classical Management Functions Useful in Describing Managerial Work?" *Academy of Management Review* 12(1) (1987): 1, 38–51.
4. Part of this is an appreciation of the effective management styles used by the Japanese. See Ouchi, William, *Theory Z* (Reading, Mass.: Addison-Wesley, 1981); and Pascall, Richard T., and Athos, Anthony G., *The Art of Japanese Management* (New York: Simon & Schuster, 1981).
5. For an analysis of the successes and failures of Japanese organizations see Drucker, Peter F., "Behind Japan's Success," *Harvard Business Review,* 59(1) (January–February 1981): 83–90. See also Van Wolferen, K., *The Enigma of Japanese Power* (New York: A. A. Knopf, 1989).
6. Drucker, Peter F., *Managing for Results* (New York: Harper & Row, 1964), p. 5.
7. Drucker, Peter F., *Management: Tasks, Responsibilities, Practices* (New York: Harper & Row, 1974).
8. For an analysis of managerial work that focuses on responsibilities, see Mintzberg, Henry, *The Nature of Managerial Work* (New York: Harper & Row, 1973).
9. Different responsibilities require different skills. For a discussion of how skill requirements change as responsibilities change see Katz, Robert, "Skills of an Effective Administrator," *Harvard Business Review* (September–October 1974): 5.
10. Orch, Charles, Wilkinson, Harry, and Benfari, Robert, "The Manager's Role as Coach and Mentor," *Organizational Dynamics* (Spring 1987): 66–74.
11. Mintzberg, Henry, *The Nature of Managerial Work* (New York: Harper & Row, 1973).
12. One highly visible example was Steven Jobs's departure from Apple Computer, of which he was a co-founder. See Uttal, Bro, "Behind the Fall of Steve Jobs," *Fortune,* August 5, 1985, p. 20.
13. Simon, Herbert A., *Administrative Behavior,* 2nd ed. (New York: Macmillan, 1957).

CHAPTER 2

1. Sören Kierkegaard as quoted in the *New York Times,* September 19, 1983.
2. The McDonald's story is told by its founder, Ray Kroc, in *Grinding It Out: The Making of McDonald's* (New York: Berkeley, 1977); see also Main, Jeremy, "Toward Service Without a Snarl," *Fortune,* March 23, 1981, p. 66.
3. Krooss, Herman E., and Gilbert, Charles, *American Business History* (Englewood Cliffs, N.J.: Prentice-Hall, 1972).
4. North, Douglass C., *Growth and Welfare in the American Past* (Englewood Cliffs, N.J.: Prentice-Hall, 1974), p. 1.
5. The term *scientific management* was used during the course of hearings by the Interstate Commerce Commission on a request by railroads to raise freight charges. Opponents claimed that if the railroads were managed more scientifically they would be more efficient in their operations, resulting in cost savings and eliminating the need to raise rates. Frederick Taylor used the phrase in his book, *Principles of Scientific Management* (New York: Harper & Row, 1911).
6. Taylor, Frederick W., *Shop Management* (New York: Harper & Row, 1983), p. 21.
7. There are excellent discussions of the Gilbreths in Boorstin, Daniel J., *The Americans: The Democratic Experience* (New York: Random House, 1973); also *The New Encyclopedia Britannica* (Macropedia) vol. 18 (Chicago: Encyclopedia Britannica, 1982), p. 1.
8. For an excellent history of Ford see Halberstam, David, *The Reckoning* (New York: Avon Books, 1986).
9. A helpful discussion of other experts in the era can be found in George, Claude, *The History of Management Thought,* 2nd ed. (Englewood Cliffs, N.J.: Prentice-Hall, 1972).
10. Sass, Steven A., *The Pragmatic Imagination: A History of the Warton School 1881–1981* (Philadelphia: University of Pennsylvania Press, 1982).
11. Wiener, Norbert, *Cybernetics: Or, Control and Communication in the Animal and the Machine,* 2nd ed. (Cambridge, Mass.: MIT Press, 1961).
12. Henri Fayol, *General and Industrial Management,* trans. Constance Stoms (London: Pittman, 1949).
13. Follett, Mary P., "Some Discrepancies in Leadership Theory and Practice," *Business Leadership,* ed. Henry C. Metcalf (London: Pitman, 1930), p. 213.

14. Weber, Max, *The Theory of Social and Economic Organization,* ed. and trans. Alexander M. Henderson and Talcott Parsons (New York: Oxford University Press, 1922–1947).

15. See Roethlisberger, F. J., and Dickson, William J., *Management and the Worker* (Cambridge, Mass.: Harvard University Press, 1956).

16. Barnard, Chester I., *The Functions of the Executive* (Cambridge, Mass.: Harvard University Press, 1938).

17. See Maslow, Abraham H., "A Theory of Human Motivation," *Psychology Review* 50 (1943): 370–396.

18. See McGregor, Douglas, *The Human Side of Enterprise* (New York: McGraw-Hill, 1960).

19. See Ouchi, William, *Theory Z: How American Business Can Meet the Japanese Challenge* (Reading, Mass.: Addison-Wesley, 1981).

20. See von Bertalanffy, Ludwig, "The Theory of Open Systems in Physics and Biology," *Science* 111 (1950): 23–28.

21. Parsons, Talcott, *Structure and Process in Modern Societies* (New York: Free Press, 1960).

22. See Thompson, James, *Organizations in Action* (New York: McGraw-Hill, 1967) for a basic discussion of the implications of open systems.

23. A valuable contribution to the integrated development of this field is Schendel, D., and Hofer, C. eds., *Strategic Management: A New View of Business Policy and Planning* (Boston: Little, Brown, 1979). A paper in that volume by H. Igor Ansoff entitled "The Changing Shape of the Strategic Problem" is a classic analysis of management history seen through the eyes of a leading strategic thinker.

24. See Luthans, Fred, "The Contingency Theory of Management: A Path Out of the Jungle," *Business Horizons* (June 1973): 67–72.

25. See Mason, Edward S., *The Corporation in Modern Society* (Cambridge, Mass.: Harvard University Press, 1959).

CHAPTER 3

1. Drucker, Peter F., *Management: Tasks, Responsibilities, Practices* (New York: Harper & Row, 1974).

2. "Decisive Ability: The Silver Medal Winners," *Financial World,* April 4–17, 1984, pp. 28, 29.

3. Lawrence Aldeman quotes in "Why Coke's Profits Suddenly Went Flat," *Business Week,* November 24, 1980, p. 46.

4. Greenwald, John, "Fiddling with the Real Thing," *Time,* May 6, 1985, p. 55.

5. "Will Things Still Go Better with Coke?" *U.S. News & World Report,* May 6, 1985, p. 14.

6. Scredon, Scott, "Is Coke Fixing a Cola that Isn't Broken?" *Business Week,* May 6, 1985, p. 47.

7. Koten, John, and Kilman, Scott, "How Coke's Decision to Offer Two Colas Undid 4½ Years of Planning," *Wall Street Journal,* July 15, 1985, p. 8.

8. Fisher, Anne B., "Coke's Brand Loyalty Lesson," *Fortune,* August 5, 1985, p. 44.

9. Koten and Kilman, op. cit., p. 1.

10. Gelman, Eric, et al., "Hey American Coke Are It!" *Newsweek,* July 22, 1985, p. 42.

11. Gelman, Eric, et al., "Coke Tampers with Success," *Newsweek,* May 6, 1985, p. 51.

12. This discussion is based on the argument presented in George P. Huber, *Managerial Decision Making* (Chicago: Scott Foresman, 1980).

13. Ackoff, Russell L., *Management in Small Doses* (New York: Wicery and Sons, 1986), ch. 27.

14. Ibid.

15. Simon, Herbert A., *The New Science of Management Decisions,* rev. ed. (Englewood Cliffs, N.J.: Prentice-Hall, 1977), pp. 47–49.

16. Knight, Frank H., *Risk, Uncertainty and Profit* (New York: Harper & Row, 1920), is a classic reference. See also Kast, Fremont, and Rosenzwerg, J., *Organization and Management: A Systems Approach* (New York: McGraw-Hill, 1979), p. 385.

17. Gelman et al., op. cit., p. 40.

18. Fisher, op. cit.

19. Simon, Herbert A., *Administrative Behavior,* 3rd ed. (New York: Free Press, 1976), pp. 38–41; 240–244.

20. For further information on the decision-making process, see Perrone, S. M., "Understanding the Decision Process," *Administrative Management* (May 1968): 88–92.

21. A broad approach to decisions and problem solving is discussed in Adams, L. L., *Conceptual Blockbusting* (New York: Norton, 1979). For other approaches to managerial problem solving, see Ackoff, Russell L., *The Art of Problem Solving* (New York: Wiley, 1978).

22. Quoted in Drucker, op. cit., p. 472.

23. For one discussion of this issue, see Celton, J. L., "Why Getting Additional Data Often Slows Decision-Making—And What to Do About It," *Management Review* (May 1984): 56–61.

24. Foltz, Kim, "Wizards of Marketing," *Newsweek,* July 22, 1985, p. 42.

25. Ibid.

26. Decision trees and other quantitative techniques for decision making are discussed in Johnson, R. D., and Siskin, B. R., *Quantitative Techniques for Business Decisions* (Englewood Cliffs, N.J.: Prentice-Hall, 1976), p. 69.

27. For one discussion on group decision making, see Holder, J. J., Jr., "Decision Making by Consensus," *Business Horizons* (April 1972): 47–54.

28. Maier, N., "Assets and Liabilities in Group Problem-Solving: The Need for Integrative Function," *Psychology Review* 74 (1967): 239–249.

29. For one discussion of this issue, see Calloway, M. R., Marriott, R. B., and Essu, J. K., "Effects of Dominance on Group Decision Making: Toward a Stress Reduction Explanation of Group Think," *Journal of Personality and Social Psychology* 49 (1985): 949–952.

30. Vroom, V., and Yetton, P., *Leadership and Decision Making* (Pittsburgh: University of Pittsburgh Press, 1973).

31. Vroom, V., "A New Look at Managerial Decision Making," *Organizational Dynamics* 1(4) (Spring 1973): 66–80.

CHAPTER 4

1. Ueberroth, Peter, *Made in America* (New York: Fawcett Crest, 1985), p. 166.

2. Ibid., p. 170.

3. Iacocca, Lee (with William Novak), *Iacocca: An Autobiogra-*

phy (New York: Bantam Books, 1984).

4. Reich, Robert, and Donahue, John, *New Deals,* (New York: Times Books, 1985).

5. As an example of assumption making and its impact, see Mason, R. O., and Mitroff, I. I., "Assumptions of Majestic Metals: Strategy Through Dialectics," *California Management Review* 22(2) (Winter 1979): 81–88.

6. Lorange, Peter, *Corporate Planning: An Executive Viewpoint* (Englewood Cliffs, N.J.: Prentice-Hall, 1980).

7. Ueberroth, op. cit., p. 131.

8. Richards, Max, *Organizational Goal Structures* (St. Paul, Minn.: West Publishing, 1978).

9. Ueberroth, op. cit., pp. 80, 81.

10. "To Build a Small Car, GM Tries to Redesign Its Production System," *Wall Street Journal,* May 14, 1984, pp. 1, 16.

11. Ueberroth, op. cit., p. 102.

12. Ibid., p. 103.

13. Hofer, Charles, and Schendel, Dan, *Strategy Formulation: Analytical Concepts* (St. Paul, Minn.: West Publishing, 1978).

14. Ueberroth, op. cit., p. 50.

15. Drucker, Peter F., *The Practice of Management* (New York: Harper & Row, 1954). See also Drucker, Peter F., *The New Realities* (New York: Harper & Row, 1989).

16. Reddin, W., *Effective Management by Objectives* (New York: McGraw-Hill, 1971).

CHAPTER 5

1. Ansoff, H. Igor, *Implanting Strategic Management* (Englewood Cliffs, N.J.: Prentice-Hall, 1984), p. 31.

2. Andrews, Kenneth R., *The Concept of Corporate Strategy,* 2d ed. (Homewood, Ill.: Dow Jones-Irwin, 1986).

3. Hamermesh, Richard G., "Making Planning Strategic," *Harvard Business Review* (July–August 1986): 115–120.

4. For a general discussion of strategic planning, see Radford, K. J., *Strategic Planning: An Analytical Approach* (Reston: Reston Publishing, 1980).

5. Mintzberg, Henry, *The Structure of Organizations* (Englewood Cliffs, N.J.: Prentice-Hall, 1979).

6. For an example of the relationship of mission and goals, see Post, James E., "The Corporation in the Public Policy Process," *Sloan Management Review* (Fall 1979): 45–52.

7. "The Fifty Largest Retailing Companies," *Fortune,* (July 1975): 122.

8. Peters, Thomas J., "Strategy Follows Structure: Developing Distinctive Skills," *California-Management Review* XXVI(3) (Spring 1984): 111–125.

9. Freeman, R. Edward, *Strategic Management: A Stakeholder Approach* (Marshfield, Mass.: Pitman, 1984), pp. 87–88.

10. Hofer, C. W., and Schendel, D., *Strategy Formulation: Analytical Concepts* (St. Paul, Minn.: West Publishing, 1978), pp. 12–45.

11. Freeman, R. Edward, *Strategic Management: A Stakeholder Approach* (Marshfield, Mass.: Pitman, 1984), p. 89.

12. See Selznick, Phillip, *Leadership in Administration* (New York: Harper & Row, 1957) for a distinction between organizations in general and organizations that are permeated with values (value-laden), which he calls "institutions." Selznick claims that the true role of leaders is to infuse values into their organizations.

13. DeParle, Jason, "Hi-Tech Trend-Speak," *The New Republic,* October 25, 1982, p. 12.

14. Ibid., p. 14.

15. Steiner, George, "Contingency Theories of Strategy and Strategic Management," in D. Schendel and C. Hofer, eds., *Strategic Management: A New View of Business Policy and Planning* (Boston: Little, Brown, 1979), pp. 405–416.

CHAPTER 6

1. There are many ways to imagine the relationship between elements of the environment. An excellent reference is Fahey, Liam, and Narayanan, V. K., *Macroenvironmental Analysis for Strategic Management* (St. Paul, Minn.: West Publishing, 1986).

2. For a basic discussion, see Samuelson, Paul, and Nordhaus, William, *Economics,* 12th ed. (New York: McGraw-Hill, 1985).

3. Ibid.

4. For a discussion of diversification strategies, see Hofer, Charles W., Murray, Edwin A., Jr., Charan, Ram, and Pitts, Robert A., *Strategic Management: A Casebook in Policy and Planning,* 2nd ed. (St. Paul, Minn.: West Publishing, 1984).

5. Ansoff, H. Igor, *Implementing Strategic Management* (Englewood Cliffs, N.J.: Prentice-Hall, 1984).

6. Ellul, Jacques, *The Technological Society* (New York: Knopf, 1964).

7. See Frederick, William, Davis, Keith, and Post, James, *Business and Society; Corporate Strategy, Public Policy, and Ethics,* 6th ed. (New York: McGraw-Hill, 1988), ch. 16.

8. Stewart Udall quoted in Norman, Colin, *The God that Limps: Science and Technology in the Eighties* (New York: Norton, 1981).

9. Fahey and Narayanan, op. cit.

10. Porter, Michael, *Competitive Strategy* (New York: Free Press, 1980).

11. Ibid.

12. This discussion is based on Porter, Michael E., "How Competitive Forces Shape Strategy," *Harvard Business Review* (March/April 1979): 137–145.

13. Ibid.

CHAPTER 7

1. Baird, L., and Frohman, A., *Acting Strategy,* AMACON, New York, 1990.

2. Mintzberg, H., *The Structuring of Organizations* (Englewood Cliffs, N.J.: Prentice-Hall, 1979), p. 2.

3. See, for example, Kanter, RoseBeth Moss, and Buck, John D., "Organizing Part of Honeywell: From Strategy to Structure," *Organizational Dynamics* (Winter 1985): 5–25.

4. Child, John, *Organization* (New York: Harper & Row, 1979).

5. For one discussion of organization charts, see Stieglitz, H., "What's Not on an Organization Chart," *Conference Board Record* 1(11) (November 1964).

6. Miles, Robert, *Macro Organizational Behavior* (Santa Monica, Calif.: Goodyear Publishing, 1980), p. 18.

7. Smith, Adam, *An Inquiry into the Nature and Causes of the Wealth of Nations* (New York: Random House, 1937).

8. For one discussion of the problems between line and staff

employees, see Logan, Hall H., "Line and Staff: An Obsolete Concept," *Personnel* (January–February 1966): 26–33.

9. Davis, Stanley M., and Lawrence, P. R., *Matrix* (Reading, Mass.: Addison-Wesley, 1977).

10. For one discussion of this issue, see Davis, Stanley M., and Paule, Lawrence, "Problems of Matrix Organizations," *Harvard Business Review* (May–June 1978): 134.

11. Herzberg, F., "The Wise Old Turk," *Harvard Business Review* (September–October 1974): 70–80.

12. For an alternative view of how to help workers cope with work structure, see Diamond, M. A., and Allcorn, S., "Psychological Dimensions of Role Use in Bureaucratic Organizations," *Organizational Dynamics* (Summer 1985): 35–59. See also Miller, Peter, and O'Leary, Ted, "Hierarchies and American Ideals, 1900–1940," *Academy of Management Review,* 1989, 14(2): 250–265.

13. Carlzon, Jan, *Moments of Truth* (Cambridge, Mass.: Ballinger, 1987), p. 60.

14. See Herzberg, Frederick, "One More Time: How Do You Motivate Employees?" *Harvard Business Review* (January–February 1968): 59.

15. Hackman, J. R., and Oldham, G. R., "Development of the Job Diagnostic Survey," *Journal of Applied Psychology* 60 (1975): 159–170.

16. For a review of these theories see Aldag, R. J., and Brief, A. P., *Task Design and Employee Motivation* (Glenview, Ill.: Scott, Foresman, 1979).

17. Galbraith, J. R., *Organization Design* (Reading, Mass.: Addison-Wesley, 1977).

18. Fayol, Henri, *General and Industrial Management,* trans, J. A. Conbrough (Geneva: International Management Institute, 1929), p. 36.

19. Urwick, Lyndall F., "The Manager's Span of Control," *Harvard Business Review* 34 (May–June 1956): 42–50.

20. Graicunas, "Relationships in Organization," in Luther Gulick and Lyndall F. Urwick, eds., *Papers on the Science of Administration* (New York: Columbia University Press, 1947), pp. 183–187.

21. Carzo, R., Jr., and Yanouzas, J. N., "Effects of Flat and Tall Organization Structure," *Administration Science Quarterly* (1969): 178–191.

22. See Druker, Peter F., "The Coming of the New Organization," *Harvard Business Review* (January–February 1988): 45–53.

23. Beres, Mary Elizabeth, "Strategic Leadership in Network Style Organizations," paper presented at the Southeast American Institute of Decisions Sciences meeting, Savannah, Ga., February 1984, pp. 2, 3.

24. Weich, Karl E., *The Social Psychology of Organizing,* 2nd ed. (New York: Random House, 1979), pp. 90–97.

25. Ibid., p. 111.

CHAPTER 8

1. Chandler, A. D., *Strategy and Structure* (Cambridge, Mass.: MIT Press, 1962); and Shwartz, H., and Davis, S. M., "Matching Corporate Culture and Business Strategy," *Organizational Dynamics* (Summer 1981): 39–48.

2. Guiles, Melinda Grenier, "Hazardous Road: GM's Smith Presses for Sweeping Changes but Questions Arise," *Wall Street Journal,* March 14, 1985, p. 27.

3. "GM: Survival of the Fittest," *Newsweek,* June 25, 1984, p. 52.

4. Weber, M., *The Theory of Social and Economic Organization,* trans. A. M. Henderson and H. T. Parsons (New York: Free Press, 1947).

5. Ibid., pp. 330–331.

6. Bennis, Warren G., and Slater, Philip E., *The Temporary Society* (New York: Harper Colophon Books, 1968), pp. 55–59.

7. Sketty, Y. K., and Carlisle, H. M., "A Contingency Model of Organizational Design," *California Management Review* (1972): 15–38.

8. Burns, T., and Stalker, G. M., *The Management of Innovation* (London: Tavistock, 1961).

9. Quoted in Guiles, op. cit., p. 27.

10. Richard Resciano's interview with Roger Smith, "What's Ahead for GM," *Barron's,* March 12, 1984, p. 11.

11. "GM Moves into a New Era," *Business Week,* July 16, 1984, p. 49.

12. Ibid.

13. For a discussion of the importance of fitting organization structure to the environment, see Yasai-Ardekani, Masoud, "Structural Adaptations to Environments," *Academy of Management Review* 11 (1986): 9–21; see also Fennell, M. L., "The Effects of Environmental Characteristics on the Structure of Hospital Clusters," *Administration Science Quarterly* 25 (1980): 485–510.

14. See Perrow, C., *Organizational Analysis: A Sociological View* (Monterey, Calif.: Brooks/Cole, 1970) and Thompson, J. D., *Organizations in Action* (New York: McGraw-Hill, 1967).

15. Alexander, J. W., and Randolph, W. A., "The Fit Between Technology and Structure as a Predictor of Performance in Nursing Subunits," *The Academy of Management Journal* 28 (1985): 844–859.

16. Woodward, J., *Industrial Organization: Theory and Practice* (New York: Oxford University Press, 1965).

17. Perrow, Charles, "A Framework for Comparative Analysis of Organizations," *American Sociological Review* 32 (1967): 194–208; and Perrow, Charles, *Organizational Analysis: A Sociological Approach* (Belmont, Calif.: Wadsworth, 1970).

18. Lawrence, P., and Lorsch, J. W., *Organization and Environment: Managing Differentiation and Integration* (Homewood, Ill.: Irwin, 1969), pp. 151–158.

19. Galbraith, J., *Organizational Design* (Reading, Mass.: Addison-Wesley, 1977).

20. Wilkins, A. L., and Ouchi, W. G., "Efficient Cultures: Exploring the Relationship Between Culture and Organizational Performance," *Administration Science Quarterly* 28 (1983): 468–481.

21. For discussions of organization culture, see Wilkins, A., "The Culture Audit: A Tool for Understanding Organizations," *Organizational Dynamics* (Autumn 1983): pp. 24–38 and Duncan, W. J., "Organizational Culture: Getting a Fix on an Elusive Concept," *The Academy of Management Executive,* 1989, III, pp. 229–236.

22. Del, T. E., and Kennedy, A. A., *Corporate Cultures: The Rites and Rituals of Corporate Life* (Reading, Mass.: Addison-Wesley, 1982).

23. Phillips, J. R., and Kennedy, A. A., *Shaping and Managing Shared Values,* McKinsey Staff paper, internal document, 1980.

24. Quote from Hewlett Packard Credo, Hewlett-Packard Corp.

25. Stieglitz, H., "The Concept of Corporate Culture," *The Conference Board* (February 1974): 10–12.

26. Schwartz, Howard, and Davis, Stanley M., "Matching Culture and Business Strategy," *Organizational Dynamics* (Summer 1981): 30–48.

27. For more information about the General Motors culture, see Wright, J. P., *On a Clear Day You Can See General Motors* (New York: Avon, 1980).

CHAPTER 9

1. Peters, Thomas J., *Thriving on Chaos: Handbook for a Management Revolution* (New York: Knopf, 1987).
2. "Tom Peters: Excellence Is No Longer Enough," interview with Michael S. Malone, *Boston Globe,* December 14, 1987, p. 18.
3. For discussions of organizational change and development, see Greiner, L., "Evolution and Revolution as Organizations Grow," *Harvard Business Review* 50 (July–August 1972): 37–38 and Zeira, Y., and Avedisian, J., "Organizational Planned Change: Assessing the Chances for Success," *Organizational Dynamics* (Spring 1989): 31–45.
4. Lewin, K., and Cartwright, D. eds., *Field Theory in Social Science* (New York: Harper & Row, 1951).
5. Thomas, K. W., and Schmidt, W. H., "A Survey of Managerial Interests with Respect to Conflict," *Academy of Management Journal* 19 (1976): 315–318.
6. Fraser, N. M., and Hipel, K. W., *Conflict Analysis: Models and Resolutions* (New York: North-Holland, 1984).
7. Likert, R., and Likert, J. G., *New Ways of Managing Conflict* (New York: McGraw-Hill, 1976).
8. Robbins, S. R., "Conflict Management and Conflict Resolution Are Not Synonymous Terms!" *California Management Review* XXI (Winter 1978). For a general discussion of competition and cooperation, see Deutsch, M. A., "A Theory of Cooperation and Competition," *Human Relations* 2 (1949): 129–150.
9. Walton, R., *Interpersonal Peacemaking. Confrontations and Third-Party Consultation* (Reading, Mass.: Addison-Wesley, 1969).
10. Pondy, L. R., "Organizational Conflict—Concepts and Models," *Administrative Science Quarterly* 12 (September 1967): 269–320.
11. Lewin, K., "Group Decision and Social Change," in G. E. Swanson, T. M. Newcomb, and E. L. Hartley, eds., *Readings in Social Psychology* (New York: Holt, Rinehart and Winston, 1952), pp. 459–473. For a further discussion of resistance to change, see Argyris, C., *Strategy, Change, and Defensive Routines* (New York: Pitman, 1985).
12. Lewin, K., and Cartwright, D., eds., *Field Theory in Social Science* (New York: Harper & Row, 1951).
13. For a discussion of choosing among change strategies, see Kotter, J. P., and Schlesinger, L. A., "Choosing Strategies for Change," *Harvard Business Review* 57 (March–April, 1979): 109–112.
14. Greiner, L., "Patterns of Organization Change," *Harvard Business Review* 45 (May–June, 1967): 119–130.
15. Leavitt, H., "Applied Organizational Change in Industry: Structural, Technological, and Humanistic Approaches," in J. March (ed.), *Handbook of Organizations* (Skokie, Ill.: Rand McNally, 1965), pp. 1144–1170.
16. Huse, Edgar F., *Organization Development and Change,* 2nd ed. (St. Paul, Minn.: West Publishing, 1980), p. 508.
17. For a comprehensive argument of why traditional OD interventions are less applicable today, see Leitko, Thomas A., and Szezerbacki, David, "Why Traditional OD Strategies Fail in Professional Bureaucracies," *Organizational Dynamics* (Winter 1987): 52–65.
18. Burgelman, Robert A., and Sayles, Leonard R., *Inside Corporate Innovation* (New York: Free Press, 1986), p. 191.
19. Ibid.
20. Sherman, Stratford P., "Eight Big Masters of Innovation," *Fortune,* October 15, 1984, pp. 66–68, 72, 76, 80, 84.
21. Burch, John G., *Entrepreneurship* (New York: Wiley, 1986), p. 5.

CHAPTER 10

1. For a discussion of leadership and influence, see Fleishman, E. A., "Twenty Years of Consideration and Structure," Fleishman, E. A., and Hunt, J. G., in *Current Developments in the Study of Leadership* (Carbondale: Southern Illinois University Press, 1973), p. 3.
2. *The Random House College Dictionary,* rev. ed. (New York: Random House, 1984), p. 683.
3. See Weber, Max, "The Three Types of Managerial Rule," *Berkeley Journal of Sociology* 4 (1953): 1–11 (orig. 1925); and O'Donnell, Cyril, "The Source of Managerial Authority," *Political Science Quarterly* 67(4) (December 1952): 573–588. See also Cohen, A. and Briarford, D., "Influence Without Authority: The Use of Alliances, Reciprocity, and Exchange to Accomplish Work," Organizational Dynamics (Winter 1989): 4–17.
4. French, J. R. P., and Raven, B. H., "The Bases of Social Power," in D. Cartwright, ed., *Studies in Social Power* (Ann Arbor: University of Michigan Press, 1959), pp. 150–167.
5. Yukl, Gary, and Taber, Tom, "The Effective Use of Managerial Power," *Personnel* 60(2) (March–April 1983): 37–44.
6. See Fisch, Gerald G., "Toward Effective Delegation" *CPA Journal* 46(7) (July 1976): 66–67.
7. Our discussion in this section is based on Monney, James D., and Reiley, Alan C., *The Principles of Organization* (New York: Harper & Row, 1939), pp. 14–19, 23–24; and Avery, S. Raub, *Company Organization Charts* (New York: National Industrial Conference Board, 1964).
8. Newman, William, "Overcoming Obstacles to Effective Delegation," *Management Review* 45(1) (January 1956): 36–41.
9. Gerber, Pat, "Success Story," *Working Women* (August 1983): 34.
10. Fabricant, Florence, "Cashing in His Chips," *Cuisine* (November 1984): 24.
11. Richman, Tom, "Mrs. Fields' Secret Ingredient," *Inc.* (October 1987): 65.
12. Ibid.
13. Gerber, op. cit., p. 34.
14. Ghiselli, E., *Explorations in Managerial Talent* (Santa Monica, Calif.: Goodyear, 1971).
15. Levinson, Harry, "Criteria for Choosing Chief Executives," *Harvard Business Review* (July–August, 1980): 113–120.
16. Ibid., p. 113.
17. Goleman, Daniel, "Successful Executives Rely on Own Kind of Intelligence," *New York Times,* July 31, 1984, p. C1.
18. Stodgill, Ralph M., "Personal Factors Associated with Leadership: A Survey of the Literature," *Psychology* 25(1) (January 1948): 35–71.
19. McManus, Kevin, "The Cookie Wars," *Forbes,* November 7, 1983, p. 152.
20. Fabricant, Florence, "Cashing in His Chips," *Cuisine* (November 1984): 17.

21. Furst, Alan, "The Golden Age of Goo," *Esquire* (December 1984): 328.
22. Ibid.
23. For a review, see Vroom, Victor H., "Leadership," in Marvin D. Dunnette, ed., *Handbook of Industrial and Organizational Psychology* (New York: Wiley, 1983), pp. 1527–1551.
24. Likert, R., *New Patterns of Management* (New York: McGraw-Hill, 1961).
25. Kerr, S., Schriesheim, C., Murphy, C., and Stodgill, R., "Toward a Contingency Theory of Leadership Based upon the Consideration and Initiating Structure Literature," *Organizational Behavior and Human Performance* 12 (1974): 62–82.
26. Howell, J. P., Dorfman, P. W., and Kerr, S., "Moderator Variables in Leadership Research," *Academy of Management Review* 11(1) (1986): 88–102.
27. Fiedler, Fred E., "Engineer the Job to Fit the Manager," *Harvard Business Review* 43(5) (September–October 1965): 116; see also Fiedler, Fred E., "The Contingency Model," in Harold Proshansky and Bernard Seidenberg, eds., *Basic Studies in Social Psychology* (New York: Holt, Rinehart and Winston, 1965), pp. 538–551.
28. See, for example, Graen, G., Orris, J. B., and Alvanes, K. M., "Contingency Model of Leadership Effectiveness: Some Experimental Results," *Journal of Applied Psychology* (1986): 555–559; and Schriesheim, C. A., and Bannister, B. D., and Money, W. H., "Psychometric Properties of the LPC Scale: An Extension of Rice's Review," *Academy of Management Review* (April 1979): 287–290.
29. See House, Robert J., "A Path-Goal Theory of Leader Effectiveness," *Administrative Science Quarterly* 16(5) (September 1971): 321–328; and House, Robert J., and Mitchell, Terence R., "Path-Goal Theory of Leadership," *Journal of Contemporary Business* 3(4) (Autumn 1974): 81–97. Also see Martin G. Evans, "Leadership and Motivation: A Core Concept," *Academy of Management Journal* 13(1) (March 1970): 91–102.
30. Schriesheim, C. A., and DeNisi, A., "Task Dimensions as Moderators of the Effects of Instrumental Leadership," *Journal of Applied Psychology* (October 1981): 589–597.
31. Greene, C., "Questions of Causation in the Path-Goal Theory of Leadership," *Academy of Management Journal* (March 1979): 22–41.
32. Hersey, Paul, and Blanchard, Kenneth H., *Management of Organizational Behavior,* 4th ed. (Englewood Cliffs, N.J.: Prentice-Hall, 1982). See also Reddin, William J., "The 3-D Management Style Theory," *Training and Development Journal* 21(4) (April 1967): 8–17, on which Hersey and Blanchard base much of their work.
33. Blanchard, Kenneth H., *Leadership and the One Minute Manager* (New York: Morrow, 1985).
34. For a discussion of transformation leadership, see Burns, F., *Leadership* (New York: Harper & Row, 1978); and Bass, Bernard M., "Leadership: Good, Better, Best," *Organization Dynamics* 13 (Winter 1985): 26–40. For another view of the role of the leader, see Zaleznik, A., "Real Work," *Harvard Business Review* 89(1) (January–February 1989): 57–76.
35. Mitchell, T. R., and Green, S. C., and Wood, R. E., "An Attributional Model of Leadership and the Poor Performing Subordinate: Development and Validation," in B. M. Staw and L. L. Cummings, eds., *Research in Organizational Behavior* (Greenwich, Conn.: JAI Press, 1981).
36. Kerr, S., and Jermier, J. M., "Substitutes for Leadership: Their Meaning and Measurement," *Organizational Behavior and Human Performance* (December 1978): 376–405.

CHAPTER 11

1. Pascarella, Perry, "Plugging in the People Factor," *Industry Week,* March 4, 1985, pp. 41–45.
2. Auerbach, Red, with Joe Fitzgerald, *On and Off the Court* (New York: Bantam Books, 1986), p. 36.
3. Ibid., pp. 46, 49.
4. For an example of how to manage people so they contribute to organization strategy, see Angle, Harold, Manz, Charles, and Van de Ven, Andrew, "Integrating Human Resource Management and Corporate Strategy: A Preview of the 3M Story," *Human Resource Management* 24(1) (1985): 51–68; and Meshoulam, Ilan, and Baird, Lloyd, "Proactive Human Resource Management," *Human Resource Management* (Winter 1987): 483–502.
5. "Uniform Guidelines on Employeed Selection Procedures," *Federal Register,* Part IV [Section 2B], August 25, 1978.
6. Patten, T. H., Jr., *Manpower Planning and the Development of Human Resources* (New York: Wiley, 1971).
7. Mills, Quinn D., "Planning with People in Mind," *Harvard Business Review* (July–August, 1985): 97–105.
8. Greer, C. R., and Armstrong, D., "Human Resource Forecasting and Planning: A State-of-the-Art Investigation," *Human Resource Planning* 3 (1980): 67–68.
9. Auerbach, op. cit., p. 20.
10. "For Celtics Fans, It's Wait Till Next Fiscal Year," *Business Week,* June 27, 1988, p. 89.
11. Schneider, B., and Schmitt, N., *Staffing Organizations,* 2nd ed. (Glenview, Ill.: Scott, Foresman, 1986).
12. Wanous, J. P., *Organizational Entry: Recruitment, Selection and Socialization of Newcomers* (Reading, Mass.: Addison-Wesley, 1980).
13. Curley, J., "More Companies Look Within for Job Managers," *Wall Street Journal,* October 28, 1980.
14. Mangum, Stephen L., "Recruitment and Job Search: The Recruitment Tactics of Employers," *Personnel Administration* (June 1982): 96–102.
15. Auerbach, op. cit., p. 36.
16. Holland, Joan, and Theodore, Curtis, "Orientation of New Employees," in Joseph Famularo, ed., *Handbook of Modern Personnel Administration* (New York: McGraw-Hill, 1972).
17. Feldman, Daniel C., "A Socialization Process that Helps New Recruits Succeed," *Personnel* 57 (March–April 1980): 11–23.
18. Auerbach, op. cit., p. 20.
19. Ibid., p. 21.
20. Moore, M. L., and Dutton, P., "Training Needs Analysis: Review and Critique," *Academy of Management Review* (July 1978): 532–545; and Wall, S., and Awal, Deepa, "Determining Managerial Training Needs," *The Training and Development Sourcebook* (Amherst, Mass.: Human Resource Development Press, 1987), pp. 38–52.
21. For an example of the many types of training programs available in one area, see Smith, D. E., "Training Programs for Performance Appraisal: A Review," *The Academy of Management Review* II (January 1986): 22–40.
22. Beer, Michael, "Performance Appraisal: Dilemmas and Possi-

bilities," *Organizational Dynamics* 9 (Winter 1981): 24–36; and Schnerer, Craig E., Beatty, Richard W., and Baird, Lloyd S., "Creating a Performance Management System," *Training and Development Journal* (May 1986): 74–79.

23. Cederblom, Douglas, "The Performance Appraisal Interview: A Review, Implications, and Suggestions," *Academy of Management Review* 7 (April 1982): 219–227.

24. Baird, Lloyd, *Performance Management* (New York: Wiley, 1986).

25. Schwab, D. P., Heneman, H. G., III, and DeCotiius, T. A., "Behaviorally Anchored Rating Scales: A Review of the Literature," *Personnel Psychology* 28 (1975): 549–562.

26. Auerbach, op. cit., p. 17.

27. Berea, Oltio, *Elements of Sound Pay Administration* (The American Society for Personnel Administration and the American Compensation Association, 1981). For a review of some of the problems in pay administration, see Folger, R., and Konousky, "Effects of Procedural and Distributive Justice on Reactions to Pay Raise Decisions," *Academy of Management Journal* 32(1) (1989): 115–130.

28. Stonich, Paul J., "The Performance Measurement and Reward System: Critical to Strategic Management," *Organizational Dynamics* (Winter 1984): 45–57.

29. Henderson, Richard, *Compensation Management*, 2nd ed. (Reston, Va.: Reston Publishing, 1983).

30. Lawler, Edward E. III, *Pay and Organization Development* (Reading, Mass.: Addison-Wesley, 1981).

31. "Red Auerbach on Management," interview with Alan M. Webber, *Harvard Business Review* (March–April 1987): 85, 88.

32. Rock, Milton L., *Handbook of Wage and Salary Administration* (New York: McGraw-Hill, 1972).

33. "Red Auerbach on Management," op. cit., p. 88.

34. Rowe, Mary P., Russell-Einhorn, Malcolm L., and Weinstein, Jerome N., "New Issues in Testing the Work Force: Genetic Diseases," *Labor Law Journal* (August 1987): 518.

35. Smothers, Ronald, "Survey Finds a Clash on AIDS in Workplace," *New York Times,* February 7, 1988, p. 28.

36. Ibid.

37. Angarola, Robert T., Esq., and Donegan, Thomas T., Jr., Esq., "Legal Issues of a Drug-Free Environment: Testing for Substance Abuse in the Workplace," paper presented to the Select Committee on Narcotics Abuse and Control, United States House of Representatives, May 7, 1986.

CHAPTER 12

1. Gronn, P. C., "Talk as the Work: The Accomplishment of School Administration," *Administrative Science Quarterly* 28 (1983): 1–21.

2. Sigband, H., *Communication for Management* (Glenview, Ill.: Scott, Foresman, 1969), p. 10.

3. Rath, G. J., and Stoyanoff, K. S., "Understanding and Improving Communication Effectiveness," in J. W. Pfeiffer and L. D. Goodstein, eds., *The 1982 Annual for Facilitators, Trainers, and Consultants* (San Diego: University Associates, 1982), pp. 166–173.

4. See also "Hitting the Communication Bull's Eye," *Personnel Administrator* (June 1974): 16.

5. See, for example, Porter, Lyman W., and Roberts, Karlene H., "Communication," in Marvin D. Dunnette, ed., *Handbook of Industrial and Organizational Psychology,* (Skokie, Ill.: Rand McNally, 1976).

6. For a discussion of personal characteristics that improve the communication process, see Klauss, Rudi, and Bass, Bernard, *Communication in Organizations* (New York: Academic Press, 1982), pp. 47, 50, 51.

7. Mahoney, Richard, *Confessions of a Street-Smart Manager* (New York: Simon & Schuster, 1988), p. 123.

8. McLuhan, Marshall, *Understanding Media* (New York: McGraw-Hill, 1964).

9. Tubbs, Stewart, and Moss, Sylvia, *Human Communication* (New York: Random House, 1977), p. 33.

10. Horn, John, "Gunfight at the Writers Guild Corral," *Los Angeles Times,* Calendar section, September 1, 1985, p. 18.

11. McCaskey, M., "The Hidden Messages Managers See," *Business Review* 57 (1979): 146–147.

12. Leavitt, Harold J., *Managerial Psychology,* 4th ed. (Chicago: University of Chicago Press, 1972).

13. Rasmussen, Jr., K. G., "Nonverbal Behavior, Verbal Behavior, Resume Credentials, and Selection Interview Outcomes," *Journal of Applied Psychology* 69 (1984): 551–556.

14. Daft, R. L., *Organization Theory and Design* (St. Paul, Minn.: West Publishing, 1983), pp. 299–302.

15. Harper, R. G., Wiens, A. N., and Matarzzo, J. D., *Nonverbal Communication: The State of the Art* (New York: Wiley, 1978).

16. Akley, S. R., "Management and Organizational Communication in Terms of the Conduit Metaphor," *Academy of Management Review* (1984): 9, 428–437.

17. Inman, J. H., and Hook, B. U., "Barriers to Organizational Communication," *Management World* 10 (1981): 34–35.

18. Rogers, Carl, *Client Centered Therapy: Its Current Practice, Implications, and Theory* (Boston: Houghton Mifflin, 1951).

19. For a discussion of the effectiveness of downward communication, see McCallister, L., "Predicted Employee Compliance to Downward Communication," *Journal of Business Communication* (Winter 1983): 67–79.

20. Planty, Earl G., and Machaner, William, "Stimulating Upward Communication," Johnson & Johnson Company Report, undated.

21. Harriman, Bruce, "Up and Down the Communications Ladder," *Harvard Business Review* (September–October 1974): 144.

22. Simpson, R. L., "Vertical and Horizontal Communications in Formal Organizations," *Administrative Science Quarterly* 4 (1959): 188–196.

23. Pondy, L., "Organizational Communication," in S. Kerrs, ed., *Organizational Behavior* (Columbus, Ohio: Grid Publishing, 1979), pp. 135–136.

24. Davis, Keith, and Newstrom, John W., *Human Behavior at Work: Organizational Behavior,* 7th ed. (New York: McGraw-Hill, 1985).

25. Simmons, Donald B., "The Nature of the Organizational Grapevine," *Supervisory Management* (November 1985): 39–42; and Davis and Newstrom, op. cit.

CHAPTER 13

1. Baird, L. S., *Managing Performance* (New York: Wiley, 1986).

2. Maslow, A., *Motivation and Personality,* 2nd ed. (New York: Harper & Row, 1970).

3. See Hall, D. T., and Nougaim, K. E., "An Examination of Maslow's Need Hierarchy in Organization Setting," *Organizational Behavior and Human Performance* 3 (1968): 12–35.

4. See Lawler, E. E., and Shuttle, J. L., "A Causal Correlation Test of the Need Hierarchy Concept," *Organizational Behavior and Human Performance* 7 (1972): 265–287; and Rauschenberger, J., Schmidt, N., and Hunter, J. E., "A Test of the Need Hierarchy Concept by a Markov Model of Change in Need Strength," *Administrative Science Quarterly* 25 (1980): 654–670.

5. Alderfer, C. P., *Existence, Relatedness, and Growth* (New York: Free Press, 1972).

6. Alderfer, C. P., Kaplan, R. E., and Smith, K. A., "The Effect of Variations in Relatedness Need Satisfaction on Relatedness Desire," *Administrative Science Quarterly* 19 (1974): 507–532.

7. Murray, H. A., *Explorations in Personality* (New York: Oxford University Press, 1938).

8. McClelland, D. C., *The Achieving Society* (New York: Van Nostrand, Reinhold, 1961); and McClelland, D., Atkinson, J., Clark, R., and Lowell, E., *The Achievement Motive* (Englewood Cliffs, N.J.: Prentice-Hall, 1953).

9. Korn, E. R., and Pratt, G. J., "Reaching for Success in New Ways," *Management World* (September–October 1986): 6–10.

10. Harrison, G., "To Know Why Men Do What They Do: A Conversation with David C. McClelland," *Psychology Today* 4 (1971): 35–39.

11. Herzberg, F., Mausner, B., and Synderman, B., *The Motivation to Work* (New York: Wiley, 1959).

12. House, R., and Widgor, L., "Herzberg's Dual-Factor Theory of Job Satisfaction and Motivation: A Review of the Evidence and Criticism," *Personnel Psychology* 20 (1968): 369–389.

13. Vroom, V., *Work and Motivation* (New York: Wiley, 1964).

14. Lawler, E. E., III, *Motivation in Work Organizations* (Monterey, Calif.: Brooks/Cole, 1973), pp. 30–36.

15. Stahl, M. J., and Harrell, A. M., "Modeling Effort Decisions with Behavioral Decision Theory: Toward an Individual Differences Model of Expectancy Theory," *Organizational Behavior and Human Performance* 27 (1981): 303–325.

16. For a discussion of how expectations differ among individuals, see Miller, L. E., and Grush, J. E., "Improving Productions in Expectancy Theory Research: Effects of Personality, Expectations, and Norms," *Academy of Management Journal* 31(1) (March 1988): 107–122.

17. Adams, J. S., "Toward an Understanding of Inequity," *Journal of Abnormal and Social Psychology* 67 (1963): 422–436.

18. Greenberg, J., "Cultivating an Image of Justice: Looking Fair on the Job," *The Academy of Management Executive* 11(2) (1988): 155–157.

19. Adams, J. S., "Inequity in Social Exchange," in L. Berkowitz, ed., *Advances in Experimental Social Psychology,* Vol. 2 (New York: Academic Press, 1965), pp. 267–300.

20. See, for example, Aikerman, K. F., "Pay Equality, Pay Satisfaction, and Work Behavior: Some Experimental Research Findings," *Management International Review* 23 (1983): 16–30.

21. For B. F. Skinner's work, see *Walden Two* (New York: Macmillan, 1948); *Science and Human Behavior* (New York: Macmillan, 1953); and *Contingencies of Reinforcement* (Englewood Cliffs, N.J.: Prentice-Hall, 1969).

22. For example, see Wallin, J. A., and Johnson, R. D., "The Positive Reinforcement Approach to Controlling Absenteeism," *Personnel Journal* (August 1976): 390–392; and Luthans, F., and Martinko, M., "An Organizational Behavior Modification Analysis of Absenteeism," *Human Resource Management* (Fall 1976): 11–18.

23. Adapted in part from Hamner, W. Clay, "Using Reinforcement Theory in Organizational Settings," in Henry L. Tosi and W. Clay Hamner, eds., *Organizational Behavior and Management: A Contingency Approach* (Chicago: St. Clair Press, 1977), pp. 388–395.

24. For a discussion of the effectiveness of participative decision making, see Cotton, J. L., Vollrath, D. A., Froggatt, K. L., Lengnick-Hall, M. L., and Jennings, K. R., "Employee Participation: Diverse Forms and Different Outcomes," *The Academy of Management Review* 13(1) (January 1988): 8–22.

25. McGregor, D., *The Human Side of Enterprise* (New York: McGraw-Hill, 1960).

26. Shaskin, M., "Participative Management Is an Ethical Imperative," *Organizational Dynamics* 12(2) (Spring 1984): 4–22.

27. Locke, E., Shaw, K. N., Saari, L., and Latham, G., "Goal Setting and Task Performance, 1969–1980," *Psychological Bulletin* 90(1): 125–152.

28. Gadon, H., "Making Sense of Quality of Work Life Programs," *Business Horizons* (January–February 1984): 42–46.

29. For an overall review of quality of work life programs, see Lawler, E. E., III, and Ledford, G. E., "Productivity and the Quality of Work Life," *National Productivity Review* (Winter 1981–1982): 23–36.

30. Meyer, G. W., and Scott, R. G., "Quality Circles: Panacea or Pandora's Box?" *Organizational Dynamics* (Spring 1985): 34–50.

CHAPTER 14

1. Miller, J., "Living Systems: The Group," *Behavioral Science* 16 (1971): 302–398.

2. Herold, D. M., "The Effectiveness of Work Groups," in Steve Kerr, ed., *Organizational Behavior* (Columbus, Ohio: Grid Publishing, 1979), p. 95.

3. Likert, R., and Likert, J. G., *New Ways of Managing Conflict* (New York: McGraw-Hill, 1976).

4. Shaw, M., *Group Dynamics: The Psychology of Small Group Behavior,* 2nd ed. (New York: McGraw-Hill, 1976).

5. Kiesler, C., and Kiesler, S., *Conformity* (Reading, Mass.: Addison-Wesley, 1969).

6. Turkman, B. W., "Development Sequence in Small Groups," *Psychological Bulletin* 63 (1965): 384–399.

7. Napier, R. W., and Gershenfeld, M. K., *Groups: Theory and Experience,* 3rd ed. (Boston: Houghton Mifflin, 1985), pp. 459–460.

8. Hare, A. P., *The Handbook of Small Group Research,* 2nd ed. (New York: Macmillan, 1976), p. 19.

9. For one discussion of this issue, see Kormanski, C., "A Situational Leadership Approach to Groups Using the Turkman Model of Group Development," in L. D. Goodstein and J. W. Pfeffer, eds., *1985 Annual Handbook for Developing Human Resources* (San Diego, Calif.: University Associates, 1985), pp. 217–226.

10. Homans, G., *The Human Group* (New York: Harcourt Brace Jovanovich, 1950).

11. Scanlan, B., and Keys, J. B., *Management and Organizational Behavior,* 2nd ed. (New York: Wiley, 1983), p. 294.

12. Hare, A. P., *The Handbook of Small Group Research,* 2nd ed. (New York: Macmillan, 1976), p. 19.

13. Feldman, D. C., "The Development and Enforcement of Group Norms," *Academy of Management Review* 9 (1984): 47–53.

14. Dyer, W. D., *Team Building* (Reading, Mass.: Addison-Wesley, 1977).

15. Ibid., pp. 55, 56.

16. Janis, I. L., "Group Think," *Psychology Today* (November 1971): 43–46; see also Janis, I. L., *Victims of Groupthink* (Boston: Houghton Mifflin, 1972).

17. This case is reported in Harvey, J. B., "The Abilene Paradox: The Management of Agreement," *Organizational Dynamics* (Summer 1974): 63–80. For an alternative point of view, see Whyte, G., "Groupthink Reconsidered," *Academy of Management Review* 14(1) (1989): 40–56.

18. Schein, E., *Organizational Psychology* (Englewood Cliffs, N.J.: Prentice-Hall, 1980), pp. 172–176.

19. Brown, L. D., *Managing Conflict at Organizational Interfaces* (Reading, Mass.: Addison-Wesley, 1983).

CHAPTER 15

1. See Mockler, R. J., *The Management Control Process* (Englewood Cliffs, N.J.: Prentice-Hall, 1984).

2. Nanni, Alfred, Jr., "Financial Versus Non-financial Measures of Performance: Barriers to Strategic Control," Manufacturing Roundtable Research Report Series, Boston University, 1988, p. 10.

3. Ashby, William Ross, *An Introduction to Cybernetics* (London: Chapman and Hall, 1964), p. 207.

4. This discussion is based on Nanni, op. cit.

5. Bettel, L. R., *Management by Exception* (New York: McGraw-Hill, 1964) is an excellent early treatment of this topic.

6. Mockler, op. cit., p. 2.

7. See Kleinfield, N. R., "Conquering Those Killer Queues," *New York Times,* September 25, 1988, sec. 3, pps.1 and 11.

8. Easterbrook, Gregg, "Why DIVAD Wouldn't Die," *Washington Monthly* (November 1984): 15.

9. Nanni, op. cit., p. 20.

10. Knight, K. E., and McDaniel, R. B., *Organizations: An Information Systems Perspective* (Belmont, Calif.: Wadsworth, 1979).

11. Easterbrook, op. cit., p. 14.

12. Peters, T., and Waterman, R., *In Search of Excellence* (New York: Harper & Row, 1982), p. 289.

13. Krajewski, L. J., and Ritzman, L. P., *Operations Management* (Reading, Mass.: Addison-Wesley, 1987), ch. 18–19.

14. Easterbrook, op. cit., p. 18.

15. Newman, W. H., *Constructive Control* (Englewood Cliffs, N.J.: Prentice-Hall, 1975).

16. Feigenbaum, A. V., *Total Quality Control: Engineering and Management* (New York: McGraw-Hill, 1961).

17. Krajewski and Ritzman, op. cit., p. 714.

18. Weston, J. F., and Copeland, T. E., *Managerial Finance,* 8th ed. (Hinedale, Ill.: Dryden, 1986).

19. Peters and Waterman, op. cit., p. 318.

CHAPTER 16

1. Buffa, E. S., *Modern Production Operations Management,* 6th ed. (New York: Wiley, and Sons, 1980); Chase, R. B., and Aquilano, N. J., *Production and Operations Management,* 3rd ed. (Homewood, Ill.: Irwin, 1981); McClain, J. O., and Thomas, L. J., *Operations Management: Production of Goods and Services,* 2nd ed. (Englewood Cliffs, N.J.: Prentice-Hall, 1985).

2. Chase and Aquilano, op. cit. Much of this section draws on their work.

3. Ibid., p. 12.

4. Lorange, P., Morton, M. F., and Ghoshal, S., *Strategic Control Systems* (New York: West, 1986), p. 106.

5. Pfeiffer, J., and Salancik, G., *The External Control of Organizations* (New York: Harper & Row, 1978).

6. Much of this discussion is based on Drucker, P. F., *Management: Tasks, Practices, Responsibilities,* abridged and rev. ed. (New York: Harper & Row, 1985).

7. Buffa, op. cit.; Chase and Aquilano, op. cit.

8. Drucker, op. cit., p. 209; and Humphrey, J., Pearce, M., Burgoyne, D., and Erskine, J., *An Introduction to Business Decision Making,* 3rd ed. (Toronto: Methuen, 1985), sect. VIII.

9. Buffa, noted in (1) above.

10. Chase and Aquilano, op. cit., pp. 155–165.

11. Many of the ideas presented in here are drawn from Wiest, J., and Levy, F., *A Management Guide to PERT/CPM* (Englewood Cliffs, N.J.: Prentice-Hall, 1969).

12. Rue, Leslie W., and Byars, Lloyd L., *Management Theory and Application,* 4th ed. (Homewood, Ill.: Irwin, 1986), p. 322.

13. Krajewski, J., and Ritzman, L. P., *Operations Management* (Reading, Mass.: Addison-Wesley, 1987), pp. 447–488.

14. See Dennis, R., "Coping with the Materials Crunch," *Factory* (August 1974): 50–51, for an example of one firm's experience in using an MRP. See also Vollmann, T. E., Berry, W. L., and Whybark, D. C., *Manufacturing Planning and Control Systems,* 2nd ed. (Homewood, Ill.: Irwin, 1988).

15. Schermerhorn, John R., Jr., *Management for Productivity* (New York: John Wiley & Sons, 1984), p. 534.

16. Humphrey et al., op. cit., pp. 329–332.

17. Ibid.

CHAPTER 17

1. Dearden, John, "MIS Is a Mirage," *Harvard Business Review* (January–February 1972): 90. Dearden has argued that MIS "is imbedded in a mishmash of fuzzy thinking and incomprehensible jargon." There has been more agreement recently; see Cheney, P. H., and Lyons, N. R., "MIS Update," *Data Management* 19(10) (October 1980): 26–32.

2. Kenneran, W. J., "MIS Universe," *Data Management* (September 1970): 63.

3. Gregory, R. H., and Van Horn, R. L., "Value and Cost of Information," in J. D. Conger and R. W. Knapp, eds., *System Analyses Techniques* (New York: Wiley, 1974), pp. 473–489. See also Epstein, B. J., and King, W. R., "An Experimental Study of the Value of Information," *Omega* 10(3) (1982): 249–258.

4. Gregory and Van Horn, op. cit., pp. 473–489.

5. Falvey, J., "Real Managers Don't Use Computer Terminals," *Wall Street Journal,* February 7, 1983, p. 24.

6. See, for example, Burch, J. G., Strater, F. R., and Grudinski, G., *Information Systems: Theory and Practice,* 2nd ed. (New York: Wiley, 1979); and Hicks, J. O., *Management Informa-*

tion Systems: A User Perspective (New York: West Publishing, 1984).

7. For other descriptions of networks, see Dreyfuss, J., "Networking: Japan's Latest Computer Craze," *Fortune,* July 7, 1986, pp. 94–96.

8. Barnett, A., "Preparing Management for MIS," *Journal of Systems Management* (January 1972): 40–43.

9. "Frito-Lay Inc.: A Strategic Transition" (#9-187-065), Harvard Business School Publishing, 1986, p. 8.

10. Herzlinger, R., "Why Data Systems in Nonprofit Organizations Fail," *Harvard Business Review* (January–February 1977): 81–86.

11. Murray, J. P., *Managing Information Systems as a Corporate Resource* (Homewood, Ill.: Irwin, 1984).

12. Hicks, J. O., *Management Information Systems: A User Perspective* (New York: West Publishing, 1984), especially ch. 22, pp. 618–651.

13. "Frito-Lay, Inc.," op. cit., p. 8.

14. Ibid.

15. Dickson, G. W., and Simmons, J. K., "The Behavioral Side of MIS," *Business Horizons* 13(4) (August 1970): 59–71.

16. "Frito-Lay, Inc.," op. cit., p. 6.

17. King, W. R., and Cleland, D. I., "Manager-Analysts Teamwork in MIS," *Business Horizons* 14(2) (April 1971): 59–68.

18. Reimann, B. C., and Warren, A. D., "User-Oriented Criteria for the Selection of DSS Software," *Communications of the ACM* 28(2) (February 1985): 166–179.

19. "Expert Systems," a Harvard Business School Note (#9-186-197), Harvard Business School Publishing, 1986.

20. Schank, R. C., and Children, P. G., *The Cognitive Computer: On Language, Learning, and Artificial Intelligence* (Reading, Mass.: Addison-Wesley, 1985).

21. "Expert Systems," op. cit., p. 2.

22. Forsyth, Richard, *Expert Systems, Principles and Case Studies* (New York: Chapman and Hall, 1984).

23. Blanning, R. W., "Knowledge Acquisition and System Validation in Expert Systems for Management," *Human Systems Management* 4(4) (Autumn 1984): 280–285 and Blanning, R. W., "Expert Systems for Management: Possible Application Areas," *Institute for Advancement of Decision Support Systems DSS-4 Transactions* (1984): 69–77.

24. "So Long, Bench Press. Thanks for the Pep Talk," *Business Week,* January 26, 1987, pp. 72, 74.

25. This discussion is based on Zuboff, Shoshana, *In the Age of the Smart Machine* (New York: Basic Books, 1988), pp. 415–422.

26. Cited in Zuboff, op. cit., p. 416.

27. Krajewski, L. J., and Ritzman, L. P., *Operations Management: Strategy and Analysis* (Reading, Mass.: Addison-Wesley, 1987), p. 204.

CHAPTER 18

1. Frederick, William C., "Theories of Corporate Social Performance," in S. Prakash Sethi and Cecilia M. Falbe, eds., *Business and Society, Dimensions of Conflict and Cooperation* (Lexington, Mass.: Lexington Books, 1987), pp. 142–161. See also Etzioni, Amitai, *The Moral Dimension: Toward a New Economics* (New York: The Free Press, 1988).

2. Edmonds, Stahrl W., "Unifying Concepts in Social Responsibility," *The Academy of Management Review* (January 1977): 38–45.

3. Friedman, Milton, and Friedman, Rose, *Free to Choose* (New York: Avon Books, 1971).

4. For a comprehensive discussion of the original case, see "An Anniversary Review and Critique: The Tylenol Crisis," *Public Relations Review* (Fall 1983): 24–34.

5. "Why Gerber Is Standing Its Ground," *Business Week,* March 17, 1986, p. 50.

6. Ibid.

7. Freeman, R. E., *Strategic Management* (New York: Pitman, 1984), pp. 52–54.

8. For one argument, see Edgerton, Jerry, "Money and Morals," *Money* (December 1985): 153–156+.

9. Cavanagh, Gerald F., Moberg, Dennis J., and Velasquez, Manuel, "The Ethics of Organizational Politics," *Academy of Management Review* (1981): 363–374.

10. This is based on Rawls, John, *A Theory of Justice* (Cambridge, Mass.: Harvard University Press, 1971).

11. The theories outlined in this section are based on Frederick, William C., "Theories of Corporate Social Performance," in S. Prakash Sethi and Cecilia M. Falbe, eds., *Business and Society Dimensions of Conflict and Cooperation* (Lexington, Mass.: Lexington Books, 1987), pp. 142–161.

12. Ibid.

13. Ibid.

14. Kavanagh, John P., "The Sinking of Sun Ship," *Business and Professional Ethics Journal* (Summer 1982): 1–13.

15. Gellerman, S., "Why 'Good' Managers Make Bad Ethical Choices," *Harvard Business Review* (July–August 1986): 85–91.

16. Hirschman, Albert O., *Exit, Voice, and Loyalty* (Cambridge, Mass.: Harvard University Press, 1970).

17. Purcell, Theodore V., and Weber, James, *Institutionalizing Corporate Ethics: A Case History,* Special Study No. 71 (New York: The President's Association of the American Management Association, 1979), p. 6; also Weber, James, "Institutionalizing Ethics into the Corporation," *MSU Business Topics* (Spring 1981): 47–52.

18. "Using Ethics to Keep Business Straight," *Security World* (September 1985): 13.

19. Cary, Frank (chairman of the board, IBM Corporation), *Business Conduct Guidelines* (Armonk, N.Y.: IBM Corporation, n.d.), p. 5.

20. Brenner, Steven N., and Molander, Earl A., "Is the Ethics of Business Changing?" *Harvard Business Review* (January–February 1977): 66–67.

21. Sethi, S. Prakash, Cunningham, Bernard J., and Miller, Patricia M., *Corporate Governance: Public Policy-Social Responsibility Committees of Corporate Board: Growth and Accomplishment* (Richardson: Center for Research in Business and Social Policy, University of Texas, 1979), pp. 7–8, 40–41.

22. Otten, Alan F., "Ethics on the Job: Companies Alert Employees to Potential Dilemmas," *Wall Street Journal,* July 14, 1986, p. 19.

CHAPTER 19

1. Fly, Richard, "A Backlash Against Business Is Building—And the Democrats Know It," *Business Week,* April 6, 1987, p. 49.

2. Ibid.

3. Welles, Chris, "The 'Competitiveness' Craze: A New Name, and Old Idea," *Business Week,* January 19, 1987, p. 31.

4. Martz, Larry, et al., "The Quest for the '88 Issue," *Newsweek,* January 19, 1987, pp. 14–16.

5. Frederick, William, Davis, Keith, and Post, James, *Business and Society: Corporate Strategy, Public Policy, and Ethics* (New York: McGraw-Hill, 1988), ch. 4.

6. Weis, W. L., Kornegay, W. R., and Solomon, L. L., "The Fiery Debate over Smoking at Work," *Business and Society Review* (Fall 1984): 4–12; for another example, see Terry, J., "Campbell Soup in Hot Water with Organized Labor," *Business and Society Review* (Summer 1983): 37–41.

7. Hamilton, John O'C., et al., "'No Smoking' Sweeps America," *Business Week,* July 27, 1987, p. 41.

8. Ibid.

9. Anderson, James E., *Public Policy-Making: Decisions and Their Implementation* (New York: Praeger, 1975), p. 35.

10. Langley, Monica, "Lagging Lobby, the Tobacco Institute Loses Power as Attitudes Change," *Wall Street Journal,* November 14, 1986, p. 20.

11. "Limiting Political Action Committees," *Congressional Digest* (February 1987): 33.

12. Miller, N. C., "The Pernicious Influence of PACs on Congress," *Wall Street Journal,* February 7, 1983, p. 1.

13. Dockser, Amy, "Nice Pac You've Got Here . . . A Pity if Anything Should Happen to It," *Washington Monthly* (January 1987): 22.

14. This view of the public-policy process is based in part on Preston, Lee E., and Post, James E., *Private Management and Public Policy* (Englewood Cliffs, N.J.: Prentice-Hall, 1975).

15. Mahon, John F., and Post, James E., "The Evolution of Political Strategies During the 1980 Superfund Debate," in Alfred Marcus, Allen M. Kaufman, and David R. Beam, eds., *Business Strategy and Public Policy* (Westport, Conn.: Greenwood Press, 1987), pp. 61–78.

16. "Dropping the Fuel Economy Standards," *Consumer Reports* (March 1987): 134.

17. Carter, Craig C., "CAFE Fight Brewing," *Fortune,* April 29, 1985, p. 238.

18. "Ford and GM Want a Federal Bailout on Fuel Economy," *Consumer Reports* (May 1985): 262.

19. "Damages Voted Against Kodak of $37.6 Million," *Wall Street Journal,* March 23, 1978, p. 5; "Berkey's Photo's Victory in Kodak Suit Is Reversed," *Wall Street Journal,* June 26, 1979, p. 2.

20. Cain, Carol, "Guilty: Execs Convicted of Murder in Worker's Death," *Business Journal,* June 24, 1985, pp. 1, 105.

21. "Can an Industrial Death Be Murder?" *U.S. News and World Report,* July 15, 1985, pp. 28–29.

CHAPTER 20

1. Goldman, Marshall J., "U.S.-Soviet Trade: What Went Wrong and What About the Future?" *Columbia Journal of World Business,* Twentieth Anniversary Issue, 1966–1986 (Fall 1986): 45–48. See also Drucker, Peter F., *The New Realities* (New York: Harper & Row, 1989).

2. "Lucky Licenses Siltec's Wafer Technology," *Electronic News,* October 14, 1985, p. 56.

3. Contractor, Farok J., "Choosing Between Direct Investment and Licensing: Theoretical Considerations and Empirical Tests," *Journal of International Business Studies* (Winter 1984): 167–187.

4. "Ford Sheds S. Africa Holdings; Workers to Benefit," *Automotive News,* November 30, 1987, p. 2.

5. Quoted in Adkins, Lynn, "New Wave of Offshore Plants," *Duns Business Month* (July 1985): 72–73.

6. Reich, R. B., and Mankin, E. D., "Joint Ventures with Japan Give Away Our Future," *Harvard Business Review* (March–April 1986): 78–86. See also Glickman, N. and Woodward, D., *The New Competitors* (New York: Basic Books, 1989).

7. Monkiewicz, Jan, "Multinational Enterprises of Developing Countries: Some Emerging Characteristics," *Management International Review* 26(3) (1986): 67–79.

8. "Columbus," *Encyclopaedia Britannica,* vol. 6 (Chicago: William Benton, 1969), p. 112.

9. Meleka, Agia Hanna, "The Changing Role of Multinational Corporations," *Management International Review* 25(4) (1985): 36–45.

10. Dymsza, William A., "Trends in Multinational Business and Global Environments: A Perspective," *Journal of International Business Studies* (Winter 1984): 25–46.

11. Wright, Peter, et al., "The Developing World to 1990: Trends and Implications for Multinational Business," *Long Range Planning* 15(4) (1982): 118, quoted in Meleka, op. cit., p. 37.

12. Meleka, op. cit., p. 40.

13. Badaracco, J. L., *Loading the Dice* (Boston: Harvard Business School Press, 1985).

14. Hofstede, Geert, "The Interaction Between National and Organizational Value Systems," *Journal of Management Studies* 22 (1985): 347–357.

15. For a comprehensive discussion of these strategies, see Stoever, William A., "The Stages of Developing Country Policy Toward Foreign Investment," *Columbia Journal of World Business* (Fall 1985): 4.

16. Fitzpatrick, M., "The Definition and Assessment of Political Risk in International Business: A Review of the Literature," *Academy of Management Review* 8 (1983): 249–254.

17. Root, Franklin R., "The Expropriation Experience of American Companies," *Business Horizons* (April 1968): 69–74.

18. Newport, John Paul, Jr., "Risky Business," *Fortune,* August 5, 1985, p. 71.

19. McKinley, Conway, "Terrorism: Growing Factor in Location Decisions," *Site Selection Handbook* (August 1986): 952–956.

20. Ibid.

21. Encarnation, Dennis J., and Vachani, Sushil, "Foreign Ownership: When Hosts Change the Rules," *Harvard Business Review* (September–October 1985): 152–160.

CHAPTER 21

1. Naisbitt, John, *Megatrends* (New York: Warner Books, 1984). See also Dertouzas, M., Lester, R., and Solow, R., *Made in America: Regaining the Productivity Edge* (Cambridge, MA: MIT Press, 1989).

2. The following examples were taken from Kirkland, Richard I., Jr., "Entering a New Age of Boundless Competition," *Fortune,* March 14, 1988, pp. 40–48.

3. The statistics in this section were compiled from the following sources: Bouvier, Leon F., "Human Waves," *Natural History* (August 1983): 6–13; "Massive Population Shift Is Foreseen in

50 years," *Geo* (May 1984): 112; Collins, John, "Global Population Growing by More than 200,000 a Day," *U.S. News & World Report,* July 13, 1984, pp. 52–53; Campon, Rita, "Building a Sustainable Society Is Possible. But It Is Not Easy," *Natural History* (April 1985): 85–86; Brown, Lester R., "The World's Population Picture at Mid-Decade Is One of Stark Contrasts," *Natural History* (April 1985): 73–76.

4. For a more complete discussion of each of these cases, see "Suddenly, A Deathwatch on the Rhine," *Business Week,* November 24, 1986, p. 52; "Why Business Is Watching this Pollution Case," *Business Week,* March 24, 1986, p. 39; and Weaver, Mary Anne, "Roiling the Holy Waters," *Forbes,* May 5, 1986, pp. 142–144.

5. The statistics in this paragraph were derived from "Rumors of Earth's Death Are Greatly Exaggerated," *U.S. News & World Report,* May 9, 1983, pp. A12–A14.

6. Thurow, Lester C., "Why the Ultimate Size of the World's Population Doesn't Matter," *Technology Review* (August–September 1986): 22, 29.

7. Davis, Stanley M., *Future Perfect* (New York: Addison-Wesley, 1987), p. 97. See Drucker, Peter, *The New Realities* (New York: Harper & Row, 1989).

8. Woodside, William S., quoted in "Seven Wary Views from the Top," *Fortune,* February 2, 1987, p. 60.

9. Labich, Kenneth, "Tracking the Two 500s over the Long Haul," *Fortune,* June 11, 1984, pp. 154–155.

10. Woodside, op. cit.

11. Berger, Joan, "The False Paradise of a Service Economy," *Business Week,* March 3, 1986, pp. 78–81.

12. Quinn, James Brian, and Gagnon, Christopher E., "Will Services Follow Manufacturing into Decline?" *Harvard Business Review* (November–December 1986): 95–103.

13. Examples and James L. Cash, Jr., quote derived from Harris, Catherine L., "Information Power," *Business Week,* October 14, 1985, pp. 108–114.

14. This section of the text is based on Davis, op. cit.

Glossary

Accountability The obligation to report back the results of the responsibilities undertaken.

Active listening Attempting to read the message beyond the words spoken.

Activities Physical movements or verbal or nonverbal behaviors in which group members engage.

Ad hoc controls Control activities undertaken apart from the routine reporting processes of the organization.

Administrative-level controls Controls that regulate and monitor technical controls, employee performance, and environmental and strategic changes.

Administrative responsibility Responsibility for directing and coordinating the work of other people.

Aggregate scheduling An approximation of how much of each type of resource must be made available to satisfy forecasted demand.

Any place A changing concept of space involving the elimination or reduction of space as a limit to human activities.

Any time A concept of operation in which less time is needed for tasks, which in the future may require little enough time to be almost instantaneous.

Artificial intelligence Information technology that attempts to mimic human thinking, seeing, talking, and listening processes.

Assembly line A production method whereby components to be worked on are cycled past a stationary worker.

Authority The right to influence others to act.

Automation The automatic handling of parts in mass production processes.

Balance sheet A report that illustrates the firm's financial position at a given point in time.

Batch processing A production process in which individual orders flow through the production facility in different patterns, starting and stopping at various points depending on what needs to be done. Also called *job shop processing.*

Behavioral standards Standards that address the way an activity is to be performed and the steps in its performance.

Benefits Noncash compensation.

Bonuses Single, lump-sum payments.

Bottom-up strategic planning Planning efforts involving managers from various levels in the development of organizational strategy.

Bounded rationality The natural limit on our ability to handle increased information.

Brainstorming A group technique used to identify alternatives.

Budgets Financial controls that present the projected and approved expenditures of an organization's financial resources.

Bureaucracy An organization structure with a clear division of labor in which positions are arranged in a hierarchy of authority and filled based on technical competence.

Canvassing Door-to-door solicitation of signatures on a petition, contributions to a campaign, or pledges of support.

Capacity planning An attempt to determine how much input will be converted into how many different products within a given time period.

Cash flow analysis The assessment of the cash sources available to a firm, their uses, and their availability in time.

Causal analysis methods Forecasting techniques in which behavior is predicted by analyzing its causes.

Centralization The degree to which decision making is concentrated at a single point in the organization.

Centralized-planning economies Economies planned and operated through a central governmental system.

Centralized processing system A system in which hardware and software are centralized in one location.

Central processing unit (CPU) The core of the computer system containing the logic that guides processing functions.

Chain of command The hierarchical reporting relationships that connect all units and levels of the organization.

Charity principle The notion that wealthier members of society should provide assistance to the poorer members.

Choice making Evaluating alternatives and selecting one that meets established criteria.

Coercive power   The ability to influence others by punishment.

Collegial (collective) structure   A structure created to allow individuals to assist each other.

Committee   A group assigned specific responsibilities on an ongoing basis.

Common law   A body of customs and legal precedents built up over time.

Communication   The exchange of ideas, opinions, and information through written or spoken words, symbols, or actions.

Comparative standards   Standards based on the experience of others.

Compensation   The financial payment package an organization provides to its employees in exchange for their work.

Competitive factors   Factors that determine what products at what prices will be successful.

Computer-based information systems (CBIS)   Information systems developed to coordinate the compilation of data and its dissemination to the appropriate individuals.

Concurrent controls   Control mechanisms used as work is being performed; also called *steering controls.*

Conditions of certainty   A situation in which the decision maker knows precisely what consequences will follow from each alternative course of action.

Conditions of risk   Circumstances in which a manager can identify several possible outcomes of decision alternatives but can only estimate the probability that each will occur.

Conditions of uncertainty   Situations in which neither the probabilities of outcomes nor even all possible outcomes can be identified.

Contingency plans   Plans that identify alternative courses of action to be taken if events disrupt the completion or accomplishment of a plan.

Contingency theory   A management philosophy that focuses on analyzing the situation and then fitting the management approach to the situation.

Contingency theory of organization   The idea that the most effective structure for an organization depends on the characteristics of both the organization and its environment.

Control   The process of monitoring performance and taking action to ensure intended or desired results.

Controlling   Setting performance standards, comparing actual performance to these standards, and taking appropriate corrective action.

Corporate social rectitude   The theory that values and ethics are part of business decisions.

Corporate social responsibility   The theory that business has responsibilities beyond the management of the organization itself.

Corporate social responsiveness   The theory that business should aggressively identify and manage social problems before they occur.

Countertrade   The exchange of goods for goods rather than the sale of goods for currency.

Crash implementation   The installation of a newly designed system all at once, completely replacing the previous system

Critical path method (CPM)   A scheduling tool that identifies the longest path in a network of activities, to determine a project's duration.

Culture   The values and beliefs that organization members hold in common as they relate to each other and do their jobs.

Cybernetics   A term used in the 1950s to describe the emerging computer field.

Data   Raw facts and figures concerning results, events, conditions, or trends.

Data channel   The connector between the input/output devices and the CPU.

Data storage devices   Devices that contain all the data to be processed by the CPU.

Decentralization   The degree to which authority and responsibility are pushed down to the lowest level in the organization.

Decision making   Identifying a problem, developing alternatives, and selecting a solution.

Decision support system   An interactive computerized information system that assists the user in making decisions.

Decoding   The process of assigning meaning to transmitted symbols.

Degree of complexity   The number of forces or influences in the environment.

Delegation   The process by which a supervisor gives a subordinate the authority to act.

Delphi technique   A forecasting technique in which a panel of experts develops a composite prediction.

Demographics   The way populations are distributed.

Demotion   A movement to a position of lesser responsibility and status.

Departmentalization   The grouping of activities and responsibilities by subunits of the organization.

Departmentalization by function   The grouping together of people who perform similar or closely related tasks.

Departmentalization by purpose   The grouping together of people who are responsible for achieving a single purpose.

Difference principle   The notion that disadvantaged people should be given proportionately more to balance out the social system.

Differentiation   The differences in structure and orientation that exist among units within an organization.

Direct foreign investment Buying or owning of property or assets in another nation.

Directing Focusing people's skills, time, and energy on the goals to be accomplished.

Distributed processing system A system in which packages of hardware and software are spread throughout the organization.

Division of labor The process of breaking a large task into components one person or group can accomplish.

Downward communication Communication initiated from upper management.

Economic factors Factors that determine the cost of production and the prices for goods.

Economic order quantity The optimum order size that balances ordering costs and carrying costs.

Effectiveness The accomplishment of proper goals.

Efficiency The best possible use of time, money, and resources.

Electronic data processing (EDP) The use of computers to process information.

Emergent behaviors Those actions group members do in addition to or in place of behaviors required by the organization.

Employee-centered behavior Leadership behavior characterized by an orientation toward human aspects of work and problems.

Encoding Selecting symbols to convey the meaning of a message.

Entrepreneur A person who undertakes a venture, organizes it, raises capital to finance it, and assumes most or all of the risk for it.

Environment The factors, forces, and influences outside the organization.

Environmental scanning The process by which managers comprehensively research and analyze the environment.

Equity theory The theory that motivation derives from the equity people perceive to exist between their circumstances and comparable situations.

Ergonomics The study of how best to design equipment to fit a worker's physical characteristics.

Executive opinion jury A forecasting technique in which a prediction is made from a composite of the opinions of a small group of executives.

Expectancy theory The theory that motivation derives from what people expect to happen as a result of their efforts.

Expert power The ability to influence others because of specialized skills or knowledge.

Expert systems Knowledge-based computer systems that try to mimic human expertise and produce decisions requiring judgment.

Exports Goods, materials, and services a country makes or grows and sells to other countries.

External control Control carried out through the organization's formal authority systems.

Feedback Built-in check-and-balance mechanisms that help managers determine whether the information generated is accurate.

Filter A limit on a person's capacity to sense or perceive stimuli.

First-line managers Those who directly supervise the technical work force.

Fixed order period An inventory control technique in which inventory is ordered on a predetermined schedule.

Fixed order quantity An inventory control technique in which inventory is reordered whenever inventory levels reach a certain predetermined point.

Flexible mass production A process in which standardized processes and parts are used to make diverse products.

Flow production The continuous production of a product or service. Also called *process production.*

Force field analysis A tool used to diagnose and plan for change.

Forecasting Predicting future circumstances.

Formal authority The right to influence others given a person because of the job he or she holds.

Formal channels Communication channels planned and established by the organization.

Formal controls Arrangements in which managers determine standards of performance, monitor performance and feedback, and take corrective action.

Formal groups Groups created by someone with formal authority.

Formal organization The organization structure put in place by management.

Formal strategic planning Planning that proceeds through a series of strategic planning steps.

Forming The first stage of group development, in which the basic ground rules and initial structure are established.

Free-market economies Economies that operate on the principles of supply and demand.

Functional regulations Laws aimed at a specific area, such as minimum wage laws.

Function layouts Layouts designed to facilitate the carrying out of a given function.

Gantt chart A scheduling tool that (1) illustrates the work planned and the work accomplished in relation to each other and in relation to time and (2) identifies work delays.

General environment The factors, forces, or influences in the environment that indirectly affect the organization— primarily social, legal, ethical, and political influences.

Global corporation A corporation that engages almost exclusively in one type of business or produces one main product line but utilizes operations around the world to do so.

Globalization To change operation and communication

as the world gets "smaller and things from all over the world affect us more and more."

Goals   An organization's primary intended accomplishments.

Grapevine   An informal, person-to-person communication network not officially sanctioned by the organization.

Group   Two or more persons working together to accomplish a common goal.

Group dynamics   The interaction patterns that evolve in a group.

Group norms   Proper or expected ways of acting in a group.

Groupthink   The tendency of group members to overemphasize the importance of agreement and thus lose their ability to evaluate and solve problems.

Hardware   The physical equipment in a computer system.

Hawthorne studies   Studies conducted by Elton Mayo and his associates in the 1920s and 1930s which attempted to measure the effects of changes in physical environment on productivity.

Hierarchical conflict   Conflict caused by differences in the nature of managers' responsibilities and frames of reference across levels in the organization.

Historical standards   Standards based on individual or corporate experience.

Human approaches to change   Approaches that attempt to improve productivity by changing employees' behavior, attitudes, skills, perceptions, and expectations.

Human relations   A management approach that emphasizes people and their feelings and attitudes.

Human resource planning   The process of deciding the type and number of employees that the organization will need.

Human resources information system   A computerized or manual filing system containing data about the skills and current responsibilities of employees.

Hygiene factors   Factors that, if present, prevent dissatisfaction but do not necessarily lead to satisfaction.

Ideologies   The beliefs, moral principles, and values that provide a basis for organizational decision making.

Implementation   The process of transforming plans into actions.

Imports   Goods, materials, and services a country buys from other countries and brings in.

Incentives   Financial payments offered for the accomplishment of specified objectives.

Income statement   A report that illustrates the money an organization made or lost during a particular period.

Individual contributors   Unsupervised technical specialists who make independent or autonomous contributions.

Industry-specific regulations   Laws passed to control the economic practices of certain industries.

Influence   The capacity or power to affect others' actions.

Informal authority   The ability to influence others without having formal authority.

Informal channels   Communication channels, such as the grapevine, that allow messages to travel outside of the formal communication structure.

Informal controls   Methods of standard setting, monitoring, and adjustment that do not conform to formal procedures.

Informal groups   Groups formed haphazardly, spontaneously, and naturally as people interact.

Informal organization   The informal network of relationships in an organization.

Informal strategic planning   Planning conducted in brainstorming sessions without adherence to steps in the strategic planning sequence.

Information   Organized, analyzed, packaged data that contains meaning beyond the individual facts and is used by managers in decision making.

Information technology   The use of computers to resolve communication needs.

Input/output devices   Communication channels between the user and the computer.

Inputs   Data from internal and external sources.

Inside/outside strategic planning   An internal analysis of strengths that assumes that the organization will continue on its present course and seeks to identify the markets the organization should serve.

Institutional-level controls   Systems or frameworks that guide action and decision making affecting the total organization.

Institutional responsibility   Responsibility for setting overall direction for the organization and managing relationships with the environment.

Integration   The degree to which separate organizational units are coordinated.

Interactions   Two-way communications between group members.

Internal control   A control method in which an individual or group sets its own standards and monitors and corrects its own performance.

International business   Financial and commercial linkages among the peoples, businesses, and governments of two or more countries.

Interpretation   The process of assigning meaning to a message.

Intrapreneurship   The act of fostering entrepreneurial spirit within an established organization.

Inventory   Stored goods including raw materials, work in process, or finished goods.

Job analysis   The method used to clearly define staffing needs.

Job-centered behavior   Leadership behavior characterized by a concern for job performance.

Job depth   The degree of control or automony an individual has over his or her own work.

Job description An outline of the specific responsibilities and duties of a job.

Job enlargement A technique used to increase the number of tasks in a job.

Job enrichment A technique that expands the number and variety of tasks in a job and expands worker responsibility.

Job posting An internal recruiting system through which information about available jobs is made publicly available in the organization.

Job rotation The moving of employees between different jobs.

Job scope The number of tasks in a job.

Job specification An outline of the education, experience, and skills necessary to perform well on the job.

Joint venture An agreement between two or more parties to share the costs and benefits of production.

Just-in-time delivery An inventory control method that schedules parts to arrive on the production line precisely when they are needed. Also called *kanban system.*

Lateral communication Information passed between persons or units at the same level in the organization.

Law of effect The principle that behavior that results in pleasant outcomes is likely to be repeated.

Layout planning The determination of the actual placement of work stations, machinery, inventory areas, and departments within the production facility.

Leadership The ability to influence people toward goal achievement.

Legitimate power The authority to influence others because of the position held.

Liaison An individual who serves as the contact between his or her unit and another unit.

Liberty principle The notion that all people have the same rights.

Licensing agreements Agreements in which a licensor in one country contracts to provide technology, skills, or trademark rights to a licensee in another country so that the licensee can produce a product similar to that of the licensor.

Line employees Workers who are directly responsible for producing the organization's goods or services.

Linking pins Group members responsible for coordinating the work of their group with the work of other groups.

Lobbyists Representatives hired to inform organizations of legislative developments and to influence legislation to protect the organizations' interests.

Local area networks Groups of computers that communicate with one another and share common resources such as data, hardware, and software.

Loosely coupled structure A structure in which two systems are weakly related.

Lose-lose conflict resolution A resolution that does not completely satisfy the needs or criteria of either party.

Mainframe A powerful computer that has extensive data-processing and storage capabilities.

Management The process of setting and accomplishing goals through the use and coordination of human, technical, and financial resources within the context of the environment.

Management agreements Agreements in which a licensor in one country agrees to provide management and direction for the licensee's enterprise in another country.

Management by exception The principle that managers should concentrate on unusual events that require their skill, expertise, or managerial experience.

Management by objectives The mutual determination of objectives and goals by employees and their supervisors.

Management decision making Identifying a problem or opportunity, developing alternatives, and selecting the best.

Management information system (MIS) An organized method of providing past, present, and projected information relating to internal and external operations.

Managerial decision making Making judgments or decisions related to the organization's goals.

Mass customizing The mass production of customized products and services.

Mass production A production process in which each worker works on one portion of a product.

Master scheduling Scheduling that details the daily and weekly resource use and production specifics for each product or service.

Material requirements planning An inventory-planning technique, based on product demand, that generates a list of the parts and subassemblies required to produce the final product along with the required amounts and the correct timing to release the orders for those items.

Matrix organization Departmentalization by two dimensions, such as function and purpose, simultaneously.

Maximax A decision that maximizes the maximum payoff.

Mechanistic organization An organization structure characterized by rules, procedures, a clear hierarchy of authority, and centralized decision making.

Middle managers Those who direct and coordinate the efforts of supervisors and are the link between the operating level and top management.

Minimax A decision that minimizes the maximum costs.

Modular implementation Direct implementation of a new system by one organizational unit at a time. Also called *pilot implementation.*

Motivation A desire and enthusiasm to act.

Motivation factors Factors that if present produce satisfaction.

Multinational corporation A corporation engaged in several types of international business participation; each affiliate in each country is considered a separate enterprise whose purpose is to serve the local area.

Need theories Theories that motivation derives from efforts people exert to satisfy needs.

Network structure A decentralized structure in which power is distributed among interdependent members.

Noise Anything that physically interferes with or distorts the transmission process.

No-matter Value that comes from intangibles.

Nonprogrammed or nonroutine decisions Decisions for which no specific policy exists by which to choose a course of action.

Norming The third stage of group development, in which the collection of people starts to see itself as a group.

Objectives The specific aims that managers accomplish to achieve organizational goals.

One-way communication Communication efforts in which a message is passed from sender to receiver without feedback from the receiver.

Operant conditioning The process of controlling behavior by manipulating its consequences.

Operating environment The factors, forces, or influences in the environment that directly and immediately affect the organization—primarily economic, technological, and competitive forces.

Operating system The activities and processes necessary to transform supplier inputs into goods and services, or outputs.

Operational planning The process through which managers design specific activities and steps to accomplish objectives.

Operations research A management approach that uses mathematical models to analyze and compare situations and alternatives.

Optimal decision A decision for which the decision maker has full knowledge of all alternatives and chooses the alternative producing the best possible outcomes.

Organic organization An organization structure characterized by flexibility, decentralized decision making, and the absence of rules and procedures.

Organizational analysis An analysis that provides information about an organization's strengths and weaknesses.

Organizational mission An organization's reason for existence and overall purpose.

Organization chart A chart that identifies the division of labor, the reporting relationships, and the levels of management in the formal organization.

Organization design The process of determining and implementing an appropriate organization structure.

Organization development An approach to planned change that applies knowledge in a continuing effort to improve the organization.

Organization structure The defined set of relationships among divisions, departments, and managers in the organization, including the responsibilities of each unit.

Organizing Identifying the work to be done, dividing it into units, and coordinating efforts to accomplish the goals.

Orientation The process of introducing new employees to the organization, their jobs, and their co-workers.

Outplacement programs Programs designed to help terminated or laid-off employees find employment in other organizations.

Output measures Indications of the results actually accomplished by the employee on the job.

Outputs Reports, printouts, charts, screen displays, or written summaries compiled and produced during the processing phase.

Output standards Standards that establish a desired level of results, such as time, quality, quantity, or cost.

Outside/inside strategic planning An analysis of the external environment that seeks to identify opportunities the organization can take advantage of through internal adaptation.

Parallel implementation Simultaneous operation of new and old systems to allow debugging of the new system and performance comparison between the two.

Participative management The involvement of all organizational members in the management decision-making process.

Performance appraisal The assessment of employee performance and potential.

Performing The final stage of group development, in which the members know how to work together to accomplish the group's goals and objectives.

Permanent groups Groups that exist over time and whose structure remains constant.

Perquisites (perks) Noncash additions to salary such as cars, expense accounts, and club memberships.

Phased implementation Segment-by-segment installation of a system throughout the organization.

Plan An agreed-upon set of means to achieve a goal within a specified time frame.

Planning The process of analyzing the environment, setting objectives, and designing courses of action to achieve them.

Policies General guidelines for managers to follow in making decisions.

Political action committee (PAC) A group formed to solicit contributions and channel funds to political office seekers.

Political risk The probability that political events and actions will endanger or negatively affect business investments in a given country.

Portfolio A group of products, businesses, or companies assembled to achieve stability and growth.

Portfolio investment The purchase of stocks, bonds, or other securities in businesses in foreign countries in order to obtain interest, dividends, or capital gains.

Postcontrols Controls undertaken when an activity or

task has reached completion and is undergoing final inspection.

Power The ability to influence others to act.

Precontrols Controls performed before work takes place; also referred to as *feed forward controls.*

Problem solving Making decisions, implementing the chosen solution, monitoring its impact, and making adjustments as necessary.

Procedures Step-by-step guides to action.

Process analysis A technique by which managers evaluate the efficiency of a process by determining whether it is level and balanced.

Process measures Indications of the way people go about their work and interact with others on the job.

Process production A production process in which several workers monitor machinery and automated or continuous production processes.

Processing The phase during which the computer transforms, organizes, and stores the data collected during input.

Production/operations management The undertaking of activities that ensure that a product is manufactured or a service performed in a manner that meets the needs of the customer and allows the organization to realize its overall objectives.

Product liability The responsibility a manufacturer has for the product it makes.

Profit sharing The distribution of a portion of business profits to a pool of employees.

Program evaluation and review technique (PERT) A scheduling tool that assumes well-defined relationships between activities, but variations in activity durations.

Programmed or routine decisions Decisions where the option to be chosen is identified by the circumstances of the situation.

Programs Plans that outline a variety of interdependent activities that must be coordinated to achieve a goal.

Projects Plans that are either smaller in scale than programs or part of a program.

Promotion A movement to a position of higher responsibility

Public policy A plan of action undertaken by government to achieve some broad purpose affecting a large segment of the citizenry.

Qualitative forecasting methods Forecasting methods based on the opinions and judgments of experts.

Quality assurance An organized attempt to ensure quality before a product or service is marketed.

Quality circles Problem-solving groups in which workers and their supervisors meet to identify, analyze, and solve productivity problems.

Quality control The process of maintaining and guaranteeing a given level of product or service quality.

Quality of work life (QWL) project An approach to improving the motivation and productivity of workers.

Quantitative forecasting methods Forecasting methods based on historic data used to project a trend or specify relationships among key variables.

Rate of change The speed or frequency with which environmental forces change in character.

Ratio analysis An assessment of a firm's performance and financial condition based on comparisons of balance sheets and income statements.

Recruitment The locating and securing of people to fill positions.

Referent power The ability to influence others based on personal magnetism and charisma.

Refreezing The process of supporting an implemented change.

Reinforcement theory The theory that motivation and behavior derive from the consequences of action.

Required behaviors Those actions a group expects from members as a condition or requirement of their membership.

Resource availability The ability of companies to get the raw materials they need to function.

Responsibility The obligation to perform a task, function, or assignment.

Responsibility center An organizational unit under the direction of a person who is responsible for its activity.

Retirement When an employee stops working in an organization and shifts to nonwork activities or a different career.

Reward power The ability to influence others by giving or withholding rewards.

Rigid mass production A process characterized by the production of large quantities of the same product following the same series of operations.

Rituals Customary and repeated actions within an organization.

Role The set of activities a group member is expected to perform.

Role ambiguity A case where a person is unsure of what others expect of him or her.

Role conflict A case where a person cannot simultaneously meet the expectations of two or more other group members.

Role overload The case where one person is expected to do more than he or she can possibly do.

Rules Specifications for actions that must be taken, or must not be taken, in particular circumstances.

Safety stock Extra inventory kept on hand in case of sudden, unpredicted changes in demand or late deliveries.

Salary The annual amount paid to an employee irrespective of the number of time units spent on the job.

Satisficing decision A decision that is satisfactory or acceptable given the limits on time and available information.

Scalar process The levels of authority and responsibility in an organization.

Scenario building A qualitative forecasting technique in which managers hypothesize future conditions.

Scientific management A systematic method of determining the best way to do a job and specifying the skills needed to perform it.

Scope The degree of impact of a decision.

Selection The process of determining which people best meet the needs of the organization.

Sentiments The feelings, attitudes, and beliefs held by group members.

Service sector The portion of the economy that focuses on delivering a service.

Single-use plans Plans prepared for unique, one-of-a-kind situations.

Social control Society's control, especially through governmental agencies, of organizational action.

Social regulations Laws passed to affect the social environment of most companies.

Social responsibility To whom and for what a modern organization is responsible.

Sociometry A process of identifying how group members interact.

Software Programs and instructions that dictate how data will be manipulated and organized.

Span of control The number of subordinates who report to a given manager.

Specialization The designing of work so that each individual undertakes a limited set of activities.

Staff employees Workers in advisory positions who use specialized expertise to support the production efforts of line employees.

Staffing The continuous process of identifying the types of jobs that need to be done, filling these positions with appropriate people, and managing their performance.

Stakeholders All groups that affect or are affected by an organization's actions or inaction.

Standard A specific criterion against which actual performance can be compared.

Standing plans Predetermined courses of action undertaken under specified circumstances.

Statistical process control The use of data and statistical information to evaluate the quality and productivity of employee performance.

Stewardship principle The notion that those in positions of power and control should use their positions for the good of society.

Stock options Rights to purchase company stock at a reduced price.

Storming The second stage of group development, in which members begin to sort out personal and operating relationships.

Strategic management Monitoring and adjusting strategic plans so that they remain current and the organization remains responsive to its environment.

Strategic planning The determination of the organization's basic mission and the means for achieving this mission.

Strategic thinking The thought process that actively creates a strategic plan and adapts it to changing circumstances.

Strategy The overall mission of the organization and the set of means for utilizing resources to accomplish the mission.

Structural approaches to change Approaches that focus on modifying reporting relationships in a firm.

Superordinate goal An overall goal that units working together can accomplish.

Symbols The names, logos, and physical characteristics used to convey an organization's image.

Systematic controls Controls that produce information about activities on a routine or predictable basis.

Systems theory A management theory that views the organization as a whole constructed of interrelated parts.

System structure The physical and spatial relationship between hardware and software.

Tactical planning The process through which managers design coherent groups of activities to accomplish a strategy.

Task approaches to change Approaches that focus on designing jobs to be as productive as possible.

Task force A temporary group assigned one problem or issue.

Technical-level controls Controls that monitor and provide feedback on operational performance and that are aimed at standardizing performance.

Technical responsibility Direct responsibility for producing goods and services.

Technological approaches to change Approaches that focus on modifying equipment and production methods.

Technological factors Factors that determine how and what products will be produced.

Technology The science and study of the practical and industrial arts.

Technology of production The tools, mechanical equipment, knowledge, and materials used to produce a good or service.

Temporary groups Groups created for a specific purpose that disband when the purpose is achieved.

Termination The final separation of an employee from the organization

Theory of justice A decision-making approach that stresses fairness, equity, and impartiality.

Theory of rights A decision-making approach that stresses minority rights or benefits.

Theory X The assumption that people inherently dislike work and must be coerced and directed at work.

Theory Y The assumption that people inherently like to work, like to accept responsibility, and are creative.

Time and motion studies Studies that attempt to make operations more efficient by finding the best way to do them.

Time series analysis A quantitative forecasting technique in which historical trends are used to project future events.

Top-down strategic planning Planning conducted by a specialized planning staff and delivered to senior executives for analysis.

Top managers Those responsible for the total organization.

Total quality control A quality control process that assigns responsibility for quality to workers rather than managers.

Trade The buying and selling of goods, materials, and services between countries.

Trade associations Groups formed by companies in the same industry to protect their interests and seek protection in numbers.

Trade-off analysis A logical method of choosing between courses of action.

Training and development Joint activities to teach people the skills, activities, and behavior necessary to perform their jobs well.

Trait measures Indications of the characteristics a person brings to the job.

Transaction-processing system EDP systems used by organizations to perform routine, recurring transactions, such as bill and invoice processing.

Transfer A lateral move into a position at the same or a comparable level of responsibility.

Transmitting Passing a message from sender to receiver.

Turnkey projects Projects set up and managed by international enterprises, then turned over to local managers after completion.

Two-way communication Communication efforts in which sender and receiver exchange feedback messages.

Unfreezing Reducing resistance to change by helping people understand the need for it.

Unique-product production A production process in which each product or service is one of a kind and is designed and produced or delivered to specifications.

Unit production A production process in which one person works on one product from beginning to end.

Unity of command A reporting relationship in which everyone reports to and receives instructions from one boss.

Upward communication Information passed from subordinates to supervisors or upper levels of management.

Utilitarian theory The notion that the goal of decisions is to do the most good for the greatest number of people.

Variable budgeting A budgeting process that recognizes that expenditures will change as the volume of sales and/or production is altered.

Wages Payments based on the number of time units a person works or on the number of units produced.

Wholly owned subsidiaries Foreign operations in which multinationals hold 100 percent ownership.

Win-lose conflict resolution A resolution in which one party wins and one loses.

Win-win conflict resolution A situation in which both parties gain from the resolution.

Work flow layouts Layouts designed to facilitate the flow of work.

Work group A group composed of a supervisor and those who report to him or her.

Yes/no controls Concurrent controls that act as checkpoints at transitional phases of an operation.

Zero-based budgeting A budgeting process that requires managers to justify their entire budget and every portion of it for the year.

Photo Credits

Company Index

ABB Company, 217–218
Airborne Express, **638**
Airplan Systems, 539
Albrecht Group, 275
Aldi, 273
Alliant Computer Systems, 180
Allstate Insurance Group, 185
Alpha Computer, 66
American Airlines, 131, 272, 515–516, 538–539
American Bell, 136, 138
American Can, 614, 646
American Express, 538, 539
American Family Association, **63**
American Honda Motor, 362
American Hospital Supply Corporation (AHSC), 516, 650, 665
American Radiator, 618
American Telephone and Telegraph (AT&T), 136, 212, 219, 237, 238–239, 240, **620**
Apple Computer, 12, 20, **76**, 272, 303, 409, 584, 633–634
Apple Corps Limited, **76**
Asea Company, 217–218
Avon Products, 129

Baby Furniture and Toy Supermarket. *See* Toys 'R' Us
Baltek Corporation, 152
Banco Brasileiro de Descontos S.A. (Bradesco), 245–247
Bank of Boston, 457
Barclays Bank, 538
Baxter Travenol Laboratories, 665–666
Bay Manufacturing, 85
Bell & Howell, 578
Bell Telephone, 144
Ben and Jerry's Foundation, 121
Ben and Jerry's Ice Cream, 119–121
Bendix Corporation, 143
Benetton, 250–252, 254–256, 265, 268–269, 270
Berkey Photo, 601
Bethlehem Steel, 37, 40
Biddle & Associates, 328n
Booz, Allen & Hamilton, 510
Borden, 276
Boston Celtics, 318–319, 326, 329, 332, 339
Bradesco. *See* Banco Brasileiro de Descontos S.A.

Brain Reserve, 166
Briggs & Stratton, 533–534
Britt Airlines, 131
Brown Boveri, 217–218
Burger Chef, 24–27
Burger King, 10, 166, 654
Burlington, **638**
Burroughs Office Machines, 618

Campbell Soup, 272
Canon, 637, 653
Caremark, 665, 666
CBS, 212, 640
Cedar Bluff Pulp Mill, 473–474
Cessna Aircraft, 510
Chiat/Day Agency, 408–410
Child World, 147
Chrysler Corporation, 100–101, 292, 596
Ciba-Geigy, 618, 619
Cimao, 616
Citibank, 204
Coca-Cola Company, 58–59, 61, 64, 68–69, 71, 73–74, 77, 78–79, 218–220, 617, 628
Coldwell Banker, 186
Compaq Computer, 314
Computervision, **42**, 520
Comumbana, 614
Continental Airlines, 131
Control Data, 178, 180
Convex Computers, 180
Coopers & Lybrand, 510
Cray Research, 178–180
Credesco, 629
Cummins Engine, 618

Dalton, B., Bookseller, 9
David's Cookies, 288–289
Dayton Hudson, 9
Dean Witter Reynolds, 58, 186, 187
Del Monte, 276
Detroit Diesel, 247, 248
DHL International, 638
Diamond Match, 618, 619
Digital Equipment, 20, 207, 546
Disney. *See* Walt Disney Company
Dow Chemical, 204
Dresser-France, 631–633
Drexel Burnham Lambert, 409
DuPont, 212, 343

Eastman Kodak, 167, 542, 543, 544, 601, 618

Edge Moor Iron, 40
Edison, 619
Electronic Data Services (EDS), 223, 224
Emery Purolator, **638**
ETA Systems, 180
Exxon Corporation, 343, 558, **620**
Exxon Shipping, 558

Factory Automation and Computer Technologies, 510
Fanuc Limited, 533
FastFax, 637, 653
Federal Express, 343, 636–639, 640, 648, 649, 651, 653, 654, 655, 656, 657
Federal Express Aviation Services, Inc. (FEASI), 637
Film Recovery Systems, 602
Finnair, 196
First Nationwide Financial, 614
First Nationwide Savings, 614
First Travel Corporation, 98
Ford Aerospace, 452–453, 456, 462
Ford Aerospace & Communications Corporation, 614
Ford Motor Company, 38, 51, 105, 212, 248, 362, 452, 461, 489, 578, 586, 587–588, 595–596, 609–610, 611, 612, 614, 616, 618, 619, **620**, 628, 629, 652
Ford Motor Land Development Corporation, 614
Frazer & Company, 619
Frito-Lay, 144, 512–514, 516, 517, 518, 519, 521, 523, 524, 525
Frontier Airlines, 131
Fuji Film, 544, 653
Fujitsu, 180, 512, 513, 525
Fuji Xerox, 544, 545, 546

Gannett Company, 125–126, 128, 129, 130, 134, 137–138, 139, 144–145
General Dynamics, 452, 672
General Electric, 141, 204, 248, 272, **401**, 409, 576–578, **620**, 653
General Motors, 72–73, 106, 222–224, 227, 229, 230, 234, 236, 237, 243, 248, 279, 303, 362, 487, 489, 578, 595–596, **620**, 661–663

Gerber Products, 170, 556–559, 562
Gerber Systems Technology, **42**
Glencoe Corporation, 85
Goodrich, B.F., Chemical, **401**
Goodyear, 583
Grace, W.R., & Company, 153, 162
Grand Metropolitan, 10
Grant, W.T., 136
Gulf Refining and Marketing, 649

Haloid Company, 541–542
Harley-Davidson, 314
Harris Corporation, 140
Hay Associates, 183
Hertz Corporation, 248
Hertz-Penski Corporation, 247–248
Hewlett Packard, 12, 20, **42**, 239–240, 465
Hillfarm Dairy, 552, 553
Honda, 620
Honeywell, 406
Hudson, J.L., Company, 9
Hutton, E.F., & Company, 602
HYL Worldwide Express, **638**

IBM (International Business Machines), 20, **42**, 43, 111–112, 123, 140, 180, 230, 252, 266–267, 303, 343, 376–377, 441–442, 542, 543, 544, 574, 614, 616, 617, **620**, 633, 653
Intel, 272
International House of Pancakes, 197
Interstate Stores, 148

Jewel Companies, 552–554, 559, 562
Johnson & Johnson, 556–559, 562, 574–575

Kama Motor Works, 628
Kawasaki, 467
Kids 'R' Us, 148
K Mart, 136, 182
Knife River Coal Company, 11
Konsberg, 669–672
Korey, Kay & Partners, 362
Korn/Ferry, 333

Laguna Madre Shrimp Farms, 153, 154
Lincoln Electric, 239
Lipper Analytical Securities, **561**
LivingWell, 531
Lloyds of London, 629
Lockheed, 343, 406
Lucky Advanced Materials, 613

McCann Erickson Agency, 59
McDonald's, 22, 32, 166, 197–198, 478–479
McKinsey & Company, 183, 544, 545
Mallinkrodt Chemical, 129
Marifarms, 153
Marin Culture Enterprises, 153, 154, 162, 163, 165
Matsushita, 651
Maytag, 314
Mazda Motor, 610
Merck, 272
Mervyn's, 9
Michigan Bell, **401**
Microelectronic and Computer Technology, 180
Midvale Steel, 35, **36**
Mills Brothers, 476–477
Minnesota Mining & Manufacturing (3M), 140–141, 272
Mitsubishi, 620
Mobil, **620**
Monongahela Power, 605
Monsanto, 341
Montana Dakota Utilities, 11
Montgomery Ward, 277
Morton Thiokol, 573
Motorola, 212
Motown Productions, 443–447
Mrs. Fields Cookies, 288–289

National Cash Register, 618
Nestlé, 619
New Jersey Bell Telephone, 47
New United Motor Manufacturing, Inc. (NUMMI), 661–663
New York Times, The, 343
Nike, 409
Nissan Motor Manufacturing, 314, 363
No Nonsense Fashions, 271

Ohio Power, 605
Osborne Computer, 122–123
Ozyx Corporation, 433–435

Parker Chemical, 614
Penney, J.C., 136, 242, 335, 649
Pennsylvania Shipping, 567
Penske Corporation, 247
People Express, 131, 515
Pepsi-Cola Company, 58–59, 61, 62, **63**, 77, 303, 512
Philip Morris, 272, 591
Phillips, NV, Gloeilampenfabrieken, 27–28
Pillar House, 197
Pillsbury, 10
Plantation Sea Farms, 152–153, 154

Plum's, 9
Polaroid, 167
POM Industries, 498–499
Primerica, 614
Prince, F.H., & Company, 153, 162
Procter & Gamble, 252
Provincetown-Boston Airlines, 131
P.T.ASEAN Aceh Fertilizer, 616
Pullman Standard, 54–56
Purolator, 618

Ralston Purina, 152, 430
Rank Xerox, 544
Reynolds, R.J., Tobacco, 583, 591
Ricoh, 637
Ringling Brothers and Barnum & Bailey Circus, 4–5, 7, **18**, 20, 89–93
Ringling Brothers' Circus, 89
RJR Nabisco, 591
Rockwell International, 572, 573
Ryder System, 248

Saturn Corporation, 223–224, 227, 230, 241
Scandanavian Airline System (SAS), 192–194, **195**, 196, 200–202, 205, 279
Sears, Roebuck, 136, 181–187, 211
Sears Merchandise Group, 185
Seraco Real Estate Group, 185
Shanghai Metallurgical & Mining Machinery Manufacturing (S4M), **42–43**
Sharp, 637
Shearson Lehman, 343
Shell Oil, 204, 649
Siltec Corporation, 613
Singer Sewing Machine, 618
Sir Speedy, 637
Solar Aquafarms, 153, 165
Sony, 324, 620, 640
Standard Oil Trust, 35, 618
Steve's Homemade Ice Cream, 121
Strategic Innovations International (SII), 164
Stratus Corporation, 651
Studebaker, 303
Sundstrand, 599–600
Sun Ship, Inc., 567–568

Tadashi Kobayashi, 545
Target, 9
Texas Air, 131, 539
Texas Instruments, 468
Texas United Fisheries, 153
Texas Utilities Electric, 570
Thornton Associates, 372
Time, Inc., 481–483, 486, 491–492
Timex, 176–178

Tootsie Roll Industries, 314
Toshiba, 667–672
Toshiba Machine, 667–672
Touchstone Pictures, 150
Toyota, 504, 662–663
Toys 'R' Us, 147–148
Trans World Airlines, 237, 343
Trans World Corporation, 237–239
Transcon Insurance, 614
Travelmation Corporation, 539
Trendy Clothing Store, 254–255
TRW, 507–509
TVSM, 483
Twentieth Century-Fox, 242–243

UniCo, 490–491
Unilever, 619

Union Carbide, 114, 212, 276, 579–580
United Airlines, 131, 343, 515
United Parcel Service (UPS), 637, **638**
United States Steel, 35. *See also* USX
United States Time, 177
Universal Studios, 444
U.S. Faxsys, 637–638, 653
U.S. Travel Systems, 539
USG Corporation, 582
USX, 640. *See also* United States Steel

Varian Associates, 14
Volvo Automobile, 230
VTS Travel Enterprises, 540

Walt Disney Company, 149–150
Warner-Lambert, 108–109
Waterbury Clock, 176–177
Western Electric, 22, 46–47
Westinghouse, 217, 653

Xerox, 541–547, 578

Yale and Towne Lock, 38
Yamaha, 409
Yamazaki Machinery Works, 532
Young, Arthur, and Company, 333
Young and Rubicam (Y&R) Advertising, 108
Yugo Automobile, 105

Zayre Department Stores, 458–459

Name Index

Abrams, C., 411
Ackoff, R.L., 494*n*
Adams, J.S., 395–396
Adolph, J., 120*n*
Agee, W., 143
Aguiar, A., 245–247
Alderfer, C.P., 385–386, **390**
Alexander, J., 152
Allen, M., 67*n*, 397
Alter, J., 125*n*
Ambrose, J., 453
Anderson, W., 579–580
Andrade, F., 397*n*, 414*n*
Ansoff, H.I., 127
Aoi, J., 667–668
Apple, J.M., 495*n*
Aquilano, N.J., 485*n*
Aquillar, F.S., 178*n*
Arbose, J., 217*n*
Archer, L., 571*n*
Arnold, S., 346*n*
Ashby, W.R., 455
Asimov, I., 394
Atchison, C., 570
Atkinson, J.W., 387
Auerbach, A., 318–319, 320, 326, 328, 332, 334, 339, 340

Bairn, B., 397
Baker, J., 298
Banks, R.J.P., 602
Barnard, C.I., **33**, 47–48
Barnes, J., 152*n*
Barnevik, P., 217–218
Barnum, P.T., 89
Barriman, B., 371
Bass, B.M., 299*n*
Beals, V., Jr., 314
Beatty, R.W., 329*n*, 338*n*
Becker, H., 542
Bedeian, A., 110*n*
Behar, R., 558*n*
Belafonte, H., 414, 415
Belkin, L., 250*n*, 349*n*
Benefield, J., 314
Benetton, C., 250, 256
Benetton, Gilberto, 250
Benetton, Giuliana, 250, 256
Benetton, L., 250, 251, 270
Bennett, D., 422
Bennett, R.K., 668*n*
Bennis, W., 226, 227
Beres, M.E., 215*n*, 279*n*, 282*n*
Bergquist, E., 316

Berube, B., 570
Best, E., 107
Bianchi, D., 245
Billingsley, L., 349*n*
Bing, S., 359*n*
Bird, L., 319, 320, 326
Bird, W., 149*n*
Black, C., 126
Blair, J.F., 152*n*
Blake, R.R., 269*n*
Blanchard, K., 308–310
Bockerstette, J.A., 510
Boesky, I., 602
Bonaparte, N., 210
Borrus, A., 28*n*
Boseman, F.G., 476*n*
Boyer, P.G., 349*n*
Bradley, B., 571*n*
Brahm, J., 314*n*
Bray, R.L., 443*n*
Brehm, W., 440
Brennan, E., 184–187
Brody, M., 661*n*
Brooks, G., 507*n*
Brown, H., 439
Brown, M.W., III, 30*n*
Brown, Walter, 334
Brown, William M., 604*n*
Brzezinski, Z., 298
Budiansky, S., 452*n*
Buggie, F.D., 164
Burch, J.G., 273
Burgelman, R.A., 270
Burns, J., 310
Burns, T., 227, 228*n*, 230
Burr, D.C., 131
Burros, M., 288*n*
Burrows, W.E., 278*n*
Bush, G., 594
Bylinsky, G., 534*n*
Byrd, R.C., 606
Byron, C., 481*n*

Caldwell, E., 394
Caler, H., 368*n*
Canion, J., 314
Carley, W., 131*n*
Carlson, C., 541–542
Carlucci, F., 422
Carlzon, J., 192–194, 200–202, 205
Carrington, T., 668*n*
Carroll, A.B., 567*n*
Carson, R.L., 588
Carter, J., 55, 439

Carter, S., 543
Caruso, C., 445
Castro, F., 629
Cauchon, D., 147*n*
Cavanaugh, J., 24–27
Chaffe, B., 345–346
Chase, R.B., 484*n*
Chemers, M., 309*n*
Chiat, J., 408–410
Child, J., 194
Christine, M., 90
Clark, C., 445
Clemens, J., 303*n*
Clow, L., 409
Cohen, B., 119–121
Colbert, B.A., 527, 528
Columbus, C., 618
Cooper, J.A., 294*n*
Cooper, W., **76**
Corelli, R., 582*n*
Cosby, B., 446
Coston, S., 445
Courbrough, J.A., 45*n*
Cousins, G., 557
Covin, T.J., 279*n*, 282*n*
Cox, J., 491*n*
Cray, S., 178–180
Cressey, D.R., 574*n*
Crews, H., 394
Crosby, P.B., 463–464
Crutchfield, R.J., 512*n*
Cunningham, M., 143
Cushman, J.H., Jr., 600*n*

Daft, R.L., 157*n*, 229*n*, 233*n*
Dahltorp, B., 333
Davidson, J., 576*n*
Davis, B., 457*n*
Davis, K., 374*n*, 588*n*, 589*n*, 594*n*, 606*n*, 631*n*
Davis, S.M., 205, 240–244, 636*n*, 648*n*, 650
Dayton, G.D., 9
Deal, T., 238
Deere, J., 186
Dennis, R., 422
DeParle, J., 125*n*
dePasse, S., 443–447
Deukmejian, G., 578
Dewar, D.L., 406*n*
Dickerson, E., 397
Dickson, G.W., 525
Dillard, A., 394

Dillingham, B., 207
Disney, W., 149
Doyle, J., 465–466
Dreyfuss, J., 409n
Drucker, P., 72, 115, 136, 182, 183, 486, 487
Dukakis, M., 590
Dunkin, A., 275n
Dylan, B., 426

Easterbrook, G., 125n, 452n
Ebert, R., 394
Edison, T.A., 640
Edmonds, S.W., 555–556
Ehrlich, A.M., 644n
Ehrlich, P.R., 536n, 644n
Eichenwald, K., 541n
Eisner, M., 150
Ellul, J., 163
Emerson, H., 38
Emmet, R., 376n
Emrich, M., 609n
Encarnation, D.J., 618n
Englemayer, P.A., 536n
Epstein, S., 394

Fabricant, F., 288n
Farnsworth, C.H., 668n
Fayol, H., 33, 44–45
Feigenbaum, A.V., 467
Feld, C.S., 512–514, 525
Feld, Irvin, 92
Feld, Israel, 92
Feld, K., 4–5, 7, 12, 13, 18, 91, 92, 93
Ferry, R., 333
Fiedler, F.E., 304–307, 309n
Fields, D., 288–289, 290, 291, 292, 294–295, 296, 299, 300, 302, 307
Finch, P., 582n
Fineberg, H.V., 88n
Fisher, A.B., 58n
Fitzgerald, J., 318n
Flatow, P.J., 166
Fleishman, E.A., 300–301, 302
Follett, M.P., 33, 44, 51
Ford, G., 87–88
Ford, H., 33, 38, 51, 487, 587–588, 609, 610
Ford, H., II, 587
Ford, N., 521
Fox, W., 207n
Frederick, W.C., 564, 566
Frederick, W.F., 588n, 589n, 594n, 606n, 631n
Freeman, R.E., 144
Freidman, J., 476–477
French, J.R.P., Jr., 292
Frydman, K., 288n

Funkhouser, G.R., 429n
Furst, A., 288n

Galbraith, J., 236
Gantt, H.L., 38
Garn, J., 672
Garson, B., 478
Gasser, T., 218
Gatza, J., 476n
Gelfond, S.M., 636n
Gelman, E., 58n
Gershwin, G., 98
Ghiselli, E., 297
Ghoshal, S., 485n
Gibson, R., 178n
Gifford, W., 238
Gilbert, S., 441n
Gilbreth, F., 33, 37, 205
Gilbreth, L., 33, 37, 205
Gitman, L.J., 497n
Glaberson, W., 600n
Glickman, A., 315n
Goizueta, R.C., 58, 61, 68, 69, 73
Golab, S., 602
Goldberg, M., 414n
Goldratt, E., 490–491
Gorbachev, M., 613
Gordon, E., 314
Gordy, B., 444, 445
Grace, R., 362
Graves, F., 120n
Green, S.G., 311n
Greenfield, J., 119–121
Greenwald, J., 58n
Gregory, R.H., 519
Greiner, L., 261, 263–264
Gruson, L., 582n
Guiles, M.G., 222n
Gundlach, B., 543
Guy, P., 152n

Hackman, J.R., 206–208
Hammer, E.R., 401n
Hammer, W.C., 401n
Hammond, B., 374n
Hammonds, K.N., 576n
Harrison, G., 76
Hartmann, T.C., 376
Harvey, J.B., 435n
Hatten, K., 133n
Hatten, M.L., 133n
Hazelwood, J., 557, 558
Hegarty, J., 362
Henderson, J., 315
Hendricks, E., 376
Henry III of France, 488
Hensen, J., 553–554
Herold, D.M., 342
Hersey, P., 308–310
Herzberg, F., 206, 390–391

Hicks, W., 543, 544–546
Hill, F.E., 609n
Hill, R., 28n, 192n
Hillkirk, J., 541n
Hinrichs, J.R., 352n
Hofer, C.W., 171n
Hofstede, G., 624–625
Holt, C.W.J., 120n
Homans, G., 425–427
Hopewell, J., 443n
Horn, J., 349n
Hougart, B., 152
House, R.J., 307–308
Houston, P., 178n, 544
Huber, G.P., 60n
Huemann, P., 67
Hunt, J.G., 388n
Hunter, J.C., 394
Huxley, A., 639

Iacocca, L.A., 100, 292, 584
Icahn, C., 253
Ikeguchi, J., 153
Inaki, J., 365

Jackson, J., 594
Jackson, M., 414, 415, 426, 640
Jacobson, A.F., 140
Jacobson, G., 541n
James I of England, 583
Janis, I., 435, 436n
Jarreau, A., 415
Jenkins, L., 26
Jennings, E.E., 212
Jermier, J.M., 312n
Jobs, S.P., 303, 584
John XXIII, Pope, 280
Johnson, C.L., 141n
Johnson, L.B., 324
Johnson, S., 85
Jones, K.C., 318n, 319
Jones, Q., 414, 415, 417, 421

Kane, D., 11
Kanongo, R.N., 294n
Katz, D.R., 181
Kearns, D., 544, 545, 547
Keider, N., 333
Kelley, P., 579n
Kennedy, A., 238
Kennedy, A.A., 239
Kenneran, J.M., 514
Kerr, P., 147n
Kerr, S., 312n
Kiely, L., 523
Kierkegaard, S., 29, 31
Killanin, Lord, 98
Kilman, R.M., 279n, 282n
King, L., 316
Kleinfeld, N.R., 571n
Knickerbocker, F.T., 176n

Knowles, A., 178*n*
Koch, E., 298
Koeki, W., 669
Koepp, S., 149*n*
Koop, C.E., 582
Kossen, S., 358*n*
Kotter, J.P., 262, **263**
Kragen, K., 218–220, 414
Krajewski, L.J., 467, 532
Kroc, R., 32
Krombeen, K., 28
Krumm, D., 314

Ladd, A., Jr., 242–423
Lager, F., 120
Lago, D., 353*n*
Lane, F.C., 488*n*
Langley, M., 239*n*
Larson, E., 120*n*
Lauper, C., 426
Lawler, E.E., 391–393, 405*n*
Lawrence, A., 153
Lawrence, P.R., 205, 234–236
Lazarus, C., 148
Leavitt, H.J., 265–267, 364
Ledford, G.E., Jr., 405*n*
Lehmkuhl, J., 176–177
Lehr, L.W., 140
Leiderman, D., 288–289, 290, 291,
    292, 294–295, 296, 299, 300,
    302, 307
Lerner, M.A., 439*n*
Letterman, D., 558
Levin, D.P., 247*n*
Levinson, H., 297
Lewin, K., 261–263, 264, 268,
    391–392
Lewis, A.S., 141*n*
Lewis, D., 86
Lewis, M., 125*n*
LiCalsi, P., **76**
Liedtke, J., 569*n*
Likert, R., 300, **302**, 417
Lincoln, A., 570
Lineback, J.R., 633*n*
Little, A.D., 542
Locke, E.A., 404
Loderand, K., 414*n*
Loggins, K., 415
Lorange, P., 485*n*
Lorsch, J., 234–236
Lowell, J., 222*n*
Lucier, C.E., 510
Lundquist, E., 365
Luter, E.R., 633
Lutz, S., 664*n*

McCarthy, M., 63*n*
McCaskey, M.B., 370*n*
McClelland, D.C., 387–389

McCullough, D., 40*n*
McDaniel, C., Jr., 497*n*
McGowan, S., 153
McGregor, D., **33**, 48–49, 402–404
Machiavelli, N., 400
McIntosh, N., 233*n*
McIntosh, S., 127
Macke, K.A., 9
McKeon, K., 362
McLuhan, M., 356
Madonna, 62, **63**
Magnet, M., 125*n*
Mahon, J.F., 481*n*, 579*n*
Mahoney, D., 293*n*
Malone, M.S., 253*n*
Maloney, J., 452
Marchese, A., 538
Mariani, J.F., 152*n*
Marriot, W.K., 400*n*
Martin, D.C., 439*n*
Martin, J., 561*n*
Maslow, A., **33**, 48, 257, 384–385,
    386, **390**
Maver, D., 303*n*
Mayo, E., 46–47
Mellon, R., 476–477
Metcalf, G., 183
Mettler, R.R., 507
Meyer, A., 476
Meyer, J.J., 14
Meyer, R.W., 510
Midler, B., 415
Mignanelli, T., 363
Miller, T., 26
Miller, W.H., 571*n*
Milutinovich, J.S., 476*n*
Mintzberg, H., 20, **21**, 128
Mitchell, R., 541*n*
Mitchell, T.R., 311*n*
Moghmer, P., 11*n*
Monden, Y., 504*n*
Moore, C.A., 574*n*
Moran, J., 184, 186
Morgan, J.H., 316
Morrow, J., 248
Mortiz, R., 520
Morton, M.F., 485*n*
Moskal, B.S., 582*n*
Mouton, J.S., 269*n*
Mullins, G., 59
Munkberg, C.-O., **203**
Murphy, J., 122*n*, 631*n*
Murray, H.A., 387
Murray, J.E., 410–412
Musser, S., 279*n*, 282*n*

Nader, R., 594
Naisbitt, J., 639
Nakasone, Y., 670
Nebuchadnezzar, King, 1

Neirenberg, G., 368*n*
Nelson, D., 326
Neuharth, A.H., 125–126, 128, 129,
    130, 134–135, 137–138, 139,
    144–145
Neustadt, R.E., 88*n*
Neveins, A., 609*n*
Newman, W.H., 465*n*
Newstrom, J.W., 374*n*
Nielsen, J., 212*n*
Nixon, R.M., 54, 355
Norris, W., 180
North, J.R., 92
Nulty, P., 558*n*
Nunn, S., 422

O'Donnel, 418*n*
O'Donnell, M., 491
Oldham, G.R., 206–208
Olds, R.E., 609
Oppenheimer, M., 647
O'Reilly, B., 222*n*, 239*n*
Orlick, T., 260
Orwell, G., 639
Osborn, R.N., 388*n*
Osborne, A., 122–123
Osipov, I.A., 669
Ott, J., 636*n*
Ouchi, W., **33**, 49
Owen, R., 34

Parker, J., 153
Parsons, T., **33**, 49
Peach, B., 490–491
Pemberton, J.S., 58
Penney, J.C., 335
Penske, R., 247–248
Perrow, C., 233, 558*n*
Perry, S., 415
Pertschuck, M., 582*n*
Peters, T., 144, 252, 253, 475
Peterson, C.R., 604*n*
Pettit, R., 378
Pfeiffer, J., 109*n*
Phillips, J.R., 239
Pickens, T.B., 253
Pines, C., 26
Pitzer, M.J., 9*n*
Plakias, G., 207
Plato, 303
Pointer, R., 415, 423
Polo, M., 618
Porter, L.W., 391–393
Porter, M.E., 173
Post, J.E., 30*n*, 98*n*, 219*n*, 588*n*,
    589*n*, 594*n*, 606*n*, 631*n*
Preston, L.E., 579*n*
Pullman, G., 54
Purcell, P., 183
Purcell, T., 573

Ramacciotti, A.R., 539
Raven, B., 292
Rawl, L., 558
Ray, M., 604n
Reagan, R., 591, 594, 596, 605, 613, 632, 671
Rehder, R.R., 661n
Reibstein, L., 636n
Reich, C., 222n
Resciano, R., 222n
Resener, M., 250n
Ricci, C., 147n
Rice, B., 271n
Richardson, A., 345
Richie, L., 414, 415
Richman, T., 288n
Ringling, Al, 89, 91
Ringling, Alfred T., 89, 91
Ringling, Charles, 89, 91
Ringling, John, 89, 90, 91
Ringling, Otto, 89, 91
Rittenmeyer, R.A., 512–514, 525
Ritti, R., 429n
Ritzman, L.P., 467, 532
Robinson, J., 397
Rodri, J., 397
Roebling, E., 38, 39–40
Roebling, J., 39
Roebling, W., 39
Roebuck, A.C., 181
Rogers, C., 369
Rogers, K., 414, 415
Rogo, A., 490–491
Rogol, M., 218
Rollwagon, J., 179, 180
Roosevelt, T., 609
Rosenberry, B., 153
Rosenwald, J., 181
Ross, D., 415, 423
Rubinfien, E., 668n
Rublin, L.R., 664n
Rukeyser, L., 322n
Russell, B., 319, 320, 326, 328, 334

Sabin, A.B., 87
Salk, J., 87
Salpukas, A., 131n
Sanchez, R., 62
Sangster, B., 590
Sashkin, M., 404
Saverin, R.F., 277–278
Sayles, L.R., 270
Schendel, D., 171n
Schermerhorn, J.R., Jr., 388n
Schlesinger, L.A., 262, **263**
Schneier, C.E., 329n, 338n
Schuster, L., 245n
Schwandt, M., 362
Schwartz, H., 240–244
Schwartz, J., 661n

Scredon, S., 58n
Sculley, J., 303
Sears, R.W., 181, 186
Sege, T.D., 14
Sencer, D., 87
Serrin, W., 323n
Shabecoff, P., 604n
Shaked, I., 67n
Sherman, S.P., 273n
Shrivastava, P., 579n
Sibbald, J., 333
Simmons, J.K., 525
Simon, H.A., 23
Simpson, J.C., 116n
Simpson, O.J., 397
Sinclair, S.W., 516n
Skevington, C., 510
Skinner, B.F., 398
Sloan, A.P., Jr., 72–73, 222, 223, 227
Smart, T., 668n
Smith, A., 196–197, 199
Smith, F.W., 636
Smith, L., 576n
Smith, M.M., 661n
Smith, R.B., 222n, 223, 224–225, 229, 243
Snow, C.P., 643–644
Socks, L.J., 533
Soekmono, R., 30n
Sokolof, M., 277–278
Sontag, P.M., 539
Sorensen, J., **42**
Springsteen, B., 426, 640
Stadtman, N., 125n
Stafford, T., 606
Stalker, G., 227, 228n, 230
Stanfill, D.C., 242–243
Stanford, B., 590
Steinberg, S., 150
Stodgill, R., 299
Stoner, J.A.F., 60n
Streufort, S., 297
Sullivan, L., 577
Szanto, 250n

Tallarigo, R., 670
Tamura, H., 671
Tannenbaum, J.A., 541n
Tarnowski, W., 193, 200
Taylor, F.W., 22, **33**, 35–37, 38, 40, 205, 265–266, 650
Taylor, J., 149n
Telling, E., 183, 186, 187
Temlock, S., 242
Terry, L., 582
Thomas, D., 393
Thomas, T.P., 159n
Thompson, L.J., 510
Thurow, R., 576n

Tita, M.A., 141
Toffler, A., 639
Towne, H., 38
Troitsky, A., 669
Tron, R., 631–633
Tsifkoff, M., 576n
Tully, S., 176n
Tunstall, W.B., 238–239

Udall, S., 164
Ueberroth, P., 98–99, 100, 101, 103, 105, 106–107, 109, 110, 113, 114, 333

Vachani, S., 618n
Vail, T., 238
Vaiser, C., 125n
Van Horn, R.L., 519
Van Leeuwen, L., 539
Vanner, B., 125n
Vitti, V., 540
Voluck, P.R., 582n
von Bertalanffy, L., **33**, 50
Voute, C., 30n
Vroom, V.H., 80, 391

Waddock, S., 344n
Wagner, T.J., 362
Wald, M., 558n
Waldron, G., 441–442
Walloran, R., 439n
Walls, D.M., 362
Wantuck, M.-M., 604n
Warner, J., 318n
Waterman, R., 144, 475
Waterman, R., Jr., 252
Webber, A.M., 318n
Weber, J., 573
Weber, M., **33**, 44–45, 225, 227
Webes, J., 668n
Weigand, R.E., 641n
Weinberger, C., 453
Weiner, N., **33**
Wells, F., 150
Wessel, D., 457n
Wheaton, L., 378
Wheeler, L., 377
Whiteside, D., 222n
Whitney, E., 618
Whitney, M., 610
Wiener, N., 41, 534
Wildmon, D., **63**
Wilkins, M., 609n
Willey, F., 604n
Williams, K., 141n
Williams, R., 508
Wilson, B., 594
Wilson, Joe, 542
Wilson, John W., 14n
Winkler, C., 512n

Winstanley, N.B., 337n
Winter, D., 222n
Witcher, G., 363n
Wolf, M.L., 582n
Wonder, S., 414, 415, 431
Wood, A., 183, 184
Wood, R.E., 181–182

Woodside, W.S., 646–648
Woodward, J., 231–233, 234
Wright, J., 585

Yager, E.G., 406n
Yang, D.J., 43n
Yetton, P., 80

Yip, P., 147n

Zeman, S., 219
Ziffren, P., 98–99
Zonana, V.F., 661n
Zuboff, S., 526

Subject Index

Accountability, 295–296
Achievement, need for, 387–389
Achieving Society, The (McClelland), 389
Acid rain, 604–606
Acquired immune deficiency syndrome (AIDS), testing for, 342–343
Acquired needs theory, 387–389
Active listening, 369
Activities, of group member, 426
Ad hoc control, 466
Administration
    issues of, 43–49
    principles of (Fayol), **45**
Administration Industrielle et Génèrale (Fayol), 44
Administrative responsibility, 16–17
Administrative search, 607
Administrative-level control, 456
Advertising, language of, 362–363
Affiliation, need for, 387–389
Affirmative action program, 322–324, 564, 601
    of Sears, 184
Age, of leader and employee, 315–316
Aggregate scheduling, 496
Air pollution, 644–645
Alternative plans, 105–106, 137–138
American Red Cross, 136
Americans for Nonsmokers Rights (ANR), 588
Analysis, of current status, 102–104
Analyzability, 233
Antismoking movement, 582–583, 588
Antitrust law, 587, 600–601
Any place concept, 651–653, 656
Any time concept, 650–651
Apartheid, 613
    and General Electric, 576–578
    opposition to, and business, **561**
Apollo reservation system (United Airlines), 515, 539
Apprentice system, 34
Aquaculture, 152–153
Arsenal of Venice, 488, 503
Artificial intelligence, 529–530, 531, 650
    and decision making, 657
Aspen Institute, 336

Assembly line production, 38, 487
    and environment, 484
    and fast food, 31–32
Attribution theory, of leadership, 310–311
Authority
    defined, 291
    delegation of, 294–295
Authority hierarchy, 45
Automation, and operations research, 41–43
Autonomy
    and job enrichment, 206
    and responsibility, 207–208
Avoidance, 398, **399**

Back injuries, and job design, 266–267
Balance, in organization, 296–297
Balance sheet, 468–469
Batch processing, 486–487
Behavior modification, organizational, 398–402
    programs for, **401**
Behavioral research, 32, 46–47
    on leadership, 299–302
Behavioral standard, 459
Behavioral theory, 396
Benefits, 340
Body language, **368,** 627
Bonuses, 340
Boss, compared to leader, 292
Bottom-up strategic planning, 143
Bounded rationality, 69
Brainstorming, 104
Bribery
    and international business, 623
    and social norms, 52
Brooklyn Bridge, building of, 39–40
Budgets, 114–115
    as control, 456, 468
Bureaucracy
    characteristics of (M. Weber), 44–45
    critics of, 226
    defined, 225
    proponents of, 225–226
Business
    priorities of, 585
    and public issues, 589–592
    and society, 559–564
Business cycles, 160
Buyers, 168

Canada, 615
Canvassing, 588–589
Capacity planning, 492–494
Capture system (American Airlines), 538–539
Career orientation, 45
Cash cow, 171–172
Cash flow analysis, 470
Causal analysis, 102–103
Cecchini Report, **67**
Center for Creative Leadership, 311
Center for Disease Control (CDC), 86–87
Central processing unit (CPU), 522
Centralization, of decision making, 213–214
Centralized processing system, 522
Centralized-planning economies, 622
Certainty, conditions of, 65
Chain of command, 209
Challenger shuttle, 572–573
Chandi Borobudur (Indonesia), 30–31, 32
Change
    anticipation of, 162
    approaches to, 265–267
    development or crisis, 252–257
    and force field analysis, 254–256
    and management, 151–187
    of organization symbols, 237–239
    planned, 261–267
    rate of, 156–157, **157**
    rate of, and complexity, 228–230
    reducing resistance to, **263**
    six-step process of, 263–264
    unfreezing, change, refreezing, 261–263
Charisma, 292
    and leadership, **294**
Charity principle, 554
Chemical leak (Bhopal, India), 579–580
Child care (British nanny), 346–347
China
    and computerization, 42–43
    trade with, 612
Choice making, 60–61
Civil False Claims Act, 570–571

Civil Rights Act (1964), 323, 564
Coercive power, 292
Cognitive complexity, 297
Cognitive theory, 396
Collective structure, 214
Collectivism versus individualism, 625, **626**
Collegial structure, 214
Commercials, language of, 362–363
Committee, 209, 417–418
    and decision making, 79–83
    on ethics, 575
    management of, **418**
Common law, 597
Communication
    barriers to, 357–364
    decoding and interpreting, 356–357
    and directing, 351
    encoding, 354–355
    face-to-face, 367–368
    formal channels of, 370–372, **373**
    of future, 659–660
    informal channels of, 372–373
    interpersonal, 366–369
    language, 361–363
    as life and death, 378–379
    nonverbal, 354–355, 368
    one-way versus two-way, 364–366
    organizational, 369–374
    as percentage of manager's work, **352**
    process of, 351–357
    and status, 363–364
    ten commandments of, **366–367**
    transmitting, 355–356
Community, as stakeholder, 561
Comparative standard, 460
Compensation, 339–340
Competition, 182
    versus cooperation, 260
    for resources, 256–257
Competitive factors, 159, 167–174
    strategic responses to, 168–169
Competitiveness, push for, 585
Competitors, as stakeholders, 560
Complexity
    degree of, 156–157, **157**
    and rate of change, 228–230
Computer(s)
    and flexibility of production, 489
    hand-held, 512–514, 516, 517, 521, 525
    and mass customizing, 654, 655

    system components, 522
    as tool, 520
Computer conferencing, 531
Computer-aided design (CAD), **42–43**, 532
Computer-based information systems (CBIS), 517
Computer-integrated manufacturing (CIM), 532
Computerization, 11, 41
Concurrent control, 461
Conditions of certainty, 65
Conditions of risk, 65–66
Conditions of uncertainty, 66–69
Conflict
    over competition for resources, 256–257
    from differences, 258
    hierarchical, 256
    intergroup, 435–437
    lose-lose resolution, 259
    managing, 257
    and matrix organization, 205
    nature of, 257–261
    role, 431
    win-lose resolution, 259
    win-win resolution, 259–261
Consensus, 423–424
Consideration, and leadership, 300–301
Consulting
    and research, 22
    technological, 164
Consumer protection, 556
Consumer rationality, 493–494
Contingency model, of leadership, 304–307
Contingency planning, 145
Contingency theory, 51–52, 227, 230–234
Control, 13–15, 451–479
    balance of, 14
    and corrective action, 462–464
    defined, 454
    effective degrees of, 474–478
    elements of, 457–464
    financial, 468–472
    in future, 660
    of inventory, 500–505
    levels of, 455–457
    methods of, 464–466
    in organizations, 454–455
    through performance management, 472–474
    of production process, 505–506
    of quality. See Quality control
    span of, 232
    timing of, 460–462

Cooperation, versus competition, 260
Coordinating mechanisms
    individual, 208–209, **210, 237**
    structural, 209–213
Coordination, 213–214
Corporate Average Fuel Economy (CAFE) standards, 595
Corporate social rectitude, **565,** 566–568
Corporate social responsibility, 564–566, **567**
Corporate social responsiveness, **565,** 566
Corporations, and political action committees, 593
Cost center, 471
Cost measure, 459
Countertrade, 611
Crash implementation, 524
Creativity
    in Benetton, 250–252
    climate for, 270
    in problem solving, **72**
Creditors, as stakeholders, 560
Critical path method (CPM), 496–497, 498–499
Crosstraining, 27
Culture
    and AT&T divestiture, 238–239
    defined, 224
    and "goodness," 52
    and individual ethics, 568
    and international business, 624–627
    managing, 240–244
    masculine and feminine, 625
    and meaning, 354–355
    and strategy, 236–244
    understanding, 237–240
Currency exchange rates, 630
Customer service, 192–194
Customers, as stakeholders, 560
Cybernetics, 41
Cyclical industry, 160

Data, 518
    and management level, **519**
Data channel, 522
Data storage devices, 522
Decentralization, 281–282
    of decision making, 213–214
Decision(s)
    defined, 60
    impact of, 76–77
    optimal versus satisficing, 69
    programmed versus nonprogrammed, 62–64
    relatedness of, 61

Decision(s) (*Continued*)
scope of, 75
Decision making, 57–93
analyzing phase, 71–74
centralized versus decentralized, 213–214
context of, 64–69
defined, 60
defining problem, 71
difficulty of, 100–101, 571–573
ethical framework for, 562–564
evaluating alternatives, 74–75
in future, 657–658
implementing decisions, 75
improving, 78–83
and management, 7–15
monitoring and evaluating, 76–77
personal versus managerial, 62
process of, 70–77
rational, 69
styles of, **83**
and U.S. Joint Chiefs of Staff, 439–440
and work needs, 404
Decision support system, 528–530
Decision tree, 78–79, 183
Vroom-Yetton model, 80–82
Decoding, 356–357
Defense contractor fraud, 599–600
Degree of complexity, 156–157, **157**
Delegation, of authority, 294–295
Delphi technique, 79, 104
Demand, 167–168
Demographic change, 642
Demotions, 341
Dental care, franchise, 277–278
DentCare Systems, 277–278
Departmentalization
defined, 200
by function, 200–202, **204**
matrix concept of, 203–205
by purpose, 202–203, **204**
Deregulation, of industry, 589–591
Diagnosis, and development, 268
Difference principle, 564
Differential pay rate, 35
Differentiation, 235
Direct foreign investment, 614–616
Directing, 12–13. *See also* Human resources, managing of
and communication, 351
compared to managing and leading, 290
in future, 659–660
overview, 284
in Ringling circus, 92

Distributed processing system, 523
Diversification, 129, 162–163, 170, 228–229
at Sears, 185–186
and structure, 234
Division air defense (DIVAD), 452–454, 456, 459, 460, 461–462, 464, 467, 468, 474
Division of labor, 44
defined, 197
and specialization, 196–208
Dog, 172
Dominican Sisters, 279–283
Downward communication, 370–371
Drugs, testing for, 342, 343, 606–607

Easy-Sabre system, 515
Economic factors, 158, 159, 160–163
strategic responses to, 162–163
Economic order quantity (EOQ), 503
Effect, law of, 398
Effectiveness, 13, 15, 136
Efficiency, 13, 14–15, 136
Electronic data processing (EDP), 516
Electronic mail, 531
Electronic Sweatshop, The (Garson), 478–479
Electrophotography, 541
Emergent behaviors, 426
Employee-centered behavior, 300
Employees
rights of, 601
as stakeholders, 559–560
Employment, and gross national product (U.S.), **648**
Enacted role, 429
Encoding, of meaning, 354–355
Entrepreneur, 22, 270
Entrepreneurship, 270–273
Environment
change in, 130
changing, and management, 151–187
complexity and change, 156–157, **157**
external, 227–230
future, forecasting of, 133–135
internal, 230–234
international, 608–634
interplay of social, political, and legal, 584–586
legal, 596–603
and management, 548
of management, 6–7, **7**

operating and general, 155, **156**
and operating system, 484
and performance evaluation, 462
political, 586–596
stakeholders as part of, **559**
Environmental protection, 589
and acid rain, 604–606
Environmental Protection Agency, 598–600
Environmental scanning, 134
Equal employment opportunity (EEO), 322–324, 560, 601
Equal Pay Act (1963), 323
Equal Rights Amendment (ERA), 589
Equity dilution, 617–618
Equity theory, 391, 395–396
Ergonomics, 266–267
ERG theory, of motivation (Alderfer), 385–386
Esteem needs, 384, **385**
Ethics
audits, 575
bribery, 52, 623
codes of, 574–575
committees on, 575
and decision making, 562–564, 566–567
foundations of, 554–559
individual, 568–573
institutionalizing, 573–575
and mutual fund yields, **561**
and technology, 165
training programs, 575
Ethics Resource Center, 574
European, Community (EC), **67**
Evaluation
of MBO program, 118
quantitative and qualitative, 78–79
of strategy, **133**
Executive opinion jury, 104
Existence needs, 385–386
Exit option, 569–571
Expectancy theory, 307, 383, 391–396
Expectancy, types of, 392
Expectation, and perception, 358
Expected role, 429
Expense accounts, 538–540
Expense Management System (American Express), 539
Experience, and management, 22
Experimental research, 22–23
Expert power, 292
Expert systems, 530, 531
Exports, 611
External control, 465

External recruiting, 331–332
Extinction, 399
Exxon Valdez oil spill, 557–558

Facilities location, 494–495
Fantasia, 252
Fast food, 31–32
Fax technology, 637–639, 652
Fear, power of, 293
Federal Bureau of Investigation (FBI), 107
Federal Election Commission, 592, 593
Federal government, and GNP, 161–162
Feed forward control, 460
Feedback, 50, 208, 365, 517–518
Feedback loop, 486
Filter, and message distortion, 356–357
Finances, and control, 468–472
Finished-goods inventory, 501
Firing, 341
First-line manager, 17–18
Fixed order period, 502
Fixed order quantity, 502–503
Flat organization, 211
Flexible manufacturing systems (FMS), 532
Flexible mass production, 487–489
Flow production, 489–491
Force field analysis, 254–256
Forecasting, 102–104, 133–135
    qualitative, 103–104
    quantitative, 102–103
Foreign Corrupt Practices Act (1977), 623
Foreign Exchange Regulation Act (India), 617–618
Foreign investment, direct, 614–616
Formal authority, 291
Formal channels of communication, 370–372, **373**
Formal control, 465–466
Formal groups, 416–418
Formal organization, 195
Formal rules and control, 45
Formal selection, 45
Formal strategic planning, 143
Forming, of group, 421–423, **425**
Free-market economics, 622
Function layouts, 495
Functional regulations, 600
Functions of the Executive, The (Barnard), 48
Future
    administrative issues in, 656
    demographic changes in, 642
    globalization in, 640–641

information technology in, 649–650
institutional issues of, 656–657
management in, 657–660
mass customizing in, 654–655
megatrends, **639**
organization responses to, 650–655
and resource availability, 642–646
service sector in, 646–649
technical issues of, 655–656
trends of, 639–650

Gantt chart, 38, 496–497
General environment, 155, **156**
Generic brands, 275–276
Global corporation, 616
Globalization, 609–610, 640–641
Goal, The (Goldratt), 490
Goals
    establishing, 104–105, 135–136
    in MBO, 115–117
    and management, 6
    organizing for, 194–196
    and structure, 192–194
    superordinate, 259–261
Going price, 167–168
Government
    incentives offered by, 641
    priorities of, 585–586
    and social responsibility, 52
    as stakeholder, 561–562
Government Accountability Project (GAP), 570
Grapevine, 372–373, **374,** 376–377
Great Depression, 43, 161, 584
    and securities law, 555, 601–602
Greed, power of, 293
Greenhouse effect, 644–645, 647–648
Gross national product (GNP), and U.S. government, 161–162
Ground-Proximity Warning System (GPWS), 378
Group(s)
    characteristics of, 416
    consensus of, 79
    and decision making, 79–83
    defined, 415
    emergent behaviors, 426
    formal, 416–418
    forming of, 421–423, **425**
    and IBM executive loan program, 441–442
    ineffectiveness of, 432–433
    informal, 418–420
    intergroup conflict, 435–437

management (USA for Africa), 414–415
norming phase, 423–424, **425**
in organization, 420–421
performing phase, 424, **425**
problems with, 431–437
required behaviors, 425
roles in, 428–431
storming phase, 423, **425**
U.S. Joint Chiefs of Staff, 439–440
Group Against Smoking Pollution (GASP), 583, 588
Group dynamics, 424–431
Group live-in experience (GLIE), 441–442
Group norms, 427–428
Groupthink, 433–435, **436**
Growth needs, 385–386

Hand and wrist injuries, 267
Hand-held computer project, 512–514, 516, 517, 521, 525
"Hands Across America," 218–220
Hanging Gardens of Babylon, 1
Hardware, 522
Hate, as motivation, 411
Hawthorne effect, 47
Hawthorne studies, 22–23, **33,** 46–47
Headhunters, 333
Hierarchical conflict, 256
Hierarchical structure, versus network, **215**
Hierarchy of human needs (Maslow), 48, 384–385, 386
Historical standard, 459–460
HIV virus, testing for, 342
Home health care, 664–666
Human approaches to change, 266–267
Human relations movement, 47–48
Human resources
    current, evaluation of, 328, **329**
    current issues, 342–343
    and external constraints, 321–324
    forecasts concerning, 102
    future availability of, 328–329, **330**
    internal guidelines, 324
    managing of, 317–347
    and needs assessment, 326–327
    orientation and training of, 334–335
    performance appraisal, 336–339
    planning, 324–330

Human resources (*Continued*)
   recruitment and selection, 331–334
   rewarding, 339–342
   selection, 332–334
   system of, 320–324
Human resources information system, 331
Human Side of Enterprise, The (McGregor), 48
Hygiene factors, 390

Ideogram, 353
Ideologies, 239–240
Images, and words, **370**
Imaging, 388–389
Immigration policy, 595
Impersonality, 45
Implementation, 106–107
   of MIS, 524–527
Imports, 611
Incentives, 340
Income statement, 469, **470**
India, 617–618
   Bhopal, chemical leak in, 579–580
Individual contributor, **17**, 18, 19–20
Individual, ethics of, 568–573
Individualism versus collectivism, 625
Industrial Revolution, 34, 279, 584
   and assumptions about human nature, 403
Industrial sector, 653–654
Industry-specific regulations, 598
Ineffectiveness, of group, 432–433
Influence
   defined, 290
   mechanisms of, 588–589
Influencing, and leading, 290–297
Informal authority, 291
Informal channels, of communication, 372–373
Informal control, 465–466
Informal groups, 418–420
Informal organization, 196
Informal strategic planning, 142–143
Information
   defined, 518
   and management level, **519**
   managerial uses of, 518–519
   value of, 519–520
Information systems. *See also* Management information systems
   hand-held computers, 512–514, 516, 517, 521, 525
   in pharmacy, 536–537
   and strategy, 515–516

Information technology, 531–534, 649–650
   in manufacturing, 532
   in service sector, 532–534
Initiating structure, and leadership, 300–301
Innovation
   eight corporate masters of, 272–273
   fostering, 270
Input, 50, 395, 517
Input/output devices, 522
Inside/outside strategic planning, 141
Insider trading, 584, 602
Instinct, and management, 21–22
Institutional responsibility, 16, 17
Institutional-level control, 456
Integration, of institutional units, 235
Intelligence, and leadership, 297
Interactions, of group members, 426
Internal control, 465
Internal recruiting, 331
International business, 611–616
   environment of, 621–627
   risks of, 628–630
International environment, **156**
   cultural factors of, 624–627
   economic factors of, 621–622
   opportunities of, 627–628
   political and legal factors of, 622–624
Interpretation, of message, 356–357
Intervention, and development, 268–269
Intrapreneurship, 273
Intuition, and management, 21–22
Inventory
   control of, 455, 500–505
   defined, 501
   ordering, 502–503
Investment center, 471–472
Ireland, 615–616
Isolation, and productivity, 508–509

Japan
   automobile industry, 222, 230, 254, 610, 662–663
   copying machines, 543, 544–547
   and human resource management, 324
   just-in-time system, 510
   kanban system, 504–505
   overseas operations of, 620
   prefabricated houses, 654
   and quality circles, 406

   and total quality control, 467
   and U.S.-Soviet relations, 667–672
Job analysis, 326
Job characteristics, 206–208
Job diagnostic survey, 206–208
Job depth, 206
Job description, 326, **327–328**
Job design, and injuries, 266–267
Job enlargement, 205–206
Job enrichment, 206, 267
Job posting, 331
Job rotation, 206
Job scope, 205
Job shop, 486
Job specification, 326
Job-centered behavior, 300
Joint venture, 614
Justice, theory of, 564, 571
Just-in-time (JIT) delivery, 504–505
Just-in-time production, 510

Kanban system, 504–505

Labor, division of and specialization, 196–208
Labor unions. *See* Unions
Language, 361–363, 627
Lateral communication, 372
Law
   and human resource system, 321–324, **325**
   impact on managers, 597–600
   making of, 590
   rule of, 596
   sources of, 597
   stages of, 586–588
Law of effect, 398
Law of the situation, 44. *See also* Contingency theory
Layoffs, of middle managers, 212
Layout planning, 494
Leader
   benevolent tyrant, 303
   compared to boss, 292
   young, and older employee, 314–316
Leadership
   attribution theory of, 310–311
   behavioral theories of, 299–302
   and charisma, 294
   compared to managing and directing, 290
   contingency approach to, 302–310
   continuing research on, 310–312
   defined, 290

Leadership (*Continued*)
  Fieldler's contingency model
    of, 304–307
  leaders' views on, **298**
  life cycle model of, 308–310
  Ohio State studies of, 300–301,
    302
  path-goal model of, 307–308
  researched traits of, **299**
  situational approaches to, 302–310
  style of, **301**, 304, 305–307
  substitutes for, 311–312
  traits of, 297–299
  University of Michigan studies
    of, 300, **302**
Leading, and influencing, 290–297
Least preferred co-worker scale
  (Fieldler), 304, **305**
Legal environment, 596–603
Legitimate power, 292
Less developed countries (LDCs),
  619. *See also* Third World Coun-
  tries
Liaison, 208–209
Liberty principle, 564
Licensing agreements, 613–614
Life cycle model, of leadership,
  308–310
Lighting, in work area, 267
Linear programming, 78
Line employees, 199–200
Linking pins, 417
Listening, 368–369
Lobbyists, 591
Local area networks, 523
Logo, change of, 237–239, 240
Loosely coupled structure, 214
Loose-tight principle, 475
Los Angeles Olympic Organizing
  Committee (LAOOC), 98–99,
  103, 105, 106–107
Lose-lose conflict resolution, 259
Loyalty, as option, 569–571

Mail-order business, 181–187
Mainframe, 522
Maintenance role, 431, **432**
Management
  basic functions of, 8
  decision making, 7–15, 57–93.
    See also Decision making
  defined, 3, 6–7
  democratic system of, 182
  and the environment, 548
  evolution of, 29–56
  in future, 657–660
  of human resources, 317–347
  importance of, 5
  in international environment,
    621–627

level of, 17–20
level of, and decisions, **64**
major themes in history of,
  31–34
by objectives (MBO), 115–118
overview, 1
participative, 402–406
process, model of, **15**
as a pyramid, **17**
responsibilities of, 15–20
scientific. *See* Scientific management
sources of knowledge about,
  20–23
span of, 210–213
strategic, 130–141
theory of, **33**
Management agreements, 613–614
Management by exception, 112,
  456
Management decision making, 8.
  See also Decision making
Management information systems
  (MIS), 514–518
  basic components of, 517–518
  defined, 514
  design of, 522–524
  establishing, 521–528
  evolution of, 516–517
  implementation of, 524–527
  as management tool, 520
  monitoring and improving,
    527–528
  planning of, 521–522
  resistance to, 525–527
Managerial decision making, 62
Managerial Grid (Blake and Mouton), 269
Managers
  advice to, 314
  compared to directing and
    leading, 290
  development programs for,
    335–336
  impact of law on, 597–600
  layoffs of, 212
  legal responsibilities of, 602–
    603
  Mintzberg's ten roles of, **21**
  planning by, 110, **112**
  process scale for, **338**
Managing, of group dynamics, 426–
  427
Man-Computer Integrative Data
  Access System (McIDAS), 637
Maquiladora Program, 615
Market, 168
  basic strategies, 169–170
  development, 170
  mass customizing of, 654–655

penetration of, 169
Market place, changes in, 653
Market saturation, 182
Market share, 544
  and foreign investment, 628
Mass customizing, 654–655
Mass production, 231, **232**
Master scheduling, 496
Material requirements planning, 503
Matrix organization, 203–205, 543
Maximax, 68
MBO (Management by objectives),
  115–118
Mechanistic organization, 227–228,
  237
Megatrends, in future, **639**
Memo writing, **359**
Mergers, transnational, 217–218
Mexico, 615, 633–634
Middle manager, 17, **18**, 19
Mind-sets, 356–357
Miniaturization, 652–653
Minimax, 68
Minorities
  and antismoking movement,
    591
  and reverse discrimination, 564
  and theory of rights, 563–564
Mission, of organization, 135–136
Modular implementation, 524–525
Moments of truth, 192–194
Money center bank, 240–244
Money laundering, 457
Motion Study (F. Gilbreth), 37
Motivation
  adversity as, 410–412
  examples of, **381–382**
  expectancy theory of, 307,
    383, 391–396
  of famous people, 394
  fear and greed as, 293
  need theories of, 383–391
  reinforcement theories of, 383
  understanding of, 382–383
Motivation factors, 390
Motivation theory, choice of, 402
Motivation-hygiene theory, 390–
  391
Multinational corporations, 616–
  621
  and apartheid, 577–578
Mutual funds, ethical, **561**

Name, as symbol, 237–239
National Aeronautics and Space
  Administration (NASA), 572–573
  Safety Reporting System, 378–
    379
National values, 625

Needs
  acquired, theory of, 387–389
  ERG theory (Alderfer), 385–386
  and groups, 420–421
  hierarchy of (Maslow), 384–385, 386
  two-factor theory (Herzberg), 390–391
Need theories, of motivation, 383–391
Negative reinforcement, 398, **399**
Network structure, 214, **215**
New Harmony, Indiana, 34–35
Niagara Institute, 336
Nixon-Brezhnev summit, 612
Noise
  and communication, 358, **359**
  effect on work, 267
No-matter concept, 653–654, 656
Nonprogrammed decision, 62–64
Nonroutine decision. *See* Nonprogrammed decision
Nonverbal communication, 354–355, 368
Norland Nursery Training College, 347
Norming phase, of group, 423–424, **425**

Objectives, **135**
  establishing, 105
  management by, 115–118
Objectivity, and perception, 359–361
Occupational Health and Safety Act (1970), 563–564
Occupational Safety and Health Administration (OSHA), 598–600
Olympic Games (1984), 98–99, 111
One-way communication, 364–366
Operant conditioning, 398–402
Operating environment, 155, **156**
  economic, technological, and competitive factors in, 157–160
Operating system, 483–486
Operational planning, 111–112, **113**
Operations research, and automation, 41–43
Optimal decision, 69
Options. *See* Alternative plans
Ordering, 502–503
Organic organization, 227–228, **237**
Organization(s)
  alternative structure, 214–215
  classical theory of, 44–45
  contingency theory of, 227

design and culture of, 221–248
diversity in, 130
formal and informal, 194–196
groups in, 420–421
growth of, 129
interdependence of, 484
legal responsibilities of, 600–602
long-term survival of, 279–283
and response to future trends, 650–655
role of, 5
size of, 230
strategic planning in, 141–145
structure of, 191–220
systems model of, **50**
tall and flat, 211
Organization chart, 195–196
Organization development, 267–273
Organization for Economic Cooperation and Development (OECD), 623, **624**
Organization of Petroleum Exporting Countries (OPEC), 158
Organization structure, 194–196
  of restaurants, 197–198
Organizational analysis, 133
Organizational behavior modification, 398–402
Organizational design, 224, 234–236
Organizational development, **269**
Organizational mission, 135–136
Organizing, 10–12
  in future, 658–659
  for goal accomplishment, 194–196
  overview, 188
  in Ringling circus, 91
Orientation, of personnel, 334–335
Outcomes, 395
Outplacement programs, 341
Output, 50, 517
Output measures, 339
Output standard, 459
Outside/inside strategic planning, 141
Overnight mail service, 636–639, 652
Overview System, 473–474
Owners, as stakeholders, 560

Parallel implementation, 524
Participative management, 402–406
Paternalism, corporate, 242
Path-goal model, of leadership, 307–308
Peer review, 20
Perceived role, 429

Perception
  differences in, 358–361
  distortion of, 360–361
Performance
  measuring and evaluating, 460–462
  objectives for, 458–460
Performance appraisal, 336–339
Performance management, control through, 472–474
Performance phase, of group, 424, **425**
Permanent groups, 417
Perquisites, 340
Personal space, 625–627
Personality-need factors, 387
Personnel department, 13. *See also* Human resources
Phased implementation, 525
Physiological needs, 384, **385**
Pictograph, 353
Piece-rate system (Taylor), **36**
Pilot implementation. *See* Modular implementation
Plan
  defined, 100
  single-use, 112, **113,** 114–115
  standing, 112–114
Planning, 8–10, 97–123
  criteria for, 107–109
  defined, 100
  in future, 658
  identifying alternatives, 105–106
  implementation, 106–107
  importance of, 100–101
  by managers, **112**
  means-ends hierarchy, **110**
  model of, **101**
  overview, 94
  Ringling circus, 91
  scope of, 109–112
  steps in process, 101–109
  strategic, 124–150. *See also* Strategic planning
  types of, 109–115
Policies, 113
Political action committees, **591,** 592, 593
Political environment, 586–596
Political risk, 629, 631–633
Pollution, 644–645
  chemical leak, 579–580
  oil spill, 557–558
Population growth, 642, 643–644, **645**
Portfolio, 171
Portfolio investment, 613
Portfolio management, 170–173
Positive reinforcement, 398, **399**

Postcontrol, 461–462
Potential limit theory, 318–319
Power, 292–294
    of fear and greed, 293
    and internal communication, 349–350
    and law, 597
    need for, 387–389
    and social responsibility, 555–556
Power distance, 625, **626**
Practice of Management, The (Drucker), 115
Precontrol, 460
Priorities
    of business, 585
    of government, 585–586
    of society, 584–585
Probability theory, 78
Problem solving, 60–61
    creative, **72**
    process of, 70–77
Procedures, 113–114
Process analysis, 505–506
Process measures, 338
Process production, 231, **232**, 489–491
Processing, 517
Product development, 170
Production
    capacity planning, 492–494
    control of, 505–506
    controlling inventory, 500–505
    designing the system, 491–495
    facilities and layout, 494–495
    process choice, 491–492
    scheduling, 495–500
    technology of, 231–233
Production/operations management, 483–486
    planning processes, 486–491
Productivity, 32
    and suppliers, 509–510
    white-collar, 507–509
Product liability, 600
Profit center, 471
Profit sharing, 340
Program Evaluation and Review Technique (PERT), 103, 496–497, 500, **501**
Programmed decision, 62–64
Programs, 114
Projects, 114
Promotions, 341
Psychographics, 74
Public issues, 586–588, **589**
Public policy
    and agenda building, 592–594
    decisions on, 595
    defined, 592

drug testing as, 606–607
    evaluation of, 596
    formulation of, 594–595
    implementation of, 595–596
    process of, **594**
Public welfare, 554–559
Public-interest groups, as stakeholders, 562
Punishment, 398–399

Qualitative forecasting methods, 103–104
Quality assurance (QA), 467
Quality circle, 405–406
    sociogram of, **419**
Quality control, 463–464, 466–467
Quality Is Free (Crosby), 463–464
Quality measure, 459
Quality of work life (QWL) project, 404–405
Quantitative forecasting methods, 102–103
Quantity measure, 459

Rate of change, 156–157, **157**
Ratio analysis, 469–470, **471**
Raw-materials inventory, 501
Reciprocal training, 193
Recruitment
    defined, 331
    external, 331–332
    internal, 331
    professional, 333
Referent power, 292
Refreezing, 261–263
Reinforcement, and organizational development, 269
Reinforcement theories, of motivation, 383, 396–402
Relatedness needs, 385–386
Reordering, 502–503
Required behaviors, 425
Research, and management, 22–23
Resources
    future availability of, 642–646
    management of, 6
    and zero-sum concept, 256–257
Responsibility, 295–296
Responsibility center, 470–472
Retirement, 341
    incentive plan (Sears), 185
Revenue center, 471
Reward power, 292
Rewards, 339–342
    intrinsic or extrinsic, 393
Rights, theory of, 563–564, 571
Rigid mass production, 487
Ripple effect, 77
Risk, conditions of, 65–66
Rituals, 239

Robotics, 532, 533–534
Rolaids, sales plan for, 108–109
Role
    in group, 428–431
    task and maintenance, 431, **432**
Role ambiguity, 431
Role conflict, 431
Role episode, **430**
Role overload, 431
Role player, 319
Roosevelt Center for American Policy Studies, 422
Routine decision. *See* Programmed decision
Rule of law, 596
Rules, 114

Sabre reservation system (American Airlines), 514–516, 538, 539
SafePlace, 344–346
Safety needs, 384, **385**
Safety stock, 503
Salary, 340
Sales forecasts, 102
Salvation Army, 116
Satisficing decision, 69
Scalar process, 209–210, 212
Scenario building, 104
Scheduling
    critical path method, 496–497, 498–499
    Gantt charts, 496–497
    program evaluation and review technique (PERT), 496–497, 500, **501**
Scientific management, 35–38
    obstacles to, 38–41
Scope, of decision, 75
Sears Tower (Chicago), 182
Securities law, 601–602
Selection, of personnel, 332–334
Selective purchasing laws, 578
Self-actualization needs, 384, **385**
Sellers, 168
Sentiments, of group members, 426
Sent role, 429
Service sector, 159
    compared to industrial sector, 653–654
    future growth in, 646–649
    and overseas expansion, 619
    productivity in, **649**
Sex roles, 625
Sexism, 315–316
Sherman Anti-trust Act (1890), 555, 600
Shrimp farming, 152–153
Single European Act (1987), **67**
Single-use plans, 112, **113**, 114–115

Situation, and leadership styles, 304–307
Size, or organization, 230
Smoking, 584–585
    antismoking movement, 582–583, 588
Social control, 456
    of managers, 598
Social needs, 384, **385**
Social regulations, 598–600
Social responsibility, 52–53
    corporate, 564–566, **567**
    defined, 556
    and food purity, 552–554
    foundations of, 554–559
    institutionalizing, 573–575
    Union Carbide, 579–580
Societal environment. *See* General environment
Society
    and business, 559–564
    priorities of, 584–585
Sociogram, **419**
Sociometry, 419
Software, 522
South Africa
    apartheid, **561**, 576–578
    investment in, 613–614
South Korea, 612
Soviet Union, 612–613
Space
    concept of, 651–653
    personal concept of, 625–627
Span of control. *See* Span of management
Span of management, 210–213
Special-interest groups, 589
Specialization, 34
    defined, 199
    and division of labor, 196–208
    and job enrichment, **206**
    unit, 201
Sri Lanka, 616
Staff employees, 199–200
Staffing, 317–347
Stakeholder, concept of, 559–562
Standards
    and corrective action, 462–464
    defined, 458
    deviations from, 462, **465**
    setting of, 13, 458–460
    types of, 459
Standing plans, 112–114
Star, 172
Statistical process control (SPC), 472–474
Status, and communication, 363–364
Steering control, 461
Stewardship principle, 554

Stock options, 340
Storming phase, of group development, 423, **425**
Strategic defense initiative (SDI), 671
Strategic management, 130–141
    and changing environment, 151–187
    and contingency theory, 51–52
    defined, 132
    process, model of, **132**
Strategic planning, 109–110, 111–112, **113**, 124–150
    approaches to, 141–143
    costs of, 130
    implementing and monitoring, 138–141
    importance of, 128–130
    levels of, 143–145
    and management, 130–141
    modes of, 128, **129**
    in oil and gas industry, 158–159
    and organizational growth, 129
    in organizations, 141–145
Strategic thinking, 127–128
Strategy
    choosing of, 173–174
    and culture, 236–244
    meaning of, 127–130
Structural approaches to change, 265
Structure
    and culture and strategy, 224–225
    defined, 194–195
    design of, 225–227
    Dominican Sisters, 279–283
    General Motors, 222–224
    and technology, 233
Students Against Smoking (SAS), 590
    subjectivity, and perception, 361
Sullivan principles, 577, 578
Supercomputer, 178–180, 529–530
Superordinate goal, 259–261
Supervisor, 17–18
Supervisory ability, 297
Suppliers, 509–510
    as stakeholders, 560
Swatch watch, 177–178
Swine flu epidemic, 86–88
Symbols, 237–239
    and communication, 353, 354–355
Systematic control, 466
System structure, 522
Systems theory, 49–51

Tactical planning, 111–112, **113**
Tall organization, 211
Task approaches to change, 267
Task environment. *See* Operating environment
Task force, 209, 417–418
Task role, 431, **432**
Task variety, 233
Team building, 432–433
Techmashimport (Soviet Union), 669
Technical issues, 34–43
Technical responsibility, 16
Technical-level control, 455–456
Technological approaches to change, 265–266
Technological factors, 158–159, 163–167
"Technological optimism," 163–164
Technological Society, The (Ellul), 163
Technology
    forecasts concerning, 102
    future issues in, 655–656
    meaning of, 163–164
    new, 164
    and organizational strategy, 165–167
    of production, 231–233
    small batch, 234
    and structure, 233
Telecommunications technology, 531
Television writers' strike, 349–350
Temporary groups, 417
Terminations, 341–342
Terrorism, 629
Theoretical research, 23
Theory of justice, 565, 571
Theory of rights, 563–564, 571
Theory X, of human nature, 403, 404
Theory X and theory Z (McGregor), 48–49
Theory Y, of human nature, 403–404
Theory Z (Ouchi), 49
Think tank, 422
Third World countries, 620
Time, concepts of, 625, 650–651
Time and motion studies, 37
Time series analysis, 102, **103**
Tobacco Institute, 591
Top manager, 17, **18**, 19
Top-down strategic planning, 143
Total quality control, 467
Trade
    defined, 611
    import-export, 611–613

Trade associations, 591, 593
Trade-off analysis, 506
Training and development, of personnel, 335
Trait measures, 337
Trait research, 297–299
Transaction-processing systems (TPS), 517
Transfers, 341
Transformational leadership, 310
Transformation process, 50, 484–485
  and any place concept, **652**
Transmitting, of message, 355–356
Transnational mergers, 217–218
Travel and expense reports, 538–540
Trusts, 555
Turnkey projects, 614
TV-Cable Week, 481–483, 484, 486, 487–489, 501, 505–506
Twelve Principles of Efficiency, The (Emerson), 38
Two-factor theory, of motivation (Herzberg), 390–391
Two-way communication, 364–366

Uncertainty avoidance, 625
Uncertainty, conditions of, 66–69
Unfreezing, 261–262
Uniform Guidelines on Employee Selection (1978), 323
Unions
  and Japanese management, 662–663
  and law, 601
  and political action committees, 593
  priorities of, 584
  and scientific management, 38–40
Unique-product production, 486
Unit production, 231, **232**
Unit specialization, 201
United Auto Workers (UAW), 662–663
Unity of command, 209, 212
Upward communication, 371
USA for Africa, 218, 414–415, 417, 423, 426
USA Today, 125–126, 128, 129, 134–135, 137, 139, 144–145
U.S. Privacy Act (1974), 564
Utilitarian theory, of decision making, 562–563, 571
Utopian experiments, 34–35

Value, no-matter concept of, 653–654
Value-added chain, 484–485
Values
  comparison of, **569**
  and corporate decisions, 566
  national, 625
Variable budgeting, 468
Venice, Arsenal of, 488, 503
Videoconferencing, 531
VNET (mail network), 376–377
Voice option, 569–571
Vroom-Yetton model, 80–82

Wages, 340

Water pollution, 645
Wealth of Nations (Smith), 196–197
Whistle-blowers Protection Act (Michigan, 1981), 564
Whistle-blowing, 569, 570–571
White-collar productivity, 507–509
Wholly owned subsidiaries, 614
Wildcat, 172
Win-lose conflict resolution, 259
Win-win conflict resolution, 259–261
Women
  employment and earnings patterns, **323**
  leader-employee relations, 315–316
  and professional couples, 333
  in workforce, statistics on, 332
Words, and images, **370**
Work flow layouts, 494–495
Work group, 417
Work-in-progress inventory, 501
World War I, and scientific management, 40–41
World War II, 161
  and human relations, 48–49
Writers Guild of America (WGA), 349–350, 351, 352, 355, 358, 371

Yes/no control, 461

Zero-based budgeting (zbb), 468
Zero-based time, 650–651
Zero-sum concept, 256–257